McGRAW-HILL YEARBOOK OF
Science & Technology

1999

McGRAW-HILL YEARBOOK OF
Science &
Technology

1999

Comprehensive coverage of recent events and research as compiled by the staff of the McGraw-Hill Encyclopedia of Science & Technology

McGraw-Hill

New York   San Francisco   Washington, D.C.   Auckland   Bogotá   Caracas   Lisbon   London   Madrid
Mexico City   Milan   Montreal   New Delhi   San Juan   Singapore   Sydney   Tokyo   Toronto

Library of Congress Cataloging in Publication data

McGraw-Hill yearbook of science and technology.
1962–   . New York, McGraw-Hill Book Co.

     v. illus. 26 cm.
     Vols. for 1962–   compiled by the staff of the
McGraw-Hill encyclopedia of science and technology.
     1. Science—Yearbooks.   2. Technology—
Yearbooks.   1. McGraw-Hill encyclopedia of
science and technology.
Q1.M13   505.8   62-12028

ISBN 0-07-052625-7
ISSN 0076-2016

McGraw-Hill

A Division of The **McGraw·Hill** Companies

This book was printed on acid-free paper.

*It was set in Garamond Book and Neue Helvetica Black Condensed by
The PRD Group, Shippensburg, Pennsylvania. The art was prepared by
The PRD Group. The book was printed and bound by R. R. Donnelley
& Sons Company, The Lakeside Press.*

Editorial Staff

International Editorial Advisory Board

Editing, Design, & Production Staff

Roger Kasunic, Director of Editing, Design, and Production

Joe Faulk, Editing Manager

Ron Lane, Art Director

Thomas G. Kowalczyk, Production Manager

Suzanne W. B. Rapcavage, Senior Production Supervisor

Consulting Editors

Prof. Eugene A. Avallone. *Consulting Engineer; Professor Emeritus of Mechanical Engineering, City College of the City University of New York.* MECHANICAL AND POWER ENGINEERING.

A. E. Bailey. *Formerly, Superintendent of Electrical Science, National Physical Laboratory, London, England.* ELECTRICITY AND ELECTROMAGNETISM.

Prof. William P. Banks. *Chairman, Department of Psychology, Pomona College, Claremont, California.* PHYSIOLOGICAL AND EXPERIMENTAL PSYCHOLOGY.

Dr. Alexander Baumgarten. *Director, Clinical Immunology Laboratory, Yale-New Haven Hospital, New Haven, Connecticut.* IMMUNOLOGY AND VIROLOGY.

Prof. Gregory C. Beroza. *Department of Geophysics, Stanford University, California.* GEOPHYSICS.

Dr. Robert T. Beyer. *Hazard Professor of Physics, Emeritus, Brown University, Providence, Rhode Island.* ACOUSTICS.

Prof. S. H. Black. *Department of Medical Microbiology and Immunology, Texas A&M University, College Station.* MEDICAL MICROBIOLOGY.

Prof. Anjan Bose. *Director, School of Electrical Engineering and Computer Science, Washington State University, Pullman.* ELECTRICAL POWER ENGINEERING.

Ronald Braff. *Principal Engineer, MITRE Corporation/Center for Advanced Aviation System Development, McLean, Virginia.* NAVIGATION.

Dr. Chaim Braun. *Bechtel Corporation, Gaithersburg, Maryland.* NUCLEAR ENGINEERING.

Robert D. Briskman. *President, CD Radio, Inc., Washington, D.C.* TELECOMMUNICATIONS.

Michael H. Bruno. *Graphic Arts Consultant, Sarasota, Florida.* GRAPHIC ARTS.

Dr. John F. Clark. *Director, Graduate Studies, and Professor, Space Systems, Spaceport Graduate Center, Florida Institute of Technology, Satellite Beach.* SPACE TECHNOLOGY.

Prof. David L. Cowan. *Chairman, Department of Physics and Astronomy, University of Missouri, Columbia.* CLASSICAL MECHANICS AND HEAT.

Dr. C. Chapin Cutler. *Retired; formerly, Ginzton Laboratory, Stanford University, California.* RADIO COMMUNICATIONS.

Dr. Michael R. Descour. *Optical Sciences Center, University of Arizona, Tucson.* ELECTROMAGNETIC RADIATION AND OPTICS.

Dr. Derek Enlander. *Internal Medicine, New York, New York.* MEDICINE AND PATHOLOGY.

Dr. Jay S. Fein. *Division of Atmospheric Sciences, National Science Foundation, Arlington, Virginia.* METEOROLOGY AND CLIMATOLOGY.

Dr. William K. Ferrell. *Professor Emeritus, College of Forestry, Oregon State University, Corvallis.* FORESTRY.

Prof. Lawrence Grossman. *Department of Geophysical Science, University of Chicago, Illinois.* GEOCHEMISTRY.

Dr. Ralph E. Hoffman. *Associate Professor, Yale Psychiatric Institute, Yale University School of Medicine, New Haven, Connecticut.* PSYCHIATRY.

Dr. S. C. Jong. *Senior Staff Scientist and Program Director, Mycology and Protistology Program, American Type Culture Collection, Manassas, Virginia.* MYCOLOGY.

Prof. Karl E. Lonngren. *Department of Electrical & Computer Engineering, University of Iowa, Iowa City.* PHYSICAL ELECTRONICS.

Dr. Philip V. Lopresti. *Retired; formerly, Engineering Research Center, AT&T Bell Laboratories, Princeton, New Jersey.* ELECTRONIC CIRCUITS.

Prof. Craig E. Lunte. *Department of Chemistry, University of Kansas, Lawrence.* ANALTYICAL CHEMISTRY.

Dr. George L. Marchin. *Associate Professor of Microbiology and Immunology, Division of Biology, Kansas State University, Manhattan.* MICROBIOLOGY.

Dr. Ramon A. Mata-Toledo. *Associate Professor of Computer Science, James Madison University, Harrisonburg, Virginia.* COMPUTERS.

Dr. Henry F. Mayland. *Soil Scientist, Northwest Irrigation and Soils Research Laboratory, USDA-ARS, Kimberly, Idaho.* SOILS.

Prof. Arnold I. Miller. *Department of Geology, University of Cincinnati, Ohio.* INVERTEBRATE PALEONTOLOGY.

Dr. Orlando J. Miller. *Center for Molecular Medicine and Genetics, Wayne State University School of Medicine, Detroit, Michigan.* GENETICS AND EVOLUTION.

Prof. Conrad F. Newberry. *Department of Aerospace and Astronautics, Naval Postgraduate School, Monterey, California.* AERONAUTICAL ENGINEERING AND PROPULSION.

Prof. Jay M. Pasachoff. *Director, Hopkins Observatory, Williams College, Williamstown, Massachusetts.* ASTRONOMY.

Prof. David J. Pegg. *Department of Physics and Astronomy, University of Tennessee, Knoxville.* ATOMIC, MOLECULAR, AND NUCLEAR PHYSICS.

Dr. William C. Peters. *Professor Emeritus, Mining and Geological Engineering, University of Arizona, Tucson.* MINING ENGINEERING.

Dr. Donald R. Prothero. *Associate Professor of Geology, Occidental College, Los Angeles, California.* VERTEBRATE PALEONTOLOGY.

Prof. W. D. Russell-Hunter. *Professor of Zoology, Department of Biology, Syracuse University, New York.* INVERTEBRATE ZOOLOGY.

Dr. Andrew P. Sage. *Founding Dean Emeritus and First American Bank Professor, University Professor, School of Information Technology and Engineering, George Mason University, Fairfax, Virginia.* CONTROL AND INFORMATION SYSTEMS.

Mel Schwartz. *Materials Consultant, United Technologies Corporation, Stratford, Connecticut.* MATERIALS SCIENCE AND ENGINEERING.

Prof. Marlin U. Thomas. *Head, School of Industrial Engineering, Purdue University, West Lafayette, Indiana.* INDUSTRIAL AND PRODUCTION ENGINEERING.

Prof. John F. Timoney. *Department of Veterinary Science, University of Kentucky, Lexington.* VETERINARY MEDICINE.

Dr. Shirley Turner. *U.S. Department of Commerce, National Institute of Standards and Technology, Gaithersburg, Maryland.* GEOLOGY (MINERALOGY AND PETROLOGY).

Prof. Joan S. Valentine. *Department of Chemistry and Biochemistry, University of California, Los Angeles.* INORGANIC CHEMISTRY.

Dr. Ralph E. Weston, Jr. *Department of Chemistry, Brookhaven National Laboratory, Upton, New York.* PHYSICAL CHEMISTRY.

Prof. Frank M. White. *Department of Mechanical Engineering, University of Rhode Island, Kingston.* FLUID MECHANICS.

Prof. Richard G. Wiegert. *Institute of Ecology, University of Georgia, Athens.* ECOLOGY AND CONSERVATION.

Prof. Frank Wilczek. *Institute for Advanced Study, Princeton, New Jersey.* THEORETICAL PHYSICS.

Prof. W. A. Williams. *Department of Agronomy and Range Science, University of California, Davis.* AGRICULTURE.

Dr. Terry L. Yates. *Chairman, Department of Biology, University of New Mexico, Albuquerque.* ANIMAL SYSTEMATICS.

Contributors

A list of contributors, their affiliations, and the titles of the articles they wrote appears in the back of this volume.

The 1999 *McGraw-Hill Yearbook of Science & Technology* provides the reader with a wide overview of the most significant recent developments in science, technology, and engineering, as selected by our distinguished board of consulting editors. At the same time, it satisfies the reader's need to stay informed about important trends in research and development that will fundamentally influence future understanding and practical applications of knowledge in fields ranging from astronomy to zoology. Readers of the *McGraw-Hill Encyclopedia of Science & Technology* will find the *Yearbook* to be a valuable companion publication, enhancing the timeliness and depth of the *Encyclopedia*.

Each contribution to the *Yearbook* is a concise yet authoritative article authored by one or more specialists in the field. We are pleased that noted researchers have been supporting the *Yearbook* since its first edition in 1962 by taking time to share their knowledge with our readers. The topics are selected by our consulting editors in conjunction with our editorial staff based on present significance and potential applications. McGraw-Hill strives to make each article as readily understandable as possible for the nonspecialist reader through careful editing and the extensive use of graphics, much of which is prepared specially for the *Yearbook*.

Librarians, students, teachers, the scientific community, and the general public continue to find in the *McGraw-Hill Yearbook of Science & Technology* the information they want and need in order to follow the rapid pace of advances in science and technology and to understand the developments in these fields that will shape the world of the twenty-first century.

Mark D. Licker

Publisher

McGRAW-HILL YEARBOOK OF
Science &
Technology

1999

A–Z

Acquired immune deficiency syndrome (AIDS)

In recent years there have been major advances in understanding the pathogenesis of human immunodeficiency virus 1 (HIV-1), as well as a dramatic increase in the number of antivirals available to treat acquired immune deficiency syndrome. The discovery of HIV-1 co-receptors has shed light on the mechanism of virus tropism. Achievement of undetectable virus levels in the plasma of AIDS patients on triple drug therapy has renewed optimism regarding the potential for long-term control of infection.

HIV-1 co-receptor. Soon after the discovery of HIV-1 as the causative agent of AIDS, CD4 was identified as the main cellular receptor for HIV-1 entry into T cells and macrophages. Further studies on the infectivity of HIV-1 suggested that viral isolates had unique affinities (tropism) for certain cell populations, leading to the characterization of HIV-1 isolates as either T-tropic, having a primary tropism for T lymphocytes, or M-tropic, having a high affinity for macrophages. It became clear that HIV-1 uses CD4 as well as a second receptor to gain entrance into the target cells. It is now known that these second receptors are members of a class of receptors for chemokines, a class of molecules normally produced during inflammatory processes.

The first indication that chemokines were playing a role in HIV-1 replication and AIDS pathogenesis came from the discovery in late 1995 that three already-known chemokines—RANTES (regulated on activation normal T cell expressed and secreted), MIP 1-α and MIP 1-β (macrophage inflammatory protein 1-alpha and 1-beta)—were able to efficiently block replication of certain strains of HIV-1. It became clear that these molecules were interfering with HIV-1 replication by blocking fusion, a critical step in entry of the viral particle into the target cell.

In 1996, it was discovered that a major co-receptor for T-tropic strains of HIV-1 was a new chemokine receptor, now called CXCR-4. The natural ligand of this receptor was a chemokine different from RANTES, MIP 1-α, and MIP 1-β. Soon, five separate groups found that another chemokine receptor, CCR-5, which can bind RANTES, MIP 1-α, and MIP 1-β, was another receptor for M-tropic strains of HIV-1. Subsequently several other chemokine receptors (among them CCR-3, CCR-2b, and STRL-33) were identified as additional co-receptors for HIV-1 entry into target cells. Thus, HIV-1 uses a second receptor for entry into cells which can be one of a number of related chemokine receptors.

Viral entry is believed to involve interactions between the HIV-1 envelope, the CD4 receptor, and the chemokine receptor. The distribution of these receptors varies among cell types. Chemokine receptors CXCR-4 and CCR-5 are expressed on activated T cells and macrophages. However, the latter is not highly expressed on quiescent cells. The microglia cells, thought to be the main target for HIV-1 in the brain, express both CCR-3 and CCR-5 receptors. It appears that in infected individuals there is a gradual and consistent pattern of change of co-receptor usage by viral isolates over time. This may represent genetic changes in the viral envelope. In early stages of infection, viral isolates predominantly use the CCR-5 receptor, consistent with previous observations that M-tropic viruses are the predominant strain transmitted. Over time, viral isolates acquire the ability to use CXCR-4 or an alternate receptor. This switch to what had been previously classified as syncytia-inducing isolates has been associated with rapid disease progression.

These discoveries not only shed light on the cell specificity of certain viral isolates but also formed the basis of new work in genetic determinants of infectivity and in therapeutics. After the discovery of HIV-1 co-receptors, it was determined that genetic modifications of the receptors may influence the rate of infection or disease progression. Analysis of the CXCR-4 receptor genetic status failed to find any genetic abnormality that correlated with protection. However, it was found that certain individuals contain a deletion of 32 nucleotides in the CCR-5 receptor. The loss of part of the gene results in the premature termination of the CCR-5 protein. Because of the presence of a truncated receptor, lymphocytes from individuals carrying this mutation in both alleles (homozygous) are not infectable with viral isolates that utilize this receptor or M-tropic isolates. Moreover, individuals who are homozygous for this deletion have extremely low rates of HIV-1, due to the fact that M-tropic viruses depending on this receptor for entry are the most commonly transmitted viruses. Interestingly, the protection appears to be independent of the route of infection, that is, whether the HIV-1-infected or -exposed individuals are hemophiliacs, drug users, or homosexuals.

Recently, however, a few cases of individuals homozygous for the CCR-5 deletion have been found to be infected with HIV-1. This suggests infection with T-tropic strains of HIV-1 whose route of infection is CCR-5 independent. Unfortunately, only a very small percentage of the population carries the mutation in both alleles. The frequency of this mutation appears to be restricted to certain genetically related populations, with the highest incidence in northern Europe. However, heterozygous carriers of the CCR-5 mutation are present with a much higher incidence (up to 20%). These individuals, although they do not appear to be protected from infection, experience a significant delay in the development of the disease (up to 3 years). The presence of only one allele mutated in the CCR-5 gene would partially protect against disease progression when patients are infected with M-tropic strains of HIV-1, that is, at the beginning of the disease. Different cytopathic T-tropic strains of HIV-1 continue to evolve. Co-receptor usage may therefore change from CCR-5 to CXCR-4, with loss of the protective effect of the CCR-5 mutation.

Recently, mutations in a related chemokine receptor, CCR-2b, have been described. This receptor is also used by certain strains of HIV-1 to gain entry into the target cell. Although homozygous carriers of the mutation in the CCR-2b gene have no protection from infection, they experience a significant delay in progression of disease once infected, with a delay of the onset of AIDS by 2–4 years. This result awaits further confirmation.

Because HIV-1 needs a chemokine co-receptor to gain entrance into the target cell, natural chemokines, or modified versions of the normally occurring chemokines, are being developed to block HIV-1 replication. For example, a chemically modified version of RANTES has shown very encouraging results in vitro. However, such chemokine antagonists would have inhibitory effects only against the viral strains that use the corresponding receptor for entry. Along with the potent antiviral effects of RANTES, several members of the chemokine family have been found to have some effect on HIV-1 replication, in-cluding MIP 1-α and MIP 1-β. A chemokinelike molecule produced by the human herpes virus 8 (HHV-8) was found to completely block HIV-1 replication of both T-tropic and M-tropic strains.

New therapies. Another major advance has been the discovery of the potent anti-HIV-1 activity of a class of agents called protease inhibitors. The protease is a viral enzyme essential for the processing of the polyprotein precursor containing structural genes (for example, GAG) and the viral enzymes protease, reverse transcriptase, and integrase. It has been demonstrated that a pharmacological approach aimed at interfering with this protein blocks HIV-1 replication. Clinical trials have demonstrated that therapeutic regimens containing a protease inhibitor not only markedly decrease HIV-1 ribonucleic acid (RNA) detected in the plasma of patients but also increase patient survival.

Until 1995, the only class of drugs available to HIV-1-infected patients targeted reverse transcriptase. Included were the nucleoside analogs Zidovudine, Didanosine, Lamivudine, Zalcitabine, and Stavudine, and the nonnucleoside inhibitor Nevirapine. Clearly, therapy with these reverse transcriptase inhibitors, particularly in combination, inhibited HIV-1 replication and improved patient survival. However, it is now evident that the very high in vivo mutation rate of the virus and the functional integrity of the resulting reverse transcriptase protein have resulted in the rapid appearance of resistant viruses in treated individuals. New regimens, combining a protease inhibitor with reverse transcriptase inhibitors, have offered the best clinical response to date. In the majority of patients experiencing these three-drug regimens, HIV-1 replication is reduced to nondetectable levels in plasma, accompanied by increasing CD4+ T cells and improvement in survival. Additionally, prompt combination therapy decreases the emergence of resistant viral variants. These optimistic results have led to discussions regarding the theoretical possibility of eradicating the virus from patients.

However, several barriers remain to achieving a cure. Similar to what was observed with reverse transcriptase inhibitors, mutations in the active site of the protease, resulting in diminished binding of the inhibitor or in a better activity of the protease, reduce the efficacy of antiprotease drugs. Indeed, a number of mutations in the protease gene have been associated with the diminished activity of the drug both in vitro and in vivo. In addition, mutations arising in the presence of one protease inhibitor may result in resistance to other protease inhibitors. Although the combined strategy of attacking the virus on two fronts, the reverse transcriptase and the protease enzymes, seems to keep the virus under detectable levels, there is always the possibility of viral rebound during the course of the therapy. Causal factors include lack of patient compliance with the difficult drug regimen, and persistence of viral replication at sites that are not easily reached by the drugs. For this reason, discovery of new and more effective drugs and strategies to halt the course of the disease continues to be imperative.

Mary E. Klotman; Andrea Cara

Bibliography. F. Cocchi et al., Identification of RANTES, MIP-1 alpha, and MIP-1 beta as the major HIV-suppressive factors produced by CD8+ T cells, *Science*, 270:1811–1815, 1995; R. W. Doms and S. C. Peiper, Unwelcomed guests with master keys: How HIV uses chemokine receptors for cellular entry, *Virology*, 235:179–190, 1997; S. J. O'Brian and M. Dean, In search of the AIDS-resistance gene, *Sci. Amer.*, 9:44–51, 1997.

Adaptive optics

Adaptive optics is a new technique to greatly enhance the resolution of an image. Imaging with adaptive optics systems is becoming common at large astronomical and military telescopes. A modern telescope is the most powerful tool for imaging distant objects at high resolution. The reason is that it can collect light over a large aperture (which is usually a curved mirror several meters in diameter) and can theoretically focus that light into a sharp image. A large-diameter mirror is significantly superior to a small one, since the exposure time is proportional to the inverse square of the diameter. Therefore, a mirror 1 m (40 in.) in diameter will detect a faint object in an 8-h exposure, but an 8-m (320-in.) telescope is 64 times greater in area and will thus image the same object in only 7.5 min. Unfortunately, telescopes of all sizes are limited to blurry images because of the Earth's turbulent atmosphere.

Atmospheric limits on imaging. Even though a large telescope can produce images much faster than a small telescope, there is little difference in the resolution (or sharpness) of the final images produced. Theoretically this should not be the case, since the diffraction of light allows a large telescope to produce a final image that is linearly sharper than a small telescope. However, small random changes in temperature in the Earth's atmosphere create turbulent convective cells, each of which has a different size and temperature. Since the air's index of refraction depends linearly on the air temperature, the resulting set of air cells of various sizes acts as a myriad of little lenses to distort the incoming wavefront from space (**Fig. 1**). To the unaided eye, these small distortions create the twinkle of stars at night because of the mixing of hot and cold air.

Another example of how convectively turbulent air distorts wavefronts is the blurring of air above a highway on a hot day. This blurring can make it difficult to see oncoming cars in the distance. Such atmospheric distortions limit all ground-based telescopes (even at mountaintop sites) to blurry images of approximately 1 arcsecond (1″.0) in angular size. (An arcsecond is 1/3600 of a degree, and corresponds roughly to the angle subtended by a thumbnail at a distance of about 3.2 km (2 mi). This atmospheric blurring, referred to as "seeing" by astronomers, is

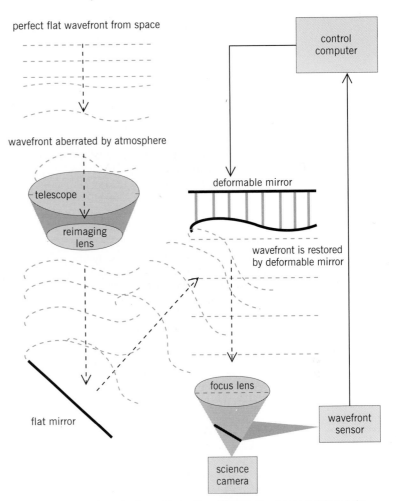

perfect flat wavefront from space

wavefront aberrated by atmosphere

telescope

reimaging lens

flat mirror

control computer

deformable mirror

wavefront is restored by deformable mirror

focus lens

wavefront sensor

science camera

Fig. 1. Schematic of an adaptive optics system. The wavefront sensor deforms the mirror to restore the original wavefront for the science camera. Diagram is not to scale.

one of the greatest limits to a large telescope in achieving optimal performance. Theoretically, a well-made (diffraction-limited) telescope should make an image of a "point-like object" (such as a star) with a diffraction-limited FWHM (full width of the star's image at half of its maximum intensity; **Fig. 2**) equal to the wavelength divided by the diameter of the telescope. Therefore, a 4-m (160-in.) telescope should be able to resolve an object just 0″.03 in size at the wavelength of yellow light (0.55 micrometer). However, seeing limits 4-m (160-in.) telescopes to resolutions of approximately 1″, which is 33 times worse than what should be possible. This loss of resolution severely limits the amount of information in astronomical images. Similar turbulent blurring occurs when spy satellites look down into the atmosphere, or when thermal blooming from the intense heat of high-energy lasers warps their beams and reduces their efficiency.

Avoiding these optical distortions from the atmosphere was the main motivation for the Hubble Space Telescope. The advantage of the Hubble Space Telescope over larger, 4- to 8-m (160- to 320-in.) ground-based telescopes is that it is above the Earth's atmosphere and so can achieve theoretical diffrac-

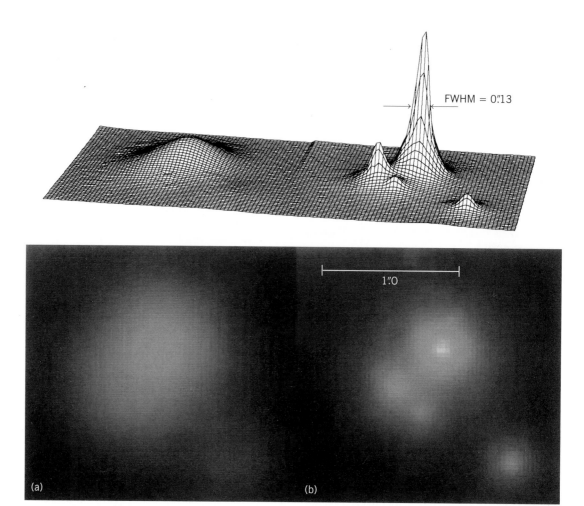

Fig. 2. Example of image improvement possible with adaptive optics. (a) Faint group of young stars imaged in the infrared by the Canada-France-Hawaii telescope. (b) Same stars imaged with the aid of an adaptive optics system using curvature sensing. Charts above photographs plot image intensity as a function of position.

tion-limited performances. The disadvantages of the Hubble are that it is a small, 2.4-m (94-in.) telescope, is heavily oversubscribed, and is very expensive to operate. Another strategy to avoid atmospheric distortions is to use the large number of existing 4- to 8-m (160- to 320-in.) telescopes but correct the images for atmospheric blurring at the telescope to restore sharp diffraction-limited images.

Technique. An adaptive optics system senses and corrects the aberrated wavefront in real time as it enters the telescope. In other words, an adaptive optics system is analogous to a pair of smart glasses placed on the telescope which can automatically change prescription to make sure the image is perfect. To do this, an adaptive optics system divides the telescope aperture into 10–300 subapertures. The subaperture size is roughly the largest area of aberrated wavefront that is "flat" or coherent at the wavelength of the science camera. This coherent patch size is commonly called r_0. The adaptive optics system then must sense the local wavefront at the position of each subaperture and use a similar number of actuators ("electronic fingers") to warp the surface of a deformable ("rubber") mirror so all the

coherent, r_0-sized patches come together as one large coherent (flat) beam across the whole aperture (Fig. 1). Although simple in concept, in practice adaptive optics systems are some of the most complex optomechanical devices ever constructed.

Part of the complexity comes from the large number of elements required. In Kolmogorov turbulence, the size of r_0 varies as the wavelength to the 6/5 power. Hence, visible wavelengths (approximately 0.55 μm) have r_0 equal to 18 cm (7 in.) at a good site, but longer infrared wavelengths have larger values of r_0 (approximately 100 cm or 40 in. at 2.2 μm)— which means the wavefront is much flatter to start with at infrared wavelengths. Thus 390 subapertures are required to correct at 0.55 μm at a 4-m (160-in.) telescope but only 12 to correct much redder (infrared) light at 2.2 μm.

The aberrated wavefront requires a very fast measurement, since it must be completed before the wavefront changes. The frequency at which the wavefront evolves (often called the Greenwood frequency) is roughly r_0 divided by the wind velocity and is found to be close to 40–100 Hz. To freeze out these aberrations requires adaptive optics systems to sample and correct a wavefront every 2.5–1.0 ms, placing harsh limits on any phase lag ("delay") in the servoloop.

Two techniques are widely used to measure the wavefront. The first wavefront sensor was the Hartmann sensor, developed simultaneously by the military and by astronomers in the 1980s. A Hartmann sensor images the light from each subaperture onto four pixels of a low-read-noise charge-coupled-device (CCD) imager (an advanced video camera). The positions of each of the spots imaged by the charge-coupled device imply the local wavefront slopes, from which the entire instantaneous wavefront can be reconstructed. Unfortunately, this technique requires a bright reference star (a guide star) to be near the science target, but has the advantage that hundreds of actuators can be used, enabling adaptive optics correction at visible wavelengths. Since sufficiently bright guide stars are rare in the sky, it is advantageous to make an artificial guide star by shining a tuned laser into the sky. Such a laser guide star is created as the laser light scatters off sodium ions in the high upper atmosphere at 90 km (55 mi). Although very complex, these laser-guide-star adaptive optics systems are close to becoming operational for general imaging.

The second technique is curvature sensing, where a map of the curvature of the wavefront is made by subtracting two out-of-focus pupil images. The advantage of this sensing technique is that it is a differential measurement, where all the light from each subaperture is piped to an individual, highly sensitive (zero-read-noise) avalanche photodiode. These avalanche photodiodes permit very faint guide stars to be used, allowing for the correction of common scientific targets without the need for laser guide stars. Curvature systems have the disadvantage of being more difficult to scale to more than 100 actuators, and so operate mainly at near-infrared wavelengths.

Figure 2 shows an example of the image improvement possible with an adaptive optics curvature system. Figure 2a shows a faint group of young stars imaged in the infrared at a wavelength of 1.65 μm at the 3.6-m (144-in.) Canada-France-Hawaii telescope. The stars have a seeing-limited FWHM resolution of approximately 0″.65 in this long, 15-min exposure. For Fig. 2b, the curvature system utilizes a brighter star located 7″.0 away (not shown) as a guide star to sample and correct the atmospherically induced aberrations at 1300 Hz. Thus the science camera is allowed to take another 15-min image but with five times the resolution (FWHM = 0″.13). This improved resolution allows several new stars to be detected for the first time.

Once the wavefront sensor has integrated for approximately 1 ms, the wavefronts at the N subapertures are read out and an $N \times N$ control matrix is used by the real-time control computer to calculate the N voltages to be applied to the deformable mirror to flatten the wavefront (Fig. 1). Once past the deformable mirror, all the photons that are to be used for imaging with the science camera are directed there, and the rest of the photons are sent to the wavefront sensor. Since atmospheric wavefront aberrations are achromatic (independent of color), it is often convenient to use all the visible photons for wavefront sensing and all the infrared light for imaging with the science camera.

New discoveries and capabilities. After intense development in the late 1980s and early 1990s, approximately 10 adaptive optics systems are in operation around the world. It is now common for diffraction-limited 0″.1 images to be obtained in the infrared with 4-m (160-in.) telescopes (Fig. 2). This resolution is a tenfold improvement over that of non-adaptive-optics images and equal to that of the Hubble Space Telescope, at a fraction of the cost. Significant new science is being carried out with adaptive optics systems. Almost all fields of astronomy benefit from the higher resolution (and better contrast) achieved with adaptive optics. Adaptive optics has made the highest-resolution images of dusty disks forming new solar systems, images of new volcanoes on Jupiter's satellite Io, images of the center of the Milky Way Galaxy, and images of the very faint host galaxies around quasars at the edge of the observable universe. These are just a few examples of the new images that current and future adaptive optics systems can produce.

For background information *see* ADAPTIVE OPTICS; OPTICAL TELESCOPE; SATELLITE ASTRONOMY; TURBULENT FLOW; TWINKLING STARS in the McGraw-Hill Encyclopedia of Science & Technology.   Laird M. Close

Bibliography. J. M. Beckers, Adaptive optics for astronomy: Principles, performance, and applications, *Annu. Rev. Astron. Astrophys.*, 31:13–62, 1993; L. M. Close et al., Adaptive optics 0″.2 resolution infrared images of HL Tauri: Direct images of an active accretion disk around a protostar, *Astrophys. J.*, 478:766–777, 1997; F. Roddier et al., A simple low-order adaptive optics system for near-infrared applications, *Pub. Astron. Soc. Pacific*, 103:131–149, 1991.

Aerodynamic decelerators

Aerodynamic decelerators are devices that are designed to produce drag and are made from textiles (as opposed to mechanical drag devices such as spoilers). The first parachute jump was in approximately 1785 and the first free-fall parachute jump, in 1919. The technology of aerodynamic decelerators is fairly mature. As with many aerospace systems, new applications require constant incremental improvement in performance and reduction in weight and volume.

Types. The most common type of aerodynamic decelerator is the traditional parachute. According to one authority, there are 29 distinct parachute types. Parachutes have evolved from the original flat, round, solid-cloth canopy. Symmetrical or asymmetrical slots can be added to a parachute canopy to change canopy characteristics. Symmetrical slots

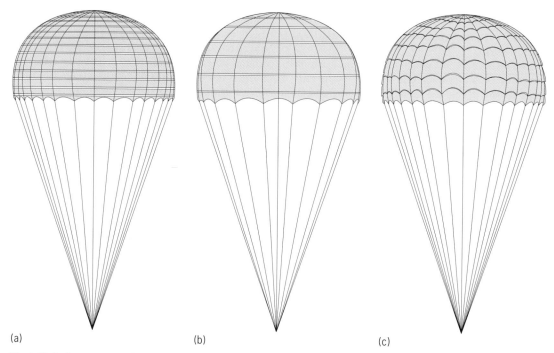

Fig. 1. Slotted-canopy parachutes. (*a*) Ribbon parachute. (*b*) Ring-slot parachute. (*c*) Ring-sail parachute. *(After Recovery Systems Design Guide, Irvin Industries Inc., Air Force Flight Dynamics Laboratory Tech. Rep. AFFDL-TR-78-151, 1978)*

add stability by reducing the coning angle of the parachute. The coning angle is the angle through which the parachute appears to oscillate from side to side. Actually, the canopy is rotating around its vertical axis along the surface of a cone with the vertex at the payload attachment point. The apparent side-to-side swing in the early troop parachutes used in World War II is a classic case of a large coning angle.

The most common types of parachutes with symmetrical slots are ribbon, ring-slot, or ring-sail parachutes. A ribbon parachute (**Fig. 1***a*) is constructed by using many ribbons, usually 2-in.-wide (5-cm) nylon, arranged in concentric circles from the center (vent) of the parachute to the skirt (lower extremity of the parachute). Between the ribbons are slots which add stability. Similarly, a ring-slot parachute (Fig. 1*b*) is constructed from rings of cloth with slots between rings. However, for a given size, a ribbon parachute would have perhaps 40 ribbons and slots and a ring-slot would have 10 rings and slots. A ring-sail (Fig. 1*c*) is similar to a ring-slot, but the lower rings have added fullness (extra cloth) along the leading edge. The sail formed thereby channels more air into the canopy and helps open the canopy mouth wider, creating more drag. The *Apollo* capsule recovery parachutes were ring-sail.

Asymmetrical slots or vents are used to provide a glide ratio (the ratio of horizontal distance traveled to the vertical distance descended) of approximately 1.1 to 1 in a round canopy. A parafoil parachute is a ram-air-inflated, square canopy, as often used by sport parachutists. Such chutes have a glide ratio of up to 4 to 1.

Applications. The landing deceleration parachute has been used on many aircraft. Ribbon parachutes were developed during World War II as durable, stable, high-speed aircraft landing decelerators. This type of parachute is currently used on F-16 fighter aircraft. The ring-slot parachute was developed to have the stability of the ribbon parachute with a lower manufacturing cost. The Euro-Fighter uses a ring-slot parachute made entirely from a synthetic fiber material notable for its tensile strength and toughness (aramid). With the emergence of thrust reversers on modern combat aircraft, parachute use will be greatly reduced. There is still a demand for landing deceleration for the space shuttle orbiter and future orbital vehicles that will return to Earth for runway landings.

A little-known use for aerodynamic decelerators is in low-level bombing from aircraft. Ballutes (ram-air-inflated tension shells; **Fig. 2**) are used as attached inflatable decelerators on 500-, 1000-, and 2000-lb (225-, 450-, and 900-kg) nonguided bombs during low-level delivery. A ballute provides high drag at a lower cost than a mechanical, high-drag bomb tail unit. High-drag bombs are required for low-level release to provide adequate separation between the aircraft and the blast.

Technology development. Applications for parachutes constantly require advancement of design and packaging. Many current systems have been in use (with minor upgrades) since the 1950s. Recent

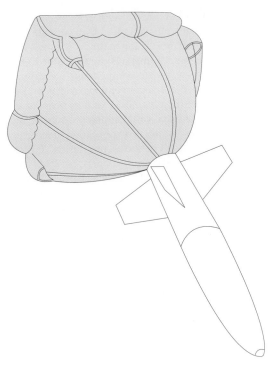

Fig. 2. Ballute attached to a nonguided bomb.

Large payload recovery. The largest-drag-area three-parachute cluster ever used to recover a payload was demonstrated in 1996. Three ring-sail parachutes with nominal diameters of 136 ft (41 m) were used to recover a 20,000-lb (9000-kg) liquid-fueled rocket-propulsion module. Work is under way on a system to recover the 40,000-lb (18,000-kg) first stage and 28,000-lb (12,700-kg) upper stage of the reusable Kistler K-1 launch vehicle. This system will utilize nine (six for the first stage and three for the upper stage) ring-sail parachutes, 156 ft (48 m) in diameter, and textile airbags that attenuate the landing impact. Modern materials will minimize weight and volume. This recovery system will be the largest developed so far.

Sustained supersonic deceleration. The upper stage of the Kistler K-1 vehicle will utilize a hemisflo parachute 23 ft (7 m) in diameter. Hemisflo parachutes are designed for supersonic deployment. This use will be unique in that the parachute will be supersonic for 20–30 s. (Supersonic payloads are usually slowed to subsonic velocities very rapidly.) This long super-

years have seen refinement to provide more stability and drag in harsher environments with less cost, weight, and volume.

Paratroop parachutes. The T-10 parachute (**Fig. 3**), developed in the 1950s, is still the predominant parachute for airborne troop insertion. The U.S. Army's Advanced Tactical Parachute program aims to reduce the descent rate of the paratrooper and allow for higher-velocity, lower-altitude drops to minimize aircraft exposure to enemy fire.

Extraterrestrial landing. The 1997 *Pathfinder* mission to Mars utilized a parachute to decelerate the landing vehicle in the Martian atmosphere. This system started with the design used on the *Viking* landers. It incorporates modern materials (an aramid structural grid with nylon cloth panels) to reduce weight and volume. Extensive research and testing refined the stability and effective drag area of the parachute under the actual conditions of Martian atmospheric pressure and chemical composition specific to the *Pathfinder* mission. The result was an advanced parachute design that was very successful during the *Pathfinder* mission and may be used on future extraterrestrial missions. *See* MARS.

Guided payload drops. Several programs have been devoted to the development of autonomously guided payloads that utilize a high-lift parafoil parachute and a control system based on the Global Positioning System to allow the pinpoint delivery of supplies. The only technical trade-off for these systems is between the need for high-precision delivery and the loss of payload due to the weight of the control system.

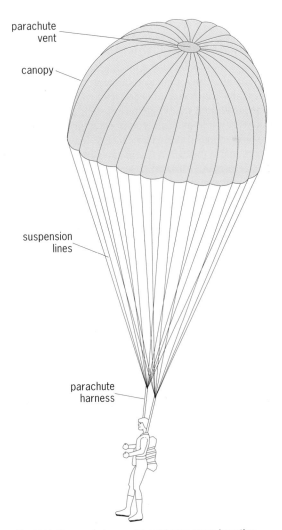

Fig. 3. T-10 parachute, used for airborne troop insertion.

sonic exposure will require high-temperature materials for the entire structure.

Aircraft spin/stall recovery. Parachute systems designed to enable aircraft to recover from spin and stall have been used on high-performance military aircraft for many years. The use of mortar-deployed parachutes in certification programs for small civil aircraft is growing. With a stall-recovery or high-speed aerobrake parachute installed on a new aircraft, its certification time can be reduced by allowing more aggressive flight-test planning. The emphasis in designing these systems is to make them as small and light as possible. These systems are installed at the aft end of the aircraft (potentially causing center-of-gravity problems) and within the fuselage mold line (requiring compact dimensions). Great efforts are being made to develop the parachute mortar, the attach-release mechanism, and the control panel as an integrated system. In the past, customers would order a parachute mortar and develop their own control system, a procedure that led to potentially dangerous system designs.

Missile test recovery. Parachutes are used extensively to recover sophisticated missiles during the flight-test phase. Modern missiles are too valuable to expend during early development testing. Missile recovery systems are challenging because the vehicle is not designed to be recovered. The parachute generally must fit in the space allocated for the warhead. Many of these vehicles are too fragile to be dropped to Earth at any practical descent rate. The air-launched cruise missile is one such vehicle. It uses a sophisticated dual-parachute system for airborne recovery by a specially equipped helicopter. This system contains five (pilot, drogue, main, engagement, and stabilization) parachutes that are packed to a density of 52 lb/ft^3 (830 kg/m^3). A self-contained unit with the pyrotechnic thrusters to initiate deployment preinstalled, it is a perfect example of a parachute system taken to the extreme in performance and packaging.

For background information *see* MISSILE; PARACHUTE in the McGraw-Hill Encyclopedia of Science & Technology.   David Reinhard

Bibliography. P. Delurgio et al., *Recovery System for the Evolved Expendable Launch Vehicle*, AIAA Pap. 97-1513, 1997; T. W. Knacke, *Parachute Recovery Systems Design Manual*, 1992.

Aerospike engine

The aerospike engine (**Fig. 1***a*) is an advanced liquid-propellant rocket engine with unique operating characteristics and performance advantages over conventional rocket engines. It combines a contoured axisymmetric plug nozzle (**Fig. 2**), an annular torus-shaped combustion chamber, conventional turbopumps, a turbine exhaust system that injects the turbine drive gases into the base of the plug nozzle, and a simple combustion tap-off engine cycle. The aerospike is one-quarter the length of a conventional rocket engine, yet it delivers comparable performance (efficiency) at high altitude and superior performance at low altitude. The low-altitude performance advantage is primarily due to the fact that the plug nozzle compensates for altitude whereas the nozzle of a conventional rocket engine does not. While the plug nozzle and its benefits are not new to the field of air-breathing propulsion, the aerospike represents the first application of this type of nozzle to the field of rocket propulsion. Typical propellants are liquid hydrogen (fuel) and liquid oxygen (oxidizer). A variation of the aerospike engine is the linear aerospike engine.

Altitude compensation. For a given set of operating conditions in the combustion chamber (pressure, temperature, and mass-flow rate) and ambient pressure, the thrust of a rocket engine is governed by the nozzle exit area, or the nozzle area ratio if the exit area is divided by the nozzle throat area. When the nozzle area ratio is specified such that the pressure at the nozzle exit is equal to ambient pressure, the flow through the nozzle is optimally expanded and the engine is operating at its maximum efficiency. This is the nozzle design point.

When the area ratio is too large, the nozzle exit pressure is lower than ambient pressure and the flow through the nozzle is overexpanded. This situation is accompanied by a decrease in thrust (efficiency). More thrust could be produced if the area ratio of the nozzle were reduced, yielding a higher exit pressure. When the area ratio is too small, the nozzle exit pressure is greater than ambient pressure and the nozzle is underexpanded. Again, thrust is reduced relative to the optimally expanded condition. Under this condition, a nozzle with a higher area ratio would produce more thrust.

Because rocket engines are required to operate over a range of ambient pressure, or altitude, and because engine efficiency is greatest at only a single altitude, selection of the nozzle area ratio (that is, the nozzle design point) for a particular application introduces a compromise. Operation at high altitude where ambient pressure is lower calls for a high area ratio to extract maximum thrust from the high-pressure, hot combustion gases, while a lower area ratio is better during low-altitude operation to avoid the reduction in thrust caused by overexpansion. Typically, the selected area ratio falls between these two limits.

Of course, if the geometry of the nozzle were not fixed, and area ratio were allowed to increase with increasing altitude, optimum performance would be obtained from the rocket engine throughout the entire flight trajectory, resulting in dramatic gains in overall vehicle performance. Since the nozzle area ratio is dependent on the nozzle exit area, changes in area ratio could be effected by simply varying nozzle exit area. This effect is referred to as altitude compensation.

Comparison with conventional engines. In a very general sense, the aerospike engine is similar to a conventional liquid-propellant rocket engine. In both

Fig. 1. Static firing tests of (a) aerospike engine with 250,000 pounds (1,112,000 newtons) of thrust, and (b) linear aerospike engine with 125,000 pounds (556,000 newtons) of thrust. Both engines use hydrogen/oxygen propellants. *(Boeing Company, Rocketdyne Division)*

cases, turbopumps are used to pressurize liquid propellants. These high-pressure propellants are then injected into a combustion chamber, where they rapidly mix and chemically react to form high-temperature, high-pressure combustion gases. Finally, these hot gases are accelerated to high velocities by expanding them through a nozzle to produce thrust.

In more specific terms, however, several key differences distinguish the aerospike engine from the conventional rocket engine. The most striking difference is the nozzle. The conventional rocket engine uses a converging-diverging nozzle, sometimes referred to as a bell nozzle owing to its shape. The hot combustion gases expand inside the nozzle in the general direction of the nozzle axis, completely contained by the nozzle wall (**Fig. 3***a*). Because the wall of a conventional nozzle forms a physical boundary between the expanding combustion gases and the surrounding atmosphere, the expansion process in the nozzle is isolated from the effect of ambient pressure. Consequently, the combustion gases will not necessarily be optimally expanded, but will be under- or overexpanded depending upon the ambient pressure.

The aerospike engine features a plug nozzle that is characterized by the combustion gases expanding on the outside of the nozzle (Fig. 3*b*). Initially, the gas flow is directed radially inward, toward the axis or center of the nozzle. The expansion process occurs about the engine cowling, controlled by the plug wall on the inside and the effect of ambient pressure on the outer jet boundary. Because the amount of expansion is controlled by ambient pressure, the aerospike engine has the ability to altitude-compensate in the absence of variable nozzle geometry. Variations in area ratio are achieved automatically by the influence of ambient pressure acting on the jet boundary, causing the effective flow area at the nozzle exit to change with altitude. Thus, ambient pressure effectively provides passive control of the expansion process in the aerospike engine, pre-

venting both under- and overexpansion and the associated loss in performance.

The plug nozzle of the aerospike engine is obtained by truncating a full-length spike nozzle. Since the amount of thrust produced by the spike nozzle drops off very rapidly toward the aft end, a significant portion of the spike nozzle can be eliminated without undue loss in thrust. By injecting the turbine drive gases into the resulting base (Fig. 2), an aerodynamic spike (thus the name aerospike) is formed.

In the combustion tap-off cycle, the turbine that powers the pumps is driven by a small amount of hot gases that are tapped from the combustion chamber. This procedure eliminates the need for an additional gas generator. Once expanded through the turbine, the gases are exhausted into the blunt base of the plug nozzle, increasing the base pressure, thrust, and overall engine efficiency. This arrangement contrasts

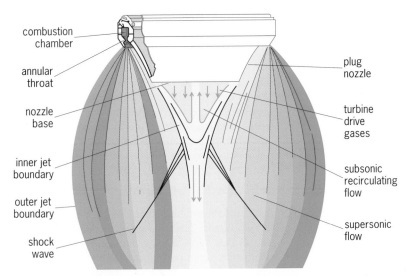

Fig. 2. Aerospike engine with plug nozzle, torus-shaped combustion chamber, and combustion gases expanding outside the nozzle. *(Boeing Company, Rocketdyne Division)*

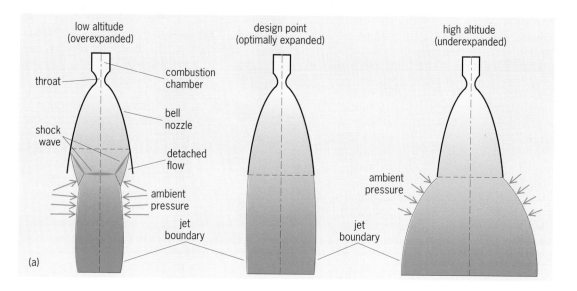

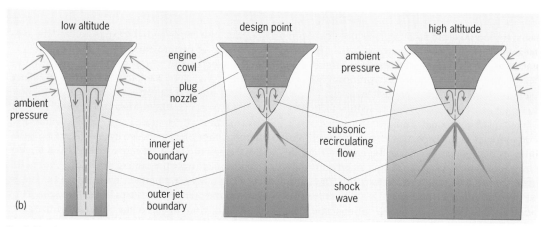

Fig. 3. Nozzle flow comparison. (a) Conventional rocket engine (bell nozzle). (b) Aerospike engine (plug nozzle). (*After R. A. O'Leary and J. E. Beck, Nozzle design, Threshold no. 8, pp. 34–43. Rockwell International Corporation, Rocketdyne Division, Spring 1992*)

with that of a conventional rocket engine, where the turbine drive gases are usually ejected through a small secondary nozzle to produce additional thrust.

To match the unique shape of the plug nozzle, the shape of the combustion chamber and the arrangement of the injectors into the aerospike engine are very different from those of the conventional rocket engine. In the conventional engine the combustion chamber is typically cylindrical and the injectors are arranged in the circular forward end of the chamber. In the aerospike engine the combustion chamber is torus shaped (Fig. 2) and the injectors are arranged in an annular pattern.

Advantages. The aerospike engine offers performance, operational, and configurational advantages over the conventional rocket engine equipped with a bell nozzle. First, altitude compensation yields higher performance at low altitude while producing comparable high performance at high altitude. Second, for the same thrust the aerospike is considerably shorter, by as much as 75%. This allows for a shorter-length, lighter-weight vehicle or, for the same-length vehicle, greater volume for higher-capacity propellant tanks or payload. For reusable winged or lifting-body vehicles, the short length moves the center of gravity forward, improving flight characteristics. Third, the altitude-compensating feature of the plug nozzle permits the safe operation of a nozzle with high area ratio at low altitude (sea level) without undesirable flow detachment in the nozzle (Fig. 3a) and the accompanying asymmetric lateral forces, or side loads, on the nozzle. Fourth, the aerospike integrates well into the base of a conventional cylindrical launch vehicle with high aspect ratio, reducing vehicle base drag and eliminating the need for a base heat shield, since the engine fills the entire base. Finally, the thrust load of the aerospike is distributed at the maximum diameter of the engine instead of concentrated at a single point (the gimbal), eliminating the need for a heavy thrust structure to distribute the load through the vehicle, and resulting in a lighter vehicle.

Linear aerospike. A variation is the linear aerospike engine (Fig. 1b). This rocket engine concept offers the same performance advantages as the annular aerospike while offering some unique configurational advantages owing to its linear shape. The combustion chamber is made up of a series of modular chamber segments, and the gas generator engine cycle is used in place of the combustion tap-off cycle.

Advanced launch vehicles. During the 1990s, interest has been renewed in single-stage-to-orbit reusable launch vehicles. Numerous studies have shown that reduced launch costs will be best achieved through the development of a fully reusable single-stage-to-orbit vehicle.

Unlike multistage launch vehicles that depend upon one rocket propulsion system for boost and others for high-altitude operation, future single-stage-to-orbit vehicles will be dependent on a single rocket propulsion system from boost to orbit insertion. While each rocket engine of a multistage vehicle can be individually tailored (for example, the nozzle area ratio) to meet the requirements of its portion of the trajectory, rocket engines for single-stage-to-orbit vehicles must provide high performance over the entire flight trajectory. Thus, advanced rocket propulsion technologies that further increase the performance of liquid-propellant rocket engines will be required. The aerospike engine is one of these advanced propulsion concepts.

For background information *see* NOZZLE; ROCKET PROPULSION; SPACECRAFT PROPULSION in the McGraw-Hill Encyclopedia of Science & Technology.

James E. Beck

Bibliography. R. I. Baumgartner and J. D. Elvin, *Lifting Body: An Innovative RLV Concept*, AIAA Pap. 95-3531, 1995; T. K. Mattingly, A simple ride into space, *Sci. Amer.*, 277(4):120–125, October 1997; I. Parker and F. Colucci, Inside-out engine, *Space*, 8(4):38–40, August–September 1992; G. P. Sutton, *Rocket Propulsion Elements*, 6th ed., 1986.

Agricultural science (plant)

Beans, corn, rice, and other grains are excellent foods for insects. Stored-grain insects, such as weevils and moths, destroy billions of dollars of grain each year throughout the world. Moreover, foods prepared with insect-contaminated grain can have unpleasant flavors, be unhygienic, or even be inedible. On subsistence farms in Africa, weevily grain may be fed to the chickens or goats in the hope of rescuing a little value from it. Insect-damaged grain germinates less well and is more subject to disease.

Traditional control of stored-grain insects. Inventiveness in protecting stored grain from insects has a long history. The ancient Celts sometimes kept grain in deep, clay-lined pits. Under these conditions, oxygen levels in the store fell low enough to prevent the insects from growing and reproducing. A modern version of the low-oxygen principle is storage of harvested grain in sealed containers. Respiration, by the grain and any insects already present, depletes the oxygen, limiting insect population growth. Low-

resource farmers in Africa sometimes store their grain mixed with ash from the cooking fires. The ash is a barrier to insect movement, retarding further infestation. Fine sand is sometimes used instead. Storing unthreshed grain is a common practice; the intact pod or husk serves as a barrier to the insect, limiting the infestation. In the developing world, botanicals or botanical products such as peanut oil are often mixed with the grain because they repel or kill the insects. In recent years, solar heating has been used to disinfest grain stores, taking advantage of the intolerance of insects to high temperatures. Modern insecticides, many of which are synthetic derivatives of botanical products, and fumigants are lethal to the insects. However, people must know how to use them safely, have access to the synthetic chemicals, have the necessary equipment for their use, and above all, have the means to buy them. For much of the world, these conditions are not met. Moreover, it was belatedly discovered that the most commonly used fumigant, methyl bromide, damages the ozone layer, so it is being phased out. It has become clear that alternatives to insecticides and the other technologies are needed.

Breeding for stored-grain resistance. Plant breeding can produce crop cultivars whose seeds resist storage insects. For example, there are lines of cowpea (black-eyed pea) which strongly resist attack by the cowpea bruchid. Stored-grain insects are actually excellent targets for selective plant breeding because it is not necessary to kill the insects to control them. When grain is first put into storage, it usually has a light infestation, often not enough to detect easily. However, the insects develop and reproduce rapidly, so the problem becomes apparent and rapidly worsens.

The cowpea bruchid serves as a good example. Under tropical conditions, a single newly mated female produces about 20 adult female offspring within approximately 3 weeks. If grain is abundant, after another 3 weeks each of these in turn produces about 20 female offspring. As reproduction continues, the female population reaches 8000, then 160,000 insects (as of week 12). However, if plant breeding results in a grain that is suboptimal for the insects (say, it provides poor nutrition), the outcome may be that one-half of the females die before reproducing; the time it takes larvae to reach adulthood doubles; and the reproductive capacity of the adult female is reduced by half. Under these conditions, a single female takes 6 weeks to produce a total of 10 female offspring; as reproduction continues, the total population is only 100 insects by week 12.

It would be ideal if stored grain could be made insect resistant through conventional plant breeding. However, any given crop species contains few, if any, resistance genes against the stored-grain pests of the crop. Appropriate plant breeding is virtually impossible without resistance genes.

Biotechnology for plant transformation. A given plant species cannot be crossed with just any other plant species because there are physical, biochemical, physiological, and cellular barriers. It would be easier to develop resistance genes in a grain crop species if these incompatibilities did not exist. The species barrier was first breached in plants in 1984, when a selected single gene was moved from one plant species to another; it was proved that the transferred gene had been stably incorporated into the chromosomes of the recipient species and the gene was expressed. In the years since, dozens of different plant species have been stably transformed with foreign genes.

Gene selection. If genetic transformation is to be used to introduce needed insect resistance into a crop species, the specific gene must be selected. Most popular has been the gene encoding *Bacillus thuringiensis* endotoxin, a protein highly toxic to certain insect species, including many pests, and practically nontoxic to most other kinds of organisms. However, the first successful transformation of a plant species to introduce resistance to stored-grain pests involved a different gene. Scientists had long known that cowpea bruchid larvae thrive on cowpea seeds but die when they feed on common beans. Eventually the factor responsible for cowpea bruchid resistance was traced to alpha-amylase inhibitor, a protein that occurs in bean seeds at a level of about 1% by weight.

Thus, alpha-amylase inhibitor became a candidate for transfer into garden pea, and into any other crop species attacked by bruchids which are susceptible to this protein. The gene, which had been cloned a few years earlier, was inserted into a transformation vector and fitted with an appropriate promoter that caused the gene to be expressed strongly in seeds; thus, the gene was transferred into garden pea and expressed in the seeds. Next, the seeds were analyzed to determine if they had bruchid resistance. The cowpea bruchid or azuki bean bruchids, both of which can grow and develop well on pea seeds, were allowed to lay their eggs on the transformed seeds. A few weeks later, when the seeds were examined, it was clear that several of the transformed lines were essentially immune to both cowpea weevil and azuki bean weevil. Biochemical analyses established that the most resistant seeds had the highest levels of alpha-amylase inhibitor. Lines with intermediate levels of alpha-amylase inhibitor exhibited a degree of resistance. Those with no expressed alpha-amylase inhibitor from common bean were as susceptible to the bruchids as untransformed pea. Subsequent studies with transformed garden pea expressing alpha-amylase inhibitor showed that the pea was also resistant to the pea weevil (*Bruchis pisorum*). Multiple existing or potential pests of a grain crop may be handled by a single process of genetic engineering.

Future. The genetic transformation of garden pea demonstrates the feasibility of introducing insect resistance through nontraditional methods. The transfer of the alpha-amylase inhibitor gene from common bean into garden pea involves moving a gene normally expressed in one human food into another food. It involves moving only a single gene, yet multiple insect pests can be controlled. It involves moving a gene whose protein product is not highly toxic to insects, as is the Bt protoxin. However, this accomplishment raises several issues concerning the consuming public. Since humans already consume alpha-amylase inhibitor in the form of foods produced from common bean, there appears to be little danger in consuming foods made from garden pea containing the inhibitor.

For background information *see* BREEDING (PLANT); ENTOMOLOGY, ECONOMIC; GENETIC ENGINEERING; INSECTICIDE in the McGraw-Hill Encyclopedia of Science & Technology.   Larry L. Murdock

Bibliography. G. S. Gasser and R. T. Fraley, Genetically engineering plants for crop improvement, *Science*, 244:1293–1299, 1989; R. E. Shade et al., Transgenic pea seeds expressing the alpha-amylase inhibitor of the common bean are resistant to bruchid beetles, *Bio/Technology*, 12:793–796, 1994.

Air pollution, indoor

Various factors contribute to indoor air pollution, a problem sometimes referred to as sick building syndrome. Formaldehyde, paint fumes, and other volatiles from construction materials can cause adverse health effects. Dust mites, dander from pets, and cockroaches are recognized sources of allergens. In addition, interest in fungi, now recognized as an important source of potentially harmful particulates and volatiles, is rapidly increasing.

Fungal allergies. Mold spores are ubiquitous in outdoor and most indoor environments. Although pollen is the most familiar cause of common allergies, many people are also subject to fungal allergy. *Cladosporium* and *Alternaria*, two common molds that are abundant in the air, are responsible for most fungal allergies. Pollen can often be filtered from air coming into structures; however, fungal spores are often produced within the interior environment, especially in damp buildings. Certain workplaces, such as bakeries or mushroom farms, may be especially liable to production of mold allergies. Nonsporulating strains of *Pleurotus* (oyster mushroom) are sometimes selected for cultivation to reduce health risks to mushroom workers. Some bakery workers are sensitized by exposure to the enzyme alpha amylase produced by yeast, or to *Aspergillus*-derived enzymes used as flour additives. Fungi have attracted most attention in homes, schools, and day-care facilities because children are especially affected by fungal allergies.

Fungal allergens. The antigens to which most people are sensitized are called major allergens. The major allergen of *Alt. alternata* is present in both spores and the threadlike mycelium. It is the spores that are commonly encountered by allergy sufferers. The same allergen is present in other species of *Alternaria* and in the related fungi *Ulocladium* and

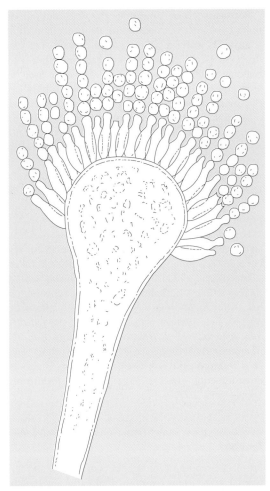

Aspergillus fumigatus.

the context of food spoilage, they are coming under scrutiny with regard to indoor air quality. Mycotoxins are present in spores of many species common in damp buildings. While evidence remains somewhat circumstantial, there is a growing consensus that prolonged respiratory exposure to spore-borne mycotoxins constitutes a health risk, especially if combined with bronchial irritation from volatiles and allergenic sensitization.

Indoor fungi. The dominant indoor fungi can be divided into the mesophiles, which grow in moist environments, and the xerophiles, which can grow in dry environments. Indoor mesophilic fungi tend to be members of the genera *Cladosporium, Penicillium, Aspergillus, Alternaria, Aureobasidium, Ulocladium, Botrytis, Epicoccum, Fusarium, Mucor,* and *Rhizopus.* Species most frequently mentioned as abundant are *C. herbarum, C. cladosporioides, Asp. niger, Asp. versicolor, Alt. alternata,* and *Aur. pullulans. Cladosporium* and *Alternaria* tend to dominate in outdoor air, and *Aspergillus* and *Penicillium* are most frequent in indoor samples. Yeasts in the genera *Rhodotorula* and *Cryptococcus* are also common in indoor samples. The xerophilic molds usually include *Asp. restrictus, Wallemia sebi,* and species of *Eurotium. Aspergillus fumigatus* is noteworthy because it can invade human tissues. *Stachybotrys atra* (=*Sta. chartarum*) produces extremely toxic metabolites; high concentrations of its spores are demonstrated to cause adverse effects, and are suspected of contributing to some cases of sudden infant death syndrome.

Sampling of indoor environments. Four principles should guide sampling of indoor environments: (1) results are extremely variable with time; (2) results vary with the culture medium and sampling device employed; (3) correct identification of recovered fungi is essential; and (4) comparisons should be made with outdoor air sampled concurrently. Many fungi respond to environmental changes with rapid spore production and release. Moreover, disturbances such as foot traffic, cleaning, construction, and air circulation can dramatically alter the number of propagules in the air. Carpets, bedding and furniture, and air-handling systems are subject to rapid disturbance that can change counts of airborne spores. Because some spores are nonviable or the media are not suitable for their growth, counting numbers of spores collected on membranes or tapes gives different results than counting colonies on agar media. Commercially available air samplers differ in method, precision, and accuracy. In addition to a medium such as malt agar or Sabouraud's agar for recovery of mesophiles, a medium with very high salt or sugar content should be used to detect xerophilic fungi. Frequently, antibiotics are added to restrict colony size, so that fast-growing fungi are not oversampled relative to others. Spores are often impacted on a membrane by an air sampler, then dilution-plated onto agar. Some researchers have attempted to avoid the problems inherent in air sampling by analyzing accumulations of house dust.

Stemphylium. The major allergen of *Asp. fumigatus* is reported only from spores and not in mycelium, but the fungus is capable of pathogenic growth (see **illus.**). Persons demonstrating antibody responses to its allergen probably have fungus germinated within the lungs. Antigens to which fewer people are sensitized are termed minor allergens. Both major and minor antigens have been characterized for a number of fungi; many appear to be glycoprotein enzymes common in fungal metabolism.

Mycotoxins and volatiles. Two other classes of fungal metabolites are potential health threats: mycotoxins and volatiles. Volatiles such as geosmin produce the musty odor in buildings with excessive fungal colonization. Microbially produced alcohols, ketones, and organic acids can constitute a health hazard as bronchial irritants and can diffuse from areas of microbial growth through water-vapor barriers. Measured indoor concentrations of such volatiles correlate with microbial activity.

Unlike volatiles, mycotoxins are located in spores. *Aspergillus* and *Penicillium,* fungi known to be dominant in colonization of building materials, often produce mycotoxins. Although these fungi and their associated mycotoxins have usually been studied in

Other researchers have emphasized the value of a thorough reconnaissance, taking note of any signs of fungal growth on walls, carpet, or basements.

Substrates for fungal growth. Most interior environments furnish ample material for fungal growth, provided suitable moisture is present. Wallpaper, gypsum-based plaster, some paints, wood, fabrics, the paper lining of sheetrock, and even some plastics support fungal growth, as does house dust. Logs, woodchips, or other fuels can function similarly. Wetted carpet, if not promptly dried, is apt to become a reservoir of fungal material. Filters in air-conditioning and humidification systems can provide an excellent growth substrate for fungi; hence, sanitization of air-handling systems has been recommended. Uncapped chimneys, leaky roofs, defective gutters or drainage, condensation, and insufficient ventilation can provide moisture requisite for fungal growth and the production of airborne spores and volatiles.

Fungal detection and diagnosis. Temporal variability of fungal propagules in the air and variability in response of individuals have greatly complicated diagnosis of health problems associated with indoor fungi. Many studies have relied on correlation between allergy symptoms or positive results of sensitization tests on the one hand, and conspicuous mold growth or odors, high spore counts, or simple dampness on the other. Diagnostic criteria for less well known maladies, such as allergic fungal sinusitis and organic toxic dust syndrome, are presently being established. Such sinusitis involves a complex of symptoms which often include nasal mucous plugs, clumps of necrotic eosinophils (a type of white blood cell), and frequently the presence of *Aspergillus* in the sinus cavities. Organic toxic dust syndrome (formerly called pulmonary mycotoxicosis) is associated with inhalation of grain dust or other agricultural materials containing high concentrations of microbes, and with inflammation of the lower respiratory system. The fungi predominantly associated with the syndrome are *Aspergillus*, *Penicillium*, *Eurotium*, and *Cladosporium*. Even less defined are diagnostic criteria for excessive exposure to mycotoxins or volatiles.

Standards for fungal exposure. Objective, quantitative tolerances for fungi in indoor air are presently lacking. Rarely, adverse health effects have been associated with low spore counts. Adverse effects are usually associated with counts of hundreds to thousands of spores per cubic meter; however, similar counts have been obtained from environments in which persons displayed no symptoms. Extreme counts of several tens of thousands (or more) of spores per cubic meter have been reported. Data on spore numbers are typically combined with cautionary statements on the necessity of identification of predominant fungal taxa. Although quantitative official standards are lacking, interior dampness, mold growth, and odors are accepted as qualitative indicators of increased risk for sensitive individuals.

Recommendations. To reduce the risk from indoor fungi, avoidance of excessive moisture accumulation is advised. Water-repellent paints or varnishes can decrease penetration of temporary moisture into building materials. Fungicidal paints can be used on areas most likely to encounter moisture; otherwise, the use of indoor biocides should be avoided. Obviously, reduction of serious moisture problems is contingent on structural changes or repairs. In the evaluation of building materials for resistance to microbial growth, xerophilic fungi should be included along with the usual mesophilic fungi in test inocula. Substantial presence of *Sta. atra* or *Asp. fumigatus* indoors should be regarded as a potentially serious problem.

For background information *see* ALLERGY; FUNGI; MYCOTOXIN in the McGraw-Hill Encyclopedia of Science & Technology.   Frank M. Dugan

Bibliography. Y. Al-Doory and J. F. Domson, *Mould Allergy*, 1984; A. Chhabra et al., Allergic fungal sinusitis: Clinicopathological characteristics, *Mycoses*, 39:437–441, 1996; R. A. Samson et al., *Air Quality Monographs*, vol. 2: *Health Implications of Fungi in Indoor Environments*, 1994; A. P. Verhoeff and H. A. Burge, Health risk assessment of fungi in home environments, *Ann. Allergy Asthma Immunol.*, 78:544–554, 1997.

Ameba

Protozoa are important members of aquatic and terrestrial ecosystems. Among them, the amebas include naked forms (without an enclosing wall or test) and testate forms (with a mineralized or organic test; **Fig. 1**). Modern techniques of culturing and enumerating have shown that amebas are far more abundant and more significant in food chains as predators of other microorganisms than was previously realized.

Soil amebas eat bacteria and in the process of digestion release waste products containing nutrients that can be used by plants. Therefore, amebas may play a major role in improving soil fertility. Some large amebas also consume algae and small protozoa. Amebas provide a link in the food chain from bacteria to larger forms of life such as roundworms and other invertebrates that prey on amebas. Amebas also combine major links in aquatic food webs: evidence has been obtained indicating the remarkable diversity and numerical significance of amebas in fresh-water and marine habitats. There are over 1 million amebas per liter in a highly productive fresh-water pond and more than 15,000 per liter in some coastal marine habitats. Testate amebas have been investigated extensively in soil and forest litters: they number 8000 per gram of soil and 10,000–24,000 per gram of surface litter in forests. They are less well documented in marine sediments. Marine sediments offer a new frontier for exploring the abundance and diversity of protozoa and other single-celled organisms.

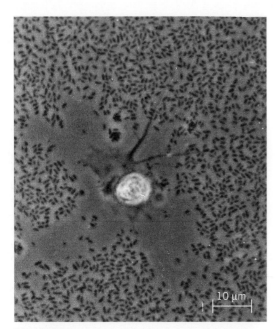

Fig. 1. Light micrograph of *Ovulinata parva* showing the translucent test and thin web of pseudopodia extending from the aperture. The pseudopodia gather bacterial prey from the surrounding surface, leaving a cleared area as shown. *(After O. R. Anderson, A. Rogerson, and F. Hanna, A description of the testate amoeba Ovulinata parva gen. nov., sp. nov. from coastal marine sediments, J. Mar. Biol. Ass. U.K., 76:851–856, 1996; reprinted with permission of Cambridge University Press)*

New marine testate ameba. A testate ameba with an organic wall (**Fig. 2**) was discovered in the sediments of the Firth of Clyde estuary in Scotland. This small protozoan (about 15 × 11 micrometers) has been named *Ovulinata parva*. The new genus name *Ovulinata* signifies that the test is somewhat egg-shaped and the species name *parva* means small. The organic wall has occasional slitlike depressions and a round-to-oval aperture (Fig. 2) that provides access to the environment. The shallow slits may allow uptake of oxygen and promote exchange of dissolved gases with the surrounding environment by diffusion. The wall is approximately 1.0 μm thick but is less than 0.5 μm at the base of the slits (**Fig. 3**). Images of the internal organization of the cytoplasm using transmission electron microscopy (Fig. 3) show that the cell has a single, large nucleus situated near the posterior. Food vacuoles containing bacteria and scattered reserves of organic food particles occur near the anterior end. Mitochondria that provide energy through metabolism of sugars and other organic compounds occur throughout the cytoplasm. The cell is surrounded by a halo of cytoplasmic strands forming a layer between the outer cell membrane and the organic wall. A thin, nonliving fibrillar envelope lining the inside of the test may protect the delicate cell surface from contact with the coarse organic wall. Pseudopodia emerge from the terminal aperture, forming a weblike network that extends into the surrounding environment. Very fine, tapered raylike pseudopodia emerge from the periphery of the pseudopodial web and project outward.

Feeding and movement. The pseudopodia are used to capture food particles and bacteria, which are carried by cytoplasmic streaming into the test and engulfed in food vacuoles. The pseudopodia collect bacteria at distances up to 50 μm from the test, forming a clear, bacteria-free zone surrounding the testate ameba (Fig. 1). It is not known what proportion of the ingested bacteria can be converted to living protoplasm during digestion or how much is lost as waste.

The pseudopodia are also used for locomotion. The web of pseudopodia attaches to the substratum and pulls the ameba forward by ameboid flowing motion. In laboratory cultures, *O. parva* moves at a rate of 25 μm/min, or a distance about two times its body length per minute. The movement is intermittent: sedentary intervals of several minutes or longer are punctuated by periods of locomotion lasting about 30–60 s. Particles of sediment in the natural environment provide large surface areas where bacteria can grow. By moving along the surfaces of the sediment particles, the ameba increases its chances of capturing suitable bacterial prey.

Reproduction. In laboratory cultures with bacteria as food, the amebas divide once in 28 h, meaning that the population can double approximately every day. Under less optimal conditions, the cultures double every 52 h. Thus, there is a potential for rapid reproductive response to highly favorable environments.

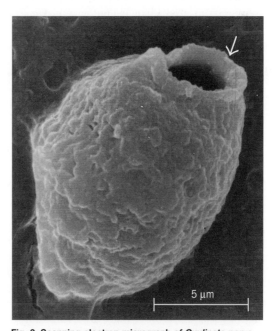

Fig. 2. Scanning electron micrograph of *Ovulinata parva* showing the surface texture of the organic (nonmineralized) test. The aperture (arrow) is oval to round. *(After O. R. Anderson, A. Rogerson, and F. Hanna, A description of the testate amoeba Ovulinata parva gen. nov., sp. nov. from coastal marine sediments, J. Mar. Biol. Ass. U.K., 76:851–856, 1996; reprinted with permission of Cambridge University Press)*

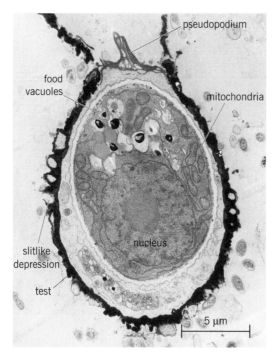

Fig. 3. Ultrathin section through the test of *Ovulinata parva* showing numerous food vacuoles containing bacterial prey near the anterior of the cell. *(After O. R. Anderson, A. Rogerson, and F. Hanna, A description of the testate amoeba Ovulinata parva gen. nov., sp. nov. from coastal marine sediments, J. Mar. Biol. Ass. U.K., 76:851–856, 1996; reprinted with permission of Cambridge University Press)*

During asexual reproduction by mitosis, the mother cell protrudes a mass of cytoplasm from the aperture. This mass expands until it approximates the size and shape of a new cell. The bulge of cytoplasm deposits a wall on its surface by secreting organic matter derived from the cytoplasm. This process creates a new test that is still connected to the mother test at the aperture. Subsequently, the nucleus of the mother cell divides and one of the daughter nuclei migrates into the new test along with a part of the cytoplasm. This step forms a complete daughter cell that detaches from the aperture of the mother cell and begins an independent existence. The test of the daughter cell is colorless at first but becomes a darker, amber color with age. Consequently, the approximate age of the cell can be determined by its color. After producing several offspring, older cells die, leaving the empty test. Sexual reproduction has not been observed in this species.

Habitat and salinity tolerance. *Ovulinata parva* was collected from sediment in an estuary near the coast of Scotland. This location suggests that the ameba may be adapted to grow in water of varying salinity: the mean salinity of the water in the sediment was 32.7‰, which is comparable to seawater (35‰), and the mean annual temperature was 47.6°F (8.7°C). Sometimes coastal species must cope with outflow of fresh water from the land. If the species are incapable of living in low-salinity water, they may perish during heavy influxes of water from rivers and watersheds. Consequently, the salinity tolerance of *O. parva* was examined in laboratory cultures. Cultures grown in bacteria-containing medium prepared with salinity varying from zero (fresh water) to 35‰ grow in all the media, indicating high adaptation to wide variations in salinity. Best growth, however, occurs in media with a salinity range of 23–35‰. When transferred from seawater into fresh-water media, *O. parva* quickly resumes growth at a pace equivalent to individuals growing in the seawater medium. This activity suggests that *O. parva* is fully capable of surviving rapid changes in salinity due to fresh-water intrusions into the estuary. The wide salinity tolerance may also indicate that *O. parva* initially was a fresh-water species that invaded the marine sediments from rivers or streams emptying into the estuary. This hypothesis requires further investigation.

For background information *see* AMEBA; ARCELLINIDA; PROTOZOA; SARCODINA in the McGraw-Hill Encyclopedia of Science & Technology.

O. Roger Anderson

Bibliography. O. R. Anderson, *Comparative Protozoology: Ecology, Physiology, Life History*, 1987; O. R. Anderson, The physiological ecology of planktonic sarcodines with applications to paleoecology: Patterns in space and time, *J. Euk. Microbiol.*, 43:261–274, 1996; O. R. Anderson, A. Rogerson, and F. Hanna, A description of the testate amoeba *Ovulinata parva* gen. nov., sp. nov. from coastal marine sediments, *J. Mar. Biol. Ass. U.K.*, 76:851–856, 1996; M. A. Sleigh, *Protozoa and Other Protists*, 1989.

Amino acids

Meteorites, specifically the carbonaceous chondrites, contain an extensive suite of amino acids. Although 8 of the 20 amino acids used by terrestrial organisms for protein synthesis are common to these meteorites, most of the meteoritic amino acids are unknown in the biosphere. They are, in general, simpler in structure than those in biological materials. Only two structural classes of amino acid have been found in meteorites: monoamino-monocarboxylic acids (structure **1**) and monoamino-dicarboxylic acids (**2**). More complex amino acids with heteroatoms (additional nitrogen or sulfur) or aromatic groups in their structures are absent.

$$NH_2—(C_nH_{2n})—COOH$$

(1)

$$NH_2—(C_nH_{2n-1})—(COOH)_2$$

(2)

Within these two classes of amino acids, complete structural diversity prevails. For example, each of the twelve 5-carbon (C_5) monoamino-monocarboxylic acids that can be formed as a result of variations in carbon-chain branching and the position of amino and carboxyl group substitution has been found in extracts of the Murchison meteorite. The abundance of individual amino acids decreases exponentially within homologous series as the carbon number increases, and at each carbon number the branched-chain isomers are more abundant than the straight-chain isomer. Amino acids with carbon chains through C_9 have been identified, and trace amounts of longer-chain species are probably present as well. The meteoritic amino acids are substantially enriched in the heavier stable isotopes deuterium (^2H), carbon (^{13}C), and nitrogen (^{15}N), compared to their terrestrial analogs.

Chirality. Meteoritic amino acids, with a few exceptions, have one or more chiral centers, that is, carbon atoms with four chemically different bonded groups. As a result, they exist as enantiomers and, when two or more chiral centers are present, as diastereomers. The L- and D-enantiomers of α-amino acid are shown as structures (**3a**) and (**3b**), respectively. The mirror plane is represented by the broken line.

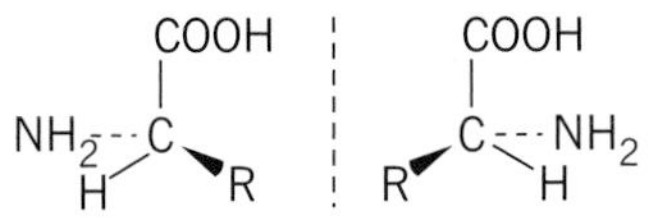

(**3a**)   (**3b**)

Determination of the enantiomer ratios has been of considerable interest, originally for the purpose of assessing terrestrial contamination. Amino acids of biological origin are almost exclusively of the L configuration. When they are present as contaminants in amino acids that are otherwise racemic (L/D = 1), the L/D ratio is greater than 1. The discovery, made soon after the fall of the Murchison meteorite in 1969, that several chiral amino acids were racemic was crucial in establishing that amino acids are indigenous to the meteorite. Furthermore, this finding, along with the structural diversity, strongly suggested an abiotic formation process.

The organic matter of carbonaceous chondrites may be representative of organic matter as it was delivered to the early Earth by asteroids, interplanetary dust, and possibly comets. Consequently, whether their chiral organic compounds are exactly racemic or exhibit enantiomeric excesses bears importantly on the fundamental question of the origin of biological homochirality, that is, whether it was achieved by chemical or biological evolution. The finding of enantiomeric excesses would suggest that some asymmetric influence was manifest in chemical evolution prior to the origin of life; thus, the question of meteoritic amino-acid enantiomer ratios has periodically been revisited. Since the initial work in 1969–1970, L-enantiomer excesses have been reported in five protein amino acids from the Murchison meteorite, and isotopic data have been presented to support the claim of an excess of the L-enantiomer in alanine extracted from this meteorite. Nevertheless, because of the ever present risk

of terrestrial contamination, the finding of enantiomeric excesses favoring the biologically preferred enantiomer (L) of ubiquitous protein amino acids, and the contradiction of the early results obtained with a fresh and presumably more pristine meteorite sample, have not made a convincing case for indigenous enantiomeric excesses.

Recently, a different approach to the question was taken. In this work, a set of α-methyl amino acids from the Murchison meteorite was targeted for analysis. These amino acids have chiral centers that are resistant to racemization or epimerization (change of configuration at a chiral center in diastereomers), and either have no known terrestrial source or are of very restricted occurrence in the biosphere. Consequently, it is unlikely that the original configuration of their chiral centers was changed during any aqueous or mild thermal processing that they might have experienced in the meteorite parent body, and unlikely that the original enantiomer ratios have been affected by terrestrial contamination.

The specific amino acids analyzed were 2-amino-2,3-dimethylpentanoic acid, which has two chiral centers (* on structures shown) and occurs as four stereoisomers: DL-α-methylisoleucine and DL-α-methylalloisoleucine (**4**), isovaline (**5**) [2-amino-2-methylbutanoic acid], and α-methylnorvaline (**6**) [2-amino-2-methylpentanoic acid].

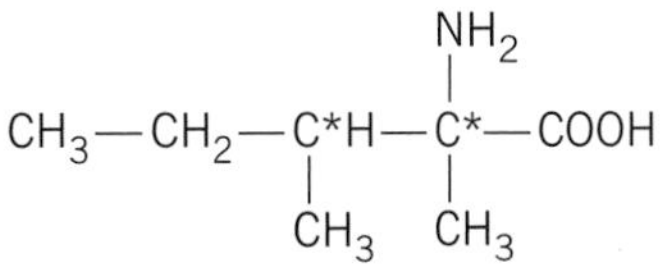

(**4**)

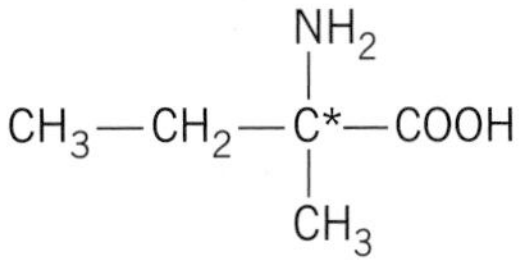

(**5**)

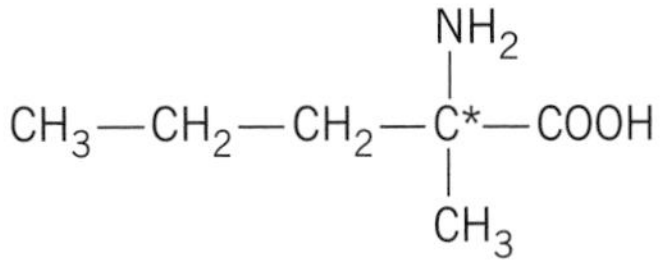

(**6**)

An L-enantiomer excess (L% − D%) was observed in each case: α-methylisoleucine (7.0%), α-methylalloisoleucine (9.1%), isovaline (8.4%), and α-methylnorvaline (2.8%). Interestingly, the α-H atom analogs of the latter two amino acids, that is, α-amino-*n*-butyric acid (**7**) and norvaline (**8**), were found to be racemic.

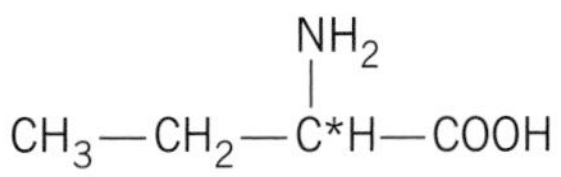

(**7**)

$$CH_3-CH_2-CH_2-\overset{\overset{\displaystyle NH_2}{|}}{C^*}H-COOH$$

(8)

It was proposed that the two analogs either underwent racemization in the parent body or are the products of a separate formation process. The failure to observe enantiomeric excesses in the α-amino acids, which have α-H atoms, contrasts with the reported L-enantiomer excess in alanine, which also has an α-H atom.

Formation mechanism. Several mechanisms have been suggested for the abiotic generation of enantiomeric excesses which invoke as the asymmetric influence, the effects of polarized light, planetary magnetic/electric fields, or the slight parity-violating energy difference conferred on enantiomers by the nuclear weak force. In the case of meteoritic amino acids, ultraviolet circularly polarized light is an attractive possibility. It has been suggested that a neutron star, the high-density residue of a supernova, produces synchrotron radiation in the ultraviolet range that is circularly polarized and of opposite handedness parallel and antiparallel, respectively, to the star's spin axis. Consequently, presolar cloud matter above (or below) such a star would be bathed in ultraviolet photons of a particular circular polarity, and enantiomeric excesses might arise from differential photolysis resulting from unequal absorption of this radiation by enantiomers. The role of interstellar cloud chemistry in the formation of meteorite organic matter [inferred from deuterium (^{2}H) enrichments], the presence of supernova products in carbonaceous chondrites, and the magnitude of experimentally observed enantiomeric excesses obtained when leucine was irradiated with ultraviolet circularly polarized light are consistent with such a possibility.

Origin of life. The discovery of enantiomeric excesses in the α-methyl amino acids of the Murchison meteorite adds a new dimension to arguments for exogenous delivery as an important contributor to prebiotic chemistry. If exogenous delivery of amino acids with L-enantiomer excesses skewed subsequent chemical evolution toward L-homochirality, more serious consideration should be given in general to the organic matter of comets and meteorites as important ingredients of the prebiotic milieu. The α-methyl amino acids are a case in point. These amino acids, which have not generally been viewed as important for the origin of life because they are relatively unimportant in contemporary biochemistry, are abundant in the Murchison meteorite and may have been well suited for a role in further amplification of the small initial enantiomeric excesses. Polymerization accompanied by formation of regular secondary structure, such as α-helices and β-sheets, has been shown to be an effective way to amplify modest initial enantiomeric excesses, and α-methyl amino acids are known to have strong helix-inducing and -stabilizing effects. Although a transition to α-H

amino acids obviously would have been required at some later evolutionary stage, the α-substituted amino acids could have played a significant role early in the development of homochirality.

For background information *see* AMINO ACIDS; METEORITE; OPTICAL ACTIVITY; PREBIOTIC ORGANIC SYNTHESIS; RACEMIZATION; STEREOCHEMISTRY in the McGraw-Hill Encyclopedia of Science & Technology.   John R. Cronin

Bibliography. J. R. Cronin and S. Pizzarello, Enantiomeric excesses in meteoritic amino acids, *Science*, 275:951–955, 1997; M. H. Engel, S. A. Macko, and J. A. Silfer, Carbon isotope composition of individual amino acids in the Murchison meteorite, *Nature*, 348:47–49, 1990; J. M. Greenberg, C. X. Mendoza-Gomez, and V. Pirronello (eds.), *The Chemistry of Life's Origins*, 1993; E. Rubenstein et al., Supernovae and life, *Nature*, 306:118, 1983.

Analytical chemistry

Charge-transfer-device detectors have become common in many systems used for chemical analysis, and are often an attractive alternative to photomultiplier tubes, photodiode arrays, and vidicons. Charge-transfer devices are solid-state, array detectors sensitive to photons from the far-infrared to the x-ray region of the spectrum. Today, most commercially available instruments use silicon-based detector technology, which has optimum sensitivity from the near-infrared to the x-ray region. Some important characteristics of properly operated scientific-grade charge-transfer devices are high sensitivity, large dynamic range, remarkably low dark current, very low read noise, and multichannel capability.

Device basics. Charge-transfer devices are two-dimensional arrays of many thousands of small detector elements called pixels. In all charge-transfer devices, photons are absorbed, producing charge carriers by promoting electrons from the valence band to the conduction band. Voltage applied to electrodes in each pixel produces potential wells which store charge carriers. The intensity of light incident on the detector is determined by measuring the charge carriers trapped in each pixel.

The two common families of charge-transfer devices are charge-coupled devices and charge-injection devices. In charge-coupled devices, charge is clocked across parallel shift registers to serial shift registers and subsequently to the amplifier gate, which determines the amount of charge that had been formed in each pixel. Because of the low gate capacitance, an extremely small amount of charge results in a significant signal, making charge-coupled devices useful for the measurement of very low light levels. In charge-injection devices, the number of charge carriers in each pixel is determined by sensing a change in voltage as the stored charge is reversibly moved between two electrodes within each pixel. The nondestructive readout allows variable integration times and random-access integration,

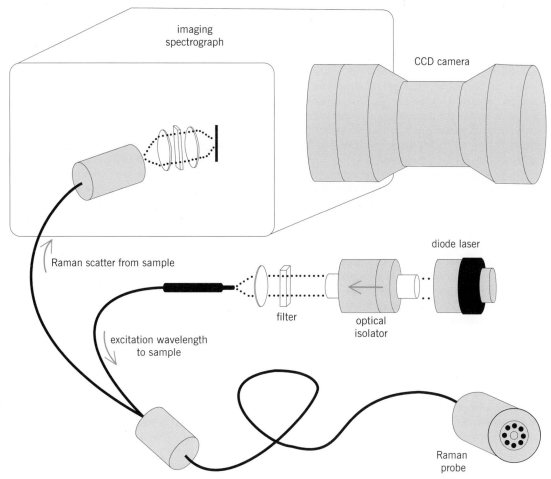

imaging
spectrograph

CCD camera

Raman scatter from sample

diode laser

filter

optical
isolator

excitation wavelength
to sample

Raman
probe

Fig. 1. Fiber-optic-probe Raman spectrometer system. The charge-coupled-device (CCD) camera is attached to a cryogenically cooled housing that contains the detector along with the controlling electronics. The fiber-optic bundle carries the excitation wavelength in a central fiber to the probe, and the Raman scatter is collected in the outer fibers of the bundle.

making charge-injection devices attractive for systems that require the simultaneous measurement of strong and weak signals.

Applications. The applications of charge-transfer devices in analytical chemistry are numerous and diverse. Charge-transfer devices have been used in phase-resolved fluorescent lifetime imaging microscopy, highly multiplexed capillary electrophoresis, liquid chromatography, thin-layer chromatography, mass spectrometry, Raman spectroscopy, x-ray crystallography, emission spectroscopy, and many other techniques. The methodologies of application range from simple replacement of conventional detectors with charge-transfer devices in well-known techniques, to transduction of other signals into photons for subsequent detection by a charge-transfer device.

For a charge-transfer device to significantly improve a measurement, the detector's advantages must be matched with a particular system's limitations. Greatest utilization of charge-transfer-device characteristics has been achieved when the design of an instrument involved the careful selection of a device, an optical train tailored to the characteristics

of that device, and a strategic choice of readout mode.

Molecular spectroscopy. Scientific-grade charge-transfer devices were first developed and used by astronomers as high-dynamic-range replacements for film. Subsequently, researchers realized the potential of these devices as detectors in various spectroscopic techniques. The use of charge-transfer devices has improved many molecular analytical techniques, including absorbance, fluorescence, and Raman spectroscopy. Furthermore, imaging techniques such as fluorescence lifetime imaging and thin-layer-chromatography plate imaging have become viable analytical tools.

Charge-transfer devices have had a profound effect in Raman spectroscopy. Raman scattering is an inherently weak effect and, prior to charge-transfer devices, was considered only a qualitative research technique with low sensitivity. Raman systems have been greatly improved by taking advantage of several charge-coupled-device properties, including quantum efficiencies approaching 100% at certain wavelengths, read noise as low as a few electrons, and dark current as low as several electrons per pixel per hour when cooled. These properties, along with the multichannel advantage of an array detector, have forced the reevaluation of Raman spectroscopy as a routine analytical technique. Raman systems can now achieve detection limits in the parts-per-million range by employing much higher throughput spectrographs and minimizing fluorescence interference through the use of longer-wavelength lasers (**Fig. 1**).

Prior to charge-coupled-device imaging technology, quantitative thin-layer chromatography required slow and expensive equipment, such as a scanning densitometer. Unfortunately, the scanning densitometer system imposed serial detection on this powerful parallel separation technique, and detector noise set detection limits. Imaging the fluorescence of the analytes on developed thin-layer-chromatography plates with a charge-coupled device eliminates many of the problems associated with the scanning densitometer. With a single exposure, a charge-coupled device can image an entire thin-layer-chromatography plate and return quantitative information from the fluorescence intensities of the analytes. This fast, multichannel detection preserves the high sample throughput inherent with the parallel separation capability of thin-layer chromatography. Because of the high sensitivity of the charge-coupled device, the minimum detectable concentration is limited by the fluorescence background of the thin-layer-chromatography plates rather than detector noise. A system has been used for sensitive detection of aflatoxins in food samples and tetracyclines in commercial antibiotics (**Fig. 2**). With simple filter sets or acoustooptic tunable filters,

both spatial and spectral information can be obtained from a series of images.

Sensitive detection of luminescent signals moving in space is often limited by the amount of time that the light source spends in view of the detector. Some techniques including separation systems have benefited from a readout mode known as time-delayed integration. In this mode, the rate of charge transfer along one dimension of a charge-coupled device is synchronized with the speed of the analyte moving through the detection window, effectively increasing the residence time of the sample in the detection region. The integration time for weak luminescent signals is increased greatly, improving detection limits. The two-dimensional nature also allows for the acquisition of full spectra for each analyte in the direction perpendicular to the synchronized charge transfer.

Atomic spectroscopy. Atomic emission spectroscopy presents the need to simultaneously measure signals that vary over 8–10 orders of magnitude. Difficulties arise when using charge-coupled devices in atomic emission spectroscopy, as the long integration times needed for weak emission lines lead to blooming in the areas of the detector exposed to more intense lines. This problem has been overcome by specialized charge-coupled-device designs, such as segmented arrays, and by the use of charge-injection devices. Charge-injection devices are uniquely suited to atomic emission spectroscopy because they are inherently antiblooming, are capable of random-access integration, and can be read nondestructively. Random-access integration means that selected pixels can be integrated for different amounts of time, such that both weak and strong signals are measured for appropriate intervals. The ability to read pixels nondestructively provides a means of interrogating individual pixels to determine the optimum integration time during analysis of an unknown and provides reduction of read noise through averaging multiple rereads of the stored charge.

Prior to charge-injection devices, high-resolution inductively coupled plasma–atomic emission spectroscopy required the use of scanning monochromators or multiple-photomultiplier-tube direct readers. High-resolution echelle spectrometer systems had been underutilized because of the lack of an appropriate two-dimensional detection system. The high full-well capacity, wide dynamic range, and nondestructive readout of charge-injection devices are ideally suited to an echelle system. Systems based on this technology have been routinely capable of parts-per-billion detection limits of atomic species.

Conventional atomic absorption in a flame or furnace relies on single-channel detection and a hollow-cathode-lamp source. Multielement analyses using hollow-cathode lamps require discrete measurements for each element of interest. In addition, since hollow-cathode lamps are rarely available with more than five elements, lamps must often be changed sequentially to complete a particular sample. By using an echelle spectrometer system with charge-

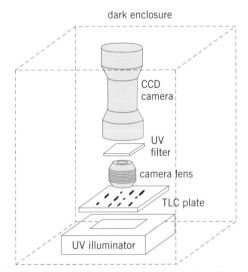

Fig. 2. Imaging thin-layer-chromatography system. The ultraviolet (UV) illuminator excites fluorescence from the analytes on the thin-layer-chromatography (TLC) plate. The fluorescent wavelengths pass through the filter and are imaged with the charge-coupled-device (CCD) camera.

injection-device detection, continuum source graphite furnace atomic absorption has been demonstrated. With an echelle spectrometer as the resolution element, simultaneous multielement analysis is possible with only a small loss in resolution, compared to hollow-cathode-lamp-based systems.

X-ray crystallography. Despite a variety of limitations, single photomultiplier tubes have been the primary detector for x-ray crystallography. Charge-transfer-device use in x-ray detection has been delayed by the availability of other two-dimensional detectors, such as image plates, multiwire detectors, and silicon-intensified targets. In recent years, however, many of the advantages of charge-transfer devices over these other two-dimensional alternatives have been realized. Charge-transfer devices are capable of much faster frame rates than image plates, their read noise is much lower than silicon intensified targets, and they are true multichannel detectors, unlike multiwire detectors.

X-ray crystallography imposes many of the same detector requirements as inductively coupled plasma–atomic emission spectroscopy. Diffraction patterns can contain thousands of tightly spaced spots with a wide range of intensities. However, because of the current availability of charge-coupled devices in buttable formats and in much larger sizes than charge-injection devices, almost all applications for the detection of x-rays have used charge-coupled devices. Several commercial instruments which employ charge-coupled devices are now available. In one application of a charge-injection device for x-ray detection, a foil-mask spectrometer was used to obtain simultaneous position, intensity, and energy of spots from a Laue diffraction pattern.

Charge-transfer-device detection of x-rays poses a unique problem in that the x-rays are of high enough energy to damage the devices. For this reason, direct detection of x-rays is usually circumvented by transducing the x-rays to optical photons by using a phosphor screen. The optical photons can then be fed through a fiber-optic taper or imaged with a lens onto the charge-transfer device.

Mass spectrometry. Mass spectrometry may seem an unlikely place for charge-transfer-device use, since ions are detected rather than photons, and mass spectrometry is not usually a technique considered to be lacking in sensitivity. However, in a conventional sector instrument, a significant portion of the ion flux is lost because the ion beam is scanned over a (typically) 50–100-micrometer-wide collector slit to select a particular mass-to-charge ratio. A significant speed and throughput advantage can be realized by removing the collector slit and simultaneously projecting a range of masses on a two-dimensional detector. Since area detectors for ions are not available at this time, an ion flux is transduced into a proportional flux of electrons by impaction of the ion beam on a microchannel intensifier plate. Ejected electrons from the intensifier are directed onto a phosphor screen, and the resulting photons are coupled with a fiber-optic bundle to a charge-coupled device without loss of spatial resolution. The photon image of the ion beam represents a range of masses. The speed advantage of such a detection scheme (as fast as 3 s per decade) has proven compatible with separation techniques and pulsed ionization sources such as fast atom bombardment and matrix-assisted laser desorption. By using time-delayed integration, signal-to-noise enhancements of 50–100 have been possible over point detection, and dynamic ranges have been extended to over three orders of magnitude.

For background information *see* CHARGE-COUPLED DEVICES; CHROMATOGRAPHY; MASS SPECTROMETRY; SPECTROSCOPY; X-RAY CRYSTALLOGRAPHY in the McGraw-Hill Encyclopedia of Science & Technology.　　M. Bonner Denton; Sean P. Madden; David A. Jones

Bibliography. Q. S. Hanley et al., Charge-transfer devices in analytical instrumentation, *Anal. Chem.*, 68:661A–667A, 1996; J. V. Sweedler et al., High-performance charge-transfer device detectors, *Anal. Chem.*, 60:282A–288A, 1988; J. V. Sweedler, K. L. Ratzlaff, and M. B. Denton, *Charge Transfer Devices in Spectroscopy*, 1994; Y. Talmi (ed.), *Multichannel Image Detectors*, ACS Symp. Ser. 236, pp. 117–132, 1983.

Animal communication

Most vertebrates and many invertebrates use sound to communicate. Many species also use light or chemical signals, and some fishes use electric signals. However, sound provides animals with the ability to communicate over long distances and to send signals whose direction is easily determined by the receiver and which are not normally impeded by objects in the environment. A disadvantage is that sound also can be detected by predators which can then find the animal emitting it.

Interest in animal bioacoustics arises not only because humans are curious about animal behavior but also because such studies provide insight into the human communication system, how it evolved, and how it develops in young humans. Moreover, investigations of hearing and biosonar in animals aid in problems as varied as understanding and dealing with human hearing loss, speech deficits, and improvement of radar and sonar technology.

Sound producers. The best-known sound producers among the vertebrates are the mammals and birds. Many frogs and toads (amphibians) and bony fishes are also known to communicate by sound. Far less is known about sound communication in reptiles. While many reptiles can detect sound, only gekkonids (gecko lizards) are known to produce sound and use it for communication during courtship. Both fishes and amphibians use sound in finding mates and in courtship, and in warning conspecifics (members of the same species) of the presence of predators. Fish and amphibian sounds, while not as complex and harmonically rich as those of birds and mammals, often contain a broad range of frequencies, and each species may use several different types of sound in different behavioral contexts. For example, toadfish and midshipman fish, species common on the coasts of the United States, have a variety of calls. While both males and females produce short pulse trains, males produce long "boatwhistle" sounds that can be heard for long distances (and even out of water). Boatwhistles are used only in the reproductive season to attract females from a considerable distance.

Evolution. An interesting question in modern bioacoustics deals with why animals that are not known to produce sound (or indeed, cannot produce sound) are able to hear; or, whether hearing evolved in association with animal communication or whether hearing evolved earlier and bioacoustic communication between animals only later. It has been suggested that animals may have evolved hearing in order to listen to the "auditory scene" and gain information about the general environment from the sounds. Animals may have evolved hearing in order to glean information from sound sources such as the rain on water, ocean waves lapping on the shore, and other environmental sounds that may help them function better in their normal habitats.

Mammalian bioacoustics. Among the mammals, researchers have probably obtained the most knowledge of the hearing systems of the primates, marine mammals, and bats. There is interest in how animals in all three groups communicate with conspecifics, and in how toothed whales (odontocetes) and bats communicate with themselves by biosonar (echolocation) systems.

Primates. Nonhuman primates are probably the best model system in which a humanlike communication system can be investigated. Their vocal repertoire is very rich, and they use sound in a wide range of behavioral situations. In fact, primates, like humans, use their complex vocalizations to convey information about their environment as well as about their own internal states. They can communicate information about finding food, details of their social relationship (dominance hierarchies), predation, and so forth. While many other species of mammals, as well as birds, often have a rich vocal repertoire, there is no evidence that they use their sounds to communicate the breadth of information provided in primate vocalizations.

Whereas it had been thought that only humans show developmental change and learning as their sounds mature to adult form, it is now apparent that at least some primates, as well as birds, go through a period of vocal maturation that is affected by the sounds they hear around them. In essence, some primates and birds learn their acoustic repertoires from their elders.

Some primates produce a range of sounds at birth that are similar to adult calls but for which the young need to learn the proper context. Thus, a young primate may use the same sound for a variety of different predators, whereas the adult uses that particular sound for a single class of predators.

In some cases the acoustic structure of the signal is closely related to a specific external event. Vervet monkeys have a different alarm call and a different behavioral response for each type of predator. For example, when a vervet sees a python, it produces a low-pitched pulsatile call which results in other vervets standing on their hindlegs so they can search the ground for the snake.

A recent observation about primate calls is germane to virtually all forms of acoustic communication. It has been demonstrated that differences in ecology strongly affect the acoustic structure of the sounds used by primates. Habitat properties and the transmission characteristics of different sound frequencies affect the acoustic components of sounds, and particularly those sounds that can be used over long distances. Thus, the acoustic components of a long-distance call may differ depending upon whether an animal lives in a desert, rainforest, or savanna, and the acoustic components of the call will be those that travel best in the particular habitat in which an animal has evolved. These same environmental factors can affect the structure of the calls used by birds and fishes.

Bats and marine mammals. Bats and marine mammals use sounds to communicate with conspecifics. Most often, these sounds are of low frequency. The call repertoires and acoustic complexity of these sounds are not nearly as rich as they are in primates. One major group of bats, the microchiroptera, and one major group of whales and dolphins, the odontocetes (toothed whales, or porpoises and dolphins), also use high-frequency sounds (above 20 kHz) in biosonar to glean information about the environment.

Other marine mammals, such as the mysticetes or baleen whales (such as blue whales and humpbacks) and the pinnipeds (sea lions and seals), cannot echolocate. However, the mysticetes produce a wide range of low-frequency sounds, some of which can be detected over hundreds, if not thousands, of miles. The nature of these very intense long-range sounds is not clear, but they may be used to keep animals in touch with one another even over distances as wide as an ocean.

Biosonar. Echolocation involves the bat or odontocete emitting a sound and the animal detecting the reflection of the sound from an object in the environment. The echo often will have a somewhat different spectrum than the emitted sound, and the animal extracts information about the nature of the object by comparing the emitted signal (presumably stored in memory) with the echo. Moreover, it should be easy for the animal to determine distance to the object by measuring the time between the emission of a signal and the receipt of the echo. This process is facilitated by the animal emitting only a single pulsed signal at a time, and then waiting long enough so that the next pulse does not interfere with detection of the echo of the earlier pulse.

Both bats and odontocetes use short-pulsed sounds in echolocation, and are able to tell a good deal about their targets from the echo. However, the sounds of the two groups are quite different, and it is not known whether the returned information is comparable in content in both groups, or if both groups process the echolocation sounds in the same way in the brain. The capabilities of both groups with respect to discrimination of target size and shape are about the same, while dolphins do better than bats at discriminating target range and the composition of different materials.

The echolocation click of dolphins is very short (70–100 microseconds), and longer in bats (0.3–100 milliseconds). The dolphin click is broadband and may contain energy over an octave in width (for example, 50–100 kHz). In contrast, bat echolocation signals either are a frequency-modulated sweep in some species or have a continuous-frequency component followed by a short frequency-modulated sweep. In the horseshoe bat, there is a long continuous-frequency component to the sound at about 83 kHz followed by a frequency-modulated downward sweep from 83 to 65 kHz.

There are substantial differences in how bats and odontocetes use their echolocation signals in pursuit of prey. When approaching its prey, a bat changes the characteristics of the sonar signal in a way that depends upon the phase of the pursuit. Thus, when a bat is flying around without a target present, it may put out a few pulses a second; but once a target is detected, the signals become shorter, the frequency-modulated sweep becomes broader, the amplitude decreases, and the interpulse interval gets shorter as the bat approaches the target. Dolphins seem to be able to decrease the interpulse interval and the signal amplitude only as they approach a target, and there is no apparent change in the frequency characteristics or the duration of the pulse.

For background information *see* CETACEA; CHIROPTERA; ECHOLOCATION; PHONORECEPTION; PRIMATES in the McGraw-Hill Encyclopedia of Science & Technology.   Arthur N. Popper

Bibliography. W. L. Au, *The Sonar of Dolphins*, 1993; D. L. Cheney and R. M. Seyfarth, *How Monkeys See the World*, 1990; M. D. Hauser, *The Evolution of Communication*, 1996; A. N. Popper and R. R. Fay (eds.), *Comparative Hearing: Fishes and Amphibians*, 1998; A. N. Popper and R. R. Fay (eds.), *Hearing by Bats*, 1995.

Antibiotic

The β-lactam antibiotics include penicillins, cephalosporins, cephamycins, carbapenems, oxapenems, and monobactams. The antibiotics of this class are characterized by the presence of a four-membered β-lactam ring (see **illus.**). Penicillins have the β-lactam ring fused to a five-membered thiazolidine ring; cephalosporins have the β-lactam ring fused to a six-membered dihydrothiazine ring; for cephamycins, carbapenems, and oxapenems, the five-membered ring contains a carbon or an oxygen instead

Chemical structure of β-lactams. (*a*) Penicillin G. (*b*) 6-Aminopenicillanic acid (6-APA). (*c*) 7-Aminodeacetoxycephalosporanic acid (7-ADCA). (*d*) Cephalosporin C. (*e*) 7-Aminocephalosporanic acid (7-ACA).

of sulfur; and in monobactams, the β-lactam ring is isolated. Substitutions of various side chains affect the solubility and the ability of the drug to be absorbed, to penetrate into various tissues, and to inhibit various bacteria. The integrity of the β-lactam ring is essential for antibacterial activity. Opening of the β-lactam ring, which can occur either chemically or enzymatically, leads to the loss of antibacterial activity. All β-lactams have a common mechanism of action, which is the inhibition of bacterial cell-wall synthesis by interfering with the biosynthesis of peptidoglycan, the essential structural component of the wall. This structural component is absent in eukaryotic cells; therefore, β-lactam antibiotics have no effect on the metabolism of fungal, plant, or animal cells.

Natural β-lactams. Natural β-lactams belong to a group of compounds called secondary metabolites because they are not essential for growth of the producing organisms. However, natural β-lactams may be critical to the producing organisms in their natural environment as they can provide competitive advantages over neighboring microorganisms. The common natural β-lactams are penicillins, cephalosporins, cephamycins, and thienamycins, which are produced by a broad spectrum of bacteria and fungi. These naturally occurring β-lactams usually possess antibacterial activity against a limited number of bacteria. The rapid increase of β-lactam-resistant bacteria, due to the production of β-lactamases, reduces the usefulness of β-lactams.

Semisynthetic β-lactams. The poor anti-gram-negative activity of naturally occurring β-lactams and the spread of staphylococcal β-lactamases drove a search for new β-lactams, but a breakthrough was not achieved until the 1950s–1970s when the chemical splitting processes of making 6-aminopenicillanic acid (6-APA) and 7-aminodeacetoxycephalosporanic acid (7-ADCA) from penicillins and 7-aminocephalosporanic acid (7-ACA) from cephalosporin C opened a new era of semisynthetic β-lactam production. Semisynthetic β-lactams are a group of antibiotics with various side chains, differing from those of naturally occurring β-lactams. Various semisynthetic β-lactams with broader spectra and excellent chemotherapeutic activities are chemically synthesized, starting with 6-APA (such as ampicillin and carbenicillin), 7-ACA (such as cefamendole and cefuroxime), or 7-ADCA (such as cephalexin and cephadroxil).

Synthetic β-lactams. Total chemical synthesis of β-lactams has been unable to compete in efficiency with the biosynthetic processes of microorganisms. Nevertheless, it has turned out to be an area in which organic chemists have made outstanding advances. Since the 1980s, the scope of research directed toward the synthesis of β-lactams has increased dramatically. Although total synthesis of some β-lactams has been developed, none of them has reached commercial application yet.

Mode of action of β-lactams. All β-lactam antibiotics have a common mechanism of action, which is the inhibition of bacterial cell-wall synthesis by interacting, in different ways, with the penicillin-binding proteins. Penicillin-binding proteins are involved in the synthesis of peptidoglycan, the essential structural component of the bacterial cell wall. Bacterial cell walls have a protective layer of peptidoglycan over the cell membrane. The peptidoglycan layer consists of chains of alternating *N*-acetylglucosamine and *N*-acetyl-muramic acid units connected by peptides. These peptides crosslink adjacent peptidoglycan chains to form a net of peptidoglycan layers. Binding of β-lactams to the penicillin-binding proteins interferes with the formation of peptide bridges between peptidoglycan chains and thus inhibits the final stage of cell-wall biosynthesis in bacteria. Microbial resistance to β-lactam antibiotics can arise via modification of the penicillin-binding proteins and via β-lactamase production. β-lactamases prevent the action of β-lactam antibiotics by hydrolyzing the β-lactam ring. The development of amoxicillin-clavulanate (augmentin), ampicillin-sulbactam (sultamicillin), and cefoperazone-sulbactam (sulperazone), which are β-lactams in conjunction with a β-lactamase inhibitor, is leading the fight against many antibiotic-resistant pathogens.

Large-scale production of β-lactams. The major precursors for semisynthetic β-lactam antibiotics include 6-APA and 7-ACA, which are produced by the enzymatic (amidase) cleavage of penicillin G/penicillin V and cephalosporin C, respectively, and 7-ADCA. Production of β-lactam antibiotics such as penicillin G/penicillin V and cephalosporin C occurs best under conditions of nutrient imbalance and low growth rates. Nutrient imbalance can be achieved by limitation of carbon, nitrogen, or phosphorus sources. In addition to these factors, amino acids such as lysine and methionine exert marked effects on the production of penicillins and cephalosporins by certain microorganisms.

Production of penicillins by fermentation is carried out in fed-batch liquid cultures of the fungus *Penicillium chrysogenum*. In modern practice, the culture volume is typically 120,000–200,000 liters (26,400–44,000 gal). The process is aerobic, and the oxygen is supplied by passing air through the culture and agitating vigorously by using turbine propellers. The medium used for penicillin fermentation contains carbon, nitrogen, sulfur, and phosphorus sources and other nutrients. A side-chain precursor, phenylacetic acid or phenoxyacetic acid, has to be included in the medium or in the feeds to the fermentor for high yields of penicillins. Approximately 28,000–30,000 tons of penicillins are annually produced worldwide, and most of the product is used for the preparation of 6-APA and 7-ADCA.

Cephalosporin C is produced by the fermentation of *Acremonium chrysogenum* using processes similar to the penicillin fermentation. The culture medium must supply carbon, nitrogen, sulfur, phosphorus, and other sources for growth. In addition, DL-methionine, which induces the differentiation of the culture, is required since differentiation is a critical stage for cephalosporin C production. DL-Methionine induces the formation of arthrospores (a specialized spore derived from the fragmentation of vegetative mycelia) which correlates with cephalosporin C production. Worldwide production of cephalosporin C is estimated at 2000–2400 tons per year for the preparation of 6-ACA.

Clinical utility. The clinical uses of penicillins are usually divided into six groups. Benzylpenicillin belongs to group 1, and is used widely against gram-positive bacteria and some gram-negative bacteria. Group 2, such as azidocillin and phenoxymethylpenicillin (pen V), comprises the orally administered penicillins resembling benzylpenicillin. Group 3, such as cloxacillin and methicillin, are less active than benzylpenicillin against gram-positive bacteria; however, they are highly resistant to staphylococcal β-lactamase. Group 4 comprises the broad-spectrum penicillins, such as ampicillin and amoxicillin. They are used for many common bacterial infections such as those of the upper and lower respiratory tract, the central nervous system, and the urinary tract. Recently, due to the spread of bacterial resistance, they have been relegated to second-line treatment for some of the diseases. Group 5 includes the penicillins active against *Pseudomonas aeruginosa*, such as carbenicillin and carfecillin. Group 6 includes the β-lactamase-resistant penicillins, such as foramidocillin and temocillin. They are used for respiratory disorders and most clinically important gram-negative bacteria, such as gonorrhea, but have no useful activity against *P. aeruginosa*.

Cephalosporins are often divided into generations according to the dates of their production. The first-generation cephalosporins include cephalexin and cephalothin, which have good activity against gram-positive bacteria and a limited number of gram-negative bacteria. The second generation, such as cephamycins, cefamandole, and cefoxitin, are more stable to β-lactamases and thus have enhanced activity against gram-negative bacteria. The third generation, such as cefotaxime, ceftazidime, ceftriaxone, and cefoperazone, have better activity against gram-negative bacteria and generally have weak activity against gram-positive bacteria. They are often used to treat meningitis and *P. aeruginosa*, an organism often encountered in the hospital. The fourth-generation cephalosporins, represented by cefepime, cefpirome, cefoselis, and cefquinome, have broad antibacterial spectra that encompass gram-negative bacteria, including *P. aeruginosa*, and gram-positive bacteria.

Continued improvements have led to highly effective, better absorbed, safe, long-acting, β-lactamase-resistant, and broader-spectrum antibiotics that are used widely today. The new β-lactam antibiotics can be considered active against almost all bacteria responsible for common infectious diseases such as sore throats, bronchitis, pneumonia, meningitis, skin infections, and urinary tract infections.

For background information *see* ANTIBIOTIC; DRUG RESISTANCE; LACTAM; PENICILLIN in the McGraw-Hill Encyclopedia of Science & Technology.

Hsing H. Hou

Bibliography. H. Aoki and M. Okuhara, Natural β-lactam antibiotics, *Annu. Rev. Microbiol.*, 34:159–181, 1980; A. M. Clark and C. D. Hufford, The rise and fall of anti-infectives, *Drug Topics*, pp. 96–104, Jan. 8, 1996; J. C. Fung-Tomc, Fourth-generation cephalosporins, *Clin. Microbiol. Newsl.*, 19:129–136, 1997; D. Hoel and D. N. William, Antibiotics: Past, present, and future—Unearthing nature's magic bullets, *Antibiotics*, 101:114–122, 1997; D. M. Livermore, Are all β-lactams created equal?, *Scand. J. Infect. Dis. Suppl.*, 101:33–34, 1996.

Antimatter

Nuclear energy has been considered as a means for the exploration of space since the early twentieth century. The pioneering rocket scientist R. H. Goddard looked at radioactive decay as a means of propulsion. Although the total energy realized from this process was high, the energy density was too low for this purpose, and he abandoned the idea for the more practical chemical rocket. By the mid-twentieth century, fission, where heavy nuclei are split, and fusion, where light nuclei are joined, were sufficiently understood to be considered for propulsion.

Fission rockets are usually examined in the form of nuclear thermal propulsion, where a nuclear reactor is used to heat a propellant. Nuclear thermal propulsion holds great promise for the crewed exploration of the inner solar system, but is not energetic enough to readily reach the outer planets in the solar system. Fusion propulsion is considerably more energetic, can easily reach all the planets, and may even be useful in sending crewless payloads to the nearer stars.

Fusion propulsion. Unfortunately, fusion systems are heavy and the accelerations are low. In magnetic confinement systems, where magnetic fields are used to confine the fusion plasma, not only are the magnets heavy, but also the components used to heat the plasma, before it is injected into the fusion reactor, are heavy. Both contribute significantly to the mass, resulting in low accelerations. The other widely examined method for generating fusion energy is inertial-confinement fusion. Inertial-confinement fusion uses a pellet of fusion fuel that is heated on its surface by lasers or high-energy particle beams. As the surface expands, it sends a compression wave into the pellet, and the wave drives the fusion reaction by compressing the pellet to a small fraction of its original volume. However, in inertial-confinement fusion the system that generates the beam is also massive, limiting the acceleration to small fractions of the Earth's gravitational pull.

Pion rockets. Fission, fusion, and radioactive decay are not the only mechanisms that yield nuclear energy; there is also the direct annihilation of matter. This can be accomplished by using antimatter in the form of antiprotons. Currently about 10 nanograms of antiprotons are created annually in high-energy accelerators. This production could easily be scaled to 100 ng, but a significant effort would be required to produce 1 microgram per year. When an antiproton is annihilated on a nucleus, the atomic weight of the nucleus is decreased by one (one neutron or proton in the nucleus is annihilated along with the antiproton). The annihilation products consist not of pure energy but mainly of pions. Pions are particles that are intermediate in mass between protons and electrons and transmit the strong force which holds the nucleus together. The pions created in the annihilation are moving at about 95% of the speed of light. The two-thirds of them that are charged can be concentrated and directed with magnetic fields. Unfortunately, a pion rocket uses kilograms of antimatter, placing it well beyond current capabilities, but the pions and the nuclear fragments can be used to heat a propellant. This process requires considerably less antimatter, on the order of 10–100 milligrams for solar-system missions; however, this amount is still beyond current capabilities.

Antiproton-catalyzed propulsion. Obviously, if antiprotons are going to be used in the near future for propulsion, they must be used as a trigger or catalyst. Muon-catalyzed fusion is an example, where muons, which are heavy, higher-energy versions of electrons, can be used to catalyze hundreds of fusion

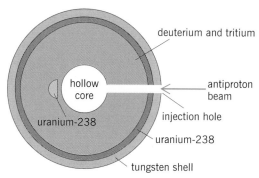

Fig. 1. Construction and geometry of the pellet in an antiproton-catalyzed fission-fusion propulsion system. *(After B. N. Cassenti, T. Kammash, and D. L. Galbraith, Antiproton catalyzed fusion propulsion for interplanetary missions, J. Propul. Power, 13:428–434, 1997)*

reactions. Muons are created when pions decay, and the pions can be created by annihilating antiprotons. Hence, antiproton annihilation provides a low-mass engineering source to support muon-catalyzed fusion.

Antiproton-catalyzed fission. There is a more effective method that could be used to drive a fusion reaction. It has been noted that when an antiproton annihilates a proton on the surface of a nucleus of uranium or plutonium the nucleus will fission, with the subsequent release of fission energy. This observation is important because antiproton annihilation heating cannot effectively heat a fusion plasma, and hence

antiprotons cannot readily be used to drive a fusion reaction directly. However, one antiproton could release the energy of a fission reaction without requiring a critical mass of uranium or plutonium, and the fission reaction products could readily heat a fusion plasma.

Fission-fusion system. A fusion spacecraft based on antiproton-triggered microfission has been designed. A pellet of fusion fuel, somewhat smaller than a tennis ball, consists of a mixture of fusion fuel (deuterium and tritium) and uranium-238. Antiprotons are injected into the pellet and preferentially annihilate protons on the uranium nuclei. The uranium nuclei fission, and the energy of the fission products is used to drive the deuterium-tritium fusion reaction.

Simulations of the system show that the fusion reaction would not propagate at ambient densities and the pellet must be compressed to about one-half its diameter to drive the fusion reaction to completion. The compression is accomplished by using a high-energy lithium beam. The result is similar to inertial-confinement fusion, but the compression required is considerably smaller. The fusion radiation products are used to heat lead propellant; lead is used because of its ability to absorb high-energy electromagnetic radiation.

The mass of the propulsion system is dominated by the mass of the lithium compression driver (which can be as much as 40% of the dry mass), and it would be very beneficial to remove the compression step in the pellet ignition. It has been noted that fusion systems may be based on the magnetic fields created when a laser ionizes the surface of solid. The surface atoms are ionized by the laser light, and the ions and electrons rush away from the surface. The much lighter electrons move more rapidly than the heavier ions, resulting in a net transient current flow. The current flow produces magnetic fields which help to confine the plasma in the same manner as the compression by the high-energy lithium beam.

Unfortunately, the mass of the laser system would now dominate the propulsion-system mass. However, a low-mass system using antiprotons can heat the surface, and this step can be accomplished by placing a chip of uranium at the annihilation site. The annihilation depth can be set by tuning the energy of the beam of antiprotons. Thus, it is possible to design a pellet based on a combination of effects (**Fig. 1**). The antiprotons are injected at the proper energy to be annihilated in a small region near the surface of the uranium. The uranium fission products heat the solid fusion fuel above and the resulting plasma in a hollow core. The magnetic fields, generated by the electron flow, develop the confinement. As a result, the plasma in the core is contained sufficiently long to complete the fusion reaction, allowing this reaction to propagate outward from the core. A heavy metal shell on the outside of the pellet helps to contain the fusion reactants and, if the shell contained uranium, addi-

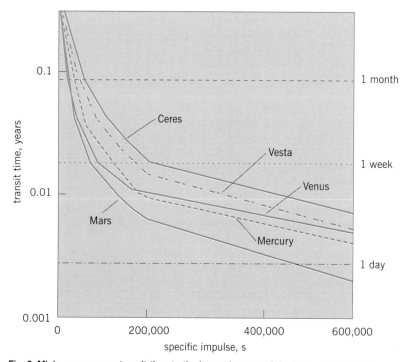

Fig. 2. Minimum one-way transit time to the inner planets and the large asteroids Ceres and Vesta for a spacecraft whose ratio of initial mass divided by final mass is 1.5. *(After B. N. Cassenti, T. Kammash, and D. L. Galbraith, Antiproton catalyzed fusion propulsion for interplanetary missions, J. Propul. Power, 13:428–434, 1997)*

tional fission reactions would help to contain the reactants. The pellet could be as small as a Ping-Pong ball and would have a yield equivalent to 20 tons of TNT.

Nuclear pulse propulsion. Nuclear explosions, much larger than the yield of the pellet, were considered for space propulsion into the 1960s, but the projects were canceled by an international agreement to ban nuclear weapons in space. Two basic propulsion concepts were examined: external-pulse and internal-pulse. In the external-pulse version, a nuclear device is exploded behind a pusher plate. A fraction of the blast is deflected by the plate and some of the pusher plate material is ablated, resulting in a thrust. In internal-pulse propulsion, the explosion occurs in a chamber and the gas, with ablated liner material, is ejected through a nozzle.

Specific impulses. The propulsion systems discussed cover a wide performance range. A measure of the performance is the specific impulse. The final speeds of a given rocket are an exponential function of the specific impulse. Hence, a small change in the specific impulse has a large effect on the final velocity. Current liquid and solid rockets are limited to a specific impulse of less than 500 s (see **table**). A nuclear thermal rocket has a specific impulse twice as large and can readily carry out crewed missions to Mars or Venus. Antiproton-triggered fusion propulsion will have a significantly higher performance than nuclear thermal systems. For example, an antiproton-triggered internal-pulse system is limited by the strength of the containment vessel to about 3000 s, but an external-pulse system can have a specific impulse as high as 600,000 s. The 600,000-s limit assumes that 100% of the fusion fuel is consumed, but it is more likely that only 5 or 10% will fuse, resulting in a specific impulse of 100,000 or 200,000 s.

Transit times. By using external-pulse propulsion, the inner planets of the solar system and the asteroids can be reached in a few days (**Fig. 2**), and would be easily accessible to tourists. The outer planets require at least 1 week to Jupiter and almost 2 months to Pluto (**Fig. 3**). The transit times are short enough for colonization and trade but are long for tourism. To reach the outer planets in a few days will require the performance of a high-thrust pion

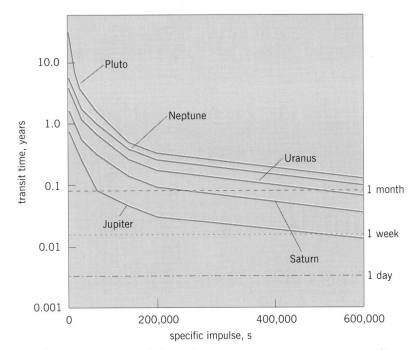

Fig. 3. Minimum one-way transit time to the outer planets for a spacecraft whose ratio of initial mass divided by final mass is 1.5. *(After B. N. Cassenti, T. Kammash, and D. L. Galbraith, Antiproton catalyzed fusion propulsion for interplanetary missions, J. Propul. Power, 13:428–434, 1997)*

rocket, which has an astounding 21,000,000 s for the specific impulse.

For background information *see* ANTIMATTER; NUCLEAR FUSION; ROCKET PROPULSION; SPECIFIC IMPULSE in the McGraw-Hill Encyclopedia of Science & Technology.   Brice N. Cassenti

Bibliography. B. N. Cassenti, T. Kammash, and D. L. Galbraith, Antiproton catalyzed fusion propulsion for interplanetary missions, *J. Propul. Power*, 13:428–434, 1997; T. Kammash and D. L. Galbraith, Antimatter driven fusion propulsion for solar system exploration, *J. Propul. Power*, 8:644–649, 1992; R. A. Lewis et al., Antiproton based microfission, *Fusion Technol.*, 20:1046–1050, 1991.

Antimicrobial resistance

After a half century of virtually complete control over infectious diseases in the developed countries, the 1990s brought a worldwide resurgence of bacterial and viral diseases. An important part of this phenomenon is the emergence of antimicrobial-resistance genes in virtually all major disease-causing bacteria.

Emergence. Bacteria are genetically versatile and can evolve genes that render them resistant to antimicrobials. A bacterium can incorporate deoxyribonucleic acid (DNA) from different bacterial species and even from different bacterial genera into its own genetic makeup. Bacteria also multiply very rapidly. Under ideal conditions, they double their numbers in less than 20 min. In the 50 years

Performance comparison of propulsion systems	
Propulsion system	Specific impulse, s
Chemical solid propellant	300
Chemical liquid propellant	450
Nuclear thermal propulsion	900
Antiproton-triggered fusion propulsion	
Internal-pulse propulsion	3,000
External-pulse propulsion, 5% burn	100,000
External-pulse propulsion, 10% burn	200,000
External-pulse propulsion, 100% burn	600,000
Pion (antiproton annihilation)	21,000,000

Key:

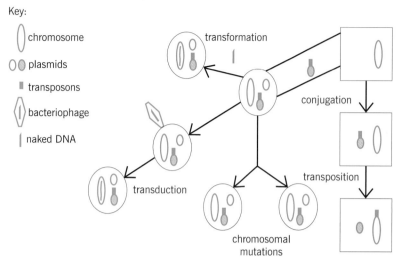

Mechanisms of genetic transfer of antimicrobial resistance in bacterial populations.

since antimicrobials were introduced, bacteria have evolved through as many generations as human beings have during the last 25 million years. If even one in a billion bacterial cells survives exposure to an antimicrobial by becoming resistant, its descendants quickly reproduce and amplify antimicrobial resistance.

In recent years, there have been major changes in human demographics and behavior that contribute to the problem of antimicrobial-resistant pathogens. The large concentrations of children in daycare centers, the increasingly global nature of the food supply, and the mobility of people and their animals contribute to the spread of antimicrobial-resistance genes. Economic development and land-use changes result in disturbances of ecosystems. In both human and veterinary medicine, there has been an increase in invasive medical interventions, and prolonged survival of many individuals with chronic, debilitating diseases. There is a tremendous increase in the number of immunocompromised individuals, such as persons with HIV, the elderly, and the intentionally immunodepressed.

Origins. Resistance to antimicrobials results either from invention and subsequent acquisition of new DNA or from mutation in existing DNA. Acquisition of DNA carrying resistance genes is the most important process in the evolution of antimicrobial resistance. Evidence suggests that the DNA acquired by resistant bacteria did not originate after the use of antimicrobials in medicine but evolved long ago in an evolutionary process. The original genes, from which resistance genes evolved, coded for proteins involved in normal bacterial metabolism. For example, *Staphylococcus aureus* possessed β-lactamase enzymes before the discovery of β-lactam antibiotics such as penicillin. The β-lactamase enzyme conferred a survival advantage by providing protection against lytic enzymes normally present in nasal secretions.

Mechanisms. Antimicrobial resistance can be mutational or transmissible. Chromosomal mutations in bacteria can occur and be passed to progeny during replication. Bacteria can also exchange or transmit antimicrobial resistance by four mechanisms: transformation, transduction, conjugation, and transposition (see **illus.**).

Transformation occurs when bacteria pick up and use naked DNA from the environment. The DNA may have come from a nearby bacterial cell that has died and ruptured. Once in a new cell, the naked DNA becomes part of the host's chromosome or a plasmid and begins to function. Transduction is a genetic exchange between bacteria by a bacterial virus known as a bacteriophage. Conjugation is the transfer of one or more plasmids from one bacterium to another via a pilus that temporarily connects the two bacteria. All bacteria contain the majority of their genetic information on a single chromosome. In addition, bacteria carry small circles of accessory DNA, called plasmids. Plasmids carry 3 to 300 genes. A bacterium may have 1 to 1000 copies of a single plasmid and may simultaneously contain many different plasmids. The cell containing the plasmid transfers it to the recipient while retaining a copy. Some plasmids have broad host ranges and can be exchanged between bacterial species (for example, from an *Escherichia coli* to a *Salmonella*). Transposition is the transfer of DNA sequences in either the same DNA strand or between independently replicating DNA strands. Thus, transposable DNA (transposons) can "jump" onto endogenous plasmids or the chromosome of a new host. Genetic resistance is greatly amplified by transposons: they are not subject to the constraints of plasmids for vector replication because they do not rely on a host cell or host DNA molecule to exist or multiply.

Population genetics. In the presence of antimicrobial usage, the transmissible mechanisms of genetic transfer in bacterial populations result in the emergence of antimicrobial-resistant bacteria. Any kind of antimicrobial use runs the risk of selecting resistant organisms and increasing the reservoir of resistance genes.

Many of the plasmids responsible for antimicrobial resistance carry genes that code for resistance to more than one antimicrobial. Enteric bacteria commonly contain plasmids for resistance to five or more antimicrobials. The plasmid that encodes resistance to a particular antimicrobial is selected by the use of other antimicrobials whose resistance is also encoded by the plasmid. In addition to the antimicrobial-associated linkage selection, resistance plasmids often carry genes for other characteristics, such as resistance to ultraviolet light, to mercury and other heavy metals, to fermentation of carbon energy sources, and to virulence. Associated linkage selection for these other plasmid-encoded characteristics contributes to the persistence of plasmid-mediated antimicrobial resistance even when antimicrobials are not used at all.

While antimicrobial therapy is usually directed at specific pathogens, the normal bacterial flora of the gastrointestinal tract, nasopharynx, and other sites in the treated host are also affected by systemic and topical application of antimicrobials. Antimicrobial treatment imposes intense selection pressure on bacteria in these populations, so that the frequencies of resistant bacteria rapidly increase and the diversity of these populations is reduced. Normally commensal bacteria such as *E. coli* and *S. aureus* serve as a reservoir for antimicrobial-resistance genes that can be transmitted to more obligate pathogens such as *Salmonella* species.

Trends. *Staphylococcus aureus* is the most frequent cause of hospital-acquired infections. Isolates of staphylococci acquired by outpatients are typically resistant to penicillin but are susceptible to most other antimicrobials. The major therapeutic difficulty is methicillin-resistant *S. aureus*, which is primarily seen in large teaching hospitals, nursing homes, and intravenous drug users. Fluoroquinolones, introduced in the mid-1980s, initially were very active against nearly all staphylococcal isolates. By 1992, fewer than 20% of methicillin-resistant *S. aureus* strains were inhibited by any of the commercially available fluoroquinolones, and the only drug that most of these strains remained susceptible to was vancomycin.

Pneumococci are the major cause of community-acquired pneumonia and a major cause of meningitis and otitis media in children. Increasing resistance in pneumococci is occurring stepwise, involving point mutations in the same as well as in independent chromosomal genes. Until recently, most penicillin-resistant pneumococci were reported from developing countries or from native populations in North America, but there are new reports of resistance in developed countries. Many of the penicillin-resistant pneumococcal strains are also resistant to other antimicrobials, including erythromycin, tetracycline, chloramphenicol, and trimethoprim/sulfonamide combinations.

The increasing resistance in hospital-acquired gram-negative infections is often due to an outbreak of a multidrug-resistant strain of a traditionally more susceptible species, such as *E. coli* or *Klebsiella* species. However, sometimes it is due to the prevalence of inherently more resistant species such as *Enterobacter, Citrobacter, Pseudomonas,* or *Serratia*. Initially, the third-generation cephalosporins were active against essentially all *E. coli* and *Klebsiella*. However, these bacteria easily became resistant, and by the 1980s they had acquired resistance to these antimicrobials.

Multidrug-resistant *Salmonella typhimurium* DT104 initially emerged in cattle in 1988 in England and Wales. Subsequently, it has been isolated from poultry, sheep, pigs, and horses. Outbreaks of human disease in the United Kingdom have been associated with poultry, meat products, unpasteurized milk, and contact with affected cattle. The United Kingdom observed a tenfold increase in the number of human cases of multidrug-resistant *Sal. typhimurium* DT104 from 1990 to 1996. Resistance is seen to ampicillin, chloramphenicol, streptomycin, sulfonamides, and tetracycline. Since 1994, an increasing number of cases with resistance to trimethoprim and ciprofloxacin has been reported. Infection with *Sal. typhimurium* DT104 is associated with hospitalization rates that are twice as high as other zoonotic food-borne salmonella infections and with case fatality rates ten times higher.

Enterococci are now common organisms in hospital-acquired infections, causing numerous problems with antimicrobial resistance. These organisms are inherently resistant to cephalosporins, penicillins, and clindamycin. In addition, they have a number of acquired resistances due primarily to plasmids or transposons. These include resistance to aminoglycosides, erythromycin, chloramphenicol, tetracyclines, and ciprofloxacin. The major clinical concerns are high-level resistance to aminoglycosides and vancomycin. Vancomycin had been in clinical use for more than 30 years without the emergence of marked resistance. Because of its activity against methicillin-resistant *S. aureus* and other gram-positive bacteria, it became very widely used for therapy and prophylaxis against such infections. However, data indicate that vancomycin resistance increased more than 20-fold from 1989 to 1995; some recently isolated strains of enterococci actually require vancomycin to grow. This demonstrates the remarkable ability of bacteria to adapt to the intense selection pressure of antimicrobial therapy.

For background information *see* ANTIBIOTIC; ANTIMICROBIAL AGENTS; BACTERIAL GENETICS; DRUG RESISTANCE; HOSPITAL INFECTION; MUTATION; PENICILLIN in the McGraw-Hill Encyclopedia of Science & Technology.   Patricia M. Dowling

Bibliography. M. L. Cohen, Epidemiology of drug resistance: Implications for a post-antimicrobial era, *Science*, 257:1050–1055, 1992; H. S. Gold and R. C. Moellering, Antimicrobial-drug resistance, *New Engl. J. Med.*, 335:1445–1453, 1996; B. R. Levin et al., The population genetics of antibiotic resistance, *Clin. Infect. Dis.*, 24(suppl. 1):S9–S16, 1997; J. Travis, Reviving the antibiotic miracle?, *Science*, 264:360–362, 1994.

Archaea

While members of the Archaea have a cellular morphology that is very similar to that of other prokaryotes (Bacteria), they are as closely related to eukaryotes as they are to prokaryotes at the genetic level. Other cellular, molecular, and biochemical evidence supports the unique nature of this group relative to all other known life forms. In recognition of the fact that the profound differences between Bacteria and Archaea represented two distinct evolutionary trajectories within prokaryotes, the Archaea were des-

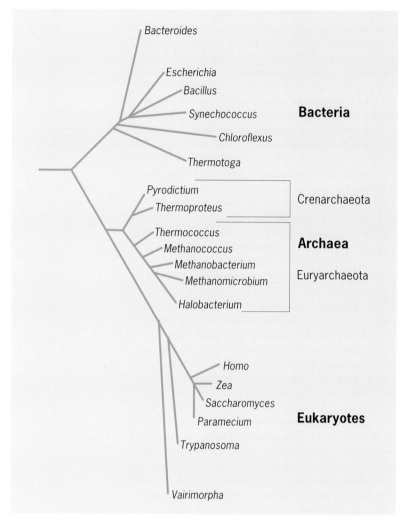

Bacteroides

Escherichia

Bacillus

Synechococcus

Bacteria

Chloroflexus

Thermotoga

Pyrodictium

Thermoproteus

Crenarchaeota

Thermococcus

Methanococcus

Archaea

Methanobacterium

Methanomicrobium

Euryarchaeota

Halobacterium

Homo

Zea

Saccharomyces

Paramecium

Eukaryotes

Trypanosoma

Vairimorpha

Universal tree of life based on ribosomal RNA (small subunit) sequence data. The rooting of the tree is based on the phylogenetic analysis of genes that duplicated prior to the divergence of the three main lineages. *(Adapted from G. Olsen and C. Woese, Archaeal genomics: An overview, Cell, 89(7):991–994, 1997)*

ing molecular hydrogen to reduce carbon dioxide to methane, a process known as methanogenesis.

Complete genome sequencing revealed that *M. jannaschii* has a circular genome of approximately 1.7 million nucleotides that encodes over 1700 genes. The cell also contains two circular extrachromosomal elements (58,000 nucleotides encoding 44 genes and 16,000 nucleotides encoding 12 genes). By using a computer-aided sequence-similarity matching algorithm, the gene sequences (and their corresponding amino acid translations) predicted from the *M. jannaschii* genome sequence were compared to archives of deoxyribonucleic acid (DNA) and protein sequences obtained from diverse prokaryotic and eukaryotic organisms. When a significant DNA or amino acid match to a gene or protein of known function was observed, the identity and function of the gene in *M. jannaschii* was inferred from the match. Over half of the genes identified in *M. jannaschii* had no significant match to any known gene or protein, and represent newly discovered genes. Many of these genes are unique to the Archaea and contain essential information for understanding the unique biochemistry and physiology of the members of this lineage.

Extrachromosomal elements. None of the 12 genes detected on the small extrachromosomal element matched any known genes or proteins. Of the 44 genes predicted for the large extrachromosomal element, two are similar to DNA restriction enzymes, and another two appear to be archaeal histone genes. While there is no direct experimental evidence to demonstrate physical interaction of extrachromosomal elements with the main chromosome in *M. jannaschii*, there are several repeated regions and genes of unknown function on the large extrachromosomal element that show a high degree of sequence similarity with the main chromosome. This suggests that an exchange of genetic material occurred between the two structures. The large extrachromosomal element contains three separate areas that are characterized by a higher-than-average (compared to the rest of the genome) content of guanine + cytosine nucleotides and that display mirror symmetry. This sequence pattern suggests that the DNA may be capable of forming a triple-stranded structure.

Similarities to bacteria. Several features of the structure, organization, and gene content of the *M. jannaschii* genome are similar to that of bacterial genomes. The genome of *M. jannaschii* is circular, the genes are densely packed, and some genes are organized into functional units called operons. Many of the genes in *M. jannaschii* associated with metabolism and cell division are clearly homologous (related by descent from a common ancestor) to those found in bacteria.

Cell processing systems. Genes involved in the cell information-processing systems of DNA replication, transcription, and translation reveal a close evolutionary affinity between Archaea and Eukaryotes. Although not all of the genes necessary for genome

ignated as a third domain of life (see **illus.**). Although the unique nature of Archaea is undeniable, many scientists believed that the group represented highly specialized bacteria. The clinching evidence to support the three-domain view of the evolution of extant life (Archaea, Bacteria, Eukaryotes) would come from the analysis of the complete genetic complement, or genome, of an archaeon.

Genome sequence. The first member of the Archaea to have its genome completely deciphered was the methanogen *Methanococcus jannaschii*. The organism was discovered in 1982 in a sediment sample retrieved from a deep-sea thermal vent 2600 m (8530 ft) below the Pacific Ocean surface. The optimal growth conditions for the organism reflect its natural habitat. It grows and reproduces best at temperatures close to the boiling point of water (100°C or 212°F) and at 200 atmospheres of pressure. The organism is an obligate anaerobe and is autotrophic. *Methanococcus jannaschii* derives its energy by us-

replication have been identified in *M. jannaschii*, the recognizable ones (based on sequence similarity to genes of known function in sequence archives) are clear homologs to eukaryotic genes. A single DNA polymerase identified in *M. jannaschii* is homologous with the epsilon member of the B family of eukaryotic DNA polymerases. Replication factor C and DNA ligase are more closely related to the eukaryotic counterparts as opposed to the analogous bacterial genes.

Transcription is catalyzed by a multisubunit ribonucleic acid (RNA) polymerase enzyme. Five core subunits of the DNA-dependent RNA polymerase complex are homologous among Archaea, Bacteria, and Eukaryotes. The archaeal and eukaryotic core subunits of RNA polymerase are more similar to each other than to the corresponding bacterial components. Archaea and Eukaryotes share additional subunits of RNA polymerase that are not found in Bacteria. Transcription initiation in *M. jannaschii* is quite different from that in Bacteria and appears to be very similar to the system in Eukaryotes. Translation (messenger RNA–directed protein synthesis) is the most universal of the three cell information-processing systems. Thus, the basic translation machinery is quite similar across all three domains of life. Most of the ribosomal protein associated with translation machinery is present in all three domains. There are, however, ribosomal proteins unique to Bacteria, and others specific to Eukaryotes. The complete ribosomal protein complement of *M. jannaschii* has all of the universal ribosomal proteins and homologs for some that are eukaryotic specific. The genome does not, however, encode any homologs of the bacterial ribosomal proteins. All the other major components of the translation mechanism, including translation initiation and elongation factors, and aminoacyl–transfer RNA synthetases resemble genes from the Eukaryote lineage more closely than those from the Bacteria lineage.

Histones. The *M. jannaschii* genome encodes a set of five histone proteins that have the typical eukaryotic histone sequence signatures. As in eukaryotic genomes, the archaeal histones are involved in DNA supercoiling and regulation of gene expression. Two of the five *M. jannaschii* histones are found on the large extrachromosomal element; three are found on the main (1.7-million-nucleotide) chromosome.

Protein secretion. The protein secretion apparatus packages proteins for transport from the cytoplasm to the cell surface. In *M. jannaschii*, some components of this system (translocation-associated protein) are more similar to bacterial genes, while others (signal recognition protein, signal peptidase, and docking protein) have greater sequence similarity to eukaryotic genes.

Energy production. All of the known genetic components necessary for methanogenesis were identified in the *M. jannaschii* genome. The organism can apparently use both elemental hydrogen and formate as substrates for energy production. However, it lacks the genetic capacity to use methanol or acetate as other methanogenic archaea do. While *M. jannaschii* can survive and reproduce by using only inorganic materials, its genome does possess several scavenging enzymes for importing small organic compounds (such as amino acids) from its environment.

Self-splicing proteins. The coding regions of 14 genes with diverse functions in *M. jannaschii* are disrupted by sequences that code for self-splicing protein segments called inteins. After inteins are excised in the mature protein, the remaining protein sequences, called exteins, are joined to form a second functional protein. Inteins were discovered in yeast, and only 10 other instances of intein-containing genes were known prior to the sequencing of the *M. jannaschii* genome. Inteins generally encode DNA endonucleases, but the sequence of the *M. jannaschii* inteins does not show significant sequence similarity to known endonucleases. The biological significance of inteins is not yet understood.

Understanding cell origins. The genome sequence of *M. jannaschii* has verified the unique nature of the Archaea and provides the best evidence to date of the close evolutionary relationship between Archaea and Eukaryotes. Metabolically and structurally, there are strong similarities between Archaea and Bacteria. However, these similarities may reflect the basic nature of the universal ancestor to all extant life rather than a specific relationship between the two prokaryotic life forms. The emerging view of the evolution suggests a universal common ancestor that gave rise to one lineage leading to the Bacteria and a second lineage shared in common by Archaea and Eukaryotes but that split into two distinct lineages within a half billion years. As additional genomes from the three domains are completely sequenced, it will be possible to more accurately trace the complex evolutionary pathways of genes and organisms and to better understand the connection between the two.

For background information *see* ARCHAEA; DEEP-SEA BACTERIA; EUKARYOTAE; GENE; METHANOGENESIS (BACTERIA); PROKARYOTAE in the McGraw-Hill Encyclopedia of Science & Technology.   Carol J. Bult

Bibliography. C. J. Bult et al., Complete genome sequence of the methanogenic archaeon, *Methanococcus jannaschii*, *Science*, 273:1058–1073, 1996; C. R. Woese, Archaebacteria, *Sci. Amer.*, 244(6):98–122, June 1981; C. R. Woese et al., Towards a natural system of organisms: Proposal for the domains Archaea, Bacteria, and Eucarya, *Proc. Nat. Acad. Sci. USA*, 87:4576–4579, 1990.

Archeological chemistry

Chemical techniques are applied in archeological research to determine the composition and isotopic makeup of biological, natural, and synthetic remains. Chemical and isotopic studies of plant and animal residues are undertaken to investigate ancient diet, nutrition, and resource use. Compositional analysis of natural or synthetic materials and residues is performed to ascertain artifact manufacturing processes and use. Archeological chemistry expertise is used to ascertain the processes that govern the preservation and decay of materials, thus providing valuable information regarding subsequent conservation and restoration. It has also been employed to determine the location of a geographical source of procurement or production of materials used in long-distance contact or trade.

Traditionally, chemical investigations in archeology focused primarily on natural (for example, stone) and synthetic (for example, ceramics, metals, glass, and glazes) inorganic materials. Organic materials derived from biological sources can be divided into amorphous residues and morphological remains. Organic residues differ in one crucial respect from the main body of organic remains: they lack the macroscopic cellular structure present in seeds, wood, leather, and pollen. Common examples of organic residues are (1) the debris associated with the remains of food and other natural products, as a result of manipulation in pottery containers, (2) the balms in the wrappings of mummified bodies, and (3) traces of coloring dyes impregnated in ancient textiles. Given the amorphous character of organic residues, the most effective approach to their identification lies in molecular composition. Characterization of organic residues generally relies upon the principles of chemotaxonomy, where the presence of a specific compound (or distribution of compounds) in an unknown sample is matched with its presence in a contemporary natural substance. The use of such molecular markers is not without its problems, since many compounds are widely distributed in a range of natural materials, and the composition of an ancient residue may have changed significantly since the time of burial. In general, molecular markers belong to the compound class defined as lipids, a heterogeneous group of molecules which includes fats, oils, resins, and waxes.

Methods. Archeological chemists have explored the application of various analytical techniques (spectroscopy and chromatography) for determining the origin of organic residues.

Gas chromatography. In this sensitive separation technique, the components of a volatile sample are partitioned between a mobile gaseous phase and a stationary solid phase. The chromatogram shows a trace of the variation in component concentration against time, and may be used to obtain qualitative and quantitative information.

Mass spectrometry. Coupling a mass spectrometer to the effluent of a gas chromatograph combines the powerful analytical capability of mass spectrometry with the high degree of separation possible with gas chromatography. At the simplest level, the mass spectrometer ionizes molecules, then identifies the ions according to their mass-to-charge (m/z) ratio, resulting in the generation of a mass spectrum (ion abundance against the m/z value). In many cases,

mass spectra allow the individual compounds present to be detected with some certainty. Gas chromatography/mass spectrometry has been used widely in the identification of ancient lipid residues, resins, and waxes.

Pyrolysis. Analytical pyrolysis is often combined with gas chromatography/mass spectrometry. Pyrolysis is the preferred method for breaking up the insoluble or polymeric fraction of organic residues that are not volatile enough for conventional analysis, thereby allowing separation and identification of the fragments. Pyrolysis–gas chromatography/mass spectrometry has been applied successfully to the study of fossil and recent higher-plant resins and to the macromolecular debris remaining from the burning of food in archeological pottery vessels.

Isotopic ratios. The recent introduction of gas chromatography–combustion–isotope ratio mass spectrometry allows the ratios of abundance of stable isotopes of elements such as carbon and nitrogen to be determined for individual compounds introduced via a gas chromatograph. Stable isotope ratios are of particular importance to studies of food webs because of the characteristic isotope signatures of plants utilizing different photosynthetic pathways. These distinctive ratios are passed along the food chain to herbivores and carnivores. The method requires very small samples, and is being applied to trace organic residues in pottery vessels to establish origin of the food source with a high degree of precision.

High-performance liquid chromatography. In high-performance liquid chromatography, the stationary phase can be a solid surface, an ion-exchange resin, or a porous polymer. The stationary phase is held in a column through which a liquid mobile phase is forced under pressure. Components separate according to interactions with the stationary phase. High-performance liquid chromatography is more versatile than gas chromatography because the sample components need not be in the vapor state. It has been used in archeology for the separation of amino acids and peptides (for the purposes of dating and amino acid racemization studies), the analysis of ancient dyes, and even the identification of alkaloids (for example, caffeine and theobromine) characteristic of cacao preserved in Mayan archeological ceramics.

Infrared absorption spectroscopy. Infrared absorption spectroscopy can be used to detect changes in vibrational movements of bonds in molecules, and is very useful for detecting the presence of specific functional groups because of the absorption of infrared radiation at characteristic wavelengths (in the range 2.5–15 micrometers). Although the technique can be limited for complex mixtures comprising many degraded components, the technique offers some possibilities for screening organic residues and "fingerprinting" certain substances. In particular, infrared spectroscopy has been very successful in characterizing Baltic amber found in prehistoric sites in

Europe and distinguishing it from other European fossil resins.

Ultraviolet/visible absorption spectroscopy. Ultraviolet/visible absorption spectroscopy has been useful in confirming the identity of dyestuffs from the New and Old worlds. Absorption of electromagnetic radiation in the ultraviolet/visible region (in the range 190–800 nanometers) transfers energy to cause transitions in the electronic energy levels of the bonds of a molecule, and results in excitation of electrons from the ground state to the excited state.

Nuclear magnetic resonance spectroscopy. Nuclear magnetic resonance spectroscopy operates on the principle of detecting the energy absorption accompanying the transition between nuclear spin states that occur when a molecule is placed in a strong magnetic field and irradiated with radio-frequency waves. Different nuclei within a molecule are in slightly different magnetic environments and therefore show absorptions at slightly different frequencies. Nuclear magnetic resonance spectroscopy has provided valuable information on the structure of highly cross-linked fossil resin samples from around the world.

Residues. Pottery vessels were extensively used in antiquity for transporting, storing, and preparing solid and liquid foods and beverages. The survival of organic molecules consistent with a particular food source provides a valuable means of determining artifact use patterns and food consumption. The survival of ancient wine residues in pottery containers from the Old World has also been suggested. *See* ANALYTICAL CHEMISTRY.

Fats and waxes. Recent research suggests that animal fats (such as adipose tissue, dairy products, and fish/marine mammal oils) and plant tissues (notably the waxy compounds coating leaf surfaces) have the ability, under favorable burial conditions, to survive either as constituents of visible surface debris or as residues absorbed into the permeable ceramic matrix (see **illus.**).

Resins. Higher plant resins, and their heated derivatives (wood tar and pitch), served as sealants and adhesives, perfumes, caulking materials, and embalming substances. The widespread use of a tar derived from heating birch (*Betula* sp.) bark has been demonstrated in prehistoric Europe from the early Holocene Epoch onward. This tar served as a ubiquitous hafting adhesive for attaching stone tools to handles of wood, bone, or antler. Birch bark tar is also the source of chewing gums excavated from bog sites of Mesolithic date in southern Scandinavia. Recent historical evidence suggests that chewing the tar may have played a role in dental hygiene and in treating throat disorders. Molecules consistent with beeswax (of *Apis mellifera*) have been identified on a pottery vessel dating to the 4th millennium B.C. in Europe, providing evidence for the collection of wax and, by assumption, honey in antiquity.

Bitumen represents the fraction of sedimentary organic matter which is soluble in organic solvents

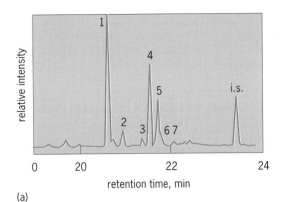

(a)

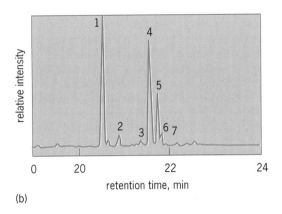

(b)

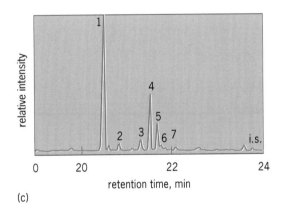

(c)

Key:

1 = *n*-nonacosane
2 = *n*-hexacosanol
3 = *n*-heptacosanol
4 = nonacosan-15-one

5 = nonacosan-15-ol
6 = *n*-hentriacontane
7 = *n*-octacosanol
i.s. = internal standard

Partial gas chromatograms of the lipid extracts from (a) an experimental pottery vessel used to cook *Brassica oleracea* (cabbage) leaves; (b) modern *Brassica* leaves; and (c) a jar (circa A.D. 1000–1150). These data demonstrate that epicuticular waxes are mobilized during cooking, resulting in their absorption into the vessel wall and survival during burial. *(From S. Charters et al., Simulation experiments for determining the use of ancient pottery vessels: The behaviour of epicuticular leaf wax during boiling of a leafy vegetable, J. Archaeol. Sci., 24:1–7, 1997)*

(the insoluble fraction is known as kerogen). The liquid or semisolid varieties of bitumen were widely used in the Near East and Middle East in antiquity, serving as a multipurpose glue and waterproofing material, a building mortar, a medicinal agent, and a constituent of the organic preparations applied to mummified bodies in ancient Egypt. Compounds consistent with a bituminous substance include saturated hydrocarbons which have linear (alkylated alkanes) or cyclic (steranes and terpanes) carbon skeletons. These molecules derive largely from microscopic plants deposited in the sediments along with bacterial inputs. It has proved possible to identify molecular and isotopic characteristics of the bitumen which enable archeological finds to be assigned to a particular source of bitumen. At the site of Susa, Iraq (dating from the beginning of the 4th millennium B.C.), bitumen was deliberately mixed and heated with mineral elements to produce a substance known as bitumen mastic, a product ideal for fashioning decorative objects by sculpture.

For background information *see* ARCHEOLOGICAL CHEMISTRY; GAS CHROMATOGRAPHY; INFRARED SPECTROSCOPY; LIQUID CHROMATOGRAPHY; MASS SPECTROMETRY; NUCLEAR MAGNETIC RESONANCE (NMR); SPECTROSCOPY in the McGraw-Hill Encyclopedia of Science & Technology.   Carl Heron

Bibliography. J. Connan and O. Deschesne, *Le Bitume à Suse: Collection du Musée du Louvre, Département des Antiquités Orientales, Musée du Louvre, Paris, France*, 1996; K. Evans and C. Heron, Glue, disinfectant and chewing gum: Natural products chemistry in archaeology, *Chem. Ind.*, 12:446–449, 1993; A. M. Pollard and C. Heron, *Archaeological Chemistry*, 1996.

Arcjet

Long-distance space flights to other planets in the solar system and beyond, such as to Mars, would involve propulsion systems that operate for long periods of time, measured in months and years, in contrast to the present chemical rocket propulsion time of a few minutes. This article discusses the need for such systems to have large exhaust velocities or specific impulses, and then focuses on the use of arcjet propulsion systems to meet these objectives. *See* MARS.

Need for large specific impulse. The characteristic velocity change necessary for planetary transfer missions is of the order of 10 km/s (6 mi/s); for example, for a mission from Earth orbit to Mars orbit and return, it is 14 km/s (9 mi/s). In order to keep the propellant mass to reasonable values, the propellant exhaust velocity should ideally be comparable to the velocity change required for the mission. This means that exhaust velocities of 10 km/s (6 mi/s) or specific impulses (defined as exhaust velocity divided by the acceleration of gravity) of greater than 1000 s are required, much higher than that which can be achieved by the best chemical rockets.

With the abundance of satellites in Earth orbit, there has been increased interest in propulsion systems capable of thrusting for long periods of time to transfer satellites from low Earth orbits to geosynchronous Earth orbits and to maintain satellite position and orientation for up to 15 years. It has been estimated that over 1000 satellites will be launched to low Earth orbit during the decade 1998–2007. For low-Earth-orbit and geosynchronous-Earth-orbit missions, characteristic velocity increments of 5–10 km/s (3–6 mi/s) are needed. In the station-keeping case, it has been shown that characteristic velocity increments of more than 1 km/s (0.6 mi/s) are required.

Thus, in the space missions now in prospect, there is an apparent need for high-specific-impulse propulsion systems, capable of providing large characteristic velocity increments and operating for long periods of time, to reduce the mass of vehicles placed in Earth orbit or propelled to other planetary systems. Since chemical rocket propulsion systems are inherently limited to specific impulses of a few hundred seconds, it is necessary to seek new methods of heating and accelerating propellant materials. One such method is to utilize electrical heating of the propellant gas and its acceleration by electric and magnetic body forces.

Electric propulsion. Electric propulsion systems may be divided into three categories: (1) electrothermal propulsion systems, wherein the propellant gas is heated electrically and the thrust is developed by thermodynamic forces produced by expansion through a nozzle; (2) electrostatic propulsion systems, often referred to as ion propulsion, wherein the electrically charged propellant particles (ions) are accelerated by electric fields; and (3) electromagnetic propulsion, often referred to as electrodynamic or magnetoplasmadynamic (MPD) systems, wherein the ionized propellant (plasma) is accelerated by internal or external electromagnetic force fields.

In the case where there is ideal conversion of electrical power into heat which, in turn, is converted without flow losses into kinetic energy, hydrogen is the optimum propellant since it has the lowest molecular weight. For the case where hydrogen is used as the propellant at a temperature of 3000 K (5000°F), an exhaust velocity of approximately 10 km/s (6 mi/s) would be produced, corresponding to a specific impulse of 1000 s. In practice, other propellant gases, such as helium, ammonia, and hydrazine, may be chosen because they are more readily storable in space (**Table 1**).

Propulsion systems. One category of electric propulsion system that employs electrical means to heat the gas to obtain an exhaust velocity (or specific impulse) higher than that achievable in chemical combustion is the arcjet (or plasma jet). Very high gas temperatures (greater than 10,000 K or 17,500°F) can be achieved with arc heating. At very high power levels, arcjets can operate as magnetoplasmadynamic systems.

TABLE 1. Performance comparison of typical propulsion systems

Engine type	Specific impulse, s	Thrust, mN (mlbf)	Specific power, W/mN	Overall thruster efficiency, %	Thrusting times
Chemical bipropellant	200–460	1 to 10^{10} (0.2 to 2×10^9)	Not applicable	80–97	Seconds to days
Resistojet	200–600	2 to 1000 (0.4 to 200)	0.5–6	50–90	Days to years
Electrothermal arcjet	280–1500	2 to 2000 (0.4 to 400)	2–2.5	20–50	Days to years*

* New systems are expected to have operational lifetimes greater than 10 years.
SOURCE: After J. D. Fillben, *Electric Propulsion for Spacecraft Applicators*, CPTR-96-64, Chemical Propulsion Information Agency, 1996.

In a simple model of the arcjet (**Fig. 1**), the propellant is heated to a very high temperature as it flows through the arc discharge. The hot gas is then expanded through a gas-dynamic nozzle to achieve thrust. In this mode the arcjet is acting in the electrothermal category. In contrast to resistojets, which are limited to temperatures of less than a few thousand kelvins because of material considerations, gas temperatures greater than tens of thousands kelvins can be achieved in the arc discharge.

System advantages. With the advent of geostationary communication satellites, arcjet propulsion systems offer many advantages, including delivery of increased payload mass to a given orbit. The use of arcjet systems for orbit insertion, satellite positioning, and deorbiting permits considerable mass to be added to the satellite. In fact, the use of arcjet systems allows inclusion of an additional satellite per launch, resulting in major overall cost savings. The big low-Earth-orbit (LEO) satellites (having masses of hundreds of thousands of kilograms) will employ 1-kilowatt-class hydrazine arcjets, producing an exhaust with a specific impulse of 585 s at an overall efficiency of 32% and a specific mass of 6.1 kg/kW.

Current status. Arcjet propulsion systems have been used for north-south station keeping on at least six different commercial satellites since 1993. During the last few months of 1997, more than 20 electric propulsion systems were successfully launched on board Iridium spacecraft. It is anticipated that more than 1000 electric propulsion systems will be employed by 2007, with many of these being arcjet systems.

In the 1980s the National Aeronautics and Space Administration initiated a research and development program with the help of industrial partners to use arcjets on commercial geosynchronous communication satellites. As of September 1997, there were 10 satellites in geostationary orbit that had arcjet propulsion systems for north-south station keeping: *Telstar 401* (now inactive), *Telstar 402R*, *Asiasat*, *Echostar 1*, *Echostar 2*, *Intelsat 801*, *Intelsat 802*, *GE-1*, *GE-2*, and *GE-3*. The *Telstars* employ MR-508 arcjet systems (**Fig. 2**), the *Asiasat*, *Echostars*, and *Intelsats* use the MR-509 system, and the *GE* units use the MR-510 arcjet system (**Table 2**). These arcjets use hydrazine as the propellant, operate at about 1.5–2 kW, and are flight qualified for 1500 h of operation, giving them a 15-year projected usable lifetime.

The MR-5100 hydrazine electrothermal arcjet system is used on the *A2100TM* satellite bus, and its on-orbit performance on the first ten *A2100TM* satellites was as predicted. The MR-5100 arcjet system uses four hydrazine arcjets for north-south station keeping. The mass of each arcjet thruster is approximately 1 kg (2.2 lb), with the power-conditioning unit and cable assembly constituting 16.4 kg (36 lb) of the total system mass of 20 kg (44 lb). The system was life-cycle tested, demonstrating a mission-aver-

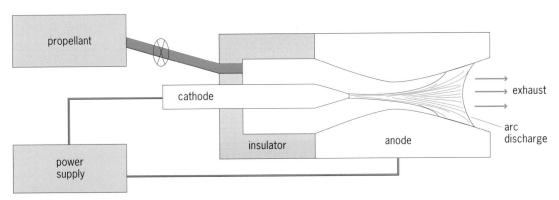

Fig. 1. Simple model of an arcjet propulsion system.

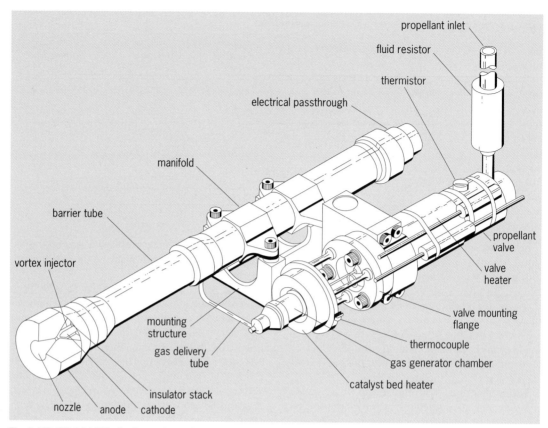

Fig. 2. MR-508 1.8-kW hydrazine arcjet and power-conditioning system. *(Primex Aerospace Company)*

TABLE 2. Typical performance parameters of selected operational arcjet systems

Thruster	Propellant	Specific impulse, s	Input power, kW	Thrust, N (lb)		Thrust efficiency, %
MR-508 arcjet	Hydrazine	~500	1.8	0.2–0.73	(0.045–0.164)	>30
MR-509 arcjet	Hydrazine	~500	1.8	0.21–0.25	(0.047–0.056)	>31
MR-510 arcjet	Hydrazine	~600	2.17	0.21–0.25	(0.047–0.056)	>31
ATOS arcjet	Ammonia	~500	0.75	0.11	(0.024)	36
ESEX arcjet	Ammonia	~800	26	1.8–2.0	(0.40–0.45)	27

SOURCE: After J. D. Fillben, *Electric Propulsion for Spacecraft Applicators*, CPTR-96-64, Chemical Propulsion Information Agency, 1996.

age specific impulse of 592 s for 1730 h, which qualified the system for a 15-year mission on the satellite. The thrust of the units is in the range 0.22–0.27 newton (0.05–0.06 pound-force). The power-conditioning unit is capable of providing 4 kW and can drive two arcjets simultaneously.

A 26-kW ammonia-fueled arcjet system with the associated power-conditioning control subsystems has been developed for the U.S. Air Force as part of the Electric Propulsion Space Experiment (ESEX) project. The system produces a thrust of 1.8–2.0 N (approximately 0.5 lbf) at specific impulse of 800 s (Table 2). The ESEX project will demonstrate an orbital transfer capability for large satellites.

In addition to the United States systems, there are active programs in Europe, Japan, and Russia. For example, the German Space Agency used a 0.75-kW ammonia arcjet system, ATOS (Table 2), on an amateur radio satellite.

For background information *see* ARC DISCHARGE; ELECTROTHERMAL PROPULSION; PLASMA PROPULSION; SPACECRAFT PROPULSION; SPECIFIC IMPULSE in the McGraw-Hill Encyclopedia of Science & Technology.   Kenneth E. Harwell

Bibliography. R. G. Jahn, *Physics of Electric Propulsion*, 1968; *Proceedings of the 33d AIAA/ASME/ SAE/ASEE Joint Propulsion Conference*, 1997; *Proceedings of the 25th International Electric Propulsion Conference*, 1997; E. Stuhlinger, *Ion Propulsion for Space Flight*, 1964.

Arterial blood flow

The flow of blood through arteries is essential for human life, providing oxygen and nutrients to the body's tissues. Understanding this delivery system requires knowledge of both biochemical and mechanical phenomena occurring in arteries. Although blood flow is mechanically complex, significant progress has been made in understanding blood flow patterns and their relationship to disease formation and progression.

Blood flow patterns very likely play a role in the development of cardiovascular diseases. Atherosclerosis, commonly referred to as hardening of the arteries, can cause heart attacks and strokes and is the most common cause of death in Western countries. It affects only certain arteries and begins to develop only in very specific locations within them. This localized nature of the disease has led to the hypothesis that mechanical factors such as flow patterns might be involved.

Modeling parameters. The investigation of blood flow is challenging to engineers. Since the human heart contracts and relaxes approximately once every second, the flow from the heart into the aorta is highly time dependent, or pulsatile. In large and medium-size arteries (diameters greater than 3 mm or 0.12 in.), this pulsatile behavior is extremely important. Another important aspect of blood flow is that the flow is in the "gray zone" between laminar and turbulent flow. In laminar flow, such as occurs at low flow rates, successive layers of fluid glide over one another without mixing. Turbulent flow occurs at higher flow rates and is characterized by highly disordered mixing of fluid. While the blood flow in healthy arteries does not qualify as being turbulent, the natural presence of curvature and branches creates disturbances in the laminar flow called vortices (**Fig. 1**). These vortices are typically regular and periodic in nature, not random or chaotic as might be observed with turbulence. The accurate reproduction of arterial blood flow depends on faithfully reproducing the pulsatile nature of the flow, the appropriate flow rate, and the vessel geometry.

Other factors that influence blood flow patterns are the flexible (compliant) nature of the vessel wall and the viscous behavior of blood. Arteries are made up of elastic fibers that stretch when blood pressure increases because of the contraction of the heart. This stretching can be fairly significant in the larger arteries such as the aorta, approaching 10% of the vessel diameter. Most of the early studies of blood flow ignored this behavior, mainly because of the difficulty in reproducing it in the laboratory. More recent research has revealed that arterial compliance has very little effect on the overall blood flow patterns. Arterial compliance is, however, very important in the overall performance of the arterial system. It aids in smoothing the pulsatile nature of the cardiac output so that the flow through capillaries is nearly steady. The coronary arteries that nourish the

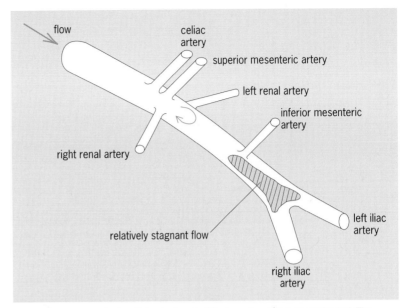

Fig. 1. Flow patterns in the abdominal aorta. The branch arteries are indicated. The curved arrow represents large vortex formation that occurs near the renal arteries. The location of relatively stagnant flow that coincides with early atherosclerosis formation is shown. (*After J. E. Moore, Jr., et al. Pulsatile flow visualization in the abdominal aorta under differing physiologic conditions: Implications for increased susceptibility to atherosclerosis, ASME J. Biomech. Eng., 114:391–397, 1992*)

heart muscle also depend on arterial compliance to receive their necessary flow.

An additional consideration is the viscous behavior of blood. Most common fluids, such as water, are classified as newtonian fluids; that is, their viscosity remains constant over a wide range of flow situations. Blood exhibits a shear-thinning behavior; that is, its viscosity increases in areas of flow stagnation and low shear rate. This behavior is due to the body's need to seal leaks in artery walls with clotting. In normal arterial flow situations, this non-newtonian behavior can affect the flow patterns. However, as with vessel compliance, the effects of this phenomenon have been shown to be minor.

Modeling techniques. Various techniques have been applied to analyze blood flow patterns, and can be classified as experimental and theoretical.

Experimental techniques. These involve the construction of a flow apparatus that accurately reproduces the important characteristics of blood flow. An artery model is typically constructed from glass, plastic, or silicone rubber. The model is then connected to a flow system consisting of one or more pumps and a reservoir. Several different techniques may be employed to obtain qualitative or quantitative information on the flow within the model. In many cases, qualitative flow visualization is the first step. This may consist of seeding the fluid within the model with small particles or injecting a thin dye stream at the entrance to the model. Using such techniques, researchers have demonstrated that blood flow in the sinus area of the carotid bifurcation (**Fig. 2**) and the posterior wall of the abdominal aorta (Fig. 1) is relatively stagnant and reverses in

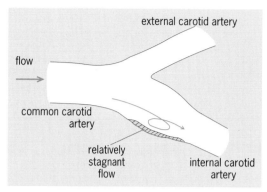

Fig. 2. Flow patterns in the carotid artery bifurcation. The curved arrow represents vortex formation that occurs in the sinus region of the internal carotid artery. The location of relatively stagnant flow that coincides with early atherosclerosis formation is shown. *(After D. N. Ku et al., Pulsatile flow and atherosclerosis in the human carotid bifurcation: Positive correlation between plaque location and low and oscillating shear stress, Arteriosclerosis, 5(3):293–302, 1985)*

direction when the heart relaxes. These are the areas where atherosclerosis begins to form in these arteries.

For obtaining detailed quantitative information on flow through arterial models, there are several methods, including laser Doppler anemometry, pulsed Doppler ultrasound velocimetry, and magnetic resonance imaging velocimetry. Researchers have used these techniques to more accurately assess the presence of flow stagnation and reversal, and have obtained statistical correlations between these particular flow patterns and early atherosclerosis development in the carotid artery and abdominal aorta.

Theoretical techniques. Theoretical methods involve the solution of the equations that govern fluid flow (Navier-Stokes equations) by using analytical or numerical techniques. These equations are inherently very difficult to solve, and are impossible to solve analytically for the complex geometries associated with the arterial system. However, if some simplifying assumptions are made, it may be possible to find exact or approximate analytical solutions. Unfortunately, the nature of these simplifying assumptions renders the results nearly inapplicable in understanding real blood flow patterns. Most current theoretical blood flow research employs numerical methods to solve the Navier-Stokes equations. The flow domain is divided into small, finite elements, allowing the derivatives in the equations to be expressed algebraically. The resulting system of algebraic equations is then solved on a computer. For complex arterial geometries, this system of equations may be quite large. The rapid increase in computing power in recent times has led to substantially increased use of numerical techniques. Still, the solution may require several days of dedicated computer time.

With numerical techniques it is possible to obtain much more detailed information on the flow field than with experimental techniques. Any desired flow variable, such as velocity, pressure, shear stress, or fluid particle paths, may be presented for any point in the flow field. Such detailed information has been used to better understand the flow field in the carotid artery and abdominal aorta. For example, numerical models of flow in these arteries were used to predict the amount of time that blood-borne cells might remain trapped in certain regions of the artery. It was found that these residence times were higher in areas where atherosclerosis forms.

Unresolved issues. Some aspects of arterial blood flow still are not well understood. The coronary arteries, attached to the surface of the heart, undergo large-scale deformation when the heart muscle contracts. The effects of this deformation on the flow patterns are not well understood. Because of the anatomical importance of the coronary arteries, a better understanding of coronary blood flow is being sought.

There is also much interest in understanding the blood flow in arteries that are already diseased with atherosclerosis. An atherosclerotic blockage in an artery has dramatic effects on the flow field. Downstream of the blockage, the flow is often turbulent. It is also possible that the blocked artery will collapse because the acceleration of the fluid through the blockage lowers the pressure within the artery (Bernoulli effect). If the artery collapses, the flow will be severely limited, and the atherosclerotic blockage may break off and lodge in a smaller artery downstream (an embolism), often with fatal consequences.

The surgical techniques to treat atherosclerosis are also being investigated from a fluid mechanics standpoint. In order to better understand the reasons why arterial bypass grafts fail, the flow patterns through graft-artery junctions are being studied. There are indications that flow patterns are of some importance in determining the locations of excessive tissue growth that may eventually block the flow through the graft.

Magnetic resonance imaging offers promise for the noninvasive assessment of blood flow. Detailed information on the blood flow patterns obtained in real time for a particular patient could greatly enhance the ability of clinicians to diagnose, treat, and even prevent arterial diseases.

For background information *see* ARTERIOSCLEROSIS; BERNOULLI'S THEOREM; CARDIOVASCULAR SYSTEM; CIRCULATION; CIRCULATION DISORDERS; COMPUTATIONAL FLUID DYNAMICS; FLOW MEASUREMENT; FLUID FLOW; FLUID-FLOW PRINCIPLES; MEDICAL IMAGING; NON-NEWTONIAN FLUID; VASCULAR DISORDERS in the McGraw-Hill Encyclopedia of Science & Technology.

James E. Moore, Jr.

Bibliography. C. G. Caro et al., *The Mechanics of the Circulation,* 1978; W. W. Nichols and M. F. O'Rourke, *McDonald's Blood Flow in Arteries,* 1990; T. J. Pedley, *The Fluid Mechanics of Large Blood Vessels,* 1980.

Atherosclerosis

Atherosclerosis is the development of yellowish plaques (atheromas) within the intima and inner media of arteries. A variety of cell types accumulate in the developing atherosclerotic plaque, including modified smooth muscle cells, monocytes/macrophages, and T lymphocytes. The presence of leukocytes in human atherosclerotic plaques suggests that atherosclerosis may be a type of subacute or chronic inflammation. The initial event in atherogenesis is generally believed to be endothelial activation or injury, which induces a local immune response. As a result, monocytes and T lymphocytes from the bloodstream invade the damaged arterial wall. An accumulation of monocytes and T lymphocytes within the intima represents the early lesion or fatty streak. The advanced atherosclerotic lesion (fibrolipid plaque) consists of a cholesterol- and lipid-rich core that contains lipid-laden macrophages (foam cells) and is covered by a fibrous cap of connective tissue (see **illus.**). Thus, the two major hallmarks of atherosclerosis are cell proliferation and blood lipid infiltration. Recent investigations have shown an association between chlamydiae, which are common bacterial pathogens, and atherosclerosis.

Chlamydiae. Chlamydiae are bacteria that grow only inside cells; that is, they are obligate intracellular parasites. Unlike most bacteria, they have an interesting developmental cycle. The two morphological forms are elementary bodies and reticulate bodies. The elementary body infects the host cell but is metabolically inactive. The reticulate body is noninfectious but metabolically active. The elementary body attaches to the host cell and is internalized. In the host cell, chlamydiae are separated from the cytoplasm into a membrane-bound vesicle, termed an inclusion. Thus, they are protected from the bactericidal mechanisms of the host cell. The mechanisms of chlamydial infection that inhibit phagolysomal fusion have not yet been elucidated. Once inside the host, the elementary body differentiates into the reticulate body, which multiplies by binary fission. Subsequently, the reticulate body reorganizes into the elementary body, which is released from the host cell and can then infect other host cells.

The four species are *Chlamydia trachomatis, C. psittaci, C. pneumoniae*, and *C. pecorum*. Several significant disease processes in humans are caused by chlamydial infection. *Chlamydia trachomatis* is a leading cause of sexually transmitted disease in the United States and the primary cause of preventable blindness in developing nations. *Chlamydia psittaci* primarily infects mammals (not including humans) and birds. For humans that come into contact with infected birds, a severe pneumonia termed psittacosis, often with systemic complications, can develop.

Chlamydia pneumoniae. *Chlamydia pneumoniae* is a human respiratory pathogen. The organism was specified on the basis of deoxyribonucleic acid (DNA) homology and antigenic and ultrastructural studies. *Chlamydia pneumoniae* has a unique pear-shaped morphology that is distinct from the round, compact elementary body of the other species. *Chlamydia pneumoniae* causes acute respiratory disease—approximately 10% of pneumonia and 5% of pharyngitis, bronchitis, and sinusitis. *Chlamydia pneumoniae* has also been associated with other acute and chronic respiratory diseases, such as otitis media, chronic obstructive pulmonary disease, and pulmonary exacerbation of cystic fibrosis. There are increasing reports on the association of *C. pneumoniae* and some diseases of immunopathology such as asthma, reactive airway disease, Reiter's syndrome, erythema nodosum, and sarcoidosis. Transmission is believed to be from person to person via respiratory droplets.

Individuals infected with *C. pneumoniae* develop specific antibodies that react with the organism. These antibodies are measured in sera by utilizing a diagnostic test, called the microimmunofluorescence test. Epidemiological studies measuring the prevalence of the antibodies in different populations have shown that virtually everyone is infected at least once in a lifetime and that reinfection is common. Antibody against *C. pneumoniae* is rare in children under the age of 5 except in developing and tropical countries. The antibody prevalence increases rapidly between the ages of 5 and 14, reaches 50% at the age of 20, and continues to increase slowly to 70–80% in older age. The frequency of occurrence of antibody specific for *C. pneumoniae* is approximately equal in both genders under 15 years of age; however, adult men have a higher prevalence of antibody than adult women, in contrast to most respiratory infections, in which women are more frequently infected than men.

Chlamydia pneumoniae and atherosclerosis. The clinical spectrum of *C. pneumoniae* infection has been extended to atherosclerosis and related clinical man-

Classic lesion of human atherosclerosis. *(From J. L. Melnick, Doctor's Infect. Newsl., 2(3):17–20, 1991)*

ifestations such as coronary heart disease (the number one killer in the United States and other developed countries), carotid artery stenosis, aortic aneurysm, claudication (occlusion of the arteries of the lower extremities), and stroke. Multiple risk factors of atherosclerosis have been well characterized, including hypercholesterolemia, cigarette smoking, hypertension, diabetes, and family history. Other possible contributing factors, such as infectious organisms, are not as well defined. The presence of inflammatory cells within the atherosclerotic lesion has led to investigation of the role of infection and the corresponding immune response in atherogenesis. Certain infectious agents have been linked with atherosclerosis. Herpes viruses have received the most scrutiny. This association was found by inoculation of chickens with Marek's virus (chicken herpes virus). The chickens developed arteritis (an inflammation of the artery leading to atherosclerosis) that could be prevented with prior vaccination against Marek's virus. Herpes simplex virus and cytomegalovirus have also been found in atherosclerotic lesions in humans. Additionally, graft arteriosclerosis is of greater severity in transplanted hearts of individuals with cytomegalovirus infection.

The evidence for the association of *C. pneumoniae* with atherosclerosis has been derived from studies showing a correlation of antibody against *C. pneumoniae* with coronary heart disease, and by direct detection of the organism within atherosclerotic lesions. Individuals with coronary artery disease and heart attacks are significantly more likely to have an antibody pattern indicative of past infection with *C. pneumoniae*. An association of *C. pneumoniae* antibody with carotid artery disease and cerebrovascular disease has been demonstrated. Compelling evidence for the association of *C. pneumoniae* with atherosclerosis has been obtained by the demonstration of the bacteria in atherosclerotic lesions by diagnostic methods that specifically detect *C. pneumoniae* deoxyribonucleic acid (DNA) and antigen. The organism has been found in atherosclerotic lesions throughout the human arterial tree. Evidence of *C. pneumoniae* has been found in atheromas in coronary, carotid, femoral, popliteal, and iliac arteries, and in the aorta. *Chlamydia pneumoniae* occurs frequently in both early lesions and developed fibrolipid plaques. The organism is found only in diseased arterial tissue and not in normal arterial tissue. The organism has been detected in tissues from persons from diverse geographical locales, in persons of different ethnic backgrounds, in males and females, and in young and older persons. Although its isolation from human specimens is difficult, the organism has been isolated from an atheroma from the coronary artery of a person undergoing heart transplantation because of advanced atherosclerosis, and from the atheromatous plaque removed by endarterectomy from a patient with carotid stenosis.

There are three possible roles of *C. pneumoniae* in the pathogenesis of atherosclerosis: the organism persists in the lesion but does not contribute to pathology; it contributes to the initiation of atherogenesis; or *C. pneumoniae* infection accelerates the progression or severity of atherosclerotic lesions. Two methods exist to investigate whether *C. pneumoniae* contributes to the disease process. The first is by proving Koch's postulates via the use of animal models of *C. pneumoniae* infection and atherosclerosis; early animal studies are promising. The second is through human intervention studies using antichlamydial therapeutics.

For background information *see* ANTIBODY; ARTERIOSCLEROSIS; CHLAMYDIA in the McGraw-Hill Encyclopedia of Science & Technology.

Lee Ann Campbell

Bibliography. J. T. Grayston et al., *Chlamydia pneumoniae* and cardiovascular disease, *Cardiologia*, 42:1145-1151, 1997; C.-C. Kuo et al., *Chlamydia pneumoniae, Clin. Microbiol. Rev.*, 8:451-461, 1995; P. Saikku, *Chlamydia pneumoniae* and atherosclerosis: An update, *Scand. J. Infect. Dis. Suppl.*, 104:53-56, 1997.

Atom cluster

Clusters are aggregates of atoms (or molecules) containing between three and a few thousand atoms that have properties intermediate between those of the isolated monomer (atom or molecule) and the bulk or solid-state material. The study of such species has been an increasingly active research field since about 1980. This activity is due to the fundamental interest in studying a completely new area that can bridge the gap between atomic and solid-state physics and also shows many analogies to nuclear physics. However, the research is also done for its potential technological interest in areas such as catalysis, photography, and epitaxy. A characteristic of clusters which is responsible for many of their interesting properties is the large number of atoms at the surface compared to those in the cluster interior. For many kinds of atomic clusters, all atoms are at the surface for sizes of up to 12 atoms. As the clusters grow further in size, the relative number of atoms at the surface scales as approximately $4N^{-1/3}$, where N is the total number of atoms. Even in a cluster as big as 10^5 atoms, almost 10% of the atoms are at the surface. Clusters can be placed in the following categories:

1. Microclusters have from 3 to 10-13 atoms. Concepts and methods of molecular physics are applicable.

2. Small clusters have from 10-13 to about 100 atoms. Many different geometrical isomers exist for a given cluster size with almost the same energies. Molecular concepts lose their applicability.

3. Large clusters have from 100 to 1000 atoms. A gradual transition is observed to the properties of the solid state.

4. Small particles or nanocrystals have at least 1000 atoms. These bodies display some of the properties of the solid state.

Geometry. Traditionally, solid-state physics describes a crystal as an infinitely extending periodic ordering of atoms with translational symmetry. Body-centered cubic (bcc), face-centered cubic (fcc), and hexagonal close packing (hcp) are the most common arrangements. These orderings are not normally found among clusters. The packing of the atoms in clusters can be investigated by electron diffraction on the cluster beam. The most favored geometry for rare-gas (neon, argon, and krypton) clusters of up to a few thousand atoms (**Fig. 1**) is icosahedral. The fivefold rotational axis of these structures, which first appears in clusters of seven atoms, is forbidden for the symmetry of the standard lattices of solid-state physics. As confirmed by computer simulation methods, the icosahedral geometry allows the atoms to be aggregated into a more compact structure with a smaller potential energy than the structures allowed in solid-state physics, such as the face-centered cubic structure of bulk rare-gas solids.

However, the preferred cluster geometry depends critically on the bonding between the monomers in the clusters. For example, ionic clusters such as those of sodium chloride [$(NaCl)_N$] very rapidly assume the cubic form of the bulk crystal lattice, and for metallic clusters it is the electronic structure rather than the geometric structure which is most important. A summary of the different kinds of clusters, classified in terms of their chemical bonding, is given in the **table**. Mercury clusters (Hg_N) are particularly intriguing since they show van der Waals, covalent, or metallic bonding, depending on the cluster size.

Production. A cluster apparatus typically consists of two separately pumped vacuum chambers which

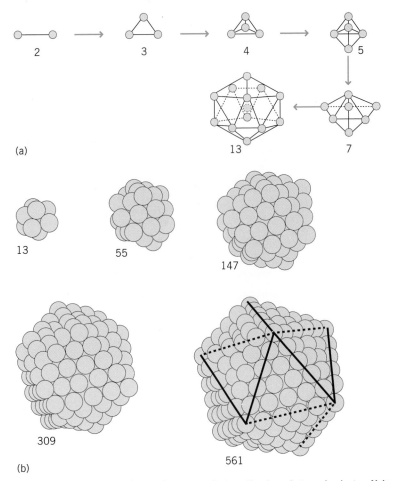

Fig. 1. Growth sequence of neutral rare-gas clusters. Number of atoms in cluster, N, is indicated for each cluster. (a) Microclusters. (b) Small and large clusters, all of which are icosahedra with fivefold symmetry. *(After H. Haberland, ed., Clusters of Atoms and Molecules, vol. 1, Springer-Verlag, 1994)*

Classification of clusters according to their chemical bonding			
Kind of cluster	Example	Average binding energy per atom, eV	Elements for which cluster type is found
Metallic clusters: half-filled band of delocalized electrons	(alkali metal)$_N$, Al$_N$, Cu$_N$, Fe$_N$, Pt$_N$, W$_N$, Hg$_N$ with $N > 200$	0.5–3	Elements of the lower-left corner of the periodic table
Covalent clusters: directed bonding by electron pairs through sp-hybridization	C$_N$, Si$_N$, Hg$_N$ with $80 \geq N \geq 30$	1–4 (Hg ≈ 0.5)	B, C, Si, Ge
Ionic clusters: bonding due to Coulomb force between ions	(NaCl)$_N$, (CaBr$_2$)$_N$	2–4	Metals from the left side of the periodic table with electronegative elements from the right side
Hydrogen-bonded clusters: strong dipole-dipole attraction	(HF)$_N$, (H$_2$O)$_N$	0.15–0.5	Molecules with closed electronic shells that contain H and strong electronegative elements (F, O, N)
Molecular clusters: like van der Waals with an additional weak covalent contribution	(I$_2$)$_N$, (S$_6$)$_N$, (organic molecules)$_N$	0.3–1	Organic molecules, some other closed-shell molecules
Van der Waals clusters: induced dipole interaction between atoms and molecules with closed electronic shells	(rare gas)$_N$, (H$_2$)$_N$, (CO$_2$)$_N$, Hg$_N$ with $N < 10$	0.01–0.3	Rare gases, closed-shell atoms and molecules

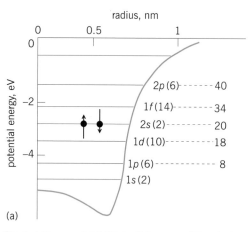

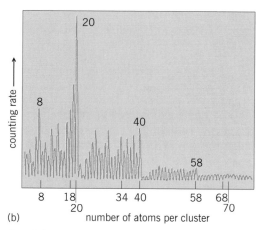

Fig. 2. Jellium model. (*a*) Potential energy of the electrons as a function of the cluster radius for a spherical sodium cluster with 20 atoms (Na_{20}). Electron energy levels are also shown, with their radial and angular-momentum quantum numbers and the degeneracies of the levels (in parentheses). The total number of electrons in a given shell is indicated on the right. Only the two electrons in the highest occupied orbital are indicated. (*b*) Mass spectrum of sodium (Na_N) clusters, showing high intensities (magic numbers) for clusters with completely filled electronic shells. (*After W. A. de Heer et al., Electronic shell structure and metal clusters, Sol. State Phys., 40:93–181, 1987*)

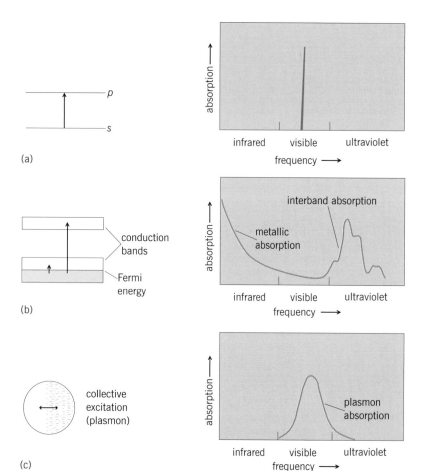

Fig. 3. Absorption of light by an alkali metal in various states of aggregation. Absorption spectra are shown on the right and schematic structures on the left. (*a*) Metal atom. (*b*) Metal crystal. (*c*) Metal cluster.

are connected by a small conical aperture, the skimmer. The central part of the cluster beam, formed in the first vacuum chamber, passes through the skimmer and is investigated in some way, ionized, and detected in a mass spectrometer in the second chamber.

There are two main types of sources for producing free cluster beams. In a gas-aggregation source, the atoms or molecules are vaporized into a cold, flowing rare-gas atmosphere. They cool by undergoing many collisions with the rare-gas atoms and aggregate into clusters. In a jet-expansion source, a gas is expanded under high pressure through a small hole into a vacuum. An extreme cooling of the rotational and vibrational degrees of freedom as well as the relative motion occurs during this adiabatic expansion, leading to cluster formation.

One crucial requirement for both these sources is to obtain a sufficient density of monomers to produce a beam with a high enough intensity of clusters for further investigation. The common way of doing this for materials with a high melting point is to use a laser-vaporization or ion-sputtering source. An intense ion or laser beam is directed onto the surface of the target material and removes material in the form of neutral or charged particles, which then cluster together. The number of clusters, their size, and their temperature can be controlled by combining this method with those of the gas-aggregation or jet-expansion source.

Properties. In most situations, the valence electrons of the atoms making up the clusters can be regarded as being delocalized, that is, not attached to any particular atom but with a certain probability of being found anywhere within the cluster. The simplest and most widely used model to describe the delocalized electrons in metallic clusters is that of a free-electron gas, known as the jellium model.

The positive charge is regarded as being smeared out over the entire volume of the cluster while the valence electrons are free to move within this homogeneously distributed, positively charged background. The calculated potential for the electrons in a spherical jellium approximation typically looks like the example in **Fig. 2***a*. Here, the inner part of the effective potential resembles the bottom of a wine bottle. The electronic energy levels are grouped together to form shells. The jellium potential is very similar to the Woods-Saxon potential, used to describe the interaction between protons and neutrons in nuclear physics, and the same classification of energy levels is found, wherein the energy levels are characterized by the radial quantum number $(1, 2, 3, . . .)$ and the angular-momentum quantum number $(s, p, d, . . .)$.

The predicted shell closures can be seen in mass spectra of alkali-metal clusters. If the neutral clusters produced from a given cluster source are hot, they can fragment on leaving the source. The intensity of relatively stable clusters will thus grow at the expense of their less stable neighbors, producing so-called magic numbers in the mass distribution. The neutral mass distribution is then probed by ionizing the clusters with a photon energy that is just slightly higher than the ionization potential of the clusters to avoid further fragmentation after ionization. This operation was used to obtain the mass spectrum of sodium clusters in Fig. 2*b*, which gives a beautiful confirmation of the electronic shell model.

The delocalized electrons can be excited by photon absorption or electron collisions into a collective motion with respect to the positively charged nuclei, which is known as a plasmon resonance. This is very analogous to the giant resonances, that is, the collective motion of neutrons and protons, found in atomic nuclei. The plasmon frequency for metal clusters depends on the cluster size and material but is generally in the visible range of the spectrum. It is the plasmon excitation of metal clusters or nanoparticles in glass that is responsible for the strong colors seen, for example, in medieval stained glass windows. The optical absorption of metal clusters is compared to that of atoms and the bulk metal in **Fig. 3**.

Fullerenes. Fullerenes are clusters of carbon atoms, C_{2N}, with N greater than 11, which have unique hollow structures. They were discovered with a laser vaporization source combined with an adiabatic gas expansion. It is now possible to produce and isolate macroscopic amounts of some of these clusters, in particular C_{60} and C_{70}. The cluster C_{60} is especially interesting because of its highly symmetrical truncated icosahedral geometry (just like a soccer ball) and a range of fascinating properties, such as a quasi-three-dimensional aromatic chemistry and superconductivity when doped with alkali atoms. The availability of macroscopic amounts of a mass-selected, neutral atomic cluster with well-defined geometrical and electronic properties has opened up a new range of experiments and theoretical treatments to probe the dynamics of a relatively simple atomic cluster system with a large but finite number of degrees of freedom.

Probing with laser pulses. A recent development in the study of atomic clusters is the use of laser pulses with durations of less than 100 femtoseconds (10^{-13} s) to probe the time scale for energy coupling between the different degrees of freedom in the cluster in real time. This work, which is presently in its infancy, will provide very detailed information on the dynamics of such complex systems and will certainly provide a stringent test of theoretical models.

Clusters on surfaces. The overall emphasis in the field is gradually shifting from gas-phase studies to the study of clusters deposited on surfaces. The aim is to produce new materials with tailor-made electrical, optical, or catalytic properties. Cluster-beam epitaxy, where large metallic clusters are deposited at high kinetic energy (greater than 10 eV per atom) onto substrates, is already producing superior-quality mirror coatings for use in high-power laser applications.

For background information *see* ATOM CLUSTER; CHEMICAL BONDING; CRYSTAL STRUCTURE; FULLERENE; GIANT NUCLEAR RESONANCES; MAGIC NUMBERS; NUCLEAR STRUCTURE; OPTICAL PULSES; PLASMONS in the McGraw-Hill Encyclopedia of Science & Technology.   Eleanor Campbell

Bibliography. M. S. Dresselhaus, G. Dresselhaus, and P. C. Eklund, *Science of Fullerenes and Carbon Nanotubes*, 1996; H. Haberland (ed.), *Clusters of Atoms and Molecules*, 2 vols., 1994; U. Kreibig and M. Vollmer, *Optical Properties of Metal Clusters*, 1995.

Atom laser

An atom laser is a device that generates an intense coherent beam of atoms through a stimulated process. It does for atoms what an optical laser does for light. The atom laser emits coherent matter waves, whereas the optical laser emits coherent electromagnetic waves. Coherence means, for instance, that atom laser beams can interfere with each other.

Properties. Laser light is created by stimulated emission of photons, a light amplification process. Similarly, an atom laser beam is created by stimulated amplification of matter waves. The conservation of the number of atoms is not in conflict with matter-wave amplification: The atom laser takes atoms out of a reservoir and transforms them into a coherent matter wave similar to the optical laser, which converts energy into coherent electromagnetic radiation (but, in contrast, the number of photons need not be conserved).

The condition of high intensity means that there are many particles per mode or quantum state. A thermal atomic beam has a population per mode of only 10^{-12} compared to much greater than 1 for an atom laser. The realization of an atom laser therefore required the development of methods to greatly enhance the mode occupation. This enhancement is accomplished by cooling the reservoir of atoms to microkelvin temperatures or below.

In the case of an ideal atom laser, the output beam should be monochromatic and directional, and have a well-defined phase and intensity. For atoms, being monochromatic means that their velocity spread is extremely small. Such beams propagate with minimum spreading, and can be focused by atom lenses to a small spot size. The minimum spreading and the minimum spot size are limited by Heisenberg's uncertainty relation in the same way as the propagation of a single-mode optical laser beam is diffraction limited. The analogy between light and matter waves is exploited in the field of atom optics.

The different nature of atoms and photons implies different properties of light and atom beams. Unlike light, an atomic beam cannot travel far through air. It scatters off air molecules in less than a micrometer. Vacuum is thus required for all atom laser experiments. Also, slow atoms are strongly affected by gravity. Furthermore, a dense atom beam will show spreading in excess of the Heisenberg uncertainty limit because of the interactions between the atoms.

Elements. A laser requires a cavity (resonator), an active medium, and an output coupler (see **table**).

Cavity. Various analogs of laser cavities for atoms have been realized. The most important ones are magnetic traps (which use the force of an inhomogeneous magnetic field on the atomic magnetic dipole moment) and optical dipole traps (which use the force exerted on atoms by focused laser beams). Confinement of atoms between two atom mirrors has been suggested and is analogous to a Fabry-Perot cavity for light. Even a single-mirror cavity is possible, where atoms perform multiple bounces off a mirror in the vertical direction and return because of gravity (an atomic "trampoline").

Active medium. The active medium is a reservoir of atoms which are transferred to one state of the confining potential, which is the analog of the lasing mode. The reservoir can be atoms confined in other quantum states of the atom cavity or an ultraslow atomic beam. The atoms are transferred to the lasing mode either by collisions or by optical pumping. The transfer of atoms is efficient only for an ultracold sample, which is prepared by laser cooling or evaporative cooling. This cooling ensures that the atoms in the reservoir occupy only a certain range of quantum states which can be efficiently coupled to the lasing mode.

Output coupler. The output coupler extracts atoms from the cavity, thus generating a pulsed or continuous beam of coherent atoms. A simple way to accomplish this step is to switch off the atom trap and release the atoms. This method is analogous to cavity dumping for an optical laser, and extracts all the stored atoms into a single pulse. A more controlled way to extract the atoms requires a coupling mechanism between confined quantum states and propagating modes.

Such a beam splitter for atoms can be realized by applying the Stern-Gerlach effect to atoms in a magnetic trap (**Fig. 1**). Initially, all the atoms have their electron spin parallel to the magnetic field, say spin up (Fig. 1*a*), and in this state they are confined in the trap. A short radio-frequency pulse rotates (tilts) the spin of the atoms by a variable angle (Fig. 1*b*). Quantum-mechanically, a tilted spin is a superposition of spin up and spin down. Since the spin-down component experiences a repulsive magnetic force, the cloud of atoms is split into a trapped cloud and an out-coupled cloud (Fig. 1*c*). By using a series of radio-frequency pulses, a sequence of coherent atom pulses can be formed (Fig. 1*d*). These pulses are accelerated downward by gravity and spread out.

Figure 2 shows such a sequence of coherent pulses. In this case, sodium atoms are coupled out from a magnetic trap by radio-frequency pulses every 5 ms. The atom pulses are observed by illuminating them with resonant laser light and imaging their shadows, which are caused by absorption of the light. Each pulse contains 10^5–10^6 sodium atoms.

Other output coupling schemes have been suggested, including optical transitions which eject atoms from the cavity because of the recoil of the absorbed photon, and tunneling through thin barriers of light.

Gain process. An atom laser is possible only for bosonic atoms. The accumulation of atoms in a single quantum state is based on Bose-Einstein statistics. Two different mechanisms have been discussed which may provide gain in an atom laser: elastic collisions and spontaneous emission of photons.

The case of elastic collisions is closely related to Bose-Einstein condensation. When a gas of bosonic particles is cooled down, it forms a Bose-Einstein condensate characterized by a macroscopic occupation of the ground state of the system. This process happens suddenly at the Bose-Einstein condensation transition temperature. The atoms in a Bose-Einstein condensate are coherent to first and higher order. An atom laser based on Bose-Einstein condensation operates in thermal equilibrium. Atom lasing is achieved simply by cooling down the gas. Below a certain temperature, nature maximizes entropy by

Analogies between an atom laser and the optical laser	
Atom laser*	Optical laser
Atoms	Photons
Matter waves	Electromagnetic waves
Atom trap	Laser cavity
Atoms in the Bose condensate	Photons in the lasing mode
Thermal atoms	Gain medium
Evaporative cooling	Excitation of the gain medium
Stimulated scattering of atoms	Stimulated emission of photons
Critical temperature for Bose-Einstein condensation	Laser threshold

* Based on evaporative cooling.

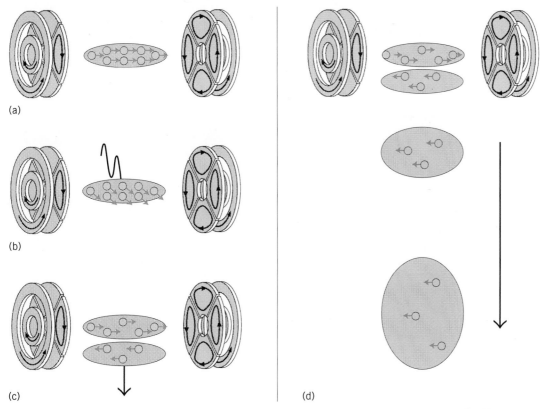

Fig. 1. Principle of the radio-frequency output coupler of an atom laser. (*a*) Bose-Einstein condensate confined in an atom trap. (*b*) Tilting of the spins of the atoms by a short radio-frequency pulse. (*c*) Splitting of the cloud into a trapped cloud and an out-coupled cloud. (*d*) Repetition of steps *a* and *c* creates a sequence of output pulses.

generating a Bose-Einstein condensate. For photons, the situation is very different: Cooling a black-body cavity reduces its energy density in proportion to the fourth power of its absolute temperature (Stefan-Boltzmann law). Thus, at very low temperatures the cavity is empty. This is how entropy is maximized when the number of particles is not conserved.

It is instructive to look more closely at the stimulated amplification process that takes place when a Bose-Einstein condensate forms. In a normal gas, atoms scatter among a myriad of possible quantum states. But when the critical temperature for Bose-Einstein condensation is reached, they scatter predominantly into the lowest energy state of the system. This abrupt process is closely analogous to the threshold for operating an optical laser. The presence of a Bose-Einstein condensate causes stimulated scattering into the ground state. More precisely, the presence of a condensate with N_0 atoms enhances the probability that an atom will be scattered into the condensate by a factor of $N_0 + 1$.

In an atom laser, the analog to excitation of the active medium can be accomplished by evaporative cooling. The evaporation process creates a cloud which is not in thermal equilibrium and relaxes toward lower temperatures. This results in growth of the condensate. After equilibration, the gain process halts and the condensate fraction remains constant until further cooling is applied. In thermal equilib-

rium, there is still stimulated scattering of atoms into the condensate. However, this process is in dynamic equilibrium with collisions that knock atoms out of the condensate.

An atom laser was realized by extracting a beam of atoms from a Bose-Einstein condensate and explicitly demonstrating its coherence. The proof of the coherence was obtained by observing a high-contrast interference pattern when two Bose-Einstein condensates overlapped. The two condensates were created by cooling a gas of sodium atoms in a double-well potential. After the condensates were released from the trap, they accelerated downward, spread out ballistically, and eventually overlapped and interfered. The interference pattern could be directly photographed. It had a period of 15 micrometers, a gigantic length for matter waves. (Room-temperature atoms have a matter wavelength of 0.05 nm, 300,000 times smaller.)

An atom laser based on Bose-Einstein condensation is a special case of macroscopic occupation of a quantum state. In this case, the atoms accumulate in the ground state and are in thermal equilibrium. More generally, atom lasers can operate in higher-order modes and also as a driven system which is not in thermal equilibrium. (This is the situation in an optical laser.) The lasing mode is distinguished by preferential population of atoms or minimum loss. It has been suggested that this condition can

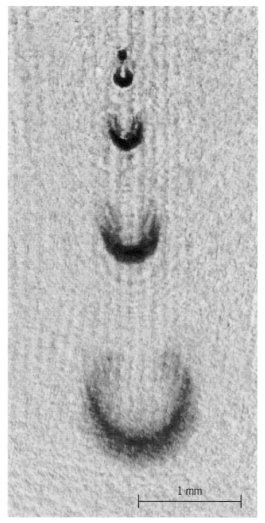

Fig. 2. Pulsed atom laser in operation, with pulses of coherent sodium atoms coupled out from a Bose-Einstein condensate that is confined in a magnetic trap.

Potential applications. Although a basic atom laser has now been demonstrated, major improvements are necessary before it can be used for applications, especially in terms of increased output power and reduced overall complexity. The atom laser provides ultimate control over the position and motion of atoms at the quantum level, and might find use where such precise control is necessary, for example, for precision measurements of fundamental constants, tests of fundamental symmetries, atom optics (in particular, atom interferometry and atom holography), and precise deposition of atoms on surfaces. Since the matter wavelength of atoms can be extremely short (it decreases in inverse proportion to the atomic velocity), the ultimate limit to the spatial resolution is not the matter wavelength but the size of the atom.

For background information *see* ATOM OPTICS; BOSE-EINSTEIN STATISTICS; COHERENCE; LASER; LASER COOLING; PARTICLE TRAP; QUANTUM MECHANICS in the McGraw-Hill Encyclopedia of Science & Technology.
Wolfgang Ketterle

Bibliography. M. R. Andrews et al., Observation of interference between two Bose condensates, *Science*, 275:637–641, 1997; B. Goss Levi, Bose condensates are coherent inside and outside an atom trap, *Phys. Today*, 50(3):17–18, March 1997; D. Kleppner, A beginner's guide to the atom laser, *Phys. Today*, 50(8):11–13, August 1997; H.-J. Miesner et al., Bosonic stimulation in the formation of Bose-Einstein condensate, *Science*, 279:1005–1007, 1998; G. Taubes, First atom laser shoots pulses of coherent matter, *Science*, 275:617–618, 1997.

be realized by optical pumping. In this case, atoms in the reservoir are optically excited. When they decay by spontaneous emission, they can reach final momentum states that differ from the initial momentum by the photon recoil. If one state within this range has a macroscopic population, then the rate of spontaneous emission into this final state is enhanced, and there is an amplification process similar to the one described above for elastic collisions. The case of optically excited atoms shows very clearly the symmetry between the optical laser and the atom laser: The rate of emission to a final state, which is specified by a particular state of the atom inside the cavity and a particular mode of the photon field, is proportional to $(N + 1)(n + 1)$, where N is the number of atoms in this level of the cavity, and n is the number of photons in this mode. The first factor in this expression is the bosonic stimulation by atoms that is responsible for the amplification process in the atom laser, and the second describes the amplification process in the optical laser.

Auditory processing

The amplitude and frequency of most sounds change rapidly over time. These changes are crucial for auditory perception and communication. Indeed, it is the pattern of these dynamic changes that conveys information in speech and music. For example, a note struck on a piano may be played backwards in time, thus reversing its dynamic pattern. It is no longer perceived as a piano note; it sounds organlike.

A fundamental question is how dynamic changes are processed by the auditory system—in particular, how well humans can detect and discriminate dynamic changes, and how this information is coded in neural activity. The primary research strategy has been to simplify a very complex situation by separating amplitude and frequency changes and studying them individually by using relatively simple stimuli.

Envelopes and modulation. Most current research has focused on the processing of amplitude changes (**Fig. 1**). A speech waveform (Fig. 1a) displays a rapidly fluctuating instantaneous amplitude, with relatively slow change in the amplitude (size) of these fluctuations, which is called the envelope. The envelope of running speech consists mainly of fluctuations of 3–4 Hz, corresponding roughly to the

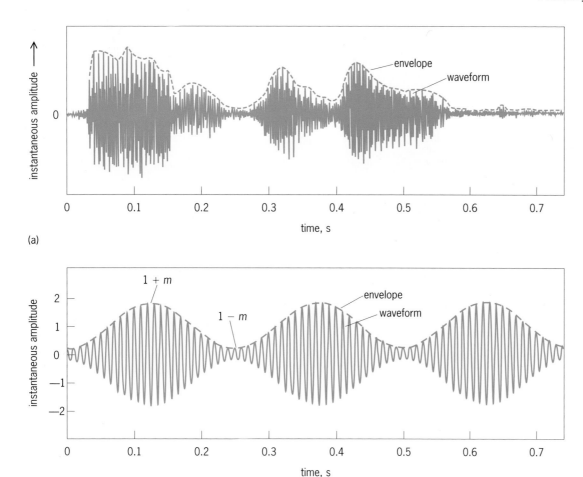

Fig. 1. Waveforms and envelopes of sound. (*a*) Speech utterance. (*b*) Sinusoidal amplitude modulation of a 100-Hz pure-tone carrier. A 4-Hz sinusoid is added to a constant and multiplied by a 100-Hz sinusoid. Modulation index, *m*, indicates the strength of the envelope fluctuations. Instantaneous amplitude is scaled so that the envelope has an average value of 1 and ranges between 1 − *m* and 1 + *m* at the points indicated.

temporal sequence of words, but there are also fluctuations above 100 Hz that are potentially important.

To understand how the auditory system processes envelopes, it is more convenient to use envelopes simpler than those of speech. Sinusoidal envelopes (Fig. 1*b*) have been extensively used. Here, a low-frequency sinusoid is added to a constant and the result is multiplied by a higher-frequency sinusoid; this is sinusoidal amplitude modulation of a higher-frequency pure-tone carrier. A modulation index, *m*, indicates the strength of the envelope fluctuations and can have any value from 0 (in the case of a flat envelope) to 1 (in the case of 100% modulation).

Transfer functions. A basic question that can be addressed by using sinusoidal amplitude modulation is how well the auditory system can follow envelope fluctuations of different frequencies. The most commonly used psychophysical approach is to measure a modulation threshold—the modulation index that is necessary to just hear the envelope fluctuations produced by sinusoidal amplitude modulation. By measuring modulation thresholds as a function of modulation frequency, a temporal modulation trans-

fer function is obtained (**Fig. 2**). To be analogous to typical transfer functions, modulation thresholds are plotted in decibels (the threshold in decibels is $20 \log_{10} m$) and increase downward; that is, 100% modulation (0 dB) is at the bottom of the vertical axis.

A typical modulation transfer function for human subjects with normal hearing (Fig. 2) has a low-pass characteristic and indicates that humans are much more sensitive to low-frequency modulation than to high-frequency modulation. Rapid envelope fluctuations appear to be smoothed or attenuated by the auditory system. This attenuation of high-frequency modulation is not as severe as in vision, where the upper frequency limit for detecting modulation is 50–60 Hz versus the 2000–4000-Hz limit suggested by the auditory transfer function. In this sense, the auditory system is fast and seems uniquely suited for processing rapid dynamic changes.

General model. Some aspects of dynamic processing, including the modulation transfer function, can be understood in the context of a frequently used, general model of the initial stages of auditory

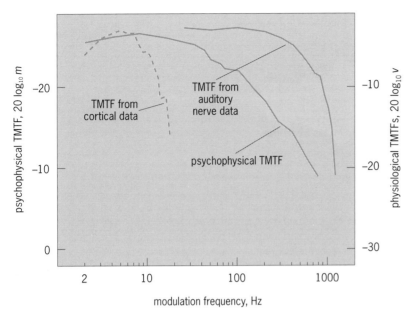

Fig. 2. Temporal modulation transfer functions (TMTFs) based on psychophysical measurement and on physiological recordings (auditory nerve data and cortical data). Psychophysical TMTF shows the modulation threshold, m, for sinusoidal amplitude modulated (SAM) noise, expressed in decibels ($20 \log_{10} m$). Physiological TMTFs show a measure of the neural envelope following, v, expressed in decibels ($20 \log_{10} v$); values near zero indicate that the neural response is highly synchronized to the envelope, while negative values indicate that the response is less related to the envelope.

processing. The model consists of a set of frequency-selective channels, with each channel tuned to different frequencies within the range of hearing. Each channel consists of a band-pass filter, followed by a nonlinearity (such as rectification), followed by a low-pass filter. The initial band-pass filters represent the cochlear filtering and tonotopic organization that is characteristic of mammalian hearing, wherein each hair-cell receptor responds maximally to sound of a particular frequency that is determined by its location along the cochlear duct. The nonlinearity is associated with transduction in the hair-cell receptors, and the low-pass filtering probably reflects the sluggishness of both synaptic transmission and later neural processing. In response to a sinusoidal-amplitude-modulated tone, the output of the channel tuned to the carrier frequency closely approximates the envelope of the input. The low-pass filter, or leaky integrator, is the primary determinant of the form of the modulation transfer function and therefore of the ability of a channel to respond to dynamic changes. Indeed, in some implementations the attenuation characteristic of the low-pass filter is chosen to mimic the transfer function.

Issues. This relatively simple model also serves to clarify some of the current issues about auditory envelope processing. A basic question concerns the role of the initial band-pass filter. That such filtering occurs in the cochlea is well established and is a cornerstone of auditory theory. But the characteristics of this filtering seem to be incompatible with the modulation transfer function. Specifically, the transfer function suggests that humans are sensitive to high-frequency envelope fluctuations that should essentially be eliminated by cochlear filtering. It has been suggested that postcochlear auditory processing somehow combines frequency-selective channels and thus overcomes the limitation that individual channels impose on envelope processing. If this is true, it necessitates a major revision of perceptually relevant models of audition.

Another issue is the possibility of a modulation filter bank. Rather than a single low-pass filter for each channel, it has been proposed that there are multiple filters tuned to different modulation frequencies. The major psychophysical evidence comes from studies of modulation masking, where it has been shown that the modulation threshold for a signal modulation frequency can be raised when another, noninformative modulation frequency is present. Thresholds are raised more when the modulation frequency of the noninformative masker is close to that of the signal. This behavior, in analogy to pure-tone masking, has led to models in which there are filters that are selective to certain modulation frequencies. The amount of modulation masking depends on how much of the masker is passed by the filter tuned to the signal modulation frequency. These models suggest that modulation filters are a biologically fixed part of auditory processing.

Physiological evidence. In addition to the psychophysical modulation transfer function, there are analogous functions based on auditory nerve recordings and on recordings from auditory cortex (Fig. 2). The modulation transfer function for the auditory nerve does not show significant tuning for modulation. It has a low-pass characteristic with a much higher cutoff frequency than that of the psychophysical transfer function. This high cutoff frequency suggests that human ability to detect envelope fluctuations for modulation frequencies up to about 1000 Hz is not determined by peripheral processing. At higher modulation frequencies, however, the psychophysical transfer function shows less attenuation than that from the auditory nerve—the transfer functions cross—and the limitation due to cochlear filtering is evident. However, the comparison of transfer functions involves very different measures, and so conclusions about the role of peripheral processing are tentative.

The cortical data (Fig. 2) are strikingly different from those derived from psychophysical and auditory nerve measurements. The modulation transfer function shows a band-pass characteristic with maximum sensitivity to a modulation frequency of 5 Hz. Different units in the cortex are, in general, tuned to different modulation frequencies. Although this is consistent with the notion of a modulation filter bank, it appears that no cortical units are tuned above 10 Hz and that no units respond to sinusoidal amplitude modulation at modulation frequencies above 100 Hz. The psychophysical data show, however, that humans can detect sinusoidal amplitude modulation frequencies much higher than 100 Hz. Also, it has been shown that humans can extract musical pitch from sinusoidal-amplitude-modulated noise up to frequencies of about 800 Hz. Although detection of modulation might be mediated by lower brain centers, which have been shown to respond to higher-frequency modulation, it is difficult to see how pitch extraction and melody recognition can be performed without cortical involvement.

Speech envelopes. A limited degree of speech recognition is possible based on only envelope information. The relevant studies have imposed the speech envelope on broad-bandwidth noise and thereby have eliminated spectral cues, which clearly are important in speech. However, the notion of a single speech envelope is somewhat misleading since it contradicts the well-established notion of frequency-selective channels, such as is incorporated in the general model described above. Thus, it is more meaningful to consider a set of envelopes, one for each channel. In general, the envelopes for channels widely spaced in frequency are different; the differences depend on the spectral content of the signal. Recently it has been shown that the envelopes from as few as four broadly tuned frequency bands are sufficient to provide good speech intelligibility, and that smoothing the envelopes in each of the channels can have a deleterious effect on speech perception. This research indicates that envelope information is extremely important and that only rather coarse spectral information is necessary for speech perception.

Other research directions. Among the other active areas of research on envelope processing is an examination of the effects of hearing loss on amplitude-modulation perception. It appears that a hearing loss caused by cochlear damage does not substantially affect envelope processing. A related research thrust is on amplitude-modulation perception by patients with cochlear implants. These prosthetic devices restore some degree of hearing to the profoundly deaf. It appears that much of the ability of such patients to understand speech is based on envelope information. Envelope information also has been shown to provide an important cue for sound localization. Research has begun to examine the difficult problem of across-channel envelope processing, where differences between the envelopes at different spectral regions provide information. This research represents an attempt to describe the properties of auditory processing of the amplitude and frequency changes that occur simultaneously as in speech and in most real-world sounds.

For background information *see* AMPLITUDE MODULATION; ELECTRIC FILTER; HEARING (HUMAN); HEARING IMPAIRMENT; MASKING OF SOUND; PHYSIOLOGICAL ACOUSTICS; SPEECH PERCEPTION in the McGraw-Hill Encyclopedia of Science & Technology.

Neal F. Viemeister

Bibliography. B. C. J. M. Moore, *An Introduction to the Psychology of Hearing*, 4th ed., 1997; R. V. Shannon et al., Speech recognition with primarily temporal cues, *Science*, 270:303–304, 1995; W. Yost, A. Popper, and R. Fay (eds.), *Human Psychophysics*, 1993.

Automated decision making

As computer technology advances, so do opportunities to use computers to automate various decision-making tasks. A decision-making task is any task requiring the generation or selection of options.

Related to automated decision making are techniques for automated control. The term control is usually applied to continuously operating systems that are constantly monitored and adjusted. The term decision making usually refers to high-level tasks with discrete decision points. For example, a control system might deal with continuous monitoring and adjustments of operating factory equipment; a decision-making system would be more concerned with the selection and scheduling of factory operations. Nevertheless, there is some relationship between technologies for automated control and those for automated decision making.

Another related area is decision support systems. These systems are intended to support human decision making, while automated decision making concentrates on completely computerized decision making. Nevertheless, there is a close connection between these two areas since many decision support systems are designed as advisory systems, recommending decisions to the user. To generate a recommendation, the decision support system invokes an automated decision model. Consequently, both automated decision making and decision support systems rely on the same underlying decision-making technology; and it is the maturity and reliability of the automated decision model which determine whether the system is used to completely automate or to support decision making.

Technology foundations. Three academic disciplines are the principal sources of techniques for automated decision making: operations research, artificial intelligence, and decision theory. Each discipline provides approaches to developing decision models.

Operations research. As an academic discipline, operations research addresses problems of systems modeling and the optimization of both the design and use of systems. Mathematical optimization (also called mathematical programming) is a component oriented toward the development of automated procedures that find optimal solutions to well-defined and mathematically representable problems. Typically, a mathematical optimization procedure decomposes a problem into an objective function and a constraint space. The objective function provides a measure of merit by which proposed solutions are rated. The constraint space mathematically defines the set of feasible solutions. The goal is to find a solution in the constraint space that is optimal with respect to the objective function.

Alternative optimization procedures can be characterized in terms of a trade-off between power and generality. A problem-solving technique is general to the extent that it can be applied to a diversity of problems. It is powerful to the extent that it quickly generates high-valued answers. Linear programming is an example of a powerful technique with little generality. For problems that can be represented as linear functions, efficient procedures exist for finding the globally optimal solution, that is, the highest-valued solution in the constraint space. However, few problems can be satisfactorily expressed in terms of a linear objective function and a set of linear inequality constraints. There are a variety of more general optimization procedures (such as nonlinear programming and integer programming) that can represent a broader range of domain constraints (for example, nonlinear inequalities), but these techniques are generally less powerful than linear optimization. For example, most of these techniques find only local optima, that is, the highest-valued solution in nearby subsets of the constraint space. Even these more general techniques, however, have limited generality in comparison with some approaches from outside operations research.

For automated decision making, mathematical optimization is usually the preferred approach. Unfortunately, because of limited expressiveness, optimization approaches are rarely adequate for fully characterizing all relevant elements of a problem domain. Consequently, optimization approaches are usually not employed.

Artificial intelligence. Artificial intelligence is dedicated to developing automated systems that exhibit intelligent behavior. Often the focus is on developing systems that exhibit problem-solving or learning abilities that are comparable to those of people (even humanlike), but there are also many applications that go beyond human abilities. Researchers have attempted to replicate human performance in almost every area of intellectual and problem-solving activity, including complex inferencing (medical diagnosis, electronic troubleshooting, military situation assessment), automated planning and scheduling (military logistics plans, financial investment planning, autonomous robots), option selection (stock evaluation, consumer product selection), natural language interaction (natural language understanding, speech recognition, machine translation), and learning. *See* NATURAL LANGUAGE PROCESSING.

There are two general approaches to developing systems that exhibit intelligent behavior: knowledge-based and computation-based. Knowledge-based approaches emphasize the importance of capturing and encoding human knowledge. The development of knowledge-based systems usually involves a substantial amount of knowledge engineering, where the engineer must work with human experts to articulate and summarize relevant expertise. Computation-based approaches attempt to avoid the knowledge engineering work by replacing knowledge with intensive computation. Typical of this genre are chess programs. Chess programs actually contain very little encoded chess knowledge, but can quickly search through billions of possible move sequences. Where feasible, computation-based approaches are preferred because they are relatively easy to develop. However, computation-based approaches require a very well defined and limited domain (like the game of chess) and are not applicable to most real-world decision-making problems. Consequently, most work on automated decision making in artificial intelligence is knowledge based.

Because of the emphasis on modeling a broad array of knowledge, artificial intelligence approaches tend to be more general but less powerful than operations research optimization approaches. Rather than seeking optimal solutions, artificial intelligence systems usually search for "satisficing" solutions, which are any solutions that satisfy all known constraints. Usually there is no defined objective function with which to evaluate solutions, much less find the optimal solution. Because of the general applicability of artificial intelligence techniques, the majority of efforts to develop automated decision-making capabilities are based on artificial intelligence.

Decision theory. Decision theory, the science of decision making, is partitioned into two fields. Normative decision theory searches for abstract characterizations of ideal decision-making behavior; the emphasis is on finding a theoretically justified approach to how judgments and decisions should be made. Behavioral decision theory is a branch of psychology that performs research on human judgment and decision making; the emphasis is on characterizing how decisions actually are made.

Normative decision theory derives ideal decision-making behavior from commonsense axioms of rational behavior. For example, it seems reasonable to assert that rational agents do not willingly select options where the best possible outcome is to break even. Yet this assertion (suitably formalized) is sufficient to logically derive that a rational agent acts as though it has a set of beliefs that conform to the probability calculus.

Similarly, it seems reasonable to assert that a rational decision maker would satisfy the following properties: (1) Transitivity: If option X is preferred to Y, and Y to Z, then X is preferred to Z. (2) Independence: If X is preferred to Y, then a chance to play X (say 50%) is preferred to an equal chance to play Y. These properties (suitably formalized with a minor addition) are sufficient to derive the fact that a rational decision maker always selects the option with the highest expected utility, which is calculated by summing the product of the probability and utility of each outcome.

Clearly, people do not always think explicitly in terms of probabilities and utilities and therefore do not satisfy the ideals of normative decision making. Much of the research in behavioral decision theory examines how people systematically deviate from this normative ideal.

Another tradition of research in behavioral decision theory focuses on the use of linear models to predict and replace human judgment. This tradition is based on three surprising, but very consistent, findings: (1) In probabilistic domains, linear models are often good predictors of human judgments. (2) This result holds true even for domains (for example, clinical judgment) where people employ a pattern-matching approach to make judgments. (3) Linear models of expert judgment usually perform better than the experts from which they were derived. Apparently, people, especially experts in a field, are much better at selecting and coding information than they are at integrating it.

Therefore, an automated decision-making system should consider the same variables that a human expert considers in making a decision, but should not emulate human expert decision-making processes. Rather, the variables should be integrated into an overall judgment or decision by using a decision-making model based on normative decision theory.

Bayesian networks and influence diagrams are emerging as preferred normative decision theory models for automated decision making. They are used in diverse applications ranging from medical diagnosis to selecting help options in applications software.

Recent trends. During the 1980s, the majority of the work in automated decision making was within a particular discipline. For example, there were numerous efforts to develop expert systems that used artificial intelligence knowledge–based approaches to emulate human expert reasoning in diverse areas (including medical diagnosis, financial decision making, engineering design, electronic troubleshooting, and military battlefield decision making), while there were efforts to develop decision-theory approaches to some of these same problems. Little attention was paid to related work in the other disciplines. In the 1990s, however, the trend was substantially reversed. Decision-theory results and perspectives now dominate much of the artificial intelligence research in automated decision making, and to less extent there has been an active interest in integrating optimization and artificial intelligence problem-solving approaches.

A second trend has to do with the relation of automated decision making to the maturing information infrastructure. With ready access to information infrastructures, such as the World Wide Web, there is a rapidly growing wealth of information available to decision makers. Indeed, the growth in information availability has led to an information overload problem: There is so much material available that it is hard to find the few items that are specifically useful to a decision maker addressing a specific decision problem. As a result, there is a rapidly growing interest in organizing materials around decision-making needs. Automated decision-making techniques can be applied to support this organization, since an automated decision-making model can be used to determine if new information substantially impacts or alters the recommendations that a decision support system makes to a user. Information that alters a decision is, by definition, important to decision making. *See* WEB RESOURCES.

A third trend is the application of automated decision making to simulation technology. Commercial computer games and many military training simulations involve interaction of players with other computer-controlled agents in a simulated world. In both cases, the value of the simulation (whether for entertainment or effective training) depends on the realism and intelligence of the simulated agents. Simulated agents must make decisions in their simulated worlds and are therefore executing automated decision making. It seems likely that a substantial investment will be made in the development of sophisticated automated decision-making capabilities in dynamic, interactive simulations.

For background information *see* ARTIFICIAL INTELLIGENCE; BAYESIAN STATISTICS; CONTROL SYSTEMS; DECISION ANALYSIS; DECISION SUPPORT SYSTEM; DECISION THEORY; EXPERT SYSTEMS; LINEAR PROGRAMMING; NONLINEAR PROGRAMMING; OPERATIONS RESEARCH; SIMULATION in the McGraw-Hill Encyclopedia of Science & Technology.   Paul E. Lehner

Bibliography. D. Brown and C. White (eds.), *Operations Research and Artificial Intelligence: The Integration of Problem-Solving Strategies*, 1990; E. Castillo, J. M. Gutiérrez, and A. S. Hadi, *Expert Systems and Probabilistic Network Models*, 1996; F. Jensen, *Introduction to Bayesian Networks*, 1996; P. Lehner and L. Adelman, Behavioural decision theory and its implications for knowledge engineering, *Knowledge Eng. Rev.*, 5(1):5–14, 1990; D. Olson and J. Courtney, Jr., *Decision Support Models and Expert Systems*, 1997.

Automotive vehicle

Electric vehicles competed head to head with gasoline cars around the beginning of the twentieth century but soon faded from the marketplace. They failed in the United States and elsewhere because electricity-recharging infrastructure was too sparse, batteries were far inferior to present ones, and the technology did not match well with the contemporary market. After batteries were made more reliable around 1907, electric vehicles made a brief resurgence, but limited-range cars had little appeal. In recent times, circumstances have changed, environmental issues are more central, and batteries continue to be improved. It remains to be seen whether the rapid pace of electric vehicle technology will continue and whether it will lead to other types of electric drive vehicles.

Technology of electric vehicles. Electric drivelines, encompassing electric motors, batteries, and power electronics, have important advantages over today's gasoline-powered internal combustion engines. They are quieter, virtually nonpolluting, and more energy efficient, reliable, and durable. Major advances have been made in various electric drive technology components since the late 1980s. For example, advances in power electronics have resulted in small, lightweight dc-to-ac inverters which, in turn, make possible ac drives that are cheaper, more compact, more reliable, easier to maintain, more efficient, and more adaptable to regenerative braking than the dc systems used in virtually all electric vehicles through the early 1990s. The electric vehicle motor-controller combination is now smaller and lighter than a comparable internal combustion engine, as well as cheaper to manufacture and maintain.

The largest hurdle holding back battery-powered electric vehicle commercialization is the battery. Batteries typically account for one-third or more of vehicle weight and one-fourth or more of the life-cycle cost of an electric vehicle. Major improvements in batteries are expected because, until recently, so little effort has been put into designing and building batteries of the size needed for vehicles, and so much progress has been made in developing new and improved small batteries for portable computers, camcorders, cellular phones, and other small consumer products.

The list of electric vehicle battery candidates includes batteries with solid, liquid, and gaseous electrolytes, high and ambient temperatures, replaceable metals, and replaceable liquids. At least 20 distinct battery types have been suggested as candidates. But what looks promising in a small cell often falls short when scaled up for a vehicle. The reality is that the underlying science of battery technology is highly complex and not well understood, rendering the engineering of large batteries difficult.

Many research efforts are under way to develop and commercialize advanced batteries. The most prominent is the United States Advanced Battery Consortium (US ABC). Launched in 1991, US ABC seeks to increase the energy and power capability, extend the life, and reduce costs of batteries as they are scaled up to sizes suitable to electric vehicles. Advanced battery development efforts in Japan and Europe have been at least as active and accomplished, but have received less publicity and have been less influenced by large consortia.

Improved versions of today's lead-acid batteries dominated through the late 1990s, because this type is relatively inexpensive and relatively reliable. In Europe, the nickel-cadmium battery and the high-temperature (250–320°C) sodium-nickel-chloride battery are also being used initially. Beyond lead-acid batteries, there is no consensus as to which batteries will prove superior for electric vehicles, though it is widely believed that nickel-metal hydride batteries will predominate over much of the next decade, and lithium-based batteries will dominate thereafter.

Environmental benefits of electric vehicles. Government support of electric vehicles in the United States has been premised primarily on air quality, but in most areas air quality by itself is probably not sufficient justification to mandate electric vehicles. Because of continuing improvements in emissions from gasoline vehicles and receding air pollution in most urban areas in the United States, electric vehicles could be justified as an air-pollution control strategy only in cities with severe pollution, such as Mexico City, Bangkok, and other rapidly industrializing metropolitan regions, plus Los Angeles and a few other metropolitan areas in the United States and Europe.

Regardless of the type of power plant, fuel, and emission controls employed, battery-powered vehicles would practically eliminate emissions of carbon monoxide and hydrocarbons (also known as reactive organic gases and volatile organic compounds) and would greatly diminish nitrogen oxide emissions. Electric vehicles would add sulfur oxides and particulate matter to the air in areas served by coal-fired power plants. However, cars and gasoline-powered trucks generally account for only a few percent of the total urban emissions of these two pollutants, so there will be critical concern only where the coal-fired plants are particularly dirty and account for a large share of the generated electricity.

The air-quality benefits of electric vehicles are largest when the electricity is produced from solar, nuclear, wind, or hydroelectric power, or when electricity is generated in well-controlled natural gas plants. Two attractive locations for battery-powered vehicles, from an air-quality perspective, are Los Angeles and France. Because over 80% of the electricity used during both daytime and nighttime in the Los Angeles area comes from outside the region, and most of the locally generated electricity comes from very tightly controlled natural gas plants, the use of electric vehicles would result in virtual elimination of all vehicle-related emissions, even particulates and sulfur oxides. In France, the benefits are large because most electricity is from emissions-free nuclear plants.

Electric vehicles are attractive antipollution strategies not only because their use results in less overall emissions but also because power plants are often located far from populated areas and a large proportion of their emissions would be at night when sunlight is not present to form ozone and when people are indoors and not exposed. Battery-powered vehicles will be an effective air-quality control strategy almost everywhere.

Other benefits of electric vehicles are dramatic reductions in oil use, and therefore petroleum imports, and reduced greenhouse gases. Battery-powered vehicles would provide small to large greenhouse gas benefits if introduced today, depending on the source of electricity. As shown in the **table**, the use of coal-fired electricity by vehicles would

Greenhouse gas impacts of electric vehicles relative to gasoline-powered vehicles	
Power source for charging	% change
Solar and nuclear electricity	−90 to −80
Natural gas power plant	−50 to −25
Current U.S. power mix	−20 to 0
New coal-fired power plant	0 to +10

cause a small increase in emissions of all greenhouse gases relative to the use of gasoline (on a per-kilometer basis), taking into account all fuel-related activities, from extraction to combustion, including energy used in vehicle manufacture. But that is a worst case; no country relies exclusively on coal. If natural gas were used in the power plant, there would be a moderate decrease in emissions of greenhouse gases, mainly because of the low carbon-to-hydrogen ratio of natural gas. Greenhouse gas emissions are reduced most when power plants do not use fossil fuels, such as in France where most electricity comes from nuclear plants. If nonfossil fuels (nuclear, solar, hydroelectric, or biomass) were used, greenhouse gas emissions would be virtually eliminated.

However, the environmental effects of electric drive are not uniformly positive. The principal concern is that increased use of batteries will lead to increased amounts of new materials released into the environment, some of which may be toxic. This concern may not be realistic, however. The more toxic materials, such as cadmium, are likely to be restricted, and others are likely to be almost completely recycled. Very little of the lead from the lead-acid batteries used in the United States ever causes a health risk, because virtually all the lead is recycled and lead-processing plants are tightly controlled. The large size and weight of traction batteries for vehicles and the high value of the materials virtually assure close to 100% recycling.

Cost of electric vehicles. An electric vehicle, minus the batteries, should cost less than a comparable gasoline vehicle, once scale economies are achieved. Since batteries are expensive, its total purchase cost is never likely to be less than that of the gasoline vehicle. Electric vehicles might eventually prove cost competitive when environmental benefits are considered. Their operating and maintenance costs should be lower than those of gasoline vehicles, and vehicle life longer. It is conceivable that on a life-cycle basis—calculating costs over the life of the vehicle and discounting them back to the present—the per-kilometer costs would be comparable. Considering the reduced environmental costs, a battery-powered electric vehicle should be economical. The most economic electric vehicles will be lighter and not required to have long driving ranges.

The most promising application of electric vehicle technology is in combination with non-battery energy storage devices and on-board generators of electricity. Devices with high power densities that can charge and discharge quickly, such as ultracapacitors and flywheels, could be used to provide surge power for short periods of time (for example, when passing or climbing hills), thus reducing battery needs. Or devices that generate electricity on board, such as fuel cells or small internal combustion engines, could be the principal energy source, with batteries used only for surge power or extended driving. Such hybridized designs have the potential to be more energy efficient, lower emitting, and less expensive than pure battery designs.

For background information *see* AUTOMOBILE; BATTERY; GREENHOUSE EFFECT; MOTOR VEHICLE in the McGraw-Hill Encyclopedia of Science & Technology.　　　　　　　　　　Daniel Sperling

Bibliography. M. B. Schiffer, *Taking Charge: The Electric Automobile in America*, 1994; D. Sperling, The case for electric vehicles, *Sci. Amer.*, 275(5): 54–59, November 1996; D. Sperling, *Future Drive: Electric Vehicles and Sustainable Transportation*, 1995.

Bacterial genetics

Humans develop the disease cholera after ingesting water or food contaminated with the bacterium *Vibrio cholerae*. In parts of the world where cholera appears in a yearly cycle (endemic areas), *V. cholerae* is constantly present in the environment even when there is no disease. During cholera epidemics the microorganisms are acquired by human hosts and rapidly transmitted via the fecal-oral route from person to person. When swallowed, *V. cholerae* colonizes the surface (epithelium) of the small intestine by using specialized adherence structures called toxin co-regulated pili or mannose-sensitive hemagglutinins (the sugar mannose specifically inhibits attachment in vitro). Then the vibrios release a potent enterotoxin that causes enterocytes to temporarily reverse their normal absorptive function and instead hypersecrete water and electrolytes. The resultant voluminous diarrhea can lead to lethal dehydration (cholera gravis); but because the infection is self limited (localized and short term), patients can be treated by simply using oral or intravenous fluid replacement. Antibiotic treatment is not necessary, but it is often employed to eliminate vibrio shedding into the environment and to decrease the amount of replacement fluids required. Unfortunately, high mortality from cholera occurs in developing countries with inadequate treatment facilities.

Vibrio cholerae are divided into biotypes, serotypes, and serogroups for identification purposes. The classical and El Tor biotypes are defined by stable, easily observable traits. Before the seventh pandemic, El Tor vibrios were considered to be avirulent or, at worst, to cause only mild, nonepidemic cholera. The current pandemic El Tor biotypes that cause cholera gravis display mannose-sensitive hemagglutinin colonization factors, no longer lyse red blood cells, and frequently acquire multiple drug resistance during outbreaks (**Tables 1** and **2**).

Antibodies directed against cell wall structures (antigens) divide the biotypes into serotypes called Inaba and Ogawa. Each biotype or serotype is further differentiated into serogroups labeled O1 through O139 according to antibodies specific for surface lipopolysaccharides called O antigens. Thus, *V. cholerae* isolates are designated classical Ogawa O1, El Tor Inaba O139, El Tor Ogawa O139, and so on.

Cholera outbreaks were thought to emanate from water contaminated by subclinically infected per-

---

TABLE 1. Cholera at the start of the seventh pandemic and in 1997

Disease parameters	Cholera before 1961	Cholera in 1997
Predominant isolate	Classical Ogawa	El Tor Inaba/Ogawa
El Tor properties	Sporadic, nonepidemic mild disease, hemolytic, agglutinates chicken red blood cells, polymyxin B–resistant	Pandemic, cholera gravis, nonhemolytic, mannose-sensitive hemagglutinins, polymyxin B–resistant, multiple-drug-resistant strains in some outbreaks
Epidemic serogroup	O1 only	O1, O139, ?
Major reservoir	Infected humans	Environment, infected humans, noncultivatable vibrios
Vehicles of transmission	Feces, contaminated water	Water, copepods, seafood, nonseafoods, ?
Distribution of epidemic strains	One major O1 serobiotype restricted to endemic areas	Seven genotypes localized worldwide, U.S. Gulf Coast and Australia clones endogenous
Colonization factors	Hemagglutinins, hemolysins	Toxin co-regulated pili, mannose-sensitive hemagglutinins, core-encoded pili, outer membrane proteins, ?
Causes of pathogenesis	Mucosal disruption by mucinase, neuraminidase, and putative "exotoxin"	Cholera toxin (CT), Zonula occludens toxin (ZOT), accessory cholera enterotoxin (ACE), toxin coregulated pili expression regulated by environmentally triggered complex regulatory cascade (*ToxR* regulon)

---

sons (infected with *V. cholerae* but not ill) and then to spread to more susceptible individuals, who developed clinical disease. The revelation in 1955 that *V. cholerae* elaborated a signature cholera exoenterotoxin (CT) established the dogma that only toxigenic *V. cholerae* O1 from humans could cause epidemic cholera. It is now known that toxigenic *V. cholerae* O1, though clearly associated with infected humans, is also prevalent in the environment on water plants and crustaceans and in other estuarine venues. Vibrios with epidemic potential can survive undetected for long periods of time in a viable but nonculturable state. Evidence is provided by recently identified endemic *V. cholerae* O1 clones (for example, isolates indigenous to local geographical regions and distinct from pandemic strains) found in locales such as the United States Gulf Coast, where there has been no epidemic cholera for over a half century.

Horizontal gene transfer. Cholera ordinarily manifests itself in either localized epidemics or worldwide epidemics known as pandemics. Since the early 1960s when the seventh pandemic emerged, *V. cholerae* has managed to constantly "leap" ahead of those trying to control its spread and develop effec-

tive vaccines. It is now clear that those leaps are assisted by horizontal gene transfer (HGT), in which large segments of deoxyribonucleic acid (DNA) encoding multiple genes pass between *V. cholerae* bacteria. The DNA clusters commonly contain genes associated with pathogenesis and are called virulence cassettes or pathogenicity islands. The phenomenon is not confined to *V. cholerae*, because similar virulence cassettes have been identified in pathogens such as *Salmonella* and *Escherichia coli*, which cause diarrheal disease similar to cholera. Frequently, the mobile DNA has a unique signature quite different from the donor or the recipient, making the true origin of the DNA uncertain (Table 2).

In addition to the mechanisms described above, vibrios have at least three other means of facilitating horizontal gene transfer. Conjugation, a process in which cell-to-cell contact promotes transfer of genetic information usually in the form of plasmids, has been used to construct a map of the *V. cholerae* genome. Transduction, where genes are moved from donor to recipient mediated by vibrio-specific bacterial viruses (bacteriophages), has been shown to be involved in seroconversion of one biotype to an-

---

TABLE 2. Mechanisms of horizontal gene transfer in *Vibrio cholerae*

Mechanism	Genetic elements involved	Examples of genes transferred
En bloc	Pathogenicity islands, filamentous bacteriophage	Toxins, pili, mannose-sensitive hemagglutinin pili, regulatory genes, phage, toxin co-regulated pili
Conjugation[a]	P and V sex factors, plasmids[b]	Nutritional markers, drug resistance, O antigens, bacteriocins, toxins
Generalized transduction[c]	Bacteriophage/defective phage?	O antigens, drug resistance, bacteriocins?, nutritional markers, agglutinins
Transposition[d]	Conjugative transposons, insertion sequences	Toxins, virulence cassettes

[a] Direct sexual contact occurs, with transfer of multiple genes from donor to recipient vibrios.
[b] Plasmids are small DNA structures that can replicate independently in the bacterial cytoplasm or in concert with the bacterial chromosome when integrated. Many plasmids promote their own transfer via conjugation.
[c] Bacterial virus-mediated transfer of donor genes to recipient vibrios occurs. During phage replication, one or more bacterial genes are incorporated into the phage genome, then carried into the recipient along with phage DNA.
[d] DNA is mobilized from donor to recipient by conjugation after excision by transposases which are part of the transposon.

other. Transposition, a complex process involving mobile units of DNA that can insert randomly into the *V. cholerae* chromosome, is clearly involved in the evolution of the cholera toxin negative O1 isolates.

In 1992 a major horizontal gene transfer event occurred when a new epidemic appeared in Bengal, India. In addition to the surface antigen (and several other new traits), this type (called O139 Bengal) produces an external coating called a capsule. This observation alarmed many scientists, because other capsulated bacteria cause invasive diseases such as meningitis, pneumonia, and septic shock. The abrupt introduction of a completely new biotype raised the specter of an eighth pandemic in which even populations with long-term exposure and natural acquired immunity to *V. cholerae* would be affected. Fortunately, O139 appears to have been replaced by O1 pandemic strains in subsequent years. Several lines of experimental evidence implicate a new style of horizontal gene transfer in the creation of a new biotype from a traditional strain.

Molecular mechanisms. In *V. cholerae* a single genetic element called a regulon controls the expression of many genes. Among such controlled genes are those for cholera toxin biosynthesis, toxic coregulated pili, and other characters. Expression of these factors is determined in response to environmental signals received through a complex sensor-activator circuit. Vaccine strains in which the gene for the toxic subunit (*ctxA*) of cholera is deleted still cause mild diarrhea. This residual ability to stimulate a negative reaction is in part due to the fact that two cholera toxin genes make up a special region of DNA referred to as a virulence (infectious) cassette. In addition, the cholera toxin genes are located by two other genes (*ace* and *zot*) whose products also exert diarrheagenic effects (**Fig. 1**). All four of these genes are located in a core region of the chromosomal DNA. Additionally, genes that encode both bacterial and phage functions (*cep* and *orfU*) are found in the core region. This entire complex is called the CTX element, and it is missing in whole or in part in nontoxigenic *V. cholerae* (Fig. 1).

The genes for cholera toxin and those that also cause diarrhea are found in various clones of vibrios, but not always together or in the same combination. In nontoxigenic strains (and in all *V. cholerae* isolates), a signature nucleotide sequence is invariably left behind following CTX excision. The universal presence of these attachment sites suggests that all vibrios can potentially serve as recipients or donors of mobile DNA such as the CTX element.

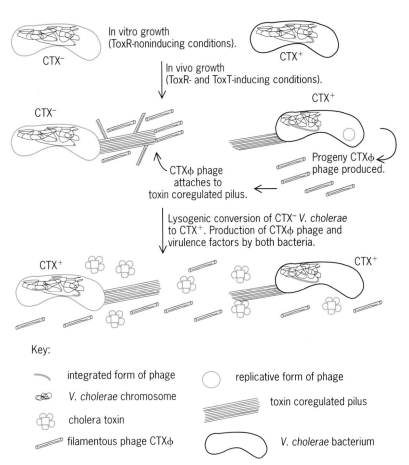

Key:

integrated form of phage   replicative form of phage

V. cholerae chromosome

cholera toxin   toxin coregulated pilus

filamentous phage CTXφ   *V. cholerae* bacterium

Fig. 2. Lysogenic conversion of CTX⁻ *Vibrio cholerae* **to CTX⁺.** *(After S. H. Richardson and D. J. Wozniak, An ace up the sleeve of the cholera bacterium, Nat. Med., 2:853–855, 1996)*

The ability to move the virulence cassette was demonstrated following the observation that the two genes (*orf* and *zot*) adjacent to the cholera toxin genes had DNA sequences homologous to certain filamentous bacteriophages (threadlike bacterial viruses that use pili to attach to the host). Soon, reproducible horizontal gene transfer between two *V. cholerae* strains was demonstrated (**Fig. 2**). The factor mediating this exchange was shown by electron microscopy and by genetic tests to be a filamentous bacteriophage containing a single-stranded DNA molecule corresponding to the coding sequence of the CTX element. Upon removal of the phage DNA from the donor chromosome, the molecule circularizes into a replicative form (Fig. 2) which occurs via a DNA recombination event between special sites (attRS1) at the ends of the CTX element. This form is capable of either replicating independently as a plasmid or integrating into the chromosome when transferred to other *V. cholerae* strains. Once the CTX element is introduced into a recipient cell, these bacteria become phenotypically CTX⁺ and are capable of producing cholera toxin and progeny filamentous bacterophages (Fig. 2).

An important observation was that no transfer of the CTX element occurred when the recipient El

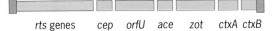

rts genes   cep   orfU   ace   zot   ctxA ctxB

Fig. 1. CTX element carries *ctx AB* genes as well as the genes *zot*, *ace*, *orfU*, and *cep*. (After S. H. Richardson and D. J. Wozniak, An ace up the sleeve of the cholera bacterium, Nat. Med., 2:853–855, 1996)

Tor biotype (responsible for the current pandemic) *V. cholerae* strains were cultured under conditions which do not favor toxin co-regulated pili production. The process of lysogenic conversion (leading to new properties expressed by the host following incorporation of phage genes into its genome) is strongly enhanced when the bacteriophage donor strain is cocultivated in mouse intestine with a recipient CTX⁻ strain. These data suggest that the bacteriophage utilizes toxin co-regulated pili receptors (Fig. 2). Mutations in two of the genes within the CTX core element abolish the ability of the bacteriophage to transfer the CTX element. Apparently, at least one protein encoded within the CTX element has a dual function, since it is required for both phage biosynthesis and *V. cholerae* pathogenesis.

A parallel example of horizontal gene transfer involving a different filamentous bacteriophage disguised as a part of the *V. cholerae* genome was reported. Filamentous phage 493, obtained from a 1994 cholera isolate, specifically lyses El Tor isolates but not classical strains. Newer El Tor biotypes reemerging after the appearance of cholera strain O139 are not lysed by phage 493; however, older El Tors, even those isolated long before the seventh pandemic, are sensitive to the phage. Like the CTX phage, phage 493 has homology to the *E. coli* filamentous phage, which replicates as part of the chromosome or independently in the cytoplasm, but uses the mannose-sensitive hemagglutinin pilus as its receptor. Spontaneous and induced mannose-sensitive hemagglutinin mutants and classical strains which do not express mannose-sensitive hemagglutinin pili are immune to the phage. Reintroduction of the mannose-sensitive hemagglutinin gene on a plasmid or by transposition makes such strains again sensitive to 493. Of related interest, 493 DNA is homologous with DNA from an encapsulated non-O1 vibrio isolated 2 years before the appearance of O139. It is possible that 493 may have been involved in the transformation of El Tor into encapsulated O139 by horizontal gene transfer and that 493-infected hosts aided O139 in replacing the indigenous El Tor strains.

In an example of horizontal gene transfer involvement in vibrio evolution, two *V. cholerae* genes, *aldA* and *tagA*, that are a part of another regulon controlled by a complex sensor-activator circuit were recently found to be located on a chromosomal virulence cassette (different from the one previously mentioned). This unique genetic unit is highly conserved in many old and new epidemic strains of *V. cholerae*, including the classical, El Tor, and O139 Bengal strains. The DNA segment includes genes for toxin co-regulated pili accessory colonization factor and *toxT*, which is a second signal in the complex sensor-activator circuit regulon. The genes are not found in nonepidemic and pandemic isolates, suggesting that the region is inherited or lost as a whole.

It is clear from these results that horizontal gene transfer is a well-established mechanism of genetic manipulation in *V. cholerae*. Horizontal gene transfer allows this versatile microorganism to adapt to myriad environments in its cycle from nature through humans and back to nature. The faces of *V. cholerae* and cholera have constantly changed throughout history, but now there is a better idea of just how those substantial changes, in the constant dual with the environment and the human host, are brought about.

For background information *see* BACTERIOPHAGE; CHOLERA; DIARRHEA; INFECTIOUS DISEASE; MOLECULAR BIOLOGY; TOXIN; VIRULENCE; WATER POLLUTION in the McGraw-Hill Encyclopedia of Science & Technology.   Stephen H. Richardson

Bibliography. E. A. Jourvleva et al., Characterization and possible functions of a new filamentous bacteriophage from *Vibrio cholerae* O139, *Microbiology*, 144:315–324, 1998; S. F. Mel and J. J. Mekalanos, Modulation of horizontal gene transfer in pathogenic bacteria by in vivo signals, *Cell*, 87:795–798, 1996; S. H. Richardson and D. J. Wozniak, An ace up the sleeve of the cholera bacterium, *Nat. Med.*, 2:853–855, 1996; I. K. Wachsmuth, P. B. Blake, and O. Olsvik (eds.), *Vibrio cholerae and Cholera: Molecular to Global Perspectives*, 1994; M. K. Waldor and J. J. Mekalanos, Lysogenic conversion by a filamentous phage encoding cholera toxin, *Science*, 272:1910–1914, 1996.

Biodiversity

Factors of evolution observed today, such as natural selection, migration, and the origin and extinction of species, have operated throughout the history of life, but the characteristic rates of these processes have varied greatly over time and from one group of organisms to another. Because of this variation, evolutionary patterns seen in the fossil record are highly episodic and irregular. Paleontological studies of biological diversity seek to document this nonuniformity and to understand it in the context of geological, environmental, and ecological change.

Approaches to studying diversity. Differences in form among organisms are essential components of biological diversity; they reflect variation in function, ecology, and architecture. Measuring such differences is central to much of evolutionary research. Because recognition of distinct species in the fossil record rests upon the documentation of morphological differences, taxonomic richness, that is, the number of species or of more inclusive categories such as genera and families, is often used as a proxy for morphological diversity. Taxonomic richness is also of interest because it reflects the difference between two fundamental processes of large-scale evolution: the origination and extinction of species. A principal advantage of taxonomic diversity data is that they can be summed across disparate biological groups, or taxa. By tallying species of mollusks, arthropods, vertebrates, plants, and so on, paleontologists can track the evolutionary success of these taxa within ecosystems, within geographic realms, and even over the entire planet.

The presence of many species during an interval of geological time implies that there must be morphological differences among them, but it says little about the magnitude of those differences. Sometimes one sees a proliferation of species that barely differ from each other, or a modest increase in richness consisting of species that are strikingly dissimilar. Taxonomic rank (degree of inclusiveness) tends to correlate with morphological difference; the dissimilarity between two species in the same genus is generally smaller than the dissimilarity between two families in the same order. The origin of taxa of very high rank, such as phyla, classes, and orders, is therefore frequently assumed to represent a very large morphological transition. Although this assumption is often valid, it is imperfect; and paleontologists have sought to quantify morphological diversity directly. To this end, recent methodological approaches have included traditional measurement of anatomical parts (such as lengths of limbs), analysis of cartesian coordinates of biological landmarks (such as junctions between different tissues), and numerical coding of traits (such as patterns of tooth sculpture). Once the form of each species is quantified, morphological diversity, or disparity, of a group is measured as the average magnitude of differences among species. The main advantage of this approach is that it is direct; no assumptions about the relationship between taxonomic rank and morphological divergence are necessary. The main disadvantage is that it limits the scope of analysis; species can be compared only if they are similar enough to allow quantification of the same traits. It may be easy to compare all snails, but comparing snails with snakes presents a challenge.

Evolutionary radiations. Comparing very disparate organisms is difficult, but recent work has broadened the scope of morphological studies with a numerical coding scheme (the skeleton space) that distills the anatomy of skeletonized animals to a few major structural features. Analysis of the skeleton space has shown that a great proportion of the anatomical designs used by animals had already evolved by the Cambrian Period (540-500 million years ago), shortly after the origin of animal skeletons. This provides evidence for rapid morphological evolution followed by the generation of small variations on the fundamental anatomical themes that had been established early. A rapid rise in disparity followed by minor innovation has recently been documented in a number of animal groups, including crinoid echinoderms during the Paleozoic Era (540-245 m.y.a.) and again during the Mesozoic Era (245-65 m.y.a.), rostroconch mollusks (extinct relatives of clams) and gastropod mollusks during the early Paleozoic, and mammals during the Cenozoic Era (the past 65 m.y.).

In the classic view of evolutionary radiations, a group of organisms enjoys vast ecological opportunities, perhaps because of the elimination of competitors (for example, the mammalian radiation after the extinction of dinosaurs), or because of an evolutionary innovation that allows new resources to be exploited (for example, the stalk and feeding apparatus that enabled many echinoderms to rise above the sea floor and filter suspended organic particles from the water). If organisms enjoy a world in which many ecological niches have not yet been filled, evolutionary changes of many kinds may yield varieties that, while perhaps not optimal, are still able to make a living in this ecologically relaxed world. The first species able to bore through a shell and eat the snail need not have been so well suited to drilling as its modern analogs that live in a competitive world of more effective predators. Morphological evolution should therefore be rapid during the early phases of an evolutionary radiation. As ecological niches progressively fill, however, opportunities should diminish and rates of morphological evolution should decrease. The analysis of ancestor-descendant transitions has allowed paleontologists to document a temporal decline in the size of these transitions within a number of animal groups, including rostroconchs, gastropods, and bryozoans. Mathematical modeling of the diversification process suggests that the observed magnitude of the decline in transition sizes is adequate to account for the observed deceleration of morphological diversification.

Inferring ecological processes from a decline in the rate of morphological change assumes implicitly that this decline reflects evolution within component lineages, but the situation may be more complicated. In rostroconchs, the overall decline in average transition size was caused only in part by a change in transition size within the two major lineages. The rest of the decline resulted simply from the extinction of the lineage with the higher characteristic transition size. It remains to be seen how frequently this situation occurs.

Ecosystem evolution. The mass extinction at the end of the Paleozoic Era yielded an early Mesozoic world with a greatly reduced number of species. Many paleontologists have argued that, at the coarsest ecological scale, the world was not quite so depauperate as species richness would suggest, since most of the major marine ecological guilds (for example, swimming carnivores and sessile suspension feeders) were present. If this were true, one might expect that morphological diversification should not have proceeded so rapidly in the Mesozoic as it had in the Paleozoic. Among crinoids, maximal Mesozoic disparity was attained as rapidly as the Paleozoic maximum, suggesting that, for crinoids at least, ecological opportunities were great. The level of disparity reached in the Mesozoic, however, was not so great as that in the Paleozoic. The reasons are unknown, but the possibilities include competition with other organisms that first appeared in the Mesozoic, as well as a hypothesized pattern of evolution in which major innovations became progressively more difficult as pathways of growth and biochemical regulation became more tightly codependent and therefore less flexible.

Sampling. Charles Darwin attributed many observations, seemingly opposed to his theory of descent with modification, to the incompleteness of the geological record. He noted that perception of evolutionary patterns changes as new fossil discoveries are made. More recently, paleontologists have argued that the stability of diversity patterns in the face of improved sampling means that these patterns are reliable. While most studies of this sort have focused on taxonomic data, analyses of morphological data suggest that, over the history of paleontology, species have in many respects been sampled randomly from the available pool of fossilized forms. Certain patterns, such as the increase in trilobite disparity from the Cambrian Period to the Ordovician Period (about 500–440 m.y.a.), are so insensitive to sampling that they could have been documented a century ago; such stable patterns are unlikely to be overturned by future sampling. Others, such as the rapid diversification of form in Mesozoic crinoids, depend more on recent discoveries; continued sampling may ultimately force rethinking of this aspect of the evolutionary radiation of crinoids.

Extinction. Episodes of mass extinction do not always entail a severe reduction in morphological diversity; survivors may represent nearly the entire spectrum of anatomical designs that existed prior to the crisis. Morphological diversity is maintained during a loss of taxonomic diversity in several cases, including trilobites and stalked echinoderms at the end of the Ordovician Period. In other examples, such as the phylum Brachiopoda, mass extinctions resulted in a conspicuous reduction in morphological diversity. Among brachiopods, the same general shell shapes appeared to be favored during different extinction events. In addition to exploring how morphological diversity responds to extinction, one can investigate its contributions to survival. Paleontologists have demonstrated that certain biological features, such as broad geographic distribution, tend to enhance survival during mass-extinction episodes. Since many important aspects of function and ecology are inherent in an organism's form, the diversity of morphology within a taxon should generally correlate with the range of ecological niches exploited by that taxon. It is therefore possible to predict that morphologically more diverse taxa would improve their prospects ecologically; that is, they would have a greater chance of surviving extinction events. Further investigation may help to identify present-day groups that are most at risk of extinction because of contemporary habitat loss and environmental change. *See* MASS EXTINCTION.

For background information *see* ANIMAL EVOLUTION; ANIMAL SYSTEMATICS; EXTINCTION (BIOLOGY); MACROEVOLUTION; ORGANIC EVOLUTION; PHYLOGENY; SPECIATION in the McGraw-Hill Encyclopedia of Science & Technology.   Mike Foote

Bibliography. D. Erwin et al., The origin of animal body plans, *Amer. Sci.*, 85:126–137, 1997; M. Foote, The evolution of morphological diversity, *Annu. Rev. Ecol. Syst.*, 28:129–152, 1997; M. Foote, Sampling, taxonomic description, and our evolving knowledge of morphological diversity, *Paleobiology*, 23:181–206, 1997; J. Jernvall et al., Molar tooth diversity, disparity, and ecology in Cenozoic ungulate radiations, *Science*, 274:1489–1492, 1996; G. R. McGhee, Jr., Geometry of evolution in the biconvex Brachiopoda: Morphological effects of mass extinction, *Neues Jb. Geol. Paläont. Abh.*, 197:357–382, 1995; R. D. K. Thomas and W.-E. Reif, The skeleton space: A finite set of organic designs, *Evolution*, 47:341–360, 1993; P. J. Wagner, Patterns of morphologic diversification among the Rostroconchia, *Paleobiology*, 23:115–150, 1997.

Brucellosis

Brucellosis, caused by *Brucella abortus,* is enzootic among the free-ranging bison (*Bison bison*) herds of Yellowstone and Grand Teton National Parks (Wyoming), Wood Buffalo National Park (Canada), and a privately owned herd in South Dakota. There have previously been numerous infected herds, both private and public. The presence of the disease in the free-ranging bison and possible control measures have led to much controversy among ranchers (who fear transmission to cattle), governmental agencies, environmentalists, and other interested individuals and organizations. Lawsuits, many meetings, media publicity, and other reactions to the problem have occurred. The climax came during the winter of 1996–1997, when over 1000 bison were slaughtered as they migrated from Yellowstone National Park and an additional 600 starved because of the severe weather.

Ranchers in Idaho, Montana, and Wyoming fear possible transmission of brucellosis from bison to cattle herds, with a subsequent reduction of the state status by the U.S. Department of Agriculture (USDA). These states are classified as free of cattle brucellosis, and a change would result in restrictions in commerce. Many people have questioned the scientific and legal consequences of this threat.

Pathology. Brucellosis in domestic animals is characterized by abortions, retained placenta, decreased milk production, and pathologic lesions in males such as epididymitis, orchitis, and decreased semen quality. Transmission occurs by ingestion, such as licking an aborted fetus or consuming contaminated forage. There is no evidence of venereal transmission in cattle or bison.

The serological evidence of brucellosis in bison of Yellowstone National Park was first reported in 1917 and bacteriologically confirmed in 1930. Since that time many workers have commented that the disease did not seem to adversely affect herd growth, in both publicly and privately owned herds. There have been many reports of clinical infections in male bison, and nearly all serological surveys have shown a higher percentage of antibodies in males than in

Comparison of effects of brucellosis in cattle and bison

Factor	Cattle	Bison
Abortions	Common	Rare
Relationship of serology to infection	High	Poor
Fecundity	May be high	Very low
Serological response to oral exposure in calves	Low	High
Public health risk	Moderate	Not confirmed
Susceptibility to infection		
Males	Low	Moderate
Females	High	Low
Uterine infection	High	Low
Response to strain 19 vaccine		
Abortions	Very low	High
Uterine infection	Rare	High
Resistance	Moderate to high	Poor

females. Abortions in infected bison appear to be rare under natural conditions. However, under experimental conditions a high percentage of bison aborted when exposed to a large dose of a virulent strain of *B. abortus* of cattle origin. From this some scientists think that brucellosis in bison mimics the disease in cattle, although this is disputed by observations of natural or farmed bison populations (see **table**).

There is a marked difference in confirmation of the presence of *B. abortus* in tissues or other specimens of seropositive cattle and bison. Cultures of specimens of seropositive cattle may yield bacterial recoveries of 85% or greater, while those of bison are approximately 20%. The true prevalence among bison populations with seroprevalences of approximately 50% may be only 10%.

Diagnosis. The diagnosis of brucellosis in bison is largely based upon the presence of antibodies in blood sera. This may be supplemented with bacteriologic cultures, usually performed on seropositive animals. The serologic tests that are used in bison were developed for cattle, and the criteria for the classification of results are usually identical. There are data showing that tests and criteria for positivity in cattle lead to a high percentage of false positive and several false negative results when used in bison.

Risks to domestic cattle. As part of the national campaign to eradicate brucellosis in cattle, bison, and swine, the USDA conducts surveillance methods to detect infected populations. The procedures are a ring test on marketed milk and tests on blood samples collected from marketed cattle, largely at slaughterhouses. Results of the tests are used to classify states relative to the known prevalence of brucellosis.

These forms of risk assessment have failed to identify any infected cattle herds as a result of commingling of cattle with free-ranging bison. A report concluded that a beef cattle herd in North Dakota became infected after purchase and introduction of an infected bison. There is anecdotal evidence of a few small cattle herds that became infected as a result of commingling with wildlife of the National Elk Refuge in Wyoming (the elk are known to have a high prevalence of brucellosis including abortions). Transmission of brucellosis occurred under experimental conditions when bison and susceptible cattle were commingled in confined areas and when bison aborted following exposure.

There is no documentation to date that transmission of brucellosis from free-ranging bison to cattle or humans has occurred. This conclusion does not preclude the eventual possibility of transmission, but is strong evidence that the many factors affecting contagiousness of disease are of minimal importance in this specific risk.

Preventive measures. Control, eradication, and prevention of contagious animal diseases are usually through three methods: hygiene (including quarantine), removal of diseased animals from the population (often referred to as test and slaughter), and vaccination.

Privately owned bison herds may be managed in a similar manner to that of cattle, and this may include quarantine, periodic herd tests, and vaccination. It is obvious, however, that management of free-ranging bison herds, and the possible commingling with cattle which graze public lands, is much more difficult.

The size of the bison population of Yellowstone National Park was controlled until 1967, when the National Park Service instituted a policy of natural regulation. In spite of the presence of brucellosis, the population grew at a rate of approximately 10% each year and reached a peak of over 4000 in 1994. The herd growth and depletion of winter range in Montana caused a migration of bison from park boundaries, with periodic slaughter and much controversy. The slaughter and starvation during the 1996–1997 winter resulted in a current estimated population of 1800. The migrations have been encouraged by the increased numbers of snowmobiles, and it has been suggested that their presence should be prohibited or greatly curtailed as part of efforts to reduce cattle-bison contacts.

Other proposed measures include buffer zones in which only nonsusceptible cattle (for example, steers) could graze; required vaccination of susceptible cattle which use public lands; and quarantine facilities where bison could be trapped and tested and seropositive animals could be slaughtered. The Greater Yellowstone Interagency Brucellosis Commission has been formed to examine possible solutions to the conflicts.

Most interested parties have concluded that periodic testing of all free-ranging bison is neither logistically nor politically possible, and that an unacceptably high level of culling would be necessary to eradicate brucellosis from these populations. Even if elimination of brucellosis from bison populations was possible, the risk of reintroduction of the disease from infected elk seems probable. Therefore, a revised policy of management, from an uncompromising one of eradication to that based upon genuine risks, is necessary.

The USDA licensed *B. abortus* strain 19 for use in young bison, and it has been administered in many privately owned bison herds and in some herds of the national parks. Also, a laboratory-derived mutant of a pathogenic strain of *B. abortus* of cattle origin, RB51, has been developed and licensed for use in young cattle; early results show that two of eight bison aborted following inoculation of the vaccine. The efficacy of strain 19 vaccine and RB51 to prevent brucellosis is unknown.

It is clear that no satisfactory vaccine exists for use in bison if administered to animals without regard for age or pregnancy status. These are important factors when attempts are made to quickly increase herd immunity. It is estimated that at least 50% of a population must be vaccinated for effectiveness, and this is unlikely to be achieved under current free-ranging conditions.

For background information *see* BRUCELLOSIS; VACCINATION in the McGraw-Hill Encyclopedia of Science & Technology.   Paul Nicoletti

Bibliography. A. Dobson and M. Meagher, The population dynamics of brucellosis in the Yellowstone National Park, *Ecology*, 77:1026–1036, 1996; R. B. Keiter, Greater Yellowstone's bison: Unraveling an early American wildlife conservation achievement, *J. Wildlife Manag.*, 61:1–11, 1997; M. E. Meyer and M. Meagher, Brucellosis in free-ranging bison (*Bison bison*) in Yellowstone, Grand Teton, and Wood Buffalo National Parks: A review, *J. Wildlife Dis.*, 31:579–598, 1995.

Calpastatin

Rheumatoid arthritis is the most frequent form of unrelenting, deforming arthritis in humans. Although its cause and mechanism are unknown and no comprehensive animal model exists, proteolytic enzymes seem to play a major role in the end result of the disease, which is the destruction of the protein matrix of articular cartilage. The enzyme families implicated are the metalloproteinases, serine proteinases, and cysteine proteinases. Normally, each enzyme is accompanied in vivo by sufficient amounts of its specific or nonspecific natural inhibitor, and the balance between them in the tissue and cell microenvironments must be tilted in favor of the enzyme in order for the disease to express itself. Recently, calpastatin, the natural inhibitor of the cysteine proteinase calpains, was identified as a human autoantigen by using autoantibodies present in the majority of rheumatoid arthritis patients. These autoantibodies may be instrumental in rupturing the equilibrium of the calpains/calpastatin system. By interfering with the function of their target autoantigen, they may provide one explanation for the aggressiveness of the rheumatoid process.

Description of calpastatin. Calpastatin is a protein found in all cells. It is both the specific inhibitor

and a substrate of calpains. It is composed of five domains (L, 1, 2, 3, and 4) of about 140 amino acids each. Domain L is different from the others and has no inhibitory activity. The four other domains are inhibitory: each contains homologous regions with highly conserved amino acid sequences exposed on the surface of the molecule and interacting specifically in the presence of calcium with the proteolytic domain II of calpains. By using recombinant calpastatin fragments, the inhibitory hierarchy of the individual domains has been established: $1 > 4 > 3 > 2$. Domain 4 possesses the immunodominant targets of rheumatoid autoantibodies, while the other domains have secondary targets. Domain L is not significantly targeted.

Calpains. Most cysteine proteinases are found in the cell lysosomes, are active at acid pH, and have been extensively studied in animal models of inflammation. In contrast, calpains are cysteine proteinases that are free ranging in the cytoplasm and are active at neutral pH. They are unique because they need calcium for activation. Calpains have two subunits. The large one has four domains: domain II contains the active site typical of all cysteine proteinases; domain IV contains the calcium-binding sites. The small subunit also has two regulatory domains: one interacts with membrane phospholipids, and the other contains additional calcium-binding sites. By mechanisms that are incompletely understood, calpains and calpastatin, which are usually

Substrates of calpains	
Target	Specific substrate in target
Enzymes	Signaling proteins and kinases
	Phosphatases
	Proteinases
	Inducible nitric oxide synthase
Cytoplasm	Spectrin in erythrocytes
	Fodrin in neural tissue and salivary gland
	Intermediate filaments: vimentin, keratin, neurofilaments
	Actin-binding proteins: tubulin, talin, filamin, a-actinin, calponin
	Profilaggrin/filaggrin of keratinized epithelia
	Calpastatin, its natural inhibitor
	Muscle myosin, troponin, and connectin
	Amyloid β p42 that accumulates in senile plaques of Alzheimer's disease
Membrane	Receptors
	Ca^{2+} ATPase pump
	PreIL-1a
	Adhesion molecules: integrin, cadherin, and N-CAM
Nucleus	Transcription factors
	p53
	Histones and histone kinase
Extracellular proteins	Proteoglycans in articular cartilage matrix
	Fibronectin, vitronectin
	Crystallins in lens
	Arrestin in retina
	Myelin
	Thyroglobulin

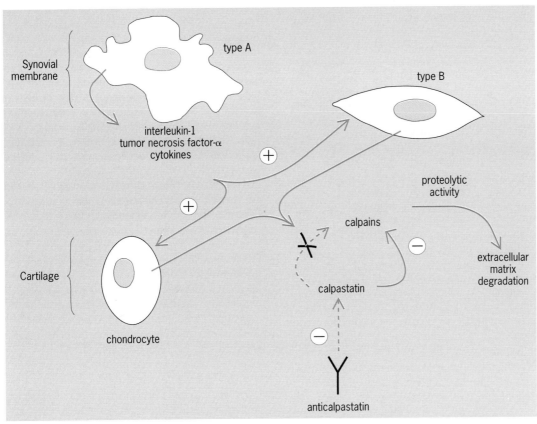

Hypothetical in vivo effect of anticalpastatin autoantibody on calpain inhibition by calpastatin in rheumatoid arthritis. Because of external factors, type A synoviocytes release interleukin-1, tumor necrosis factor-α, and other cytokines which stimulate type B synoviocytes, the lymphomonocytic pannus cells, and articular chondrocytes to produce calpains and calpastatin. In the presence of anticalpastatin autoantibodies, calpastatin interaction with calpains is prevented, and unopposed calpain proteolytic activity acts as a disease amplification loop (dotted arrow). *(From H. A. Ménard and M. El-Amine, The calpain-calpastatin system in rheumatoid arthritis, Immunol. Today, 17:545–547, 1996)*

present diffusely in the cytoplasm, can, upon cell activation, move to the plasma membrane, to specific cytoplasmic areas, or to the nucleus where they interact with phospholipids and deoxyribonucleic acid (DNA). This interaction reduces to physiologic range the calcium concentration needed for activation. Usually, calpastatin and calpains would be essentially intracellular molecules that should not be seen by autoantibodies. In microenvironmental conditions inducing cell stimulation, synthesis of calpains increases and they are exported outside the cell by an undetermined mechanism. Calpains and calpastatin can be found extracellularly in blood or other biological fluids, such as joint fluid, where they are accessible to autoantibodies.

Calpains are biomodulators that are not by themselves very aggressive molecules. As enzymes, they are more activating and permissive than digestive. Thus, the end result of the activation of calpains can be quite drastic. Calpains are central to most processes in cell biology: plasma membrane–associated signaling events; cell proliferation, differentiation, activation, and communication; and programmed cell death. Some of their many targets have been identified (see **table**). Overactivation of calpains has been observed in many human diseases:

muscular dystrophy, Alzheimer's disease, AIDS, cataract formation, multiple sclerosis, and arthritis.

Calpains and calpastatin in arthritis. Calpains are present in increased quantity in the accumulated fluid and diseased synovial membrane of swollen rheumatoid joints. In these fluids, specific enzymatic activity of calpains is much greater than calpastatin inhibitory capacity. Calpains (and calpastatin) are secreted in vitro when synovial cells are stimulated by the cytokines tumor necrosis factor-α and interleukin-1, which are central to the disease process in rheumatoid arthritis. This stimulation makes the autoantigen accessible to autoantibodies. Calpains are capable of degrading proteoglycans (a component of articular cartilage), and calpastatin can inhibit this effect. If arthritis is induced in mice by immunizing them with articular collagen, the appearance of calpains in the joint tissues correlates with the clinical manifestations of arthritis. In synovial fluid, calpains can directly degrade the extracellular matrix of articular cartilage.

The same result can be achieved indirectly via activation of other proinflammatory substrates. A therapeutic role for synthetic cysteine proteinase inhibitors has been shown in rat and mouse models of arthritis. Calpains have substrates that are central to the physiopathology of rheumatoid arthritis (see table). Calpastatin is recognized by autoantibodies in 85% of rheumatoid sera versus less than 30% and 5% of sera from patients with other autoimmune diseases and from normal individuals, respectively. This rheumatoid immunoreactivity against calpastatin raises the possibility of specific immune interference with the interaction between calpastatin and calpains (see **illus.**). In vitro evidence has shown that release of calpains in the presence of calpastatin and purified anticalpastatin autoantibodies causes immune interference as originally hypothesized.

Prospects. Under normal conditions, proteinases from each major family are neutralized by natural inhibitors. It has been suggested that an enzyme/inhibitor imbalance in the metalloproteinase family could be responsible for cartilage breakdown in degenerative joint disease (arthrosis). In that case, the imbalance is attributed to a deficit in the production of inhibitor. In the case of rheumatoid arthritis, the imbalance may be attributed to a net increase in enzyme concentration or to a functional decrease or blockade of the inhibitor or to both. If the actual concentration of calpastatin was equal to that of calpains, autoantibodies to calpastatin could be entirely responsible for tilting the balance toward an uncontrolled activity of calpains (see illus.). This inflammatory amplification loop would be associated with an accelerated and much more destructive arthritic process. This concept has been validated in vitro, but further in vivo documentation of the putative role of the calpain/calpastatin system in articular target cells is needed.

For background information *see* ARTHRITIS; AUTOIMMUNITY; CELL (BIOLOGY); CELL ORGANIZATION; ENZYME INHIBITION in the McGraw-Hill Encyclopedia of Science & Technology.

Henri-André Ménard; Moustapha El-Amine

Bibliography. D. E. Croall and G. N. DeMartino, Calcium-activated neutral protease (calpain) system: Structure, function, and regulation, *Physiol. Rev.*, 71:813–847, 1991; R. L. Mellgren and T. Murachi, *Intracellular Calcium-Dependent Proteolysis*, 1991; H. A. Ménard and M. El-Amine, The calpain-calpastatin system in rheumatoid arthritis, *Immunol. Today*, 17:545–547, 1996; T. C. Saido, H. Sorimachi, and K. Suzuki, Calpain: New perspectives in molecular diversity and physiological-pathological involvement, *FASEB J.*, 8:814–822, 1994; K. K. W. Wang and P.-W. Yuen, Calpain inhibition: An overview of its therapeutic potential, *Trends Pharmacol. Sci.*, 15:412–419, 1994.

Cancer (medicine)

This article discusses the application of viruses utilized in gene therapy to combat cancer, and the use of computer-assisted radiation therapy to treat tumors.

Gene Therapy

Because cancers arise from abnormal proliferation, migration, invasion, and death of cells, treatments directed against any single feature generally fail. Surgery, conventional chemotherapy, and radiotherapy have been unable to cure many highly malignant tumors. Therefore, gene therapy and immunotherapy are being pursued as potential treatment avenues. The efficacy and safety of these new anticancer approaches are being tested in numerous clinical trials.

Gene delivery. The basic features of gene therapy are a gene delivery vehicle (vector) and an anticancer gene. Current vectors are based on chemical carriers or genetically modified viruses. The chemical constructs include liposomes, which are charged lipid membranes capable of gene transfer through the formation of deoxyribonucleic acid (DNA)-liposome complexes (lipoplexes). The advantages of liposomes are the low toxicity and lack of immunogenicity. A disadvantage is the low efficiency of gene transfer. Another form of nonviral gene therapy comprises antisense approaches that employ specific oligonucleotides to shut off the expression of specific undesirable genes within a tumor cell. In fact, there have been promising attempts at targeting and reducing the expression of tumor genes (oncogenes) through antisense technology.

Vectors that use genetically modified viruses include adenoviruses, herpes simplex virus, and retroviruses.

Adenoviruses. Adenoviruses are double-stranded linear DNA viruses that do not generally integrate their DNA into that of the host cell. A disadvantage is that an immune response is elicited. Advantages include the ability to infect replicating and nonreplicating cells, and high efficiency of gene transfer into target cells.

Herpes simplex virus. Herpes simplex virus is a large DNA virus which can potentially transfer very large segments of foreign DNA. It does not integrate and can infect both proliferating and quiescent cells. Notwithstanding these favorable characteristics, its potential neurotoxic side effects have limited its experimental and clinical applications. However, recent work has shown that replication-incompetent herpes simplex virus vectors can allow long-term nontoxic transgene expression in brain tumor cells and that replication-conditional nonneurovirulent herpes simplex virus-1 (HSV-1) strains have shown efficacy against experimental brain tumors.

Retroviruses. Derived from the Moloney murine leukemia virus, retroviruses remain the most widely used vectors for cancer gene therapy. Retroviruses integrate their genetic material [consisting of diploid, positive-strand ribonucleic acid (RNA) encoding for the structural *gag, pol,* and *env* gene products] into the genome of target cells. This process requires the retroviral enzyme reverse transcriptase and occurs only during the mitosis of target cells.

Therefore, retroviral vectors cannot deliver a gene into nondividing cells. Once integrated, the viral genetic material is inherited by progeny cells. Since the initial integration event is random, the possibility of inactivating desirable cellular genes (such as tumor suppressor genes) remains a concern. However, this has not been a factor in clinical trials, and the low toxicity of the vector remains appealing. To increase the range of retroviral vectors, current technological advances employ hybrid vectors, consisting of desirable features from different viruses. For example, in the vesicular stomatitis virus G system, the envelope glycoprotein substitutes for the conventional retroviral envelope (*env*) protein. This process is designated as pseudotyping. This new hybrid vector can now be generated to very high concentrations, and it can infect many cell types resistant to conventional retrovirus vectors. Another recent advance involves a hybrid vector composed of retroviral and lentiviral sequences to allow gene transfer into noncycling cells. The vectors described above can be used to deliver anticancer genes into tumor cells such as those genes that will sensitize cells to drugs or to an immune response.

Drug-sensitivity genes. Drug-sensitivity genes encode enzymes which catalyze the conversion of a prodrug into active anticancer metabolites. One such gene encodes the enzyme HSV-1 thymidine kinase, which converts the prodrug ganciclovir into an active phosphorylated nucleoside analog. This metabolite selectively disrupts DNA synthesis, leading to toxicity of dividing tumor cells. Since nonproliferating tumor cells are relatively spared, there may be the potential for limited anticancer effects. This system also has toxic effects on neighboring tumor cells even if they do not express HSV-1 thymidine kinase. Termed the bystander effect, this mechanism allows for an amplification of the antitumor effect by the converted drug metabolites. A second drug-sensitivity gene encodes the enzyme *Escherichia coli* cytosine deaminase. The enzyme deaminates the prodrug 5-fluorocytosine into the highly toxic metabolite 5-fluorouracil. The cytosine deaminase/fluorocytosine system inhibits both RNA and DNA synthesis and also exhibits a powerful bystander effect. A third drug-sensitivity gene encodes the liver-specific enzyme cytochrome P450(2B1), which converts the chemotherapeutic agent cyclophosphamide into phosphoramide mustard. This metabolic end product produces cross-links in cellular DNA, leading to tumor cell toxicity independent of cell cycle status. A different approach involves transferring drug-resistant genes (such as the multiple-drug resistant gene *MDR1* or the alkyltransferase gene) into normal hematopoietic stem cells in order to render them less susceptible to the toxic side effects of chemotherapy agents and thus allow increases in their doses.

Immuno-gene therapy. Human cancers can stimulate immune reactions directed against tumor surface antigens. Tumor-infiltrating lymphocytes and cytotoxic T lymphocytes are T cells that become activated against tumor major histocompatibility complexes and co-stimulatory surface molecules. In passive immuno-gene therapy, autologous T cells are repeatedly sensitized in culture by exposure to cytokines or by transfer of cytokine genes and then are transferred back into the patient. The adoptive transfer of these modified autologous tumor-infiltrating leukocytes and interleukin-2 has shown evidence of cancer regression in metastatic melanoma patients. Additional progress in passive immunotherapy has been made in terms of specificity and targeting efficacy by improvements in monoclonal antibody engineering. This has led to the development of bispecific monoclonal antibodies that are specific for tumor-associated antigens. These can activate cytotoxic T lymphocytes and can target tumor-specific receptors. In active immuno-gene therapy, the tumor is directly altered with cytokine genes in order to induce an endogenous reaction against it. For example, retroviral-mediated transfer for genes encoding cytokines such as interleukin-2, interleukin-4, interleukin-12, interferon-γ, and granulocyte-monocyte colony-stimulating factor has provided evidence of tumor regression in experimental models.

Thomas S. Deisboeck; Griffith R. Harsh IV; E. A. Chiocca

Radiation Therapy

Radiation therapy is the clinical specialty involved in the treatment of malignant neoplasms (and, rarely, benign conditions) with ionizing radiation. The goal is to deliver a precise dose of high-energy radiation to a tumor while minimizing the exposure of surrounding normal tissue. It is estimated that approximately 60% of individuals diagnosed with cancer will require radiation therapy as part of their overall treatment. Radiation therapy possesses extraordinary palliative capabilities. Moreover, a significant percentage of patients are successfully treated with radiation to achieve a curative outcome. Major advances in technology and computerized treatment planning have revolutionized the field of radiation oncology to allow for the delivery of superhigh radiation doses with exquisite precision and minimal associated toxicity. In addition, there is a trend to employ chemotherapy in conjunction with radiotherapy in order to enhance the tumor-cell kill potential. Such treatment programs are now routinely used for squamous tumor of the larynx and tongue, soft tissue sarcomas of extremities, and cancer of the bladder (as well as at other sites) as effective organ preservation alternatives to aggressive surgical approaches.

External-beam therapy. Most external-beam treatment units or machines deliver x-rays in a range of 1–25 million volts. The source of these x-rays is linear accelerators, wherein high-speed electrons moving through a vacuum tube are rapidly accelerated. Megavoltage x-ray therapy has several ideal features for curative radiation therapy. High-energy x-rays deliver their peak energies deeper within tissue, creating a skin-sparing effect. High radiation doses can be delivered more safely to deep-seated tumors within the chest, abdomen, or pelvis, with less dose delivered to the surrounding organs and improved tolerance of the therapy. Because of the physical features associated with high-energy x-rays, less differential absorption between soft tissue and bone is observed, resulting in less potential for osteonecrosis.

The isotope cobalt-60 functions in the same manner as a megavoltage x-ray unit. X-rays arise from several thousand curies of radioactive cobalt-60 which is housed in the shielded head of a machine with collimating devices to focus the high-energy gamma rays (1.17–133-MeV x-rays). Cobalt therapy is especially suitable for patients with superficial tumors such as in the head and neck. In particular, there are reports of improved cure rates among patients with early glottic tumors when cobalt therapy is used as compared to high-energy, more-penetrating x-ray beams.

Linear accelerators are by far the most frequently used treatment units for radiation therapy. These machines can deliver x-rays in the range of 4–50 million volts at very high outputs of 2–10 grays per minute. In addition to x-rays that are produced from such units, electrons can be generated which are frequently used in cancer therapies. Depending upon the type of linear accelerator, different electron energies in the range of 6–35 million electronvolts can be used. The physical characteristics of the electron beam make it extremely suitable for superficial tumors. The electron beam is associated with a rapid buildup to its maximal dose as it traverses skin and underlying tissue. It is also associated with a rapid dose fall-off, whereby the normal structures beyond the intended target receive substantially reduced irradiation.

Another form of irradiation comprises heavy particles in the form of protons and alpha particles. Protons are positively charged particles whose individual mass is 200 times greater than that of electrons. These massive particles require complex and expensive equipment to accelerate the particles to clinically therapeutic energies (160 megavolts). The advantage of this heavy particle for cancer therapy lies in its ability to deposit maximum ionizations deep within tissue immediately prior to the beam coming to a sudden halt (Bragg peak phenomenon). Thus, high doses can be safely delivered to tumors with less effect on the surrounding normal tissue structures. Certain tumors (choroidal melanomas and chordomas) in proximity to sensitive normal organs have been effectively treated with proton-beam therapy.

Brachytherapy. Depending upon the radioisotope and the type of tumor, radioactive sources can be placed within the tumor as permanent or temporary implants. Currently, early-stage prostate tumors can be effectively treated by using a permanent iodine-125 or palladium-103 implantation. The half-lives of these two radioisotopes are 60 and 17 days, respectively. By using computerized tomography or ultra-sound-based guidance, multiple radioactive pellets are deposited within the prostate gland to ultimately achieve a homogeneous distribution of the radiation dose. The seeds remain active for approximately five half-lives; a high cumulative dose is received by the gland while the surrounding tissues are spared. Permanent-implant approaches have been used to treat tumors located in other anatomic sites, such as the lung, brain, and head and neck. Temporary interstitial (within tissue) or intracavity (within a body cavity) implants entail the placement of high-energy radioactive sources for several days to deliver high radiation doses confined to a limited area. With the aid of computerized treatment planning, the placement of radioactive sources can be optimized to achieve the necessary distribution of the radiation dose required for tumor control. Temporary-implant approaches have often been used to treat gynecologic tumors as well as soft tissue sarcomas and head and neck tumors (among other cancers).

Recent innovations. With the availability of improved computer technology, radiation oncologists now can more accurately target high doses of irradiation onto tumors. High-precision three-dimensional conformal radiation therapy uses sophisticated computer-aided treatment planning to accurately distribute a prescribed radiation dose to the anatomical surface of a three-dimensional region. A rapid decrease in the dose delivered to the surrounding normal tissues has permitted increases in the tumor doses to levels far beyond those feasible with conventional two-dimensional radiotherapy. Recently, intensity-modulated treatment planning has been introduced to help deliver radiation beams with different intensity profiles to the tumor. This major technological advance is expected to enhance the ability to deliver high radiation doses with improved tolerance. In addition, brachytherapy delivery via high-dose-rate systems makes it feasible to deliver high-precision, high-dose radiotherapy to tumors in several minutes with less exposure of surrounding normal tissues.

For background information *see* CANCER (MEDICINE); CELL (BIOLOGY); CHEMOTHERAPY; GENE; GENE ACTION; HUMAN GENETICS; ONCOLOGY; RADIATION BIOLOGY; RADIATION THERAPY; TUMOR; X-RAYS in the McGraw-Hill Encyclopedia of Science & Technology.

Michael J. Zelefsky

Bibliography. E. A. Chiocca and X. O. Breakefield (eds.), *Gene Therapy for Neurologic Disorders and Brain Tumors*, 1997; V. T. DeVita and S. A. Hellman (eds.), *Cancer Principles and Practice of Oncology*, 5th ed., 1996; M. G. Kaplitt and A. D. Loewy (eds.), *Viral Vectors: Gene Therapy and Neuroscience Applications*, 1995; C. A. Perez and L. W. Brady (eds.), *Principles and Practice of Radiation Oncology*, 2d ed., 1992; R. E. Sobol and K. J. Scanlon (eds.), *The Internet Book of Gene Therapy: Cancer Therapeutics*, 1995; M. J. Zelefsky et al., The feasibility of dose escalation with three-dimensional conformal radiotherapy in patients with prostatic carcinoma, *Canc. J. Sci. Amer.*, 1:42–50, 1995.

Carbonatites

Volcanic activity on Earth is dominated by the eruption of silicate melts, as might be expected from the abundance of silicon in the outer regions (for example, 66 weight percent of silicon dioxide in the mantle and crust). In this volcanism, carbon dioxide (CO_2) is one of the important gases, but the amount is tiny compared with the melts and ashes, so that molten carbonate might not be expected. Carbonate eruptions, although minute in quantity, are the only important exception to silicate magmatism, and this unanticipated composition and the nature of the activity afford insights into Earth processes.

Nature and amount. Igneous rocks with a content of carbonate exceeding 50% are known as carbonatites. About 350 carbonatites have so far been recorded, most consisting of calcium carbonate. Less common than calcio carbonatites are magnesio (containing magnesium) and ferro (containing iron) carbonatites, and all three types may occur in the same complexes, most of which are subvolcanic intrusions.

Many carbonatites form parts of alkali-rich silicate magmatic complexes (typically of the uncommon compositions nephelinite/melilitite/phonolite). First discoveries of carbonatite were in such complexes, and in the 1920s–1960s this led to controversy as to whether carbonatites were merely sedimentary limestones that had been mobilized by the heat from silicate magmas moving through the Earth's crust. It is now clear from their chemistry, however, that the ultimate source of carbonatites must lie below the crust, in the mantle. Most carbonatites are small, with areas of the order of 0.4 mi² (1 km²), with none yet recorded in excess of 7.7 mi² (20 km²). In age they range from mid-Precambrian (2000 million years ago) to present, but most are younger than 150 million years. In northern Tanzania, a volcano built largely of alkali silicates is currently (late 1997) erupting sodium calcium potassium carbonates as lava and ash. Being the only active example, it has been intensively studied and has helped to promote a strong consensus that carbonatites form by separation, at high levels in the crust, from a CO_2-rich alkali silicate melt during its passage from the mantle.

Special features of chemistry. An outstanding, distinctive feature of carbonatites is their high levels of elements that are otherwise rare in the outer layers of the Earth, and in other igneous rocks. In addition to the high carbon content, elements such as phosphorus, normally found in trace amounts, reach percent levels. In general, high levels of volatiles (such as phosphorus, fluorine, chlorine, and alkalis) and elements with large ionic radii or high field strengths (for example, barium, strontium, and niobium) characterize carbonatites. Such elements cannot be accommodated in the crystal lattices of normal mantle mineralogy and are referred to as incompatible or large-ion lithophile elements. This exotic aspect of carbonatite chemistry (as well as a similar global distribution) is shared with the kimberlites and lamproites, and all three are widely regarded as small-volume partial-melt extracts from the mantle, whereby incompatible elements would be concentrated. Kimberlites also contain carbonate and, with increasing amounts, grade into carbonatite. A feature not shared with kimberlites/lamproites is that carbonatites provide commercial deposits of some rare elements, such as niobium, phosphorus, and rare-earth elements; most of the world demand for niobium is supplied by a carbonatite in Brazil. A major

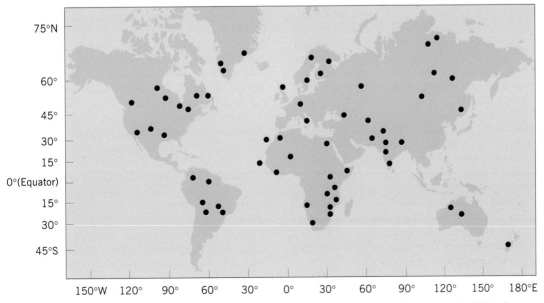

Fig. 1. World distribution of carbonatite and alkali-rich silicate magmatic complexes represented by circles. Kimberlites and lamproites have a similar distribution.

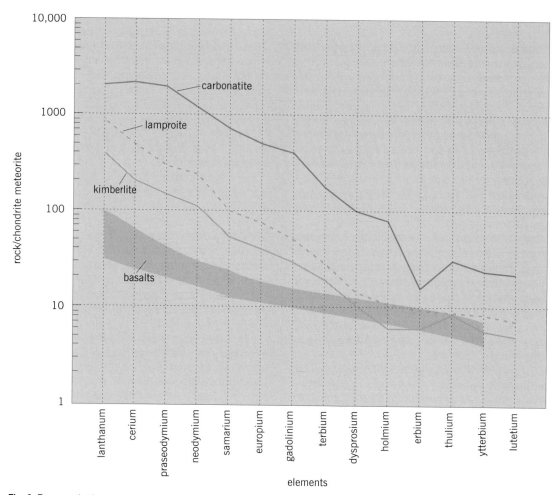

Fig. 2. Rare-earth element profiles for average carbonatites, kimberlites, and lamproites compared with a range of typical basalts from central volcanoes. The vast bulk of igneous silicate rocks have even lower profiles. All values are normalized against a chondrite meteorite.

surge in discoveries of new carbonatites in the 1950s and 1960s resulted from an intensified search for these types of deposit. In most areas of geologically young/recent carbonatite (and alkali silicate) activity, there are still strong emissions of CO_2 today, often in the form of CO_2-rich springs (some of commercial importance) but also as subsurface economic resources of pure CO_2 (high-pressure gas in Kenya; liquid CO_2 in South Australia). These serve to emphasize the importance of carbonatite (and alkali silicate) centers as zones of major release of CO_2 from the Earth's interior.

A distinctive feature of carbonatite intrusions is that surrounding rocks are subject to intense chemical alteration, best distinguished by the introduction of sodium or potassium, with new alkali minerals replacing the older ones. This process of alkali metasomatism is referred to as fenitisation.

Location. Nearly all carbonatites are located in the continental plates, very commonly in the rift zones of the stable interiors, with Africa containing about half the recorded cases (**Fig. 1**). Only two are in a stable oceanic region, the Cape Verde Islands and the eastern Canaries, both now part of the African

plate. A few exceptional cases are in fold mountain belts, representing a double anomaly in their uncharacteristic tectonic setting, in that they are completely at odds with typical fold-belt magmatism. These eruptions seem to be connected to extensional interludes (rifting) between the compressive phases that give rise to the folding. More study is needed to reveal their relationships (if any) with the more typical intraplate setting of the majority of carbonatites.

Possible origins. Although carbonatites are associated with alkali silicate magmas in many classic examples of the activity, this is by no means universal, but has nonetheless assumed prominence in hypotheses of carbonatite origins. Many carbonatites have little or no associated silicate magmas, and the association, although characteristic, cannot be an essential prerequisite for carbonatite generation. Furthermore, there are increasing reports of isotopic decoupling of carbonatite and silicate rocks in the same complex. As with most natural phenomena, there is no simple prescription, and carbonatites can form in a variety of ways. Some may separate from CO_2-rich alkali silicate magmas as they pass from the mantle to the surface, while others are erupted directly from the mantle, adding an entirely new perspective to the knowledge of the mantle. These latter carbonatites obviously command special attention.

Mantle implications. All types of carbonatite reveal an ultimate mantle source in their chemistry, notably in the isotope ratios which are in the same ranges as found in mantle fragments, and in other magmas with undoubted mantle sources. Some carbonatites are found in ultramafic intrusive complexes, pointing to another link with the mantle source. The same is true of alkali silicate magmas found in association with carbonatite. Carbonatites erupted directly from the mantle are now further recognized by their content of mantle debris (minerals and rock fragments) entrained en route to the surface. A rapidly growing list has already stretched to 16 cases, as opposed to only one in 1989. Typical fragments are composed of clinopyroxene/olivine/phlogopite, in different proportions, having similar compositions to those recorded in other eruptions (such as alkali basalts and kimberlites) from which stem most current direct insights into mantle compositions. Carbonates have recently been reported in some mantle fragments and in diamonds, confirming their existence in the mantle. Important differences in the mantle debris in carbonatites (and alkali silicate magmas) are the absence of orthopyroxene (a common mineral in normal mantle) and abundant signs of replacement of an earlier mineralogy by new minerals containing essential alkalis and volatiles (exemplified by the potassium, hydroxyl, and fluorine in phlogopite), a process now generally referred to as mantle metasomatism. Experimental studies at high pressure and temperature show that such modified mantle (carbonate-phlogopite peridotite) would be required to produce carbonate and alkali silicate melts (in that order) at the onset of melting. Such melts would represent minute volumes of the bulk mantle and would incorporate most of the alkalis, volatiles, and other incompatible elements. Consistent with this scenario, carbonatites show the highest levels of incompatible trace elements of any igneous rocks, closely followed by the alkali silicate magmas with which they are characteristically associated (**Fig. 2**). The typical location of carbonatite activity in regions of thick lithosphere implies that this provides favorable conditions for mantle metasomatism and, ultimately, carbonate melt formation. A further characteristic of carbonate melts is their exceptionally low viscosity compared with other magmas, such that minute melt fractions (0.01%) could separate from the enclosing solids, segregate, and then rise to the surface. Recognition of directly erupted carbonatite represents an important expansion to the range of known mantle melt products.

Earth dynamics. A further dimension in carbonatite activity is gradually emerging as more radiometric age determinations reveal patterns in the ages of eruption. Not only is the activity repeated in the same areas over periods extending back into the Precambrian time period, but there is mounting evidence that the repeated episodes are synchronous at widely separated locations across stable tectonic plates. Across Africa, for instance, during the last 150 million years of Earth history, sufficient eruption ages have been determined to show at least four peaks in activity, affecting the same sites scattered across the continent. These four platewide episodes coincide with major events in the collision history of Africa and Europe and with other major igneous events worldwide. In addition to providing information on mantle compositions and transformations in regions of stable lithosphere, carbonatite activity (and alkali silicate magmatism) are imposing powerful constraints on a global scale, which may necessitate radical reappraisal of current hypotheses of mantle and, indeed, whole-Earth dynamics.

For background information *see* CARBONATE MINERALS; CARBONATITE; IGNEOUS ROCKS; MAGMA; NIOBIUM in the McGraw-Hill Encyclopedia of Science & Technology.   D. K. Bailey

Bibliography. D. L. Anderson, S. R. Hart, and A. W. Hofmann, Convenors, Plume 2, *Terra Nostra,* 3:15–19, 1995; K. Bell (ed.), *Carbonatites,* 1989; M. J. Le Bas (ed.), Milestones in geology, *Geol. Soc. Mem.,* 16:249–263, 1995.

Catalyst

An object is defined as chiral if it is not superimposable on its mirror image. Chirality takes on great significance in organic chemistry. Many molecules, natural and synthetic, possess chirality and perform a special function which their enantiomer (the nonsuperimposable mirror image) cannot accomplish. Chiral molecules may act as catalysts; that is, a small amount of a chiral catalyst, when added to a reaction, may accelerate or make possible the reaction, while remaining unchanged itself. Research in the design and synthesis of chiral ferrocene derivatives has provided catalysts to perform specific functions. The importance of this class of molecules is increasing in research and in industrial applications.

Chirality in ferrocenes. Molecules may possess one or more different types of chirality (**Fig. 1**). The most common type is due to a center of chirality, resulting from an atom with four different substituents, A, B, C, and D. Axial chirality occurs when there is hindered rotation about a bond. Planar chirality occurs when there are two or more different substituents, A and B, in the same ring of a metallocene or related molecule. In each of these examples, the mirror images are nonsuperimposable.

A large number of ferrocene molecules are known to exhibit chirality in one or more of the types discussed above. For ferrocenes, centers of chirality and planar chirality are the most important ones to consider. For a given function, either a plane or center of chirality in the ferrocene unit may provide the required chiral environment to produce the desired catalytic effect (**Fig. 2**).

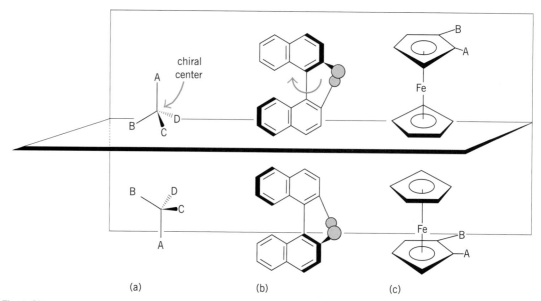

Fig. 1. Chiral molecules and their enantiomers showing the different chirality types: (*a*) center of chirality, (*b*) axial chirality [the substituents cannot move past each other when one tries to rotate about the bond indicated by the arrow], and (*c*) planar chirality.

Design. In designing a chiral catalyst, the desired function of the catalyst and how it should interact with its environment to perform that function must be considered. Many ferrocene catalysts are designed to work in conjunction with another metal center; that is, they act as ligands on another metal. Since the ferrocene molecule contains a chiral component—be it from a center or plane of chirality—a chiral environment is created about the reactive metal center when the molecule binds to the metal.

Other reactions involve the direct participation of the ferrocene molecule without first complexing to another metal. Regardless of the type of catalytic reaction being considered, highly coordinating groups must be included in the ferrocene unit. This is usually accomplished through the inclusion of groups containing heteroatoms such as phosphorus, nitrogen, sulfur, and oxygen. Phosphorus, usually in the form of a diphenylphosphino (—PPh$_2$) group

(Fig. 2*b* and *c*), is the most frequently used. Since triphenylphosphine (PPh$_3$) is widely used as a ligand in a number of achiral catalytic processes, the change to chiral analogs of triphenylphosphine for the purpose of chiral catalysis is a logical progression. While diphenylphosphino groups are the most popular, many other coordinating groups, such as other phosphines, amines, alcohols, and thiols, may also be used.

Synthesis. In view of the importance of chiral ferrocenes, several methods have been developed for their synthesis. Most start with a ferrocene core and then proceed through a series of derivatizations to put in the appropriate substituents and the required elements of chirality. An exception is the synthesis of ferrocenes with a chiral center by using chiral cyclopentadiene derivatives [reaction (1)]. In this strategy, an oxygen-containing chiral cyclopentadienyl molecule, obtained through asymmetric synthesis, is treated with iron(II) chloride (FeCl$_2$) to give

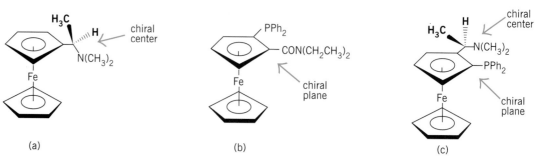

Fig. 2. Chiral planes and centers in ferrocenes.

the chiral ferrocene product. This synthesis provides symmetrically substituted ferrocenes with two chiral centers.

(1)

Syntheses starting from a ferrocene molecule may be classified into two types: those imparting a center of chirality, and those imparting planar chirality.

Chiral center. The inclusion of a chiral center in the alpha position, that is, directly bonded to the ferrocene ring, is one of the most popular ways to incorporate chirality into a ferrocene molecule. This can be accomplished in a number of ways. The classical, and popular, way to prepare many chiral ferrocene derivatives is through resolution techniques. In these techniques, a mixture of both enantiomers is prepared through standard procedures, and then an appropriate method is applied which allows the two to be separated. Since both enantiomers of a chiral compound have the same physical properties, sophisticated techniques must be used to separate them. Frequently, this is accomplished by resolution using enzymes. For example, a mixture of two enantiomers (racemic mixture) is treated with vinyl acetate and an enzyme such as *Pseudomonas cepacia* [reaction (2)]. The enzyme is stereoselective, meaning that it reacts with only one of the enantiomers such that two chiral products are formed—one which is an acetate derivative, and one which is unreacted starting material which the enzyme has resolved to a single enantiomer.

(2)

Asymmetric synthesis techniques may also be used to introduce the chiral center [reaction (3)]. In this case, a chiral reduction of the ferrocenyl diketone takes place to give a chiral ferrocene diol which is the enantiomer of that produced in reaction (1).

(3)

Chiral plane. The introduction of planar chirality in ferrocenes may be accomplished through resolution techniques similar to those described above for molecules containing chiral centers. Thus, a racemic mixture of planar chiral ferrocenes may be separated into its two enantiomeric components when treated with an appropriate enzymatic catalyst, such as *Candida cylindracea* [reaction (4)].

(4)

In a diastereoselective reaction, a ferrocene molecule which already contains a chiral center is substituted in an ortho position to impart the planar chirality. This is usually accomplished through a metalation procedure in which a chiral directing group is responsible for the asymmetric substitution leading to planar chirality. Typically, the chiral directing group bears coordinating atoms allowing the substitution step to occur with high selectivity with consequent high induction of planar chirality.

A conceptually similar procedure involves substitution of one of the ortho hydrogens in an achiral ferrocene enantioselectively. In this case, however, the induction comes from the presence of a chiral additive rather than from within the ferrocene molecule. The products from this type of reaction have only planar chirality and may be obtained with a high degree of induction.

Applications. Catalytic processes are of increasing importance in modern chemical industry. The attractiveness of such a process lies not only in the cost effectiveness but also in environmental considerations. The catalysts are usually highly selective for specific processes, resulting in minimal side reactions and reducing the production of unnecessary waste.

Laboratory-scale uses of chiral ferrocene catalysts and ligands are numerous, and their success is exemplified by today's industrial applications. A chiral ferrocene ligand is used in conjunction with rhodium as a catalytic system in the production of a key intermediate in the synthesis of (+)-biotin. The asymmetric hydrogenation reaction is the crucial step in the synthesis of this biologically important compound. Similarly, a related chiral ferrocene ligand is used in the reduction of the imine functionality, a key step in the synthesis of a herbicide which introduces the only chiral center in the molecule. Both of these commercial applications involve ferrocenes with planar and central chirality. It is not clear whether the central or planar chirality or a combination of both is responsible for the chiral induction of the catalysts.

For background information *see* CATALYSIS; CATALYST; FERROCENE; METALLOCENES; STEREOCHEMISTRY; STEREOSPECIFIC CATALYST in the McGraw-Hill Encyclopedia of Science & Technology.

Victor Snieckus; Brian J. Chapell

Bibliography. S. Borman, Ferrocene derivatives find use as chiral catalysts, *Chem. Eng. News*, 74:38, 1996; A. Togni, Planar-chiral ferrocenes: Synthetic methods and applications, *Angew. Chem. Int. Ed. Engl.*, 35:1475, 1996; A. Togni and T. Hayashi (eds.), *Ferrocenes: Homogeneous Catalysis, Organic Synthesis, Materials Science*, 1995.

Ceramics

Advanced ceramic materials that can withstand temperatures over 1500°C (2732°F) without degradation or oxidation are needed for applications such as structural parts for motor engines, gas turbines, catalytic heat exchangers, and combustion systems. Ceramic composites and coatings that are hard and oxidant resistant are in demand for use on aircraft and spacecraft.

Much present research effort is directed toward ultrahigh-temperature ceramics with properties surpassing those of conventional materials such as carbon, silicon carbide (SiC), and silicon nitride (Si_3N_4). A major aim is to develop novel ceramics with extraordinary thermomechanical stability even in oxidative or corrosive environments. The study of precursor-derived multicomponent ceramics based on the silicon-boron-carbon-nitrogen (Si-B-C-N) system indicates that there might exist compounds exhibiting significantly improved ultrahigh-temperature resistance. Advanced processing techniques on new ceramic materials and composites have had an enormous impact on the technological development of novel ultrahigh-temperature ceramics.

Composition and properties. Industrial manufacturing of advanced ceramic components is accomplished by the conventional powder process. Because of the use of low-melting-temperature metal oxide systems for enhanced densification of silicon nitride or silicon carbide, the mechanical properties of these powder processed materials are excellent at room temperature, whereas the strength and creep at elevated temperatures are impaired. Consequently, the application of silicon-based nonoxide ceramics is limited to temperatures up to 1300°C (2372°F). Moreover, in oxidizing environments at higher temperatures conventional liquid-phase sintered silicon nitride creeps and corrodes. Improved thermomechanical properties are expected for newly synthesized Si_3N_4/SiC composites. However, the processing of dense Si_3N_4/SiC-based ceramics is difficult and requires hot pressing of mixtures of Si_3N_4 and SiC powders at temperatures greater than 1800°C (3272°F).

Alternatively, ternary and multicomponent amorphous or polycrystalline ceramics composed of multiple carbides or nitrides can be obtained by the novel hybrid technology which involves silicon polymers as the starting materials and their subsequent thermally induced transformation into ceramics. This polymer-to-ceramic transformation route operates at lower temperatures (800–1600°C or 1472–2912°F) than the conventional powder process, and the corresponding elements can be distributed homogeneously on a molecular level. As a result, single-phase and multiphase ceramics are obtained by the ceramization of polymeric precursors and by their subsequent in situ crystallization of amorphous intermediates at higher temperatures, respectively. The low polymer-to-ceramic transformation temperature enables the formation of metastable amorphous ceramics, as well as thermodynamically stable polycrystalline ceramic composites which cannot be obtained by traditional synthetic methods.

Ceramic fibers composed of silicon, boron, carbon, and nitrogen exhibit significantly increased tensile strength up to very high temperatures (1500°C or 2732°F) compared to what is commercially available. Different synthetic routes have been developed which allow the formation of boron-containing polysilazanes. The polymer-to-ceramic conversion of these polyborosilazanes provides single-phase amorphous silicoboron carbonitrides which show outstanding stability in terms of crystallization and thermal degradation. Accordingly, the materials decomposition in 0.1-megapascal (14.5-lb/in.²) helium or argon atmosphere is shifted from 1400°C (2552°F) for Si_3N_4 to about 2000°C (3632°F) for the nonstoichiometric compounds $Si_3B_1C_{4.3}N_2$ and $Si_2B_1C_{3.4}N_{2.3}$, which are the most stable nitride-based nonoxide silicon ceramics to date.

Synthesis of polyborosilazane. Generally, the synthesis of boron-modified polyorganosilazanes is performed by two different schemes: (1) reaction of polyorganosilazane with borane or boron compounds; or (2) synthesis of (organochlorosilyl)chloroboranes or (organochlorosilyl)boranes and their subsequent polycondensation with ammonia or primary amines. In the resulting Si-B-C-N polymer of scheme 1, boron will be inhomogeneously distributed; while the silicon, nitrogen, carbon, and boron atoms in the polyborosilazane as well as in the final ceramic obtained by scheme 2 will be mixed on a molecular level (homogeneous). Reaction types that can be applied to form boron-containing compounds suitable for the synthesis of silicoboron carbonitrides are salt elimination, transamination, dehydrogenation, and hydroboration. In salt elimination, transamination, and dehydrogenation, the boron distribution is not necessarily homogeneous (scheme 1), thereby limiting the high-temperature properties of the silicoboron carbonitride. Homogeneous distribution of silicon and boron atoms is obtained in the hydroboration reaction (scheme 2), thereby increasing the high-temperature properties of the silicoboron carbonitride.

The Si/B ratio of the monomer can be changed from 3:1 to 2:1 or 1:1 by the hydroboration of chlorovinylsilanes with borane- and chloroborane-complex compounds. The Si/B ratio of the synthesized monomer is retained after its ammonolysis to the polyborosilazane and final ceramization to silicoboron carbonitride (**Fig. 1**). Moreover, copolycondensation of the obtained monomer with various chlorosilanes enables the fabrication of polyborosilazanes with varying degrees of cross-linking and Si/B ratios differ-

ent from 3:1, 2:1, and 1:1. Disproportion can occur during the polycondensation as a side reaction, which then leads to inhomogeneities in the produced ceramics.

Transformation into ceramics. The polymer-to-ceramic transformation process opens the door to new materials, ceramic processing technologies, and applications. The polyborosilazanes produced are fusible and soluble in common organic solvents. Thus, these physical properties can be utilized to form fibers, films, ceramic matrix composites, porous matrices, or multicomponent bulk materials which cannot be realized by traditional powder processing. Each application requires the adjustment of the polymer viscosity by thermal or chemical cross-linking.

The thermally induced polycondensation and subsequent ceramization of the polyborosilazanes takes place in the range between room temperature and 1200°C (2192°F). The outgassing of amines or ammonia between 300 and 500°C (572 and 932°F) is due to intermolecular and intramolecular transamination reactions and further polycondensation enhancing the cross-linking. Thus, the fusible poly-

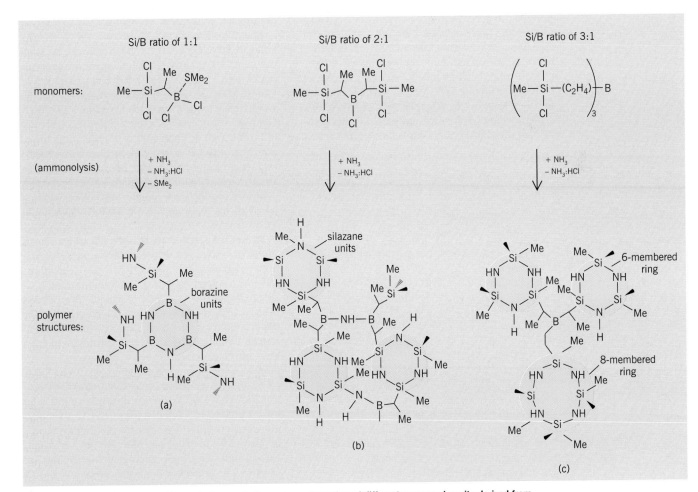

Fig. 1. Structural environments of boron before and after polycondensation of different monomeric units derived from hydroboration of dichloromethylvinylsilane (Me = CH$_3$). Polymeric structures are shown for (a) Si$_{1.2}$B$_1$C$_4$N$_2$H$_{11}$, (b) Si$_2$B$_1$C$_6$N$_3$H$_{19}$, and (c) Si$_3$B$_1$C$_9$N$_3$H$_{25}$.

mer can be transformed into a preceramic polymer with a rigid three-dimensional network. The polymer viscosity can be modulated from being a liquid at room temperature to becoming infusible by controlled cross-linking. At temperatures exceeding 500°C (932°F), hydrogen and hydrocarbons such as methane are evolved, leaving behind an amorphous solid network composed of silicon, boron, carbon, and nitrogen atoms. The ceramization is completed at 1000–1200°C (1832–2192°F). Besides the molecular structure of the polyborosilazane, the pyrolysis atmosphere determines the elemental composition of the Si-B-C-N ceramic formed. The polymer-to-ceramic conversion in ammonia instead of argon decreases the carbon content, while the amount of nitrogen is increased. However, the silicon-to-boron ratio remains unaffected and is fixed by the stoichiometry of the molecular precursor.

Thermal stability. Ceramics based on silicon nitride are thermodynamically stable up to 1400°C (2552°F) in vacuum or argon, and resist a temperature of 1775°C (3227°F) in nitrogen without decomposition. At higher temperatures silicon nitride decomposes into silicon and nitrogen (**Fig. 2**). In amorphous silicon carbonitride the thermal stability is improved up to 1500°C (2732°F). At higher temperatures the polymer-derived Si-C-N ceramics decompose (Fig. 2) with the loss of nitrogen and crystallize to form the binary phases SiC and Si_3N_4. In boron-containing silicon carbonitrides, the crystallization onset is shifted to temperatures above 1700°C (3092°F) and the resistance to thermal degradation is enhanced up to 2000°C (3632°F) even in nitrogen-free atmospheres (Fig. 2). Transmission electron microscopy and x-ray investigations of precursor-derived silicoboron carbonitride heat-treated at tem-

peratures greater than 1700°C (3092°F) exhibit the presence of nano-sized β-Si_3N_4 and β-SiC crystals embedded in a metastable amorphous matrix. In particular, the composition $Si_3B_1C_{4.3}N_2$ (Fig. 1c) synthesized from polyborosilazane partitions to the above-mentioned phases with the evolution of nitrogen after 50 h of annealing at 1700°C (3092°F) or 2 h at 2000°C (3632°F) in argon. Chemical analysis and x-ray measurements show the retarded crystallization and decomposition of β-Si_3N_4 at temperatures above 1700°C (3092°F) and the predominant formation of β-SiC at 2000°C (3632°F). The negligible isothermal weight loss of the silicoboron carbonitride $Si_3B_1C_{4.3}N_2$ between 1500 and 1700°C (2732 and 3092°F) confirms the high thermal stability of the novel ceramics.

Structure and thermal stability. The excellent thermal resistance of boron-containing Si-C-N ceramics compared to commercial silicon nitride and silicon carbonitride ceramics has been demonstrated by thermal gravimetric analysis in a nitrogen-free atmosphere. Investigations of various Si-B-C-N ceramics with different Si/B and C/N ratios have shown that the enhanced thermal stability is strongly related to the structural environment of the boron atoms rather than to the Si/B ratio. The carbon and nitrogen contents also play a minor role in the decomposition of the Si-B-C-N materials, but significantly affect their crystallization behavior. Therefore, the particular molecular structure of the polyborosilazane is essential for the synthesis of high-temperature-resistant silicoboron carbonitride. Polycondensation of Cl_2CH_3Si-$CH(CH_3)$-BCl_2 by ammonolysis or aminolysis can result in the formation of borazine rings interconnected with cyclic silazane units with a Si/B ratio of 1:1 (Fig. 1a). In contrast, the borazine-ring formation is impossible in the case of the polyborosilazanes with ratios of 2:1 (Fig. 1b) and 3:1 (Fig. 1c). The thermal stabilities of these two silicoboron carbonitride products are significantly enhanced compared to the behavior of the $Si_{1.2}B_1C_{1.7}N_2$ ceramic with a ratio of 1:1 (Fig. 2).

These findings indicate that the borazine units in the $Si_{1.2}B_1C_{1.7}N_2$ ceramic are prone to phase separation, resulting in boron-enriched and silicon-enriched carbonitrides during the ceramization.

Silicoboron carbonitride ceramics synthesized from molecular precursors have a high potential for application as a structural material that can withstand ultrahigh temperatures in harsh environments. This novel ceramic can resist degradation up to 2000°C (3632°F), crystallization up to 1700°C (3092°F), and oxidation up to 1500–1600°C (2732–2912°F). The Si-B-C-N alloys probably have the highest crystallization temperature of any supercooled glass known so far. It is evident that boron plays a decisive role in stabilizing the amorphous silicon carbonitride. This high metastability is strongly related to the precursor molecular structure and to the boron environment.

For background information *see* BORON; CARBON; CERAMICS; COMPOSITE MATERIAL; NITROGEN; POWDER

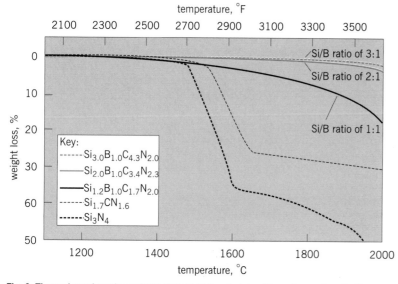

Fig. 2. Thermal gravimetric analysis of Si-B-C-N materials with various ratios. As the ratio of Si/B increases, thermal degradation (weight loss %) decreases. Note the increased thermal stability of boron-impregnated ceramics.

METALLURGY; SILICON in the McGraw-Hill Encyclopedia of Science & Technology.

Ralf Riedel; Lutz Ruwisch

Bibliography. W. Dressler and R. Riedel, Progress in silicon-based non-oxide structural ceramics, *Int. J. Refract. Met. Hard Mater.*, 15:13–47, 1997; R. Riedel et al., A silicoboron carbonitride ceramic stable to 2,000°C, *Nature*, 382:796–798, 1996; R. Riedel, J. Bill, and A. Kienzle, Boron-modified inorganic polymers: Precursor for the synthesis of multicomponent ceramics, *Appl. Organometal. Chem.*, 10:241–256, 1996; T. Wideman et al., Reactions of monofunctional boranes with hydridopolysilazane: Synthesis, characterization, and ceramic conversion reactions of new processible precursors to SiNCB ceramic materials, *Chem. Mater.*, 9:2218–2230, 1997.

Chemical dynamics

Bimolecular reactive collisions play a key role in macroscopic chemical processes such as combustion, formation of pollutants in engines and heat generators, and reactions in the Earth's atmosphere. The concept of close molecular encounters of reagents also applies to heterogeneous catalysis and reactions in liquids. Mechanisms of these fundamental processes are understood on the basis of quantitative models founded on contemporary research. The formulation of these models and their examination require detailed experimental information.

The bulk of empirical data results from investigation of energetic properties. It has become a central goal of modern chemistry to characterize the molecular-level changes that occur during a chemical reaction. As a result, laser-based spectroscopic methods are important tools for research of this type. The outcome of a reactive collision depends on the relative orientation of the reagents prior to the encounter as a consequence of the anisotropy of the molecular structure. Orientation and energy-dependent properties of reactive collisions provide complementary information, and knowledge of both is required to develop a detailed picture of how reactants evolve to products.

Molecular Orientation

The orientation of a molecule is determined by the directions of the unit vectors of a body fixed-coordinate frame relative to a space fixed-coordinate frame; the most suitable molecular frame is defined by the body's three principal axes of inertia. Consider an ensemble of molecules, such as a molecular beam. Perfect orientation of the ensemble is achieved if all corresponding axes are parallel. But this ideal case is far from attainable. A more realistic situation is where the corresponding axes are directionally distributed. An unperturbed ensemble in thermal equilibrium features an isotropic distribution for all axes. Distortion of the equilibrium or perturbations by external fields may lead to anisotropic distributions. The term orientation is then used in context with a distribution that favors a certain axial direction (**Fig. 1***a*). Another significant type of axis distribution, termed alignment, is characterized by the property that both a given direction and its reverse occur with the same probability (Fig. 1*b*).

Experimental techniques. In the pioneering studies on orientational effects in reactive scattering, electrostatic hexapole fields were employed to prepare an oriented beam of reagents. A severe drawback of the technique is that only symmetric top or symmetric top–like molecules can be oriented. This circumstance forced the research on orientation effects to concentrate on molecular reagents such as methyl iodide (CH_3I), carbon trifluoroiodide (CF_3I), nitric oxide (NO), and hydroxide (OH). In recent years, a new method (''brute force'' technique) has been

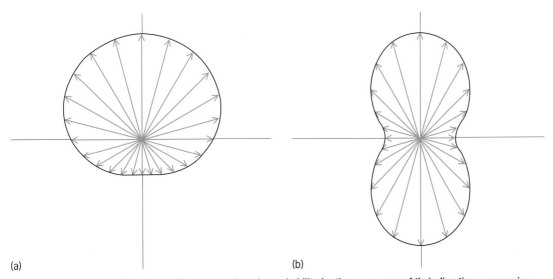

(a)   (b)

Fig. 1. Axis distributions. The length of the arrows gives the probability for the occurrence of their directions concerning (*a*) orientation and (*b*) alignment.

developed that overcomes these limitations. Generally applicable to all kinds of polar molecules, it has been used in current research to orient beams of linear molecules without electronic angular momentum, such as iodine monochloride (ICl), and with asymmetric tops, such as iodobenzene (C_6H_5I), iodotoluene (C_7H_7I), iodoethane (C_2H_5I), and 2-iodopropane (C_3H_7I). The brute force technique manipulates the orientation of the molecular frame via the interaction of an external electrostatic field with the molecule's permanent electric dipole moment that is rigidly attached to the molecular structure. The interaction exerts a torque on the molecule which distorts or even disrupts molecular rotation and tends to steer the dipole (brutally) toward the direction of the field (**Fig. 2**). The axis distributions show how the orientation evolves while the molecules move from the field free region through the fringing field into the orientation field. In particular, the rotational ground state ($J = 0$) develops a very marked orientation with rising field strength. With increasing rotation, the orientation in a given field becomes weaker and eventually vanishes. Thus the extent of orientation depends crucially on the population of low rotational states. Use of a state selector for low rotational states or of a highly expanded rotationally cold supersonic nozzle beam is mandatory. In a similar way, alignment can be created for nonpolar molecules via the field-induced electric dipole moment and for paramagnetic molecules via the magnetic dipole moment; in the latter case, a magnetic field is required.

Orientational studies. The significance of experiments with oriented molecules can be assessed most easily for the ideal situation of an ensemble prepared with a sharp orientation of the axes. Neglecting reorientation of the axes during the approach of an incoming parallel flux of reagent particles, the atoms would interact essentially with the constituents of the molecule exposed to the flux. By control of the axes' directions, any domain of the molecular surface can be selected for probing by the reagent flux. In this way can be determined the reactivity, dynamics, and energetics of reactions with molecular constituents, the effect of shielding of active groups by inactive ones, and the anisotropy of intermolecular forces. If the orientation of one or both axes is not sharp but distributed, the experimental data represent an average over all exposed areas. The resulting loss of orientational information grows with the width of the distributions and becomes complete for isotropic ones. Both the brute force and the hexapole technique allow preparation and control of the directional distribution of one axis only; the two other axes are distributed at random in a plane perpendicular to the oriented axis. Properties of the two domains at the molecular surface surrounding the molecular axis (head-versus-tail reactive asymmetry) and averaged properties of the domains perpendicular to the axis are accessible to experiments. In the case of an alignment, the individual head or tail information is lost and replaced by an averaged one.

Applications. One of the first applications of the novel brute force technique was a crossed-molecular-beam study of orientational effects in the reaction $K + ICl \rightarrow KCl + I$. ICl is a polar molecule that can be oriented by this technique only. The prepared axis distribution favors a certain direction (Fig. 1a). The probabilities for finding the axis parallel and antiparallel to the electric field depart only by $+5\%$ and -5% (orientation parameter) from unity. The crucial axis distribution can be calculated provided the population of molecular rotational states is known; the latter has been obtained through laser-induced fluorescence, beam deflection by inhomogeneous electric field, or translational temperature of the nozzle beam. It has also been determined experimentally by studying the anisotropic angular distributions of the atomic fragments following photodissociation of iodine monochloride in the field.

In this technique, product flux from collisions

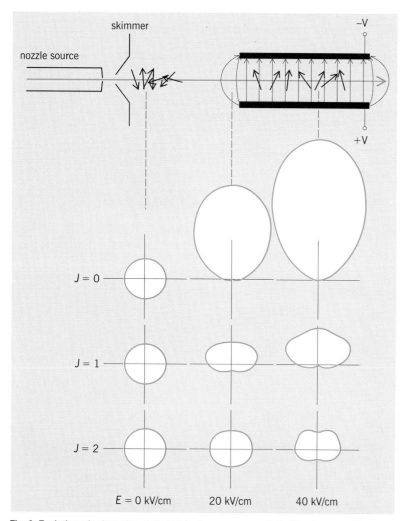

Fig. 2. Evolution of orientation. Axis distributions are presented without arrows. They demonstrate how orientation evolves with rising electric field strength (E) as molecules in the indicated rotational state move from the field free region into the orientation field. The beam is generated by a supersonic nozzle and collimated by a skimmer; the field is created by two parallel plates to which voltages ($\pm V$) are applied.

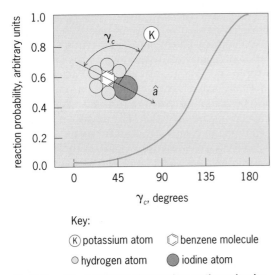

Key:

Ⓚ potassium atom   ⬡ benzene molecule

○ hydrogen atom   ⬤ iodine atom

Fig. 3. Reaction probability of potassium on the molecular surface of iodobenzene. The location on the molecular surface is described by the angle γ_c; the probability is averaged with respect to rotations around the figure axis â. (From H. J. Loesch and J. Möller, Reactive scattering from brute force oriented asymmetric top molecules: K + $C_6H_5I \rightarrow KI + C_6H_5$, J. Phys. Chem. A, 101:7461–7690, 1997)

with brute force–oriented molecules is measured at various scattering angles (Θ). The scattering angle is between the nominal direction of one beam and the direction of the flux velocity entering the detector. Product angular distributions are obtained for the orientation field parallel and antiparallel to the relative velocity of the reagents. Product angular distributions are obtained for the orientation field parallel and antiparallel to the relative velocity of the reagents. The ratio of the difference of the signals over their sum defines the differential parallel steric effect [$S_\parallel(\Theta)$]. Product angular distributions are obtained for the orientation field perpendicular to the relative velocity pointing to the detector and pointing away from the detector. The ratio of the difference of the signals over their sum defines the differential perpendicular steric effect [$S_\perp(\Theta)$]. Both steric effects are proportional to the orientation parameter, and their magnitude must always be smaller or equal to the parameter's value. In addition, angular and velocity distributions are measured for products from collisions with randomly oriented molecules.

Provided the molecular axis keeps its initially prepared direction during the approach of the reagents, the steric effects can be interpreted quite easily. The parallel steric effect probes the difference of reaction probabilities for products that appear at a given scattering angle of the chlorine end and the iodine end. The perpendicular steric effect characterizes the correlation of the product flux at the scattering angle created by side-on attacks with the direction of the molecular axis. The effect reaches the upper limit if the products are ejected along the molecular axis; it vanishes if the differential flux is independent of the direction of the axis. The experiments with the

reaction K + ICl → KCl + I indicate that the potassium chloride (KCl) flux is ejected essentially along the direction of the axis and, surprisingly, attacks to the iodine end form products most favorably. The reaction probability then decreases rapidly for sideways and chlorine-end attacks. For potassium + methyl iodide (K + CH_3I), iodobenzene (C_6H_5I), and the other iodine-containing molecules previously mentioned, encounters with the iodine end are most favorable; in iodobenzene it is obvious that the carbon group effectively shields the reactive iodine atom (**Fig. 3**). The correlation of the product flux with this axis is similar to iodine monochloride. It is consistent with the assumption of a rapid electron migration from the atom to the molecule during the approach of the reagents ("harpooning" mechanism), followed by an impulsive dissociation of the anion into the iodide ion (I^-), the neutral fragment along the axis, and the final formation of the potassium iodide (KI) product.   Hansjürgen Loesch

Laser Spectroscopy

Lasers are used to create reactants with well-characterized energies and to monitor how energy is distributed among the motions of the products. The product energy distributions are used to test models of the mechanism, or pathway, for the reaction. There are two possible reaction mechanisms for the generalized reaction of ABC with D to produce AB and CD (**Fig. 4a**). The horizontal axis of the diagram represents the course of the reaction and is called the reaction coordinate. The vertical axis is the potential

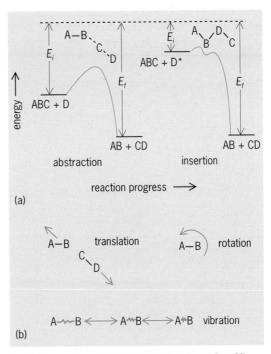

Fig. 4. Energetics of the reaction ABC + D → AB + CD. (a) Two possible mechanisms, abstraction and insertion. (b) Different forms of energy in the product molecules (translational, rotational, and vibrational motions).

energy (E) along the reaction coordinate. As the reactants move along the reaction coordinate, ABC approaches D until they are close enough to react, with a corresponding rise in the potential energy to a maximum at the transition state. The potential energy then falls as the atoms rearrange, ultimately reaching a value characteristic of the products.

In each case, the reactants are provided with initial energy (E_i), and final energy (E_f) is available for partitioning between the products. In the first mechanism where D abstracts C from ABC, the reactants must have sufficient energy to reach the ABCD transition state. Alternatively, if D is formed in some high-energy initial state (D*) that can insert between B and C, an intermediate species ABDC will be formed, which would subsequently decompose into the products. Each of the two possible reaction pathways should result in different distributions of the energy E_f among the various product motions. Determining how many molecules are created with specific amounts of vibrational, rotational, and translational energy can therefore be used to provide insight into the mechanism for the reaction (Fig. 4b).

Experimental methods. Various experimental approaches are used for characterizing product energy distributions, with most consisting of a low-pressure reaction chamber, a source of reactive species, a laser for probing product states, and detectors for molecular fluorescence or absorption. Lasers may also be used to prepare the reactants with specific energies prior to reaction. For simple reactions, it is possible to completely characterize the initial reactant states and final product states. These elegant state-to-state studies represent the ultimate in a detailed view of the dynamics of a model chemical reaction.

Infrared spectroscopy. One method for characterizing product state distributions is the use of infrared absorption spectroscopy. An infrared laser produces radiation at a wavelength that corresponds to the difference in energy between specific rotational (J) and vibrational (v) levels of a product molecule (**Fig. 5**). The experimental measurement involves monitoring the change in transmitted infrared intensity following the initiation of the reaction. The observed change in intensity is used to determine the populations of the specific vibration-rotation levels. Rotational distributions can be obtained by tuning the laser to transitions involving different rotational levels of the same pair of vibrational states. Vibrational distributions are measured by tuning the laser to transitions between different pairs of vibrational states. The average translational energy of a fragment can also be determined by measuring the spectral width of a given infrared probe transition. Translational excitation will lead to broadening of the transition line width due to the Doppler effect.

Laser-induced fluorescence spectroscopy. Another powerful probe technique is laser-induced fluorescence (LIF). A visible or ultraviolet laser is used to excite a product molecule from a specific vibration-rotation level of the ground electronic state to an excited electronic state. The intensity of the fluorescence from the excited state is monitored as a function of excitation wavelength to obtain the relative population of the initial vibration-rotation states (Fig. 5). Analogous to infrared absorption spectroscopy, the products' vibrational, rotational, and translational energies can be characterized by laser-induced fluorescence. The technique is more sensitive, that is, it is capable of detecting lower concentrations of products, than the infrared absorption method, but requires that the product of interest have an accessible electronic state which fluoresces.

Ionization spectroscopy. Other laser-based detection methods have been developed which utilize the absorption of more than one photon. One example of this type of nonlinear probe technique is resonance-enhanced multiphoton ionization spectroscopy, which uses one or more high-powered pulsed lasers to selectively ionize a species. Product state distribution information is again obtained by tuning the excitation laser, and in this case monitoring either the yields of ions or electrons, which are proportional to the initial product state populations. The advan-

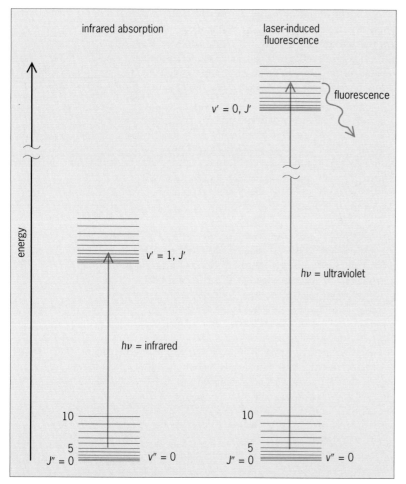

Fig. 5. Energy-level diagram showing a vibrational transition used for infrared absorption detection, and an electronic transition used in laser-induced fluorescence detection. Infrared or ultraviolet radiation with energy $h\nu$ is used to probe the vibrational and rotational distribution of the reaction products.

tage of this technique is its high sensitivity, but obtaining quantitative information about product state populations is difficult.

Product monitoring. One of the many examples of laser-based spectroscopic monitoring of product state distributions is the investigation of the mechanisms involved in the reaction of oxygen atoms with hydrocarbons. This class of reactions plays an important role in atmospheric and combustion chemistry, motivating numerous experimental and theoretical studies. Oxygen (O) atoms can be produced in either the ground (^3P) or excited (^1D) electronic states by photolysis of an appropriate precursor molecule. Both O(^3P) and O(^1D) react with methane (CH_4) to produce hydroxide (OH) and methyl (CH_3) radicals. The mechanism for the reaction, however, depends on the nature of the oxygen electronic state. The O(^3P) reaction follows an abstraction mechanism, while the O(^1D) reaction is thought to proceed by way of an oxygen atom insertion into a C-H bond followed by unimolecular decomposition of the highly excited methanol (CH_3OH) intermediate (Fig. 4a). In principle, these two mechanisms should result in different patterns of energy distributions among the products.

For the oxygen + methane reactions, laser-induced fluorescence has been used to monitor the hydroxide product rotational and vibrational populations. Infrared absorption spectroscopy has been applied to characterize the rotational motions and one of the vibrational motions of the methyl fragment. In addition, multiphoton ionization spectroscopy has been used to identify methyl vibrational excitation induced via the O(^1D) reaction.

One possible outcome for product energy partitioning is that the available energy (E_f) is distributed among the various product states in a statistical fashion. A statistical distribution is expected for mechanisms with long-lived intermediate species, such as insertion reactions. If the intermediate does not live long enough to allow complete randomization of energy into all possible product states, deviations from the statistical distribution will be observed. The abstraction reaction is expected to have a highly nonstatistical distribution since the reactants go directly to products with no intermediate species.

The hydroxide products from the O(^3P) reaction are formed with a higher-than-statistical degree of O-H stretching energy, consistent with the abstraction mechanism. The observed hydroxide and methyl energy partitioning for the O(^1D) reaction with methane is closer to the statistical prediction, supporting the insertion mechanism. O(^1D) reactions with larger hydrocarbons, such as C_3H_8, appear to occur by way of a mixture of both the abstraction and insertion mechanisms. The uniquely detailed perspective of laser-based spectroscopic monitoring of product energy distributions holds great promise for increasing the understanding of the fundamental, molecular-level changes that occur during chemical reactions.

For background information *see* CHEMICAL DYNAMICS; COLLISION (PHYSICS); EXCITED STATE; GROUND STATE; INFRARED SPECTROSCOPY; LASER SPECTROSCOPY; MOLECULAR BEAMS; SCATTERING EXPERIMENTS (ATOMS AND MOLECULES) in the McGraw-Hill Encyclopedia of Science & Technology.

Marsha I. Lester; Jeanne M. Hossenlopp; David T. Anderson

Bibliography. W. Demtröder, *Laser Spectroscopy: Basic Concepts and Instrumentation*, 1996; R. D. Levine and R. B. Bernstein, *Molecular Reaction Dynamics and Chemical Reactivity*, 1987; G. Scoles (ed.), *Atomic and Molecular Beam Methods*, vol. I, 1988; H. J. Loesch, Orientation and alignment in reactive beam collisions: Recent progress, *Annu. Rev. Phys. Chem.*, 46:555–594, 1995; R. Schinke, *Photodissociation Dynamics*, 1993; Special issue on dynamical stereochemistry, *J. Phys. Chem. A*, 101:7461–7690, 1997.

Chemotherapy

It has long been known that deoxyribonucleic acid (DNA) binds heavy metals. Thus, it is not surprising that compounds containing a metal ion would be tested for their ability to bind to DNA to produce cancer chemotherapeutic effects. An example is cisplatin, or *cis*-DDP [*cis*-diamminedichloroplatinum II; **Fig. 1**], a compound containing platinum. It was described in 1965 and is now a widely used anticancer agent.

Cisplatin. Cisplatin is a transition-metal complex containing a central platinum atom bound to two chlorine atoms and two stable amine groups. *Trans*-DDP is not a clinically effective isomer of *cis*-DDP. Cisplatin's use in therapy has revealed several problems. It has side effects such as neurotoxicity and kidney toxicity, and leads to the development of resistance by tumor cells. This resistance may be due to an increased ability of the tumor cell to repair or to tolerate the cisplatin DNA. Extensive efforts have been made to develop new platinum compounds that avoid these problems, but success has been very limited. Only one other therapeutically useful compound, carboplatin, has been developed. In order to improve the chances of success in making useful new platinum compounds, it is necessary to understand the mechanism of action of cisplatin at the molecular level.

Research has shown that cisplatin interaction with DNA leads to a number of structural changes involving unwinding, formation of cross-links, and bending. The first step in the reaction between cisplatin and the purine bases of DNA yields a monofunctional adduct (combination of two or more stable chemical compounds), which reacts further with a second purine base to form bifunctional intrastrand and interstrand cross-links (**Fig. 2**). The reaction between cisplatin and DNA produces approximately 70% N7,N7 cisplatin cross-links between two intrastrand adjacent guanines (N7,N7 indicating that nitrogen in the seventh position of one guanine is linked to

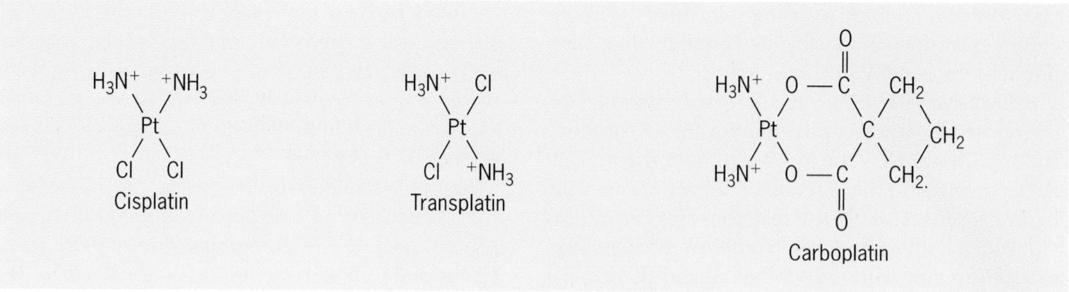

Fig. 1. Structures of *cis*-diamminedichloroplatinum II, or cisplatin, and related compounds.

a nitrogen in the seventh position of the ring of the adjacent guanine). A minor product (about 15%) is the intrastrand cross-link to the adenine-to-guanine (ApG) sequence. There are small amounts of intrastrand 1,3 cross-links to guanine-to-guanine (G-G) sequences, and interstrand guanine-to-guanine cross-links at guanine-to-cytosine (GpC) sequences. There are 1,2 intrastrand adducts which produce a rigid bend of 30–35° directed toward the major groove of the DNA helix and a localized unwinding of the double helix of 13°. The 1,3 intrastrand adducts produce a similar bend and an unwinding of the double helix of 23°. The structural image obtained from nuclear magnetic resonance (NMR) imaging shows

the cross-link in the minor groove. There is a change in hydrogen bonding and in base stacking, and a reversal of the double helix at the cross-link. The therapeutically inactive trans isomer of cisplatin forms intrastrand adducts having one or more intervening nucleotides. The 1,2 cisplatin interstrand cross-linked product produces a 20–45° bend directed toward the minor groove of the DNA helix and an unwinding of 80–90°. This change in the DNA configuration results in the inhibition of DNA replication, the inhibition of transcription, and the induction of programmed cell death (apoptosis).

Intrastrand and interstrand cisplatin DNA adducts can isomerize. Intrastrand cross-links can be transformed into interstrand cross-links in vitro, but such an occurrence in vivo has not been proven. The major adduct formed by the interaction of cisplatin and DNA is the intrastrand cross-link between cisplatin and the N7 of adjacent guanine bases with the loss of two chloride ions from cisplatin.

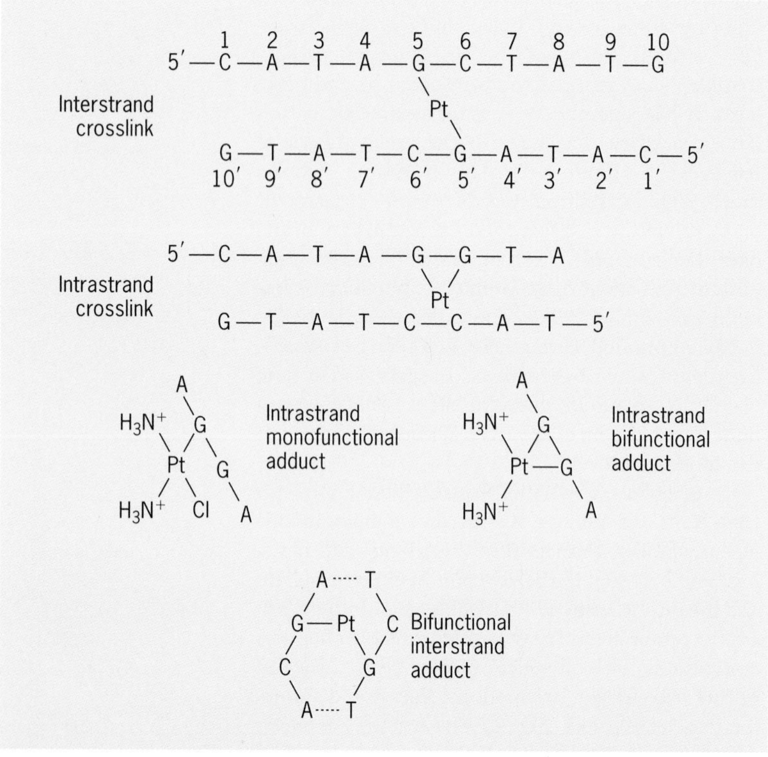

High-mobility-group proteins. Bent or kinked DNA formed by the interaction of cisplatin and DNA is recognized by high-mobility-group proteins. High-mobility-group-1 proteins are members of a class of chromatin proteins that are present in all vertebrate nuclei. They are involved in a number of DNA reactions. High-mobility-group-1 proteins do not interact with DNA modified with *trans*-DDP. The *trans*-DDP interstrand cross-link bends the double helix toward the major groove by 26° and unwinds it by 12°. High-mobility-group protein domains interact with DNA, with most contacts being made in the minor groove of DNA. These proteins have three structural areas: a positively charged *N*-terminal A-domain, a positively charged central B-domain, and a negatively charged C-domain. The positively charged A and B areas interact with negatively charged groups of DNA, and the negatively charged C area reacts with positively charged histones (small basic proteins, to which DNA is tightly bound, and which are components of chromosomes). High-mobility-group-1 proteins bind preferentially to bent DNA such as cisplatin-modified DNA. The A- and B-domains are homologous to each other and to units of approximately 70 amino acids called the high-mobility-group protein box. The A and B box bind to *cis*-DDP-modified double-stranded DNA that contains a single intrastrand cross-link at

Fig. 2. Interstrand and intrastrand cross-links and adducts result from the reaction of cisplatin and DNA. The DNA bases are A (adenine), G (guanine), C (cytosine), and T (thymine). *(After M. J. Pillaire et al., Replication of DNA containing cisplatin lesions and its mutagenic consequences, Biochimie, 77:803–807, 1995)*

the guanine-to-guanine (GpG) site. Structure-specific recognition protein (SSRP) is a high-mobility-group protein that interacts with kinked DNA, which is the irregular structure formed by the interaction of DNA with cisplatin that binds to the N7 portions of adjacent guanine bases in a DNA strand. High-mobility-group-1 proteins bind cisplatin DNA with greater affinity than linear DNA. This preference may be related to the ability of the high-mobility-group proteins to bend linear DNA.

The elucidation of the molecular binding of cisplatin offers clues to the mechanism by which tumor cells are prevented from multiplying. Perhaps, even more effective therapeutic agents can be designed by utilizing the information obtained from these studies.

Resistance. The development of resistance to cisplatin is a major reason for treatment failure. Acquired resistance can be demonstrated in patients receiving chemotherapy and in cell lines exposed to increasing concentrations of the drug. Intrinsic resistance is seen in tumors that have never been exposed to cisplatin. Some of these tumors had cell lines that were more proficient at removing cisplatin adducts than normal cisplatin-sensitive lines. The nucleotide excision repair pathway removes 1,2 and 1,3 intrastrand cisplatin adducts. Proteins of the nucleotide excision repair pathway (such as ERCC1) are also involved in cisplatin resistance.

The many mechanisms of resistance to cisplatin include DNA repair, signal transduction pathways, increased detoxification, and changes in drug transport. Cisplatin is much more toxic to cells that have decreased DNA-repair capacity, suggesting that DNA repair can overcome the effect of cisplatin and is one mechanism of cellular resistance to the drug. The protein metallothionein may play a role in cisplatin resistance in some cells. Metallothionein binds 10 platinum atoms per molecule. Each molecule of metallothionein has 20 sulfhydryl groups. It can bind both *cis*- and *trans*-DDP. Glutathione, which has one sulfhydryl group per molecule, also reacts with alkylating agents and with cisplatin. Glutathione may intercept cisplatin before it can react with DNA. Increased glutathione concentrations can be found in some cisplatin-resistant cells but not in others.

Combination chemotherapy with cisplatin, bleomycin, etoposide, and vinblastine is curative in 85% of patients with advanced testicular cancer. In combination with paclitaxel, cyclophosphamide, or doxorubicin, cisplatin is beneficial in carcinoma of the ovary. Cisplatin sensitizes cells to the cytotoxic effects of radiation therapy. Cisplatin's kidney toxicity has been largely overcome by the use of hydration and diuresis, but ototoxicity remains. (Ototoxicity involves high-frequency hearing loss and tinnitus.) The marked nausea and vomiting that occur with cisplatin can be controlled by high doses of cortisone. Cisplatin causes peripheral neuropathy and electrolyte disturbances. The magnesium concentration of patients' blood must be carefully monitored.

Anaphylactic-type reactions to cisplatin must be treated with epinephrine, steroids, and antihistamines.

The precise mechanism of cisplatin inhibition may vary from one tumor cell type to another, but most experimental evidence points to cisplatin's interaction with DNA. Further modifications or changes of the groups linked to the platinum atom may lead to more therapeutically useful drugs. Perhaps new platinum compounds can be designed to overcome toxicity and resistance problems.

For background information *see* CANCER (MEDICINE); CHEMOTHERAPY; COORDINATION COMPLEXES; DEOXYRIBONUCLEIC ACID (DNA); ORGANOMETALLIC COMPOUND in the McGraw-Hill Encyclopedia of Science & Technology.   Herbert W. Felsenfeld

Bibliography. R. Grosschedl, K. Giese, and J. Pagel, HMG domain proteins: Architectural elements in the assembly of nucleoprotein structures, *Trends Genet.*, 10(3):94–99, 1994; H. Huang et al., Solution structure of a cisplatin-induced DNA interstrand cross-link, *Science,* 270:1842–1845, 1995; D. Locker et al., Interaction between cisplatin-modified DNA and the HMG boxes of HMG 1: DNase I footprinting and circular dichroism, *J. Mol. Biol.,* 246:243–247, 1995; K. J. Mellish et al., Effect of geometric isomerism in dinuclear platinum antitumor complexes on the rate of formation and structure of intrastrand adducts with oligonucleotides, *Nucl. Acids Res.,* 25(6):1265–1271, 1997; M. J. Pillaire et al., Replication of DNA containing cisplatin lesions and its mutagenic consequences, *Biochimie,* 77:803–807, 1995.

Clinical pathology

Raman spectroscopy offers a powerful new way to look at atherosclerotic tissue. Rather than categorizing disease in terms of arterial luminal diameter reduction, Raman spectroscopy allows a qualitative and quantitative biochemical description of the diseased vascular segment. The clinical implications are enormous, inasmuch as plaque composition rather than plaque volume appears to be the most important predictor of clinical outcome. Knowledge of plaque composition is likely to improve the physician's ability to predict plaque behavior, and it may also provide a means to monitor the effects of medical interventions.

Atherosclerosis. Atherosclerosis is a chronic, progressive, degenerative disease of the vascular system which predominantly affects middle-aged men, but it is also being recognized with increasing frequency among postmenopausal women. By occluding major arteries throughout the body, atherosclerosis eventually leads to heart attack, stroke, kidney failure, limb loss, and death. Despite many advances in the diagnosis and treatment of atherosclerosis, it remains the number one cause of premature death in the United States. Atherosclerosis of the coronary arteries alone accounts for almost one-half million deaths annually.

The etiology of atherosclerosis is not known, but it is hypothesized that a genetic predisposition in combination with a mixture of environmental (risk) factors causes the focal accumulation of lipids within the vascular wall. These lipid-laden plaques develop slowly, gradually narrowing the arterial lumen and thereby reducing blood flow to vital organs. During maturation, some plaques grow too rich in lipids and become unstable, with a propensity to rupture rather than slow growth. Rupture into the arterial lumen can cause formation of a thrombus which acutely occludes the vessel, depriving critical organs such as the heart, brain, or kidneys of blood flow. This results in damage to the involved end organ and can cause death. Plaque rupture is particularly difficult to manage medically because its occurrence is difficult to predict.

There has been a national effort to alter the onset and progression of atherosclerosis through the vigorous use of laboratory testing to identify individuals with abnormally elevated levels of blood cholesterol, considered by many to be a major risk factor for this disease. Once identified, these patients are aggressively treated with diet, exercise, and hypolipemic drugs in an effort to reduce blood lipid levels. It has been noted, however, that simply screening the blood for elevated cholesterol will miss 50–80% of the patients who develop atherosclerotic heart disease. In addition, physicians now recognize that traditional diagnostic techniques used to quantify the clinical severity of established atherosclerosis, including thallium stress testing, vascular cine-angiography or arteriography, and intravascular ultrasound, are poor predictors of the sudden vascular events such as stroke or heart attack, which are more closely related to plaque instability than to plaque volume. Clearly, a new technique, such as Raman spectroscopy, is needed to allow the physician to more closely monitor the development and progression of the atherosclerotic process at the biochemical level in situ and in vivo. The result can be a better understanding of the factors that lead to the initiation of new plaques and the instability of existing plaques. *See* ARTERIAL BLOOD FLOW; ATHEROSCLEROSIS.

Raman effect. In the Raman effect, light impinging on biological tissue sets the molecules within it into vibration. As a result, a small portion of the light scattered from the surface of the tissue is shifted in frequency by the vibrational frequency of the molecules. Since different molecular species vibrate at distinct frequencies, the Raman shifts are a direct indication of molecular composition.

Raman signal enhancement. Raman signals are, however, quite weak. Visible laser light is known to produce Raman spectra in tissue, but it also excites fluorescence. This fluorescence is a million times more intense than the Raman signals, obscuring them. In contrast, infrared laser light excites Raman tissue spectra with little or no fluorescence, resulting in Raman signals which are free of background. The combination of infrared excitation and Fourier-transform Raman detection demonstrates that important information about the biochemical makeup of the tissue can be provided. However, although fluorescence is absent, data collection times of 30 min or more are required, because as the wavelength increases from the visible to the infrared, detectors become less sensitive. This suggests a trade-off in which near-infrared laser light is used to excite the Raman spectra. Using near-infrared excitation and charge-coupled-device (CCD) detector arrays, Raman detection times can be greatly reduced. Advanced deep-depletion CCD/spectrometer systems have reduced collection times to seconds while maintaining excellent signal-to-noise ratios, making intravascular applications clinically feasible.

Quantification. Near-infrared Raman spectroscopy can be used to quantify the chemical composition of coronary arteries. Finely ground minces of coronary artery taken from the explanted hearts of cardiac transplant patients are excited with short pulses of 830-nanometer light from an argon-ion-pumped titanium:sapphire laser, and the Raman light emitted from the samples is collected and analyzed. Collection times of approximately 60 s are sufficient for analysis. Computer modeling allows the recognition of seven major spectral components, including unesterified cholesterol, esterified cholesterol, triglycerides, phospholipids, calcium salts, and two types of delipidized residuals. A linear combination of these individual component spectra is then used to estimate the relative concentrations of each component. These concentrations are compared to those obtained by analyzing the same samples with standard chemical assays and are found to be in close agreement, thus providing an in situ method for quantitative biochemical assay of atherosclerosis.

Classification in situ. Near-infrared Raman spectroscopy can also be used to classify atherosclerosis within a vessel segment. Traditionally, the degree of atherosclerotic disease, from mild to severe, is determined by a pathologist after the segment has been removed from the patient, fixed, sectioned, and stained for examination under a microscope. Quantitative Raman spectroscopy can classify tissue in situ without the need for tissue removal and processing. This method is based on the correlation of biochemical constituents with disease type. Samples of coronary artery tissue are classified into three histopathologic categories: nonatherosclerotic, noncalcified atherosclerotic plaque, and calcified atherosclerotic plaque. The cholesterol concentration of nonatherosclerotic vascular tissue is found to be less than 8%, whereas atherosclerotic tissues consistently contain higher cholesterol concentrations, sometimes as large as 45%. Similarly, calcified atherosclerotic tissue consistently contains large amounts of calcium salts, an average relative weight of about 41%, far greater than that present in noncalcified plaques.

These correlations were used to develop a diagnostic scheme based on the concentrations of cholesterol and calcium salts, measured by Raman spectroscopy. This scheme was tested in a prospective study in which 68 arterial samples were first analyzed by Raman spectroscopy and then by a highly trained pathologist. The Raman diagnosis agreed with that of the pathologist in 64 of the 68 samples (94% agreement), thus demonstrating the accuracy and robustness of the method.

Classification in vivo. In order to test the concept of spectral diagnosis in vivo, a Raman spectroscopy system with special features has been designed for hospital use. The system consists of a laser, CCD/spectrometer, and fiber-optic catheter. A 500-mW air-cooled diode laser is used to produce 830-nm excitation light. Pulses of this light are focused into the central fiber of a seven-fiber, 3-m-long (10-ft) optical catheter which has been advanced through the patient's vascular system and into the artery of interest, such as a coronary artery, to contact a diseased segment. A 1-mm-diameter spot of laser light delivered to the tissue excites molecules within it, resulting in weak Raman signals, which are collected by the six fibers in the catheter surrounding the excitation fiber. Collected light is coupled into a spectrograph and dispersed onto a cooled, deep-depletion CCD array detector. A notebook computer controls the system, displays spectra, and analyzes data. The system can be safely used in an operating room or catheterization laboratory; the apparatus is electrically insulated and the laser beam is fully enclosed. The entire system fits onto a small cart that can be moved from room to room in the hospital and brought close to the patient during diagnostic procedures. In preliminary experiments employing this system during peripheral vascular surgery, Raman spectra were collected in vivo. Percutaneous experiments using optical catheters optimized for the collection of Raman signals are planned in the near future.

Clinical applications. Once spectroscopic catheters are refined for routine clinical use, physicians will have a new tool for studying the initiation and progression of the atherosclerotic process percutaneously. With minimal invasion, it will be possible to look at the biochemical makeup of diseased tissue directly, rather than making assumptions about the disease process on the basis of an analysis of circulating-blood samples. Direct knowledge of changes in plaque composition following the initiation of drugs specifically designed to retard or prevent plaque growth will allow the clinician to make earlier and more effective adjustments in medical regimens for individual patients.

There are also preliminary indications that near-infrared Raman spectroscopy will be a useful diagnostic tool in many other organs of the body. By using fibers within biopsy needles or spectral endoscopes, rather than catheters, this technology should be particularly useful for the detection and classification of premalignancies and malignancies of the mouth, colon, bladder, and breast.

For background information *see* ARTERIOSCLEROSIS; RAMAN EFFECT in the McGraw-Hill Encyclopedia of Science & Technology.

John R. Kramer, Jr.; Michael S. Feld

Bibliography. J. J. Baraga, M. S. Feld, and R. P. Rava, Rapid near-infrared Raman spectroscopy of human tissue with a spectrograph and CCD detector, *Appl. Spectrosc.*, 46:187–190, 1992; J. F. Brennan III et al., Determination of human coronary artery composition by Raman spectroscopy, *Circulation*, 96:99–105, 1997; J. R. Kramer, R. R. Dasari, and M. S. Feld, Shedding laser light on the subject, *Nat. Med.*, 2:1079–1080, 1997; R. P. Rava, J. J. Baraga, and M. S. Feld, Near infrared Fourier transform Raman spectroscopy of human artery, *Spectrochim. Acta*, 47A(3/4):509–512, 1991.

Coal

Because of the sulfur dioxide (SO_2) emissions when coal is burned, sulfur levels in coal are important. Coal supplies 32% of the world's energy. In 1995, United States electric utilities used coal to generate 55% of the nation's net electric power, and this approach is projected to remain virtually the same through 2005. In the United States, the utility and industrial sectors are the largest emitters of sulfur oxides, and in 1985 accounted for 22.3 million tons, or 96%, of the total SO_2 emitted. In the presence of particulate matter, sulfur oxides have been related to irritation of the human respiratory system, reduced visibility, materials corrosion, and varying effects on vegetation. The reaction of sulfur oxides with moisture in the atmosphere contributes to acid rain.

The Clean Air Act of 1970 and amendments in 1977 and 1990 aimed to reduce the amount of acid rain. Beginning in 1990, it was mandated that SO_2 emissions from all coal-fired power plants be capped at 8.9 million tons by the year 2000. From 1970 to 1988, SO_2 emissions in the United States diminished from 28.4 to 20.7 million tons per year. During this same period, coal consumption by utilities increased from 320 to 758 million tons. Had there not been any emissions control, it is estimated that SO_2 emissions would have grown to 34.7 million tons per year by 1998.

Use of high-sulfur coals. Sulfur occurs in coal in three forms: organic sulfur, which is part of the coal's molecular structure; pyritic sulfur, occurring as the mineral pyrite; and sulfate sulfur, primarily from iron sulfate. The principal sulfur source is the sulfate ion, which is found in water. Fresh water has a low sulfate concentration while salt water has a high sulfate content. Bituminous coal, deposited in the interior of the United States when seas covered this region, is high in sulfur. In 1989, 67% of the coal consumed was bituminous coal, which is mined primarily from the Appalachian region and the Central states. Two-thirds of the coal reserves lie in the Great Plains, Rocky Mountains, and Western states, and are mostly subbituminous and lignitic and have low sulfur content.

High-sulfur bituminous coal has been traditionally used for a variety of reasons. Its proximity to the industrial and populace regions during the growth periods of the nation led to the construction of power plants throughout the East and Midwest in order to minimize coal transportation costs. The majority of these power plants were designed to burn high-sulfur bituminous coal.

Clean Air Act compliance. Today, utilities with plants that burn high-sulfur coal must comply with the Clean Air Act and are forced to look at several emissions control options. The two primary technological strategies that utilities are using to control SO_2 emissions are switching to low-sulfur coal and installing flue-gas cleanup equipment. The Clean Air Act specified 261 plants that had to comply by 1995, and all plants must comply with an even tighter set of specifications by 2000. Of these 261 plants, 52% switched to low-sulfur coal and 10% built flue-gas scrubbers, 3% were retired, and 3% either were repowered or switched to gas or oil.

The use of low-sulfur coal permits utilities to comply. Fuel switching is attractive because it can be implemented in a relatively short time span and without major capital investment. Low-sulfur coal will cost more primarily because of rail transportation from the mines in the western states to the eastern plants. Fuel cost is a plant's largest contributor to generating cost and must be considered carefully. Burning a coal different from what the power plant was designed to fire can be detrimental to the plant's reliability and availability. Consideration must be given to the fuel preparation equipment, as low-sulfur coals typically have a lower heat content requiring that more fuel be processed to maintain the plant's rated design output. The higher ash content of the low-sulfur coal will increase maintenance of equipment to grind the coal. Higher slagging and fouling of the boiler's heat-transfer surfaces can be expected with the higher ash loading and lower fusion temperatures inherent with low-sulfur coals. Usually, the utility will perform a test burn of a fuel to determine how it will behave. The utility must thoroughly study all of the plant's systems to determine the impact on operations and generating costs before opting for low-sulfur coal.

Compliance options with high-sulfur coal. Power plants using high-sulfur coals need to comply with the Clean Air Act. To meet emission requirements, utilities can look at several technologies: coal benefication, coal gasification, in-furnace capture, and postcombustion cleanup.

Coal benefication. A variety of proven techniques and processes can remove the sulfur and mineral matter from the coal prior to combustion. The advanced cleaning processes to achieve the sulfur removal required by emissions standards usually involve grinding the coal to a fine particle size and then washing it. This process allows the pyritic sulfur and other minerals to be removed. The clean coal

product must be dried, and can be pelletized and then processed as raw coal feed. Benefication currently is not cost competitive with other sulfur removal techniques.

Coal gasification. By converting coal to a gaseous fuel through partial oxidation, undesirable substances such as sulfur and ash can be removed. To gasify the coal, incomplete combustion is controlled by limiting the amount of oxygen supplied. Less heat is released, and new gaseous reaction products (hydrogen, carbon monoxide, and methane) are formed and captured as a gaseous fuel. The heat generated during the process is absorbed by the heat recovery boiler downstream of the gasifier to produce steam. Sulfur in the coal is predominantly converted to hydrogen sulfide, referred to as sour gas. There are several gasifier types, and some require cleanup of the fuel gas for further removal of the undesirable materials. The sulfur compounds in the fuel gas from a gasifier are more efficiently removed than is possible with a wet scrubber, with better than 99% sulfur recovery achievable.

In-furnace capture. Fluidized-bed combustion features a mixture of particles (fuel and usually sand) suspended in an upwardly flowing gas stream where combustion takes place in the bed. Heat transfer to the combustor furnace can be achieved at relatively low combustion zone temperatures, 1500–1600°F (816–871°C). These low operating temperatures allow the use of sorbent, such as limestone or dolomite, to calcinate the SO_2, which then can be removed as a solid for disposal. Depending on the sulfur content and the amount of sorbent used, fluidized-bed combustion can remove 90% or more SO_2 from the flue gas. Fluidized-bed combustion technology is commercially available on boilers of industrial and small utility size. On conventional boilers, sorbents and additives injected into the furnace have been tested since the late 1970s, but SO_2 capture efficiencies of only 50–60% have been achieved. *See* FLUIDIZED BED.

Postcombustion cleanup. The strategy is to remove the sulfur generated as a product of combustion from the flue gas before it vents through the stack to the atmosphere. Flue-gas desulfurization systems, such as wet and dry scrubbers, rely on reagents added to the flue gas to react with and thereby capture the sulfur. Wet scrubbers spray the reagent into the flue gas in the scrubber tower, and the slurry by-product is then dewatered. Dry scrubbers spray the reagent into the reactor module, where it reacts with the flue gas. Dry scrubbers produce a dry by-product which can be collected downstream in an electrostatic precipitator or baghouse. Of the 180,000 megawatts of worldwide flue-gas desulfurization capacity, 85% are wet scrubbers.

The wet-scrubber system consists of four process steps: reagent preparation (lime or limestone), SO_2 absorption, slurry dewatering, and final disposal or utilization. The reagent preparation process differs slightly, depending on whether lime or limestone is used. In the absorption step, the calcium in the reagent reacts with the flue gas to precipitate out the sulfur as calcium sulfite in a wet slurry. The slurry either is sent to ponds where the water evaporates and the sludge cake is landfilled, or is dewatered by using dryers, centrifuges, presses, and filters. In some wet-scrubber system designs, oxygen can be added to the sulfite formed in the reaction to produce gypsum.

Dry scrubbing involves spraying a highly atomized aqueous solution of an alkaline reagent into the hot flue gas to absorb the SO_2. Unlike the wet scrubber, the dry scrubber is positioned before the particulate collector. Dry scrubbing is predominantly used on low-sulfur fuels, is less costly to construct, produces a dry waste product, and is easier to operate.

Advanced technologies. Research is under way within the United States industrial sector to develop technologies and processes to further reduce emissions produced by power plants. Most of the work involves refining or combining the various technologies described above. For example, considerable work has been done toward designing a new pulverized-coal-powered generating system equipped with improved combustion and heat-transfer subsystems and advanced environmental control technologies capable of achieving emissions far below current environmental standards. These designs achieve higher cycle efficiencies, lowering fuel consumption and pollutants emitted; apply advanced combustion concepts to lower nitrous oxide emissions; and couple in-furnace sorbent injection with dry scrubbing for SO_2, air-pollutant, and particulate removal.

For background information *see* ACID RAIN; AIR POLLUTION; COAL; COAL GASIFICATION; FLUIDIZED-BED COMBUSTION; SULFUR in the McGraw-Hill Encyclopedia of Science & Technology.   Patrick G. Whitten

Bibliography. R. M. Davidson, *Sulfur in Coal*, IEA Coal Research, August 1993; T. J. Feeley III and L. A. Ruth, The U.S. Department of Energy's Advanced Environmental Control Technology Program, presented at the 22d International Technical Conference on Coal Utilization and Fuel Systems, March 1997; J. S. Khingspor and D. R. Cope, *FGD Handbook: Flue Gas Desulphurization Systems*, IEA Coal Research, May 1987; S. Stultz and J. Kitto, *Steam, Its Generation and Use*, 40th ed., 1992.

Comet Hale-Bopp

The study of comets, which were once regarded, at best, as atmospheric exhalations and, at worst, as harbingers of doom sent by angry gods, has advanced tremendously during the past few centuries. The successful prediction in the eighteenth century by E. Halley of the return of the comet that now bears his name established that comets are true members of the solar system, subject to the same laws of physics as are other celestial bodies. Twentieth-century developments in cometary studies include investigations of the physical structure of comets, in particular, the "dirty snowball" model of the comm-etary nucleus developed by F. Whipple; theoretical and observational examinations of cometary populations, such as the Oort Cloud and, more recently, the Kuiper Belt; and space-based and on-site investigations of cometary environments. Recent studies have also examined the role that comets played in the formation of the planets, including the Earth, and the ways that they continue to affect the solar system's evolution.

The population of known comets is now close to 1000. During a typical year, up to a dozen previously unknown comets may be discovered, some as a result of deliberate photographic or charge-coupled-device (CCD) searches for near-Earth asteroids, some during the course of large-scale survey programs at various observatories, and still others (perhaps three per year, on the average) by amateur astronomers engaged in visual search programs. Most comets remain dim telescopic objects throughout their period of visibility, which typically ranges 3–6 months; perhaps one comet per year, on the average, will attain dim naked-eye visibility. So-called great comets, objects brilliant enough to attract the attention of casual nonastronomers, are significantly less common, occurring only once every 10–20 years, on the average.

Discovery. The most recent great comet, Hale-Bopp, was discovered by A. Hale and by T. Bopp on July 23, 1995. (The two discoveries were independent and accidental.) Subsequent orbital calculations soon revealed that the apparently unremarkable 11th-magnitude object was located at the enormous distance of 7.15 astronomical units from the Sun, between the orbits of Jupiter and Saturn, and was unprecedentedly bright for a comet at such a distance. (An astronomical unit is the average distance between the Earth and the Sun, equal to 1.5 $\times$ 10^8 km or 9.3 $\times$ 10^7 mi.) Furthermore, the comet would not reach its perihelion (its closest approach to the Sun) until April 1, 1997, at which time it would be located at a heliocentric distance of 0.91 astronomical unit (**Fig. 1**). This suggested that Comet Hale-Bopp had the potential, during the first few months of 1997, of becoming one of the brightest comets of the twentieth century.

Brightness prediction. The brightness of comets, especially of those not previously recorded, is notoriously difficult to predict, since this is dependent upon the activity level of their nuclei, which is to some extent a stochastic process. Comets that are making their first visit into the inner solar system from the Oort Cloud, notably, Comet Kohoutek in 1973–1974, are often covered by a crust of organic substances, which is itself covered by a thin layer of volatiles picked up during its 4.5 $\times$ 10^9 years in near-interstellar space. A comet discovered during the blow-off of these volatiles that occurs when it first experiences solar heating, as was the case with Comet Kohoutek, may show promise of becoming a bright object when it rounds perihelion. However, once these volatiles have dispersed, the organic crust causes the comet to all but "shut down." Usually

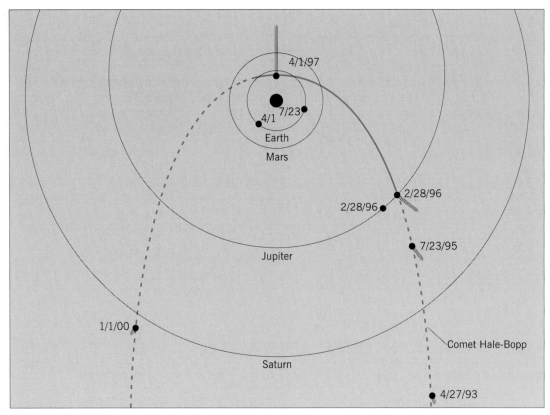

Fig. 1. Orbit of Comet Hale-Bopp, viewed from directly north of the Earth's orbital plane. Those sections of the comet's orbit north of the Earth's orbit are shown as a solid line, those which are south as a broken line. The comet's position is shown for April 27, 1993 (prediscovery photograph), July 23, 1995 (discovery), February 28, 1996 (ascending node), April 1, 1997 (perihelion), and January 1, 2000. The positions of Jupiter and Earth are shown for some of these dates.

the first perihelion passage is sufficient to disperse this crust, and the comet is a much better performer at subsequent returns.

There initially was concern that Comet Hale-Bopp might be a first-time visitor from the Oort Cloud, but a prediscovery image located on a photograph taken from Siding Spring Observatory in New South Wales in April 1993, at which time the comet was 13.1 astronomical units from the Sun, soon showed that this was not the case. Orbital calculations now suggest that Hale-Bopp last visited the inner solar system some 4200 years ago.

Volatiles. The dominant volatile in the nuclei of most comets is water ice. However, the ambient temperature in the solar system is not high enough for water sublimation beyond approximately 4 astronomical units from the Sun. With Hale-Bopp being active beyond 7 astronomical units, some other volatile had to be present in sufficient quantities to drive this activity, and observations in August 1995 revealed that the activity was due to the sublimation of carbon monoxide. Once Hale-Bopp had closed to within 4 astonomical units of the Sun (in mid-1996), water sublimation became the dominant activity generator.

Brightening. As it approached the Sun and Earth, Comet Hale-Bopp brightened more or less as predicted, being close to 9th magnitude when it reap-

peared in February 1996 after solar conjunction, near 6th magnitude at midyear, and 4th magnitude near the end of 1996. In January 1997, it was visible in the morning sky and near 3d magnitude, and it brightened rapidly after that, being close to magnitude 0 by early March. Closest approach to the Earth (1.32 astronomical units) occurred on March 23 (**Fig. 1**), and thereafter Hale-Bopp was an evening sky object for the Northern Hemisphere. During late March and early April, it reached a peak brightness of −1 (**Fig. 2**) and displayed a straight ion tail and a broad, curving dust tail, both of which reached apparent lengths of approximately 20° (corresponding to true lengths of several tens of millions of kilometers) as seen from dark rural sites. (Even casual viewers in major metropolitan areas were able to enjoy good views of the comet.) After this time, it began to fade as it commenced its exit from the inner solar system, but in late July 1997 it was still a 4th-magnitude object, visible from the Southern Hemisphere.

Scientific observations. The long lead time provided by Hale-Bopp's early discovery allowed an almost unprecedented battery of scientific observations to be planned and obtained. One objective was a determination of the size of its nucleus, a task rendered difficult by the dense cloud of gas and dust that continued to enshroud it. Hubble Space Telescope

Fig. 2. Approximate naked-eye view of Comet Hale-Bopp near perihelion. The photograph was taken from Cloudcroft, New Mexico, on April 1, 1997. *(Courtesy of Alan Hale)*

precise role that comets have played in the Earth's geological and biological evolution.

Third tail. Other scientific findings include the detection of a third tail composed of sodium atoms which, based upon its structure and the chemistry that is involved, probably originated from sodium-containing molecules that separated from dust grains that had already been ejected from the icy nucleus. X-rays from the coma of Comet Hale-Bopp were detected by the *Extreme Ultraviolet Explorer* (*EUVE*) and *BeppoSAX* satellites. This phenomenon was first detected with Comet Hyakutake (a bright comet which passed near the Earth in March 1996) and has since been observed in a handful of other comets.

Future evolution. Now on its way into the outer reaches of the solar system, Hale-Bopp should re-

images obtained in October 1995 suggest a diameter of approximately 40 km (25 mi), a value which is necessarily uncertain but which would appear to be consistent with the comet's high intrinsic brightness. Another area of investigation was the rotation period of the nucleus, and this quantity remained uncertain until near the time of perihelion, when several investigators determined this period to be 11.5 h. Like Comet Halley in 1986, however, the nucleus of Hale-Bopp appears to exhibit a relatively short precessional period, with the result being a somewhat tumbling motion. Jets of material emitted from the rotating nucleus produced dramatic hoods or ripples in the inner coma, which were readily detectable in even small telescopes (**Fig. 3**).

Molecules. A wide variety of molecules were detected in the coma and nucleus of Comet Hale-Bopp, including hydrogen sulfide, methyl alcohol, formaldehyde, formic acid, formamide, methyl cyanide, and acetylene. These and other organic compounds are thought to have played a significant role in the development of life on the early Earth, and suggest that impacts by comets may have provided at least some of the materials which allowed life to begin. At the same time, recent findings suggest that the deuterium-to-hydrogen ratio in the water molecules in Comet Hale-Bopp (and a couple of other recent comets) is about twice that of the Earth's seawater, challenging the idea that Earth has received a significant amount of its water as a result of cometary impacts throughout its history. Much work thus remains to be done in attempting to understand the

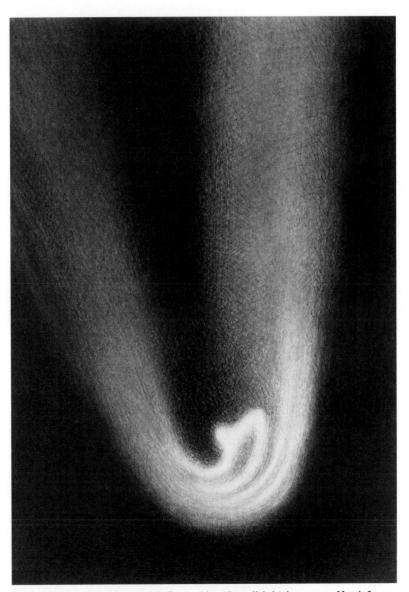

Fig. 3. Closeup view of Comet Hale-Bopp with a 15-cm (6-in.) telescope on March 9, 1997. The barred spirallike feature represents multiple dust shells emitted from the rotating nucleus of the comet. *(Drawing by Greg Mort)*

main visible in large backyard telescopes until perhaps early 1999, and in large observatory instruments for several years after that. Space-borne platforms such as the Hubble Space Telescope may be able to image the comet until about 2020 or later. Eventually it will reach its aphelion point some 355 astronomical units from the Sun, nine times the distance of Pluto, and then will begin heading sunward again. A close approach to Jupiter (0.77 astronomical unit) on its inbound leg in April 1996 shortened its orbital period to about 2390 years; thus observers around the year 4387 will have the opportunity to study and enjoy this celestial wanderer.

For background information *see* COMET in the McGraw-Hill Encyclopedia of Science & Technology.   Alan Hale

Bibliography. E. L. Aguirre, The great comet of 1997, *Sky Telesc.*, 94(1):50–57, July 1997; A. Hale, *Everybody's Comet: A Layman's Guide to Comet Hale-Bopp*, 1996; R. J. M. Olson and J. M. Pasachoff, *Fire in the Sky: Comets and Meteors, the Decisive Centuries, in Art and Science*, 1997; D. K. Yeomans, *Comets: A Chronological History of Observation, Science, Myth, and Folklore*, 1991.

Command and control

With its origins in the military, command and control may be defined as the exercise of authority and direction by a properly designated commander over assigned and attached forces in the accomplishment of a mission. Command-and-control functions are performed through an arrangement of personnel, equipment, communications, facilities, and procedures. Command and control relies heavily on communication and computer equipment.

The explosive growth in communications and computer applications in modern society simultaneously enables and necessitates the use of command-and-control systems to manage large, distributed, and complex operations. Many command-and-control concepts and practices have spread into commercial arenas, as the private sector is increasingly reliant on communications and computers to conduct business. Command and control is also critical in civilian and local government activities, such as firefighter and police dispatching.

Information management. Military command and control illustrates the general, underlying concept of information management, independent of modern (electronic) communications and computers. Before the electronic age, commands were issued and intelligence gathered by physically carrying, for example by horseback, handwritten messages. Two characteristics of command and control have remained constant: the human element and the need for relevant, timely, and accurate information. For example, during the U.S. Civil War, General Robert E. Lee relied heavily on Major General J. E. B. Stuart's cavalry unit as much for its intelligence gathering as for its fighting. Indeed, Stuart's tardy arrival at Gettysburg seriously hampered Lee's ability to assess the enemy's movements, strength, and position, because he lacked the relevant, timely, and accurate information he had come to rely on from Stuart.

The elements of modern command and control, and how they are employed, are illustrated by the life cycle of a typical military operation: planning (establishing mission needs), establishing objectives, developing courses of action, assessing courses of action, making decisions, implementing decisions (issuing commands), and determining results. This process is analogous to steps of the general systems engineering process. The systems engineering process comprises the following steps: define the problem, establish objectives, develop options, perform systems analysis, rank alternatives, and plan for action. The military adaptation adds a sizable component of communications and computer gear to implement the decisions, while the general systems engineering process steps rely more on reviews and documentation (specifications).

In the military process, intelligence gathering is stepped up and focused as a situation develops. Information gathered through various sources (human assets, space-based sensors, and so forth) is communicated up through a reporting hierarchy embedded in the command-and-control structure. At several steps, information is analyzed, interpreted, and fused with other data, and then relayed up the hierarchy through various media. Throughout this process, raw information is progressively transformed into knowledge, understanding, and ultimately a planned response.

Based on the knowledge gained during planning, objectives are established at the upper echelons of the command structure, along with multiple potential courses of action. These courses of action, themselves large collections of data, are assessed, possibly with complex computer models and simulations (war games). At the appropriate command level, a course of action is selected and the flow of information reverses from bottom-up to top-down. The top-level commands are translated, generally with much computer support, into numerous orders and are communicated down the command-and-control structure.

Military assets are assigned as appropriate to the commander in order to execute the mission (implement the decisions made above). All but the simplest of military operations involve multiple services and multiple elements within those services in an arrangement known in the business world as a matrixed organization. Hence the term control is used, because elements are assigned to (controlled by) commanders outside their chain of command.

During an engagement, military commanders may redirect the forces via new commands. The engagement is closely monitored, again using an elaborate information gathering and management system. Following the operation, the cycle begins anew as intelligence is gathered to perform battle damage assessments, and a new planning cycle ensues.

Dominant battlespace knowledge. The emerging concept of dominant battlespace knowledge involves leveraging advantages in information gathering, processing, and dissemination possessed by a nation's armed forces to gain a strategic and tactical advantage in the battlespace. If information is not effectively employed, simply possessing it is of little value. As an example, during the Persian Gulf War the concepts of smart bombs and precision or surgical strikes were publicized. Accurate and timely data are required to arm these smart weapons with the information they need for geographical positioning, identification and targeting, and precision guidance. These weapons serve as a vivid example of leveraging information dominance, employed through a command-and-control network, to achieve battlefield dominance.

Command and control provides commanders with tools needed to combat the inevitable uncertainties and confusion in battle known as the fog of war. Incorrect decisions based on faulty or incomplete information can have deadly results, so the military's command-and-control apparatus is designed to be conservative and to minimize downside risk. The systems must simultaneously support centralized planning and decentralized execution. Command and control strives to reduce the fog of war, exercise control over forces to accommodate the fog of war, exploit the enemy forces' and commanders' fog, and increase the fog for the enemy. Again, since command and control relies heavily on intelligent exploitation of relevant, timely, and accurate information, the information itself becomes a key strategic and tactical component in the war.

Information warfare. Increasingly heavy reliance on information in modern command-and-control systems entails vulnerability to attack or disruption of information systems themselves by the enemy. Well-publicized cases of computer hacking into classified military systems, as well as private and commercial systems, hint at the havoc that could be wreaked during armed conflict. Although a separate field, computer and communications security plays a crucial role in command-and-control systems. For instance, a well-placed computer virus in such a system during conflict could greatly increase the fog of war. *See* COMPUTER SECURITY AND PRIVACY.

In response to this growing threat, the U.S. Joint Chiefs of Staff has established the Information Warfare Division under the Command, Control, Communication, and Computer Systems Directorate. Service-level organizations implement the policy initiatives from the Joint Staff. The military colleges also address information warfare. In addition, the U.S. Congress has passed several laws defining, for instance, the criminality of computer fraud and abuse. Of course, the most serious threat to military information security is from outside the borders of a given country, where international legal action is typically limited and has practically no impact in a real-time sense during active conflict.

The U.S. Air Force recently created the Air and Space Command and Control Agency. Its mission is to consolidate command and control across the Air Force by integrating air and space command-and-control systems, modernizing them, and increasing commonality and interoperability of existing and planned systems. A much more complex problem is the integration and interoperability of these systems across the services to achieve joint command-and-control systems, doctrines, and procedures. The services tend to compete rather than cooperate on major systems acquisitions. To avoid parochial systems with limited interoperability, the United States military is building a large Global Command and Control System to provide an integrated, joint command-and-control capability around the world.

Commercial applications. Many large commercial enterprises, particularly those involved in logistical activities (such as transportation, distribution, and scheduling), employ command-and-control systems similar to those in the military. An example is the United Parcel Service (UPS), the world's largest package distribution company, transporting over 3.1 billion parcels and documents annually and utilizing over 500 aircraft, 147,000 vehicles, and 2400 facilities in 200 countries. Completely analogous with military planning, UPS conducts both long-range and short-range planning (establishing mission needs and objectives), develops and executes daily plans through a complex system of computers and communications (developing and assessing courses of action, making decisions, and implementing them), and measures on-time delivery and customer feedback (determining results).

As with military command and control, UPS relies on centralized planning and decentralized execution. For example, the UPS Airline operation relies on the Computerized Operations Monitoring, Planning, and Scheduling System (COMPASS), an automated scheduling and decision aid supporting flight planning, scheduling (deliveries and crew), and load handling. Having a more predictable mission, commercial enterprises such as UPS are generally more concerned with optimization, whereas military planning is more concerned with mission accomplishment. However, both activities rely heavily on command-and-control systems supported by computers and communications. Also, both military and commercial command-and-control systems are fueled by information gathering, management, and intelligent utilization.

A final example of nonmilitary command and control, on a worldwide basis, is the international environmental concern related to global warming. A policy objective is to control greenhouse gas emissions, which some scientists say cause global warming. The country-by-country restrictions mandated (commanded) by international treaty and controlled by monitoring and enforcement organizations constitute a very slow, diffuse command-and-control process.

For background information *see* COMPUTER SECURITY; ELECTRONIC WARFARE; SYSTEMS ENGINEERING in the McGraw-Hill Encyclopedia of Science & Technology.   Maurice A. Roesch III; John F. King

Bibliography. S. E. Johnson and M. C. Libicki (eds.), *Dominant Battlespace Knowledge*, 1996; National Research Council, *Star 21: Strategic Technologies for the Army of the 21ˢᵗ Century*, 1992; U.S. Joint Chiefs of Staff, *Information Warfare, Legal, Regulatory, Policy, and Organizational Considerations for Assurance*, 1995.

Communications

Over the past century the technological means of communication have expanded to include the telegraph, telephone, facsimile machine, data modem, and the Internet. The modalities of communication have also expanded to include the transmission of voice, data, document images, graphics, and video. Meanwhile, the computer has evolved from a device suitable for large computations, to a manipulator of large bodies of information (enabled by mass-storage technologies), and then to a tool for communications (enabled by computer networking). Looking to the future, depending on the perspective chosen, there will be a strong trend toward incorporating communications as an integral part of computing applications, or incorporating information access and manipulation as an integral part of communications applications.

Integrated media. Recently, the infrastructure for both communications and computing has enabled integrated media, in which voice, audio, images, video, and data can coexist within the same network and be manipulated within the same networked desktop computer in real time. This capability enables multimedia applications, those that mix different media such as data, audio, and video. Thus, both telecommunications networks and desktop computers now support a full range of applications, including computation, information access, and communications. More significantly, integrated media allow these modalities to be mixed freely within the same application.

Horizontal, layered model. The communications portion of this infrastructure, like computing before it, is evolving from a vertical model (which dedicates an infrastructure to each of data, voice, and video communications) to a horizontal, three-layered model comprising applications (top), services, and bitways (bottom). An application may be defined as a collection of functionality that provides direct value to a user (a person). The applications relevant to this discussion are networked applications, implying that they are distributed across a distributed telecommunications and computing environment. Examples are electronic mail, telephony, database access, file transfer, World Wide Web browsing, and video conferencing. A service is functionality of a generic or supportive nature, provided as a part of a computing and telecommunications infrastructure, that is available for use in building any application. Examples include audio or video transport, file-system management, printing, electronic payment mechanisms, encryption and key distribution, and reliable data delivery. Bitways are network mechanisms for transporting bits from one location to another. Examples of bitways with sufficient flexibility for integrated multimedia applications are asynchronous transfer mode (ATM) networks, or internets interfaced with the Internet Protocol (IP).

By design, bitways should not be cognizant of the significance of the bits they transport, but only of quality-of-service parameters, such as the reliability and delay with which they deliver bits. Bitways also need to be configurable as to both bit rate and quality of service if they are to properly support integrated media and the full range of applications. Also by design, services should be configurable to support a wide range of applications with different quality parameters, such as audio bandwidth, video resolution, and subjective quality (as interpreted by the user), so that they can satisfy different user needs with regard to price and quality.

A horizontal, layered architecture strongly encourages a diversity of applications, since new applications can be deployed to a mostly existing infrastructure with low incremental effort and cost. Increasingly, applications are defined by software that is executed on programmable terminals (such as desktop computers and even hand-held devices), and as a result can be transported over the bitway itself. Such software is called mobile code, and will become increasingly common.

Taxonomy of networked applications. A taxonomy of networked applications can be constructed, with four categories (see **table**). Each user in a networked application interacts with a local terminal, which communicates in turn with remote terminals at the other edge of the network, as well as with servers (computers not associated directly with users). One classification of applications comprises user-to-user and user-to-information-server. In user-to-user applications, two (or more) users each participate in some shared functionality. This arrangement supports remote collaboration among users. In user-to-information-server applications, a user (or sometimes two or more users) interacts with a remote system in order to access, receive, or interact with information stored on that system. Increasingly, applications will combine these two modes, as it is natural to include

Taxonomy of networked applications with examples		
Category	Immediate	Deferred
User-to-information-server	Video on demand World Wide Web browsing	File transfer
User-to-user	Telephony Video conferencing	Electronic mail Voice mail

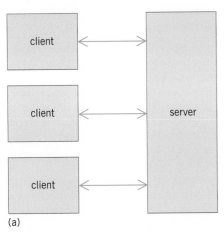

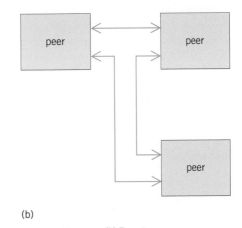

(a) (b)

Fig. 1. Comparison of architectures for networked applications. (*a*) Client-server architecture. (*b*) Peer-to-peer architecture.

information access in a collaborative application, and collaboration with information access.

There are also two observable temporal relationships in the interaction of the user with a server or with another user, namely, immediate and deferred. In immediate applications, a user interacts with a server or another user in real time, typically with requirements on the maximum latency or delay. Examples include telephony, video conferencing, and World Wide Web browsing.

Deferred applications are those in which a user interacts with another user or a server in a manner that implies no fixed temporal relationship and for which the delay is typically not critical. Examples include electronic mail and voice mail.

Architectures for networked services. Networked applications are realized by adding functionality (either permanently or by mobile code) to terminal nodes (often simply called terminals) interconnected by the bitway. Two basic architectures are common for networked services, namely, peer-to-peer and client-server (**Fig. 1**).

In peer-to-peer architecture, two (or more) peer terminals, each associated with a local user, communicate directly over a bitway to provide a user-to-user networked application. The common telephone is a peer, as is a facsimile machine or a desktop computer providing networked telephony. This architecture is almost ubiquitous in traditional telecommunications.

In client-server architecture, a client terminal associated with a user communicates over the bitway with a server computer, which is not associated directly with a user but realizes an information-server function. Examples of this architecture include the World Wide Web server and many other traditional distributed computing applications.

Often the peer-to-peer or client-terminal functions will be realized in software in a desktop computer, or they may be realized in dedicated-function terminals (such as a telephone or video conference set), also known as information appliances. The distinction

between terminal and bitway is primarily a physical partitioning of functionality between a terminal at the edges of the bitway and the bitway itself. The horizontal, three-level architecture discussed above is a logical separation of functionality, where application software will typically be executed in the terminals, and services in terminals or servers. Especially with mobile code, there is considerable freedom as to where each software function executes, depending on performance parameters such as interactive delay and available processing power.

A user-to-information-server application is usually realized with the client-server architecture, but a user-to-user application can be realized in either the peer-to-peer or client-server architecture. In the latter case, the two clients communicate through the server, which may realize additional applications or control functionality. The client-server architecture is particularly appropriate for deferred user-to-user applications, since the server provides a convenient location to carry out the necessary buffering, with guaranteed availability.

Sophisticated multimedia applications will increasingly mix these application types and architectural models. Typical collaborative applications will combine user-to-user and user-to-information-server functionality, as in a collaborative design involving two or more users and a common information server (**Fig. 2**).

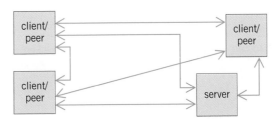

Fig. 2. Example of a networked application that combines user-to-user and user-to-information-server functionality in a mixed peer-to-peer and client-server architecture.

Advantages of mobile code. All client/peer and server terminals or hosts can include repositories of mobile code that can be opportunistically provided to other terminals or servers. This arrangement ensures interoperability, and it yields the flexibility that allows computations to be carried out at whatever location results in the best responsiveness and lowest latency, and wherever the needed data can be accessed.

Mobile code has a more subtle but very important impact in this environment. An obstacle to establishing new user-to-user applications has been network externalities, an economics term referring to the limited value that early adopters of such applications derive from them because of the paucity of other participants in the application. If the application code can be opportunistically transported to another user and executed there, this obstacle is removed.

Integration of communications and computing. Before computers became tools for communications, telecommunications and computing shared many common technologies, but were distinguished in two primary ways. First, telecommunications focused on immediate user-to-user applications (principally telephony and facsimile), while computing focused on initially stand-alone and subsequently deferred user-to-user and immediate user-to-information-server applications, each on dedicated and separate infrastructures. Second, telecommunications focused on continuous media such as audio and video, while computing focused on computation and information storage, retrieval, and manipulation. These distinctions are no longer useful, because all applications and media will share an integrated-media, horizontal, layered infrastructure; and because, largely as a result of this infrastructure, networked applications will increasingly combine user-to-user and user-to-information-server elements. Mobile code will make this integration much easier, especially by making opportunistic user-to-user collaboration components available to applications without the obstacles of network externalities. As a result, collaborative features can be expected in an increasing number of distributed applications.

For background information *see* COMPUTER SYSTEMS ARCHITECTURE; DATA COMMUNICATIONS; DIGITAL COMPUTER; ELECTRICAL COMMUNICATIONS; ELECTRONIC MAIL; INTEGRATED SERVICES DIGITAL NETWORK (ISDN); LOCAL-AREA NETWORKS; MULTIMEDIA TECHNOLOGY; TELECOMMUNICATIONS; TELEPHONE SERVICE; TELEPROCESSING; WIDE-AREA NETWORKS in the McGraw-Hill Encyclopedia of Science & Technology.

David G. Messerschmitt

Bibliography. D. G. Messerschmitt, The convergence of telecommunications and computing: What are the implications today?, *Proc. IEEE*, 84:1167–1186, 1996; D. G. Messerschmitt, The future of computer telecommunications integration, *IEEE Commun. Mag.*, 34(4):66–69, April 1996; National Academy of Sciences, *Realizing the Information Future: The Internet and Beyond*, 1994; National Academy of Sciences, *The Unpredictable Certainty: Information Infrastructure Through 2000*, 1996.

Communications platform

There are four general telecommunications architectures that can deliver broadband wireless local-loop service to consumers. Two of these architectures are space based: geostationary satellites and nongeostationary satellites. The other two are considered terrestrial: rooftop cellularlike millimeter-wave repeaters and stratospheric relay platforms. *See* RADIO COMMUNICATIONS.

Considerations of intrinsic geometry and hardware engineering lead to the conclusion that the greatest amount of communications capacity over metropolitan areas, for an equivalent investment in equipment and bandwidth, will come from the stratospheric architecture. Accordingly, the greatest amount of broadband Internet capacity for the lowest cost can be provided to consumers via stratospheric telecommunications. Stratospheric platforms have some of the best attributes of satellite systems, such as wide-area coverage, and some of the best attributes of millimeter-wave repeaters, such as short path lengths.

Stratosphere. The Earth's atmosphere is divided into four major layers or shells: the troposphere, stratosphere, mesosphere, and ionosphere. Humans live in the troposphere, the lowest layer. It is characterized by the presence of weather and decreasing temperature with increasing altitude. The stratosphere begins at an altitude of approximately 12 mi (20 km) and extends to 31 mi (50 km). This region is characterized by a lack of weather and increasing temperature with increasing altitude.

Only a few planes, such as the Concorde or the Lockheed SR71, can fly in the stratosphere because the air is so thin there. The stratosphere is also beyond the 12-mi (20-km) limit, and hence above controlled airspace for commercial and military aircraft.

Recently, there has been increased interest in the stratosphere by environmental scientists. The National Aeronautics and Space Administration (NASA) has been flying a modified SR71 through the stratosphere, taking on-site atmospheric measurements in support of studying the greenhouse effect and the ozone layer. High-altitude, crewless drones are also being prepared to monitor coral reef degradation and deforestation around the island of Kauai, Hawaii, from the stratosphere.

Stratospheric infrastructure. The technology now exists to set up a stratospheric platform by providing a low-drag airship with adequate propulsion power to maintain a stationary position against winds aloft that range from under 22 mi/h (10 m/s) in the summer to over 110 mi/h (50 m/s) in the winter. The airship would have a multilayer skin containing buoyant helium-filled cells. A station-keeping system, a telecommunications payload, integrated solar arrays for daytime power, and fuel cells for nighttime power would be aboard the platform. The platform would be at an altitude of approximately 14 mi (23 km), above the weather and above controlled airspace. Numerous studies have demonstrated a mini-

TABLE 1. Stratospheric platform parameters (of an example system)

Parameter	Customary units	Metric units
Operating altitude	14 mi	23 km
Lift at altitude	0.0039 lb/ft^3	0.062 kg/m^3
Hull volume	6,000,000 ft^3	170,000 m^3
Gross lift at altitude	11.5 tons	10.5 metric tons
Hull area	270,000 ft^2	25,000 m^2
Envelope weight	12,407 lb	5628 kg
Payload	10,829 lb	4912 kg
Engine force	225 lbf	1000 newtons

mum in the wind speed at this altitude. Baseline platform characteristics of an example system are provided in **Table 1**.

Although stratospheric platforms are an old idea, they only recently have become practical through the invention of station-keeping technologies. The enabling technologies are high-efficiency propulsion systems for station keeping, the Global Positioning System (GPS) for accurate position keeping, and ultrathin fabric hulls for long-duration buoyancy.

A global network of stratospheric platforms is deployed in a population-based manner instead of the orbital dynamics-based spacing of low-Earth-orbit satellites. Gateway earth stations, located in each coverage area, connect each stratospheric platform to the public telephone network. Portable and fixed communication devices are used to send and receive digital information via the stratospheric platforms and gateway earth stations.

Stratospheric stations remain stationary because of the use of high-efficiency propulsion systems to counteract winds for accurate station keeping. Solar-power panels able to produce 200 W/kg are currently available. Approximately 1000 kg of solar panels can produce adequate power to keep a stratospheric platform stationary. Such a mass requirement represents only 20% of the payload capacity listed in Table 1. Newer-technology solar panels, with efficiencies of 300 W/kg or more, will allow even greater percentages of stratospheric payloads to be devoted to communications equipment.

From the stratosphere, communication links with high angles of elevation can be established across large land areas. For example, at 14-mi (23-km) altitude, links with angles of elevation of 30° extend to a radial distance of 25 mi (40 km) from the center of coverage. Throughout any urban area centered around a stratospheric platform, the angles of elevation exceed 50–60°. Each stratospheric platform will limit its service to one country, except for cities located near border areas.

Longevity and safety. Current airship skin materials virtually eliminate helium leakage, and double layering effectively precludes leakage through inadvertently manufactured micropores. The principal factor that limits longevity is now power production losses brought about by ultraviolet degradation of solar-cell efficiency, cumulative losses in the regener-

ative fuel-cell system, or mechanical fatigue. Airships are being designed for multiyear lives between refurbishment of a preexisting platform.

Safety concerns are manageable since the technology of bringing airships down in a controlled landing has been perfected over the past 50 years. The stratospheric platforms operate above controlled airspace except during ascent and descent, which will occur at a remote location. Airship fabric is tear resistant, and small pinholes do not pose a danger of rapid decompression.

Broadband wireless capacity. If the bandwidth, antenna aperture, power, and other technical factors are held constant, the metropolitan capacity of a telecommunications system is proportional to the number of spot beams with high elevation angles that the system provides. At low elevation angles between transmitter-receiver pairs, most capacity is lost to ground clutter. A single building-top repeater can generate at most six spot beams using a 60° sectorial antenna. The angles of elevation of these beams become too low within a distance of 2–3 mi (3–5 km). At the other end of the continuum, a geostationary satellite cannot generate more than one spot beam per metropolitan area using typical advanced-technology antenna apertures of 16 ft (5 m) at 20/30 GHz. However, a single stratospheric telecommunications platform at 13 mi (21 km) altitude can generate approximately 700–1000 spot beams within a single metropolitan area, whereas a nongeostationary satellite at 300 mi (500 km) altitude would generate only six to nine spot beams out to 60 mi (100 km) from the center of a metropolitan area. The stratospheric architecture thus yields approximately 100 times greater metropolitan-area capacity than the nongeostationary satellite orbit architecture (**Table 2**).

High- and low-density architectures. Stratospheric and other broadband systems can be differentiated into high-density and low-density architectures. All space systems (geostationary and networked nongeostationary) are low-density architectures. They do an excellent job of providing some bandwidth everywhere, but cannot compete with terrestrial architectures in providing maximum capacity in metropolitan areas. Stratospheric and ground-based millimeter-wave systems are high-density architectures. These designs excel at delivering metro-

TABLE 2. Broadband capacity in metropolitan areas

Technology	Urban capacity	Angle of elevation
Terrestrial wireless	6 spot beams per tower	Low
Stratospheric platform	700 spot beams per city	High
Low-Earth-orbit network	6 spot beams per city	High
Geostationary-Earth-orbit satellite	Fractional spot beam per city	Low

politan consumers the greatest value in terms of cost per unit bandwidth, but are not cost effective when it comes to rural service.

In planning for national broadband networks, it is wise to consider the complementary capabilities of high- and low-density system architectures. The best mix of service appears to come from layering a space-based system for rural low-density broadband service with a stratospheric system for metropolitan high-density broadband service. In addition, ground-based millimeter-wave equipment should be considered for ultrahigh-reliability links in either metropolitan or rural geographic areas.

It is important not to confuse low-density market segments with developing parts of the world. Indeed, most of the world's rapid metropolitan growth is expected to come from the developing world. The developing world's megacities, such as Cairo, Lagos, Jakarta, and Bombay, are high-density market segments which need terrestrial and stratospheric architectures in order to ensure mass access to the broadband channels essential to rapid economic development.

For background information *see* AIRSHIP; ATMO-SPHERE; COMMUNICATIONS SATELLITE; MOBILE RADIO; SO-LAR CELL in the McGraw-Hill Encyclopedia of Science & Technology.　　　　Martine A. Rothblatt

Bibliography. Federal Communications Commission, *Second Report and Order*, FCC 97–153, July 21, 1997; Y. C. Lee and M. Rothblatt, Stratospheric telecommunications service: An opportunity to close the information gap, *ITU News*, pp. 25–29, 1997; M. Lewyn, Space case, *Wired*, pp. 112–116, September 1996.

Compact disk

The compact disk digital audio (CD-DA) format is an optical disk media system for storing binary data. It was originally developed as a music carrier providing high fidelity, random access, convenience, durability, and low cost. Subsequently, the compact disk format was extended to include the CD-ROM (read-only memory) format for computer applications. Newer formats that use the compact disk as their basis include the recordable CD-R and CD-RW formats, and the multimedia DVD format.

CD-R. The CD-R (recordable) format allows users to record audio or other digital data on a compact disk; it is also called the CD-WO (write-once) format. The recording is permanent and may be read indefinitely, but cannot be erased. CD-R disks with up to 74 min (or about 650 megabytes) of playing time are available. A recording is complete when a lead-in area (with table of contents), user data, and lead-out area have been written.

CD-R disks are built on a polycarbonate substrate and contain a reflective layer and a protective top layer. Sandwiched between the substrate and the reflective layer is a recording layer composed of an organic dye polymer, generally either cyanine or phthalocyanine. To achieve appropriate reflectivity, a gold reflective layer must be used. Unlike regular compact disks, CD-R disks are manufactured with a pregrooved track, which is used to guide the recording laser. This practice simplifies recorder hardware design and promotes disk compatibility. The organic dye recording layer is a photoabsorption surface that absorbs energy from the recording laser as heat. The laser passes through the polycarbonate substrate and heats this layer, causing the substrate layer to expand into the absorption layer and mix with the dye materials there. The polycarbonate mixed with dye, which has been decomposed from the heat, acts to form a pit in the substrate. These pits create the change in reflectivity required by compact disk player pickups. During readout, the same laser, reduced in power, is reflected from the pits and its changing intensity is monitored. In this way, CD-R disks can be played in most CD-DA and CD-ROM drives.

CD-RW. The CD-RW (rewritable) format allows data to be written, read, and rewritten. A CD-RW drive can read, write, and erase CD-RW media, read and write CD-R media, and read CD-DA and CD-ROM media. The data can comprise computer programs, text, pictures, video files, or audio files. Altogether, five layers are built on a transparent polycarbonate substrate: a dielectric layer, a recording layer, another dielectric layer, a reflective aluminum layer, and a top acrylic protective layer. As in the CD-R, the writing and reading laser follows a pregroove across the disk radius. However, whereas the CD-R uses a dye recording layer, the CD-RW format employs a phase-change mechanism. The recording layer is composed of an alloy of silver, indium, antimony, and tellurium, which exhibits a reversible crystalline-amorphous phase change when recorded at one temperature and erased at another. Data are recorded by directing a laser to heat an area of the crystalline layer to a temperature slightly above its melting point. When the area solidifies, it becomes amorphous, and the decreased change in reflectivity can be detected. Because the crystalline form is more stable, the material will tend to change back to this form. Thus, when the area is heated again (at a slightly lower laser power), it will return to a crystalline state, providing rewritability. A very low power laser is used to read data.

This phase-change recording technology allows thousands of rewrite cycles. The disk capacity is 650 megabytes. Since the reflectivity of CD-RW disks is only about 15 and 25% in the amorphous and crystalline states respectively, they cannot be played in conventional compact disk players. A CD-RW drive is required, or one of the recently introduced CD-ROM drives capable of reading lower-reflectivity disks. The CD-UDF (universal disk format) specification modifies the CD Red Book file format so that nonaudio data can be written in data packets. With CD-UDF–compliant drives, CD-R and CD-RW disks can be used in a personal-computer environment much like other storage media; in addition to audio recording, nonaudio data files can be dragged and dropped from the personal computer to disk storage.

DVD. The DVD (digital video disk or digital versatile disk) standard includes formats for video, audio, and computer applications. DVD-video was the first DVD format to be developed. One disk digitally stores a complete feature film with digital audio sound tracks. As with the compact disk, DVD-video uses a pit-and-land structure to store data. The track pitch is 0.74 micrometer, compared to 1.6 μm on a compact disk. The pits and lands are as short as 0.4 μm, compared to 0.83 μm on a compact disk. These reduced dimensions are possible because the laser beam uses a visible red wavelength of 635 or 650 nanometers, compared with 780 nm in a compact disk. The standard specifies a lens with a numerical aperture of 0.6, compared with 0.45 in the compact disk standard. These specifications provide a large storage capacity.

Data storage. A DVD-video disk is the same diameter (120 mm or 4.75 in.) and thickness (1.2 mm or 0.05 in.) as a compact disk. Whereas a compact disk uses a single polycarbonate substrate, a DVD-video disk employs two 0.6-mm substrates, bonded together, with the data layers placed near the internal interface.

A single-layer, single-sided DVD-video disk uses one substrate with a data surface, and one blank substrate; the disk holds 4.7 gigabytes of data. Two substrates with data surfaces can be bonded together to form a single-layer, double-sided disk holding 9.4 gigabytes of data; the disk is turned over to access the opposite layer.

The DVD-video standard also allows data to be placed on two layers in a substrate, one embedded beneath the other to create a dual-layer disk that is read from one side. The layers are separated by a semitransparent (semireflective) metal layer. Both layers can be read from one side by focusing the reading laser on either layer. The beam either reflects from the lower semireflective layer or passes through it and reflects from the top reflective layer. Together, the dual layers hold 8.5 gigabytes of data. The DVD-video standard allows for a double-sided, double-layer disk, in which two dual-layer substrates are bonded together, creating a capacity of 17 gigabytes.

Data compression. A motion picture may comprise 200 gigabytes of data; to fit this program on a single disk, data reduction must be employed. The DVD-video standard uses the MPEG-2 (Motion Picture Experts Group-2) algorithm to encode its video program. Image data that are redundant, not perceived, or marginally perceived are removed. This analysis is carried out for both individual video frames and series of frames. MPEG-2 allows for a variable bit rate. Simple pictures are given a low bit rate, and complex pictures a high bit rate. The maximum output bit rate is 10.08 megabits per second, and the average bit rate is about 3.5 megabits per second, in contrast to the compact disk's fixed rate of 1.41 megabits per second. With MPEG-2, a single-layer DVD-video disk can store up to 133 min of high-quality digital video with digital audio sound tracks; longer motion pictures can use the dual-layer disk design. The video program is stored at 4:2:0 component video; 4:2:0 refers to the ratios of frequencies used to record the different video components (one luminance and two color-difference), and the luminance and color-difference data are kept separate for higher fidelity. *See* TELEVISION.

Audio. The audio portion of the DVD-video standard provides both multichannel and stereo sound tracks. DVD-video disks can accommodate three independent 5.1-channel sound tracks, each with five main channels and a low-frequency effects channel. The DVD-video standard recognizes two multichannel formats. In one, the sampling frequency is 48 kHz, and the normal output bit rate is 384 kilobits per second. Disks also carry linear pulse-code-modulation (PCM) digital stereo sound tracks employing sampling rates of either 48 or 96 kHz, and word lengths of 16, 20, or 24 bits. Up to eight independent pulse-code-modulation channels are permitted.

Features. A DVD-video player is connected to a home theater system and can also play CD-DA disks. DVD-video disks cannot be played in compact disk players. The DVD-video standard provides features such as normal (4:3) and wide-screen (16:9) aspect ratios, an automatic pan-scan feature, up to nine camera angles and interactive story lines, up to eight language tracks, and up to 32 sets of subtitles. These features are options, and implementation is left to the content provider. The DVD-video format also uses copy protection to prevent digital or analog dubbing of disks. Disks and players are tagged with regional flags so that players will play only disks intended for certain geographical markets.

Formats. In addition to the DVD-video format (formally known as Book B), the DVD family includes DVD-read only (Book A), DVD-audio (Book C), DVD-write once (Book D), and DVD-rewritable (Book E). The DVD format uses the Universal Disk Format (UDF) file structure. The DVD-audio format will be used to store high-quality multichannel music programs. The other DVD formats are employed in computer applications; Books A and E are often called DVD-ROM and DVD-RAM (random access memory), respectively. In its initial implementation, a DVD-RAM disk with phase-change technology holds 2.6 gigabytes per side. DVD-ROM and DVD-RAM drives are connected to personal computers, and function much like CD-ROM drives.

Other optical disk formats are under development, many of them providing greater capacity and performance. The compact disk and the DVD will further integrate the audio and video industry with the computer industry, acting as a driving force toward their convergence.

For background information *see* COMPACT DISK; COMPUTER STORAGE TECHNOLOGY; DATA COMPRESSION; OPTICAL RECORDING in the McGraw-Hill Encyclopedia of Science & Technology.   Ken C. Pohlmann

Bibliography. A. E. Bell, Next-generation compact disks, *Sci. Amer.*, 275(1):28–32, July 1996; K. Pohlmann, *The Compact Disk Handbook*, 1992; K. Pohlmann, *Principles of Digital Audio*, 1995.

Computer security and privacy

In an information system the goal of computer security is to provide computer-system components that exhibit accuracy, availability, and confidentiality. Such computer systems must be developed, implemented, and operated with a combination of managerial, operational, and technical components. A computer system cannot provide adequate service if any component is inappropriate to the user requirements.

The managerial component of security in computer systems is centered on the statement of security policy goals and the monitoring of compliance to these goals. The critical elements of computer security policy are the avoidance of unnecessary risks, the deterrence of behaviors which place computer systems at risk, the detection of detrimental acts on or with the computer components of an information system, and the correction of system components in response to actual or potential detrimental acts.

Definitions. The protection of data in a computer is essential to security. Database security is the protection of data against unauthorized disclosure, alteration, or destruction. Database security mechanisms strive to ensure privacy of data in computer systems. Privacy is a broad term defining all the legal and ethical aspects of personal data systems, that is, systems that contain information about specific individuals. Authorization is the specification of rules about who has what type of access to what data. The data owner determines access rules for the users of the data. Protection refers to the absolute systems that control access to executing programs on stored data. System integrity is the ability of a system to operate according to specifications in spite of deliberate attempts to make programs behave differently. Integrity also is applied to data and to the mechanisms that help ensure stability. Access control is the process of ensuring that data and other protected objects are accessed only in authorized ways. Internal resolution controls the actions performed on the data once programs have access. Dataflow control prevents security leakage as data flows through the communication subsystems. Semantic integrity is concerned with the correctness of data structures in the presence of user modifications.

Evaluation and risk assessment. In an effort to determine how much cost in time, equipment, training, and operational constraints is appropriate for a given computer system, management has the responsibility to evaluate the data in the system, the threats against the system, and the cost of countermeasures to those threats. Only with such analysis can appropriate levels of protection for a computer system be determined.

Computer systems exist to store and process data for the user. The most valuable component of a computer system should be the data in that system. Evaluating data may involve quantifying the competitive edge provided by owning the data set. Certain data obtain value in that the data must be kept confidential for ethical or legal reasons. Data may have quantifiable value derived through the cost involved in obtaining or replacing the data. Data that are disclosed improperly or data that are used to commit fraud raise issues of liability for the owner.

The data owner has the responsibility of acknowledging ownership of the data, authorizing criteria for access to the data, understanding and approving controls on access to and storage of the data, and monitoring compliance with these criteria. The implementation of the owner responsibilities may involve applying both procedural and technical controls to the computer system. The owner must balance the need for control of the data with the cost of implementing security practices in both economic and human terms. This balance is achieved through applying the principles of risk assessment to the evaluation process. Risk assessment provides a means of justifying the implementation and controls to provide assurance against unacceptable risk and to assess compliance with regulation, laws, and corporate policy. Risk assessment should identify vulnerabilities of the computer system and determine the likelihood that they will be exploited.

Access control. Access to the computer system must be controlled both physically and logically.

Physical access. Physical access to the computer system means the access to input devices such as terminals, keyboards, communication lines, and disk drives. Where access must be monitored closely, employees are required to wear identification cards at all times. Physical controls might include the removal of outside knob hardware on all doors on the perimeter of the installation that are not to be used as emergency exit points, installation of panic-door opening hardware on all interior doors in place of knobs, attachment of audible exit alarms to all emergency doors, and control of the locks to rooms and devices with smart cards or biometric devices.

Logical access. Logical access to the computer system may be controlled and monitored through the use of auditing software. Security audit trails should be available to track and identify users who update sensitive information files. If the sensitivity of information stored on networked microcomputers requires audit trails, the host computer, not the terminal, is where the audit trails should be located. Auditing software should not be switched off to improve processing speed. Audit-trail printouts should be reviewed regularly.

Logical access to computer systems is often controlled through the use of identification systems and password systems. Users must identify themselves to the computer with some quantity known only to the system and the user. This is accomplished by using something that the user is (via biometrics), something the user has (smart card), or something the user knows (a password). These techniques demand that the computer have some method of storing securely the data necessary to identify each user. Each of these techniques has implementation difficulties and can be defeated. Access to networked and communicating computers is now also controlled by firewall approaches.

Firewalls. The firewall approach to restricting access to computer systems requires that the computer system be isolated from other computer systems or networks except for a communication channel that is under the control of a firewall. The firewall is a suite of hardware and software devices that monitor communication traffic into and out of the system it guards. The firewall is programmed to accept only traffic that meets criteria determined by the system owner. Often such criteria are based on a list of permitted addresses for incoming and outgoing message traffic. The firewall program must know both the sender and the receiver of a transmission to permit its passage. The firewall separates the inside and the outside computer world. Work is under way on incorporating many other parameters into the firewall suite to improve its functioning.

A fundamental flaw in firewalls is that the internal system must be completely isolated from the nonsystem components. Computer communication devices are now so inexpensive and so readily available that users of large systems often invalidate the firewall concept by establishing their own communications without passing through the firewall.

Software security. The protection of the internal computer system may rely heavily on software security. Software security can be defined as the protection of data and programs in a computer system through the use of special-purpose computer programs. There are three major categories of software security programs: Certain programs protect systems by detecting suspicious program sequences; computer virus checkers are of this type. Certain computer programs and program functions protect data with in-line routines; programs that ask the user for permission to write over an existing file or data element are of this type. Certain programs protect systems by maintaining internal checks on data consistency; programs that perform range checks are of this type.

Cryptography. Cryptography is the manipulation of data by some technique that results in the data being transformed into patterns not recognizable, while maintaining the ability to reverse the transformation process. Modern cryptographic techniques rely on mathematical manipulation of data controlled by a key value. Cryptographic programs allow knowledge of the algorithm, but without possession of the key value the algorithm provides no aid in the decryption of data. Cryptographic programs and hardware are strictly controlled by most governments.

In symmetric cryptosystems, the most pervasive, only one key exists that will allow the message to be solved. The safeguarding of keys is a major vulnerability of such encryption systems. Although the unauthorized disclosure of a key may be devastating to an organization, the loss of a key to the organization itself is more common and is also devastating. Data stored in an encrypted form have greatly enhanced security, but subject to the perils of key unrecoverability.

Public-key cryptography is a system to solve the distribution or sharing of keys between the message sender and the recipient. The public-key system suffers from major flaws: By design, the system relies on large prime numbers, creating transmission distribution difficulties. The implementation of the system, as illustrated in the RSA system developed by R. L. Rivest, A. Shamir, and L. Adleman, results in relatively slow encryption and decryption. Digital signatures are derived from other encryption systems, often the RSA system, and are used to verify the message originator. Using the public-key–private-key protocol, senders use their private keys to encrypt their signatures and these signatures can be verified only with the use of the corresponding public key. The implementation of these key-exchange protocols often relies on a "trusted" third party. Finding acceptable trusted parties has been a great difficulty in implementing strong key-based cryptographic systems.

Data protection techniques. Techniques implemented in data protection including performing such activities as audit programs to record changes made to data, logs of access to data, user authentication, maintaining checks that data values are within permissible ranges, and transition constraints. The proper control of data involves considering the cost effectiveness of the techniques employed in terms of economic and people costs. People costs include considering the effectiveness of data restrictions when balanced against the need of the user to employ the computer systems and the level of difficulty introduced into the operation by these security restrictions.

Configuration management. Computer security involves control over both the physical and logical components of the computer system. This area of computer security is known as configuration management. Configuration management involves identifying hardware and software components of the computer system, controlling changes to the systems, accounting for the operational status of systems components, and auditing any changes to the systems hardware and software components.

For background information *see* COMPUTER SECURITY; CRYPTOGRAPHY; RISK ANALYSIS in the McGraw-Hill Encyclopedia of Science & Technology.

John R. Cordani

Bibliography. E. Amorous, *Fundamentals of Computer Security Technology*, 1994; M. E. Kabay, *The NCSA Guide to Enterprise Security: Protecting Information Assets*, 1996; *Proceedings of the 19th*

National Information Systems Security Conference, Baltimore, MD, October, 1996; Proceedings of the 20th National Information Systems Security Conference, Baltimore, MD, October, 1997.

Computer storage

Once considered novelties, small, portable pen-based computers (sometimes called personal digital assistants or PDAs) are growing in popularity, fueled by the demands of an increasingly mobile information society. This situation is the direct result of advances in component miniaturization, improvements in user interface design, and progress in pattern recognition research.

As an input device, the pen has numerous advantages over a keyboard, beyond the familiarity gained from conventional ink pens. For languages such as Chinese which have thousands of characters in everyday use, keyboards are complicated devices accessible only to highly trained specialists. Even in the case of the Latin alphabet, the keyboard becomes a limiting factor as notebook computers continue to shrink in size. Moreover, some people just find a keyboard intimidating.

This migration to pen computers for many day-to-day activities also opens up the possibility of another shift: from character-based information systems to those that treat electronic ink as first-class data.

Pen-based computing. In a pen-based computer, the user writes on a digitizing surface with a stylus. The surface may be a passive graphics tablet, or a transparent digitizer overlaying an active flat-panel display. The trajectory of the pen tip is sampled over time and transmitted to the host system as a sequence of points specified by their cartesian (x and y) coordinates. This sampling must be fast enough to capture the shape of the ink; 100 samples per second is usually sufficient. It is not necessary that the sampling take place at a constant rate. (Indeed, the ink is often resampled during a later normalization step anyway.)

To provide feedback to the user, a two-dimensional bitmap must be created in real time to display the ink. This is a simple mapping process from the point data to the screen memory (**Fig. 1**). However, these two representations are fundamentally different. The point sequence is dynamic, since it contains the points in the order in which they were drawn, whereas the bitmap is static, since it simply shows the final result. Certain useful information, such as precisely when a letter "i" was dotted, is present in the point sequence but absent in the bitmap. This distinction becomes important in the search of a database of previously stored ink.

Traditionally, the next step is to apply handwriting recognition to translate the input ink into a predefined character set. In the case of English, for example, the American Standard Code for Information Interchange (ASCII) serves as the standard. This set consists of 128 characters including the upper- and lowercase letters, digits, punctuation, and control codes. The range of allowable inputs is constrained by what can be represented in the underlying character set. *See* COMPUTERIZED DOCUMENT ANALYSIS.

For the most part, today's pen computers operate in a mode which might be described as eager recognition. Pen strokes are translated as soon as they are entered, the user corrects the output of the recognizer, and then processing occurs as if the characters had been typed on a keyboard. Chief among the advantages is that existing techniques can be used for storing and searching the data. Hence, few changes need to be made to the underlying system software.

The technology of handwriting recognition has progressed significantly over the past several years. Still, this problem has proved more difficult than was anticipated because of the large variation in the way people write. Humans can make use of past experience and semantics when attempting to read ambiguously written text; machines are not yet as adept. As a result, handwriting recognition is still an area of active research. Some work has focused on techniques to make it easier for the user to correct the inevitable errors. A recent approach is to make the problem simpler for the computer by changing the input alphabet so that confusing characters can be better disambiguated. For example, the user might be forced to add a tail when writing a "V" to distinguish it from a "U."

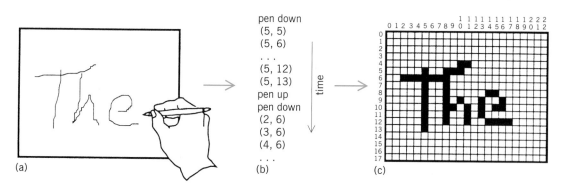

Fig. 1. Pen input and display. (*a*) User writes on the digitizer. (*b*) Point sequence. (*c*) Two-dimensional bitmap display.

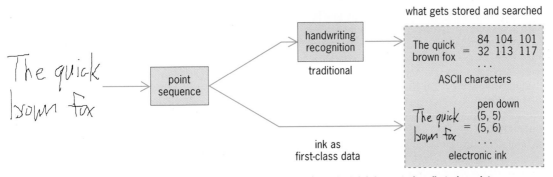

what gets stored and searched

Fig. 2. Comparison of traditional handwriting recognition with a system in which ink is treated as first-class data.

Ink as first-class data. Instead of taking a very expressive medium such as ink and immediately mapping it into a small, predefined set of alphanumeric symbols, an alternative is to support it as a first-class datatype. With the ink left untranslated, new functionality must be developed to replace what is lost by shunning the standard, character-based representation. These two competing approaches are depicted in **Fig. 2.**

There are compelling arguments for deferring or even eliminating handwriting recognition in certain applications:

1. Many of a user's day-to-day tasks can be handled entirely in the ink domain by techniques more accurate and less intrusive than handwriting recognition.

2. No existing character set captures the full range of graphical representations that a human using a pen can create (for example, sketches, maps, diagrams, equations, and doodles). By not constraining pen strokes to represent valid symbols, a much richer input language is made available.

3. Whereas handwriting recognizers must be customized to a specific language, language independence is a natural by-product of first-class ink.

Storing ink data is relatively straightforward, but memory demands are great. The sequence of points corresponding to a single handwritten word may be a hundred samples long, whereas the word itself could be encoded in ASCII in fewer than ten bytes. Fortunately, handwriting tends to be highly compressible by a variety of methods. Moreover, memory densities are continually increasing.

A bigger concern is losing the existing infrastructure for searching previously stored data. Efficient, well-known algorithms exist for locating keywords in ASCII text files; some form of "Find" command is a basic feature of all modern word-processor software. The key to reproducing this functionality in

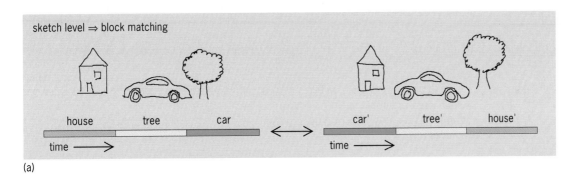

(a)

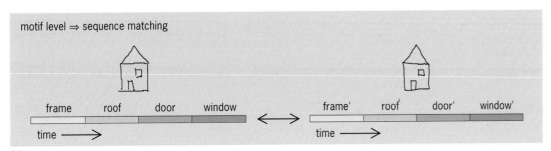

(b)

Fig. 3. Sketch matching problem. (a) High level of abstraction. (b) Low level of abstraction.

the ink domain is observing that, despite much variation across users, a particular individual tends to be self consistent. Hence, ink data can be searched by matching the pen strokes of the query to what was written before.

Textual ink matching. Ink that is primarily textual can be searched by using an adaptation of a well-known dynamic programming algorithm. First, the incoming points are grouped into strokes. These might be delimited at, say, local y-minima and pen-up—pen-down events. The strokes are then converted into vectors of descriptive features: the length of the stroke, the total angle traversed, and the angle and length of the bounding-box diagonal, for example.

Next, the feature vectors are classified by using vector quantization, in which the multidimensional space is mapped into a small number of clusters. Each vector in turn is placed in the proper cluster (the one whose centroid is nearest to the vector) as determined by using an appropriate distance measure. From then on, a stroke is represented by the index of the cluster to which it belongs.

Finally, an edit distance is computed between the query and each entry in the database. Under this model, five basic operations are permitted: delete a stroke, insert a stroke, substitute one stroke for another, split one stroke into two, and merge two strokes into one. Each of these is assigned a cost, and the edit distance is defined as the minimum chosen from all combinations of operations that transform the query into the database item.

Determining the edit distance between two ink sequences is a problem solvable with dynamic programming. Starting from the initial strokes, the sequences are aligned step by step; longer alignments are built up from earlier, shorter ones through the use of the basic editing operations. The final distance value is a measure of the similarity between the two sequences in question. A small distance means that the sequences are good matches, and a large one means that they are dissimilar.

Sketch matching. The approach described above works well for writer-dependent searching of textual ink. Sketches present more of a challenge, however, as a user might vary the order in which constituent objects are drawn. **Figure 3**a demonstrates this; the house on the left is drawn first, while in the similar sketch on the right it is drawn last. The standard edit-distance algorithm does not permit this sort of flexibility.

Hence, sketch matching must be viewed at two levels of abstraction. At the high level (Fig. 3a), long subsequences of the ink string (called blocks or motifs) may be interchanged and repeated to allow for variations in drawing order (for example, house → tree → car versus car → tree → house). At the low level (Fig. 3b), a single motif is treated as a sequence of strokes that, for a given user, are always drawn in a consistent order, just as in textual ink matching (for example, frame → roof → door → window). The algorithm for solving this problem, also based on dynamic programming, exploits this

structure by partitioning the query ink into blocks adaptively and matching each to a block in the database ink such that the sum of the distances between corresponding blocks is minimized. As before, this approach quantifies the similarity between the query and each entry in the database, allowing the best match to be returned to the user.

For background information *see* CHARACTER RECOGNITION; DATA COMPRESSION in the McGraw-Hill Encyclopedia of Science & Technology.

Daniel Lopresti

Bibliography. S. Jajodia and V. S. Subrahmanian (eds.), *Multimedia Database Systems: Issues and Research Directions*, 1996; M. L. Simner, G. Leedham, and A. J. W. M. Thomassen (eds.), *Handwriting and Drawing Research: Basic and Applied Issues*, 1996; C. C. Tappert, C. Y. Suen, and T. Wakahara, The state of the art in on-line handwriting recognition, *IEEE Trans. Pattern Anal. Mach. Intellig.*, 12(8):179–190, August 1990.

Computer-supported collaborative work

There are varied definitions of computer-supported collaborative work (CSCW) depending on the nature of the application. Primarily, it is an environment where computers provide support to a group of people in order to accomplish a common goal or task. Computer-supported collaborative work consists of hardware and software utilizing communication parameters and procedures. Support is provided in various decision-making processes. A typical CSCW system consists of five principal components: a database module, a model base module, a computer network module, an interface module, and a facilitator.

Cooperative team-based activities are changing the way that people collaborate and share information across an enterprise. Competition has forced enterprises to improve product development and decision-making processes and to explore concurrent engineering, collaborative design, integrated product development, and total quality control. All these engineering-related activities have a common focus of reducing cost and increasing quality by having people cooperate more effectively. Computer-supported collaborative work is viewed as an excellent tool to apply.

Characteristics. The CSCW field has emerged from a growing interest of software product developers in supporting networked groups and from a common interest among researchers in various disciplines in how the productivity of workgroups can be improved. In the 1990s, research and development in the human-computer interaction field has shifted from single-user applications such as word processing to group support applications such as integrated product design and development. The mechanism to support the activity of a group of people working on a product, research area, topic, or scholarly endeavor with the help of computers is CSCW.

For instance, brainstorming to generate ideas, structuring these ideas, and then evaluating them can be facilitated by a CSCW system. CSCW systems should provide interaction in a synchronous and asynchronous manner among team members and coordinate the various tasks performed by them. These systems enable people to interact from remote places, while providing visualization and accessibility of data by team members. They are set up to separate public and private data. Successful implementation of CSCW should incorporate these features to give a complete architecture to support the decision-making process.

Types and classification. The time and place dimensions of a team are the basic determinants of the type of CSCW, and distinguish among the different types of interactions based on these dimensions. Group interactions may take place in the same place (face to face) or geographically dispersed locations (distributed). They may take place at the same time (synchronous) or different times (asynchronous).

A three-level CSCW taxonomy has been proposed, based on the system's functions. Level 1 CSCW provides technical features aimed at removing common communication barriers such as large screens, voting and aggregation, anonymous inputs of ideas and preferences, and electronic message exchange between members. Level 2 systems contain decision aids such as multiple criteria tools, nominal group techniques, planning models, and modules supporting idea generation procedures such as brainstorming and idea organization. A Level 2 CSCW is envisioned as an enhanced system including a wide range of decision-modeling tools and group decision-making techniques. At Level 3, the system includes machine-induced and -controlled communication, with facilities for rule writing and selection. These facilities are intended to assist the negotiation process in the later stages of the group decision-making process.

Groupware. Groupware is multiuser software that addresses a variety of CSCW applications through digital media, bringing significant improvement and transformation to organizations. Groupware builds upon the latest advance in information technology, utilizing local- and wide-area networking, the World Wide Web, and recent advances in software and hardware technologies to achieve collaboration goals. Technologies that enable routing, networking, communication, and concurrent sharing are important to groupware. Hundreds of commercial groupware products are available in the market in the areas of (1) communications (electronic mail and messaging, desktop video and data conferencing, and electronic meeting systems and audio conferencing); (2) planning and scheduling (group calendaring and scheduling, workflow process diagramming and analysis tools, and electronic forms and routing products); and (3) specific projects (group document handling including group editing, workgroup utilities and groupware development

tools, and collaborative–internet-based applications and products).

The workgroup computing market is still small. It is about a decade old, and many groupware products have been applied to specific business problems. These applications support sales force automation, human resource management, customer service, product design and development, strategic planning, business process reengineering, and supplier management. Research and development in CSCW are now focused on the inclusion of collaborative tools to support workgroups geographically distributed. This mode of development is particularly significant since companies either are becoming more global in their operations or are required to collaborate with a network of global suppliers and partners.

Benefits. Computer-supported collaborative work is designed to increase the effectiveness of a group of decision makers by facilitating information retrieval, sharing, and use. It encourages interactive information exchange and can reduce the counterproductivity sometimes associated with decision makers meeting in groups, that is, disorganized activity, member dominance, social pressure, and inhibition; participation by members is increased; fewer meetings are required. Through decision aids, CSCW can increase the efficiency of the decision-making process and the quality of the resulting decision, so that there is greater satisfaction among members.

Owing to the parallel nature of the communication channel, CSCW can support multiple input to a greater degree than can traditional meeting systems. The spontaneity gained through CSCW allows for immediate group reactions during collaborative sessions. The elimination of meeting-related travel time and expenses and easier scheduling of meetings are immediate consequences of decentralized CSCW. CSCW efficiencies can lead to improved competitiveness through faster times to market. Computer-supported collaborative work achieves integration of geographically dispersed teams, and better coordination globally. Through CSCW, application of professional expertise can be enhanced. Finally, the quality of management programs can be upgraded through automation of routine processes.

Manufacturing applications. The design of manufacturing systems is an engineering activity that requires inputs from several stakeholders. A CSCW system can assist in resolving the conflicts that are likely to arise among a cross-functional team dealing with such a manufacturing application.

A recent study focused on the development and testing of an intelligent CSCW system to assist teams of engineers faced with evaluating and selecting the best manufacturing configuration from a number of design alternatives. Twelve multidisciplinary design teams of four members each were organized. Some teams used a CSCW with Level 2 enhancements, while others were exposed to a CSCW with Level 3 tools. The design task was based on the reorganization of state-of-the-art computer numerical control equipment to facilitate manufacture of a wide range of precision components. The groups were also presented with the design and operational objectives that must be satisfied by the final design of the manufacturing system. The task of the multifunctional design team was to select the layout configuration that would best satisfy a predetermined set of agility and flexibility criteria.

The teams using the enhanced CSCW recorded a significantly higher level of satisfaction with the final decision, displayed a significantly higher level of agreement with the final solution, and perceived the level of consensus attained by the team to be significantly higher. These results corroborate most recent studies that CSCW technology can successfully produce decisions of a higher quality, particularly for complex tasks such as product design and development and manufacturing systems design.

Internet. The long-term goal of CSCW developers has been to create a system that will enable engineers, managers, and executives to conduct and manage product design and development activities as a unified and collaborative process. The emergence of internet-based groupware could provide the long-needed infrastructure for managing a range of collaborative projects as single business units. One advantage of web-based projects is that all the documentation about the design process can be available to all participants regardless of geographical location.

Web-based CSCW attempts to integrate three main components using a shared workspace: on-line decision-making tools, World Wide Web server and browser, and collaborating workgroups. The shared workspace will consist of a groupware kernel and a toolkit containing a variety of engineering project management tools. The web server and browser provides the interface to other project management tools such as spreadsheets, simulation programs, financial planning templates, project scheduling, computer-aided design tools, and shared whiteboard tools. Project teams will be able to access and execute applications on their local networks and bring the results into the shared workspace environment for further analysis and discussion. The advent of the virtual company with concomitant co-located teams has significant implications for the application of the CSCW technology. This development will ultimately drive the utilization of CSCW for a myriad of business applications ranging from strategic planning, to product design, to remote production operations.

For background information *see* COMPUTER; DATA COMMUNICATIONS; DATABASE MANAGEMENT SYSTEMS; SOFTWARE in the McGraw-Hill Encyclopedia of Science & Technology.   Leslie Monplaisir

Bibliography. G. DeSanctis and R. B. Gallupe, A foundation study of group decision support system, *Manag. Sci.*, 33(5):589–609, 1987; J. Grudin, Groupware and social dynamics: Eight challenges for developers, *ACM*, 37(1):92–105, 1994; L. F. Monplaisir, An Intelligent GDSS for Multiple Criteria Evaluation of Agile Manufacturing Systems Designs, unpublished Ph.D. Dissertation, University of Missouri-Rolla, 1995.

Computerized document analysis

Digital imaging is a mature technology that involves the acquisition, indexing, compression, storage, authentication, transmission, retrieval, and display of entire pages of documents by means of computers. Document image analysis attempts to go a step further, to extract the content of the digitized documents and convert it into a form suitable for digital processing. Document image analysis includes the processing of graphic documents such as engineering drawings, circuit schematics, and organization charts and maps, but this discussion is restricted to mostly-text documents. The extraction of content from the digital image requires two major phases. The first phase, identification of the logical or functional components of a document, is called layout analysis. The second phase, encoding of the glyphs (letters, numerals, mathematical symbols, and punctuation) into a computer representation such as the American Standard Code for Information Interchange (ASCII), rich-text format (RTF), or UNICODE (a new international standard) is called optical character recognition. Both of these steps require prior knowledge of the underlying script. Furthermore, the accuracy of text recognition can be improved by postprocessing that applies linguistic constraints.

Digitization. The device used to convert light reflected from the paper to digital form is called an optical scanner. Most current scanners use fluorescent illumination and charge-coupled-device (CCD) arrays, but there are many other possible scanning configurations. The most common scanners are hand-held devices, small-footprint roller-feed transports, flatbed page scanners, and one- or two-sided autofeed scanners which may digitize over 50 pages per minute. Specialized scanners are available for calling cards, credit-card slips, microforms, 35-mm slides, bound volumes, and large-format applications such as maps and engineering drawings. Some scanners produce only a binary (black-and-white) rendition of the page, but gray-scale and color scanners are increasingly common.

The digitized document is an array of pixels (integer-valued picture elements), which can assume the values 0–1 for black and white, 0–255 for gray scale, or $3 \times (0–255)$ for the red-blue-green (RBG) representation of color. The spatial scanning resolution varies from 200 dots per inch for hand-printed documents, through 300–600 dots per inch for printed documents, to 1000 dots per inch for maps. With a 300-dots-per-inch binary representation, a letter-sized page yields about 1 megabyte (MB) of data. At the same scanning resolution in color, it requires 24 MB; therefore, compression mechanisms may be an integral part of the scanner. Efficient lossless compression schemes can reduce the storage requirement for a printed page by a factor of 10–20. An old idea, symbol-based image compression, is undergoing a revival.

Identification of logical components. The first task here is the separation of text, line art, and halftones. This can be readily accomplished by analysis of the distribution of size, aspect ratio, local density, and relative orientation of isolated foreground (usually black) elements on the page. The line art and photographs are usually stored without further processing, while the text regions are subjected to more detailed layout analysis and eventually to optical character recognition. Potential sources of difficulty include interference effects between the halftone patterns and the scanner sampling grid, and confusion between line art and hand-printed or cursive notations. It is also difficult (but not always necessary) to isolate lettering within illustrations, and large capital letters at the beginning of a paragraph (drop caps or decorative majuscules) may be mistaken for figures.

Once the text regions have been isolated, it may be necessary to estimate and correct skew, possibly at reduced resolution for the sake of speed. Next, columns, paragraph blocks, text lines, and words are located.

Extraction of the document content requires additional information that human readers derive from long-established layout conventions. These conventions allow identification of titles and subtitles, footnotes, references, page numbers, figure captions, dates, authors, destinations, and so forth. The conventions are so complex that so far they can be interpreted automatically only for restricted, specific families of documents. Publication-specific systems have been successfully demonstrated on newspaper pages, business letters, printed tables, resumes, technical journal articles and reviews, patent applications, typed business forms, and, strikingly, the periodical *Chess Informant*. Highly specialized knowledge-based systems are widely used for postal-address location and interpretation.

Optical character recognition. It is traditional to divide the recognition of individual glyphs into two subtasks, feature extraction and classification. Features are usually designed by experts to represent local pixel configurations corresponding to horizontal and vertical strokes, stroke junctions and intersections, serifs, and holes, protrusions, and indentations. The presence or absence of specific features is associated with each character class by using automated structural or statistical pattern-recognition techniques or neural networks. The association process is based on a large sample of labeled glyphs (typically over 1 million). During the recognition phase, new character samples are mapped onto the class identities (which may include, in addition to the alphabetic label, the type size and font) according to the presence or absence of features.

The recognition of difficult material can be enhanced by context, that is, the application of common-letter n-gram statistics (for example, the fact that "ing" is more common than "uiq"), lexicons of words, and word associations (syntax). Low-level contextual aids are incorporated into most optical character recognition devices. The amount of context ordinarily and subconsciously used by human readers can be appreciated by attempting to transcribe a postcard in a foreign language. However, contextual clues tend to be least available when accuracy is most important, as on proper nouns, numerical amounts, part numbers, or e-mail addresses.

The recognition accuracy of an optical character recognition system is measured by the fraction of misrecognized or rejected glyphs, words, or phrases. The character recognition accuracy ranges from above 99.5% for large, well-spaced, high-contrast pages in a simple layout to below 70% for multigeneration copies of small, crowded, and smudged print in an unusual typeface. If the recognition accuracy is below 98%, it is usually more effective to keyboard the entire document than to correct the errors. Some applications (such as textual information retrieval) are much less sensitive to errors than others (such as constructing a database from a printed directory).

Processing of degraded documents. Degraded copy can often be traced to facsimile, old copiers and computer printers, poorly maintained typewriters, high-speed tabloid presses, coarse paper, or heavy handling. The processing of degraded documents can be improved by multilevel gray-scale quantization and a high spatial sampling rate. Adaptive local thresholding of the gray tones helps cope with uneven contrast, but fine, faint connecting strokes and other small features can be more easily detected on the gray-scale image than on any binarized version. High-resolution spatial sampling reduces edge effects due to the unpredictable location of the sampling grid. Localized skew correction is necessary for hand-set pages and for line curl on pages copied from bound books.

Touching type, fragmented type, and cursive script require elaborate line and word segmentation methods that do not rely on white space between items. Because character-level segmentation is unreliable, the smallest unit that can be interpreted is an entire word. Even better results can be obtained by decoding larger units such as printed lines or entire pages. Some methods combine layout analysis and optical character recognition.

On degraded material, feature extraction and recognition methods customized to the dominant typeface of the document perform much better than omnifont or multifont systems. Except for essentially single-font applications, such customization requires in-the-field training using segmented and labeled training samples. Trainable systems (called supervised adaptation) have not proved popular because users of optical character recognition systems are reluctant to segment and label a training sample of characters for every new document. Perhaps, however, the training process can be simplified: character segmentation takes more time than labeling, and this step can be circumvented by taking advantage of multiple occurrences of the same character. Unsupervised adaptation, which relies on the observation that even in a degraded document there are many characters that can be easily recognized by a multifont classifier, may also be incorporated in future optical character recognition devices.

Unsolved problems in optical character recognition include the proper interpretation of tables and mathematical formulas, and the accurate recognition of kerned text and of display type used in headlines and advertising.

Script and language identification. The script and language of a document cannot be taken for granted, particularly outside the United States, where mixed-language documents abound. Because most optical character recognition systems are tuned to a single script and even a single language, it is important to identify them accurately.

The first step is to determine the orientation of the lines of text (horizontal or vertical) from the spatial distribution of the glyphs. The script can often be identified by cues such as the uniform spacing and block structure of Han (Chinese) ideographs, the presence of ascenders and descenders in lowercase Latin and Cyrillic, a strong headline in Sanskrit, and dots and connectors in Arabic and Farsi. European languages based on the Latin script can be identified by character shape codes that match the characteristic outlines of the most common words (typically articles and pronouns). The diversity of diacritic marks (accents) is also useful. The separation of Chinese from Japanese is more difficult. Once the language is known, the reading order (left to right, or right to left) can be easily determined.

Because most of the attributes used for script and language identification are statistical in nature, it is much easier to identify a whole page of text than an isolated passage. However, European documents often include phrases or sentences in another language, Japanese text may be interspersed with English words and Arabic numerals, and Bengali and Devanagari are sometimes mixed. Experimentation with document script and language identification requires an enormous database and significant computing resources (although some of the statistical features may be derived from compressed images). Reliable identification of short passages has not yet been demonstrated. Even if the script and language are correctly identified, the recognition of text in languages other than English has received less attention and is more error prone.

Applications. The motivation for converting paper documents to digital form includes fast, global access and distribution over digital networks; inexpensive storage on electronic media; automated workflow management; security and privacy through encryption; and information processing (such as bibliographic search, data mining, financial records, and inventory management). Some of these benefits can be obtained through digital imaging, but document image analysis technology has an even wider range of potential applications. Organizations that handle claims for health care must process more than 50,000 forms per day. Hospital records bulge with hundreds of pages per patient that, if converted to computer-readable form, could be used for improved case management and medical research. Corporate litigation requires searching immense files. Most airline accounting is still based on ticket stubs. Electronic libraries require the conversion of massive archival holdings: 2000 technical journals amount to about 20 million pages per decade. Millions of postal addresses must be read daily. Although computerized applications such as electronic transaction processing, on-line magazines, and the World Wide Web are making inroads, the volume of paper is still growing. *See* DATA SYSTEMS.

At present, the conversion of arbitrary documents to computer-readable form requires considerable manual intervention. Some operator actions are required initially to adjust the parameters of the system to a particular family of documents, but the most costly aspect is the correction of errors. The design of the workflow and of the interactive graphical user interface for corrections is therfore at least as important as that of the automated components.

Research on the recognition of hand-printed and cursive writing (intelligent character recognition) is extensive, but progress has been elusive. However, highly constrained vocabularies that are used in forms processing and postal-address reading can already be recognized accurately enough to reduce overall data-entry costs. On-line recognition on palmtop devices equipped with a stylus (which generate data known as electronic ink) is also viable because most people can quickly adapt and learn to write in such a way that automated systems can interpret their writing. *See* COMPUTER STORAGE.

For background information *see* CHARACTER RECOGNITION; DATA COMPRESSION; IMAGE PROCESSING in the McGraw-Hill Encyclopedia of Science & Technology.   George Nagy

Bibliography. M. Nadler and M. E. P. Smith, *Pattern Recognition Engineering*, 1993; G. Nagy, At the frontiers of OCR, *Proc. IEEE*, 80(7):1093–1110, 1992; J. Schurmann et al., Document analysis—from pixels to contents, *Proc. IEEE*, 80(7):1111–1119, 1992; A. L. Spitz, Determination of the script and language content of document images, *IEEE Trans. PAMI*, 19(3):235–245, 1997; I. H. Witten, A. Moffat, and T. C. Bell, *Managing Gigabytes: Compressing and Indexing Documents and Images*, 1994.

Conflict analysis

Strategic conflict is a sociological phenomenon that seems to occur whenever human beings interact. The types of conflict range from outright hostility, such as warfare, to highly cooperative situations in which disputants form coalitions or jointly attempt to reach resolutions in which everyone gains—the "win/win" solutions. The key ingredients of any conflict are the various decision makers who are in disagreement over some issue, and each participant's multiple objectives, which influence what that decision maker would prefer to do as he (or she) strategically interacts with his competitors in the process of reaching a resolution.

Conflict analysis consists of methodologies and techniques for systematically studying multiple-participant–multiple-objective decision situations in order to enhance understanding and communication so that better and fairer resolutions can be achieved. The most comprehensive approach for modeling and analyzing conflict is the graph model for conflict resolution, which constitutes a significant expansion and improvement over earlier ideas from conflict analysis, metagame analysis, and classical game theory. The graph model is designed for application to both simple and complex real-world disputes, and is based upon sound theoretical foundations formulated through set theory, logic, and graph theory, that is, the mathematics of relationships. The decision support system called GMCR II permits practitioners, researchers, teachers, and students to conveniently apply the computerized version of this unique decision technology to virtually any kind of social conflict. A practical application will be employed to illustrate the main features of the graph model.

Ground-water contamination conflict. Elmira, a town of about 7400 inhabitants, is located in southwestern Ontario, Canada. In late 1989, a serious controversy arose when a known carcinogen, *N*-nitroso dimethylamine (NDMA), was discovered in the aquifer beneath the town and in the related municipal water supply. Suspicion fell on the pesticide and rubber products plant of Uniroyal Chemical Ltd., which had a history of environmental problems. In August 1990, the Ontario Ministry of the Environment issued a control order under the Environmental Protection Act of Ontario stipulating that Uniroyal implement a long-term collection and treatment system, undertake studies to assess the need for a cleanup, and carry out any necessary cleanup under Ministry supervision. Uniroyal immediately appealed. Various interest groups formed and attempted to influence the process through lobbying and other means. The Regional Municipality of Waterloo and the Township of Woolwich (the Local Government) took common positions in the dispute and, encouraged by the Ministry, hired independent consultants and obtained extensive legal and technical advice at substantial cost. Negotiations involving the Ministry, Uniroyal, and the Local Government began in mid-1991. The Ministry's objective was to execute its mandate as efficiently as possible, Uniroyal wanted the control order modified or rescinded, and the Local Government wanted to protect its citizens and industrial base.

General application procedure. The graph model for conflict resolution can be applied to the Elmira dispute (**Fig. 1**). Initially, a dispute may appear to be confusing and difficult to comprehend, but by systematically applying a sequence of modeling and analysis stages in an iterative fashion (Fig. 1), a con-

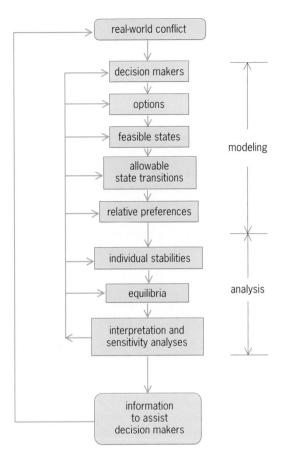

Fig. 1. Applying the graph model for conflict resolution.

flict can be understood and analyzed in terms of its essential characteristics and possible resolutions. The procedure is implemented by GMCR II.

Modeling. It is necessary to first identify the decision makers in the dispute, as well as the option choices or courses of action that fall under the control of each one. In the Elmira dispute, each of the three decision makers can exercise the option(s) immediately below its name (**Table 1**). The Ministry

TABLE 1. Feasible states in the Elmira conflict

Decision makers and options	Feasible states								
Ministry									
1. Modify	N	Y	N	Y	N	Y	N	Y	—
Uniroyal									
2. Delay	Y	Y	N	N	Y	Y	N	N	N
3. Accept	N	N	Y	Y	N	N	Y	Y	N
4. Abandon	N	N	N	N	N	N	N	N	Y
Local Government									
5. Support	N	N	N	N	Y	Y	Y	Y	—
State number	1	2	3	4	5	6	7	8	9

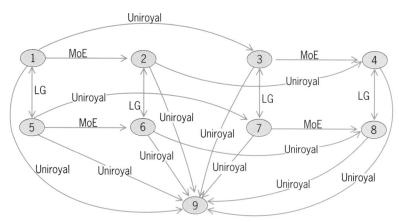

Fig. 2. Integrated graph of the Elmira conflict. MoE is the Ontario Ministry of the Environment; LG is the Local Government.

has the option of modifying the control order to make it acceptable to Uniroyal (the option is called Modify in the table). Uniroyal can lengthen the appeal process (Delay), accept responsibility for implementing the control order (Accept), or close down its Elmira factory (Abandon). Finally, the Local Government has the option of supporting the Ministry's control order (Support).

The nine feasible states or scenarios that could arise in the dispute are given as columns of Y's, N's, and dashes (Table 1). Y indicates yes (the option is taken by the decision maker controlling it), N means no (the option is not selected), and a dash means either Y or N. For example, state number 5 is the scenario where the Ministry does not modify the control order, Uniroyal decides to delay the appeal process, and the Local Government supports the original control order.

From some states in a conflict model, a particular decision maker may unilaterally cause a transition to other states by changing his or her option selection to form allowable state transitions. For instance, by changing from N to Y for the fifth option, the Local Government can create a state transition from the status quo given as state 1 (Table 1) to state 5. The integrated graph model for the Elmira dispute (**Fig. 2**) shows all allowable state transitions for the conflict. Each node represents a state, designated by its state number, and each arc stands for an allowable state transition. Because the Local Government controls the movement from state 1 to state 5, LG is written on the arc joining these two states. Arrowheads at each end of the arc point out that this is a reversible move, since the Local Government can cause a transition from state 1 to state 5 or from state 5 to state 1. However, if there is an irreversible move, transition can occur in only one direction, and only one arrowhead is used on the arc. For example, the movement from state 1 to state 3 is controlled by Uniroyal and considered to be irreversible, because if Uniroyal decides to stop delaying the proceedings and instead to accept responsibility, it could not reverse this decision at a later date.

A distinct advantage of the graph model for conflict resolution is that it requires only relative preferences among states for each decision maker. Accordingly, it is necessary to know only whether one state is more preferred than another, less preferred, or equally preferred; it is never necessary to know by how much a state is preferred. This feature is useful because absolute preference information may be difficult or impossible to obtain, especially in social conflicts.

A decision maker who can rank-order the states (from most to least preferred) has ordinal preferences. States may be equally preferred, so that the decision maker is indifferent in that he or she does not favor any state over any other within the equally preferred set. If the preferences for a decision maker are strictly ordinal, the states are ranked from most to least preferred and there are no sets of equally preferred states. A common assumption underlying preferences is transitivity. If a decision maker's preferences are transitive, it is necessary that if state p is preferred to q and q is preferred to r, then p must be preferred to r. When preferences are intransitive, this conclusion need not follow. A key design feature of the graph model is that it can be used with transitive or intransitive preferences. Moreover, if by chance cardinal utility values are available—that is, real numbers to represent payoffs or preference values for the states—the graph model for conflict resolution can still be employed, since ordinal preference information is always contained within the cardinal payoffs. For most practical applications in conflict resolution, preference information is ordinal; the decision support system GMCR II assumes ordinal preferences, implying transitivity.

In the Elmira conflict model, the states can be ranked from most preferred on the left to least preferred on the right, for each of the three decision makers (**Table 2**). For example, state 7 is most preferred for the Ministry, since at state 7 the Ministry does not have to modify the control order, which is accepted by Uniroyal and supported by the Local Government. State 9 is least preferred by both the Ministry and the Local Government, because Uniroyal abandons its Elmira facilities. Since preferences are strictly ordinal for all three decision makers, the Elmira conflict is strictly ordinal.

Analysis and results. When a conflict model has been constructed, it can be used as a basic framework within which potential strategic interactions among the decision makers can be analyzed in detail. The systematic examination of the permissible moves and countermoves by the decision makers during

TABLE 2. Ranking of states for each decision maker									
Decision makers	Most preferred	$\rightarrow$					Least	preferred	
Ministry	7	3	4	8	5	1	2	6	9
Uniroyal	1	4	8	5	9	3	7	2	6
Local Government	7	3	5	1	8	6	4	2	9

TABLE 3. Strategic movement from the status quo through transition states to the final equilibrium

Decision makers and options	Status quo	Transition equilibrium		Transition state		Final equilibrium
Ministry						
1. Modify	N	N	→	Y		Y
Uniroyal						
2. Delay	Y	Y		Y	→	N
3. Accept	N	N		N	→	Y
4. Abandon	N	N		N		N
Local Government						
5. Support	N	→ Y		Y		Y
State number	1	5		6		8

possible evolutions of the conflict and the calculation of the most likely resolutions are carried out at the stability analysis stage. Stability analysis is executed by using a solution concept, or stability definition, which constitutes a mathematical description of a decision maker's behavior in a strategic conflict. Different solution concepts model different patterns of behavior, including different levels of foresight and different attitudes to strategic risk. In GMCR II, each state is analyzed for stability for a range of stability types for each decision maker. If a state is individually stable for a given decision maker according to some solution concept, it is not advantageous for that decision maker to unilaterally change his or her option selections in order to move to another state. When a state is stable for all decision makers in a conflict, it is referred to as a compromise resolution or equilibrium.

For the Elmira conflict (Tables 1 and 2), stronger and longer-term equilibria occur at states 5, 8, and 9. Transitions to state 9, in which Uniroyal abandons its Elmira plant, are completely controlled by Uniroyal (Fig. 2). It is not surprising that state 9 did not arise, as in this model Uniroyal prefers both state 5 and state 8. Historically, the status quo in mid-1991 was state 1 (**Table 3**), in which Uniroyal was delaying the proceedings, the Ministry was not modifying the control order, and the Local Government was not supporting the control order. The Local Government shifted to supporting the original control order, resulting in state 5 for a protracted interval of time (Table 3). As shown by the transitions from state 5 to 6 and from 6 to 8 (Table 3; Fig. 2), the Ministry and Uniroyal together control transitions from state 5 to 8. Moreover, both the Ministry and Uniroyal are better off at state 8 than at 5 (Table 2), and hence from their viewpoint state 8 is superior to state 5. This incentive to form a coalition for these two decision makers explains what actually took place. Specifically, on October 7, 1991, the Ministry and Uniroyal announced an agreement on a modified version of the original control order, thus moving to the equilibrium at state 8. This agreement caught the Local Government by surprise; protesting to no avail, it was forced to reach a separate and unfavorable arrangement with Uniroyal. The coalition made both the Ministry and Uniroyal better off, and the outcome was no less stable than before. The Local Government was harmed by the deal, but could do nothing to prevent it.

Interpretation and sensitivity analyses. Conclusions from a graph-model stability analysis can be interpreted by analysts, decision makers, or interested parties. The graph model for conflict resolution is applied in an iterative fashion (Fig. 1). Whenever new insights or information becomes available during the modeling and analysis stages, it is possible to return to the appropriate location to make any required changes before continuing with the study.

In sensitivity analyses, systematic changes in the model parameters are used to assess the robustness of the stability results. In other words, sensitivity analyses are used to answer "what-if" questions. Which sensitivity analyses are appropriate is usually dictated by the specific problem being studied. For instance, when there is uncertainty about the preference of one of the decision makers, a reasonable range of possible preference rankings can be analyzed to determine whether and how the equilibria are affected. If, for example, the equilibria do not change after preference ranking is modified, the equilibrium results are robust with respect to those preferences and greater confidence can be placed in them. However, when the equilibria change dramatically after small preference changes, the analyst should ensure that the most reliable preference information is included in the model.

For background information *see* DECISION SUPPORT SYSTEM; DECISION THEORY; GAME THEORY; GRAPH THEORY in the McGraw-Hill Encyclopedia of Science & Technology.   K. W. Hipel; D. M. Kilgour; L. Fang

Bibliography. L. Fang, K. W. Hipel, and D. M. Kilgour, *Interactive Decision Making: The Graph Model for Conflict Resolution*, 1993; K. W. Hipel, D. M. Kilgour, L. Fang, and X. Peng, The decision support system GMCR in environmental conflict management, *Appl. Math. Computation*, 83:117–152, 1997; D. M. Kilgour, L. Fang, and K. W. Hipel, Negotiation support using the decision support system GMCR, *Group Decision and Negotiation*, 5:371–383, 1996.

Conformal optics

Conformal optical systems have outer surfaces whose shape is chosen to optimize the interaction with the environment in which the optical system is being used. The imaging through such conformal optical windows is likely to suffer from extreme aberration, requiring special techniques for correction.

For example, a conformal optical window might relate to the nose of an infrared-seeking missile. These conformal surfaces permit a beneficial interface with the environment and allow substantial improvements in the overall performance of the vehicle. Recently there has been considerable research into methods of compensating for the aberrations produced by such windows. Computer-intensive methods of design, fabrication, and testing of optics have reached a level where the development of cost-effective methods for insertion of these conformal optics concepts into operational systems appears to be practical.

Applications. Important applications of conformal optics are found in missile and aircraft systems. Missiles and aircraft carry optical sensors for imaging, detection, and ranging that must look at the world through the outer skin of the vehicle. Traditionally, the windows for viewing through the skin of missiles and aircraft have had simple optical forms, such as flats or spheres, that enable the optical tracking systems to operate by using well-known technology. But these optically advantageous windows degrade the performance of the vehicle through increased drag, aerodynamic heating, or other undesirable effects. One example is the use of an optical tracker or seeker on the front end of a missile. These optical systems, usually used with infrared sensors, need to have a wide and unobstructed field of view. The classical solution for the window for these optics is a hemispherical dome mounted at the front of the missile. An optical tracker located within the dome is scanned around the field of view to keep track of a target. The spherical-surfaced-dome approach is easy to accommodate in the design, fabrication, and testing of the system, but the blunt spherical form adds considerable aerodynamic drag to the missile. The use of a conformal window, whose shape conforms more closely to the optimal, pointed ogival shape, reduces the drag of the missile and provides significant gains in the missile's performance. Such ogival shapes produce considerable optical aberration, however.

Similar considerations apply to aircraft. The optical sensors of most combat aircraft are mounted in pods that attach to the wings or other outer surfaces. These pods increase drag and reduce maneuverability and stealth properties of the aircraft. Location of the sensors within the body of the aircraft using traditional flat windows limits their field of view. The use of windows that have surfaces conforming to the desirable aerodynamic shapes of the aircraft is necessary to permit internal, drag-free location of these sensors.

One example of the benefits to be obtained through the appropriate use of conformal optics is a typical missile. Replacement of a hemispherical front-end window by an optimal-shaped ogival window can reduce the drag coefficient by as much as 25%. This reduction of the drag will lead to an increase in range for the same fuel consumption. There are additional advantages such as improved maneuverability of the missile.

The **illustration** shows one possible implementation of a conformal window to replace a conventional optical spherical window. It is a diagram of a conformal window, shaped to provide an improved drag profile for the missile. The optical tracker behind the conformal window can be seen looking toward the side of the missile. The optical tracker no longer sees a simple and constant spherical form for the window at any angle of view. The aspheric shape of the window produces a significant amount of aberration that must be compensated at some location in the optical system. The variation of the aberration with direction of view requires that this correction be dynamic.

There are other applications in which general aspheric optical surfaces are needed. Compact illumination systems require many unique forms of conformal surfaces, sometimes for utilitarian reasons and frequently for design or styling reasons. One growing area of interest comprises unique compact headlight systems for automobiles. Unobscured reflecting imaging systems used in spacecraft or microlithographic optics require nonconventional aspheric shapes for packaging or aberration correction purposes.

Challenges. The most desirable form for the front end of a missile is a pointed shape called an ogive. This ogival shape reduces the aerodynamic drag on the missile but produces a greatly distorted view of the scene that is viewed through the ogival dome. An optical tracker looking through the dome will see large amounts of aberration. A conformal optical surface is extremely aspheric and cannot be described by traditional surface prescriptions. Traditional optical design and fabrication methods cannot cope with the large amount of aberration that is generated by such conformal shapes. There are no established guidelines for the incorporation of these extreme aspheric conformal surfaces in the design of optical systems.

Fabrication of these conformal surfaces provides a new set of challenges. Traditional optical fabrication is based on the generation and polishing of spherical or flat surfaces by a lapping process. The surface eventually converges to the final required shape as a natural result of the process. Most aspherics used in lenses are minor deviations from these base spherical surfaces. Conformal surfaces require significant departures from traditional optical surfaces. New techniques for shape generation and polishing need to be developed so that conformal surfaces can be successfully fabricated.

Test and measurement of these surfaces provide a new set of challenges. There are no natural nulling tests, which provide an absolute reference for the surface shape. Testing requires new methods of numerically constructing reference surfaces for defining, aligning, and calibrating the conformal surface. The use of these new surfaces as windows for optical systems also provides some new challenges in operation. The alignment between the window and the tracking optics is very critical. Therefore, alignment

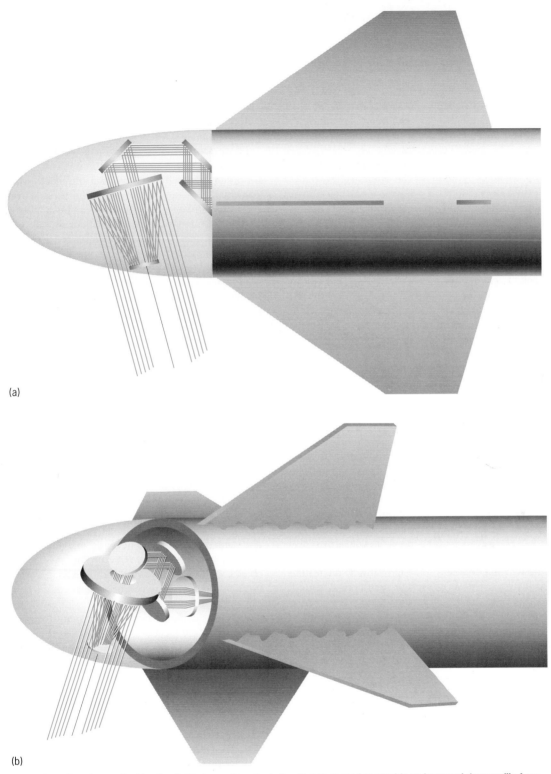

(a)

(b)

Geometric optics of an optical tracker behind a conformal window that is shaped to provide an improved drag profile for a missile. Paths of rays through the optical system are shown. (*a*) Side view. (*b*) Oblique view. *(Optical Research Associates)*

during installation and field operation must frequently be carried out by new adaptive optical techniques.

All of these new approaches require novel technical solutions within the framework of economic real-ity. None of these conformal techniques can be inserted into operational practice unless they are cost effective. Thus the cost of introducing conformal surfaces into missiles and aircraft must not exceed a small fraction of the cost benefit.

Design approach. The approach to design with conformal optics does not call for complete abandonment of current understanding of the image-formation process. Optical design methods are based on the description of the wavefront passing through surfaces by use of numerical ray tracing. The understanding of the aberrations arising at surfaces is obtained from an analytic method for describing the surface and the wavefront to stated levels of accuracy. The aberrations produced by general aspheric surfaces defy simple analytic descriptions but can be obtained by fitting of the numerical ray-tracing results. It is found that for most conformal surfaces the local aberration for a wavefront passing through a conformal window can be well described in terms of combinations of simple aberration shapes such as focus, astigmatism, and coma. The variation of these aberrations with location on the window becomes very difficult to describe analytically, leading to a design process in which the numerical ray tracing is used to establish the aberration level.

An intuitive grasp of the aberration content of conformal windows can be obtained by graphical presentations of the behavior of the aberrations with respect to the angle of view through the window. New design approaches permit expressing the targets of the design programs in terms of combinations of the sets of aberrations that naturally describe the effect of the conformal windows. New types of nonsymmetric aspheric components are required to compensate these sets of aberrations and are incorporated into the tracker optics. New approaches to tolerancing and assembling of these unusual optical systems are being investigated.

Research and development. In the United States, conformal optics is the subject of intense development under two academic and industrial consortia. These 4-year-long investigations are directed toward developing a full capability in design, fabrication, testing, and system integration in this new optical field.

For background information *see* ABERRATION (OPTICS); GEOMETRICAL OPTICS; OPTICAL SURFACES in the McGraw-Hill Encyclopedia of Science & Technology.   Robert R. Shannon

---

Correlation (physics)

Correlation is the tendency of two or more systems that independently exhibit simple behavior to show complex and novel behavior together because of their interaction. In a wide sense, correlation is responsible for most of the complex behavior of matter observed at all scales. Examples include the forces that confine quarks inside a particle such as the proton, the interactions responsible for superconductivity, the energy landscapes that govern chemical reactions of molecules, and the principles that govern the shapes and functions of giant protein molecules in living systems.

Simple systems. Recent progress has been made in a fundamental problem of correlation, that of small quantum systems. An example is three-body systems, such as the electrons and nucleus of the two-electron atom helium. The apparent simplicity of this system is notoriously deceptive. The three-body problem has been of fundamental interest from the early days of celestial mechanics. Its fascination still holds in classical planetary systems, and also in systems where quantum mechanics holds sway, such as atoms and molecules.

Electron correlation in atoms. The atom is usually thought of as a planetary system, with the nucleus playing a role analogous to the Sun, and the electrons to planets. If the atom obeyed classical mechanics, the electrons in the planetary model might be thought of as moving in independent orbits. Because quantum mechanics rules at the atomic level, the electrons must be thought of as occupying quantum-mechanical orbitals, or clouds of electron density, rather than classical orbits. In this quantum analog of the planetary atom, the question arises as to whether the electrons in their orbitals can really be considered independent of each other, or whether their mutual electrical repulsion renders this picture invalid. If so, there is a further question as to whether some other simple picture is possible, with physical immediacy, or whether massive computer calculations of the Schrödinger wave equation are the best that can be hoped for in the way of intuitive understanding. The interest here arises not only from the fundamental nature of the problem, but also for the reason that its understanding is essential for larger systems of more practical interest, such as the electrons in molecules undergoing chemical reactions.

Motions of atoms in a molecule. Besides the problem of the electrons in an atom, an important correlation problem is the motions of the atoms in a molecule. The standard picture is of heavy atomic nuclei, held together in a nearly rigid structure by the electron clouds, with small vibrations of this molecular structure, and overall rotation of the molecule as a whole. These vibrations are usually thought of as regular motions, or harmonic normal modes. But the situation is more complicated if the vibrations are excited with a great deal of energy, perhaps enough to break one or more of the bonds. It is known that, because the normal modes are not truly harmonic, especially at high energy, chaotic motion can result. It is not even certain whether a rational description of such motion is possible. Moreover, bearing in mind that the vibrations of a molecule are also quantum mechanical, it is not clear what happens to the quantum description that corresponds to the intuitive, classical understanding of the molecule. These issues constitute the problem of correlated motion of the atoms in a molecule.

Highly excited states. A surge of new knowledge, experimental and theoretical, of highly excited quantum states of few-body systems is leading to a new view of the motion of electrons in atoms, and of atoms in molecules. The planetary model of the atom is most nearly valid for the atom in its lowest energy, or ground, quantum-mechanical state. As described above, the normal-modes model of molecules is most nearly valid for the ground vibrational state. However, extensive research in recent years shows that in highly excited states each system shows characteristics of the behavior that describes the other at low energy. At high energy, the motion of electrons in atoms takes on attributes of molecular rotation-vibration modes, while the motion of atoms in highly excited vibrational states shows drastic departure from the low-energy normal-modes picture.

Molecular-model atoms. The quantum-mechanical ground state of the helium atom is denoted by the electronic configuration $1s^2$, meaning both electrons are in the $1s$ orbital, the lowest orbital possible for an atom such as hydrogen with just one electron. This orbital configuration description is the quantum analog of the planetary model of electrons moving in independent orbits. Excited states were also once thought to be described by this simple configuration picture. For example, one possible excited state could have both electrons in a $2p$ orbital, the configuration $2p^2$. Evidence has accumulated in recent decades that this configuration description is severely inadequate for highly excited states. Nonetheless, it came as a great surprise to discover that the excited atom had many properties in common with the motion of a triatomic molecule. There is now compelling evidence that in states with both electrons excited from the ground level, the atom behaves according to a molecular model, similar to a highly nonrigid linear XYX molecule. The electrons are correlated on opposite sides of the nucleus, with concerted motions like those of molecular normal modes.

The atomic structure of an excited quantum state of the electrons in such a molecular atom is that of an elongated cloud or blob of charge, with the density of the electrons concentrated at the ends (**Fig. 1**). This structure is understood by saying that the electrical repulsion of the electrons tends to correlate them on opposite sides of the nucleus. At the same time, a residual effect of the configuration description is to concentrate the electrons very loosely but symmetrically at a favored distance from the nucleus. This structure of the electron cloud is that of a highly nonrigid system. Nonetheless, the correlation gives the atom a distinct shape. In fact, the symmetry of the two-electron cloud is like that of a linear triatomic molecule, with the atomic nucleus taking the role of the central atom of the molecule, and the electrons taking the role of the outer atoms.

If the atom really has this kind of shape, it is natural to suppose that it could exhibit motions like those of the molecule, that is, normal modes of vibration and overall rotation of the system (Fig. 1). In fact, detailed comparisons of the patterns of quantum-mechanical energy levels of the highly excited atom, viewed through the necessary lens of a proper classification of the quantum states, show remarkable agreement between experiment and the pattern expected for the molecular atom.

Highly excited molecules. As discussed above, the spectrum of a highly excited two-electron atom resembles that of a linear molecule undergoing vibration and rotation. This resemblance can be turned around to ask what happens to a real molecule when it is excited high above the ground state, and what is the correct description of the changes that must occur from the low-energy picture of regular vibrations about a near-rigid structure.

At high energies, the modes can become strongly coupled to each other. As the atoms perform progressively larger excursions from the ground structure, the motion can become chaotic. The traditional normal-modes description is then no longer physically valid. But this is where the quantum vibrational spectrum may become extremely complex. The spectrum provides a window on the molecular world through which to obtain important information such as the forces between atoms which govern molecular dynamics and reactivity. The search for new ways to extract the information encoded in spectra has been a concerted effort of fundamental chemical science since the 1970s.

A principal object of this research has been to determine what happens when the normal modes are destroyed or modified on the route to molecular chaos. From the viewpoint of classical mechanics, the modes undergo branchings in a process mathematically described as bifurcation. When a normal mode bifurcates, new types of motions arise in place of the original modes. For example, before bifurcation, ordinary bend and stretch normal modes govern an H_2O (water) molecule (**Fig. 2a**). After bifurcation, new motions called resonant modes dominate (Fig. 2b). Recent work has shown how to characterize the bifurcations in specific molecules, as evidenced by analysis of new kinds of patterns observed in their experimental spectra.

Further similarities at higher energy. As discussed above, the two-electron atom at high energy has properties similar in certain ways to a molecule, while in actual molecules at high energy the vibrational modes are transformed in bifurcations because of resonant couplings. To a certain extent, the planetary atom has

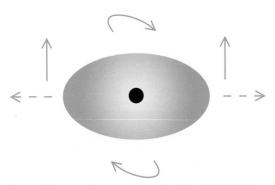

Fig. 1. Molecular structure and motion of a highly excited two-electron atom. The structure has bending and stretching vibrations, with overall rotation, all indicated by arrows.

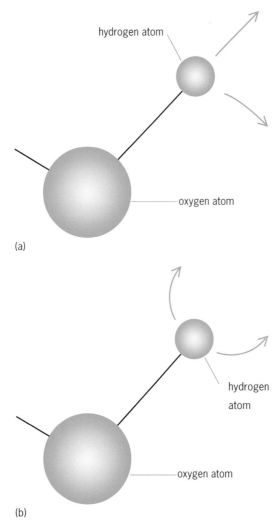

(a)

(b)

Fig. 2. Vibrational modes of the H$_2$O (water) molecule. Motion of one of the hydrogen (H) atoms, bonded to the central oxygen (O) atom, is indicated by arrows. (a) Before bifurcation. The stretch (a long bond) and bend (perpendicular to bond) are shown. (b) After bifurcation. One of two resonant collective modes is shown.

lation in truly nonrigid molecules and that in highly excited atoms. In fact, the mathematical tools used to describe high-energy behavior are beginning to give signs of a unified formal description of the two systems.

For background information *see* ATOMIC STRUC-TURE AND SPECTRA; CHAOS; MOLECULAR STRUCTURE AND SPECTRA; QUANTUM MECHANICS in the McGraw-Hill Encyclopedia of Science & Technology.

Michael E. Kellman

Bibliography. M. E. Kellman, Algebraic methods in spectroscopy, *Annu. Rev. Phys. Chem.*, 46:395–421, 1995; M. E. Kellman, Symmetry in chemistry from the hydrogen atom to proteins, *Proc. Nat. Acad. Sci. USA*, 93:14,287–14,294, 1996.

Corrosion

Various metals and treatment processes have been used throughout history in an effort to minimize the effects of surface erosion (corrosion). Increased corrosion protection can be accomplished by coating the outer surface of one metal with another which acts as a barrier preventing oxidation of the inner metal. One example of oxidation is when iron is exposed to water and air and forms iron oxide, or rust. Some oxidized metals have certain characteristics making them less desirable, such as iron oxide which forms flakes; other metals can form a relatively stable film, such as zirconium oxide, which is resistant to further corrosion. The first section of this article discusses the benefits of using zirconium.

Aluminum alloys are normally coated with chromium, forming a passive layer (chromium oxide) that is highly resistant to corrosion. However, uncoated aluminum undergoes oxidation, forming aluminum oxide, and in the presence of certain salts undesirable cavitation occurs. The second section of this article discusses a pretreatment process utilizing cerium and molybdenum that has been developed for aluminum alloys in place of coating with chromium.

Zirconium. This metallic element has a density somewhat less than that of carbon steel. After the corrosion-resistant properties of zirconium were defined in a nuclear environment, it was recognized that the material could be used in many other applications involving corrosive media.

Zirconium oxide film. Most engineering metals and alloys are passive. The corrosion resistance of passive metals relies on the presence of a surface oxide film. Zirconium, a passive material, forms a protective oxide film by reaction with oxygen. Necessary oxygen can be removed from surrounding media (air, water, carbon monoxide, or carbon dioxide), and this capability of zirconium is less conditional than the capability of most passive metals. The corrosion resistance of zirconium is due to a tenaciously adherent, chemically inert, thermodynamically stable film of zirconium oxide which forms naturally on the metallic surface. This dense oxide film pro-

become like a molecular atom, and the rigid molecule less regular. Still, the two systems could come to seem more similar. A real molecule can have excursions of the atoms completely out of its equilibrium configuration, as in isomerization, an important type of chemical reaction. A natural question is whether the motion of these wandering atoms could resemble the correlated but nonrigid motion of the electrons in an atom; or whether the electrons in atoms could show multiple molecular configurations, analogous to isomers of a real molecule. There is evidence that two-electron atoms have "frozen-planet" states in which the electrons really are locked into a second molecular configuration, with the electrons on the same side of the nucleus. Furthermore, there are indications that the electronic normal modes sometimes bifurcate, just as in a molecule. At hand is the prospect of understanding the similarities and correspondences between the corre-

tects the metal from both chemical and mechanical attack at temperatures up to about 752°F (400°C). Its thickness can vary, depending on the method of formation: natural films are in the range of less than 10 nanometers to over 100 nm in thickness; anodization produces films in the range of 400 nm to about 700 nm. Since the thickness of the zirconium oxide film is in the visible light spectrum, selected wavelengths are reflected from the metallic surface, depending on the film thickness. Decorative colors ranging from yellow to blue can be produced readily via anodization.

Oxide films due to anodization and those occurring naturally are formed at room temperature and do not have the coherence that thermally produced films exhibit. Oxide films can also be formed in autoclaves containing high-pressure, high-temperature water or steam. They are very similar to the surface films formed in air at elevated temperatures. Thermally produced films are formed at temperatures of 1022–1427°F (550–775°C) and range in thickness from 0.0002 to 0.0012 in. (0.005 to 0.030 mm). These films are equivalent to sapphire in hardness and are diffusion-bonded to the base metal; that is, oxygen diffuses into the metal matrix. These thermally produced films are black.

Corrosion resistance. Zirconium is resistant to corrosion in most mineral and organic acids. It is unique among highly corrosion-resistant metals, such as tantalum and niobium, in that it also resists attack by alkaline materials. Localized forms of corrosion such as pitting, crevice corrosion, and stress corrosion cracking are very rare in zirconium applications in the chemical industry. Since zirconium and many of its compounds are nontoxic and biocompatible, the metal is used to manufacture surgical tools and instruments. Zirconium vessels are extremely important in the manufacture of the organic acids, such as formic, acetic, lactic, and glycolic; the largest single use for zirconium in the chemical industry is acetic acid production. Other instances where zirconium containers are used is organic synthesis operations (in which sulfuric acid is a primary raw material) and production of nitric acid.

Electronics. Electronic component manufacturing involves a complex and intricate series of operations using ultrapure, quite corrosive chemicals. Exclusion of impurities is essential for electronic component quality, reliability, and profitability. The corrosive chemicals (for example, sulfuric acid, nitric acid, hydrogen peroxide, and various organic solvents) must be delivered to the component surface free of contaminants. Using a zirconium container helps to maintain purity. Phenolic resins, used to manufacture circuit boards, are formulated in zirconium reactors to maintain impurity levels in the parts per billion range. Disposal of mixed waste is another application in which zirconium containers have been very successful. Many electronic companies are located where water is an expensive commodity, so water reuse may be tantamount to the economic viability of the operation. Removal of ions resulting

from corrosion is necessary whether the water is reused or discharged. Aqueous discharges must meet imposed environmental standards; however, the standards for reuse are far more stringent. The use of zirconium can minimize or eliminate the need for expensive downstream aqueous waste treatment. The Japanese electronics industry uses zirconium even in areas where corrosion by normal standards is not a problem: zirconium is used primarily to keep the necessary contaminant levels at a minimum.

Paper products. Chlorine-free paper products are becoming very important as the environmental issues associated with chlorine usage become more pronounced. Zirconium has a role in the manufacture of chlorine-free paper by allowing the use of formic acid and hydrogen peroxide in paper production. The use of zirconium in paper production will become more important in the future as the world populace exerts environmental pressure to reduce or eliminate the use of chlorine.

Food and pharmaceuticals. Zirconium receptacles are used in the food industry to handle acidic media such as citric acid and ketchup, or to produce acidulants and food preservatives, such as maleic acid (acidulant), acetic acid (vinegar), and sorbic acid (food preservative). Most pharmaceutical formulations are manufactured in small batches by multistep synthesis reactions (with pH adjustments performed via acids or bases). Zirconium has proven to be an excellent material for many of these operations, as it withstands corrosive attack over a wide range of media and operating conditions. The use of zirconium in the pharmaceutical sector will continue to grow as more complex and varied formulations are devised.   Kenneth W. Bird

Aluminum alloys. Corrosion protection of aluminum alloys is usually achieved through chromate conversion coatings, anodizing, or polymer coatings. Using chromate conversion coatings, anodizing in chromic acid, or sealing of anodized layers with dichromate solutions needs to be restricted in the near future since hexavalent chromium is a human carcinogen. In the search for replacements of hexavalent chromium in corrosion protection of aluminum alloys, surface modification in rare-earth metal salt solutions has become quite successful. The cerium-molybdenum process, in which aluminum alloys are immersed in hot cerium salt solutions and anodically polarized in a molybdate solution, has been successfully applied to comercial aluminum alloys.

Cerium chloride addition. Corrosion of aluminum alloys in neutral media occurs as a result of the reduction of oxygen at intermetallic compounds which leads to anodic dissolution of the aluminum matrix. In the presence of chloride ions, aluminum alloys undergo localized corrosion in the form of pitting. It has been found that the addition of cerium salts such as cerium chloride to sodium chloride reduces corrosion rates by lowering the rate of oxygen reduction. Similar results have been obtained after the immersion of aluminum alloys in cerium chloride solutions at room temperature or in boiling cerium chloride or cerium nitrate solutions. The resistance of commercial aluminum alloys to localized corrosion was greatly increased after these pretreatments.

Cerium-molybdenum process. Further refinement of this method of corrosion protection led to the cerium-molybdenum process. This process differs from conventional conversion coatings insofar as cerium and molybdenum oxides (or hydroxides) are incorporated in the natural surface oxide instead of forming a surface coating. The details of this process differ slightly for different aluminum alloys. In general, the alloys are immersed in boiling solutions of cerium chloride, cerium nitrate, or cerium acetate and polarized anodically in a sodium molybdate solution. For Al 6061, the sample is immersed in a boiling solution of cerium chloride for 2 h, followed by immersion in a boiling solution of cerium nitrate for 2 h, and finally by anodic polarization in a sodium molybdate solution for 2 h at a potential of 500 mV versus a saturated calomel reference electrode.

Aluminum-copper pretreatment. Alloying with copper greatly improves the mechanical properties of aluminum alloys but reduces their corrosion resistance by providing additional sites for oxygen reduction. For copper-containing aluminum alloys, a pretreatment step is therefore used in the cerium-molybdenum process in which copper-containing intermetallic compounds are removed from the outer surface layers by a chemical or electrochemical procedure without affecting the mechanical properties. In the electrochemical pretreatment step, the applied potential is adjusted to a value at which copper compounds dissolve at high rates but the aluminum matrix remains passive. In the chemical pretreatment step, the oxidizing power of the solution is adjusted to provide the same potential.

Corrosion resistance. Immersion of aluminum alloys in a sodium chloride solution after treatment in the cerium-molybdenum process has demonstrated the excellent resistance to localized corrosion of these alloys after surface modification. The corrosion behavior of surface-modified aluminum alloys has been evaluated with electrochemical impedance spectroscopy, which is a nondestructive technique so that the corrosion characteristics can be observed as a function of time. These surface-modified alloys have also passed the salt spray test. Cathodic polarization curves recorded in aerated sodium chloride solutions have shown that the rate of oxygen reduction has been greatly reduced by treatment in the cerium-molybdenum process. From anodic polarization curves, it can be concluded that the passive properties have been greatly improved and that the pitting potential, which is the potential at which pits initiate and grow, has been significantly increased. Samples that had been scratched after surface modification and then immersed in a sodium chloride solution did not show any indication of corrosion for extended time periods. These results are considered to be due to the insulating nature of the modified surface layers. Since the rate of the cathodic reaction, which provides the driving force for the initiation and growth of pits, is greatly reduced, localized corrosion does not occur.

Surface analysis has shown that the excellent corrosion resistance of aluminum alloys treated in the cerium-molybdenum process is due to the coverage of cathodic intermetallic compounds by cerium and molybdenum oxides and hydroxides. During immersion in the hot cerium salt solutions, reduction of oxygen occurs at these sites, leading to an increase of the local pH value and precipitation of cerium oxides and hydroxides. During anodic polarization in the molybdate solution, deposition of molybdate compounds occurs only at these sites since the alumina matrix is not conductive. The precipitated cerium compounds are highly insoluble and eliminate any electrochemical reactions on the surface-modified alloys. The role of the molybdenum compounds in the surface-modified layers is not entirely clear. It is possible that electrostatic effects retard the adsorption of chloride ions and therefore increase the pitting potential.

For background information *see* ALUMINUM ALLOYS; CORROSION; METAL COATINGS; PAPER; ZIRCONIUM in the McGraw-Hill Encyclopedia of Science & Technology.   Florian Mansfeld

Bibliography. K. W. Bird, Zircadyne Zr, an alternative to costly corrosion maintenance, *Wah Chung Outlook Newsletter*, 17:2, 1996; B. Lustman and F. Kerze, Jr., *The Metallurgy of Zirconium*, 1955; F. Mansfeld and Y. Wang, Corrosion protection of high-copper aluminum alloys by surface modification, *Brit. Corros. J.*, 29:194, 1994; F. Mansfeld and Y. Wang, Development of "stainless" aluminum alloys by surface modification, *Mater. Sci. Eng.*, 198A:51, 1995; F. Mansfeld, Y. Wang, and H. Shih, The Ce-Mo process for the development of stainless aluminum, *Electrochim. Acta*, 37:2277, 1992; F. Mansfeld, Y. Wang, and H. Shih, Development of stainless aluminum, *J. Electrochim. Soc.*, 138:L74, 1991; J. H. Schemel, *Manual on Zirconium and Hafnium*, 1977.

Cosmic distance scale

The big bang model of the universe makes a number of profound and testable predictions. In a uniformly expanding universe, galaxies would have been closer together in the past. Early in the universe, the density (and temperature) of matter would therefore have been very high. The discovery of the expansion of the universe by E. Hubble in 1929, the discovery of a (now) cool remnant cosmic background radiation by A. Penzias and R. W. Wilson in 1965, and the observed relative abundances of the lightest elements (notably, hydrogen and helium) provide compelling evidence in support of the big bang model.

Importance of distance measurements. In a uniform and isotropic universe, the relative expansion rate, V, is proportional to the relative distance, d, so that $V = Hd$. The Hubble constant, H, thus characterizes the expansion rate of the universe and is required to determine its age. A reliable measurement of the expansion rate, together with an independent estimate of the ages of the oldest objects in the universe, and a further measurement of the average density in the universe, are separately required in order to determine the parameters that govern the evolution of the universe, and ultimately provide constraints on cosmological models.

In addition to providing tests of cosmological models, measurement of the cosmic distance scale and the expansion rate of the universe is important for many other reasons. Knowledge of the Hubble constant is required to determine many of the intrinsic properties of galaxies and clusters of galaxies (such as their masses, luminosities, and radii), and hence provides a necessary foundation for the eventual understanding of how these objects formed and evolved to their present states. Understanding the growth of structure throughout the universe, estimating the abundances of light elements formed in the early universe, and determining the size and age of the visible universe require a determination of the Hubble constant. The expansion rate, size, and age of the universe have been outstanding problems since 1929, but no conclusive answers have been obtained despite half a century of serious efforts at major observatories around the world. Because of the impasse reached by ground-based observations, and because of the obvious importance of these outstanding questions, the Hubble Space Telescope was built in large part to resolve them.

Observing programs. In the mid-1980s a panel of astronomers reviewing the top-priority science for the Hubble Space Telescope designated the determination of the extragalactic distance scale as one of the key projects to be undertaken and completed by the telescope. A team of about 20 astronomers has been actively involved in this effort. This key project involves determining accurate distances to about two dozen galaxies. In addition, at least two other groups have been awarded time on the Hubble Space Telescope to observe several additional galaxies for complementary calibrations. These galaxy distances will be used to establish an accurate and precise value for the Hubble constant.

From Earth orbit, the vacuum of space provides an unhindered view of the sky, free from the blurring by the Earth's atmosphere that plagues ground-based telescopes. The large aperture and fine-tuned optics of the Hubble Space Telescope allow details to be seen with such clarity that a volume of space that is 1000 times larger than is comparably available to most Earth-bound telescopes can now be surveyed. With this vast reach, the Hubble has been programmed to undertake a rapid survey of distances to once-remote galaxies. The Hubble is so efficient that in 3 years it has almost tripled the number of nearby galaxies whose distances have been accurately measured, compared to a half century of observations at the world's largest telescopes on the ground.

Measurement technique. Remarkably, the technique employed to obtain distances with the Hubble Space Telescope is the same as the one used when Hubble first demonstrated that spiral galaxies, such as the Milky Way, are major constituents of the universe. The key to this effort is in discovering a class of variable stars called Cepheids. These supergiant stars are known to obey a precise relation between their period (or frequency) of oscillation and the total luminosity of the star. Discovered by H. Leavitt in 1912, this period-luminosity relation for Cepheids means that, given a measure of the period of a Cepheid, the star's intrinsic brightness can be predicted. Then, if the observed brightness of the Cepheid is measured and compared with the predicted brightness, the distance is obtained by applying the inverse-square law of light.

Results. Even at the midterm of the key project, with only half of the target galaxies observed, it is possible to obtain a number of independent estimates of the Hubble constant derived from the new Cepheid distances. The Cepheids are being used to tie into several other methods that operate at greater distances than the Cepheid measurements themselves, and two major efforts in pushing the Hubble Space Telescope to its detection limit have resulted in Cepheid distances to two major clusters of galaxies, each probing the Hubble flow at large distances. The two clusters are called Virgo and Fornax, after the constellations in which they are found. Virgo is in the northern hemisphere, Fornax in the southern. Although Virgo is massive and complex, by mid-1997 the Cepheid distances to five of its galaxies had been independently measured by the Hubble Space Telescope; Fornax has one Cepheid distance measured, and two additional galaxies had just been observed with the Hubble Space Telescope in 1998. The galaxies with Cepheid distances are used to calibrate the expansion rate by employing a number of independent distance techniques. One example is the Tully-Fisher relation, which uses the empirical correlation of total galaxy luminosity with its distance-independent rotation rate. This method gives a Hubble constant of 75 kilometers per second per megaparsec. (1 Mpc equals 3.26×10^6 light-years, 1.9×10^{19} mi, or 3.1×10^{19} km.) Another method is the use of type Ia supernovae as standard candles, again calibrated by Cepheids, gives 68 km/(s)(Mpc). The uncertainties in these measurements are both statistical (which decrease as the sample size increases) and systematic (due, for example, to large-scale flow motions or uncertainties in the foundations of the Cepheid distance scale itself), and are currently estimated to be at the ± 10 km/(s)(Mpc), or 15%, level.

Age of the universe. Once both a measure of the expansion rate or Hubble constant and the value of the average density of matter in the universe have been obtained, the expansion age of the universe can be estimated. This age can then be compared with the ages measured for stars in the Milky Way Galaxy. If the universe has a high enough density of matter to exactly balance the outward Hubble flow, the value of the Hubble constant implied by the current Hubble Space Telescope measurements suggests that the universe is only 9 billion years old. Even if the density of the universe is very low, the age of the universe can only be as large as 12 billion years, unless there is a nonzero value for the cosmological constant, as some preliminary results have suggested. (In that case the universe could be expanding more rapidly than in the past and the age of the universe could be somewhat larger than 12 billion years.) However, the oldest stars have been calculated to have present-day ages of 15 ± 2 billion years. At face value it would appear that the oldest objects of the universe are older than the universe itself, obviously a paradox that must be solved. The astrophysicists who work on stellar evolution theory and who calculate the ages of stars are confident that their calculations, and the observations on which the ages are based, are secure. However, recent results from the *Hipparcos* parallax satellite may be indicating that the ages of the oldest stars have, in fact, been overestimated.

Although great strides have been made in measuring the expansion rate of the universe, the question is still not settled. It will take several years of continued work with the Hubble Space Telescope, including measurements in the infrared using the new Near-Infrared Camera and Multi-Object Spectrometer (NICMOS) instrument, to increase the precision in the value of the Hubble constant. It will then be seen whether the new observations from Hubble will make it necessary to rethink some of the basic properties of the universe. Nevertheless, these first results are noteworthy, and there is reason to believe that in the next few years an accurate cosmic distance scale and value of the expansion rate of the universe can be determined. *See* INFRARED ASTRONOMY.

For background information *see* BIG BANG THEORY; CEPHEIDS; COSMOLOGY; HUBBLE CONSTANT; SATELLITE ASTRONOMY; UNIVERSE in the McGraw-Hill Encyclopedia of Science & Technology.

Wendy L. Freedman; Barry F. Madore

Bibliography. D. Goldsmith, *Einstein's Biggest Blunder*, 1995; S. W. Hawking, *A Brief History of Time*, 1988; E. Hubble, *The Realm of the Nebulae*, 1958, reprint 1991; D. Overby, *Lonely Hearts of the Cosmos*, 1991.

Crab

Recent investigations of crabs have focused on their social and sexual interactions which involve use of special long-stalked eyes and chemical communication.

Long-Stalked Eyes

In theory, to respond to potential predators, an animal needs information about its immediate risk. If this information is costly to obtain, evolution will favor fixed responses to small amounts of information. Fiddler crabs live in open, flat habitats such as sandflats and beaches. When they emerge at low tide from their underground burrows to feed and court, they are at considerable risk from predators. While fiddler crabs do not require vision for foraging, they rely heavily upon vision for their intraspecific social interactions, and they rely almost exclusively on vision for predator detection. They must, therefore, make unambiguous discriminations between conspecifics and predators; and to minimize risk of predation and to maximize mating opportunities, they must do this at as great a distance as possible.

In principle, the visual characteristics that might allow identification of predators and conspecifics are shape, size (predators are usually larger than their prey), and speed (predators are often fast moving). These cues are useful within only a short range and place the crab at risk if they must be used to distinguish, for example, hungry seagulls from potential mates. It has been shown that fiddler crabs greatly reduce their risk by taking advantage of the unique geometry of their flat habitat in a way that extends their capacity to identify predators and conspecifics well beyond what is possible with these cues. The results discussed below are mainly from the species *Uca pugilator* of eastern North America.

Eye resolution and movements. The use of the cues mentioned above is ultimately limited by the resolution of the crab's eyes. The eyes are of the apposition compound type, and the ommatidial array of each eye views an impressively large proportion of the world: from about $+85°$ to $-70°$ altitude at the front of the eye, and $360°$ horizontally. There is a narrow band of high resolution, or acute zone, extending around the eye at its equator. In this region, the vertical angular resolution decreases from a peak at the eye equator of about $1°$ to twice that value at $\pm25°$ altitude. The horizontal angular resolution remains fairly constant over the whole eye, about $2-3°$.

The eyes are set on long stalks that protrude above the carapace. They are held in a stereotyped position, with the plane of the acute zone parallel to the flat substrate, by using gravitational cues and by fixating the visible horizon with the acute zone. When the substrate is tilted, such as on a sloped beach, fixation of the local horizon dominates gravity as the orientational cue, allowing the acute zone to remain parallel to the tilted substrate. Thus the eyes are designed, both in their morphology and in their movements, to sample preferentially the region of space around the horizon.

Shape, size, and speed. Using shape to identify objects requires the crab to have sophisticated pattern recognition abilities, which ultimately depend on visual resolution. Since each ommatidium represents a single pixel of the retinal image, a grid representing the resolution of the fiddler crab eye can be overlaid on a scene with objects of potential interest (**Fig. 1**). It is clear that unless objects are very large they must be quite close before their shape can be resolved.

Size and speed cues have ambiguity related to distance. The eye sees only the angular size and speed of objects; distance is required to convert these to absolute terms. Distance can be measured stereoscopically within a range that depends on horizontal resolution and interocular distance, and is limited to about 4.5 in. (12 cm). One way that larger distances could be measured, if the substrate is assumed to be flat, is by measuring the angle of declination of the base of an object (angle δ in **Fig. 2**). The effective range of this mechanism depends on vertical resolution and the height of the eye above the ground, both of which are enhanced in fiddler crabs, and would increase the radius of distance perception to about 8 ft (2.5 m). However, crabs readily respond to predators at greater distances. While stereoscopic and declination mechanisms may be used for social interactions, all of which occur within 12 in. (30 cm) or so, they are useless in predator identification because of their limited range.

Use of visual horizon. That distance may be acquired via the declination angle demonstrates that relations between objects in a flat habitat have a certain geometrical predictability. Another example of this principle, more important for the problem of predator–conspecific discrimination, is that any object which appears above eye level is larger than oneself (Fig. 2). Fiddler crabs use this situation: the only difference between stimuli eliciting intraspecific behavior, such as the claw-waving display, and escape is the part of the visual field in which they occur. Objects below the horizon elicit waving, while objects above the horizon prompt escape. In the laboratory, crabs escaped from stimuli presented above eye level with a frequency that was dependent on angular size, but they almost never escaped from identical stimuli below eye level. This result demonstrated that the crucial feature of a stimulus was its position relative to the horizon.

There are two possible strategies for determining whether an object has penetrated the horizon: (1) the eye is not specially aligned with the horizon, but the crab knows from gravity or visual cues where the horizon lies across the eye; (2) the crab aligns its eye with the horizon and uses its anatomical horizon (corresponding to the acute zone) to determine whether objects occur in the upper or lower hemisphere. In the latter case, threatening objects will always occur in the distal part of the retina, and thus the response can be "hard wired." In the former case, threatening objects may occur in any part of the retina, and only after computing the eye's relation to the substrate can they be verified as threatening. Behavioral experiments indicate that the second case is true: when crabs are presented with a visible horizon-stripe that is tilted away from horizontal, some fixate it with their acute zones, and some do not (their eyes remain parallel with gravity). However, whether they fixate the stripe or not, crabs escape only from objects which are imaged in the distal portion of the retina. Thus, escape depends

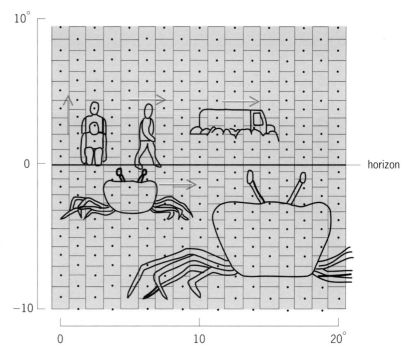

Fig. 1. Angular sizes of various objects, projected onto the ommatidial array in the center of the eye of *Uca pugilator*. Each rectangle represents the area of space that corresponds to a single ommatidium, and thus represents the pixelation of the image. Above the horizon, objects caused escape if they moved vertically or horizontally through one ommatidial angle. Below the horizon, the moving crab at left caused an increase in mating display behavior of the male; the crab at right is of the size when sexes are distinguished. The acute zone is assumed to be centered vertically at the horizon. *(After M. F. Land and J. E. Layne, The visual control of behavior in fiddler crabs, I. Resolution thresholds and the role of the horizon, J. Compar. Physiol., 177A:81–90, 1995)*

only on the object's position on the retina, not on an object's position relative to gravity or to the visible stripe.

John E. Layne

Sexual Behavior

The shore crab, *Carcinus maenas*, is a decapod crustacean commonly found on the coasts of northwest Europe and the northeast United States. It occurs on all shore types from the high water mark to a depth of 200 ft (60 m), feeding on a wide variety of invertebrates including mollusks, polychaete worms, and other crustaceans. In order to grow, shore crabs periodically shed, or molt, their exoskeleton to reveal soft, folded cuticle tissue which subsequently expands and hardens to form a new, larger exoskeleton. It takes several days for the new exoskeleton to fully harden, and during this early postmolt period crabs have a limited capacity for movement and so are unable to actively defend themselves from predators. Throughout this hazardous time, solitary male crabs attempt to hide from danger beneath rocks or weed until full mobility returns. For sexually mature female crabs, however, the situation is different because during their molt mating takes place. A female pairs with a hard-shelled male in a bond that lasts 4–10 days, and thus gains the protection of the attendant male throughout the dangerous postmolt period. The male defends his partner against compet-

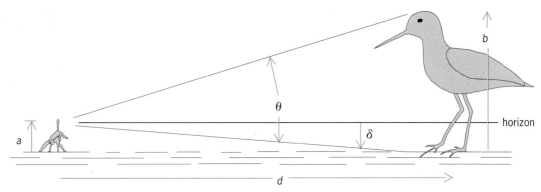

Fig. 2. Penetration of the horizon characterizes objects larger than the self. Unlike judgments of size and distance, this relation can be used for objects at any distance. In principle, at close range distance d may be obtained from a/δ, and the height b of the intruder is then $d\theta$. This mechanism is restricted by the visual resolution to about 8 ft (2.5 m). *(After J. E. Layne, M. F. Land, and J. Zeil, Fiddler crabs use the visual horizon to distinguish predators from conspecifics: A review of the evidence, J. Mar. Biol. Ass. U.K., 77:43–54, 1997)*

ing males and predators, often burying himself and his mate in sediment.

Mating behavior. Sexual behavior between pairs of crabs normally starts several days before the molt of the female. When in proximity to mature premolt females, sexually receptive males exhibit highly stereotyped behavior, rising up on extended walking limbs with their claws extended forward. The fifth pair of walking limbs are often held in an elevated posture at the rear of the crab, and if sufficiently stimulated, the male commences a slow forward searching motion. Once physical contact is established, a period of precopulation pairing commences, often lasting for several days, with the male settling onto the back of the female and cradling her with his walking limbs. Copulation usually takes place immediately following the female molt, with the pair of crabs adopting a posture in which the male overlies the female with their ventral surfaces touching. The female abdomen is extended, overlapping that of the male, whose underlying pair of pleopods, the structures used for transferring spermatophores, are then inserted into the female genital openings. Paired crabs typically remain in this position for 2–3 days, after which there may follow a short period of postcopula guarding in which the male adopts the cradling posture seen at precopula pairing. When the female is eventually released by the male, her exoskeleton is hard and she is capable of normal motion.

Chemical communication. Pheromones are externally released, biologically active chemicals that

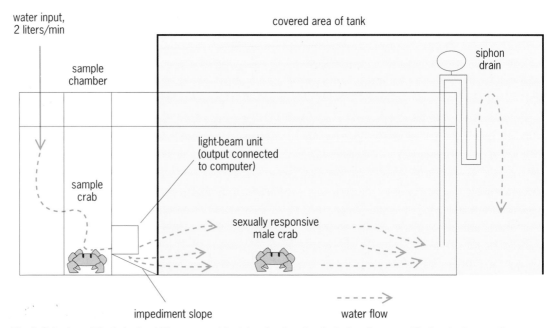

Fig. 3. Side view of the behavioral bioassay used to determine the chemical attractiveness of test crabs to sexually receptive males.

function as a means of communication between members of the same species. Evidence that pheromones are involved in the sexual behavior of shore crabs is provided by the observation that male crabs exhibit a full sexual behavioral response when exposed to water taken from a vessel that has previously contained premolt females. A sexual response is also generated when premolt female urine is introduced into tanks containing receptive males.

Behavioral bioassay. In order to investigate the nature of pheromone communication in shore crabs, the characteristic sexual display of stimulated males can be incorporated into a behavioral bioassay (**Fig. 3**). A chamber is constructed within a tank into which test crabs can be placed without visual or physical contact with a sexually receptive male held in the main chamber. A constant unidirectional flow of seawater is directed through the sample chamber before entering the main tank area through a series of small holes in a horizontal plane. When chemically attracted, males in the main tank area exhibit the characteristic sexual response and move upcurrent toward the sample chamber, typically remaining nearby for as long as the attractive source persists. The continued presence of male crabs in the region adjacent to the sample chamber is used as a positive indicator of chemical attraction. In order to deter crabs that are not sexually stimulated from approaching the chamber, a slope is positioned across the width of the tank which provides a physical challenge. In addition, the slope is illuminated by ambient light, in contrast to the remainder of the main tank area which is shaded. The combination of these factors is normally sufficient to deter nonstimulated males from climbing the slope but does not prohibit the approach of sexually stimulated males. Crabs reaching the top of the slope break an infrared light beam, the output of which is connected to a computer that records the duration of each breakage. Each crab to be tested for chemical attractiveness is preceded and followed by a premolt female to allow the receptivity of males to be assessed and to provide a comparative level of response intensity to that obtained for the test crab in each individual assessment.

Plots obtained from the bioassay show that males climb the deterrent slope in response to the presence of premolt females in the sample chamber but fail to respond to intermolt females or premolt males presented in the same fashion (**Fig. 4**). This behavior demonstrates both temporal and sexual specificity of chemical attraction and shows that the pheromone is not a direct by-product of the biochemistry associated with molting but has sexually specific origins elsewhere. Further investigations using the bioassay have shown that postmolt females remain chemically attractive to receptive males up to 8 days after the molt. In order to test the relationship between chemical attractiveness and reproductive capability, previously unmated females of known postmolt age were offered to males. It was shown that males were successful in inserting their pleopods

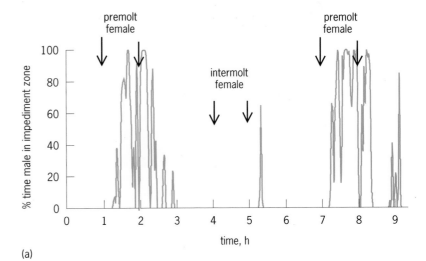

(a)

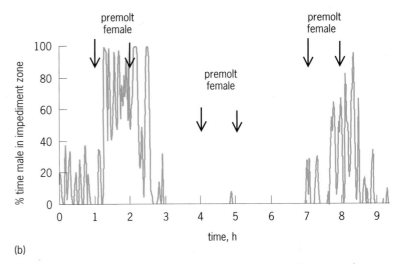

(b)

Fig. 4. Percentage of time that a sexually receptive male shore crab spent on the impediment slope (*a*) for each successive 2-min period following the addition of premolt and intermolt females to the sample chamber of the test tank; and (*b*) in response to premolt females and a premolt male. Arrows delimit the time period that each crab remained in the sample chamber.

into all of the tested females up to 10 days after the molt, with reduced success thereafter. It appears that increased hardening of the female exoskeleton eventually denies full penetration of male pleopods into the female genital openings. Even though it is likely that the majority of females will copulate immediately following their molt, the potential for extended sexual receptivity could be important in areas where crab density is low or where suitable males are in short supply because of a temporary glut of molting females. If only a brief period of sexual receptivity were available, unaccompanied molting females would lose reproductive potential until their next molt many months later.

Detection of pheromone. Manipulation of the antennules, the site of detection of pheromone in males, has given further insight into the role of chemical communication in shore crabs. With a nondestructive technique it is possible to temporarily disable the paired antennules so that sexual behavior between pairs of crabs can be observed in the absence of pheromone stimulation. Individual components of sexual behavior proceed in the absence of sex pheromone detection, with crabs responding to tactile and possibly visual stimuli. However, there is evidence that pair bond reinforcement throughout the prolonged mating period is dependent on detection of sex pheromone by the male and in its absence the normal sequence and duration of sexual behavior components is disrupted.

For background information *see* CRAB; EYE (INVERTEBRATE); MOLTING; PHEROMONE; VISION in the McGraw-Hill Encyclopedia of Science & Technology.   Shaw D. Bamber

Bibliography. S. D. Bamber and E. Naylor, Sites of release of putative sex pheromone and sexual behaviour in female *Carcinus maenas* (Crustacea: Decapoda), *Estuar. Coastal Shelf Sci.*, 44:195–202, 1997; J. H. Christy, Competitive mating, mate choice and mating associations of brachyuran crabs, *Bull. Mar. Sci.*, 41:177–191, 1987; J. E. Layne, M. F. Land, and J. Zeil, Fiddler crabs use the visual horizon to distinguish predators from conspecifics: A review of the evidence, *J. Mar. Biol. Ass. U.K.*, 77:43–54, 1997; J. Zeil, G. Nalbach, and H.-O. Nalbach, Eyes, eye stalks and the visual world of semiterrestrial crabs, *J. Compar. Physiol.*, 159A:801–811, 1986.

Crumpling

The haphazard complexity of a crumpled sheet or membrane has recently been shown to be governed by a simple mathematical law. Other things being equal, an eightfold increase in the size of a sheet implies a twofold increase in its energy.

When a flat sheet of metal, paper, rubber, plastic, or cloth is strongly distorted, the sheet typically does not bend uniformly. The bending gets concentrated into sharp points and narrow ridges. Understanding such deformations is important since deforming sheets of material is a central feature in creating and manipulating many objects in everyday life. Points and ridges appear whenever a container is crushed, a vehicle crashes, or a garment is worn. They also appear on a molecular level in large fullerene molecules and in shriveled cell membranes. On a geological scale, when the Earth's crust buckles to form mountain ranges, points and ridges appear. Despite the prevalence of points and ridges, there has been little quantitative understanding of them. There has been no simple way to judge how narrow the ridges should be, or how much energy they contain, or how severely the material there is stressed. The newly discovered law provides such understanding for the first time.

Crumpling occurs when a two-dimensional sheet is confined within a small volume. A sheet may be crumpled by enclosing it within a hollow sphere and then gradually shrinking the sphere. A thin sheet may be crushed to a tiny fraction of its original size before the sphere is full of material. The resulting pattern of sharp points and ridges appears similar whether the sheet has been compressed by a factor of 10, 100, or 1000. Recent studies have sought to characterize the size-independent features of these crumpled patterns by considering the limiting behavior of sheets that are very thin relative to their size. These studies have used experimental measurement and computer modeling. They complement the new approach described below.

Energy minimization. A deformed sheet takes on a shape that minimizes its energy. There are two kinds of deformation: bending and stretching. The energetic cost of a given amount of bending or stretching depends on the thickness of the sheet. When the thickness is halved, the cost of stretching halves, but the cost of bending is divided by eight. Thus a very thin sheet of any material becomes arbitrarily easier to bend than to stretch, as everyday experience confirms. To analyze very thin sheets, they may initially be supposed to be unstretchable.

Conelike deformations. The unstretchability condition strongly limits how a confined sheet can deform as its confining sphere gradually shrinks around it: Each point on the sheet can curve in only one direction. This statement confirms the everyday knowledge that a flat piece of paper cannot be wrapped over a rounded shape without stretching it. An unstretchable sheet can accommodate to its confining sphere by distorting into a conelike shape (**illus.** *a*). A point on a cone has no curvature in the direction toward its vertex. Thus, every element curves in only one direction, and no stretching is necessary. (The vertex itself must curve in more than one direction, but the local stretching that results can be neglected.) The energy cost of this conelike deformation is readily found. It grows logarithmically, that is, very gradually, with the size of the sheet.

As the confining sphere continues to shrink, there comes a point when the conelike distortion of the sheet is no longer sufficient to keep it within the sphere. Then a second cone becomes necessary. The second vertex alters the shape and energy of a sheet (illus. *b*). The unstretchability of the sheet limits the curvature at a generic point *p*. The sheet cannot curve in the direction of the left vertex because it is part of the left cone, nor can it curve in the direction of the right vertex. Thus the sheet at *p* has no curvature in two independent directions. This means that the entire sheet on each flank of the two cones must be completely flat. Only on the line joining the two vertices can there be curvature. Since the flanks are flat, there must be a sharp crease along this connecting ridge. All the bending energy is concentrated on this ridge. If the crease were really infinitely sharp, the bending energy would be infinite.

Stretching ridges. To avoid this infinite energy, a sheet with two (or more) vertices must stretch. To see where and how much stretching occurs, a simpler situation may be analyzed (illus. *c*), wherein a kite shape is formed by clamping a sheet in a rigid, diamond-shaped frame and then bending down the two

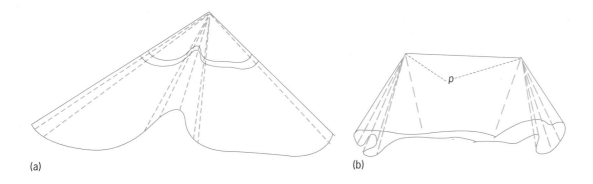

(a) (b)

sharply creased line

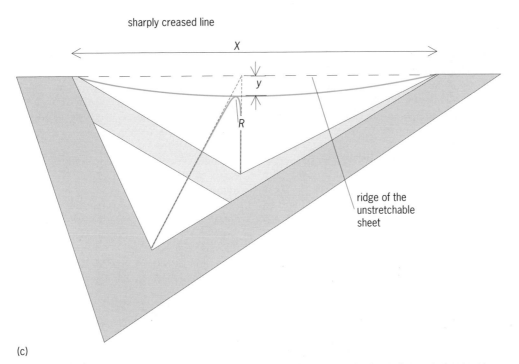

(c)

Stages in the deformation of an elastic sheet. (a) Conelike shape resulting from moderate confinement of a sheet in a sphere. (b) Two-cone shape resulting from further confinement. Here p is a representative point on the sheet. (c) Kite shape, illustrating how the stretching ridge arises. The ridge length X, the transverse radius of curvature R in the middle, and the resulting deflection y are indicated, and a sharply creased line of the unstretchable sheet is shown.

sides, holding the long axis fixed. If the sheet were unstretchable, it would be obliged to form a sharp crease (illus. c). But since the sheet has some small stretchability, it can stretch to avoid the infinite energy of this sharp crease. The optimal amount of curvature and stretching is found by supposing that the sheet has some transverse radius of curvature R in the middle of the ridge. This quantity R is gradually increased from zero until the value of R with the least total energy is found. As R increases, the bending energy decreases.

The transverse diagonal perpendicular to the ridge line is now considered. Near the midpoint this line may be approximated as a circular arc of radius R. Elsewhere it is essentially straight, as it would be for an unstretchable sheet. If it is supposed that this line does not stretch, its total length will remain the same as that of the sharply creased line of the

unstretchable sheet (illus. c). In order to curve smoothly without increasing its length, this line must move away from the sharp ridge of the unstretchable sheet. As R is increased, the distance y of the midpoint from its original position (illus. c) must increase. The ridge line, deflected a distance y, is now lengthened. The ridge line must be increasingly stretched as R increases from zero, adding stretching energy to the sheet.

As R is increased from zero, there comes a point where the decrease in bending energy is just compensated by the increase in stretching energy. At this point the total energy is minimal and R is optimal. By analyzing this configuration quantitatively, it is found that the optimal value of R grows as the ridge length X to the ⅔ power. This means that as X becomes large, R also grows large in an absolute sense, but relative to the length X, R becomes indefinitely small. The energy is concentrated in the long, narrow ridge zone. This zone becomes a smaller and smaller fraction of the sheet as the size X increases. The same trade-off between bending and stretching seen in the kite example (illus. *c*) occurs in the confined sheet with the two-cone configuration (illus. *b*). The line joining the two vertices has the same properties as the ridge of the kite. The optimal shape of the sheet necessarily involves stretching. As the sheet is confined to a smaller and smaller sphere, more vertices appear, and these are connected by ridges, each behaving quantitatively like the kite ridge.

Power-law increase in energy. These stretching ridges have a dramatic effect on the energy of a crumpled sheet. Without considering these ridges, it might be supposed that the energy of a crumpled sheet was the bending energy in the conelike skirts around the vertices. Then the energy of each such region would grow only logarithmically with its size, as noted above. But the stretching ridges make the energy grow faster, as the $\frac{1}{3}$ power of the size. Thus an eightfold increase in the length X of a ridge implies a twofold increase in its energy. The ridge properties also dictate the apportionment of this energy into $\frac{5}{6}$ bending energy and $\frac{1}{6}$ stretching energy. These properties of ridges do not presuppose any special properties of particular materials. They depend only on the common behavior of all gently stressed solid sheets. Thus these conclusions apply to all materials, from soft rubber to stiff paper, provided these are made into large, thin sheets.

Computer studies. Computer studies have corroborated the predicted properties of stretching ridges in a variety of deformed sheets. The predicted thin-sheet behavior sets in when the thickness becomes less than about a thousandth of the distance between vertices. If a brittle material such as glass or a malleable one such as solder is chosen, the constraints on size and thickness become more stringent.

Strength properties of sheets. Even with these restrictions, the power-law properties of stretching ridges provide a new, quantitative insight regarding the energy, strength, and shape of crumpled and other strongly deformed sheets. To deduce the energy in a crumpled sheet to a good approximation, it is necessary to know only the bending modulus and thickness of the sheet, and the number of ridges of various lengths. In deliberately constructed ridge structures, the ridges are expected to add strength and rigidity to membranes in the same way that prestressing adds strength to concrete. With knowledge of the ridge behavior, these strength properties can potentially be understood and controlled.

For background information *see* CELL MEMBRANES; ELASTICITY; FULLERENES in the McGraw-Hill Encyclopedia of Science & Technology.   T. A. Witten

Bibliography. G. Gompper, Mechanics: Patterns of stress in crumpled sheets, *Nature*, 386:439, 1997; A. E. Lobkovsky and T. A. Witten, Properties of ridges in elastic membranes, *Phys. Rev. E*, 55:1577–1589, 1997; D. Nelson, T. Piran, and S. Weinberg (eds.), *Statistical Mechanics of Membranes and Surfaces*, 1989; Z. Zhang et al., The asymptotic shape of elastic networks, *Phys. Rev. B*, 52:5404–5413, 1995.

Data systems

Increasingly, organizations recognize that in order to remain competitive and grow profitably they need to leverage their informational assets, in addition to their operational assets such as inventory and manufacturing. Until recently, few organizations could take advantage of their informational assets. Because of technology limitations, high costs, and even the marketing conditions of the time, information exploitation was always low priority. Since 1995 several conditions have changed: relevant technologies (databases, processors, analytical tools, and visualization) have improved, costs have significantly decreased, and market conditions have changed (competition has increased, along with the homogenization of the market in the eyes of the consumer). These factors have led to the emergence of business intelligence, an umbrella term comprising three processes whose goal is to facilitate the extraction of information from databases and its application to decision making: data warehousing, data mining, and decision support. This article outlines the processes that make up business intelligence, describes the various generations of business intelligence systems, and provides examples from application domains where business intelligence has been successfully used.

Business intelligence. Each business intelligence process includes a set of technologies and implementation methodologies.

Data warehousing. This term refers to the process of extracting, cleaning, augmenting, and organizing operational data, that is, preparing it for analysis. The resulting database is called the data warehouse. Building a data warehouse involves (1) extracting data from transactional databases, for example, point-of-sale data from a supermarket's cash register; (2) cleaning the data, for example, supplying missing values, removing duplicate records, and identifying incorrect records; (3) enriching the data set with outside data, for example, credit reporting data and credit scoring data; and (4) organizing the resulting data set in ways that expedite downstream processing and desired user interaction, for example, running a set of batch reports to establish the effectiveness of marketing campaigns, interactively querying the database to establish the profitability of particular customers, or applying data mining techniques to automatically segment a set of customers.

Data mining. This term (and more generally, knowledge discovery) refers to the extraction of structure (patterns, models, and relations) from the warehoused data. The two forms are verification-driven data mining, which enables a user to verify patterns and relations (expressions of a hypothesis) against a data set; and discovery-driven data mining, where patterns and relations are extracted automatically. During the mining process, data may need to be transformed, enhanced, and otherwise preprocessed. These operations are separate from the corresponding ones which have taken place during the creation of the data warehouse, since they are task specific rather than organization specific. Present-generation data-mining systems combine verification-driven and discovery-driven data-mining operations. Verification-driven data mining allows the decision maker to express and verify knowledge in both the organizational and personal domains, while discovery-driven data mining is used to refine this knowledge and identify information not previously hypothesized by the user.

Decision support. This term refers to the process of filtering, optimizing, and organizing mined information to support decision making. The decision maker must (1) assess the value of each extracted pattern in relation to a set of objectives related to a goal, for example, to increase the response rate of a telemarketing campaign by 60%; (2) decide whether patterns will need to be combined, and how; and (3) select the most appropriate patterns and use them to formulate an action plan. For example, after the identification of a pattern wherein lower-middle-class consumers in metropolitan areas prefer purchasing supermarket-brand orange juice, supermarkets serving these areas decide to stock larger quantities of their brand of orange juice, whereas national consumer packaged goods companies decide to run advertising campaigns in the same areas to counter this trend.

Evolution of systems. Business intelligence systems appeared in the early 1980s in the form of custom-developed decision support and executive information systems. These systems provided application-specific front ends for querying small, carefully crafted databases that contained summaries from operational databases. They were followed by warehouses which enabled large-scale what-if analysis. These warehouses were accessed through a new generation of interactive query and reporting tools which eliminated the need for the user to know the SQL database language and thus made data warehouses more approachable by business analysts. By the mid-1990s, business analysts were asking for more sophisticated data analysis capabilities to deal with the ever-increasing sizes of the data warehouses. This demand has resulted in a series of business intelligence innovations:

1. Multitiered data architectures. While initial warehouses contained summary data, organizations came to realize that better understanding could be obtained if unsummarized (or atomic) data were used instead. In addition, organizations started implementing warehouses to simultaneously support several functional areas (sales, marketing, distribution). This shift resulted in explosive growth in the size of data warehouses. To draw value from such warehouses, organizations began creating data marts, topic-specific data warehouses which address only the data and informational needs of a single organization, or even one group. An enterprise's business intelligence architecture may contain several levels of data marts.

2. Warehouses storing complex data. First-generation warehouses contained only numeric data, such as per-month sales by department and store. Building on the increased sophistication of database management systems, data warehouses under development store time-series data, for example, the set of automatic teller machine transactions that a customer executes over a moving window of 6 months; image data, for example, images of the merchandise that a customer selected (but not necessarily bought) from a retailer's Web site; and so forth.

3. Scalable data-mining algorithms. Most modeling and clustering algorithms now in use are computationally expensive, inhibiting their application on very large data sets. New data-mining algorithms are linear or near linear, thus overcoming this problem. Many of these new algorithms have also been parallelized.

4. Interactive data-mining toolkits that can be embedded in databases. Present-generation data-mining tools include a variety of pattern extraction techniques and sophisticated visualization tools, thus enabling multistrategy data mining.

5. Applications that are implemented on top of the developed data-mining toolkits. These applications couple sophisticated analysis techniques with business rules enabling business analysts to interact with the created data warehouses to address complex problems such as attrition analysis, fraud detection, and sales analysis.

6. Web-enabled analysis software. Such software uses the ubiquity and low cost of the Internet and the World Wide Web to provide business users with broad access to the information in data warehouses. It is estimated that through such software the users of data warehouses will grow from 400,000 in 1997 to over 10 million by the year 2000. *See* WEB RESOURCES.

Applications organizations. While the interest in business intelligence is strong in every industry, three dominant applications have emerged: database marketing, category management, and fraud detection. The interest in these applications is fueled by the need of organizations to better understand customers: their behaviors, their needs (stated and inferred), and their attitudes toward a company, a product, and so forth. These applications are deployed on top of data marts and include a query component, a predictive modeling component, and a clustering component, and a set of application-specific and industry-specific reports, providing, for example, the response of a particular marketing campaign per geographical area, or the sales of a specific item per department.

Database marketing involves analysis of databases that include customer data (for example, demographic data) and behavior (for example, purchases made over a particular time period) to identify homogeneous customer groups and predict their response to a marketing campaign (for example, their propensity to buy a particular product, or to accept a product offer if contacted by mail).

Category management examines data on movement of retail stock, recorded at a point of sale, to support decisions on shelf space allocation for a particular product (for example, 16-ounce frozen orange juice packages of brand X) or a category of products (for example, frozen orange juice), store layout and product location (for example, where the 16-ounce frozen orange juice packages of brand X should be placed), and promotion effectiveness (for example, whether the campaign to sell a particular type of frozen orange juice through coupons distributed in the store has paid off).

Fraud detection applications compare data describing a transaction (for example, a claim submitted to an insurance company) with information describing past behavior of the individual executing the transaction, or of a group that shares a set of characteristics similar to those of the individual executing the transaction, to establish the probability of the transaction being fraudulent. Transactions that are flagged as potentially fraudulent can then be investigated in greater detail so that a decision can be made.

Advantages of data warehouses. By the turn of the century, business intelligence systems will be fully integrated with the rest of an organization's informational infrastructure. Coupled with appropriate applications and accessible over the Internet, the data warehouse will provide the foundation for this integration because it has three basic advantages over other methods of organizing data for analysis: (1) It results in a clean database which positively impacts the quality of the mined information. (2) It integrates static data (for example, a patient's demographic and life-style data) with behavioral data (for example, how many times a patient took a particular drug during the prescribed period). (3) It provides a "single version of the truth"; that is, every department in an organization accesses exactly the same data.

For background information *see* DATABASE MANAGEMENT SYSTEMS; DECISION SUPPORT SYSTEM in the McGraw-Hill Encyclopedia of Science & Technology. Evangelos Simoudis

Bibliography. U. M. Fayyad et al. (eds.), *Advances in Knowledge Discovery and Data Mining*, 1996; J. R. Quinlan, *C4.5: Programs for Machine Learning*, 1993.

Deoxyribonucleic acid (DNA)

Advanced analytical techniques are available to determine physical and electronic properties of deoxyribonucleic acid. Experiments on single DNA molecules have shown that their physical properties are described quite well by classical elasticity theory. Whether DNA is a good electron conductor is still open to debate, but recent experiments indicate that electron transport in DNA does occur.

Elasticity

As the twentieth century began, the reality of atoms and molecules was still vigorously debated. The patient accumulation of indirect evidence for the molecular hypothesis finally left no room for doubt, but molecules remained unseen actors in a strange world governed by bizarre laws (quantum theory) totally unlike the classical physics of the nineteenth century. By the 1930s, when this picture was firmly in place, it would have seemed as foolish to treat molecules by classical physics as to apply quantum theory to the motions of the planets. The two domains were viewed as entirely divorced; molecules were just too small for classical physics to apply.

By midcentury, however, it became clear that enormous single molecules exist in living cells. Indeed, some animals contain single molecules of DNA up to a meter (3 ft) in length. Biomolecules such as DNA, actin, and proteins are polymers, long chains of similar, repeated units. Moreover, since each unit contains dozens of individual atoms, there is a question as to whether the molecule itself could behave effectively as a continuum object, governed by the rules of matter in bulk. If so, DNA would respond to applied forces as an elastic body—an enormous simplification over the complex and unintuitive underlying quantum laws.

Recently it has become possible to test this hypothesis directly in a new class of experiments on single molecules of DNA. Besides its conceptual value, the elastic picture offers the promise of detailed understanding of the binding of DNA to drugs, genetic regulation, and the compact packaging of DNA in living cells.

Testing the elastic hypothesis might seem farfetched. DNA is a long, thin rod, only 2 nanometers in diameter. Certainly there is no "vise-and-pliers" apparatus with which to stress DNA, nor any suitable microscope to observe how it deforms. Instead, experimentalists have constructed a micrometer-scale apparatus, many thousands of times bigger than the actual length scale of interest, indirectly finding the intrinsic elastic parameters by using simple ideas from statistical physics. (Even more ingenious, but more indirect, means had been used earlier to obtain rough estimates of these parameters.)

Rubber-tube model. To see how this approach might be possible, it is helpful to imagine a long, thin elastic object, such as a length of rubber tubing 1 cm (0.4 in.) in diameter. Scaled to this human size, the DNA in a typical experiment would be almost a kilometer (0.6 mi) long. A rubber tube resists bending, but clearly it is easier to make a 90° bend of large radius than one of small radius. Indeed, the energy cost of a 90° bend can be as small as desired if a long enough segment of the tube is chosen.

The significance of this remark lies in the fact that at room temperature molecules are in constant motion. Specifically, every possible molecular motion, including bending deformations, is constantly taking place, and each independent kind of motion has an average energy equal to 4×10^{-21} joule. This seems like a tiny amount of energy, and indeed thermal motion is scarcely noticeable in everyday life. But the previous remarks imply that for any elastic rod there is a length scale beyond which the elastic cost of bending is negligible compared to the thermal energy. This scale is called the bend-persistence length. The stiffer the rod, the longer the scale. The significance of the name may be understood by reconsidering the image of the rubber tube and imagining that it is being randomly shaken. Any particular point on the tube will be pointing in a random direction; but nearby points will be pointing in roughly the same direction if they are close enough—this is "persistence." Points farther away than the bend-persistence length will be uncorrelated, because large-radius bends are easy to create.

For DNA the stiffness corresponds to a bend-persistence length of about 50 nm; in the tube analogy this corresponds to 25 cm (10 in.), much shorter than the total tube length. Thus, pure DNA in water will be a random, tangled mess. It can be straightened, however, by pulling on the ends. This procedure can be understood by simplifying the model still further. Since bends longer than 25 cm (10 in.) are easy to create, the image of the rubber rod is replaced by a chain of straight links, each about 25 cm (10 in.) long and completely free to pivot at the linkage points. If the ends of this chain are pulled and friction is ignored, the chain will straighten without any resistance until fully extended, and then resist further straightening. (Knotting will be ignored in this simplified discussion.)

Experiments with single molecules. Remarkably, the experiment sketched above can now be performed with single DNA molecules. Researchers have succeeded in attaching one end of the molecule to a wall and the other end to a large bead, then applying small forces to the bead by a variety of techniques (hydrodynamic drag, optical tweezers, or small magnetic fields) and observing its displacement as the force is varied. Since individual molecules are fragile, the forces must be extremely small, in the range of 10^{-12} newton (10^{-13} pound-force). This force corresponds roughly to the weight of a single bacterium; nevertheless, the techniques just mentioned are delicate enough to apply such forces accurately.

Entropic effects. The observed behavior (total length versus applied force) turns out to be totally different from the simple expectation just sketched, which was appropriate for a macroscopic chain (**Fig. 1**). The difference arises from entropic effects; they hold the key to using these experiments to learn about DNA elasticity.

The problem with the simple chain model is that it includes thermal fluctuations only incompletely. There are very few possible ways for the chain to be, say, 99.9% of its full length: every link must be nearly straight. However, there are an enormous number of ways for the chain to be 10% of its full

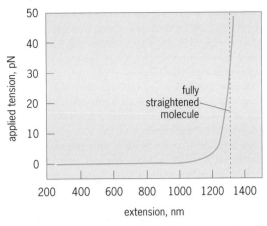

Fig. 1. Extension of a single DNA molecule as a function of applied tension. 1 pN = 10^{-12} newton = 2.25×10^{-13} pound-force. The curve represents both the experimental data and the theoretical prediction for a chain with thermal bend fluctuations, a bend-persistence length of about 50 nm, and some intrinsic stretchiness. *(After M. D. Wang et al., Stretching DNA with optical tweezers, Biophys. J., 72:1335–1346, 1997)*

length: every link can have any angle in a vast number of combinations. In other words, the unstretched state has far more entropy than the stretched one. Statistical physics then says that the free energy of the chain is effectively lower than the stretched state, even though there is no energy cost in bending each individual link. The size of this effect is again proportional to Boltzmann's constant and the temperature, which explains why the effect is not observed in daily life: 4×10^{-21} J is a tiny energy. For polymers, however, this effect is crucial. It implies that even a freely jointed chain resists elongation, an effect called entropic elasticity. The field of polymer physics began with the realization that this effect is the origin of elasticity in rubber. Since the strength of the effect is proportional to the temperature, the theory predicts that a rubber band should get stiffer, and shorter, if it is heated—a well-known effect.

It is now a simple mathematical calculation to determine how the entropic elasticity effect depends on the unknown bend-persistence length of the chain, to compare it to experimental data (Fig. 1), and to find the persistence length. Dividing by 4×10^{-21} J then gives the desired elastic constant for DNA, or equivalently the persistence length mentioned above, 50 nm.

Success of elasticity theory. It is now possible to investigate how well classical elasticity theory describes DNA. The experimental data indeed fall on the theoretical curve. Moreover, further experiments at higher applied force (up to 50 times greater than mentioned above) reveal another phenomenon: in addition to getting straighter, DNA can stretch. The elastic resistance to stretching a rod is related to the bend stiffness by a formula from classical elasticity theory; DNA obeys this formula remarkably well.

Recently it has become possible to take the model one step farther. Besides resisting bending, a rubber rod resists twisting. While traditional simple polymers do not exhibit any appreciable twist resistance, complicated ones such as DNA and actin do. To measure this effect, researchers have succeeded in stretching long DNA strands while keeping the ends from rotating. The extension of the molecule then depends on both the applied tension, as before, and the amount of extra twist, if any, imposed on the molecule beyond its natural helical twist. Analyzing these experiments by a generalization of the scheme sketched above yields values for both the bend- and the twist-persistence length, two independent parameters controlling the behavior of DNA in vivo.

Philip Nelson

Electron Transfer

The periphery of the deoxyribonucleic acid double helix contains the negatively charged sugar phosphate backbone while, in the center of the double helix, the aromatic heterocyclic base pairs are stacked together providing substantial stability to the DNA duplex. Analogous doped-stacked arrays in the solid state are known to be efficient conductors along the stacking direction. The DNA helix, as a molecular-stacked array, might serve as an efficient medium to promote charge transport over long molecular distances. A fundamental issue of electron transport is the migration of radicals through the DNA helix. Since the first proposal of the structure of DNA, scientists have debated whether and how far radicals might migrate through the helix to effect damage. Whether such long-range charge transport occurs is critical with respect to mutagenesis and carcinogenesis.

Synthetic DNA assemblies have been applied to probe long-range electron transfer chemistry. These assemblies contain metallointercalators (metal complexes), as donors or acceptors, which are bound at fixed positions. Intercalation is the process in which metal complexes are stacked between the base pairs along the DNA backbone (**Fig. 2**). Electron transport in DNA depends upon the intervening distance between donors and acceptors, the intervening sequence, and the manner in which the donor and acceptor are coupled into the DNA stack. Aromatic complexes, in stacking directly with the DNA base pairs, provide a critical probe of π stacking (that is, stacking of π orbitals in the interior of the helix). DNA-mediated charge transport is extremely sensitive to the stacking of donor and acceptor, as well as the stacking of intervening bases within the DNA double helix. Spectroscopic techniques and direct assays of chemical reactivity were used to study and describe systematically how DNA-mediated electron transfer occurs.

Intercalation. A variety of octahedrally coordinated metallointercalators have been designed that bind strongly with DNA. Ruthenium intercalators containing the dipyridophenazine ligand are useful luminescent probes of DNA in both chemical and

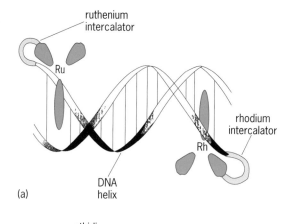

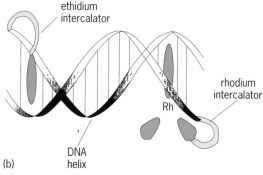

Fig. 2. Intercalators and DNA assemblies used to explore photoinduced electron transfer with the DNA helix as a bridge. Intercalator combinations used were (a) ruthenium and rhodium and (b) ethidium and rhodium.

diagnostic applications. Rhodium intercalators containing phenanthrenequinone diimine have allowed exploration of site-specific recognition of DNA. Once bound to DNA by intercalation, with photoactivation, these rhodium intercalators promote DNA direct strand cleavage and, in so doing, mark their sites of binding. Some of the intercalators prepared have specificities (selective binding between two sequences) comparable to DNA-binding proteins.

In a prepared 15-base-pair synthetic DNA assembly, a ruthenium intercalator was tethered covalently near one end. Photoinduced electron transfer over long range was examined in this DNA assembly. The ruthenated duplex tethered near one end of the DNA helix showed luminescence characteristic of DNA-bound ruthenium. Next, in the same 15-base-pair synthetic DNA assembly, ruthenium and rhodium intercalators were tethered covalently to opposing ends (Fig. 2a). In this mixed-metal 15-mer oligonucleotide duplex, containing the ruthenium intercalator tethered to the 5' end of one strand and the rhodium intercalator tethered to the 5' end of the other strand, no luminescence was evident. The presence of rhodium served to quench the emission from ruthenium by long-range electron transfer. Photocleavage studies on the rhodium-modified duplex indicated stacking of the intercalators at most two base pairs in from the end. Therefore, in the mixed-metal assembly the quenching results were consistent with fast photoinduced electron transfer over a donor or acceptor separation of greater than 4 nm (40 angstroms).

Ethidium is a well-characterized organic intercalator and has also been used in experiments as the photoinduced donor. In fact, significant quenching of ethidium emission was also evident in the mixed intercalator assemblies containing tethered rhodium near one end of the duplex and tethered ethidium bound near the other end (Fig. 2*b*). In a 10-mer duplex, where the donor/acceptor separation was approximately 2 nm (20 Å), approximately 30% quenching was observed, whereas for a 13-mer duplex with a separation of about 3 nm (30 Å) 10–15% quenching was seen. In all cases, the quenching occurred on a time scale which was fast compared to the resolution of the instrumentation ($>10^9$ s^{-1}). Thus, fast photoinduced electron transfer was observed at long range between donors and acceptors intercalated in a DNA duplex.

With these ethidium and rhodium assemblies, the sensitivity of the photoinduced electron transfer to stacking of the donor, acceptor, and intervening base pairs was demonstrated in a mismatch experiment. While 24% quenching was observed in the 11-mer duplex containing tethered ethidium and rhodium, if a thymine-adenosine (TA) base pair was mutated to a cytosine-adenine (CA) base pair at the center of the duplex, the photoinduced quenching observed was only 4%. In contrast, if the TA base pair was mutated to a guanine-adenine (GA), 28% quenching was observed. This mismatch experiment also established that the quenching must be mediated by the DNA helix; the quenching could not arise as a result of an interaction of donor and acceptor outside the duplex because of unraveling. DNA-mediated electron transfer between intercalators appeared to be only weakly sensitive to distance, yet extremely sensitive to stacking.

Photoinduced damage. Different synthetic DNA assemblies were constructed to explore oxidative damage to DNA from a remote site. In the first such assembly, the rhodium intercalator was tethered to the 5′ end of one strand with a tether length sufficient to allow intramolecular intercalation. The site of intercalation was determined in photocleavage experiments, since high-energy irradiation serves to mark the site of binding. However, these complexes of rhodium can also serve as potent photooxidants when irradiated at lower energy ($\geq$360 nm). The tethered rhodium complex was able to oxidize the DNA duplex directly. Both empirical studies and theoretical calculations indicated that the site most easily oxidized on DNA is the guanine base, and in particular the 5′-G of guanine doublets or triplets.

The tethered rhodium complex could be utilized to promote oxidative damage to 5′-GG-3′ doublets away from the site of intercalation. Moreover, the yield of such oxidative damage appeared to be relatively insensitive to the distance separating the 5′-GG-3′ doublet from the rhodium intercalator. Experiments indicated that the photoinjected hole, once

introduced into the helix by the rhodium intercalator, can promote oxidative damage to DNA over 0.2 micrometer (200 Å) away. Analysis showed that the base product of this oxidative damage was 8-oxo-guanine, which is a common oxidative lesion in cellular DNA. It is likely that upon oxidation by one electron in these reactions, the guanine radical is first formed, and that subsequent chemistry, trapping the radical by dioxygen or water, must then occur to give the final stable 8-oxo-guanine.

This rhodium oxidation chemistry was valuable in demonstrating for the first time in a chemically well-defined system that oxidative damage to DNA could be promoted from a distance. But the quantum yields and efficiencies of this rhodium photochemistry were quite low. A more efficient long-range reaction called a flash-quench methodology was developed for studies of protein electron transfer. This strategy utilized tight-binding ruthenium intercalators to generate Ru(III), a potent oxidant, by oxidative quenching. Photoexcited Ru(II) bound to DNA can be quenched by electron transfer to a groove-bound species, such as methyl viologen. This quenching process generates Ru(III) in situ, and this ground-state oxidant, intercalated into the helix, can then be harnessed to promote oxidative damage to DNA.

The intercalating Ru(III) oxidant could also promote oxidative damage to DNA from a distance. Oxidative damage to DNA was explored with tethered ruthenium. A single 5′-GG-3′ doublet was included in the sequence; in this case, oxidative damage was evident at the 5′-G of the 5′-GG-3′ doublet. But when a single base mutation was made in this DNA assembly, such that only single G sites were present, oxidative damage was observed essentially equally at all guanine positions. Hence, the yield of oxidative damage did not depend sensitively upon distance, nor upon reactive characteristics which are particular to a 5′-GG-3′ site. Instead, the site oxidized depended upon base oxidation potential. The result graphically underscored the notion of migration of the injected hole across the DNA duplex on a time scale which was fast compared with trapping of the hole to form the irreversible oxidized product.

By utilizing the flash-quench technique, transient absorption spectroscopy was able to identify for the first time the neutral guanine radical in duplex DNA as the primary oxidative intermediate. In addition, the yield of oxidative damage with Ru(III) is substantial and several orders of magnitude greater than that seen with rhodium photochemistry, depending upon the quencher employed. The yield of this long-range electron transfer chemistry appeared to be relatively insensitive to distance, yet exquisitely sensitive to the base-pair stack.

Oxidative repair. The oxidative repair of thymine dimers represents an excellent system for studying long-range electron transfer in DNA. In bacteria systems, the enzyme photolyase, containing a bound flavin cofactor, repairs thymine dimers in a reductive

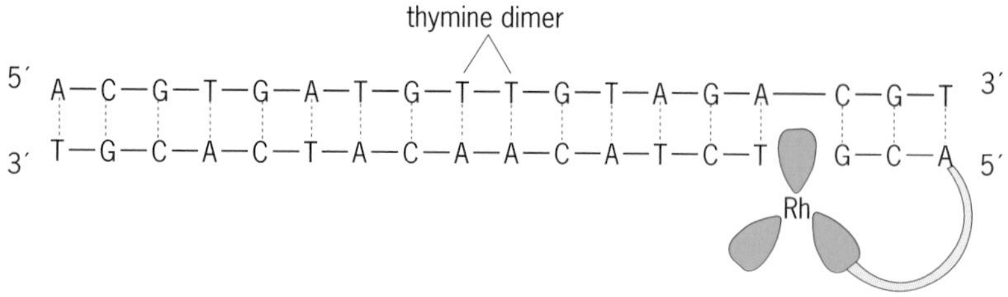

thymine dimer

5′ A—C—G—T—G—A—T—G—T—T—G—T—A—G—A——C—G—T 3′

3′ T—G—C—A—C—T—A—C—A—A—C—A—T—C—T G—C—A 5′

Rh

Fig. 3. A DNA assembly prepared to test the repair of thymine dimers in DNA from a distance.

catalytic cycle upon photoactivation with visible light; model studies on thymine dinucleotides had shown that thymine dimers could also be repaired in an oxidative cycle. Therefore, it is considered that rhodium intercalators containing phenanthrenequinone diimine, given their high oxidative potential and their photoactivation with visible light, might be particularly amenable to studies of oxidative thymine dimer repair. Moreover, the thymine dimer represents the primary photochemical lesion of the cell, and its repair is of therapeutic importance. By incorporating tethered rhodium intercalators into assemblies containing thymine dimers, a reaction on DNA involving electron transfer from a distance can be explored.

An assembly was tested to determine the oxidative repair of a thymine dimer in DNA from a distance. DNA duplexes were constructed containing a single thymine dimer site-specifically incorporated in the center of the DNA oligomer, with the rhodium intercalator covalently tethered to the opposite strand (**Fig. 3**). Upon photoactivation with visible light, the rhodium complex could promote the quantitative repair of the thymine dimers to the native unmodified form. The reaction, moreover, yielded no secondary products and could even be carried out with sunlight.

The efficiency of thymine dimer repair was found to be relatively insensitive to the distance separating the thymine dimer from the intercalated rhodium. Quantitative repair could proceed over >3 nm (30 Å). Again, however, long-range repair was sensitive to the stacking of the thymine dimer within the duplex, the covalently bound intercalator, and the intervening base pair. Experiments carried out with a bulged base intervening between the rhodium intercalator and the thymine dimer demonstrated substantial decreases in repair efficiency.

The DNA double helix serves as a novel medium for long-range electron transfer. Factors are being defined in establishing DNA-mediated electron transfer by systematically appending donors or acceptors onto DNA duplexes and monitoring a range of electron transfer reactions, utilizing both spectroscopic methods and chemical assays of reactivity. Stacking is a key parameter modulating this long-range chemistry, whether it is the stacking of the donor, the stacking of the acceptor, or the intervening stacking of the DNA duplex. In fact, chemistry at a distance can be accomplished through the DNA helix. Elec-

tron transfer chemistry depends upon DNA sequence, structure, and the dynamics of base stacking. The issue of electron mobility through DNA therefore should now be carefully considered in developing an understanding of cellular DNA damage and its control.

For background information *see* DEOXYRIBONU-CLEIC ACID (DNA); ELASTICITY; ELECTRON-TRANSFER REACTION; ENTROPY; PHOTOCHEMISTRY; POLYMER; STATISTICAL MECHANICS in the McGraw-Hill Encyclopedia of Science & Technology.   Jacqueline K. Barton

Bibliography. C. Bustamante et al., Entropic elasticity of lamdaphage DNA, *Science,* 265:1599–1600, 1994; C. Calladine and H. Drew, *Understanding DNA,* 1992; P. J. Dandliker, R. E. Holmlin, and J. K. Barton, Oxidative thymine dimer repair in the DNA helix, *Science,* 275:1465–1468, 1997; D. B. Hall, R. E. Holmlin, and J. K. Barton, Oxidative DNA damage through long range electron transfer, *Nature,* 382:731–735, 1996; R. E. Holmlin, P. J. Dandliker, and J. K. Barton, Charge transfer through the DNA base stack, *Angew. Chem. Int. Ed. Engl.,* 36:2714–2730, 1997; P. O'Neill and E. M. Fielden, Primary free-radical processes in DNA, *Adv. Radiat. Biol.,* 17:53–120, 1993; S. B. Smith, L. Finzi, and C. Bustamante, Direct mechanical measurements of the elasticity of single DNA molecules by using magnetic beads, *Science,* 258:1122–1126, 1992; T. R. Strick et al., The elasticity of a single supercoiled DNA molecule, *Science,* 271:1835–1837, 1996.

Design engineering

Design is a creative process of engineering synthetic solutions to satisfy human needs. In this sense, design is synonymous with engineering. Engineering design is undergoing a transition, driven by two complementary factors: the creation of the scientific basis of design, and industrial needs to shorten lead time, improve quality, and reduce the cost of new products. Many engineering problems can be solved when the basic scientific principles of design are applied. The science base enables designers of products and large engineering systems to perform their tasks on a logical, rational, and systematic basis (minimizing the trial-and-error process and empiricism). These changes have affected both design education and the practice of engineering in industry.

Four elements of design. There are several different activities and subspecialties within the design field. The first element of the design field is associated with the design process, which is largely empirical and heuristic. The second element deals with the tools used in the design processes (for example, computer-aided design, or CAD). As a result of this effort, many commercial computer-aided-design codes are widely used as design aids. The third element deals with design methodologies (for example, robust design) which have helped to improve the reliability of industrial products. The fourth element is the axiomatic approach, which has been founded on a set of fundamental principles that can be applied universally to all design problems. The premise of this science element is that design can be done correctly, cheaply, and faster when founded on basic principles that can be generalized and codified to all synthetic processes.

Computers in design. Computers are used primarily for graphic representation, solid modeling, product modeling, and optimization of design solutions. Designers use computers as a tool to augment human capability. This requires the codification, generalization, and abstraction of human design knowledge. Without the use of generalized systematic design knowledge, the power of computers will be either wasted or not fully utilized. The ultimate outcome of such design research combined with computational power may be a "thinking" design machine that can design products, software, systems, and processes with limited human inputs.

Universality of design. Design is done in all engineering fields. Manufacturing engineers design new manufacturing processes and systems, ranging from manufacturing cells to a complete factory. Electrical engineers design analog or digital circuits, communication systems, and computer hardware. System architects design technical or organizational systems where many parts must work together to yield a system that achieves the intended goals. A software engineer designs the architecture of the software before coding. Similarly, managers design organizations to achieve organizational goals.

All of these design activities involve knowledge that is field specific. Although each field utilizes different databases and different design practices, all the fields share many design characteristics. Common activities include: know the customers needs; define problems to be solved and determine functional requirements; conceptualize solutions through synthesis, which involves the task of satisfying several different functional requirements by using a set of inputs within given constraints; perform analysis to optimize the proposed solution; and check the resulting design solution to see if it meets the original customer needs. Design parameters can be specified to satisfy the functional requirements after the design solutions are conceptualized.

Science of design. The axiomatic approach to design, in contrast to algorithmic approaches, has been advanced to establish a scientific base for design. One goal is to improve design activities by providing the designer with a theoretical foundation based on logical and rational criteria for good design, design processes, and methodologies. Another goal of axiomatic design is to make human designers more creative, reduce the random search process, minimize the iterative trial-and-error process, determine the best designs among those proposed, and endow the computer with creative power. Axiomatic design deals with principles and methodologies rather than simply algorithms or methodologies. It derives theorems and corollaries, and develops methodologies based on functional analysis and information minimization leading to robust design. Axiomatic design is applicable to all designs: products, processes, systems, software, organizations, materials, and business plans.

Design is made up of four domains: customer, functional, physical, and process. The customer domain is characterized by customer needs or the attributes that the customer is looking for in a product, process or system. In the functional domain, the customer needs are specified in terms of functional requirements and constraints. In order to satisfy the specified functional requirements, design parameters are conceived in the physical domain. Finally, to produce the product specified in terms of design parameters, the process domain is developed and characterized by process variables. All designs fit into these four domains and can be generalized in terms of the same principles. Because of this logical structure, generalized design principles can be systematically and concurrently applied to all design applications.

All designers go through similar thought processes. In mechanical engineering, design is often thought of in terms of product and hardware design. However, mechanical engineers also deal with other important designs such as software, manufacturing processes, systems, and organizations. In materials science, the design goal is to develop materials with certain properties or functional requirements. This is done through the design of microstructures (or design parameters) to satisfy these functional requirements, and through the development of material processing methods (or process variables) to create the desired microstructures.

Design axioms. The basic postulate of the axiomatic approach to design is that there are fundamental axioms that govern the design process. Two axioms were identified by examining the common elements that are always present in good designs, be it a product, process, or systems design. They were also identified by examining actions taken during the design stage that resulted in dramatic improvements. The first axiom is called the independence axiom, and the second the information axiom. Based on these design axioms, theorems and corollaries can be derived.

Independence axiom. This axiom states that the independence of functional requirements must always be maintained during mapping, where functional requirements are defined as the minimum number of independent functional requirements that characterize the design goals. It also states that when there are two or more functional requirements, the design solution must be such that each one of the functional requirements can be satisfied without affecting the other functional requirements; that is, a correct set of design parameters must be chosen to satisfy the functional requirements and maintain their independence. The independence axiom requires that the functions of the design be independent from each other, but design can reside in the same physical part. Based on the independence axiom, designs can be classified into uncoupled, decoupled, and coupled. Coupled designs do not satisfy the independence axiom. The best design is an uncoupled design, where each functional requirement can be changed by changing a specific design parameter. Decoupled designs require that the design parameters be changed in a specific sequence to satisfy the independence of functional requirements. There are many theorems that help the designer to make right decisions.

Information axiom. This axiom states that among those designs that satisfy the independence axiom, the design that has the smallest information content is the best design. Because the information content is defined in terms of probability, the axiom also states that the design that has the highest probability of success of achieving functional requirements is the best design. The probability is defined for each functional requirement in terms of the designer-specified probability distribution and the probability distribution that the system provides. The information axiom suggests that physical integration is desirable to reduce the information content, if the functional independence can be maintained; that is, both functional independence and physical integration are necessary features in a good design.

Mapping. To go from the functional domain to the physical domain requires mapping, which involves creative conceptual work. Once the overall design concept is generated by mapping, design parameters must be identified to complete the mapping process. It is convenient to think about a specific design parameter to satisfy a specific functional requirement, repeating the process until the design is completed. There are many theorems that help this process.

Robust design. A design that can accommodate large variations in design parameters and process variables and yet satisfy the functional requirements is called a robust design. There are four different ways of reducing the bias and variance of a design to achieve a robust design, provided that the design satisfies the independence axiom. The reduction of the information content is accomplished by choosing small magnitudes for the elements of the design matrix of an uncoupled design, designing a system that is immune to variations, fixing the values of extra design parameters, and increasing the design range.

Concurrent engineering. The mapping from the physical domain to the process domain is called the product design. After certain design parameters are chosen, a map from the physical domain to the process domain (that is, process design) is created by choosing the process variables. This process design mapping also must satisfy the independence axiom. When existing processes must be used to minimize capital investment in new equipment, the existing process variables must be used and thus act as constraints in choosing design parameters. In developing a product, both the product design and the process design (or selection) must be done at the same time. This is called concurrent engineering, or sometimes simultaneous engineering.

System architecture. Once the design hierarchies are established in the functional requirements and the design parameter domains, a system architecture is created that shows the relationship among modules (representing the elements of the design matrix) and the operational sequence of the design. The system architecture provides the fundamental basis for documentation, which is important in describing the design of complex systems. It also provides the roadmap for controlling the system.

For background information *see* COMPUTER-AIDED DESIGN AND MANUFACTURING; COMPUTER-AIDED ENGINEERING; ENGINEERING DESIGN; ENGINEERING DRAWING; MANUFACTURING ENGINEERING in the McGraw-Hill Encyclopedia of Science & Technology.

Nam P. Suh

Bibliography. B. A. Bras and F. Mistree, A compromise decision support problem for robust design and axiomatic design, *ASME J. Mech. Des.*, 117(1):10–19, 1995; N. P. Suh, *The Principles of Design*, 1990; N. P. Suh and S. Sekimoto, Design of thinking design machine, *Ann. CIRP*, 39:145–148, 1990.

Diamond

Diamond is a very versatile material. Although it has remarkable characteristics, for example, high thermal conductivity, very low electric conductivity, and extreme hardness, its other properties have limited its use. Since the first production of high-pressure synthetic diamond in 1955, industrial diamond has been manufactured in large amounts, and it is now widely used. In 1976, a film of diamond was formed for the first time by chemical vapor deposition. It is now possible to make thin films with sizes larger than those made by high-pressure synthesis. Consequently, diamond can be used in new applications, such as surface coating. The techniques for using diamond, like those for using silicon, have rapidly progressed as diamond has been transformed from a bulk material into a high-quality thin film.

The methods that have been developed for synthesizing high-quality crystals and controlling their impurity levels have been applied to diamond, which can be made to behave as a semiconductor (like silicon) by adding small amounts of impurities. Since diamond is also a good insulator and has excellent thermal conductivity, diamond substrates can be used in integrated-circuit chips to suppress leakage current through the substrate as well as stray capacitance, and to alleviate high heat loads. These characteristics have all been serious problems for very large scale integrated circuits and high-speed devices made with silicon substrates. The barriers preventing the attractive properties of diamond from being utilized have been lowered considerably by the successful production of synthetic diamond by low-pressure deposition. Various low-pressure dry-etching techniques have been tested for micromachining diamond.

Ion-beam sputtering. Surface atoms of diamond can be physically removed by sputtering with positive argon (Ar^+) ions, accelerated to 0.5–2 keV. The directional dependence of incident ions has been observed. When ions bombard the surface in the [110] direction, along which the crystalline structure is open, they penetrate deep into the crystal, and thus the desorption rate becomes low. When ions undergo multiple collisions with surface atoms, desorption rates of surface atoms increase.

Reactive ion-beam etching. If positive molecular oxygen (O_2^+) ions accelerated to about 300 eV are incident on diamond, surface carbon atoms are desorbed by chemical reactions forming volatile compounds such as carbon monoxide (CO) and carbon dioxide (CO_2). The ion energies used for reactive ion-beam etching are lower than those used for sputtering with positive argon ions. Electron energy loss spectroscopy of diamond surfaces bombarded with ions at energies equal to or higher than a few hundred electronvolts indicates the formation of a graphitized layer on the surface. Irradiation with low-energy ions can even repair a surface that previously suffered damage at higher ion energies so that it regains the characteristics of a natural diamond surface. Depending on various experimental parameters, etch rates ranging from tens of nanometers to several hundred nanometers per minute have been achieved by using oxygen ions.

In the case of beam sputtering by 1-keV ions formed in an environment of xenon and nitrogen dioxide (NO_2) gas, the etch rate exhibits a maximum when the substrate temperature is held at $-10°C$ (14°F). This result suggests that an effective way of removing carbon from a diamond surface is to allow an energetic ion beam to attack an oxidation layer of suitable thickness. In order to avoid damage to surface layers (which degrades electrical properties), diamond has been etched by an electron-cyclotron-resonance plasma of molecular oxygen (O_2), which produces only low-energy ions at about 50 eV. In this case, an etch rate of 8.6 nm/min has been attained for boron-doped diamond formed by chemical vapor deposition.

Another approach has been tried in which an intentionally damaged layer is removed. An etch rate of 100 nm/min has been obtained when the surface is exposed to a hydrogen plasma at a substrate potential of -250 V for 1 h at a substrate temperature of 450°C (850°F). There is speculation that in this technique the diamond surface is first graphitized by a large amount of electron flux, and then etched by hydrogen atoms.

In all these techniques, suitable mask materials are needed to protect the diamond surface from etching by the energetic particles, so that the surface can be selectively etched.

Laser-excited etching. Laser-excited etching of diamond has been carried out by using an argon-fluorine excimer laser. This laser operates at a wavelength of 193 nm, in the ultraviolet region. At this wavelength, the photon energy is greater than the band gap of diamond, 5.4 eV. Carbon is sublimated when a focused laser beam with an energy fluence equal to or higher than 3 mJ/cm² irradiates a diamond surface that has been placed in oxygen or chlorine gas or even in vacuum. The deposition of a graphitized region occurs only when the laser fluence is lower than 3 mJ/cm². In the case of ultraviolet-laser excitation, as well as charged-particle-beam bombardment, a process of graphitization followed by removal of carbon atoms or carbon compounds from the surface is apparently important for diamond etching. Spatially selective etching is possible by scanning the irradiation site using pulsed light.

Etching with synchrotron radiation. Recently, diamond has been etched by using synchrotron radiation as a light source. This process differs from ion-beam sputtering, reactive ion-beam etching, and laser-excited etching in the following respects: (1) diamond is well etched in the irradiated area; (2) etchant oxygen is essential to this process, and thus the diamond surface reacts neither in vacuum nor in an etchant gas environment containing fluorine atoms; (3) the etch rate is almost invariant from $-140°C$ to 100°C ($-220°F$ to 212°F); and (4) the etch rate of graphite is lower than that of diamond when excited by synchrotron radiation at low temperatures, at which the thermal reaction hardly proceeds. When a diamond surface is etched by synchrotron radiation that has passed through a nickel mesh a few millimeters above the surface (**Fig. 1**), the shadow area due to the mesh wires is not etched but the irradiated area is strongly etched. In the area irradiated by the synchrotron, the etching reaction proceeds on any type of diamond, including single-crystal natural diamond, high-pressure synthetic diamond, and polycrystalline thin-film diamond deposited by the chemical vapor method.

The energy and the number of photons in the synchrotron light used for etching (**Fig. 2**) are quite different from those of the ultraviolet argon-fluorine laser mentioned above. The synchrotron light includes not only photons of the same energy as those from the argon-fluorine laser but also higher-energy photons. However, the total number of photons in the synchrotron radiation source is much lower than in the laser beam that is used to etch diamond. *See* SYNCHROTRON RADIATION.

The synchrotron radiation used in etching is focused by reflection from a platinum-coated mirror. In two other experiments, the spectrum of this light is then modified before it irradiates the diamond surface (Fig. 2). In one of these experiments this is done by passing the radiation through a carbon filter 100 nm thick, and in the other experiment by reflecting it from a silicon carbide (SiC) mirror. In a fourth experiment, the diamond surface is exposed to undulator radiation, which is quasimonochromatic light that is emitted when relativistic electrons pass through undulator magnets, where they are made to follow a wavy (undulatory) path.

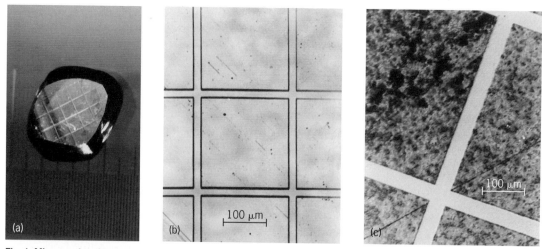

Fig. 1. Micrographs of typical diamond surfaces etched by synchrotron radiation that has passed through a nickel mesh 5 mm (0.2 in.) above the surface, with wires 20 μm wide. Pressure of etchant oxygen (O_2) gas is 13 pascals (0.1 torr), and substrate temperature of the specimen is $-60°C$ ($-76°F$). (a) Single-crystal natural diamond. (b) Synthetic diamond. (c) Polycrystalline diamond film deposited by chemical vapor.

The rates of etching are compared in the four experiments. The light that has passed through a carbon filter retains relatively high-energy photons, which can excite inner-shell electrons of carbon. Its etching rate is down from that of the undispersed synchrotron radiation by less than half. However, the spectrum of light reflected from silicon carbide has a cutoff at an energy of about 300 eV, above which photons are practically absent, and its etching rate is reduced from that of the undispersed radiation by a factor of about 13. Finally, the etching rate of the undulator light, which is quasimonochromatic at 36 eV, is down by a factor of about 60.

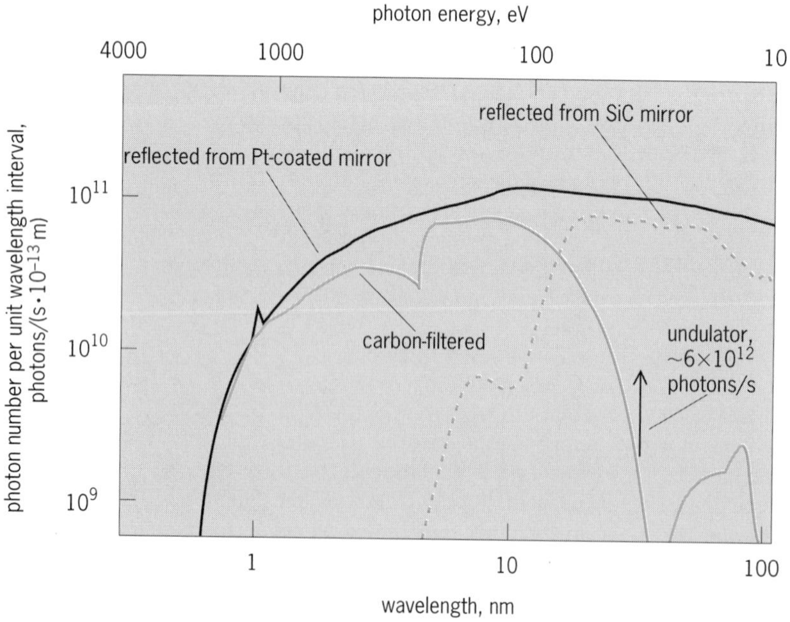

From the analysis of these results and of the absorption cross section of diamond in each energy range, the energy region of the photons that are effective for diamond etching has been found to be over 285 eV. At this energy, inner-shell electrons of carbon can be excited. However, measurements that could support inner-shell excitation as the mechanism of reaction have not yet been carried out. Following inner-shell excitation by synchrotron radiation, the formation of multiply charged ions is expected. There is speculation that strong repulsion between such multiply charged ions causes local disorder of the surface atoms of diamond, and that this disorder, in turn, may enable oxygen radicals or ions to react with surface carbon atoms or to diffuse into the subsurface layer. As a result, volatile compounds are readily produced near the surface, and thus carbon atoms are desorbed from the diamond surface.

Diamond and silicon. In the case of silicon, the success of the semiconductor industry has been fostered by the existence of an electrically complementary material, silicon dioxide, which can be prepared simply by oxidizing the silicon substrate. By selecting appropriate processes, silicon can be converted into a *p*-type or an *n*-type semiconductor, or even into an electric insulator by oxidation. This behavior is quite different from that of gallium arsenide (GaAs) and germanium. By contrast, pure diamond is an excellent insulator but can become a semiconductor by doping. Through a phase transition, diamond can be easily converted into graphite, which is a good electric conductor. Since the properties of diamond can be well controlled by doping with impurities or by graphitization, its usefulness may come to equal or even surpass that of silicon in some applications. Silicon is widely used for micromachines and ultra-

Fig. 2. Spectra of synchrotron radiation used for light-excited etching: with synchrotron radiation focused by reflection from a platinum-coated mirror; with the same light, but also passed through a carbon filter; with the same light, but also reflected from a silicon carbide mirror; and with undulator light at a photon energy of 36 eV.

high-density devices because of the ever-increasing number of devices that are manufactured and the realization of microfabrication. Once the technology for microfabrication of diamond is established, there will be a possibility of creating new, diamond-based industries.

For background information *see* DIAMOND; GRAPH-ITE; ION-SOLID INTERACTIONS; PLASMA (PHYSICS); SPUT-TERING; SURFACE AND INTERFACIAL CHEMISTRY; SYN-CHROTRON RADIATION in the McGraw-Hill Encyclopedia of Science & Technology.

Haruhiko Ohashi; Kosuke Shobatake

Bibliography. S. A. Grot et al., Oxygen based elec-tron cyclotron resonance etching of semiconducting homoepitaxial diamond films, *Appl. Phys. Lett.*, 61:2326–2328, 1992; H. Ohashi et al., Synchrotron radiation excited etching of diamond, *Appl. Phys. Lett.*, 68:3713–3715, 1996; M. Rothchild, C. Arnone, and D. J. Ehrich, Excimer-laser etching of diamond and hard carbon films by direct writing and optical projection, *J. Vac. Sci. Technol.*, B4:310–314, 1988; B. R. Stoner, G. J. Tessmer, and D. L. Dreifus, Bias assisted etching of diamond in a conventional chemi-cal vapor deposition reactor, *Appl. Phys. Lett.*, 62:1803–1805, 1993.

Diamond film

Diamond is the crystalline form of carbon with a wide range of unique and desirable properties. Dia-mond is the hardest substance known; it is the best conductor of heat at room temperatures; it expands or contracts less than nearly all other materials when exposed to temperature changes; and it is optically transparent to a very wide range of visible light and other electromagnetic radiation. Such properties have made diamond a useful material for precise and durable cutting and grinding tools, for optical windows for various sensor technologies, and for heat sinks to help draw away the energy and heat generated by closely packed electronic components. As such markets for diamond products have devel-oped, considerable interest has been generated in finding and perfecting methods to synthesize di-amond.

Diamonds were first produced artificially in the early 1950s by recreating the very high pressures and temperatures at which diamond forms naturally. A breakthrough came during the 1970s, when dia-mond was produced by the chemical vapor deposi-tion process. In this process, diamond films are formed by flowing a reactive stream of gas-phase chemicals over a heated substrate surface. Through the reaction of highly energetic growth species, dia-mond can be formed at temperatures and pressures that are much less than those necessary for natural diamond formation.

The diamond chemical vapor deposition process can be produced with several different technolo-gies, including dc-arc plasma torches, microwave-induced plasmas, hot-wire filaments, and combus-tion. All of these techniques combine a heat source with an energetic stream of reactive growth species.

In the combustion technique, also referred to as diamond flame synthesis, the flame provides the source of heat and the source of reactants, known as flame radicals. The important growth species pro-duced in the flame for diamond deposition are the methyl radical (CH_3) and atomic hydrogen (H). The methyl radical is the primary source of carbon, while atomic hydrogen maintains surface stability during growth, preventing the formation of nondiamond carbon such as graphite.

With flame synthesis, diamond can be formed from simple acetylene/oxygen shop torches by im-pinging the flame against a surface such as molybde-num, although the resulting diamond films are not uniform. As an alternative to conventional torches, flat-flame configurations show promise for uniform, large-area diamond deposition with high growth rates, but are more complex to engineer.

Nozzle design for deposition. To achieve the uniform deposition of diamond, it is necessary to provide evenly distributed fluxes of both heat and growth species to the substrate surface. A suitable flat-flame profile can be realized based on stagnation-point flow (**Fig. 1**). In an idealized stagnation-point flow, a vast flow of fluid is directed against an equally vast solid surface. The resulting flame is situated above the stagnation point and is radially uniform about the central region. Such an ideal stagnation-point

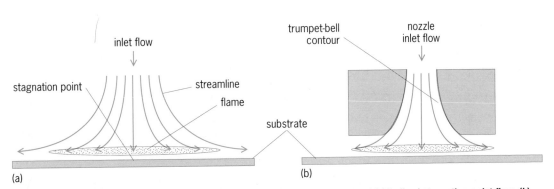

Fig. 1. Distribution of fluxes of both heat and growth species by nozzle geometry. (*a*) Idealized stagnation-point flow. (*b*) Actual chemical vapor deposition reactor showing contoured nozzle based on ideal streamlines.

flow is impractical for actual diamond deposition because of the large flow rates of gas that would be necessary. In practice, however, a stagnation-flow flame reactor can be realized by replacing the vast flow field with a carefully designed nozzle. Specifically, if natural flow contours, called streamlines, are replaced with an identically shaped nozzle, the inner fluid flow will behave as the ideal flow. The shape of the resulting nozzle resembles the bell of a trumpet (Fig. 1). By using detailed computer codes that simulate the fluid flow and combustion processes, the contour of a trumpet-bell nozzle can be designed to optimize reagent gas usage for a predetermined deposition area.

Nozzle and substrate cooling. In addition to the nozzle geometry, other design considerations are necessary for a practical diamond chemical vapor deposition reactor. To promote efficient combustion, the inlet fuel and oxygen gases are well mixed, often using turbulent-flow-producing screens, prior to entering the trumpet-bell nozzle. Cooling ensures that the large amounts of heat generated by the flame are removed from the nozzle assembly and the diamond deposition surface. The nozzle is cooled by water flowing through small channels. The best substrate material for diamond flame deposition is the metal molybdenum, which has a high melting temperature (4750°F or 2620°C) and good heat conductivity. Substrate cooling is achieved by spraying water beneath the deposition surface. Temperature of the deposition surface, typically around 1850°F (1000°C), can be maintained by adjusting the flow rate of the coolant water spray.

Reagent gas. As discussed above, the flame provides both the source of heat and the necessary growth species for chemical vapor deposition of diamond. Diamond has been deposited successfully by using several different fuels, including ethylene, propylene, methane, and acetylene. Acetylene flames produce the highest diamond deposition rates, approaching 0.004 in./h (100 micrometers/h), and the highest-quality diamond films of these four fuel types. The acetylene/oxygen flames perform best because their high flame temperatures (5550°F or 3075°C) generate large pools of methyl radicals and atomic hydrogen, and because the high burning velocity of acetylene/oxygen mixtures enables the flame to be pressed very close to the substrate surface without extinguishing it, making the large pool of growth species available for diamond formation.

The necessary amount of reagent gas for diamond growth is dependent on the substrate surface area targeted for deposition. For a 2-in.-diameter (5-cm) diamond film (this is considered a useful diameter for many diamond applications), a chemical vapor deposition reactor (Fig. 1) would require about 8.5 ft³/min (240 liters/min) of premixed acetylene, oxygen, and hydrogen gas. The acetylene and oxygen are used in approximately equal amounts, with 2–4% more acetylene than oxygen. Hydrogen accounts for about 25% of the total flow and is added primarily to lower the flame temperature and burning velocities of the mixture, thereby producing a more stable flame.

Substrate. With flame synthesis, diamond films are usually deposited on a molybdenum substrate because of its desirable high-temperature properties, although diamond is also deposited on silicon and other materials. The substrates are prepared by polishing them to a very fine finish and then pasting the surface with a slurry of diamond powder and alcohol. Particular surface preparation can vary greatly, and much experimentation is required to determine the optimal conditions. In general, the pasting step scratches the surface of the molybdenum and may actually deposit microscopic fragments of diamond. Both processes are believed to be important in providing surface sites for the nucleation and formation of small diamond clusters during the initial stage of the chemical vapor deposition process. The individual nucleation centers then grow and spread over the substrate surface, creating a continuous thin diamond film that grows thicker throughout the remaining deposition process.

Film removal. After the desired growth period is completed, the diamond films freely pop off the substrate surface because of the difference in thermal contraction between the substrate and film. Cracking may occur in thinner film (especially if residual stresses are present) if the film has adhered too much to the substrate; this is avoided by proper surface preparation. Approximately 0.001-in.-thick (25-μm) films can be grown in 1 h in a chemical vapor deposition reactor as described above (**Fig. 2**). High-quality chemical vapor deposition diamond

Fig. 2. Scanning electron microscope images of diamond films. (a) Typical diamond morphology shows continuous well-formed facets throughout. (b) By varying various conditions, the diamond morphology changes.

comprises many almost randomly oriented crystals that have grown together. The individual crystal facets represent separate nucleation sites on the substrate surface. The surface morphology of thin diamond films is determined by the orientation of the diamond crystalline structure and which crystallographic facets form the surface. The {111} facets are most prevalent with diamond flame synthesis (Fig. 2*a*). Small changes in the substrate surface temperature or in the ratio of acetylene to oxygen can alter the resulting film morphology. In this case, {100} diamond facets sometimes exist in a localized region of an overall {111} faceted film (Fig. 2*b*).

Characteristics. The growth rates of diamond films, the resulting diamond quality (the ratio of diamond to nondiamond carbon), and the diamond surface morphology are complex functions of the chemical vapor deposition parameters. These diamond film characteristics can be controlled by adjusting the fuel-to-oxygen ratio or the amount of hydrogen addition, by adding gases such as nitrogen or argon, and by adjusting the deposition temperature. Experimentation is used to determine the optimal growth conditions for a desired set of diamond film characteristics. Because experimentation is costly and time consuming, computer simulations are useful for analyzing the chemical vapor deposition process and for providing data to assist in the selection of appropriate experiments.

For background information *see* DIAMOND; VAPOR DEPOSITION in the McGraw-Hill Encyclopedia of Science & Technology. David W. Hahn

Bibliography. M. W. Geis and J. C. Angus, Diamond film semiconductors, *Sci. Amer.*, pp. 84–89, October 1992; M. Murayama, S. Kojima, and K. Uchida, Uniform deposition of diamond films using a flat flame stabilized in the stagnation-point flow, *J. Appl. Phys.*, 69:7924–7926, 1991; W. A. Yarbrough and R. Messier, Current issues and problems in the chemical vapor deposition of diamond, *Science*, 247:688–696, 1990.

Dinosaur

The origin of birds and their flight capability is a highly debated issue in vertebrate evolution. Most paleontologists accept that birds descended from bipedal, swift, predatory dinosaurs called Theropoda. However, the transformations involved in the origin of flight are poorly understood. The Patagonian theropod dinosaur, *Unenlagia comahuensis*, partially fills the morphological gap between dinosaurs and birds, and sheds light on the acquisition of avian flapping flight.

Unenlagia. *Unenlagia comahuensis* (**Fig. 1***a*), the "half-bird" from northwest Patagonia nearly 90 million years old, was discovered in Upper Cretaceous rocks. The partial but almost articulated skeleton corresponds to a medium-sized carnivorous dinosaur roughly 2 m (6 ft) long. The scapula (the shoulder blade; Fig. 1*b*) is a straplike bone, and the humerus

(bone of the upper arm) is slender but not particularly elongate. The trunk vertebrae are dorsoventrally (toward the surface of the back) deep and, as seen in many theropod dinosaurs, a pair of large foramina (openings) perforate their centra. The sacrum (a series of fused vertebrae that articulate with the hip) is made up of at least seven fused vertebrae, indicating strong connections with the pelvic girdle. The pubic bone ends in a large distal "foot," and the hindlimb bones (for example, the femur and the tibia) are long and slender, suggesting that *Unenlagia* was fleet footed. The pelvic girdle (hip bones) is noteworthy (Fig. 1*c*); it is characterized by an ilium (upper bone of the pelvic girdle) cranially (anteriorly) extensive but caudally (toward the tail) short, a pubis ventrally oriented, and a short, platelike ischium (the caudal and ventral bone of the pelvic girdle), triangular in side view. This set of pelvic features supports the membership of *Unenlagia* in the Maniraptora, a theropod lineage that includes birds and their most immediate forerunners (**Fig. 2**). The adaptive meaning of this peculiar kind of pelvis is not easily understood, although increased capability for jumping and landing is a possibility.

Unenlagia represents a critical stage in dinosaur evolution, between terrestrial bipedal dinosaurs and flying birds (Fig. 2). Stratigraphic distribution of fossils suggests that birds originated, minimally, during the Late Jurassic, and that *Unenlagia* constitutes a Late Cretaceous survivor of a critical evolutionary stage during which cursorial, terrestrial dinosaurs evolved toward flying birds. In agreement with concepts from phylogenetic systematics, birds are considered not only theropod derivatives but also living dinosaurs. Seminal works emphasized the numerous and prominent anatomical similarities between the Upper Jurassic *Archaeopteryx lithographica*, the oldest known bird, and the Dromaeosauridae, a group of Cretaceous maniraptorans that includes *Velociraptor* and *Deinonychus*. Until 1997, no other dinosaur had been discovered that closed the morphological gap between these theropods and birds. *Unenlagia*, in spite of its relatively late record in the Mesozoic, presents features that are more advanced toward birds than does any other theropod dinosaur.

Anatomy of flight. Notable in this morphological transition is the shoulder girdle (Fig. 1*b*), which exhibits a novel orientation of the glenoid cavity, an articular socket for the reception of the humerus. The orientation of this socket has important consequences in forelimb movements. In most dinosaurs the glenoid cavity orientates posteroventrally (from front back and down), thus restricting the range of forelimb movements laterally (to the side) and below the body (**Fig. 3**). In *Unenlagia*, however, the glenoid socket is laterally faced, a condition that closely resembles that of birds. This modification bears two significant functional implications: One is the ability to elevate the humerus almost vertically during maximum upstroke, thereby increasing the dorsoventral (up and down) excursion of the forelimbs (Fig. 3). The other consequence is the ability of the forelimbs

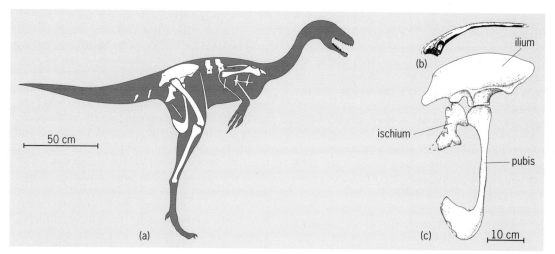

Fig. 1. Patagonian dinosaur *Unenlagia comahuensis*. (*a*) Skeletal reconstruction, (*b*) left scapula in lateral view, and (*c*) pelvic girdle in right lateral aspect. (*After F. E. Novas and P. F. Puerta, New evidence concerning avian origins from the Late Cretaceous of Patagonia, Nature, 387:390–392, 1997*)

to fold against the body, a unique postural activity that in living birds is usually related to both the possession and protection of feathers. Although no epidermal structures have been preserved in the sandstone in which *Unenlagia* was found, the almost avian postural activity of its forelimbs, deduced from the morphology of the shoulder girdle, opens the possibility that the Patagonian dinosaur was also feathered.

Unenlagia used its arms not only to hold and tear prey (as other theropods are thought to have done) but also probably to control the body attitude while running, turning, and leaping. If *Unenlagia* was feathered, its forelimbs could have acted as brakes. The large size of *Unenlagia*, along with its proportionally short forelimbs, suggests that this animal was flightless, and its phylogenetic position suggests that it was not derived from a flying form (Fig. 3). Yet, *Unenlagia* had already acquired extended elevatory range of humeral movements that could have prepared the wing for a powerful downstroke, characterizing incipient flapping activities.

Such anatomical and functional transformations of the shoulder girdle and forelimbs distinguish a paramount aspect in bird evolution: the acquisition of flapping, powered flight. The advanced morphology of the shoulder girdle of *Unenlagia* clearly indicates that outstanding functional attributes present in modern birds (namely, the wide arc of dorsoventral forelimb movements) evolved prior to the acquisition of flight. This extensive, avianlike forelimb elevation (upstroke) constitutes a capital adaptation for a winged theropod to generate thrust to lift off from the ground. Birds inherited this condition, suggesting that the extensive forelimb elevation constituted a prerequisite for powered flight.

Among flying (*Archaeopteryx*) and grounded (*Unenlagia*) dinosaurs, no major osteological modifications involved with flight are recognized, except for a reduction in body size and mass (facilitating body maneuverability), as well as changes in relative proportions in forelimbs and integument (skin). Basal birds inherited almost the same kind of shoulder girdle as did nonflying maniraptorans, while also maintaining the wide arc of forelimb movements and flapping abilities evolved in their dinosaurian

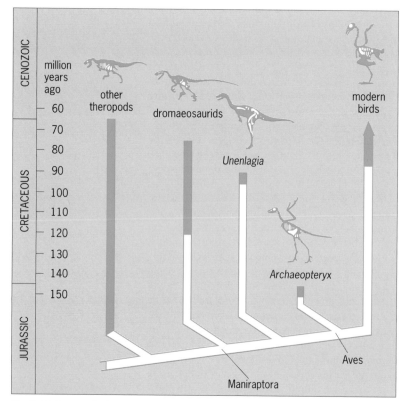

Fig. 2. Cladogram depicting the phylogenetic relationships of *Unenlagia comahuensis*, and indicating the actual record of each theropod lineage (solid bars).

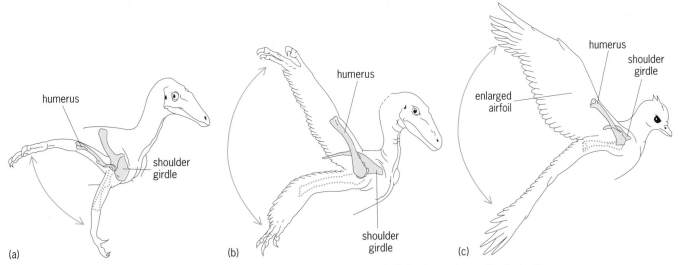

Fig. 3. Anterolateral view of the left shoulder girdle and forelimb in several dinosaurs, depicting its maximum elevation and depression. (*a*) Basal Triassic theropod *Coelophysis*, (*b*) avianlike *Unenlagia*, and (*c*) modern bird (not to scale). (*After C. Sanchez, El hombre que hizo volar a los dinosaurios, Viva, magazine from Clarin newspaper, Buenos Aires, pp. 20–30, June 1997*)

ancestors. Birds experienced both forelimb elongation and enlargement of their feathers, thus increasing the power of thrust of wings.

Living flying birds taking off from the ground after a short run (swans, for example) may represent a good source of information to interpret the function of protowings, and the emergence of flapping flight. Three observations may be made: First, young swans extend their wings outward to keep the body equilibrium as the speed conferred by their hindlimbs increases. Second, as wing feathers develop, swans progressively use their wings as aerodynamic propellers to increase running speed through vigorous flaps. Third, when the speed supplied by the forelimbs surpasses that of the hindlimbs, takeoff occurs. Protowings of theropods such as *Unenlagia*, with an increased arc of downstroke, can be envisaged as aerodynamically performing to increase speed on land and then, in phylogeny, evolving into enlarged airfoils allowing takeoff from the ground. Thus, the evolution of flying capabilities can be envisaged as an aerial extension of displacement on the ground by using forelimbs as propellers.

For background information *see* ANIMAL EVOLUTION; ARCHAEORNITHES; AVES; DINOSAUR; FLIGHT; SKELETAL SYSTEM in the McGraw-Hill Encyclopedia of Science & Technology.   Fernando E. Novas

Bibliography. G. Caple et al., The physics of leaping animals and the evolution of preflight, *Amer. Nat.*, 121:455–476, 1983; J. A. Gauthier, Saurischian monophyly and the origin of birds, *Mem. Calif. Acad. Sci.*, 8:1–46, 1986; F. E. Novas and P. F. Puerta, New evidence concerning avian origins from the Late Cretaceous of Patagonia, *Nature*, 387:390–392, 1997; J. H. Ostrom, *Archaeopteryx* and the origin of flight, *Quart. Rev. Biol.*, 49:27–47, 1974.

Earth interior

Recent research has shown that the Earth's inner core, a solid iron sphere comparable in size to the Moon, is rotating eastward faster than the rest of the solid Earth, at a rate of about 1° per year. This rotation is driven by magnetic coupling to convection patterns in the Earth's fluid outer core.

Core formation. The Earth was formed about 4.6 billion years ago by violent processes in which large numbers of solid objects in the solar system coalesced. As these objects crashed together, mutually attracted by gravitational forces, the protoplanet became very hot and large amounts of available iron melted. Iron is one of the most common elements in the solar system. The Earth's fluid iron, being very heavy, sank to the center of the new planet and formed a liquid iron core whose diameter was more than half the planet's radius. Over time, slow cooling of the planet's deepest interior led to solidification of part of the Earth's iron core, and a solid inner core began to grow inside the fluid core. The solid inner core now has a mass of about 10^{20} tons (30% more than the mass of the Moon).

The resulting stratification gives an Earth with a solid iron inner core having a radius of about 760 mi (1220 km) inside a fluid iron core with a radius of about 2160 mi (3480 km). Though the fluid core is mostly iron, about 10% of it is made from lighter constituents. These cores lie inside a solid mantle that makes up most of the Earth's volume. A thin crustal layer of low-density rocks makes up the outermost stratum, with an outer radius of 3960 mi (6370 km).

Inner-core rotation. The Earth's core rotates eastward with the rest of the Earth, going around once each day; however, the Earth's inner core has an extra spin. Recent evidence from seismology has shown that this extra spin amounts to about 1° per year, above the daily rotation of the mantle and crust. This differential rotation leads to a complete revolution of the inner core about once per 400 years inside the Earth—a rate that is fast enough to be observed on a human time scale.

The rotation of the inner core of the Earth is driven by motions in the fluid core that generate the Earth's magnetic field. Observations of the inner-core rotation rate will help in understanding more about this magnetic field.

The search for inner-core rotation was prompted by scientists looking for an explanation for the Earth's magnetic field. Since the late 1940s, the leading candidate to explain geomagnetism has been some type of self-sustaining dynamo motion, mostly associated with convection in the fluid core, as motions take place that reduce its internal heat. There is a link between electric current, magnetic field, and forces that generate motion in a conducting fluid. In 1995, computers were used to solve the dynamo equations. The numerical solution reproduced the principal observed properties of the Earth's geomagnetic field—overall strength, tendency to drift westward about 0.2° per year, dipole pattern over the Earth's surface, and tendency to change polarity from time to time. These phenomena are driven by the fluid core's need to cool by convection. As a by-product of the numerical solution, it was found that the inner core in the computer model was rotating at a rate of a few degrees per year. This rate was linked to the rate of cooling of the fluid core.

The challenge to find observational evidence for such inner-core rotation was a matter for seismology, which has long been the principal technique for detailed studies of the Earth's interior. Seismology is so successful for studying deep Earth structure because the seismic waves generated by earthquakes travel throughout the planet's interior and can then be recorded at the Earth's surface, where their arrival time and frequency content carry information about the affected interior regions. The inner core itself was discovered in 1936 by interpreting certain seismic signals recorded in Europe as faint echoes from a deep internal surface (far below the core-mantle interface), the signals originating from an earthquake in New Zealand. That reflecting surface had to be the top of an inner core.

The most useful seismic waves are like sound waves, but in order to detect the rotation of an almost spherical object such as the inner core it is necessary first to identify a marker, that is, some feature that moves with the inner core and influences the seismic waves traveling through the slowly moving object.

Fortunately, there is such a marker, associated with the fact that the inner core is composed of a special type of crystalline solid iron which transmits seismic waves (sound waves) that have different speeds in different directions. Seismologists showed in the 1980s and early 1990s that sound waves travel about 4% faster if they go through the inner core in a direction close to the north-south axis than if they go through in an equatorial direction. Even better, for purposes of finding a marker that could be tracked, it was discovered in the mid-1990s that the fastest direction for waves in the inner core was not exactly north-south but was tipped over about 10°.

Thus, the inner core has an innate special direction, like the grain in a piece of wood, but in this case the grain is tipped over 10°. This meant that if the inner core were rotating about a north-south axis, there would be a systematic change in the time it took for earthquake waves to travel from a localized source region, where many earthquakes occur, to a fixed station on the other side of the Earth. Seismologists looked for such a change, using a series of earthquakes over a 30-year period in the southernmost Atlantic Ocean, recorded at a seismic station in central Alaska, and found that the travel time had become shorter by a few tenths of a second. For other paths through the Earth, the travel time through the inner core was getting longer.

It remained to find an overall motion of the inner core that would lead to a consistent explanation of all these changes. The orientation of the fast-direction seismic waves traveling through the inner core at different dates became the key marker. Over the 30-year period covered by the data, the measured travel times could be explained by a rotation (about the north-south axis) of the crystalline structure of the inner core, and hence of the inner core itself. As the fast axis was moved by this rotation, some

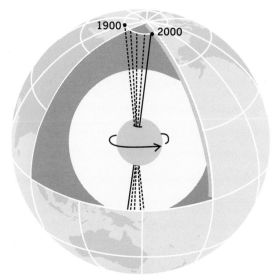

Relative sizes of the Earth's fluid core (the lightest sphere) and the solid inner core (arrow indicates direction of rotation). Broken lines show a marker, a special direction that moves with the inner core, at different times during the twentieth century.

paths through the inner core became faster over time as the fast axis came into better alignment with such paths, and some paths became slower as the fast axis moved to a worse alignment. The position can be found by measuring the time that seismic waves take to travel through the inner core. As the inner core rotates about the north-south axis, the marker also moves. Extrapolating for the whole period from the year 1900 to 2000, the marker appears to have gone about a quarter of a complete revolution (see **illus.**). This indicates that the inner core makes a complete revolution, inside the Earth, in about 400 years.

This motion may be contrasted with the Moon, which goes around the Earth roughly once every 28 days while keeping the same fixed face toward the Earth. The inner core is more massive and about 80 times closer to the Earth's surface than the Moon, but it does not keep the same fixed face as it rotates inside the Earth.

Mechanism for rotation. The Earth's deepest interior is losing its primordial heat and cooling down. The inner core is growing in radius at a rate of about an inch (2.5 cm) per century, as iron from the fluid core solidifies and is plated onto the inner core's surface. This process releases the lighter constituent into the fluid core, generating a rising column of material that is strongest in the directions upward toward the north and south poles. Material elsewhere in the fluid core moves downward, and then inward along the base of the fluid core, toward points underneath the two poles. As it moves toward the axis of daily rotation, its eastward motion (derived from the daily rotation) has to speed up, like the speeding spin-up of a skater whose arms are drawn to an inward position. The result is a pair of ring jets at the base of the fluid core, one in the Northern and one in the Southern Hemisphere, each moving eastward. The inner core is magnetically linked to these ring jets, so its own eastward motion is an expression of what is going on in the fluid core, the place where the geomagnetic field is generated.

For background information *see* EARTH INTERIOR; EARTH ROTATION AND ORBITAL MOTION; GEOMAGNETISM; SEISMOLOGY in the McGraw-Hill Encyclopedia of Science & Technology.   Paul G. Richards

Bibliography. G. A. Glatzmaier and P. H. Roberts, Rotation and magnetism of the Earth's inner core, *Science*, 274:1887–1891, 1996; R. Jeanloz and B. Romanowicz, Geophysical dynamics at the center of the Earth, *Phys. Today*, pp. 22–27, August 1997; X. Song and P. G. Richards, Seismological evidence for differential rotation of the Earth's inner core, *Nature*, 382:221–224, 1996.

Earthquake

The eastern Mediterranean region is one of the most actively excavated areas in archeology. Typically, sites there are in the form of tells (large, flat-topped artificial hills) comprising the accumulated layers of human habitation. Since this region also experiences earthquake activity, it is inescapable that earthquakes and archeology be intimately related. However, only recently have earth scientists and archeologists come together to formally address the evidence for earthquakes in archeological remains. As a result, there has been much disagreement through the years over the role that earthquakes played in ancient society.

Although earthquakes have often been associated with unexplained past societal disasters, their impact has been thought to be only secondary for two reasons: inconclusive archeological interpretation of excavated destruction, and misconceptions about patterns of seismicity. However, new and revised archeological evidence and a better understanding of the irregularities of the time-space patterns of large earthquakes suggest that earthquakes have been instrumental in shaping the history of humankind.

Rise and fall of cities. Not only do earthquakes periodically damage cities, but they also create the landforms that make some of those cities politically and economically important. Ancient Armageddon (Megiddo), the most excavated archeological site in Israel, is a fascinating example of this: it is situated next to the Mount Carmel-Gilboa fault system, which according to recent geophysical measurements is seismically active. Earthquakes are caused by a sudden motion of faults. Depending on the configuration of the faults in an area, this motion may cause the uplift of mountains or the formation of deep rifts. For instance, motion on the complicated Carmel-Gilboa fault has created, over time, the topography which made Megiddo strategically important. The accumulated motion created both the Carmel-Gilboa mountain range and the Nahal Iron Pass, which controlled ancient traffic between Syria and Egypt. Megiddo's strategic location at this pass led to some of the greatest ancient battles in this region, and was the reason for the maintenance of its fortifications.

Unfortunately for ancient builders, the recurrence of the same earthquakes that shaped the land, possibly three or four per millennium, also explains the repeated destruction of Megiddo—destruction sometimes assigned, for lack of a better explanation, to unproved battles. For example, King David's often-assumed (but not documented) conquest and destruction of Megiddo actually may have been a destructive earthquake in northern Israel around 1000 B.C. An earlier earthquake about 1400 B.C., which damaged many sites around the countryside, also destroyed Megiddo.

Indicators. There is some disagreement about what constitutes archeological evidence for earthquake destruction. A list of the most telling features would include fallen columns, fallen walls, slipped keystones, and crushed skeletons.

Fallen columns. An attacker may, by the application of a great deal of human force or ingenious leverage, topple the columns of a building. However, when an entire row of columns is found toppled in the same direction, the sudden concerted ground motion of an earthquake is the likely explanation.

Fallen walls. The uniform toppling of walls is a sign of earthquakes. When many similarly oriented walls at a site fell in the same direction—particularly when they buried grain, gold, or other valuables in their fall—the action of an army is an unlikely cause.

Slipped keystones. When an earthquake completely destroys a building, it is often difficult to unscramble the jumbled stones to determine the cause of the destruction. However, for buildings with unreinforced arches, partial earthquake damage leaves a distinctive signature. When one side of an arched doorway slips relative to the other, the stones in the arch are loosened. As a result, one or more of the wedge-shaped stones drop down until the arch is again wedged tight. If the slip is large enough, the entire arch collapses; if not, the dropped keystone remains as clear evidence of the disruption.

Crushed skeletons. People do not often bury their dead in the rubble of collapsed buildings. Also, when a building is under attack and soldiers are laboring to topple a wall, they would try to avoid being crushed beneath the stones. Thus, the presence of crushed skeletons beneath ruined buildings is accepted by most archeologists as evidence of collapse by earthquake.

Regional damage. Although some of these effects of earthquake destruction have been recognized in archeological excavations for decades, opinions regarding their greater significance have varied. Few archeologists have dared to apply their theories of earthquake destruction outside the boundaries of their own excavations, even to towns only a short distance away. However, the nature of ground motion in earthquakes makes it natural to apply these interpretations more widely.

Large and moderate earthquakes may cause widespread damage, especially to vulnerable architecture and in areas with unstable soils; it is uncommon that a large earthquake will damage only a single town. Large and moderate earthquakes are not isolated events; a large earthquake will trigger aftershocks, some of which may be nearly as large as the main seismic event. Furthermore, the stress increase that results from releasing one section of the fault without releasing adjacent fault segments can make the stuck segments more likely to slip.

The modern history of large and moderate earthquakes on the North Anatolian Fault illustrates this phenomenon. A series of earthquakes, starting in 1939 and propagating roughly westward in 1942, 1943, 1944, 1951, 1957, and 1967, ruptured this entire plate boundary. Over approximately 30 years, an average slip of 7-13 ft (2-4 m) occurred along the plate boundary.

Using what is known about the long-term plate motion across the boundary, if this earthquake "storm" is typical of how plate motion is accommodated along this fault, a recurrence should be expected every few hundred years, with relatively quiet periods in the interim. Indeed, there are other historically recorded instances of seismic activity on the North Anatolian Fault in the seventeenth and eighteenth centuries, and at the beginning of the eleventh century. Unfortunately, it cannot yet be predicted exactly when earthquakes will occur, nor can it be ascertained when they occurred in the past without precise geological evidence dug from the fault itself. The modern sequence of earthquakes caused tremendous death and destruction in Turkey, with some towns completely wiped out. While the sections of the fault that slipped were fairly discrete, the areas of damage extended far from the fault, and often an area damaged in an earlier earthquake was struck again a year or two later. This phenomenon helps explain how many sites throughout an area could be destroyed within the span of 50 years or so. The extent of the destruction by such rare but powerful earthquake clusters may have been far greater in ancient times than today because of poorer construction and the lack of any concept of earthquake preparedness.

Contribution to historical conflicts. Earthquakes have been used by archeologists to explain the physical destruction of various sites. However, the prevailing opinion among archeologists has been that such destruction is not sufficient to substantially affect the social order. It is true that a healthy city with a robust economy and a fairly broad support network can, if unchallenged, rebuild quickly after an earthquake, possibly achieving complete recovery within a few decades. However, in areas of social tension or economic decline, an earthquake can be the trigger for social overturn.

For instance, the Holy Land earthquake of 31 B.C., occurring during a war between the Arabs and the Jews, prompted an Arab attack on Jewish-held Jerusalem. In this case, the Jews successfully defended the city, but had the earthquake damage to the city walls been slightly greater, the outcome could have been different. In another scenario, the slave uprising at Sparta in about 469 B.C. may have been triggered by an earthquake, which greatly damaged the grand homes of the ruling elite. An earthquake has been proposed (and refuted) as the cause of the end of the Hittite Empire. The Hittite capital, Hattusa, would have been severely damaged if it had been functioning during the modern earthquake storm on the North Anatolian Fault. Indeed, if Hatussa existed long enough in its current location, it must eventually have suffered extreme seismic damage. Depending on the political and economic situation at the time, the Hittites might have recovered and rebuilt. In any case, it is expected that the crude huts of survivors or of squatters would be seen atop the rubble of the buildings beneath. Such is seen in excavations all over earthquake country.

The conjunction of earthquake science and archeology is a field that is ripe for further study. Improvements in both archeological method and geophysical understanding should allow a much better understanding of how earthquakes affected ancient civilization. Both disciplines would benefit from such collaborative work. Earthquake prediction efforts may be helped by extending the earthquake record back into prehistory, and archeologists will gain a new understanding of what type of damage earthquakes or earthquake sequences can cause.

For background information *see* ARCHEOLOGY; EARTHQUAKE; FAULT AND FAULT STRUCTURES in the McGraw-Hill Encyclopedia of Science & Technology.   Amos Nur; Dawn Burgess

Bibliography. N. N. Ambraseys, Value of historical records of earthquakes, *Nature*, 232:374–379, 1971; A. Nur and H. Ron, Earthquake! Inspiration for Armageddon, *Biblical Archaeol. Rev.*, pp. 48–58, July/August 1997; D. Soren, An earthquake on Cyprus, *Archaeology*, 38(2):52–59, 1985.

Electric power transmission

Until 1996 the electric power utility industry in the United States was a regulated monopoly that controlled all portions of the electric power system, including the generation and transmission of electric power. In recent years the federal government has successfully deregulated portions of other industries, such as the gas pipelines and the telephone system. On April 24, 1996, the Federal Energy Regulatory Commission (FERC) issued two orders that ushered in the deregulation of electric power generation, permitting electric power to be generated by companies other than regulated electric power utilities. The electric power transmission system is still a regulated monopoly, but the utilities must sell transmission rights at a fair price to those needing to transmit power to customers. There was a need to communicate the available transmission capacity and prices to everyone in a fair and equitable manner. Therefore, an electronic system, the Open-Access Same-time Information System (OASIS), was developed that would post this information and allow for purchasing and reselling of transmission rights.

Electronic information system. In order to provide access to the transmission grid, the transmission providers must use the OASIS to post information about the available transmission capability and the cost of purchasing transmission services, such as capacity. This information must be posted for each major interstate transmission line of the transmission grid that is near capacity. In addition, the OASIS allows transmission customers to purchase and resell transmission services.

A transmission provider is the public electric power utility that owns, operates, or controls facilities used for the transmission of electric energy in interstate commerce. These groups are generally the electric power utilities. However, in 1997 new organizations called independent system operators began to form, and they will operate the transmission grid for a number of electric power utilities.

A transmission customer is any eligible company that has a contract with a utility to purchase transmission rights. These companies may be utility companies, independent generation companies, or power marketing companies. There are power marketing agents both within the utility companies in subsidiary organizations, called affiliated marketers, and in power trading companies that are not connected to any utility. Power marketers buy, sell, and trade generation to provide energy to large industrial customers or to other electric power utilities. These purchases and sales can be within a state or region, or across a large portion of North America. Many electric utility companies have recently set up their own independent affiliated power marketing organizations. These organizations can communicate with the transmission portion of a utility only through the OASIS, so that they receive information at the same time as nonaffiliated marketing organizations.

OASIS specifications. The Electric Power Research Institute and the North American Electric Reliability Council helped electric power industry groups to decide how this electronic system would work and what information needed to be conveyed between transmission providers and transmission customers. The resulting OASIS specifications became part of the FERC order that established the OASIS.

The OASIS electronic information system for posting and ordering transmission capacity consists of 22 Internet Web modes. The 10 regions served by the regional reliability councils of the North American Electric Reliability Council provide a rough guide to the location and geographic area covered by these nodes (see **table**). There is at least one OASIS node in each of these regions. In the Western States Coordinating Council (WSCC) region, there

Division of OASIS nodes among regional reliability councils	
Regional reliability councils	OASIS nodes
East Central Area Reliability Coordination Agreement (ECAR)	ECAR OASIS
Electric Reliability Council of Texas (ERCOT)	AEP OASIS ERCOT OASIS
Florida Reliability Coordinating Council (FRCC)	Florida OASIS Network
Mid-Atlantic Area Council (MACC)	PJM OASIS
Mid-America Interconnected Network Inc. (MAIN)	MAIN OASIS
Mid-Continent Area Power Pool (MAPP)	MAPP OASIS
Northeast Power Coordinating Council (NPCC)	NEPOOL OASIS NYPP OASIS
Southeastern Electric Reliability Council (SERC)	Southern Co. OASIS VACAR OASIS
Southwest Power Pool (SPP)	SPP OASIS
Western States Coordinating Council (WSCC)	APS OASIS ENX OASIS Idaho Power OASIS LADWP OASIS Northwest OASIS PacifiCorp OASIS Puget OASIS Rocky Mountain Area OASIS SWOASIS Western OASIS

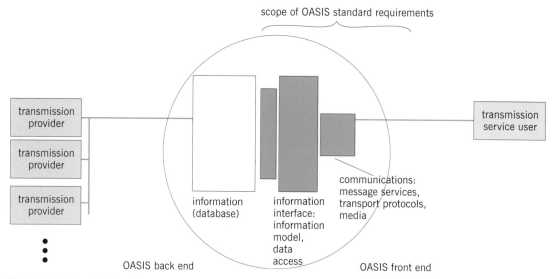

Fig. 1. Model of an OASIS node.

are 10 OASIS nodes. Each OASIS node has information for one or more transmission providers. There are about 178 transmission providers in North America, which include almost all electric power transmission companies.

Use of the World Wide Web for posting and transacting transmission services started in January 1997. Thousands of transactions take place daily using OASIS.

OASIS node model. An OASIS node is a computer web site with a database for storing information and communication links (**Fig. 1**). The OASIS front end has communication links over the Internet in order that customers can make queries for information or transact business. The OASIS back end has communication links to enable one or more transmission providers to upload prices and information about available transmission capability into the database and to allow confirmation of sales, billing, and the actual scheduling of energy to take place. Back-end processes that are supported include billing and reconciliation, calculation and posting of total transmis-

sion capability and available transmission capability, confirmation or denial of a request for transmission services, computation of the price for each transmission service, validation that a request for transmission service is correct and made from a valid transmission customer, and scheduling the actual energy flow on the transmission grid.

Security. Security has been an important issue. Each OASIS node has firewalls, passwords, and other security measures to protect its information. The firewalls provide security limits as to how the data can be accessed to prevent unauthorized users from modifying the data. Each node has a database that is organized by transmission provider. Transmission customers can access the OASIS node through the public Internet or by using modems or leased lines. The transmission customer must pay for the cost of these modem or leased-line services (**Fig. 2**). *See* COMPUTER SECURITY AND PRIVACY.

Internet use. The use of the Internet provides any transmission customer with an inexpensive means of entry to the OASIS, and gives the transmission providers an inexpensive and high-function node. In addition, for most people the required training is reduced, since they are already familiar with the use of the World Wide Web. Information can be accessed through web pages or downloaded as files after making a query. *See* WEB RESOURCES.

OASIS Phase IA. In 1997, the electric power industry submitted changes to the OASIS specification to the FERC for its approval. These changes, called OASIS Phase IA, were based on the FERC's request that the OASIS nodes be more consistent and allow for additional functions such as price negotiations. Some of the new additions include the following:

1. Bidding capability to allow transmission customers and transmission providers to negotiate a new price that is different than the posted offering price.

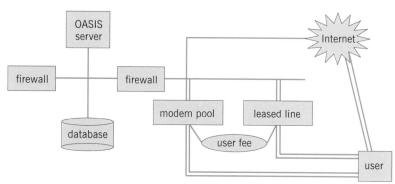

Fig. 2. OASIS node with provisions for access and security.

2. Allowing for a capacity profile when making a request for transmission services. This would allow a transmission customer to request a different capacity at each hour of a single request for transmission service.

3. Ability to offer transmission services on a sliding window. That is, for daily service, a day could be any 24-h period, rather than from one second past midnight to the next midnight. Weekly service could be any 7 days of service.

4. Ability to link requests for ancillary services to transmission services. Ancillary services are generation services that support transmission services. Some ancillary services are frequency control and voltage control.

5. Dynamic notification of the status of a request for transmission service. This will allow transmission customers to be notified of changes in the status of their reservations automatically through the Internet.

6. Standardization of transmission services to indicate features such as the length of service, whether the service is provided for peak hours, and whether the service is firm or nonfirm. Firm service is transmission service that is guaranteed to happen, while nonfirm service, which is usually provided at lower cost, may be curtailed if the transmission line is at full capacity.

Future use. There are plans to improve OASIS beyond the changes in OASIS Phase IA. These improvements would include scheduling energy interchange transactions and communicating transmission line constraints. Plans are being designed to create OASIS Phase II, which would allow both generation capacity and transmission services to be offered and reserved using OASIS, rather than just transmission services. This system would keep track of resales and curtailments.

For background information *see* COMPUTER SECURITY; ELECTRIC POWER SYSTEMS; ELECTRIC POWER TRANSMISSION; TELEPHONE SERVICE in the McGraw-Hill Encyclopedia of Science & Technology.   Peter M. Hirsch

Bibliography. G. Cauley et al., Information network supports open access, *IEEE Comput. Appl. Pow.*, pp. 12-19, July 1996; L. Lamarre, Deregulating in the information age, *EPRI J.*, pp. 18-25, May/June 1997.

Electrochemistry

Electrochemistry is emerging as an important technique for selective and sensitive detection in ultrasmall environments. The growth in use of electrochemical techniques can be attributed to improvements in instrumentation as well as miniaturization of the electrodes. Individual microelectrodes are being used to conduct cellular investigations in vitro and in vivo that require detection of minute amounts of material. Analyzing a sample released upon stimulation of a single cell is extremely difficult because of the sample's small volume and the femtomole (10^{-18}) to zeptomole (10^{-21}) levels of analyte present. To realize the full potential of electrochemical techniques, further developments in small-volume sample handling are needed to prevent dilution by restricting the low analyte levels present in single cells to picoliter (10^{-12}) volumes.

This article focuses on the development of picoliter microstructures and on characterization of the electrochemical properties in these tiny "beakers." Combining nanotechnology with electrochemical detection for the analysis of chemical release from single cells provides a substantial improvement in small-sample handling. Thus, opportunities will immediately be created for biological and chemical analyses previously unexplored in the solution phase.

Fabrication of microvials. Microvials have been fabricated for several applications in various sizes. Microvials have been constructed in silicon wafers (1 nanoliter to 9 picoliters) to solve sample handling and dilution problems for small-volume samples injected into separation systems. Silicon microvials are very useful in applications where it is not necessary to visually observe the material in the microvial. For work involving cells, however, the silicon microvials are not sufficient, so microvials have been constructed in polystyrene. In contrast to silicon microvials, polystyrene vials are transparent, which is advantageous for use with single cells since transmission optical microscopy can be used to view the cell.

Standard photolithographic and wet chemical etching techniques are used in the fabrication process. A photomask is utilized to transfer a pattern by using ultraviolet irradiation onto a silicon wafer. The silicon wafer is processed by plasma etching procedures, and then wet chemical etching is performed to anisotropically etch the silicon, leaving square pyramidal structures protruding from the surface. The pattern on the completed silicon wafer template is then transferred into polystyrene by heating. After cooling, the polystyrene microvials are removed from the template. The polystyrene wafer that is produced contains hundreds of microvials spaced 1 mm apart.

The vial size can be easily manipulated by changing the photomask or by controlling the etch depth. Sizes fabricated in polystyrene range 310-0.4 pL. The microvials are characterized structurally by using standard transmission optical microscopy and scanning electron microscopy (SEM) to image them. Microvial volumes have been calculated from the measured dimensions.

Picoliter volumes. The small vial sizes developed in polystyrene are well suited for investigations that require extremely low sample volumes. However, the main difficulty in handling liquid samples in the picoliter regime is rapid evaporation. The rate of evaporation is proportional to the surface area-to-volume ratio of the sample, which is extremely large in a picoliter vial. Under normal laboratory conditions, an aqueous sample evaporates in a matter of seconds from a 16-pL vial. Methods to prevent evaporation in microvials have included coating the vial

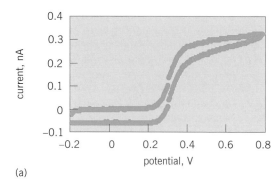

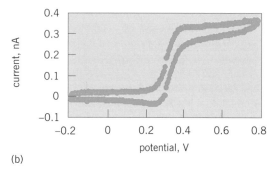

(a)

(b)

Fig. 1. Cyclic voltammograms of 1.0 *mM* ferrocene carboxylic acid in (*a*) a 16-pL microvial and (*b*) bulk solution. The scan rate is 1.0 V/s and a 5-μm-diameter carbon fiber electrode is used.

with an oil or membrane lid, saturating the headspace with water, and adding glycerol to lower the vapor pressure. With these methods, evaporation is not observed over the time scale of the electrochemical experiments performed (1–5 min).

Electrochemistry in microvials is performed by using the two-electrode mode normally used for microelectrodes. The working electrode is made from a 5-μm carbon fiber, and the reference is a miniature silver chloride (Ag/AgCl) electrode (1-μm tip diameter). Experiments are conducted on the stage of an inverted microscope equipped with three micromanipulators for positioning the electrodes and an injector. High-precision micromanipulators are necessary to move the electrodes around, considering the micrometer dimensions of the vials. Experiments are conducted by initially filling a picoliter vial with solution by pressure injection with a microinjector. Once the microvial is filled, the miniature Ag/AgCl reference electrode and the working carbon-fiber electrode are manipulated into it for subsequent electrochemistry.

The basic utility of microvials for electrochemical analysis has been demonstrated by performing cyclic voltammetric analysis on an electrochemical standard, ferrocene carboxylic acid. Voltammograms have been collected in a variety of microvial sizes. Cyclic voltammograms show the onset of oxidation of ferrocene carboxylic acid at approximately 0.3 V and reach maximum oxidation quickly (the current levels off). Once the potential reaches 0.8 V, the

scan is reversed and ferrocene continues to be oxidized until the formal potential is passed where the current returns to zero. The cyclic voltammograms in the 16-pL vial at scan rates of 1 V/s display the normal sigmoidal response expected for steady-state diffusion at a microelectrode. The formal potential and current response measured in the microvials are identical to those for ferrocene carboxylic acid in bulk solution (**Fig. 1**).

To push the limits for electrochemical measurements to the smallest volumes, experiments have been conducted in 1-pL vials with smaller carbon-fiber (1-μm tip diameter) electrodes. For these experiments, measurements must be carried out rapidly (approximately 30 s) to alleviate evaporation problems. At the appropriate scan rates, sigmoidal voltammograms are again observed for 1 *mM* ferrocene carboxylic acid solutions in only 1 pL.

Variations are observed in the cyclic voltammetric response at slower scan rates in the microvials compared to bulk-solution conditions. Electrochemical measurements obtained for ferrocene carboxylic acid as a model system have provided critical information about the electrochemical response in these small volumes.

Cellular isolation. Nerve and hormonal cells are known to communicate by releasing chemicals that the neighboring cells use as cues to continue or discontinue specific functions. Previously, research in this area focused on studying the cells by electrochemical means in petri dishes with volumes of 3–4 milliliters. Successful development of voltammetric measurements in picoliter microvials will provide a means to investigate single-cell systems and reactions in extremely small and restricted volumes. The goal of these experiments is to place a single cell (approximately 15 μm in diameter) in a microvial (7 or 16 pL) where the extracellular environment will be restricted and released materials can be monitored with minimum dilution. To accomplish this goal, methods to transfer cells into the microvial have been developed. Two methods are currently used to isolate single cells. One method involves transfer of a cell into a microvial by using a microinjector, and the other uses culturing procedures to isolate the cell. Cells have been isolated in 16- and

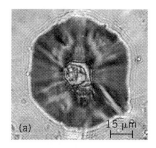
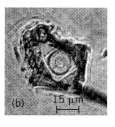

Fig. 2. Single bovine adrenal cells microinjected into (*a*) 81-pL microvial and (*b*) 16-pL microvial. (*From R. A. Clark and A. G. Ewing, Experimenting in picoliter microvials, Chemtech, 28:20–25, 1998*)

81-pL vials. The cell in the 81-pL vial still has a substantial volume around it; however, the cell in the 16-pL vial is very close to the vial dimensions. In this case, the cell diameter is approximately 15 μm and the bottom of the vial is 20 μm. Single cells and groups of cells have been transferred into microvials (**Fig. 2**), and the electrochemistry is beginning to be studied in the picoliter volumes.

In preliminary experiments, groups of cells (6–10) have been placed into 390-pL vials and voltammetry carried out in the microvial solution surrounding the cells. Bovine adrenal cells which contain large amounts of norepinephrine and epinephrine (easily oxidized catecholamines) were used with the voltammetry expected to resemble that for catecholamines in standard solution. This is in fact the case; catecholamines measured in a 390-pL microvial give similar cyclic voltammograms to catecholamine standards in bulk solution. Based on the current, the concentration of catecholamine is approximately 60 μM and appears to represent a background amount of these substances released from these cells.

For background information *see* ELECTROCHEMICAL TECHNIQUES; ELECTROCHEMISTRY; ELECTRODE in the McGraw-Hill Encyclopedia of Science & Technology.   Rose A. Clark

Bibliography. A. J. Bard (ed.), *Electroanalytical Chemistry*, 15:267–351, 1988; R. A. Clark, H. P. Beyer, and A. G. Ewing, Electrochemical analysis in picoliter microvials, *Anal. Chem.*, 69:259–263, 1997.

Evolution

There is overwhelming evidence that all existing creatures on Earth are descended from a common ancestor. All organisms are composed of the same biochemical units—the same 20 amino acids, the same four nitrogen bases, and the same simple sugars. All organisms synthesize and assemble these units into long chains (polymers or macromolecules) to make proteins out of the amino acids, and nucleic acids [ribonucleic acid (RNA) and deoxyribonucleic acid (DNA)] out of the bases and sugars. Each organism assembles these units into macromolecules according to its own genetic blueprint in the form of the inherited order of units in its DNA. It is the occasional errors in copying DNA from one generation to another that lead to individual differences and eventually to new species. This sameness of composition but uniqueness of arrangement is often referred to as biochemical unity and diversity.

Prokaryotes and eukaryotes. Until relatively recently, biologists tended to divide the living world into two major groups, the prokaryotes and the eukaryotes, depending on whether or not their cells had a nucleus. Prokaryotes, which do not have a visible nucleus, are single-celled creatures whose DNA is in the form of a simple circle. Eukaryotes may be either single celled or multicellular; their DNA is in the form of linear chromosomes that are compacted with proteins and stored inside a membrane-enveloped body called the nucleus. In prokaryotes, cell division is a simple process: the duplicated circles of DNA are attached to the cell membrane and are simply pulled away into the new cells. Cell division in eukaryotes takes place by a much more complicated process called mitosis, which sorts recently duplicated chromosomes into new daughter cells. There are numerous other distinctions that can be made between prokaryotes and eukaryotes.

In the 1970s it became possible to determine the order, or sequence, of biochemical units in nucleic acids (RNA and DNA). A large-scale study of ribosomal RNA in a wide assortment of prokaryotes and eukaryotes gave rise to a surprising result. Although, for the most part, organisms that were thought to be similar on the basis of many biological properties did indeed have similar RNA sequences, taken as a whole, the sequences fell into three large and distinct groups instead of the anticipated two. Based on the RNA sequences, there are two major subgroups of prokaryotes. One group is composed of common and well-studied bacteria. The other group comprises an exotic cluster of organisms, many of which live under harsh conditions that some scientists consider a reflection of the environment on the early Earth, including high temperatures or very high concentrations of salt. Accordingly, prokaryotes are now divided into the eubacteria and the archaea. *See* ARCHAEA.

Eukaryotes are usually divided into four subgroups, including a large and diverse kingdom of single-celled creatures called protists. Protists include algae and amebas and many other organisms previously called protozoa. Like other eukaryotes, most of these creatures have cytoskeletons, as well as intracellular bodies called organelles, the most common of which are mitochondria. These organelles are descendants of bacteria that came to live within eukaryotic cells. Although this idea of an endosymbiotic origin for organelles had become well established on the basis of other evidence, the similarity of mitochondrial ribosomal RNA sequences to those of bacteria further strengthened the case.

The most familiar eukaryotes occur in three kingdoms—plants, fungi, and animals—distinguished by morphological and physiological features. For example, plants and fungi have cell walls and animals do not. With regard to ribosomal sequences, analysis indicates that the plant lineage branched off first, then fungi, and finally animals. Animals first make their appearance in the fossil record about 600 million years ago (m.y.a.). A family tree of animals can be constructed on the basis of morphological characters shared between existing species and reliably dated fossils. For example, vertebrate animals first appear in the fossil record about 450 m.y.a. Vertebrates include fish, amphibians, reptiles, birds, and mammals. The first appearance of amphibian fossils occurs in geologic strata dated to 385 m.y.a., whereas fossils corresponding to the last common ancestor of reptiles and birds are dated to about 290 m.y.a.

Divergence times. The time of divergence of the principal biological groups—archaea, eubacteria, and eukaryotes—from their common ancestor remains to be determined with certainty. This is difficult to resolve because bacteria are so small that fossil evidence of their existence can be made only by painstaking electron microscopy. For the most part, the macrofossil record (fossils from multicellular creatures that can be seen with the naked eye) extends back only to the Cambrian Period, about 600 million years before the present (m.y. B.P.). It is well established that the Earth is 4600 million years old, but very high temperature and intense bombardment by other bodies early in Earth history make it seem unlikely that any form of life could have existed before 4000 m.y. B.P. That leaves about 3400 million years bereft of a macrofossil record during which life originated and diverged into the principal groups in existence today.

Microfossils. Microfossils that look very much like bacteria have been found in rocks that have been reliably dated to 3450 m.y. B.P. Many resemble modern-day bacteria called cyanobacteria, photosynthetic organisms that convert carbon dioxide and water into a simple sugar and oxygen. The chloroplasts found in green plants are descendants of an endosymbiont that was also the common ancestor of modern cyanobacteria. As in the case of mitochondria, chloroplasts still retain their eubacteria-like ribosomal RNA.

Macromolecular sequencing. Computers can be used to align ribosomal RNA sequences and cluster them according to their similarities in the form of a phylogenetic tree. In general, there is good correspondence between the branching order of the tree and that determined from other biological characteristics. However, placing the root of the tree has proved troublesome. Which of the three major groups the common ancestor gave rise to initially cannot be determined on the basis of the ribosomal RNA sequences alone.

However, the same kinds of sequence analysis used for RNA can be applied to protein sequences, and several advantages accrue. For one, new proteins tend to come about by the duplication of genes for existing proteins. By comparing the sequences of sets of proteins that resulted from gene duplications that occurred before the divergence of archaea, eubacteria, and eukaryotes, several groups of workers were able to show that archaea are more akin to eukaryotes than are eubacteria.

Sequence of events. Thus, current views have eubacteria and archaea diverging from the common ancestor at some early point, and the eukaryotes diverging from archaea at some later time. Subsequently, a particular oxygen-utilizing eubacterium established residence inside a eukaryotic cell. Its descendants eventually became entirely dependent on the host cell and evolved into a mitochondrion. At some later point, a similar endosymbiosis developed between a plant cell and a cyanobacterium destined to become the chloroplast.

It is of great interest to determine when all these events took place. One approach is to compare pro-

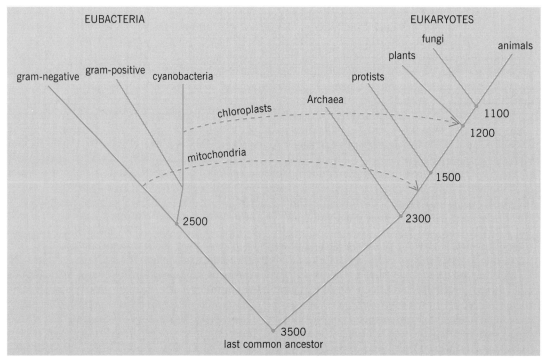

Tree of life diagram based on analysis of protein sequences. Numbers at nodes indicate approximate divergence times in millions of years.

tein sequences from extant multicellular organisms, correlate their differences with divergence times determined from the fossil record, and then extrapolate backward in time to find the divergence times for those creatures for which there is a scant fossil record but for which protein sequences are available for their present-day counterparts. When this is done for eukaryotes, it appears that fungi and animals diverged a little more than 1000 m.y.a. and plants just a little before that (1200 m.y.a.). Protists may have diverged from the main line numerous times to give their present-day members, but taken as a whole the divergence occurred about 1500 m.y.a. (see **illus.**).

The farther back one goes, the less reliable this method may be, and there is much debate about the times of the earliest eukaryotes. One interpretation of the protein sequence data suggests that eukaryotes first appeared between 2000 and 2500 m.y.a. This date tends to be supported by the microfossil record, the oldest generally accepted eukaryote-like specimens dating to 2100 m.y. B.P. The protein sequence data suggest that numerous proteins were transferred to the eukaryote host from an endosymbiont, probably the mitochondrion, during this same period. The protein sequence data also suggest that the divergence of eubacteria and archaea occurred much earlier, probably between 3000 and 4000 m.y.a. A similar interpretation may be made for the ribosomal RNA data. In either case, alternative scenarios can be drawn.

One controversial point has to do with the 3450-million-year-old microfossils that resemble cyanobacteria. Both the protein and ribosomal RNA phylogenetic trees have modern cyanobacteria appearing high on the tree (see illus.). If the ancient microfossils truly represent this group, the divergence of eukaryotes from archaea had to have been even earlier. If it is presumed that life originated on Earth some time after 4000 m.y. B.P., then the available window of time for evolving the three major lineages is only 500 million years, after which for some unknown reason there was a great slowdown in molecular evolution.

Reconstructing the history of life on Earth, whether from microfossils or macromolecular sequences, is still a matter of some uncertainty, but the unanticipated availability of enormous amounts of sequence data from recent genome projects offers the prospect that many of the arguments and inconsistencies will be resolved in the near future.

For background information *see* ARCHAEA; CELL DIVISION; CYANOBACTERIA; EUKARYOTAE; NUCLEIC ACID; PREBIOTIC ORGANIC SYNTHESIS; PROKARYOTAE in the McGraw-Hill Encyclopedia of Science & Technology.   Russell F. Doolittle

Bibliography. D. F. Feng, G. Cho, and R. F. Doolittle, Determining divergence times with a protein clock: Update and re-evaluation, *Proc. Nat. Acad. Sci. USA*, 1997; A. H. Knoll, The early evolution of eukaryotes: A geological perspective, *Science*, 256:622–627, 1992; J. W. Schopf, Microfossils of the early Archaen apex chert: New evidence of the antiquity of life, *Science*, 260:640–646, 1993; M. L. Sogin, The phylogenetic significance of sequence diversity and length variations in eukaryotic small subunit ribosomal RNA coding regions, in L. Warren and H. Koprowski (eds.), *New Perspectives in Evolution*, 1991; C. R. Woese and G. E. Fox, Phylogenetic structure of the prokaryotic domain: The primary kingdoms, *Proc. Nat. Acad. Sci. USA*, 74:5088–5090, 1977.

Fluid-flow visualization

Air and water are the media in which humans and all other living organisms spend their lives, the media by which heating and cooling are accomplished, and the media through which all means of transportation must pass. Fluid-dominated phenomena are critical for the operation of aircraft, sailboats, cars, and trucks, and they play an important role in energy efficiency and combustion.

Over the years, most insight into fluid motion has been gained from various methods of visualizing air and water flows. Until recently, these methods of visualization have been qualitative in nature. Early work relied mostly on light passing through the flow, and flow structures were observed by the deflection of that light. Shadowgraphs of supersonic flows taken in the 1880s clearly showed shock structure and other features of supersonic jets. By incorporating a knife edge at the focal point of the collection optics, the schlieren method produces much greater sensitivity than the shadowgraph, and has become a common tool for fluid-dynamics research. More recently, interferometry has been used to give more quantitative measurements of flow structure. In all these cases, however, the images represent the integration of features along the light path, and cannot, in general, give localized values of fluid properties.

With high-power lasers it is now possible to image the flow molecules themselves, so that quantitative information can be acquired. This imaging is accomplished primarily by laser-induced fluorescence and by Rayleigh scattering. Laser-induced fluorescence occurs when a laser is tuned so that the laser light overlaps an absorption frequency of the molecule. The molecule is excited, and emits light as it relaxes back to the ground state. This emission is called laser-induced fluorescence, and the strength of the emission is related to the number of the particular

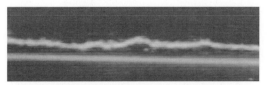

Fig. 1. Turbulent air visualized by line tagging. Lines are tagged into turbulent air by vibrational excitation of oxygen and are observed with 0- and 7-μs time delays.

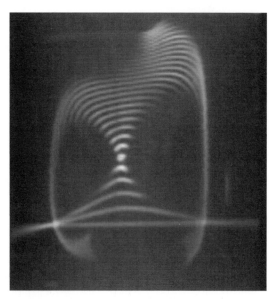

Fig. 2. Rotating water visualized by line tagging. Lines are tagged at 1-s intervals into a cylinder of water which has a rotating top.

molecular species that were excited, as well as to other factors such as the temperature or the presence of collisions with other species. Rayleigh scattering is, in a sense, the reflection of light from a molecule, and occurs because any light impinging on a molecule causes the electrons in the molecule to oscillate at the frequency of the light wave. The electrons then act as small antennas and reradiate some of this energy. This reradiated light is at the same frequency as the incident light and is called Rayleigh scattering. Scattering is stronger at higher frequencies, so a white light source illuminating a volume of molecules generates more scattering at blue wavelengths than at red wavelengths, and it is this phenomenon that causes the sky to appear blue.

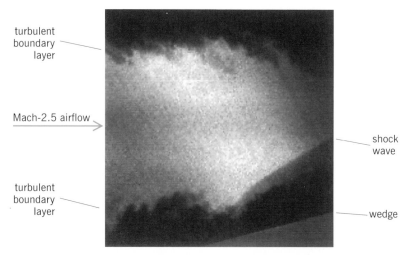

Fig. 3. Mach 2.5 airflow over a wedge, visualized by Rayleigh scattering. Instantaneous boundary-layer and shock-wave structure in the vicinity of a 14°-angle wedge are visible in the flow.

Laser-induced fluorescence. In air, laser-induced fluorescence from oxygen molecules can be used. The illumination source is usually an argon-fluoride laser operating with a wavelength of 0.193 μm and expanded to a thin sheet of light by using lenses. By carefully tuning the frequency of the argon-fluoride laser, vibrationally hot oxygen molecules can be excited and imaged. The brightness of this image is a quantitative measure of the number of hot oxygen molecules illuminated by the ultraviolet laser light sheet. An application of oxygen laser-induced fluorescence is flow tagging of air. In this case, oxygen molecules are driven into their vibrationally excited state by a high-power, pulsed (two-color) laser beam. This laser beam leaves a track of vibrationally excited molecules which appear as a straight line. After the molecules have moved for some short period of time, the argon-fluoride laser is fired, and an image of the vibrationally hot molecules is recorded (a procedure known as interrogation). The displaced line segment gives a picture of the air motion. If the displacement between tagging and interrogation is accurately recorded and divided by the time delay, the flow velocity can be measured.

Figure 1 shows a line 100 μm in diameter written into a turbulent airflow, and that same line displaced after 7 microseconds. The average displacement gives the average flow velocity, and the waviness of the line gives a measure of the turbulence scale and structure. If the line is observed with two cameras, a stereoscopic view of it can be generated, and two components of the velocity field can be recorded. A pair of lines can be made to form a cross to yield point velocity and vorticity measurements, and a group of lines can be formed into a grid for a more complete measurement of the flow-field characteristics. Since the profile of the flow can be seen as well as quantified, it is possible to get a very good intuitive sense of flow properties, even before the necessary calibration and computation steps required for quantification have been performed.

A similar approach to flow tagging has been developed for water flows. In this case, a small quantity (a few parts per million) of a dye must be mixed into the water. The dye is activated with an ultraviolet laser beam, and, anytime thereafter, if it is illuminated with blue light it will fluoresce. Thus, a pulsed ultraviolet laser beam is used to tag the flow by writing a pattern such as a line, a cross, or a grid. Then, after a short period of time, the flow is illuminated by a pulsed blue laser, and the fluorescence (in the green-to-orange region) is photographed with a videocamera.

Figure 2 shows the internal circulation in a cylinder of water with a rotating top. The lines have been written at 1-s intervals, and the interrogation laser is focused to a rather thick sheet of light intersecting the central portion of the cylinder. The most recent tagged line is at the bottom and appears long and straight. The line tagged 1 s before has moved up toward the center, and this motion is further indicated by the lines tagged at previous 1-s intervals.

Since the fluid is rotating, the line appears shorter as it turns orthogonal to the field of view, and lengthens again as it swings around to 180°. At the edges of the cylinder the fluid is forced down, as can be seen from the earliest tagged lines. This set of lines gives both a qualitative and a quantitative view of the circulation in the cylinder of water.

Rayleigh scattering. Imaging the Rayleigh scattering from airflows by illuminating with a sheet of light from a high-power pulsed laser produces an instantaneous picture of the air density. The reason is that the Rayleigh-scattered signal is directly proportional to the number of molecules in each resolvable element. The problem with Rayleigh scattering has always been that the scattering intensity is very low, and the background scattering from windows and walls is at approximately the same frequency, so it tends to obscure the Rayleigh-scattered image. Thus, capturing images of a free jet has been relatively straightforward, since there are no windows or walls to contend with, but imaging more complex flows in ducts or wind tunnels has been virtually impossible.

There are three approaches to overcoming this background signal problem: seeding the air with a particulate fog or some molecular species that has a large Rayleigh-scattering cross section, using an ultraviolet illumination source to enhance the Rayleigh scattering, or using an optical filter with a very sharp cutoff to eliminate background scattering and transmit the scattering from the air molecules. An example of the first approach is the imaging of high-speed turbulent boundary layers and shock-wave–boundary-layer interactions by introducing a small amount of carbon dioxide (CO_2) gas into the air. This carbon dioxide freezes into a fog of submicrometer-scale particles in the core of a supersonic flow because the temperature drops far below the sublimation point. In the boundary layers, however, the temperature remains high, so the fog does not appear.

Figure 3 shows a shock-wave–boundary-layer interaction in a Mach 2.5 airflow passing over a 14°-angle wedge. Here the core of the flow is bright because of the fog of condensed carbon dioxide particles, and the boundary layer is dark. The shock wave shows up because it creates a change in flow velocity which is highlighted by observing the scattered light through a narrow-linewidth molecular-vapor filter. In a high-speed flow, the light that is scattered from the molecules is slightly shifted in frequency because of the Doppler effect. If the filter cutoff is sharp enough, this Doppler-shifted light can pass through the filter and be imaged with a camera. Typically, this method is accomplished by using a cell filled with an atomic or molecular vapor and by tuning the laser onto the resonant absorption line of that atom or molecule. In Fig. 3, the lower speed of the flow behind the shock leads to reduced transmission through the filter, so the flow is darker.

For background information *see* BOUNDARY-LAYER FLOW; FLUID FLOW; FLUORESCENCE; LASER; SCATTERING OF ELECTROMAGNETIC RADIATION; SCHLIEREN PHOTOG- RAPHY; SHADOWGRAPH; SHOCK WAVE in the McGraw-Hill Encyclopedia of Science & Technology.

Richard B. Miles

Bibliography. R. S. Adrian et al., *Developments in Laser Techniques and Applications to Fluid Mechanics*, 1996; R. B. Miles and W. R. Lempert, Quantitative flow visualization in unseeded flows, *Annu. Rev. Fluid Mech.*, 29:285–326, 1997; R. Pitz, Special section on aerodynamic measurement technology, *AIAA J.*, 34:433, March 1996; M. Van Dyke, *An Album of Fluid Motion*, 1982.

Fluidized bed

A fluidized bed consists of discrete particles through which a gas or liquid flows upward. Fluidization is achieved when the gas or liquid velocity is sufficiently high that the drag on the particles is equal to their weight. The particles are suspended in the fluid flow, without being transported, over a significant range of fluid flow rates. Fluidization occurs primarily because of a dynamic balance between forces resulting from the flow of a fluid through a bed of discrete particles and gravitational forces. Practical realization of the fluidized state is achieved in a container having an appropriately constructed porous bottom, termed a distributor. Examples of distributors include a porous plastic sheet, or a steel plate with drilled holes.

In gas-solid fluidization, several operating regimes are possible. The type or regime of fluidization depends on the physical properties of the solid and gas, the gas flow rate, and the physical size of the system. For systems where the fluidizing medium and the particles have much different densities, instabilities locally create pockets of very high void fraction termed bubbles. This fluidization regime is known as the bubbling regime. In the bubbling regime, the gas flow in excess of that required to achieve fluidization creates regions of high void fractions that have the appearance of bubbles in a boiling liquid. Gas-flow rates high enough to transport the particles constituting the bed are employed in circulating fluidized beds.

Both the bubbling and circulating regimes have advantages in a variety of applications. Fluidized beds are employed, for example, in heat treating, as chemical reactors, and in plastic coating operations. Gas-fluidized beds also have great potential for application in the combustion of coal for steam generation. Bubbling-bed coal combustors, consisting of limestone and coal with air as the fluidizing gas, provide highly efficient heat-transfer rates within the fluidized bed and excellent emission characteristics. Combustion is stable at temperatures around 870°C (1600°F), allowing operation with very low nitrous oxide emissions. Further, limestone reacts with sulfur in the coal, greatly reducing the potential for acid rain. *See* COAL.

Experimental chaos. Advances in chaos theory and nonlinear dynamics have made possible an increased

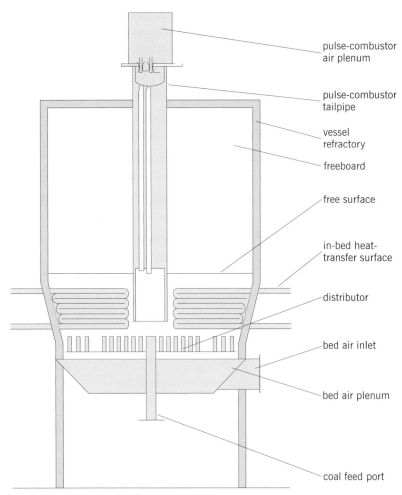

pulse-combustor
air plenum

pulse-combustor
tailpipe

vessel
refractory

freeboard

free surface

in-bed heat-
transfer surface

distributor

bed air inlet

bed air plenum

coal feed port

Fig. 1. Pulsed atmospheric fluidized-bed combustor.

understanding of fluidized beds. Fluidized beds may be accurately described as self-excited nonlinear systems. Although the flow rate of the fluidizing gas is completely steady, density-wave instabilities create complex hydrodynamics within the fluidized bed. These complex behaviors provide significant advantage for chemical reactions and heat transfer because of the high degree of mixing and solid-to-fluid contact. However, design and scale-up from laboratory studies are difficult. Chaos analysis techniques provide the means to characterize the dynamics of a non-linear system from the time-accurate measurement of variations in one of the state variables. In fluidized beds, such measurements have been made for pressure, void fraction, and local heat-transfer rates. The measurements are recorded as digital signals, and appropriate chaos analysis techniques are applied.

Chaotic systems exhibit strange attractors associated with a state or phase space representing the dynamics. The existence of such an attractor and an extreme sensitivity to initial conditions indicate the possible existence of underlying chaotic dynamics in an observed behavior. The quantitative measure most often used to describe the degree of chaos present in a system is the entropy. This entropy is

related to information theory, and measures the rate at which information is changed by the chaotic dynamics. A positive finite entropy value indicates behavior consistent with chaos.

Chaos control in fluidization. Fluidized beds have been shown to display chaotic dynamics. The degree of chaotic behavior as measured by the entropy varies significantly with operating conditions, physical size of the system, and physical location within the bed. The recognition that fluidized beds are chaotic systems presents two important possibilities for advances in the applications that use fluidized beds. Chaos theory has shown promise for the scale-up of fluidized beds using entropy as one of the scaling parameters. In addition, the extreme sensitivity to initial conditions associated with chaotic systems suggests the possibility of controlling, enhancing, or suppressing chaos. Two broad categories exist for chaos-control schemes. Chaos control, in the present context, refers to elimination, minimization, or enhancement of the chaotic nature of the system. The two categories are control through suppression by invoking a periodic or stochastic perturbation of a relevant parameter, or control through exploitation by incorporating small perturbations of a relevant parameter. To date, chaos has been successfully controlled in a number of nonlinear biological, electrical, and mechanical systems. Many chaos-control techniques do not require a prior knowledge of the system dynamics.

Pulse-stabilized fluidization. Recently, the development of a combustor that combines a fluidized bed with a pulsed combustor as a hybrid combustor has provided dramatic indication of the potential for exploiting chaos in physical systems. In traditional bubbling beds, very fine coal particles, a by-product of coal processing, are transported outside the defined region of the fluidized bed, and burn in an inefficient manner. This method causes a loss in thermal efficiency and increases emissions. The pulsed atmospheric fluidized-bed combustor (PAFBC) provides significant advantages for the combustion of these very fine coal particles, and the reduced emissions and high heat-transfer rates of a bubbling fluidized bed. In the PAFBC, the smallest coal particles are burned in a pulsed combustor that faces vertically downward in the bubbling fluidized bed (**Fig. 1**). The pulsed combustor introduces a secondary flow of high-temperature combustion gases into the bed. This secondary flow has an exit velocity that consists of a sinusoidally oscillating component superimposed on a steady mean flow. This hybrid combustor is very efficient because the fluidization is strongly affected by the presence of the flow from the pulsed combustor. Stable operation and very high steam-production rates have been demonstrated for this technology. Heat-transfer rates can be enhanced by as much as 50% over typical fluidized beds.

Stabilization occurs in the fluidized system as a result of the interaction between the oscillating secondary flow and the bubbling fluidized bed. This

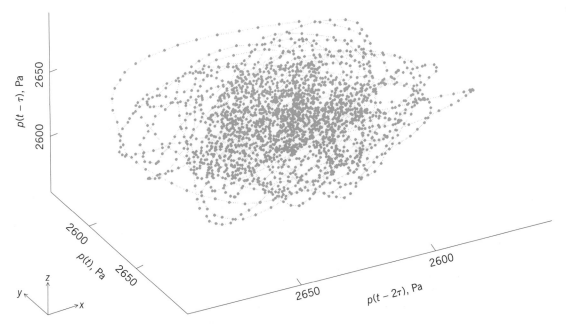

Fig. 2. Pressure phase-space attractor representing fluidized-bed dynamics. Each coordinate is constructed by time-delaying the pressure signal by $\tau = 38$ ms. Thus the coordinates represent the pressure, p, measured at times t, $t - \tau$, and $t - 2\tau$. Gas flow is 10% above that required for fluidization.

stabilization is associated with chaos suppression. Such suppression can be demonstrated by using time-series data representing local, instantaneous pressure at the surface of a horizontal cylinder submerged in a bubbling fluidized bed. **Figure 2** is an attractor representing the chaotic dynamics in a typical bubbling fluidized bed. The pressure signal used to construct this attractor was measured in a laboratory model of the PAFBC. **Figure 3** represents the attractor associated with pulse-stabilized fluidization, measured with vertically downward, oscillating secondary flow. The presence of the secondary flow has clearly reduced the complexity of the system dynamics and has suppressed the degree of

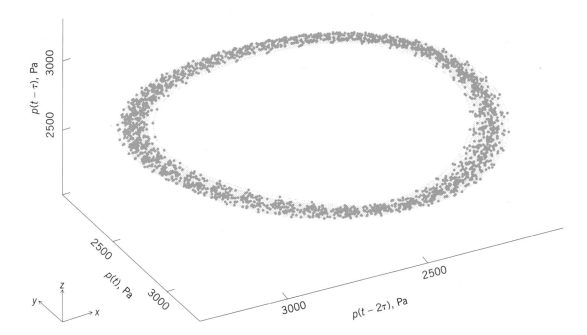

Fig. 3. Pressure phase-space attractor representing pulse-stabilized fluidized-bed dynamics. Each coordinate is constructed by time-delaying the pressure signal by $\tau = 12$ ms. Thus the coordinates represent the pressure, p, measured at times t, $t - \tau$, and $t - 2\tau$. Gas flow is 10% above that required for fluidization, with a downward flow and oscillations at 15 Hz.

chaos present in the system. This chaos suppression is confirmed quantitatively by entropy values calculated under these conditions.

Advanced clean-coal technologies. Construction of power plants in the United States has slowed markedly, and there is currently a strong preference for natural gas as an energy source. However, worldwide electrical generation requirements will increase significantly over the next several decades, with coal providing a more significant fraction of the total energy capacity. Highly efficient coal technologies will be required. Clean-coal technologies incorporating fluidization can provide significant enhancement in the efficiency of conversion, while yielding very low emissions. The two basic technologies involve full gasification of coal, with the resulting fuel providing the energy source for a gas turbine, or pressurized fluidized-bed combustion, where coal is burned directly in an advanced fluidized-bed combustor.

Recently, it has become clear that distinct advantages in capital cost and efficiency may be achieved through a combination of these ideas. These technologies are based on combined cycles. This novel class of power plants employs partial gasification of coal to produce fuel for a gas turbine. Not all of the coal is converted to gaseous fuel; the remaining, unconverted coal is carbon rich, and is burned in a fluidized-bed combustor to provide steam or to preheat combustion air for the gas turbine. Advances in both gas turbines and gasification processes make such combined cycles feasible and economically attractive. It is projected that such integrated power cycles may reach thermal efficiencies greater than 60% by the year 2020.

Fundamental research. The hydrodynamics of discrete-particle systems continues to present significant challenges to modeling and scale-up. A current research area is the prediction of the behavior of discrete-particle systems using direct numerical simulation of the individual particles behavior. This research has already had significant impact on understanding the behavior of granular materials, and holds promise for fluidization. As computers become more powerful, more particles can be included in direct simulations.

For background information *see* CHAOS; COAL GASIFICATION; ENTROPY; FLUIDIZATION; FLUIDIZED-BED COMBUSTION in the McGraw-Hill Encyclopedia of Science & Technology.   Donald E. Beasley

Bibliography. R. P. Behringer and J. T. Jenkins (eds.), *Powders and Grains 97*, 1997; W. L. Ditto and L. M. Pecora, Mastering chaos, *Sci. Amer.*, 269(2):78–84, August 1993; E. Ott, *Chaos in Dynamical Systems*, 1993.

Food biotechnology

New varieties of foods and food substances are being produced through modern biotechnological methods (for example, genetic engineering or recombinant DNA methods), whereby scientists introduce one or a few copies of genes into organisms used as sources of food to improve processing, nutritional, or agronomic characteristics. These new methods permit more precise, directed improvements than can be achieved through conventional methods that rely on the random processes of mutagenesis or mating between closely related organisms. Because the genes can be obtained from any organism (plant, animal, or microbe), questions have been raised about the safety and proper labeling of foods and food substances developed by modern biotechnology.

Food law. In the United States, the Food and Drug Administration (FDA) has federal oversight, under the Federal Food, Drug, and Cosmetic Act, for all domestic and imported foods and food ingredients, except for meat and poultry, which are regulated by the U.S. Department of Agriculture. Although foods such as fruits, vegetables, cereals, flour, oils, milk, fish, and shellfish are not required to be approved by the FDA prior to marketing, the Act places a legal duty on purveyors to offer consumers foods that are safe and wholesome. The FDA has broad authority to take legal action against anyone (or any product) in violation of the Act (postmarket authority). The FDA has premarket authority to approve food additives, that is, substances intentionally added to food that are not generally recognized as safe (GRAS). GRAS ingredients are exempt from premarket clearance and include substances such as flour, sugar, spices, and many flavors and enzymes. Foods and food ingredients developed by modern biotechnology are regulated under the same effective system and stringent safety standards that apply to all other food products under the FDA's authority.

Chymosin. Rennet (now called chymosin), the milk-clotting enzyme used to produce cheese, has been obtained for centuries from the stomach of calves. The gene for rennet was introduced into microorganisms, and now over half of the chymosin produced in the United States is made by fermentation. Chymosin was the first food substance developed by modern biotechnology that the FDA reviewed and affirmed as GRAS in 1990. The FDA's decision was based on the sponsor's data demonstrating that the new enzyme had the same milk-clotting properties as the conventionally produced enzyme; that the microorganism used to produce the enzyme was safe; and that the production and purification of the final enzyme product removed any potentially harmful substances, including the gene for antibiotic resistance used to develop the microorganism that produces chymosin.

Food crops. In 1992, the FDA published a policy that explained how it regulates foods (including animal feeds) derived from new plant varieties, including foods developed by conventional breeding and modern biotechnology. The policy is based on current developments in agricultural research and is intended to be flexible to accommodate rapid advances in modern biotechnology. The scientific principles that underpin the FDA's policy are consistent with principles published jointly by the Food and Agricultural Organization and the World Health Organization of the United Nations and by the U.S. National Academy of Sciences' National Research Council.

The policy explains that foods produced by modern biotechnology will be regulated primarily under the agency's postmarket authority of the Act. Further, the policy makes clear that a substance introduced into food as a result of breeding or genetic engineering is subject to the same premarket approval requirements for food additives incorporated during processing or manufacture, unless the substance is GRAS.

Safety assessment. The policy also describes scientific and regulatory issues that should be addressed during the development of new crop varieties. This guidance establishes a standard of care for developers of foods derived from new plant varieties based on current agricultural practices and fundamental food safety considerations, taking into account both intended and unintended or unexpected changes in the food. Developers should initially consider the characteristics of the host plant that is being modified, the donor organism that is contributing genetic information, and the genetic material and substances that are being introduced or modified. Based on this information, other information may be needed to evaluate the safety and regulatory status of food derived from the new plant variety. For example, the developer should evaluate whether any significant changes have occurred in the level of important nutrients, toxicants, or antinutrients associated with the plant, and if so, the developer should ensure that the levels of these substances in the new variety are within acceptable limits. Similarly, if the donor organism produces toxicants, the developer should ensure that the genes for these toxicants are not transferred or that the new variety does not produce unacceptable levels of such toxicants.

The policy also assists developers in determining whether a substance intentionally introduced or altered by genetic modification will require premarket approval as a food additive. The policy states that newly introduced or modified substances of known function will not require the FDA review if they have been safely consumed at comparable levels in other foods or are substantially similar to safely consumed food substances. Presently, the substances introduced into food via genetic engineering are proteins, fats and oils, and carbohydrates that have been safely consumed in other foods or are substantially similar to safely consumed food substances so that premarket approval has not been required. However, new proteins or carbohydrates with unusual structural or functional groups or oils that contain new, unusual fatty acids may require premarket approval as food additives. In general, modifications to carbohydrates do not raise safety questions that would warrant consultation with the FDA, unless digestibility or nutritional value of a carbohydrate has been al-

tered and the substance is likely to be a major constituent of the diet.

Allergenicity. The FDA also identifies other instances where developers should consult with it. For example, developers should discuss with the FDA possible allergens that may be introduced into the food when genetic material is derived from an allergenic source. In one case, a developer discontinued work on a soybean modified to contain a protein from the Brazil nut after skin tests showed that the introduced protein caused a reaction in individuals sensitive to the nut. To date, no commercially available genetically engineered foods have proteins derived from sources known to cause food allergic reactions, and developers routinely test newly introduced proteins to be sure that they are not similar to proteins known to be allergens.

Food labeling. The Food, Drug, and Cosmetic Act prescribes specific labeling requirements. Labeling must be truthful and not misleading, and a food must be identified by its common or usual name. Labeling must reveal all facts that are material in light of representations made or suggested by labeling (for example, significant alterations in nutritional content) and must also inform consumers about any consequences that may result from the use of the product (such as the presence of an unexpected allergen or altered storage or preparation conditions). For example, if wheat gluten were introduced into potatoes, labeling would be required so that consumers sensitive to gluten, such as those with celiac sprue, could avoid those potatoes and any products that contain them.

The FDA's policy does not contemplate special labeling of the method of development (genetically engineered) for foods derived from genetically engineered plants. Historically, the FDA has not considered plant breeding techniques to be material information subject to labeling, and the agency is not aware of any information that genetic engineering techniques result in foods that differ in safety or quality from foods developed via other methods of plant breeding. Mandatory, process-based labeling would not provide information about the composition of the food and often would be impractical. Voluntary labeling that a product is or is not genetically engineered could be used to inform consumers, provided the information is not misleading.

Animals. Food derived from animals modified through modern biotechnology has not reached the market. However, a growth hormone, recombinant bovine somatotropin, is approved for administration to cows to increase milk production in the dairy industry. Experimental fish that express fish genes for growth hormone are under development. Growth hormones used in milk production and fish farming are regulated under the FDA's authority over new drugs used in animals.

Prospects. Because of the consequences that may occur if the FDA challenges a product on safety or legal grounds, producers routinely consult with the agency before marketing new products. The FDA encourages such consultations, especially when new technologies are used in food production and processing. At this stage of biotechnology, the FDA believes that it is prudent for producers to consult with the agency prior to commercial distribution. The FDA has established procedures to facilitate consultations on genetically engineered products.

The FDA has carefully evaluated the use of genetic engineering techniques to produce food and food ingredients and has not found that these new techniques present any unique safety concerns. The agency intends to be vigilant as the technology advances, and will make any necessary adjustments in its policy to ensure that foods that reach consumers are safe, wholesome, and properly labeled.

For background information *see* ALLERGY; BIOTECHNOLOGY; BREEDING (PLANT); FOOD ENGINEERING; FOOD MANUFACTURING; GENETIC ENGINEERING in the McGraw-Hill Encyclopedia of Science & Technology.   James H. Maryanski

Bibliography. E. L. Flamm, How FDA approved chymosin: A case history, *Bio/Technology*, 9:349–351, 1991; J. C. Juskevich and C. G. Guyer, Bovine growth hormone: Human food safety evaluation, *Science*, 249:875–884, 1990; D. A. Kessler et al., The safety of foods developed by biotechnology, *Science*, 256:1747–1749, 1992; D. D. Metcalf et al. (eds.), Allergenicity of foods produced by genetic modification, *Crit. Rev. Food Sci. Nutrit.*, vol. 36, special suppl., 1996.

Food safety

The safety of meat—pork, beef, and lamb—begins at the farm, the feed lot, and the ranch. Yet, little is known about how to prevent apparently healthy livestock from leaving the farm with food-transmissible hazards outside or inside their bodies. Admittedly, brucellosis in cattle and swine and tuberculosis in cattle have been practically eradicated from the United States, resulting in the disappearance of these human infections acquired through milk or meat. Brucellosis and tuberculosis are serious diseases in both livestock and humans. Currently, about 15 bacterial diseases, 7 parasitic diseases, and 4 viral diseases may be meat-borne to people but cause little or no illness in the livestock carriers.

Meat-borne hazards that may affect humans are classified as physical, chemical, or microbiological. They may enter the food chain anywhere from the farms to the eating implements. Included at farm-production level are breaks in bones, slivers of wood or metal or glass, broken injection needles, and shotgun pellets, which can all be prevented by good management practices. Progress is being made, but metal detectors in processing plants still find broken needles in meat, or even gun pellets from irresponsible shooters.

Chemical hazards enter meat and milk supplies almost exclusively during production. Animal drug and antibiotic residues occur when farmers do not observe an adequate withdrawal time between treating animals and selling them to be butchered. Agricultural and pest-control chemical residues, which livestock should never encounter in their feed or water, also occur. Livestock raisers are making some progress toward good production practices.

Microbiological hazards are of great concern. Microbes enter the food chain along its entire length from "pig sty to stir fry" and from "stable to table." They include infecting parasites, toxin-producing molds, infecting and carrier-state bacteria, and contaminating viruses in and on meat. Category 1 microbiological hazards include pathogens that enter only living animals. If farm animals are protected from infection by *Trichinella*, *Toxoplasma*, and *Cysticercus*, these parasites will never be in the meat. Great progress is being made in eliminating *Trichinella* from pork, and in keeping swine farms free of rats, which may carry these worms from pig to pig. *Trichinella* also infects bears, walrus, and some other wild animals which must be prevented from infecting swine; preventing such *Trichinella* from infecting people is more difficult. *Toxoplasma* can be excluded from the meat supply if hog lots, cattle feed lots, and sheep lots are kept free from cats and cat feces, and if cannibalism in hogs can be totally prevented. Cysticercosis occurs in swine or cattle only when these animals eat feed contaminated by human feces—still an unfortunate occurrence.

Category 2 pathogens enter the food chain in living farm animals, but may also multiply on meat and may be spread by contact between, or handling of, animal carcasses. These pathogens are the most hazardous causes of food-borne illness, and include *Salmonella*, *Escherichia coli* O157:H7, *Yersinia*, and *Campylobacter*. If it were possible to keep these organisms from causing carrier states in livestock animals, concern about them would be minimal. Through a group of universities called the Food Safety Consortium, studies are in progress on the prevention of *Salmonella* infections in swine. A first step is to provide *Salmonella*-free feeds to swine of all ages. Commercially milled feeds, especially pelleted feeds prepared at sufficient pressure to heat-pasteurize them, have been found to have no *Salmonella* or fewer *Salmonella* than farm-formulated feeds. Acidification of swine feeds as well as addition of nonstarch polysaccharides reduces *Salmonella* in feeds. Competitive exclusion is a system of exposing baby pigs to desired intestinal bacteria which will compete with pathogenic bacteria to which the young may be exposed and thus keep the harmful bacteria from infecting the pigs. A similar system is used in the broiler poultry production industry. *Salmonella*-free hogs can be produced by early weaning of baby pigs before they become infected from their mothers, with physical removal to cleaned and sanitized segregated nurseries in which all pigs in the same building are less than a week's difference in age, followed by transferring the pigs as single groups into cleaned and sanitized segregated units to grow to market weight. This system uses all-in-all-out movement of swine between buildings as well as age-segregated rearing. Many swine farmers are adopting these systems both for production efficiencies and for prevention of infections, including contamination by meat-borne pathogens. In the northern United States, *Salmonella* infections in swine occur more frequently during June–December than January–May. Swine raising, however, is a year-round farm enterprise, so raising swine only in winter and spring is not a practical option. Some swine farms have specially constructed ponds called lagoons for disposing of the wastes of swine; pump systems may draw recycled wastewater back from the lagoons to flush wastes from gutters in the swine production units. Swine raised in these buildings are more frequently infected with *Salmonella* than swine raised in buildings where gutters are flushed with fresh water. Prompt removal of any pigs which die in production units helps to prevent the spread of *Salmonella*. Rodents and flies, and less commonly sparrows, starlings, and other birds, which get into buildings with swine not only may bring *Salmonella* into the units but may also spread infections within the units. Swine farmers following best production practices to prevent all of these mechanisms of exposure are far more likely to market hogs free of *Salmonella* or with reduced prevalence of infection. Development of effective vaccines to prevent *Salmonella* infections in swine is a priority; one vaccine protective against certain serotypes of *Salmonella* is becoming widely used.

Category 3 pathogens are environmental bacteria and parasites which enter the food chain wherever animals live in unsanitary environments, eat contaminated feeds, drink contaminated water, or become covered with soil and feces. The important environmental pathogens are *Listeria monocytogenes*, *Clostridium perfringens*, and *Bacillus cereus* which live in soil, and *Cryptosporidium parvum* which may be found in contaminated water. Control consists in keeping livestock clean in sanitary production units where they are provided uncontaminated feed and water. Improvements are being made, but protection of livestock from all environmental pathogens throughout production is still a distant goal.

Category 4 pathogens are principally pathogens which are carried by people; contaminate livestock, carcasses, or meat during handling or by contact with human wastes; and multiply on or within the animal tissues. *Staphylococcus aureus*, frequently carried in nasal passages or on the skin of people, is the most frequent cause of human food poisoning; it passes from a carrier person to an animal product, where it multiplies and produces a toxin which is ingested in the food or milk and causes disease. Hepatitis A virus, present in the feces of infected persons during incubation, clinical illness, and convalescence from infection, can contaminate meats and other foods through unsanitary personal habits. Unlike bacteria, the viruses do not multiply on meat, but may remain viable for a long time. Prevention

of meat-borne diseases by these pathogens requires animal caretaker and food-handler sanitation.

Progress is being made in food safety at the production level. Meat-borne disease prevention should emphasize origin of the contamination, as research is proving. For chemical hazards and *Trichinella*, *Toxoplasma*, and *Cysticercus*, protection of livestock at farm level is the only preventive control point. For physical hazards and *Salmonella*, *Escherichia coli*, *Yersinia*, and *Campylobacter*, protection at the farm is the first control point. For the environmental and human-carried pathogens, the farm is one of the preventive links in the food chain.

For background information *see* BEEF CATTLE PRODUCTION; FOOD MICROBIOLOGY; FOOD POISONING; MEDICAL BACTERIOLOGY in the McGraw-Hill Encyclopedia of Science & Technology.   George W. Beran

Bibliography. N. H. Bean and P. M. Griffin, Foodborne disease outbreaks in the United States, 1973–1987: Pathogens, vehicles, and trends, *J. Food Protect.*, 53:804–817, 1990; F. L. Bryan, Risk of practices, procedures, and processes that lead to outbreaks of foodborne diseases, *J. Food Protect.*, 51:663–667, 1988; P. J. Fedorka-Cray et al., Alternate routes of invasion may affect pathogenesis of *Salmonella typhimurium*, *Infect. Immun.*, 63:2658–2664, 1995; Food and Drug Administration Food Code, U.S. Department of Health and Human Services, P.H.S., 1997; D. L. Harris, Alternative approaches to eliminating endemic diseases and improving performances of pigs, *Vet. Rec.*, 123:422–423, 1998.

Fuel cell

Promising high efficiency and low environmental impact, fuel cell electric generator power plants have entered the commercial marketplace. A broad spectrum of fuel cell applications are envisioned, including stationary power generation, transportation, and portable devices.

A fuel cell is a device that electrochemically converts chemical energy to electrical and thermal energy. The chemical reaction in the fuel cell combines hydrogen and oxygen through this electrochemical process to produce water and heat. The major components of a fuel cell are two electrodes and an electrolyte. The electrodes are the anode, where the fuel is oxidized, and the cathode, where the oxygen (either from air or pure oxygen) is reduced. The electrolyte, which can be either a liquid or a solid, has three primary roles: it separates the reactants, electronically isolates the anode and cathode, and provides an ionic bridge between the two electrodes. The electrochemical reactions produce an operating voltage of 0.5–1.2 V for an individual cell. The electrons from the anode flow through an external circuit and back to the cathode, providing the external electric current. In most cases, multiple cells are stacked to achieve a practical operating voltage. The area of the cell determines the amount of current that can be produced. A fuel cell differs

TABLE 1. Fuel cell types

Type	Electrolyte	Operating temperature
Proton exchange membrane fuel cell	Perfluorinated ionomer polymer membrane	176°F (80°C)
Alkaline fuel cell	Concentrated potassium hydroxide	248°F (120°C)
Phosphoric acid fuel cell	Concentrated phosphoric acid	392°F (200°C)
Molten carbonate fuel cell	Alkali carbonate salts typically retained in lithium aluminum oxide matrix	1202°F (650°C)
Solid oxide fuel cell	Typically zirconia-based ceramic	1832°F (1000°C)

from a battery by its reactant sources. A battery contains a finite amount of reactants and is discarded or recharged after use, while a fuel cell can be supplied with reactants continuously to produce electricity indefinitely.

Types. The five commonly recognized fuel cell types are proton exchange membrane, alkaline, phosphoric acid, molten carbonate, and solid oxide. They are classified by their electrolyte and operating temperature (**Table 1**). Each type is in a different stage of development and commercial readiness. Alkaline fuel cells have been used throughout the U.S. Manned Space Program since the mid-1960s, providing both electric power requirements and water for the astronauts. These cells have been used in all the Apollo and space shuttle missions; at the present time, three independent alkaline fuel cell power plants are used in the shuttle spacecraft. Commercial application of alkaline fuel cells is prohibited by their intolerance to carbon dioxide which precludes their use with air and processed hydrocarbon fuels. Phosphoric acid fuel cell power plants are the only fuel cell type that is presently commercially available. Their principal applications are as on-site cogenerators and as an uninterruptible, assured power source. Molten carbonate fuel cells are in the early demonstration phase as stationary power generators in sizes ranging from 250 kW to 2 MW. Solid oxide

fuel cells have been demonstrated in 25-kW size. Proton exchange membrane fuel cells are also in the demonstration phase, primarily as an alternative power source for transportation vehicles.

Phosphoric acid fuel cell. A 200-kW phosphoric acid fuel cell power plant includes all the components necessary to convert natural gas to electric utility-quality power and provide heat suitable for domestic water heating, or space heating to 167°F (or 75°C). Electricity is generated at greater than 40% efficiency. When the thermal energy is fully utilized, the overall efficiency can exceed 80%. The power plant consists of three major subsystems: a fuel processor, a power section containing the fuel cell stack, and a power converter (**Fig. 1**). The fuel processor combines the fuel gas with steam (generated from power section heat) to reform the fuel into a hydrogen-rich mixture for use by the fuel cell stack in the power section. The most common fuel is natural gas. However, the power plant can operate on other hydrocarbon fuels such as propane, gases from wastewater treatment or landfills, light liquid hydrocarbons, or hydrogen. In the power section, the fuel mixture, rich in hydrogen, is combined with oxygen from the air to produce direct-current electricity. The overall process generates heat and produces carbon dioxide and water as exhaust gases. The power converter changes the direct current from

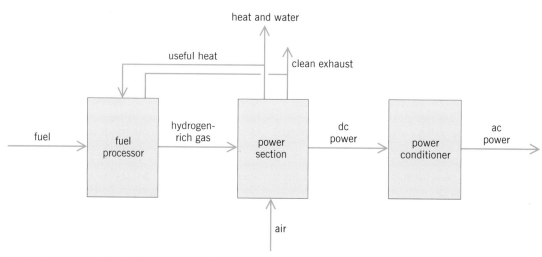

Fig. 1. Phosphoric acid fuel cell power plant schematic showing the integration of the three major subsystems.

the fuel cell stack to usable alternating current. The excess heat from the stack is removed and used for cogeneration or discharged through a cooling module.

The features of the conversion process are associated with the static nature of the power plant. Movement is confined to gas molecules, electrons, and ions. The processes produce very little noise, no pollution, and high efficiency, and have very little inertia. Consequently, the power plant can be located in densely populated areas near the electrical load requirement. The electrical output is of extremely high quality, and maintenance requirements are minimized. The emissions from the phosphoric acid fuel cell power plant are 10 times less than those produced by conventional electric utility generating systems (**Table 2**).

The most common application of the power plant has been as an on-site cogenerator system. In the cogenerator application, the fuel cell power plant is located near both the electric load and cogenerator heat requirements. Electrically, the power plant can be connected to the utility grid, supplementing the load requirements, or can be connected directly to the load, independent of the utility grid. Separate from the grid, the power plant automatically follows the load demand as it varies throughout the day. Similarly, the cogenerating heat system follows the customer demands; any heat not used by the customer is automatically ejected to the atmosphere.

As economic enterprise and communication become more dependent on electronic systems that cannot tolerate electric power disturbances, and as the electric utility industry restructures, there is a rapidly growing demand for distributed generation to minimize transmission requirements and for uninterruptible electric power generators. The fuel cell's high reliability and long life make it ideal for uninterruptible power application. As an uninterruptible power source, the power plant is directly connected to the vital electrical loads.

Proton exchange membrane. Vehicles powered by fuel cells using conventional fuels could double the fuel efficiency of today's comparable conventional vehicles while meeting the most stringent anticipated emissions standards, retaining the current internal combustion engine operating characteristics,

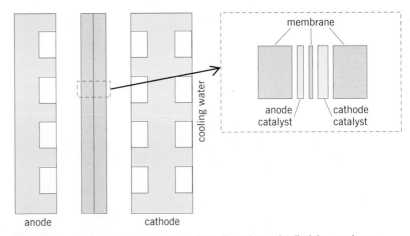

Fig. 2. Proton exchange membrane fuel cell configuration; a detail of the membrane-electrode assembly is shown.

and costing no more to own and operate than today's vehicles. The proton exchange membrane is considered the most attractive fuel cell type for transportation applications because of its compact packaging and ability to start and stop quickly; the membrane properties provide the enabling factors.

The membranes presently used in proton exchange membrane fuel cells generally consist of a perfluorinated polymer with side chains terminating in sulfuric acid moieties. This material is unique in that it possesses the three essential characteristics for fuel cell application: chemical stability, proton conductivity, and gas impenetrability. The chemical stability provides stable power generation over the life of the power plant. The conductivity of the material is excellent even at ambient temperatures, permitting rapid startup. Rapid starting capability is critical to automobile application. Very thin membranes have been capable of maintaining gas impenetrability (necessary to prevent direct fuel and air combustion). These thin membranes enhance the conductivity, permitting high-power-density production per unit cell area.

The proton exchange membrane cell operating temperature ($\sim$176°F or 80°C) is similar to the cooling system temperature for current internal combustion engines. Water cooling can be used to maintain the operating temperature. This cooling approach permits thin cell designs. A typical proton exchange membrane cell contains anode and cathode separator plates, which are part of the membrane-electrode assembly (**Fig. 2**). The cathode plate also contains the water coolant cavity. This thin cell design permits a high cell stacking density, consistent with automobile design criteria.

A 50-kW demonstrator proton exchange membrane power plant has been configured for installation in an automobile (**Fig. 3**). This power plant, which weighs less than 300 lb (136 kg), operates on hydrogen fuel and air, and produces direct current. The power plant would replace the present internal combustion engine. Electric power from the

TABLE 2. Comparison of utility generated pollution*

Contaminant	Avg. U.S. utility emissions	Phosphoric acid fuel cell emissions
Nitrogen oxides (NO$_x$)	7.65	0.016
Carbon monoxide	0.34	0.023
Reactive organic gases	0.34	0.0004
Sulfur oxides (SO$_x$)	16.1	0.0
Particulates	0.46	0.0

*Emissions are measured in pounds of contaminant per megawatt-hour.

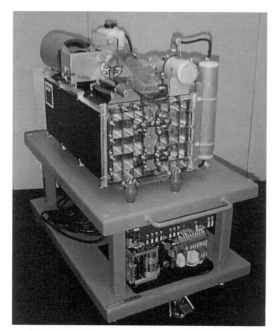

Fig. 3. A 50-kW proton exchange membrane power plant. (International Fuel Cells Corporation)

fuel cell would power electric motors located near the automobile's drive wheels. The power plant is approximately 2½ ft long, 2 ft wide, and 2 ft high (76 cm × 61 cm × 61 cm). This includes, in addition to the cell stack, the coolant pump and associated piping, the air delivery system, and the engine control system. The air is delivered by a simple blower at nearly ambient pressure and temperature conditions. Other elements (not shown in Fig. 3) are the radiator and the fuel storage and delivery system. The radiator is similar to that used on conventional vehicles powered by internal combustion engines since the coolant is water at an operating temperature and pressure nearly identical to the conventional engine coolant. The fuel delivery system depends on the type of fuel used. The efficiency (based on a lower heating value using H_2) is approximately 50% at maximum power and 60% at cruise power. *See* AUTOMOTIVE VEHICLE.

A significant issue for automobiles powered by fuel cells is the type of fuel to be used. Since the fuel cell operates on hydrogen, any common transportation fuel, such as gasoline, diesel, or methane, needs to be converted to a hydrogen-rich gas prior to being introduced to the fuel cell. Placing the converter on board the automobile adds to the complication of the power system and its cost. An alternative is to make hydrogen as easily accessible as other fuels are today (perhaps by a hydrogen filling station that uses a fuel processor from a power plant to generate hydrogen from natural gas or from other renewable energy sources) and carry the hydrogen in a storage device on the car. A vehicle using this approach would readily qualify as a zero-emission vehicle since the only emission product would be water.

For background information *see* COGENERATION; ELECTRIC POWER GENERATION; FUEL CELL; HYDROGEN; INTERNAL COMBUSTION ENGINE; MOTOR VEHICLE in the McGraw-Hill Encyclopedia of Science & Technology.   Murdo J. Smith

Bibliography. A. J. Appleby and F. R. Foulkes, *Fuel Cell Handbook*, 1989; T. F. Fuller, *Is a Fuel Cell in Your Future?*, 1997; S. S. Penner et al., *Commercialization of Fuel Cells*, 1995; U.S. Department of Energy, *Fuel Cells for Transportation, Program Implementation Strategy*, 1996; U.S. Department of Energy, Federal Energy Management Program, *Natural Gas Fuel Cells*, 1995.

Fungi

Three types of fungi occur in the rumen of herbivores. (1) The aerobic and facultatively anaerobic fungi are described as transient because they enter the rumen continuously in the feed and do not necessarily thrive under the conditions of the rumen environment. (2) A fungus type that parasitizes ciliate protozoa comprises two species. (3) Unlike all other known fungi, the obligately anaerobic zoosporic fungi are saprophytic on plant material.

Microbial diversity in the rumen. Bacteria, protozoa, and fungi are the major groups of microorganisms that occur in the gastrointestinal tract of herbivores. These microorganisms are suspended in the liquid phase, attached to plant fragments, or attached to the epithelial lining of the rumen. The plant material is composed of structural polysaccharides, cellulose, hemicelluloses, and pectic compounds arranged in a variable and complex order. Digestion of plant materials by microorganisms provides easily utilizable forms of carbon, energy, some vitamins, and microbial protein. Herbivores can be considered as walking microcosms with communities of different species of microorganisms that have evolved together with their host.

Discovery of rumen fungi. In 1913 a multiflagellate rumen protozoon, *Callimastix frontalis*, was described. Several years later, a different species of *Callimastix* was isolated from a copepod, but it was suggested that this protozoon was a zoospore of a fungus. This hypothesis was confirmed when the vegetative stage of this fungus was demonstrated. Subsequently, the other species of *Callimastix* were placed in a new protozoan genus, *Neocallimastix*, with *N. frontalis* as the type species. In 1975 the multiflagellate cells previously considered as protozoa were conclusively shown to be zoospores of an anaerobic chytrid-like fungus. This was the first strictly anaerobic fungus; its discovery contradicted the long-standing mycological belief that all fungi required oxygen for growth.

Morphology and development of rumen fungi. The life cycle of the rumen fungi consists of a zoospore stage, a zoosporangial stage, and a resting sporangial stage. Depending on the genus, the zoospore has 1–24 flagella. The flagella of multiflagellate zoospores beat together in a clockwise motion that propels the zoospore forward in a spiral manner. Zoospores can also move in an ameboid manner. They shed their flagella, encyst, and develop to form a thallus (fungal plant) by one of three methods. (1) The cyst may enlarge into a single vegetative sporangium in which mitosis takes place (endogenous, monocentric). (2) The cyst produces a second outgrowth that develops into the sporangium (exogenous, monocentric). (3) The cytoplasm migrates from the cyst into the germ tube, which develops into an extensively branched rhizomycelium with nuclei; several sporangia are produced from the rhizomycelium (exogenous, polycentric). Sexual reproduction has not yet been described in the rumen fungi.

Classification of rumen fungi. On the basis of their life cycle and the presence of chitin in the cell wall, these fungi are considered to be chytrids. Five genera comprising 18 species of the rumen fungi have been described. Taxonomic classification is as follows:

Division Eumycota
Class Chytridiomycetes
Order Neocallimasticales
Family Neocallimasticeae
Genera and species:
Monocentric
Piromyces (zoospore with 1-4 flagella)
   P. communis (in sheep)
   P. minutus (in deer)
   P. mae (in horse)
   P. dumbonica (in elephant)
   P. spiralis (in goat)
   P. citronii (in horse)
   P. rhizinflata (in ass)
Neocallimastix (zoospore with 4-24 flagella)
   N. frontalis (in sheep)
   N. patriciarum (in sheep)
   N. elegans (in cattle)
   N. variabilis (in cattle)
   N. hurleyensis (in sheep)
Caecomyces (zoospore with 1 or 2 flagella)
   C. communis (in sheep)
   C. equii (in horse)
Polycentric
Anaeromyces (zoospore with 1 flagellum)
   A. elegans (in cattle)
   A. mucronatus (in sheep)
Orpinomyces (zoospore with 6-18 flagella)
   O. joyonii (in sheep)
   O. intercalaris (in cattle)

Genera of rumen fungi are characterized on the basis of the number of flagella per zoospore, thallus morphology (monocentric or polycentric), and rhizoid type (filamentous or a vegetative cell). Species are described on the basis of zoospore ultrastructure and source of isolate.

Physiology and metabolism of rumen fungi. The rumen fungi are saprophytes with nutritional requirements that are similar to those of other fungi. They can use a wide range of carbohydrates and amino acids.

They grow optimally under conditions similar to the rumen environment. The temperature range for growth is 30-42°C (86-108°F), but they grow best at 39°C (102°F); they can survive for extended periods at temperatures below 30°C (86°F) in the form of a resting sporangium. Oxygen is toxic to the vegetative stages of the rumen fungi, but the resting spore can survive aeration. The pH range for optimal growth of these fungi is 5.8-6.8.

Rumen fungi produce mixed acids from the fermentation of carbohydrates. They convert glucose to pyruvic acid by the Embden-Meyerhof-Parnas pathway, and the end products of their fermentation include carbon dioxide, hydrogen, formate, acetate, lactate, succinate, and ethanol. Formate and succinate are produced in the hydrogenosomes, which are mitochondrialike organelles found in obligately anaerobic eukaryotes. Lactate and ethanol are produced by the dehydrogenases that occur in the cytoplasm. Lipids are synthesized from long-chain fatty acids derived from glucose and acetate. The fatty acids have a high amount of *cis*-monoenoic fatty acid, which is not found in aerobic chytrids. The presence of sterols in the membrane is a controversial issue since it has been found in some taxa but not in others.

Distribution of rumen fungi. Species of rumen fungi have been isolated from the gastrointestinal tract of a diverse array of domesticated and wild herbivores, as shown in the taxonomic classification above. Isolates have been obtained from small herbivores such as the blue duicker, as well as from large herbivores such as the elephant. However, most of the detailed work has been carried out on domestic ruminants such as sheep and cattle. Specific sources from which isolates have been obtained include saliva; partially digested plant material from the rumen, reticulum, omasum, abomasum, and cecum; and freshly voided and dry feces. There are herbivores from which these fungi have not been isolated. The geographical distribution of the anaerobic zoosporic fungi is worldwide and coincides with the distribution of host animals. Isolates have been obtained from all continents.

Fiber degradation by rumen fungi. The role of rumen fungi in plant fiber degradation has been extensively examined. The rhizoids of vegetative thalli penetrate plant tissue better than bacteria and protozoa, allowing access to plant material not available to other rumen microorganisms. This penetration leads to more rapid and complete degradation of fiber that enters the rumen. Degradation of lignin-containing walls of plant cells is an important characteristic of rumen fungi. Zoospores of many species appear to preferentially colonize the lignin-containing tissues and to establish colonies localized on sclerenchyma and xylem cells. These lignified cell walls are degraded to a greater extent by rumen fungi than by bacteria or protozoa. The rhizoids or rhizomycelia penetrate lignified cell walls, with initial colonization of the secondary wall layer occurring from the lumen of the cell. The rhizoids are also able to partially degrade highly recalcitrant cell walls such as the mestome sheath of leaf blades. Some rumen fungi solubilize small amounts of phenolic compounds from plant cell walls. These fungi can penetrate the cuticle, which is a rigid structural barrier on the outside of the plant epidermis. Though this barrier is impenetrable to other microorganisms, the rumen fungi often enter the leaf interior through the stomata in the epidermal layer. Attack on recalcitrant plant cell walls by rumen fungi weakens the textural strength of the residue. The greater ability of rumen fungi, as compared with rumen bacteria, to weaken forage fiber may be important to the host animal in forage utilization.

For background information *see* CARBOHYDRATE METABOLISM; DIGESTIVE SYSTEM; FERMENTATION; FUNGI in the McGraw-Hill Encyclopedia of Science & Technology.   Daniel A. Wubah

Bibliography. C. G. Orpin, Studies on the rumen flagellate *Neocallimastix frontalis, J. Gen. Microbiol.*, 91:249–262, 1975; D. A. Wubah, D. E. Akin, and W. S. Borneman, Biology, fiber degradation and enzymology of the anaerobic zoosporic fungi, *Crit. Rev. Microbiol.*, 19:99–115, 1993; D. A. Wubah, M. S. Fuller, and D. E. Akin, *Neocallimastix*: A comparative morphological study, *Can. J. Bot.*, 69:835–843, 1991.

Gamma-ray bursts

About once per day an intense burst of gamma rays is detected, coming from a random direction in the sky. Often, the burst outshines all other sources of gamma rays in the sky combined. The original observations of these bursts were made serendipitously in the 1960s. Today, gamma-ray bursts are one of the most enigmatic phenomena observed in astronomy. Even their distance (and thus their intrinsic luminosity) has been hotly debated in recent years. Their brief, random appearance only in the gamma-ray region has made their study difficult. Several breakthrough observations in 1997, made possible by the orbiting satellite *BeppoSAX*, have opened up new avenues of gamma-ray-burst research and have virtually solved the distance debate.

Discovery and observations. The initial discovery of gamma-ray bursts was tied closely to the space program and to the cold-war activities of the 1960s. The *Vela* series of spacecraft was developed to detect clandestine nuclear explosions above the atmosphere. In the first years after their discovery, gamma-ray bursts were observed at the rate of about 10–20 per year. Now, with more complete coverage of the sky and larger detectors, gamma-ray bursts are detected at a rate of over 300 per year. At this sensitivity, the corrected, all-sky burst rate is about 800 per year.

Since the launch of the BATSE (Burst and Transient Source Experiment) instrument on the *Compton Gamma-Ray Observatory* in 1991 and the launch of *BeppoSAX* in 1996, the field of gamma-ray burst research has undergone a dramatic change. Prior to observations by these spacecraft, the sources of gamma-ray bursts were believed by most workers in the field to be relatively nearby neutron stars in the galactic plane. Beginning in 1991, burst locations were determined for a large sample of weak bursts. Over 1800 bursts have been observed by BATSE in over 6 years of operation (**Fig. 1**). The isotropic distribution of the bursts and the relative deficiency of weak gamma-ray bursts have led many to believe that the bursts originated from distant parts of the universe, but this could not be conclusively determined until the recent observations.

Several breakthrough observations seem to have settled the distance question. It is now generally agreed that the gamma-ray bursts originate from the most distant regions of the universe and represent the most powerful explosions seen in nature. However, their energy source and the mechanism by which the bursts convert this energy into gamma rays are subjects of intense current research.

Counterparts. In 1997, for the first time, afterglow radiation was seen from a gamma-ray-burst source in another wavelength region. Although searches for such emission had been carried out for over 20 years, these searches were never fast enough or sensitive enough to capture the rapidly fading, faint x-ray and optical emission that follows some (but apparently not all) gamma-ray bursts. Both x-ray and optical afterglow emissions were seen from two well-located gamma-ray bursts observed on February 28 and May 8, 1997. The May 8 burst was observed to be associated with or behind an object that was observed to be at cosmological distances, as determined from optical spectral measurements of a redshift. At last, the direct observation of a distance indicator had been associated with a particular gamma-ray burst.

The *BeppoSAX* spacecraft, launched in April 1996, has the unique capability of quickly and accurately locating the position of x-ray emission from a gamma-ray burst that happens to be within the field of view of a wide-field x-ray camera. On February 28, 1997, a gamma-ray-burst monitor on *BeppoSAX* detected a strong gamma-ray burst lasting about 80 s. The wide-field x-ray camera determined the location of the burst to an accuracy of about 3 arc-minutes. Such a rapid, accurate location had never before been attained. This achievement allowed a narrow-field instrument on the spacecraft to be pointed at the burst location within 8 h, where a faint x-ray source was found.

About 3 days later, the same region of the sky was observed with the same instrument. It was found that the weak x-ray source had faded to an undetectable level, less than 1/20 as bright as it had been earlier. This afterglow x-radiation could be located by *BeppoSAX* even more precisely than the initial burst, to an accuracy better than 1 arc-minute. Precise timing measurements of the burst by the distant, interplanetary spacecraft *Ulysses* further constrained the position of the burst. *See* SPACE FLIGHT.

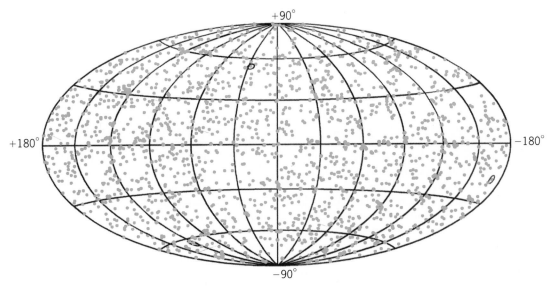

Fig. 1. Sky distribution of 1828 gamma-ray bursts observed by the BATSE instrument on the *Compton Gamma-Ray Observatory*. The map is plotted in galactic coordinates.

Following the initial report of the February 28 burst, an optical photograph of the region was taken via William Herschel Telescope in the Canary Islands. A follow-up photograph was taken of the same region about 8 days later. A comparison of the two images revealed a single faint object at the burst location which had faded dramatically over the 8 days (**Fig. 2**). This was the first discovery of an optical afterglow from a gamma-ray burst. Another photograph, taken by the New Technology Telescope of the European Southern Observatory in Chile, showed that this optical object was associated with, but not centered on, a faint extended object. Images taken by the Hubble Space Telescope confirmed this observation. This extended object may be a distant galaxy.

BeppoSAX made two additional x-ray afterglow observations of gamma-ray bursts, on April 2 and

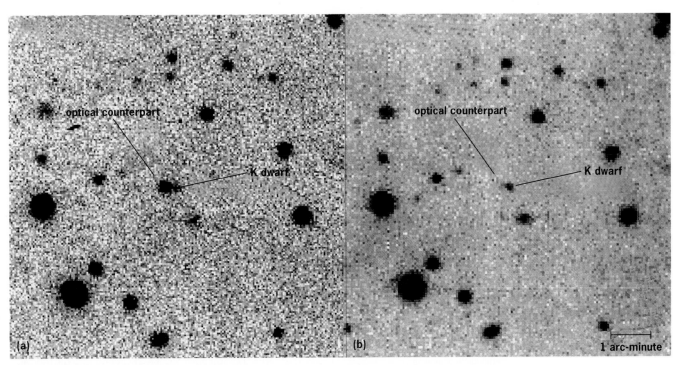

Fig. 2. Photographs, via the William Herschel Telescope, of the fading optical counterpart to a gamma-ray burst of February 28, 1997. (*a*) Image taken about 1 day after the burst. (*b*) Same region about 8 days later. The counterpart object has faded greatly.

May 8, 1997. Both again showed the presence of fading x-ray afterglow emission. Extensive searches for optical afterglow objects turned up no object for the April 2 burst. However, at the location of the May 8 burst, a faint optical object was observed by a telescope at the Kitt Peak National Observatory. The object increased in brightness for 2 days after the burst and then faded. This optical object was also observed with the Keck Telescope in Hawaii. This telescope showed the presence of absorption and emission spectral lines in the object which gave an indication of its distance, about 3×10^9 light-years. If the optical emission and the gamma-ray burst are in fact from the same source region, then for the first time the distance to the source of a gamma-ray burst has been determined by a direct observation. This same region was also found to contain a weak, rapidly varying radio source. This variability was seen to disappear after a few months, although a steady radio source remained. This behavior is expected for a distant, expanding source.

Time profiles and spectra. The most striking feature of the time profiles of gamma-ray bursts is the diversity of their time structures and the wide range of their durations. Coupled with this diversity is the difficulty of placing many gamma-ray bursts into well-defined types, based on their time profiles. Many bursts have multiple characteristics, and many other bursts are too weak to classify. Some burst profiles are chaotic and spiky with large fluctuations on all time scales, while others show rather simple structures with few peaks. No periodic structures have been seen from gamma-ray bursts. There is, however, one general characteristic: At higher energies, the overall burst durations are shorter, and subpulses within a burst tend to have shorter rise times and fall times (sharper spikes). Most bursts also show an asymmetry, with the leading edges being of shorter duration than trailing edges (**Fig. 3**). The durations of gamma-ray bursts range from about 30 milliseconds to over 1000 s. However, the duration of a gamma-ray burst, like the burst morphology, is difficult to quantify since it is dependent upon the sensitivity and the time resolution of the experiment.

Almost all of the power from gamma-ray bursts is emitted at energies above 50 keV. Most bursts have a simple, smooth continuum spectrum which appears somewhat similar in shape when integrated over the entire burst and when sampled on various time scales within a burst.

Prospects. It is expected that *BeppoSAX* will continue to make several precise locations per year that will allow rapid afterglow observations to be made in the x-ray, optical, and radio regions. BATSE has had a quick-alert capability since 1991 that was developed to provide burst locations within several hours under favorable conditions. A near-real-time burst location system utilizing BATSE data, called BACODINE (BATSE Coordinates Distribution Network), is also in operation. The BATSE-BACODINE system can provide gamma-ray-burst locations to external sites within about 5 s of their detection by BATSE. However, these locations are typically accurate to only a few degrees, too imprecise to permit follow-up observations by most telescopes. When BACODINE is linked to a rapid-slewing, wide-field optical telescope, there is the possibility of obtaining optical images of burst regions while the burst is in progress. Recently, a rapid-slewing, robotic telescope dedicated to gamma-ray burst follow-up observations has gone into operation near Livermore, California. Another possibility for future observations is the rapid scanning of the region by the *Rossi X-ray Timing Explorer* spacecraft to observe a fading x-ray afterglow radiation.

At their tremendous distance, gamma-ray bursts represent the most powerful explosions in the universe. Some of them produce more energy than that of a million galaxies combined. The source of this energy and the means by which much of it is converted into gamma rays is much debated, and has become a very active area of research in astrophysics. Most current theories describe the burst as a rapidly expanding fireball, powered by some central explosive event, perhaps the merging of two massive, compact objects. Continued observations by space observatories and ground-based facilities, as well as new space missions and increased use of robotic and dedicated instruments for optical and radio observations, promise to shed light on these enigmatic bursts of radiation.

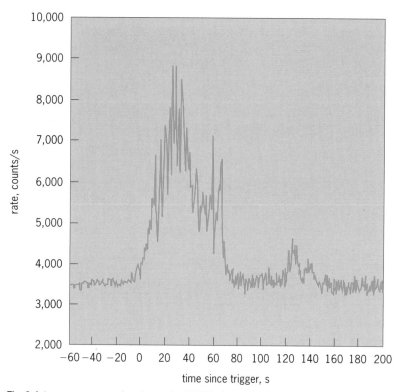

Fig. 3. Intense gamma-ray burst seen by **BATSE** aboard the *Compton Gamma-Ray Observatory* on February 17, 1994.

For background information *see* GAMMA-RAY AS-TRONOMY; SATELLITE ASTRONOMY in the McGraw-Hill Encyclopedia of Science & Technology.

Gerald J. Fishman

Bibliography. G. J. Fishman and D. Hartmann, Gamma-ray bursts, *Sci. Amer.*, 277:34–39, July 1997; G. J. Fishman and C. A. Meegan, Gamma-ray bursts, *Annu. Rev. Astron. Astrophys.*, 33:415–458, 1995; C. Kouveliotou, M. Briggs, and G. Fishman (eds.), *Gamma-Ray Bursts*, AIP Conf. Proc. 384, 1996.

Grass endophytes

An endophyte is an organism, usually a fungus or bacterium, that lives inside a plant during most or all of its life cycle. Many grass species contain endophytic fungi belonging to the order Ascomycetes (family Clavicipitaceae, tribe Balansieae). Endophytes of the genus *Balansia* are found in various warm-season grass genera such as bluestems (*Andropogon*), lovegrasses (*Eragrostis*), and dallisgrass and bahiagrass (*Paspalum*). Endophytes of the genus *Epichloe* and its asexual descendant *Neotyphodium* are found in the cool-season grasses—bentgrasses (*Agrostis*), fescues (*Festuca*), ryegrasses (*Lolium*), and bluegrasses (*Poa*).

Grass–endophyte symbiosis. A symbiosis consists of two different species living in intimate association. The relationship may be antagonistic (harmful), neutral, or mutualistic (beneficial). *Neotyphodium* endophytes form mutualistic symbioses with their grass hosts. The endophyte enhances the survival and vigor of the grass by protecting it against feeding by some parasites, wildlife, and grazing livestock through the production of toxic compounds. The endophyte also promotes grass survival during drought. In turn, the grass host provides protection, nutrition, and a means of dissemination for the endophyte.

Fungal endophytes of grasses have attracted substantial attention from agriculturalists and biologists since the late 1970s. In 1977, *N. coenophialum* growing in tall fescue (*F. arundinacea*) was reported to occur in a pasture in north Georgia and was positively associated with toxicosis symptoms in grazing cattle. This discovery was key to unlocking the mystery of fescue toxicosis. This syndrome of maladies has been frequently observed in cattle grazing tall fescue since it became widely planted in the east-central and southern United States after World War II. Later research showed that ergot alkaloids, especially the peptine type, are most likely responsible for symptoms in herbivores such as poor blood flow to extremities, high body temperature, poor appetite, and reduced reproduction. These maladies can cause poor weight gain, low milk production, and reduced calf production in cattle, resulting in substantial economic loss to the United States beef industry. Reproduction, birthing, and lactation problems in horses can also be severe.

Perennial ryegrass (*L. perenne*) forms a symbiosis with the endophyte *N. lolii*. This grass is commonly used for sheep and cattle pasture in New Zealand and is widely infested with its endophyte. Lolitrem alkaloids are produced by the endophyte at the base of the plant and are translocated to leaf blades, which are available for grazing. The lolitrems cause ryegrass staggers in the animals, a neuromuscular disorder manifested by neck and limb tremors, staggering gait, and falling down. The endophyte produces an anti-insect alkaloid, peramine, which deters feeding by larvae of the Argentine stem weevil (*Listronotus bonariensis*). Endophyte-free ryegrass pastures do not cause staggers symptoms in the animals; however, weevil damage quickly decimates the plants. A similar dilemma exists in tall fescue in the United States. Removing the endophyte from tall fescue (by planting new pastures with aged seed) alleviates fescue toxicosis, but fescue stands can thin or die out. Endophyte-infected tall fescue produces peramine and loline alkaloids, which confer host resistance to some insects. However, instead of a single, serious insect predator as in perennial ryegrass, the major threats to stand longevity of endophyte-free tall fescue are drought stress and overgrazing.

Grasses and *Neotyphodium* coevolved such that the endophyte lost the pathogenicity and ability to sexually reproduce outside the plant possessed by its ancestor *Epichloe*. *Neotyphodium* is transferred to new grass seedlings by growing up the stem with a developing flower and infecting the newly developing seed. After seeds ripen, fall to the ground, and germinate, the endophyte is reactivated and grows into the young shoot, thereby infecting a new generation.

Growth. The effect of the endophyte on grass growth is complex because of interactions among host genetics, endophyte genetics, and environment. It is frequently generalized that endophyte infection enhances grass growth. Indeed, several researchers have reported greater aboveground plant mass (biomass yield), number of tillers, number of belowground stems (rhizomes), and amount of seed production owing to endophyte presence. These traits contribute to greater competitiveness and reproductive success of infected grasses and help explain, along with antiherbivory, why endophyte presence is so prevalent in wild and naturalized stands of these grasses.

There are reports, however, that with some individual plants *Neotyphodium* has no effect on growth or, in fact, depresses growth. This could occur because, with each annual cycle of seed production, genetic recombination results in some seedlings being produced which have low compatibility with the endophyte. In a field environment, with the typical levels of weather extremes and interplant competition, those less fit plants would die out and the more compatible and aggressive grass–endophyte combinations would prevail. In fact, research shows that the advantages of endophyte infection on grass growth and persistence

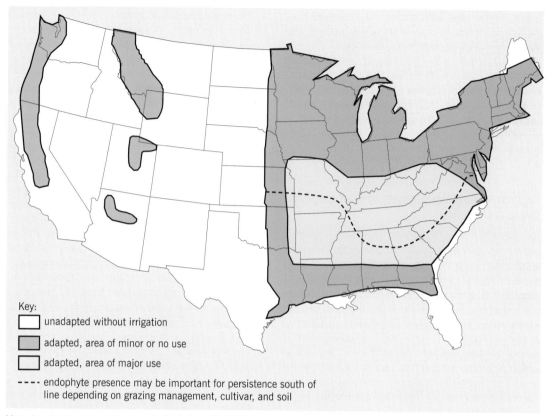

Map showing the areas of use and adaptation of tall fescue in the United States. Tall fescue can be grown for pasture in the dark-colored area without the benefit of the fungal endophyte *Neotyphodium coenophialum* if good management, soils, and cultivars are used. Infection with the endophyte is important to assure tall fescue persistence in the light-colored area. Tall fescue is unadapted or is of minor use in other areas.

are greater in harsh field environments (high temperature, deficient water) than in mild climates. For example, tall fescue is more likely than perennial ryegrass to benefit from endophyte infection because tall fescue is grown in warm, continental climates whereas ryegrass is more prevalent in mild, maritime climates where environmental stresses are less likely.

Where endophyte stimulates grass growth even in the absence of environmental stresses, the involvement of plant hormones is strongly suggested. Auxin is a key hormone controlling plant growth, cell division, branching (tillering), and leaf elongation, and is produced in the shoot meristem and expanding leaves. The endophyte is more frequently found near these organs. In fact, endophytes isolated from tall fescue plants which exhibited a large growth advantage over their identical endophyte-free clones were found to produce auxin in test tubes. This suggests that the endophyte may produce hormones in the plant which then alter growth.

Drought tolerance. During the 1980s, when the toxic effects of the endophyte on livestock were being confirmed in grazing trials, it was observed that endophyte-free stands of tall fescue recovered poorly and thinned out after dry summers. This phe-

nomenon was especially common in states such as Georgia, Arkansas, Louisiana, and Texas. These states constitute the southern and western extremes of the zone of adaptation of tall fescue and are typified by high temperature and soil moisture deficit during summer. The endophyte expands the range of adaptation of tall fescue into more stressful environments (see **illus.**).

Controlled studies in greenhouses have confirmed that the endophyte enhances drought tolerance. In annual crops, such as wheat and corn, drought tolerance is measured by how well the plants can continue to grow and produce harvestable grain in the face of water deficit. In a perennial grass used for grazing and turf, where maximum growth may not be necessary or even desirable and where grain yield is irrelevant, stand survival during prolonged drought is the main criterion for drought tolerance.

Many traits have been observed, directly or indirectly, that may explain how the endophyte enhances tall fescue survival during drought. Suggested mechanisms include water conservation, protection of meristems, root stimulation or protection, and antiherbivory of shoots.

Water conservation. The endophyte enhances the plant's ability to sense the early stages of soil water deficit, perhaps via the production of the hormone abscisic acid. As a result, leaf pores (stomata) close, thus reducing the loss of water from leaves.

Protection of meristem. During summer, the tiller meristem is deep within the whorl of leaf sheaths, at or below ground level. This meristem must survive in order to assure rapid and complete stand recovery after extended drought. Endophyte-infected plants may position their meristems lower in the soil, thereby buffering them from temperature extremes and desiccation. The sheaths of old leaves wrap around the meristems and growing zones of the young leaves. The endophyte stimulates the accumulation of various solutes in the cells of the sheaths, causing osmotic adjustment. These solutes increase the power of the cells to retain water against the forces of desiccation. Greater water retention in the leaf sheaths slows down water loss in the inner growing zone and meristem, and delays the lethal desiccation of these critical tissues.

Root stimulation or protection. The endophyte generally does not grow in grass roots; however, certain hormones may be produced by the endophyte, or stimulated in the grass, which promote deeper and denser rooting. This would benefit the grass during drought by allowing the plant to explore and scavenge water from greater soil volume. The endophyte deters root parasitism by a wide range of microscopic worms in the soil. These nematodes drain the plant's energy reserves and stunt root growth, thereby increasing susceptibility to drought stress. Some nematode species are prevented from entering roots of endophyte-infected plants. Other nematodes can enter but cannot reproduce and proliferate in the roots. So far, no nematicidal alkaloid has been identified that is produced by the endophyte and translocated to the roots. Therefore, the mechanism of nematode resistance is probably quite different from that of insect resistance. The endophyte, by virtue of its presence as a mutated, now-benign pathogen, may stimulate a process resembling an immune response that lends the plant generalized resistance to other invading organisms.

Antiherbivory of shoots. Endophyte-produced alkaloids are prevalent in the leaves of the grasses and deter feeding by mammals and insects. Intact leaves allow the plant to continue photosynthesizing and providing energy for vigorous growth of roots, new tillers, and seed. In turn, this robust growth provides the plant additional buffers from periodic water deficits.

For background information *see* FUNGI; GRASS CROPS; HERBIVORY in the McGraw-Hill Encyclopedia of Science & Technology.   Charles P. West

Bibliography. C. W. Bacon and J. F. White, Jr. (eds.), *Biotechnology of Endophytic Fungi of Grasses*, 1994; A. E. Glenn et al., Molecular phylogeny of *Acremonium* and its taxonomic implications, *Mycologia*, 88:369–383, 1996; R. Joost and S. Quisenberry (eds.), *Acremonium/Grass Interactions: Agriculture, Ecosystems and Environment*, 44:1–324, 1993.

Hearing (human)

Psychological studies of human hearing show that infants exhibit sensitivity to musical sounds. These studies employ a variety of experimental techniques to uncover infants' auditory abilities and preferences. One frequently used method reinforces the infant when it turns its head in response to a sound. Fortunately, even young infants have relatively good motor control of the eyes and head. This method measures whether a head turn occurs when the infant hears a specific sound. If the infant responds with a head turn, the response is reinforced by an interesting visual event (for example, a mechanical toy moves). If the infant turns its head during the absence of the specific sound (when either no sound or another sound is presented), the head turn is not reinforced (the mechanical toy does not move). In this way, the experimenter can determine which sounds the infant is able to detect and discriminate.

This method, and variants of it, has been used extensively to measure general perceptual capacities. Infants are more sensitive to high pitches (frequencies above 4000 Hz) than are adults. They are also more sensitive to high pitches than to low pitches. This sensitivity to high pitches may arise because they are more attention-getting or alerting. In other measures of auditory capacities, infants are similar to adults. They are almost as accurate in detecting a change of pitch. They can detect a pitch change when the frequency differs by about 1%. Infants are also similar to adults in perceiving changes of loudness (detecting a change of about 3 dB) and sound quality (timbre). Since infants have good auditory abilities, it is interesting to examine their sensitivity to music.

Consonance and dissonance. Consonance in music refers to the effect produced by combinations of tones that sound pure, smooth, or pleasing. Dissonance is the opposite of consonance. The cause of consonance is the subject of debate. Consonance may be a consequence of the way that the ear processes sounds or it may depend on an individual's experience with music. That consonance may be at least partially influenced by experience is supported by the fact that different pitch combinations are preferred in different musical cultures around the world, and in different historical periods within Western music. However, pitch combinations are not arbitrary. Most musical styles employ octaves (frequencies in a 2 : 1 ratio), considered the most consonant interval. Interval refers to a combination of two tones (sounded either simultaneously or one after the other). Many musical styles also employ fifths (frequencies in a 3 : 2 ratio), considered to be the next most consonant interval. These near-universals suggest that the auditory system may influence the selection of musical intervals. If so, infants would be expected to show a preference for consonant tone combinations.

Exposing infants approximately 4 months old to melodies played in two versions allowed examination of preferences for consonant tone combinations. The consonant version played the melody in parallel thirds; thirds are considered moderately consonant intervals. The dissonant version played the melody in parallel minor seconds; minor seconds are considered highly dissonant. The loudspeaker playing the music was covered with an attractive visual pattern (concentric circles). The length of time that the infants looked at the visual pattern during the music was recorded. The time that the infants looked at the pattern was longer for the consonant versions than for the dissonant versions. The infants waited longer before moving their arms or legs during the consonant melodies. There was no relationship between the infants' responses and their previous exposure to music. This study demonstrated that infants discriminate between consonance and dissonance, and also suggested that infants prefer the consonant intervals.

These findings support the idea that consonance depends on the way that the auditory system processes sounds. Consonant intervals have harmonics that either coincide or are far enough apart not to interfere. Dissonant intervals have harmonics that are close enough in frequency to interfere with one another. This could account for the infants' preference for consonant intervals. It could also explain why consonant intervals appear in many different musical styles. Thus, auditory processing may influence the selection of sounds in music. This does not exclude the possibility that experience could lead to preferences for other intervals. Some musical styles, such as the music of the Javanese gamelan, do not include such consonant intervals as fifths and thirds. Also, some Western twentieth-century music exhibits a high degree of dissonance.

Memory for pitch. Infants may also remember consonant intervals better than dissonant intervals. One study tested this with infants 6 to 8 months old. Using sine-wave tones that do not have nearby harmonics eliminated sensory dissonance caused by interfering harmonics. The method was the visual reinforcement of head turns described earlier. The infants heard a series of intervals (two tones sounded simultaneously). These intervals were all the same except that they were shifted up and down in pitch (called transposition in music). For example, if the interval was a fifth, it might be sounded first as C and G, then as D and A, then as A and E, and so on (called the background interval). The background interval was then increased or decreased in size by a semitone (the smallest step on the musical scale), and the experimenter measured whether the infant turned its head to receive reinforcement. This study also had adults perform a similar task for comparison with the infants.

The background interval was either consonant or dissonant. The consonant intervals were octaves (with a 2:1 ratio of frequencies) and fifths (with a 3:2 ratio of frequencies). The dissonant intervals were major sevenths and minor ninths that differ from an octave by a semitone, and tritones (also called diminished fifths or augmented fourths) and minor sixths that differ from a fifth by a semitone. When the background interval was consonant, infants and adults easily detected the change to a dissonant interval. For example, changing from a fifth to a tritone was detected quite accurately. When the background interval was dissonant, both infants and adults had greater difficulty detecting the change. Thus, a change from a tritone to a perfect fifth was relatively difficult to detect. This suggests that memory is more accurate for the consonant intervals.

To investigate memory for intervals in short melodies, 6-month-old infants heard melodies based on either Western major and minor scales or a Javanese scale (called pélog). The issue addressed in this experiment was whether infants have a predisposition toward the Western major and minor scales; that is, if the melodies based on these scales are easier to remember than those based on the Javanese scale. The infant first heard the well-tuned version repeated a number of times. Then the fifth tone in the melody was mistuned by raising its frequency. The infant response of turning its head toward the loudspeaker to receive visual reinforcement was measured. Adults, who were also from Western culture, performed a similar task for comparison.

As would be expected, adults were better at detecting the mistuned tone when it was in a Western major or minor melody context than when it was in a Javanese scale context. In contrast, the infants were equally good on all three kinds of melodies. This suggests that infants are not influenced by the familiarity of the underlying scale of the melodies. Unlike adults, infants were able to detect the tuning change in the Javanese scale context as accurately as the other melodies. This finding suggests a parallel with language learning. Infants appear to be born with the ability to learn the speech sounds of any language; with experience, they select those sounds used in their own language. Similarly, infants appear to be born with the ability to learn the interval patterns of any scale; with experience, they develop greater skill with the scale of their own culture.

For background information *see* HEARING; PHONO-RECEPTION; PSYCHOACOUSTICS; SOUND in the McGraw-Hill Encyclopedia of Science & Technology.

Carol L. Krumhansl

Bibliography. I. Deliège and J. Sloboda (eds.), *Musical Beginnings: Origins and Development of Musical Competence*, 1996; M. P. Lynch et al., Innateness, experience and music perception, *Psychol. Sci.*, 1:272–276, 1990; L. J. Trainor, Effect of frequency ratio on infants' and adults' discrimination of simultaneous intervals, *J. Exp. Psychol. Human Percept. Perform.*, 23:1427–1438, 1997; M. R. Zentner and J. Kagan, Perception of music by infants, *Nature*, 383:29, 1996.

Helicopter aerodynamics

The helicopter is a flight vehicle using two or more rotor blades fixed to a common drive shaft rotated by an engine. In contrast to fixed-wing aircraft, the helicopter can take off vertically, land vertically, and hover. It can move forward, backward, and sideways. The helicopter is designed for effective operation in hover for long periods of time, for high-speed cruise, and for high range and payload. Helicopter aerodynamics usually refers to rotor-blade aerodynamics. Proper design of the rotor blades is essential.

Flow problems. The air velocity around the rotor blades can reach very high speeds, close to and exceeding the speed of sound, while neighboring regions have much lower air velocities, perhaps only one-third of the speed of sound. Generally, the speed of the rotor tip is somewhat less than the speed of sound because the blade lift decreases and the blade drag increases at the higher subsonic Mach numbers. Many complex fluid-dynamics problems occur simultaneously (**Fig. 1**).

On the advancing side of the rotor (**Fig. 2a**), where the rotor-blade motion is in the same direction as the forward flight speed, the velocity relative to the blade is high. Since the lift is proportional to the square of the relative speed of the blades, a high lift is generated at a small pitch angle. When the blade speed is opposite to the direction of the flight speed, a lower lift is obtained, generating a force and moment imbalance. To counter this effect, the angle of attack of each blade is adjusted throughout the blade cycle to provide a balance of lift; this is called cyclic pitch. Often the angle of attack is approximately equal to the pitch angle (Fig. 2b; if the velocity of the air is purely horizontal, the two angles are nominally equal).

On the retreating side of the blade, since the velocity is lower, a higher angle of attack is required to

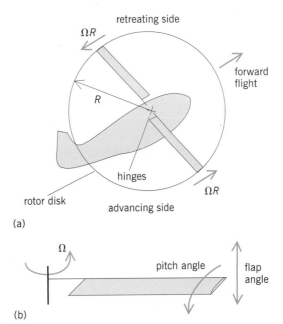

(a)

(b)

Fig. 2. Geometry of motion of helicopter rotor blades. (*a*) **Top view of the rotor disk illustrating its advancing and retreating sides. The linear velocity of the blade tip is the product of the radius of the rotor, *R*, and its angular velocity, Ω.** (*b*) **Pitch and flap angles of a rotor blade.**

balance the forces and moments. This can lead to dynamic stall, in which the flow breaks away from the surface, generating a large region of reversed flow (Fig. 1). This separation vortex grows and eventually leaves the blade surface, causing a significant loss of lift. Dynamic stall can thus lead to a significant decrease in performance. A rotor in a state of a balance of forces and moments is said to be trimmed.

The helicopter is unusual because it operates in the wake of its own blades. Thus the flow field around a helicopter is unsteady in contrast to fixed-wing aircraft, in which the wake of the wings trails the aircraft. Two major problems associated with helicopter aerodynamics are the occurrence of dynamic stall and interactions of vortices with rotor blades. These complications make it difficult to formulate any sort of prediction scheme for the air velocities around a helicopter.

Rotor wake. The wake of the blades is complicated, consisting of a vortex sheet and a tip vortex (**Fig. 3**). Both these structures are very thin regions of highly three-dimensional and rapidly rotating flow, and are part of the family of flows called vortical flows. The tip-vortex creates large loads on the rotor blades. A major consideration in the design of the rotor blades is maximizing the blade lift, which is the force that keeps the helicopter in the air, and minimizing the drag, which is the force that acts opposite to the direction of flight. Determining the lift and drag requires knowledge of the fluid velocities in the wake.

Rotor blades have a large span-to-chord ratio, and thus severe stresses can be communicated to the

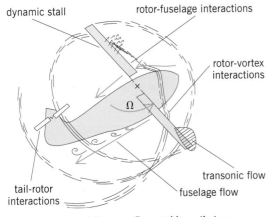

Fig. 1. Summary of the many flow problems that can occur simultaneously when a helicopter is in forward flight. The arrow indicates the direction of the rotor and Ω its angular speed. (*After F. X. Caradonna, The Application of CFD to Rotary Wing Aircraft, NASA, TM 102803, 1992*)

hub if the blades are not permitted to flap (Fig. 2*b*). The reason is that the forces and moments on the blades are much larger near the blade tip than near the root. Thus the rotor blades must be permitted to bend out of the rotor disk plane or flap, in addition to the pitching motion. Also, because of the large span-to-chord ratio, blade aeroelastic effects play a major role in determining helicopter performance. Because the rotor blades can bend out of the plane, the tip vortex shed from a blade can interact with the trailing blade and cause significant changes in load and a significant amount of noise. The periodic slapping sound which often precedes the appearance of a helicopter is largely due to rotor-blade–vortex interactions.

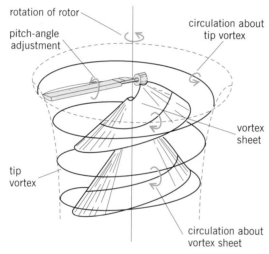

Fig. 3. Sketch of a helicopter rotor wake for a single blade. *(After R. Gray, An aerodynamic analysis of a single-bladed rotor in hovering and low-speed forward flight as determined from smoke studies of the vorticity distribution in the wake, Princeton Univ. Aero. Eng. Dep., Rep. 356, September 1956).*

Determining the motion. The major component of the lift and drag on the entire helicopter is the lift and drag on the rotor blades. To determine these quantities, the distribution of pressure on the blades must be known, and this distribution is a strong function of the position of the rotor wake at each point in the cycle. Thus, great effort must be expended to determine the fluid velocity at a large number of points in the wake.

To design the blades, most modern computer programs for helicopter rotors determine the blade loads by using a free-wake calculation in which the motion of the vortex system is calculated directly from the effects of all the other wake components and the influence of the blade. In this description, which is the most common design tool, the wake is allowed to develop in time, and the fluid velocities in the rotor wake are calculated by solving compli-

cated and nonlinear partial differential equations which result from the conservation of mass, momentum, and energy. There are two methods of using these equations to determine the fluid velocities in the wake of the rotor blades, termed lagrangian and eulerian.

Lagrangian description. In lagrangian methods, a specified formula for the velocity field is usually the starting point and individual fluid particles are followed forward in time. The velocity induced by the vortex is usually described by the Biot-Savart law for the velocity due to an arbitrary patch of fluid containing vorticity. By using the definition of the fluid velocity at a point as the time rate of change of position, the vortex system is moved sequentially in time. The distribution of pressure on the blades is calculated at each instant of time, and the lift and drag on the blades is determined from this pressure distribution. The tip vortex is usually approximated by a line vortex, and the vortex sheet is often approximated by a lattice of vortex segments. A deficiency of the method is that the initial value of the circulation which is shed into the wake must be modeled, usually as a lifting line. Blade designs are usually performed for an isolated rotor. This type of computation is often used for blade design because of its relative computational efficiency.

Eulerian description. In an eulerian description, the solution for the entire velocity field is calculated on a spatial grid system, which is not required in a lagrangian description. The Navier-Stokes equations govern fluid flow and are an expression of the conservation of linear momentum; there is one equation for each of the three spatial dimensions. These equations are the analog of Newton's law in fluid dynamics. The laws of conservation of mass, momentum, and energy comprise five nonlinear partial differential equations which, along with an equation of state, must be solved for the three velocity components: temperature, pressure, and density.

The Navier-Stokes equations for an isolated rotor in hover are usually solved with the rotor started from a given state; the equations are integrated forward in time, and the blade pressure is calculated as described above. An advantage over typical lagrangian techniques is that the amount of circulation shed into the wake is calculated directly. However, the problem is very difficult, especially in hover and low-speed forward flight, because of the number of grid points required to resolve the flow for a relatively large number of time steps. Typically, a minimum of two turns of the rotor is required for a good representation of the rotor wake, and by this time the tip vortex and the vortex sheet are much weaker than those seen in experiments, because of numerical inaccuracy. Nevertheless, these methods are very powerful, and recent research has allowed flows past entire configurations to be calculated. While most blade designs are performed with lagrangian computations, eulerian calculations using the Navier-Stokes equations are beginning to be applied to both blade and fuselage design.

Experiments. A full-scale helicopter may have rotor blades on the order of about 15 ft (5 m) in length, and most wind tunnels are too small to accommodate these blades even when they are tested in isolation. Thus, many rotor experiments are done at model scale with blades that are much shorter than the full-scale blades and with aeroelastic properties that can be considerably different.

The measurement of the flow field around a rotating blade is a significant challenge even at relatively low rotational speeds. Model rotor speeds generally exceed 1000 revolutions per minute, and if the rotor-hinge mechanism fails, the blade will acquire a velocity in the plane of the rotor disk comparable to that of a handgun bullet.

Four methods of measuring various quantities associated with the rotor wake are common: flow visualization of the rotor wake by smoke or some other nonintrusive means such as wide-field shadowgraphy; direct measurement of the distribution of pressure on the blades; measurement of velocities at the inlet to the rotor disk; and direct measurement of the velocity field of the wake, using techniques such as hot-wire probes, laser-Doppler velocimetry, and particle-image velocimetry. Velocities at the inlet to the rotor disk are termed rotor inflow conditions, and experimentally generated rotor inflow conditions are generally used as boundary conditions for computational fluid dynamics studies.

Experimental research is focused primarily on the wake structure and dynamic stall. Recent studies have sought to more accurately measure the position and the strength of the rotor wake as well as the local flow field in and around the tip vortex. These properties have a significant effect on blade loads. Measured quantities are often used in computational predictions of performance. Active control of the dynamic stall process is also an important research area. Efforts to achieve higher lift at low angles of attack using leading and trailing edge flaps (so-called smart structures) are also being investigated.

For background information *see* AERODYNAMIC FORCE; AERODYNAMICS; AEROELASTICITY; COMPUTATIONAL FLUID DYNAMICS; FLOW MEASUREMENT; FLUID-FLOW PRINCIPLES; HELICOPTER; NAVIER-STOKES EQUATIONS; VORTEX; WIND TUNNEL in the McGraw-Hill Encyclopedia of Science & Technology.   A. T. Conlisk

Bibliography. A. T. Conlisk, Modern helicopter aerodynamics, *Annu. Rev. Fluid Mech.*, 27:515–567, 1997; B. W. McCormick, *Aerodynamics of V/STOL Flight*, 1967; J. Seddon, *Basic Helicopter Aerodynamics*, 1990; W. Z. Stepniewski and C. N. Keys, *Rotary-Wing Aerodynamics*, 2 vols., 1984.

Hibernation

Hibernation is a seasonal period of extremely low metabolic activity that permits certain animals to survive winter, when little or no food is available. Most hibernators accumulate large amounts of fat over the summer and fall to use as the primary fuel source during the hibernation season. By also reducing energy expenditure and living below ground in burrows, they can survive winter when there is heavy snowfall and air temperature hovers near freezing. Hibernation is, however, only one type of winter dormancy. A season of relative inactivity occurs in a vast array of plants and animals. A type of winter dormancy occurs in several species of insects, amphibians, reptiles, birds, and mammals. Only one avian species is known to hibernate, although other species become hypometabolic for several hours each day during the winter. It is generally agreed that the primary function of winter dormancy, and hence hibernation, is to conserve energy during an energetically challenging time of year when little or no food is available. Dormant ectotherms remain hypometabolic throughout the entire winter and become active again in the spring when high ambient temperatures return. In contrast, in mammals a season of hibernation is characterized by prolonged intervals (days or weeks) of hypometabolism that alternate with brief intervals of high metabolism (less than 24 h) over the course of 5–6 months.

Mammalian hibernation. A comprehensive understanding of mammalian hibernation comes from field and laboratory work on golden-mantled ground squirrels (*Spermophilus lateralis*). During the hibernation season, these squirrels live individually in burrows underground. At the end of the season, females come above ground shortly before the males emerge. The breeding season begins immediately and lasts no more than 2 weeks. For the remainder of the spring and summer, males spend much of their time foraging in order to accumulate the large amounts of fat they will need to fuel the next hibernation season. Females must complete parturition and lactation and then wean the litter before they can begin to accumulate enough fat to survive winter.

The hibernation season starts in early fall when squirrels enter their burrows and undergo short torpor bouts that last only several hours. Within a few weeks, the entrance to the burrow is plugged and squirrels begin to cycle through much longer bouts of torpor. As a squirrel begins to enter torpor, it moves into the center of the nest and covers itself with additional nesting material. It then enters into a curled-up posture with the tail lying flat over the snout and the legs tucked in along the sides of the abdomen, a position that maximizes heat distribution during the arousal process. During entry into hibernation, body temperature declines over the course of 10–12 h from 37°C (98°F) to as low as 2–3°C (36–37°F) in midwinter. Animals remain at this body temperature for 2–14 days before they initiate the rewarming process and arouse from deep torpor. Individual torpor bouts are longest in midwinter and shortest at the beginning and end of the hibernation season. Deep torpor is also characterized by infrequent breathing; two or three breaths per minute are typical, but apneas (lapses in breathing) may be as long as 10 min. During arousal, or exit, from torpor, rewarming can occur as fast as 1°C (1.8°F) per minute and brain temperature can be as much as 15°C (27°F) higher than core body temperature. Arousal from deep torpor is completed within 90–120 min. Squirrels stay fully rewarmed (body temperature ~37°C or 98°F) for about 12–20 h before initiating the next torpor bout. During this period of euthermia, squirrels spend 80% of their time asleep and remain relatively motionless until the next torpor bout begins.

Brain regulation of hibernation. An important feature of hibernation is that neural regulatory centers must be able to function across a broad range (more than 30°C or 54°F) of tissue temperatures. The hypothalamic suprachiasmatic nucleus is one brain structure that is well adapted to function at these temperatures. The suprachiasmatic nucleus is known as the site of a pacemaker that controls circadian rhythms of sleep-wake cycles in mammals. Circadian rhythms are daily cycles in physiology and behavior that are endogenously generated by an organism. The periods of these rhythms generally range from 23 to 25 h. Environmental cycles of light and dark synchronize the pacemaker in the suprachiasmatic nucleus, which, in turn, adjusts behavioral rhythms so that animals stay synchronized to environmental cycles of 24 h. Ablation of the suprachiasmatic nucleus completely eliminates circadian organization of physiological and behavioral events. The suprachiasmatic nucleus in squirrels consists of a bilateral pair of ovoid nuclei approximately 500 micrometers in diameter. These nuclei consist of about 10,000 cells each that are located at the base of the hypothalamus immediately above the optic chiasm and along the walls of the third ventricle.

During deep torpor, metabolism is greatly slowed down throughout the entire brain. Metabolic activity in the suprachiasmatic nucleus declines, however, much less than in other brain structures so that the suprachiasmatic nucleus remains more active than the rest of the brain during torpor. The role of the suprachiasmatic nucleus in hibernation has been evaluated by comparing hibernation patterns in female ground squirrels in which the suprachiasmatic nucleus has been surgically ablated with those of neurologically intact squirrels (control group). Miniature temperature-sensitive transmitters implanted in the abdomen were used to monitor hibernation. Transmitter signals were detected by a small receiver placed underneath the animal's nest area and were converted into core body temperature measurements by a computer that recorded the signals at 10 min intervals over a 2.5-year period.

The loss of suprachiasmatic nucleus regulation produced striking changes in hibernation patterns. Normally, squirrels hibernate for about half the year and maintain their body at temperatures typical of nonhibernating mammals (~37°C or 98°F) for the other half of the year. In the absence of the suprachiasmatic nucleus, however, hibernation was continuous with no seasonal modulation of body temperature. Torpor bouts still alternated with brief intervals of euthermia in these animals as in other hibernators, but over a 2-year period there was no time of year when hibernation completely stopped; torpor bouts were never separated by more than a few days. Not all squirrels extended their hibernation season in this manner after removal of the suprachiasmatic nucleus. In those cases, however, the hibernation season was much longer than in control animals. Thus, in all squirrels removal of the suprachiasmatic nucleus resulted in a hibernation season that was extended to well beyond what other squirrels normally experience.

Several additional features of torpor bout regulation were also disrupted in the absence of the suprachiasmatic nucleus. The average torpor bout is over 5 days long in control animals. Without the suprachiasmatic nucleus, torpor bouts shortened to an average duration of 3 days and the euthermic intervals between bouts were about 50% longer. Torpor bouts typically increase in duration from the beginning to the middle of the season and then progressively shorten until springtime. This pattern, normally very predictable, was replaced by a random progression of torpor bout duration in which the length of time of a single bout was unrelated to the one before or after it. Similar changes in torpor bout expression also occurred in squirrels in which suprachiasmatic nucleus ablation was substantial but incomplete. In those animals, circadian rhythms were normal but torpor bouts and euthermic intervals were disrupted just as much as they were in the absence of the suprachiasmatic nucleus. Thus, the suprachiasmatic nucleus is important in regulating the duration of the hibernation season as well as the structure and timing of individual torpor bouts and the intervals between those bouts. No other treatments have ever produced similar disruptions.

Implications. Because hibernators spend the entire winter underground, where they are not exposed to cycles of light and dark, the need for circadian organization is not apparent and makes it difficult to understand why the suprachiasmatic nucleus has such a striking influence on hibernation. The suprachiasmatic nucleus may serve other functions during hibernation in addition to its role as a circadian pacemaker. In squirrels in which the suprachiasmatic nucleus was only partially intact, circadian rhythms persisted despite disruptions in torpor patterns. Similar disturbances in torpor patterns in squirrels with complete loss of the suprachiasmatic nucleus, therefore, could not have been due to elimination of their circadian organization. Thus, the suprachiasmatic nucleus may have a novel role in hibernation that is unrelated to its known role as a circadian pacemaker. Additionally, a relation to temperature compensation in the suprachiasmatic nucleus is possible. Circadian pacemaker period is stable over a range of physiological temperatures. The suprachiasmatic nucleus generates a circadian rhythm of neuronal activity that requires large populations of neurons to discharge synchronously. In hibernators, individual neurons must be able to discharge and remain synchronized at low tissue temperatures in order to drive circadian rhythms during torpor. Throughout the evolution of hibernation, neurons of the suprachiasmatic nucleus may have been coopted by natural selection for these characteristics as a means of regulating the structure and timing of torpor bouts precisely because these cells are able to function synchronously at low tissue temperatures.

For background information *see* ADIPOSE TISSUE; BIOLOGICAL CLOCKS; ENERGY METABOLISM; HIBERNATION; METABOLISM in the McGraw-Hill Encyclopedia of Science & Technology.   Norman F. Ruby

Bibliography. D. Grahn et al., Persistence of circadian rhythmicity in hibernating ground squirrels, *Amer. J. Physiol.*, 266:R1251–R1258, 1994; C. P. Lyman et al., *Hibernation and Torpor in Mammals and Birds*, 1982; N. F. Ruby et al., Ablation of suprachiasmatic nucleus alters timing of hibernation in ground squirrels, *Proc. Nat. Acad. Sci.*, 93:9864–9868, 1996; N. F. Ruby and H. C. Heller, Temperature sensitivity of the suprachiasmatic nucleus of ground squirrels and rats in vitro, *J. Biol. Rhythms*, 11:126–136, 1996.

High-temperature superconductor

The discovery of high-temperature superconducting materials in 1986 unleashed a worldwide flurry of research with high hopes for an ensuing technological revolution in electronics, transportation, and energy fields. In the 10 following years, valuable scientific knowledge was acquired which is beginning to lead to these expected technological advances. The essential property of superconductors, namely infinite electrical conductivity (zero resistance) in steady current flow, leads to many possible applications, including faster electronics requiring less power; smaller, more efficient motors and generators; and more efficient transfer and storage of electrical energy.

The drawback to superconductivity has always been that the materials require a low-temperature, or cryogenic, environment. Previously known superconducting materials, mainly niobium-titanium (NbTi) for magnets and niobium for electronics, were cooled with a liquid-helium bath to the extremely low temperature of 4.2 K ($-452°$F). The constant maintenance, costly refrigerants, and bulky thermal containers (dewars) needed to maintain the low temperature restricted such materials to a few applications (magnets for magnetic resonance imaging, high-energy physics research, and materials research). High-temperature superconducting materials offered the same beneficial attributes but at considerably higher temperatures and thus with much less demand on refrigerators and cryogenic systems. Indeed, high-temperature superconductivity has completely eliminated the need for an expensive liquid-helium environment. Wider use of superconductivity was envisioned after the discovery of high-temperature superconducting materials in 1986.

Lessening of the cryogenic burden for superconductivity, however, came with a price: The materials are much more difficult to fabricate and manufacture in the required geometries with useful properties. The new high-temperature superconducting materials contain four or five elements which form compounds with complex crystal structures at high temperatures. These materials react with many other materials and gases, and their properties are very sensitive to the precise chemical composition. To make matters worse, the ceramic oxide materials are brittle. They usually form as collections of small crystallites (grains), and the supercurrent flow across grain boundaries is severely degraded by minute impurities and crystalline misalignment. It has taken considerable time and effort to develop instrumentation and techniques to manufacture these materials with forms and properties that are useful for specific applications. Commonly used high-temperature superconducting compounds are yttrium-barium-copper oxide ($YBa_2Cu_3O_7$-), bismuth-strontium-calcium-copper oxide ($Bi_2Sr_2Ca_2Cu_3O_{10}$ or $Bi_2Sr_2Ca_1Cu_2O_8$), and thallium-strontium-calcium-copper oxide ($Tl_2Sr_2Ca_1Cu_2O_8$).

Materials development has progressed to the point where specific applications of high-temperature superconducting materials are being demonstrated and in some cases actually being used commercially.

Current leads. One of the first applications of high-temperature superconducting materials is the current lead since it is easy to form, being typically a short cylindrical rod, and does not require high supercurrent density. Since the thermal conductivity of the high-temperature superconducting materials is poor while the electrical resistance is essentially zero, these current leads provide a much improved interface between low-temperature superconducting magnets used in magnetic resonance imaging, high-energy physics, or materials research and the room-temperature electronics. With the improved thermal isolation, it is now possible to cool niobium-titanium magnets by conduction with small, closed-cycle refrigerators, thereby eliminating the need for liquid helium and its associated logistics. This simple application is already used in many commercially sold superconducting magnet systems. All of the common high-temperature superconducting materials have been used as current leads.

Filters for cellular communications. Microwave filters fabricated from films of high-temperature superconducting materials (typically $YBa_2Cu_3O_7$ or $Tl_2Sr_2Ca_1Cu_2O_8$) possess sharper band cutoff and smaller insertion losses than conventional filters. Early filters degraded at high power levels, but improvement in film growth has now produced single-crystal or highly textured films over large surface areas (5–10-cm or 2–4-in. squares). Improved material quality and new filter designs fully meet requirements for in-service performance at an operating temperature of around 70 K ($-334°$F). High-temperature superconducting filters are presently manufactured by several companies and are used in cellular base stations where improved performance is essential, that is, in remote regions where increased range is important and in high-density regions where improved discrimination is needed. Small, inexpensive, low-maintenance refrigeration systems and complementary cryogenic packaging are being developed specifically for these devices, and increased use of such filters for cellular communication systems is expected.

Magnetometers. Superconducting quantum interference devices (SQUIDs) form the basis for making extremely sensitive magnetometers for measuring magnetic waves emanating from the Earth (in mineral exploration), from the human body (in heart or brain scans), or from manufactured products (in nondestructive evaluation). Improved logistics of operation at 70 K ($-334°F$) with a small, compact refrigerator or with inexpensive, environmentally friendly liquid nitrogen (at 77 K or $-321°F$) offer great advantages for high-temperature SQUID technology. High-temperature SQUIDs are fundamentally more difficult to fabricate than filters because SQUID performance depends on fabrication of a high-quality junction between two high-temperature superconducting materials as well as high-temperature superconducting coupling transformers (with multilayer crossovers) to concentrate the magnetic signals onto the junction. Nevertheless, material advances and special designs have recently led to $YBa_2Cu_3O_7$ SQUID magnetometers with the sensitivity required for application in geophysics, nondestructive evaluation, and medical diagnosis. All of these applications have been demonstrated, and in some cases (particularly for heart or brain scans) complete systems have been developed. Widespread use of SQUID magnetometers now depends on clinical studies in the case of heart and brain scans and on greater demand for the other applications.

Underground transmission lines. Transmission of electrical power, especially in large cities, increasingly relies on underground cables, which are being operated at close to maximum capacity in many cases. Replacement of conventional oil-cooled cables with high-temperature superconducting cables will result in three to four times more capacity due to higher currents and lower losses. Furthermore, the liquid-nitrogen coolant is more environmentally friendly than oil in the event of cable rupture. Several partnerships have been formed to develop and install high-temperature superconducting cables using silver-clad $Bi_2Sr_2Ca_2Cu_3O_{10}$ as the conductor operating at 77 K ($-321°F$), the boiling temperature of liquid nitrogen. Technical issues involved in this development include increasing the superconducting current capacity through improved processing techniques, increasing quality control of long-length production runs, decreasing alternating-current electrical losses in the cable, improving the flexibility of cables for installation, and developing techniques for joining and terminating the conductors. These issues are being successfully addressed, and installation of the first underground transmission lines is expected by the year 2000.

Transformers. Electrical transformers are major components in the utility system. Present transformers use copper windings, and the majority of the larger transformers use internal oil coolants, which create potential environmental contamination problems and fire hazards. Furthermore, many of the high-capacity transformers are large and difficult to transport and conveniently site. Because of the lower resistance of high-temperature superconducting windings ($Bi_2Sr_2Ca_2Cu_3O_{10}$ or $Bi_2Sr_2Ca_1Cu_2O_8$ are presently used), superconducting transformers offer lower electrical losses, smaller size, and an environmentally friendly coolant (liquid nitrogen). The major technical barriers to developing high-temperature superconducting transformers are the need to increase the current-carrying capacity of the conductor, reduce the alternating-current losses, and reduce the overall cost of the transformer. As with underground cables, several partnerships have been formed to develop high-temperature superconducting transformers, and at least one such transformer has been field tested.

Fault-current limiters. Protection of electrical systems against current surges produced by downed power lines, lightning strikes, or other damage is a major concern of electric utilities. Failures produced by surges can damage customer and utility equipment and shut down an entire power-distribution system until damaged equipment is replaced. High-temperature superconductors (presently $Bi_2Sr_2Ca_2Cu_3O_{10}$ or $Bi_2Sr_2Ca_1Cu_2O_8$) are uniquely suited to provide protection against these faults, since current surges exceeding the limit of the conductor will rapidly switch the conductor from the zero-resistance superconducting state to a high-resistance normal state, and hence immediately reduce the magnitude of the current surge. Superconducting fault-current limiters are under development, and will be used either separately or in conjunction with superconducting transformers.

Motors. Large electrical motors account for two-thirds of the power consumption in the United States. Development of more efficient motors, using high-temperature superconducting windings for the motor magnet system, will improve the efficiency of large electrical motors and significantly reduce wasted power consumption. Superconductivity increases the efficiency of motors because the energy losses in the high-temperature superconducting magnets are considerably lower than those in normal copper magnets. (Losses in high-temperature superconducting magnets are not zero in high magnetic fields because of magnetic flux motion, but losses are much smaller than in copper when the supercurrent is less than a critical current.) Furthermore, a superconducting magnet can generate a more intense magnetic field and, hence, greater power density. Because of the low critical currents in magnetic fields, high-temperature superconducting motors using $Bi_2Sr_2Ca_2Cu_3O_{10}$ are presently limited to power ratings of around 150 kW, but because of material improvements which are being implemented in advanced conductors, it is expected that 1500-kW high-temperature superconducting motors will be available by the year 2000.

Magnetic energy storage. In addition to generating magnetic fields, magnets store the energy in these fields. Thus, a large magnet can store electrical energy in an almost lossless manner for future use. Because of the small losses in high-temperature superconducting magnets, only small superconducting magnetic energy storage units (called micro-SMES units) are presently envisioned with such magnets. (Niobium-titanium magnets are being built for larger SMES units.) These micro-SMES units are used for power quality improvements. Small, momentary fluctuations in electrical power can damage computers or shut down processing lines, causing major investment losses. The rapid response of a micro-SMES unit can compensate for these fluctuations and preserve power quality for short periods of time or until alternate power sources can be turned on. Present micro-SMES units use niobium-titanium magnets (operating at 4.2 K or $-452°F$) with high-temperature superconducting current leads, but high-temperature superconducting systems using $Bi_2Sr_2Ca_2Cu_3O_{10}$ and operating at higher temperatures (20 to 30 K or -424 to $-406°F$) are under development.

Other potential applications. There are several other areas of potential application of high-temperature superconducting materials whose commercial development is in the future. Among them are digital electronics (where material issues remain to be solved); electrical generators (whose large size and high magnetic fields lead to materials-related problems); and possible military applications, such as ship propulsion, magnetic mine sweeping, and underwater magnetic-moment detection (of magnetic mines).

For background information *see* ELECTRIC POWER TRANSMISSION; ENERGY STORAGE; MAGNETOMETER; MICROWAVE FILTER; MOTOR; SQUID; SUPERCONDUCTING DEVICES; SUPERCONDUCTIVITY; TRANSFORMER in the McGraw-Hill Encyclopedia of Science & Technology.   Donald U. Gubser

Bibliography. B. Batlogg et al., *Proceedings of the 10th Anniversary HTS Workshop of Physics, Materials, and Applications*, 1996; P. F. Dahl, *Superconductivity: Its Historical Roots and Development from Mercury to the Ceramic Oxides*, 1992; F. J. Owens and C. P. Poole, *The New Superconductors*, 1996.

Hormone

The thymus gland is a primary lymphoid organ located in the neck or upper thorax of all vertebrates. It is a site of lymphocyte development. T-cell precursors (prothymocytes) migrate from the bone marrow to the thymus gland, where they undergo a stringent selection process. The microenvironment of the thymus is composed of nonlymphoid cells (epithelial cells, macrophages, dendritic cells, and fibroblasts) and extracellular matrix components. This environment stimulates the differentiation (maturation) of prothymocytes. The maturation includes the acquisition of T-cell function, leading to the mature and self-tolerant T cells that are found in the peripheral lymphoid organs. Classical hormones and neural innervation also affect lymphoid development and function.

Thymic peptides. The many polypeptides isolated from the thymus gland include thymulin, thymopoietin, thymic humoral factor, and thymosins. These substances demonstrate immunobiological activity. All promote the acquisition of antigenic markers which are connected with T-cell function. Whether these substances possess only intrathymic activities or are secreted to act on distal sites is still largely unknown. Only thymulin is recognized as a hormone in accordance with the classical endocrine and physiological criteria because it is thymus-restricted and regulated in its secretion. In a similar fashion, lymphocytes produce serotonin and other neural peptides that once were thought to be confined to the nervous system. Thymectomy or thymic involution does not remove the presence of the other thymic factors (such as cytokines and growth factors) from serum, and their genes are expressed in nonthymic tissues.

Thymulin. Thymulin is a nonapeptide originally called thymus serum factor that requires zinc for full biological activity. Its production is under multiple control involving the levels of thymulin itself and other classical hormones (for example, prolactin, growth hormone, adrenocorticotropic hormone). Thymulin secretion regulates the differentiation of the immature thymocyte subpopulation and the function of mature T and natural killer cells. Thymulin also functions as a transmitter between the neuroendocrine and immune systems. The serum levels of this peptide decrease with age parallel to thymic atrophy. However, the aged thymus maintains the capacity to increase thymulin secretion in response to stimulation by other hormones (for example, growth hormone).

Thymopoietin. Thymopoietin binds cell membrane receptors present on prothymocytes, mature T cells, and certain T-cell lines. Three distinct thymopoietin messenger ribonucleic acid strands (mRNAs) have been described, each suggesting that the proteins have unique functions and may be directed to specific subcellular localizations; also indicated is a nuclear but not endocrine function for thymopoietin. Thymopentin is a pentapeptide derivative of thymopoietin that has unique biological properties. In many countries, thymopentin has been approved as a drug for treatment of primary immunodeficiencies. Thymic humoral factor γ_2 is an octapeptide that retains essentially all the activity of thymic humoral factor, including stimulating effects on myeloid and erythroid hematopoietic progenitor cells. However, thymic humoral factor γ_2 has not been detected in thymic epithelial cells grown in culture.

Thymosins. Thymosins promote the maturation and function of T cells, and possess neuroendocrine activity. From a thymic extract known as thymosin fraction V (TF5), at least 30 different peptides, including thymosin α_1, thymosin β_4, and MB 35, were identified. These three components produced the most potent activity. The presence of other peptides structurally related to thymosin α suggested the existence of a larger precursor molecule called prothymosin α. The relative physiological roles of prothymosin α and thymosin α_1 have not been determined. The prothymosin α gene belongs to a family of six members. Prothymosin α has been highly conserved through evolution and is found in a variety of tissues, suggesting an essential role. Possible functions of prothymosin α include nuclear activity and involvement with cellular proliferation events.

Immunoregulators. The early studies of thymic peptides were linked to their role in the maturation of T lymphocytes within the thymus. More recent investigations have focused upon the effects of thymic peptides on mature effector cells. These investigations are based on several facts: (1) All thymic peptides have been detected in human plasma. Except for thymulin, their levels are not reduced by thymic involution. In some groups of sick patients or monkeys, thymosin α_1 levels are decreased or augmented. (2) Except for thymic humoral factor, all are secreted specifically by some thymic epithelial cells. (3) They bind to different receptors on T cells (and other tissues). (4) Thymic peptides stimulate various T-cell functions in normal and partly T-cell-deficient rats, mice, and humans. In general, thymic peptides tend to normalize the immune balance, either by enhancing suppressed systems or by stimulating suppressor mechanisms in hyperresponsive states. Thymic peptides have been used extensively to regulate T-cell deficits to permit specific clinically useful immunotherapeutical approaches. Data show that thymic peptides may act as fine physiological immunoregulators contributing to the maintenance of T-cell subset homeostasis.

Further investigations on the physiological relevance of these data are required because of the contradictory reports on the possible nuclear roles for thymic peptides. Many hypotheses have emerged, ranging from the assumption that thymic peptides are a result of cellular damage or cell death to the possibility that certain nucleoproteins targeted during cellular activation are secreted. Additionally, peptides may act as components of the extracellular matrix.

Thymic factors and therapy. The functions and pharmacological effects of thymic peptides have promoted intense laboratory and clinical research. A large body of clinical evidence had been obtained from allergic, autoimmune, and neuroendocrine diseases; various malignancies; acquired immunodeficiencies; infections; and immunorestorative effects after chemotherapy. However, only a few drugs containing thymic peptides have been approved by regulatory authorities worldwide because of the lack of convincing clinical studies.

As initial trials have often shown, crude thymic extracts achieve a better response than a single peptide. It is well recognized that in the hematopoietic process an early cytokine induces a receptor to permit the action of the next. New immunotherapeutic strategies are employing combinations of cytokines and thymic peptides. Various clinical trials have been conducted with combination therapies. Thymosin α_1 combinations have been used in treating diseases such as HIV, chronic hepatitis B or hepatitis C, tumors such as head and neck cancer, and advanced non-small-cell lung cancer or metastatic melanoma.

Numerous trials have shown that thymostimulin (a combination of thymic peptides) improves the efficacy of the standard regimen alone in metastatic colon cancer and hepatocellular carcinoma (in liver cirrhosis patients). Thymostimulin and thymopentin show more positive effects than conventional corticosteroid therapies on atopic dermatitis (neurodermitis).

For background information *see* CELLULAR IMMUNOLOGY; ENDOCRINE SYSTEM (VERTEBRATE); IMMUNITY; IMMUNOLOGICAL ONTOGENY; THYMOSIN; THYMUS GLAND in the McGraw-Hill Encyclopedia of Science & Technology.   Oscar J. Cordero; Montserrat Nogueira

Bibliography. O. J. Cordero, H. R. Maurer, and M. Nogueira, Novel approaches to immunotherapy using thymic peptides, *Immunol. Today,* 18:10–13, 1997; E. Garaci and A. L. Goldstein (eds.), *Combination Therapies: Biological Response Modifiers in the Treatment of Cancer and Infectious Diseases,* 1992; G. Goldstein, J. F. Bach, and H. Wigzell (eds.), *Immune Regulation by Characterized Polypeptides,* 1986; M. D. Kendall and M. A. Ritter (eds.), *Thymus Update 1: The Microenvironment of the Human Thymus,* 1988.

Human genetics

Genomic imprinting refers to a phenomenon whereby one of the two alleles at a gene locus is preferentially expressed depending upon the parent of origin. Imprinting manifests at the level of the genome, the individual chromosome/chromosomal region and the gene. For many years it has been recognized in the mouse, and more recently has been identified in humans. The mechanisms of imprinted gene expression are not fully understood, but deoxyribonucleic acid (DNA) methylation and asynchronous replication of the parental alleles (allele-specific replication) are common characteristics of imprinted genes. DNA methylation and allele-specific DNA replication are involved in both the somatic cell expression and inheritance of the imprint. Abnormalities related to genomic imprinting have been observed in several human disorders, marked by alterations in prenatal and/or postnatal growth. The best-characterized disorders that result from abnormal genomic imprinting include triploidy, complete hydatidiform moles (a condition in which the placenta degenerates and the fetus is reabsorbed), ovarian teratomas, and the Beckwith-Wiedemann, Angelman, and Prader-Willi syndromes.

Triploidy, moles and teratomas. Triploidy accounts for approximately 15% of chromosomal causes in early pregnancy loss. In such pregnancies, an additional haploid set of 23 chromosomes is present; that is, 69 chromosomes are observed in each cell, instead of the normal total of 46. An additional set, often paternal in origin, arises from fertilization of an ovum by two sperm. An additional maternal set may arise from fertilization of an egg that failed to extrude the second polar body. An extra paternal set results in poor fetal development, whereas an extra maternal set has a more severe effect on placental development.

In complete moles and teratomas, 46 chromosomes are present but all chromosomes are from a single parent. Complete moles often arise by fertilization of an enucleated egg by an X-bearing sperm and a subsequent doubling of the paternal chromosome complement. Abnormal placental development is observed in complete moles, but no embryo is found. Complete moles occur in about 0.05% of pregnancies, and 10% of complete moles become malignant. In contrast, ovarian teratomas are exclusively maternal in origin and result in formation of disorganized embryonic tissue.

Beckwith-Wiedemann syndrome. Beckwith-Wiedemann syndrome is a congenital, generalized overgrowth syndrome that consists of visceromegaly (enlargement of the organs in the abdomen, such as the liver, spleen, pancreas, stomach, or kidneys) and predisposition to childhood tumors, especially Wilms' tumor (abdominal tumor that usually affects the kidneys). Beckwith-Wiedemann syndrome is localized to chromosome 11. About 85% of the cases are sporadic, and a small number of patients have maternally inherited cytogenetic abnormalities or paternal uniparental disomy (the presence of two copies of a chromosome or a part of a chromosome from the father) or duplication of a region of chromosome 11. Beckwith-Wiedemann syndrome is attributed to a relative deficiency of maternally derived genes, and the clinical severity is increased when the affected chromosomal region (11p15) is transmitted by the mother. Several imprinted loci have been observed in this region and may include insulinlike growth factor 2 (IGF2), insulin 2 (INS2), cyclin-dependent kinase inhibitor (p57KIP2), tumor suppressor (H19), and human achaete-scute 2 (HASH2/ASCL2). In normal individuals, insulinlike growth factor 2 and insulin 2 are expressed solely from the paternal chromosome; and tumor suppressor (H19), cyclin-dependent kinase inhibitor (p57KIP2), and human achaete-scute 2 from the maternal chromosome. Expression of both insulinlike growth factor 2 alleles (biallelic expression) has been observed in some Beckwith-Wiedemann syndrome patients, along with repression and DNA methylation of the maternal (otherwise active) copy of the neighboring tumor suppressor (H19) gene.

Loss of imprinting is seen in Wilms' and other tumor tissues. In Wilms' tumor, tumor suppressor H19 is frequently inactivated by loss or hypermethylation of the maternal allele, and insulinlike growth factor 2 is then biallelically expressed. In these tumors, cyclin-dependent kinase inhibitor expression is also reduced, but in contrast to tumor suppressor H19, the alleles are hypomethylated, thereby indicating differences in maintenance of imprinting for the two loci.

Other syndromes. Angelman syndrome and Prader-Willi syndrome are clinically distinct syndromes caused by genetic defects that localize to chromosome 15. Angelman syndrome is characterized by severe mental retardation, absence of speech, microcephaly, facial dysmorphism, seizures, neonatal hypotonia, ataxic movements, and inappropriate laughter. Prader-Willi syndrome is characterized by mild mental retardation, neonatal hypotonia, hypogonadism, compulsive overeating, childhood onset obesity, and mild facial dysmorphism. About 70% of patients with Angelman syndrome or Prader-Willi syndrome have deletions of regions of chromosome 15, with the only difference being the parental origin of the deletion. The deletion is on the maternally derived chromosome in Angelman syndrome and on the paternally derived chromosome in Prader-Willi syndrome. The remaining 30% of patients are described as nondeletion or nonclassical deletion, but their different causes are consistent with Angelman syndrome resulting from a maternal deficiency of chromosome 15 and Prader-Willi syndrome from a paternal deficiency of the same chromosomal region. Paternal uniparental disomy for chromosome 15 is present in less than 5% of Angelman syndrome patients, and maternal uniparental disomy is present in most nondeletion Prader-Willi syndrome patients, with the remaining Prader-Willi syndrome patients showing imprinting center mutations. Mutations that involve germline genetic elements which control imprinting (that is, imprinting center mutations), and mutations in the ubiquitin-protein ligase E3A gene (UBE3A) account for the molecular findings in many nondeletion Angelman syndrome patients. These findings reveal that familial cases of Angelman syndrome are consistent with an autosomal dominant phenotype expressed only when the mutant allele is maternally inherited.

Duplications of 15q11q13 have also been described. They include interstitial and supernumerary duplications with one and two extra copies of the region, respectively. Most duplications are maternally derived and are associated with an abnormal phenotype distinct from Angelman syndrome and Prader-Willi syndrome. Paternally derived duplications are not detected until transmitted through a germline.

There are consistent differences in genomic methylation in Angelman syndrome, Prader-Willi syndrome, and normal individuals at zinc finger 127 (ZNF127), region D15S63, and small nuclear riboprotein N (SNRPN)—three loci which span more than 1 million base pairs of DNA. Parent-of-origin-specific DNA replication differences between alleles are consistently seen in normal individuals but not in patients with uniparental inheritance. Diagnostic tests based on these allele-specific characteristics have been developed for Angelman syndrome and Prader-Willi syndrome. Paternally expressed [zinc finger 127, small nuclear riboprotein N, pseudoautosomal region 5 (PAR5), imprinted Prader-Willi region (IPW), pseudoautosomal region 1 (PAR1), necdin NDN)] genes are associated with Prader-Willi syndrome, and a maternally expressed (ubiquitin-protein ligase E3A) gene has been identified in Angelman syndrome. The paternally expressed genes are located over a large interval (2 million base pairs of DNA), and allele-specific expression is regulated by the imprinting center, a sequence in the promoter region of small nuclear riboprotein N. A small number of Prader-Willi syndrome or Angelman syndrome patients are deleted for the imprinting center. Prader-Willi syndrome individuals with imprinting-center mutations do not express small nuclear riboprotein N and other imprinted loci in this interval despite the presence of both maternal and paternal alleles at several of these loci. Imprinting-center mutations require transmission through the maternal germline to produce Angelman syndrome or through the paternal germline to produce Prader-Willi syndrome. In such mutations, the imprint is not reset during gametogenesis. Sequences within the imprinting center appear sufficient to confer either maternal or paternal genomic imprinting in chromosome 15.

Other imprinted chromosomes/chromosomal regions. In the diploid cells of most individuals, half of all chromosomes are inherited from each parent. In uniparental disomy, however, both copies of one chromosome pair are derived from one parent. This results from nondisjunction and may involve two copies of a single homolog (isodisomy) or one copy of two homologs (heterodisomy). Uniparental disomy results from correction of a monosomy to a disomy (isodisomy) or a trisomy to a disomy (isodisomy or heterodisomy). Uniparental disomy has been observed for most chromosomes. In addition to uniparental disomy for chromosomes 11 and 15 (as in Beckwith-Wiedmann syndrome, Angelman syndrome, and Prader-Willi syndrome), only chromosomes 7 and 14 currently have a potential imprinting effect. In one study, maternal uniparental disomy for chromosome 7 has been reported in about 10% of patients with Russell-Silver syndrome, a disorder with significant prenatal and postnatal growth retardation. It has also been reported in isolated cases of short stature and intrauterine growth retardation, including an individual with an isochromosome for the long arm of chromosome 7. Maternal uniparental disomy for chromosome 14 is associated with growth retardation, hypotonia, motor delay, and mild facial dysmorphology. It is likely that other autosomes/regions with imprinting effects will also be identified as studies are extended.

The X sex chromosome is also implicated in imprinting. In females, one X chromosome undergoes inactivation and shows the asynchronous replication and hypermethylation characteristic of imprinted regions. (X inactivation serves as a gene dosage mechanism between sexes, where males and females have one and two X chromosomes, respectively.) Specific imprinted chromosomal regions on the X chromosome and the autosomes will undoubtedly be identified as more cases are investigated.

For background information *see* CHROMOSOME; CHROMOSOME ABERRATION; GENE; HUMAN GENETICS in the McGraw-Hill Encyclopedia of Science & Technology.   Joan H. M. Knoll

Bibliography. S. D. Cheng et al., Cytogenetic and molecular characterization of inverted duplicated chromosomes 15 from 11 patients, *Amer. J. Hum. Genet.*, 55:753–759, 1994; M. Lalande, Parental imprinting and human disease, *Annu. Rev. Genet.*, 30:173–195, 1996; D. H. Ledbetter and E. Engel, Uniparental disomy in humans: Development of an imprinting map and its implication for prenatal diagnosis, *Hum. Mol. Genet.*, 4:1757–1764, 1995; W. Reik and E. R. Maher, Imprinting in clusters: Lessons from Beckwith-Wiedemann syndrome, *Trends Genet.*, 13:330–334, 1997; S. Saitoh et al., Minimal definition of the imprinting center and fixation of chromosome 15q11q13 epigenotype by imprinting mutations, *PNAS*, 93:7811–7815, 1996.

Human immunodeficiency virus (HIV)

Recent advances in the study of the human immunodeficiency virus involve determining the molecular mechanisms in the binding of the virus to cells, and the biological basis of natural resistance to HIV.

Virus Binding to Cells

Like all viruses, the human immunodeficiency virus is an intracellular parasite. In order for HIV to multiply, it needs to subvert cellular machinery. HIV has to gain access to the cytoplasm and nucleus of the cells in which its multiplication will take place. New virus particles will then be produced and subsequently be released at the cell surface. These particles are enveloped in a membrane, derived from the membrane that surrounds the cell. Therefore, the virus surface will have many of the properties of the cell surface. Cell plasma membranes tend to repel each other, a mechanism to avoid useless clumping of cells in the body. Thus, for the virus to attach to the surface of the target cell, a strong interaction is required to overcome these repulsive forces. For this reason, viruses use molecules present at the surface of target cells as docking sites, also termed virus receptors. Many different molecules have been identified as virus receptors, including carbohydrates associated with proteins and lipids, and proteins themselves. The first identified target of HIV infection was a white blood cell (leukocyte) termed a CD4+ T lymphocyte. T lymphocytes are a population of leukocytes that are central to the regulation and function of the immune system. It is in large part the elimination of T lymphocytes that leads to immunodeficiency in AIDS. CD4 is a molecule in the membrane of these cells that not only defines this population but has specific activities that are essential for the correct function of these cells. An important component of the HIV receptor, the CD4 molecule determines to a great extent the susceptibility to HIV infection of cell types both in infected individuals and in the laboratory. Other molecules that are important for HIV infection have also been identified, and their role in the binding of virus to cells is discussed below.

CD4. There is strong evidence that in the body, HIV infects only cells that carry CD4 on the surface. This molecule is therefore considered to be the principal receptor for the virus. At least three different cell types carry CD4: T lymphocytes, macrophages, and some populations of dendritic cells. All of these cell types are natural targets for HIV infection, and are also important for immune system function. The CD4 molecule binds a carbohydrate-containing protein, glycoprotein 120, on the virus envelope. The attachment of HIV to cellular CD4 triggers structural changes in glycoprotein 120 and also in viral glycoprotein 41, that allow entry of the virus into the cell cytoplasm. The structure of CD4 is known; it is clear that glycoprotein 120 binds to the part of CD4 that is farthest from the cell membrane, known as CD4 domain 1 (**Fig. 1**). The glycoprotein 120 structure has not been determined, and little is known of the attachment site for CD4. Soluble forms of CD4 and glycoprotein 120 have been prepared by genetic engineering, allowing measurement of the affinity (strength) of the interaction between these two molecules. The strong binding indicates that the virus may be capable of adhering to the cell surface by virtue of this interaction alone. However, glycoprotein 120 is present on the virus as a cluster of three molecules (a trimer); it is unlikely that this trimeric complex interacts with the same strength as soluble glycoprotein 120 with cellular CD4. The technical difficulties involved in carrying out direct binding studies between HIV particles and cellular CD4 means that no precise measurements of this interaction are available. However, the fact that other molecules in addition to CD4 are generally required for efficient attachment of HIV to its target cells provides indirect evidence that the CD4–glycoprotein 120 interaction is probably not sufficient for strong virus-cell binding.

Other molecules. Several years ago, a phospholipid termed galactosyl ceramide was shown to act as a receptor alternative to CD4 for HIV infection of cells in laboratory culture. The affinity between soluble glycoprotein 120 and galactosyl ceramide was found to be strong, suggesting that this receptor might bind HIV rather tightly to the cell. Galactosyl ceramide is negatively charged, and interacts via charge attraction with a region of glycoprotein 120 termed the V3 loop (corresponding to the third variable

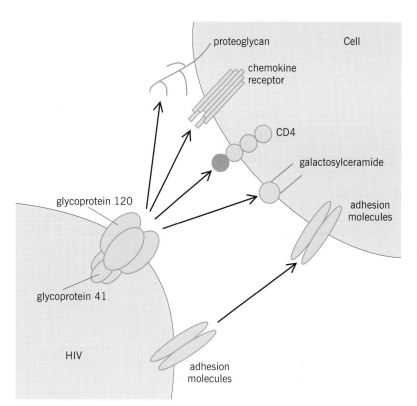

Fig. 1. Different cellular receptors used by HIV for attaching to target cells.

domain of glycoprotein 120) that has, in many HIV-1 strains, a strong positive charge. However, there is no conclusive evidence that HIV uses this molecule to bind and infect cells during a natural infection; therefore, it is unlikely to function as a physiologically relevant receptor. Many cell types carry a family of molecules called proteoglycans on their surfaces, which in turn express negatively charged carbohydrates, termed heparans. Because of strong negative charge, heparans have an attraction for positively charged molecules. It has been shown that glycoprotein 120 can interact directly with cell-surface heparans (Fig. 1). Removal of these molecules reduces the ability of HIV to attach to cells in a cell type–dependent manner; for some cells the relative contribution of heparans is minor, while for others heparan appears to be the principal binding receptor.

Another family of cell-surface molecules implicated in HIV binding comprises adhesion molecules. These allow close contact between cells that need to communicate, and are found on many different cell types, including those of the immune system. As described above, the virus envelope is of cellular origin, and it contains adhesion molecules derived from the infected cell (Fig. 1). These virion-associated adhesion molecules have the capacity to bind cell-associated adhesion molecules, and therefore can reinforce virus-cell binding. As is the case for galactosyl ceramide and the heparans, adhesion molecule expression is cell type dependent, meaning that the contribution of these molecules will depend on the cell type in which the virus multiplied, and on the cell type that the virus is attempting to infect. Finally, a family of cell-surface proteins called chemokine receptors, which bind small soluble protein messengers called chemokines, has recently been shown to be important in HIV tropism and infection. At present it is not clear whether these molecules mediate HIV attachment to target cells, whether they allow entry of the virus into the cell, or both.

Implications for therapy. Since binding of HIV to its cellular receptor is the initial step in infection of a target cell, interference with this would save the cell from infection and probable early death, and prevent production of new virus particles. Several possible ways of interfering with virus binding have been explored over the last few years. Soluble CD4 was considered to be a way to compete with cell-surface CD4 for virus binding. Soluble CD4 has been tested not only in the laboratory but also in the clinic with disappointing results. The problem was that the affinity between the soluble CD4 and virus glyco-protein 120 was too low to effectively compete with cell-associated CD4. Novel forms of soluble CD4 are currently being developed that may bind virus more strongly and thus be more efficient competitors. Antibodies are soluble protein molecules that are produced by the body to combat infection and that bind specifically to invading microorganisms such as viruses. Antibodies to HIV have been found to interfere with virus binding to cells in the laboratory. Several different antibodies are currently being tested in the laboratory and clinic for their ability to prevent or reduce infection in humans. Ultimately, the resolution of the structure of glycoprotein 120 may allow for development of small molecules that are able to insert into the CD4 binding site and inhibit virus binding to target cells.

Quentin Sattentau

Biological Basis of Natural Resistance to Virus

Researchers have known since 1984 that human immunodeficiency virus enters cells by docking onto a receptor protein known as CD4, located on immune cell surfaces. Two years later, it was found that CD4 alone was insufficient for HIV infectivity; some unknown cofactor, found only in human cells, was also required. The identity of the cofactor remained unknown despite much investigation. In 1996, the cofactor of CD4 was distinguished as, for at least some strains of HIV, a member of the seven-transmembrane, G-protein-coupled receptor family, and more specifically a member of the chemokine receptor family. This cofactor, termed fusin, mediated entry of T-cell-lines-adapted (T-tropic) HIV-1 strains, but not of macrophage tropic (M-tropic) strains. M-tropic strains that infected monocytes, macrophages, and primary T cells predominate during the asymptomatic phase of the disease, and are responsible for the virus transmission. It was demonstrated that CCR5, a new cofactor belonging to the seven-transmembrane chemokine receptor family, is

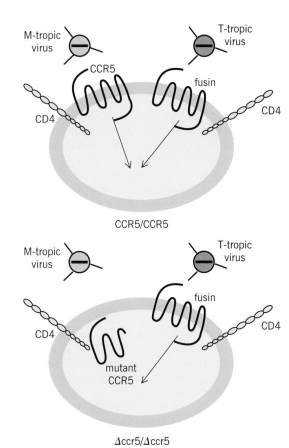

Fig. 2. HIV infection of target cells is dependent on CD4 and chemokine receptors. Macrophage-tropic (M-tropic) viruses bind to CD4 on the surface of target cells via the virus envelope glycoproteins. Entry of the virus into the cell is then dependent on the chemokine receptor CCR5. Similarly, T-cell-line-tropic (T-tropic) viruses bind to CD4 and are then dependent on the CCR-like molecule fusin for entry into cells. In people who are homozygous for a mutation of CCR5, T-tropic viruses can still enter target cells via fusin, but entry of M-tropic viruses is impaired.

the major cofactor for primary macrophage-tropic HIV-1 strains (**Fig. 2**).

Chemokine receptor CCR5. Some individuals remain uninfected despite repeated exposure to HIV. A proportion of these exposed, uninfected individuals results from the relatively low risk of contamination after a single contact with the virus. However, it has been postulated that truly resistant individuals do exist. In fact, lymphocytes expressing CD4 (CD4+) isolated from exposed, uninfected individuals are highly resistant to infection by primary M-tropic, but not T-tropic, HIV-1 strains. Also, peripheral blood mononuclear cells from different donors are not infected equally with various HIV-1 strains. Given the role played by CCR5 in the fusion event that mediates infection by M-tropic viruses, researchers have postulated that variants of CCR5 could be responsible for the relative or absolute resistance to HIV-1 infection exhibited by some individuals, and possibly for the variability of disease progression in infected patients. In order to test this hypothesis, researchers have sequenced CCR5 genes from deoxyribonucleic acid (DNA) of different donors. The frequent allele corresponded to the known CCR5 sequence, while the minor one displayed a 32-base pair deletion within the CCR5 gene, in a region corresponding to the second extracellular loop of the receptor. The deletion causes a frame shift, which is expected to result in premature termination of CCR5 protein. The protein encoded by this mutant allele ($\Delta ccr5$) therefore lacks the last three transmembrane segments of the receptor.

Truncated receptor Δccr5. The truncated protein has been tested for its capacity to function as an HIV-1 cofactor, and its ability to support membrane fusion by primary M-tropic virus. In contrast to CCR5, the truncated receptor ($\Delta ccr5$) fails to support either membrane fusion or virus infection. Individuals expressing the truncated receptor ($\Delta ccr5$) have been identified, and peripheral blood mononuclear cells (lymphocytes and monocytes) of these people were tested for the capacity to be infected by HIV viruses. These cells were found to be infectable by T-tropic, but not by M-tropic, HIV-1 strains. Using two informative families, it was confirmed that the CCR5 gene and its $\Delta ccr5$ variant are alternative forms of the same gene (alleles), and are segregated in a normal mendelian fashion. Interestingly, both a cohort of DNA samples originating from West and Central Africa (collected from Zaire, Burkina Fasso, Cameroun, Senegal, and Benin) and samples of Japanese and Venezuelan origin did not reveal a single $\Delta ccr5$ mutant allele, suggesting that this form is absent in Africa, Venezuela, and Japan. The consequences of the existence of a null allele of CCR5 in the normal Caucasian population were then considered in terms of susceptibility to infection by HIV-1. If, as predicted, CCR5 plays a major (not redundant) role in the entry of most primary virus strains into cells, individuals holding two copies of $\Delta ccr5$ should be particularly resistant to HIV-1 challenge. The frequency of homozygous $\Delta ccr5$ genotype should therefore be significantly lower in HIV-1 infected patients, and increased in exposed, uninfected individuals. These hypotheses were tested and confirmed by genotyping a large number of seropositive Caucasian individuals. The absence of individuals homozygous for the $\Delta ccr5$ allele in the seropositive Caucasian population shows that homozygous individuals are highly resistant to HIV-1 infection. Heterozygotes could also be partially protected, although this has to be clarified further. The heterozygotes for this mutation were found to be more frequent among slow progressors in some cohorts.

Outlook. The discovery of the biological basis of natural resistance to HIV describes the first human genetic polymorphism that may affect the spread of HIV-1. This is a big step in understanding the critical relationship between chemokine receptors and HIV infection. These observations suggest that blockade of CCR5 receptor by peptides, antibodies, or pharmacologic means could interfere with the binding of macrophage-tropic HIV-1 to CCR5 receptor without significant toxicity. The potential implications for the design of therapeutic and vaccine strategies based on these observations are of considerable interest.

For background information *see* ACQUIRED IMMUNE DEFICIENCY SYNDROME (AIDS); CELL (BIOLOGY); CELL MEMBRANES; CELLULAR ADHESION; CELLULAR IMMUNOLOGY; RETROVIRUS; VIRUS in the McGraw-Hill Encyclopedia of Science & Technology.   Michel Samson

Bibliography. M. Dean et al., Genetic resistance of HIV-1 infection and progression to AIDS by a deletion allele of the CCR5 structural gene, *Science*, 273:1856, 1996; D. S. Dimitrov and C. C. Broder, *HIV and Membrane Receptors*, 1997; R. Liu et al., Homozygous defect in HIV-1 coreceptor accounts for resistance of some multiply-exposed individuals to HIV-1 infection, *Cell*, 86:367, 1996; M. Samson et al., Resistance to HIV-1 infection of Caucasian individuals bearing mutant alleles of the CCR5 chemokine receptor gene, *Nature*, 382:722, 1996.

Hydrogen

Hydrogen has been the prototypical system of the insulator-to-metal transition ever since it was predicted in 1935 that the insulating molecular solid would transform to a conducting monatomic solid at sufficiently high pressure and density at absolute zero temperature (0 K). So far, metallization of solid hydrogen has not been observed. However, fluid hydrogen has recently been observed to become metallic at pressures above 140 gigapascals (1.4 megabars) and temperatures of about 3000 K (4900°F).

Solid hydrogen. The prediction of a transformation to a monatomic solid was based on the fact that at sufficiently high density the internal energy of the monatomic solid would become less than that of the diatomic one and the monatomic solid would then become the stable phase. The monatomic solid would have one electron per unit cell and, thus, a half-filled conduction band typical of a metal. Substantial pressure is required to effect this transition because solid molecular hydrogen is an insulator with a wide band gap (15 eV) at ambient pressure. The original theoretical estimate of the required pressure was 25 GPa (0.25 Mbar). Since that time, the estimated pressure has ranged up to 2000 GPa (20 Mbar) at 0 K. The best recent theoretical estimate is 300 GPa (3 Mbar). Extrapolation of recent pressure-volume experimental data at static pressures up to 120 GPa (1.2 Mbar) in a diatomic solid phase yields a predicted dissociative transition pressure of 620 GPa (6.2 Mbar). Metallization in the solid has not been observed by optical measurements up to 250 GPa (2.5 Mbar).

It is also possible that metallization occurs within the diatomic solid, without a transition to the monatomic phase. In this case, metallization would be achieved by reduction to zero of the electronic energy gap separating filled valence-band states from the empty conduction-band states. Such a metallization process within the molecular solid phase has been predicted to occur at lower pressures than is the case in which metallization is accompanied by the transition to the monatomic phase. However, the pressure required for metallization depends on crystal structure, and the structure at metallization at 0 K is not known.

The basic conclusion is that solid hydrogen at temperatures below 300 K (80°F) has not been observed experimentally to transform to the metallic state and the pressure required to do so is not known, although it must be greater than 250 GPa (2.5 Mbar).

Fluid hydrogen. The failure of solid hydrogen to metallize at static high pressures up to 250 GPa (2.5 Mbar) is thought to be a result of phenomena that occur in the ordered solid, namely, structural and molecular orientational phase transitions. Thus, a logical place to look for hydrogen metallization is in the disordered fluid at temperatures just above melting at high pressures. In this case, metallization is expected when pressure reduces the band gap, E_g, to approximately $k_B T$, where k_B is Boltzmann's constant and T is the absolute temperature. That is, pressure reduces the electronic energy gap, and disorder and temperature fill it in. When E_g is approximately $k_B T$, a metallic density of states is achieved and the electronic system has a Fermi surface, as required for a metal.

Hydrogen in the fluid phase at high pressures and temperatures is also of great importance for planetary science because of the cosmological abundance of hydrogen. About 90% of all atoms in the universe are hydrogen. Jupiter and Saturn contain over 400 earth masses, most of which is hydrogen. Jupiter-size planets now being discovered close to nearby stars probably contain massive amounts of hydrogen as well. The interiors of giant planets are at high pressures and high temperatures in the fluid phase because of their large mass and low thermal conduc-

tivity. Magnetic fields of giant planets are produced by the convective motion of electrically conducting fluid hydrogen by dynamo action. Thus, the electrical conductivity characteristic of metallic hydrogen is needed to understand the magnetic fields of the giant planets.

Nonzero temperatures. It is extremely difficult to produce a stable hydrogen sample at high temperatures. Hydrogen is so mobile that when it is heated statically it rapidly diffuses into the solid walls of the sample holder. Thus, it is essential that hydrogen be heated for only a very brief time, say about 100 nanoseconds, which is sufficiently fast that hydrogen cannot be lost by rapid diffusion. Heating hydrogen in such a brief time is extremely difficult. For example, hydrogen at accessible static high pressures is an insulator and optically transparent. Thus, pulsed laser heating cannot be used without adding a dark optical absorber, which would probably react chemically with the surrounding hydrogen at high temperatures. Shock compression is ideal because the sample is compressed to high pressures and simultaneously heated adiabatically and uniformly. In this way a stable hydrogen sample was achieved at temperatures of about 3000 K (4900°F) and pressures of about 100 GPa (1 Mbar). A melting temperature of 1500 K (2200°F) is estimated at 140 GPa (1.4 Mbar), the observed pressure of metallization. A hydrogen temperature of 3000 K (4900°F) is relatively low because the equivalent energy is 0.26 eV, which is much smaller than the energy gap at ambient pressure (15 eV), and is comparable to the zero-point energy of the molecule (0.3 eV). The time duration of about 100 ns is more than sufficient to obtain thermal equilibrium, as well as the equilibrated configuration of electrical current flow.

Experiment. Recently, an experiment was set up to study fluid hydrogen at high pressures (**Fig. 1**). A layer of liquid hydrogen or deuterium was compressed dynamically by a high-pressure shock wave reverberating between two stiff, electrically insulat-

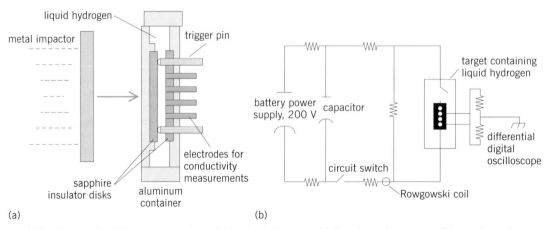

Fig. 1. Electrical conductivity measurements on fluid metallic hydrogen. (a) Experimental apparatus. Trigger pins activate the recording system. (b) Electronic circuit to which the four electrodes are connected. The differential digital oscilloscope has 1-ns time resolution. All cables are coaxial.

ing sapphire (single-crystal Al_2O_3) disks, or anvils. The two sapphire anvils were contained between two aluminum plates, which were part of a cryostat at 20 K ($-424°F$). The sapphire disks were 25 mm (1 in.) in diameter, and the liquid hydrogen layer between the sapphire disks was 0.5 mm (0.02 in.) thick. The compression was initiated by a shock wave generated when a metal plate launched by a two-stage light-gas gun at velocities up to about 7 km/s (15,000 mi/h) impacted one of the aluminum plates. This shock was amplified when it was transmitted into the first sapphire disk. The initial shock pressure in the liquid hydrogen was about 30 times lower than the shock incident from the sapphire (**Fig. 2***a*). The shock then reverberated quasi-isentropically between the two anvils. The pressure-density states achieved in this way (Fig. 2*b*) are relatively close to the 0 K isotherm and at much higher densities than those on the Hugoniot curve, the locus of states achieved by single-shock compression.

The electrical resistance of the hydrogen sample versus time was measured by inserting electrodes through one of the anvils (Fig. 1*a*). Either hydrogen or deuterium samples were used, depending on the final density and temperature desired. Because the initial mass densities of liquid hydrogen and deuterium differed by a factor of 2.4, their final shock-compressed densities and temperatures also differed substantially, with hydrogen giving lower temperatures than deuterium. The loading path, which describes the evolution of pressure with time (Fig. 2*a*), consisted of an initial weak shock followed by the quasi-isentrope associated with the successive reverberations. This quasi-isentrope is represented by a ramp over a period of about 50 ns from the pressure $P_f/30$ associated with the initial weak shock up to P_f, where P_f is the incident shock pressure in sapphire. After reverberation was complete, the pressure P_f was held for about 100 ns. The final temperature was about one-tenth of what it would be for a single shock to the same final pressure. In order to relate measured electrical resistance to electrical resistivity, the current flow in the sample was simulated by representing the hydrogen as a three-dimensional network of resistors and solving Kirchhoff's laws with the appropriate boundary conditions. In this way the cell constant, which gives the ratio of resistance to resistivity, was calculated.

In this experiment, pressure can be determined with an uncertainty of about 1% from measurement of the impactor velocity and from previously measured shock-wave equations of state of the impactor, aluminum base plates, and sapphire anvils. However, at present there is no way to measure density and temperature in this experiment because the high-rate deformations caused by the reverberating shock render the sapphire anvil opaque. Thus, density and temperature were calculated by using two reasonable equations of state. The results did not vary significantly. That is, although use of a computational model introduces systematic uncertainties, the results are sufficiently accurate to determine the

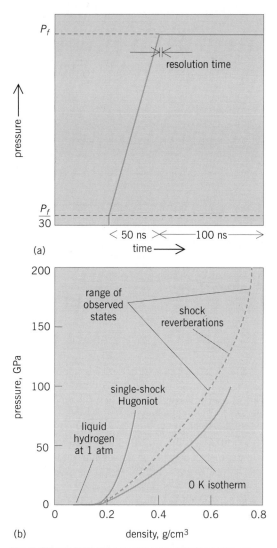

Fig. 2. Effect of rise time on pressure-density states. (*a***) Loading curve, showing evolution of pressure with time during and after shock reverberations.** P_f **is the incident shock pressure in sapphire and the final pressure in the hydrogen. The experimental resolution time is a few nanoseconds, which is small compared to the duration of the experiment. (***b***) Equation-of-state curves plotted as pressures versus densities: 0 K isotherm, points reached by shock reverberations, and single-shock Hugoniot. The range of actual states observed in the experiments is indicated. The initial point is liquid hydrogen (H₂) at pressure of 1 atm (101.3 kPa).**

cause of the slope change at 140 GPa (1.4 Mbar) observed in a graph that plots the electrical resistivity versus the final pressure, P_f (**Fig. 3**).

Semiconducting range. In the semiconducting range, 93–135 GPa (0.93–1.35 Mbar), the resistivity data were fit to the dependence of a thermally activated semiconductor. This fitting procedure yielded an expression for the density dependence of the mobility gap in the electronic density of states of the fluid. The energy gap derived in this way and k_BT are equal at a density of 0.32 mol/cm³ and a temperature of about 2600 K (4200°F), corresponding to an energy of 0.22 eV. At 0.32 mol/cm³ and 2600 K, the pressure

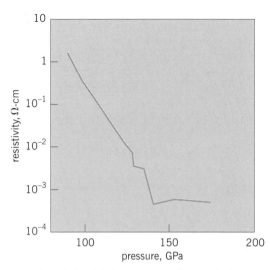

Fig. 3. Electrical resistivity of hydrogen (H_2) and deuterium (D_2) samples plotted on a logarithmic scale versus pressure. The slope change at 140 GPa (1.4 Mbar) is the transition from semiconducting to metallic fluid.

is 120 GPa (1.2 Mbar), which is close to the 140-GPa (1.4-Mbar) pressure at which the slope of the electrical resistivity changes (Fig. 3).

Metallic resistivity. At pressures of 140–180 GPa (1.4–1.8 Mbar), the measured hydrogen resistivity is essentially constant at a metallic value of 500 microohm-centimeter. This value is essentially the same as that of the fluid alkali metals cesium and rubidium undergoing the same transition at 2000 K (3100°F). This metallic resistivity of cesium, rubidium, and hydrogen is achieved at the same Mott-scaled density of $D_m^{1/3}a^* = 0.30$, where D_m is the density of hydrogen at metallization in molecules per unit volume, and a^* is the Bohr radius. The Mott-scaled density at an insulator-metal transition is roughly the ratio of the size of an atom supplying conduction electrons to the average distance between the atoms, and the value of 0.30 measured at nonzero temperatures is consistent with N. Mott's estimate of this quantity at 0 K, based on his analysis of the overlapping of charge distributions on adjacent atoms. As discussed below, hydrogen is primarily molecular H_2 in this case. The measured resistivity of 500 $\mu\Omega$-cm is reasonable because it is bracketed by simple theoretical values. For example, the maximum electrical resistivity of a metal at the calculated density of metallization is 250 $\mu\Omega$-cm. The electrical resistivity of liquid metallic hydrogen calculated in the strong-scattering free-electron model is 1500 $\mu\Omega$-cm. A preliminary calculation of the electrical resistivity using the Ziman model for a molecular liquid metal yields a resistivity of about 100 $\mu\Omega$-cm. Thus, fluid hydrogen becomes metallic at about 140 GPa (1.4 Mbar) and 3000 K (4900°F) via a continuous transition from a semiconducting to metallic fluid.

The free-electron Fermi energy of metallic fluid hydrogen is about 12 eV. Since the temperature at

metallization is equivalent to about 0.22 eV, the ratio of the actual temperature to the Fermi temperature is about 0.02, and this system is highly degenerate condensed matter.

Mostly proton-paired metal. This fluid is most likely molecular with about 5% of the hydrogen molecules dissociated into atoms at metallization. At 3000 K (4900°F) in the fluid, molecular and atomic hydrogen (H_2 and H) are probably miscible and the measured energy gap is that of the mixture. Molecular-dynamics simulations show that protons are paired transiently and exchange on the time scale of a few molecular vibrational periods, about 10^{-14} s. When averaged over times long compared to the lifetime of a pair, the system behaves as though there is an equilibrium concentration of molecules and monomers. These simulations also show that rotational energies of the transient pairs are comparable to their kinetic and vibrational energies. This picture of a fluid in which protons comprising transient pairs and monomers are continually exchanging on a dynamical time scale of about 10^{-14} s and in which characteristic times for collisions, vibrations, and rotations are comparable describes a new state of condensed matter.

For background information *see* BAND THEORY OF SOLIDS; EXCHANGE REACTION; FREE-ELECTRON THEORY OF METALS; HIGH-PRESSURE PHYSICS; HYDROGEN; JUPITER; PLANETARY PHYSICS; SHOCK WAVE in the McGraw-Hill Encyclopedia of Science & Technology.

William J. Nellis

Bibliography. W. J. Nellis, S. T. Weir, and A. C. Mitchell, Metallization and electrical conductivity of hydrogen in Jupiter, *Science*, 273:936–938, 1996; S. T. Weir, A. C. Mitchell, and W. J. Nellis, Metallization of fluid molecular hydrogen at 140 GPa (1.4 Mbar), *Phys. Rev. Lett.*, 76:1860–1863, 1996.

Hydrothermal vent

Submarine hydrothermal vent environments span the temperature range from 2°C (36°F) for ambient deep seawater to over 400°C (750°F) for some hydrothermal fluids. These high-temperature fluids remain liquid because of the hydrostatic pressure at deep-sea vent depths (2–4 km or 1–2.5 mi). The microbial world at hydrothermal vents includes organisms capable of growing at 2°C (36°F) or lower to above the boiling point of water (100°C or 212°F at atmospheric pressure). The ability to grow above 60°C (140°F) is confined to prokaryotes (cells that lack a nucleus) divided into two groups: moderate thermophiles that have maximal growth temperatures of 50–60°C (122–140°F), and hyperthermophiles that grow optimally at 80°C (176°F) or higher with maximal growth temperatures of 90°C (194°F) or higher. The highest temperature for growth by a pure culture (*Pyrolobus fumaris*) is 113°C (235°F), although there is some evidence that deep-sea vent hyperthermophiles may grow and survive at higher temperatures under elevated pressures.

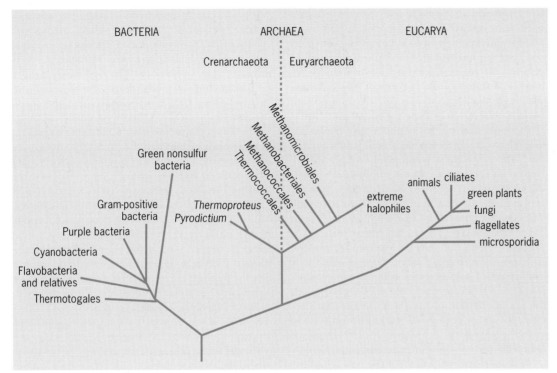

Rooted universal phylogenetic tree based on 16S rRNA sequence analyses, showing the domains Bacteria, Archaea, and Eucarya, and the Crenarchaeota and Euryarchaeota kingdoms within the Archaea. *(After C. R. Woese et al., Towards a natural system of organisms: Proposal for the domains Archaea, Bacteria, and Eucarya, Proc. Nat. Acad. Sci. USA, 87:4576–4579, 1990)*

Thermophiles and hyperthermophiles. Thermophiles fall within the extremophiles, a group that includes microorganisms capable of growing in very acidic or alkaline environments, in brines, and at high pressures. Many extremophiles, including most hyperthermophiles, belong to the domain known as Archaea. Although the archaea have many characteristics similar to the bacteria, their evolutionary location on a phylogenetic tree of living organisms (see **illus.**), based on differences in nucleotide sequences of 16S ribosomal ribonucleic acid, indicates that they are distinct from bacteria. Another indication is that the oldest extant organisms in both the bacteria (Thermotogales) and the archaea (*Pyrodictium*, *Thermoproteus*, and Thermococcales) are hyperthermophiles. This implies that the first microorganisms on Earth would have also been hyperthermophilic.

The most common hyperthermophiles isolated from hydrothermal vent environments include heterotrophs and methanogens. Both are inhibited by oxygen and are referred to as obligate anaerobes. Most of the heterotrophs are pleomorphic cocci and require elemental sulfur, which they reduce to hydrogen sulfide. Marine hyperthermophiles require salt. Among the hyperthermophilic species tested, hydrostatic pressure equivalent to the pressure of the depth of isolation can raise both the optimal and maximal growth temperatures.

Ecology of hyperthermophiles. Hyperthermophiles have been isolated from many of the habitats associated with hydrothermal vents, including sulfide structures that form around source sites of hydrothermal fluids, hot and warm waters, microbial mats, hot sediments, and guts and surfaces of animals that live on sulfides. One of the most extensively studied hyperthermophilic habitats at submarine hydrothermal vent sites is the black smoker, sometimes referred to as a chimney since the particle-rich fluid emissions look like smoke, or related sulfide structures found at most deep-sea vent sites. These structures form when metal sulfides precipitate from hot anaerobic fluids on contact with cold oxidic seawater. In addition to the small chimneys, extremely large sulfide structures, about 45 m (148 ft) high and more than 20 m (65 ft) in diameter, are found on the Juan de Fuca Ridge in the northeastern Pacific Ocean. Characteristic of these large structures is the presence of sulfidic ledges called flanges. Underneath these flanges are hot hydrothermal fluid (>300°C or 570°F) pools, a portion of which diffuses upward through the ledges, creating internal thermal and chemical gradients. The remaining hot fluid flows over the edge of the flange, mixing with cold seawater to create small smokers. It has been estimated that more than 100 million hyperthermophilic archaea cells per gram of sulfide live in discrete mineral layers within these flanges. The hyperthermophiles isolated from these layers include sulfur-dependent Thermococcales and methanogens. The sulfidic surfaces of chimneys and flanges usually harbor high numbers of several species of polychaete worms, including *Alvinella* and *Paralvinella* that have been observed to survive exposure to near-boiling-water temperatures (at 1 atmosphere of pressure) and thus may dwell at the highest temperature of any animal. Heterotrophic hyperthermophiles have been isolated from the guts of these animals, suggesting that these worms may derive a portion of their nutrition from hyperthermophiles.

The presence of thermophilic and hyperthermophilic microorganisms has been demonstrated in the deep subsurface environment. Evidence includes the presence of hyperthermophiles in deep oil wells, in deep cores from oceanic sediments, and in fluids released from the sea floor following volcanic eruptions. Eight new eruptions have been observed since 1982. Massive amounts of microbially produced white floc material referred to as snow have been observed at many of these sites. It is estimated that subsurface environments may penetrate to depths greater than 1000 m (3280 ft) through the porous portion of the Earth's crust. Few data exist on the physiology of microorganisms living in the sub-sea floor, although there are reports of hydrogen- and iron-utilizing microorganisms.

Many mysteries remain about the ecology of hyperthermophiles in hydrothermal vent environments. For example, little is known about the sources of organic nutrients, ammonia, phosphorus, and sulfur, which are required by most deep-sea vent hyperthermophiles, or the phylogenetic diversity of these organisms as a function of habitat. The significance of hyperthermophiles to the geochemistry of sea-floor sulfide structures and subsurface crustal environments is completely unknown.

Isolation and cultivation of thermophiles. Sampling at submarine hydrothermal vent environments requires the use of submersibles. Hot water is sampled by the submersible using titanium syringes. Smoker sulfides and flange solids are sampled by breaking apart the structures with an arm of the submersible. Solid samples, including animal specimens and sediment cores, are placed in an insulated box attached to the submersible.

Thermophiles isolated from hydrothermal vent environments are anaerobic. It is advisable to inoculate samples into special anaerobic tubes capped with gas-impermeable stoppers. However, most hyperthermophilic species are generally stable in the presence of oxygen, at least for a short time, if temperatures are below their minimum for growth. Hyperthermophiles have been cultured from cold seawater weeks after being released into the ocean during a deep-sea volcanic eruption.

Most heterotrophic hyperthermophiles can grow on media containing various protein preparations, including soy and casein, supplemented with yeast extract, which provides essential trace nutrients such as vitamins. The methane-producing hyperthermophiles will grow on a sea-salt-based medium with carbon dioxide and hydrogen or, in some cases, will use simple organic compounds such as a formate instead of carbon dioxide. Hyperthermophile cultures are usually enriched at incubation temperatures of 80–90°C (176–194°F). Many species will divide every 25–30 min at their optimal temperature and reach densities greater than 100 million per milliliter.

Thermophiles and the origin of life. The universal phylogenetic tree (see illus.) suggests that the oldest extant organisms are hyperthermophilic. By inference, the common ancestor to all living organisms was also hyperthermophilic. The implications are that the earliest microbial ecosystems on Earth were thermophilic and the setting for the origin of life was hot. This is a contentious issue, since different models of the early Earth indicate different temperatures that range from frigid (ice-ocean) to hot conditions (100°C or 212°F) during the first 600 million years. However, most estimates of global temperatures predict high enough carbon dioxide levels during the first 600 million years to result in significant greenhouse heating. During this period the Earth was relentlessly bombarded by large asteroid bodies (bolides), some of which would have been large enough to evaporate a 3-km-deep (2-mi) ocean and exterminate aquatic and terrestrial life; the bombardment significantly delayed the removal of carbon dioxide and the weathering of continental rocks and thus delayed cooling. An unavoidable conclusion is that the deep-sea or sub-sea-floor zones would have been the least negatively impacted environments on the early Earth, increasing the likelihood that they were also habitats for the earliest microbial communities. Hydrothermal activity during the first 500 million years of Earth history was significantly elevated over present levels, suggesting that thermophilic or hyperthermophilic microbial communities, with metabolisms similar to hyperthermophiles that thrive in present-day vent environments, were among the earliest organisms to evolve.

It has also been suggested that the sub-sea-floor environment associated with hydrothermal systems would have offered the greatest range of chemical and physical conditions for initiating the sequence of chemical and biochemical reactions leading to the origin of carbon-based life.

For background information *see* ARCHAEA; BACTERIA; HYDROTHERMAL VENT; LIFE, ORIGIN OF; MARINE ECOLOGY in the McGraw-Hill Encyclopedia of Science & Technology.   John A. Baross

Bibliography. J. A. Baross and J. W. Deming, Growth at high temperatures: Isolation and taxonomy, physiology, and ecology, in D. M. Karl (ed.), *The Microbiology of Deep-Sea Hydrothermal Vents*, 1995; T. Gold, The deep, hot biosphere, *Proc. Nat. Acad. Sci. USA*, 89:6045–6049, 1992; S. V. Liu et al., Thermophilic Fe(III)-reducing bacteria from the deep subsurface: The evolutionary implications, *Science*, 277:1106–1109, 1997; N. H. Sleep et al., Annihilation of ecosystems by large asteroid impacts on the early Earth, *Nature*, 342:139–142, 1989; K. O. Stetter, Hyperthermophilic prokaryotes, *FEMS Microbiol. Rev.*, 18:149–158, 1996; T. O. Stevens and J. P. McKinley, Lithoautotrophic microbial ecosystems in deep basalt aquifers, *Science*, 270:450–454, 1995; C. R. Woese et al., Towards a natural system of organisms: Proposal for the domains Archaea, Bacteria, and Eucarya, *Proc. Nat. Acad. Sci. USA*, 87:4576–4579, 1990.

Icing

Aircraft icing encompasses a range of conditions during which frozen precipitation forms on an aircraft. It is usually separated into two broad classifications, ground icing and in-flight icing. Icing can compromise flight safety by affecting the performance, stability, and control of the aircraft, and as a result the ability of the pilot to maintain the desired flight path. The primary effect of icing is its adverse impact on the aerodynamics of the airplane. Ice accretion results in increased drag and reduced maximum lift which reduce the performance and safety of the flight. While ice does add weight to the aircraft, the amount is usually a very small percentage of the aircraft gross weight, and its effects are insignificant compared to the aerodynamic effects.

Ice accretion. Ground icing occurs when the aircraft is on the ground, and becomes significant when it affects the aircraft's ability to take off. This form of icing occurs when ice, snow, or freezing rain collects on the upper surfaces of the aircraft or when frost forms on the aircraft.

The formation of in-flight icing is much more complex. In-flight icing forms when an aircraft flies through a cloud of supercooled precipitation. Icing clouds usually contain water droplets with diameters of 2–50 micrometers and have concentrations, or liquid water content, of up to 2.5 grams of water per cubic meter of air. Water droplets approach the aircraft, approximately following the air streamlines. Near the surface of the aircraft, large changes in velocity exist. The droplets, because of their inertia, cannot change velocity rapidly enough to follow the air around the aircraft, and strike or impinge on the aircraft surface. Because of the role played by the aerodynamic velocity gradients and the droplet size in this process, more droplets impinge when they are large and the forward-facing aircraft surface has a small leading-edge radius. Ice forms on the leading or forward-facing edges of the wings, tail, antennas, windshield, radome, engine inlet, and so forth.

Once the droplets have impinged, the freezing process determines the actual size and shape of the ice accretion. The two most common types of ice accretions are rime ice (**Fig. 1***a*) and glaze ice (Fig. 1*b*). Rime ice occurs at low temperature, low liquid water content, and low flight velocity so that the droplets freeze on impact. As a result, rime ice grows into the direction of the incoming droplets and forms an opaque, streamlined shape. Glaze ice occurs at temperatures near freezing with high liquid water content and high flight velocity. In this type of accretion, the impinging water droplets do not freeze on impact with the surface. Liquid water forms as a

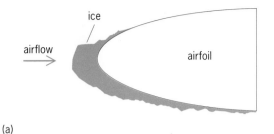

(a)

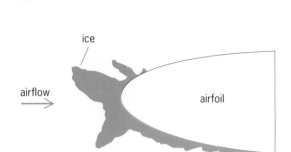

(b)

Fig. 1. Ice accretion on an airfoil leading edge. (*a*) Rime ice. (*b*) Glaze ice. *(NASA)*

film or as hemispherical beads on the surface and eventually freezes, resulting in ice that is clear in color. The formation of beads, and sometimes larger ice roughness due to water flowing on the surface, augments the droplet impingement and accretion process, causing the large ice protrusions referred to as horns (Fig. 1*b*). Mixed ice accretions contain features of both rime and glaze ice, with glaze accretion occurring near the leading-edge stagnation point (where the air is stationary with respect to the wing), and rime ice accretion occurring farther back on the airfoil.

Droplets much larger than 50 μm may exist in some meteorological situations, including freezing drizzle and freezing rain. These larger drops are referred to as supercooled large droplets. Ice formations from these droplets can extend very far back on the wing or other aircraft components and can pose serious safety hazards.

Aerodynamics. Icing affects the propulsion system by reducing the thrust of the engine and thus the ability of the aircraft to climb and maintain speed or altitude. This thrust reduction is usually due to the restriction of airflow into the engine by ice formation in the carburetor of piston-engine-powered light aircraft or ice formation on the inlet of larger jet aircraft. On a propeller-driven aircraft, ice formation on the propeller can also result in reduced thrust.

Probably the most dangerous way that ice acts on an aircraft is through its effect on the aerodynamics, which results in degraded performance and control. Small amounts of ice or frost add roughness to the airplane surfaces. The roughness increases the friction of the air over the surface; this is called skin

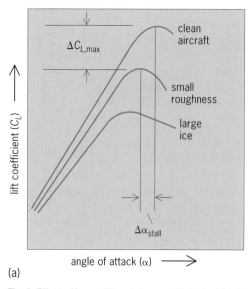

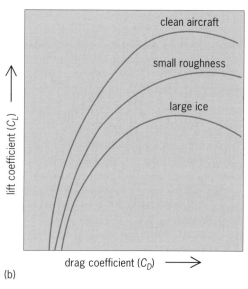

Fig. 2. Effect of ice on lift and drag coefficients. (*a*) Lift coefficient (*C_L*) versus angle of attack (*α*). $\Delta C_{L,max}$ is the reduction in maximum lift coefficient. $\Delta \alpha_{stall}$ is the reduction in the angle of attack at which stall occurs. Both are shown for small roughness case only. (*b*) Lift coefficient versus drag coefficient (*C_D*). (*After Effects of Adverse Weather on Aerodynamics, Proceedings of the AGARD Fluid Dynamics Specialists Meeting, AGARD-CP-496, 1991*)

friction. Higher-than-usual levels of skin friction cause additional drag and also affect the lift (**Fig. 2**). The effect of small ice accretions or frost on lift is a reduction in the maximum lift coefficient and a reduction in the airplane angle of attack at which it is reached. Higher drag is also seen, which reduces the ability of the aircraft to climb and reduces its maximum speed. Reduced maximum lift coefficient increases the stall speed of the aircraft and thus increases the takeoff distance. Safety is compromised if ice is present and landing and takeoff speeds are not increased, since the margin between flight speed and stall speed is reduced.

Large accretions can drastically alter the shape of the wing (Fig. 1). Then, in addition to skin friction, flow separation results in a further reduction in aerodynamic performance of the aircraft. For larger ice accretions, there is a larger reduction in maximum lift coefficient and a larger increase in drag coefficient (Fig. 2). Large ice accretions may also reduce the lift coefficient at angles of attack below stall.

Aircraft control can be seriously affected by ice accretion. Ice accretion on the tail can lead to reduced elevator effectiveness, reducing the longitudinal control (nose up and down) of the aircraft. In some situations, the tail can stall or lose lift prematurely, resulting in the aircraft pitching nose down. Similarly, ice on the wing ahead of the aileron can result in roll upset. Ice is often asymmetric and affects one wing more than another. This leads to unexpected roll, which can be difficult to control. For aircraft with unpowered controls, the pilot directly opposes the hinge moment produced by aerodynamic forces through the force applied to the control wheel. The ice-induced flow separation causes a redistribution of the air pressure on the

wing or tail surface, which results in a large change in hinge moment and, therefore, in the control force required to maintain the desired flight condition. Both tail stall and roll upset are thought to be the cause of recent aircraft icing accidents.

Ice protection. All large aircraft and many light aircraft are equipped with in-flight ice protection systems to reduce the effect of ice. Ice protection systems are classified as de-ice or anti-ice systems. De-ice systems allow some ice to accrete, and then they periodically remove the ice. The most common system is the pneumatic boot, in which inflatable tubes are placed on the wing leading edge or other surfaces. The inflating boot expands, breaking the bond between the ice and the surface. The ice fractures into small pieces, which are carried downstream by aerodynamic forces and away from the aircraft. Anti-ice systems prevent ice from forming either by heating the surface above 0°C (32°F) or through the use of freezing-point depressants. The most common systems are electrothermal, used to protect small surfaces, and hot-air systems, used on most jet aircraft where engine bleed air is available. Wing and tail leading edges, engine inlet lips, propellers, air data system components, and windshields are typically ice protected.

Ground icing is usually dealt with by ground-based de-icing systems. Freezing-point depressant fluids are applied to the upper surface of the aircraft to remove ice and frost, and a coating remains to prevent the formation of additional ice. The fluid is effective for some period of time after application, referred to as holdover time, which depends on the type of fluid, atmospheric temperature, and rate of precipitation. The fluid is designed to flow off the aircraft wing due to aerodynamic shear during takeoff so that the fluid itself does not act as surface roughness and reduce the performance and safety of the flight.

Supercooled large droplets. Until very recently, aircraft ice protection systems were tested and certified only for icing cloud droplet sizes between 2 and 50 μm. The area of the aircraft to be protected was set by the impingement location of these drops. However, during the investigation of a commuter aircraft accident which occurred in 1994, the probable cause was determined to be the resulting aerodynamic effect of ice accretion due to supercooled large droplets, which have diameters from 50 to 500 μm. Supercooled large droplets impinge much farther back from the leading edge and can cause ice to accrete aft of the ice protection systems. Research is under way to characterize the atmosphere, improve computer models, understand aerodynamic effects, and improve ice protection systems for the supercooled-large-droplet icing environment.

For background information *see* AERODYNAMIC FORCE; AERODYNAMICS; AERONAUTICAL METEOROLOGY; CLOUD PHYSICS in the McGraw-Hill Encyclopedia of Science & Technology.   Michael B. Bragg

Bibliography. M. B. Bragg et al., Effect of underwing frost on a transport aircraft airfoil at flight Reynolds number, *J. Aircraft*, 31:1372–1379, 1994; A. Heinrich et al., *Aircraft Icing Handbook*, DOT/FAA/CT-88/8-1, 1991; A. Khodadoust and M. B. Bragg, Aerodynamics of a finite wing with simulated ice, *J. Aircraft*, 32:137–144, 1995; *Proceedings of the FAA International Conference on Aircraft Inflight Icing*, DOT/FAA/AR-96/81, vol. 2, 1996.

Immunization

The prophylactic use of vaccines has contributed significantly to the decrease in morbidity and mortality associated with many common infections. Diseases such as measles, polio, and tetanus have been largely eliminated from most developed countries, and since about 1950 their incidence has been declining globally because of widespread vaccination programs. However, with the AIDS pandemic and the appearance of antibiotic-resistant bacteria, humankind is once again challenged with developing vaccines to combat both human and veterinary pathogens. Recently a new class of vaccines has been developed, composed not of living organisms or purified proteins as are conventional vaccines, but of nucleic acids.

Advantages of DNA immunization. Deoxyribonucleic acid (DNA) vaccines offer many of the advantages sought in an ideal vaccine. They are relatively cheap, easy to produce, heat stable, simple to administer, and when lyophilized have an unlimited shelf life. However, questions regarding their efficacy and safety for widespread human use remain unanswered. Successful vaccination hinges upon the ability of a vaccine to evoke a strong and appropriate immune response capable of protecting the host from disease if the pathogen is encountered later.

Protection against extracellularly replicating bacteria requires a strong antibody response, whereas protection against most viruses and some intracellularly replicating bacteria is mediated predominantly by cytotoxic T lymphocytes. Conventional human vaccines consist of attenuated live or killed pathogens, or pathogen-derived proteins. The replication of live vaccines within the vaccinee results in the induction of strong cytotoxic T-cell and antibody responses. Some live vaccines can regain pathogenicity during growth, and even nonpathogenic forms pose a danger to immunocompromised individuals. Killed vaccines or purified proteins cannot replicate or revert to a more pathogenic form, so they pose little risk to the vaccinee. Although killed vaccines can induce strong antibody responses, they are rather ineffective at inducing cytotoxic T cells. Both types of vaccines are costly to produce and most are heat labile, limiting their availability among developing nations where the need for vaccines is greatest. DNA vaccination results in foreign protein expression within the cells of the vaccinee, but the vaccine itself is unable to replicate. DNA vaccines offer the advantages of a live vaccine, inducing both cellular and humoral immunity combined with the safety of a killed vaccine.

Mechanisms of action of DNA vaccines. The DNA vaccines are composed of circular molecules of bacterial DNA known as plasmids into which a gene encoding an immunogenic protein has been inserted. When introduced into the body, plasmids can be taken up by certain cell types and transported to the nucleus. Eukaryotic control sequences inserted in the plasmid are recognized by the host cell's genetic machinery, which then transcribes the gene into messenger RNA (mRNA). This mRNA is exported from the nucleus and translated into protein by the host cell's ribosomes. The protein or fragments of it are complexed with a major histocompatibility molecule, exported to the cell surface, and presented to the immune system. Presentation by major histocompatibility complex (MHC) class I or class II molecules leads to the induction of cytotoxic T-cell or antibody responses, respectively. The immune response directed against the plasmid-derived protein can also act against a pathogen encoding that protein and protect against disease caused by the pathogen. It is not known why only certain types of cells take up and express plasmid DNA or how the plasmid transverses the cell and nuclear membranes. The specific cell type that presents plasmid-derived proteins to the immune system also remains unidentified. Recent evidence suggests that cells derived from bone marrow precursors play a critical role in the induction of immune responses to plasmid DNA vaccines.

Modes of delivery of DNA. Naked plasmid DNA can be injected intradermally or intramuscularly. By using a gene gun, DNA can be dried onto submicrometer-sized gold beads and propelled through the surface of the skin by an explosive or electrical charge. Plasmid DNA can also be embedded into a protective biodegradable matrix and taken orally. Immune responses against plasmid proteins have also been detected when lipid-coated plasmids are administered intravenously or intranasally. Gene expression from plasmids delivered by these methods has been observed in skeletal and smooth muscle (intramuscular and intravenous), keratinocytes (intradermal), endothelial cells lining blood vessels (intravenous), alveolar cells in the lung (intranasal), and specialized antigen-presenting dendritic cells (intradermal and oral). Although a wide variety of cell types can take up and express foreign DNA, with the exception of dendritic cells, their ability to effectively present antigens and stimulate immune responses has not been shown.

Immune responses to DNA. Animal studies have proven that plasmid DNA can provoke protective immune responses against a number of viral, bacterial, and protozoan pathogens as well as certain forms of cancer. The types of immune responses induced by DNA immunization appear to depend upon the method of DNA delivery. In the influenza virus model system, intradermal or intramuscular injection of naked DNA in saline leads to a Th1 T-helper cell response and antibodies of the immunoglobulin IgG2a subclass. In contrast, gene-gun immunization results in a Th2 helper cell response and antibodies of the IgG1 subclass. Reimmunization by an alternative method does not alter the predominant T-helper or antibody responses. The mechanism responsible for this skewing of T-helper and antibody responses remains unknown. It has been suggested that different antigen-presenting cells or different mechanisms of DNA uptake may lead to the production of cytokines that promote either a Th1 or a Th2 type of response. The uptake of plasmid following direct injection is most likely an active process, whereas transfection of cells with the gene gun is passive. The gene gun may transfect antigen-presenting cells, which may not have the capacity to spontaneously take up DNA. These cells may secrete a different cytokine repertoire than cells which can take up and express exogenous DNA.

In an attempt to engineer specific immune responses to DNA vaccines, a variety of cytokines and immunostimulatory molecules have been coexpressed from plasmids. Coadministration of a plasmid encoding an immunogenic protein along with plasmids expressing either the interleukins IL-2, IL-7, IL-10, or IL-12, or the co-stimulatory molecules B-7.1 or B-7.2 has been used in attempts to enhance cellular immune responses by providing an additional source of T-cell stimulation. Expression of granulocyte-macrophage stimulating factor has been shown to lead to an increase in antigen-specific antibody levels and cytotoxic T-cell responses against carcinoembryonic antigen and rabies virus glycoprotein. These techniques may make it possible to design future vaccines which induce exquisitely specific immune responses tailored to combat individual pathogens.

Safety of DNA immunization. As with any new scientific development, DNA immunization raises a number of safety issues that are being actively addressed. There is a need to know whether the DNA itself is capable of eliciting a damaging immune response. Specific immunostimulatory sequences found in bacterial DNA have been shown in laboratory experiments to enhance the activity of natural killer cells, promote polyclonal B-cell activation, and stimulate the release of the inflammatory cytokines interleukin-12, interferon alpha/beta, and tumor necrosis factor. In addition, certain mouse strains develop symptoms of the autoimmune disease lupus erythematosus when injected with bacterial DNA. However, there is no evidence that plasmid DNA immunization causes any injurious immune system dysfunction in healthy animals. On the contrary, certain plasmid DNA sequences may act as adjuvants, enhancing the immune response against the plasmid-encoded antigen.

One potentially serious risk of DNA immunization is that plasmid DNA will recombine with the host cell's chromosomes, disrupting key regulatory genes and causing cancer. Detectable levels of plasmid DNA can remain in the nucleus for over a year, yet integration into the host's chromosomes has been difficult to detect. There is presently no evidence that vaccinated animals have an increased risk of developing cancer. The only potential risk of DNA immunization that has been substantiated experimentally is the development of a localized antigen-specific inflammatory reaction among individuals intramuscularly injected with a plasmid encoding a viral protein to which they are already immune. The inflammation is self limiting and does not appear to result in any long-term adverse consequences to the vaccinee. It is notable that intramuscular inflammatory reactions of this type are also associated with tetanus vaccination, and although they can cause discomfort they pose little risk to the vaccinee.

Research in this field is still in its infancy. There are a number of limited human trials under way to assess the safety and effectiveness of DNA vaccines against human immunodeficiency virus (HIV), influenza, tuberculosis, and some human cancers. Although presently it seems unlikely that DNA vaccines will quickly supplant currently available human vaccines, in the future they may offer a cheaper, safer, and in some cases a more effective alternative. In addition, DNA vaccines may prove effective against pathogens for which no vaccine is currently available.

For background information *see* CELLULAR IMMUNOLOGY; CYTOKINE; DEOXYRIBONUCLEIC ACID (DNA); HISTOCOMPATIBILITY; IMMUNOLOGY; PLASMID; VACCINATION in the McGraw-Hill Encyclopedia of Science & Technology.   Daniel E. Hassett

Bibliography. D. M. Feltquate et al., Different T helper cell types and antibody isotypes generated by saline and gene gun DNA immunization, *J. Immunol.*, 158:2278–2284, 1997; D. E. Hassett and J. L. Whitton, DNA immunization, *Trends Microbiol.*,

4(8):307–311, 1996; J. J. Kim et al., In vivo engineering of a cellular immune response by coadministration of IL-12 expression vector with a DNA immunogen, *J. Immunol.*, 158:816–826, 1997; J. B. Ulmer, J. C. Sadoff, and M. Liu, DNA vaccines, *Curr. Opin. Immunol.*, 8:531–536, 1996.

Immunoselective adsorption processes

Immunoselective adsorption processes exploit biospecific interactions between antibodies and their corresponding antigens in order to separate pure high-value bioactive products from biological sources (for example, blood, food materials, and products of genetically engineering organisms). Enzymes, hormones, vaccines, interferons, and antibodies have been purified by using immunoselective adsorption processes. The purified products find applications in therapeutics, diagnostic tests, drug targeting, food immunoassays, research, and clinical examinations, and as ligands for the preparation of highly selective immunoadsorbents. Immunoassays are rapidly becoming important for the detection and quantification of components in foods such as additives, fungal and bacterial contaminants, antinutritional factors, pesticide residues, and hormones. Purified antibodies have potential use in infant formulas to prevent intestinal infections.

General principles. The technique, generally referred to as immunoaffinity adsorption or immunoaffinity chromatography, involves the immobilization (attachment) of an antibody, the ligand, to an insoluble matrix to form the bioselective adsorbent. In an affinity adsorption separation process, the mixture containing the desired product is contacted with adsorbent. The compound of interest, the adsorbate, binds to the adsorbent as a consequence of its high affinity to the ligand. The ligand-adsorbate interaction is highly specific. Other compounds are unbound and can be removed by washing. In the final step, known as elution or desorption, eluents are used to dissociate the adsorbate from the ligand, so that the adsorbate can be recovered. Eluents are generally solutions with appropriate pH, ionic strength, polarity, or other properties that can serve to detach the adsorbate from the adsorbent. High pressure may also be effective in accomplishing ligand-adsorbate dissociation. The adsorbent can be used over a number of sorption and elution cycles until its adsorption capacity diminishes to an unacceptable level.

When the ligand is coupled to a polymer in solution (for example, dextran) and an immiscible solvent is used to form two phases, the technique is called immunoaffinity partitioning. The dissolved compound is drawn to the polymer-ligand phase, while the impurities with no affinity to the ligand remain in the other phase. In immunoaffinity precipitation, a precipitate forms as noncovalent cross-links form between the product and the ligand. The product-ligand complex may be recovered through filtra-

tion or sedimentation. These immunoselective separation techniques do not involve adsorption at the surface of a solid support, but they are useful complements to immunoadsorption chromatography.

Immunoadsorbents. Immunoadsorbents are prepared by immobilizing antibodies (or antigens) to inert solid matrices (supports). The support should satisfy certain characteristics regarding its rigidity, porosity, surface chemistry, chemical stability, biocompatibility, and ease of ligand immobilization. Supports frequently used in immunoadsorption include agaroses, celluloses, polyacrylamides, porous glass, silica, and polystyrenes. The ligand attaches to a matrix as amino groups in the antibody react with active sites on the support. The support is activated to bind the ligand by treatment with cyanogen-bromide (CNBr). When the ligand is a small molecule, another compound, known as an arm, is generally used. This spacer arm attaches to the support by one end, while the other end is coupled to the ligand (**Fig. 1**). Spacer arms are usually hydrocarbon chains that minimize steric hindrance by the matrix, thereby ensuring attachment of the desired product to the absorbent. When the ligand is a large molecule such as an antibody (molecular weight around 150 kilodaltons), the use of spacer arms is not necessary.

Equipment. Immunoadsorption separation could be carried out in a batch process or continuously by using a packed column. A continuous immunoaffinity chromatography system generally includes a column; pumps; tanks for feed solutions, buffers, and washing solutions; tubing or piping and fitting; valves; an ultraviolet detector and monitor; and other instrumentation to verify safe and consistent operation of the system. Some systems include fraction collectors when several fractions are of interest, while others include only a valve to divert product from the waste stream to a collection vessel. On-line dialysis using hollow-fiber ultrafiltration is sometimes included in the system for fast separation of product from eluent. Other designs combine immunoaffinity chromatography and ultrafiltration to separate the antibody-antigen complex from impurities. Samples can be taken automatically and analyzed by using high-performance liquid chromatography (HPLC) or an enzyme-linked immunosorbent assay (ELISA).

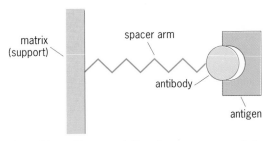

Fig. 1. Schematic representation of a spacer arm coupled to a matrix and to an antibody.

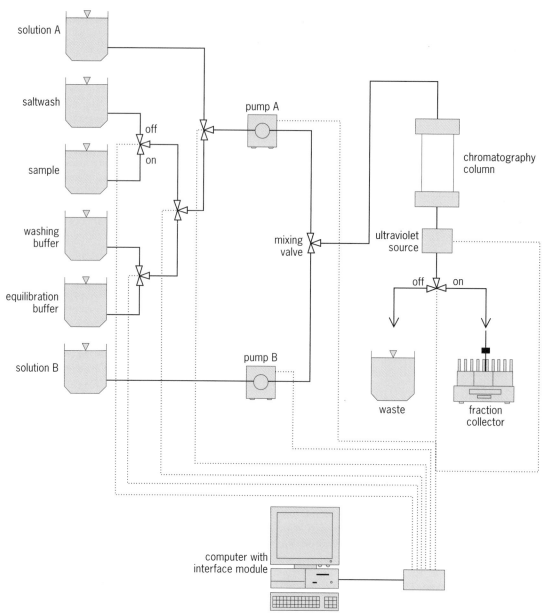

Fig. 2. Schematic diagram of a computer-controlled chromatography system. Dotted lines represent computer control. *(After J. Fichtali et al., Separation of egg yolk immunoglobulins using an automated liquid chromatography system, Biotechnol. Bioeng., 40:1388–1394, 1992)*

Immunoaffinity chromatography can be readily automated in order to more efficiently control, adjust, and monitor the process (**Fig. 2**). A suitable control system operates valves, regulates flow rates at various stages of the cycle, diverts product from the waste stream, and analyzes chromatograms obtained during operation.

Modeling. The simplest approach to modeling an immunoselective adsorption process for purposes of performance evaluation and scale-up is through an analysis of breakthrough curves. A breakthrough curve for the adsorbate is obtained by plotting the change in adsorbate concentration leaving the packed bed (that is, ratio of the concentration of adsorbate of the outlet of the bed to the inlet concentration) as a function of contact time. The curves generally fit the Langmuir adsorption isotherm, where the concentration of adsorbate bound to the support, q, is related to the concentration of adsorbate in the feed solution, C_o, by the equation $q = q_m C_o/(K_d + C_o)$, where q_m is the maximum capacity of the adsorbent, and K_d is the dissociation constant of the antigen-antibody complex. Values of q_m and K_d can be determined by using small-scale experiments and then can be employed to predict performance of large-scale immunoadsorption columns. Typical values of K_d range from 10^{-10} to 10^{-5} M, with small values indicating higher affinity between the antigen and the antibody. It is also important to have a high value for the ratio C_o/K_d, so that the available column capacity is used efficiently.

The shape of breakthrough curves provides information about the binding strength and the capacity of the adsorbent for the product. In large-scale packed columns, breakthrough curves are needed to determine the point when the adsorbent needs to be renewed. Several factors affect the shape of the breakthrough curve, including flow rate, the values of C_o and K_d, and the adsorbent capacity. In some situations, specifically when dealing with complex systems, the Langmuir adsorption isotherm may not be able to accurately describe immunoadsorption processes; consequently, more complex models may be required.

Scale-up. Much of the information that is useful for predicting large-scale operation of an immunoaffinity adsorption process can be obtained by running small-scale experiments. Scale-up of batch processes is relatively straightforward, provided that the procedure has been optimized at laboratory or pilot plant scale. Although packed columns are more common in large-scale operations, batch modes are often more suitable in situations where the feed stream is highly viscous or contains particulates, or when the concentration of the desired product is very low.

In packed-bed systems, increasing the volume to be processed may generally lead to an increased flow rate and scaling-up of the cross-sectional area. Increasing the column length causes an increase in pressure drop across the column, which may lead to bed compaction. Increasing the column diameter, however, generally broadens the product elution with consequent reduction in product concentration and purity. In practical operation, it is often easier to maintain a constant bed height, increase column diameter to allow increased capacity, and then connect several other scaled-up columns in series in order to counteract peak broadening effects.

All steps of immunoselective adsorption processes (adsorption, washing, elution) are carefully considered in large-scale applications, with the cost and stability of immunoadsorbents being the major concern. Equipment for large-scale production is available commercially.

For background information *see* ADSORPTION; ANTIGEN-ANTIBODY REACTION; FOOD ENGINEERING; IMMUNOASSAY in the McGraw-Hill Encyclopedia of Science & Technology.　　　　Jaouad Fichtali

Bibliography. J. Fichtali et al., Separation of egg yolk immunoglobulins using an automated liquid chromatography system, *Biotechnol. Bioeng.*, 40:1388–1394, 1992.

Industrial ecology

Many studies indicate that if the world population continues to grow, if the material standard of living improves throughout the world, and if attempts are made to meet the demands for consumption and products in the same way that they are currently met, the result will be a highly polluted environment and insufficient production because of natural-resource shortages. But if technology growth declines along with its economic basis, the likely result will be increased pollution and economic stagnation arising from population increases alone, prompting a number of regional and perhaps global conflicts. There are two major hopes: humans could change their consumption attitudes toward less product-oriented satisfaction; and technological innovations could enable sustainable world growth and development through the evolution of products, processes, and systems management procedures that provide simultaneously for human need satisfaction and natural-resource conservation.

Definition. The term industrial ecology suggests that models of biological systems and their interactions in nature are useful in the definition, development, and deployment of industrial systems. The ecological model is compelling because of the way in which evolution has enabled biotic and abiotic elements to live off the by-products and wastes of one another. Ecosystem resilience is often achieved, and industrial ecosystem resilience is a major need today as well. All properties of natural ecosystems are not necessarily and always appropriate; natural ecosystem efficiency is often quite low, for example. The term industrial ecology is used not because of the desire for an environmentally friendly industry, but because there is inherent insight in the concept of an ecosystem that can be beneficially used in the definition, development, and deployment of industrial systems. The primary objective of industrial ecology is to interpret and adapt understanding of natural ecological systems and to apply the most beneficial concepts to the acquisition of human-made systems such that they become efficient, effective, and sustainable. Industrial ecology involves integrated management of technological and economic resources on the one hand and environmental resources on the other as a basis for the development of policies and strategies.

Simply defined, industrial ecology is the development and use of industrial processes that result in products based on simultaneous consideration of product functionality and competitiveness, natural-resource conservation, and environmental preservation. Sometimes, industrial ecology is also called green design, or design for environment.

Principal elements. There are three essential pillars of sustainable development: technological and economic progress; nonconsumptive use of the world's natural resources, and environmental preservation; and social and cultural human progress throughout the world in ways that are sustainable.

The realization of these goals requires (1) industrial ecosystems, in which the wastes of one production process become input sources for others; (2) balancing the industrial inputs and outputs to the constraints of natural systems; (3) dematerialization of industrial outputs, primarily by reducing the quantity of materials in the resulting product, especially the nonrecyclable components and nonrenewable-resource components; (4) full utilization of information technology and knowledge-management-based supports; (5) improving the efficiency and effectiveness of industrial processes; (6) development and use of renewable natural resources; (7) integration of economic and ecological cost accounting in consideration of policy options; and (8) sublimation of a product-oriented, consumption-based economy to a functionally oriented economy.

These eight elements of industrial ecology involve such considerations as knowledge management and the development of learning organizations. Implementation of industrial-ecology-based principles may be enabled through the principles and practices of systems engineering and systems management.

Relation to biological ecology. Industrial ecology is related to biological ecology. In a biological ecosystem, virtually nothing is wasted in the ecosystem as a whole. The products of metabolism of one organism are useful to another, and the external supply to a specific organism comprises sunlight, water, and minerals. These enable a specific organism in the biological ecosystem to grow. Other organisms in the ecosystem consume the first, or its products, and also use sunlight, water, and minerals. Each process and network in the biological ecosystem is a dependent and interactive part of the larger ecosystem. Similarly, an ideal industrial ecological system would produce no waste and would be fueled by natural resources, including energy from sunlight. The waste from one industrial ecosystem process would be used as inputs for another, and at the end of their useful lives final products would be recycled into their original form or into something else that was used in another process, such that the overall industrial ecosystem system would not dissipate resources.

Types of industrial ecosystems. Three types of industrial ecosystems have been defined:

In a traditional type I system, the input natural resources and output wastes are not, fundamentally, considered except in an economic fashion, and there is no flow of materials from one life-cycle production process to the other. The system is essentially an inactive approach to sustainability, although it can become reactive through imposition of command-and-control-like pollution restraints to ensure environmental protection or restraints on use of natural resources.

In a type II industrial ecological system, there is recycling of wastes and reuse of by-products of one process, either in the same process or in another one, in order to reduce the requirements for resource inputs and the output waste by-products of the several processes. This system embodies an interactive approach to industrial ecology. It can be strongly supported through such free-market mechanisms as emissions trading as well as technological recycling.

Process redesign and reengineering can potentially enable the type II system to become a type III system, in which the overall industrial ecological system is closed and there are no nonrenewable resource requirements and no waste products. This system is a proactive approach to industrial ecology and ultimately leads to simultaneous human socioeconomic development and sustainability. While the ideal of no wastes may not be fully achievable, the wastes that are generated may be capable of utilization in a type II industrial ecosystem.

Industrial ecosystem life cycles. All industrial ecosystem life cycles comprise natural-resource, or materials, extractors; a materials processor or production process; consumers of the products; and waste products. The major challenge in industrial ecology is to identify appropriate life-cycle processes that minimize resource inputs and that are capable of using the potentially reprocessed wastes or by-products of other production life cycles. This objective also requires attention to recycling processes. In order to render the overall process ultimately sustainable, the culture and sociology of the consumer society must be examined and potentially reengineered such that attention is focused more on obtaining needed functionality of products and services and not just on the possession and consumption of products. This redirection requires attention to socioeconomic, political, and cultural issues. Thus, the subjects of industrial ecology and sustainable development have natural multidisciplinary interactions, and this is one reason why systems-engineering and systems-management perspectives on these subjects are of value.

Scope of field. Industrial ecology concerns more than the specific technical efforts that occur inside a factory. It encompasses the interrelationships among extraction of raw materials, transportation of these materials, manufacture of products, and disposition of wastes from manufacture and packaging. It also concerns the transportation and disposition of the final products, whether they become useful raw materials for new products, and whether they harm humans or nonhuman parts of ecosystems while they are being used. Most importantly, it concerns consumer values and attitudes toward products and toward the environment.

A large number of issues are associated with systems engineering as a catalyst for innovation, quality, and sustainable development. Four principal benchmarks for a sustainable industrial ecology and for systems engineering and management efforts are as follows:

1. Much contemporary thought concerning innovation, productivity, sustainability, and quality can be easily cast into a systems-engineering framework.

2. Industrial ecology, information-ecology and knowledge-management efforts, and organizational and infrastructure reengineering efforts are a natural complement to systems engineering and management perspectives.

3. The overall framework for sustainability can be valuably expressed within systems engineering and management.

4. The information technology revolution provides the necessary tool base that, together with systems engineering and systems management, allows the needed process-level improvements for the development of sustainable systems of all types.

Many challenges remain unmet. They concern the basic principles of systems engineering and management, and industrial ecology for sustainable development. Industrial ecology has a number of interactions with the social and behavioral sciences. One major need is the development of appropriate life cycles for processes that assist in the attainment of simultaneous human resource development and need satisfaction, natural-resource conservation, and environmental preservation; this development is the primary objective of industrial ecology.

For background information *see* CONSERVATION OF RESOURCES; ECOLOGY; ECOLOGY, APPLIED; ENVIRONMENT; ENVIRONMENTAL ENGINEERING; SYSTEMS ENGINEERING in the McGraw-Hill Encyclopedia of Science & Technology.　　　　Andrew P. Sage

Bibliography. J. H. Ausubel and H. D. Langford (eds.), *Technological Trajectories and the Human Environment*, 1997; J. Fiskel (ed.), *Design for Environment: Creating Eco-Efficient Products and Processes*, 1996; T. E. Graedel and B. R. Allenby, *Industrial Ecology*, 1995; E. A. Lowe et al., *Discovering Industrial Ecology*, 1997; P. C. Schultz (ed.), *Engineering within Ecological Constraints*, 1996; R. Socolow et al. (eds.), *Industrial Ecology and Global Change*, 1994; P. C. Stern et al. (eds.), *Environmentally Significant Consumption*, 1997.

Industrial facilities

Spatial layout is an integral part of the process of facilities planning. Facilities planning is concerned with how a specific activity can best be used to obtain a specific goal. One such activity is manufacturing, where the goal is the fabrication of a product. Facilities planning can be divided into a location component and a design component. The latter can be subdivided into systems design, spatial layout design, and material-handling design. Because of the complexity of the problem of facilities planning, each component is usually studied individually and then integrated into the complete system.

Spatial layout. Spatial layout, more generally referred to as facility layout, is concerned with the determination of the arrangement of the physical facility and its resources so as to best meet the desired goal of an activity. In an industrial setting, it generally relates to the arrangement of machines, work cells, and resources.

The key to determining a facility layout is the objective that is to be met. If the objective is to minimize material-handling cost, the layout might differ from one where the objective is to maximize flexibility or minimize maintenance costs. Most current research deals with only one objective, but it is clear that in many cases a layout may need to meet several objectives at the same time. However, regardless of the objectives, facility layout involves the arrangement and manipulation of resources, making the problem combinatorial in nature and difficult to solve.

The most commonly used objectives for facility layout are the maximization of an adjacency score and the minimization of material-handling costs inside the facility. The adjacency score can also be normalized and used as an efficiency score. Even though the adjacency objective is intuitive, that is, departments with large flows from one to another should be close together, it does not truly reflect the efficiency of a layout since it does not consider distances between departments. The material-handling cost objective is based on distance. Distance is usually defined as the distance from a pickup/delivery point of a department to the pickup/delivery point of another or the distance from the centroid of one department to the centroid of another. The metrics for these distances are normally rectilinear or euclidean distance.

The constraints on the problem are generally related to the area requirements of the individual departments and the overall facility and to the location restrictions of the resources such as fixed locations and whether certain departments can be contained in other departments. Constraints for the model also depend on whether a discrete or continuous representation is being used for the layout. A discrete representation uses a grid to which departments must match. The grid size determines the flexibility and complexity of the layout. The continuous representation allows departments to be placed at any point in the facility. The continuous case is more difficult to model and requires more constraints. It also does not easily handle irregular-shaped departments, such as L shapes and U shapes. Other constraints can be added to the model, depending on the level of integration of the facility layout with the other design components.

Solution techniques. Techniques to solve the layout problem can be either exact or heuristic. Because of the complexity of the problem, exact procedures do not generally work well for realistically sized problems, but they can form the basis for heuristic approaches. Three analytical methods are the quadratic assignment problem approach, the graph-theoretic approach, and the mixed-integer programming approach. Since the exact approaches are computationally infeasible for realistically sized problems, heuristic methods have dominated the solution approaches to facility layout.

Quadratic assignment problem. In this approach the layout problem is modeled by using a distance-based cost objective whereby departments are assigned to locations so as to minimize the overall cost. It is assumed that all departments are of equal size. Quadratic assignment is a well-known problem with existing solution techniques. However, exact solution procedures become computationally prohibitive for problems with more than 15–20 departments. The quadratic assignment problem can be adapted for departments of unequal sizes, but then only small-sized problems can be solved.

Graph-theoretic. Another approach is to view the problem as a graph with nodes representing either the pickup/delivery points or the centroids of departments, and arcs representing the adjacency scores for departments. To solve a layout problem, the adjacency-graph representation of the problem must be formed, and the dual graph of the adjacency graph must be determined and then translated into a block layout. The construction of the dual graph depends on the number of arcs in the original graph and the number of regions they enclose. The dual graph is difficult to derive and can be computationally taxing when there are a large number of arcs, making this approach for finding an optimal solution unsuitable for even average-sized problems.

Mixed-integer programming. This approach is similar to the quadratic assignment problem. A distance-based objective is used and department shapes are restricted to rectangles, but departments do not have to be of equal size. This yields more flexibility but requires more constraints to describe the problem. To date, optimal solutions for this problem have been reported for only six or fewer departments. The biggest advantage of this approach is that it provides the basis for a variety of new models that better integrate and capture the true nature of facility layout.

Computer algorithms. The heuristic development of computer algorithms is an approach using discrete representation, distance-based objective, and centroids. This method requires an initial layout that is improved by exchanging department locations. Two-way or three-way exchanges are used. The exchanges are allowed only for adjacent or equal-size departments, and departments are exchanged only when there is a reduction in the distance-based cost. When there are no more exchanges that can reduce the cost, the algorithm stops. Other heuristics are based on this algorithm, allowing nonadjacent departments to be exchanged (within predetermined bands of departments).

There are algorithms that use space-filling curves and increase the number of exchanges allowed. These algorithms can be used for a single-floor or multiple-floor facility. Exchanges are based on those that most decrease the distance-based objective. Variations of this approach provide improvement by allowing a more generic search for the department exchanges through the use of simulated annealing.

Another algorithmic approach sequentially divides (cuts) the facility into smaller portions. With each cut, affected departments are assigned to one side or the other of the cut. The determination of which side is based on the distance objective. The cuts continue until all departments are separated and lie in their own portion of the facility. The layout solution can also be improved by exchanging departments for each cut to find the best separation.

Meta-heuristics. It is also possible to heuristically solve the models of the exact approaches described through the use of meta-heuristics, including genetic algorithms, tabu search, and simulated annealing. Each of these meta-heuristics is based on the concept of allowing solutions that do not improve the current solution in the hope that they will lead to a better solution later. Each of these three methods employs a different approach to allow the nonimproving solutions, and each has its drawbacks and advantages. All have been successfully applied to the quadratic assignment problem and mixed-integer programming. Likewise, they can be applied within each of the described methods to improve the exchange process and produce potentially better solutions.

Adjacency graphs. All three methods are for distance-based objectives. There are also heuristic approaches for the adjacency-based objective. These approaches are based on different techniques to find the dual graph and the resulting block layout. The most successful of these uses different relationships to construct the adjacency graph. These relationships are maintained in a "relationship tuple." These tuples are also used to reduce the number of arcs in the original graph, resulting in a more easily determined dual graph.

With the improvement in solution algorithms, model representation, and computer processing speed, facility layout will become an integrated part of facilities planning, resulting in better solutions and economic savings.

For background information *see* INDUSTRIAL FACILITIES; MATERIALS HANDLING in the McGraw-Hill Encyclopedia of Science & Technology.   Cerry M. Klein

Bibliography. R. D. Meller and K. Y. Gau, The facility layout problem: Recent and emerging trends and perspectives, *J. Manuf. Sys.*, 15(5):351–366, 1996; R. L. Rardin, *Optimization in Operations Research*, 1998; J. A. Tompkins et al., *Facilities Planning*, 1996.

Inflammation

The four cardinal signs of inflammation of tissues are swelling, redness, pain, and heat. Inflammation is caused by a complex network of mediators, receptors, and white blood cells that interact with the vasculature and nerve fibers. In recognizing inflammation histologically, the swelling and redness come from localized edema secondary to enhanced vascular permeability in the postcapillary venules and tissue infiltration by leukocytes. When the leukocytes are predominantly polymorphonuclear neutrophils, the process is usually acute. In chronic inflammation, in contrast, the infiltrating cells are lymphocytes and mononuclear phagocytes. The answer as to why inflammatory response exists lies in the nature of innate and acquired immunity, and the complex response of multicellular organisms to threats from the environment.

Innate and acquired immunity. Mammals have evolved two overlapping and interactive systems for host defense: innate immunity and acquired immunity. In general, innate immunity is nonspecific, while acquired immune response is exquisitely selective. The innate immune response is capable of recognizing foreign substances such as unmethylated deoxyribonucleic acid (DNA) with cytosine-guanine-rich sequences (found in bacteria, but not eukaryotes, in the unmethylated form), carbohydrates unique to fungi and bacteria, and bacterial lipopolysaccharide (endotoxin) which is a component of bacterial gram-negative membranes. Effectors in the innate immune response include amebalike phagocytic cells, which ingest foreign matter; among them are the macrophages and the polymorphonuclear neutrophils. Other blood-borne proteins known as the complement system coat foreign bodies to make them more attractive to the phagocytes, and form lytic pores in foreign cells which result in lysis and cell death. Small peptide fragments from the complement system known as anaphylatoxins are potent stimulators of phagocytes and cause leakage of the small blood vessels for access of other innate immune effector proteins. Most cells in the body can react nonspecifically to trauma, foreign cells, or non-self biomolecules by releasing potent substances known as cytokines. In general, cytokines serve as a bridge between innate and acquired immunity. Cytokines are short-lived proteins which are synthesized or released, or both, during activation of various immune response effectors. The innate immune system also includes lipid mediators such as prostaglandins and leukotrienes, both derived from the 20-carbon fatty acid, arachidonic acid. Signs of inflammation may be suppressed by nonsteroidal anti-inflammatory drugs or aspirin, which inhibit the formation of arachidonic acid metabolites. Finally, the amino acid metabolites serotonin and histamine may be stored and released from specialized white blood cells such as platelets, basophils, and mast cells. These mediators alter local blood flow, contract smooth muscle, and stimulate secretion of other biomolecules such as cytokines and mucus.

The acquired immune response involves both T and B lymphocytes. It may result in the production of highly selective cellular and humoral (that is, antibody) processes. There are over 30 examples of cytokines. Some are known as interleukins because of their ability to cause cooperation between various types of white blood cells in the formation of an acquired immune response. In general, the acquired immune response involves communication between a number of cell types, including monocytes, macrophages, dendritic or antigen-presenting cells, and T and B lymphocytes. The nature of acquired immunity requires education of the immune system; that is, the specificity of the response increases after repeated exposure.

The processes of host defense and inflammation are linked, as the same mediators and mechanisms apply in both. Leukocytes are recruited from the vasculature in a multistep fashion. Chemoattractant molecules may be peptides, nucleotides, or lipids. Once outside the bloodstream, the recruited cells may injure host tissues via bystander effects, wherein their toxic contents, meant to destroy non-self substances, are released locally into the tissue.

A seemingly redundant array of chemoattractants bind to members of a family of G-protein-coupled seven-transmembrane-segment receptors. These receptors uniquely recognize leukotrienes, platelet-activating factor, complement anaphylatoxins C5a and C3a, nucleotides, bacterial N-formylated peptides, and chemoattractant cytokines (chemokines). The signal transduction mechanisms are common to these receptors; differences in biological responses likely relate to differences in coupling to a limited family of G proteins.

Chemokines and receptors. The chemokines are positively charged, heparin- and proteoglycan-binding polypeptides that are synthesized and secreted by most cells of the body. While some chemokines are constitutively stored in granules and are secreted by exocytosis upon cell activation (for example, RANTES is released upon platelet aggregation), all are products of cytokine- or growth-factor-inducible genes. Thus, interleukin-1 or platelet-derived growth factor can initiate de novo synthesis of chemokines from responding cells.

Biologically, a great deal of information has been gathered supporting a role for chemokines as key mediators of leukocyte trafficking. Chemokines may regulate basal (or constitutive) trafficking of leukocytes, as well as margination of leukocytes in acute or chronic inflammatory sites (see **illus.**). In addition to their role as leukocyte chemoattractants, chemokines have unresolved functions on hematopoietic cells, endothelial cells, and neurons.

Biochemically, the chemokines may be defined by their content and pattern of cysteine residues. Alpha chemokines, typified by interleukin-8, possess four cysteine residues which form two intramolecular disulfide bonds. The first two cysteines are separated by an intervening amino acid. Beta chemokines, typified by macrophage inflammatory proteins (MIPs), also possess four cysteine residues, but in these chemokines the first two cysteines are adjacent. Genomic analyses have suggested that each of these two major classes of chemokines may possess as many as several dozen members. Less well-characterized are the gamma, or C, chemokines, which possess only a single intrachain disulfide bond. These molecules, called lymphotactins, are specified by two nonallelic genes and act as chemoattractants for subpopulations of lymphocytes and other mononuclear cells.

Several representatives of alpha and beta chemokines have had nuclear magnetic resonance (NMR) structure or crystal structure, or both, determined. In each instance, a similar pattern is seen for the

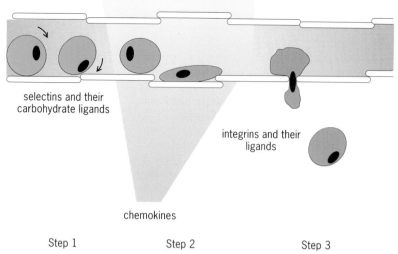

selectins and their
carbohydrate ligands

integrins and their
ligands

chemokines

Step 1   Step 2   Step 3

Three-step model of leukocyte emigration. Step 1: The cell rolls along the pavement of endothelial cells lining blood vessels through low-affinity Velcro-like interactions between adhesion molecules called selectins and their cognate carbohydrate ligands on the cell. Step 2: The tractor beam of chemoattractant acting through a G-protein-coupled receptor causes the upregulation of cell surface molecules called integrins, which mediate firm interactions with adhesion molecules called ICAMs via protein-protein interactions. The cell flattens out on the endothelial surface. Step 3: The cell crawls in between endothelial cells up a concentration gradient of attractant to emerge into the tissue spaces. *(Courtesy of Jose-Carlos Gutierrez-Ramos)*

monomeric chemokines, with a disordered amino terminal region followed by a compact structure involving three-stranded beta sheets stabilized by the two disulfide bonds. Both classes of chemokines possess a carboxy-terminal alpha helix that projects from the disulfide knot.

Receptors for the major alpha and beta chemokines have been identified through molecular cloning and expression in transfected cells. All are members of the large superfamily of G-protein-coupled receptors.

Unusual features of the chemokine receptors are their individual recognition of an array of different ligands, and redundancies in ligand-binding specificity among unique receptors. For example, CCR5 recognizes and transduces signals upon binding MIP-1α, MIP-1β, and RANTES. At the same time, CCR1, CCR4, and CCR5 are MIP-1α receptors. The biologic significance of these overlapping specificities is unknown at present. However, one feature of this ligand/receptor overlap is that the expression of a given receptor regulates the ability of a particular cell type to respond to a particular array of chemokines. While chemokine receptor expression is constitutive in some cells (for example, interleukin-8 receptors on neutrophils), induction of chemokine receptors by interleukin-2 has been demonstrated on lymphocytes and other mononuclear cells. Thus, the regulation of leukocyte trafficking by chemokines in a particular environment will likely be governed by the expression pattern of the receptors on responding cells.

Gene knock-outs. Gene knock-outs of chemokines and receptors have confirmed the role of the latter in cell trafficking and host defense. The first chemokine receptor knock-out, for murine (mouse) CXCR2 (which binds the chemokines KC and MIP-2), demonstrates a dramatic phenotype which develops leukocytoses, hyper immunoglobulin E (IgE), enlargement of the lymphoid organs (lymph nodes and spleen) with plasma cells, high serum levels of interleukin-4, and impaired emigration of neutrophils to peritoneal irritants. Surprisingly, when these barrier-facility mice are surgically delivered and bred in an absolutely sterile environment, this phenotype exhibits no overt features different from the wild type. These data suggest that resident commensal pathogens in the mouse stimulate the host defense network in a manner which is downregulated by CXCR2 under normal conditions. In the absence of CXCR2 receptor (found on myeloid cells, macrophages, and lymphoid cells), there is a tonic inflammatory stimulus (derived from nonpathogenic flora) which stimulates a T-helper-cell-type response as well as a leukocytosis.

Deletion of the MIP-1α gene resulted in animals with no overt immunologic or developmental defects. However, these animals were shown to be partially protected from the inflammatory sequellae of coxsackie B myocarditis and influenza pneumonia. In each of these models, tissue damage and lethality may result from leukocyte activation within the target organ. However, no immunologic evidence was provided to determine whether the immune response to the viral infection was altered, viral clearance was altered, or the enhanced injury was solely due to an abnormal leukocyte response in the absence of the chemokine. Additionally, in the mouse there are at least four chemokine receptors for MIP-1α; thus, this phenotype may reflect an absence of a number of important regulatory responses determined by CCR1, 3, 4, and 5 which are found in an overlapping series of cells including monocytes, macrophages, mast cells, eosinophils, lymphocytes (both CD4 and CD8 positive), and neutrophils.

Finally, gene targeting of CCR1, the MIP-1α/RANTES receptor, demonstrates a role for this receptor in host defense and inflammation. CCR1 null (−/−) mice were shown to be more susceptible to neutrophil-mediated pulmonary injury following experimental pancreatitis, to have difficulties clearing aspergillus antigen, and to have modifications in the T-helper Th-1/Th-2 cytokine balance following experimental immunization. With respect to MIP-1α and Coxsackie myocarditis, no differences in viral clearance or inflammatory myocarditis in mice lacking CCR1 have been found.

For background information *see* ANTIGEN; CELLULAR IMMUNOLOGY; CYTOKINE; IMMUNITY; INFLAMMATION; PHAGOCYTOSIS in the McGraw-Hill Encyclopedia of Science & Technology.   Craig J. Gerard

Bibliography. M. Dean and S. J. O'Brien, In search of AIDS-resistance genes, *Sci. Amer.*, September 1997; B. J. Rollins, Chemokines, *Blood*, 90(3):909–928, August 1, 1997.

Infrared astronomy

The Hubble Space Telescope was placed in Earth orbit in April 1990 by astronauts aboard space shuttle *Discovery*. The telescope, high above the Earth's atmosphere, is designed to receive new observational instrumentation at regular intervals. It was first serviced by astronauts in 1993 as part of a series of planned missions to keep it operating at peak performance. In February 1997, another space shuttle crew placed two new scientific instruments into the Hubble Space Telescope. One, the Near-Infrared Camera and Multi-Object Spectrometer (NICMOS), gives the telescope its first infrared observing capability. (Infrared light is emitted at longer wavelengths than human eyes can see.) The NICMOS operates in a wavelength range from 0.8 to 2.5 micrometers.

NICMOS instrument. The NICMOS is primarily a combination of three cameras, each with a different spatial resolution. It records images of astronomical objects at infrared wavelengths in the same way that optical cameras, such as the second Wide-Field and Planetary Camera (WFPC2), on the Hubble Space Telescope take images.

Two of the NICMOS cameras have very high spatial resolution, while the third camera has a wider field of view with lower spatial resolution to observe extended objects such as individual galaxies or galactic clusters. Each camera has 19 different filters; images recorded through the filters cover different infrared wavelengths.

Total infrared emission of an object can be observed by the NICMOS, but some of its narrow filters record light from a particular type of atom or molecule (such as hydrogen). Several observations can be combined to determine an object's temperature or measure how much light has been absorbed by interstellar dust. Observations can also be combined by three different filters to produce a color picture much like a television image. The NICMOS also performs spectroscopy, polarimetry, and coronagraphic imaging.

Spectroscopy and polarimetry. The NICMOS utilizes instruments called grisms to take spectra of objects in its wide-field camera's view. Grisms combine a light-dispersing grating and a prism. In the NICMOS, the grating spreads light out into its rainbow colors, while the prism moves the spectrum's position to the point in an image where the object appears.

The NICMOS higher-resolution cameras have devices to measure light polarization from an astronomical object. This measurement indicates whether light has been scattered by interstellar dust or was produced by an emission mechanism associated with the source.

Coronagraphic imaging. Coronagraphs were first used to observe the Sun's relatively faint coronal halo through telescopes when the Sun was not eclipsed by the Moon. Within the NICMOS, a coronagraph blocks out bright light from a star or other objects, allowing astronomers to search for fainter components, such as planets around nearby stars, or to see structure within galaxies containing bright quasars that emit light so bright that they hide structural details of the galaxy from view.

The NICMOS detectors were designed specifically for installation on the Hubble Space Telescope; however, they are also used at ground-based observatories worldwide. These detectors are 256×256 arrays of mercury cadmium telluride (HgCdTe) sensors, read out by a silicon multiplexing chip bonded to the detector's array. For maximum sensitivity, they must operate at very low temperatures. The NICMOS uses a dewar (essentially a large thermos bottle) to keep the detectors at $-352°F$ (60 K). The cooling agent, or cryogen, is a 230-lb (105-kg) block of nitrogen ice kept cold by the NICMOS dewar. As the NICMOS mission progresses, the nitrogen ice slowly sublimates to vapor and is vented out the back of the Hubble Space Telescope.

Scientific program. With its capability to observe infrared light, the NICMOS has two research goals: to study the expanding universe, and to study the formation of planets, stars, and galaxies.

Expanding universe. As the universe expands, the wavelengths of light observed in it expand at the same rate. Astronomical objects observed at extreme distances from Earth shine with light emitted long ago. As a result, light wavelengths detected from these more distant objects are longer, or redder, a phenomenon referred to as redshift. The more distant an object is, the more time its light has taken to reach the Earth; consequently it has a larger redshift.

Very distant objects have most of their light shifted from optical ranges that human eyes see to much redder light that the NICMOS observes. Therefore the NICMOS can see more distant objects than other instruments in the Hubble Space Telescope. *See* COSMIC DISTANCE SCALE.

Formation of planets, stars, and galaxies. Planets, stars, and galaxies are born in areas of high concentrations of dust and gas within the universe. Astronomers usually cannot see this formation process because dust blocks or scatters the shorter wavelengths of emitted light. But longer light waves, such as infrared, get through the dusty material. (This phenomenon also makes sunsets red: Earth's atmospheric dust scatters away blue light, but red light penetrates and can be seen.) The NICMOS, with its longer-wavelength view of the universe, peers through dust blocking optical wavelengths to observe new planets and stars being born, and even hidden quasars at the centers of galaxies.

Other NICMOS applications. Though designed to excel in studies of very distant cosmological objects, the NICMOS also explores infrared emissions from solar system objects: planets, their satellites, and comets.

Hubble Deep Field. The NICMOS instrument plays a significant role in cosmological research, probing the origin and fate of the universe. Near the pattern of bright stars in northern skies commonly called the Big Dipper (part of the constellation Ursa Major, the Great Bear) lies a small section of sky that researchers have observed with the WFPC2 aboard the Hubble Space Telescope. In astronomical terms, it is now known as the Hubble Deep Field. The WFPC2 images, recorded in four optical colors, combined to probe further back in time than any other previous observations and showed the faintest, and therefore the farthest, galaxies ever found. The NICMOS will observe part of this region to add infrared imaging data, and perhaps will reveal more about the origins of the universe.

Researchers using the NICMOS have specific goals regarding observations of the Hubble Deep Field. One goal is to determine whether galaxies appear in the NICMOS images that do not appear in previous optical images. This behavior is a signature of a very distant galaxy that has all of its light redshifted into the near-infrared spectral range. (Redshifts are measured in terms of a factor z, where the observed wavelength is $1 + z$ times the original wavelength. At a z equal to approximately 5, most of the light of a galaxy has been shifted out of the optical region and into infrared. Galaxies at a z of 5 existed when the universe was only about 5% of its present estimated age.)

The NICMOS also looks for galaxies undergoing high star-formation rates. Scientists want to know when galaxies coalesced from merely extended gas clouds to star-filled galaxies. Redshifted spectral emission lines from hydrogen atoms and ions of oxygen are signatures for star formation in distant galaxies. The grisms within the NICMOS detect these lines in all galaxies in the field of view.

In combination with optical images, the NICMOS data are used in statistical analysis of numbers and brightnesses of observed galaxies. These statistics are compared with various models of the universe and the Hubble constant to measure the mass of the universe. If the Hubble constant and the mass can be determined, they dictate whether the universe will expand forever (a theory of an open universe), stop expanding at an infinite time (a flat universe), or collapse upon itself (a closed universe).

Observations. The NICMOS has begun scientific observations after testing while on orbit within the Hubble Space Telescope, and published results reveal its ability to peer through obscuring interstellar and intergalactic dust.

Star formation. Study of star formation around Allen's Source in NGC 2264 (found within the constellation Monoceros, the Unicorn) combines the abilities of the NICMOS to see through obscuring dust with its imaging capabilities. Allen's Source is a bright young star, visible only at infrared wavelengths. Six much fainter stars appear in the image of Allen's Source recorded by the NICMOS (**Fig. 1**); they are invisible at optical wavelengths because of dust obscuration. It is probable that these six infant stars resulted from triggered star formation, a process where the birth of a massive star induces star formation within dust and gas in the region around it. Stellar wind from the more massive star moves surrounding gas and dust away, compressing them to much higher density. The higher-density material then has enough

Fig. 1. Composite of three NICMOS images, showing Allen's Source at left and six fainter stars around this parental source. Images were taken with filters centered at wavelengths of 1.1, 1.6, and 2.2 μm. The crosslike pattern is a normal effect of light diffraction from the mounts of the secondary mirror of the Hubble Space Telescope.

gravitational potential to trigger formation of new stars. The central star in this case (Allen's Source) is a brilliant star (spectral type B2) of about 15 solar masses. Each of the six individual stars triggered by its birth probably has less mass than the Sun.

Colliding galaxies. Individual stars rarely collide, but galaxies often do. When galaxies collide, stars are generally unaffected, except that their orbital paths become deflected by the different gravitational field they encounter. The gaseous material in galaxies, however, is very much affected.

Figure 2 is a NICMOS picture of the galaxy Arp

Fig. 2. NICMOS composite of the galaxy Arp 220, actually a merger of two galaxies. In this image, east is to the left and north is up. Two bright areas lie on an east-west line. The western bright area is arc shaped because of obscuration by a dusty disk.

220, actually a merger of two galaxies. Although this picture shows two main components along an east-west line, these are not the true galactic nuclei. The true nuclei lie south of the bright infrared structures. The western arc-shaped structure is part of one galactic bulge, but its nucleus is hidden by a dark dust disk that is opaque at even near-infrared wavelengths. The eastern nucleus is visible as a faint area south of the eastern bright spot. In about 100 million years the two nuclei will probably have merged into one.

For background information *see* ASTRONOMICAL SPECTROSCOPY; GALAXY, EXTERNAL; INFRARED ASTRONOMY; POLARIMETRY; SATELLITE ASTRONOMY; STELLAR EVOLUTION; UNIVERSE in the McGraw-Hill Encyclopedia of Science & Technology.

Rodger I. Thompson; Lauray D. Yule

Bibliography. J. Barbree and M. Caidin, *A Journey Through Time*, 1995; D. Fischer and H. Duerbeck, *Hubble: New Window to the Universe*, 1995; C. C. Peterson and J. C. Brandt, *Hubble Vision*, 1995; R. W. Smith, *The Space Telescope*, 1989; R. I. Thompson et al., *Astrophys. J. Lett.*, 492: L95–L98, 1998.

Integrated circuits

As integrated circuits have become more complex, testing them has become more challenging. Tests are required in three situations. The earliest test is applied at the wafer stage of fabrication to ascertain that the manufacturing process has succeeded and that packaging of the individual integrated circuits, one of the most expensive stages of manufacture, is worthwhile. The second phase is when the integrated circuit has been incorporated into an electronic product. This test, which is often applied at the board stage, when the printed-circuit card is tested, also checks for faults in the board and in its assembly. The final test situation is when the circuit is in operation, to check whether a fault has occurred and to indicate to the user that the system is functioning correctly.

The methods used to test circuits depend on the type of circuit, the test coverage required, and when the test is to be applied. Increasingly, reference to the physical mechanisms of device failure is required to assess the efficacy of the test methods employed.

Fault mechanisms, effects, and models. An integrated circuit comprises many layers of materials in or on the surface of a silicon substrate into which the circuit has been fabricated. These layers are patterned by photolithographic techniques to define the shapes of the electronic components and their interconnections. Most commonly, faults occur either when some additional material is present, for example, it has not been properly removed during the manufacturing process; or when some material is missing, because it has not been deposited or has been incorrectly removed in the processing. These physical fault mechanisms give rise to electrical fault

effects, the most common of which are the existence of short or open circuits in the electronic network.

To analyze the effects of such defects, the technique of inductive fault analysis may be used. In this approach, a computer scatters at random faults in the form of additional or missing areas of material on the set of drawings of the masks from which the circuits are fabricated. Examples of such faults are a small area of additional metal causing a short between two interconnections (**illus.** *a*), missing material affecting an interconnection or contact hole [known as a via] (illus. *b*), and a pinhole defect, where material is missing from an insulating layer (illus. *c*).

Dependent on the type of circuit under consideration, these effects can be incorporated into fault models that describe the electrical behavior of a faulty circuit in a way that can be used by a computer program to analyze the circuit's performance, and by automatic test pattern generation (ATPG) to devise tests to detect all the likely faults.

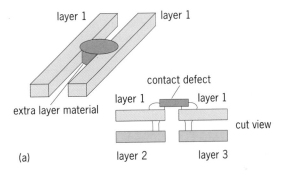

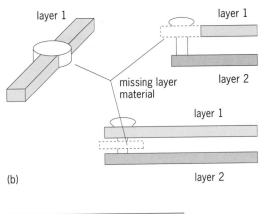

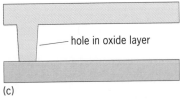

Typical defect types causing faults in an integrated circuit. (*a*) Extra layer material, causing a short circuit. (*b*) Missing layer material replaced by oxide, causing an open circuit. (*c*) Pinhole defect, in which a hole in the insulating oxide layer is filled with material from the upper layer, causing a vertical short circuit.

Digital circuit testing. The development of complex circuits was dominated by digital technology for many years, with complexity increasing exponentially. In the early stages of the development of digital integrated circuits, a very simple fault model was adequate to describe many situations. This model, which was dependent for its usefulness on the technology of the time, has been extended to cover more recent logic families, in particular complementary metal oxide semiconductor (CMOS). Known as the stuck-at model, it derives its effectiveness from the behavior of many circuit types, in which a node within the circuit goes to either the upper or lower logic level and remains there if commonly occurring faults have been introduced in manufacture.

Simple theory shows that the number of test stimuli required to exhaustively test a digital circuit increases exponentially with circuit complexity and rapidly becomes prohibitive. For this reason, test techniques were devised to reduce the time taken to test the circuit. It was recognized that a test that caused each node to be toggled or switched between the upper and lower logic levels could detect stuck-at nodes. By identifying a limited number of paths through the circuit that incorporated all of the circuit nodes, the problem was reduced significantly.

Division of the circuit into sections to provide a means to introduce and detect test conditions or vectors at intermediate points in the circuit provided a method to reduce the complexity of test programs. Further progress was made by recognition of the fact that consideration of the test requirements of integrated circuits at the design stage could enhance their overall testability and the efficiency of the tests.

Analog and mixed-mode testing. Analog circuits and mixed-mode circuits, comprising both analog and digital elements, present a more difficult challenge to the test engineer. Since the late 1980s, many methods have been suggested to provide effective test methodologies for these families of circuits. The fundamental problem is that the voltages and currents in the circuits can have a continuous range of values which, taken together with normal component spreads, makes it difficult to set criteria for failure. Methods have been derived to introduce and observe signals at intermediate points in the analog sections of circuits, and often a very simple low-frequency test can reveal a high proportion of the probable faults.

Supply-current testing. A recent test method, which has been used for both digital and analog circuits, is based on the measurement of the supply current drawn by the circuit under test. Many faults give rise to an anomaly in this current which, in the case of CMOS digital integrated circuits, can often be substantial and easily detected against the background of the low quiescent current drawn by such circuits. By exercising the circuit with external stimuli during the test, it is possible to get much greater fault coverage. In this procedure, each transistor in the circuit is made to contribute to the supply-current anomaly by ensuring that the electrical conditions for the individual transistors include a situation where an anomalous current is observable.

Built-in self test. In many applications it is important not only to know that the circuit is working when installed into a system but also to be assured of its continuing health in operation. To achieve this assurance, various methods of providing test signals on-chip, which continuously test the circuit, have been developed.

In safety-critical applications, for example, where integrated circuits are used in a system where failure could be catastrophic, as in aerospace and automobile applications, this provision is clearly important. Less obvious but equally important is a situation where the machine in which the integrated circuit is being used could be hazardous if a failure occurs. Extensions of failure-mode effects analysis (FMEA), in which the effect of the fault mechanisms and effects described above are analyzed, have been suggested to provide enhanced assurance of safe operation of the system when internal faults occur.

Test economics. The economics of testing has recently become a major consideration. As circuit complexity rises, the facilities required to carry out tests become more expensive, and the time required to complete the requisite tests becomes longer at a given test frequency. This makes the expense of testing of circuits a greater proportion of their cost, and as prices are driven downward the targets to be met become more stringent. The requirement to ship fewer defective devices to improve product reliability in non-safety-critical applications also drives the need for more efficient and effective testing methods.

An approach to improving the overall efficiency of the test is to effectively build a tester into the simulation environment at the design stage. This allows efficient design of the test methodology to be developed as the design proceeds. This method of virtual test allows the designer to optimize the test requirements at the design stage, reducing cost and enhancing testability.

Increasing test requirements. There is no sign that the exponential growth in integrated-circuit complexity that has been observed since the 1960s is about to abate. Circuits that provide more user facilities and are incorporated into systems that use this complexity will increasingly include a wider variety of functions. To provide for this greater complexity, new processes with critical dimensions well below 1 μm will become necessary. Associated with these processes, there will be new fault mechanisms, and factors such as heat dissipation will require consideration. In many applications, higher clock speeds will create new challenges, particularly for the design of the necessary test equipment. The demand for greater reliability in use and higher quality, as reflected in the delivery of fewer faulty circuits, will continue to create a need for greater and more comprehensive test coverage.

For background information *see* ELECTRONIC TEST EQUIPMENT; FAULT ANALYSIS; INTEGRATED CIRCUITS in the McGraw-Hill Encyclopedia of Science & Technology.   A. P. Dorey

Bibliography. *Proceedings of the International Test Conference*, IEEE Computer Society, annually; A. M. Richardson and A. P. Dorey (eds.), Special section on mixed signal and analogue IC test technology, *IEE Proc.—Circuits Devices Syst.*, 143(6):357–407, 1996.

Local Area Augmentation System (LAAS)

The U.S. Federal Aviation Administration (FAA) is developing two augmentations to the Global Positioning System (GPS) to enable civil aviation to make the transition from ground-based radionavigation aids to space-based navigation. Well along in development, the Wide Area Augmentation System (WAAS) will provide service beginning in 1999, meet the vast majority of user needs, and obviate the need for most conventional, ground-based radionavigation aids for aviation in the United States. The Local Area Augmentation System (LAAS) will follow the introduction of the WAAS and meet precision approach and landing requirements that are presently provided by the Instrument Landing System (ILS) and are beyond the capabilities of the WAAS. It will complement, and be interoperable with, the WAAS.

Both systems make use of differential techniques, whereby reference stations at surveyed locations observe the performance of the GPS on a continual basis and provide corrections for errors that occur in common between the reference stations and airborne receivers (for example, satellite ephemeris errors). Such errors constitute most of the error budget, and their elimination produces superb accuracy. The WAAS is a network of these reference stations spaced hundreds of miles apart. It transmits its correction information via geostationary communications satellites. The LAAS will serve individual airports. It will consist of reference stations spaced tens of meters (1 m = 3.3 ft) apart and a line-of-sight data broadcast with a service volume of approximately 50 km^3 (12 mi^3).

Advantages. The FAA, in conjunction with aviation industry, is presently specifying the LAAS. Differentially corrected GPS service, from the WAAS or the LAAS, could provide global, uniform navigation services for all types of aircraft operations and all phases of flight. Differentially corrected GPS services can simplify navigation for aviators, reduce costs, and provide more efficient, flexible procedures. In particular, significant cost reduction is obtained because the same receivers are used for en route, terminal, and approach navigation. Benefits and savings are also available through satellite navigation, achieved mainly by the minimization of terrestrial-based assets that have to be procured and maintained.

RNP parameters. LAAS service will improve upon basic GPS service. Error models for GPS have been developed over the years, revealing limitations in GPS coverage, accuracy, and integrity. Integrity constitutes the most important system safety parameter for aviation and is one of four required navigation performance (RNP) parameters, along with accuracy, continuity, and availability. System integrity is vital, since it encompasses the system's response to component failures or other rare events, which constitute major system safety concerns. Any breach of integrity could result in loss of life or property. The integrity function detects failures and alerts pilots in sufficient time to avoid hazardous situations.

The required navigation performance parameters are further defined as follows.

Accuracy. The position accuracy requirements are given in terms of the navigation sensor error, and are sufficient for automatic landing guidance. Navigation sensor error encompasses both the signal-in-space errors (such as errors in the differential data and any satellite signal errors that may not be removed in the differential data) and errors local to the aircraft (such as receiver noise and signal-reflection errors at the aircraft antenna).

Integrity. The integrity of the differential GPS data must meet the requirement for the probability of hazardously misleading information, which is reflected in the integrity requirements. For a landing system, this probability is of the order of 1 in 10^9 per approach. The probability of hazardously misleading information drives the fault-tree probability requirements of the ground station and the alert limits that are guaranteed for obstacle avoidance and path following in an aircraft. A system fault tree breaks the system down into its components and examines failure modes and their effects for each component, and the effect such failures would have on overall system performance.

The accuracy requirements for integrity are more stringent than those for the position accuracy needed to perform successful automatic landings, because the magnitude of the maximum permissible navigation sensor error is small. Therefore, the integrity alarm threshold has to be set at a low value. The higher the accuracy, the lower the probability of exceeding the threshold and generating an alarm. Simulation has shown that a landing system with an accuracy of 2.0 m (6.5 ft) with 95% probability is sufficient to land aircraft; however, for the purpose of integrity an accuracy of the order of 0.6–1.0 m (2.0–3.3 ft) is needed.

Continuity. Loss of continuity encompasses both disruption of the differential GPS broadcast data and disruption of the satellite signals. Continuity is related to integrity through the alarm threshold setting that is chosen in the integrity monitoring of the differential GPS data.

Availability. Availability is the percentage of time that the system is available for approach and landing. It encompasses meeting the other three performance requirements simultaneously. Therefore, it accounts for those outages of the ground and space segments caused by equipment failure and poor satellite geometry. The LAAS availability analysis considers outage duration, as well as outage and restoration rates. There is a range of values for availability to match individual airport requirements. The nominal availability requirement is 99.9%. (The equivalent loss of service is 8.8 h per year.)

Design requirements. Several other LAAS design requirements have been established by the FAA and the aviation industry:

1. The LAAS will be an Instrument Landing System look-alike. This assumption has profound implications. It means not only that cockpit instrument scaling and procedures will emulate the present Instrument Landing System but also that the service provider (the FAA or another civil aviation authority) will have primary responsibility for integrity (safety) of the signal in space. The signal in space is a combination of both the GPS signal and any corrections generated by the LAAS.

2. The LAAS incorporates multiple ground reference stations.

3. As necessary, to increase system availability, the LAAS incorporates additional ranging sources through means other than the satellites themselves.

4. LAAS data will be broadcast to user aircraft in existing navigation bands.

5. LAAS ground systems for approaches in categories I, II, and III will be interoperable with each other, and interoperable with the WAAS but independent of it. (Approaches in categories I, II, and III are defined by minimum-visibility criteria. Category III has the lowest visibility minima, and therefore includes the most difficult approaches.)

6. The LAAS will be based upon the GPS Standard Positioning Service but will allow growth through the incorporation of elements of other global navigation satellite systems (GNSS), such as the Russian GLONASS.

7. LAAS service will not be dependent upon use of aircraft inertial navigation systems or upon onboard radio altimetry, although the use of such altimetry is implicit within category III requirements.

The **illustration** shows the architecture of the LAAS and its operation at an airport.

Enhancements. LAAS design is a synthesis of the best ideas, including measurement averaging, carrier smoothing, multipath limiting, and the addition of pseudolites, that have emerged from the basic research into differential GPS in the past few years.

Measurement averaging. The power of measurement averaging among several spatially separated reference receivers has been shown to provide improved accuracy and a means for integrity monitoring through internal consistency checks among receivers. This averaging concept has helped improve positioning accuracy and establish realistic alert limits for integrity monitoring without sacrificing continuity. The concept is simple: Several GPS receivers, serving as reference stations with independent antennas (see illus.), are separated

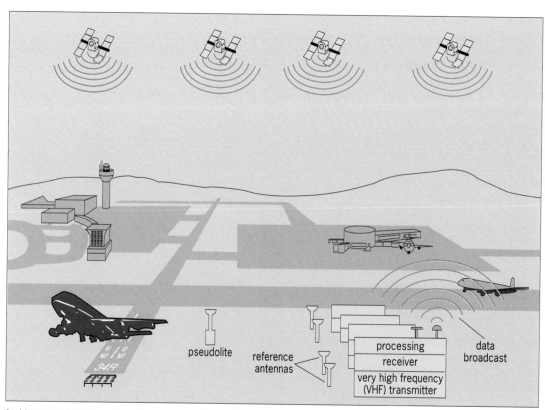

Architecture of the Local Area Augmentation System (LAAS), showing its operation at an airport.

sufficiently to protect against common environmental errors. A mini-network results, with the measurements from the individual stations being averaged to improve accuracy, to provide an averaged correction against which individual reference-station measurements can be compared for integrity, and to add system robustness, since the loss of any one reference station would only degrade performance slightly.

Carrier smoothing. This technique combines the code measurements (based on a pseudorandom noise code for each satellite that is used for range determination) with the carrier phase measurements (based on the GPS carrier at 1575.42 MHz that is modulated by the pseudorandom noise code) in order to reduce errors. This combination averages code range measurements with the carrier phase changes, accounting for the motion of the aircraft between code measurements.

Multipath limiting. Multipath is a reflection of a satellite's signal from a surface in proximity to the receiving antenna (at a distance of tens of meters at most). Multipath can distort receiver measurements because the reflected false signal distorts measurement of the true direct GPS broadcast. The design and development of a special dual-antenna configuration have helped limit multipath to a reasonable level consistent with required system performance. This configuration has a top element shielded from ground-induced multipath. It receives GPS signals from 30° above the horizon up to the zenith. A lower array of vertically stacked dipole antennas is designed to receive GPS signals from 5° up to 30° from the horizon, while rejecting multipath on those signals because of the total antenna gain pattern achieved by the dipole array.

Addition of pseudolites. Finally, limitation in GPS coverage, as measured by dilution of precision (DOP), a geometric error multiplier, has the effect of limiting overall LAAS performance. This problem is temporal in nature because of the motion of the satellites, and could be dealt with through operational restrictions on aircraft flying during periods of marginal coverage. The economic impacts of these limitations preclude LAAS service as a public-use system, unless they can be mitigated or eliminated. Additional satellites or other ranging sources could be used, as long as they did not add to the complexity or cost of system design.

A simple, modular approach appears feasible in the addition of pseudolites or pseudosatellites. Pseudolites, ground transmitters of GPS-like signals, will be placed on the airport surface to provide the best geometry for the principal runways (see illus.). The broadcast will be at the GPS frequency using a GPS-like code and a pulsing scheme to ensure that the pseudolite does not overpower reception of the GPS satellites. The pseudolite will act like a satellite on the ground, and its signal will be differentially corrected by the LAAS reference stations and will be received by aircraft, just as the signals of GPS satellites will.

Insurance of system integrity. All of the developments described above have been carefully analyzed for their respective impacts on system integrity. This critical safety parameter will be met in the LAAS as follows: Prior to broadcast, the initial integrity monitoring of the correction data will be accomplished by comparisons of the corrections from the different reference receivers. The avionics will be responsible only for (1) computing the vertical and horizontal position protection levels using standard equations whose parameters are error-data and statistical-error parameters contained in the ground station's broadcast and (2) comparing the position protection levels to their respective alert thresholds. Signal-quality monitoring will also be used to monitor critical GPS signal parameters at the reference stations, such as code correlation functions and signal levels. The monitoring of critical signal parameters is characteristic of existing aviation radionavigation aids. Its purpose is to ensure that any approved airborne receiver will derive correct measurements from the satellite signals.

For background information *see* AIR NAVIGATION; INSTRUMENT LANDING SYSTEM (ILS); RISK ANALYSIS; SATELLITE NAVIGATION SYSTEMS in the McGraw-Hill Encyclopedia of Science & Technology.

Raymond J. Swider, Jr.

Bibliography. B. W. Parkinson and J. J. Spiker, Jr. (eds.), *Global Positioning System: Theory and Applications*, vol. 2, American Institute of Aeronautics and Astronautics, 1996.

M-theory

A fundamental goal of physics is to describe and understand all the forces appearing in nature. All the phenomena occurring in the universe can be traced to the action of just four fundamental forces or interactions, namely, the gravitational, electromagnetic, strong, and weak interactions. This classification, although it greatly simplifies the picture of different interactions, does not provide real understanding of the nature of the different forces. Recent theoretical work suggests the existence of an M-theory, which would unify and explain all the interactions in a natural way.

Elementary particles. Since the time of the ancient Greeks, matter was treated as being composed of indivisible atoms. About 1900, it was shown that atoms are built from smaller units, electrons and nuclei. The atomic nucleus was soon shown to consist of still smaller units, protons and neutrons. Electrons, protons, and neutrons were called (not quite properly) elementary particles. Since 1930, many new elementary particles have been discovered. Elementary particles are assumed to be structureless, pointlike objects characterized by mass, electric charge, spin, and other quantum numbers. Any particle with mass is a source of the gravitational field, and when it carries an electric charge it creates its own electromagnetic field.

The electromagnetic field, weak interaction, and strong interaction are quantum in nature; that is, such interactions are transmitted by the exchange of special particles called quanta. A photon, which is a massless, spin-1, electrically neutral particle, moving with the speed of light, is a quantum of the electromagnetic field. The strong and weak interactions are transmitted by massive quanta. Despite many efforts, physicists have not been able to formulate a consistent quantum theory of gravity. It is believed, however, that gravitational interactions are transmitted by a massless, spin-2 particle, called the graviton.

The range of an interaction is inversely proportional to the mass of its quantum. Thus, the gravitational and electromagnetic interactions, transmitted by massless quanta, are of infinite range, while the strong and weak interactions, transmitted by massive quanta, are short range.

Renormalization. Promptly after quantum mechanics was discovered, physicists started to describe and calculate interactions between charged particles. It soon became clear that such calculations led to infinite results and that the main reason for this unexpected and unrealistic outcome was the assumption that elementary particles are pointlike. A very complicated procedure called renormalization was devised to extract finite results from these infinite expressions. It was surprising that the finite results obtained in such a way were in very good agreement with observations. Quantum electrodynamics, the quantum theory describing interactions between charged particles, is the most successful theory created so far. It is not considered, however, a complete theory because it is supplemented by a set of rules necessary to obtain finite results. For many years, quantum electrodynamics was used as a model of a quantum theory describing interactions between elementary particles.

Gauge theories. In 1954, using classical electromagnetic theory as a model, C. N. Yang and R. L. Mills constructed a classical gauge theory allowing in its simplest versions two or three different electric and magnetic fields. Quantum versions of gauge theories were soon applied to describe the weak and strong interactions. However, like quantum electrodynamics, the quantum gauge theories lead to infinite results, and to obtain finite results it is necessary to properly manipulate infinite terms. In 1971, G. t'Hooft showed that there exists a consistent set of rules leading to finite results in quantum gauge theories.

Quarks. Meanwhile, in 1963, M. Gell-Mann and independently G. Zweig, by unraveling a hidden symmetry between elementary particles, postulated that protons and neutrons, among other elementary particles, are not truly elementary but are composed of smaller units, which were named quarks. To explain the observed properties of elementary particles, six different types of quarks are needed. The existence of all six quarks has been observationally confirmed.

Standard model. In the late 1960s, the weak and electromagnetic interactions were unified into a new type of interaction, now called the electroweak interaction. This unification means that at sufficiently high energies of the interacting particles it is not possible to distinguish between the weak and electromagnetic interactions. The theory describing interactions between quarks and their strange properties was combined with the electroweak theory, which in the meantime was successfully tested observationally, into the standard model of elementary particles. So far, the standard model has survived all the observational tests that have been carried out, but because it contains several parameters that must be specified by fitting observational data, it is not considered a fundamental model. The standard model, for example, does not include the gravitational interaction.

String theory. Meanwhile, a new, radically different approach slowly emerged. The first point of departure was the assumption that elementary particles are not pointlike objects but one-dimensional extended strings. A string could be open, like a piece of thread, or closed, like a rubber band. The typical length of a string is only about 10^{-35} m. To test this length scale, it is necessary to reach very high energies. Different states of vibration of a string correspond to different elementary particles.

In 1984, M. Green and J. Schwarz discovered that a consistent quantum theory of interacting strings can exist only in a spacetime with either 10 or 26 dimensions. To obtain the 4-dimensional physical space that is observed, it is necessary to assume that the additional 6 or 22 dimensions are compactified or "wrapped around" at a very small scale, comparable to the size of a string and therefore unobservable at low energy. There was great interest when the low-energy limit of string theory was shown to very closely resemble the standard model. New versions of string theory were soon proposed which, at the low-energy limit, resembled the standard model even more closely. Each of these theories contained massless spin-2 particles, that is, gravitons, and in the low-energy limit also reproduced the classical theory of general relativity. However, the great excitement of the mid-1980s faded when it proved impossible to derive observationally tested predictions from string theory.

So far, five different string theories containing general relativity in an appropriate limit have been proposed. The type I string theory allows open and closed strings, while other string theories are based on closed strings only. To this list, string theorists also added the 11-dimensional supergravity theory.

String duality. During the last few years, it has been shown that the six theories are interrelated. This surprising result is connected with a recently discovered duality relating different string theories. This duality was discovered when E. Witten and then others realized that one string theory at a strong-coupling limit is equivalent to another string theory at a weak-coupling limit. It was therefore possible

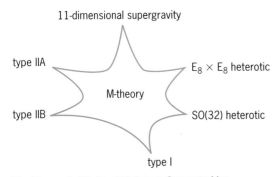

11-dimensional supergravity

type IIA

$E_8 \times E_8$ heterotic

M-theory

type IIB

SO(32) heterotic

type I

Weakly coupled limits of M-theory. Connected by dualities, each weakly coupled theory can be interpreted as strong-coupling limits of others. (After E. Witten, Duality, spacetime and quantum mechanics, Phys. Today, 50(5):28–33, May 1997)

to perform calculations at the strong-coupling limit. For example, in 10-dimensional Minkowski spacetime, the strong-coupling limit of the type I string theory is equivalent to the weakly coupled SO(32) heterotic string. The five string theories and the 11-dimensional supergravity theory are different weak-coupling limits of a more general, yet to be discovered, M-theory (see **illus.**). The M-theory is now the prime candidate for the theory of everything, unifying all interactions that appear in nature.

D-branes and black holes. Very little is known about the M-theory. Probably, the M-theory resides in an 11-dimensional spacetime. If so, there is an interesting possibility that strings are actually 2-dimensional membranes.

J. Polchinski showed that duality between different string theories requires existence not only of strings but also of higher-dimensional objects, named D-branes (short for D-dimensional membranes). D-branes are a kind of topological defect, similar to dislocations in crystals, with the distinctive property that the end points of strings can be attached to them. D-branes carry charges and vibrate, move in spacetime, and interact with strings and other D-branes.

By using string theory and D-branes, it was possible to solve one of the mysteries of black holes. Black holes form at end points of evolution of sufficiently massive stars. The central core of such a star is unable to counterbalance its own gravitational attraction and collapses to form a black hole; the energy released during the collapse causes a dramatic expulsion of the outer layers of the star (a supernova explosion). S. Hawking showed that, if quantum processes are taken into account, black holes radiate energy in the same way as a black body whose temperature is inversely proportional to the mass of the black hole. The black hole can be characterized by a temperature, and hence by an entropy, which is proportional to its surface area. For a standard system, the entropy is proportional to the logarithm of the number of quantum microstates of the system. Recently, several groups of researchers were able to calculate the number of quantum microstates for

a class of black holes and confirm that the entropy of a black hole is indeed described by the formula given by quantum-statistical mechanics. This result indicates that black holes behave as standard quantum-mechanical systems, and that the process of formation of a black hole, contrary to Hawking's assertion, is not connected with loss of information.

The recent developments in string theory have revived prospects for formulating the theory of everything. However, since the M-theory has not been discovered yet, the present situation is similar to the early development of quantum mechanics when N. Bohr formulated the basic rules for finding energy levels in an atom.

For background information *see* BLACK HOLE; ELEMENTARY PARTICLE; FUNDAMENTAL INTERACTIONS; GAUGE THEORY; QUANTUM ELECTRODYNAMICS; QUANTUM FIELD THEORY; QUARKS; RENORMALIZATION; STANDARD MODEL; SUPERSTRING THEORY in the McGraw-Hill Encyclopedia of Science & Technology.

Marek Demianski

Bibliography. J. Polchinski, String duality, *Rev. Mod. Phys.*, 68:1245–1258, 1996; E. Witten, Duality, spacetime and quantum mechanics, *Phys. Today*, 50(5):28–33, May 1997; E. Witten, Reflections on the fate of spacetime, *Phys. Today*, 49(4):24–30, April 1996.

Machining

The machining of metals requires planning to decide which types of tools are to be used for a particular application. Conditions vary as to type of material, surface finish desired, and type of cut to be made. Much research is being done regarding the selection of strategies and approaches for establishing tool paths. Improvements in techniques, such as high-speed machining, provide more flexibility in planning machining operations.

Tool Path Planning

Various types of milling processes are considered when planning a tool path. The choice is dependent on the type of metal and how it is to be machined. The metal can be cut by various processes such as face milling, peripheral milling, and end milling.

Milling processes. A variety of sizes and shapes of cutters are employed in milling, with more diversity added by tooth configurations and materials. Milling is considered a multitooth or multipoint operation; rarely, a single-tooth fly cutter may be employed.

Face. Face milling typically uses a flat-end cutter, with multiple teeth. The face end of the tool is involved in the removal of material from a workpiece. Multiple passes are required over a surface when the cutter diameter is smaller than the object dimensions.

Peripheral. In peripheral or slab milling, material removal is achieved by using cutting edges mounted on the cylindrical surface of the cutter.

End. End milling utilizes cutting edges on the periphery of the cutter as well as the teeth on the face end of the tool for material removal. The machining of pockets is an example employing end milling. The sides of the pocket are machined by the circumferential edges, while the bottom is finished by the face-end teeth. Pockets may be fabricated by using flat-end mills as well as ball-end mills. When the cutter diameter is smaller than the pocket dimensions, more than one (radial) pass of the cutter is required to machine the pocket.

Path operations. Milling is considered a path-dependent operation, as opposed to drilling. The specific path followed by the cutter in milling is critical in the determination of the path length, cutting forces, and surface finish.

Drilling. In this operation, the cutter can completely exit a workpiece after one hole is drilled, move rapidly to another location, and resume drilling at that location. As long as no obstacles are presented in the path, rapid movement between hole locations may be achieved, with little dependence on the path taken to reach the next hole to be drilled. In drilling, the selection of alternate paths pertains to the selection of the hole-location-visiting sequence, and is analogous to the well-known traveling salesman (travel path) problem.

Turning. In this operation, the path to be followed during the course of cutting is typically dependent on the desired component geometry and the cut allocation, whereby the number of roughing and finishing passes must be determined. Selection of alternate paths is seldom a major problem in turning.

Milling. In milling with a smaller tool, after the cutting has begun, the cutter cannot be retracted until the entire object is machined. Milling is similar to lawn mowing, where a rotary cutter traverses a path governed by the user until every blade of grass is removed. The milling cutter rotates about a vertical axis, while simultaneously translating in a linear fashion, along a prescribed path. Thus, the path followed by the individual teeth of the cutter is a trochoid; for slower speeds of translation, it may be considered as a series of discrete circles, from end to end, along the linear path.

Path patterns. Typically, several cutting path patterns are used in face milling and pocketing, of which the most common are staircasing or wafering, and windowing or spiraling. In staircasing (**Fig. 1***a*), the cutter is moved from end to end, turned, and brought back in an opposite direction along the adjacent layer of material. A zigzag path is followed until all of the desired object is machined. In windowing (Fig. 1*b*), a spiral-in or spiral-out pattern may be employed. In spiral-in, the cutter starts from the periphery and spirals inward (toward the center of the object), with adjacent passes made until the object is machined completely. In all strategies, sufficient overlap must be maintained between adjacent passes to ensure good finish of the object. In addition, in face milling proper edge (end) clearance must be provided by the cutter, so as to completely

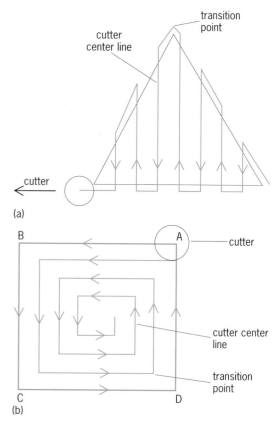

Fig. 1. Face-milling techniques: (*a*) staircasing; (*b*) windowing.

exit the object on its periphery. This is required to ensure proper removal of metal at the edges of the object; and a prudent allowance also minimizes burrs and other artifacts at the edges of the object. In pocket milling, staircasing may result in gouges at the end of a linear pass, along nonturn directions, due to the lack of an edge clearance. This gouge must be removed by a subsequent finishing pass along the periphery of the pocket.

The strategy or pattern selected to cut an object is important since it governs the machining time of the object, which in turn controls the production rate. Many more alternate paths may be generated in staircasing by varying the orientation of the cutter with respect to the object geometry, the starting point of cut, the cutter size and type, and the cutter overlap. Following alternate paths may result in differences in path length which, considered over a large lot size of objects machined, can result in significant differences in productivity. Hence, prior path planning can be very advantageous. Off-line path planning with computer-aided design (CAD) systems or dedicated computer-aided manufacturing (CAM) software can further reduce the amount of physical experimentation involved in path planning.

Many recent improvements have been made in the development of such programs for face milling, polygonal pocketing, and sculptured surface machining. The last is the most complex, and hence face milling of convex polygonal parts is the program most used as the test-bed for promoting the benefits of path planning. However, most existing systems are limited to the generation of a good path or selection of a path based on path length alone. Notably, this simulated path may not be applicable in actual cutting because of certain possible process violations. An optimal orientation with regard to path length may result in the breakage of the cutter due to undesirable engagement and disengagement of the tool with the object being machined. Hence, the process must be adequately represented in these computer models through consideration given to as many process variables as possible. These process variables include cutter entrance and exit angles, cutting forces, temperatures, tool wear, tool breakage, surface finish, and surface errors.

Planning in milling. When the cutter suddenly meets the edges of the workpiece during engagement and disengagement, significant damage can be caused to the tool due to impact loads. If the direction of entry and or exit of the tool into the work is controlled to some prescribed orientations, the severity of the impact may be minimized. Different tool and work materials, tool and work geometry, speeds of cutting, depths of cut, and feeds play a role in determining these prescribed orientations. Minimizing the number of severe impacts can reduce the possibility of failure of the cutting tool. Moreover, when a tool rotates and travels across the workpiece, cutting forces are generated. These forces act on the cutting edge, leading to tool and work deflections and reduced tool life. The forces also affect the temperature and heat generation in the cutting tool and work, leading to more adverse effects. These process effects are common to the actual cutting process and must be adequately represented in computerized tool-path planning studies to achieve realistic planning. Hence, a tool-path analysis may be conducted through a comprehensive evaluation of multiple variables, and a good path selected based on a user prioritization of these variables.

Shivakumar Raman

High-Speed Machining

In machining of metals, material removal occurs via a concentrated shear flow initiated at the point of contact between the workpiece and a wedge-shaped tool (such as a turning insert or milling flute) to remove a chip and produce a machined surface. On the majority of machines, the cutting action is generated by the rotation of the machine spindle. The axes of the machine (typically ranging from three to five) are used to position the workpiece relative to the tool and are generally capable of complex contouring motions. Increasing the power and speed of the spindle and axes has several advantages, including shorter machining time, improved surface finish, reduced thermal and mechanical stresses on the workpiece and tool, and increased dynamic stability. These potential

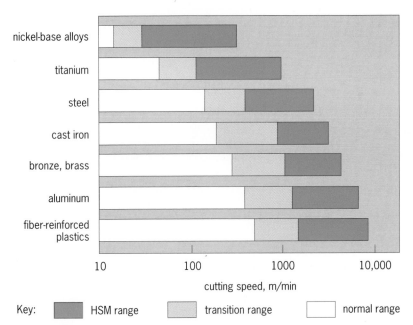

Fig. 2. Machining speeds as a function of material. *(After P. Shultz and T. Moriwaki, High-speed machining, Ann. CIRP, 41(2):637–643, 1992)*

advantages have driven a recent, rapid increase in the industrial adoption of high-speed machining processes and technology.

The definition of high-speed machining depends upon a number of factors that include the characteristics of the material being machined, the availability of suitable tool materials, and the speed and power of available machines. The highest attainable machining speeds are a strong function of the material being machined (**Fig. 2**). In general, machining speeds on difficult-to-machine materials such as titanium and hardened steel are limited by the availability of suitable tool materials, whereas machining speeds in more machinable materials such as aluminum and plastic are limited by the availability of machines. To increase machining speeds and hence production rates, research effort is aimed at improving the characteristics of tool materials, workpiece materials, and machines.

Recent years have seen a rapid increase in the speed and power of production-grade machining centers. These improvements are geared toward increasing machining speeds in easy-to-machine materials such as aluminum, which make up a large portion of the manufactured products in the aerospace and automotive industries. Reliable machining spindles capable of running continuously at speeds of up to 40,000 revolutions per minute (rpm) with a power output of 30 kW (40 horsepower) are now available on production equipment. In addition, axis speeds attainable during machining now exceed 15 m/min (49 ft/min) with accelerations of greater than 10 m/s² (33 ft/s²). The marked increase in material removal rates and the reduction in production time and costs afforded by this new technology have the potential to drastically alter the manufacturing process for aluminum components.

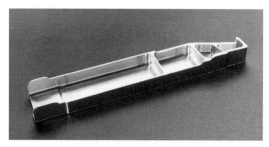

Fig. 3. Aluminum aerospace component where the material remaining after machining is less than 5% of the volume of the original workpiece stock. Machining chips are typically recycled and reused.

Parts that benefit. A great variety of machined parts can benefit from the use of high-speed machining. Because high-speed machining frequently allows dramatic increases in material removal rates, parts which require extensive removal of material (**Fig. 3**) spend significantly less time on the machine. With high-speed machining, it has recently become economically viable to machine parts with tall (100 mm or 4 in. or more), thin (0.5 mm or 0.02 in. or less) walls and similar thin floors from solid blocks. Such monolithic components are now competitive with sheet metal buildups only because of the reduction in machining time associated with high-speed machining. In addition, replacing sheet metal parts with high-speed-machined components reduces costs associated with the need for creating and managing fixtures, assembly, and carrying costs (associated with residence of components on the assembly line).

High-speed machining has become a competitive process in the die and mold industry as well. In this application, parts which were previously rough-machined in the soft state, hardened, and then finished by grinding or electrodischarge machining are now machined directly to the finished dimension in the hardened state. The reduction in processing time and post-polishing work required to manufacture the die can lead to a significant cost savings, which makes the production of smaller lot sizes of dies and molds economically feasible.

Machine requirements. The ability to machine with higher speeds has placed demands on all components of machine tool technology. Spindles must be dynamically stiff and must maintain bearing preload throughout the operating range. Hybrid bearings (such as ceramic balls and steel races) and fluid bearing technology have resulted in commercially available, 40,000-rpm, 30-kW (40-hp) spindles. Because the centrifugal forces are proportional to the square of the rotational speed, rotating components must be well balanced. The tool retention system must provide rigid clamping and accurate tool location at all spindle speeds. These concerns become more important as spindle speeds continue to increase. This trend toward higher spindle speeds shows no sign of abating, as spindle designs have recently been proposed which might allow speeds

of 100,000 rpm with 100 kW (134 hp) of continuous power output.

The machining feeds (feed rate during machining) of the axes required to fully utilize existing high-speed spindles is greater than 20 m/min (66 ft/min). In addition, to save time on the noncutting motions (during a tool change, for example) feeds of up to 60 m/min (197 ft/min) are desirable. More importantly, to reach such high axis velocities within a reasonable working volume, the axes must have high accelerations. Commercial machines are available with accelerations of up to 10 m/s^2 (33 ft/s^2), and higher accelerations exist in experimental machines. Higher accelerations are achieved through more powerful servomotors, improved control strategies, and reduction in the mass of moving components. If a 100,000-rpm, 100-kW (134-hp) spindle becomes available, the corresponding machine would need machining feeds of 40 m/min (131 ft/min), accelerations of up to 40 m/s^2 (131 ft/s^2), and substantially higher noncutting feeds. Attaining these higher speeds and accelerations may require the development of entirely new drive system technology. For long-travel drives and very high speeds, traditional lead-screw and ball-screw systems have dynamic and thermal limitations. Linear motors capable of higher speeds and accelerations have been proposed as an alternative to traditional drive systems. There are challenges associated with the development of linear motor drives, including inadequate force capability, greater heat production, the need to isolate the strong magnets from ferrous metal chips, and the need for more sophisticated control systems. These issues require additional research and development before linear motors will be widely used on machine tools.

Tool materials. In many applications, the use of high-speed machining is limited by the lack of suitable tool materials. In general, the higher the yield strength and melting temperature of the material being machined, the greater the stresses and temperatures generated at the tool-chip interface. These increased stresses and temperatures cause increased rates of chemical and mechanical tool wear that may make the high-speed machining of certain materials impractical. Solid carbide and diamond-coated carbide tools have essentially eliminated this limitation when machining soft nonferrous materials such as aluminum and copper. The development of cubic boron nitride tooling has allowed manufacturers to machine hardened ferrous materials (with hardnesses of up to 65 Rockwell-C), but cutting speeds are limited to approximately 300 m/min (984 ft/min). Because of their chemical reactivity, titanium and its alloys also remain very difficult to machine at high speeds. For example, in machining titanium 6Al4V, a common alloy used in industry, maximum speeds of 120–180 m/min (394–590 ft/min) are attainable only with special titanium-carbide and titanium carbonitride–coated carbide milling tools. For these reasons, the application of high-speed machining will continue to increase only if improvements in machine technology are accompanied by corresponding improvements in tool materials.

Controllers and data processing. The increased complexity of machined parts leads to a similar increase in the size and complexity of the programs required to generate the machine motion. The flow rate of the data required to control tool motions over complex surfaces has grown dramatically as machine speeds have increased. This is especially true as high-speed machining becomes practical in the die and mold industry, where the tool motion over the workpiece is described in a series of point-to-point movements and the volume of data required to geometrically define a part is quite large. As a result, machine-tool controllers must be able to store large amounts of data and process the data quickly. Most high-speed machines are now equipped with powerful computers and network connections.

Dynamics of high-speed machining. Because the machine, tool, and workpiece are not infinitely stiff, the cutting forces cause time-varying deflections which are imprinted on the workpiece. Subsequent cutting encounters the variable surface, which results in time-varying forces and deflections (**Fig. 4a**). This feedback mechanism is the cause of regenera-

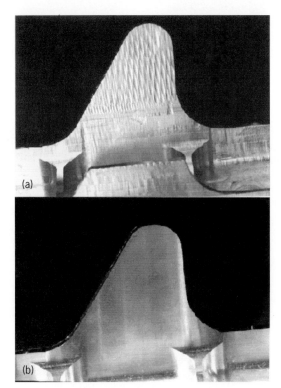

Fig. 5. Thin rib produced under (*a*) unstable (chattering) conditions and (*b*) stable high-speed machining.

tive machine tool chatter, which is a dominant problem in high-speed machining. Chatter results in unacceptable surfaces and potential damage to the tool or workpiece (**Fig. 5**). Generally, combating this phenomenon demands that the components of the machining system be as stiff as possible and possess as much damping as possible. The dynamic characteristics of the machine, tool, and workpiece result in a complex relationship between cutting conditions and performance in high-speed machining.

The milling process is a complex dynamical system. The feedback effects associated with regenerative chatter and nonlinearities associated with the intermittent cut result in complex stability behavior. For the case of regenerative chatter, the stability behavior is characterized by a stability chart. On such a chart, the regions of stable (nonchattering) and unstable (chattering) behavior are plotted as a function of practical machining parameters such as spindle speed and (axial) depth of cut. The chart is characterized by large lobes of instability separated by narrow tongues of stable behavior that lie approximately at spindle speeds corresponding to fractions of the dominant natural frequencies of the system. The stable tongues become more pronounced at higher spindle speeds, and the ability to take advantage of these regions is one of the major potential benefits of high-speed machining. A conventional milling machine with spindle speeds up to 6000 rpm can achieve a stable axial depth of cut of approximately 100 mm (4 in.), whereas a high-speed machine with a 30,000-rpm spindle can achieve a stable

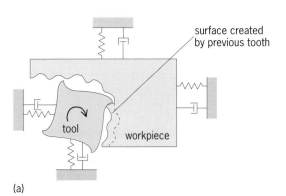

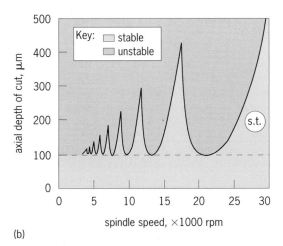

Fig. 4. High-speed machining. (*a*) Feedback effect in milling operation. (*b*) Stability chart for a long, slender milling cutter typical of those used in aerospace machining operations. Note the complex stability behavior that results (s.t. = stability tongue).

axial depth of cut more than five times greater by taking advantage of the stability tongue (Fig. *4b*). The combined increase in spindle speed, feed rate, and depth of cut associated with this increased stability provides a potential increase in metal removal rate of over 25 times.

In order to maximize the metal removal rate, it is necessary to use knowledge of the stability lobe diagram for each tool. Without this knowledge, users may stabilize machining operations by reducing the axial depth of cut, thus sacrificing metal removal rate for stability. With the stability diagram, it can be seen that each tool has a spindle speed which is best, and an axial depth of cut which should not be exceeded. If this information is available at the time that the program defining the tool path is created, then the part is machined without chatter the first time, and the material removal rate can be maximized for each given tool. In this way the machine tool can be utilized to its full potential.

For background information *see* ALLOY; ALUMINUM; IRON; MACHINABILITY OF METALS; MILLING MACHINE; POLYMERIC COMPOSITE; STEEL; TITANIUM; TOOLING in the McGraw-Hill Encyclopedia of Science & Technology.   M. A. Davies; S. Smith

Bibliography. N. Balasubramanian and S. Raman, A comprehensive evaluation tool for tool path planning in engineering technology, Conference Papers, Book IV, *Tribology*, 4:368–375, 1996; R. I. King, *High-Speed Machining Technology*, 1985; R. Lakkaraju, S. Raman, and S. A. Irani, An analytical model for optimization of NC tool cutting path, *Int. J. Prod. Res.*, 30(1):109–127, 1992; M. Nallakatla and S. Smith, A verification system for NC programming for quality in milling, in D. Dutta et al. (eds.), *Concurrent Eng.*, ASME PED, 59:165–178, 1992; K.-W. Ng and S. Raman, Forces, surface error and path length in tool path planning, *Proceedings of the 6th IE Research Conference*, pp. 948–953, 1997; S. Raman and R. Lakkaraju, The effect of tool life and other process variables in NC path planning, *Comput. Ind. Eng.*, 24(2):315–328, 1993; P. Shultz and T. Moriwaki, High-speed machining, *Ann. CIRP*, 41(2):637–643, 1992; S. Smith and J. Tlusty, NC programming for quality in machining, *Trans. NAMRI/SME*, 21:483–488, 1993; S. Smith and J. Tlusty, An overview of modelling and simulation of the milling process, *ASME J. Eng. Ind.*, 113:169–175, 1991; H. Soons and S. Yaniv, *Precision in Machining: Research Challenges*, NIST Internal Rep. 5626, 1995; J. Tlusty et al., High-speed machining, *Ann. CIRP*, 42(2):733–738, 1993.

Macroevolution

Environments such as lakes, caves, or mountaintops provide fascinating opportunities for studying evolution in isolation and determining rates and modes of evolutionary processes. Lying in the Great Rift Valley of Central Africa, Lake Tanganyika is such an evolutionary marvel. Tanganyika is one of the oldest, largest, and deepest lakes in the world. It is also a hot spot of biological diversity, harboring hundreds of species found nowhere else.

Geology of Lake Tanganyika. In order to understand the origins of this extraordinary biodiversity, it is necessary to first explore the geological evolution of the lake, because the two processes are closely linked. Lake Tanganyika and the rift valley as a whole owe their origins to the process of continental rifting, which split the African continent into two distinct tectonic plates, part of the global system of massive, 60-mi-thick (100-km) plates that cover the Earth. In some parts of the world these plates move past one another, are destroyed by sliding under one another, or collide in great mountain belts. In Africa new plate material is being created as two plates separate from one another, leaving behind a deep depression as a scar of that separation. This depression, the rift valley, has filled over time with both water and sediment, forming a vast chain of both fresh-water and saline lakes. This process has been going on in various parts of East and Central Africa for the past 45 million years. In the Lake Tanganyika region, however, the rifting began much later, starting about 10 million years ago, during the Miocene Epoch. One or more lakes have existed in what is today the Lake Tanganyika basin for most or all of the time since then.

The process of rifting is also responsible for the extraordinary depth of Lake Tanganyika, nearly 4900 ft (1500 m) at its deepest part (it is the second deepest lake in the world, after Lake Baikal in Russia). As rifting proceeds, it causes the bottom of the rift valley to sink along great fault systems that form the margins of the rift. Subsidence of the Earth's crust within the rift valley causes the lake floor to deepen over time, a process that is partly countered by sediment infilling the lake. Most of the world's deepest lakes have formed in this fashion. Because the Lake Tanganyika region has had high rainfall throughout its history, the lake has filled to a great depth and today spills out of its basin into a tributary of the Congo River. This great depth has ensured that even in times of aridity the lake has remained a harbor of fresh water for aquatic life and has made it possible for evolutionary processes to proceed throughout that time period. In contrast, many other rift valley lakes that exist today actually formed earlier in Earth history but were so shallow that they dried up repeatedly, causing the extinction of any species restricted to those lakes. However, changes in climate and tectonic activity have caused lake level in Tanganyika to fluctuate greatly over time, often rising and falling several hundreds of meters. During times of lake level falls, the lake basin can become divided into several lakes, isolating the populations of aquatic species in each lake for periods of thousands of years. This isolating mechanism is thought to play a major role in the evolution of new species and diversification in the lake, since some species are restricted to regions of the modern lake that once were separate lakes.

Structuring evolution in Lake Tanganyika. The faults that bound Lake Tanganyika are not continuous along the entire rift valley, but are divided into segments, broken by relatively unfaulted regions of lake shore. This geological factor has also played a role in structuring biological evolution in the lake. Faulted shorelines are associated with rocky lake bottoms, whereas unfaulted shorelines are sandy or muddy. Therefore, animals and plants that are restricted to either rocky or sandy lake floors find themselves restricted in their geographic ranges to relatively small segments of shoreline, separated from similar habitats and populations elsewhere in the lake. Again there is evidence that this process has played a role in driving the evolution of new species from separated populations through long periods of isolation. Many species in Lake Tanganyika have such poor capacities to disperse their offspring that even minor barriers to the spread of populations (or even sheer distance) may have been significant factors in isolating populations and driving evolution. Data from deoxyribonucleic acid (DNA) sequences in isolated populations of rock-dwelling fish and snails around the lake have shown that there are indeed genetic differences between populations living across both substrate barriers and old lake boundaries.

Biodiversity of Lake Tanganyika fauna. Lake Tanganyika is known to house over 1500 species of animals, plants, and single-celled organisms, and new species are being described from the lake every year, making it (along with Lake Baikal) one of the biologically richest lakes on Earth. Among these species, over 600 are found nowhere else (these are said to be endemic to the lake). Most of this endemic diversity is concentrated in a small number of groups of animals. These include the fish family Cichlidae (the cichlids, popular fish among aquarists), several families of the ostracod crustaceans (small crawling or swimming animals that are distantly related to crabs or shrimp and possess two calcium carbonate shells covering the body, similar in appearance to a clam shell), and the gastropod (snail) family Thiaridae. Within all three groups, evolution has proceeded in the lake for such a long time interval that the animals are extremely distinct from their fresh-water relatives in other parts of Africa. For example, among the endemic snails found in the lake are many species with extremely thick shells and spines, both very unusual features for fresh-water snails. For many years following discovery of the snails by early European explorers, scientists actually speculated that these snails might be related to fossil snails from the deposits of ancient seas, because of a superficial resemblance between the two. However, anatomical studies have shown that this similarity is actually a result of convergence in form rather than common evolutionary ancestry. Snails in Lake Tanganyika are under intense selective pressure from a wide variety of specialized predators, such as crabs and fish. Over time an "evolutionary arms race" has ensued, driving the snails to evolve heavier shells and their predators

to counter these changes with more effective shell-crushing abilities. Similar evolutionary changes have occurred independently in the world's oceans over hundreds of millions of years, but the young age of Lake Tanganyika illustrates that this process can occur in much shorter intervals of time.

Groups of closely related species that are restricted to a single lake (or other environment such as a mountaintop, cave, or island) and owe their evolution to a single ancestor species are referred to as species flocks. Evolutionary biologists have debated the question of whether species flocks in lakes arise suddenly, in a burst of speciation, or gradually over the history of the lake. Some evidence from both ancient lake deposits and genetic data supports the idea of sudden bursts of speciation as the dominant mode of diversification in lakes. In Lake Tanganyika, however, a resolution of this problem will have to await the collection of extremely long cores from the lake bottom that will provide a record of the lake's geological and paleontological history.

Genetic evidence from comparative studies of the DNA sequences of Lake Tanganyika species and their relatives outside the lake also illustrate how divergent the Lake Tanganyika species have become over the lake's long history. For example, comparisons of variability in DNA sequences from Lake Tanganyika cichlids have been made with cichlids from other large lakes of Africa which also harbor immense numbers of endemic species. These studies show that the degree of variability in DNA sequences of Lake Tanganyika cichlids far surpasses that of cichlids of other lakes. In fact, the variation seen in these other lakes is actually encompassed in one small part of the evolutionary tree of the Lake Tanganyika cichlids.

Species diversity in Lake Tanganyika is not only high on a lakewide basis but also at individual locations. It is not unusual to find more than 50 species of fish or ostracods living around a single area of rocks. The mechanisms that support such high diversity are controversial. Some scientists studying cichlid fish communities think that, through the lake's long evolution, species have been able to finely subdivide their use of habitat and food resources to the point where many species can coexist. However, other scientists point to data on modern ostracod species distribution as well their distribution in the recent past (inferred from sediment cores); they argue that species associations have been highly variable over the past few hundreds of years, suggesting that tightly interconnected species associations are not required to maintain high local diversity, and that other mechanisms to promote the maintenance of diversity must be sought.

This last point has an applied significance for conservation management of the lake as well. Lake Tanganyika today is under threat of various human impacts, notably the deforestation of its watersheds by heavy human population pressure and subsequent erosion. Massive quantities of silt entering the lake as a result of this erosion may be transforming ecosystems in unknown ways. An understanding of how stable or unstable the communities of Lake Tanganyika are naturally will help scientists to better predict the outcome of human disturbance and thereby allow them to make appropriate conservation recommendations for this remarkable storehouse of biological diversity and evolutionary history.

For background information *see* ECOSYSTEM; LAKE; PLATE TECTONICS; RIFT VALLEY; SPECIATION in the McGraw-Hill Encyclopedia of Science & Technology.   Andrew S. Cohen

Bibliography. A. S. Cohen et al., New palaeogeographic and lake level reconstructions of Lake Tanganyika: Implications for tectonic, climatic and biological evolution in a rift lake, *Basin Res.*, 9:107–132, 1997; G. W. Coulter, *Lake Tanganyika and Its Life*, 1991; A. Meyer, Phylogenetic relationships and evolutionary processes in East African cichlid fishes, *Trends Ecol. Evol.*, 8:279–284, 1993; K. West and A. S. Cohen, Shell microstructure of gastropods from Lake Tanganyika, Africa: Adaptation, convergent evolution and escalation, *Evolution*, 50:672–681, 1996.

Manufacturability

Manufacturability refers to the ease with which a product can be manufactured. More specifically, it is defined as the feasibility and ease of producing a part based on a judgment of whether the specifications stipulated for the part can be achieved by the manufacturing process that has been chosen to produce the part. The manufacturability assessment of the part occurs in different domains such as sheet metal, machining, casting, and injection molding. Manufacturability encompasses all of the more specific terms such as machinability, formability, and castability, which are, respectively, design for machining, design for forming, and design for casting. During preliminary design, the design specifications are often flexible, and knowledge of the manufacturing capability constraints can influence design specifications in a positive way with respect to final cost and quality. The methodology is based on the postulation that the early consideration of manufacturing will reduce the cost, improve the product quality, and shorten the time to market. There is extensive empirical evidence to justify the conclusion that design decisions are the most important in terms of costs.

Product realization process. The product realization process occurs in stages. The first stage is clarification of task, which involves a formal specification of the requirements that the new product must satisfy. The second stage is the creation of concepts that satisfy the product requirements. The final stage is the evaluation and analysis of the alternative concepts and the selection of a single concept. This concept is further refined until a complete design specification is created. Similarly, manufacturability evaluation and analysis should occur in stages that

correspond to the product development stages. Two of the earliest product development decisions that are relevant to manufacturing are material selection and process selection. These decisions are highly correlated since a decision concerning material often limits the choices for process selection. For example, in automotive design two material options for a door panel are plastic and sheet metal. Selecting plastic limits the manufacturing process to one of the molding processes, while selecting sheet metal limits the manufacturing process choice to forming. Following material and process selection, the part must be assessed against the intended process in the process manufacturability evaluation. After each individual part is evaluated, the assembly evaluation is performed.

Integrated material selection. Material choices are important decisions affecting the final product cost and quality. The material, the manufacturing process, and product geometry are closely related such that any decision about one will have significant repercussions on the others. Moreover, developments in materials science and improvements of manufacturing processes have greatly increased the number of material alternatives that designers must consider. Selection problems such as material selection are called multiattribute decision-making problems.

Material attributes critical to product design can be classified as either mechanical properties or physical properties. Mechanical properties include strength, hardness, and stiffness. Physical properties consist of density and conductivity. To aid designers in selecting the most suitable material, software systems have been developed that utilize both database technology for storing the tremendous amount of material data and decision support systems that help the designer to state the product requirements with respect to materials.

Process selection. Process selection is similar to material selection in many respects but can be more difficult. Often, several processes are used to fabricate a part. Process selection is facilitated by using a classification such as a primary, a secondary, and a tertiary process. Primary processes are the main shape-generating processes and include casting, injection molding, forging, machining, and such. Secondary processes form features on the parts such as holes or refine existing features. This category includes machining, drilling, and broaching. Tertiary processes do not affect the part geometry but improve surfaces or tolerances. Examples include lapping, plating, or heat treatment.

Process selection factors are the shape-generating ability, size limitations, tolerance capabilities, surface finish capabilities, power consumption, production volume, and production rate capabilities. Process selection is aided by several observations. Many combinations of materials and processes are not possible. For example, aluminum and injection molding are not a feasible combination. Many combinations of processes are not possible. The overall geometry often dictates which processes are compatible. For example, axisymmetrical parts are often turned on a lathe. These observations facilitate selection of the primary process. Secondary processes are selected based on the future geometry required, tolerances required, and surface finish required. Tertiary processes are selected based on the enhancement desired such as a better surface quality.

Process manufacturability evaluation. Following process selection, the design must be evaluated against the capabilities of the intended manufacturing process. Manufacturability is concerned with the design of a single part. It is during this stage that modifications can be made to the design to improve its manufacturability. Manufacturability usually refers to the feasibility of fabricating a part given a particular manufacturing process. Equally important is a cost comparison between alternative design solutions. The manufacturing cost is a significant factor in developing new products. A cost estimate is often performed, and different processing alternatives can be compared to determine the lowest-cost alternative.

Assembly evaluation. Most products are composed of many parts that are assembled together. Considerations during the design phase can result in creating a design that is easy to assemble and less costly. Design for assembly is conducted with heuristics. A primary assembly heuristic is to reduce the total number of parts. Assembly evaluation should occur early in product realization since the design team may be able to eliminate some parts and thus avoid engineering evaluations of those parts.

Information issues in product design. The front loading of the design process poses significant strains on existing methodologies and design systems. Manufacturability evaluation is knowledge and information intensive. Knowledge is contained in rules that usually involve one or more design features or attributes. An example of a rule is to make the corner radii of pockets equal to the radius of one of the available milling cutting tools. Handbooks have organized much of this knowledge. Designers who utilize these handbooks can achieve manufacturability improvements in their design with little effort. However, the broad knowledge and information provided in handbooks is difficult to use. Designers must determine applicability of rules to their case, and exceptions to the rules are difficult to handle in this format. Information is more data intensive and is exemplified by material databases that may contain information on up to 100,000 different materials. The tremendous amount of data involved in performing these evaluations requires support, usually in the form of databases.

Manufacturability software applications address these needs. These systems incorporate knowledge with large databases to aid designers in following guidelines of good design practice that will result in manufacturable products. Since the manufacturing domain is so broad, the systems developed typically concentrate on a single manufacturing process such as machining, casting, or injection molding. Many of these systems provide manufacturability ratings,

make recommendations, and identify difficult-to-manufacture product features. Consequently, designers can determine the effect of their decisions on the manufacturability of the product. The use of such systems is becoming more widespread and is regarded as an important technique for competing in the markets of today.

For background information *see* COMPUTER-AIDED DESIGN AND MANUFACTURING; COMPUTER INTEGRATED MANUFACTURING; MACHINING; MANUFACTURING PROCESSES; PRODUCT DESIGN; PRODUCTION ENGINEERING in the McGraw-Hill Encyclopedia of Science & Technology.   Ronald E. Giachetti

Bibliography. J. G. Bralla, *Handbook of Design for Manufacturability*, 1999; J. R. Dixon and C. Poli, *Engineering Design and Design for Manufacturing*, 1995.

Mars

On July 4, 1997, the spacecraft *Mars Pathfinder* landed in Ares Vallis, an ancient flood channel in the northern hemisphere of Mars. In addition to returning spectacular multispectral images (**Fig. 1**) and weather data, *Pathfinder* (renamed the Sagan Memorial Station) and its mobile robot, *Sojourner Truth*, measured the chemistry and composition of rocks and found that Mars had a more active geologic history than previously believed, and that Mars shows evidence of having had liquid water on the surface for an extended time.

On September 11, 1997, *Mars Global Surveyor* entered a 45-h elliptical orbit and began aerobraking toward a 2-h polar, Sun-synchronous orbit that will take it over the Sun-facing hemisphere of the planet at 2 p.m. local Mars time. When it achieves this mapping orbit in March 1999, *Mars Global Surveyor* will begin a one-Mars-year (two-Earth-year) mapping mission to study the surface and atmosphere of the planet. Valuable science data have been obtained by *Global Surveyor* since shortly after entering Mars's orbit, including the discovery of magnetic anomalies in the crust and the correction of altitudes and map locations of major features.

Pathfinder and *Global Surveyor* are the first two missions in a long-term program of Mars exploration which will feature launches every 26 months, in the time windows when Mars and the Earth are favorably placed for space missions.

Mars Exploration Program

The Mars Exploration Program, initiated in 1994, is launching two missions to Mars at every opportunity, to study the planet from orbit and from the Martian ground. The program, managed by the Jet Propulsion Laboratory (JPL) for the National Aeronautics and Space Administration (NASA), is pioneering NASA's thrust in "better, faster, cheaper" space science missions. The scientific focus of the program is on accumulating knowledge about Mars's climate and resources, and to address the question of

Fig. 1. First panorama from the surface of Mars by the *Mars Pathfinder* spacecraft on July 4, 1997. *(NASA; Jet Propulsion Laboratory)*

whether life ever originated on the planet. This question has been of great interest since the announcement in August 1996 of the possibility that evidence of past life was discovered in the Martian meteorite ALH84001, found in Antarctica in 1984.

Carry-over of knowledge. One key to the low-cost Mars Exploration Program is that each mission will do less science than previous missions such as *Mars Observer*; but a steady stream of information about Mars and about how well spacecraft designs or technology are working will allow the following missions to be designed and operated with the advantage of that knowledge. For example, information obtained by *Mars Pathfinder* on the atmospheric characteristics of Mars is being used by *Mars Global Surveyor* to conduct aerobraking activities.

Mars Global Surveyor, in turn, will provide a backup radio relay link to Earth for the *Mars Surveyor 1998* lander (the *Mars Polar Lander*) and the primary link for its two microprobes. *Pathfinder*'s demonstration of entry and descent techniques, plus its computer, is also being used by the *Mars Polar Lander*. *Pathfinder*'s rover, *Sojourner*, is a technology demonstration which is providing data necessary for the design of long-range rovers in 2001 and 2003.

Redesign of processes. The second key to low cost for the Mars Exploration Program is the redesign of processes. For example, the Jet Propulsion Laboratory uses the following processes to reduce cost:

1. Unnecessary paperwork and reviews are eliminated. For instance, the program office has imposed no additional reviews on the projects, but attends project reviews to provide oversight and evaluation of the projects' progress.

2. New computer technology is utilized to communicate between team members and to do quick and efficient designing.

3. Rapid prototyping is used; that is, whole systems are built up quickly and tested to find problems before moving on to the next version.

4. End-to-end system design and testing is employed so that the way in which the parts work together can be understood before the detailed design proceeds too far.

5. The Jet Propulsion Laboratory teams up with an industrial partner to manufacture a series of spacecraft.

6. The Laboratory teams up with other NASA centers, universities, and so forth, to capture expertise.

7. The Laboratory teams up with other countries to add to the science that can be collected within a fixed cost to the United States.

Utilization of existing technology. The third key to low cost is to take advantage of the new technology that has already been developed by NASA, the military, and especially commercial enterprise. For instance, the commercial hardware-based computer on *Mars Pathfinder* exceeded the combined capability of all previous flight computers. Of course, commercial elements require extensive test and flight qualification to ensure their reliability and robustness in space environments.

Mars Surveyor 1998. An orbiter and a lander that make up the *Mars Surveyor 1998* mission set are being built by the Jet Propulsion Laboratory's industrial partner, Lockheed Martin Astronautics. The *Mars Climate Orbiter* will focus on the atmosphere of Mars; the *Mars Polar Lander*, on the soil near the south polar cap. The lander will investigate how much water is in the soil, the form in which it resides there, and the effect of the Martian seasons on the water content.

This water search will be augmented by the two microprobes, provided through NASA's New Millennium Program. The microprobe project, called Deep Space 2, is developing basketball-sized, advanced-technology heat shields to carry the probes to the surface without parachutes. The probes, shaped like missiles, are about the size of a quart milk bottle. They are expected to plunge up to 2 m (6.5 ft) into the soil and make subsurface measurements of the water content.

In addition to the United States missions, Japan is

flying an aeronomy orbiter in 1998, called *Planet B*. A Program Science Group has been formed which comprises all project scientists from all the Mars missions, including *Planet B*.

Search for evidence of life. NASA has devised a plan to look intensively, beginning in 2001, for evidence of past (or even extant) life by flying a series of orbiters, rovers, and sample returns. This program, which augments the 1994-initiated Mars Exploration Program, began in fiscal year 1998. In the current program plan, the orbiters will reveal environments which might have harbored life to which rovers can be targeted. In 2001 and 2003, rovers will be sent to select, collect, and cache samples; and in 2005, the first sample return mission will be launched to bring one of these caches back to Earth for analysis in 2008. Earth analysis is required to look for indications of chemistry with possible links to life because the traces are too small to be detected by instruments that can be carried to Mars. Sample returns are several missions in one: a Mars orbiter; a Mars lander; a small rover to retrieve the cached samples; a rocket to launch from Mars; a spacecraft to bring back the samples to Earth; and an Earth entry, landing, and collection-storage system to safely allow the samples to be archived and analyzed. Therefore, the new program involving sample returns is significantly more expensive than the original program.

Robots and humans in partnership. In 2001, in addition to finding out about how Mars evolved by sending a long-range rover to explore and collect samples for later return, the orbiter and lander missions are planned to carry instruments to find out whether Mars is safe for humans to visit. Another experiment proposes to derive oxygen from the Martian atmosphere, which is primarily carbon dioxide. The Johnson Space Center is working with the Jet Propulsion Laboratory to carry out a joint venture between the Human Exploration and Development of Space Enterprise and the Space Science Enterprise. This relationship is planned to extend for decades, and demonstrates that humans and robots can be partners rather than competitors in the exploration of space.

International cooperation. In 2003 the European Space Agency is contemplating an orbiter and lander mission, and the United States is working with the Agency to define cooperation and roles for missions launched within the 2003 time window. For example, the 2003 European orbiter might provide a communications relay for the 2003 United States lander and rover. The 2005 sample return mission, which will undoubtedly have international participation, is intended to be the first of three such missions, interspersed with rover missions, through 2016. With three samples of Mars being analyzed on Earth, scientists believe that there is a good chance to identify whether life ever existed on Mars, as well as to understand the climate and history of the planet.

Donna L. Shirley

Pathfinder Test and Verification

The *Mars Pathfinder* mission embodies NASA's faster, better, cheaper mode of operation. It required 3 years from project start to launch (compared with 5–10 years for previous missions); it embodied three spacecraft in one (cruise, entry, and a lander plus a rover for the surface of Mars); and it cost about ¹⁄₁₅ as much as the *Viking* mission of 1976. In order to succeed within the constraints of this mission, the *Mars Pathfinder* project had to develop and implement a design that inherently takes risk without significantly increasing the likelihood of failure. The key to meeting this challenge was robust design, thorough analysis and simulation, and an extensive test program.

Spacecraft system testing. The assembly, test, and launch operations phase began in June 1995, 18 months prior to launch. Its unusually long duration was necessary to reduce risk. Considerable time was needed to operate and test the electronics (over 2700 h on most electronics, almost half the trip time to Mars) and to assemble the complex mechanical system. The delivery of the avionics, structure, and cabling was followed by a sequential buildup and test of hardware and software leading to the first complete lander assembly (**Fig. 2**) in February 1996. Along with the buildup, major system tests were conducted in the various spacecraft operating modes: prelaunch, launch, cruise, entry, descent and landing, and surface operations.

Completion of the spacecraft assembly was followed by the environmental and functional test phase. Tests were conducted in the launch configuration to simulate the launch and deep-space cruise environments. During the simulation of deep-space conditions, the solar array ran 30°C (54°F) hotter than predicted. This problem was related to a lack of detailed analytic modeling of the significant blockage of the back of the solar array by the propulsion system and electronic hardware. Changes were made in the thermal blanket design, and some loss of power was accepted. In flight the solar array performed exactly as expected. The process concluded

Fig. 2. Fully assembled *Mars Pathfinder*, ready for test. (*NASA; Jet Propulsion Laboratory*)

with a test of the deployed (petals opened) lander under simulated Mars surface conditions: gaseous nitrogen at a pressure of 10 kilopascals (0.1 atmosphere) and temperatures ranging from 0 to −100°C (32 to −148°F). These tests included the rover waking up on the first day and driving off the lander petal. On August 10 the spacecraft was shipped to Kennedy Space Center for the final full-up assembly and verification process. The final assembly and test was completed on October 28. *Mars Pathfinder* was launched by the Delta II rocket on December 4, 1996.

Verification. Any mission designed to land on the surface of a planet from space carries higher inherent risk than a fly-by or orbiting mission. The risk comes largely from the entry, descent, landing, and surface operations phases, where the complexities of the required hardware and software and the uncertainties in the environment make such missions extremely challenging.

Entry, descent, and landing. The entry, descent, and landing test program, completed in June 1996, grew significantly from its start in 1993 with the first set of scale-model airbag tests. The hardware test program was tied together with a sophisticated set of computer analyses and simulations.

The computer master simulation used a probabilistic model (a Monte Carlo model) to account for all the uncertainties in the hardware performance and the environment. This simulation included all the elements of the entry, descent, and landing sequence, starting with the dynamics and thermodynamics of entry, including all the dynamics of decelerations from the parachute and deceleration rockets, and ending with the impact of the airbags on the Martian surface. The simulation was used to verify the test conditions applied to each of the hardware elements. For example, prior to the final qualification drop test of the airbags, the simulation was run to predict the 99.99%-probable fastest landing condition. This number, 28 m/s (63 mi/h), was then used in the final airbag test.

While the spacecraft was undergoing its testing at the Jet Propulsion Laboratory, three entry, descent, and landing subsystems were completing qualification testing. The parachute, deceleration rockets, and airbags were functionally tested at special facilities suited to their unique characteristics.

In the case of the parachute test program, the simulation model predicted a range of dynamic pressures that the parachute could be expected to experience as it opened in the Mars atmosphere. One of the qualification units was subjected to a dynamic overpressure test at greater than three times the highest predicted value, and the parachute survived undamaged. *See* AERODYNAMIC DECELERATORS.

The rocket-assisted deceleration subsystem is required to decelerate the parachute-lander system from an average terminal velocity of 65 m/s (145 mi/h) to zero by using three solid rockets. The key to success was in the precise timing and duration of the firing. The simulation program predicted the

Fig. 3. Full-scale *Mars Pathfinder* airbag assembly. *(NASA; Jet Propulsion Laboratory)*

firing conditions, and a successful live fire test of the rockets was conducted at the China Lake Naval Air Warfare Center in the California desert.

The airbag subsystem is a completely new design that uses gas-pressurized bags made of high-tensile-strength-fiber material. The four airbags envelop the lander and cushion its landing on the rocky Martian terrain. The design was tested at Lewis Research Center's Plum Brook Station in Ohio, which has the world's largest vacuum chamber with a ceiling height of about 37 m (120 ft). Here the full-scale assembly, consisting of four segments forming a spheroid with overall diameter of about 5.8 m (19 ft; **Fig. 3**), was dropped onto a rock field representative of the expected landing site. In order to simulate the horizontal velocity in a vertical drop test, the rocky surface was rotated 60° off the floor. The final test was conducted in March 1996 with a completely successful drop at the predicted velocity of 28 m/s (63 mi/h).

Flight and surface operations. In order to verify the flight and surface performance of the *Mars Pathfinder*, an extensive set of end-to-end tests of the flight and ground hardware and software was conducted. The most important tests were the lifelike simulations of entry, descent, and landing and of the first few days of surface operations. These tests were conducted in a manner as close to the expected flight conditions as possible, including the actual start times and round-the-clock activities.

For example, Operational Readiness Test #5 was conducted for 5 days in March 1997. The test used the engineering model spacecraft, located in a sandbox built to roughly simulate a Mars terrain, running the most current flight software. The test was designed to address every aspect of the approach, entry, and first 5 days of surface operations. The initial conditions for the test were set up by a small group that kept them secret from the rest of the team. The test began with a simulated approach to Mars that required the navigation team to prepare for and conduct a last-minute trajectory correction maneuver. The simulated entry and landing used realistic data for the software to operate on. The simulated landing occurred at 10:07 a.m. local time, or 3:00 a.m. on Mars, just as the actual landing would on July 4. Once on the surface the on-board software, which runs completely autonomously from days before entry until 4 h after touchdown, sensed the orientation of the lander and proceeded to right the vehicle. During all this activity the operations team was stationed at their consoles, in the same way as anticipated on July 4, looking for the few signals that the lander would normally send at this time in the mission. At about 2:00 p.m. (7:00 a.m. on Mars) the spacecraft transmitter turned on and sent the team the first full set of telemetry, indicating that the lander was healthy but tipped at a fairly steep angle. At 4:30 p.m. the team turned on the lander camera to see what their simulated world looked like. The test went on uninterrupted for the next 4 days. The same type of test was repeated three more times, with each test teaching the team more about spacecraft operations and how they would have to perform.

Performance. The performance of the *Mars Pathfinder* exceeded all expectations. The entry, descent, and landing and the early surface operations phase were completely successful as illustrated by the first image sent back from *Pathfinder* on the afternoon of July 4, 1997 (Fig. 1). The lander and rover operated until September 27, when it is believed that the lander battery, designed to operate for 30 days, finally failed, and normal communications were lost. At that time the lander had operated about three times and the rover about twelve times their design life, and the total science data return was about four times the original expectations.

Brian K. Muirhead

Pathfinder Scientific Results

The *Mars Pathfinder* mission investigated the geology and meteorology of Mars and tested several engineering tasks. It operated for more than 80 sols, or Martian days, and returned vast amounts of scientific and engineering data, including more than 16,000 images from the lander and 550 images from the rover.

Weather. The weather at Ares Vallis, the *Pathfinder* landing site, was warmer than expected, with morning clouds and even a few storms. The Atmospheric Structure Instrument/Meteorology Package measured daily temperatures ranging from a predawn low of about 200 K (~ −100°F) to a daytime high of about 260 K (~10°F). These temperatures are on average about 10 K (18°F) warmer than those measured at the *Viking* lander sites. The air temperatures measured on descent (**Fig. 4**) were on the

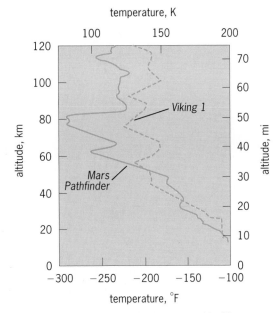

Fig. 4. Atmospheric temperatures measured by *Mars Pathfinder* during its descent compared to similar measurements by *Viking 1*. (NASA; Jet Propulsion Laboratory)

order of 30–50 K (54–90°F) colder than the *Viking* descent temperatures. The different latitudes and different times of day for the entry and landing of *Pathfinder* and *Viking 1* could be a factor in the temperature differences. At an altitude of 80 km (50 mi), the atmospheric temperatures were below the condensation level of carbon dioxide (CO_2), indicating that some of the high clouds may be composed of dry ice rather than water ice. Below about 50 km (30 mi), the *Viking* and *Pathfinder* temperatures were very similar.

Morning clouds were seen on several days in the hours before sunrise. It is difficult to determine their altitude. If they were lit directly by the Sun over the horizon, they could have been quite high, on the order of 120 km (75 mi), and possibly then they were a mix of water and carbon dioxide ices. If the lighting was a more complex, scattered illumination, then they could have been as low as 15 km (9 mi).

The storms that rolled over the Sagan Memorial Station, as the *Pathfinder* lander was named, were large dust devils. In all, 16 were detected based on short-term, highly correlated variations in temperature and wind measurements. Early analysis shows that they can be as large as 200 m (650 ft) in diameter and up to perhaps 10 km (6 mi) tall. Their frequent occurrence indicates that they may be a contributor to the high level of background dust.

Atmospheric pressure at the landing site was slightly less than that seen in 1976 at the *Viking* sites, but with the same daily variations. This 10–20% difference is due mostly to the altitude variations between the sites. The pressures were on average 675 pascals (6.7 mbar or 0.2 in. of mercury), com-

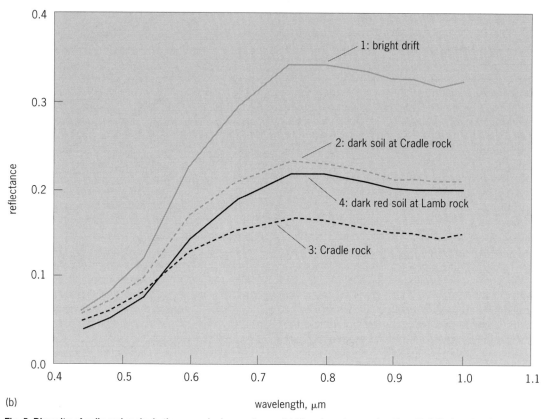

Fig. 5. Diversity of soils and rocks in the rover deployment area. (a) View from Imager for *Mars Pathfinder,* showing four areas of study. (b) Twelve-color spectra showing similarities and differences among these four regions. Low values and steep slope in the visible range (0.4–0.62 μm) indicate that all the features appear red to the human eye. Higher values of the bright drift at all wavelengths indicate that it is brighter than the other three regions. *(NASA; Jet Propulsion Laboratory)*

pared to the average Earth atmospheric pressure of 101.3 kPa (1013 mbar or 30 in. of mercury). The wind directions appear to be controlled by local slopes. In general the winds blow upslope during the day (toward the south) and downslope during the night (toward the north), with the direction rotating clockwise almost continuously between these two conditions. The wind-sock experiment suggests that in general the winds were light and less than about 10 m/s (~20 mi/h).

Imager results. The Imager for *Mars Pathfinder* had several tasks. First was a general survey of the area around the lander. The Imager built up a panorama of the landing site, taking pictures in at least three

of the twelve filters for a full-color view. It was also to take an image of *Sojourner*, the rover, at the end of each day so that the rover team would have a definite position from which to start moving the next morning. The Imager also obtained images of the magnetic properties experiment. This experiment consisted of a metal plate in front of several bull's-eye magnets. The magnetic particles of dust adhered to these targets over time. Since each magnet was of a different strength, the amount of dust at each one, as well as the pattern created, indicated that at least some of the dust is a mineral composed partially of magnetic material with a mean size of 1 micrometer.

Many of these images were taken at relatively low resolutions and with a good deal of data compression so that the information could be transmitted back to Earth more quickly. However, the Imager was capable of taking very high resolution images and sending them back to Earth with no data compression. This was done early in the mission for several small areas through all twelve color filters. These colors range from the visible to the near-infrared. The spectral images (**Fig. 5**), once fully calibrated, will allow the mineral composition of the rocks to be constrained. So far it has been determined that there are four types of soil (bright, red, global dust; dark, coarser-grained, less-oxidized soil; darker disturbed soil found in rover tracks; and intermediate-brightness soil with a higher abundance of crystalline material) and three types of rocks (bright, red, weathered rocks; dark, less weathered rocks, perhaps crater ejecta; and pink rocks possibly formed by cementation of water-rich soils).

After the end of the primary mission, the Imager began to take a full panorama of the site at the highest resolution, in all twelve colors, and to send it back to Earth with very little data compression. This so-called Super Pan was over 80% complete when the lander finally failed.

Geology and geochemistry. The elemental abundances of Martian rocks and soils (**Fig. 6**) were measured by *Sojourner*, using the Alpha Proton X-Ray Spectrometer. The elemental abundances of the soils measured were very similar to the elemental abundances of the soils measured at the sites of the *Viking* landers, indicating a similar origin for the soils of these three sites.

Elemental abundances of rocks could not be measured by the *Viking* landers. However, several meteorites, known collectively as the SNCs (after three types: shergottites, nakhlites, and chassignites), are believed to originate from Mars, and their elemental abundances have been measured. The rocks at the Ares Vallis site do not match these at all. Based upon diagnostic abundance ratios, the rocks at the *Pathfinder* site look more like terrestrial andesites, which are volcanic rocks found in, among other places, the Andes mountains of South America. Andesites can be texturally similar to volcanic basalts, such as the rocks found in the Hawaiian islands, but they contain less aluminum and more silicon.

The cameras of the rover imaged many small rocks that appear to be rounded pebbles. One way that pebbles are rounded is by being carried along a stream or river. Another way is by waves crashing on a beach. Three rocks, Shark, Half Dome, and Prince Charming, may be conglomerates, composed of rounded pebbles cemented together by what was once Martian mud. Although this is one interpretation based on the texture seen by the rover camera, there is still much debate about it. If correct, these interpretations would require a warm, wet period on Mars far longer than current theories suggest.

One other geological experiment was performed to measure the core of Mars. By tracking the radio

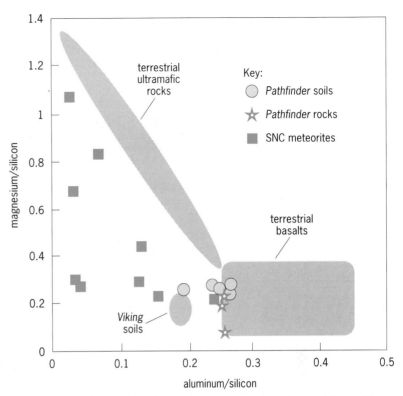

Fig. 6. Plot of the elemental abundances of magnesium and aluminum, relative to silicon, for some of the soils and rocks measured by *Sojourner*. Also plotted are the same abundances for the SNC meteorites, thought to come from Mars, and terrestrial volcanic rocks. The Mars rocks, if volcanic, are more like terrestrial basalts than the Martian meteorites. *(NASA; Jet Propulsion Laboratory)*

signals from the lander and comparing them to similar measurements made in 1976 with the *Viking* landers, it was determined that the rotational axis of Mars had precessed slightly. This precession allows the measurement of the planet's moment of inertia, the property of rotating bodies that resists changes in rotation. This parameter is the key, along with the mass and radius, to understanding the planet's density distribution. The *Pathfinder* measurements show that the planet is differentiated with a core radius ranging from at least 1300 km (800 mi), if it is pure iron, up to about 2000 km (1250 mi), if it is less dense by the inclusion of larger amounts of sulfur.

For background information *see* ANDESITE; BASALT; COSMOCHEMISTRY; MARS; METEORITE; MONTE CARLO METHOD; SIMULATION; SPACE PROBE; X-RAY SPECTROMETRY in the McGraw-Hill Encyclopedia of Science & Technology.   David Klassen

Bibliography. M. Carr, *Water on Mars,* 1996; H. Kieffer (ed.), *Mars,* 1992; B. K. Muirhead, Mars Pathfinder flight system design and implementation, *1995 IEEE Aerospace Applications Conference Proceedings,* 1995; B. K. Muirhead, Mars Pathfinder flight system integration and test, *1996 IEEE Aerospace Conference Proceedings,* 1996; Reports on Mars Pathfinder, *Science,* 278:1734–1774, 1997; D. Shirley and D. McCleese, *Mars Exploration Strategy: 1995–2020,* AIAA 96-0333, 1996.

Mass extinction

Recent advances in technology are allowing researchers to gain new insights into the causes of extinction among several life-forms millions of years ago, notably during the Paleozoic Era and the Cretaceous-Paleogene boundary.

A Theory of Marine Mass Extinction

The most severe mass extinction of all time occurred at the end of the Paleozoic Era, 250 million years ago, when 50% of the families and 75% of the genera of marine animals became extinct. To calculate the loss at the species level on a global scale from that distant time requires extrapolation from the data of higher taxonomic levels. Approximately 95% of the species would have had to go extinct to eliminate the high percentages of families and genera lost in the late Permian, the period ending the Paleozoic Era.

Permian Period. The Permian was an unusual time in geologic history. Collisions from plate tectonic motion had sutured most of the continental blocks into Pangaea, a supercontinent that extended from pole to pole. Because of the grouping together of the continents, there was only one large ocean basin, called Panthalassa, instead of the several partially isolated ocean basins of today. In the late Permian, the sea level was lower than at any other time in the last half billion years, and sharp changes in carbon-13/carbon-12 ($^{13}C/^{12}C$) isotopic ratios indicate that unusual oceanographic events characterized the late Permian. Exceptional amounts of volcanism occurred in South China and Siberia.

In 1995 it was first recognized that large amounts of chemical precipitates of calcium carbonate, which can form only if unusually high concentrations of carbon dioxide drive the alkalinity of the water to high levels, occur in late Permian rocks. Such conditions existed in very ancient Precambrian times, when carbon dioxide was an abundant constituent of the atmosphere, but carbonate precipitates present in great quantity are almost unknown in the last 500 million years except in the late Permian. It was suggested that overturn of a stratified ocean with a huge reservoir of carbon dioxide, accumulated from the decay of organic matter settling from the surface plus other sources, could have made surface waters carbon dioxide rich. Evidence for deep-sea anoxia (which implies high levels of carbon dioxide) has now been obtained from late Permian rocks in Japan and British Columbia, flanking the Panthalassic basin. Shifts in $^{13}C/^{12}C$ isotope ratios at the end of the Permian also suggest that a reservoir of isotopically light carbon (from organic fractionation) was fed into the surface waters of the oceans at that time, and evidence for a brief episode of sea-level glaciation at the end of the Permian in Siberia indicates that high-latitude cooling and freezing could have triggered increased thermohaline circulation and oceanic overturn.

Aquatic organisms differ from air-breathing organisms in having few physiological adaptations for controlling exchange of carbon dioxide with the external environment. The reason is that carbon dioxide is highly soluble in water but is in very low concentration in most environments. Therefore, metabolically produced carbon dioxide easily diffuses across cell membranes from body fluids into the surrounding water and never builds up in concentration in the bodies of aquatic animals, whereas carbon dioxide must reach internal concentrations 20–40 times higher than atmospheric concentration before it will readily leave solution in the body fluids of air breathers and diffuse into the atmosphere as a gas.

Because aquatic organisms have so little physiological control over carbon dioxide, when the concentration of carbon dioxide increases in water the carbon dioxide diffuses into aquatic animals and causes severe effects, mostly in acid-base balance. One effect is a narcotizing acidosis in which metabolic activity slows down. Also, carbon dioxide can interfere with the secretion of calcium carbonate skeletons, the most common type of hard parts in marine animals. In addition, carbon dioxide can reduce the ability of some respiratory pigments to hold oxygen, so that there is a decrease in the ability of the pigments to acquire oxygen and transport it into the animal if excess carbon dioxide is present externally. All these effects are dangerous for any aquatic organism and potentially fatal. In the late Permian, ocean overturn apparently brought high concentrations of carbon dioxide into surface waters on a global scale. Since overturn of the world ocean would have taken about 1000 years, the disruption of the physiology of most marine animals would have lasted far longer than their individual life spans, resulting in widespread death of marine life.

Hypercapnia. The various groups of organisms dominant in the Permian ocean may be grouped into those with no potential physiological buffering from hypercapnia (elevated carbon dioxide) and those with some potential buffering or ability to physiologically adapt to hypercapnia. The groups with no predicted potential resistance to hypercapnia include organisms that conduct gas exchange by diffusion over the whole body surface and lack specialized respiratory tissues. These sensitive groups also lack internal circulatory systems capable of regulating the rates of movement of metabolites in the body. The sensitive group included calcareous foraminifera, corals, bryozoa, brachiopods, and heavily calcified echinoderms. The groups predicted to be buffered or less sensitive to hypercapnia include animals with specialized gills, active internal circulation, and active life habits for which adaptation to exercise metabolism and short-term metabolic increases in carbon dioxide is part of their normal life. The less sensitive group included most mollusks, large arthropods, chordates, protozoa that do not secrete calcium carbonate tests, and the burrowing holothurians (sea cucumbers) in the Echinodermata.

Hypercapnia would have stressed all marine animals, elevating their extinction rates, but if hypercapnia were involved in the Permian extinction a selectivity of extinction also should have been present, with more extinction in the sensitive than in the less sensitive groups. The effect of the Permian extinction on the two physiologically different groups was examined by tabulating the extinction and survival of genera in the taxa constituting the two groups. An unpublished database of time ranges of about 36,000 genera of marine animals was used as the information source. During the Permian extinction the less sensitive group had extinction of about 40% of its genera in each interval, whereas the sensitive group had 63% generic extinction at the start and 87% extinction at the height of the Permian extinction. In fact, no similar two-to-one selectivity, as seen at the end of the Permian Period, occurs in any of the other intervals of very high extinction rate over the last 500 million years. This marked selectivity is consistent with an elevated concentration of carbon dioxide in late Permian oceans as the kill mechanism for this remarkable event.

Overturn of a stratified ocean bringing carbon dioxide–rich water to the surface would also affect the Earth's atmosphere and climate. The carbon dioxide–enriched oceanic surface waters would have equilibrated with the atmosphere as oceanic overturn occurred, and the carbon dioxide content of the atmosphere would have increased up to sixfold, causing a severe greenhouse warming of the climate far more extreme than that predicted for the doubling of atmospheric carbon dioxide from human burning of fossil fuels happening today. This may have driven the major climate changes and extinction events also seen on land at the end of the Permian Period.

Comparison with other theories shows that hypercapnia is most likely to have been the major kill mechanism for the Permian marine extinction among other possible causes. The three most recently proposed theories—nutrient limitation with collapse of the food chain, anoxia, and multiple mechanisms—do not produce the observed selectivity of extinction. In fact, nutrient limitation would have damaged most severely the active organisms that survived best and would have favored passive, sedentary organisms with low metabolic rates; yet the passive organisms were the most devastated. The same is true for anoxia. Passive groups should have been less affected than active organisms, yet just the reverse was true. The wrong groups suffered high extinction and were less affected for anoxia to have been the major cause of extinction in the late Permian. The idea of multiple mechanisms contains no predictions of selectivity, but would produce a selectivity consonant with the kill mechanisms involved. The selectivity predicted for hypercapnia successfully predicts which groups actually declined most and least in the end-Permian extinction event.   Richard K. Bambach

Cretaceous-Paleogene Impact Event

The Cretaceous-Paleogene (K-P) boundary (equivalent with the K-T boundary of older usage) was originally recognized because of the extinction of numerous species of organisms, including the dinosaurs and large marine reptiles. Detailed studies of both the terrestrial and deep-sea record demonstrate that about 50% of marine genera and about 70% of all species disappeared at or close to the end of the Cretaceous Period. There appears to have been considerable selectivity in the extinction, with terrestrial plants, stream and pond dwellers, and bottom-dwelling species in the deep sea suffering far lower extinction rates than other groups of organisms. There may also have been regional differences in extinction rates since land plants experienced much greater extinction in North America than in the rest of the world.

The record of all fossil groups displays biases produced by sampling effects which obscure the rate of extinction (see **illus.**). For example, dinosaurs appear to decline in diversity over several million years prior to the end of the Cretaceous Period, but this gradual extinction may simply reflect the uncommon occurrence of dinosaur remains. Rare species such as most dinosaurs are unlikely to be found up to the end of the Cretaceous even if they really died out right at the Cretaceous-Paleogene boundary. It is notable that very abundant fossils such as deep-sea planktic foraminifera show a much more rapid decline in diversity at the Cretaceous-Paleogene boundary than dinosaurs. In turn, the extremely abundant calcareous nannofossils (the prime constituent in chalk) display an even more abrupt extinction level than the planktic foraminifera. Therefore, it is likely that sampling biases related to the abundance and preservation potential of different fossil groups may partly account for the prevalence of apparently gradual losses of biological diversity before the Cretaceous-Paleogene boundary. After accounting for these sampling biases, the fossil record is generally consistent with an abrupt extinction, although the possibility that some groups of organisms had been in significant decline prior to the Cretaceous-Paleogene boundary cannot be eliminated.

Cretaceous environment. There was a long-term decline in global temperatures during the last several million years of the Cretaceous Period as seen in both the deep sea and records of terrestrial climate. These climatic changes were probably responsible for the extinction of typical Cretaceous groups such as the reef-associated rudist bivalves, the inoceramids, and the distinctive high-latitude species of calcareous nannofossils in the 6 million years prior to the Cretaceous-Paleogene boundary. An abrupt warming event occurred a half million years before the boundary, as reflected by changes in the relative abundance of species in both deep-ocean and terrestrial communities. However, this warming was not

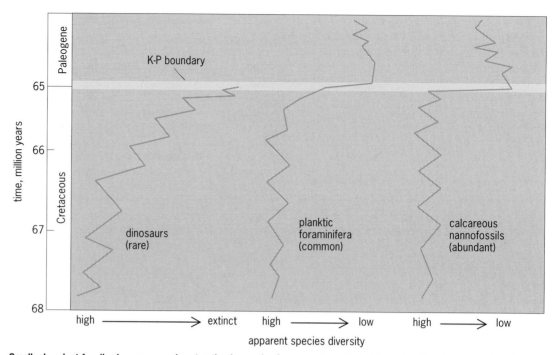

Small, abundant fossils show a more abrupt extinction at the Cretaceous-Paleogene boundary than large, rare fossils.

associated with unusually high extinction rates. Detailed studies of dinosaur assemblages suggest that there were no major changes in dinosaur communities in the 2 million years prior to the Cretaceous-Paleogene boundary, although some analyses suggest that an overall decline in dinosaur diversity occurred.

Impact at K-P boundary. Evidence for a large extraterrestrial impact at the Cretaceous-Paleogene boundary includes varieties of quartz, diamonds, and glass spherules produced by the extreme heat and pressures of an impact; quartz grains with multiple sets of deformation planes resembling grains known only from impacts and nuclear blasts; and a (now buried) crater on the Yucatán Peninsula of Mexico about 113–188 mi (180–300 km) in diameter. An iridium enrichment has been reported from over 100 Cretaceous-Paleogene boundary sections, and reflects the abundance of platinum group elements such as iridium and osmium in asteroids relative to Earth surface rocks. The concentration of iridium at the Cretaceous-Paleogene boundary suggests that the extraterrestrial object was about 6 mi (10 km) in diameter. Bits of iron compounds recovered from deep-sea cores suggest that the bolide was an asteroid rather than a comet. The size and abundance of tektites (glass beads produced by condensation of the impact vapor plume) increase toward the Yucatán. In addition, Cretaceous-Paleogene boundary tektites and melt rocks in the crater have similar radiometric ages (which date between 64.98 and 65.01 million years) as well as geochemical similarities that suggest a common source. In turn, the impact debris is overlain directly by sediments containing the earliest representatives of Paleocene Epoch fossils, including abundant fern spores in terrestrial sections and short-lived abundance peaks of disaster species of dinoflagellates and planktic foraminifera in the deep sea.

Deep-sea localities adjacent to the impact structure and on Haiti contain thick sequences of tektites mixed together with fossils of diverse ages, rock debris that includes granitic and metamorphic rocks like those known to underlie the crater, and large grains of impact-deformed quartz. The impact debris forms a thinner blanket to the south of the Yucatán, lending support to the recent idea that the asteroid arrived at a relatively low angle from the south and caused much of the impact debris to be blown northward. Around the Gulf of Mexico, most Cretaceous-Paleogene boundary sites contain thick layers of sandstone that include large boulders of locally derived rock as well as features indicative of strong waves. These sandstones often occur in what were relatively deep marine environments during the late Cretaceous and the early Paleocene, and have been cited as evidence of either a short-lived drop in sea level or the deposits of tidal waves kicked up by the impact. Drilling off northeastern Florida and in New Jersey has revealed unexpectedly thick layers of impact debris (1–7 in. or 3–17 cm thick), suggesting that the ejecta may have been flung out of the crater in long rays like those surrounding many lunar craters. Finally, records of the Cretaceous-Paleogene boundary in Europe, the Pacific Ocean, Antarctica, and New Zealand typically display only a sharp break between Cretaceous and Paleocene sediments that coincides with elevated concentrations of iridium. Many of these rock sequences have been partly homogenized by burrowing of deep-sea organisms which obscures the exact sequence of events and contributes to uncertainty about how rapidly the extinction and recovery took place.

Sequence during K-P boundary impact. Computer simulations and modeling with high-velocity cannons suggest that major impact events pack both short-term and long-term killing punches. Initially, an asteroid or comet roughly 6 mi (10 km) in diameter not only would have produced a blast crater several hundred kilometers across, but also would have generated a rapidly expanding shock wave with pressures greater than that produced by a large hurricane. The heat of impact would convert much of the bolide to a hot vapor plume that would incinerate plants and animals that survived the catastrophic winds. An impact in the ocean like that covering the Yucatán in the Cretaceous would also generate a large tsunami with wave heights 3–33 ft (1–10 m) or more in the deep sea that could travel over an ocean the size of the Pacific and decimate coastal areas far from the impact site. Following closely behind the vapor plume and tsunamis would be a shower of returning tektites whose heat of reentry through the atmosphere would set wildfires over much of the Earth's surface. The wave of tektites would begin to rain down on the surface 600 mi (1000 km) from the crater within 12–14 min after the impact, and debris from the asteroid would begin to rain out shortly thereafter. Furthermore, both the heat produced by reentering tektites and the initial impact would generate nitrogen oxides that could deplete the Earth's ozone layer.

Aftermath of impact. Over several weeks to years, dust lofted into the high atmosphere by the impact would blot out the sunlight on the Earth's surface and drastically alter the food chain. Fine-grained debris from the asteroid as well as rock excavated from the crater would reflect incoming sunlight, causing the Earth to cool. A similar phenomenon would result from a large-scale nuclear war and so has been named nuclear winter. Dust lofted by impact-generated winds, soot from fires, and carbon dioxide and sulfur dioxide from rocks vaporized by the impact would exacerbate global cooling. Surface temperatures over the continental interiors would plummet, although the temperature decline in coastal areas would be less because of the heat stored by the ocean. It is notable that extinctions were heaviest among groups of herbivorous animals as well as among organisms living in the continental interiors. Removal of the ozone screen might eventually lead to an increase in mutation rate among organisms exposed to infrared radiation from the Sun as the dust cleared from the sky.

The deep-sea record suggests that the recovery of marine ecosystems occurred over several million years. Productivity in the ocean was depressed, and the export of organic carbon from the surface waters to the bottom was either crippled or fundamentally altered for about 3–4 million years. Oceanic ecosystems did not recover their former species diversity for nearly 10 million years following the impact.

For background information *see* ANIMAL EVOLUTION; ASTEROID; BRECCIA; CARBON DIOXIDE; COUNTERCURRENT EXCHANGE (BIOLOGY); CRETACEOUS; DINOSAUR; EXTINCTION; FOSSIL; MACROEVOLUTION; MARINE ECOLOGY; ORGANIC EVOLUTION; PERMIAN; PHYSIOLOGICAL ECOLOGY; PHYTOPLANKTON; RESPIRATION; SEAWATER in the McGraw-Hill Encyclopedia of Science & Technology.   Richard D. Norris

Bibliography. D. H. Erwin, *The Great Paleozoic Crisis: Life and Death in the Permian*, 1993; T. Gehrels (ed.), *Hazards due to Comets and Asteroids*, 1994; J. P. Grotzinger and A. H. Knoll, Anomalous carbonate precipitates: Is the Precambrian the key to the Permian?, *Palaios*, 10:578–596, 1995; A. H. Knoll et al., Comparative earth history and Late Permian mass extinction, *Science*, 273:452–457, 1996; D. M. Raup, Size of the Permo-Triassic bottleneck and its evolutionary implications, *Science*, 206:217–218, 1979; D. M. Raup and D. Jablonski (eds.), *Patterns and Processes in the History of Life*, 1986; O. B. Toon, R. P. Turco, and C. Covey, Environmental perturbations caused by the impacts of asteroids and comets, *Rev. Geophys.*, 35:41–78, 1997; O. H. Walliser (ed.), *Global Events and Event Stratigraphy in the Phanerozoic*, 1995.

Materials handling

Materials handling is concerned with moving, storing, and controlling material. It covers a wide range of applications, such as luggage handling at an airport or parcel handling by an overnight delivery service. However, it is especially associated with parts flow in manufacturing systems or warehousing/distribution systems, where controlling the material flow and ensuring that parts (or unit loads) are available is a critical task. In some cases, it can be maintained that manufacturing and distribution are predominantly materials-handling activities (interrupted by processing of materials or parts/loads).

Automated systems. Much of the progress made in materials-handling systems engineering has occurred in fully automated or semiautomated, computer-controlled equipment used for parts storage/retrieval or movement in manufacturing and distribution. There has also been considerable improvement in manual systems, such as industrial lift trucks. However, such improvements are aimed primarily at the ergonomics and safety associated with materials handling.

Storage/retrieval systems. Developments continue in automated storage/retrieval systems, which can store and retrieve loads under complete computer control. A typical automated system consists of a storage/retrieval machine (which is often aisle captive) and a rectangular storage rack located on either side of the aisle. The storage/retrieval machine is fully automated; load movement in and out of the rack is accomplished through a telescoping shuttle mechanism. The storage/retrieval machine has three separate drives: a horizontal motor to move the mast up and down the aisle, a vertical motor to move the shuttle mechanism up and down the mast, and a shuttle drive to move the load in and out of the rack on either side. The horizontal and vertical drives are activated concurrently to position the shuttle mechanism in front of the appropriate rack opening. Once the storage/retrieval machine is positioned, the shuttle mechanism is activated to store or retrieve a load. An on-board, dedicated computer controls the storage/retrieval machine movements and communicates with a central computer, which keeps track of the activities of all the storage/retrieval machines and also maintains an inventory map (that is, the status and contents of all the rack openings).

Well-known examples of automated storage/retrieval systems include unit load (for palletized loads), miniload (for small to medium parts stored in special trays), microload (for small to medium parts stored in tote boxes), person-on-board (which allows an operator to ride the machine and have direct access to individual rack openings), and deep lane (where each rack opening is two or more loads deep). For example, in unit-load automated storage/retrieval systems, palletized drums are stored and a roller conveyor is used to bring loads to or from the system.

Input/output. Loads to be stored in or retrieved from the automated storage/retrieval system are brought to or taken away from the system typically via either conveyors or automated guided vehicles. The interface point between the automated storage/retrieval system and conveyors or automated guided vehicles is the input/output point, which is located typically at the lower left corner of the storage rack. Each aisle has its own input/output point, which often consists of a short segment of chain conveyor or roller conveyor that can hold a load while it is transferred to or from the storage/retrieval machine.

Work-in-progress. Engineering developments concerned with automated storage/retrieval systems have occurred in both the application domain and system hardware. For the former, the primary trend has been toward building smaller systems (that is, smaller number of rack openings and fewer aisles) and at the same time moving the automated storage/retrieval system for raw-material or finished-goods storage to work-in-process (or work-in-progress) storage. In other words, rather than building large automated storage/retrieval systems at the front or back end of manufacturing plants, the trend is to build smaller systems, sometimes at multiple locations, to store unfinished parts/loads (work-in-progress) within a factory. Such a trend is a natural consequence of the just-in-time operation principle, which drives inventory levels down throughout the system but also requires tighter control of work-in-progress (that is, knowing the exact quantity and status of all the parts, loads, or jobs on the factory floor). Since automated storage/retrieval systems run under computer control, they provide the right work-in-progress visibility required to implement just-in-time effectively.

When an automated storage/retrieval system is used for work-in-progress storage, it is also important to size the system correctly (that is, the number of rack openings to be provided). Certain analytical models (based on queuing theory) may be used to estimate the total expected work-in-progress in the system so the automated storage/retrieval system is sized properly. Furthermore, with work-in-progress storage, the storage and retrieval requests from the work centers will, generally speaking, arrive randomly. Providing the right number of aisles (and storage/retrieval machines) to meet the storage and retrieval requests is crucial. Although simulation has been the primary tool used for automated storage/retrieval system design and analysis, there are some analytical models which can quickly narrow down the alternatives.

Parts movement. In parts movement, while industrial lift trucks continue to play a significant role, shrinking load sizes (that is, smaller quantities of parts being moved from one work center or machine to the next) has led to an increased emphasis on one-piece-flow automated conveyors, automated electrified monorails, and unit-load (or multiload) automated guided-vehicle systems. Even if the same production rate is maintained, moving the parts in smaller quantities increases the frequency with which loads are transferred between the work centers or machines. In fact, the highest frequency is reached when parts are transferred one at a time, resulting in the highest demand placed on the handling system.

One notable development in parts movement is three-dimensional handling systems based on monorails, which have been used successfully in Japan. A typical monorail is positioned overhead, and it moves the loads in a horizontal (x,y) plane. By modifying the carrier (that is, the self-powered unit that moves the load on the monorail), vendors are able to move the load vertically (in the z dimension) as well. With such an approach, loads can be transferred more readily to floor-bound entities (such as machines or automated guided vehicles), and vertical handling in multifloor buildings is facilitated.

Vehicle dispatch. Advances in automated guided-vehicle systems include more sophisticated dispatching rules (that is, deciding which load is to be moved by which vehicle), guidewire-free vehicles, and remote diagnostics. Vehicle dispatching is important in automated guided-vehicle systems in that it reduces empty-vehicle travel and improves the response time of the system. A new dispatching concept based on bidding was shown to improve the system response time considerably. Each time a load that needs to be transferred (that is, a move request) arrives at the system, each vehicle places a bid for that load based on the vehicle's current workload and status. The load either is assigned to the lowest-bidding automated guided vehicle or is offered for bidding again shortly thereafter. While previous dispatching rules assigned a load only when a vehicle became empty, with the bidding approach the status of all vehicles is considered and it is not necessary to wait until a vehicle becomes empty.

Guidewire-free automated guided vehicles have been available for some time and are inherently more flexible and adaptable as flow patterns in the facility change. Remote diagnostics allows the vendor to log into the client's computer and monitor the automated guided-vehicle system as if the engineer were on-site. Problems associated with the control system or bottlenecks can often be diagnosed and fixed without having the engineer travel to the client site.

New developments. As for system hardware, a notable development is preengineered automated storage/retrieval systems. Although such systems allow very little or no tailoring to meet exact specifications, they can considerably shorten the lead time (primarily the time required to engineer, install, and test the system) while reducing overall system cost. Preengineered systems come in user-selectable modules that offer specific storage and throughput capacities.

Another development is the enhancement of the storage/retrieval machine itself, including the use of faster and lighter-weight drive motors and twin-shuttle (or multishuttle) machines which can handle more than one load at the same time. Typical speeds for unit-load storage/retrieval machines is 450–550 ft/min (137–168 m/min) horizontally and 80–120 ft/min (24–37 m/min) vertically. The acceleration/deceleration rate in both directions is approximately 1.5 ft/s² (0.46 m/s²). Some twin-shuttle storage/retrieval machines are now commercially available, and there is ongoing work on storage/retrieval machines with multiple shuttles. These shuttles are installed vertically between the twin masts of the machine; and an entire column of loads is moved in and out of the aisle as opposed to moving the loads one at a time. Also under development are even smaller, low-cost automated storage/retrieval systems which resemble vertical enclosures (or towers) that are located at multiple points throughout the factory.

For background information *see* AUTOMATION; BULK-HANDLING MACHINES; CONVEYOR; INDUSTRIAL FACILITIES; MATERIALS HANDLING; MATERIALS-HANDLING EQUIPMENT; MONORAIL in the McGraw-Hill Encyclopedia of Science & Technology.   Yavuz A. Bozer

Bibliography. Y. A. Bozer and C. Yen, Intelligent dispatching rules for trip-based material handling systems, *J. Manuf. Sys.*, 15(4):226–239, 1996; J. A. Tompkins et al., *Facilities Planning*, 1996.

Medical imaging

Diagnostic imaging techniques such as magnetic resonance imaging (MRI), ultrasound, and computerized tomography (CT) have had an enormous impact in clinical applications. Magnetic resonance imaging offers a noninvasive means to map brain structure and function by sampling the amount, flow, or environment of water protons in vivo. Intrinsic contrast can be augmented by the use of paramagnetic contrast agents in both clinical and experimental settings. However, these agents are little more than anatomical reporters which can at best label individual fluid compartments or distinguish tissues that are magnetically similar but histologically distinct. To permit a more direct imaging of the physiological state of cells or organs, an entirely new class of smart magnetic resonant imaging contrast agents has been developed that change their influence on the nearby water protons in a conditional fashion. The agents modulate fast water exchange, yielding distinct "on" and "off" states.

Magnetic resonance imaging. Magnetic resonance imaging is a technique that generates three-dimensional images of a specimen. It is a nondestructive technology that employs nonionizing radiation, with energies in the microelectronvolt range. It does not require optically transparent samples, and detailed structural information in three dimensions is obtainable in relatively short time spans (minutes). For these reasons, magnetic resonance imaging has emerged as a powerful diagnostic tool in clinical settings.

The most abundant molecular species in biological tissues is water. It is the quantum-mechanical spin of the water proton nuclei that ultimately gives rise to the signal in magnetic resonance imaging experiments. The subject to be imaged is placed in a strong, static magnetic field (1–12 tesla) where the spins of the water protons are excited with a pulse of radio frequency (RF) radiation to produce a net magnetization. The image is created by imposing one or more orthogonal magnetic field gradients upon the specimen while exciting nuclear spins with radio-frequency pulses as in a standard nuclear magnetic resonance (NMR) experiment. Typically, the image is based upon the nuclear magnetic resonance signal from the protons of water where the signal intensity in a given volume element is a function of the water concentration and relaxation times (T_1 and T_2). Local variations in these parameters provide the vivid contrast observed in a magnetic resonance image.

For example, the low water content of bone makes it appear dark, while the short relaxation

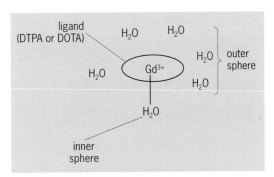

Fig. 1. Inner- and outer-sphere water molecules associated with a gadolinium complex.

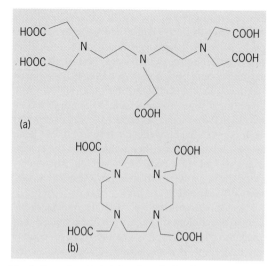

(a)

(b)

Fig. 2. Examples of chelating ligands that form contrast agents with gadolinium: (a) diethylenetriaminepentaacetic acid (DTPA), and (b) 1,4,7,10-tetraazacyclo-dodecane-*N,N',N",N'''*-tetraacetic acid (DOTA).

tons. Some paramagnetic ions decrease the T_1 without causing substantial line broadening [for example, gadolinium(III), (Gd^{3+})], while others induce drastic line broadening [for example, superparamagnetic iron oxide]. The mechanism of T_1 relaxation is generally a through-space dipole-dipole interaction. This interaction is between the unpaired electrons of the paramagnet, such as Gd^{3+}, and water molecules that are in fast exchange within the metal's inner coordination sphere (**Fig. 1**).

Regions associated with a Gd^{3+} ion (nearby water molecules) appear bright in a magnetic resonance image where the normal aqueous solution appears as a dark background. The lanthanide atom Gd^{3+} is by far the most frequently chosen metal atom for magnetic resonance imaging contrast agents because it has a very high magnetic moment and a symmetric electronic ground state. Transition metals such as high-spin manganese(II) and iron(III) are also candidates for use as contrast agents because of their high magnetic moments.

Since paramagnetic ions are generally toxic, a suitable ligand or chelate must be found to render the complex nontoxic. Diethylenetriaminepentaacetic (DTPA) chelates and thus acts to detoxify lanthanide ions (**Fig. 2a**). The stability constant (K) for $Gd(DTPA)^{2-}$ is very high (log K = 22.4) and is more commonly known as the formation constant (the higher the log K, the more stable the complex). The water-soluble $Gd(DTPA)^{2-}$ chelate is stable and nontoxic, and one of the most widely used contrast-enhancement agents in experimental and clinical imaging research. It is an extracellular agent that accumulates in tissue by perfusion-dominated processes. Image-enhancement improvements using $Gd(DTPA)^{2-}$ are well documented in a number of applications, including visualizing blood-brain bar-

time (T_2) of clotted blood affords it a higher signal intensity than that from nonclotted blood. Moreover, the magnetic resonance image may be acquired in a variety of ways to emphasize differences in one or more of the water proton properties.

Contrast agent. A magnetic resonance imaging contrast agent is called a dye. Unlike optical dyes such as fluorescent compounds, magnetic resonance agents are detected in an image because of their influence on nearby water protons. Paramagnetic metal ions, as a result of their unpaired electrons, act as potent magnetic resonance imaging agents. They decrease the T_1 and T_2 relaxation times of nearby water pro-

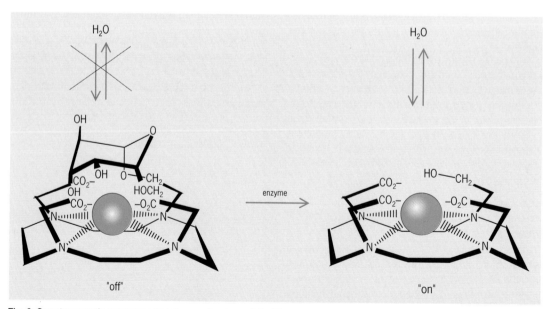

Fig. 3. Smart magnetic resonance imaging contrast agent that is an enzyme reporter. The substrate is a galactopyranosyl bond, and the sugar resides above the water coordination site. *β*-Galactosidase cleaves the substrate, allowing water to bind to the Gd^{3+} ion and thereby turn the agent on.

rier disruptions caused by space-occupying lesions and detection of abnormal vascularity. It has recently been applied to the functional mapping of the human visual cortex by defining regional cerebral hemodynamics.

A second type of ligand commonly used for chelating paramagnetic ions is the macrocycle 1,4,7,10-tetraazacyclo-dodecane-N,N',N'',N'''-tetraacetic acid (DOTA) [Fig. 2b]. It has been thoroughly studied in laboratory tests involving animals and humans. The complex is conformationally rigid, has an extremely high formation constant (log $K = 28.5$), and at physiological pH possesses very slow dissociation kinetics. The smart contrast agents described here are derivatives of this ligand framework.

Smart agents. The agents described thus far have the common property of being "on" or detectable by magnetic resonance at all times. A smart agent is one where there are two distinct states: an agent which is "off" in one state and turned "on" by a metabolic or physiological event (**Fig. 3**). The design of this new class of agents exploits the fundamental means by which a paramagnetic species affects the intensity of an image acquired by magnetic resonance imaging. In other words, the "trigger" for the detection of a metabolic species by these agents is the presence or absence of an inner-sphere water molecule which will ultimately be controlled by the presence or absence of a metabolite.

The protons of water molecules that are in the inner-coordination sphere (bound to the metal) of the paramagnetic ion display a net decrease in their T_1 (Fig. 1). The agents described in the preceding discussion provide eight coordinating ligands to the metal atom. Gd^{3+} has the potential to bind a ninth ligand and therefore has one open coordination site available for water molecules. This characteristic is the origin of the high relaxivity exhibited by these complexes.

A smart magnetic resonance imaging contrast agent was designed to permit an in vivo assay of enzymatic activities (Fig. 3). The contrast agents are synthesized with protection groups that are designed to prevent water from accessing the first coordination sphere by sterically blocking the approach to the Gd^{3+} ion (or paramagnetic center). The protection groups are themselves enzyme substrates. By limiting the access of water, the unprocessed agent is an ineffective contrast agent (magnetic resonance imaging is "silent" in the absence of a selected enzyme) and hence serves as a reliable marker for regions of enzyme activity. When exposed to an enzyme, the "walls" or protection groups of the complex are cleaved, and the contrast agent is then detectable by magnetic resonance imaging.

The Gd^{3+} ion is inaccessible to water until the enzyme removes the galactopyranose blocking group. The difference in observed intensity is revealed by an in vitro experiment with two capillary tubes containing active and inactive forms of the enzyme. This class of magnetic resonance imaging agents offers the promise of direct, three-dimen-sional visualization of gene expression, metabolic activity, and neuronal activation in the form of an acquired magnetic resonance image. The ability to obtain in vivo magnetic resonance images that report on metabolic activity could represent a substantial leap in existing diagnostic techniques, from quantifying heart attack victims to diagnosing brain disorders.

For background information *see* COMPUTERIZED TOMOGRAPHY; MAGNETIC RESONANCE; MEDICAL IMAGING; NUCLEAR MAGNETIC RESONANCE (NMR) in the McGraw-Hill Encyclopedia of Science & Technology.

Thomas J. Meade

Bibliography. J. W. Belliveau et al., Functional mapping of the human visual cortex by magnetic resonance imaging, *Science*, 254:716–719, 1991; S. C. Jackels, Enhancement agents for magnetic resonance and ultrasound imaging, *Pharmacological Medical Imaging*, Sec. III, Chap. 20, pp. 645–661, 1990; R. M. Moats, S. E. Fraser, and T. J. Meade, A smart magnetic resonance imaging contrast agent that reports on enzymatic activity, *Angew. Chem. Int. Ed. Engl.*, 36:726–728, 1997.

Melatonin

The role of biological clocks in physiology has focused attention on melatonin for treatment and prevention of disease. Discovered in 1958, melatonin was named for its ability to disperse pigments in skin cells of the frog. Derived from the dietary amino acid tryptophan, it is synthesized primarily in the pineal gland and, to less extent, in the retina and small intestine. In most animals the pineal gland resides at the confluence of the two cerebral cortices and the cerebellum. In the human it is centrally located deep within the brain just above the thalamus. In 1965, studies in the Syrian hamster demonstrated that the pineal could influence reproductive function. Within a decade, scientists realized that melatonin production follows a true circadian rhythm, occurring with a 24-h pattern that is remarkably similar in organisms as diverse as unicellular dinoflagellates, rodents, and primates. In a variety of vertebrate species, melatonin production by the pineal gland and retina occurs at night. The pronounced rise in synthesis each night elevates both melatonin concentrations in the circulation and the excretion of its principal metabolite in urine, 6-sulfatoxymelatonin. Virtually no melatonin is produced by the pineal gland during daylight, and concentrations in the circulation are nearly undetectable.

Melatonin rhythm. When animals or people are in constant darkness for long periods of time, the melatonin rhythm is still present. The rhythm is also evident in most blind subjects, but the onset of the melatonin rise in circulation drifts slightly out of phase each day with respect to the environmental photoperiod—a so-called free-run. Persistence of the melatonin rhythm in the absence of light-dark information is a clear indication that the 24-h hormone profile is generated by an internal biological clock. The neuroanatomical location of such a master biological clock appears to be a group of neurons in the anterior hypothalamus, the suprachiasmatic nuclei. These neurons receive information about the ambient environmental light-dark cycle by way of a direct projection from the retina. Suprachiasmatic neurons have a daytime peak in metabolic activity, which oscillates with a period of about 24 h. This pattern of neuronal activity drives a variety of internal rhythms in hormone secretion and behaviors, such as the surge in luteinizing hormone secretion that induces ovulation, locomotor activity, and sleep-wake cycles. Lesions of the suprachiasmatic nucleus or its connections to other parts of the brain disrupt most of these circadian rhythms, including the pineal melatonin rhythm.

Removal of the pineal gland also has significant effects on behaviors and physiology. In reptiles and birds, pinealectomy abolishes such diverse circadian rhythms as locomotor activity, feeding, and body temperature. Many of these rhythms are completely restored by daily timed administration of melatonin. One of the most profound effects in pinealectomy is that it abolishes seasonal patterns of reproduction. Most species reproduce in spring and summer to ensure that offspring are born and reared during favorable conditions. The melatonin rhythm plays a critical role in the mechanism by which photoperiod regulates seasonal breeding. The daily melatonin rhythm serves as the hands of an internal clock because concentrations of this hormone are increased at night. Moreover, the rhythm represents an endogenous calendar because the annual change in day length is directly reflected by the duration of time that melatonin is elevated in the circulation. An extended melatonin profile indicates that days are getting shorter, while an abbreviated nighttime rise signifies that day lengths have increased—the approach of winter or of spring, respectively. The change in the duration of the nightly melatonin rhythm in circulation appears to be the crucial variable that defines the functional role for this hormone. Neither the amplitude of the rhythm nor the absolute concentration at a particular clock time mediates the known effects of melatonin on reproduction. In the wild, information about day length, as provided by the pineal melatonin rhythm, is critical because survival for most animals depends upon their ability to adjust to changes in seasonally limited resources. Based upon the needs of each species to adapt to its unique habitat, many other seasonal physiological processes are modulated by the melatonin rhythm, including mating behavior, puberty onset, milk production, prolactin secretion, hair follicle activity, and brown fat metabolism.

Physiology. Specific receptors are thought to mediate the diversity of melatonin effects on physiological functions. Sites for melatonin action have been identified in the suprachiasmatic nucleus region and several other hypothalamic areas, the pituitary and the pars tuberalis (a region just above the pituitary),

as well as a portion of the thalamus that may modulate states of attention, alertness, and thermoregulation. Except for the pars tuberalis, the distribution of melatonin-specific binding sites varies among species. One or more of these brain loci may be responsible for the ability of melatonin to regulate gonadotropin hormone secretion and seasonal reproduction. In addition, focus on the brain does not exclude the possibility for specific actions by melatonin on other organ systems. For example, melatonin receptors on human lymphocytes and monocytes implicate this hormone as a potential regulator of immune cell function.

In higher vertebrates, melatonin conveys information about time that influences reproduction and circadian physiology. Photoperiod control of the duration of nighttime melatonin rhythm in humans may not be as dramatic as that in seasonal breeding mammals or other primates, such as the Siberian hamster, sheep, or rhesus monkey. In artificial photoperiods, changes in duration of the melatonin rhythm are evident. Light exposure at night suppresses nocturnal melatonin in circulation, but the intensity required to depress production in humans is manyfold greater compared with that in other species. In fact, typical indoor lighting does not normally affect the nighttime rise in melatonin. Even so, melatonin has been implicated in the photoperiodic mechanism that controls seasonal reproduction in the monkey. Data also suggest that melatonin suppresses human reproduction at high doses in combination with gonadal steroids. Melatonin reinforces behavioral and environmental cues that promote sleep. Melatonin advances the phase of its own endogenous rhythm, and advances sleep onset, reduces core body temperature, and enhances prolactin secretion as well. In addition, administration of melatonin hastens adaptations of endogenous rhythms to an abrupt phase shift. Timed melatonin treatments promote sleep onset in most sighted humans and in some blind subjects. Thus in humans, melatonin may protect the endogenous pacemaker that generates circadian rhythms against random occurrences of daytime darkness or exposure to light at night. Collectively, evidence suggests that melatonin acts as a coupling agent for specific physiological processes that, to some extent, depend upon entrainment of the endogenous circadian pacemakers to the light-dark cycle.

Therapeutic applications. Uses of melatonin for insomnia or relief from jet lag are under investigation in humans. Melatonin can induce drowsiness and may improve the quality of sleep. Melatonin administration has been proposed as a treatment to reverse an age-associated decline in melatonin rhythm amplitude, a potential contributing factor to sleep disorders. For many people, transmeridian travel is commonly associated with loss of sleep, disruptions in other circadian rhythms, and flulike symptoms that are commonly known as jet lag. Timed treatments with melatonin are considered as one way to reset the internal biological clock, hasten adjustment of normal sleep patterns, and synchronize attendant physiological rhythm. Melatonin also acts to shift the circadian temperature rhythm in a predictable way, advancing or delaying the peak depending upon the time of day for administration. With a rapid clearance from circulation and few known side effects, melatonin may be a natural way to maintain adaptation and help the body adjust to environmental challenges.

There are indications that melatonin has oncostatic and antioxidant capabilities in animal or tumor cell lines. The initiation and promotion of certain cancers, hormone-dependent neoplasms in particular, have been found to be influenced by photoperiod and inhibited by melatonin. Some of these antitumor effects on mammary carcinomas may be mediated by suppression of prolactin or gonadal steroid hormones. In the context of melatonin as a timekeeping hormone, there is evidence that winter depression may be controlled in patients with seasonal affective disorder with a combination of bright light and timed melatonin administration. Such optimism for therapeutic uses of melatonin as a chronobiotic must be counterbalanced with the fact that very little is known about the long-term effects related to time-, dose-, or age-dependency of treatments. Possible adverse side effects or drug interactions, and long-term consequences of hormone treatments that influence endogenous biological timekeeping require further investigation.

For background information *see* BIOLOGICAL CLOCKS; PHOTOPERIODISM; PINEAL BODY in the McGraw-Hill Encyclopedia of Science & Technology.   Steven M. Yellon

Bibliography. J. Arendt, *Melatonin and the Mammalian Pineal Gland*, 1995; C. A. Czeisler and F. W. Turek (eds.), Melatonin, sleep and circadian rhythms: Current progress and controversies, *J. Biol. Rhythms*, 12:485–708, 1997; R. J. Reiter and J. Robinson, *Melatonin*, 1995; S. M. Reppert and D. R. Weaver, Melatonin madness, *Cell*, 83:1059–1062, 1995.

Memory

Understanding the cognitive function of memory raises many questions about the types of memories and the impact of aging on the brain. This article discusses the dissociation of memory of self from other types of memories, and the relation between memory loss and aging.

Memory and the Self

The intriguing relation between the self and memory has been a topic among philosophers for more than 300 years. One's sense of self is said to consist of memories of one's past experiences and the capacity to recall those memories. Conversely, the ability to remember a personal past logically presupposes a sense of self. A personal memory (as opposed to, say, an imagined event) is identified as such by virtue

of its having occurred not just in the past but in one's own past. Thus the concepts of self and memory are inseparable. In the field of psychology, however, the self and memory historically have been approached as separate areas of inquiry. Beginning in the late 1980s, psychologists have come to appreciate that an account of one area cannot be fully realized without an account of the other.

Types of memory. Memory stores three general types of information, only one of which contributes to knowledge about the self. Broadly speaking, procedural memory includes motor, perceptual, and cognitive skills (such as how to ride a bike, or how to read), semantic memory stores generic, context-free knowledge (such as 2 plus 2 is 4, or owls are nocturnal), and episodic memory stores information about specific past events that involved the self and occurred at a particular time and place (such as remembering the specific day one learned to ride a bike, or remembering hearing an owl last night).

Only episodic memory had been considered as a source of self-knowledge, because it has a self-referential quality—it is a record of the individual's past experiences—thought to be missing from procedural and semantic memorial experience. In recent years, however, evidence from clinical neuropsychology has forced memory theorists to consider the possibility that other types of memory experiences also might be self-referential. Several supporting cases will be discussed.

A college student suffered a concussive blow to the head shortly after completing her first term. As a result, she showed profound amnesia for specific events and experiences that occurred during the year prior to the accident. Despite this loss of episodic memory, her memory for general facts about her life during that period seemed largely intact. For example, she knew which classes she had attended, although she could not recall a specific occasion of attendance or a specific classroom event; she knew the names of teachers and friends she had met since beginning college, but could not remember meeting them or sharing particular experiences with them.

A similar dissociation between types of self-knowledge was seen in the case of a man who had contracted a severe case of herpes simplex encephalitis in his late thirties. As a result, he was unable to consciously bring to mind personal experiences from any point in his life. Despite this near-total loss of episodic memory, he still knew a variety of facts about himself. For example, he knew where he worked and the jobs he performed, but he could not recall a particular occasion when he was at work, or a single event that occurred there.

To explain these dissociations between event and factual self-knowledge, psychologists have suggested broadening the concept of self-referential memory to include semantic as well as episodic memory. By this view, semantic memory consists of generic knowledge about the world, including facts about one's life, such as one's name, occupation, residence, or family members.

Independent systems of self-knowledge. The finding that an individual has access to personal facts about his or her life, yet is unable to remember particular episodes on which that knowledge supposedly is based, suggests that factual and event self-knowledge are served by different memory systems. The episodic memory system has become dysfunctional as a result of brain damage, whereas the semantic memory system remains unimpaired. A further implication is that in addition to personal facts an individual could have in semantic memory knowledge of his or her personality, and that this information could remain available even if episodic memory is impaired. By this view, a person could have detailed knowledge of what he or she is like, despite the loss of behavioral memories from which that knowledge is derived.

Such a notion has been counterintuitive for many philosophers and psychologists, who have long assumed a link between memory for behavior and knowledge of personality. Nonetheless, recent research with amnesic patients casts serious doubt on the necessity of this linkage.

In the above case of the amnesic student, interviews conducted shortly after her accident revealed that she had forgotten much of what had happened in her life during the preceding 12 months—a period that included her first term at college. To document her deficit in episodic memory, the investigators asked her to try to recall a specific personal event related to each of a list of cue words (for example, car, sing, lonely) and to provide for each recollection as precise a date as possible. This initial testing showed that she had little memory for personal events from recent years. Over the next month, however, her amnesia remitted completely, and when she was retested 4 weeks later, her performance had improved to the point that it was indistinguishable from that of three neurologically healthy women who served as controls.

Both during her amnesia and after its resolution, she was asked to provide personality ratings describing what she was like during her first term at college. In contrast to the change in her episodic memory performance over the month following her accident, her own personality ratings did not change at all over the same period: her ratings made during her amnesic period agreed with those she made afterward. Thus, while she was amnesic, she knew what she had been like in college despite the fact that she could not recall any of her behavior from that period of time.

Admittedly, it is possible that her ratings were based not on semantic knowledge of her personality during her time at college but on recollection of episodic memories from high school (or earlier) that were not covered by her amnesia. However, other evidence suggests that accurate self-description can occur even with total episodic memory loss.

For example, following a motorcycle accident a man lost all access to episodic memory and underwent a marked personality change, yet could de-scribe his current personality with considerable accuracy even though he had no memories of what he had experienced in the course of his life. This means that he had acquired generic, semantic knowledge of what he was like following his accident without retaining any episodic knowledge of the specific actions and experiences on which that knowledge was based.

Although theorists differ concerning the precise interpretation of such findings, this much is clear: neurally impaired individuals who have lost the ability to recall personal experiences show no obvious impairment in the ability to make accurate personality judgments about themselves, and may even maintain the ability to revise those judgments based on new episodes that they cannot remember. It seems that one does not need to remember how one behaved in the past to know what one is like.

Summary. The fact that a loss of episodic memory does not necessarily lead to a complete loss of self-knowledge has prompted theorists to expand the basis of self-knowledge to include both episodic and semantic memory. The finding that individuals can have accurate and detailed knowledge of their personalities despite no access to behavioral episodes suggests that these two aspects are represented independently in memory and perhaps mediated by separate cognitive systems.

The relation between memory and self is being increasingly well mapped experimentally. The improvement began when psychologists interested in the self started contemplating evidence from mainstream memory research and psychologists interested in memory began to note the impact of catastrophic memory loss on patients' personal identities. This collaboration ultimately may bridge the gap in mainstream psychology between theories of memory function and theories of self.

Stanley B. Klein

Memory Loss and Aging

Healthy adults above the age of 60 often cannot remember newly learned information as well as young adults. This observation has been demonstrated repeatedly in experimental and naturalistic studies of recall and recognition that use a variety of materials ranging from totally meaningless, such as nonsense syllables, to highly relevant, such as information contained on simulated medicine labels.

A cognitive neuroscience approach attempts to associate age-related changes in specific memory processes with alterations in distinct brain regions. With this approach, researchers can draw upon studies of amnesic patients with damage to the hippocampus, a small structure embedded deep within the temporal lobes of the brain. These patients display profound impairments in declarative memory, the ability to consciously recall or recognize newly learned information. Other intellectual functions, however, remain relatively intact. Thus, evidence from amnesic patients supports the idea that the hippocampus is part of a declarative memory system of the brain. The milder declarative memory impairment associated with normal aging suggests that a decline in the function of the hippocampus may underlie memory problems in late life.

Aging and the hippocampus. Researchers have long assumed that aging is associated with some process that leads to loss of neurons in the hippocampus, and that this loss of neurons negatively affects the ability of the hippocampus to support declarative memory. However, recent evidence using new methods of counting neurons has challenged this assumption, suggesting that age-related hippocampal neuron loss is much less extensive than previously thought. Thus, memory problems experienced in old age may not be due to hippocampal neuron loss per se, but may be associated with subtle changes in the way that existing neurons interconnect or communicate with one another. How age-related factors affect the integrity of the hippocampus has not been determined, but the issue remains highly salient in the neurobiology of aging.

Although neuron number may not decline in old age, some studies suggest that the hippocampus does undergo age-related change in size, and that this change is detrimental to declarative memory. For example, magnetic resonance imaging scans of the brain can be used to estimate the overall volume of the hippocampus; many studies have reported that the size of the hippocampus is smaller in older adults than in young adults. Using this technique, a recent study reported that older adults who performed poorly on tests of declarative memory tended to have smaller hippocampi than older adults who performed well. This suggests that individuals with poor declarative memory experience more hippocampal atrophy than others whose declarative memory is maintained.

Although some characteristics of memory decline in old age resemble those of amnesic patients, others resemble those of patients with lesions of the frontal lobes of the brain. For example, frontal-lobe patients are often disproportionately impaired on memory tasks that require temporarily storing information, such as rehearsing a string of numbers, while carrying out other cognitive tasks, such as comprehending a complex sentence. Such tasks tap working memory, a cognitive system involved in simultaneous storage and processing of information necessary to comprehend language, to reason, and to learn. Frontal-lobe patients are also impaired on memory tasks that require individuals to remember the source, appearance, or frequency with which information was first learned. These strategic memory tasks require the use of plans in order to retrieve this information successfully. Deficits in working memory and strategic memory are also found in old age, and are exacerbated in some age-related degenerative diseases such as Parkinson's disease. Parkinson's disease primarily affects the basal ganglia, a collection of structures that lies deep within the brain and makes connections with various frontal-lobe regions. Functional decline in frontal regions, or in connections between the frontal lobes and the basal ganglia, may contribute to age-related decline in working memory and strategic memory. Indeed, there is a great deal of neuroanatomical evidence to suggest that the frontal lobes are particularly vulnerable to the aging process.

Old age is also associated with memory deficits in experiments that require individuals to form new associations between previously unrelated stimuli. For example, older adults are impaired in some forms of eye-blink classical conditioning. In these experiments, an auditory tone is paired repeatedly with the presentation of an air puff to the eye, which reflexively causes the subject to blink. Over time, subjects begin to associate the tone and air puff, becoming conditioned to a point where presentation of the tone without the air puff is enough to produce the eye-blink response. The conditioned eye-blink response is evidence for an association formed in memory between the tone and the air puff. Some forms of eye-blink conditioning are abolished following lesions to the cerebellum (located at the base of the cerebrum), suggesting that eye-blink classical conditioning is critically dependent on the integrity of the cerebellum. The parallel between older adults and patients with cerebellar lesions suggests that the integrity of the cerebellum is compromised in old age.

Spared memory processes. Fortunately, some forms of memory do not decline substantially as people age. For example, semantic memory, which consists of factual information such as general world knowledge, or relationships among various concepts, remains largely unaffected until extremely late in life. Other forms of relatively preserved memory are more subtle. In some memory experiments, a list of stimuli (words, pictures, and so forth) is processed in an initial study phase, and these stimuli are intermixed with new, unstudied stimuli in a later test phase. The test phase often involves using the stimuli in a cognitive task. Often, the studied stimuli are processed faster, identified easier, or come to mind quicker than unstudied stimuli, reflecting a change in the way that studied information is processed as a result of a prior exposure. This is known as repetition priming, and changes very little across the life span, even though older adults typically recall or recognize fewer words from the study phase than young adults. This suggests that the multiple brain regions that underlie semantic memory and repetition priming operate relatively normally in old age, despite age-related changes in other structures (such as the hippocampus, frontal lobes, basal ganglia, and cerebellum) that are critical for declarative memory, working memory, strategic memory, and conditioning.

For background information *see* AMNESIA; BRAIN; COGNITION; LEARNING; NEURAL MECHANISM; NEUROBIOLOGY; PERCEPTION in the McGraw-Hill Encyclopedia of Science & Technology.   Matthew W. Prull

Bibliography. L. S. Cermak and M. O'Connor, The anterograde and retrograde retrieval ability of a patient with amnesia due to encephalitis, *Neuropsychologia*, 21:213–234, 1983; J. Golomb et al., Hippocampal formation size in normal human aging: A correlate of delayed secondary memory performance, *Learn. Memory*, 1:45–54, 1994; S. B. Klein, J. F. Kihlstrom, and J. Loftus, Self-knowledge of an amnesic patient: Toward a neuropsychology of personality and social psychology, *J. Exper. Psychol. General*, 125:250–260, 1996; E. Tulving, Self-knowledge of an amnesic individual is represented abstractly, in T. K. Srull and R. S. Wyer (eds.), *Advances in Social Cognition*, vol. 5, pp. 147–156, 1993; M. J. West, Regionally specific loss of neurons in the aging human hippocampus, *Neurobiol. Aging*, 14:287–293; R. L. West, An application of prefrontal cortex function theory to cognitive aging, *Psychol. Bull.*, 120:272–292, 1996; D. S. Woodruff-Pak, *The Neuropsychology of Aging*, 1997.

Metal coating

Coatings are applied to metal parts used in many applications, and serve functions such as decoration, insulation, corrosion protection, and lubrication. Various techniques are used to apply such coatings, including spray coating, powder coating, dip coating, electrodeposition, and autodeposition. Coating an object with a complex topography is a challenging task, especially around the edges and inside the cavities. Traditional coating processes often involve environmentally hazardous or toxic substances, such as chromates and phosphates. New coating methods need to be developed to overcome these technological and environmental challenges.

Spontaneous polymerization. A novel process has been developed to form protective polymer coatings on metals such as aluminum, steel, and copper. With this process, called spontaneous polymerization, polymer chains can be directly initiated and grown on the metal surface when a metal sample is immersed in a solution of certain monomers. The solution in the tank is made slightly acidic by addition of dilute mineral acid, such as sulfuric acid. When a cleaned metal substrate is immersed in this solution, the metal surface reacts with the solution monomers to generate highly reactive free radicals. The monomers then react with these free radicals to form long polymer chains. These polymer chains precipitate on the metal surface as they are being formed, resulting in a layer of swollen coating on the metal. The process, which is relatively independent of the shape of the object, is conducted at room temperature in a single tank of monomer solution, and no external driving force or initiator is required. Polymerization, deposition, and cross-linking can be achieved in a single step. A variety of monomers can be copolymerized so that the final coating properties can be tailored easily by adjusting the monomer feed composition according to the specific needs.

This process differs from conventional coating processes in that the polymer chains "grow" on the metal surface instead of being deposited. Significant advantages are that the coatings are conformal and pinhole free and are formed uniformly on objects with complex topographies. The process results in very good adhesion of the polymer coating to the metal substrate, because wetting of the metal surface is easier by monomers as compared with wetting by polymers. The monomers typically are in an aqueous or partially aqueous solution; the process is environmentally friendly.

Monomers. The monomer systems tested so far involve phenyl maleimides and related compounds. These compounds are very electrophilic because of the two strongly electron-withdrawing carbonyl groups on the imide ring. Since it is very difficult for phenyl maleimide to homopolymerize by a free-radical mechanism, the presence of some nucleophilic monomers, such as styrene, is necessary. The reaction is completely quenched when a free-radical scavenger (inhibitor) is added to the solution. This result establishes the polymerization as being free-radical type. Two mechanisms have been proposed to explain the process as it occurs on steel and aluminum.

Redox mechanism. When steel is used as the substrate, a redox mechanism is responsible for the spontaneous initiation. The metal and the monomer form an electrochemical cell. The iron surface is oxidized and loses electrons. The monomer accepts the electron and is reduced to radical form to initiate polymerization. The process is thermodynamically favored. Such a mechanism is reasonable, considering the low reduction potential of phenyl maleimide and the ease of oxidation of iron. 4-Carboxyphenyl maleimide was used extensively for studies on steel. By the spontaneous polymerization process, 4-carboxyphenyl maleimide copolymerizes with electron-rich monomers, such as styrene, to form an alternating copolymer (because styrene is electron rich and forms a charge transfer complex with 4-carboxyphenyl maleimide). The copolymerization of 4-carboxyphenyl maleimide with electron-deficient monomers, such as methyl methacrylate, yields random copolymers. Propagation through both a charge-transfer complex and free monomer at the same time is possible, as demonstrated by the 4-carboxyphenyl maleimide styrene/acrylonitrile system. Such propagation allows considerable flexibility in the design of monomer systems.

Free-radical mechanism. On aluminum substrates, the polymerization reaction on the substrate is initiated by the interaction of the monomers in solution with the metal surface. For the reaction to occur, it is important that there are two types of monomers: one that is electrophilic in nature, such as *N*-phenyl maleimide, and another that is nucleophilic, such as styrene. In solution, such monomer combinations show an affinity to associate with each other, like opposite poles of a magnet, depending on the extent of charge separation. In some cases, this leads to the formation of alternating copolymers. If the pairs are weakly polar, they do not react by themselves, but require some additional external driving force. This driving force is provided by surface aluminum ions, when the metal is immersed in the acidic monomer solution. Once the metal ions interact with the monomers, reactive free radicals are produced and polymer is formed. A proof of a free-radical mechanism for the chain growth was obtained simply by adding free-radical scavengers, which quench the reaction completely.

Process variables. Some process variables that influence the kinetics of the process and the properties of the coatings obtained are polymerization time, monomer concentration, solution pH, solution temperature, and monomer feed composition. These variables can be easily adjusted in order to obtain the desired coating rate and properties. In general, coating rates are higher on steel by a factor of 2–5, as compared to aluminum, while the rate on copper is somewhere in between.

In order to retain the polymer chains on the surface of the metal, the solvent quality of the solution is adjusted such that, while all the monomers are soluble, their polymers are not, and the polymers exist in a swollen state. Once the conditions for forming the polymer coatings are established, other monomers are introduced into the solution in order to modify the properties of the final polymer coating. The 2-(methylacryloyloxy)ethyl acetoacetate monomer has the potential of forming chelates with several important metals and thereby enhances the adhesion of the polymer coating, while bis-maleimide helps to cross-link the coatings, making them suitable for high-temperature applications and increasing the coating uniformity.

Corrosion resistance. Coatings made by a combination of the monomers 2-(methylacryloyloxy)ethyl acetoacetate and bis-maleimide show excellent corrosion resistance when subjected to salt spray testing. While the coatings on aluminum have surpassed exposure times of 4000 h, coatings on steel are stable up to 1000 h. Most commercial coatings require extensive pretreatment operations in order to obtain good corrosion performance. Another advantage is the very low dielectric constant of these coatings, which encourages their use in electronic applications.

For background information *see* METAL COATINGS; POLYMER; POLYMERIZATION; SURFACE COATING in the McGraw-Hill Encyclopedia of Science & Technology.   James P. Bell; Rajat Agarwal; Xu Zhang

Bibliography. R. Agarwal and J. P. Bell, Protective coatings on aluminum by spontaneous polymerization, *Polym. Eng. Sci.,* 38:299–310, 1998; R. Agarwal and J. P. Bell, Spontaneous polymerization on aluminum to form quality protective coatings, *Proc. Amer. Chem. Soc.,* PMSE, 75:341–342, 1996; X. Zhang and J. P. Bell, The formation of protective coatings on steel by spontaneous polymerization, *Proc. Amer. Chem. Soc.,* PMSE, 76:519, 1997; X. Zhang and J. P. Bell, The in-situ synthesis of protective coatings on steel through a surface spontaneous polymerization process, *J. Appl. Polym. Sci.,* 66:1667–1680, 1998.

Milky Way Galaxy

Gamma-ray astronomy, a new window for viewing the universe, is providing important opportunities for testing current understanding of the evolution of stars and galaxies. Recently, using a gamma-ray telescope in orbit around the Earth, scientists discovered a cloud of positrons—the antimatter counterpart of the electron—in a part of the Milky Way Galaxy where there are no known sources of positrons. This discovery is causing scientists to rethink the theories for the production and transport of positrons in the Milky Way Galaxy, and may provide clues to improve understanding of the creation of elements in stars and the history of stellar evolution in the central region of the Galaxy.

Positron annihilation. All known subatomic particles have antiparticles, often referred to as antimatter. The antiparticle of the normal-matter electron is called the positron, which has the same mass as an electron but is positively charged. When a positron and an electron interact they annihilate, converting all of their mass into energy, following Einstein's equation $E = mc^2$, where E is the total energy released, m is the combined rest-mass of the positron and electron, and c is the speed of light. The total amount of energy released when a positron and an electron annihilate is 1.022 MeV. The energy is released in the form of photons, and the number of photons released depends on exactly how the positron and electron annihilate.

A positron and electron can annihilate either directly in a process that is like a head-on collision, or through the formation of positronium, a hydrogenlike atom composed of a positron and an electron in which the positively charged positron takes the place of the proton in a normal hydrogen atom. If the positron and electron annihilate directly, two photons are produced, each having an energy of 0.511 MeV, or about 250,000 times the energy of normal visible light. If positronium is formed, the annihilation produces either two 0.511-MeV photons or three photons, all of which have energies less than 0.511 MeV.

The shape of the resulting three-photon annihilation spectrum is roughly triangular, increasing in intensity from zero at zero energy to a peak intensity near 0.511 MeV. Detecting photons with an energy of 0.511 MeV is direct evidence for positron annihilation.

Possible positron sources. There are several possible ways in which positrons can be created. One way is through a form of naturally occurring radioactivity called positron beta (β^+) decay. When a radioactive nucleus decays via β^+ decay, a positron is produced. Certain radioactive isotopes, such as sodium-22, aluminum-26, scandium-44, and cobalt-56, are known to decay via β^+ decay and are believed to be produced by nucleosynthesis processes occurring in novae and supernovae. For example, about 0.6 $M_\odot$ ($M_\odot$ corresponds to the mass of the Sun, about 2×10^{30} kg or 4.5×10^{30} lb) of radioactive nickel-56 is believed to be produced by a kind of supernova called type Ia. Since nickel-56 decays to cobalt-56, which subsequently decays producing a positron, type Ia supernovae could be an indirect source of positrons.

Another possible source of positrons is a process called pair production, in which high-energy photons in the vicinity of a massive black hole can spontaneously create a positron and electron. Matter spiraling into a black hole will increase in temperature as it gets closer to the black hole. The material can become hot enough that it emits high-energy photons, which then can interact in the extremely high gravitational field near the black hole, producing pairs of positrons and electrons. The positron and electron pairs are created with very high energies, and so rapidly stream away from the black hole in two antiparallel jets of high-energy particles.

Observing gamma rays. Since the Earth's atmosphere is not transparent to gamma rays, gamma-ray telescopes must be placed on high-altitude balloons or on spacecraft in order to observe and study them. The *Compton Gamma-Ray Observatory* spacecraft, one of the Great Observatories of the National Aeronautics and Space Administration, was launched into low Earth orbit by the space shuttle *Atlantis* in April 1991. It carries four separate gamma-ray instruments, each designed to observe a different range of gamma-ray energies. One instrument, the Oriented Scintillation Spectrometer Experiment (OSSE), is primarily sensitive to gamma rays over the energy range 0.05–10 MeV.

Unlike visible light, gamma rays cannot be focused with lenses or mirrors, making direct imaging of gamma-ray emission impossible with present technology. Instead, gamma-ray instruments such as OSSE can measure only the total number of gamma-ray photons coming from within a specific region in the direction in which they are pointed—like a view through a short cardboard tube. The size of this region, called the field of view, generally varies for different instruments.

Observations of positron annihilation. Positron annihilation radiation was discovered from the direction of the galactic center in the early 1970s. Subsequent observations by numerous balloon and satellite gamma-ray instruments confirmed the presence of the annihilation radiation, but were not able to determine the exact location or distribution of the emission. After the galactic center region had been observed by instruments with fields of view of different sizes, it was noticed that instruments with large fields of view observed a higher number of 0.511-MeV photons. This was believed to indicate that the distribution of the positrons was very diffuse, and that instruments with large fields of view were seeing a larger portion of the emission than the small-field-of-view instruments. The total flux of 0.511-MeV photons observed from within about 30° of the galactic center was found to be about 2.4×10^{-3} photon cm^{-2} s^{-1}. If the source of the positrons is at the distance of the galactic center, about 8000 parsecs

or 25,000 light-years away, this flux corresponds to the annihilation of about 3×10^{42} positrons per second.

Discovery of antimatter cloud. Soon after the launch of the *Compton Gamma-Ray Observatory*, the OSSE instrument began observing the galactic center region to try to determine the distribution of the positron annihilation emission. These observations were concentrated along the plane near the center of the Milky Way Galaxy, where novae and supernovae are primarily located. Observations soon showed that the emission in the plane of the Galaxy was concentrated within about 10° to 15° of the galactic center. Surprisingly, the total flux near the galactic center observed by OSSE was found to be much lower than that observed by other instruments with large fields of view. This indicated that additional annihilation radiation was located near the galactic center, but in regions away from the plane of the Galaxy that had not been well observed by OSSE.

To try to identify where this excess emission might be located, a team of scientists began developing methods for generating images of the annihilation radiation using the available overlapping OSSE observations. Various imaging methods were investigated, all of which suggested the presence of some excess emission above the plane of the Milky Way Galaxy. To search for this excess emission, a series of OSSE observations was performed in November and December 1996 which included exposures both above and below the galactic plane. These new observations confirmed the excess emission above the plane of the Galaxy, and helped produce the image of the central region of the Galaxy in the 0.511-MeV positron-annihilation line shown in the **illustration**.

The map of the 0.511-MeV positron-annihilation line has three general components: a diffuse feature along the galactic plane, an extended region centered near the center of the Milky Way Galaxy, and an extended feature or cloud located about 10° above the central region of the Galaxy. The first two components correspond to the disk and the nuclear bulge of the Galaxy, which are known features. The cloud of emission, however, does not correspond to any known features of the Galaxy, and there are no known objects in this region which could have produced the observed positrons.

Implications of discovery. The discovery of a cloud of positron annihilation emission above the plane of the Milky Way Galaxy is surprising because it indicates the presence of positrons far from the currently understood sources. In addition, since positrons cannot annihilate without electrons, and most normal matter in the Galaxy is found in or near the galactic plane, there must also be some mechanism for transporting normal-matter electrons so far out of the plane of the Galaxy.

One theoretical model developed to explain the excess positrons above the plane suggests that up to 1000 supernovae may have exploded in the central region of the Milky Way Galaxy within the past few million years. This type of activity, which has been

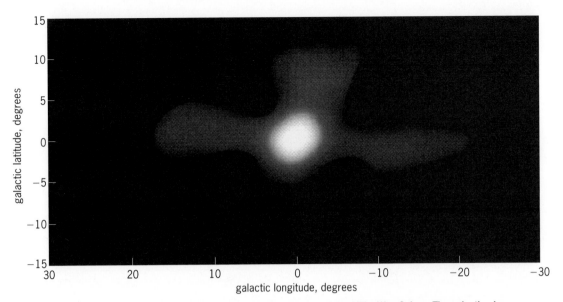

Map of 0.511-MeV positron annihilation emission from the inner region of the Milky Way Galaxy. The galactic plane corresponds to a galactic latitude of 0°. The galactic center is at latitude 0°, longitude 0°. The feature above the galactic center is the newly discovered cloud of positron annihilation emission. *(D. D. Dixon, University of California, Riverside, and W. R. Purcell, Ball Aerospace & Technologies Corp.)*

seen in some other galaxies called starburst galaxies, might produce a bubble of expanding gas from the combined supernovae. The bubble would tend to expand above and below the plane of the Galaxy, where the pressure is lower. Slight asymmetries in the initial supernovae explosions might have caused the bubble to have expanded preferentially above the galactic plane, carrying with it the radioactive nuclei created in the supernova explosions. Some of these radioactive nuclei would β^+-decay, producing positrons which would then be carried along with the other normal matter to great distances above the galactic plane.

Overall, the discovery of this new cloud of positrons has raised more questions than it has answered. These questions concern the source or sources of the positrons; how the positrons got into the cloud; the age, size, shape, and distance of the cloud; whether the cloud is directly connected to the galactic center; whether the cloud was produced by a single event or many separate events; and whether there are other clouds in the Milky Way Galaxy. The answers require further observations by OSSE and future gamma-ray instruments.

For background information *see* ANTIMATTER; BLACK HOLE; GAMMA-RAY ASTRONOMY; MILKY WAY GALAXY; NOVA; NUCLEOSYNTHESIS; POSITRON; RADIOACTIVITY; SUPERNOVA in the McGraw-Hill Encyclopedia of Science & Technology.   William R. Purcell

Bibliography. C. D. Dermer and J. G. Skibo, Annihilation fountain in the galactic center region, *Astrophys. J. Lett.*, 487:57–60, 1997; N. Gehrels et al., The *Compton Gamma Ray Observatory, Sci. Amer.*, 269(6):68–77, December 1993; W. R. Purcell et al., OSSE mapping of galactic 511 keV positron annihilation line emission, *Astrophys. J.*, 491:725–748, 1997; R. Ramaty and R. E. Lingenfelter, Diffuse galactic annihilation radiation, *Astron. Astrophys. Suppl.*, 97:127–131, 1993.

Mining

This article will discuss two techniques used in mining: longwall mining and ground-penetrating radar.

Originating in England in the seventeenth century, longwall mining has been the predominant coal mining method in Europe. Since its adoption in the United States in the early 1960s, it has been gaining in popularity. In 1996, total longwall production in the United States was 194 million tons (175 million metric tons) out of the total annual underground coal production of 410 million tons (370 million metric tons).

Ground-penetrating radar is a new high-resolution imaging tool that sees into the shallow subsurface. It is efficient, inexpensive, and noninvasive (that is, it does not disturb subsurface objects or artifacts). These attributes make ground-penetrating radar a good choice for rapid subsurface surveying to replace or guide expensive excavation through drilling and trenching.

Longwall Mining

Longwall mining is a caving method in which a long panel is prepared with entry systems on both sides. The method employs a movable set of cutting tools that cut coal along the face, with the broken coal being discharged on an armored face conveyor belt. The roof receives hydraulic supports which advance as the face moves forward, allowing the roof to cave behind the supports to create gob (mined-out area).

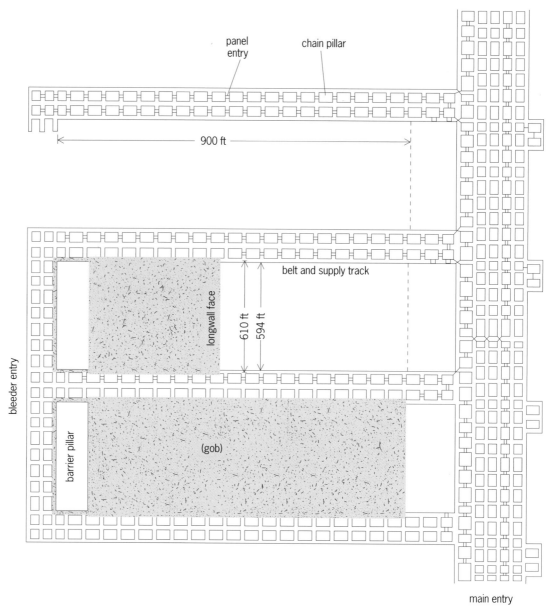

Fig. 1. Typical longwall retreat system.

In this method, there are two systems: advancing and retreat. The advancing system is widely used in Europe, while the retreat system is used exclusively in the United States. In the advancing system, one entry is continuously developed on each side of the panel simultaneously ahead of the production face. The entries have to be maintained through the gob as the face advances to transport the coal produced and to ventilate along the face. Pack walls and yieldable arches are used for maintaining the entries. The major advantage of the advancing system is that longwall production does not have to be delayed until entries are completely developed. However, the advancing system has inherent health and safety problems and fails to meet mining regulations in the United States. In the retreat system, entries are developed before coal is cut in the panel using the room-and-pillar mining technique. Because all the coal seams employing longwall mining in the United States are nearly flat, the entries are open in the coal seam. The entries are open on both sides of the panel length, with the common width ranging 12–22 ft (4–7 m). Three entries and two chain pillars are the minimum requirement. These entries are connected to the main entries and bleeder entries, and are used for ventilation and transporting coal. The panel width ranges 500–1100 ft (150–335 m) and panel length 2500–14,000 ft (760–4270 m). Longwall mining starts at the bleeder entry side and proceeds toward the main entries. Usually, a barrier pillar is installed on each end of the panel to protect the main and bleeder entries (**Fig. 1**).

There are two types of face-cutting machines: plough and shearer. Plough machines are equipped with a set of bits that can cut soft coal with a scratching action along the face. Their usual cutting depth is 6 in. (15 cm). Shearer machines feature a rotating drum cutter equipped with drag bits that can cut 2–4 ft (0.6–1.2 m) of coal thickness (**Fig. 2**). In most cases, double drums are used and can reach as high as 17 ft (5 m). The cutting machine discharges coal onto the armored face conveyor belt installed parallel to the longwall face. The conveyor belt is pushed forward by the hydraulic rams connected to the face supports aligned along the face behind the belt and spill plate as the coal is mined. The coal from the armored face conveyor belt is discharged onto an entry conveyor which carries the coal to the main entry conveyor. In the United States, almost all longwall faces (except two panel types) presently uses shearer machines.

The modern longwall system employs self-advancing hydraulic supports that support the roof along the face line. In the past, frame and chock types were used; however, these have basically been replaced by two- or four-leg shields. A shield is composed of legs, base, canopy, and gob shield (**Fig. 3**). The legs are generally inclined to make the shield resistant to the horizontal roof stress. Each shield can support up to 1000 tons (900 metric tons) of a roof load covering a 5-ft (1.5-m) width.

Longwall coal production is expected to continuously increase in the United States because of the following advantages: improved safety; higher extraction rate; better subsidence control; and cost saving from the elimination of the need for bolting, rock dusting, and many ventilation controls. Longwall mining also has disadvantages, such as higher capital costs for equipment; high moving costs; and inflexibility where there are gas or oil wells, and irregular geologic conditions.

Fig. 2. Longwall face area. *(Joy Mining Machinery)*

Trends. Longwall panels are becoming larger and production efficiency is enhanced because of equipment improvement. Total longwall production has been increasing, in 1996 reaching about half of the total underground coal production in the United States. The production rate per shift has also been increasing. Many mines are producing more than 5000 tons (4500 metric tons) per shift. The width of a longwall panel has been increasing for the last several decades. It was 400–500 ft (122–152 m) in 1977, whereas in 1997 the average panel width was

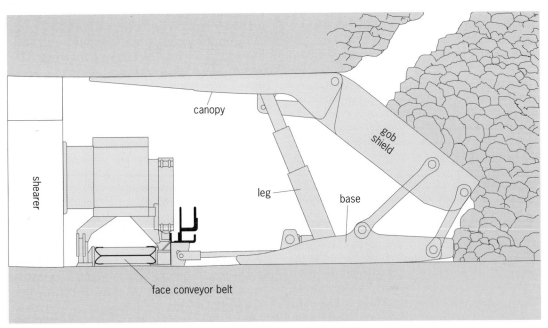

Fig. 3. Typical two-legged shield, comprising base, legs, canopy, and gob shield.

824 ft (251 m). The same trend applies to panel length, with the average being 8430 ft (2569 m) in 1997, compared with 7750 ft (2362 m) in 1996.

New developments. The complexity of longwall mining demands a more sophisticated control of the system and a thorough understanding of interactions of the longwall components and geology. Two recent developments are the longwall strata control and maintenance system, and seismic tomography for longwall faces.

The longwall strata control and maintenance system (LoSCoMS) includes a software package designed to monitor shield leg pressure, interpret the data, and predict forthcoming roof loads and the existence of geological anomalies. It can also detect maintenance problems of the face equipment. This system was installed underground and connected to the surface terminals at a coal mine. It has proven to be a useful and practical system for improving safety and efficiency in coal mining operations.

A seismic tomography technique was developed to image the longwall panel ahead of the face. It has the capability of imaging stress concentrations influenced by the presence of a fault zone.

Duk-Won Park

Ground-Penetrating Radar

A ground-penetrating radar survey involves pulling a relatively small radar antenna across the ground surface. The antenna emits a low-energy pulse of electromagnetic radiation within the radar frequency band. The ground-penetrating radar frequency band ranges from approximately 10 MHz to 2 GHz. The energy of this pulse corresponds approximately to that of a hand-held ultrahigh-frequency (UHF) radio transmitter. The radar pulses (approximately 50,000 per second) are directed into the earth and occasionally reflect from materials having electrical properties that differ from the surrounding soil or rock. The subsurface electrical properties that cause the radar to reflect to the surface are the electrical conductivity and the dielectric constant (indicating the efficiency of a material to act as an insulator).

Radar signals reflected to the surface are recorded for display by a second antenna. The resulting record provides a cross-sectional image of the subsurface beneath the radar profile. The raw signals appear similar to the sonic fish-finder records used by fishing crews to locate schools of fish.

Limitations. Although ground-penetrating radar has received much attention, it has some limitations. The higher the frequency of electromagnetic radiation used, the less penetration into the rock or soil achieved. Sunlight, an example of very high frequency electromagnetic radiation, does not penetrate rock and soil at all; if it did, the interior of the Earth would be visible to the eye. Hence, the depth to which the subsurface may be viewed greatly depends on the radar frequency chosen and the type of soil or rock at the site. A frequency of 10 MHz, for example, penetrates to a depth of 330 ft (100

m) in granite, whereas the same frequency energy penetrates only 33 ft (10 m) in shale. At a frequency of 1 GHz, radar penetration in granite is only 33 ft (10 m) and in shale is only 1–2 in. (2.5–5 cm). So, it is unlikely that a single frequency will suffice for all purposes.

Higher frequencies (shorter wavelengths) provide good spatial resolution but are limited to shallow depths. Lower frequencies (longer wavelengths) provide poor spatial resolution but penetrate deeper. The sacrifice of spatial resolution for depth of penetration is an insurmountable trade-off.

The pulses of energy emitted into the Earth by the radar antenna have a three-dimensional shape, or antenna pattern. The form of this pattern influences the signals that are returned to the radar receiver. The three-dimensional nature of the antenna pattern means that objects do not have to be directly below the antenna to be recorded; they can be in front, behind, or to the side. This characteristic can result in confusion as to precisely where a given anomaly is located.

Interpretation of radar. Typical features of ground-penetrating radar records include vertical dashed lines which are impressed upon the record at specified intervals along the profile. These lines are done by hand or automatically by a meter wheel. Horizontal lines partition the vertical scale (two-way travel time for the reflected radar beam) into depth segments. Each segment corresponds to a subsurface slice of the earth along the radar profile.

One major advantage of ground-penetrating radar is its insensitivity to surface clutter, such as fences, overhead transmission lines, and trash. However, there are some site-preparation activities, discussed below, that greatly enhance ground-penetrating radar results and improve the cost effectiveness of the survey.

Topography. Topography has a major influence on the ground-penetrating radar patterns (and hence the ability to accurately interpret them). Preparing an accurate topographic map of the site greatly helps the interpretation of the ground-penetrating radar patterns. Later, the topographic effects can be removed from the profiles with standard computer processing techniques.

Vegetation. Vegetation at the site influences the ground-penetrating radar survey in at least two ways. First, the radar signal reflects strongly from healthy vegetation, severely limiting radar penetration. Sparse grasses, even if green and healthy, are not as severe a problem as broadleaf weeds and plants. At a minimum, broadleaf vegetation should be removed prior to a ground-penetrating radar survey. Second, large bushes and trees require deviation from the survey profile lines, and can slow survey progress significantly. The site should be brushed (cleared) to eliminate all but the largest trees. At a minimum, bushes should be pruned to permit maximum freedom of movement.

Site calibration. Sites can be calibrated by using a target at a known depth. Then the dielectric constant at the site can be computed so that the precise depth of subsurface objects can be calculated.

Surface clutter. Although ground-penetrating radar is insensitive to most surface clutter, the signal that results when the radar antennas pass directly over metallic objects may obscure deeper reflections. It will speed the survey if metallic objects (for example, wire or cans) are removed from the survey profile lines beforehand.

Developments. A new hardware development called micropower-impulse radar consists of small radar antennas less than 1.5 in. (38 mm) mounted onto a circuit board. The small size and low power requirements permit large arrays of antennas (100 or more) to be employed for subsurface profiling. These arrays make three-dimensional images of the subsurface possible, eliminating the antenna pattern problems.

New software developments will likely be geared toward postacquisition processing and visualization. Software development to produce three-dimensional subsurface images using conventional radar and micropower-impulse radar technology are already under way, and scientific visualization of the three-dimensional subsurface environment is rendered by using models in animations and in real-time virtual reality settings.

For background information *see* COAL MINING; MINING; RADAR; RADAR-ABSORBING MATERIALS; REFLECTION OF ELECTROMAGNETIC RADIATION; UNDERGROUND MINING in the McGraw-Hill Encyclopedia of Science & Technology.   Charles E. Glass

Bibliography. D. Deb et al., Longwall control at Shoal Creek, *Min. Eng.*, 49(7), 1997; J. A. Doolittle and M. E. Collins, Use of soil information to determine application of ground penetrating radar, *J. Appl. Geophys.*, 33(1–3):101–108, 1995; S. Fiscor, The 1997 U.S. Longwall Census, *Coal Age*, February 1997; J. S. Mellett, Ground penetrating radar applications in engineering, environmental management, and geology, *J. Appl. Geophys.*, 33(1–3):157–166, 1995; R. Stefenko, *Coal Mining Technology, Theory and Practice*, 1983; R. Stefenko, *Longwall Mining: Shearer and Ploughs and System Considerations, Longwall-Shortwall Mining, State of the Art*, 1981.

Molecular electronics

Modern electronics is based largely on the inorganic semiconductor silicon. In contrast, molecular electronics is concerned with the exploitation of organic compounds. Its many current commercial applications include liquid-crystal displays, conductive-polymer sensors, and pyroelectric plastics. Longer-term developments might include molecular computational devices.

Organic semiconductors. Since the discovery of semiconducting behavior in organic materials, considerable research effort has been aimed at exploiting these properties in electronic and electrooptic devices. Organic semiconductors can have significant advantages over their inorganic counterparts. For example, thin layers of polymers can easily be made by inexpensive methods such as spin coating. High-temperature deposition from vapor reactants is generally needed to fabricate layers of inorganic semiconductors. Synthetic organic chemistry also offers the possibility of designing new materials with different band gaps.

The electrical properties of the organic devices cannot be directly compared to those based on single-crystal silicon and gallium arsenide. The mobilities (carrier velocity per unit electric field) of the charge carriers in organic field-effect transistors are low and similar to those found in amorphous silicon. Nevertheless, the simple fabrication techniques for polymers have motivated research on polymer transistor applications, such as data storage and thin-film device arrays to address liquid-crystal displays. Other commercial applications include battery electrodes, antistatic protective coatings, and replacements for conventional electrolytes in electrolytic capacitors. An early problem with conductive polymer materials was their limited stability. To some extent this difficulty has been resolved, and a few conductive polymers are now displaying adequate storage and operating lifetimes.

Polymer light-emitting diodes. Light emission from organic materials in response to the application of an electric field has been reported for many years. The simplest type of device structure is an organic semiconductor sandwiched between metals of high and low work functions. On application of a voltage across the structure, electrons are injected from one of the metallic electrodes and holes are injected from the other. These charge carriers recombine within the organic material with the consequent emission of visible radiation. The internal quantum efficiencies (ratio of number of photons generated to the number of carriers injected) of the original devices were quite low, about 0.01%. However, an improvement of three orders of magnitude has been obtained by applying techniques developed for inorganic light-emitting diodes. **Figure 1** shows the use of a heterostructure to allow carrier confinement at the interface between two polymers, based on polyphenylenevinylene (PPV). This device arrangement increases the likelihood of radiative electron-hole recombination because of the energy-band structure shown in **Fig. 2**. Besides increases in efficiency, light-emitting polymers have advanced to the stage where the range of colors covers the spectrum from blue to the near infrared, all at efficiencies of over 1%. These polymer devices have reached a performance comparable to that of inorganic light-emitting diodes. They also have fast switching speeds, higher than 1 MHz, that are typical of light-emitting diodes.

Electronic nose. Gas detectors with high sensitivity, reversibility, and the appropriate selectivity continue to be sought for process control and environmental monitoring. Inorganic materials such as the oxides of tin and zinc have been favored as the sensing element. However, a disadvantage of sensors

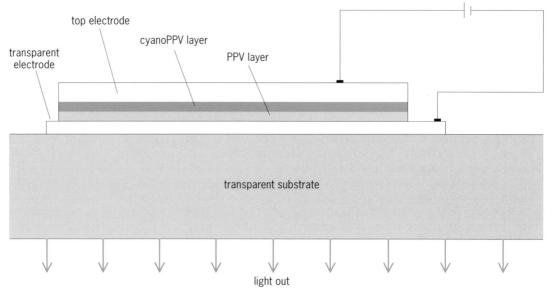

Fig. 1. Structure of a light-emitting diode composed of two polymer layers. The polymer materials are based on polyphenylenevinylene (PPV). *(After P. May, Polymer electronics: Fact or fantasy, Phys. World, 8(3):52–57, March 1995)*

based on metallic oxides is that they usually have to be operated at elevated temperatures (several hundred degrees), limiting some applications. As an alternative, there has been considerable interest in trying to exploit the properties of organic materials. Many such substances are known to exhibit a high sensitivity to gases and vapors, and their selectivity can be varied by simple chemical modification.

For most gas sensors, advantages accrue by using the sensing element in thin-film form (one such advantage is the high surface-to-volume ratio). Methods of film deposition include electrodeposition, thermal evaporation, and spinning. The Langmuir-Blodgett technique, in which monomolecular films are lifted off a water surface and deposited on a solid substrate, is a further means of producing layers of certain organic materials; it allows ultrathin films to be engineered at the molecular level. By combining these fabrication processes with synthetic chemical techniques, it may be possible to tailor a thin-film element to respond to a particular gas or range of gases.

A simple sensor exploits the resistance change of a thin layer of a gas-sensitive material, for example, a phthalocyanine or conductive polymer. The conductivity of such organic semiconductors changes in the presence of oxidizing or reducing gases. This effect is analogous to the doping of an inorganic semiconductor, such as silicon, with acceptor or donor impurities. A problem associated with these chemiresistor devices is that the resistance of the organic layer is usually very high. Consequently, the current outputs are low (typically picoamperes), requiring elaborate detection electronics and careful shielding and guarding of components. This difficulty may be overcome by incorporating the organic sensing layer into a diode or field-effect transistor structure.

To improve the selectivity of these gas sensors, an array of sensing elements may be used. This is the method favored by nature. The human olfactory system has many sensors, which are individually nonspecific. Signals from these sensors are fed to the brain for processing. As a result, the olfactory system is a highly sensitive and selective detector of odors.

The electronic nose is an attempt to mimic the human olfactory system. Individual sensors are usually based on organic polymer films. Each element is treated in a slightly different way during deposition

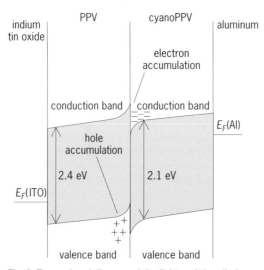

Fig. 2. Energy-band diagram of the light-emitting diode shown in Fig. 1. Fermi energies of the indium tin oxide [E_F(ITO)] and aluminum [E_F(Al)] electrodes are shown; the applied voltage is E_F(ITO) − E_F(Al). (After P. May, Polymer electronics: Fact or fantasy, Phys. World, 8(3):52–57, March 1995)

so that it responds uniquely on exposure to a particular gas or vapor. The pattern of resistance changes in the sensor array can then be used to "fingerprint" the vapor.

Infrared camera. Pyroelectricity is the release of electric charge as a result of a temperature change. Perhaps the main use of pyroelectrics is in sensors for electromagnetic radiation. Their application in intruder alarms, working in the infrared, is widespread, as these devices have certain advantages (broad wavelength response, no need for cooling) over semiconductor photon detectors.

A well-known organic pyroelectric is polyvinylidene fluoride (PVDF). The PVDF molecules have a repeat unit of ($-CH_2\text{-}CF_2$) in which the carbon-hydrogen and electrically polar (that is, possessing a finite dipole moment) carbon-fluorine bonds take on several stable configurations determined by the polymer's treatment. In the pyroelectric phase (formed by mechanical stretching and electrical poling), all the carbon-fluorine bonds (dipoles) point in the same direction, producing a polarization in the material. PVDF may also be mixed with related polymers to form copolymers with improved properties. The pyroelectric coefficients of these materials are modest compared to those of some ceramics. This characteristic is, to some extent, offset by the low permittivities of the polymers (important in determining the figure of merit for a pyroelectric sensor). Polymer materials also lend themselves to easy processing, as discussed above.

To make a simple radiation sensor, the pyroelectric element is generally fabricated in the form of a thin film with electrodes on either side of it. Radiation incident on the sensor is absorbed, producing a small temperature change. This releases charge into the external circuit. The resulting electric current will flow only while the temperature of the pyroelectric element is changing; that is, the sensor responds to the rate of change of the incoming radiation. Although this system is satisfactory for monitoring variations in infrared intensity (for example, in an intruder alarm), it is unsuitable for thermal imaging. For the latter, the incoming radiation must be mechanically chopped or panned across the pyroelectric element to provide a flux that varies with time.

The reduction or elimination of thermal crosstalk in thermal detector arrays is important to obtain a clear image. One pixel must be thermally insulated from the next, but electrical contacts must be made to the individual elements. **Figure 3** shows a structure developed for use with a copolymer of PVDF. In the design (Fig. 3*a*), the lateral heat flow is contained within the pixel repeat area by means of an array of gold busbars that serve as thermal ground lines. Each pixel consists of an octagonal detection area supported by four polymer webs attached to an array of solid metallic pillars. These pillars are directly below the thermal ground lines, ensuring that the latter are adequately heat-sunk to the silicon substrate. The electrical readout track is carried by one

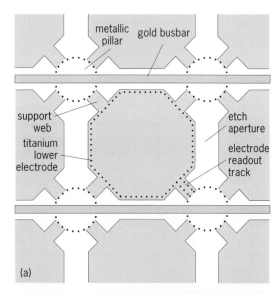

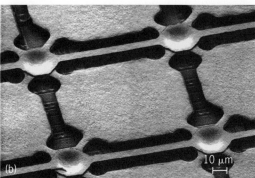

Fig. 3. Pyroelectric pixel. (*a*) Cross section. (*b*) Scanning electron micrograph.

of four corner straps. A scanning electron micrograph of the pixel structure is shown in Fig. 3*b*. The substrate circuitry is visible through the aperture between the suspended copolymer elements.

For background information *see* BIOELECTRONICS; ELECTRON-HOLE RECOMBINATION; FILM (CHEMISTRY); LIGHT-EMITTING DIODE; ORGANIC CONDUCTOR; PYRO-ELECTRICITY in the McGraw-Hill Encyclopedia of Science & Technology.   M. C. Petty

Bibliography. J. W. Gardner, *Microsensors: Principles and Applications*, 1994; J. W. Gardner and P. N. Bartlett, A brief history of electronic noses, *Sensors and Actuators B*, 18:211–220, 1994; P. May, Polymer electronics: Fact or fantasy, *Phys. World*, 8(3):52–57, March 1995; M. C. Petty, M. R. Bryce, and D. Bloor (eds.), *Introduction to Molecular Electronics*, 1995.

Molecular imprinting

Molecular imprinting is a highly attractive approach for producing binding sites in polymeric materials. It can be described as a way of making artificial locks for molecular keys. With this technique, lock-building elements are assembled in the presence of a molecular key and subsequently are made transfixed by cross-linking. The prepared lock becomes selective for the chosen molecular key and will not effectively recognize other keys. The molecular key may, in principle, be any type of molecule—from small molecules such as drug substances, amino acids, or steroid hormones to large molecules such as nucleic acids or proteins. Molecular assemblies such as cells and viruses can also be perceived. The lock-building elements consist of different monomers capable of forming three-dimensional network polymers.

Approaches. The selected key or print molecule first interacts with one or more functional monomers. This bond formation takes place freely in solution. The resulting complexes are subsequently copolymerized with a large excess of cross-linking monomers to give a rigid, insoluble polymer. Following removal of the print molecule, specific recognition sites are left in the polymer, complementary in shape and functionality to the print species (see **illus.**). Association and dissociation of the print molecule may then occur by plain diffusion in and out of the sites.

Two basic approaches to molecular imprinting may be distinguished: the self-assembly approach, where the prearrangement between the print molecule and the functional monomers is formed by noncovalent or metal coordination interactions; and the preorganized approach, where the aggregates in solution prior to polymerization are maintained by (reversible) covalent bonds. Both imprinting procedures make use of a high level of cross-linker, resulting in polymers which are of substantial rigidity and completely insoluble.

Systems. A wide variety of print molecules can be used in molecular imprinting. Compounds such as drugs, amino acids, carbohydrates, proteins, nucleotide bases, hormones, pesticides, coenzymes, and whole cells have been successfully used for the preparation of selective recognition matrices. With respect to the chosen target molecule, a toolbox of different polymer systems can be employed. The most readily used are polyacrylate-based or polyacrylamide-based systems. Other approaches include polystyrene-based systems and polysiloxane-based strategies, used to a lesser extent. Typical functional monomers used are acidic/hydrogen bonding (for example, methacrylic acid) or basic (vinylpyridine, vinylimidazole). For metal chelating interactions, an iminodiacetic acid derivative is commonly used in conjunction with metal ions such as copper (Cu^{2+}) and zinc (Zn^{2+}).

A very high degree of cross-linking (70–90%) is necessary for achieving specificity. Originally, isomers of divinylbenzene were used for cross-linking of styrene and other functional monomers into polystyrenes. Later, it was found that acrylic acid– or methacrylic acid–based systems could be prepared with higher specificity. Ethylene glycol dimethacrylate (EDMA) and trimethylolpropane trimethacrylate (TRIM) are commonly employed in several systems.

Configurations. Molecularly imprinted polymers can be developed in several configurations. The most commonly used technique involves the preparation of bulk polymer monoliths which, after fragmentation and particle sieving (giving particles of usually about 25 micrometers), are employed in several applications. This approach is commonly used in the laboratory scale, and for chromatographic applications other configurations have been developed. Thus, polymers can be prepared in situ in chromatography and electrophoresis columns. Since the flow properties in chromatography are dependent on particle size and shape, attempts have also been made to acquire molecularly imprinted polymer particles that are homogeneous in dimensions and morphology. This can be accomplished following either grafting/coating of the imprinted polymer on preformed particles, such as silica particles, or preparation of beads through suspension, emulsion, or dispersion polymerization. In this manner, spherical molecularly imprinted polymer particles with narrow size distribution can be obtained, providing good flow performances in chromatography. For an-

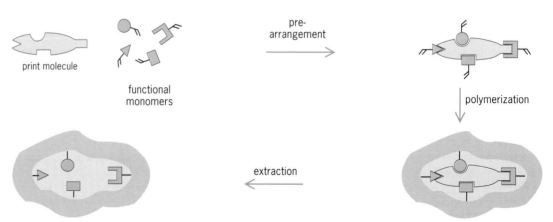

Schematic representation of the preparation of a molecularly imprinted material following the self-assembly approach.

alytical or sensor-device applications, thin layers or polymer membranes have been developed. In this case, either the polymer is directly cast as a thin layer on a surface or chip, or molecularly imprinted polymer particles are glued together by using a particle-binding agent, obtaining, for example, coated glass plates. Another technique, which may be denoted surface imprinting, can be envisaged as a two-dimensional variant of imprinting.

Characteristics. Apart from the more obvious recognition properties of molecularly imprinted polymers, their physical and chemical characteristics are highly appealing. These materials exhibit high resistance toward various external degrading factors. Thus, molecularly imprinted polymers are remarkably stable against mechanical stress, elevated temperatures, and high pressures; resistant against treatment with acid, base, or metal ions; and stable in a wide range of solvents. The shelf-life of the polymers is also very high: storage for several years at ambient temperature leads to no apparent reduction in performance. Furthermore, the polymers can be used repeatedly, well in excess of 100 times, without loss of recognition. In comparison to biological recognition sites, which are often proteins, these properties are highly advantageous.

Applications. In addition to studies where the nature of the recognition events has been the major issue, several application areas have been developed for imprinted materials.

Separations and isolations. Molecular imprinting chromatography (MIC) has been the most extensively studied application, and several intriguing separations have been accomplished. Imprinting is highly suitable for separation, allowing the preparation of tailor-made supports with predetermined selectivity. Of special interest are chiral separations. By using self-assembly imprinting protocols, highly efficient chirally discriminating phases may be produced. Characteristic of these materials is the elution order of the enantiomers, depending only on which enantiomeric form was used as print molecule. For instance, when the *R*-enantiomer is used as antigen, the *S*-form will be eluted first, and vice versa if the *S*-enantiomer is used as the template.

Molecular-imprinting solid-phase extraction (MISPE) is also a very efficient tool. The selectivities of the imprinted materials in combination with their robustness offer a great advantage in adsorbing a selected analyte from a complex (biological) matrix. The selectively adsorbed analyte can subsequently be easily separated from the polymer.

Antibody-binding mimics. Molecularly imprinted polymers can be used as substitutes for antibodies in immunoassays. These molecularly imprinted sorbent assays (MIAs) have been based on competitive radioligand binding protocols, and their recognition of related structures may be either nonexistent or far below that of the original print molecule. Furthermore, the cross-reactivity of these molecularly imprinted polymers may be similar to those reported for monoclonal antibodies.

The polymeric nature of molecularly imprinted polymers results in several advantages over natural antibodies. For instance, the physical and chemical resistance of imprinted polymers leads to the possibility of sterilizing the polymers, the high durability ensures a high stability of the recognition properties, and the production cost is considerably lower. Another advantage is the obviation of the need for host animals in the antibody production.

Plastizymes. Molecularly imprinted polymers can be designed to possess catalytic properties. These enzyme mimics, or plastizymes, can be prepared in several ways. The most common approach has been to use transition-state analogs (TSAs) in the imprinting protocol, thus stabilizing the reaction transition and enhancing the rate of product formation. Special emphasis has been put on the hydrolysis of active esters, using phosphonate transition-state analogs as the print molecule. Other strategies involve the use of coenzyme analogs, coordination compounds, and designed bait-and-switch strategies for introducing catalytic groups in the sites.

Sensors. Molecularly imprinted polymers can be used as recognition elements in biosensorlike devices. Normally, a sensing element, such as an enzyme, antibody, or receptor, is immobilized at the interface between the sensor and the analyte sample. A selective chemical signal, resulting from the binding process of the analyte to the recognition element, is subsequently transduced into an electrical signal, amplified, and converted to a manageable format. By substituting natural sensing elements with molecularly imprinted polymers, a number of advantages can be obtained. Thus, the sensing elements are far more stable and can perform in harsh environments. Furthermore, in cases where no biological recognizing elements can be found, they offer a useful alternative.

Others. Molecular imprinted materials can be utilized to guide or enhance a selected reaction pathway in (bio)chemical syntheses. This can be accomplished either by using the polymer as a reactant per se or by taking advantage of its selective adsorption properties.

The special characteristics of the materials can also be used to give controlled release matrices. By fine-tuning the binding conditions of the polymers, a bound analyte can be released as a response to external actions.

For background information *see* ANTIGEN-ANTIBODY REACTION; MOLECULAR RECOGNITION; POLYMER in the McGraw-Hill Encyclopedia of Science & Technology.   Olof Ramström; Klaus Mosbach

Bibliography. R. J. Ansell, O. Ramström, and K. Mosbach, Towards artificial antibodies by the technique of molecular imprinting, *Clin. Chem.*, 42:1506–1512, 1996; D. Kriz, O. Ramström, and K. Mosbach, *Anal. Chem.*, 69:A345–A349, 1997; K. Mosbach and O. Ramström, The emerging technique of molecular imprinting and its future impact on biotechnology, *Bio/Technology*, 14:163–170, 1996.

Mushroom

Mushrooms possess nutritional, commercial, and medicinal values, as evidenced in oyster, maitake, and shiitake mushrooms.

Oyster Mushrooms

Oyster mushrooms are widely distributed throughout the world and belong to the genus *Pleurotus* (Fungi: Basidiomycetes). Their cap is normally shell-like, about 1.9–7.8 in. (5–20 cm) in diameter, and fleshy, with eccentric or lateral stipe; and their color is white, cream, yellow, pink, brownish, or dark gray. As primary decomposers having the ability to degrade lignocellulose, oyster mushrooms grow in the wild on dead organic matter in tropical and temperate regions. Several species are also capable of acting as parasites of living trees and attacking nematodes or bacterial colonies.

Empirical cultivation of *Pleurotus* started around 1917 in Germany, using natural spawn for inoculation of wood logs and stumps. The first large-scale cultivation on logs was achieved in Hungary in 1969. Later, a variety of lignocellulosic by-products from agriculture or forestry were also found to be good growing substrates, and several species were brought into cultivation throughout the world, such as the tree oyster mushroom (*P. ostreatus*), the gray oyster mushroom (*P. pulmonarius*), the abalone mushroom (*P. cystidiosus*), the white oyster mushroom (*P. florida* nomen nudum), the golden oyster mushroom (*P. citrinopileatus*), the pink oyster mushroom (*P. djamor*), and the black oyster mushroom (*P. sapidus*). The oyster mushroom is the second most important cultivated mushroom in terms of world production.

Taxonomy. The extraordinary genetic diversity of oyster mushrooms, involving adaptation to a broad range of environmental conditions and substrates, makes clear taxonomic delimitation of *Pleurotus* species difficult. Conventional methods (fruit-body morphology, microscopic observations, mating studies between populations, biochemical analyses) have not provided clear-cut results. Thorough molecular studies have been shown to be more informative: intraspecific and interspecific heterogeneity was determined by using ribosomal and mitochondrial deoxyribonucleic acid (DNA) analyses, and phylogenetic studies of ribosomal DNA sequences indicated geographic speciation in several groups. However, a present research problem is to obtain isolates that represent authentic indigenous populations, because many commercial strains, now widely distributed throughout the world, may have already escaped from cultivation. In general, the taxonomy and systematics of *Pleurotus* species remains far from being solved, and requires not only the identification of effective classical and molecular characters but also a basic consensus on speciation processes and species concepts within the genus.

Breeding potential. *Pleurotus* mushrooms show the typical life cycle of Basidiomycetes, a major fungal group (**Fig. 1**). The cycle begins with the germination of a basidiospore in a suitable substrate. The basidiospore gives rise to a monokaryotic mycelium containing genetically identical nuclei (*n*) and capable of indefinite independent growth. When two compatible monokaryotic mycelia are in close contact, they are able to establish a fertile dikaryon by hyphal fusion or plasmogamy. This dikaryon (*n* + *n*), having clamp connections and binucleate in each hyphal compartment, contains two genetically different nuclei (one from each monokaryon) throughout the mycelium. When environmental conditions are appropriate (temperature, light, and relative humidity), the dikaryotic mycelium will differentiate into fruit bodies having specialized structures called basidia. In these club-shaped, binucleate cells, which are formed in the lamellae (hymenium) of each fruit body, karyogamy (fusion of the paired nuclei; 2*n*) and meiosis (recombination and segregation) take place. The four resulting haploid nuclei move to the sterigmata on the basidium to form four new basidiospores. When the fruit bodies are mature, basidiospores are discharged, starting the sexual life cycle again. A few species, such as *P. cystidiosus*, also have an asexual cycle through the production of structures (0.03–0.4 in. or 1–10 mm high) called synnemata.

The pattern of sexuality of oyster mushrooms studied has been described as bifactorial heterothallism, in which two multiallelic mating-type factors (*A* and *B*) act synchronously to control mating between monokaryons to produce a fertile dikaryon, in the absence of morphological differentiation. This pattern has advantages in breeding programs because compatible matings having different *A* and *B* factors are reliably recognized by the formation of clamp connections in the dikaryotic mycelium. Oyster mushrooms are easily handled in the laboratory on culture media, spore germination is close to 100%, and mutants can be obtained by direct mutagenic treatment (for example, x-rays and ultraviolet radiation) of basidiospores or by hyphal fragments. These features make it possible to obtain suitable combinations of selected characters through simple mating techniques. Recombinant DNA technology is increasingly important in breeding oyster mushrooms, providing outstanding information and powerful tools at the molecular level. Most studies are concentrated in *P. ostreatus*, *P. cornucopiae*, and *P. sajor-caju*. The nuclear and mitochondrial DNA has been isolated and characterized. Uniparental inheritance and recombination of mitochondrial DNA has been shown to occur. Reliable genetic markers were recently developed, such as enzyme markers and DNA restriction fragment length polymorphisms. DNA transformation has already been reported for *P. ostreatus*, and a molecular analysis to study the role and properties of important enzymes in the life cycle of oyster mushrooms is being carried out. A systematic combination of classical and molecular genetics meets the main breeding challenges of oyster mushrooms: (1) sporeless strains and strains with reduced

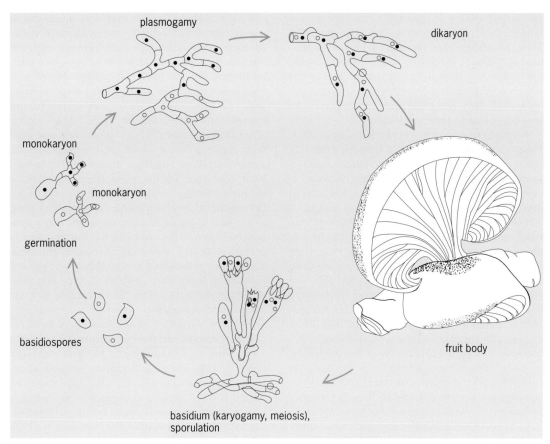

Fig. 1. Life cycle of the oyster mushroom *Pleurotus ostreatus*. *(Courtesy of D. Martinez-Carrera)*

sporulation, (2) tolerance to elevated temperatures, and (3) genetic resistance to competitor molds, especially *Trichoderma*. Further genetic manipulation may be focused on increasing the nutritional value and postharvest quality of fruit bodies, and increasing degradation efficiency of extracellular enzymes.

Spawn preparation. Commercial strains of oyster mushrooms with a range of fruiting temperatures (59–86°F or 15–30°C) are available. Modern methods of spawn preparation use cereal grains, which are sterilized in glass jars or polypropylene plastic bags, inoculated with a selected strain, and incubated at appropriate temperatures for complete colonization. An alternative small-scale method uses serial dilutions of basidiospores from a spore print to prepare grain spawn. Other organic raw materials (for example, straw, coffee pulp, cotton waste, and sawdust), alone or combined in different mixtures, are also used to make spawn.

Substrate preparation. After homogenizing particle size and adjusting water content (about 70%) and pH (5–6), many substrates have been shown to be suitable for cultivation. Substrates include straw, coffee pulp, cotton waste, wood shavings, banana pseudostem, cotton seed hulls, waste paper, diverse plant leaves, cardamom pulp, sawdust mixtures, corncobs, tequila bagasse, pulp mill sludges, cocoa shell waste, and *Cassia* by-products. The direct use of

some of these substrates, without any further treatment, for rustic cultivation in the field was reported from China. However, five methods have been developed to make substrates more suitable for growing oyster mushrooms on a large or small scale: (1) sterilization; substrates are autoclaved at 100–121°C (212–250°F) for 1–2 h; (2) pasteurization; substrates are placed in an appropriate room or tunnel and pasteurized with steam at 60–100°C (140–212°F) for 6–24 h, or immersed in hot water at 70–90°C (158–194°F) for 1–2 h; (3) aerobic fermentation; substrates are aerobically fermented for 2–6 days, and then pasteurized with steam at 60–82°C (140–180°F) for 12–24 h; (4) semi-anaerobic fermentation; substrates are immersed in water 7–10 days to induce lactic acid fermentation; and (5) xerothermic process; dry substrates are treated with steam at 100°C (212°F) for 1 h in a small tunnel, and then cool water is added. Supplementation may be carried out before treatment to increase nutrient content and yields.

Production systems. Prepared substrates are homogeneously inoculated with the spawn, either by hand or mechanically, at the rate of 0.5–3% of fresh substrate weight. The spawned substrate is placed in a variety of containers. In the tunnel process, the substrate is colonized in bulk under controlled conditions and then transferred to smaller containers. The use of plastic bags of different sizes containing

15-66 lb (7–30 kg) of spawned substrate is a common practice. Horizontal trays, shelves, vertical plastic sacks, and pressed rectangular blocks are also used. Containers are placed inside growing rooms for incubation. After complete colonization of the substrate by the mushroom mycelium (15–40 days), light, ventilation, and watering are increased in the growing rooms to promote fruiting.

Harvesting and processing. Production of fruit bodies varies according to each species, spawn quality, substrate quality, environmental conditions, impact of pests, and impact of diseases (fungi, bacteria, viruses). Average biological efficiencies (yield of fresh mushrooms as a percentage of the dry weight of substrate at spawning) reported from diverse substrates range 35–159%, considering a whole production cycle of about 70–80 days. Recent cultivation of *P. tuber-regium* has opened up the possibility to extend commercial production from fruit bodies to edible sclerotia (a firm, frequently rounded mass of mushroom tissue, resistant to unfavorable environmental conditions). A processing technology is fundamental for commercial production because oyster mushrooms undergo rapid postharvest deterioration at room temperature. Mushrooms are normally cooled in specific facilities to retard fruit-body metabolism, and then sent to the fresh market. Further processing, such as canning or drying, can be carried out depending on marketing strategies. After mushroom cultivation, spent substrates can be recycled as organic fertilizer, animal feed, or substrate for other cultivated mushrooms, as well as for biogas or enzyme production, vermiculture, paper manufacture, and cardboard production.

World production. The cultivation of oyster mushrooms has spread rapidly worldwide as a result of their remarkable biological features and the versatile technology available. In general, two main trends can be identified: (1) private commercial enterprises operating primarily on a large or small scale for accumulation of capital, and involving intensive cultivation tending to be highly mechanized (**Fig. 2**); and (2) rural production for satisfying regional needs, which is performed through rustic cultivation methods. Developing countries have benefitted by the latter trend in terms of its local contribution to food production, rural development, and sustainable agriculture. China, South Korea, Japan, and Indonesia are major producers. The oyster mushroom has become an important cultivated mushroom, accounting for about 22% of the total world production.

Nutritional and medicinal attributes. The protein content of oyster mushrooms can be considered their main nutritional attribute. Average values ranging 10.5–30.4%, on a dry weight basis, have been reported. The concentration of essential amino acids varies from 33.4 to 46.0 g per 100 g of corrected crude protein, showing significant amounts of lysine, leucine, and methionine. The fat content reported is 1.1–2.2% on a dry weight basis, having a high proportion of unsaturated fatty acids (79.3%). The carbohydrate content varies from 46.6 to 81.8% on a dry weight basis. Main vitamins present in 100 g dry weight of oyster mushrooms are thiamine (1.16–4.80 mg), niacin (46.0–108.7 mg), and ascorbic acid (7.4 mg). Fiber (7.4–27.6% on a dry weight basis) and minerals (potassium, phosphorus,

Fig. 2. Intensive cultivation of oyster mushrooms in a vertical container. *(Courtesy of D. Martinez-Carrera)*

iron, copper, zinc) are also present in good proportion. Several compounds from oyster mushrooms, potentially beneficial for human health, have been isolated and studied: polysaccharides showing strong antitumor activity, a lectin called pleurotolysin with hemolytic properties, and extracts with hypotensive action on renal functions.

Disadvantages. Oyster mushrooms release enormous amounts of spores into the atmosphere of growing rooms. The inhalation of these spores induces allergic reactions in about 30–40% of farm workers. Spore allergy is characterized by influenzalike symptoms, which disappear without treatment in a few days if exposure is prevented. This major drawback, which has not discouraged the worldwide development of oyster mushroom cultivation, can be reasonably controlled by wearing effective masks and having efficient ventilation systems.
                                            D. Martinez-Carrera

Maitake Mushroom

Also known as hen-of-the-woods, *Grifola frondosa* occurs in nature in large, clustered masses of grayish-brown, fleshy caps. It somewhat resembles a small hen and is often found covered with leaves. The caps have whitish pores and lateral, white stalks branching from a compound base. The caps are 0.8–2.76 in. (2–7 cm) wide; are velvety, being covered with small clusters of radial fibrils; and are 0.08–0.18 in. (2–3 mm) thick with white flesh. Tubes (0.08–0.18 in. or 2–3 mm long) line the underside of the caps and descend the stalk of the mushroom. The tubes contain the basidia that produce the basidiospores. Spore prints of *Grifola frondosa* are white. Maitake is considered a white-rot fungus because of its preference to attack lignin, a major component in woody plant cells.

Natural habitat. In North America, maitake is found fruiting throughout the fall at the base of stumps or dead or dying deciduous hardwoods. Clusters as large as 100 lb (45.5 kg) have been harvested from the base of oak trees. Some mushroom hunters return to the same stump each fall to harvest additional clusters of maitake. In North America, the mushroom is distributed from Canada to Louisiana, the Midwest, and Idaho. It is found in northeastern Japan and the temperate hardwood regions of China and Europe.

Commercial production. Japan is the major producer and consumer of maitake. Commercial production in Japan began in 1981 (716,625 lb or 325 metric tons) and by 1994 reached 30,870,000 pounds (14,000 metric tons), a 43-fold increase. Maitake is produced primarily in the provinces of Niigata, Nagano, Gunnma, and Shizuoka. Other countries, such as the United States, began maitake production in the early 1990s.

Most maitake is marketed as food. However, maitake has been shown to have both antitumor and antiviral properties. Powdered fruit bodies are used in the production of many health foods such as maitake tea, whole powder, granules, drinks, and tab-

Fig. 3. Maitake mushroom (*Grifola frondosa*) may be produced on synthetic substrate contained in polypropylene bags. *(Courtesy of Dr. Daniel Royse)*

lets. Maitake also is believed to lower blood pressure, reduce cholesterol, and reduce the symptoms of chronic fatigue syndrome.

Commercial production of most *G. frondosa* is on synthetic substrate contained in polypropylene bottles or bags (**Fig. 3**). A common substrate is hardwood sawdust supplemented with rice bran or wheat bran in a 5:1 ratio, respectively. Other formulas include hardwood sawdust supplemented with white millet and wheat bran. Some growers may add soil to the mix to stimulate fruit-body formation. For bottle production, the containers are filled with moistened substrate and sterilized prior to inoculation. For production in bags, the moistened substrate is filled into microfiltered polypropylene bags and sterilized to kill unwanted competitive microorganisms. After cooling 16–20 h, the substrate is inoculated and the bags are heat sealed and shaken to uniformly distribute the spawn throughout the substrate. Spawn run lasts about 30–50 days depending on strain and substrate formulation. Some growers use a cold shock (4°C or 39°F) for 1–4 days to ensure fruiting induction. For growers not using a hard cold shock, temperatures may be lowered more gently from about 72°F (22°C) during spawn run to 57°F (14°C) to induce fruiting and fruit-body maturation.

During production, humidity management is important to maintain optimum-quality fruit-body development. Primordia may die if the humidity is too low. If the humidity is too high, moisture may condense on the fruit body and cause death of the immature mushroom. Excessive humidity may also result in malformed mushrooms with pore formation on the surface of the fruit body. Expected yields are in the range of 0.75–1.5 lb (340–680 g) per 5.5-lb (2.5-kg) bag. Yields are lower for the 0.85–1.06-qt (800–1000 ml) bottles. Production of a second break is possible, but results are highly variable. Most growers discard the substrate after harvesting the first break, although some bury the substrate in soil outdoors to produce a second flush of mushrooms.
                                            Daniel J. Royse

Shiitake Mushroom

The shiitake mushroom (*Lentinula edodes*) is the second most widely cultivated mushroom in the world. Because of its unique flavor, nutritional value, and purported medicinal properties, it has been a traditional ingredient of the culinary art of the Far East for centuries and is now becoming more popular in the Western world.

Lentinula edodes is a white-rot fungus, capable of decomposing all the important structural components of wood, including cellulose and lignin. It grows as a saprophyte on dead hardwood in moist climates and is found throughout Asia (**Fig. 4**). Japan is the leading producer of this mushroom.

Cultivation and production. Shiitake reproduces by means of spores, which develop on special structures within the fruit body (mushroom) and are spread by air currents to new wood substrates. After the spores germinate, logs become colonized by a threadlike mycelium that permeates the wood. When environmental conditions are suitable, new fruit bodies will be produced and the cycle is repeated.

Traditional shiitake production on logs is seasonal. Fruiting occurs during the spring and fall when rainfall and temperature are most favorable. Since hardwood logs are becoming scarce or are unavailable in some countries, alternative substrates have been developed. The cultivation of shiitake on artificial or synthetic logs is increasing in popularity and permits year-round production in areas unsuited to natural outdoor cultivation. Compared to natural log production, cultivation on artificial logs produces higher yields on a regular basis in a shorter time.

Artificial logs differ from natural logs in the particulate nature of their composition. Virtually all artificial logs are produced by the same basic technology. The substrate is usually composed of hardwood sawdust. In addition, straw, corncobs, sugarcane bagasse, citrus-peel wastes, and grain chaff have been used either alone or combined with sawdust. Supplements added to the basic substrate contribute nutrients or improve the chemical or physical composition. Sawdust-based substrates have been commercialized independently in several regions of the world. Each area has adopted methods reflecting locally available resources, technologies, and traditions.

Cultivation methods using artificial substrate require pure culture spawn; sterilization of the substrate; aseptic inoculation techniques; a container, usually plastic bags, to protect substrate from contamination; and skilled personnel. As with log cultivation, the grower can control temperature and humidity to provide optimum conditions for growth and fruiting. However, as the climate becomes less favorable, greater capital investment is needed for protective structures and systems for heating, cooling, humidification, and ventilation.

Use. According to Chinese medical tradition, eating shiitake is recommended for good health and longevity. The shiitake is also regarded as an elixir. Because of its protein, fiber, vitamin, and mineral content, shiitake is considered to be a nutritious food. Shiitake mushrooms contain all essential amino acids, as well as most commonly occurring nonessential amino acids and amides.

A number of biologically active compounds have been isolated and purified from the fruit body, the mycelium, and the liquid culture medium of shiitake. Eritadenine is a unique amino acid that reduces cholesterol in the blood and lowers blood pressure. More than one hundred derivatives of eritadenine have been synthesized and tested, and several patents capitalizing on its effect have been issued. Lentinan is a high-molecular-weight glucose polymer extracted from the fruit body of shiitake. It is a potent host defense potentiator that stimulates nonspecific host resistance and exerts inhibitory effects against experimental tumors. In Japan and other Asian countries, lentinan is a commercially available drug used in the treatment of stomach cancer.

Antithrombotic compounds (low-molecular-weight nucleosides or other nucleic acid derivatives), an antibiotic (Cortinellin), and interferon-inducing substances from the ribonucleic acid (RNA) fraction extracted from the fruit bodies and spores have also been identified in shiitake.

For background information *see* BASIDIOMYCOTINA; FUNGI; MEDICAL MYCOLOGY; MUSHROOM in the McGraw-Hill Encyclopedia of Science & Technology.   Jeannette M. Birmingham

Bibliography. S. T. Chang, Mushroom research and development: Equality and mutual benefit, *Mush-*

Fig. 4. Shiitake mushroom (*Lentinula edodes*) colonizes and grows on logs. (*Courtesy of Jeannette Birmingham*)

room Biol. Mushroom Prod., 2:1-10, 1996; T. J. Elliott (ed.), *Science and Cultivation of Edible Fungi*, 1995; K. Esser and P. A. Lemke (eds.), *The Mycota*, 1994; H. Hadeler, *Medicinal Mushrooms You Can Grow for Health, Pleasure and Profit*, 1995; S. C. Jong and J. M. Birmingham, The medicinal value of the mushroom *Grifola*, *World J. Microbiol.*, 6:227-235, 1990; T. Mizuno and C. Zhuang, Maitake, *Grifola frondosa*: Pharmacological effects, *Food Rev. Int.*, 11(1):135-149, 1995; P. Przybylowicz and J. Donoghue, *Shiitake Growers Handbook: The Art and Science of Mushroom Cultivation*, 1988; D. J. Royse, Specialty mushrooms and their cultivation, *Hort. Rev.*, 19:59-97, 1997; P. Stamets, *Growing Gourmet and Medicinal Mushrooms*, 1993.

Natural language technology

Computers that can speak and understand natural language have long appeared in science fiction. Endowing computers with linguistic capabilities in practice, however, has proven to be exceptionally difficult. Efforts to build automatic translation machines started in the early days of functional computers in the 1950s, and the complex problems thwarted researchers for decades. Recently, however, significant progress has been made, and while machines are far from fully understanding language, useful applications involving language are now possible. Linguistic capabilities can be expected to appear in a wide range of products and applications and to transform the way people think about and interact with computers.

The stages of understanding language consist of transforming sound into words (speech recognition), words into meaning (parsing), and meaning into intention and action (pragmatics [see **illus.**]). For instance, a woman might come up to a man on the street and speak to him. Using speech recognition, the man would identify the words as "Do you have a watch?" Using parsing, he would identify the meaning as a question about whether he possessed a watch. Using pragmatics, he would decide that the woman wanted him to tell her the time. The stages of language generation involve the opposite process of generating a response, and map intention to meaning (content planning), meaning to words

(generation), and words to sound (speech synthesis).

While full understanding of any natural language will not be feasible in the foreseeable future, there are many specialized tasks in which natural language processing can be of great benefit. This article explores some applications that already exist or that are close to development, organized by the phases of processing defined above.

Speech recognition. Speech-recognition systems, which map sounds to words, have reached the stage where many applications are feasible. The factors affecting the performance of recognition systems include the size of the vocabulary to be recognized, the range of speakers to be handled, and whether people must speak one word at a time with pauses (isolated word recognition) or can speak naturally (continuous word recognition). There are already many applications of speech recognition in commercial products that range from very high accuracy, isolated-word-recognition systems to viable-accuracy, continuous-speech, single-speaker, large-vocabulary systems. An example can be found in systems that allow a person to make long-distance, calling-card calls entirely by voice. These systems can handle a wide range of the population using a small vocabulary of numbers and words such as "yes" and "no" (typically less than 50 words) and speaking one word at a time. Such applications are saving telephone companies substantial operator costs. On the other end of the spectrum are programs available on personal computers for dictating letters and documents. After adaptation to a single speaker, these systems can attain up to 95% word accuracy on carefully spoken continuous speech with a vocabulary of 30,000 words or more.

These systems only map sounds to words. They do not understand what is being said. Speech recognition is likely to become a pervasive technology and appear in a wide range of products.

Speech synthesis. Speech synthesis is opposite to speech recognition, and maps words to sounds. Speech synthesis is clearly economical and feasible, since nearly every large company is presently using it in receiving telephone calls. However, while intelligible, it is still not very natural.

Two main techniques are used in speech synthesis. The most common systems use prerecorded

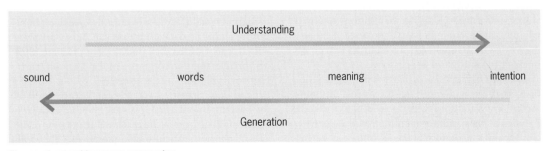

Stages of natural language processing.

words and phrases spoken by a human which are then assembled by the computer to produce the desired sequence of words. While easy to construct, such systems sound unnatural because the individually recorded words do not have the appropriate intonation or pacing for the sentence. The second method involves synthesizing a signal that sounds like speech, much as early music synthesizers generated musical sounds. Because of the better control over the entire process, this technique can do a better job of producing the correct intonation, emphasis, and pacing. There are commercial systems that can take a sentence in text form and produce intelligible speech with reasonable intonation. However, the synthesized voices still take some listening experience to get used to. The technique is constantly improving, however, and soon will reach the stage where it will become the synthesis method of choice.

Parsing. As higher levels of language processing are attempted, a difficult problem arises. With speech recognition, the desired result is clearly known, namely to ascertain what words were spoken. But a clearly defined notion of what meaning and understanding are does not exist. In the early decades of research, it was believed that machines would have to acquire a capability for deep understanding of language before the technology could be useful. In the 1990s, however, researchers found that shallow analysis techniques that capture only some structure and content can be useful in a wide range of applications. Most researchers in the field now take a pragmatic approach and consider how well language systems can perform a specific task. For example, the task might be to find relevant pages on the World Wide Web, given natural language input such as "I want to find sources that deal with the economic growth in the late nineteenth century." It is possible to evaluate how well such an application performs the task by checking, for example, how many relevant pages it finds (the recall) and what proportion of the pages found are relevant (the precision).

A wide range of practical applications are becoming feasible by using structural approaches that fall far short of deep understanding. Included are (with an example of each) document retrieval (searching a database for existing patents that might relate to a new invention), information extraction (generating a database of merger and acquisitions activity from newspaper reports), information retrieval (using speech over the telephone to obtain information on airline schedules), machine translation (automatically translating equipment maintenance manuals), and writing tools (spelling-correction and grammar-checking tools in word processors).

Generation. The reverse process of parsing is generation, transforming meaning to words. In these cases, the meaning to be expressed is in the form of some database of information, or a more general representation of information as found in knowl-edge-based systems developed in artificial intelligence. The challenge is to capture a given meaning in a natural-sounding sentence of extended discourse. Such technology is critical for providing responses in telephone-based information retrieval (for example, planning a response to a query about airline schedules), as well as in longer-term applications such as automated help and tutorial systems.

Dialogue. The two areas of transforming meaning to intention and back to meaning are combined, as they naturally go together. Most potential applications involve building intelligent language-based computer interfaces. Specifically, the work involves relating the language used to the tasks that the human (and machine) is attempting to accomplish. Many of the parsing applications discussed above involved performing tasks (such as information extraction). But in all these applications there was one fixed task that the person was performing in every interaction, so it could be encoded directly in the programming. As more complex tasks are attempted, such as interactive design, diagnosis, planning, or control applications, there are many different specific tasks that may need to be accomplished. Work in this area generally uses an explicit model of the task to drive techniques for identifying the most likely subtask that the person wants to perform, given what is said. Currently, fairly robust experimental conversational systems can be constructed, but only in very limited tasks (for example, defining efficient routes on a map for a set of trains).

Approaches. While a diverse set of methods are used in the field of natural language processing, the techniques can generally be classified as statistical methods, structural and pattern-based methods, and reasoning-based methods. These approaches are not mutually exclusive; in fact, the most comprehensive models combine all three. The approaches differ in the kind of processing tasks they can perform and in the degree to which systems require handcrafted rules as opposed to automatic training and learning from language data.

Statistical methods. These involve using large databases of language or speech to compute statistical properties such as word co-occurrence and sequence information. For instance, the probability that one word might follow another might be estimated from a corpus of language, and then this information might be used to help predict what words are likely in speech-recognition task. Good statistical word-prediction algorithms can double the word-recognition accuracy rate in current speech-recognition systems. Statistical models can be surprisingly effective in a wide range of tasks. For instance, they can predict the correct part of speech (noun, verb, and so forth) for words over 95% of the time in general text. Statistical models can also be used as the basis for information retrieval, and for producing rough, first-cut drafts in machine translation. The advantage of statistical techniques is that they can be automatically trained from databases of language data. The challenge for statistical models concerns how to capture higher-level structure such as meaning, and structural properties such as sentence structure. In general, the most successful solutions to these problems involve combining statistical approaches with other approaches.

Structural and pattern-based approaches. These have the closest connection to linguistic theory. These approaches involve defining structural properties of language in formalisms such as finite-state machines and context-free grammars. Structural approaches are not constrained solely to analyzing sentence structure, however. Some work dispenses with fully analyzing sentence structure, and uses simpler semantically based patterns to match sentence fragments. Such techniques are especially useful in limited-domain, speech-driven applications where errors in the input can be expected. Structural models provide a capability for detailed analysis of linguistic phenomena; but the more detailed the analysis, the more it becomes necessary to rely on hand-constructed rules rather than automatic training from data.

Reasoning-based approaches. These involve modeling the knowledge and reasoning processes of humans and applying them to interpret language. By trying to capture the knowledge that a human may have in a situation, and modeling commonsense reasoning, these techniques have the potential to come closest to human levels of understanding of language in context. The disadvantage is the complexity of the models required to define the conversational agent.

For background information *see* NATURAL LANGUAGE PROCESSING; SPEECH RECOGNITION; VOICE RESPONSE in the McGraw-Hill Encyclopedia of Science & Technology.   James F. Allen

Bibliography. J. F. Allen, *Natural Language Understanding*, 2d ed., 1995; E. Charniak, *Statistical Language Learning*, 1993.

Near-Earth Objects

Asteroids and comets that closely approach or cross the orbit of the Earth are called Near-Earth Objects (NEOs). The potential of these objects to collide with the Earth has increased interest in them. The effort to study Near-Earth Objects has grown substantially, but much remains to be done considering the tragic consequences they pose to humankind.

Nature and importance. Near-Earth Objects are natural objects in the solar system whose orbits take them within 1.3 astronomical units (1 AU equals 1.5×10^8 km or 9.3×10^7 mi) of the Sun, or no more than 0.3 AU outside Earth's orbit. Since all Near-Earth Objects orbit the Sun, and their periods generally do not exceed a few tens of years, they can be searched for and observed depending on the capability and extent of the effort.

The study of Near-Earth Objects expands as their potential hazard to life is more fully understood. The discovery and recognition of an increasing number of impact features and craters serve to show what can happen when collisions occur. Examples include the Chicxulub crater in Yucatán, Mexico, creating the impact believed responsible for the extinction of the dinosaurs 6.5×10^7 years ago; Meteor Crater in Arizona, which has existed about 50,000 years; and the Tunguska event in Siberia in 1908. Near-Earth Objects are important for other reasons, ranging from offering raw material to support space exploration to revealing more about the origin of life and adding to the understanding of the universe. *See* MASS EXTINCTION.

Discovery. Near-Earth asteroids have been recognized since the early 1930s, when the asteroid (1862) Apollo was discovered and shown to cross the Earth's orbit. It was later realized that (433) Eros and (887) Alinda, discovered in 1898 and 1918 respectively, were also near-Earth asteroids. Starting in the 1970s, the pace of near-Earth asteroid discoveries increased when several were found each year, usually by systematic search programs. By the 1980s, approximately two dozen asteroids per year were discovered, mostly by purposeful searches, with some contribution from amateur astronomers. As of April 1998, the number of known near-Earth asteroids was 460.

Asteroid population. Most asteroids orbit the Sun in the region between Mars and Jupiter. Near-Earth asteroids are exceptions. The asteroids that approach the Earth's orbit are called Amors, and those that cross, Apollos; a small group, Atens, have orbits smaller than the Earth's and orbital periods of less than one year (**Fig. 1**).

As many as 50% of the near-Earth asteroids may be degassed and defunct comets that survive in their cometary orbits but have become inactive over time and appear noncometary, masquerading as asteroids. One object, (4015) Wilson-Harrington, was photographed in 1949, displaying a cometary tail; yet it was discovered as an asteroid in 1979. This object of cometary nature had lost its ices and volatiles after many orbits around the Sun and had evolved into an asteroid. Another apparent example of a comet transitioning to an asteroid is 1996 PW, which has an orbit similar to a long-period comet but shows no cometary activity. It may be the first asteroid discovered that is a member of the Oort Cloud.

Potential hazard. Gravitational perturbations of an object's orbit over time can bring it to or across the Earth's orbit even if it is currently 0.3 AU outside the Earth's orbit. As discoveries of near-Earth asteroids increased, the term "potentially hazardous asteroids" was introduced to classify objects 200 m (650 ft) or larger in diameter that, over the next 200 years, approach the Earth by 8×10^6 km (5×10^6 mi) or less. Of the 448 known near-Earth asteroids, over 100 are potentially hazardous asteroids. Short- and long-period comets can closely approach and cross

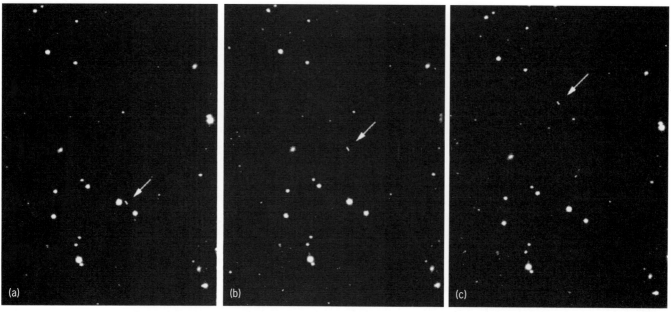

Fig. 1. Images of Aten asteroid 1997 AC11 obtained with the Near-Earth Asteroid Tracking (NEAT) camera. Images, taken at 12-min intervals, show rapid apparent motion. (Position of the asteroid is indicated by the arrow.) The asteroid was the first Aten discovered with the NEAT system, on January 10, 1997. When these images were taken on January 15, it was at a distance of 0.134 astronomical unit (20 ×10⁶ km or 12.5 × 10⁶ mi) from the Earth and came within 0.107 AU (16 × 10⁶ km or 9.95 × 10⁶ mi) on January 22. *(NASA; Jet Propulsion Laboratory; U.S. Air Force NEAT Team)*

the Earth's orbit, contributing an additional concern. *See* COMET HALE-BOPP.

Of greater worry is the large number of Near-Earth Objects that are as yet undiscovered. The realization that only a small percentage of the estimated near-Earth-asteroid population has been discovered is adequate reason to accelerate search efforts. Answers are needed as to what are or what will be in near-Earth space and how close an undiscovered asteroid may be to striking the Earth, causing a major extinction. The only sure way to establish the degree of risk involved in an object encounter with the Earth is to conduct a full-sky survey and find the larger objects that are the greater threat. It is estimated that, with an extension of present search efforts using charge-coupled devices, 90% of the population of near-Earth asteroids that are 1 km (0.6 mi) or larger in diameter can be found within a decade. An essentially complete mapping of these objects and their orbits will provide the basis for assessing the collision potential for each and the opportunity to take diversionary actions, vastly reducing the hazard. If objects that are determined to be a potential danger to the Earth are found early enough, measures can be taken to divert them from collision courses with the Earth.

Occasionally, long-period comets suddenly appear in proximity to the Earth. Not only are they difficult to detect, particularly if heading directly toward the Earth, but the time to impact may be only months or even days—little time in which to take evasive action.

Mitigation or deflection. Many interception techniques and strategies are being investigated. If an asteroid is found on a collision course with the Earth, the primary consideration is the time available before probable impact. Various types of sensing must be carried out on the incoming body, characterizing its composition, mass, density, and structure. With the orbital data, an evaluation can be conducted to determine the amount of diversionary force required to adequately alter the orbit and cause the asteroid to pass at a safe distance from the Earth, and the form that force must take.

Other considerations involve the actual effects of the collision. A stony-ice object up to 50 m (160 ft) in diameter would simply burn up in the atmosphere, while an iron-nickel one of comparable size would produce on land another Arizona Meteor Crater (1.2 km or 0.75 mi in diameter, and 230 m or 750 ft deep) with local devastation. An impact by an object 1 km (0.6 mi) in diameter would result in a global catastrophe.

Search programs. Two programs make monthly searches for Near-Earth Objects in the United States: the Spacewatch program in Tucson, Arizona, and the Near-Earth Asteroid Tracking (NEAT) program in Maui, Hawaii.

Spacewatch program. The Spacewatch Camera Telescope uses a 0.9-m (35-in.) telescope with a charge-coupled-device camera attached to image the sky for Near-Earth Objects. It scans the sky in a planned pattern, and the images are displayed on a computer screen. This program discovers not only large bodies but also small asteroids, tens to hundreds of meters in diameter, and approaching as close as 100,000 km (60,000 mi). The Spacewatch project is adding a 1.8-m (70-in.) telescope which is expected to expand its sky coverage and capability of imaging faint objects.

NEAT program. The Near-Earth Asteroid Tracking program uses a 1-m (39-in.) telescope equipped with a charge-coupled-device camera. It is autonomously operated and has been in use since December 1995. Over 21,500 detections have been made, about 60% being new objects. As of March 1998, it had discovered 30 near-Earth asteroids (Fig. 1) and two long-period comets, as well as the unique object 1996 PW, of record-breaking eccentricity (0.992). This program has found objects that are of sufficient brightness to be followed and observed by other types of analytical instruments. Such instruments measure the light reflected from the asteroid surface and provide information about the color, composition, rotational period, and other physical properties important to establishing the nature of the small body.

Other programs. Planned search programs include LINEAR, LONEOS, ODAS, and the International Spaceguard Survey coordinated from Rome, Italy. There are also intermittent, limited, photographic survey programs such as the Bigelow Sky Survey in Arizona, which concentrates on the discovery of high-inclination objects. This program discovered 1996 JA1, a fast-moving near-Earth asteroid, which appeared and crossed the sky in 5 days, coming within 1.05×10^6 km (6.5×10^5 mi) of the Earth (**Fig. 2**).

Detection and observation. All means of detection for Near-Earth Objects use the same sensing criteria. The objects, when discovered, are relatively close to Earth, and appear to be moving rapidly with respect to the Earth-bound observer and the background of apparently fixed stars. In all cases, photographs or electronic images are examined for streaks or compared to detect relative movement. Initially this was accomplished by visually examining exposed film for trails, or by comparing two films with a blink comparator or stereomicroscope (in which the moving object would appear in the third dimension).

Most serious observers now employ electronic detectors and computers in place of film and labor-intensive examination. Moreover, charge-coupled devices permit an increase by orders of magnitude in sensitivity and speed with which the data can be acquired, reviewed, and analyzed. The result is both more sky coverage and an increased rate of discovery.

Radar observation. Photographic or electronic images are positionally accurate in two dimensions in the sky. The distance from the observer must be assumed in the orbital calculation and checked against additional observations of the object. The reflected radar signal provides an accurate distance measure-

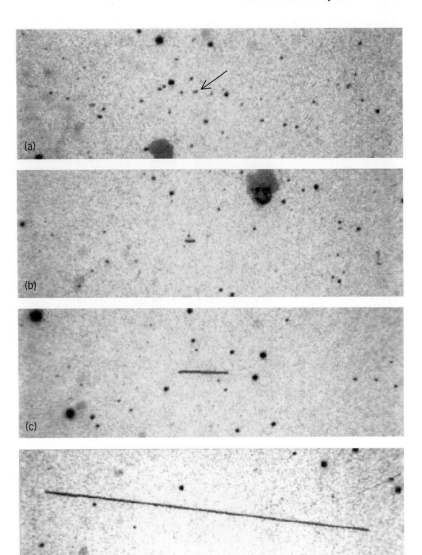

Fig. 2. Bigelow Sky Survey discovery of the asteroid 1996 JA1. (*a*) One of the discovery images taken on May 14, 1996, when the object (position indicated by the arrow) was 0.065 AU from the Earth. (*b*) May 16 at 0.043 AU. (*c*) May 18 at 0.018 AU. (*d*) May 19 at 0.007 AU. All images are to scale and are 8-min exposures, so that the asteroid appears as a streak. Each field is roughly 27 arc-minutes wide. (*Courtesy of T. B. Spahr and C. W. Hergenrother*)

ment from the observer, a third dimension, making possible a more precise orbital computation with very few observations. In addition, since the late 1980s appropriate interpretation of the initially focused reflected radar signal has provided the first images of near-Earth asteroids. One of the first near-Earth asteroids imaged with radar, (4769) Castalia, was shown to be a double-lobed asteroid (**Fig. 3**), suggesting the impact and sticking of two asteroids.

Photometry. The science of photometry is another essential remote means of obtaining information about a body by measuring its light, reflected or emitted, for both color and changes in intensity over time. These changes provide clues about the shape

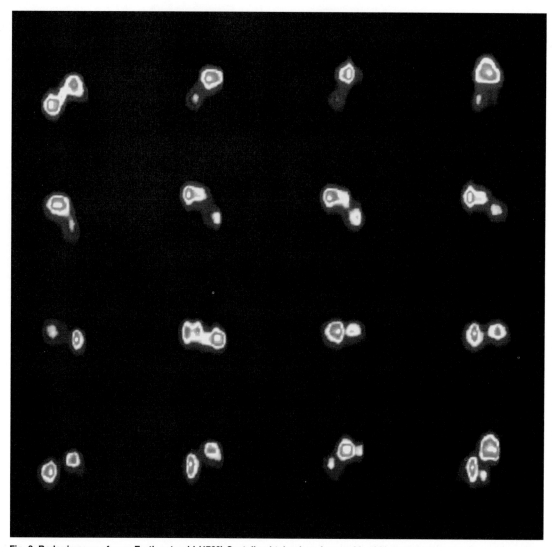

Fig. 3. Radar images of near-Earth asteroid (4769) Castalia obtained on August 22, 1989, by using the Arecibo radar-radio telescope in Puerto Rico. Images were obtained about 9 min apart, and the asteroid was at a distance of 5.64×10^6 km (3.5×10^6 mi). The rotational period of the two lobes is approximately 4 h. *(NASA; Jet Propulsion Laboratory)*

of the object, its reflectivity (helpful in estimating size), and its rotational speed. Color provides information about the surface composition of the object, and perhaps more importantly a means of comparing objects and investigating whether they could have come from the same source.

For background information *see* ASTEROID; CHARGE-COUPLED DEVICES; COMET; RADAR in the McGraw-Hill Encyclopedia of Science & Technology.

Eleanor Helin

Bibliography. C. J. Cunningham, *Introduction to Asteroids*, 1988; T. Gehrels (ed.), *Hazards Due to Comets and Asteroids*, 1995; E. F. Helin and R. S. Dunbar, Search techniques for near-Earth asteroids, *Vistas Astron.*, 33(1):21–37, 1990; J. L. Remo (ed.), *Near-Earth Objects: The United Nations International Conference*, 1997; G. L. Verschuur, *Impact!: The Threat of Comets and Asteroids*, 1996.

Neutrino astrophysics

Neutrino astronomy involves the detection of neutrinos from the Sun and from extrasolar astronomical sources. Except for the historic neutrino burst from Supernova 1987A, no signal of extrasolar neutrinos has been detected so far. Neutrinos are also produced locally by the interaction of primary cosmic rays with the atmosphere. This article focuses on neutrino astrophysics with the Super-Kamiokande detector.

Super-Kamiokande detector. The Super-Kamiokande detector is a 50,000-metric-ton (55,000-ton), ring-imaging, water-Cerenkov detector located at a depth of 1000 m (3300 ft) of rock in the Kamioka Mozumi mine in Japan. It consists of a cylindrical stainless steel tank, 39 m (128 ft) in diameter and 41 m (135 ft) high, filled with purified water. The detector is optically segmented into an inner volume, 34 m (112 ft) in diameter and 36 m (118 ft) in height, and an outer (anticoincidence) region, 2.5 m (8 ft) thick, on the top, bottom, and sides of the inner volume. The inner detector is viewed by 11,200 photomultiplier tubes, 50 cm (20 in.) in diameter, uniformly distributed on the inner boundary, giving a 40% photocathode coverage. The total mass of water inside the surface of the inner detector defined by the photomultiplier tubes is 32,000 metric tons (35,000 tons). The fiducial mass, defined to be 2 m (6.5 ft) inside the photomultiplier-tube plane, is 22,000 metric tons (24,000 tons).

The outer annulus of the detector is an anticoincidence region used to tag entering muons and low-energy components as well as to attenuate low-energy gamma rays and neutrons, which cause undesirable background events in the sensitive volume. It also complements calorimetry in the inner detector by measuring the energy loss due to exiting particles. This outer detector region is viewed by 1860 photomultiplier tubes, 20 cm (8 in.) in diameter, with additional light collection afforded by attached wavelength-shifter plates. The walls of the anticoincidence region are reflective to enhance light collection. The photomultiplier tubes are mounted facing outward on the same superstructure as the 50-cm (20-in.) photomultiplier tubes of the inner volume. Also, an optical barrier is mounted on the same structure to separate the inner and outer regions.

Observation of Cerenkov light. When a charged particle passes through a transparent material with a speed faster than the speed of light in that material, it emits light (Cerenkov light). The light is given off at a constant angle to the particle track. The angle is determined by the particle speed and the index of refraction of the medium. For a charged particle traveling in water at a speed close to that of light in vacuum, this angle is about 42°. In the case of a track which begins and ends in the detector, a ring of Cerenkov light is formed on the detector wall (see **illus.**).

By measuring the time of arrival of each photon at a photomultiplier tube, and by knowing the angle that this photon made with the particle track, it is possible to fully reconstruct the particle track, including its direction and its beginning (vertex) and ending points. The extraordinary photocathode coverage and time resolution of the Super-Kamiokande detector allows the detector to attain an energy threshold of 5 MeV and a vertex resolution of 10 cm (4 in.) for processes that emit light isotropically. For through-going tracks, the photomultiplier-tube configuration yields an angular resolution of 1°.

Solar neutrinos. The solar neutrino problem is an important issue in particle physics. It results from the discrepancy between the observed flux of solar neutrinos and the combined predictions of the standard model of particle physics and the standard solar model.

There is at present one solution for this problem, the Mikheyev-Smirnov-Wolfenstein (MSW) effect.

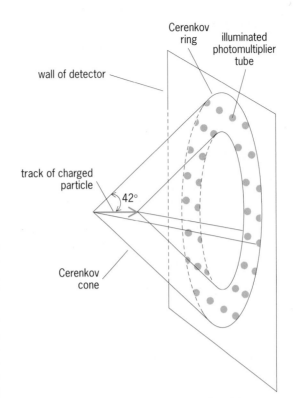

Ring of Cerenkov light formed by a charged particle traveling through water.

This theory invokes finite neutrino mass and neutrino flavor mixing, enhanced by the high matter density in the solar interior. The MSW mechanism has the effect of transforming an electron neutrino produced in the core of the Sun into another neutrino flavor (a muon neutrino or a tau neutrino). Since the detectors on Earth are sensitive only to electron neutrinos, this transformation would produce an observational deficit. The MSW predictions, if verified, would have profound implications for particle physics. Nonzero neutrino mass, neutrino oscillations, and lepton-number violation would be verified. Such a result must be put to the most stringent tests.

The accurate measurement of the solar neutrino flux is thus an urgent task for particle physics. The results of the Homestake and Kamiokande experiments yield a flux which is less than half the value predicted by the combined standard models. The SAGE and GALLEX experiments, sensitive to even lower-energy neutrinos from the main solar cycle, support the deficit.

Apparently, either the models of the Sun's interior are incomplete or present understanding of neutrino physics is deficient. In order to distinguish between these two possibilities, it is necessary to go beyond the current generation of experimental results by studying detailed characteristics of the effects.

Super-Kamiokande detects solar neutrinos by using the elastic scattering reaction of neutrinos on electrons and observing the recoil electrons. Up to now, experiments have simply compared the total number of recoil electrons with that predicted by the standard solar model. The current efforts are concentrated on studying the energy spectrum of these recoil electrons. Any distortion of the expected spectral shape would be positive evidence of oscillations.

Extrasolar neutrinos. The large mass of the Super-Kamiokande detector and the cosmic-ray shielding afforded by its great depth provide the opportunity to use neutrinos as probes of the universe, a role in which they offer unique advantages.

Since neutrinos are neutral particles, they travel in straight lines from source to detector, undeflected by magnetic fields. Charged cosmic rays, however, have arrival directions that are completely distorted by the galactic magnetic fields.

Furthermore, neutrinos have a very small interaction cross section. This gives neutrino telescopes the ability to see through optically thick dust clouds and deep into the cores of stars. Since gamma rays can be absorbed in the source or on the way from the source to the Earth, neutrinos enable a totally new observational window with the potential of revealing previously unknown point sources.

Finally, neutrinos are a unique tracer of energetic hadron acceleration in sources. Whereas photons can be produced by hadronic or electromagnetic processes such as inverse Compton scattering or synchrotron radiation of energetic electrons, the neutrinos can be produced only by hadronic interactions. Neutrinos (or the lack of them) can therefore be used as a diagnostic tool to understand the acceleration mechanism.

A promising neutrino source is expected to be binary systems containing compact objects. In the most popular model, matter from a neutron star's companion forms a flat accretion disk in the plane of the orbit, where high-energy protons (accelerated by the intense rotating magnetic field of the neutron star) interact.

Neutrinos from these sources can interact in the rock surrounding the detector. The interactions produce particles which enter the detector. These particles are mainly muons with some contamination by charged pions and electrons. By reconstructing the track of the muon in the detector, it is possible to point back to the neutrino source. In order to eliminate contamination from muons produced by cosmic-ray interactions in the atmosphere, only those tracks originating from below the horizon are normally accepted. This sample is still dominated by atmospheric neutrino interactions and, so far, no compelling evidence of a source of extraterrestrial origin in this signal has been found.

Supernova signals. Supernova 1987A, at a distance of 50 kiloparsecs (160,000 light-years), was just within the sensitive range of current detectors. The 24 events recorded at the same time in the Kamiokande, IMB, and Baksan detectors provided unique data for both astrophysics and elementary particle physics. The large number and variety of physical and astrophysical results that ensued from the detection of neutrinos from Supernova 1987A has motivated experimental preparations for the next stellar collapse. An event within the Milky Way Galaxy, closer by a factor of 2–10 than Supernova 1987A, would produce an extremely large signal in Super-Kamiokande.

Several thousand events are expected from the inverse beta decay reaction, in which a proton absorbs an electron antineutrino, resulting in its conversion to a neutron and the emission of a positron. The positrons are emitted almost isotropically with respect to the incoming antineutrino and take almost all of its energy. In addition, several hundred events resulting from elastic scattering on electrons can be predicted. The recoil electrons follow the neutrino directions, while their energy on the average is only half of the neutrino energy.

The vast majority of neutrinos are emitted as a result of cooling of the protoneutron star. However, the instant of core collapse is initiated by the core's neutronization due to the process in which protons absorb electrons and are converted to neutrons with the emission of electron neutrinos. This event is signaled by a very short pulse of electron neutrinos. The Super-Kamiokande detector is likely to detect this pulse by observing interactions of the electron neutrinos within the first 10 ms, before the onset of the thermal electron antineutrinos.

A supernova is also an abundant source of muon and tau neutrinos, and provides a unique opportunity to study their properties. Time dispersion resulting from the long distance that would be traveled by massive neutrinos offers the possibility for a significant improvement in the laboratory limits on the neutrino masses. It is therefore vital to separate the massive neutrinos from the dominant interactions of electron antineutrinos. The directionality of the elastic scattering on electrons provides a means to observe these events by using the angular distribution measured with respect to the direction from the supernova. The higher energies of the muon and tau neutrinos will be helpful in estimating their contribution to the forward peak.

The forward peaking of these events allows the Super-Kamiokande detector to estimate the source's direction with an accuracy of about 2°. This measurement may be particularly vital for a supernova in an optically opaque region of the Milky Way Galaxy, where such an event is most likely to occur. The determination of the supernova's direction would allow others to orient their detectors to study the supernova.

The thousands of events due to inverse beta decay will allow detailed tests of models of the core collapse and protoneutron star formation. Some models predict an oscillatory time profile of the electron antineutrino flux within the first 500 ms. An abrupt end to the neutrino emission could be a signature of the formation of a black hole.

For background information *see* CERENKOV RADIATION; NEUTRINO; PHOTOMULTIPLIER; SOLAR NEUTRINOS;

SUPERNOVA in the McGraw-Hill Encyclopedia of Science & Technology.   Henry W. Sobel

Bibliography. J. N. Bahcall, *Neutrino Astrophysics*, 1989; N. Hata, S. A. Bludman, and P. Langacker, Astrophysical solutions are incompatible with the solar neutrino data, *Phys. Rev. D*, 49:3622–3625, 1994; K. Hirata et al., Observation of a neutrino burst from the supernova SN1987A, *Phys. Rev. Lett.*, 58:1490–1493, 1987; S. P. Mikheev and A. Y. Smirnov, Resonance enhancement of oscillations in matter and solar neutrino spectroscopy, *Sov. J. Nucl. Phys.*, 42:913–917, 1985.

Nitric oxide

Nitric oxide (NO) is an important and diverse messenger molecule in mammals and other animals. It can be toxic or beneficial, depending on the amount and where in the body it is released. Initial research into the chemistry of nitric oxide was motivated by its production in car engines, which results in photochemical smog and acid rain. Then, in the late 1980s, researchers in immunology, cardiovascular pharmacology, neurobiology, and toxicology discovered that nitric oxide is a crucial physiological messenger molecule. Nitric oxide is now thought to play a role in blood pressure regulation, control of blood clotting, immune defense, digestion, the senses of sight and smell, and possibly learning and memory. Nitric oxide may also participate in disease processes such as diabetes, stroke, hypertension, impotence, septic shock, and long-term depression.

Most cellular messengers are large, unreactive biomolecules that make specific contacts with their targets. In contrast, nitric oxide is a small molecule that contains a free radical—that is, an unpaired electron—making it very reactive. Nitric oxide can freely diffuse through aqueous solutions or membranes, reacting rapidly with metal centers in cellular proteins and with reactive groups in other cellular molecules. The half-life of nitric oxide in living cells is only 5 s. The chemical reactivity of nitric oxide determines the fate of this molecule.

Production. Nitric oxide is produced in the body by an enzyme called nitric oxide synthase, which converts the amino acid L-arginine to nitric oxide and L-citrulline (see **illus.**). There are three types of nitric oxide synthase: brain, endothelial, and inducible. Both brain and endothelial enzymes are constitutive, that is, they are always present in cells, while the production of inducible nitric oxide synthase can be turned on or off when a system needs nitric oxide. Nitric oxide synthase contains two heme groups and utilizes NADPH (nicotinamide adenine dinucleotide phosphate, reduced form), an electron donor, and oxygen to form nitric oxide from the terminal nitrogen (N) atom of L-arginine. The constitutive forms of nitric oxide synthase are activated by the binding of calcium to the cofactor calmodulin, which can then bind to and activate the enzyme. After nitric oxide is produced in specific areas of the body by nitric oxide synthase, it diffuses to nearby cells. Nitric oxide then reacts preferentially in the interior of these cells with the metal centers of proteins. Nitric oxide binds specifically to the iron (Fe) atom of the heme group in proteins; it can also interact with other metal sites in proteins as well as with the thiol group (SH) of the amino acid cysteine. The interaction of nitric oxide with these proteins causes a cascade of intracellular events that leads to specific physiological changes within cells.

Blood pressure regulation. In the cardiovascular system, nitric oxide is produced by nitric oxide synthase in the endothelial layer, the cells that line the blood vessels. The activation of nitric oxide synthase is triggered by the binding of hormones to receptors on the surface of these cells, opening up calcium channels that release calcium ions into the endothelial cells. The calcium then attaches to the cofactor calmodulin, which binds to and activates nitric oxide synthase. The nitric oxide that is produced diffuses to the smooth muscle that surrounds blood vessels and binds to the iron atom of the heme group in the enzyme soluble guanylyl cyclase. This enzyme converts guanosine triphosphate to cyclic guanosine monophosphate and pyrophosphate within cells. The binding of nitric oxide to the heme of soluble guanylyl cyclase leads to a structural change in the enzyme which causes a dramatic increase in the production of cyclic guanosine monophosphate. It is thought that the cyclic guanosine monophosphate

Conversion of L-arginine to L-citrulline and nitric oxide (NO) catalyzed by the enzyme nitric oxide synthase. *(After P. L. Feldman et al., The surprising life of nitric oxide, C&EN News, 71(51):26–38, 1993)*

activates a protein kinase (an enzyme that adds a phosphate group to another protein) that phosphorylates calcium transporters, causing calcium to be returned to its cellular storehouse within the smooth muscle cells. The decrease in calcium levels causes relaxation of blood vessels since the muscle cells require calcium for contraction. The treatment of hypertension, heart attacks, and other blood pressure abnormalities often involves using chemical compounds that can release nitric oxide in the body. These compounds, which include nitroglycerin, the active ingredient in dynamite, are thought to bypass the nitric oxide synthase pathway and directly release nitric oxide into smooth muscle cells, causing relaxation and thus decreasing the blood pressure.

The protein hemoglobin, the oxygen carrier in the blood, has also been implicated in nitric oxide transport and regulation of blood pressure. Hemoglobin contains four heme groups that function as oxygen-binding sites. Nitric oxide reacts with hemoglobin in several distinct ways. First, it reacts rapidly with oxygen bound to the iron atom of the heme to form nitrate (NO_3^-) and methemoglobin, which is hemoglobin that cannot bind oxygen. Second, the iron atom of the heme in hemoglobin can bind nitric oxide when oxygen is not bound. Since hemoglobin is present in high concentrations in the vascular system and hemoglobin can scavenge nitric oxide, it has been a mystery how enough nitric oxide can reach the smooth muscle cells to cause blood pressure relaxation. There is now evidence indicating that hemoglobin may protect nitric oxide by forming S-nitrosothiols (R-S-NO compounds, where R represents a carbon side chain). Research suggests that two conserved cysteine residues in hemoglobin react with nitric oxide to form nitrosothiols, preventing the oxidation of nitric oxide to nitrate. The nitric oxide could then be released to the smooth muscle cells, causing blood vessel relaxation. The physiological relevance of protein S-nitrosothiols is controversial and may or may not be important in the delivery pathway for nitric oxide.

Neurotransmitter. Nitric oxide plays an important messenger role in the central and peripheral nervous systems; it may even be the neurotransmitter involved in long-term memory formation. The overproduction of nitric oxide in brain tissues has been implicated in stroke and other neurological problems. The peripheral nervous system also utilizes the production of nitric oxide in neurons to regulate blood flow. Neurons sensitive to nitric oxide have been found in many peripheral tissues, including those of the cardiovascular, urogenital, respiratory, and digestive systems. Nitric oxide has also been implicated in vision and the sense of smell. In contrast to the vascular system, these systems produce nitric oxide without using hormone activators. The production of nitric oxide in the peripheral nervous system dilates the blood vessels in the penis, causing an erection. Thus, the use of drugs that stimulate release of nitric oxide has been suggested as a noninvasive way of treating impotence.

Immune system. Nitric oxide functions as an important agent in the immune system by killing invading bacterial cells. The body uses cells called macrophages that are found in every type of tissue to destroy these foreign microorganisms by engulfing them through the process of phagocytosis or killing them by injecting toxic substances. Macrophages have the inducible form of nitric oxide synthase that produces a larger quantity of nitric oxide than the constitutive form of the enzyme found in blood vessels because the nitric oxide is released over a longer period of time. Nitric oxide released by macrophages can inhibit important cellular processes, including deoxyribonucleic acid (DNA) synthesis and respiration, by binding to and destroying iron-sulfur centers in key enzymes in these pathways. Nitric oxide is thought to react with the iron center of these proteins either to remove the iron or to form dinitrosyl iron [$Fe(NO)_2$] species. Thus, nitric oxide kills the invading microorganism by disrupting its essential cellular processes.

Although nitric oxide production in the immune system serves a crucial biological function, there can be adverse effects when too much nitric oxide is produced. During a massive bacterial infection, excess nitric oxide can go into the vascular system, causing a dramatic decrease in blood pressure, which may lead to possibly fatal septic shock. Thus, scientists are working on drugs that can selectively inhibit the inducible form of nitric oxide synthase in order to avoid the harmful effects produced by excess nitric oxide without interfering with useful nitric oxide pathways.

For background information *see* HEMOGLOBIN; IMMUNOLOGY; NEUROBIOLOGY; NITROGEN OXIDES in the McGraw-Hill Encyclopedia of Science & Technology.   Judith N. Burstyn; Mark F. Reynolds

Bibliography. A. R. Butler and L. H. Williams, The physiological role of nitric oxide, *Chem. Soc. Rev.*, 22(4):233–241, 1993; P. L. Feldman et al., The surprising life of nitric oxide, *C&EN News*, 71(51):26–38, 1993; R. Rawls, Bioinorganic reactions of nitric oxide underlie diverse roles in living systems, *C&EN News*, 74(19):38–42, 1996; S. H. Snyder and D. S. Bredt, Biological roles of nitric oxide, *Sci. Amer.*, 266(5):68–77, 1992.

Nobel prizes

The Nobel prizes for 1997 included the following awards for scientific disciplines.

Physics. Professor Steven Chu at Stanford University in California, William D. Phillips at the National Institute of Standards and Technology in Gaithersburg, Maryland, and Professor Claude Cohen-Tannoudji at the Collège de France and École Normale Supérieure in Paris were awarded the prize for the development of methods to cool and trap atoms with laser light. They cooled assemblies of isolated atoms to temperatures very close to absolute zero, sufficiently reducing the speeds of the atoms that they could be trapped, manipulated, and studied with great accuracy.

Atoms in a laser beam that is tuned to their characteristic absorption frequency experience a net force in the direction of the beam. If the laser is tuned to a slightly lower frequency, atoms moving against the beam will absorb laser photons because of the Doppler effect and will be slowed down. In 1985, Chu (then at Bell Laboratories in Holmdel, New Jersey) and colleagues constructed a system with six such laser beams directed at a common target. Atoms in the target region were slowed and nearly stopped in whatever direction they tried to move, so that the laser light functioned as a viscous liquid, termed optical molasses. Sodium atoms were cooled to 240 microkelvins, a temperature that was then thought to equal a theoretical Doppler limit. In 1987 the system was augmented by a magnetooptical trap, which prevented atoms from falling from the optical molasses.

Phillips devised a similar experiment, and in 1988 measured sodium atoms at 40 μK, a temperature much lower than the Doppler limit. This limit had been calculated from an oversimplified atomic model. Cohen-Tannoudji and his colleagues explained Phillips's results in terms of the structure of the lowest energy levels of the sodium atom. Phillips and Cohen-Tannoudji's group then cooled atoms even further.

Finally, Cohen-Tannoudji's group overcame the recoil limit, associated with an atom's recoil velocity from emitting a single photon, by converting the slowest atoms to a dark state in which they do not absorb photons. In 1995, helium atoms were cooled to 180 nanokelvins, a temperature at which their velocities are only about 2 cm/s (0.8 in./s).

The numerous current and potential applications of laser cooling and trapping include atomic clocks with a hundredfold greater precision than at present, atom interferometers for ultrahigh-precision measurements of the gravitational acceleration, atomic lithography of integrated circuits, and atom lasers. The discovery in 1995 of Bose-Einstein condensation in dilute gases is also related to this technique. *See* ATOM LASER.

Chemistry. Paul D. Boyer and John E. Walker shared one-half of the prize for their elucidation of the enzymatic mechanism underlying the synthesis of adenosine triphosphate (ATP). Jens C. Skou received the other half for the discovery of an ion-transporting enzyme, sodium, potassium-adenosine triphosphatase (Na^+,K^+-ATPase). Boyer is professor of chemistry at the University of California, Los Angeles; Dr. Walker is senior scientist at the Medical Research Council Laboratory of Molecular Biology, Cambridge, United Kingdom; and Skou is professor of physiology at Aarhus University, Denmark.

The synthesis of adenosine triphosphate occurs in cells and involves the enzyme adenosine triphosphate synthase. In 1960, researchers identified this enzyme in mitochondria. A few years later, it was proposed that hydrogen ions moving through the cell membrane play a key role in causing adenosine triphosphate synthase to create adenosine triphosphate. Before 1970, it was determined that adenosine triphosphate synthase consisted of three sets of protein assemblies identified as wheel, rod, and cylinder. The mechanism governing the relationship between the three assemblies was not known.

Boyer postulated that hydrogen ions moving through the cell membrane spin the wheel structure (like a waterwheel) as well as the attached rod. The various structural conformation changes that occur in the F_1 unit as the rod rotates within the cylinder, thereby altering catalytic sites, is called Boyer's binding change mechanism. Three active sites within the cylinder catch the building blocks of adenosine triphosphate until a whole molecule is created.

In 1994, Walker established the structure of adenosine triphosphate by using x-ray crystallography. The catalytic portion (consisting of rod and cylinder) was portrayed as a three-dimensional structure. The resultant conformational structures of the F_1 unit (which rotates) allowed researchers to see even more clearly the mechanism behind the structure, thus verifying the mechanism proposed by Boyer.

In 1957, Skou discovered the first enzyme that uses energy stored in adenosine triphosphate to pump ions across cell membranes. In work with cell membranes from crab nerves, this enzyme broke down adenosine triphosphate when sodium and potassium were both present in the surrounding medium. By altering the concentrations of these ions and observing the effects, Skou determined that an enzyme in the membrane pumps sodium out of the cells, and potassium in. This enzyme was later identified as sodium, potassium-adenosine triphosphatase. This enzyme uses about one-third of all the adenosine triphosphate produced in the human body, transporting ions from one side of the cell membrane to the other.

Physiology or medicine. Stanley B. Prusiner was awarded the Nobel prize for the discovery of prions, the infectious agents that cause transmissible spongiform encephalopathies. Prusiner is a neurologist and biochemist at the University of California, San Francisco.

During the 1960s, Tikvah Alper found that brain tissue from sheep afflicted with scrapie remained infectious following exposure to radiation. Ultraviolet radiation, which was capable of destroying deoxyribonucleic acid (DNA) and ribonucleic acid (RNA), did not obliterate the scrapie infectivity. A proteinaceous agent for transmissible spongiform encephalopathies was first hypothesized at that time. Subsequently, J. S. Griffith of Bedford College, London, England, suggested that the infectivity may be attributed to the altered conformation of a normal cellular protein.

In 1972, inspired by a patient who died from Creutzfeldt-Jakob disease, Prusiner began to investigate the causative agent of this brain-wasting disease. In 1982, he and his colleagues found a protein unique to the brain of scrapie-infected hamsters. The protein was identified one year later. The protein-aceous infectious particles were termed prion proteins. Prusiner continued to demonstrate that prion protein is normally present in healthy animals and humans, but in diseased brains it appears in an altered form. Conclusive evidence showing the participation of the prion protein in producing brain disease was obtained when the gene encoding prion protein in mice was eliminated. These "prion knockout" mice were completely resistant to infection when exposed to disease-causing prion protein preparations. Reintroduction of the gene rendered the mice susceptible to the infection.

This work by Prusiner established the most widely accepted explanation of diseases such as kuru, scrapie, Gerstmann-Straussler, Creutzfeldt-Jakob, and mad-cow, as well as the biological mechanisms upon which drug and therapeutic strategies may be developed.

For background information see ADENOSINE TRI-PHOSPHATE (ATP); LASER COOLING; PARTICLE TRAP; PRION DISEASE; SCRAPIE; VIRUS INFECTION, LATENT, PER-SISTENT, SLOW; X-RAY CRYSTALLOGRAPHY in the McGraw-Hill Encyclopedia of Science & Technology.

Nondestructive testing

Nondestructive testing (or nondestructive evaluation) is often used to determine whether a newly manufactured product meets acceptable quality standards established by the producer. In the past, success in identifying defects by such testing has caused conflict between inspectors and management because of lower overall production yield. In recent years, management has found that using nondestructive testing during manufacturing can improve quality during the fabrication process and enhance yield by providing process feedback and control.

Methods. Nondestructive evaluation methods encompass a variety of ways to probe and sense material structure and properties without causing damage. Some methods employ acoustic and ultrasonic waves, infrared and visible light, or x-rays.

Acoustic and ultrasonic waves. One method employs mechanical waves of audible sound, called acoustic waves (at frequencies of typically a few kilohertz), ranging up to ultrasonic waves (at frequencies up to or beyond 20–30 megahertz). Information can be obtained from such waves propagating through the bulk of a material or along a free surface from wave amplitude attenuation, wave velocity, or locations of sources of wave reflections.

Infrared imaging. In this method a special camera detects distributions of the heat flux being radiated from a surface by using infrared light. In many cases, this pattern can be converted directly to an image representing the temperature distribution on the surface.

Visible light. Optical techniques include ordinary imaging using visible light which has been either transmitted through or reflected by an object. Optical techniques also can be used to implement noncontact ultrasonic wave measurements. A very short time laser pulse can nondestructively initiate an ultrasonic wave. Laser interferometry can be used for noncontact detection of ultrasonic waves arriving at a point on an object's surface.

X-rays. Another method utilizes x-ray radiography, x-ray computed tomography, or x-ray diffraction. Radiography is like a medical x-ray, where the image is a shadowgraph and contrast comes from differences in amounts of attenuation of the x-rays as they pass through the flesh, bone, muscle, and cavities in the body. Computed tomography is similar to a medical computed axial tomography scan (CAT scan), and x-ray diffraction is sensitive to crystal structure flaws in single crystals (such as silicon chips or single-crystal jet engine turbine blades).

Visual images. Each of the generic inspection methods listed above can display data in the form of an image correlated with (or mapped into) the surface of the object under examination. Visual inspection using nondestructive testing methods is not limited to images seen with ordinary light. Visual images covering two-dimensional fields of view can be displayed, representing all manner of interior material properties or interior flaws. Various defects include delaminations or lack of bonding in composites, voids, cracks, inclusions, porosity, and other inhomogeneities. Material property characterizations include elastic moduli (from ultrasonic velocity), grain size distribution in metals and alloys, surface temperature distributions, variations in thermal diffusivity due to lack of subsurface uniformity, and fluorescent emission from surfaces under ultraviolet illumination.

Some methods instantly produce complete full-field visual two-dimensional images at 30 frames per second (for example, optical imaging, infrared imaging, and real-time x-ray radiography). Another way to produce images by sequential scanning takes more than the 33 milliseconds required for 30 frames per second. This technique can build a full-sized image from ultrasonic data in a few minutes, with delaminations or cracks in an aerospace composite represented by false colors.

A newly developed air-coupling technique for noncontact detection of ultrasonic waves has been shown to be a practical solution for noncontact ultrasonic monitoring of resin curing during on-the-fly prepreg (that is, pre-impregnated material) tape lay-up when using a robot for the tape placement. This development is significant as it represents another step toward automated fabrication of large and complicated composite structures without the need for vacuum autoclaves large enough to hold the product for curing. Traditional lay-up of prepreg material is done by hand and is extremely labor intensive, raising the cost considerably and creating problems with regard to reproducibility.

Full-field images. Raw data for ultrasonic measurements are generally in the form of time-based waveforms or frequency domain spectra. In scanning to build a full-field image, these measurements are correlated with the location of the transmitting and receiving transducers for each data point. Algorithms to compute velocity, attenuation, and positions of sources of anomalous reflections are commonly used to construct false color images representing the desired information in a full-field two-dimensional computer screen display. Specialized software is written to address particular data display needs. X-ray image data are readily converted to real-time visible images by using appropriate phosphor screens to convert the x-ray photons to visible photons (an image intensifier is used to brighten the visible image, facilitating faster recording with a camera). Infrared images are acquired by a special camera with a two-dimensional detector array which is constructed to be sensitive to infrared wavelengths. Otherwise, the data are processed just the same as visible-light images, and are displayed as a full-field two-dimensional image.

Detectors. Virtually all cameras use solid-state imaging detectors as their light-sensitive element. These detectors provide an array of sites, and each site accumulates a charge proportional to the intensity of the light falling on it and the duration of exposure. The sites (pixels) are the picture elements which will constitute the image. Line-scan detectors have a one-dimensional string of pixels. To generate a two-dimensional image, the line (of pixels) is swept along in the direction perpendicular to its axis, much like a broom sweeping a floor. Two-dimensional arrays of pixels generate an image by staring at the scene to be recorded for an appropriate duration while a charge accumulates at each pixel. The most common cameras are of three types: charge-coupled devices, n-type metal-oxide-silicon devices, and charge injection devices. These cameras differ according to the construction of their visible-light-sensitive detectors.

Charge-coupled devices. Charge-coupled devices have two-dimensional arrays of pixels which are all exposed to the incident image simultaneously, and are read destructively. If too much incident flux accumulates at a pixel site, the capacity of the well at that site (which collects photoelectrons) is exceeded. The result is an overflow into adjacent well sites, an undesirable effect known as blooming which destroys intensity data collected in the neighboring pixel sites.

N-type metal-oxide-silicon. N-type metal-oxide-silicon devices are arrays of photodiodes. Capacitance associated with each pixel site is precharged to a fixed level prior to exposure. During exposure, the photoelectrons generated by the incident light discharge these capacitors by some amount. Then each pixel site is destructively read to determine how much charge is left. Finally, each site is recharged by charge injection to reset the initial state.

Charge injection devices. Charge injection devices are very similar to n-type metal-oxide-silicon devices, except the charge at the pixel site is read nondestructively. Image data can be allowed to accumulate at pixel sites by inhibiting the charge injection cycle, which resets the initial state of charge. Although not as commonly used, charge injection devices are less susceptible to blooming and more resistant to radiation damage than charge-coupled devices.

In general, all but the high-end scientific cameras use detectors providing an image in the standard National Television Standards Committee (NTSC) format. For example, a nominal charge-coupled-device camera with an NTSC format has 575 pixels in a horizontal line and 425 horizontal lines. This format produces a vertical spatial resolution of about 16 line pairs per millimeter, presuming an image diagonal on the detector of 16 mm. Detectors with larger arrays are becoming more readily available, making higher spatial resolutions easier to acquire. Of course, there are many other design parameters whose selection must be consistent with the use of a larger array in order to achieve its full benefit (for example, the proper selection of the lens which couples the image to the detector).

Image capture. Although some high-end scientific cameras (particularly ones with slower scans than 30 frames per second) provide a digitized image output, most solid-state video cameras provide an analog output. To be of use in most process control applications, video camera images must be digitized to enable subsequent processing, analysis, and interpretation. A frame grabber board in a computer is needed to capture, digitize, and control these analog outputs. There are four classes of frame grabbers: the original hardwired type (which is outdated and will not be discussed), modular image processing systems, programmable processors, and direct image transfer.

Modular image processing. Modular image processing systems contain a pipelined video bus. Digitization operations are performed much faster than in the original hardwired frame grabbers, and can serve well for many industrial applications, particularly since their dedicated processors are continually improving in capabilities.

Programmable processors. Frame grabbers utilizing programmable processors are extremely adaptable and flexible. However, they are limited in their ability to keep up with data at 30 frames per second, because of the need for intervention of the central processing unit (CPU) chip located on the computer motherboard to direct storage of acquired images.

Direct image transfer. Frame grabbers with direct image transfer should have all the advantages of those with programmable processors, as well as being able to run faster. Images are stored directly in the computer's random access memory (RAM), without requiring intervention by the CPU chip.

Image processing. Once digitized and stored, the image can be operated upon by using a multitude of tools to achieve the desired form for analysis. Among these tools are image averaging to improve the image's signal-to-noise ratio; image subtraction to retain only those features which are changed with regard to some reference image; edge enhancement routines to define and sharpen faint or blurred edges; and various kinds of filtering operations to eliminate unwanted noise and to aid in defining features and shapes important in subsequent computer interpretation of images. Under the right conditions, a very effective tool to enhance contrast of poorly differentiated features is histogram equalization. In this operation, software computes a histogram of pixel count for each gray level in a representation with a linear gray scale. The integral of the profile of this histogram is then defined as a nonlinear gray scale for replotting the image. The result very effectively maximizes the contrast between formerly faint differences.

Image interpretation by a computer requires software that establishes a procedure to extract features of an appropriate type from the image, to then identify shapes, to conduct reorientations, and finally to define objects defined adequately enough to allow numerical measurements. As the interaction of the process variables is better understood through experience with a growing nondestructive testing database, control of the process will become more automated. While some cases will certainly evolve to interpretation by machine vision, most image interpretations will require human intervention to provide decisions on the status of a process.

For background information *see* ACOUSTICS; CHARGE-COUPLED DEVICES; IMAGE PROCESSING; INFRARED RADIATION; INSPECTION AND TESTING; NONDESTRUCTIVE TESTING; PROCESS CONTROL; QUALITY CONTROL; ULTRASONICS; X-RAY DIFFRACTION in the McGraw-Hill Encyclopedia of Science & Technology.   John M. Winter, Jr.

Bibliography. P. I. Corke, *Visual Control of Robots: High Performance Visual Servoing*, 1996; B. Jahne, *Practical Handbook on Image Processing for Scientific Applications*, 1997; R. Jain, R. Kasturi, and B. Schunck, *Machine Vision*, 1995; A. K. Sood and H. Wechsler (eds.), *Active Perception and Robot Vision*, 1992.

Nuclear reactor

The CANDU pressurized heavy-water reactor (PHWR) is based on more than 50 years of nuclear technology development. An ongoing comprehensive product development program is advancing all aspects of CANDU technology, with a focus on improving economics, enhancing safety, and ensuring fuel-cycle flexibility to secure fuel supply for the foreseeable future. The development program retains the essential features of CANDU reactors: high neutron economy, utilization of natural rather than enriched uranium, modular core components for easy upgrading and plant life extension, simple fuel bundle designs for on-power fueling, and emphasis on passive safety.

The reactor (**Fig. 1**) consists of fuel channels within a large vessel (the calandria) filled with heavy-water moderator, which is maintained at low operating temperatures (about 70°C or 158°F) and near atmospheric pressure. Each fuel channel contains 12 fuel bundles of simple design (only 0.5 m or 1.6 ft long) that can be replaced on-power, resulting in high capacity factors since the reactor does not have to be shut down. High-pressure coolant (also heavy water) passes through the pressure tubes and removes heat from the fuel. The coolant then passes through a steam generator, where heat is transferred to the secondary light-water system to produce steam. The steam drives a turbine generator to produce electricity, as in conventional thermal plants. The pressure tubes are located inside a second set of tubes in the calandria. A small gas annulus between the two concentric tubes separates the hot pressure tube from the external tube facing the cooler moderator. The use of heavy water as the moderator and low-cross-section materials in the core allows the design to be optimized for neutron economy.

Reactor size. Two CANDU reactors are commercially available. The 700-MWe-class (700 megawatts of electric power) CANDU 6 is a robust, proven design. Six plants are operating and five are under construction. The four original CANDU 6 plants have reached the midpoint of their design life, but their capacity factors have remained high, exceeding 85% on average during 1987–1997. A 900-MWe-class reactor, the CANDU 9, has evolved from other 900-MWe-class plants operating in Canada.

Improved economics. Nuclear reactor economics depend on several factors, including initial capital costs, capacity factors, operating and maintenance costs, fuel costs, and output power.

Capacity factors. CANDU reactors already enjoy high capacity factors. Nevertheless, improvements are possible by using more advanced information-technology systems, reducing the complexity of systems, and ensuring long-lived components. A good example of how knowledge evolution has led to improvements over the years is the CANDU fuel channel. Elucidation of the mechanisms affecting such phenomena as corrosion, fracture toughness, and creep and growth has resulted in substantial improvements in fuel channels. Current fuel channels have higher resistance to corrosion than previous channels, are less affected by radiation, and contain smaller amounts of initial hydrogen that could adversely affect performance. Fuel channels in new CANDU reactors are designed to operate for more than 30 years without requiring replacement. By understanding basic phenomena affecting component lifetime and operability, and by enhancing materials properties, similar progress is being made for all CANDU components.

Output power. Power increases have a large effect on the unit cost of electricity, especially if they can be accomplished with relatively small changes in plant costs. One approach to increasing the power of

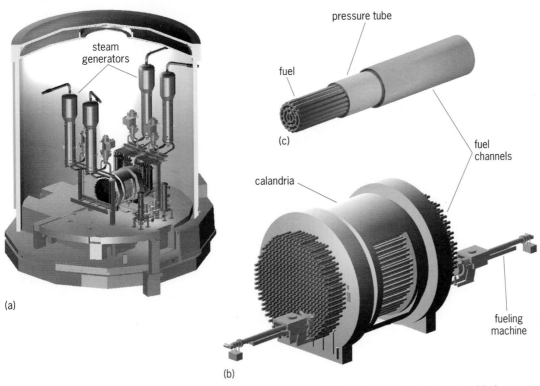

Fig. 1. CANDU pressurized-heavy-water reactor. (*a*) Reactor power plant. (*b*) Reactor core, with calandria and fuel channels. (*c*) Detail of a fuel channel.

CANDU reactors is to switch from natural uranium to slightly enriched uranium fuel containing 0.9–1.2% uranium-235. The slightly enriched uranium can be used to flatten the power distribution over the core to produce about 15% more power, without changing the core design. Alternatively, the modular nature of the core allows the addition of fuel channels, which are relatively inexpensive. For example, the 700-MWe-class CANDU 6 contains 380 fuel channels, while the 935-MWe CANDU 9 increases the number to 480. The number of channels can be further increased to 640 in a similarly sized calandria, providing 1275 MWe power. In the longer term, it may be possible to operate the primary heat transport system at much higher temperatures, thereby substantially increasing the power plant's thermodynamic efficiency. Such a change would require considerable advances in the understanding of materials at elevated temperatures under reactor core conditions, but the efficiency gains could have a significant impact on unit energy costs.

Enhanced safety. The low-temperature heavy-water moderator within the calandria surrounding the fuel channels mediates the impact of postulated severe accidents. If primary coolant is lost from the system, and if the emergency core cooling system fails, heat is transferred out of the fuel channels and into the moderator water. As a result, fuel does not melt when emergency cooling is impaired. From the moderator, heat can be transferred to the environment by way of the normal moderator-water cooling system.

Even if the moderator were unavailable, the shield tank surrounding the calandria would be capable of containing and maintaining a collapsed core in a cooled state for a long period of time.

In the future the moderator system can be used even more effectively as a passive heat sink, so that all fuel damage can be avoided. New fuel channels are being tested that can transfer even larger amounts of heat to the moderator under loss-of-cooling conditions. New fuels are being developed that have higher thermal conductivity and that operate at lower temperatures. New moderator cooling systems are being examined for highly efficient heat removal based on natural circulation as opposed to forced convection using pumps. Such improvements could also lead to greater ease of operation and lower capital costs because of the simplification and elimination of components.

Fuel-cycle flexibility. High uranium utilization and fuel-cycle flexibility result from excellent neutron economy, on-power fueling, and simple fuel design. The exploitation of this flexibility results in fuel cycles that can optimize the use of uranium resources, recycle light-water-reactor (LWR) reprocessing wastes, exploit the natural LWR-PHWR synergism, and secure very long term fuel supplies through the development of the thorium fuel cycle. All these fuel cycles (**Fig. 2**) are part of the overall strategy for sustainable development using CANDU technology.

There is a natural synergism between light-water-

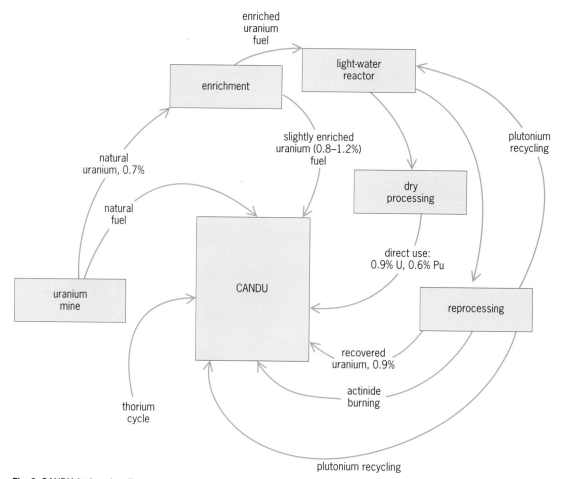

Fig. 2. CANDU fuel cycles. Percentages of uranium-235 (and also of plutonium in the case of direct use) are indicated.

reactor and pressurized-heavy-water-reactor fuel cycles. Light-water reactors are designed to burn enriched uranium (about 3.5% uranium-235) fuel down to a fissile content of 1.5% (0.9% uranium-235, 0.6% plutonium). CANDU natural uranium fuel starts with 0.7% uranium-235, which is burned down to concentrations of enrichment plant tailings (about 0.2%). Therefore, CANDU reactors are in a unique position to take advantage of the relatively high fissile content of spent light-water-reactor fuel. A number of strategies for the use of this fuel in CANDU reactors are possible.

Use of recovered uranium. In conventional reprocessing, uranium and plutonium are separated from the fission products and other actinides in the spent fuel. The recovered uranium from conventional reprocessing still contains valuable uranium-235 (typically around 0.9%, compared to 0.7% in natural uranium fuel). This can be burned as-is in pressurized heavy-water reactors, without reenrichment, to obtain about twice the burn-up of natural uranium fuel. Also, approximately twice the energy would be extracted using CANDU reactors, compared to reenrichment of recovered uranium for recycle in a pressurized-water reactor (PWR). The uranium-235 would be burned down to low levels (that is, 0.2%) in pressurized heavy-water reactors compared to pressurized water reactors (0.9%), so there may be

no economic incentive for further recycle of this material. The CANDU spent fuel would then be ultimately disposed of, after a period of dry storage, in a deep geological repository. Recovered uranium is currently a liability to many owners of pressurized water reactors, who have no plans to recycle it in these reactors because of the complications in fuel fabrication with reenriched recovered uranium and the marginal, if any, economic benefit. Therefore, the use of recovered uranium in CANDU reactors would appear to be an extremely attractive way of dealing with an otherwise waste product while at the same time extracting additional energy.

Use of mixed-oxide fuel. The other major product from conventional reprocessing is plutonium. Plutonium is currently mixed with depleted uranium to form mixed-oxide (MOX) fuel, which is recycled by loading up to one-third of a pressurized-water reactor core with this fuel. However, mixed-oxide fuel can also be utilized in pressurized heavy-water reactors using a full core load. While fabrication of mixed-oxide fuel will be much more expensive than using natural uranium, the simplicity of the CANDU fuel bundle will result in lower mixed-oxide fuel fabrication costs than those of mixed oxides in pressurized-water reactors. A high-burn-up CANDU mixed-oxide fuel, therefore, has the potential of considerably lowering fuel-cycle costs. Up to 50% more energy could be extracted from the fissile uranium and plutonium in spent pressurized-water-reactor fuel through recycling in CANDU compared to recycle in a pressurized-water reactor. This has important advantages in improving uranium utilization, in reducing enrichment requirements, and in reducing the amount of spent fuel for ultimate disposal.

Direct use of spent fuel. The direct use of spent pressurized-water-reactor fuel in CANDU (DUPIC) involves converting the spent fuel into CANDU fuel without any wet chemical processing. Only dry processes are used, in which there is no selective removal of fission products. This, along with the high radiation fields associated with the spent pressurized-water-reactor fuel, offers a very high level of proliferation resistance. Several possible DUPIC cycles have been examined.

Use of nuclear waste. CANDU reactors can be extremely efficient eliminators of nuclear waste. Simulations for CANDU reactors fueled with a mixture of plutonium and actinide waste in an inert matrix carrier show that over 63% of the actinides can be destroyed in a single pass through the reactor, and over 91% of the initial fissile plutonium. The high thermal conductivity of the inert matrix carrier would result in extremely low fuel operating temperatures.

Thorium cycle. All fissile material for nuclear reactors is ultimately derived from uranium-235. This is a finite resource that must be carefully managed. Therefore, the applicability of CANDU reactors for burning thorium, which is about three times more abundant than uranium in the Earth's crust, is under study. In this cycle, thorium-232 is used as a fertile material to form the fissile isotope uranium-233. The conversion ratio (the rate of formation of fissile nuclei divided by the rate of destruction of fissile nuclei) can exceed 0.95, which means that CANDU reactors can be near-breeders using this cycle. Modifications to increase the neutron economy even higher would result in a closed self-sufficient thorium cycle in which no external source of fissile material would be required. This would obviate the need to develop expensive new breeding technology.

Use of liquid-metal-reactor products. In the long term, the CANDU/liquid-metal-reactor (LMR) system may also be attractive. In this system, a small number of efficient liquid-metal breeder reactors could provide the fissile material that would fuel several lower-cost CANDU reactors that are already installed. If the plutonium were used to drive a thorium-based cycle in CANDU, about nine CANDU reactors could be supported by using one liquid-metal reactor. Owing to the high cost of the latter, this could be of substantial economic benefit to countries developing a liquid-metal-reactor program.

Conclusions. The future sustainability of nuclear power will depend on three main criteria: improved economics, enhanced safety, and fuel-cycle flexibility. For example, the product development program of Atomic Energy of Canada Limited has been structured to focus on these key areas over the next 25 years. CANDU technology is sufficiently flexible that enhancing the product to meet the objectives can be achieved by retaining all the essential characteristics of the current pressurized heavy-water reactor design.

For background information *see* NUCLEAR FUEL CYCLE; NUCLEAR FUELS; NUCLEAR FUELS REPROCESSING; NUCLEAR POWER; NUCLEAR REACTOR; RADIOACTIVE WASTE MANAGEMENT in the McGraw-Hill Encyclopedia of Science & Technology.   David F. Torgerson

Bibliography. *Proceedings of the 5th International Conference on Nuclear Thermalhydraulics (NUTHOS-5),* Beijing, China, 1997; *Proceedings of the 1997 CNA/CNS Annual Meeting,* Toronto, Canada, 1997; *Proceedings of the 12th KAIF/KNS Annual Conference,* Seoul, Korea, 1997.

Olivine

It is generally accepted that the Earth's upper mantle consists mainly of olivine, an orthorhombic silicate with the composition $(Mg_{1.8},Fe_{0.2})SiO_4$, together with some pyroxene and garnet. The natural occurrence of two high-pressure forms (polymorphs) of olivine—orthorhombic wadsleyite, and cubic ringwoodite (with a spinel structure)—was predicted from high-pressure experiments and was later confirmed by meteorite investigations. The names olivine, wadsleyite, and ringwoodite refer only to naturally occurring compositions $[(Mg,Fe)_2SiO_4]$. Chemical analogs with the same crystallographic structures but different compositions, such as Mg_2GeO_4, are more generally called α phase, β phase, and γ phase, respectively. Some authors also use the terms spinel for γ phase, and β-spinel or modified spinel for β phase.

Because of their abundance in the Earth's mantle, knowledge of physical and chemical properties of olivine, wadsleyite, and ringwoodite is of great geophysical importance. Until recently, many of these properties had to be inferred from theoretical considerations and from experiments on chemical analogs, which transform at lower pressures. With the development of new experimental apparatus capable of generating very high pressures and temperatures (multianvil press and diamond anvil cell), a growing number of experimental studies are being performed on phases of natural composition. Such studies, investigating elastic properties, densities, rheology, phase transformations, water solubilities, and diffusivities, substantially contribute to a better understanding of the dynamics of the Earth's mantle.

Polymorphic transformations in mantle. Experimentally determined thermodynamic phase equilibria data indicate that in the Earth's mantle olivine transforms to wadsleyite, then to ringwoodite, and finally to compositions of magnesiowüstite plus perovskite (see **illus.**). Estimated transformation pressures correspond closely to the discontinuities of seismic velocities at, respectively, 246, 322, and 417 mi (410, 520, and 670 km) depth in the mantle. However, to obtain reliable mineralogical models of the mantle

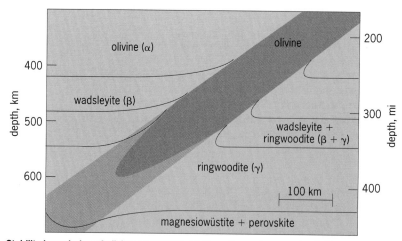

Stability boundaries of olivine, wadsleyite, ringwoodite, and magnesiowüstite + perovskite in the mantle as a function of depth, and the metastable olivine wedge (dark color) in subducting slabs (light color). *(After S. H. Kirby, W. B. Durham, and L. A. Stern, Mantle phase changes and deep-earthquake faulting in subducting lithosphere, Science, 252:216–225, 1991)*

and evaluate the seismic effects of the olivine to wadsleyite to ringwoodite transformations, not only are the well-constrained phase diagrams required, but also the characterization of the elastic properties of all three phases.

Progress has been made in determining elastic moduli of olivine and wadsleyite at pressures up to 2.3×10^6 lbf·in.$^{-2}$ (16 gigapascals) for olivine and 2×10^6 lbf·in.$^{-2}$ (14 GPa) for wadsleyite by using ultrasonic interferometry, impulsive stimulated scattering, and Brillouin scattering measurements in a high-pressure apparatus. These measurements have been performed at room temperature, thus requiring large extrapolations of elasticity data to mantle temperatures. An advanced technique for acoustic wave measurements in the multianvil press at both high pressures and high temperatures is currently being developed, and will help eliminate these problems. Recent in-situ x-ray diffraction measurements performed in multianvil apparatus and diamond anvil cells yielded precise unit cell volumes of olivine, wadsleyite, and ringwoodite at pressures up to 3.8×10^6 lbf·in.$^{-2}$ (26 GPa) and moderate temperatures at approximately ~1160°F (900 K). These data help to evaluate the pressure effect on thermal expansivities and the temperature effect on isothermal bulk moduli of all three polymorphs.

On the basis of these new constraints on elasticity, it has been inferred that the depth and magnitude of the seismic discontinuity at 246 mi (410 km) can be adequately explained by the olivine to wadsleyite transformation in a mantle model with 60–65% olivine. In contrast, a possible connection of the wadsleyite to ringwoodite transformation with the seismic discontinuity at 322 mi (520 km) remains controversial because temperature dependencies of the bulk moduli of the two phases have been found to be almost identical.

Subduction zones. In general, temperatures in the Earth's mantle are high and changes in pressure-temperature conditions are slow, so that the olivine to wadsleyite to ringwoodite transformations will occur close to the equilibrium phase boundaries. However, the kinetics (mechanisms and rates) of the olivine to wadsleyite to ringwoodite transformations become important for the cold regions in the mantle, that is, in subduction zones, where it is assumed that because of slow transformation rates olivine can persist metastably down to depths far below 246 mi (410 km; see illus.). Transformation of highly metastable olivine deep in subduction zones would affect subduction dynamics and might cause deep earthquakes. Kinetic results of earlier experimental studies on analog compositions (most of which do not contain a β phase) are currently being replaced or confirmed by direct investigations of the transformation behavior of natural olivine. Transmission electron microscopy techniques have proven to be most useful for determining transformation mechanisms and kinetic data.

It is commonly accepted that the olivine to wadsleyite to ringwoodite transformations can occur either by an intercrystalline mechanism involving nucleation of incoherent (crystallographically randomly oriented) product phase grains on parent phase grain boundaries, or by an intracrystalline mechanism, resulting in thin product phase lamellae in the interior of the parent phase lattice that have a definite crystallographic orientation. Intercrystalline transformation has been observed in the majority of experimental studies and is expected to occur in subduction zones. Kinetic data show strongly temperature-dependent (sluggish) transformation rates, thus confirming the hypothesis of metastable olivine wedges in subduction zones.

Intracrystalline transformation has commonly been assumed to be similar to (athermal) martensitic transformations, to require high levels of differential stress, and to be unlikely to occur in subduction zones. These assumptions have recently been contradicted by a detailed transmission electron microscopy study of microstructures and reaction rates of intracrystalline ringwoodite lamellae in olivine. Results reveal that lamellae form by thermally activated nucleation on olivine stacking faults (two-dimensional lattice defects) and grow in much the same way as grain boundary nucleated grains. High differential stress is not required for the intracrystalline olivine to ringwoodite transformation, but could affect transformation rates by enhancing stacking fault formation in olivine. Details of the intracrystalline wadsleyite to ringwoodite transformation remain to be investigated. However, preliminary transmission electron microscopy results on intracrystalline ringwoodite in wadsleyite crystals also appear to contradict martensitic transformation models.

Recent results on transformation mechanisms indicate that both intercrystalline and intracrystalline transformation mechanisms occur in subduction zones. Both mechanisms probably compete and interact with each other, thus complicating models of the transformation kinetics of the olivine to wadsleyite to ringwoodite transformations in subduction zones.

Rheology. Understanding mantle dynamics and related subduction zone processes requires precise knowledge of the rheology (that is, plastic deformation behavior) of mantle minerals, especially of olivine, since it is the dominant and least viscous mineral in the upper mantle and is therefore expected to control the rheological behavior of the upper mantle. Information on the relative strengths of mantle minerals and the depths of changes between different deformation mechanisms (dislocation creep and diffusion creep) in the mantle can be obtained by combining experimentally determined creep strengths, characterizations of dislocation structures, and diffusivity measurements with observations of seismic anisotropies.

In terms of rheological properties, olivine is the most intensively studied mineral. In contrast, no deformation studies of ringwoodite exist. However, from intensive transmission electron microscopy investigations of dislocation structures and creep strengths of γ phase with analog compositions, it has been inferred that ringwoodite is stronger than olivine in the dislocation creep regime. In the case of wadsleyite, only very preliminary transmission electron microscopy results of dislocation structures exist. Although no direct rheological data in the diffusion creep regime of high-pressure phases exist, occurrence of diffusion creep in mantle regions can be deduced from the absence of seismic anisotropy. It has been proposed that in the Earth's mantle a change from dislocation creep (shallow mantle) to diffusion creep (deep upper mantle) occurs.

The rheological structure of the mantle is affected by phase transformations, mainly through associated changes in grain size. Weakening due to grain size reduction can be particularly important for the fate of subducting slabs. However, quantification of the effect of grain size reduction, as well as of the effect of water, remains a goal for future studies.

Water solubility. The water content of the Earth's mantle has been estimated to be on the order of a few hundred parts per million by weight of water (H_2O), but it remains to be clarified whether water is present as a free phase, is dissolved in nominally anhydrous phases, or requires special hydrous minerals. Furthermore, even small amounts of water can substantially influence mineral properties such as mechanical strength, seismic wave velocities, rates of phase transformations, electrical conductivities, diffusivities, and melting temperatures. Consequently, constraining amounts and possible structural sites of hydrogen (H) atoms or hydroxyl (OH) groups (colloquially "water") in olivine, wadsleyite, ringwoodite, and other mantle minerals is of great geophysical importance.

Recent experimental studies at high pressures and temperatures have observed very high solubilities of water in olivine, wadsleyite (up to 3% by weight), and ringwoodite. While water can be stored in olivine as hydroxyl point defects, it has been proposed that the wadsleyite structure provides a suitable crystallographic site for hydrogen incorporation. Indeed, a new hydrogen-bearing phase, wadsleyite II, has

recently been synthesized and has been structurally characterized with x-ray diffraction. In the case of ringwoodite, no obvious crystallographic sites suitable for hydrogen incorporation exist in its structure. Detailed transmission electron microscopy investigations of water-bearing ringwoodite might provide information of a possible connection between lattice defects and water storage.

High solubilities of water in mantle minerals suggests that a free fluid phase should not be stable in the upper mantle and that special hydrous phases (such as the currently intensively investigated dense hydrous magnesium silicates) are not required. Furthermore, the very high solubility of water in wadsleyite indicates that the transition zone [the mantle region between 246 and 417 mi (410 and 670 km) depth] can be enriched with water, compared to the upper mantle.

For background information *see* MAGMA; METEORITE; OLIVINE; PERIDOTITE; POLYMORPHISM (CRYSTALLOGRAPHY); SERPENTINITE; SILICATE MATERIALS in the McGraw-Hill Encyclopedia of Science & Technology.
Ljuba Kerschhofer

Bibliography. L. Kerschhofer, T. G. Sharp, and D. C. Rubie, Intracrystalline transformation of olivine to wadsleyite and ringwoodite under subduction zone conditions, *Science*, 274:79–81, 1996; D. L. Kohlstedt, H. Keppler, and D. C. Rubie, Solubility of water in the α, β, and γ phases of $(Mg,Fe)_2SiO_4$, *Contrib. Mineral. Petrol.*, 123:345–357, 1996; Y. Meng et al., In situ high P-T x-ray diffraction studies on three polymorphs (α, β, γ) of Mg_2SiO_4, *J. Geophys. Res.*, 98:22199–22207, 1993; J. R. Smyth and T. Kawamoto, Wadsleyite II: A new high pressure hydrous phase in the peridotite-H_2O system, *Earth Planet. Sci. Lett.*, 146:E9–E16, 1997.

Ontogeny

Ontogeny is the developmental history of an organism from its origin to maturity. It starts with fertilization and ends with the attainment of an adult state, usually expressed in terms of both maximal body size and sexual maturity. Fertilization is the joining of haploid gametes (a spermatozoon and an ovum, each bearing half the number of chromosomes typical for the species) to form a diploid zygote (with a full chromosome number), a new unicellular living being which will grow through a series of asexual reproductions. The gametes are the link between one generation and the next: the fusion of male and female gametes is the onset of a new ontogenetic cycle. Many organisms die shortly after sexual reproduction, whereas others live longer and generations are overlapped. Species are usually conceived as adults, but in most cases the majority of their representation in the environment is as intermediate ontogenetic stages.

In unicellular organisms, each asexual reproduction leads to the formation of new individuals, the cells deriving from a first sexually derived individual forming a clone of genetically identical individuals.

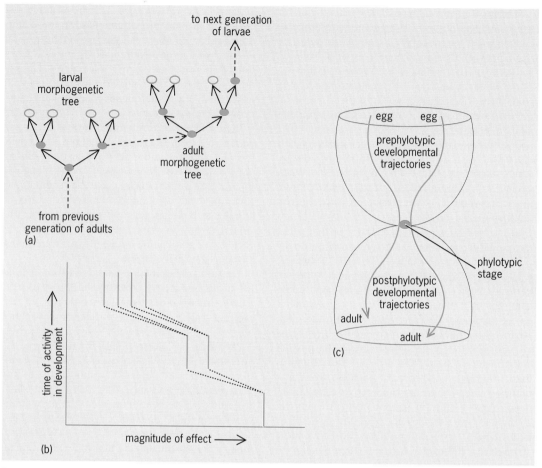

Fig. 1. General theories of ontogeny. (*a*) Morphogenetic trees for larval and adult stages showing development through a two-stage life cycle. (*b*) Locus-based version of a morphogenetic tree. The loci acting early in ontogeny have a greater effect on the rest of development than those acting later. (*c*) Developmental hourglass showing the phylotypic stage, a rigid body architecture through which the development of phylogenetically related organisms must pass. Ontogeny is "elastic" in earlier and later stages. *(Parts a and b after W. Arthur, A Theory of the Evolution of Development, John Wiley & Sons, 1988; c after R. A. Raff, The Shape of Life, University of Chicago Press, 1996)*

In multicellular organisms, the products of the asexual reproductions starting with the first division of the zygote remain connected, and the clone they form is a single individual. Clonation of individuals occurs even in humans, when the first results of asexual reproduction of the zygote separate from each other, leading to twin formation.

The ontogeny of a multicellular organism involves segmentation (or cleavage): the zygote divides into two, four, etc., cells which continue to divide. These cells are initially similar to the zygote, although smaller in size. They soon start to differentiate from their ancestors, acquiring special features, and forming specific tissue layers and, eventually, organs. These processes lead to the formation and growth of an embryo. Embryos can develop freely, within egg shells, or within the body of one parent; they can grow directly into juveniles (as in humans) or into larvae (with an indirect development, as in insects). Ctenophores, commonly known as comb jellies, are marine organisms that are paradoxical in having sexually mature larvae which transform into sexually mature adults.

Juveniles are similar to adults but are smaller in size and not sexually mature. Their ontogeny contin-

ues until they reach a maximal size and reproductive ability. Larvae have different morphology, physiology, and ecology from adults; they become juveniles through a metamorphosis (that is, an abrupt change). Usually ontogeny is interrupted at adulthood, but some organisms can grow throughout their life, so that ontogeny ends with their death.

Disciplines. The study of ontogeny, comprising most aspects of biology, splits into disciplines: Embryology, often referred to as developmental biology, is the study of embryonic development from fertilization to the beginning of independent life of the new individual. Larval biology is the study of postembryonic and prejuvenile or preadult organisms. Developmental genetics is the study of genetic regulation and specification of development. Life cycle biology and ecology involve the study of all the general aspects dealing with postembryonic transformation to adult organisms. Evolutionary biology and phylogeny encompass the patterns and processes of evolution, often inferred from ontogenetic patterns and processes.

Theories. The morphogenetic tree theory states that ontogeny starts with a cell (the zygote) which has the potential to produce a whole adult organism.

Further developmental steps—from cleavage to tissue and organ formation—restrict the possibilities of expression of the new cells (**Fig. 1***a*). A mutation in any of the first ontogenetic steps (at the base of the morphogenetic tree) will thus affect the rest of development, with a sharp modification of the mutated organism, whereas a change in late ontogeny produces a slight modification in the terminal branches of the morphogenetic tree (Fig. 1*b*). Organisms with direct development have a single morphogenetic tree, whereas those with complex life cycles have a morphogenetic tree for every developmental stage.

The theory of the developmental hourglass (Fig. 1*c*) allows freedom of change at most ontogenetic stages except for a conservative phylotypic stage (some sort of general body plan). The finding of similar adults having much different larval development has been taken as a falsification of the morphogenetic tree theory, because major changes at the beginning of development do not involve great changes in adult structures. This seeming discrepancy can be explained when considering that species with complex life cycles have different morphogenetic trees which are almost independent of each other. Thus, both the morphogenetic tree and developmental hourglass theories are subject to integration into some future general theory of development.

Heterochrony. Heterochrony is a change in the sequence of ontogenetic events within a lineage and is a major evolutionary mechanism, leading to reelaboration of preexisting structures. The evolution of new body plans requires subtraction or reassemblage of old structures as well as the introduction of novel structures added to the ancestral ones. Fossil records show that early organisms were simple and that complex organisms are the products of the addition of structures. Since almost no new body plans are known to have evolved after the Cambrian radiation, it is reasonable to presume that most of post-Cambrian evolution occurred via modification of preexisting structures.

Developmental genetics. The discovery of HOX genes in almost all animals investigated shows that the genes of development are conserved, even though their expression in different lineages leads to different body plans. In the past, embryology had a separate evolution from genetics, but this gap will be bridged by the understanding of ontogenetic processes through an integrated approach. In fact, every cell contains all the information that is necessary to specify a whole organism (the very basis of clonation). However, it is also a fact that, during differentiation, the cells of an organism differentiate from each other despite their uniform genetic information. It is for this reason that embryology flourished separately from genetics. Apparently, there is a reciprocal information flux through genotype and phenotype.

Ontogeny reversal. Ontogeny is considered a one-way chain of events from fertilization to death. Dedifferentiation and redifferentiation of cells and tissues were known to occur but these were not radical changes. The conversion of an adult into a larva has been shown in the hydrozoan *Turritopsis nutricula*, whose adult medusae can become reduced to a mass of dedifferentiated cells which transdifferentiate into other cell types and form a hydroid colony. This colony is the developmental stage preceding the medusa (**Fig. 2**). Hydroids are normally formed by medusae through sexual reproduction, involving fertilization and planula formation, that is, through an embryonic development. Most medusae die after sexual reproduction, but those of *T. nutricula* are able to reverse their ontogeny and, if under stress or after spawning, go back to a hydroid stage, escaping death. These medusae transformed into hydroids are able to produce new medusae, redirecting ontogeny in its normal flow. Transdifferentiation demonstrates that a differentiated cell can still use the whole potential of its genome. This usually occurs at a cellular level and has almost no bearing on the architecture of the individual organism. In *T. nutricula* it is the whole adult organism which reassembles its transdif-

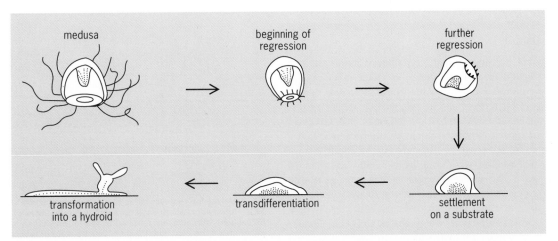

Fig. 2. Ontogeny reversal in the hydromedusa *Turritopsis nutricula*. *(After S. Piraino et al., Reversing the life cycle: Medusae transforming into polyps and cell transdifferentiation in Turritopsis nutricula (Cnidaria, Hydrozoa), Biol. Bull., 190(3):302–312, 1996)*

ferentiated cells, metamorphosing into an earlier on-togenetic stage.

Ecology of ontogeny. Life cycles allow the persistence of species from one generation to the other. The study of ecology has been centered mainly on both interspecific (food webs) and inter-extraspecific (biogeochemical cycles) fluxes. The importance of intraspecific fluxes (life cycles) has been neglected in the explanation of ecosystem functioning, having been restricted to populational approaches. The widespread occurrence of ontogenetic patterns involving the presence of resting stages leading to the formation of seed banks in terrestrial ecosystems and of resting egg–embryo and cyst banks in aquatic ecosystems is a way of tackling the problem of how matter is maintained in a living state. Ontogeny can be put into an ecological framework (and ecology into a development framework). Ontogeny interruption, usually caused by the onset of adverse conditions, with the formation of resting-stage banks, leads to the formation of a potential biodiversity which is then realized at the onset of a new favorable period when the resting organisms become active again to complete their ontogeny. This process explains sharp discontinuities in the occurrence patterns of many organisms in their adult stage, from terrestrial plants and insects to planktonic protists and metazoans.

For background information *see* ANIMAL GROWTH; DEVELOPMENTAL GENETICS; ECOLOGY; EMBRYOLOGY; FERTILIZATION; HETEROCHRONY; PHYLOGENY; REPRODUCTION in the McGraw-Hill Encyclopedia of Science & Technology.   Ferdinando V. Boero

Bibliography. W. Arthur, *A Theory of the Evolution of Development*, 1988; F. Boero et al., The continuity of living matter and the discontinuities of its constituents: Do plankton and benthos really exist?, *Trends Ecol. Evol.*, 11(4):177–180, 1996; L. Buss, *The Evolution of Individuality*, 1987; S. Piraino et al., Reversing the life cycle: Medusae transforming into polyps and cell transdifferentiation in *Turritopsis nutricula* (Cnidaria, Hydrozoa), *Biol. Bull.*, 190(3):302–312, 1996; R. Raff, *The Shape of Life*, 1996.

Opal

Opal is a fine-grained, crystalline to noncrystalline silica phase that is common in a wide range of low-temperature environments. The composition of opal is often represented as $SiO_2 \cdot nH_2O$, where SiO_2 is silicon dioxide and nH_2O indicates that chemical analysis of most opals includes the presence of water. Water contents can range up to about 20% of total weight (wt %) but are generally less than 10 wt %. The nature of water in opal remains poorly understood. Infrared spectroscopic analysis and dehydration analysis show that most of the H_2O in opal occurs as molecular water (that is, an H_2O molecule) as opposed to a hydroxide anion (OH^-) associated with the silica framework. Some of these water mole-

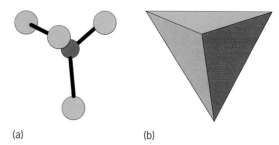

(a)   (b)

Fig. 1. The SiO_4^{4-} molecules as (*a*) ball-and-stick and (*b*) tetrahedral representations. The dark sphere is a Si^{4+} ion, and the colored spheres are O^{2-} ions.

cules appear to exist inside the silica framework, whereas others appear to exist as pockets of water in tiny void spaces within the material (for example, the water is a part of a separate fluid phase along the boundaries between grains).

Opal can also contain small amounts of other impurities, principally aluminum (Al^{3+}), which likely substitutes for silicon (Si^{4+}) in the tetrahedrally coordinated sites in the opal structure. These impurities may constitute up to a few weight percent of a chemical analysis, but generally the impurities (other than H_2O) are less than 1 wt %.

Molecular structure. The molecular structure of opal consists of a silicon cation (Si^{4+}) surrounded by four oxygen anions (O^{2-}) arranged to form a tetrahedron (**Fig. 1**). This tetrahedral arrangement also forms the basis for most other silicates. In opal, as is common in many other silicates, these tetrahedra are partially polymerized (linked to one another by having one oxygen in common to both tetrahedra). The three-dimensional polymer network that exists in some opals can be visualized as consisting of two-dimensional sheets of polymerized polyhedra (**Fig. 2**) that

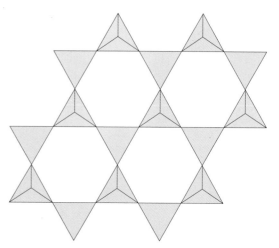

Fig. 2. Polyhedral representation of a polymerized sheet of SiO_4^{4-} tetrahedra, where each tetrahedron shares three of its oxygens with adjacent tetrahedra. The fourth oxygen is either above the page (the triangles with spokes) or below the page and will be shared with tetrahedra in adjacent sheets.

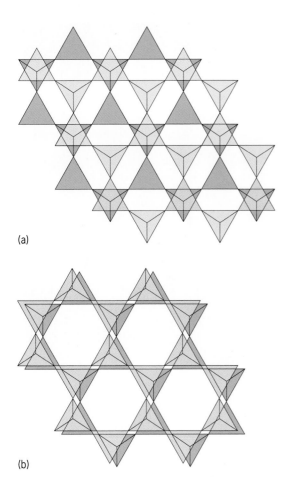

(a)

(b)

Fig. 3. Polyhedral representations of the stacking of polymerized silica sheets as found in (a) cristobalite and (b) tridymite.

are stacked together along the third dimension (much like a deck of cards). Within each individual sheet, the tetrahedra are linked in a honeycomb, hexagonal mesh pattern with each hexagonal ring formed by tetrahedra that alternately point up and down. These sheets can be attached to one another by stacking in one of two ways (**Fig. 3**): Adjacent sheets can be shifted relative to one another to allow tetrahedra to align (and hence to share oxygens); or adjacent sheets can be rotated 180° relative to one another to allow tetrahedral alignment. The first case is the pattern followed by the high-temperature silica mineral cristobalite, and the second is the pattern followed by the high-temperature silica mineral tridymite. Some types of opal exhibit both types of stacking patterns within an individual crystal.

It has long been recognized that some opals are structurally similar to cristobalite and tridymite, as evidenced by x-ray diffraction patterns. These opals have traditionally been designated opal-C and opal-CT, depending on whether the x-ray diffraction pattern contains elements of cristobalite or cristobalite-tridymite. Other opals produce x-ray diffraction patterns with no distinct peaks, as is typical of noncrystalline (amorphous) materials, and these have been designated opal-A.

Opal crystals are very small (for example, tens of nanometers; by comparison, the smallest objects that can be seen by light are hundreds of nanometers). Within each of these small crystals, both cristobalite and tridymite patterns are found for the polymerized silica sheets described above. In some opals the sequence of stacking is partially ordered (that is, within a crystal, cristobalite sheets tend to follow tridymite sheets, and vice versa), whereas in other opals the sequence of stacking is disordered (random). The significance of stacking order in opal likely relates to the conditions under which the material formed, but the details remain to be investigated. The very small size of the individual crystals combined with the occurrence of both stacking patterns within a crystal makes opal-C and opal-CT appear to be poorly crystalline by x-ray diffraction, when, in fact, on an atomic scale these opals have regular arrangements of atoms.

Opal-A, which appears amorphous by x-ray diffraction, may be less well ordered on an atomic level or may consist of even smaller crystals than opal-C and opal-CT. Regardless of its atomic-level order, some opal-A exhibits order at a scale commensurate with the wavelength of light. These opals have formed spherical particles with diameters in the range of light waves (for example, 400–800 nm). The spherical particles are stacked in a regular way such that the assemblage of particles acts as a diffraction grating for light, producing the fiery appearance of gem opals.

Classification. Opal (particularly opal-C and opal-CT) exemplifies a material that challenges the definition of a mineral. The standard definition for a mineral requires it to be a crystal (that is, to possess translational periodicity at an atomic scale in much the same way that a brick wall possesses translational periodicity in the form of a brick repeated in a regular pattern). This definition reflects, to a large extent, one of the mineralogist's primary tools over the last several decades: x-ray diffraction. Crystals that are sufficiently large (that is, that contain at least thousands of translationally repeating ''bricks'' or unit cells) will diffract x-rays, which can be monitored by an x-ray diffractometer. New analytical techniques (for example, transmission electron microscopy) and improvements in abilities to use computers to model x-ray diffraction patterns have allowed mineralogists to investigate smaller volumes of material. The result is a new recognition that many materials that do not produce well-defined diffraction peaks by x-ray diffraction are, in fact, orderly at scales below the resolution of x-ray diffraction. These materials challenge the current definition of mineral by showing that describing a material as crystalline depends on the scale of the description (that is, on the analytical technique used).

The definition of crystalline also has important implications for opal because crystalline silica (in particular quartz, cristobalite, and tridymite) has been designated as a human carcinogen by the International Agency for Research on Cancer

(IARC). A description of some types of opal as crystalline could have a significant impact on the use of materials that contain even small amounts of opal. In its review of the published literature, the IARC concluded that there is sufficient evidence that some types of crystalline silica can pose a risk but the data on noncrystalline silica (including opal) are inconclusive.

The regulatory classification of opal is particularly important given the widespread distribution of opal and the occurrence of opal with a number of commercially important materials (for example, clays and zeolites). In general, opal is associated with both biogenic and abiogenic processes. Biogenic processes include the precipitation of opal-A by silica-secreting plants and organisms (including some grasses, diatoms, radiolaria, and sponges), which can result in the deposition of opal simultaneously with the deposition of clays as the organisms die and their tests fall to the ocean floor. During diagenesis (a metamorphic-like process that occurs at relatively low temperatures following burial), opal-A converts to opal-CT, then opal-C, and finally quartz. Abiogenic processes include low-temperature dissolution-re-precipitation processes that redistribute silica within rocks near the Earth's surface.

For background information *see* CRYSTAL; CRYSTAL STRUCTURE; CRYSTALLOGRAPHY; GEM; OPAL; SILICATE MINERALS in the McGraw-Hill Encyclopedia of Science & Technology.   George D. Guthrie

Bibliography. S. L. Cady, H. R. Wenk, and K. H. Downing, HRTEM of microcrystalline opal in chert and porcelanite from the Monterey Formation, California, *Amer. Mineralogist*, 81:1380–1395, 1996; J. M. Elzea and S. B. Rice, TEM and x-ray diffraction evidence for cristobalite and tridymite stacking sequences in opal, *Clay Clay Miner.*, 44:492–500, 1996; C. Frondel, *The System of Mineralogy*, 1962; H. Graetsch, Silica: Physical behavior, geochemistry, and materials applications, *Rev. Mineralogy*, 29:209–232, 1994; G. D. Guthrie, Jr., D. L. Bish, and R. C. Reynolds, Modeling the x-ray diffraction pattern of opal-CT, *Amer. Mineralogist*, 80:869–872, 1994.

Open pit mining

Traditional open pit mining methodologies and processes are being modified by new technologies. The personal computer now allows mines of varying size and capacity to increase productivity and efficiency through the use of software. Computer-based monitoring and control systems are being used to measure and optimize, in real time, the performances of operating equipment. This capability forms the foundation of a more comprehensive, dynamic management and planning facility, where ultimately information acquired from the producing equipment will be used to optimize and control machine and human activities. The technologies will eventu-

Fig. 1. Blasthole drill used in open pit mining.

ally serve as the basis for more robotic and autonomous mining operations.

As the large, high-grade ore bodies are exhausted in developed countries, mining companies will need to find other mineral sources. Exploration efforts or advanced technologies should allow the economic exploitation of marginal ore bodies. An exploration program defines the extent and nature of the ore body to determine the economic viability of starting a mine. Once the mine is operational, a typical mining sequence consists of drilling holes in the rock with large blasthole drills (**Fig. 1**) and filling these with explosives. The distance separating the drilled holes, hole depth, type of explosives used, and the geology determine the size of the resulting broken rock fragments, or muckpile. This size is critical and influences the digging and excavating requirements to load this material into large haulage trucks (**Fig. 2**).

Monitoring systems. A mine must constantly deal with variable factors. For example, open pit mine planning needs to be active as market conditions fluctuate, equipment fleets age, and variations in the quality and composition of the ore contribute to changing production targets. Monitoring these external and internal variables is essential in efficient mine planning. Monitoring and control systems make it possible to collect operating data on mining equipment identifying any change in use, perfor-

Fig. 2. Large electric cable shovel loading rock into a haulage truck. Such trucks can carry up to 240 metric tons (260 tons).

mance, maintenance, or location. Feedback from these systems permits the mobile mining equipment to become the means by which the overall status of the mine can be measured.

Much like process control in a mine concentrator, monitoring the condition and output of the mining equipment, such as drills and excavators, can indicate changes in the in-situ rock conditions. This application of advanced technology enables the collection of detailed operating information concerning geological structures and discontinuities, workforce utilization and productivity, rock strength and blastability, muckpile diggability, dilution and mining loss, machine maintenance and diagnostics, production statistics, equipment optimization and control, and machine location and guidance.

Integrated monitoring of the performance of key equipment provides data necessary to successfully maximize the benefits derived from all these components. By having such data readily available in a centralized database, on-line or real-time decision making becomes a possibility, thus permitting improved control over the nature and quality of the recovered ore.

The communication network required to achieve such a capability will need to have an open and flexible architecture so that many existing data and voice systems can be interfaced. This wireless network will need to readily accommodate future application modules and hardware. In addition, its design will need to facilitate the integration of future remote control and autonomous operation of various mobile mining machines, such as drills, front-end loaders, shovels, and trucks.

Until recently, equipment locations were estimated by traditional optical or laser-based surveying methods. The time and effort required to collect this information limited its usefulness in day-to-day

planning applications. The recent introduction of Global Positioning System (GPS) technology into mines permits accurate, real-time position information to be available upon demand. This same information can be used for guiding a machine from one location to another. The operator can safely guide a machine based on a computer screen displaying the precise location of mobile mining equipment relative to color-coded, geographic and geologic features.

Information management. As monitoring, control, and guidance technology systems are more routinely used as production tools in open pit mines, the information generated by them will need to be readily and simultaneously available to many users. To ensure this capability, a key component of an information system will be a broadband, high-speed communication network to facilitate seamless and timely two-way transfer of information from the field to the office, and between machines in the field. With the system in place, the response time to changing mining conditions will be reduced. Better control of mining activities will be realized because of enhanced knowledge of the quality and location of the mineral resources in a mine. In addition, adjustments can be made more frequently to optimize mineral extraction based on market conditions.

The information management system will consist of the following subcomponents:

Computer-based monitoring, control and guidance systems on-board mobile and stationary equipment.

A production control system capable of proactive (very short term) planning and scheduling.

An integrated database and business management system, permitting ready access by operations, production, maintenance, or management departments and suppliers.

A comprehensive mine planning system that uses an open-architecture, object-oriented modeling and GIS (Geographical Information System) that can be updated in real time, based on data and information from mobile or stationary equipment.

A bidirectional mobile communications network with sufficient data rates and bandwidth to meet both current needs and future system enhancements.

The unique constraints and conditions of the surface mining environment, as well as the projected evolution of communication systems toward ever-increasing levels of supervised autonomy of mobile machines, require a complex network to handle data and control functions. The requirements for broadband voice, video, and data transmission for such applications far exceed the capability of any communication or dispatching system used currently in open pit mines. A possible solution is one in which data and control networks are integrated to fulfill all the requirements of a wireless communication network. Such a hybrid system will do more than simply manage the data and information flow between mobile equipment and a central office location, and will permit remote control and supervision from the same office personal computer or workstation.

To obtain the required functionality for open pit mines, the following preliminary design requirements for a communication system have been identified: integrated, bidirectional communication of data, voice, and video signals; easy integration with different third-party monitoring, control, and guidance systems; data security and network integrity; and capability to simultaneously handle in excess of 200 individual machines. General specifications for the communications network have been outlined based on using an open system interconnect model. The physical layer would consist of radio frequencies in the ultrahigh-frequency to microwave range. This layer would have sufficient bandwidth for the concurrent operation of more than 5 real-time video channels at 800 kilobits per second for remote control and supervision, 150 channels at 64 kbps for bidirectional data flow to and from the in-pit equipment and a central office, and 150 channels at 16 kbps for wide voice communications.

The data link and network layer would be based on a broadband integrated services digital network. Issues to be assessed before this solution is considered viable would be those related to media access control, collision avoidance and detection, roaming, data encoding, error checking, priorities, and the most suitable types of media transceivers. In addition, specific issues related to the network layer that need better definition are addressing—for example, unicast, multicast, or broadcast—and router technology and type. Transport layer issues involve achieving the most reliable data transfer methodologies, including end-to-end acknowledgment, duplicate detection, and automatic retries. Issues related to the session, presentation, and application layers would be specified on an equipment-, user-, or site-specific basis.

Communication technologies. A number of commercially available communication technologies partially meet the above specifications. Spread spectrum radios offer the desired functionality at the physical and data link layers, but support at the network layer is currently lacking. In addition, application of this technology is restricted to line of sight, not generally characteristic of an open pit mine. However, spread spectrum radios are affordable and offer high data-transfer rates at low power outputs, with minimal licensing requirements in most countries.

Network architectures utilizing asynchronous transfer mode communications are becoming more commonly used for high-bandwidth and high-data-rate communications in many industries. An integration of network architectures and spread spectrum communications may offer a solution in some open pit mines. There are network architectures that provide support for various types of media, including radio-frequency and power-line transmission in mines using electric drills and cable shovels. A radio-based system would, however, offer the solution with the widest range of application.

A cellular telephone network enables most of the communication requirements to be met. Either analog or digital cellular networks can provide voice, video, and data transmission throughout a mine at rates and bandwidths suitable for most applications. In addition, such networks permit the mine to be connected to the outside world via standard cellular phones. Global connectivity is possible by integrating to a T1 link or regional telephone service provider. Limitations to using cellular networks are their high cost for equipment and service (air time), low data rates (analog system), and spectrum management and allocation restrictions depending upon the particular country. However, recently introduced personal communications services technologies will provide readily available communications for open pit mines. These systems are currently being implemented in most countries, and provide a range of services and capabilities previously unavailable via analog cellular systems. Over the next few years, these types of communication facilities will be greatly enhanced by low-Earth-orbiting (LEO) satellite systems to provide even higher bandwidth and data-rate capabilities. An example is the SkyBridge system, scheduled to begin service in 2001. This system will use 64 LEO satellites to provide a range of two-way services, including data transmission, Internet access, and video conferencing. The system will offer downlink bandwidths up to 60 megabits per second and a maximum uplink speed of 2 Mbps. Similar systems are being developed or planned by other large aerospace or communications companies.

For background information *see* COMMUNICATIONS SATELLITE; CONTROL SYSTEMS; DATA COMMUNICATIONS; MINING; MOBILE RADIO; OPEN PIT MINING; PROCESS CONTROL; ROBOTICS; SPREAD SPECTRUM COMMUNICATION; SURFACE MINING; TELEPHONE SERVICE in the McGraw-Hill Encyclopedia of Science & Technology.

Jonathan Peck

Bibliography. J. H. Gray, F. B. Amon, and J. P. Peck, Integrated mine planning and production, *Bull. Can. Inst. Min. Metallurgy*, September 1991; J. P. Peck and J. H. Gray, The Total Mining System (TMS): The basis for open pit automation, *Bull. Can. Inst. Min. Metallurgy*, 88(993):38–44, September 1995; Sharp joins Alcatel in satellite project, *Infoworld*, November 24, 1997.

Optical imaging devices

Complementary metal-oxide semiconductor (CMOS) technology has been used to produce a high-performance electronic "camera on a chip." CMOS technology is used for most microelectronic circuits such as microprocessors, memory, and application-specific integrated circuits. The main advantages of the CMOS-based approach to image capture, compared to charge-coupled-device technology, are reduced system power consumption, greater system miniaturization, and lower cost. Pixel arrays as large as 1024 × 1024 elements and pixel sizes as small as 5.6 × 5.6 micrometers have been demonstrated. On-chip, analog-to-digital converters that have 8-bit resolution and permit video-rate (30-frames-per-second) operation have been developed.

Overall architecture. The CMOS image sensor (**Fig. 1**) consists of an array of pixels that are typically selected a row at a time by row-select logic. The array can be covered by a mosaic of color filters, one per pixel, such as red, green, and blue, that permits reconstruction of the original color image after readout and interpolation. The pixels are read out to vertical column buses that connect the selected row of pixels to a bank of analog signal processors. These processors perform functions such as charge integration, sample and hold, correlated double sampling, and suppression of fixed pattern noise.

More advanced CMOS image sensors contain on-chip analog-to-digital converters. Column-parallel analog-to-digital converters are frequently used; that is, each column of pixels has its own analog-to-digital converter (Fig. 1). There are certain benefits to this approach, but a single-analog-to-digital-converter or three-analog-to-digital-converter (one for each color) architecture is also viable. The digital outputs of the analog-to-digital converters (or analog output of the analog signal processors) are selected for readout by column-select logic.

Also integrated on-chip is a timing and control logic block. This digital block is readily defined at a high level by using tools such as a hardware description language, is synthesized into physical circuits, and is placed on the chip.

The CMOS image sensor architecture (Fig. 1) permits several modes of image readout. Progressive-scan readout of the entire array is the common mode. A window readout mode is readily implemented, where only a small region of pixels is selected for readout, increasing access rates to windows of interest. A skip readout mode is also possible, where every second (or third, and so forth) pixel is read out. This mode allows for subsampling of the image to increase readout speed at the cost of resolution. Combination of skip and window modes allows electronic pan, tilt, and zoom to be implemented.

Pixels. CMOS image sensors can have either active or passive pixel circuits. Active pixels contain an amplifier circuit within the pixel, whereas passive pixels are used for very low cost, low-performance applications. In CMOS active pixel sensors, two main types of pixels are used: the photodiode and the photogate (**Fig. 2**). Other types of pixels, such as logarithmic, floating-gate, and pinned-photodiode, are also possible for specialized applications.

Photodiode type. In the photodiode-type active pixel sensor, a reverse-biased *pn* junction is attached to a source-follower buffer amplifier in the pixel. The pixel is selected for readout by turning on a row-

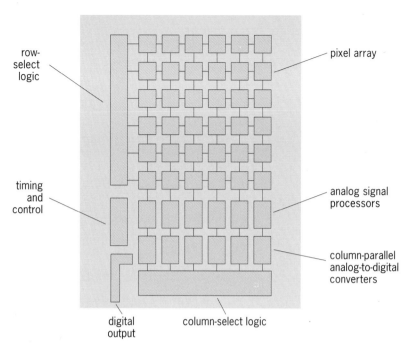

row-select logic

timing and control

digital output

pixel array

analog signal processors

column-parallel analog-to-digital converters

column-select logic

Fig. 1. Block diagram of a CMOS active-pixel-sensor camera on a chip.

select transistor. The voltage on the *pn* junction is driven onto a vertical column bus by the source-follower through the row-select transistor. At the bottom of the column (not shown in Fig. 2*a*) is a load transistor and the analog signal processor for that column. Once the voltage on the *pn* junction is sampled, the junction is reset by pulsing a reset transistor, and returns to its original condition. This new voltage is also sampled by the analog signal processor. The difference between the two sampled voltages is the photosignal from the pixel. During the next frame period, photogenerated electrons are integrated on the *pn*-junction capacitance, reducing its voltage. At the end of the frame period, the pixel is selected again for readout.

Photodiode-type active pixel sensors have high quantum efficiency since there is no overlying poly-silicon. The read noise is limited by the reset noise on the photodiode and is typically 75–100 electrons root-mean-square. The photodiode-type active pixel sensor uses three transistors per pixel and has a typical pixel pitch (distance between corresponding points on adjacent pixels) of 15 times the minimum feature size. It is suitable for most mid- to low-performance applications.

Photogate type. In the photogate-type active pixel sensor, the photogenerated electrons are integrated under the photogate. When the pixel is selected for readout by using the row-select transistor, the floating diffusion attached to the reset transistor is reset to a high level by pulsing this transistor. The voltage on the floating diffusion is then sensed by the source-follower and driven onto the column bus, as is the case with the photodiode-type active pixel sensor, and sampled by the analog signal processor.

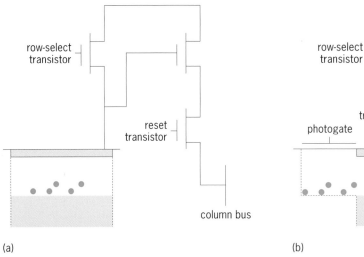

Fig. 2. Active pixels. (*a*) Photodiode type. (*b*) Photogate type.

The photogate is then pulsed, forcing the signal charge over a transfer gate barrier onto the floating diffusion. The new floating diffusion voltage is also sampled by the analog signal processor. The difference between the two samples is the photosignal from the pixel.

The photogate-type active pixel sensor uses five transistors per pixel and has a pitch typically equal to 20 times the minimum feature size. Thus, to achieve a 10-μm pixel pitch, a 0.5-μm process must be employed. The floating diffusion capacitance is typically of the order of 10 femtofarads, yielding a conversion gain of 10–20 microvolts per electron. Subsequent circuit noise is of the order of 150–250 μV root-mean-square, resulting in a readout noise of 10–20 electrons root-mean-square, and noise as low as 5 electrons root-mean-square has been reported. The advantage in read noise for the photogate pixel is offset by a reduction in quantum efficiency, particularly in the blue, due to the overlying polysilicon.

Analog signal processing. On-chip, column-parallel analog signal processing can be used to improve the performance and functionality of the CMOS image sensor. Sample-and-hold circuits are typically employed for active pixel sensors. A delta-difference sampling approach to suppress fixed pattern noise to 0.15% of saturation level has been developed. Other examples of signal processing demonstrated in CMOS image sensors include smoothing by using neuron MOSFETs (metal-oxide-semiconductor field-effect transistors), motion detection, programmable amplification, multiresolution imaging, video compression, dynamic-range enhancement, discrete cosine transform, and intensity sorting. Continued improvement in analog signal processing performance and functionality is expected.

Analog-to-digital conversion. To implement a camera on a chip with a full digital interface requires an on-chip analog-to-digital converter. This device must support video-rate data that range from 0.92×10^6

samples per second for a 320×288-format sensor operating at 10 frames per second for videoconferencing, to 55.3×10^6 samples per second for a 1280×720-format sensor operating at 60 frames per second. The analog-to-digital converter must have at least 8-bit resolution with low integral nonlinearity and differential nonlinearity, so as not to introduce distortion or artifacts into the image. Analog-to-digital conversion can be implemented as a single serial analog-to-digital converter (or several analog-to-digital converters, for example, one per color) that operates at nearly video rates (10^7 samples per second). As mentioned above, in column-parallel architecture, each (or almost each) column in the pixel array has its own analog-to-digital converter (Fig. 1), so that each analog-to-digital converter operates at the row rate (for example, 15,000 samples per second). In this architecture, single-slope analog-to-digital converters work well for slow-scan applications but dissipate too much power for video rates. Oversampled analog-to-digital converters require significant chip area when implemented in column-parallel formats. A successive-approximation analog-to-digital converter has a good compromise of power, bit resolution, and chip area. On-chip analog-to-digital conversion enables on-chip digital signal processing for sensor control and compression preprocessing.

Capabilities. CMOS active-pixel-sensor technology has achieved low noise (as low as 5 electrons root-mean-square), ultralow-offset fixed pattern noise (less than 0.1% of saturation), and high dynamic range (80 dB), comparable to the best commercial charge-coupled-device sensors. Gain variation is less than 1.5%, the same as for charge-coupled devices. Sensors as large as 1024×1024 pixels and higher have been demonstrated. It is clear that yield in modern CMOS foundries will allow the realization of array sizes at least up to 2048×2048 pixels, or 4×10^6 pixels.

CMOS image sensors are well poised both to replace charge-coupled devices in many traditional applications and to enable new ones. The low system power enables new portable applications, and the low system cost enables semidisposable applications. Rapid advancement is expected over the next few years.

For background information *see* ANALOG-TO-DIGITAL CONVERTER; CHARGE-COUPLED DEVICES; INTEGRATED CIRCUITS; OPTICAL DETECTORS; PHOTOELECTRIC DEVICES; TRANSISTOR in the McGraw-Hill Encyclopedia of Science & Technology.   Eric R. Fossum

Bibliography. E. R. Fossum, CMOS image sensors: Electronic camera on a chip, *IEEE Trans. Electr. Devices*, 44:1689–1698, 1997; R. H. Nixon et al., 256 × 256 CMOS active pixel sensor camera-on-a-chip, *IEEE J. Sol. State Circ.*, 31:2046–2050, 1996; P. Wong, Technology and scaling considerations for CMOS imagers, *IEEE Trans. Electr. Devices*, 43:2131–2142, 1996.

Optoelectronic device

Single-crystal silicon is the material of choice for most semiconductor electronic applications, such as computer microprocessors, computer memory chips, or power transistors. However, silicon has not been used in applications which require the electronic production of light. For applications such as digital calculator displays, light-emitting diodes (LEDs) used as indicator lights, semiconductor lasers used in compact-disk players to read the digital data by reflection of light, or phosphors for television picture tubes, III-V and II-VI semiconductor alloys are used. Examples are gallium arsenide (GaAs), formed from atoms from columns three and five of the periodic table, and cadmium sulfide (CdS), from columns two and six. Popular solid-state light emitters such as light-emitting diodes and lasers are presently made from these direct-band-gap compound semiconductors. Bulk silicon itself cannot be used as a light emitter because its indirect band gap leads to low optical efficiency.

In 1990, room-temperature light emission from silicon etched in a special way was first observed. Porous silicon is prepared by anodic electrochemical etching, which produces a surface that is porous and either spongelike or dendriticlike depending on the etching conditions. A very active research area has developed from this first experiment, with the goal of fabricating conventional light-emitting solid-state devices from porous silicon. Integrating porous-silicon light-emitting devices with conventional electronics on the same silicon wafer would provide advantages for such diverse fields as fiber-optic communications and flat-panel display technologies.

Luminescence. Light emission in semiconductors is called luminescence. Photons of light with energies corresponding to the semiconductor band-gap energy are emitted from the semiconductor when electrons in the conduction band recombine with holes in the valence band. If these excess electrons and holes are produced by optical absorption of light greater than the band gap, the emission is called photoluminescence. If the excess electrons and holes are produced in a semiconductor diode by foward-biasing the diode with a voltage to inject these excess carriers into the diode junction, the emission is called electroluminescence.

Not all electron-hole recombination leads to the emission of light. Several nonradiative recombination processes, particularly at the semiconductor surface, compete with the radiative recombination process so that fewer photons are emitted than the number of electron-hole pairs which recombine. The ratio of the number of radiative recombinations to the total number of recombinations, expressed as a percentage, is called the luminescence efficiency.

The band structure is important in determining luminescence efficiency. In direct-band-gap semiconductors, such as the III-V and II-VI alloys, the conduction-band minimum, where most electrons reside, and the valence-band maximum, where most holes reside, occur at the same value of particle momentum. Since the momentum of a photon of visible light is quite small, optical transitions are nearly vertical. Momentum and energy for all particles (electrons, holes, and photons) must be conserved during recombination. In direct-band-gap semiconductors, conservation of momentum is easily attained since the electron and hole momenta are the same and the photon carries little momentum.

In an indirect-band-gap semiconductor, such as silicon, the conduction-band minimum and valence-band maximum occur at different values of particle momentum. To conserve momentum in an optical recombination, the momentum of another particle is needed to make up for this momentum difference between the electrons and holes. This need is usually met by the emission of a phonon, a quantum of lattice vibration. This process is much less likely than direct recombination since the electron must scatter off the proper phonon before it can recombine with the hole.

Typical room-temperature photoluminescence efficiencies in silicon are therefore less than 0.001%. In direct-band-gap semiconductors, such as gallium arsenide, efficiencies approaching 30% are obtained for specialized light-emitting diodes. Interestingly, room-temperature photoluminescence efficiencies near 10% have been observed in porous silicon. Furthermore, the wavelength of this photoluminescence is tunable through most of the visible range of wavelengths by varying the etching process. Thus, it is likely that the band structure of porous silicon is direct and that the band gap can be varied by variation of the etching process.

Porous silicon. Porous silicon is a network of nanometer-sized silicon regions surrounded by void space. A porous-silicon film is prepared by electrochemical anodization of the surface of a silicon wafer (**Fig. 1**). The silicon electrode and a platinum electrode are immersed in an electrolyte which is a mix-

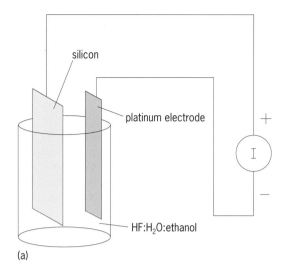

(a)

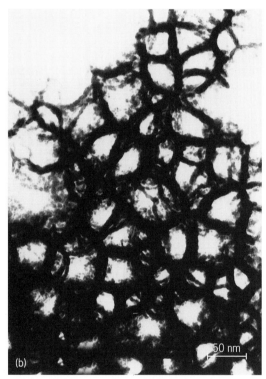

Fig. 1. Porous silicon. (*a*) Electrochemical cell used in preparation *(after R. T. Collins, P. M. Fauchet, and M. A. Tischler, Porous silicon: From luminescence to LEDs, Phys. Today, 50(1):24–31, January 1997).* (*b*) Transmission electron micrograph showing open pore structure *(from A. G. Cullis and L. T. Canham, Visible light emission due to quantum size effects in highly porous silicon, Nature, 353:335–337, 1991).*

ture of water, ethanol, and hydrofluoric acid (HF) [a typical ratio would be 2 : 1 : 1 respectively]. A current source is attached between the silicon and platinum, with the positive potential attached to the silicon. Porous silicon is formed at the surface of the wafer upon application of an appropriate current in the range of 1–100 mA/cm².

The structural, electronic, and optical characteristics of porous silicon strongly depend on the fabrica-

tion conditions. The main processing parameters are the resistivity and conductivity type of the wafer, the concentration of hydrofluoric acid in the electrolyte, and the current density. Illumination during anodization also alters the properties of the porous layer. In general, porosity increases with increasing current density and decreasing hydrofluoric acid concentration, and is higher for *p*-type than for *n*-type silicon.

Porous silicon contains a distribution of pore and feature sizes typically ranging 1–30 nanometers. Since the distance between atomic planes is 0.18 nm, the porous-silicon features contain 5–170 planes of atoms. Probably, then, the electrons and holes are confined to small regions of crystalline material. Porous silicon also has a very high surface density compared with that of silicon wafers.

Surface states. Freshly prepared porous silicon contains a high density of hydrogen, which terminates dangling bonds at the surface. This point is important, since unterminated bonds produce nonradiative recombination of electrons and holes at the surface. The first problem with porous silicon as an optoelectronic material thus arises. A freshly formed surface exhibits high-efficiency photoluminescence. However, with time, this luminescence degrades as the surface oxidizes, forming silicon dioxide on the surface features.

Band structure. Porous silicon appears to be a direct-band-gap material. The peak of the luminescence can be adjusted from blue-green to the near-infrared by controlling the preparation conditions of the surface (**Fig. 2**). This phenomenon has suggested to most scientists that the size distribution of the small crystallites controls the peak position of the luminescence spectrum.

This dependence is based on a strict quantum-mechanical effect called quantum confinement. Electrons and holes behave as waves. If each crys-

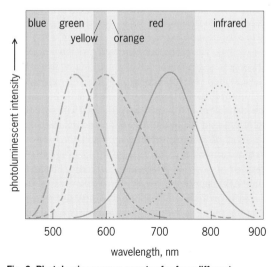

Fig. 2. Photoluminescence spectra for four different samples of porous silicon. By varying the preparation conditions, the luminescence wavelength has been varied from the infrared to the green.

tallite of the porous silicon is thought of as a small particle or box, the electrons and holes are confined to this box. The largest wavelength that will fit in this box is determined by the rule that a half wavelength of the electron must be of the same size as the smallest dimension of the box or silicon particle. The electron momentum is inversely proportional to its wavelength by the Planck relationship, $p = h/\lambda$, where p is momentum, h is Planck's constant, and λ is the electron wavelength. Thus, as the size of the porous-silicon particle decreases, momentum increases and the minimum electron energy increases in proportion to the square of the momentum. Holes also exhibit this quantum property, except that energy is decreased. Both effects contribute to an increase in band gap with decreasing box size. The lowest possible electron energy is moving upward while the highest hole energy is moving downward, thus increasing the band gap. This quantum confinement also explains the high luminescence efficiency observed. Since the wavelengths of the lowest-energy electron and the highest-energy hole must be the same, a phonon is not needed to conserve momentum during the optical transition.

Although most researchers believe that quantum confinement is required to explain the high efficiencies and change in emission energy with average particle size, mechanisms involving surface states have also been proposed.

Light-emitting diodes. Luminescence can be obtained electrically by the injection of charge carriers (electrons or holes) into the junction region of a semiconductor diode. The technology problem is how to make electrical contact to each silicon particle of the porous silicon. Electroluminescence was observed shortly after the first room-temperature photoluminescence was reported. In early experiments, liquid-electrolyte contacts were used to make contact with the porous silicon surface, but this arrangement is not a practical solution for a commercial device. Problems of luminescence stability were encountered as the electrolyte interacted with the porous silicon surface, chemically replacing the hydrogen terminating the surface states with other chemical species, thereby causing a reduction of the luminescence efficiency.

Researchers quickly tried to switch to solid-state contacts. Gold was evaporated on the porous silicon surface. However, it was found that stability was still a problem, probably due to solid-state chemical reactions with the surface. Light-emitting diodes formed in this manner demonstrated external quantum efficiencies (which take into account all light losses, including absorption in both the porous silicon and the underlying substrate, and internal reflections) of approximately 0.2%. However, voltages of 20–30 V were required because of the high series resistance of the devices, and efficiencies dropped by a factor of 3.5 in twelve days.

Recently, a stable electroluminescent device based on porous silicon has been reported. The sur-

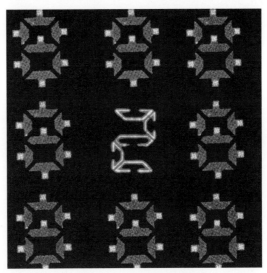

Fig. 3. Digital diplay made from porous silicon.
(Photograph by K. Hirschman and L. Tsybeskov, cover of Phys. Today, vol. 50, no. 1, January 1997)

face of the porous silicon is given a very thin oxidation at high temperature (800–900°C or 1500–1650°F). A top contact is then formed by depositing heavily doped polysilicon. These light-emitting diodes have been integrated with conventional driver electronics and fabricated into digital displays (**Fig. 3**).

For background information *see* ELECTROLUMINESCENCE; ELECTRON-HOLE RECOMBINATION; LIGHT-EMITTING DIODE; LUMINESCENCE; SEMICONDUCTOR; SEMICONDUCTOR DIODE; SILICON in the McGraw-Hill Encyclopedia of Science & Technology.

Jon M. Meese

Bibliography. L. T. Canham, Silicon quantum wire array fabrication by electrochemical and chemical dissolution of wafers, *Appl. Phys. Lett.*, 57:1046–1048, 1990; R. T. Collins, P. M. Fauchet, and M. A. Tischler, Porous silicon: From luminescence to LEDs, *Phys. Today*, 50(1):24–31, January 1997; R. T. Collins and M. A. Tischler, Porous silicon sheds a new light on OEICs, *IEEE Circuits and Devices*, 9(5):22–28, September 1993; L. Tsybeskov et al., Stable and efficient electroluminescence from a porous silicon-based bipolar device, *Appl. Phys. Lett.*, 68:2058–2060, 1996.

Organometallics

This article discusses the synthesis and structure of $[Os(CO)_4(SnPh_2)]_6$—a molecular bracelet.

Organometallic compounds containing unbridged, covalent bonds between a transition-metal atom and a second metal atom were first identified in the early 1960s. The second metal atom may be either another transition-metal atom, which is the same as or different from the first metal, or a nontransition (main-group)-metal atom. Examples are

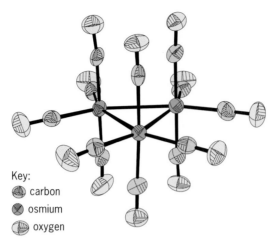

Key:
🔘 carbon
🔘 osmium
🔘 oxygen

Fig. 1. Structure of $Os_3(CO)_{12}$ drawn from the coordinates obtained by x-ray crystallography.

$Mn_2(CO)_{10}$, which contains two $Mn(CO)_5$ units bound together by an unbridged manganese-manganese bond of length 290 picometers; $(OC)_5MnNi(CO)(C_5H_5)$, with a manganese-nickel bond (261 pm); and $(OC)_5MnSnMe_3$ (Me is a methyl group or CH_3), which contains a manganese-tin bond (267 pm). Compounds are also known that contain several metal atoms bound together in a closed unit surrounded by organometallic ligands; for example, *closo*-hexadodecacarbonylpentaosmium, $Os_5(CO)_{16}$, contains a trigonal bipyramid of five osmium atoms to which are bound 16 carbon monoxide (CO) ligands.

Structural characterization. Each year the syntheses of hundreds of new compounds containing metal-metal bonds are reported. Many of these compounds

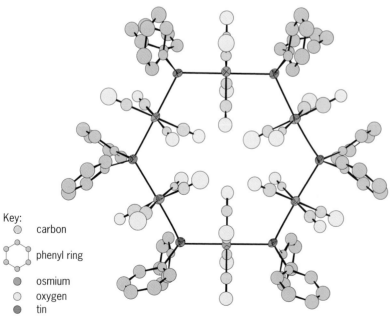

Key:
🔘 carbon
⬡ phenyl ring
⚫ osmium
⚪ oxygen
⚫ tin

Fig. 2. Molecular structure of $[Os(CO)_4(SnPh_2)]_6$ as determined by x-ray crystallography.

are structurally characterized by x-ray crystallography. In this technique a minute single crystal is subjected to a beam of monochromatic x-rays, and from the three-dimensional diffraction pattern about the crystal the molecular structure (with accurate bond lengths and angles) can be deduced. In the 1990s, advances in computing greatly shortened the time needed for the determination of x-ray structures. The development of the charge-coupled-device detector has also significantly reduced the time needed to collect the diffraction data, such that now a typical data set for an organometallic compound can usually be collected within 6 h. By comparison, a conventional diffractometer requires several days to collect an equivalent data set. Diffractometers with charge-coupled-device detectors can also work with much smaller crystals than the earlier diffractometers. *See* ANALYTICAL CHEMISTRY.

Carbonylosmium compounds. Osmium (element 76) is a rare metal like platinum. It exhibits formal oxidation states from −II (as in the tetracarbonylosmate(−II) anion, $[Os(CO)_4]^{2-}$) to VIII (in osmium tetroxide, OsO_4). Mononuclear compounds of osmium have coordination numbers ranging from four to eight, for example, OsO_4 and bis(diisopropylphenylphosphine)hexahydridoosmium, $OsH_6[P(C_3H_7)_2Ph]_2$, respectively (Ph is a phenyl group or C_6H_5). Osmium has a particular propensity to form metal cluster compounds for reasons that are not entirely understood. For example, whereas other transition metals form at the most 3 neutral binary carbonyls (that is, containing only the metal and carbonyl ligands), osmium forms 13 known binary carbonyls that have from one (in pentacarbonylosmium, $Os(CO)_5$) to eight osmium atoms (in $Os_8(CO)_{23}$). There are also binary carbonyl anions of osmium of still higher nuclearity (for example, $[Os_{17}(CO)_{36}]^{2-}$ and $[Os_{20}(CO)_{40}]^{2-}$). As verified by x-ray crystallography, some of the osmium atoms in these high-nuclearity cluster compounds have a coordination number of 10. In the pure metal the coordination number of each osmium atom is 12.

The starting material for most of the organometallic chemistry of osmium is dodecacarbonyl-*triangulo*-triosmium, $Os_3(CO)_{12}$, which is prepared in nearly quantitative yield by treating osmium tetroxide in methanol with carbon monoxide (100 atm or 8.1 MPa) at 150°C [reaction (1)]. It is found that the

$$3OsO_4 + 24CO \rightarrow Os_3(CO)_{12} + 12CO_2 \quad (1)$$

majority of metal cluster compounds are based on the fusion of triangular metal (M_3) units; $Os_3(CO)_{12}$ is therefore a relatively simple compound (**Fig. 1**) that contains this fundamental building block of this class of compounds.

Synthesis and structure of $[Os(CO)_4(SnPh_2)]_6$. The osmium precursory compound used in the synthesis is the salt $Na_2[Os(CO)_4]$, which is prepared by the treatment of $Os_3(CO)_{12}$ with sodium metal in liquid ammonia [reaction (2)]. Addition of $Na_2[Os(CO)_4]$

$$Os_3(CO)_{12} + 6Na = 3Na_2[Os(CO)_4] \quad (2)$$

to diphenyltin dichloride [Ph_2SnCl_2] in tetrahydrofuran at or below room temperature gives a mixture of Os-Sn–containing products and sodium chloride [reaction (3)]. One of the products is the expected

$$Na_2[Os(CO)_4] + Ph_2SnCl_2 \xrightarrow{<25°C}$$
$$[Os(CO)_4(SnPh_2)]_2 + [Os(CO)_4(SnPh_2)]_6$$
$$+ \text{ other Os-Sn products} + NaCl \quad (3)$$

$[Os(CO)_4(SnPh_2)]_2$. The x-ray structure of the methyl analog ($[Os(CO)_4(SnMe_2)]_2$) reveals that it contains a four-membered ring of alternating osmium and tin atoms. This compound can be readily converted into higher-nuclearity cluster compounds such as $Os_4(SnMe_2)_4(CO)_{14}$.

The compound of interest, $[Os(CO)_4(SnPh_2)]_6$, is separated (as air-stable, pale yellow crystals) from the other products by size-exclusion chromatography, followed by crystallization. The x-ray structural determination of $[Os(CO)_4(SnPh_2)]_6$ employed a crystal with dimensions $0.08 \times 0.16 \times 0.01$ mm. The molecule possesses a 12-membered ring of alternating osmium and tin atoms, which is an unprecedented bonding arrangement for an organometallic compound with metal-metal bonds (**Fig. 2**). The Os-Sn lengths in $[Os(CO)_4(SnPh_2)]_6$ range 273–275 pm. The molecule has been likened to a bracelet with the phenyl (C_6H_5) rings acting as charms dangling from the central metal ring. Another feature of interest is that ^{13}C nuclear magnetic resonance (NMR) spectroscopy indicates that in solution there is rapid rotation about the Os-Sn bonds so that the inner and outer CO ligands on the osmium atoms are equivalent by this spectroscopic method.

It is believed that the hexameric, rather than the dimeric, osmium-tin ring compound is formed because it results from the reaction of $[Os(CO)_4]^{2-}$ with the intermediate $Os(CO)_4(SnPh_2Cl)_2$, in which the $SnPh_2Cl$ groups are opposite (trans) to one another in the six-coordinate intermediate and not adjacent (cis) to each other. In the previously studied methyl derivative, the intermediate $Os(CO)_4(SnMe_2Cl)_2$ has a predominantly cis configuration in solution and, furthermore, there is rapid interconversion between the cis and trans forms so the further reaction of $Os(CO)_4(SnMe_2Cl)_2$ with $[Os(CO)_4]^{2-}$ yields only the dimeric $[Os(CO)_4(SnMe_2)]_2$, with cis Sn-Os-Sn units. Note that in $[Os(CO)_4(SnPh_2)]_6$ the Sn-Os-Sn linkages have a trans orientation.

There are no immediate practical applications for $[Os(CO)_4(SnPh_2)]_6$, but its synthesis and structure suggests a number of intriguing possibilities. For example, pyrolysis of $[Os(CO)_4(SnPh_2)]_6$ may yield still larger cluster compounds with Os-Sn skeletons; it may be possible to prepare other rings with the same or different metal atoms. On the more practical side, it is known that molecules with rings often have polymeric analogs, for example, the polymeric analog of cyclohexane, C_6H_6, is polyethylene, $-[CH_2\text{-}CH_2]_n-$. It may be that $[Os(CO)_4(SnPh_2)]_6$ can be converted into a polymer with an Os-Sn backbone with useful physical properties (for example,

metal conductivity in one dimension). Theory suggests that both the $SnPh_2$ and $Os(CO)_4$ molecular fragments have similar bonding properties to CH_2 (they are said to be isolobal). An important use of compounds of transition metals is as catalysts to facilitate useful chemical reactions under mild conditions. The compound $[Os(CO)_4(SnPh_2)]_6$, with its six osmium atoms in proximity to one another, may be able to catalyze reactions that mononuclear transition-metal catalysts with their one active site cannot.

For background information *see* CHEMICAL BONDING; COORDINATION CHEMISTRY; COORDINATION COMPLEXES; INORGANIC CHEMISTRY; METAL; OSMIUM in the McGraw-Hill Encyclopedia of Science & Technology.   Roland K. Pomeroy

Bibliography. E. W. Abel, F. G. Stone, and G. Wilkinson (eds.), *Comprehensive Organometallic Chemistry II*, vol. 7, 1995; F. A. Cotton and G. Wilkinson, *Advanced Inorganic Chemistry*, 5th ed., 1988; W. K. Leong et al., Synthesis and structure of $[Os(CO)_4(SnPh_2)]_6$: A compound with an unprecedented 12-membered ring of metal atoms, *Organometallics*, 16:1079–1082, 1997; D. M. P. Mingos and D. Wales, *Introduction to Cluster Chemistry*, 1990.

Perception

It is commonly believed that vision is a unified, coherent sense; that people perceive objects and surfaces, manipulate objects under visual guidance, and move around using visual information that is seamless and integrated. This notion, however, is false. There are at least two pathways for visual information in the brain, each with its own representation of visual space. These representations have distinct functions, and under some conditions they can hold contradictory spatial information.

Cognitive and sensorimotor pathways. The cognitive pathway supports normal perception. Since this pathway manages visual experience, people report the contents of its representation when asked what they see. The cognitive pathway specializes in pattern recognition: identifying and remembering objects, people, and places in the environment. This requires fine-grained, high-resolution information from the retina. The cognitive pathway detects very small motions by using relative motion of one texture against another as a cue, and as a result its representation of visual space cannot be calibrated relative to the body. For example, people experience illusions such as induced motion, when the Moon appears to be rushing past clouds, when in fact it is the clouds that are moving and the Moon that is still. The cognitive pathway cannot ignore context information, even when context gets in the way.

The sensorimotor pathway has a complementary set of capabilities. It is sensitive mainly to low-resolution retinal information and insensitive to visual context. As a result, it can support a body-centered calibration, providing information about locations of objects relative to the body that the cognitive pathway lacks. The sensorimotor branch has very limited pattern-recognition abilities, possessing information about the locations of objects but little about their features. This pathway also works in the here and now, and has a memory only long enough to execute a movement.

Neurophysiological evidence. Single nerve cells in the cognitive pathway, in the temporal lobe of the brain, tend to be sensitive to stimuli in large parts of the visual field, but are excited only when those stimuli possess particular features. Many of the cells are affected by the meaning of a visual stimulus. For example, they are more active when an object has acquired a learned meaning. Some of the cells seem specialized for distinguishing faces, and others for making difficult visual discriminations.

In the sensorimotor pathway, cells are sensitive to aspects of visual information which are relevant for action. In the posterior part of the parietal lobe, some cells respond to objects that are visually present, but only when they are within reach. Other cells respond only to stimuli that are the focus of visual attention. Many of the cells are sensitive to motion, in depth as well as in the frontal plane. To code position relative to the head, cells in one brain area respond more strongly when the eyes are looking in a certain direction than when they are oriented in other directions. The direction varies from cell to cell, so that all directions of gaze and all retinal locations are coded in one cell or another. These cells as a group can code position of an object relative to the head, even though each individual cell's responsive area is tied to a particular retinal location.

Experimental lesions in primates also reveal a dissociation between cognitive functions in a temporal brain region and sensorimotor functions in a parietal region. Monkeys with lesions of the inferior temporal cortex have difficulty in performing visual discriminations but have good hand-eye coordination, while animals with parietal lesions have good discrimination skills but are clumsy and uncoordinated in reaching and grasping.

Clinical evidence. Brain-damaged humans show patterns similar to those found in lesioned monkeys. Many neurological patients show the symptom of visual apraxia, an inability to reach for and grasp objects appropriately. The deficit is not a general damage to motor ability, for grasp that is not guided by vision can remain normal. In apraxia patients, information in the perceptual pathway is not available to control accurate grasping and reaching. A less common group of individuals has difficulty with perception and object identification but can reach for and grasp objects accurately even though their properties cannot be identified. One such individual, whose brain was damaged by carbon monoxide poisoning, could not identify the orientation of a slot cut into a disk held before her. However, when asked to extend her flattened hand through the slot, she did so accurately, rotating the hand to pass

through the slot. This is a demonstration of the sensorimotor pathway possessing knowledge that is not available to perception.

An extreme form of the preservation of motor capability in the absence of perception is a deficit called blindsight. These individuals have blind spots in parts of their visual fields, due to damage to the visual cortex. However, they can still locate targets in the blind field. Though perception is blocked, sensorimotor information reaches the parietal lobe of the brain through alternate pathways. Both the apraxia and blindsight individuals show a double dissociation of cognitive and sensorimotor information: one group has cognitive but not motor ability, while the other has motor but not cognitive ability.

Psychophysical evidence. To know how these two pathways normally operate and cooperate, they must be studied in normal humans. Such study has become possible with the development of psychophysical methods that isolate the two pathways and measure separately the spatial information in each representation. Early experiments on this issue showed that subjects were unable to perceive jumps of targets that take place during changes of eye fixation. However, the subjects could still point accurately to the new locations of the same targets, even if they could not see their hands during the pointing movements. This showed that information about the new locations of the targets was stored accurately but was not available to perception.

A more rigorous method of separating cognitive and motor systems is to introduce a signal only into the sensorimotor pathway in one condition and only into the cognitive pathway in another. A fixed target was projected in front of a subject, with a frame surrounding it. When the frame was laterally displaced, subjects had the illusion of stroboscopic induced motion: the target appeared to jump in the opposite direction. Target and frame were then extinguished, and the subject pointed to the last target position. Subjects pointed to the same location regardless of the direction of induced motion, showing that the illusion did not affect pointing: the displacement signal was present only in the cognitive system.

In another experiment, displacement information was inserted selectively to the motor system by nulling the cognitive signal. Each subject adjusted the real-target motion until the target appeared stationary. Thus, the cognitive pathway specified a stable target. Nevertheless, subjects pointed in different directions when the target was extinguished in the left or the right positions, showing that the difference in real-target positions was still represented in the sensorimotor pathway. This is another example of a double dissociation, for in the first experiment the target displacement affected only the cognitive measure, while in the second experiment the displacement affected only the sensorimotor measure.

Another method has been developed that can test dissociations of cognitive and sensorimotor function without possible confounding effects of motion. The dissociation is based on the Roelofs effect, another perceptual illusion: if a target is seen inside a rectangular frame that is presented off center, the target's location tends to be misperceived in the direction opposite the offset of the frame. The effect can be measured reliably by asking subjects to describe the target's position verbally. If their task is simply to jab the target as soon as it disappears from view, however, they almost never miss. Motor behavior remains accurate despite the perceptual mislocalization. The result is different if a delay is imposed between the disappearance of the target and the jabbing movement. If the delay is more than a few seconds, the subjects jab in a direction that is biased by the cognitive illusion. Having lost the accurate representation in the sensorimotor pathway, they must import the remembered spatial information in the perceptual pathway. In the process, they import the illusion as well, and the illusion serves as a marker for the source of the information.

Together, these studies reveal a perceptual system for vision and a parallel system that controls visually guided behavior.

For background information *see* COGNITION; INFORMATION PROCESSING; NEURAL NETWORK; PERCEPTION; VISION in the McGraw-Hill Encyclopedia of Science & Technology.   Bruce Bridgeman

Bibliography. B. Bridgeman, S. Peery, and S. Anand, Interaction of cognitive and sensorimotor maps of visual space, *Percept. Psychophys.*, 59:456–469, 1997; A. D. Milner and M. A. Goodale, *The Visual Brain in Action*, 1995.

Phenacene

Until recently, four compounds constituted the only known members of the family of polycyclic aromatic compounds whose molecular structures have an extended phenanthrene-like motif (**Fig. 1**). For this family, a naming system has been invented in which each member is designated as "phenacene" preceded by a bracketed number specifying fused aromatic rings. For example, phenanthrene is [3]phenacene and picene is [5]phenacene.

Graphite, which consists of very large flat layers of fused aromatic rings stacked together in parallel planes, is of practical importance because of its electrical conductivity. Phenacenes are related structurally to graphite roughly in the way that ribbons are related to sheets. This structural relationship suggests that [*n*]phenacenes with large values of *n* might be of practical importance as electrically conducting "graphite ribbons" or "molecular wires."

Synthesis. A key requirement in the synthesis of large phenacenes is the construction of new aromatic rings. This construction can be accomplished by a two-step sequence: a Wittig reaction to produce a 1,2-diarylethylene, followed by photocyclization of the resulting diarylethylene (**Fig. 2**). Ultraviolet irradiation of solutions of either *trans-* or *cis-*stilbene, dissolved in a solvent such as cyclohexane or benzene, produces a mixture of three isomeric species:

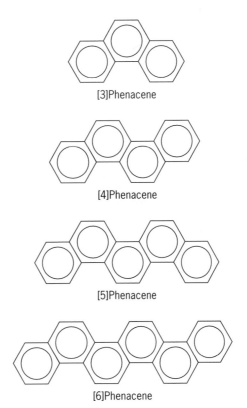

Fig. 1. Molecular structures of some small [*n*]phenacenes.

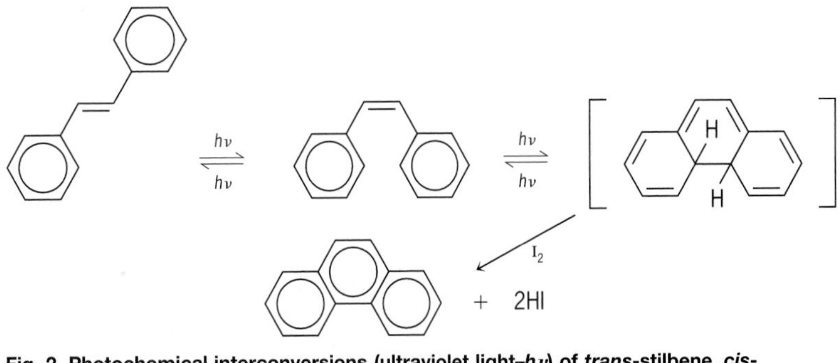

*trans-*stilbene, *cis-*stilbene, and the nonaromatic compound 4a,4b-dihydrophenanthrene. This dihydrophenanthrene cannot be isolated because it is unstable, both thermally and photochemically, with respect to ring opening to regenerate *cis-*stilbene. If the solution being irradiated also contains molecular iodine, the resulting 4a,4b-dihydrophenanthrene can be trapped by reaction with iodine to produce phenanthrene (along with hydrogen iodide). An adaptation of this method was used to synthesize the previously unknown [7]phenacene (**Fig. 3**).

The solubilities of the unsubstituted [*n*]phenacenes decrease dramatically with increasing *n*; [7]phenacene, for example, has almost no solubility in common organic solvents and is therefore almost

Fig. 2. Photochemical interconversions (ultraviolet light–*hν*) of *trans-*stilbene, *cis-*stilbene, and 4a,4b-dihydrophenanthrene, and trapping of the last by iodine (I_2) to give [3]phenacene plus hydrogen iodide (HI).

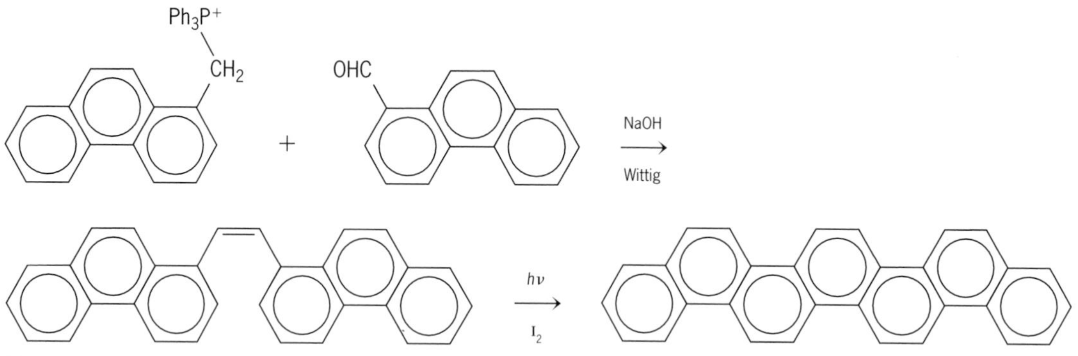

Fig. 3. Synthesis of [7]phenacene.

intractable. It is clear that the objective of synthesizing and characterizing [n]phenacenes with very large values of n is not feasible unless the solubilities of large phenacenes can be enhanced sufficiently to permit them to be handled experimentally with ordinary chemical techniques. This solubility problem has been solved by incorporating n-pentyl, tert-butyl, 1,1-dimethylpentyl, or phenyl groups as substituents along the polycyclic carbon framework. For example, an [11]phenacene derivative that is solubilized by four n-pentyl substituents has been synthesized by the double photocyclization approach (**Fig. 4**). This [11]phenacene derivative represents the largest known [n]phenacene that has been synthesized.

An iterative divergent-convergent synthesis strategy (**Fig. 5**) seems particularly well suited in principle for the synthesis of some very large [n]phenacenes. Each four-step iteration in this strategy transforms a substituted aromatic system containing n fused rings into an analogously substituted aromatic system containing $2n + 1$ fused rings. The individual steps in each iteration consist of (1) transformation of a methyl substituent on the starting aromatic system to a benzylic triphenylphosphonium (Ph$_3$P$^+$) group by treatment with N-bromosuccinimide (NBS) followed by triphenylphosphine; (2) transformation of a bromo substituent on the starting aromatic system to an aldehyde group by treatment with butyllithium (BuLi) followed by N,N-dimethylformamide (DMF); (3) Wittig coupling of the two compounds obtained from steps 1 and 2 to give a diarylethylene; and (4) photocyclization of the diarylethylene obtained from step 3. The first two iterations (Fig. 5) have been carried out successfully to produce the [7]phenacene derivative, and the third iteration is expected to produce the corresponding [15]phenacene derivative. The extension of this iterative synthesis to a fourth, fifth, and sixth iteration, if successful, would yield dramatically larger [n]phenacenes with $n = 31$, 63, and 127, respectively.

Physical properties. One physical property of interest for these large phenacene derivatives is the longest-wavelength band (the p band) in each of their ultraviolet-visible absorption spectra. For a particular [n]phenacene molecule, this wavelength is inversely related to the magnitude of the difference between the energy of the highest occupied molecular orbital and the energy of the lowest unoccupied molecular orbital. This energy difference, known as the band gap, would need to be small (ideally zero) in order for the phenacene to exhibit electrical conductivity. Experimentally measured wavelengths of the p bands indicate that the band gap is continually decreasing with increasing n (**Fig. 6**). The observation that the band gap shows no sign of leveling off, at least up to $n = 11$, encourages the hope that very large phenacenes might prove to have small band gaps.

Another physical property of interest for phenacene derivatives is the extent to which these molecules deviate from coplanarity of their polycyclic carbon frameworks, a structural feature that would be revealed by x-ray crystallographic measurements. As a rule, most polynuclear aromatic systems (ranging from benzene to graphite) exhibit strict coplanarity of their carbon frameworks, but the generality of that rule has been severely challenged by discover-

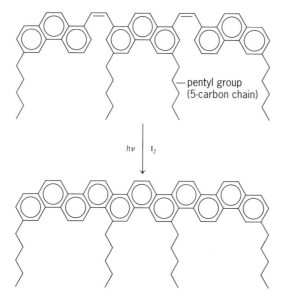

Fig. 4. Synthesis of a tetra-n-pentyl[11]phenacene by a double photocyclization.

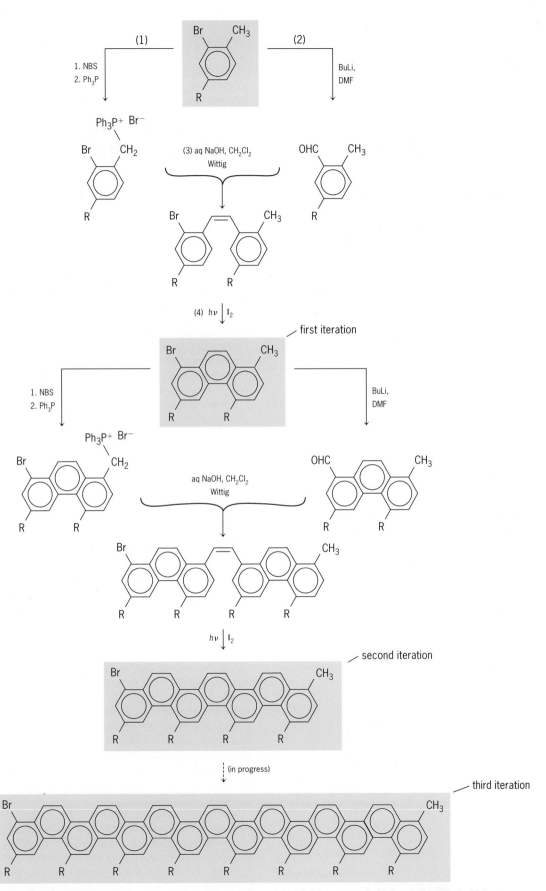

Fig. 5. Divergent-convergent approach for the synthesis of a series of [*n*]phenacene derivatives substituted with bromo and methyl functional groups, and also substituted with various bulky groups (R = *tert*-butyl, 1,1-dimethylpentyl, or phenyl) to enhance solubility.

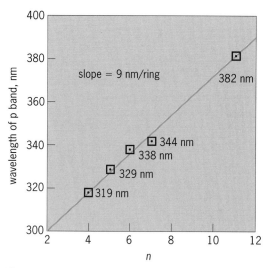

Fig. 6. Wavelength of the p band for five [*n*]phenacenes in benzene solution plotted as a function of *n*. Background correction was done for [11]phenacene by subtracting 18 nanometers from the p band observed at 400 nm for the tetra-*n*-pentyl-[11]phenacene derivative, thereby compensating for the four *n*-pentyl groups.

ies of polycyclic aromatic systems whose carbon frameworks are either curved (for example, the fullerenes) or twisted. The carbon frameworks of phenacenes are predicted to be twisted in a helical sense (**Fig. 7**), because that kind of molecular twisting relieves some of the significant intramolecular steric crowding that exists in the bay regions of these molecules that contain one R substituent and one hydrogen substituent. The extraordinarily long [*n*]phenacenes that the synthesis approach (Fig. 5) is designed to produce have many of these crowded bay regions. As a consequence, these molecules may possess extraordinarily large extents of end-to-end helical twisting. These large [*n*]phenacenes may therefore contribute new insights regarding the effects of noncoplanarity on the properties of polycyclic aromatic systems.

For background information *see* AROMATIC HYDRO-CARBON; BENZENE; CARBON; FULLERENE; GRAPHITE; MO-

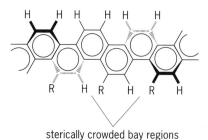

sterically crowded bay regions

Fig. 7. Representation of a six-ring segment located in the interior region of a long [*n*]phenacene, illustrating the postulated helical twist of the carbon skeleton resulting from steric crowding between R and H groups located in bay regions.

LECULAR ORBITAL THEORY; NANOCHEMISTRY in the McGraw-Hill Encyclopedia of Science & Technology.   Frank B. Mallory

Bibliography. F. B. Mallory et al., Phenacenes: A family of graphite ribbons: 1. Syntheses of some [7]phenacenes by stilbene-like photocyclizations, *Tetrahed. Lett.*, 37:7173–7176, 1996; F. B. Mallory et al., Phenacenes: A family of graphite ribbons: 2. Syntheses of some [7]phenacenes and an [11]phenacene by stilbene-like photocyclizations, *J. Amer. Chem. Soc.*, 119:2119–2124, 1997; F. B. Mallory and C. W. Mallory, Photocyclization of stilbenes and related molecules, *Org. React.*, 30:1–456, 1984.

Photochemistry

Solar radiation is a powerful and plentiful energy source that needs to be harnessed more efficiently. Only approximately 0.3% of the incident solar flux is being used by the entire flora of the Earth. Photochemistry involves the reactions of molecules excited by the absorption of light. Photosynthetic techniques involving synthetic light-harvesting antennas are being developed to capture solar radiation for energy production.

Energy and electron transfer. It is imperative to completely understand the mechanism of energy transfer and the subsequent electron transfer in the photosynthetic reaction center to optimally design an artificial photosynthetic device to harness solar energy. Energy transfer is the process in which the excitation energy gained by the absorption of light by a molecule (donor) is transferred to another molecule (acceptor). The acceptor molecule receives the energy and enters an excited state. Electron transfer is the process in which an excited state of a molecule donates an electron to (or accepts an electron from) another molecule.

Various model compounds have been synthesized to mimic the energy transfer and electron transfer aspects of photosynthesis. The potential for these devices is enormous in that they may be used not only to convert solar energy into chemical potential energy but also to gain insight into the fabrication of molecular photonic devices based on organic materials.

Techniques such as fluorescence spectroscopy, time-resolved laser spectroscopy, and x-ray and electron crystallography have been used to examine and characterize the various units and the functions of the photosynthetic system. The result is a better understanding of the mechanism behind the light-harvesting process.

Natural light-harvesting complexes. The photosynthetic process consists of three basic photochemical reactions: singlet-singlet energy transfer, triplet-triplet energy transfer, and photoinduced electron transfer (**Fig. 1**). Singlets have paired electron spins, whereas triplets have unpaired electron spins. The conversion of the singlet to the triplet is called the intersystem crossing. Light-harvesting antenna sys-

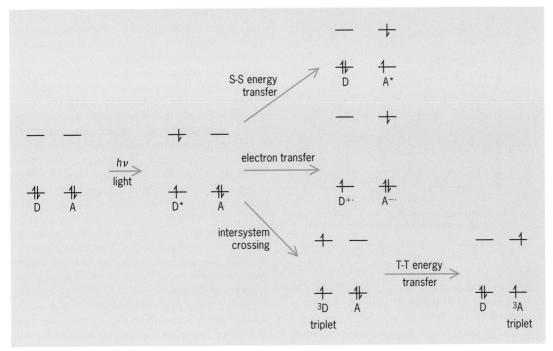

Fig. 1. Three basic photochemical reactions in a photosynthetic system: singlet-singlet (S-S) energy transfer, photo-induced electron transfer, and triplet-triplet (T-T) energy transfer.

tems consisting of chlorophylls and carotenoids collect light and transport the excitation energy to the reaction center via singlet-singlet energy transfer. The photoinduced electron transfer involving chlorophylls and quinones transforms the excitation energy into chemical potential in the form of a long-lived charge-separated state. Light-harvesting molecules such as chlorophylls and carotenoids are collectively called pigments, and they exist as pigment-protein complexes because of noncovalent interactions between them. The green pigments, chlorophylls, are derivatives of tetrapyrrole ring systems complexed with a metal atom (magnesium; Mg) at the center. The yellow or orange pigments, carotenoids, belong to the conjugated polyene family. The color of the carotenoids in the plant is normally masked by chlorophylls, but in the fall season when the chlorophyll disintegrates the yellow/orange color becomes distinctly visible. In a photosynthetic system, only a few chlorophyll molecules make up the reaction center and participate in the direct photochemical reactions, while most of the chlorophyll molecules serve as light-gathering antennas capturing sunlight and funneling it to the reaction centers.

The antenna function in photosynthesis allows metabolically valuable reaction centers to turnover at optimal rates and permits organisms to harvest light where the extinction coefficients of the reaction center are relatively low. For instance, carotenoids in the light-harvesting complexes augment the absorption of light in the 450–550-nanometer region, where the chlorophylls have very weak absorption. Thus, these pigments enlarge the reaction center's absorption cross section for capturing solar radiation and thereby enable the organism to grow even in low light intensities.

The photosynthetic bacteria contain two types of antenna complexes. Type LH1 is intimately associated with the reaction center, forming the core or inner complex. Arranged more peripherally than LH1 without any direct association with reaction centers is type LH2, called the outer complex. With the aid of x-ray crystallography, the structure of the LH2 complex of a photosynthetic bacterium was determined to a resolution of 0.25 nm. The complex contains bacteriochlorophyll *a* and rhodopsin (carotenoid)–glucoside pigments. The bacteriochlorophyll *a* molecules in this complex are divided into two categories based on their absorption spectral properties. One type of bacteriochlorophyll *a* molecule, called B800, has absorption maximum at 800 nm whereas the other, called B850, has a peak at 850 nm. Both units have a ninefold symmetry. The B800 unit contains nine bacteriochlorophyll *a* molecules arranged in a ring, and the interaction between the bacteriochlorophyll *a* molecules is rather weak. The larger B850 unit has 18 bacteriochlorophyll *a* molecules also arranged in circular fashion, with very strong interaction among bacteriochlorophyll *a* molecules leading to exciton coupling (that is, the excitation energy is delocalized over the interacting molecules). The B850 unit is 1.8 nm away from the B800 unit.

When energy is deposited in the B800 unit of the peripheral LH2 complex, a cascade of energy transfer steps is initiated (**Fig. 2**), the first being that the excitation energy is transferred to the B850 in 0.7 picosecond. This transferred excitation energy

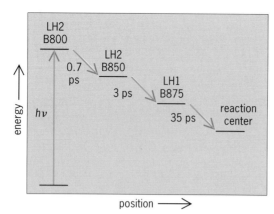

Fig. 2. Excitation energy transfer from the outer complex (LH2) to the reaction center via the inner complex (LH1).

is delocalized within the B850 unit in about 130 femtoseconds. From the B850 unit, the energy is transferred to the inner LH1 complex in about 3 ps. The LH1 ring contains 16 bacteriochlorophyll *a* molecules and has absorption maximum at 875 nm. The excitation energy eventually reaches the reaction center from LH1 in about 35 ps, which is relatively a slow process because of long separation between the two units (~4.5 nm). The bacteriochlorophyll *a* molecules have different absorption spectra, depending on the nature of the protein environment in which they are embedded and the strength of the interactions between bacteriochlorophyll *a* molecules and the proteins. Nature's light-harvesting complexes are ingeniously designed in that there is an energy gradient from the periphery to the core which facilitates the ultrafast energy transfer.

The carotenoids in the LH2 complex have van der Waals contact with both the B800 and B850 units and transfer energy to them efficiently. Besides transferring excitation energy to bacteriochlorophyll *a* molecules through singlet-singlet energy transfer, carotenoids act as photoprotective agents. The triplet of bacteriochlorophyll *a*, if formed during photosynthesis, can sensitize the formation of highly reactive singlet oxygen ($^1O_2$) which is injurious to the organism. Carotenoids intercept the bacteriochlorophyll *a* triplets and thus prevent the formation of singlet oxygen.

Artificial light-harvesting compounds. Synthesis of model compounds to mimic the photosynthetic system has been an active area of research. The study of such compounds serves the dual purpose of gaining more insight into the mechanism of elementary processes in the complex photosynthetic system and checking the viability of efficient photo-driven devices. Studies have been conducted on the photon-harvesting properties of polymeric antenna molecules with naphthalene and anthracene pendant groups. With fluorescence spectroscopy, it has been shown that selective excitation of the naphthalene moiety induces fluorescence from anthracene groups, indicating energy transfer. The polymeric systems are not suitable for such studies, as they tend to collapse to a random coil conformation and form excimers which act as energy traps.

Extensive research has been carried out with model compounds containing carotenoids and porphyrins which, like chlorophylls, are derivatives of tetrapyrrole. Several caroteno-porphyrin compounds with ester, ether, and amide linkage between carotenoids and porphyrins have been synthesized. Fluorescence spectroscopy and time-resolved laser spectroscopy have been used to look at the singlet-singlet as well as triplet-triplet energy transfer in these compounds. From these studies, information has been obtained involving the dependence of the rate constant and efficiency of the energy transfer with the nature of the linkage and the orientation of the groups. A pentad (five units) molecule containing two porphyrins, two quinones, and one carotenoid was reported to undergo efficient electron transfer upon irradiation to form a charge-separated state with a lifetime of 0.5 millisecond and an efficiency of 83%. These systems can be used to effect further chemical reactions.

A series of dendrimers with phenylacetylene repeat units and perylene at the core have been synthesized. Dendrimers are a type of polymer with branching at each repeat unit. Their functionality and molecular architecture can be easily controlled. Thus, these dendrimers can be site-selectively functionalized to obtain the desired electronic properties. They differ from linear polymers in that dendrimers have more rigid structure and the possibility of entanglement is avoided. Irradiation of the phenylacetylene moiety induces fluorescence from perylene, indicating intramolecular energy transfer. By using steady-state as well as time-resolved fluorescence spectroscopy, the quantum yields and the rate constants of the energy transfer in these dendrimers were measured. Among this series of dendrimers, there is a unique dendrimer that possesses an inherent energy gradient from the periphery to the core (**Fig. 3a**), like a natural light-harvesting antenna complex. In this dendrimer the intramolecular energy transfer occurs within 5 ps with an efficiency of 98%. Because of the energy gradient, the excitation energy cascades from the high-energy moiety to lower-energy ones, just like a ball rolling down the stairs (Fig. 3b). The photon-harvesting properties of phenylacetylene-based dendrimers have been clearly established by these studies. Other dendrimers based on metal-ligand complexes have also been shown to possess this light-harvesting property.

Applications. Light-harvesting antennas can photosensitize the reaction of a remote moiety by excitation energy trap. The reaction centers in the photosynthetic system are in fact photovoltaic devices at the molecular level. A low-cost, high-efficiency solar cell based on a dye-sensitized semiconducting titanium dioxide (TiO_2) thin film has been fabricated. The dye which is absorbed on the TiO_2 film collects the solar energy.

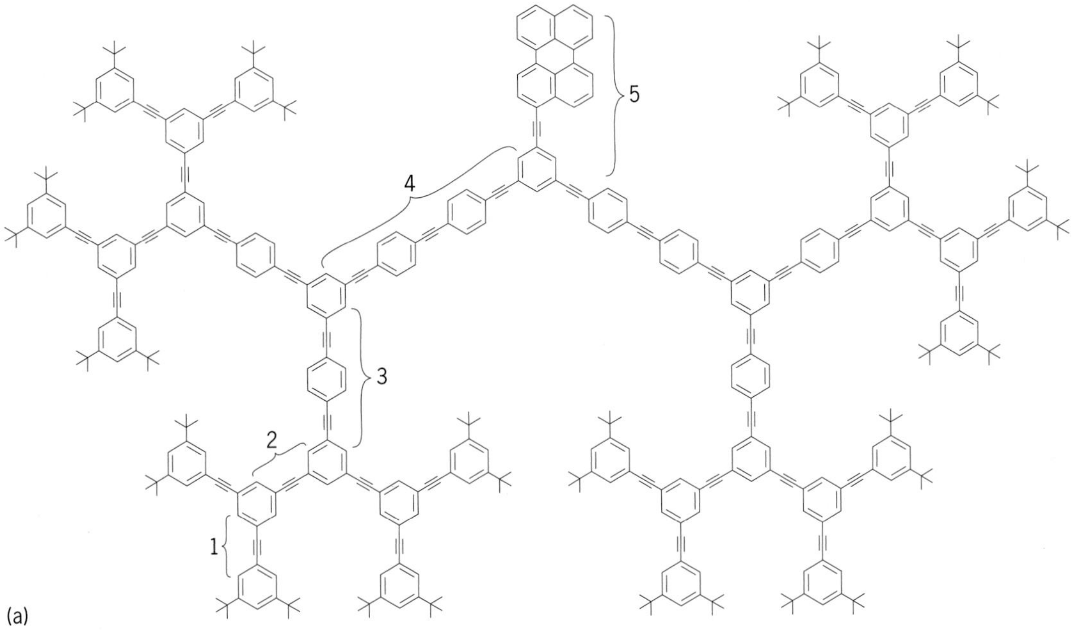

Fig. 3. Dendrimer-based light-harvesting molecular system with (*a*) built-in energy gradient and (*b*) cascading of excitation energy (from the periphery to the core). The excitation energy of the sections gradually decreases from positions 1 through 5.

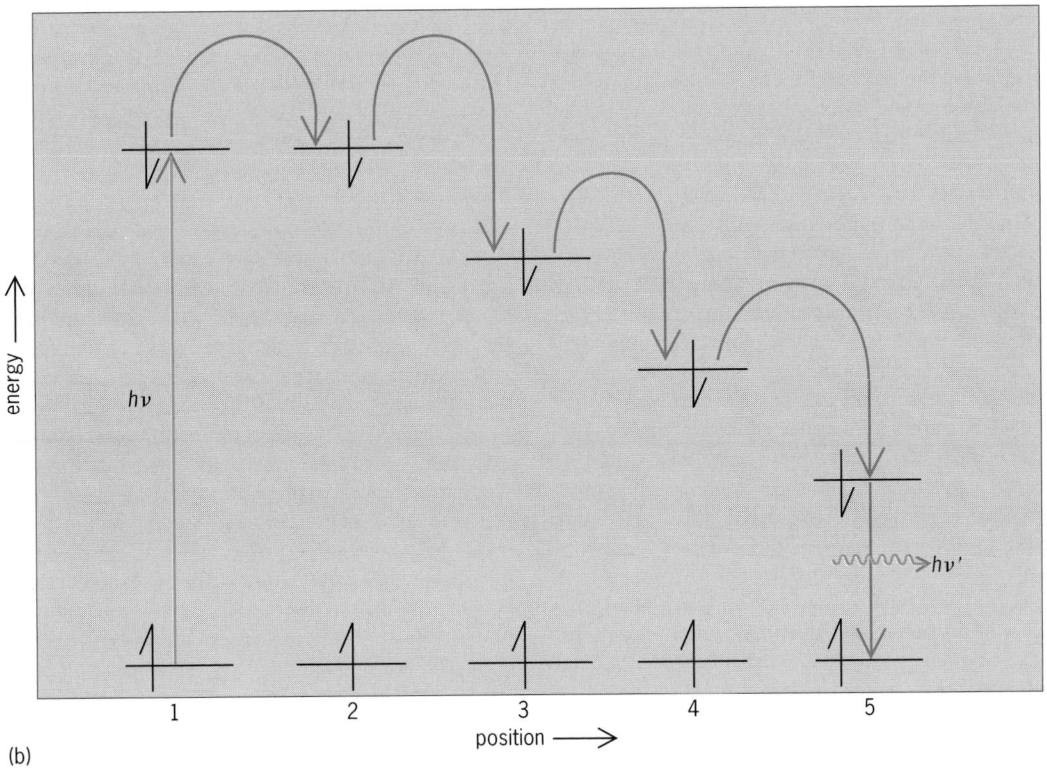

In the microelectronic industry, there is a growing need for new photoresists which can absorb at short wavelengths. Since the resolution of the integrated circuit device is proportional to the excitation wavelength, the resolution can be improved with photoresists which absorb at short wavelengths. The excitation energy can be transferred to a photoactive group in the molecule which absorbs at a long wavelength. Thus, photosensitization provides a way to obtain high-resolution features. The cascading energy transfer has been utilized to obtain high-gain light amplification in organic systems.

For background information *see* ELECTRON-TRANS-FER REACTION; INORGANIC PHOTOCHEMISTRY; PHOTO-

CHEMISTRY; PHOTOSYNTHESIS; SOLAR ENERGY in the McGraw-Hill Encyclopedia of Science & Technology.   Jeffrey S. Moore; Chelladurai Devadoss

Bibliography. C. Devadoss, P. Bharathi, and J. S. Moore, Energy transfer in dendritic macromolecules: Molecular size effects and the role of an energy gradient, *J. Amer. Chem. Soc.*, 118:9635–9644, 1996; J. E. Guillet, Prospects for solar synthesis, *Pure Appl. Chem.*, 63:917–924, 1991; D. Gust and T. A. Moore, Mimicking photosynthetic electron and energy transfer, *Adv. Photochem.*, 16:1–65, 1991; X. Hu and K. Schulten, How nature harvests energy, *Phys. Today*, pp. 28–34, August 1997.

Pipeline flow

Transport of viscous materials, such as heavy crude oil, through a pipeline is a subject of interest to the oil industry. Since the beginning of the twentieth century, it has been known that introducing a small amount of water into the pipeline to form an annulus surrounding the crude results in significant savings in the pumping power. Several water-lubricated pipelines were operated by oil companies in various capacities in the past, and there is renewed interest in the potential use of this technology in the petroleum industry, including the transport of bitumen froth.

Core-annular flow. Co-current, pressure-gradient-driven flow in a circular pipe with one fluid occupying the core region encapsulated by an annulus of a second fluid is called core-annular flow. When the core fluid is more viscous than the encapsulating fluid in the annulus, the flow is termed lubricated core-annular flow. Lubricated pipeline flow is an example. In a core-annular flow, the driving force, which is the applied pressure gradient, balances the viscous shear force at the pipe wall (drag). In lubricated pipeline flow, the less viscous lubricating fluid is usually water which is located adjacent to the pipe wall. Since the viscosity of water is much lower than that of the crude, the benefit of a lubricated pipeline flow is that the wall shear force is several orders of magnitude smaller than its value without such a lubricating annulus, with oil directly sticking to the pipe wall. Thus, lubricated pipelines provide an energy-efficient transport of crude oil because of the much lower pumping power required. In the ideal situation when there are no waves appearing at the oil-water interface, the pumping energy required for a water-lubricated pipeline is only a fraction of that needed to transport the same amount of crude oil alone (of the order of $1/1000$, approximately twice the water-to-oil viscosity ratio). The lubrication of the oil core benefits from the tendency of water to migrate toward the high-shear region near the wall—a fluid-dynamic phenomenon. Fluid mechanics analysis shows that if the annulus fluid is more viscous than the core fluid, core-annular flow becomes hydrodynamically unstable. Only under restricted conditions are lubricated core-annular flows

hydrodynamically stable and thus observable in practice.

Lubricated core-annular flows can be formed by introducing the less viscous fluid from the circumference at the inlet of the pipe, for example. Hydrodynamically stable, lubricated core-annular flows, however, are possible only when the annulus is thin. Even for a thin annulus, stable lubricated core-annular flows are very difficult to achieve. At very low speeds, surface tension can break the core fluid into slugs or drops. Lubricated transport of these slugs and drops is not as efficient as lubricated transport of a coherent core. The breakup of the core fluid can be prevented by increasing the flow speed. At higher flow speeds, however, waves which can increase the drag force are formed at the interface of the two fluids. Thus, lubricated core-annular flows without interfacial waves can be realized only for intermediate flow speeds. In many practical applications, this speed window is very narrow, and the most frequently observed flows are lubricated core-annular flow with finite interfacial waves and lubricated flow with slugs and drops of the more viscous fluid. Detailed flow charts as well as drag coefficients have been obtained experimentally. These data can serve as a general guideline for lubricated pipeline flow operations.

Interfacial waves. Several technical issues are associated with lubricated pipeline flows. The first is the formation of waves at the water-oil interface. Whenever two different fluids are set into a co-current motion, the interface separating them can become wavy because of hydrodynamic instabilities. The origin of the wave formation is the incompatibility of the fluid properties at the interface. For two fluids with a large difference in their viscosities, interfacial waves always appear in lubricated core-annular flows (**illus.** *a*). The shape and amplitude of these interfacial waves determine the drag on the pipe wall, and thus determine the energy efficiency of the lubricated pipeline. These characteristics of the interfacial waves in a core-annular flow can be determined from fluid mechanics analyses. Hydrodynamic stability theory and direct numerical simulation have been used to obtain this information. For very viscous oils, the waves appearing at the water-oil inter-

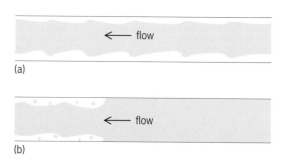

Core-annular flows. (*a*) Flow with interfacial waves. (*b*) Flow with fouling of pipe wall. (*After D. D. Joseph et al., Core-annular flows, Annu. Rev. Fluid Mech., 29:65–90, 1997*)

face travel with the same speed as the oil core, and the waves are stationary when viewed from a frame moving with the oil core. Furthermore, if the density of the oil nearly matches the density of water, the waves are axisymmetric. The shape of these waves, and therefore the wall shear force, can be computed numerically for a given set of data for flow rates and volume percentages of oil and water. The interfacial waves are nonaxisymmetric and highly three dimensional when the density difference between oil and water is not too small. Experiments have shown that these flows with nonaxisymmetric interfacial waves are a robust form of lubricated pipeline flows, although there is as yet no comprehensive analysis of these nonaxisymmetric waves. Although lubricated core-annular flows without interfacial waves are the most energy-efficient form of lubricated transport through pipelines, lubricated, wavy core-annular flows are the most encountered mode of lubricated pipeline operation, and are also very energy efficient.

Levitation of oil core. The second issue associated with lubricated pipeline flow is the levitation of the oil core in horizontal flows when the densities of oil and water are quite different. In this case, the flow has to generate enough lift force to overcome the buoyancy force which tends to move the oil core toward either the upper or the lower portion of the pipe wall, depending on whether the oil is lighter or heavier than water. This lift force is required to keep the oil core from contacting and contaminating the pipe wall, which in turn can cause the fouling and blockage of the pipe wall. To generate a levitation force large enough to lift off the oil core from the pipe wall, the pipeline has to operate at a flow speed above a certain limit and the water-oil interface has to become wavy and nonaxisymmetric. This requirement, in turn, has a major effect on the drag force. The fluid mechanics analysis of this situation is very complicated since the flow becomes three dimensional. Physical mechanisms for generating this lift force have been discussed, and inertia is found to be a necessary mechanism for the levitation of the oil core. Direct numerical computation to obtain wave characteristics, however, requires further investigation.

Fouling and restart. Another technical issue involved in lubricated pipeline flow is the potential fouling and blockage of the pipe wall by the crude oil (illus. *b*). Fouling can occur when oil wets the pipe wall, which can happen when the pipe wall is hydrophobic. The surface chemistry of a hydrophobic pipe wall is such that the intermolecular forces between the pipe material and water are repulsive. Thus the pipe wall "hates" water and attracts oil. This is a problem of surface chemistry, and it cannot be studied by fluid mechanics alone. The pipe can also be fouled when lighter oil floats and sticks to the upper portion of the pipe wall (or when heavy oil sinks and sticks to the bottom of the pipe wall) when the pipeline is stopped for maintenance. This fouling can lead to a large surge in the pressure drop during pipeline operation or when the pipeline is restarted after maintenance. If oil cannot be removed immediately from the pipe wall under an applied pressure drop, fouling can build up and eventually lead to the complete blockage of the pipeline. To remedy this problem, the inner surface of the pipe wall must be treated so that it has the desired hydrophilic properties. For example, it was found that the addition of sodium silicate to water can prevent fouling of carbon steel pipes. Another possibility is to use cement-lined pipelines, since mortars of portland cement form strongly hydrophilic calcium silicate hydrate gels naturally in curing.

For background information *see* FLUID FLOW; PIPE FLOW; PIPELINE; SURFACE TENSION; VISCOSITY in the McGraw-Hill Encyclopedia of Science & Technology.   Kang Ping Chen

Bibliography. M. S. Arney et al., Cement lined pipes for water lubricated transport of heavy oil, *Int. J. Multiphase Flow,* 22:207–221, 1996; R. Bai, K. Kelkar, and D. D. Joseph, Direct numerical simulation of interfacial waves in a high viscosity ratio and axisymmetric core annular flow, *J. Fluid Mech.,* 32:1–34, 1996; D. D. Joseph et al., Core-annular flows, *Annu. Rev. Fluid Mech.,* 29:65–90, 1997; D. D. Joseph and R. R. Renardy, *Fundamentals of Two-Fluid Dynamics,* 1992.

Plant development

Although the basic body plan of flowering plants—similar to that of animals—is established during embryogenesis, plants continue to generate organs throughout their life cycle from groups of undifferentiated cells called meristems. In a typical flowering plant, two meristems are laid down during embryogenesis: the shoot meristem, which produces the aerial part of the plant, and the root meristem, which produces the subterranean root system. Several genes that control establishment and function of meristems have been discovered. The essential mechanisms, discovered in *Arabidopsis thaliana,* a relative of mustard, have been found to hold true for many other species as well, including snapdragon, tomato, petunia, and maize.

Establishment and maintenance of shoot meristem. During the second half of embryogenesis the shoot meristem becomes morphologically distinct as a group of unvacuolated cells between the cotyledons. Following germination, new meristems and organ primordia form in the peripheral zone of the shoot meristem, while the central zone serves to replenish cell number in the peripheral zone (**Fig. 1**). The size of shoot meristems remains more or less constant during the whole plant life cycle, indicating that the generation of undifferentiated cells in the central zone and the loss of cells from the peripheral zone through differentiation are tightly balanced.

Of the genes affecting the establishment and maintenance of the shoot meristem, the greatest amount

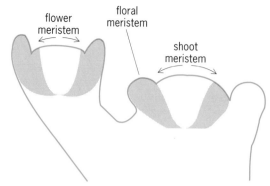

Fig. 1. Shoot apex configuration, highlighting the similarities of shoot and floral meristems. New cells are generated in the central zone (white area). The arrows indicate displacement of these cells toward the peripheral zone (gray area), where new organs or meristems are initiated, including floral meristems on the flank of the shoot meristem.

of information is known about the mutants *CLA-VATA1* (*CLV1*) and *SHOOT-MERISTEMLESS* (*STM*). The *clv1* mutant seedlings start out with an enlarged shoot meristem which continues to grossly overproliferate during postembryonic growth; mature plants have a shoot meristem whose volume is thousands of times larger than that of a normal plant. In contrast, *stm* mutants do not form a functional shoot meristem during embryogenesis. In addition to establishment of the shoot meristem, *STM* must play a role in maintaining the shoot meristem, since new, ectopic meristems, which form spontaneously on the stem of *stm* mutants, are immediately consumed by the production of leaves.

A major question in examining any developmental pathway is the functional relationship between the genes in such a pathway. Because of the opposite effects of *STM* and *CLV1*, two regulatory scenarios may be anticipated. If the genes acted sequentially, inactivation of one gene should mask the consequences of inactivating the other gene. Conversely, if the genes acted in parallel, an additive effect is expected. It turns out that *stm clv1* double-mutant seedlings lack a normal shoot apical meristem, confirming that the *STM* gene is absolutely required for the establishment of this structure during embryogenesis. As with *stm* single mutants, the double mutants form ectopic shoot meristems which can go on to form complete shoots rather than just one or two leaves. Therefore, *STM* does not control *CLV1* activity, or vice versa. Instead the two genes appear to affect a common target in opposite ways. The activity of both genes is needed to assure the correct balance between proliferation and differentiation in the shoot meristem.

In order to understand the molecular function of *STM* and *CLV1*, both genes were cloned, and it was found that the respective proteins are very different: STM protein is a transcription factor capable of binding deoxyribonucleic acid (DNA) in the nucleus, while CLV1 protein is a transmembrane kinase that

might function in the reception of extracellular signals. In contrast to their divergent structure, the expression patterns of both genes are quite similar, with both genes being expressed in the center of shoot and floral meristems. However, neither gene is confined to the central zone, where new, undifferentiated cells are generated. It remains unclear whether these genes control the rate with which undifferentiated cells are generated in the central zone or whether they control the rate with which the number of undifferentiated cells is depleted by differentiation in the peripheral zone.

Identity of meristems. The newly formed meristems that are derived from the shoot meristem can become either leaves with associated lateral shoots or flowers that can be considered specialized lateral shoots that produce floral organs instead of vegetative leaves. In most plants, the shoot apical meristem produces leaves with associated lateral shoots during the initial vegetative phase, while the production of flowers is confined to the later reproductive phase. The switch from the vegetative to the reproductive phase is caused by a complex process termed floral induction which is governed both by endogenous signals such as plant age and by environmental signals such as day length. One consequence of floral induction is the activation of a group of genes called flower-meristem-identity genes, which include *LEAFY* (*LFY*) and *APETALA1* (*AP1*). Inactivation of these genes by mutation causes flowers to be replaced by shoots or shootlike structures, indicating that *LFY* and *AP1* are required for floral identity.

The hypothesis is that these genes are not merely required for floral identity but also might function to impart floral fate. This has been tested with transgenic plants in which *LFY* or *AP1* genes were expressed under the control of a constitutively active viral promoter. Plants that overexpressed either *LFY* or *AP1* had solitary flowers whereas lateral shoots would appear in normal plants, with the consequence that these plants flower precociously. In addition, the main shoot is converted into a flower after producing a limited number of vegetative leaves and lateral flowers. Thus, *LFY* and *AP1* encode genetic switches, since in their absence flowers are transformed into shoots with associated leaves, while their overexpression has the opposite effect of transformation of shoots into flowers.

The finding that *LFY* encodes a genetic switch controlling floral fate has been extended to other species, including trees, which normally go for years before flowers are produced for the first time. When the constitutively active version of *LFY* was introduced into hybrid aspens, they began to produce flowers after only a few months. Furthermore, this occurred while the aspen plants were still very small, only a few inches tall.

Patterning of flowers. While genetic experiments have shown that *LFY* and *AP1* can induce the normal floral program in a meristem, it is not clear how this is actually done at a mechanistic level. Both genes appear to encode transcription factors that are capa-

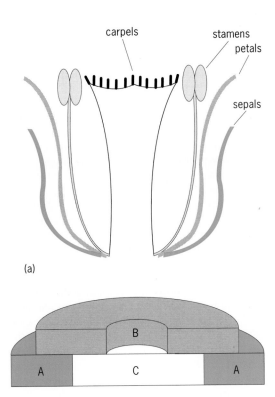

carpels

stamens
petals

sepals

(a)

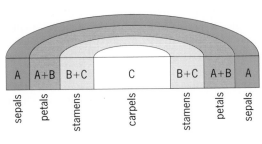

(b)

Fig. 2. Regulation of floral organ fate based on the ABC model. (a) Cross section of a mature flower, indicating the four types of organs forming the central gynoecium. (b) Half section of an early flower primordium with the domains of ABC homeotic gene activities, which generate four unique combinations that specify organ fate.

ble of directly regulating the expression of other genes. Once individual flowers have been initiated, floral organs arise in four concentric rings termed whorls, with sepals in the outermost whorl, followed by petals and stamens and finally carpels in the central whorl. The fate of individual floral organs is controlled by organ-identity or homeotic genes, which fall into three classes termed A, B, and C. Each class specifies organ fate in two adjacent whorls, and regulates floral organ fate as summarized in the ABC model (**Fig. 2**).

The central tenet of this model is that the particular combination of ABC gene activities in a given whorl specifies the type of organ in that whorl. Thus, in whorl one, A-function alone causes sepals to develop; in whorl two, A + B-function causes petals to develop; in whorl three, B + C-function causes stamens to develop; and in whorl four, C-function

alone causes carpels to develop. In *Arabidopsis*, at least four genes are known to control ABC functions, including *APETALA2* (*AP2*) [A-function]; *APETALA3* (*AP3*) and *PISTILLATA* (*PI*) [B-function]; and *AGAMOUS* (*AG*) [C-function]. All four genes encode again transcription factors. Furthermore, with the exception of *AP2*, these genes also function as genetic switches; that is, they are both necessary and sufficient to impart a particular organ fate. For example, the *AG* gene is normally active in the center of the flower, where it promotes stamen fate in combination with *AP3* and *PI*, as well as carpel fate on its own. If *AG* is inactivated by mutation, a flower that consists only of sepals and petals results. Conversely, if *AG* is made to be active in both the periphery and the center, a flower that produces only carpels and stamens results.

Interestingly, homeotic genes in both animals and plants encode transcription factors, but they belong to different gene families. Homeotic proteins in animals contain a very highly conserved sequence of 60 amino acids, the homeo domain, while most homeotic proteins in plants contain a different conserved amino acid sequence, the MADS domain. A further similarity between plant and animal homeotic genes was found in the discovery that the *CURLY LEAF* gene, which keeps the homeotic gene *AG* shut off in inappropriate places such as leaves, is structurally related to regulators of animal homeotic genes.

While much has been learned about the genes that are required for the initiation of flowers and about the genes that control organ fate, important questions remain. The next few years may bring answers as to how meristem-identity genes are involved in setting up the pattern of homeotic gene activities and how homeotic genes in turn control target genes that make the characteristic structures typical for each floral organ.

For background information *see* FLOWER; GENE; PLANT GROWTH; PLANT MORPHOGENESIS in the McGraw-Hill Encyclopedia of Science & Technology. Detlef Weigel

Bibliography. J. Goodrich et al., A Polycomb-group gene regulates homeotic gene expression in *Arabidopsis*, *Nature*, 386:44–48, 1997; J. A. Long et al., A member of the KNOTTED class of homeodomain proteins encoded by the *STM* gene *Arabidopsis*, *Nature*, 379:66–69, 1996; E. M. Meyerowitz, The genetics of flower development, *Sci. Amer.*, 271:56–65, 1994; D. Weigel and O. Nilsson, A developmental switch sufficient for flower initiation in diverse plants, *Nature*, 377:495–500, 1995.

Poliomyelitis

There are an estimated 1.6 million survivors of acute poliomyelitis in the United States today. A significant percentage of them have experienced the onset of new weakness, fatigue, and pain many years after recovering from paralytic poliomyelitis. The causes of these new symptoms have not been fully elucidated. An underlying physical overuse etiology is the most widely accepted explanation.

Postpolio syndrome. The viruses that cause the polio infection attack anterior horn cells, the nerve cell bodies in the spinal cord which control movement. These cells project axons which connect to muscles. When anterior horn cells are destroyed by the virus, paralysis results. A unique aspect of the polio virus is that it does not attack sensory cells; therefore, no sensory impairment is present either during or after the acute attack of poliomyelitis. The degree of paralysis is determined by the inoculum, or the amount of the virus present; the virility of the strain; and the level of the person's immune defenses.

In most cases of paralytic polio, a variable degree of recovery occurs up to 2 years after the acute attack for several reasons. Shortly after the acute attack subsides, a carefully graduated physical therapy program is started. Over a period of months, partially as a result of this physical conditioning program, strength improves. Hypertrophy of the remaining viable muscles occurs, a process rather like that in weight training. A state of deconditioning makes a small contribution to the weakness after the acute illness. If muscles are not utilized, as in a situation of enforced bed rest during and shortly following acute viral attack, muscle atrophy results. With the training already noted, this condition has been reversed. During the acute period, rest has been essential to prevent exacerbation of the paralysis.

Collateral sprouting. By far the most significant factor in partial or apparently complete clinical recovery from paralytic poliomyelitis is a physiologic process known as collateral sprouting. An axon, projecting from the anterior horn cell, reaches to the muscles in a distant part of the body. When the axon gets very near a muscle, many small innervations are formed and make the final connection to the muscle tissues, which the nerve activates. This part of the nerve is termed the terminal sprouts or the motor end plate. The entire anatomical unit—the anterior horn cell, the axon, the terminal sprouts, and the muscle fibers activated by this nerve—is defined as the motor unit. When the polio virus kills an anterior horn cell, its axon and terminal sprouts will also die, leaving muscle fibers devoid of nerve supply.

Collateral sprouting occurs over a period of months, depending on how many adjacent anterior horn cells have survived. Adjacent motor units, in the areas of terminal sprouts, form collateral sprouts which effectively reinnervate these areas of muscle tissue. Very large motor units are formed which, by some estimates, are up to 10 times normal size. Clinically significant muscle function returns, and in some cases complete clinical recovery results.

Typically, many polio survivors remain functionally and neurologically stable for many years after recovery. Then, 25–60% experience new fatigue, weakness, and in many cases pain. This can occur 20–40 years after recovery and is not recognized as an age-related phenomenon. A number of studies have implicated dysfunctioning motor units, particularly at the area of the terminal sprouts: a portion of the collateral sprouts are dropping off, and nerve conduction blocks are occurring in other places in the area of the terminal sprouts. Another indication is that entire motor units may be under physiologic stress. Such studies have led to the hypothesis that postpolio syndrome is an overuse syndrome.

Diagnosis. No objective test is available which will specifically identify the presence of postpolio syndrome. The diagnosis is made clinically: Reasonable alternative diagnoses which can cause similar symptoms in a person with a history of paralytic polio are first considered. After additional historical information and testing results are obtained, these other diagnoses are excluded from consideration, finally arriving at a diagnosis of postpolio syndrome.

The primary approach in managing a patient with postpolio syndrome entails the attenuation of the physical activities that are contributing to the overuse. This requires examining the life-style and daily activities of the patient and determining those factors that are most likely responsible for these physical overuse patterns.

Overuse factors. Many factors may potentially contribute to physical overuse; some of the most common will be discussed. Polio survivors who have extensive residual paralysis are more likely to experience postpolio symptoms, although those who have less apparent paralysis but are very active physically are also at significant risk. Overweight patients are at risk as well. Many polio survivors have been highly driven in terms of career pursuits and often have pushed themselves physically, ignoring fatigue and pain. Many have discarded braces injudiciously early after recovery, and many years later have begun experiencing significant weakness and pain.

Overuse factors may be grouped into those which primarily result in neurologic overuse or in musculoskeletal overuse. Neurologic overuse involves excessive chronic metabolic overuse of the surviving motor units. Musculoskeletal overuse results in excessive stresses on muscles, joints, and ligaments without necessarily or directly placing extreme stress on the motor units. A clear delineation between these two categories cannot always be made. When a musculoskeletal overuse factor is present, for example, it may lead immediately, or after a variable period of time, to neurological overuse, or overstress on the surviving motor units.

In the absence of paralysis in weight-bearing joints in the legs, joint stability is maintained by a combination of ligaments and intact muscle action. If significant muscle paralysis is present, chronic stresses often are placed on ligaments, resulting in their stretching. With the progressive deformity that results, gait dynamics are adversely affected. The combination of the unprotected joint and abnormal forces placed on the joint often leads to degenerative arthritis. The net effect in many cases is that increasing fatigue results from abnormal gait mechanics. Coexisting joint pain may typically develop because of ligamentous strain, abnormal joint alignment, and degenerative arthritis. Further, if pain is experienced when walking, regardless of preexisting paralysis, increased energy demands are expended in an attempt to minimize discomfort.

If a person who has paralysis in one leg, for example, is having difficulty clearing the toe because of foot drop, a brace enclosing the ankle and foot is recommended. Once the brace is fitted, gait dynamics improve markedly in stability and walking requires less energy expenditure. If the paralysis in the leg is more extensive, a larger brace is fitted. With bracing, joint malalignments are reduced and gait dynamics are improved. Almost invariably the level of fatigue and pain is reduced.

In many cases, patients who have already been wearing braces and walking with crutches begin experiencing fatigue and pain in their arms, shoulders, and hands. Over many years these persons have been "walking on their arms." While the braces and crutches have served as a functional solution to the paralysis, the arms were never intended for this type of long-term activity and fatigue and pain symptoms of arthritis, tendinitis, and myalgias have become increasingly severe. The common solution is to have these persons utilize either a powered wheelchair or other powered assistive device. Thus the chronic stressors on the arms are eliminated, with a commensurate reduction in symptoms of fatigue and pain. Often polio survivors with less extensive paralysis may also benefit from a powered assistive device, at least part time. In most cases, not only are fatigue and pain symptoms well contained, but these persons are then able to do more.

Another factor commonly present in many polio survivors, especially after they reach middle age, is being overweight. Polio survivors with residual paralysis tolerate excessive weight very poorly. In many cases, the gradual onset of fatigue and pain is directly correlated with weight gain. The difficulty in losing weight is greater for polio survivors than for the general population, because polio survivors usually cannot increase physical exercise as an adjunct to a weight loss program. For those able to achieve the target weight loss, the improvement in symptoms of fatigue and pain can be dramatic.

The greatest anxiety of many polio survivors is that the progressive weakness and pain will worsen to the point that they will become confined to wheelchair or bed. Unfortunately, no long-term studies are available to elucidate the likelihood of further symptom progression. One earlier theory hypothesized that postpolio syndrome is a mild form of amyotrophic lateral sclerosis. However, a number of factors indicate that postpolio syndrome is a distinct entity, and that the prognosis for postpolio syndrome individuals is much more optimistic. Most importantly, the motor units in postpolio survivors are not dying off. Anecdotal clinical reports and re-

search studies indicate that if the overuse patterns are controlled, the prognosis for long, productive, and relatively symptom-free life is quite good.

In some cases, the biggest obstacle to controlling the progressive fatigue and pain are polio survivors themselves. Many have great resistance to returning to the use of braces or to making life-style changes, for with great courage and determination over the years, they have overcome the physical and social limitations imposed by the paralysis. However, once physical and emotional adjustments are made, the quality of life of postpolio syndrome patients will almost invariably improve.

For background information *see* CENTRAL NERVOUS SYSTEM; JOINT (ANATOMY); MOTOR SYSTEMS; NERVOUS SYSTEM (VERTEBRATE); PAIN; POLIOMYELITIS; SKELETAL SYSTEM; SPINAL CORD; VIRUS in the McGraw-Hill Encyclopedia of Science & Technology.   Paul E. Peach

Bibliography. A. Alba et al., Exercise testing as a useful tool in the physiatric management of the postpolio survivor, *Birth Defects*, 23:301, 1987; P. E. Peach, *Late Effects of Poliomyelitis in Rehabilitation Medicine: Contemporary Clinical Perspective*, 1992; D. Trojan and N. Cashman, *Current Trends in Post-Poliomyelitis Syndrome*, Milestone Medical Communications, New York, 1996; D. O. Wiechers, Acute and latent effects of poliomyelitis as revealed by electromyography, *Orthopedics*, 8:870, 1985.

Polymorphism (genetics)

Polymorphism is the occurrence of two or more forms of a gene in a population in such frequencies that the presence of the rarest of the forms cannot be explained by mutation alone. The implication is that polymorphic alleles confer some selective advantage on the host. Individuals who have two identical genes at a polymorphic locus are homozygous for the gene; those who have two different alleles are heterozygous. Possession of nonidentical alleles at a single locus generally gives the advantages of both polymorphic forms. In some cases, however, nonfunctional alleles have been maintained in the population, resulting in relative or complete deficiency of the function encoded by the gene product. Polymorphisms have been described in both the coding regions and the noncoding regions (for example, upstream promoters) of genes. In humans, at least 30% of structural genes are polymorphic. Perhaps the most widely known example of polymorphic genes is the ABO blood group system. The most polymorphic genes in the genome, however, belong to the immune system.

Immunity. The mammalian immune system has evolved over hundreds of millions of years to protect the host from infection by the myriad of disease-causing microorganisms in the environment. Thus, the immune system has been placed under strong pressure to evolve a system of genes that confer a selective advantage on the host. The result has been a very high degree of polymorphism of a number

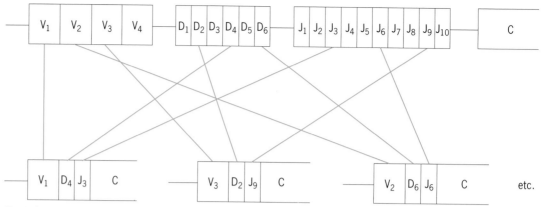

Fig. 1. Combinatorial joining of short gene segments to generate antigen receptor diversity.

of genes involved in immunity. The immune system has the ability to recognize a vast range of foreign substances, known as antigens, through genetically encoded antigen-specific receptors on B and T lymphocytes. For the recognition of an antigen by T lymphocytes, the antigen must be presented to the T cell's antigen receptor in association with self molecules encoded in the highly polymorphic major histocompatibility complex (MHC). A large number of proteins that do not themselves exhibit antigen specificity cooperate in the elimination of antigens. A number of the genes encoding these proteins have been shown to have more limited, but nonetheless functionally significant, polymorphism.

Antigen receptors. At their cell surface, both B cells and T cells express antigen-specific receptors [surface immunoglobulin on B cells, and T-cell receptors (TcR) on T cells], with each lymphocyte expressing only a single specificity of receptor. To protect against the possible range of antigens, the overall diversity of antigen receptors must be enormous. If each antigen receptor were encoded by a unique gene, most of the genome would be taken up with these genes. In order to get around this problem, the immune system has evolved a mechanism (**Fig. 1**) for encoding the antigen receptors of B and T cells, whereby multiple small gene segments are rearranged and joined in different combinations to generate the huge diversity of antigen receptors required effectively to fight any infection. It has been estimated that, by this mechanism, each individual has the potential to generate approximately 10^{11} different B-cell antigen receptors and 10^{18} different T-cell receptors. This mechanism of combinatorial joining of small gene segments is unique to the immune system. It is fascinating in terms of its genetic strategy for the generation of maximum diversity from a minimum of genetic material, but this mechanism is not strictly genetic polymorphism, although there is polymorphism in the germline coding sequences for these genes.

Major histocompatibility complex. For T-cell recognition of antigen, the protein antigen must be broken down into short peptides by an antigen-presenting cell, and then presented to the T-cell receptors in association with a self protein encoded in the host's MHC. These MHC-encoded antigen-presenting molecules represent the most polymorphic gene products in the genome. The MHC consists of three subregions (**Fig. 2**). The MHC class I and class II regions contain the genes that encode antigen-presenting molecules for cytotoxic T cells (which kill virally infected cells) and helper T cells, respectively. In humans, the MHC (termed HLA, for human leukocyte antigen) class I and class II regions each contain three loci encoding antigen-presenting molecules: HLA-A, -B, and -C in class I, and HLA-DR, -DP, and -DQ in class II. In the population as a whole, there are over 600 different alleles which encode the gene products of these loci. Polymorphism of these genes arose through a combination of point mutations, gene conversions, and recombination events. The structures of the MHC class I and class II gene products are similar, with the membrane distal domains forming a groove into which peptides fit and are bound. The majority of the polymorphisms in MHC genes encode amino acid substitutions which cluster in and around the peptide-binding groove. Different MHC molecules bind a different subset of peptides. The MHC type of an individual, therefore, determines the range of peptides that are presented to the individual's T-cell receptors. The high degree of polymorphism of these MHC genes is believed to have resulted from the selection throughout evolution of mutations in MHC genes which offered the host an advantage by protecting against specific pathogens. This view is supported by the finding that one HLA allele (*HLA-B53*), which is found at high frequency in certain African populations, is associated with protection against severe malaria. The arrival of new pathogens, such as human immunodeficiency virus (HIV), allows the effect of selection to be studied in a dynamic situation by observing whether any HLA alleles or haplotypes are associated with a better or worse prognosis. While a protective role for individual HLA molecules is not clear in HIV

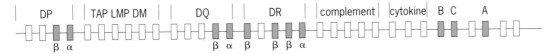

Fig. 2. Human major histocompatibility complex.

infection, some HLA haplotypes have been associated with more rapid progression to acquired immune deficiency syndrome (AIDS).

In addition to these antigen-presenting molecules, the class I and II regions of the MHC contain other genes encoding molecules that are involved in the processing of antigen (Fig. 2) and that show limited polymorphism. The functional significance of these polymorphisms is not yet clear.

MHC and disease association. In addition to their roles as antigen-presenting molecules, the polymorphic MHC gene products act as transplantation antigens; in other words, non-self MHC molecules are the major antigenic determinants in organ transplant rejection (hence the name major histocompatibility complex). Individual MHC molecules and certain MHC haplotypes have also been associated with specific autoimmune diseases. Perhaps the best example is the association between the HLA type *HLA-B27* and ankylosing spondylitis (a type of arthritis). Individuals who are *HLA-B27* positive are nearly 100 times more likely to develop this disease than individuals who are *HLA-B27* negative. Many diseases that have an immunological basis have been associated with polymorphic MHC genes. Some of these associations may be quite complex. For example, in diabetes mellitus the MHC region contains the major genetic component of the disease, with some class II loci contributing. Different combinations of MHC alleles at these loci may either predispose or protect.

The class III region of the MHC also contains genes encoding proteins of immunological significance, for example, components of the complement system and certain cytokines. Defective, or null, alleles have been described in the MHC genes encoding complement components C2 and C4, and are associated with an increased incidence of infection and with development of the autoimmune disease systemic lupus erythematosus. Polymorphisms in the cytokine gene *TNFα* and its promoter have been associated with a wide range of infectious and autoimmune diseases and with certain tumors.

Other genes of immune system. While the MHC encompasses the most polymorphic genes of the immune system, there are also polymorphic, non-MHC encoded proteins that contribute to immunity and that have significant clinical implications. A polymorphism in a chemokine receptor gene which offers protection against infection with HIV has recently been described. The chemokine receptor acts as a coreceptor for some strains of the virus, facilitating viral entry and infection of the cell. The polymorphic variant does not act as a coreceptor for the virus. Individuals who are homozygous for this variant are much less likely to become infected with HIV following exposure. In addition, individuals heterozygous for the variant gene progress more slowly to AIDS than individuals who are homozygous for the wild-type receptor gene. Several polymorphic variants of the mannose-binding lectin, a component of the complement system, that encode dysfunctional mannose-binding lectin proteins have been described. Individuals who are homozygous for variant mannose-binding lectin genes are more prone to a wide range of infections, including HIV infection and progression. Similarly, a polymorphism in a gene encoding a cell surface receptor for the antibody Fc region is associated with an increased incidence of infections with a wide range of bacteria.

Although polymorphic genes may confer a selective advantage on individuals in a population through protection against infectious diseases, at least some polymorphisms are associated with potentially harmful side effects. An example is the hemoglobin gene (*HbS*) which encodes for sickle cell anemia: while the gene is potentially harmful in terms of its poor oxygen-carrying capacity, its presence protects the individual against infection with malaria.

For background information *see* ANTIBODY; ANTIGEN; AUTOIMMUNITY; CELLULAR IMMUNOLOGY; CYTOKINE; HISTOCOMPATIBILITY; HUMAN GENETICS; IMMUNOLOGY; POLYMORPHISM (GENETICS); TRANSPLANTATION BIOLOGY in the McGraw-Hill Encyclopedia of Science & Technology.   Michael Browning

Bibliography. M. Browning and A. McMichael, *HLA and MHC: Genes, Molecules and Function*, 1996; M. Dean et al., Genetic restriction of HIV-1 infection and progression to AIDS by a deletion allele of the *CKR5* structural gene, *Science*, 273:1856–1861, 1996; A. V. S. Hill et al., Common West African HLA antigens are associated with protection from severe malaria, *Nature*, 352:595–600, 1992; S. M. Lewis, The mechanism of V(D)J joining: Lessons from molecular, immunological and comparative analyses, *Adv. Immunol.*, 56:27–150, 1994.

Positron emission tomography

Positron emission tomography is a medical imaging method which measures the concentration of positron-emitting radioisotopes in a volume element of tissue. The positron-emitting isotopes that are used typically have short half-lives. In addition, their chemical character allows labeling of organic compounds and drugs so that this technique is ideally suited for imaging drug action and biochemical transformations in living systems. Positron emission tomography grew out of the integration of many disciplines such as physics, chemistry, mathematics, physiology, anatomy, pharmacology, and medicine. All these fields are needed to develop and apply positron emission tomography to problems in biology and medicine. In the study of how drugs of abuse affect brain chemistry, positron emission tomography allows researchers to track these drugs in the brain and to measure their effects on the brain and on behavior.

Producing positron emitters. Positron-emitting radioisotopes typically have short half-lives and are produced near the site of use by means of a charged particle accelerator such as a cyclotron. A typical cyclotron accelerates protons or deuterons to an energy of 10–20 MeV. Protons are produced by ionizing hydrogen gas, and by using a strong magnetic field and radio-frequency energy they are accelerated to a very high energy and guided into a target. The protons deposit their energy in the target, giving rise to a nuclear reaction. For example, carbon-11 is produced when the beam of protons impinges on nitrogen gas; an alpha particle is also produced: $^{14}N(p,\alpha)\,^{11}C$ (as $^{11}CO_2$). The carbon-11 has an atomic mass of 11 (6 protons and 5 neutrons) and a half-life of 20.4 min. The carbon-11 atoms react with the trace oxygen present within the target to give rise to carbon dioxide ($^{11}CO_2$) gas. Many other positron emitters are useful in medicine, such as nitrogen-13, oxygen-15, and fluorine-18 (see **table**).

Rapid radiotracer synthesis. After the positron emitting isotope has been produced, it is rapidly converted into a labeled drug or some other radiotracer whose distribution in the body provides information on a particular biochemical process. The synthesis of carbon-11-labeled cocaine is a good example. Here carbon-11-labeled carbon dioxide is rapidly converted to carbon-11-labeled methyl iodide by reduction with lithium aluminum hydride (LiAlH$_4$), followed by reaction with hydrogen iodide (HI) [reactions (1) and (2)]. Methyl iodide is then trans-

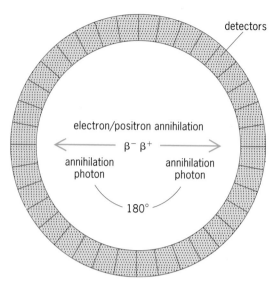

Fig. 1. Positron emission tomography scanner is used to detect protons emitted by electron/positron annihilation.

$$^{11}CO_2 + LiAlH_4 \rightarrow {}^{11}CH_3OH + \text{various products} \qquad (1)$$

$$^{11}CH_3OH + HI \rightarrow {}^{11}CH_3I + H_2O \qquad (2)$$

ferred to a reaction vessel containing norcocaine (the cocaine molecule minus a methyl group). Carbon-11-labeled methyl iodide reacts with norcocaine to produce carbon-11-labeled cocaine [reaction (3)].

The reaction mixture is purified and formulated in sterile saline solution for positron emission tomography studies. The amount of carbon-11-labeled cocaine produced is a few micrograms, very far below the amount which causes a behavioral effect (usually about 40 milligrams). The sequence of events constituting a radiotracer synthesis, from unloading the target gas to placing the final product in a sterile vial, is done very quickly. For carbon-11-labeled cocaine, the synthesis is accomplished in just under 40 min, which is the equivalent of two half-lives. At this time, for carbon-11, the radioactivity has decayed to one-quarter of its initial activity.

Imaging. Positron decay is at the heart of positron emission tomography imaging. When a positron-emitting radioisotope decays, it emits a positron (a positive electron). The positron travels a very short distance from the nucleus and annihilates with an electron. As a result, two energetic photons (511 keV) are emitted about 180° apart. The annihilation photons penetrate the body barrier and are detected in coincidence by a ring of detectors (**Fig. 1**). By

Most common positron emitters used in tomography		
Positron emitter	Half-life, min	Decay product
Carbon-11	20.4	Boron-11
Nitrogen-13	10.0	Carbon-13
Oxygen-15	2.1	Nitrogen-15
Fluorine-18	109.7	Oxygen-18

using mathematical algorithms, a tomographic map can be created to depict the location and concentration of the positron-emitting isotope within the field of view, typically the human brain. For example, once carbon-11-labeled cocaine has been synthesized, it is transported to the positron emission tomography imaging laboratory. Positron emission tomography studies are approved by an ethical review board, and the individual who has given informed consent to participate in the study is positioned in a custom-fitted head holder to prevent movement inside the positron emission tomography scanner (**Fig. 2**). The radiotracer is injected into the subject's bloodstream and scanning is started. The 511-keV photons resulting from positron decay interact with the detectors and send signals to a computer to display a visual representation of distribution of the radioisotope. The region of interest, usually the brain, is presented as a series of slices, and the distribution of the radioisotope is shown as various colors (representing areas of high and low concentrations of radioisotope). The positron emission tomography scan lasts for approximately one-half hour, with signals being sent from the detector/scanner to a computer which accumulates data at various time intervals. The regions under investigation are stored as two- or three-dimensional images and are reviewed and quantitated to visualize the movement of the drug or the functional status of the brain.

By utilizing various radiotracers, positron emission tomography studies can determine blood flow, glucose metabolism, oxygen metabolism, neurotransmitter and enzyme activity, and drug concentrations in the human brain. Consequently, scientists can learn a great deal about the neurochemistry and physiology of the active human brain. Positron emission tomography scans are used to help identify the regions in the brain where drugs and neurotransmitters are most active. Other useful information is obtained, such as the amount of time for a drug to reach a neurotransmitter receptor, the drugs that activate certain receptors, and the length of time required for the drug to leave the brain.

Drug addiction. Dopamine is a chemical compound (neurotransmitter) involved in physical movement, motivation, and reward. Because of its involvement in reinforcing behaviors, significant drug abuse research is centered on the study of the brain dopamine system. Cocaine, marijuana, amphetamine, heroin, alcohol, and nicotine elevate dopamine levels in the nucleus accumbens, located deep in the brain. Because dopamine plays a central role in human behaviors such as eating and drinking, specific drugs that control dopamine levels could help correct addictive behavior.

Cocaine is one of the most addictive drugs. Indeed, animals given free access to cocaine will self-administer the drug at the expense of life-preserving behaviors such as eating and mating. Positron emission tomography has been used since the mid-1980s to study both the distribution of cocaine in, and its effects on, the human brain. The synthesis of carbon-11-labeled cocaine and other radiotracers made it possible to carry out these investigations. Cocaine was found to localize in the basal ganglia, a brain region containing the nucleus accumbens. Positron emission tomography imaging showed that cocaine blocks a large fraction of the dopamine transporters (protein molecules which terminate the action of dopamine by removing it from the synapse and storing it in the dopamine nerve cell). This information is significant because high dopamine levels in the synapse are associated with the euphoria induced by cocaine and because drugs which block the transporter are important targets in the development of treatments for cocaine abuse.

Another crucial piece of information gleaned from positron emission tomography was the speed with which cocaine binds in the brain. Cocaine reaches its peak concentration in the basal ganglia within 3–5 min after it is injected, and within 30 min most of it has disappeared from the brain. This time course coincides well with the description by addicts who report a very rapid subjective high which declines by 30 min after they inject the drug. This information supports the notion that for a drug to be reinforcing it must be rapidly delivered to the brain. Routes of administration such as intravenous injection or smoking provide the brain with rapid access to a drug.

Although direct labeling of cocaine gives valuable information, it does not provide the complete picture. Other radiotracers are needed to study the diverse effects of drug addiction on the brain. The most commonly employed radiotracer uses fluorine-18 and is called [^{18}F]fluoro-deoxyglucose (^{18}FDG) which is an analog of glucose. Glucose is the major source of energy in the brain, and thus ^{18}FDG provides a map of glucose metabolism there. With ^{18}FDG, abnormalities of glucose metabolism in the

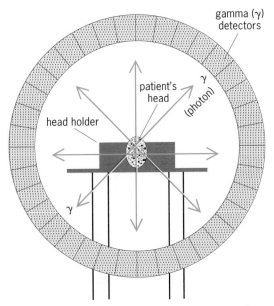

Fig. 2. With the patient positioned inside the scanner, the detectors (in pairs) pick up concurrent signals (coincidence detection).

brains of cocaine abusers have been pinpointed. Positron emission tomography scans show the drastic differences in brain activity of chronic cocaine abusers and normal (control) volunteers, particularly in the orbital-frontal cortex, a brain region important in controlling behavior.

The uses of positron emission tomography to understand the human brain and drug abuse are limited to the highly specific radiotracers being developed. With more radiotracers available than ever before, the maps of underlying biochemical and physiological processes are becoming more complete. Positron emission tomography is not the only technique that can see into the brain, but it is the only way to see where a drug enters the brain and to measure how much. It provides a unique opportunity to understand the link between human brain chemistry and behavior. Positron emission tomography is also applied in clinical diagnosis in heart disease, epilepsy, and cancer.

For background information *see* ADDICTIVE DISORDERS; COCAINE; COMPUTERIZED TOMOGRAPHY; MEDICAL IMAGING; NEUROBIOLOGY; POSITRON; RADIOLOGY in the McGraw-Hill Encyclopedia of Science & Technology.   Joanna S. Fowler; Nora D. Volkow

Bibliography. J. S. Fowler et al., Inhibition of monoamine oxidase B in the brains of smokers, *Nature*, 379:733–736, 1996; J. S. Fowler and N. D. Volkow, Mapping the human brain: Positron emission tomography traces brain metabolism, *Sci. Spectra*, 6:20–27, 1996; J. S. Fowler and A. P. Wolf, New directions in positron emission tomography, Part I, *Annu. Rep. Med. Chem.*, 24:277–286, 1989; J. S. Fowler and A. P. Wolf, Working against time: Rapid radiotracer synthesis and imaging the human brain, *Acct. Chem. Res.*, 30:181–188, 1997; J. S. Fowler, A. P. Wolf, and N. D. Volkow, New directions in positron emission tomography, Part II, *Annu. Rep. Med. Chem.*, 25:261–269, 1990.

Pressure-sensitive paint

The measurement of the pressure on the surface of an object with fluid flow present is important in determining the behavior of fluid flow and calculating the forces imposed by the flow on an object. For example, the shock wave that forms on the upper surface of a commercial transport wing in cruise conditions can be located by knowing the surface pressure distribution. By knowing the pressure distribution over the surface of an automobile, ventilation inlets can be appropriately placed. Aircraft designers determine expected loads by measuring surface pressures on wind-tunnel models and integrating the corresponding forces over the entire surface of the model.

Until recently, the standard method for determining the surface pressure on an object has been to install pressure taps (small round holes in the surface, typically on the order of 0.02 in. or 0.5 mm in diameter) and run tubing from each hole to a transducer. The surface pressure is thus transmitted to the transducer, where it is converted to an electrical signal and recorded by using an analog-to-digital converter interfaced to a computer. Before computers became available, manometer tubes were used, in which the height of a column of mercury or water was visually determined and manually recorded.

Pressure taps have two primary limitations. First, they provide the pressure at only one point on the surface. Obtaining a good understanding of how the pressure changes over a surface requires many pressure taps. A typical fighter wind-tunnel model might have 1000 pressure taps, with associated tubing and transducers. Second, it is often impossible to install pressure taps in regions where knowing the pressure is critical. For example, pressure taps generally cannot be located in the rotating compressor blades in a turbine engine or the thin wing-tip of a wind-tunnel model.

The pressure-sensitive-paint technique overcomes these limitations and allows the measurement of pressure over an entire surface by using a surface coating and optical detection. It is a global measurement rather than a point measurement so the entire surface pressure distribution can be determined, not just the pressure at individual pressure taps. It can also determine pressure on very thin surfaces as well as rotating surfaces.

Basic principle. The basic principle of the pressure-sensitive-paint technique is the oxygen quenching of fluorescence. The surface coating is made up of two components, a probe molecule and an oxygen-permeable binder. When the probe molecule is illuminated by light of an appropriate frequency, typically in the blue to ultraviolet range, it fluoresces at a lower frequency, typically red to orange. In this process, the probe molecule absorbs a photon and is excited to a higher electronic state. There are two ways for the probe molecules usually used in pressure-sensitive paint to relax back to the ground electronic state. One way is to emit a photon of lower energy, in which the orange to red light is produced. The other way is to transfer the energy to an oxygen molecule, in which case no light is produced.

As the concentration of oxygen molecules increases in the paint layer, the probability of probe molecules transferring their energy to an oxygen molecule increases, and thus the fluorescence intensity is reduced. This process is referred to as oxygen quenching. Air is made up of 20.9% oxygen, and therefore, as the air pressure increases, so does the oxygen number density in the paint layer, and thus the fluorescence intensity is reduced.

For a given formulation of pressure-sensitive paint, a relation can be developed between air pressure, luminescence, and incident illumination. However, if only the intensity of the luminescence were to be measured, additional information would be needed to determine the pressure since there are two unknowns, the pressure and the incident illumination. Presently, most pressure-sensitive-paint measurement systems rely on the following technique. The pressure can be determined if two measurements are taken, one at the desired conditions, where the pressure is unknown, and one where the pressure is known. If it is assumed that the temperatures of the two measurements are the same, the ratio of the two luminescence intensities is strictly a function of pressure. Luminescence itself is also a function of temperature, but to a lesser degree. Thus, if the surface temperature varies, errors can be introduced in the pressure measurement.

Alternatively, if a measurement of the incident illumination can be obtained, a reference condition is not required. A technique where two probe molecules are used in the binder is under development. One probe is the standard pressure-sensitive molecule, and the other is a pressure-insensitive probe that has an emission separated far enough in wavelength from the illumination and pressure-sensitive molecule emission so that it can be separated by using optical filters. Thus, no reference condition is required, but two measurements in the run condition must be taken. This discussion focuses on the standard technique that requires a reference measurement.

Measurement setup. In a typical wind-tunnel pressure-sensitive-paint setup (**Fig. 1**), blue lights illuminate the model and the orange luminescence is captured by digital cameras. The blue light is obtained by using narrow-bandwidth filters placed in front of a simple tungsten-halogen light source. Narrow-band filters are also required in front of the digital cameras to eliminate the blue excitation light so that they receive only the orange luminescence from the paint.

Digital cameras currently used have spatial resolutions of 512 by 512 or 1024 by 1024 pixels with 12- to 14-bit gray-level resolution at each pixel. A 14-bit camera yields 1-in-16,384 resolution of the intensity. Such resolution is required for accurate pressure measurements.

All surfaces on which pressures are to be measured must be visible to at least one camera. Thus, with complex wind-tunnel models, as many as 8–10 cameras may be required to determine surface loads on the entire model. Personal computers control the digital cameras and provide images to a graphics workstation, where processing of the images takes place.

In a typical wind-tunnel test, the tunnel is started and the model is positioned in the desired attitude. Then each camera takes an image, called the run image. Multiple run images at various model attitudes may be taken. Then the flow is stopped in the tunnel, allowing the pressure around the model to return to atmospheric pressure, and a reference image is taken with each camera.

Data reduction. The ratio of the luminescence intensities in the reference and run conditions must be determined for each point on the model surface to determine the corresponding pressure. In principle, this is straightforward. The intensity at each pixel of the image for the reference condition can be divided by the intensity of the corresponding pixel of the run image. However, in practice, the model moves with respect to the camera and deforms because of the aerodynamic loads. Thus a pixel-by-pixel ratio is not possible because a given pixel may represent one point on the model in the run image and an entirely different point in the reference image.

To solve these problems, fiducial (alignment) marks are placed on the model. These are small round black dots that are easily identifiable in the image. By using these dots, a biquadratic mapping between the two images can be determined that aligns the fiducial marks in the run image to those in the reference image. Then the ratio can be formed between the reference and run intensities.

To compute loads or to determine the location of

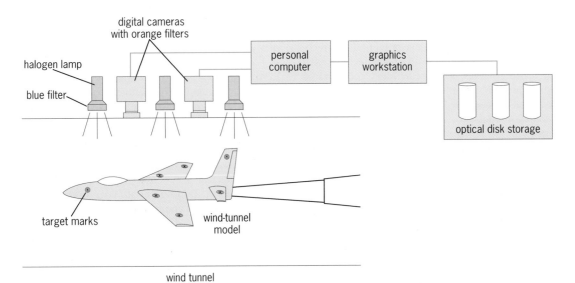

Fig. 1. Typical pressure-sensitive-paint measurement system installed in a wind tunnel.

the pressure measurements for each pixel, a transformation must be determined between the pixel location on the charge-coupled device (CCD) of the digital camera, (m,n), and the coordinate system of the model, (x,y,z). Here, m and n represent integers that locate the particular pixel on the charge-coupled device; for example, the pixel 125 to the left and 30 up from the lower left corner would be $(125,30)$. The values (x,y,z) represent the target location in physical units, such as $(100.5,32.4,76.3)$ inches relative to the origin of the model coordinate system.

Present techniques use target marks placed on the model. These marks are similar to fiducial marks except that the exact location of the dot is known in the model coordinate system for targets. By using the principles of photogrammetry with the information of the target (x,y,z), and the target (m,n), the location of the camera relative to the model when the reference image was obtained can be determined. Once this three-dimensional camera location is found, the transformation from the three-dimensional model surface to the two-dimensional charge-coupled device is known.

A three-dimensional representation of the model surface is required that specifies the locations of points where the pressure is desired. Such a representation is referred to as a grid for the model. It is similar to a computational-fluid-dynamics grid used to compute the flow around an aircraft. Each point in the model grid, (x,y,z), is then projected into the charge-coupled device, (m,n), using the transformation determined for the particular image. Once the location of the point is known in the charge-coupled device, the pressure can be determined by interpolation with the neighboring pixels. Upon completion of this process for each point of the model grid, the surface pressure is known at each desired point on the model surface. Loads can then be determined by integrating the pressures over the various components of the model.

Applications. The pressure-sensitive-paint technique has been successful in a wide variety of applications ranging from the automotive industry to the aircraft industry. Wind-tunnel testing has been the primary driver behind the development of the technique (**Fig. 2**). Pressure-sensitive paint has been used on rotating blades of propellers and compressors where pressure taps are extremely difficult to utilize. It has also been used on internal ducts, such as ventilation ducts.

Most of the applications have been for the measurement of pressure in a steady flow where the pressure is not varying as a function of time. The time response of the technique depends primarily on the diffusion time for oxygen through the binder. Presently, the response of most paints is on the order of 0.5 s, but faster paints are being developed.

Problems. The primary error source in current pressure-sensitive-paint measurement systems is the variation of temperature over the surface of the model. In the above discussion, it was assumed that

Fig. 2. Pressure distribution on the surface of an advanced fighter aircraft wind-tunnel model.

the temperatures were constant between the reference and run conditions to obtain the pressure. In practice, they are not, and an in-situ calibration is employed where several pressure taps on the model are used to determine a calibration for the paint. This technique accounts for changes in temperature from reference to run, but not for a nonuniform temperature distribution over the model surface in either image. Techniques to correct for this variation are under development.

Paint thickness and texture can affect the flow. Usually this is not a problem unless the model is highly polished so as not to promote boundary-layer transition, or if the paint thickness becomes a significant fraction of the local radius of curvature, such as near a sharp leading edge.

The application of the pressure-sensitive-paint technique to typical low-speed wind-tunnel testing presents a particular problem because the technique provides an absolute pressure measurement. In low-speed facilities, the pressure over the model surface changes by only a small percentage of atmospheric pressure. For example, a 100-ft/s (30-m/s) facility may produce only 0.08 lb/in.^{2} (550 pascals) change in pressure relative to an absolute pressure of 14.7 lb/in.^{2} (101,300 Pa), or 0.5% of the absolute pressure. Even with this limitation, quantitative measurements have been obtained at speeds as low as 120 ft/s (37 m/s).

For background information *see* CHARGE-COUPLED DEVICES; FLUORESCENCE; LUMINESCENCE; PRESSURE MEASUREMENT; WIND TUNNEL in the McGraw-Hill Encyclopedia of Science & Technology.   John F. Donovan

Bibliography. J. Donovan et al., Data analysis techniques for pressure and temperature sensitive paint, *AIAA Pap.*, 93-0176, 1993; J. Kavandi et al., Luminescent barometry in wind tunnels, *Rev. Sci. Instrum.*, 61:3340–3347, 1990; M. Morris et al., Aerodynamic applications of pressure sensitive paint, *AIAA J.*, 31:419–425, 1993.

Prion disease

Prion diseases, also known as spongiform encephalopathies, are a group of transmissible disorders that affect the brains of humans and animals and are invariably fatal. The nature of the pathogenic agent is unique. In contrast to all other known infectious agents (for example, viruses, bacteria, yeast), which contain nucleic acids as information carriers, the infectious prion pathogen seems to lack this component. The prevailing view is that the molecule responsible for the transmission of the spongiform encephalopathies is the structural isoform of a protein, named prion protein (the term prion is a skewed acronym for proteinaceous infectious agent). The identification of an infectious agent that apparently does not require a nucleic acid for replication presents a fascinating puzzle in modern biology and medicine.

Molecular basis. A hallmark of spongiform encephalopathies is the cerebral accumulation of an abnormal prion protein which is resistant to proteolytic enzymes. This aberrant protein is derived from a cellular (nonpathogenic) form of prion protein that is normally present. The two forms of the protein have identical sequences of amino acids (the building blocks of proteins) but appear to have markedly different physicochemical properties. While the normally occurring prion protein is soluble in water and easily degradable by proteolytic enzymes, the abnormal prion protein forms insoluble aggregates resistant to enzymatic proteolysis. Furthermore, recent structural studies revealed profound differences in the conformation (three-dimensional shape) of the two protein isoforms: the normal cellular prion protein contains three helices and only two very short strands; the proteolytic enzyme-resistant prion protein has a high content of sheet structure (**Fig. 1**). According to the protein-only hypothesis of prion disease, the sole causative agent is the pathogenic form of the protein (proteolytic enzyme-resistant), and the central event in the transmission of the disease is the conversion of the benign conformation of normally occurring prion protein into the pathological conformation.

In view of the pathogenic mechanism, prion diseases may be classified as conformational diseases. Other examples of this diverse group of otherwise-unrelated disorders, which appear to arise from abnormal folding of an underlying protein (that is different in each case), include Alzheimer's disease, various forms of systemic amyloidosis, Huntington's disease, sickle cell anemia, and cystic fibrosis. However, the unique feature of prion diseases is that they are transmissible.

The mechanism of prion disease propagation is not fully understood. However, rapidly accumulating data support the protein-only hypothesis. The key evidence in this respect was obtained from experiments showing that (1) upon infection with the aberrant prion protein-containing material, transgenic mice devoid of normal prion protein are

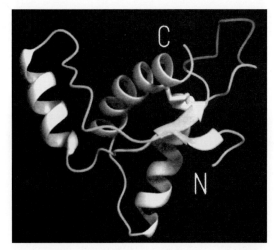

Fig. 1. Ribbon diagram of the structure of the mouse prion protein (domain 121-231), determined by nuclear magnetic resonance spectroscopy. Three α-helices are represented by ribbons and two short β-strands by arrows. (From Riek et al., NMR structure of the mouse prion protein domain PrP (121-231), Nature, 382:180–182, 1996)

completely protected against the pathogen, whereas the wild-type animals (for example, those containing the normal prion protein gene) develop disease; (2) the abnormal prion protein expressed by animals challenged with exogenous prion particles reproduces the physicochemical characteristics of the injected proteolytic enzyme-resistant prion protein. Two distinct models have been proposed for the molecular mechanism of the standard-to-aberrant prion protein conversion (**Fig. 2**). The template-assisted refolding model postulates that, because of a very high energy barrier, the spontaneous conversion of normal prion protein into a resistant form is very unlikely. However, in the presence of the abnormal protein (either acquired by infection or formed spontaneously), the two isoforms interact, generating a proteolytic enzyme-resistant/nonresistant heterodimer. The proteolytic enzyme-resistant prion protein in this complex would act as a template, inducing (or catalyzing) the conversion of normal prion protein to the resistant conformation. The newly formed protein resistant to proteolysis could, in turn, engage in a similar interaction with another responsive (normal) prion protein molecule, resulting in an exponential conversion cascade. According to the seeding model, the infectious unit is not the abnormal prion protein monomer but only a prion protein aggregate, and the conversion occurs as a nucleation-dependent polymerization process. Thus, in the absence of preexisting aberrant prion protein aggregate, the transition between normal and abnormal prion protein is reversible, but the proteolytic enzyme-resistant monomer is less stable than the prion protein susceptible to proteolysis. Stabilization of the resistant conformation occurs only in the presence of a protein oligomer which acts as a template; the monomeric protein can suc-

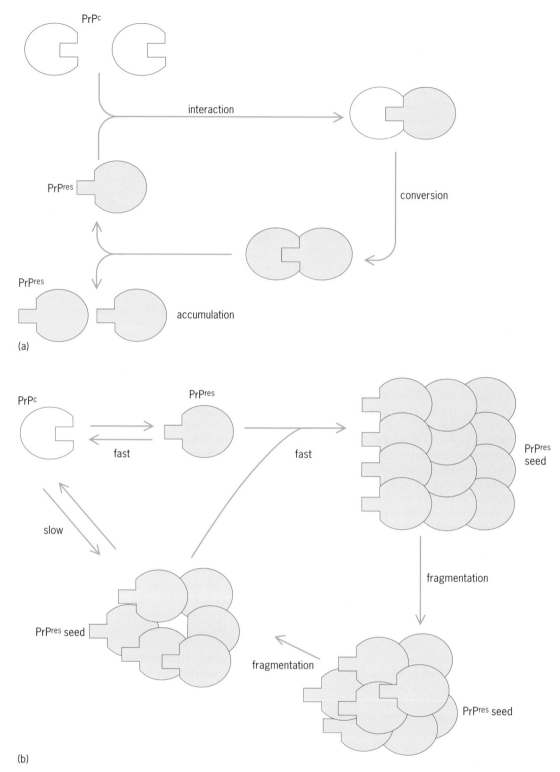

Fig. 2. Models for the conversion of normal prion protein (PrP^C) into prion protein resistant to proteolytic enzymes (PrP^{res}).
(*a*) **The heterodimer model postulates the formation of dimers between PrP^C (open symbols) and PrP^{res} (filled symbols).**
Upon binding, PrP^{res} induces refolding of PrP^C into PrP^{res}, which in turn can induce formation of additional PrP^{res} molecules
by an autocatalytic process. (*b*) The seeding (nucleation-dependent polymerization) model postulates that PrP^{res} aggregate
serves as a seed onto which monomeric protein deposits, adopting its conformational structure. The polymer can then be
fragmented, and the new seeds generated by this process can start nucleation-dependent polymerization again.

cessively deposit onto this template, adopting its conformational structure.

Classification. Prion diseases can be classified according to the mechanisms by which they develop (that is, the forms) and the characteristics of the disease that they cause (that is, the phenotype). Thus, the sporadic form is thought to be caused by the random misfolding of normal prion protein, resulting in the spontaneous formation of the aberrant protein. The inherited form includes diseases linked to one of a number of mutations in the prion protein gene; these mutations are likely to facilitate the spontaneous conversion of prion protein into the resistant form by destabilizing the native structure of the protein. Finally, the acquired forms occur as a result of an infectious process initiated by the introduction of abnormal prion protein–containing material from the outside.

Forms and phenotypes. All inherited forms of prion disease are associated with specific mutations (changes in amino acid sequence) of prion protein. These mutations include replacement of a single amino acid with another, deletion of part of the prion protein molecule, and addition of one or more units of an eight-residue-long amino acid sequence. An important feature of the prion protein is the polymorphism at amino acid residue number 129, which can be either methionine or valine. This polymorphism modulates the risk of acquiring the sporadic and the transmitted forms and can modify the disease phenotype. The mutation at codon 178 causes a disease called fatal familial insomnia when associated with a methionine codon at position 129, and a familial form of Creutzfeldt-Jakob disease when associated with the 129 valine codon. The mutation at codon 200 resulting in the substitution of the amino acid glutamic acid with lysine is the most common mutation associated with familial Creutzfeldt-Jakob disease, while the 102 mutation replacing proline with leucine is commonly associated with Gerstmann-Straussler-Scheinker disease. Overall, prion diseases are rare, with the incidence of about one case per million persons a year. About 85% of the cases are sporadic. All inherited and sporadic forms occur in adults; the age at onset of the acquired form depends on the time of infection. The incubation time varies between 16 and 28 months when the brain tissue is directly contaminated, and 5 and 15 years when the infection occurs peripherally. The Creutzfeldt-Jakobs disease phenotype associated with the familial, sporadic, or iatrogenic forms is characterized by dementia and disturbances of gait and vision. Brain tissue changes can be detected only under the microscope and are characterized by the presence of small spongelike holes, referred to as spongiform degeneration. Features of fatal familial insomnia include inability to sleep and severe loss of nerve cells in a region at the center of the brain called the thalamus. The Gerstmann-Straussler-Scheinker disease phenotype most often includes a slowly progressive gait disturbance and other disturbances due to cerebellar dysfunction; the microscopic pathology is distinct for the presence of amyloidlike deposits. The capacity to spread through an infectious mechanism potentially makes prion diseases a serious threat to public health.

Prion epidemics. Over 200 cases of the infectious form of the disease have been transmitted through medical interventions; these cases are commonly referred to as iatrogenic (pertaining to a secondary condition arising from treatment of a primary condition) Creutzfeldt-Jakob disease. The carriers of the infection are implants of contaminated human tissues, such as the cornea and the external layer of the brain covering called dura mater, the hormones extracted from the pituitary gland, and contaminated surgical instruments. The first evidence that prion diseases can be acquired by the ingestion of contaminated food was provided in the 1950s by the discovery of kuru, a disease affecting endemically a New Guinea tribe that practiced cannibalism. A prion disease of sheep and goats called scrapie has been known for over two centuries, but no cases of human transmission have been recorded. A major epidemic of a prion disease affecting cattle, called bovine spongiform encephalopathy or mad cow disease, broke out in the United Kingdom in 1986. Bovine spongiform encephalopathy was transmitted by meat and bone meal derived from infected cattle and other ruminants that had not undergone appropriate denaturing treatment during the rendering process. The epidemics peaked in 1992 and are now rapidly receding. To date, mad cow disease has affected approximately 200,000 cows from over 34,000 herds. A few years after the bovine spongiform encephalopathy epidemics, a new human prion disease with a phenotype distinct from that of sporadic Creutzfeldt-Jakob disease was observed in the United Kingdom. To date, 21 cases of new variant Creutzfeldt-Jakob disease have been reported in the United Kingdom and one in France. The major features that distinguish new variant Creutzfeldt-Jakob disease from the typical type include earlier onset and the widespread presence in the brain of microscopic prion protein deposits surrounded by vacuoles, named daisy plaques. Substantial evidence has been accumulated to indicate that new variant Creutzfeldt-Jakob disease might have been acquired from bovine spongiform encephalopathy–affected cattle. The link between animal and human forms of the disease justifies the precautionary measures that have been instituted throughout Europe and the United States.

For background information *see* MUTATION; NERVOUS SYSTEM DISORDERS; VIRUS INFECTION, LATENT, PERSISTENT, SLOW in the McGraw-Hill Encyclopedia of Science & Technology.

Pierluigi Gambetti; Witold Surewicz

Bibliography. A. Aguzzi and C. Weissmann, Prion research: The next frontiers, *Nature*, 389:795, 798, 1997; H. Büeler et al., Mice devoid of PrP are resistant to scrapie, *Cell*, 73:1339–1347, 1993; P. Gambetti, B. Ghetti, and P. Parchi, Human prion diseases, in *Progress in Pathology*, 1997; S. B. Prusiner, Novel proteinaceous infectious particles causing scrapie, *Science*, 216:136–144, 1982; G. C. Telling et al., Evidence for the conformation of the pathologic isoform of the prion protein enciphering and propagating prion diversity, *Science*, 274:2079–2082, 1996.

Propellant modification

Liquid rocket propellants often require the largest component volume aboard a rocket vehicle. They must be contained by very bulky and heavy tanks that keep the liquids at the right pressure and temperature until they are used in a rocket engine. An increase in the propellant density, or mass per volume, can reduce the mass of the tanks, structure, and other parts of the rocket that depend upon the propellant volume. The use of higher-density propellants is therefore an excellent way to improve the performance of rocket vehicles. Reducing the mass of the rocket will lead in turn to a reduction in the weight of fuel needed to move the rocket, so there is a powerful cascade effect.

Reducing the weight of a rocket is also made possible by using a higher-energy fuel, because less fuel is needed. This energy is related to the exhaust velocity or specific impulse of the rocket engine, which is essentially a miles-per-gallon analogy for rockets. The higher the energy of the fuel, the higher the specific impulse. Adding energy to the fuel by changing its chemistry, gelling the fuel, or gelling and adding particles of metal or other higher-energy compounds can increase the specific impulse.

Several methods of increasing the density of the propellants have been used in the past. One method adds small metal particles, or frozen liquid particles, and suspends them in the fuel or oxidizer. A gelling agent is used to thicken the fuel and allow the suspension of the solid particles. The gelling agent may be frozen liquid particles, solid particles, or long-chained liquid polymers. Gelling the fuel without adding metal particles can also increase the density and change the energy of the fuel. The gelling agent itself can add energy and increase the density, but the energy and density increases are much larger if metal additives are also used.

This article outlines the methods of gelling propellants, the methods of increasing their energy with metal combustion, and the overall vehicle and mission benefits of these procedures. Several propellant types are illustrated, and the benefits of gelled hydrogen with no added metal and of metallized gelled propellants are described.

Gelling propellants. Gelling is a way of increasing the viscosity or thickness of a liquid propellant. A shear-thinning liquid is a desirable choice for the gelled fuel consistency. When such a liquid begins to flow, its viscosity drops, and the lower viscosity allows the liquid to flow more easily, and be easily pumped from the propellant tank to the rocket engine. When the liquid is not flowing, the thickened liquid helps to suspend the additives. Thus, the additives or metal particles are uniformly distributed in the fuel, and can remain there until needed by the engine.

Metal combustion. Metal is typically added to the fuel in the form of fine particles. The finer the particle, the better the combustion properties. Particle sizes of 5–10 micrometers are used in metallized gelled fuels. Many different metal additives have been investigated, but aluminum is an excellent overall choice. In most cases, aluminum metal additives improve the specific impulses of rocket propellants (see **table**). Though the performance benefits may seem small, these increases in specific impulse have a powerful effect on reducing the overall mass of rocket vehicles, as discussed below. Even though the specific impulse decreases in some cases, the increase in propellant density that results from metal additives can still improve overall rocket payload capability.

Carbon and boron are also candidates for metal additives, having good combustion properties. Metal atoms, as well as molecules, are also potential fuel additives. The atoms would be stored in a solid cryogenic ice, made of hydrogen at 4 K ($-452°$F), a very low temperature. In the more traditional liquid rocket propellants, only metal molecules are desirable. The metal atoms are very unstable at temperatures above 10 K ($-441°$F), and will tend to recombine into molecules before their energy can be used in the rocket engine. These very advanced propellants have not been demonstrated and are far in the future, but their potential is very promising, as their specific impulse can be greater than 750 s, more than 50% higher than traditional oxygen/hydrogen propellants (that is, propellants that use oxygen as the oxidizer and hydrogen as the fuel).

Studies of gelled propellants. Metallized gelled rocket propellants have been considered for many different applications. Numerous studies have shown the potential benefits of gelled fuels and oxidizers. While operational usage has not yet occurred, many technology programs are under way to eliminate the unknowns with gelled propellants and the propulsion systems that will use them. Technology programs to prove the combustion performance of gelled propellants have been conducted most recently for tactical missile applications. Metallized

Specific impulses for metallized gelled propellants with aluminum metal additive*			
Propellant (oxidizer/fuel)	Specific impulse, s		Metal loading in fuel, weight percent
	Without metal	With metal	
Oxygen/hydrogen	419	428	60
Oxygen/kerosine (RP-1)	325	319	55
Nitrogen tetroxide/ monomethyl hydrazine	308	319	40
* For first-stage booster engines with an expansion ratio of 30:1.			

gelled propellants have also been investigated for missions of the National Aeronautics and Space Administration (NASA), and experimental programs have been conducted to validate elements of the combustion and fuel technology. The propellants studied for NASA missions were oxygen/hydrogen/aluminum and oxygen/kerosine/aluminum (with the notation oxidizer/fuel/metal additive), where the kerosine was in a highly refined form called rocket propellant 1 (RP-1). Gelled and metallized gelled hydrogen and kerosine have been emphasized because hydrogen and kerosine are typical propellants for NASA launch vehicles and upper stages. Derivatives of these propellants are therefore preferred to minimize the incremental risk for a newly introduced propulsion concept.

Benefits of gelled hydrogen. Gelled hydrogen's most likely applications would be for rocket-powered launch vehicles and upper stages; rocket-based, combined-cycle, air-breathing vehicles; and combination (rocket and air-breathing) propulsion options. Air-breathing space vehicles will typically have a large hydrogen tank, making up the largest portion of the volume of the vehicle. Any method of reducing the volume of that tank will benefit such space vehicles.

There are five major benefits of gelled hydrogen propellants: safety increases; boil-off reductions; density increases, with the attendant area- and volume-related mass reductions for related subsystems (the thermal protection system, structure, insulation, and so forth); slosh reductions; and increases in the specific impulse (in some cases).

Safety can be significantly increased with gelled fuels, compared to conventional propellants. A higher viscosity reduces the spill radius of the gelled hydrogen and limits the potential damage and hazard from a fuel spill. Another advantage is the potential for leak reduction or elimination. The leak paths from the feed systems would be minimized, and the possible explosion potential would be reduced. Boil-off reduction is another feature of gelled hydrogen, and boil-off would be reduced up to a factor of 2 to 3 over ungelled liquid hydrogen. This feature would assist in long-term storage of hydrogen for upper stages that must remain in orbit for long periods of time or require long coast times between firings. Also, lunar and interplanetary missions with large hydrogen fuel loads would derive a benefit.

Significant density increases are possible and have been demonstrated with gelled hydrogen. A 10% density increase is possible for hydrogen with an ethane or methane additive constituting 10% of the mixture by weight. These gellants are introduced as frozen particles that form a gel structure in the hydrogen. A material called a nanoparticulate can also be used for gelling, and it can reduce the amount of gellant needed to 7–8% by weight. Further theoretical studies have shown that the addition of metal particles can achieve much greater increases in density (to over three times the density of liquid hydrogen with a 70% aluminum loading by weight), but

the complexities of metal combustion must be overcome to make this fuel fully successful.

Applications. Many different applications of metallized gelled propellants have been investigated. The vehicle types include launch vehicles, which take payloads to low earth orbit; upper stages, which help move payloads from low Earth orbits to high orbits; and missions to Mars.

Space shuttle boosters. One way of using higher-density fuels is to replace a rocket booster by using an alternative technology. For example, studies have been carried out to determine the effects of replacing the solid rocket boosters of the space shuttle with liquid rocket boosters using propellants such as oxygen/kerosine/aluminum. These analyses were conducted to find ways to improve the shuttle's payload performance to the International Space Station. The performance can be increased several ways. Very significant reductions in booster length are possible with these high-density metallized fuels (see **illus.**). These length reductions can ease the ground handling of the boosters, and reduce the drag during ascent, thus improving the shuttle's performance. Alternatively, the metallized gelled booster length can be allowed to grow to that of the solid rocket booster, and the payload performance of the space shuttle then increases by 14% for kerosine (RP-1) fuel with 55% aluminum loading by weight, and by 35% for monomethyl hydrazine fuel with 50% aluminum loading by weight. Additional increases in payload performance are possible with small increases in the diameter of the metallized gelled liquid rocket booster. A 1-ft (0.3-m) increase in diameter, from 12 to 13 ft (3.7 to 4.0 m), increases the shuttle payload in low Earth orbit from 50,000 to 70,500 lb (22,680 to 31,980 kg), using kerosine (RP-1) fuel with 55% aluminum loading by weight.

Upper stages. Special, very fast (high-energy) missions can use metallized gelled fuels to the greatest

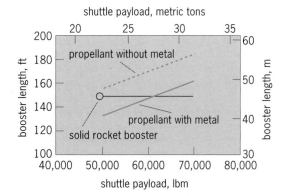

Graph of length of liquid rocket booster versus payload mass of space shuttle. The liquid rocket booster carries the oxidizer/fuel combination oxygen/kerosine (RP-1), with or without 55% aluminum metal loading by weight. Length and payload performance of a solid rocket booster now in use are also shown. *(After B. Palaszewski and J. Zakany, Metallized Gelled Propellants: Oxygen/RP-1/Aluminum Rocket Heat Transfer and Combustion Experiments, AIAA Pap. 96-2622, 1996)*

advantage. On any fast mission, very high velocity changes are needed, and an increased specific impulse is required to make the size of the upper stage manageable and affordable. On high-speed missions, metallized gelled propellants can sometimes double the payload of robot missions. Studies of fast missions to Uranus showed that oxygen/hydrogen/aluminum propellants would allow transport of heavy payloads that are beyond the capacity of current chemical propellants.

Mars missions. By using metallized propellants for human Mars missions, more payload can be delivered on each mission. This increase is made possible by the higher specific impulse of the oxygen/hydrogen/aluminum propellants. The baseline payload for a fast expedition or sprint flight to Mars, using an oxygen/hydrogen propellant without metal additives, is 55,000 lb (25 metric tons), and the specific impulse of this propellant is 470 s. A metal loading of 60% aluminum by weight increases the specific impulse only by about 1%, to 475 s, but increases the payload by 22%. With a 70% aluminum loading, by weight, which improves the specific impulse to 480 s, the payload increase is 33%, with over 73,000 lb (33 metric tons) of payload delivered to Mars. *See* MARS.

For background information *see* METAL-BASE FUEL; PROPELLANT; ROCKET PROPULSION; SPECIFIC IMPULSE in the McGraw-Hill Encyclopedia of Science & Technology.   Bryan Palaszewski

Bibliography. B. Palaszewski, Metallized propellants for the human exploration of Mars, *AIAA J. Propul. Pow.*, 8:1192–1199, 1992; B. Palaszewski and R. Powell, Launch vehicle propulsion using metallized propellants, *AIAA J. Propul. Pow.*, 6:828–833, 1994.

Prosthesis

Total knee replacement is the substitution of the knee joint with a mechanical device called a prosthesis that provides relief of pain, stability of motion, and correction of the deformity. It is particularly appropriate for individuals with painfully disabling arthritis that is no longer responsive to nonsurgical treatment. An estimated 129,000 of these procedures are performed in the United States alone each year. Successful outcome depends on candidate selection, careful surgical technique, postoperative rehabilitation, and prevention of complications.

Biomechanics of the knee. Kinematics, stability, normal alignment, and balance through weight distribution are important considerations in the design and development of the knee prosthesis. The material of the prosthesis must be biologically compatible, as well as resistant to friction and wear. Early prosthesis designs failed because they considered the knee as a simple hinge, with flexion and extension limited to a single axis. Kinematic studies have shown that the knee is extremely complex, providing multicentered, polyaxial movements during the course of a normal gait cycle. In addition to kinematics, static magnitude and distribution of forces in a variety of positions and activities must be considered. It has been calculated that the load applied to the knee while walking on a level surface equals three times the body weight. In climbing stairs or running, these forces are increased to between four and seven times the body weight.

The alignment of the lower limb determines the distribution of weight across the joint. Deformities such as bow legs or knock knees can cause the mechanical axis and the transmission of weight to be moved, to the inside in bow legs and to the outside in knock knees. This increased strain on one side of the joint, with all the forces concentrated in a much smaller area, accelerates wear and tear and promotes the arthritic process. Similarly, if alignment is not correct after knee prosthesis, there will be a tendency to loosen and fail. Careful surgical technique is extremely important in obtaining correction of the deformity, proper alignment of the extremity, and equal distribution of weight.

Original prosthesis designs consisted of metal bearing on metal. This created very high friction and excessive wear, resulting in painful loosening, much infection, and an unacceptable rate of failure. In 1960, a low-friction hip replacement was developed that consisted of a stainless steel femoral component bearing on a high-density polyethylene pelvic component, both being fixed to bone with polymethylmethacrylate cement. Soon after, a knee prosthesis based on this concept was developed. Many improvements and modifications have appeared over the years, but the basic principle of metal bearing on polyethylene still applies.

Materials. The metals used must be biocompatible and of sufficient mechanical strength to withstand cyclic body forces. The common ones are alloys based on cobalt, titanium, and iron. Iron-based alloys or stainless steel have a low fatigue strength and are susceptible to corrosion inside the body. Although used for the original hip prosthesis, they are currently employed only for temporary devices such as bone plates, bone screws, and intramedullary nails. In the case of cobalt and titanium alloys, two components must be considered: the stem and the bearing surface. Cobalt alloys have high wear resistance that makes them desirable for load supporting and as bearing surfaces. Titanium alloys have a low density that makes them stronger than any other metal, with a high modulus of elasticity; that is, their stiffness is most similar to that of bone. However, their poor shear strength and low wear resistance make titanium alloys unsuitable for bearing surfaces. Hence, a titanium alloy stem is combined with a cobalt-chrome alloy bearing surface in both hip and knee prostheses.

Ultrahigh-molecular-weight polyethylene is a plastic whose viscoelastic properties give it limited flexibility under loading conditions, thus imparting a remarkable resistance to wear.

Fixation. There are three methods of fixing a prosthesis to the bone: polymethylmethacrylate cement, a porous coated metal surface that allows fixation by bony ingrowth into the implant, and press-fit design.

Cement. Polymethylmethacrylate is a cold-curing acrylic polymer. It is self-curing, having a catalyst in the powder and an accelerator in the liquid. In joint replacement, it is used as a filler to fix the component securely to the bone—much like the quality of mortar between bricks—and to transfer stress from the surface of the component to the larger bone surface, thus reducing pressure per unit of surface. This polymer can withstand considerable compression, although it fails under tension or shear stresses. The surface or bone cavity is prepared by washing to eliminate debris, blood, and clots, and then drying it. The polymethylmethacrylate is introduced to the cavity or surface with pressure, and the prosthesis is inserted. Excess cement that flows out from the sides is removed, and the prosthesis is held in position until the cement cures to a solid state. This can take 8–13 min, depending on the formulation of the cement and the temperature of the room.

Coated metal. Polymethylmethacrylate-fixed implants have a relatively high risk of loosening, especially in young, active people. Therefore, alternative methods of fixation have been developed. Porous coated metal prostheses have an irregular surface, allowing ingrowth of new bone into the irregularities. The fixation becomes biological, since bone grows into the interstices of the prosthesis; the greater the stress, the stronger the fixation. This technique uses porous metals, created by sintering cobalt-chrome powder or beads and by diffusion-bonding titanium wire mesh. Most porous coatings are composed of multiple layers up to 800 micrometers thick, with interconnecting open pores between the various particles, allowing for ingrowth of bone. The ingrowth occurs if the pores are greater than 40 μm in diameter, if micromotion is absent, and if the porous surface is in intimate contact with the bone.

Press fit. Press-fit designs achieve fixation by interference fit; the surgical technique and preparation of the bone must be very precise. The bone is whittled down to fit the prosthesis and then jammed into it. However, there is always the risk of bone fracture.

Conditions for use. Arthritis that has not responded to medical treatment and produces severe pain and disability requires total knee replacement. Medical management such as anti-inflammatory compounds, physical therapy, and restriction of activity should be continued as long as possible. In young individuals, and depending on the degree and severity of the arthritis, alternative surgical methods should be considered. These include arthroscopy of the knee with cleaning out of the joint, and elimination of tissue damaged by arthritis. Osteotomy, which involves cutting the bone, can correct the deformity (bow legs or knock knees), realign the extremity, and transfer weight to the unaffected side of the joint. However, there are numerous reasons for doing total replacement, including end-stage joint destruction due to osteoarthritis, rheumatoid arthritis

and other inflammatory processes such as systemic lupus erythematosus and juvenile rheumatoid arthritis, osteonecrosis, arthritis due to injury (traumatic arthritis), and arthritis due to crystal deposition diseases such as gout or pseudogout.

With advances in technology, surgical skill, and understanding of joint replacement, many former reasons for not doing this procedure have become less absolute. Infections of the knee used to be a reason, but they can now sometimes be treated by radical surgical cleaning out of the joint, plus antibiotic therapy. Once the infection is cleared, the knee usually has enough bone and ligamentous support to allow reconstruction. If the infection cannot be adequately controlled, replacement should not be attempted.

One condition that remains a problem is marked weakness of the musculature. Unless the individual has active muscular control of knee function, including straightening and bending, it is unlikely that the procedure will be successful. Surgical stiffening of the knee that was converted to a total knee replacement has not usually been successful because the muscle integrity around the knee had been significantly compromised by the stiffening itself.

Complications. For a major surgical procedure, there are relatively few complications associated with knee replacement. However, replacement is usually done in persons of advanced age, and careful evaluation of overall health is essential. Possible complications include formation of blood clots that can travel to the lungs, and superficial infection of the skin at the edges of the wound. The latter can be treated without difficulty, but infection deep in the knee joint is a devastating complication that requires intravenous antibiotics and removal of the prosthesis in order to clean the wound. Depending on the causal bacteria, a new prosthesis can be implanted either immediately or after 6–8 weeks of antibiotic therapy, when the infection is completely eradicated. Fortunately, the incidence of infection is less than 1%. Other complications include fracture of the bone, stiffness of the knee, nerve injury, and damage to the major arteries. The last, fortunately, is rare.

For background information *see* ALLOY; ARTHRITIS; BIOMEDICAL ENGINEERING; JOINT (ANATOMY); PROSTHESIS in the McGraw-Hill Encyclopedia of Science & Technology.   Enrique Ergas

Bibliography. J. J. Callaghan et al. (eds.), *Orthopedic Knowledge Update: Hip and Knee Reconstruction*, 1995; A. H. Crenshaw, *Campbell's Operative Orthopedics*, 1992; J. N. Insall et al., *Surgery of the Knee*, 1993; W. Petty, *Total Joint Replacement*, 1991.

Protein

Proteins are heteropolymers built from the 20 naturally occurring amino acids. These molecules, which may contain fewer than 50 or as many as several hundred amino acids, adopt unique three-dimensional structures (folds) determined by the sequence of amino acids in the polymeric chain. In the late 1960s, C. Levinthal formulated the paradox that an impossibly long period of time is required to fold an average-sized protein by a random search of all possible conformations. The fact that proteins fold quite rapidly demonstrates that they follow folding pathways to reach their equilibrium conformations. Understanding how proteins form their unique structures from nonnative conformations remains a challenge for both theory and experiment.

Time scales. The complex process of protein folding involves dynamics on time scales that range from picoseconds to minutes. Until recently, however, studies of whole-protein folding have been limited to the millisecond and longer time regime. Rapid mixing techniques, including stopped-flow kinetic spectroscopy and pulsed deuterium-exchange nuclear magnetic resonance methods, have provided the vast majority of the available experimental data on whole-protein folding kinetics. In many proteins, a submillisecond burst phase is observed during folding. It has been speculated that during the burst phase there is a collapse to a compact denatured state with partial secondary-structure formation. These burst-phase dynamics have spurred the development of new techniques for studying protein folding on submillisecond time scales.

Techniques. Multiple spectroscopic methods are required to monitor all steps in the folding process. The simplest probe, ultraviolet-visible absorption spectroscopy, provides little structural information, but has excellent time resolution and can be quite sensitive to some steps in the folding process, particularly for intensely colored heme proteins. Far-ultraviolet circular dichroism spectroscopy is a valuable tool for evaluating the secondary structure content of proteins, and can provide vital information about the folding process. The time resolution of conventional circular dichroism spectrophotometers is limited to about 10 milliseconds, but microsecond and faster techniques have been developed. Infrared absorption arising from C=O bond vibrations in the peptide backbone is also sensitive to secondary structure, and has been applied recently to time-resolved measurements of protein folding. Another vibrational spectroscopy, resonance Raman, has been useful for characterizing the environment of heme prosthetic groups during protein folding. The intensity of fluorescence from aromatic amino acids (such as phenylalanine, tyrosine, and tryptophan) depends on the environment of the fluorophore. In addition, fluorescent labels that report on folding can be attached to specific sites on protein surfaces. Time-resolved fluorescence spectroscopy (often with laser excitation of the fluorophore) is used to measure the folding dynamics of specific regions in a protein. The greatest detail about the folding process comes from nuclear magnetic resonance spectroscopy, which can provide information about individual amino acids in a protein and has been used to provide residue-specific insight into protein folding.

Light-scattering provides information on the global dimensions of a protein in solution. Dynamic laser light scattering and small-angle x-ray scattering are used to measure the radii of folded and unfolded proteins, and could provide critical information about protein-folding pathways. Thus far, these techniques lack the sensitivity or time resolution required for measurements of fast protein-folding kinetics.

Kinetics. In order to understand more fully the kinetics behind protein folding, various technqiues are used, such as rapid mixing, temperature jumps, and photochemical triggers.

Rapid mixing. Many proteins can be reversibly unfolded by high concentrations of chemical denaturants (for example, urea and guanidine hydrochloride). Mixing a denatured protein solution with diluent will initiate refolding. Stopped-flow mixing is the traditional method employed to study protein-folding kinetics. With mixing times on the order of a few milliseconds and with ultraviolet-visible, circular-dichroism, and fluorescence probes, stopped-flow investigations of protein folding have provided a wealth of data on protein-folding kinetics. Stopped-flow investigations of site-specific mutants of barnase and chymotrypsin inhibitor 2 have been used to measure the degree of native structure formation about individual amino acids in the folding transition state. New techniques that employ smaller solution volumes have pushed the experiment dead time below 100 μs. These methods, employing Raman spectroscopic probes, have revealed that some of the earliest events in the folding of a heme protein, cytochrome c, involve changes in ligation to the heme.

In a folded protein, the amide protons of the polypeptide backbone exchange very slowly with those of the solvent (water), but in an unfolded protein these protons exchange very rapidly. Protection from amide-proton exchange forms the basis of a particularly powerful method for studying protein folding. Pulsed deuterium-exchange measurements provide information about the degree of protection from exchange of individual amino acids during the folding process. This approach, which depends on conventional mixing methods to initiate folding and quench the exchange reactions, has been used to describe in great detail the folding of cytochrome c on millisecond and longer time scales.

Temperature jump. The position of the equilibrium between a folded and unfolded protein is a sensitive function of temperature. Most proteins will unfold at elevated temperatures (heat denaturation), and some at low temperatures as well (cold denaturation). Folding and unfolding processes can, therefore, be initiated by rapid temperature jumps. Temperature jumps initiated by Joule heating can achieve microsecond time resolution. The early events in the folding of a cold-denatured 89-residue ribonuclease inhibitor (barstar) have been investigated by this approach. By using protein fluorescence as a probe, the denatured form of the barstar was found to collapse in less than 500 μs upon raising the temperature from 2 to 10°C (36 to 50°F), yielding a discrete intermediate with some fluxional secondary structure. Folding to the fully native form of the protein requires hundreds of milliseconds.

Pulsed lasers can heat protein solutions in nanoseconds or even picoseconds. Nanosecond time-resolved laser temperature jump has been used to trigger the folding of cold-denatured apomyoglobin. These experiments, in which tryptophan fluorescence was used to monitor folding, suggest that the collapse of the unfolded protein to a compact denatured state requires just 20 μs.

Measurements of the rates of peptide and protein unfolding can provide information about the dynamics of the folding process. If there are only two states involved (folded and unfolded), the ratio of the rates of folding to unfolding must equal the equilibrium constant for folding. Investigations of temperature-jump-induced unfolding of proteins and small peptides have been aimed at characterizing the time scales for secondary structure formation. Time-resolved infrared spectroscopy has been used to probe the secondary structure of a 21-residue helical peptide following a laser temperature jump from 9 to 27°C (48 to 81°F). The time constant for unfolding was found to be 160 nanoseconds, implying a folding time constant of less than 20 ns. Laser temperature-jump unfolding of apomyoglobin at 60°C (140°F), again probing with time-resolved infrared, reveals that the rate of α-helix formation is three orders of magnitude faster than the rate of formation of tertiary contacts between helical segments. The data suggest that the folding process involves disordered intermediates comprising a heterogeneous mixture of structures.

Photochemical triggers. A common approach for fast kinetics studies involves the use of laser-initiated photochemistry to trigger the chemical process of interest. This approach is just beginning to find applications in protein-folding research.

Binding carbon monoxide to the heme of ferrocytochrome *c* destabilizes the protein toward denaturants. Within the range of denaturant concentrations in which the carbon monoxide–bound protein is unfolded and the native form of the protein is folded, carbon monoxide can be dissociated from the heme in a few nanoseconds (or less) by pulsed-laser photolysis to initiate protein folding. Studies using time-resolved ultraviolet-visible and tryptophan fluorescence spectroscopies suggest that heme-ligand binding processes dominate the submillisecond folding kinetics.

Thermodynamic analyses point to another photochemical approach for initiating the folding of many redox-active proteins. The formal potentials of redox cofactors in proteins are often shifted substantially from their aqueous-solution values. If the active-site reduction potentials are different for the folded and unfolded states, the free energies of folding the oxi-

dized and reduced proteins will differ by a comparable amount. This method has great promise for folding investigations because of the many well-established techniques for rapidly injecting and removing electrons from proteins on time scales as short as a few nanoseconds. The oxidized form of cytochrome *c* unfolds more readily than the reduced form, and there is a wide range of denaturant concentrations where the oxidized protein is unfolded and the reduced protein is folded. Laser-initiated electron injection into unfolded oxidized cytochrome *c* rapidly generates the reduced unfolded protein, which then proceeds to fold. Electron-transfer-triggered folding studies, using time-resolved ultraviolet-visible spectroscopy as a probe, have revealed processes that likely arise from changes in heme ligation. The rate constant for the subsequent formation of fully folded cytochrome *c* has been shown to be a sensitive function of the folding driving force.

For background information *see* AMINO ACIDS; PEPTIDE; PHOTOCHEMISTRY; PROTEIN; SPECTROSCOPY in the McGraw-Hill Encyclopedia of Science & Technology.   Jay R. Winkler

Bibliography. R. L. Baldwin, Why is protein-folding so fast?, *Proc. Nat. Acad. Sci. USA*, 93:2627–2628, 1996; T. E. Creighton (ed.), *Protein Folding*, 1992; K. A. Dill and H. S. Chan, From Levinthal to pathways to funnels, *Nature Struc. Biol.*, 4:10–19, 1997; K. W. Plaxco and C. M. Dobson, Time-resolved biophysical methods in the study of protein-folding, *Curr. Opin. Struc. Biol.*, 6:630–636, 1996.

Proton radioactivity

Proton radioactivity is a process by which an unstable nucleus spontaneously decays by the emission of a proton. Other common types of radioactivity include beta decay (the emission of electrons or positrons), alpha decay (the emission of a helium-4 nucleus), and gamma decay (the emission of high-energy photons). Proton decay is simpler than other forms of radioactivity since the proton is one of the constituents of the nucleus, and thus provides an opportunity to study details of nuclear structure.

All atomic nuclei are composed of protons and neutrons. The number of protons, Z, determines the element of the atom, and the total number of nucleons (protons and neutrons) determines the mass. The nucleons are bound together to form the nucleus by a strong interaction called the nuclear force. The stability of a particular nuclide depends critically upon the relative numbers of protons and neutrons of which it is composed. Only 262 nuclides are found in nature that are stable. The dependence of stability on the number of protons and the number of neutrons, N, can be seen in a chart of the nuclides (**Fig. 1**), in which every possible nuclide is allocated a box. The stable nuclides lie in a particular region of the chart, called the valley of stability. Nuclei in the regions adjacent to the valley of stability have been experimentally observed, and some of their

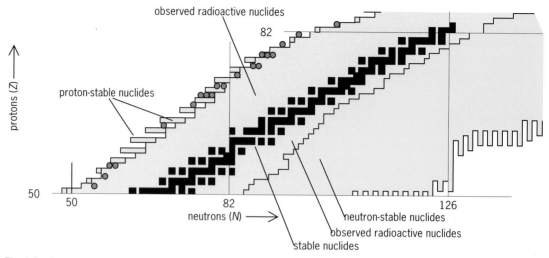

Fig. 1. Portion of the periodic chart of the nuclides for neutron number (*N*) and proton number (*Z*) greater than 50. The black boxes represent the stable nuclides. Observed radioactive nuclides have had some properties measured. Nuclides termed proton-stable or neutron-stable are predicted to be stable to spontaneous proton or neutron emission in their ground states. Known proton emitters are indicated with circles.

properties have been measured. They decay toward the valley of stability by the emission of electrons, positrons, or alpha particles or the capture of an orbital electron. Adjacent to the regions of observed nuclides, in turn, are regions of nuclides that are predicted to be stable to spontaneous proton or neutron emission in their ground states. Beyond these regions, whose limits are called the proton and neutron drip lines, nuclei are unstable toward the emission of a neutron or proton. The location of the neutron and proton drip lines is not completely known because of the lack of experimental data in these regions far from stability. Theoretical mass formulas can predict the location of the drip lines. Only nuclides that are beyond the proton drip line can decay by proton radioactivity. Thus, proton radioactivity is limited to nuclei that are very far from stability, and can be studied only for a very limited selection of isotopes. The exploration of this region of the periodic chart at the limits of nuclear stability had to await the development of powerful heavy-ion accelerators and sophisticated detection techniques. Recent proton radioactivity measurements are beginning to establish the location of the proton drip line.

Mechanism and controlling factors. Protons are attracted to the nucleus by the nuclear force, while they are repelled by the Coulomb (electric) force. Thus, there is a competition between these forces in the determination of whether a proton will be spontaneously emitted from the nucleus. This competition can be seen in a cross-sectional view of the potential energy of a proton in the presence of a nucleus (**Fig. 2**). A curve can be drawn to indicate the Coulomb potential energy, that is, the potential energy that a proton would have if only the Coulomb force were active. The nucleus would look like a tall mountain, and a proton would have considerable

energy at the top (the center of the nucleus). Another curve (Fig. 2) shows the Coulomb and nuclear potential, that is, the potential energy that a proton will have if the strong nuclear force on it is also included. The attraction of the nuclear force produces a deep crater in the top of the Coulomb mountain. Protons caught deep inside the crater are effectively trapped. If the highest-energy proton has an energy less than zero relative to the potential energy at large distances, there is no possibility of its escape unless the nucleus receives energy from outside. However, for nuclei beyond the proton drip line, the least-bound proton has a positive energy, and hence, if it can get over the rim of the crater, it will be accelerated toward large radii by the repulsive Coulomb force.

A horizontal line (Fig. 2) can be used to represent the energy of the least-bound proton in thulium-145, about 1.7 MeV. The energy is much smaller than the potential energy of a proton at the rim of the crater, and thus classically, one would expect this proton to be trapped. However, because of the uncertainty principle in quantum mechanics, there is a finite chance that the proton can tunnel through the barrier. The barrier penetration probability depends very critically on the total energy of the proton; if the proton has an energy near the potential energy at the rim of the crater, the decay will occur very rapidly, while for small decay energies, the decay will occur very slowly. In the first case the decay would possibly be too fast to give experimenters a chance at measuring it, while in the second case the decay may be too slow to compete with the normal beta (β^+) decay of the nucleus. Thus, there is a very narrow band of energies (and nuclei) where proton radioactivity can be successfully observed.

If the least-bound proton in a nucleus has a non-

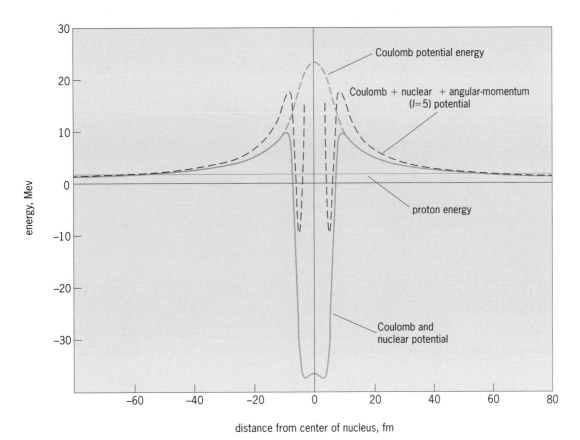

Fig. 2. Cross-sectional view of the potential energy of a proton in the presence of a nucleus, in comparison to the total energy of the most-unbound proton in thulium-145. Curves represent the Coulomb (electric) energy, the sum of the Coulomb and nuclear potentials, and the added effect of having the proton in the angular momentum state $l = 5$. The horizontal line shows the total energy of the proton.

zero angular momentum, the effect is to increase the barrier through which the proton must tunnel (Fig. 2). Because of the sensitivity of the half-life to barrier height, it is often possible to determine the angular momentum of the emitted proton, and thus the angular momentum (spin) of the proton-emitting nucleus. In addition to the dominating angular momentum factor, there is a small dependence of the half-life on details of the nuclear structure, which permits determination of the nuclear shell-model parameters in this region at the limits of nuclear stability.

Production of nuclei. The production of nuclei far from stability is accomplished by the bombardment of a nuclear target with energetic heavy ions. The bombarding energy must be large enough to overcome the large repulsion between the two highly charged nuclei and reach a radius where the nuclear force can cause the two to merge into a single system. A compound nucleus formed in such a heavy-ion collision is quite excited, and evaporates several nucleons in the process of cooling. For example, when molybdenum-92 is bombarded with krypton-78 at various energies, the platinum-170 compound nucleus sometimes evaporates one proton and two, three, or four neutrons, resulting in the production

of iridium-167, iridium-166, or iridium-165, respectively. These three proton emitters, and several others with different beam and target combinations, have been produced in recent experiments at the Argonne National Laboratory by utilizing the Argonne Tandem Linac Accelerator System (ATLAS). One proton emitter was recently produced at the Oak Ridge National Laboratory by utilizing the nickel-58 beam from the Holifield Radioactive-Ion Beam Facility (HRIBF).

Isotope separation. In order to observe proton radioactivity of these nuclei formed in heavy-ion reactions, it is necessary to separate the radioisotopes of interest from the much more intense incident beam and from a plethora of other reaction products, and rapidly deliver the proton emitters to the site of a detector because of the very small half-lives. Since the reaction products are formed with a relatively high energy, this step is most easily accomplished by using electric and magnetic devices to separate the reaction products from the beam and disperse them according to their mass and charge. The recent experiments at Argonne and Oak Ridge utilize recoil mass spectrometers to accomplish this task (**Fig. 3**). The time required for recoils to pass through these machines is typically a few microsec-

Fig. 3. Recoil Mass Separator at the Holifield Radioactive-Ion Beam Facility at Oak Ridge National Laboratory.

onds, thus constituting a lower limit on the half-lives that can be observed.

Detection method. Proton radioactivity is observed by use of a silicon detector which produces a charge pulse proportional to the energy of the proton. In the Argonne and Oak Ridge experiments, double-sided silicon strip detectors were utilized. Charge-collecting electrodes on the fronts and backs of the detectors have been sectored into strips, vertical on the front and horizontal on the back. The recoiling proton emitters are implanted in the detector, yielding a large pulse which is used to determine the time that the implant occurred, and the detector is then monitored for a subsequent decay at the same location. The half-life is determined from the time between the implant and the decay. A count-rate limitation on this technique results from the necessity to await the decay after a radionuclide has been implanted before another implant can be accepted. The use of strips to subdivide the detector has the effect of producing 1600 separate detectors so that the decay of many implants can be awaited simultaneously. Another limitation on the smallest half-life observable results from the necessity of having the detector and electronics recover from the deposit of an energetic recoil before it can effectively measure the small energy of a proton. The smallest half-life measured by this technique so far is 3.5 microseconds for thulium-145.

Proton energies and half-lives. Proton radioactivity from nuclear ground states has been observed in many odd-Z elements from $Z = 51$ to 81 (Fig. 1). The proton energies have been useful in testing and improving the predictions of nuclear mass formulas. The proton half-lives have been used to determine the shell from which the proton decayed. For example, the predicted half-life for thulium-145, if it is assumed to be spherical, is about 1.7 μs if the last nucleon resides in the $h_{11/2}$ angular momentum state, but would be more than 1000 times faster if in the $d_{3/2}$ or $s_{1/2}$ spin states. The 3.5-μs experimental half-life clearly indicates that the nucleus must be in the $h_{11/2}$ state and that the spherical shell model works fairly well for this nucleus. Proton decay data have been useful in determining the nuclear shell-model characteristics of many nuclei beyond the proton drip line.

Deformed nuclei. Of the known proton emitters, the only ones that cannot be reasonably described in terms of the spherical shell model are those for $Z = 53$, 55, 63, and 67. Nuclear structure models predict that these nuclides are in a deformed region which encompasses drip-line nuclei between $Z = 53$ and 67. The deformation of the nuclei causes a mixing of shell structures such that the least-bound proton will not always reside in a single angular momentum state. Proton radioactivity provides a tool to investigate the nature of the mixing of shell-model orbitals in this interesting deformed region. One of the plans for radioactive-ion beams is to produce several deformed proton emitters which have eluded study with stable heavy-ion beams.

For background information *see* EXOTIC NUCLEI; MASS SPECTROSCOPE; NUCLEAR STRUCTURE; RADIOACTIV-ITY in the McGraw-Hill Encyclopedia of Science & Technology.   Carrol Bingham

Bibliography. J. C. Batchelder et al., Observation of the exotic nucleus ^{145}Tm via its direct proton decay, *Phys. Rev. C,* 57:R1042–R1046, 1998; C. N. Davids et al., New proton radioactivities in ^{165,166,167}Ir and

Phys. Rev. Lett., 76:592–595, 1996; D. N. Poenaru (ed.), *Nuclear Decay Modes*, 1996; P. J. Sellin et al., A double-sided silicon strip detector system for proton radioactivity studies on the Daresbury recoil separator, *Nucl. Instrum. Meth. Phys. Res. A*, 311:217–223, 1992.

Quantum chromodynamics

With the advent of accelerators that could probe the structure of the nucleon, it was soon found that hadrons are composed of quarks, spin-½ particles with fractional electric charges $\pm\frac{1}{3}$ or $\pm\frac{2}{3}$ of the electron charge. In addition, there was strong evidence that quarks carry a new quantum number which can take on three distinct values. This new property was called color, because just as ordinary colors can be combined to yield white, bound states of quarks form colorless hadrons. Three quarks of different color form a baryon; a quark and an antiquark carrying color and anticolor form a meson.

Quantum chromodynamics (QCD) is based on the assumption that color is a new kind of charge which is the source of a field between particles carrying the charge. The situation is largely analogous to the case of quantum electrodynamics (QED), where the electric charge is the source of the photon field. The quantum-chromodynamic field quanta were named gluons because they "glue" quarks together into hadrons. Like the photon, the gluon is a spin-1 boson. Formally both theories are Yang-Mills theories, which explain forces between particles as a consequence of certain continuous symmetries, for example, the rotational symmetry of a sphere. In mathematical language, quantum electrodynamics is based on an underlying U(1) symmetry, while quantum chromodynamics is based on an SU(3) symmetry. Given the underlying symmetry, there remains only one free parameter. In the case of quantum electrodynamics, this is the fine-structure constant α, and for quantum chromodynamics it is the strong coupling α_s.

In the last few years, a wide variety of experimental findings have given strong support for quantum chromodynamics as the fundamental theory of strong interactions. The strong coupling was found to be a universal parameter in all interactions between quarks and gluons, and color was shown to exhibit an SU(3) symmetry. The experimental measurements are described below, after a short introduction to the basic phenomenology of quantum chromodynamics.

Phenomenology. The central feature of quantum chromodynamics is the fact that gluons are color-anticolor states. A red quark, for example, can emit a red-antigreen gluon, thereby changing its color from red to green. Given three fundamental quark colors, nine possible combinations would be expected for a gluon. In actuality, only eight are allowed by the SU(3) symmetry. The ratio of the number of color states for quarks and gluons thus is predicted to be $N_Q/N_G = 3/8$. In addition, being a color-anticolor state, the color charge of a gluon is larger than that of a quark. For the squares of the color charges, quantum chromodynamics predicts a ratio of $C_G^2/C_Q^2 = 9/4$.

Since gluons couple to color charges, gluons couple also directly to gluons. As a consequence of this gluon self-interaction, vacuum fluctuations of quantum-chromodynamic fields have completely different characteristics than the vacuum fluctuations in the electrically neutral photon field of quantum electrodynamics. In quantum chromodynamics, the net effect is an antiscreening of color charges; that is, the interaction between quarks becomes stronger with increasing distance. As discussed in detail below, this behavior explains why free color charges have never been observed. However, at small distances or correspondingly large energies, the color force becomes sufficiently weak to be analyzed in the framework of perturbation theory, which predicts a decrease of the strong coupling with energy. Measurements of the strong coupling performed at different energies thus have to be compared by evolving the result to a fixed reference energy. In the past years the energy corresponding to the mass of the Z boson has emerged as the most commonly used reference point.

Accelerator facilities. Precision tests of quantum chromodynamics require experiments to be done at very short distances or high energies. The highest-energy accelerators currently in operation are listed in the **table**. All of these machines operate with colliding beams, and the energy given in the table is the center-of-mass energy. The resolution, which is inversely proportional to the center-of-mass energy, gives some indication of the distance scale at which scattering experiments probe the interaction between quarks and gluons. For comparison, the radius of the proton is roughly 1 femtometer, and the energy contained in the rest mass of a proton is about 1 GeV.

Measurements of strong coupling. Although strong interactions at microscopic distances are being probed, the scattered quarks and gluons have to travel macroscopic distances in order to be seen in a detector. Because of the antiscreening property of quantum chromodynamics, the potential between separating color charges starts to grow indefinitely, with the gluon self-interaction bundling the field lines into flux tubes. As soon as the energy stored in those flux tubes is large enough to create additional quark-antiquark pairs, the field energy is transformed into quarks via a quantum-mechanical tunneling process. The quarks ultimately combine into long-lived hadrons, which can be recorded in the detector. As a consequence, the dynamics of quarks and gluons can be seen only in the form of jets of particles, which are emitted in the directions of the primary color charges.

An example is given in **Fig. 1**, where three jets of hadrons from an electron-positron annihilation are clearly visible. The electron and the positron

Parameters of highest-energy accelerators in operation			
Accelerator (institution; location)	Particles	Energy, GeV	Resolution, fm
CESR (Cornell University; Ithaca, New York)	positron-electron (e^+e^-)	12	2×10^{-2}
SLC (SLAC; Stanford, California)	positron-electron (e^+e^-)	100	2×10^{-3}
LEP (CERN; Geneva, Switzerland)	positron-electron (e^+e^-)	183	1×10^{-3}
HERA (DESY; Hamburg, Germany)	electron-proton ($e^- p$)	314	6×10^{-4}
SppS (CERN; Geneva, Switzerland)	proton-antiproton ($p\bar{p}$)	630	3×10^{-4}
Tevatron (Fermilab; Chicago, Illinois)	proton-antiproton ($p\bar{p}$)	1800	1×10^{-4}

collide in the center of the detector and form a Z boson, which then decays into a quark-antiquark pair and a high-energy gluon. The jets of hadrons materialize from these three primary particles. Historically, events of this type helped to prove the existence of the gluon. Angular correlations between the jets show that gluons are indeed spin-1 particles. Since the probability for gluon radiation off a quark is proportional to the strong coupling, the study of three-jet events is also one important way to determine this quantity.

Z-boson decays. The strong coupling can also be inferred from inclusive measurements, which do not require the explicit reconstruction of jets. An example is the ratio of the number of Z-boson decays into hadronic final states over the number of decays into muon pairs. Hadronic final states arise from Z decays into a quark-antiquark pair. In the absence of strong interactions, this ratio would be determined by the electroweak couplings of the Z. In quantum chromodynamics, the primary quarks will emit gluon radiation, which opens up additional final states and thus

enhances the decay rate into hadrons. The enhancement is proportional to the strong coupling.

Nucleon structure. Studying the structure of the nucleon offers another way to measure the strong coupling. Only at low energies can a nucleon be described as a bound state of three quarks. High-energy electron-nucleon scattering experiments, which probe the structure of the nucleon with high spatial and time resolution, are also sensitive to vacuum fluctuations in the gluon fields. The number of resolved particles increases with energy. In quantum chromodynamics this increase is predicted in terms of the strong coupling, α_s.

Heavy-quark bound states. Bound states of heavy quarks are sensitive to the quantum-chromodynamic potential at short distances and thereby to the strong coupling. The strong coupling can be inferred, for example, from the level splitting between P and S states of the upsilon meson, which consists of a b quark and its antiquark.

Combined results. The combined result from a compilation of measurements of the strong coupling is

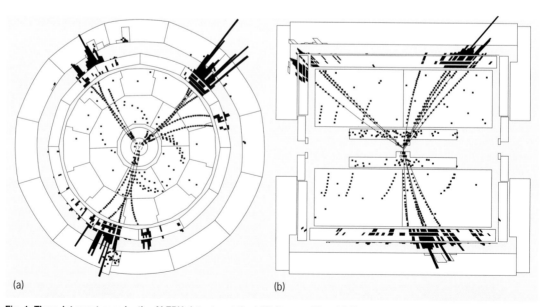

(a)   (b)

Fig. 1. Three-jet event seen by the ALEPH detector at the LEP Storage Ring. (a) View along the electron-positron beam direction. (b) View orthogonal to the beam. The tracks are bent in a magnetic field which allows the momenta of the particles to be measured. Histograms at the periphery of the detector visualize the energy emitted into the respective angular regions.

shown in **Fig. 2**. Consistent results were obtained over two orders of magnitude in energy, between 1.5 GeV and 161 GeV, in such diverse reactions as lepton-nucleon scattering experiments, proton-antiproton collisions, and electron-positron annihilation, using the methods explained above as well as other ways to determine the strong coupling. The energy dependence found for the strong coupling is in perfect agreement with the quantum-chromodynamic prediction based on a reference value $\alpha_s(M_Z) = 0.118 \pm 0.003$, $\alpha_s(M_Z)$ denoting the strong coupling at the energy corresponding to the mass of the Z boson. The global consistency between measurements from widely different sources is one of the strongest arguments in favor of quantum chromodynamics.

Tests of symmetry. Another important test of quantum chromodynamics is the demonstration that strong interactions indeed are described by a Yang-Mills theory based on an SU(3) symmetry. This has been done in studies of the angular correlations in four-jet events from hadronic Z decays, where two gluons are emitted in addition to the primary quark-antiquark pair. The correlations between the resulting jets are sensitive to the number of color states of quarks and gluons, and to the relative strengths of the quark-gluon and the gluon-gluon coupling. The combined result shown in **Fig. 3**, $N_Q/N_G = 0.33 \pm 0.12$ for ratio of the number of color states and $C_G^2/C_Q^2 = 2.22 \pm 0.22$ for the ratio of the squares of the color charges, is perfectly consistent with the SU(3) prediction, $N_Q/N_G = 3/8$ and $C_G^2/C_Q^2 = 9/4$. The measurements show unambiguously that gluons carry color charge ($C_G^2 > 0$) and are consistent with the assumption of eight distinct color states for a gluon. The experimental findings are consistent with only a very small number of possible symmetries,

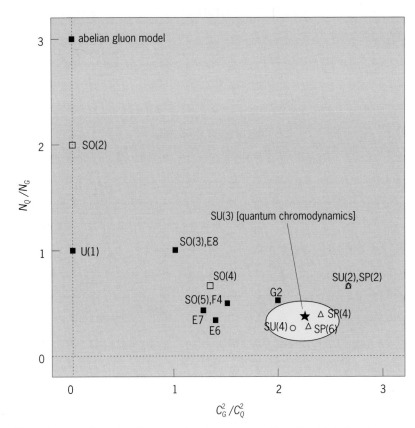

Fig. 3. Testing of the underlying symmetry of strong interactions. The labeled markers indicate the predictions, for various types of continuous symmetries, of the ratio of the number of color states for quarks and gluons (N_Q/N_G) and of the ratio of the squares of the color charges of gluons and quarks (C_G^2/C_Q^2). The ellipse is the 68%-confidence-level combined result for these quantities from measurements by four experiments at the LEP Storage Ring.

out of which SU(3) is the only candidate that allows three colors for the quarks.

Prospects. Current research focuses on further refinements in the determination of the strong coupling and toward a better understanding of the long-distance behavior of strong interactions. One approach is based on extensive numerical calculations in the framework of lattice gauge theories, which aims at solving quantum chromodynamics from first principles. This program aims also at the calculation of the hadron masses and at a quantitative understanding of the nuclear force, which in the framework of quantum chromodynamics is a residual van der Waals–type interaction between bound states of quarks. The ultimate goal is to understand all of strong-interaction physics, whether it is interactions between quarks and gluons at small distances, hadron spectroscopy, or nuclear forces, as the consequence of a Yang-Mills theory based on an SU(3) symmetry with only one free parameter, the strong coupling.

For background information *see* ELEMENTARY PARTICLE; GLUONS; PARTICLE ACCELERATOR; QUANTUM CHROMODYNAMICS; QUARKS; SYMMETRY LAWS (PHYSICS) in the McGraw-Hill Encyclopedia of Science & Technology.

Michael Schmelling

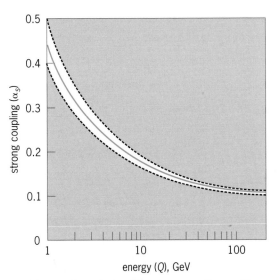

Fig. 2. Energy dependence of the strong coupling, α_s. The error band reflects the precision of a combined result based on a large variety of measurements. At the scale of the Z-boson mass, all measurements are consistent with a central value $\alpha_s(M_Z) = 0.118 \pm 0.003$.

Bibliography. R. M. Barnett et al., Quantum chromodynamics, *Phys. Rev. D*, 54:77–84, 1996; H. Fritzsch, *Quarks: The Stuff of Matter*, 1983; M. Rozanska and K. Rybicki (eds.), *Physics in Collision: Proceedings of the 15th International Conference*, 1996.

Radio communications

For the first 100 years of telephony, each telephone required a wire from the home or office to a central location in the telephone network (the central office). After radio was invented, car telephones became available, but only since the early 1980s could large numbers of people have car telephones, now called cellular phones. In the 1990s, there has been an explosion in wireless communications. Wireless technology has expanded from high-tier systems for vehicles and individuals to low-tier systems for the home and office. The design of high-tier systems differs from that of low-tier systems.

The **table** compares the key features of high-tier and low-tier technologies. High-tier radio systems support base stations with large coverage areas and low traffic densities. The trade-off, however, is low-quality voice service and limited data-service capabilities with high delays. The low-tier systems have the advantages of high quality and low-delay voice and data capabilities, but have small cells.

High-tier systems. Traditional wireless services (called cellular systems) use the same frequencies repetitively across the coverage area of the system over a regular grid. A simplified architecture for the cellular system consists of a mobile switching center, several base stations, and the mobile or portable telephones (**Fig. 1**). The base station consists of radio transmitters and receivers that are connected to a common antenna mounted on a tower 15–50 m (50–150 ft) tall. Each base station is connected to the mobile switching center by copper wires, fiber-optic cables, or microwave links. The base stations are distributed over the coverage area of the system and are designed to have a radio range from 1–2 km to tens of kilometers (1 km = 0.6 mi). The base is often located inside a specially constructed building at the foot of the tower. Some small base stations may be mounted on the tower or on a building roof.

Protocols. Several radio protocols are in use worldwide for cellular telephony. The Advanced Mobile Telephone Service (AMPS) was the original analog cellular phone protocol used in the United States and many other areas. Europe had its own set of analog protocols and frequencies that varied among countries. In the mid-1980s, the European nations adopted a new digital protocol, the Global System for Mobile (GSM) Communications, that used the same frequencies throughout Europe. In the United States, two digital protocols have been adopted for cellular telephony, one based on time-division multiple access (TDMA) and the other based on code-division multiple access (CDMA). While CDMA and TDMA are generic terms, often their use is meant to describe the two specific United States standards. All three digital systems (CDMA, GSM, and TDMA) are in use around the world. Other systems also have seen limited deployment.

Characteristics. The traditional cellular systems (or high-tier systems; Fig. 1) are based on serving small numbers of users who primarily communicate with wireline users but can, of course, communicate with other cellular users. Base stations are typically expensive; it is therefore necessary to minimize their number in a system. To maximize the number of users per base station, it is important to minimize the bandwidth for each conversation. The service cost is often high, and users tend to make few calls on the system. Thus, users often choose the cellular system only when there are no less expensive options available.

Comparison of high- and low-tier wireless systems		
Property	High-tier system	Low-tier system
Base station/radio port size	Large	Small
Base station/radio port cost	Expensive	Inexpensive
Base station/radio port range	1–10 km (0.6–6 mi)	100 m to 2 km (300 ft to 1.2 mi)
Density of base stations/radio ports	Low	High
Antenna location and size	Large antenna mounted on a 15–50-m (50–150-ft) tower	Small antenna mounted on the radio port
System capacity	Low	High
System economics		
Low traffic density	Low cost per subscriber	High cost per subscriber
High traffic density	High cost per subscriber	Low cost per subscriber
Coverage area	Everywhere	Only high-traffic areas
Primary use	Vehicles and portables	Fixed users (home and office) and portables
Voice quality	Poorer than wireline	Equal to wireline
Expected usage	Low	High
Representative systems	AMPS, GSM, CDMA, TDMA	DECT, PACS, PHS
Voice services	Same as wireline	Same as wireline
Data services	Circuit- and packet-switched data	Voice-band modems and fax, circuit- and packet-switched data
Data speeds	1.2–115.2 kbps with data adapter	1.2–28.8 kbps with voice-band transparency, 32–512 kbps with data adapter
Data users supported	Few	Many

Voice services. The cellular network provides the full range of voice services provided by the wireline network. Voice services range from call waiting, caller identification, and voice mail to multiline hunt groups (which search for a line in the group that is not busy) consisting of combinations of wireless and wireline phones. In addition, many systems offer integrated paging, thus eliminating the need for a separate pager.

Voice coders. The voice coders used for CDMA, GSM, and TDMA are designed to operate at the lowest possible bit rate. To accomplish low-bit-rate encoding, they digitize speech by using encoding schemes that model the human vocal tract. The decoder in the receiver is an electronic representation of the vocal tract. The voice coding necessary to digitize the conversation can add as much as 100 milliseconds of delay for each modulation and demodulation step. Thus, a wireless-to-wireless call could have up to 400 ms of round-trip delay. Experience with satellite communications demonstrates that this much delay causes conversations to become awkward. Since there are few wireless-to-wireless calls, the excessive delay is rarely noticed.

Data transmission. When digital cellular phones are used for data, the speech encoder-decoder does not correctly reproduce the signals sent by wireline voice-band modems. Therefore, data transmission over digital cellular systems requires that the digital data from the sending-receiving device be accepted and used directly by the phone. Voice-band modems and speech encoder-decoders are thus removed from the data transmission path. Data transmission rates from 1200 bits per second to as high as 115 kilobits per second (kbps) can be sent over cellular connections. In the late 1990s, systems supporting data rates as high as 14.4 kbps were being deployed. Data rates of greater than 14.4 kbps are not expected until 1999 or later. Since speech is encoded at rates of 8–13 kbps, data transmission rates have become higher than the speech encoding rates, and therefore reduce the capacity of the system. One data user can use capacity equivalent to that of 2–10 voice users. For each data communications protocol supported by the high-tier systems, a pool of wireless modems must be installed so that wireline-to-wireless networking can be supported.

Low-tier systems. Low-tier wireless systems (**Fig. 2**) are designed to support wireless local loops and portable telephones for indoor and neighborhood environments. Two key differences in low-tier system design are the cost of the base stations and the quality of the voice services. The base stations (radio ports) are designed to have a radio range of few hundred meters to a few kilometers and are designed for low cost. A wireless access fixed unit (WAFU) is mounted in the home or office and provides an interface to the wiring there. Telephones, modems, and facsimile machines can be plugged in and function in the same manner as in a traditional wired loop. The radio ports are connected to a radio-port controller that is connected to the central office.

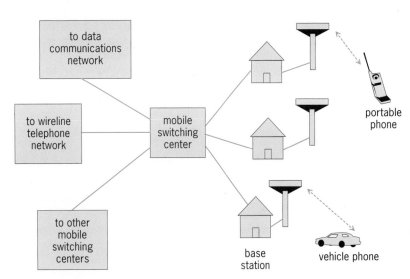
Fig. 1. Architecture of a high-tier wireless system.

Since the cost per radio port is low, many radio ports can be deployed over a given area, and spectrum utilization per port is less of an issue than in a high-tier system. The radio ports are often mounted on telephone poles or light poles for outdoor use and on the walls of office buildings for indoor use. The deployment of inexpensive radio ports over a wide area results in a high-capacity, inexpensive system that can offer services to the user at an economical cost. High-tier systems can reduce cell sizes, but the higher cost of the base stations results in an expensive system.

In low-tier systems, the cost per call is low. Thus, users are apt to make calls more frequently and often may choose the wireless phone even where wireline phones are available. Some users

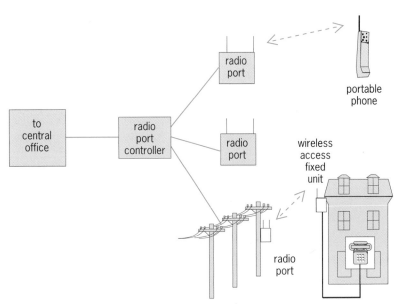
Fig. 2. Architecture of a low-tier wireless system.

may not even be aware that the loop is wireless. The low-tier systems can also support portable telephones for use by pedestrians. While the portable telephones can be used in vehicles, the small cell sizes and radio system design may limit the speed at which the vehicle can move and still support good voice and data quality.

Waveform voice coders. The wireless local loop systems use waveform voice coders similar to those in the digital wireline telephone network. Two different types of voice coders are commonly used; one type uses pulse code modulation (PCM) at 64 kbps, and the other type employs adaptive differential pulse-code modulation (ADPCM) at 32 kbps. Both of these waveform coders reproduce any waveform offered to them and therefore have low coding delay and high-quality speech and data reproduction.

Common systems. The three most common low-tier systems are the Digital Enhanced Cordless Telephone (DECT), the Personal Access Communications System (PACS), and the Personal Handyphone System (PHS). All are based on digitizing the signal and sending it by using time-division multiple access. Each system defines time slots and data speeds differently, and all are different from the high-tier TDMA and GSM systems. Since many users of the low-tier systems may not know that they are using a wireless system, feature transparency is important. The interface that the WAFU presents to the wiring in the home or office is almost identical to that presented by the wired loop.

Voice and data services. As local loop replacements, low-tier systems can offer the same set of voice services as their wireline counterparts. The voice services for low-tier radio systems depend on the design of the radio port controller and the services supported by the connecting central office. They are traditionally the same as those offered by the wireline network.

Low-speed data services (1.2–14.4 or 28.8 kbps) can be obtained by connecting a facsimile machine or modem directly to the WAFU by using the in-building wiring. Since the voice coders reproduce waveforms rather than speech, the user is unaware of the wireless nature of the loop. However, at data rates higher than 28.8 kbps, low-tier systems must also bypass the waveform coders and send the digital data directly. By combining time slots, data rates as high as 512 kbps are possible. Data support for high-speed data requires terminal adapters in the home or office that digitally interface to the WAFU. Similar to their use in the high-tier systems, modems are required to interconnect to the various wireline services. Since radio ports are inexpensive, additional ports can be added to support high-speed data without impacting system capacity. Thus, low-tier systems typically support high data rates without seriously reducing system capacity.

For background information *see* DATA COMMUNICATIONS; ELECTRICAL COMMUNICATIONS; MOBILE RADIO; MODEM; MULTIPLEXING AND MULTIPLE ACCESS; RADIO SPECTRUM ALLOCATIONS; TELEPHONE SERVICE in the McGraw-Hill Encyclopedia of Science & Technology.   Joseph E. Wilkes

Bibliography. V. K. Garg and J. E. Wilkes, *Principles and Applications of GSM*, 1998; V. K. Garg and J. E. Wilkes, *Wireless and Personal Communications Systems*, 1996; W. C. Jakes, Jr., *Microwave Mobile Communications*, 1974; A. Mehrotra, *GSM System Engineering*, 1997; T. S. Rappaport, *Wireless Communications, Principles and Practice*, 1996.

Resonant ionization mass spectrometry

Resonant ionization mass spectrometry (RIMS) is an emerging analytical technique that can accomplish very sensitive and unambiguous identification of elemental impurities in bulk materials, on surfaces, and in particulates. Because the technique combines high sensitivity and selectivity, the concentration of various contaminants may be determined at and below the part-per-billion (ppb) level. Moreover, such determinations can be quantitative even in complex matrices, and concentration maps at high lateral resolution have been obtained.

Sensitivity and discrimination. The increasingly stringent demands of the electronic industry for quantitative identification of trace impurities in semiconductor materials at high lateral resolution require both sensitivity and discrimination. Particulate analysis, the isotopic and elemental analysis of micrometer-sized grains, is receiving much attention from the analytical community. The difficulty in both cases arises from the need to make the measurement before consuming the few atoms of the element of interest while discriminating against the vast excess of bulk atoms. An example is the trace analysis of zirconium (Zr) at the part-per-million (ppm) level in a 1-μm-sized silicon carbide (SiC) grain. For terrestrial isotopic composition, this grain contains about 11,000 zirconium atoms, half of which are the major isotope zirconium-90 (^{90}Zr) and approximately 300 are ^{96}Zr atoms. Analysis is complicated by the need to discriminate bulk species, some of which have nominally the same mass as the analyte. In order to demonstrate the power of resonant ionization mass spectrometry, the analysis of stardust will be discussed.

Stardust analysis. Primitive chondritic meteorites contain small amounts of presolar dust grains (such as graphite, silicon carbide, microdiamonds, and corundum) which have survived the formation of the solar system. It is generally believed that these grains condensed in stellar outflows before being incorporated into meteoritic material of the solar system, and that the elemental and isotopic compositions of these grains preserve a nucleosynthetic record of the parent star. These presolar grains can be considered as stardust (**Fig. 1**). Measurements of their elemental composition and isotopic anomalies provide information about stellar nucleosynthesis and conditions during circumstellar grain formation. The first hints of such exotic matter in meteorites surfaced

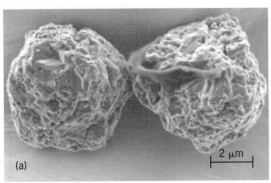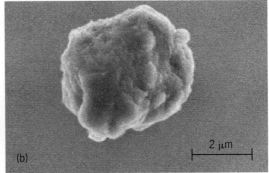

Fig. 1. Stardust. (*a*) Electron micrograph of a pair of silicon carbide presolar grains. (*b*) Graphite presolar grain.

in the 1960s, when isotopic anomalies were observed for the noble gases xenon and neon, but their carriers (grains of graphite, silicon carbide, and diamond no larger than a few micrometers) were discovered much later.

Silicon carbide. Silicon carbide is the best-studied type of presolar grain, because it contains a number of minor and trace elements. Most silicon carbide grains fall into the so-called mainstream group and have properties suggesting condensation around low-mass asymptotic-giant-branch stars. These grains have carbon-12 (^{12}C) depletions, nitrogen-14 (^{14}N) enrichments, enhanced silicon-29 (^{29}Si) and ^{30}Si relative to ^{28}Si compared to solar system isotopic compositions, and high initial aluminum isotopic (^{26}Al/^{27}Al) ratios; and aggregates of silicon carbide grains show enrichments in heavy-element isotopes produced by *s*-process nucleosynthesis. In the *s*-process, nucleosynthesis occurs by slow neutron capture, where neutron densities are low enough that short-lived radionuclides produced by neutron capture decay before another neutron capture can occur.

Graphite. Graphite grains are another form of presolar dust grains and exhibit a wide range of ^{12}C/^{13}C ratios, suggesting a variety of possible stellar sources for circumstellar graphite grains (for example, asymptotic-giant-branch stars, novae, supernovae, and Wolf-Rayet stars). A significant fraction of these grains may have been produced in a high-neutron-density and high-temperature stellar environment where neutron captures are faster than β^- decays, even for neutron-rich unstable nuclei up to 10–20 units from stability. Historically, this rapid neutron capture, or *r*-process, has been identified with supernovae.

Measurement. Whereas isotope ratios of a number of light elements (carbon, nitrogen, magnesium, silicon, calcium, and titanium) have been measured in individual presolar grains, isotope ratios of heavy elements have been measured only in aggregates of many grains to date. Since each presolar grain may have come from a different star, resonant ionization mass spectrometry has begun the difficult process of analyzing such material for trace heavy elements.

Resonant ionization mass spectrometry measurements may be based on laser-induced or ion-induced

desorption, resonant laser postionization, and time-of-flight mass spectrometry (**Fig. 2**). The instrument operates in a pulsed mode where each cycle consists of the following sequence: (1) A pulsed ion beam or a short-pulsed ablation laser is focused through an optical microscope onto the sample (silicon carbide grain or standard) and produces a cloud of laser-desorbed neutral atoms, ions, and molecules. (2) An electrostatic field is applied in front of the target in order to suppress the emission of secondary ions; neutral species are not affected and move away from the surface. (3) Multicolor resonant laser radiation (usually from two or three lasers) intersects the cloud of desorbed neutral species and ionizes resonantly a specific element with high efficiency. (4) The photoions produced are extracted by a positive

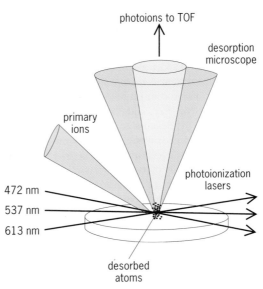

Fig. 2. Extraction region of a surface resonant ionization mass spectrometry instrument. The measurement sequence begins with either a laser desorption pulse through the microscope or a burst of energetic primary ions. Atoms are desorbed from the sample surface and are subsequently photoionized with three lasers. For zirconium these three lasers are tuned to wavelengths of 472 nanometers, 537 nm, and 613 nm. The photoions produced are extracted by electric fields into a time-of-flight (TOF) mass spectrometer for analysis.

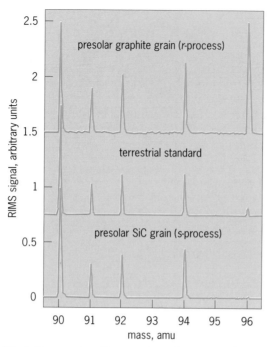

Fig. 3. Mass spectra of two presolar grains compared to a terrestrial standard. There is dramatic variation in the relative abundance of ^{96}Zr. This abundance clearly indicates that these grains are not of terrestrial origin and that the nucleosynthetic environment experienced by the silicon carbide grain is very different from that experienced by the graphite grain.

2000-V target pulse and mass-analyzed in a re-flectron-type time-of-flight mass spectrometer. (5) Photoion arrival times are measured at a particle-counting detector, producing a mass-versus-abundance graph.

Zirconium is one of the elements first successfully measured on these grains and is interesting for several reasons: (1) Zirconium is the most abundant heavy element in mainstream silicon carbide grains. (2) Zirconium has four predominantly s-process isotopes, ^{90}Zr, ^{91}Zr, ^{92}Zr, and ^{94}Zr, and one r-process isotope, ^{96}Zr. (3) Because of the relatively long half-life of ^{95}Zr, the production of ^{96}Zr by the s-process is a sensitive indicator of neutron density.

Isotopic analysis of zirconium is challenging because of a number of isobaric interferences from other elements that occur in presolar silicon carbide. Zirconium has five stable isotopes, 90, 91, 92, 94, and 96, and has the following isobaric overlaps: molybdenum at masses 92, 94, and 96; ruthenium at mass 96; and titanium at masses 92, 94, and 96 (with the most abundant isotope of titanium and the least abundant isotope of zirconium at mass 96). Titanium, molybdenum, and ruthenium are present in silicon carbide and as grains within presolar graphite spherules. The mass resolution needed for these interferences is beyond the capability of currently available secondary ion mass spectrometers. Resonant ionization mass spectrometry gets around this difficulty by resonantly ionizing ablated zirconium atoms while leaving molybdenum and ruthenium atoms and titanium molecules in the ground state and undetected. Three xenon chloride (XeCl) excimer-pumped dye lasers generate the resonant laser radiation.

Presolar grains. An enormous range of isotopic anomalies was observed for zirconium. The resonant ionization mass spectra of a terrestrial reference material, a silicon carbide grain, and a graphite grain demonstrate the extreme range of zirconium isotopic anomalies found (**Fig. 3**). The silicon carbide grain has virtually no ^{96}Zr whereas the graphite grain shows ^{96}Zr as the most abundant isotope. The isotopic abundances of both these grains differ from terrestrial sources, which have slight deviations across the Earth. The diversity of isotopic abundances measured in these grains indicates that the material forming the solar system condensed from many stellar sources. On Earth the zirconium produced in these diverse sources mixed to produce the terrestrial zirconium isotope abundances. Only resonant ionization mass spectrometry possesses sufficient sensitivity and discrimination to be able to make isotopic measurements on parts-per-million impurities in micrometer-sized grains.

For background information see MASS SPECTROMETRY; NUCLEOSYNTHESIS; RESONANCE IONIZATION SPECTROSCOPY; TRACE ANALYSIS in the McGraw-Hill Encyclopedia of Science & Technology.

Michael J. Pellin; Günther K. Nicolussi

Bibliography. E. Anders and E. Zinner, Interstellar grains in primitive meteorites: Diamond, silicon carbide, and graphite, *Meteoritics*, 28:490, 1993; G. Nicolussi et al., s-Process zirconium in presolar silicon carbide grains, *Science*, 277:1281, 1997; M. J. Pellin et al., Secondary neutral mass spectrometry using three-color resonance ionization: Osmium detection at the p.p.b. level and iron detection in silicon at the <200 p.p.t. level, *Phil. Trans. Roy. Soc. London, Ser. A*, 333:133, 1990.

Scanning tunneling microscope

This article discusses recent work on use of a scanning tunneling microscope to break single chemical bonds, one at a time. The possible applications of such work, and the importance of scanning tunneling microscope studies that treat atoms as building blocks in a construction set, are considered. This discussion requires a review of the ways in which scanning tunneling microscopes and other proximal probes make it possible to visit the submicrometer world, the properties of surface atoms and electrons that scanning tunneling microscopes have revealed, and the possible impact of a technology capable of atom-by-atom manipulations.

Visiting the nano-world. Scanning tunneling microscopes are pointed electrodes that are scanned over the surface of a conducting specimen, with help from a piezoelectric crystal whose dimensions can be altered electronically. Scanning tunneling micro-

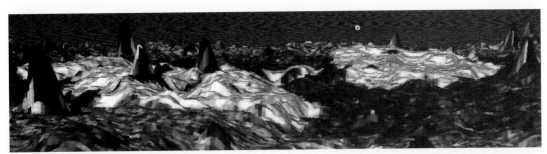

Fig. 1. Unexpected slippery patches (white) less than a nanometer high, from a nano-human's viewpoint in an atomic force microscope image of freshly cleaved and etched mica. The peaks are particles lying on the mica surface. Landscape shading was provided by lateral force measurements during the scan which, in this case, are dominated by coefficient-of-friction variations on the surface. *(P. Fraundorf, University of Missouri, St. Louis)*

scopes normally generate images by holding the current between the tip of the electrode and the specimen at some constant (set-point) value by using a piezoelectric crystal to adjust the distance between the tip and the specimen surface, while the tip is piezoelectrically scanned in a raster pattern over the region of specimen surface being imaged. By holding the force, rather than the electric current, between tip and specimen at a set-point value, atomic force microscopes similarly allow the exploration of nonconducting specimens. In either case, when the height of the tip is plotted as a function of its lateral position over the specimen, an image that looks very much like the surface topography results.

It is becoming increasingly possible to record other signals (such as lateral force, capacitance, scan-related tip displacement, temperature, light intensity, or magnetic resonance) as the tip scans. For example, modern atomic force microscopes can map lateral force and conductivity along with height, while image pairs from scanning tunneling microscopes scanning to and fro can provide information about friction as well as topography. Ray-tracing programs make it possible to combine such inputs, putting three-dimensional pattern recognition capabilities to work in the nano-world, and facilitating human-viewpoint explorations, increasingly in real time (**Fig. 1**).

Observing atoms and electrons. These explorations have revealed that the scanning tunneling microscope views more than just atoms. For example, an oxygen atom on a metal surface appears as a depression in the scanning tunneling microscope image, even when the atom is positioned above the metal surface. The reason is that the tip needs to press closer to the specimen to maintain the set-point current when an oxygen atom is in the way. The growing library of molecules whose scanning tunneling microscope images either have been seen or can be predicted now includes many small hydrocarbons. Some of the detail in scanning tunneling microscope images of molecules comes from the bonding electrons themselves. For example, ripples have been discovered near step edges on a copper surface from electrons hanging out on the surface. Further, iron atoms have been positioned, one at a

time, to build "electron corrals" of various shapes. These observations have resulted in some of the most striking images of quantum-mechanical phenomena ever produced (**Fig. 2**).

Scanning tunneling microscopes have also revealed that atoms on surfaces behave differently from atoms contained within three-dimensional solids. For example, some metal atoms (such as silver) on a substrate surface (such as platinum) hang together and avoid the differing atoms of the substrate, while other atoms (such as gold on certain silver surfaces) form unexpected alloys or layer configurations. Moreover, atoms do not always behave in the ways that researchers desire. For example, elemental semiconductors (such as silicon, whose chips dominate the world of digital logic) end up with their

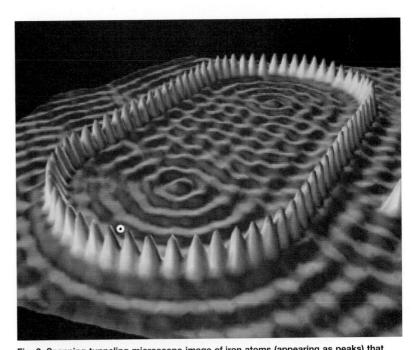

Fig. 2. Scanning tunneling microscope image of iron atoms (appearing as peaks) that have been positioned on a copper surface to form a stadium-shaped corral, so as to force some surface-state electrons into quantum states of that shape. The ripples inside the wall of atoms are the density distribution of a particular set of quantum states for electrons in the corral. *(M. F. Crommie, C. P. Lutz, and D. M. Eigler, IBM Almaden Research Center)*

surface atoms scrambled on newly cleaved surfaces, making it difficult to use scanning tunneling microscopes to monitor atomic arrangements in cross section beneath a wafer surface. Compound semiconductors such as gallium arsenide, however, more readily yield information such as the location of subsurface dopant atoms.

Nano-manipulations. Scanning tunneling microscopes make it possible not just to view atoms but to push them and even to rearrange them in unlikely combinations (sometimes whether or not these rearrangements are desirable). A few considerations of scale are important in understanding this process. Atoms comprise a positive nucleus and a surrounding cloud of negative electrons. These charges rearrange when another atom approaches, with unlike charges shifting to give rise to the van der Waals force of attraction between neutral atoms. This force makes gravity (and most accelerations) ignorable when contact between solid objects in the micrometer size range and smaller is involved, since surface-to-volume ratios are inversely proportional to object size. On the nanoscale, the fact that sizes are down by a factor of 1000 from the micrometer scale means that volumes are down another factor of 10^9. On this size scale, the wave nature of electrons and the quantum nature of angular momentum become more evident. What can be expected from attempts to move objects around, therefore, is less obvious.

An ability to see surface atoms was demonstrated with the first scanning tunneling microscope, but the ability to move xenon atoms around on nickel at liquid-nitrogen temperature was first demonstrated in 1989. The mechanism for sliding these atoms is called the van der Waals atom trap, because it involves competition between the van der Waals attractions of neutral xenon to both the nickel surface and the electrode tip. The electron corral work mentioned above involved the sliding of strongly adsorbed (chemisorbed) iron atoms on copper by a similar process, with smaller tip-sample distances.

The electric field in the scanning tunneling microscope allows plucking as well, in which adsorbed or substrate atoms are removed and transferred to the electrode tip with a suitable voltage pulse. Because the electric field from the tip falls off less rapidly with separation than do van der Waals forces, the most weakly attached nearby atom rather than the nearest may end up being removed. One solution to this problem is a hybrid approach. By invoking the tip electric field for bond breaking only when the tip is sufficiently close to the target atom that the van der Waals forces contribute as well, atoms on silicon could be singly removed and redeposited at will.

A third kind of selective bond breaking was also demonstrated. It involved the selective breaking of silicon-hydrogen bonds using electron energies (that is, pulse voltages) below those necessary to break bonds directly. Since the desorption probability was observed to vary exponentially with the tip-specimen current, it is believed that vibrational heating from inelastic electron tunneling mediated the chemical transition in this work. This work involves bond alteration at the level of single atoms, the ultimate frontier for lithographic miniaturization.

The mechanism used for modifying silicon surface bonds is effective at room temperature, unlike the work with xenon atoms on nickel. However, the electrical pulses used would likely cause problems if delicate molecules were to be repositioned. Recently, researchers have succeeded in positioning individual molecules at room temperature by purely mechanical means. They first carefully chose an organic molecule with 173 atoms based on its promise for this experiment. By selecting six such molecules from a set randomly positioned on a copper surface, they pushed each individually into position to form a ring which would not normally be found in nature. Other molecules in the vicinity were not disturbed.

Prospects. The work discussed here is incomplete, and the results are less practical than informative. Scanning tunneling microscope images are better understood, and some surprising and some annoying behaviors of atoms have been uncovered in recent years. Mechanical forces can serve to slide single atoms on cold metal surfaces, and to move selected large molecules around at room temperature as well. Voltage pulses can be used to break single silicon bonds. Electric current can even free a hydrogen atom of choice from a silicon surface. However, it is difficult to be sure exactly what the scanning tunneling microscope tip looks like during each scan. A toolbox of methods to assemble designer molecules from an assortment of many atoms is not yet in hand. And of course, anything that can be done one atom at a time will seem extremely slow if the goal is to work on a macroscopic quantity of matter.

The scanning tunnel microscope and the related proximal-probe instruments are the vehicle for a widening range of explorations taking place in worlds on the size scale of atoms and molecules. The interface to these microscopes is becoming less abstract, allowing the application of pattern recognition skills developed in the macro-world. In the near future, it may be possible to apply the technology of virtual reality to immerse oneself in the landscape of molecules attached to a specimen's surface.

For background information *see* NANOCHEMISTRY; NANOSTRUCTURE; NANOTECHNOLOGY; SCANNING TUNNELING MICROSCOPE; VIRTUAL REALITY in the McGraw-Hill Encyclopedia of Science & Technology.

Philip B. Fraundorf

Bibliography. Ph. Avouris, Manipulation of matter at the atomic and molecular levels, *Acc. Chem. Res.*, 28:95–101, 1996; S. Chaing (ed.), Force and tunneling microscopy, *Chem. Rev.*, 97(4):1015–1230, 1997; M. F. Crommie et al., Waves on a metal surface and quantum corrals, *Surf. Rev. Lett.*, 2(1):127–137, 1995; T. A. Jung et al., Controlled room-temperature positioning of individual molecules: Molecular flexure and motion, *Science*, 271:181–184, 1996; T. C. Shen et al., Atomic-scale desorption through electronic and vibrational excitation mechanisms, *Science*, 268:1590–1592, 1995.

Sea-floor imaging

New, detailed images of the sea floor are revealing terrains as remarkable as those being radioed back to Earth by planetary probes. Modern technologies have revolutionized sea-floor mapping. The greatly improved sea-floor imagery is aiding scientists and engineers in endeavors ranging from locating and managing offshore natural resources to furthering understanding of the dynamics of the Earth.

Sea-floor panoramas. Diverse sea-floor terrains, covering some 70% of the Earth's surface, are concealed from view by the oceans. Images have been produced that show the ocean stripped away and the sea floor laid bare. This has been accomplished with the use of computers by mathematically fitting a continuous surface to numerous, closely spaced, high-resolution depth measurements to render a detailed model of what the sea floor in various regions looks like (**Fig. 1**).

A wide range of submarine terrains border the continental United States. Continental slopes are where the sea floor drops at a relatively steep angle (on average, 2–6°) from the edge of the shallow shelf plateaus (on average, <400 ft or 120 m water depth) that rim the continents down to the gradually dipping (≤0.5°) rise and abyssal plains that underlie the deep sea (generally, >2 mi or 3000 m water depth). The continental slope off New Jersey (Fig. 1a) is scarred by numerous submarine canyons. A primary agent in cutting the canyons has been subsea avalanches of shelf-edge and slope sediments that became unstable and failed.

On the continental slope off Louisiana (Fig. 1b), the movement of buried salt has deformed the sea floor to create a lunarlike surface. The salt was deposited earlier in geologic time when the Gulf of Mexico was first forming. It became buried by the massive amounts of sediments eroded from North America and dumped into the Gulf of Mexico by the Mississippi River. Under the great weight of these sediments, pockets of salt are being squeezed upward and seaward, rearranging the seascape above them like groundhogs burrowing through soil.

On the continental slope off Oregon (Fig. 1c), the North American plate, which is one of the 12 lithospheric plates forming the Earth's outer shell and in which the United States is embedded, is overriding the Juan de Fuca plate, which lies beneath flat sea-floor sediments extending from the base of the slope. As the plates collide, the overthrusting North American plate is bulldozing the sediments off the downgoing Juan de Fuca plate and folding them into the ridges that run parallel to the continental slope.

Mapping technologies. Highly detailed images of the sea floor have been made possible by sophisticated mapping technologies. The most commonly used are the four technologies described below, each of which provides a unique viewpoint of the sea floor.

Satellite altimetry. The technology that provides the broadest perspective but the lowest resolution is satellite altimetry (**Fig. 2a**). A laser altimeter is mounted on a satellite and, in combination with land-based radars that track the satellite's altitude, is used to measure variations in sea-surface elevation to within 2 in. (5 cm). Removing elevation changes due to waves and currents, sea-surface height can vary up to 660 ft (200 m). These variations are caused by minute differences in the Earth's gravity field, which in turn result from heterogeneities in the Earth's mass. These heterogeneities are often associated with sea-floor topography. For example, the gravitational attraction of a massive undersea volcano pulls water toward it, producing a local bulge in the ocean surface. If the volcano is 6600 ft (2000 m) high and has an average radius of 12.5 mi (20 km), the sea surface above will typically form a bulge 6.6 ft (2 m) high. By using a mathematical function that equates sea-surface height to bottom elevations, global areas of the sea floor can be mapped within a matter of weeks. However, this approach has limitations. Sea-floor features less than 6–9 mi (10–15 km) in length are generally not massive enough to deflect the ocean surface, and thus go undetected. Furthermore, sea-floor density also affects the gravity field; and where different-density rocks are found, such as along the margins of continents, the correlation between Earth's gravity field and sea-floor topography breaks down.

Side-scan sonar. This provides a higher-resolution view of the sea floor, but one which is a bit different

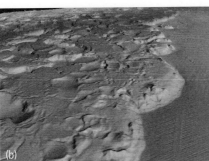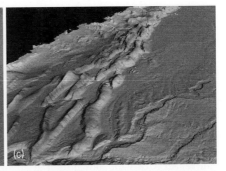

Fig. 1. In the original images, colors are used to portray sea-floor depth. Here, white represents the shallowest depths and dark gray the deepest; land is represented by black. (*a*) New Jersey continental slope. (*b*) Louisiana continental slope. (*c*) Oregon continental slope.

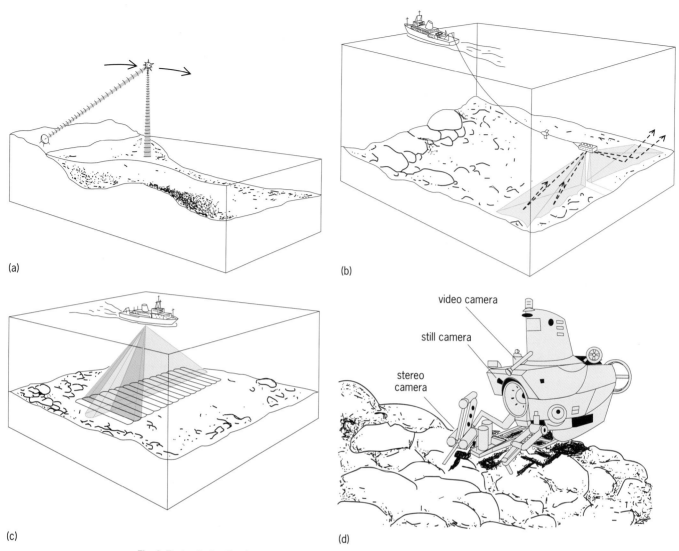

(a)

(b)

(c)

video camera

still camera

stereo camera

(d)

Fig. 2. Technologies that have revolutionized sea-floor mapping; (*a*) satellite altimetry; (*b*) side-scan sonar; (*c*) multibeam sonar; (*d*) submersibles. *(Courtesy of Roberto Osti)*

from other technologies. In general, a side-scan sonar consists of two sonar units attached to the sides of a sled tethered to the back of a ship (Fig. 2*b*). Each sonar emits a burst of sound that insonifies a long, narrow corridor of the sea floor extending away from the sled. Sound reflections from the corridor that echo back to the sled are then recorded by the sonar in their arrival sequence, with echoes from points farther away arriving successively later. The sonars repeat this sequence of "talking" and listening every few seconds as the sled is pulled through the water so that consecutive recordings build up a continuous swath of sea-floor reflections, which provide information about the texture of the sea floor. For example, if the sea floor is flat and smooth, none of the sound from the sonars is reflected back to the instrument, just as a mirror does not reflect back light shown on it at an angle. But if the sea floor has a roughness, the sound will be

reflected in multiple directions; and similar to light reflecting off broken glass, some of the reflections return to the sonar. By equating the amplitude of the returning echoes to different levels of gray, and the time that the echoes arrive back at the sled to distance, an image is obtained of sea-floor textures that looks like a black and white photograph. The textures in the image reflect a combination of sea-floor morphology and bottom sediment type; but like a single photograph, they cannot be used to determine sea-floor depths.

Multibeam sonar. The best technology for mapping sea-floor depths or bathymetry is multibeam sonar (Fig. 2*c*). These systems employ a series of sound sources and listening devices that are mounted on the hull of a survey ship. As with side-scan sonar, every few seconds the sound sources emit a burst that insonifies a long, slim strip of the sea floor aligned perpendicular to the ship's direction. The listening devices then begin recording sounds from within a fan of narrow sea-floor corridors that are aligned parallel to the ship and that cross the insonified strip. Thus, sound reflections received at the listening devices are only from relatively small sea-floor regions where the insonified strip and listening corridors intersect. The timing of these reflections yields a profile of sea-floor depth, and successive profiles collected as the ship moves build up a continuous swath of sea-floor bathymetry along the ship's track. By running the survey the same way that one mows a lawn, adjacent swaths are collected parallel to one another to produce a complete sea-floor map of an area.

Direct visual imaging. The most modern swath mapping systems now collect both bathymetry and side-scan sonar imagery. But the most accurate and detailed view of the sea floor is provided by direct visual imaging through bottom cameras, submersibles (Fig. 2*d*), remotely operated vehicles, or if the waters are not too deep, scuba diving. Of these, bottom cameras were the first widely used means of getting an upclose view of the sea floor. However, because light is scattered and absorbed in waters greater than about 33 ft (10 m) deep, the sea-floor area that bottom cameras can image is no more than a few meters. This limitation has been partly overcome by deep-sea submersibles and remotely operated vehicles, which provide researchers with the opportunity to explore the sea floor close-up for hours to weeks at a time. But even the sea-floor coverage that can be achieved with these devices is greatly restricted relative to side-scan sonar, multibeam sonar, and satellite altimetry. Hence, with each technology there is a trade-off in sea-floor coverage with resolution, and which technology is used depends on what information is needed.

Uses. Ever since large ships began plying the oceans, there has been a need to know what the sea floor looks like. At first this need was simply to avoid dangerous shoals upon which a ship could wreck. In the mid-1800s, the need increased with the first laying of transocean communication cables. World War II and the initiation of submarine warfare elevated the need to a matter of national defense, and mapping of the world's ocean floors was greatly accelerated. The vast body of information accrued by this effort went far beyond aiding militaries. It also led to the theory of plate tectonics, the backbone of modern geology that explains volcanoes, earthquakes, mountain chains, and many other Earth features. At present, sea-floor mapping is also aiding a variety of societal endeavors. High-resolution images of the sea floor are being used to locate and manage marine resources such as fisheries and oil and gas reserves, identify offshore faults and the potential for coastal damage due to earthquakes, and map out and monitor marine pollution. The greatly improved sea-floor imaging is providing information on what processes are affecting the sea floor, where these processes occur, and how they interact.

For background information *see* ACOUSTIC SIGNAL PROCESSING; ECHO SOUNDER; HYDROPHONE; MARINE GEOLOGY; SONAR; SONOBUOY; UNDERWATER SOUND in the McGraw-Hill Encyclopedia of Science & Technology.   Lincoln F. Pratson

Bibliography. L. F. Pratson and W. F. Haxby, Panoramas of the seafloor, *Sci. Amer.*, 276(6):66–71, 1997; L. F. Pratson and W. F. Haxby, What is the slope of the U.S. continental slope? *Geology*, 24(1):3–6, 1996; D. T. Sandwell, Geophysical applications of satellite altimetry, *Rev. Geophys. Suppl.*, pp. 132–137, 1990; R. Vogt and B. E. Tucholke (eds.), *Imaging the Ocean Floor: History and State of the Art—Geology of North America: The Western North Atlantic Region*, 1986.

Semiconductor

Semiconductors are an important class of materials with unique and attractive properties. By controlling the amount and type of impurities in a semiconductor, its electric conductivity can be varied by more than seven orders of magnitude. Because of their peculiar properties, some semiconductors can detect and generate light efficiently. These properties make semiconductors the basic materials for microelectronics and optoelectronics, which provide the technological foundations for the computer and communications industries.

Thin films versus substrates. Almost all electronic and optoelectronic devices use the properties of semiconductor thin films rather than the bulk semiconductor crystal. However, high-quality semiconductor bulk crystal is critical since it will be made into substrates as platforms to support the growth of semiconductor thin films. Semiconductor thin films in their most useful form are single crystals made of periodic arrays of atoms spaced by a distance called the lattice constant. To grow high-quality, defect-free semiconductor thin films, the lattice constant of the thin films must be equal to that of the substrate, a condition called lattice match. If these two lattice constants differ by as little as 1%, stress builds up rapidly with increasing film thickness. As soon as the thickness of the thin film exceeds about 10 nanometers, the high built-in stress due to lattice mismatch will create defects such as dislocations. Although most of the dislocations are located at the interface between the thin film and the substrate, the dislocations leave traces in the film as they are first nucleated in the thin film and then propagate toward the interface. Those traces are called threading dislocations and are detrimental to device performance and reliability.

Since semiconductor devices cannot tolerate threading dislocations, only lattice-matched thin films have been used so far to build them. In spite of the tremendous success in doing this, as demonstrated by fast computer chips and laser chips, a severe limitation on both device performance and device variety will remain if the constraint of lattice match cannot be lifted.

Need for a compliant substrate. Semiconductors can be divided into two groups: silicon and compound semiconductors. Silicon is the workhorse for microelectronics, and compound semiconductors are pivotal to optoelectronics and high-speed electronics. There is a growing need for integration of silicon with compound semiconductors to enhance the performance and functionality of silicon-based devices. For example, silicon-germanium compound semiconductors with a higher germanium composition than the silicon host crystal can normally tolerate are desirable for a new generation of integrated circuits. For compound semiconductors, the constraint of lattice match imposes more immediate challenges to device development. Antimonide compound semiconductors for infrared sensing cannot be grown without a large number of defects because their lattices are highly mismatched to that of gallium arsenide (GaAs) substrates, the prevailing substrates for compound semiconductors. The lasers used in fiber-optic systems have to be made on small, fragile, expensive indium phosphide (InP) substrates simply because silicon and gallium arsenide substrates do not meet the lattice-match requirement. Worst of all, gallium nitride (GaN) compound semiconductor thin films, which generate green, blue, and ultraviolet light for display and optical storage and have superior high-temperature, high-power characteristics, have no lattice-matched semiconductor substrates on which to grow. To remove this major roadblock to semiconductor research, a compliant substrate has been proposed.

Sacrificial compliant substrates. A compliant substrate is a new type of substrate converted from a traditional semiconductor substrate by engineering means to support the growth of defect-free semiconductor thin films of essentially any lattice constant. A substrate could conceivably become compliant if it were made extremely thin and free standing, so that it was flexible enough to accommodate the stress from lattice mismatch. However, such freestanding thin substrates cannot be realized with enough robustness and uniformity to be of practical use, so this concept does not offer a viable solution to the problem. An alternative design is based on the concept of a sacrificial substrate. In this case, defects such as dislocations still occur when the stress due to lattice mismatch is above the critical value. However, special sacrificial substrate techniques can make the dislocations form in the substrate instead of in the thin film. As a result, all stress-releasing dislocations leave their traces in the substrate rather than in the thin film. This state of affairs is highly desirable since for nearly all applications it is the quality of the thin film rather than that of the substrate that is of interest. In other words, high-quality thin films are achieved at the expense of the substrates, which are plastically deformed by dislocations. The concept of a sacrificial compliant substrate is relatively easy to realize and has become the focus of research.

When a semiconductor thin film is grown on a conventional semiconductor substrate, dislocations tend to form not in the substrate but in the thin film, which is energetically more favorable. In the design of a compliant substrate, an artificially formed interface is introduced within and near the surface of the substrate. Detailed analysis has shown that when the interface in the substrate is close (say, within 10 nm) to the free surface and has a particular interface structure, the part of the substrate between the free surface and the embedded interface tends to be more easily deformed to generate dislocations than the single-crystal semiconductor thin film, and hence serves as an effective compliant substrate.

Fabrication. A special technique to create a sacrificial compliant substrate is shown in the **illustration**. The embedded interface within the substrate is formed by first bonding two substrates together with an intentional angular misalignment and then etching back most of one substrate except for a very thin (around 10 nm) layer. Such an embedded interface in the substrate is called a twist boundary. As with many semiconductor grain boundaries that separate two parts of otherwise perfect single crystals, dislocations can terminate at the boundary or be attracted to it. When such a substrate is used as a compliant substrate for the growth of thin films with a different lattice constant, the growth interface and the twist-boundary interface interact in such a manner that stress-releasing dislocations prefer to be nucleated in the region between these two interfaces. As a result, the thin substrate region is badly plastically deformed whereas the grown semiconductor thin film becomes defect free; this result is precisely what

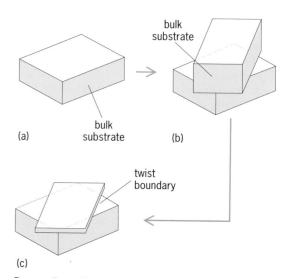

Process flow of forming a semiconductor compliant substrate containing a twist boundary. (*a*) Initial bulk substrate. (*b*) Result of bonding two substrates at an angle. (*c*) Compliant substrate with a twist boundary, created by removing most of one substrate.

a sacrificial compliant substrate is supposed to achieve.

Theoretical models. The use of embedded twist boundaries to form compliant substrates is such a new concept that very little research has been done on this technique so far. It is believed that the interaction between the lattice stress and the twist boundary is very complicated. One proposed model assumes that the embedded twist boundary migrates to the surface during the thin-film growth, and the atomic motions associated with the twist-boundary migration create dislocations suitable for strain release, without leaving traces of threading dislocations in the thin film. Other models assume that dislocation kinetics are responsible for the production of defect-free semiconductor thin films. More research is necessary to fully understand the physics of compliant substrates.

Experimental results. Compliant substrates have produced very encouraging experimental results. On gallium arsenide compliant substrates containing twist boundaries, high-quality quantum wells (1.5% mismatched to gallium arsenide) and thin films of indium antimonide (InSb; 15% mismatched to gallium arsenide) have been demonstrated, among other materials with different degrees of lattice mismatch. The quantum wells, which are special semiconductor thin-film structures showing pronounced quantum effects, are used to make 1.3-micrometer laser diodes for optical-fiber communication; and the indium antimonide thin films are used for infrared sensing, imaging, and solid-state sensors. The films grown on the compliant substrates have a defect density at least four orders of magnitude lower than those grown on conventional gallium arsenide substrates. Because indium antimonide thin film has the largest lattice mismatch with gallium arsenide next to gallium nitride, the demonstration of defect-free indium-antimonide on gallium arsenide compliant substrates indicates the possibility that any semiconductor thin film of interest can be grown on gallium arsenide. This makes the long-sought goal of a compliant universal substrate appear more attainable than ever before.

In addition, silicon compliant substrates containing twist boundaries have been fabricated. Experimental results have shown that high-quality germanium (4% mismatched to silicon) thin films can be grown on silicon compliant substrates. The demonstration of silicon compliant substrates is particularly significant, offering the possibility of integration of compound semiconductors with silicon. Such integration has the potential of revolutionizing the fields of microelectronics and optoelectronics.

For background information *see* CRYSTAL DEFECTS; CRYSTAL GROWTH; CRYSTAL STRUCTURE; INTEGRATED CIRCUITS; SEMICONDUCTOR; SEMICONDUCTOR HETEROSTRUCTURES in the McGraw-Hill Encyclopedia of Science & Technology.   Yu-Hwa Lo

Bibliography. F. E. Ejeckam et al., Dislocation-free InSb grown on GaAs compliant universal substrates, *Appl. Phys. Lett.*, 71(6):776–778, 1997; F. E. Ejeckam et al., Lattice engineered compliant substrate for defect-free heteroepitaxial growth, *Appl. Phys. Lett.*, 70:1685–1687, 1997.

Silicon

Silicon and oxygen are the most abundant elements in the Earth, excluding the metallic core. The Earth's crust and mantle are dominated by silicates, which are chemical compounds formed by silicon and oxygen. Changes in coordination of silicon by oxygen in the minerals with increasing pressure result in changes of physical properties, such as density, and transport properties of the silicates. The density changes, in particular, can be associated with seismic discontinuities within the Earth.

Tetrahedral silicon. Silicate minerals formed at the relatively low pressures typical of the Earth's crust and upper mantle are usually coordinated by four oxygen atoms. Together the oxygen and silicon atoms form tetrahedra whose apices are defined by the positions of the oxygen atoms (**illus.** *a*). Because the SiO_4 tetrahedron is a charged species with a net ionic charge of -4, it cannot exist in isolation. Charge balance in crystal structures occurs through two mechanisms: (1) Linking of tetrahedra by sharing oxygen atoms between them produces more complex silicate anions, but of lower charge. For example, if every SiO_4 tetrahedron shares all of its four oxygens with other tetrahedra, a neutral three-

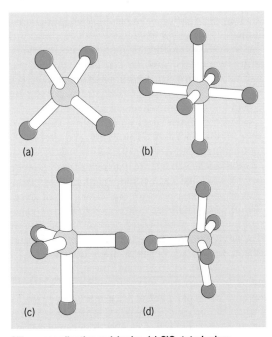

Silicon coordination polyhedra. (*a*) SiO_4 tetrahedron. (*b*) SiO_6 octahedron. (*c*) SiO_3X_2 trigonal bipyramid found in organosilicon compounds. (*d*) SiO_5 square-based pyramid found in $CaSiSiO_5$.

dimensional framework can be formed, such as that found in the low-pressure polymorphs of silicon dioxide (SiO_2), such as the minerals quartz and coesite. (2) Other cations may be introduced into the void spaces between the silicate tetrahedra. For example, the dominant mineral of the Earth's upper mantle, olivine, is formed of isolated SiO_4 tetrahedra connected together and charge-balanced by Mg^{2+} cations in octahedral coordination. *See* OLIVINE.

Octahedral silicon. Low-pressure silicates become stable and more dense as they are transformed under high pressure. In order to increase the density, the coordination number of the silicon is increased to six (illus. *b*), and the connectivity of the polyhedral units in the structure is therefore also increased. Stishovite, the high-pressure form of SiO_2, was the first mineral discovered to have silicon in octahedral coordination by oxygen. It occurs only in rocks that have been shocked to high pressures by meteorite impact. Other silicates with octahedrally coordinated silicon can be synthesized in the laboratory only at very high temperatures and pressures. The advent of an apparatus such as the multianvil press, capable of generating pressures of up to 3.6×10^6 lbf $\cdot$ in.$^{-2}$ (25 gigapascals) and temperatures of up to $4530°F$ ($2500°C$), has enabled silicates typical of the Earth's transition zone and lower mantle to be synthesized, recovered to room conditions, and characterized. In compounds of more complex chemical composition, especially those including alkali metal cations such as sodium (Na) and potassium (K), the steric requirements of the other cations in the structure result in some of the silicon forming SiO_4 tetrahedra and some SiO_6 octahedra.

Five-coordinated silicon. Since silicon occurs widely in four-coordination by oxygen in silicates at low pressures and in six-coordination at high pressures, it might be naively expected that silicon should occur in five-coordination at intermediate pressures. However, until recently, five-coordinated silicon was known only in a small number of organic crystal structures; indeed, the majority of organosilicon compounds contain silicon in five-coordination by a mixture of oxygen and other anions. This difference in behavior has been attributed to the relatively high difference in electronegativity between silicon and oxygen, which is more than twice the difference between silicon and carbon. In more ionic compounds the anions tend to form close-packed arrays within which there are only tetrahedral and octahedral interstices available for occupation by cations (including silicon). Thus, silicates normally contain silicon with these coordination environments.

In organosilicon compounds the silicon is coordinated by a mixture of oxygen atoms belonging to organic molecules and at least one atom such as carbon or nitrogen or a halide that is more electronegative than oxygen. The electronegative anions tend to form the apices of a trigonal bipyramid around the silicon, with oxygens occupying the equatorial positions (illus. *c*). The axial bonds from the silicon are always longer than the equatorial

bonds, and the average Si-O bond lengths in these compounds fall between those of SiO_4 tetrahedra and SiO_6 octahedra in silicates.

In 1996 the first inorganic silicate structure to contain silicon in five-coordination by oxygen was synthesized at high pressures and temperatures. The compound has the chemical formula $CaSi_2SiO_5$, and the structure contains SiO_4 tetrahedra and SiO_6 octahedra in addition to the SiO_5 groups. In contrast to the trigonal bipyramidal coordination found in organic compounds, this SiO_5 group forms a square-based pyramid (illus. *d*), which resembles an octahedron with one corner removed.

Role. The significance of five-coordinated silicon for the earth sciences does not lie in its occurrence as a structural element in one crystal structure. Its true importance is the role it is believed to play as a reaction intermediate or activated state in such dynamic processes as oxygen diffusion in minerals under high pressures, and the flow of silicate melts. Insights into the details of these processes at the atomic level can be obtained through using the structures described above as models for the local coordination of silicon, especially through the methods of computer simulation.

Diffusion in minerals. Solid-state diffusion is the process by which individual atomic species, such as silicon or oxygen, are transported through a bulk solid. Such transport is required when minerals react chemically with one another in the absence of fluid, or when a mineral decomposes into two or more other minerals as a result of a change in pressure or temperature. Diffusion on a local scale or atomic rearrangements are also necessary during isochemical changes in structure. Silicon diffusion in low-pressure structures containing tetrahedra probably occurs through displacement of the silicon through one face of its tetrahedron, into a neighboring but initially vacant tetrahedral site. The reaction intermediate that exists while the silicon is on the face of the tetrahedron is a SiO_5 group. Similarly, oxygen diffusion can proceed by attack of a fifth oxygen upon the tetrahedral silicon to form a SiO_5 group, followed by expulsion of one of the original oxygens.

Magnesium silicate perovskite ($MgSiO_3$) is the dominant phase in the Earth's lower mantle. Its structure is based upon SiO_6 octahedra. Computer simulations suggest that the dominant diffusion process in perovskites involves oxygens and vacancies. A small concentration of vacancies is formed by removal of oxygens from their normal sites, leaving SiO_5 square-based pyramids. Oxygen atoms can then transfer from adjacent complete octahedra, resulting in bulk transport.

Amorphization. When low-pressure silicates containing SiO_4 tetrahedra are compressed at room temperature, they do not transform to the equilibrium crystalline phases with octahedral silicon, because of lack of thermal energy to drive the required structural changes. Instead they transform to amorphous materials. Computer simulations of the amorphous state suggest that it is denser than the crystalline material because of the formation of SiO_5 trigonal bipyramids.

Amorphization also occurs on pressure release in some materials. Calcium silicate perovskite ($CaSiO_3$) is the second major component of the Earth's lower mantle. But when it is synthesized at high pressures and temperatures, the material recovered to room conditions is a glass containing tetrahedrally coordinated silicon. Computer simulations of the process of decompression suggest that the structure first partially disintegrates by loss of an oxygen from each SiO_6 octahedron to form partially connected SiO_5 groups with the square-based pyramid configuration. Exactly the same process is responsible for the formation of the SiO_5 groups in $CaSiSiO_5$ from the octahedra in the high-pressure phase, but in $CaSiSiO_5$ the process stops at this point. In calcium silicate perovskite, each of the SiO_5 groups expels a second oxygen to form chains of SiO_4 tetrahedra. The randomness of this process destroys the crystal structure, thereby producing an amorphous glass.

Density of melts. The ascent of magmas and the crystallization and separation of magmas once they are emplaced within the Earth's crust are controlled primarily by the temperature- and pressure-dependent densities and transport properties of silicate melts. Unlike crystalline structures, glasses possess no long-range structural order. Therefore, in addition to the mechanisms of compression available to crystal structures, such as bond shortening and bond bending, glasses and melts can increase their density by a continuous increase in the average coordination number of silicon. Even some silicate glasses formed at room pressure by quenching melts from high temperatures have been shown to contain small but significant amounts of five-coordinated silicon by nuclear magnetic resonance spectroscopy. The concentration of SiO_5 units increases with pressure. Computer simulations suggest that it reaches a maximum at pressures in the range of 1.5–3.0×10^6 lbf $\cdot$ in^{-2} (10–20 GPa). At higher pressures the dominant coordination for silicon is octahedral, as in crystalline materials. Because the SiO_5 group will be a reaction intermediate in the processes of both flow and diffusion, there is expected to be a maximum in the diffusion rates and a minimum in the viscosity of melts in this pressure range. The geometry of the SiO_5 groups in glasses appears to be trigonal-bipyramid, similar to the silicon coordination found in organosilicon compounds.

For background information *see* SILICA MINERALS; SILICATE MINERALS; SILICON in the McGraw-Hill Encyclopedia of Science & Technology.   Ross J. Angel

Bibliography. R. J. Angel et al., Structural characterisation of pentacoordinate silicon in a calcium silicate, *Nature*, 384:441–444, 1996; P. J. Heaney, C. T. Prewitt, and G. V. Gibbs (eds.), *Silica: Reviews of Mineralogy*, vol. 29, 1994; F. Liebau, *Structural Chemistry of Silicates*, 1985; J. F. Stebbins, P. F. McMillan, and D. B. Dingwell, *Structure, Dynamics and Properties of Silicate Melts: Reviews of Mineralogy*, vol. 32, 1995.

Single-electron transistor

Single-electron transistors are devices whose critical dimensions are extremely small: tens of atoms to a hundred atoms across, that is, in the nanometer range. Associated with these dimensions is an extremely small capacitance. This small capacitance, in turn, magnifies the energy required for a single electron to charge the volume defined by the critical dimension, causing this charging energy to become comparable to or larger than the thermal energy. Consequently, conduction is prevented if not enough energy is available to the electron attempting to traverse this island, and the transistor exhibits characteristics sensitive to transport and storage of single electrons. In semiconductors, at these small dimensions, device operation also becomes sensitive to quantum confinement effects. Hence, both single-electron and quantum effects help determine the device behavior, and result in a large nonlinearity in the relation of current to applied voltage and the quantization of electrons in a small volume. Such devices can be coupled to a less confined region, namely, a channel of a field-effect transistor, resulting in a memory element. Because of their smaller dimensions, low voltages, operation with a limited number of electrons, and use of silicon as the semiconductor medium, these memory elements offer a very high areal density of storage, compatibility with present-day microelectronic practice, and low-power operation. The devices cover a large design range, including high-speed elements (with write times measured in tens of nanoseconds) that require refreshing similar to that of dynamic random-access memories, and medium-speed elements (having microsecond write times) that display nonvolatility similar to that of electrically erasable and programmable memories and flash memories. Conventional dynamic memories now in production are 64 megabits in size and occupy approximately 1 cm^2 (0.16 in.^{2}) of silicon chip area. Because of their significantly smaller size, the density of the new memories can exceed tens of gigabits in the same chip area; that is, they offer improvement in density by many orders of magnitude, and a large reduction in power density.

Single-electron and quantum effects. For a small surface area and hence a small volume, confined by a barrier (**Fig. 1a**), the capacitance of a device can become small enough that the electrostatic energy required to place an electron in the volume from adjacent reservoirs (the source, a region that provides the electrons for conduction; and the drain, a region where electrons go) becomes larger than the thermal energy. For example, for a capacitance of 10^{-18} farad, the charging energy ($e^2/2C$, where e is the fundamental charge and C is the capacitance to the surroundings) is 80 millielectronvolts, which is larger than the thermal energy at room temperature of 26 meV. This implies that there is a range of applied voltage around zero for which no current flows through this structure. This phenomenon is

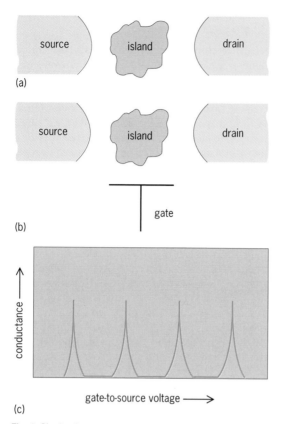

(b)

gate

(c)

conductance ⟶

gate-to-source voltage ⟶

Fig. 1. Single-electron transistor. (*a*) **Island whose size and surrounding barrier impose a Coulomb blockade.** (*b*) **Same structure with an additional electrode, the gate electrode.** (*c*) **Resulting conductance characteristic as a function of gate-to-source voltage.**

known as the Coulomb blockade effect. The number of electrons in the confined volume, called the island, is constrained to be a small integer in a semiconductor because of the reduced density of states resulting from the small volume. The addition of a gate (Fig. 1*b*) makes it possible to influence the electrochemical energy of the island and hence obtain the condition where the charge in the island is allowed to fluctuate by $\pm e$. This voltage bias point with a fluctuating charge, due to the shifting of the Coulomb blockade range by the applied gate potential, is a charge degeneracy point and causes the conductance between the reservoirs to display periodic peaks as a function of the gate voltage (Fig. 1*c*).

In order for this behavior to be observed at room temperature, the dimensions of the island must be less than 10 nm for silicon as the semiconductor and silicon dioxide as the barrier. This is a dimension range of the order of the electron de Broglie wavelength in semiconductors. Hence, confinement effects are also substantial, and the island is sometimes referred to as a quantum dot. An orthodox single-electron transistor consists of this small island (usually silicon) connected to a source region of electrons (usually silicon) and a region where the electrons can be drained (usually silicon) upon their transit through this small island. This connection is

provided by a barrier through which the electron must be able to tunnel; that is, it must have specific characteristics conducive to observation of the single-electron effects. The transistor can also be fabricated from compound semiconductors, in which case it requires the use of depleting Schottky barriers that confine a two-dimensional electron gas in order to create the island coupled to the reservoirs.

In either case, a gate electrode controls the potential of the island and thus the current flow through the island. The device is a miniaturized field-effect transistor with some substantial differences: a finite and small number of electrons are involved, a large nonlinearity arises from the Coulomb blockade effect, and the gate-voltage dependence of the drain-to-source conductance is periodic. In order that the change in system energy be much larger than the thermal energy and the energy width of the eigenstate in the island, the barrier tunneling resistance should be much larger than the resistance quantum (more precisely, $\hbar/e^2 \approx 4.1$ kiloohm, where $\hbar$ is the reduced Planck's constant). Barrier resistance and single-electron transport result in small currents (typically several nanoamperes or less) and large time constants in charging the interconnections of integrated-circuit devices.

Sensitivity to imperfections. Single-electron sensitivity also implies sensitivity to stray charged defects in the vicinity of a device, and quantum confinement implies sensitivity to variations in the dimensions of islands through their effect on the bound-state energy. For example, in the case in which the source, the drain, and the gate are grounded, the electrochemical potential of the small island can still differ from that of the surrounding by up to $e^2/2C$. The gate influences the island through only a fraction of the total capacitance, while the rest of the capacitance represents coupling to the rest of the environment. As an example, a charged defect in the vicinity of the island also produces a fractional polarization charge on the island—an offset charge. Such defects are known to exist at semiconductor interfaces and in insulators such as silicon dioxide with a finite but low probability. The change in electrochemical potential means that there is a variation in the gate voltage at which the Coulomb blockade is overcome.

Another source of variation is that of dimension. Quantum confinement leads to a variation in the energies that electrons are allowed to have when they are in the quantum dot. The energy levels in a confined medium follow an inverse-square dependence on dimension. The charging energy of the island is related to the energy of the states allowed as well as the electrostatic charging energy, $e^2/2C$. The capacitance is proportional to linear dimension, hence the electrostatic charging component of the electron energy also has an inverse dependence on length. Thus, reproducible conduction in such single-electron devices requires control of dimensions on the atomic scale and elimination of stray charge.

Solution to sensitivity problem. A solution to this dilemma of sensitivity and the needs of microelectronics is to couple the quantization of the electrons to the flow of electrons in a conventional field-effect transistor. Either a single quantum dot (an island) can be placed on the channel of a conventional transistor (**Fig. 2a**), or multiple quantum dots can be placed there (Fig. 2b). Now, a single electron or multiple electrons on the tiny islands act as a screen between the gate and the channel. The placement of these electrons is still controlled by the Coulomb-blockade and size-quantization effects, and their injection from the inversion channel region to the dot occurs because of the lowering of the gate electrochemical energy. But the effect of these electrons is observed through their influence on the electrons

in the channel. The presence of electrons in the dot or dots reduces the number of electrons, and hence the current, in the channel. But this current is not limited by a barrier such as that of an orthodox single-electron transistor and can be much larger than a few nanoamperes. Such devices can also be insensitive to random charged defects because statistics can be improved by increased numbers. More than one electron can be stored in a single quantum-dot memory, and more than one quantum dot can be occupied in a multiple-quantum-dot memory, the nanocrystal memory.

The quantum-dot memory (Fig. 2a) consists of a silicon channel of a silicon-on-insulator substrate. Between the channel and the gate exists a tunneling layer of silicon dioxide, a silicon quantum dot, and

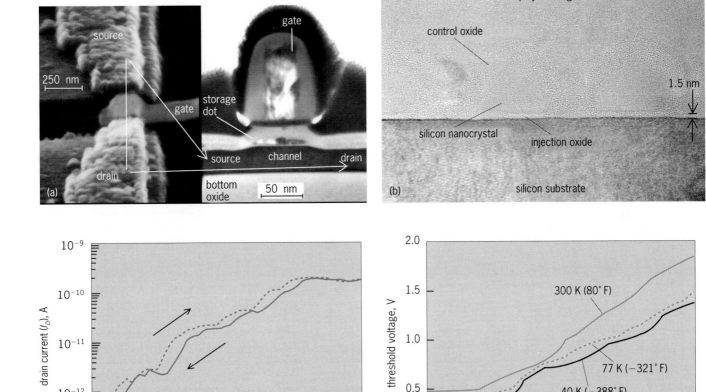

Fig. 2. Quantum-dot and multiple-quantum-dot (nanocrystal) memories. (a) Transmission electron micrographs of quantum-dot memory. The picture on the right is a cross section along the line on the left. The picture on the left is angled, so its scale bar applies only to horizontal dimensions. (b) Transmission electron micrograph of nanocrystal memory with three single-crystal islands (silicon nanocrystals). (c) Changes in drain current of a quantum-dot memory as the gate voltage is increased and electrons are stored on the quantum dot. Measurements were made at a temperature of 90 K (−298°F) and a drain-source voltage of 0.2 V. (d) Shift in threshold voltage of the nanocrystal memory as the gate voltage is varied and an increasing number of electrons is placed on each nanocrystal. *(After S. Tiwari et al., Single charge and confinement effects in nano-crystal memories, Appl. Phys. Lett., 69:1232–1234, 1996)*

a controling layer of silicon dioxide. The tunneling oxide allows charging of the quantum dot by the channel. The nanocrystal memory (Fig. 2b) consists of a multitude of single-crystal silicon quantum dots between the silicon channel and the gate electrode of polysilicon along with the tunneling (injection) oxide and the control oxide.

In either memory, the source and drain regions, which are doped, form the reservoirs for the flow of electrons in the channel. When the gate is sufficiently positively biased with respect to the source and drain, an inversion region forms in the channel, and provided the Coulomb blockade and the size quantization allow it, a finite and small number of electrons are injected into the quantum dot or dots. If the current due to the flow of electrons in the channel were now to be sensed by applying a drain-to-source voltage, a significantly reduced current would be measured because the presence of electrons in the dot or dots reduces the number of electrons in the channel. This change in the current can be very substantial, amounting to orders of magnitude (Fig. 2c).

The most important property of a transistor is usually the condition for the onset of conduction, a threshold gate voltage at which the channel begins to conduct. The presence of electrons in the dot or dots changes this condition. In the case of a nanocrystal memory, this variation in threshold voltage as the gate-to-source voltage is changed and one, two, three, and more electrons are stored in the dots, leads to a characteristic staircase shape (Fig. 2d).

Advantages. Reduction in size produces large advantages in density for these microelectronic structures. Another advantage is in power, which is an equally important constraint in the progress of microelectronics. Powers per bit need to be reduced to nanowatts and below in order to make the power consumption and energy distribution of multigigabit and terabit devices managable. By using very few electrons and low voltages for operation, the power dissipation for storage and sensing are minimized.

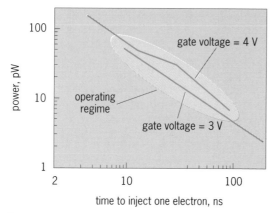

Fig. 3. Power-delay behavior resulting from storage of a single electron in a single-electron memory.

Calculations (**Fig. 3**) show that this minimization is likely to become feasible with these memories while providing continuity with the current practice of microelectronics.

For background information *see* CAPACITANCE; NANOSTRUCTURE; QUANTIZED ELECTRONIC STRUCTURE (QUEST); SEMICONDUCTOR; SEMICONDUCTOR MEMORIES; TRANSISTOR; TUNNELING IN SOLIDS in the McGraw-Hill Encyclopedia of Science & Technology.

Sandip Tiwari

Bibliography. T. A. Fulton and G. J. Dolan, Observation of single-electron charging effects in small tunnel junctions, *Phys. Rev. Lett.*, 59:109–120, 1987; H. Grabert and M. H. Devoret (eds.), *Single Charge Tunneling: Coulomb Blockade Phenomena in Nanostructures*, 1992; L. Guo, E. Leobandung, and S. Chou, A silicon single-electron transistor memory operating at room temperature, *Science*, 275:649–651, 1997; S. Tiwari et al., Single charge and confinement effects in nano-crystal memories, *Appl. Phys. Lett.*, 69:1232–1234, 1996.

Software engineering

Software reuse and software metrics are rapidly developing areas in the field of software engineering. In recent years, both have contributed to the productivity of the software development process as well as the quality of computer software.

Software Reuse

Moore's law notes that the performance doubles every 18 months for semiconductor devices with approximately constant price. There is also a doubling phenomenon that applies to software. The size of new versions of any particular unit application has doubled at about the same rate as for hardware. For example, the size of new versions of a particular document-processing program has increased from 40 kilobytes to 200 kilobytes, 1 megabyte, and 5 megabytes over a decade. Such increase in size of a software product occurs by adding new features to the core functionality of the product or to some related product. The way that software developers can achieve this ever-increasing productivity (some measure of software produced per unit development time) is by reuse of software parts, either from previous versions of software products or from libraries of reusable parts. Just as a new model car does not have all newly designed parts, so new software will not have all newly designed parts if it is to be developed in a timely manner. Growth in productivity cannot be achieved by just adding numbers of software developers, because the overhead of communication and interference between interacting workers increases as the number of workers and the amount of interaction increases. Productivity cannot be achieved by just good design, but good design is necessary in order to allow reuse of parts to occur. The kinds and sizes of reusable parts for software have changed as the size of software has increased.

Reuse of components will also improve the quality of new software. Components that have been tested through use will have fewer residual errors than newly developed code.

Reuse of procedure libraries. All programming languages provide libraries of commonly used functions and procedures. Examples include mathematical functions such as "cos," string functions such as "substring," and system utilities such as "date." These are characterized by the property that procedures do not retain state information from previous calls to either the same or other procedures.

Reuse of class libraries. Procedure libraries are not suited for defining related operations with retained state information, but that is exactly what classes and objects encapsulate. Object-oriented languages help in structuring new software, and they provide even greater benefits in the definition of reusable parts. Standard data structures (such as lists, queues, tables, and vectors) and graphical user interface (GUI) parts are common, reusable classes provided with object-oriented languages. Other domain-specific or device-specific classes are maintained by individual development groups. The development of such proprietary components provides a competitive advantage for building new software.

Languages with strict type checking provide a safer base for software development, but also a more restrictive base for definition of standard data-structure classes. For such languages, parametrized classes provide a kind of generator that can be reused to make specific classes. For general classes, sharing has been enhanced by access via the File Transfer Protocol (FTP) and the World Wide Web, and by distribution via CD-ROM drives. For reuse in client-server architectures, objects can be provided for use by client applications. CORBA (common object request broker architecture) defines a structure for reuse of distributed objects.

Reuse of assemblies. Classes define single objects rather than subsystem assemblies (even though the class may use subcomponent classes). Frameworks and construction systems are contrasting mechanisms to allow reuse of an assembly of several parts.

Frameworks. A framework is a working assembly, typically a working program or a working collection of tasks, for which it is intended that very simple component classes will be extended to provide greater functionality. For example, a simple compiler framework program can be extended by redefining classes of the grammar components. The key point is that extended components must have the same interface to the assembly as the original components. The extended component classes must be compiled and then linked with the framework (static linking). Frameworks for common applications (such as a graphics editor and simple games) may be included as example files within programming-language development systems. Frameworks for specialized applications are usually proprietary, and benefit the owners.

Frameworks are related in structure to the use of dynamically linkable components and plug-in components. Dynamically linkable components are separately compiled and not linked to any main program. They provide an interface whereby programs that support the same interface can call the component and receive back results. This is like a remote procedure call, but without the component being remote. Dynamically linkable components can be shared by several application programs. For example, a word-processing program and a spreadsheet program may use the same spelling checker component. Plug-in components are similar, but differ in the mechanisms by which they are connected to an application program. For example, a Web browser can use different plug-in components to view different kinds of images. The plug-in parts can be separate applications which are accessed via a dynamically linkable reference component.

Construction systems. In contrast with frameworks, construction systems (or kits) are auxiliary programs, together with libraries of reusable components, that enable a user to build an assembly of some of the components. The construction system then generates code for the constructed application.

The most common construction system is the graphical user interface builder. It uses a visual interface to manipulate visual components so as to compose a new visual interface tailored for the user application. The user must then extend the generated framework with the application functions. Graphical user interface builders are incorporated within several visual program development systems.

Construction systems may use a textual, domain-specific language to describe an assembly of components. For example, the Estelle language is used to describe protocols, and then the Estelle description is compiled to create an executable language. Various computer-aided software engineering (CASE) tools are also construction systems. The CASE tool is used to construct a visual model of a program or database, and then it is able to generate a code framework from this model.

Patterns. Whereas class libraries, frameworks, and construction systems aid the reuse of components of executable code, patterns are a description of a more abstract design structure of a group of components. Patterns support reuse at the design level rather than at the code level. The use of patterns appears to help software productivity almost as much as reuse of components.

Classification and retrieval. At present, the reuse of components is often limited to general domains (such as data structures and graphical use interfaces) for which components are publicly available, or to proprietary components for specialized domains (such as for point-of-sale systems). Before much larger numbers of specialized components can be widely shared, there need to be more public archives of components and better methods of classification and description (specification) of components in order to support browsing and retrieval by potential users.   William Hankley

Software Metrics

Measurement is the process through which some aspect or characteristic of an object or an event is quantified. Measurements are used to answer questions such as how much and how many. Measurements help to determine such things as how much a person is paid, how much a person weighs, how much the government spends, and how fast an automobile is traveling.

Every measurement process begins with a definition of the characteristic to be quantified, that is, the property or condition of the object or event that is to be associated with a number, such as salary, weight, or speed. In the area of software engineering, software metrics have emerged as a way of measuring some attributes or characteristics of both the software being produced and the process to produce that software. In this sense, embedded in any software metric is the idea of assigning quantitative values to the characteristics of a program during its entire life cycle. The ultimate goal of measuring these process and product characteristics is to provide managers and practitioners with a definite set of criteria that are meaningful, reasonable to collect, and capable of measuring progress and predicting results throughout the entire life cycle.

In a narrower sense, the term software metrics has been used to denote a set of techniques whose aim is to measure the quality of a computer program. A quality program is defined as one that is correct, reliable, efficient, usable, maintainable, flexible, testable, portable, and reusable. In other words, a quality program should satisfy the user's specifications, function with precision, use a minimal set of resources to perform its function, be maintainable and testable with minimum effort, and be transferable to another platform without significant changes, while at the same time being easy to learn.

In this narrower sense, the focus is on the program, its components, and how these components interact with each other. Here, for example, are identified metrics that attempt to capture the psychological complexity of a program module or pro-

gram unit. In this context, a complex program means one that is difficult to read and understand—hence, a program that is difficult to modify and maintain later on.

Intraprocedure and interprocedure. Also in this narrower sense, metrics can be divided into two categories: intraprocedure and interprocedure. Among the intraprocedure metrics are found those concerned with the flow and use of control structure in a module. There is considerable agreement among computer professionals that complicated, or "spaghetti," code should be minimized or avoided completely. Interprocedure metrics determine the complexity of a program as a function of the relationships of the different modules constituting a program.

Intraprocedure metrics tend to expose the control flow by representing programs as directed graphs (flow graphs), where a node in the graph corresponds to a block of sequential code and branches correspond to decisions taken in the program. The complexity of the code is then derived from its flow graph. Most of the widely used metrics fall in this category. For example, within a flow graph, McCabe's cyclomatic number is calculated as the total number of decision statements plus one. If this cyclomatic number exceeds a predefined value, say 10, then the code of the module is considered to be too complicated to understand it and the entire module needs to be rewritten.

Interprocedure metrics, in contrast, tend to estimate the complexity of a module or program based on the way that data are used, organized, and allocated in relationship with some other modules. Here the degree of association of the modules (coupling) can be measured by how they interact through a common environment of data. Now, among M objects, there are $M \cdot (M - 1)$ different ways of interacting with each other. This relationship makes it very difficult to understand the interactions between M modules that may share a common environment of, say, N data elements. In this case, there are $N \cdot M \cdot (M - 1)$ paths along which errors or changes can propagate. For example, in a program that has 10 modules and 25 common variables, there are $(10) \cdot (25) \cdot (10 - 1)$, or 2250, paths through which an error can propagate. It should be clear from this

Software metrics and their applications to activities of the software life cycle

Activity	Quantity to be measured or estimated	Selected input to the metric
Analysis model	Size of the program or system	Number of user inputs, user outputs, user inquiries, files, external interfaces
Specification quality	Completeness, correctness, understandability, verifiability, traceability, reusability	Number of functional requirements, nonfunctional requirements, requirements with identical interpretation by technical reviewers
High-level design	Structural complexity, data complexity, system complexity	Number of modules controlled by the module (fan-out), modules that control the given module (fan-in), input and output variables
Source code metrics	Size in terms of lines of code	Non-comment lines of code, size of design
	Size in terms of functional content of the software	Number of user inputs, user outputs, user inquiries, files, external interfaces
Testing measures	Testing effort	Program volume, program level, number of distinct operators and operands, total number of operands and operator occurrences
Maintenance	Effort required to develop new software and maintain old software	Number of modules in current release, modules in current release that have changed or been added, modules of preceding release that were deleted

example that, because of the high number of cases that need to be considered, finding an error in this type of environment may be quite difficult. Some common measurements considered in this interprocedure category include characteristics such as the number of procedure calls, the number of references to global variables, and the number of input and output parameters.

Need for metrics. The need to produce high-quality software at lower cost is a very powerful economic incentive in light of the percentage costs associated with the software development process. In fact, more than 50% of all software projects have schedule slips and cost overruns. In addition, within the software life cycle, studies show that, on the average, up to 60% of the development effort may be consumed in the testing and maintenance of the programs. Software metrics are intended to alleviate this situation. However, in order to accomplish this a metric should satisfy a minimal set of criteria which require that the metric be simple and computable, consistent and objective, and programming-language independent, and provide effective feedback. That metrics are considered promising and useful can be seen by their wide use in the different phases of the software life cycle (see **table**).

Performance. Since their introduction in the mid-1970s, many complexity metrics have been developed as a result of the efforts of the research community. These measures have focused on the problems and methods of producing high-quality software. Experiences in the use of complexity metrics in the computer industry have been mixed. Many companies have been successful; others have reported failures. Sometimes the reason for failure has been the unrealistic expectation that a single metric can be used as a panacea to solve all software maladies. No single metric will suffice. On other occasions, the reluctance of managers and practitioners to apply the metric and gather data has proven insurmountable. Metrics, in such cases, are sometimes seen as a tool to evaluate individual performance, and not a product or a process. These fears and doubts may not be entirely unjustified. Despite the fact that numerous metrics exist, none has gained widespread acceptance as a good measure. In addition, developers sometimes feel overwhelmed by the volume of data, and it is not always clear what program characteristics need to be considered to improve the quality of the software being produced. However, in spite of all the failures that may have occurred, most practitioners and researchers are convinced that metrics are a valuable tool to improve the overall process of producing quality software.

For background information *see* MATHEMATICAL SOFTWARE; OBJECT-ORIENTED PROGRAMMING; SOFTWARE; SOFTWARE ENGINEERING in the McGraw-Hill Encyclopedia of Science & Technology.

Ramon A. Mata-Toledo

Bibliography. A. Behforooz and F. J. Hudson, *Software Engineering Fundamentals*, 1996; S. N. Cant, D. R. Jeffrey, and B. Henderson-Sellers, *Information and Software Technology*, 37(7):351–362, 1995; N. E. Fenton and S. L. Pfleeger, *Software Metrics*, 1997; E. Gamma et al., *Design Patterns: Elements of Reusable Object-Oriented Software*, 1995; R. S. Pressman, *Software Engineering: A Practitioner's Approach*, 4th ed., 1997; Special issue on object-oriented application frameworks, *Commun. ACM*, vol. 40, no. 10, October 1997; Special issue on object-oriented reuse, *IEEE Comput.*, vol. 30, no. 10, October 1997.

Soil chemistry

Soil nutrients taken up by plants are conveyed to animals and humans in food; thus soil chemistry has significant effects on the quality of life. At times, levels of mineral nutrients or soil conditions (such as pH, which affects removal of the nutrients from the soil) are not optimal, and difficulties ensue. Thus, there may be deficiency disorders at one end of the supply spectrum or toxicities at the other. The soil relationships of the micronutrient element selenium are a case in point. Selenium is recognized, at levels of less than 1 part per million (ppm) in the diet, to be an essential nutrient, yet in excess quantities a potent poison.

Problems with dietary selenium. Selenium toxicity was confirmed in 1937, when selenium was identified as the active principle in poisonings of horses and other livestock in states of the northern Great Plains. Locally called alkali disease, the sickness involved loss of hair, sloughing of hoof tissue, and sometimes death. An aggravating factor was the presence of unique range plants, including members of the genus *Astragalus*, a wild vetch, which can accumulate high levels of selenium from the soil. Such plants are called selenium indicators, since they grow only where soil selenium is high. They clearly contribute to the instances of livestock poisoning.

In very small amounts, selenium is an essential nutrient. Insufficiency of selenium in an animal's diet results in problems such as liver necrosis in pigs; white muscle disease, a type of myopathy, in young calves and lambs; and exudative diathesis in baby chicks. Selenium deficiency also has broad, detrimental effects on the major metabolic processes of growth and reproduction. Livestock producers now routinely include selenium supplementation in their operational technology worldwide. Biochemists have attributed much of selenium's beneficial activity to its presence in enzymes that counteract oxidative damage; there is evidence that selenium is an integral part of the enzyme glutathione peroxidase. The extent of the benefits attained from dietary selenium supplementation reflects the seriousness of the dietary deficiency of the element. In the severely deficient grazing lands of New Zealand, spectacular improvement of lambing percentages followed selenium supplementation of ewes pastured on them. Similarly, positive results have been seen in elimination of losses of young beef calves in the

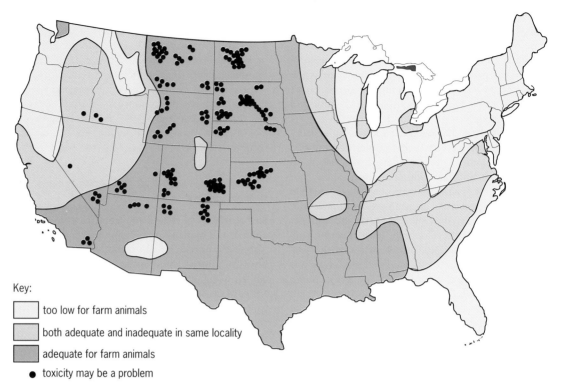

Key:

▢ too low for farm animals

▢ both adequate and inadequate in same locality

▢ adequate for farm animals

● toxicity may be a problem

Map showing the selenium status of soils and forages in the United States. *(After Council for Agricultural Science and Technology, Selenium: An essential poison, Sci. Food Agric., pp. 22–26, 1986)*

volcanic range area of central Oregon. Judicious supplementation with selenium has also been found to have a protective effect against livestock problems such as mastitis in dairy cows and retained placentas after calving. To aid in determining areas of usefulness for selenium supplementation, selenium-status maps have been prepared for a number of countries, including the United States (see **illus.**).

Methods of selenium supplementation. Where a need for additional selenium in animals is indicated by presence of selenium-responsive disease or by substandard growth or reproductive performance, several technologies have been developed for supplementation. Selenium can be made available orally to animals, usually as sodium selenite (Na_2SeO_3), either in their feed or in mineral mixtures consumed with the feed. The level is usually adjusted to supply 0.1–0.3 ppm of selenium in the total diet dry matter; however, local feed control or veterinary authorities should be consulted for the best level to use in specific local circumstances. Selenium may also be given by intramuscular injection, and several products are commercially available which often also contain vitamin E that tends to support selenium's protective function. In grazing ruminants (cattle, sheep), an ingenious heavy pellet, or bolus, has been developed which lodges in the forestomach and gradually dispenses selenium for as long as a year. Elemental selenium is used, which is sparingly soluble and useful over extended time periods. Earlier versions of this treatment employed iron filings to give added weight. Later products include a soluble glass bolus which is impregnated with selenium, and an osmotic-pump device which releases measured amounts of selenium over time.

A further alternative supplementation method, which works directly in the soil chemistry, is the addition of selenium to fertilizers, usually in the form of sodium selenate (Na_2SeO_4). This method counteracts natural soil deficiencies of the element and supports the growth of feed or forage crops with adequate levels of selenium for normal health. The amount most frequently used supplies 10 g (0.35 oz) of selenium per hectare (2.5 acres). This method has been applied successfully on a commercial scale in New Zealand and Finland, small countries with extensive areas of selenium-deficient cropland. In New Zealand, soil amendment with selenium was requested by the livestock industry, an important part of the nation's economy. In Finland, it was prompted by concerns for the health of the human population. In both countries, this practice has been in use for over a decade, and careful monitoring indicates that it does provides an adequate supply of selenium and is safe from the viewpoint of the maintenance of the quality of the environment.

Human implications of selenium. The dramatic responses by animals to selenium led to interest in possible benefits to human health. In industrialized countries, interregional shipment of foods tends to lessen the possibility of selenium deficiency or toxicity. Nevertheless, instances of selenium deficiency in humans have been reported, notably in China, where Keshan disease is selenium responsive. Keshan disease is a cardiomyopathy, affecting mostly young people from rural families which produce their own food. First seen in Heilongjiang province in northeast China, the disease extends southwesterly through a belt of low-selenium soils. Research in a number of countries suggests that selenium may exert an important, protective effect against some human health problems, including certain types of cancer and coronary disease.

Selenium in environment. It is important to remember that in excess quantities selenium can become a potent toxin. This aspect was given new prominence when deformities and deaths among nesting waterfowl at the Kesterson reservoir in California's San Joaquin Valley were attributed to excess selenium in irrigation runoff water. The source of the high selenium was found to be a rocky outcrop on the west side of the valley from which the selenium leached to the valley floor and was ultimately picked up in the irrigation runoff. The runoff was released into some shallow wetland ponds at Kesterson, where the selenium and some other soil nutrients were concentrated to toxic levels. With this incident in one of the United States' most productive agricultural areas, concern was voiced about the environmental safety of selenium and whether livestock supplementation practices might contribute to a soil buildup that could become dangerous. However, data were assembled attesting to the safety of approved animal uses of selenium. Although the use of selenium in food animal production is recognized as desirable in areas of deficiency, the presence of excess selenium in Kesterson and in some other areas is a serious matter. One proposal is to use plants as scavengers of excess selenium, thus lowering soil levels when they are harvested, then using this plant material for purposes such as livestock feeding or industrial applications.

Regulation of selenium. Since selenium is used in the production of food animals, its use in the United States is regulated by the Food and Drug Administration (FDA). Initially, such regulation was complicated by experimental data showing that selenium, fed at high levels to laboratory rats, was carcinogenic, but subsequent studies invalidated this concept. In 1974, the FDA authorized supplementation of animal diets with not more than 0.1 ppm selenium for pigs and growing chickens and 0.2 ppm for turkeys. The authorization has since been extended to all classes of food animals and poultry, and the permissible level has been raised to 0.3 ppm.

The remarkable amount of research with selenium over the last half century has shown that its metabolic activity can bring significant health benefits to animals and humans. The research has also lent emphasis to the importance of soil chemistry to the food supply.

For background information *see* SELENIUM; SOIL CHEMISTRY in the McGraw-Hill Encyclopedia of Science & Technology.   James E. Oldfield

Bibliography. E. D. Andrews, W. J. Hartley, and A. B. Grant, Selenium-responsive diseases of animals in New Zealand, *N.Z. Vet. J.*, 16:3–17, 1968; J. A. Moore, R. Noiva, and I. C. Wells, Selenium concentrations in plasma of patients with arteriographically defined coronary arteriosclerosis, *Clin. Chem.*, 30:1171–1173, 1984; A. A. Nelson, O. G. Fitzhugh, and H. O. Calvery, Liver tumors following cirrhosis caused by selenium in rats, *Cancer Res.*, 3:230–236, 1943; H. M. Ohlendorf et al., Embryonic mortality and abnormalities of aquatic birds: Apparent impacts of selenium from irrigation drainage water, *Sci. Total Environ.*, 52:49–63, 1986; J. T. Rotruck et al., Selenium: Biochemical role as a component of glutathione peroxidase, *Science*, 179:588–590, 1973.

Soil variability

Agronomic production, the growing of plants for food and fiber, is undergoing a technological revolution. Farmers and ranchers are using many of the same advanced and elaborate tools used in industry. Computer technology is driving this revolution. For the food and fiber producer, a significant development is real-time positioning capability, which means that a portable computer is able to determine its position on Earth almost instantaneously. The primary method of position acquisition used by agriculture is the Global Positioning System (GPS). This system is composed of computerized ground receivers and 24 satellites in orbit around the Earth. The satellites emit signals that allow a receiver on Earth (or in space, for that matter) to precisely determine its location (latitude, longitude, and elevation) through a mathematical method known as triangulation. GPS receivers mounted on tractors, sprayers, or combines (see **illus.**) or carried by hand allow farmers or ranchers to know their location in a field or pasture or rangeland to an accuracy of 10–16 ft (3–5 m) at present and a future accuracy of 1–2 in.

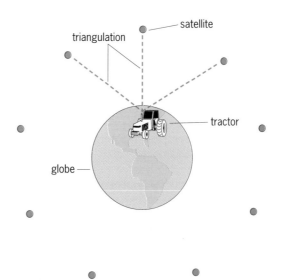

Global Positioning System (GPS) with the receiver mounted on a tractor.

(3–5 cm). This real-time positioning capability is resulting in a significant increase in the intensity of farm and ranch management. This intense management is referred to as site-specific farming or precision farming.

This technological advancement is important because soil profiles that are only centimeters to meters apart exhibit much variability in chemical and physical makeup. The chemical and physical variabilities result in variable crop-yield potential from one place in a field to another. Soil physical parameters are particle size (texture), composite particle configuration (structure), and pore configuration (porosity). Soil chemical parameters involve the basic chemical composition of the dissolved and undissolved material in the profile.

Soil differences. Farmers and ranchers have long known that there is a significant difference in the yield potential of soil from one place in a field to another. The physical and chemical differences in soil result from site-specific variable geological soil-forming processes. With the exception of tile drainage systems, pH-regulating compounds, and fertilizer, in most cases it is not economically feasible to manually alter the soil's physical or chemical properties. Tile drainage systems, when installed, lower the water table and significantly reduce the salinity concentration of soil water. Limestone (calcium carbonate) is effectively used to raise the pH of acid soils. Waste acids are used to lower the pH of alkaline soils. Fertilizers increase the amount of a specifically needed nutrient. Physical and chemical properties of soil determine its inherent ability to supply water and nutrients to plants.

The physical makeup of soil is complex and changes greatly across short distances. For example, granite bed rock is found at the surface in some locations, but it is almost impossible for plants to grow in granite. Plants growing on granite outcroppings have their roots in the formation cracks. It is not unusual to find soil profiles that are 20 ft (6 m) deep made up of rich silt loam soil (a desirable mix of sand, silt, and clay-sized particles). These are usually the most highly productive soil profiles. The water-holding capacity and the ability of the soil to supply nutrients have significant impact upon the productivity of the soil. Granite has limited ability to hold water or to supply plants with water and nutrients. A deep silt loam soil, in contrast, usually has significant potential to store water for future plant needs, release stored water to plants, and supply plants with adequate amounts of essential nutrients.

Chemical properties of a soil profile are as dramatically different as physical properties but are not as obvious to the untrained observer. Soils of different geological origin but the same textural class (the same mix of sand, silt, and clay) have different abilities to release nutrients. Soils that initially appear to be similar may have salt concentrations in the soil water that vary from close to the concentration of sea water to almost that of rain water. Soils that appear similar may have hydrogen ion concentrations (pH) that vary from very acid to quite alkaline. The geological parent material can have a significant impact upon the soil's ability to provide nutrients essential to plant growth. The fact that soils are formed from a variety of minerals in proximity can lead to very different physical and chemical properties within the same field.

Changes in farming. Before the twentieth century, farmers typically cultivated with hand tools or with equipment drawn by animals. Around 1900 the average full-time farmer with horse or oxen intensively cultivated 40 acres (16 hectares) or less of land. Today, the typical farmer using high-power machinery intensively farms single-handedly as much as 1000 acres (405 hectares). If this area is translated into familiar city blocks, about 1/8 mi (0.2 km) square, put in perspective, a modern farmer is intensively cultivating the equivalent of 100 blocks. In the nineteenth century, when farmers harvested their 40 acres (16 hectares) by hand, they knew where the high- and low-yield-potential parts of the field were. Farmers intensively managed these different parts by variably applying fertilizer, usually livestock manure, according to soil need and matching the selection of crop and plant population to the soil. As machinery increased the number of acres that a farmer could plant, cultivate, and harvest, the farmer's ability to determine the nutrient need, plant variety need, or plant population need of a particular portion of the acreage diminished. By the middle 1990s, a western corn belt farmer would typically treat a 160-acre (65-hectare) field as a uniform field. One soil test would be used to determine antecedent nutrient levels, and a uniform application of fertilizer and pesticide would be used to treat the field. The farmer would harvest the field with a combine that cut a 14–30-ft (4–9-m) swath at 3–5 mi/h (5–8 km/h).

Technology driver. Computer technology in general and GPS in particular are revolutionizing agronomic production. New combines, grain harvesters, have features such as yield and moisture sensing, GPS, and data acquisition and storage capability. As the combine harvests a field, the position, the yield, and the moisture content of the grain are stored every second or several seconds. Grain-quality parameters such as protein content, selenium content, or other specific-ion content may soon be added to the array of information that is being stored by its precise location of acquisition. When soil samples are taken by the farmer who simultaneously is using a handheld GPS receiver, the precise location of the soil nutrients can be documented. Field scouting, that is, walking through the field and documenting pest concentrations, signs of nutrient deficiencies, plant populations, and other noteworthy visual information, is accomplished with a handheld GPS. As this significant information is recorded, the location of the subarea is documented.

Fertilizer and pesticide application equipment is beginning to get computer-controlled multiple product, variable rate application, and GPS positioning capability. Field maps of variable-product and -rate recommendations are loaded onto precision application equipment. The product with the greatest probability of resolving the nutrient or pest problem is applied at the desired rate to the precise place in the field where it is needed. The GPS receiver and computer on a tractor are coupled with multibox (more than one variety of a particular species of crop will be carried by the planter) variable-rate planters, giving farmers the ability to match specific genetic material and variable population rates to soils within the field to achieve the highest positive response. Data sensed remotely via satellites, aerial scanners, and aerial cameras are being used to improve the efficiency of field scouting. Airborne data-acquisition equipment gains information from reflected energy waves from very small portions of the electromagnetic spectrum. Images from specific spectral bands provide the field scout with the referenced location of significant anomalous areas within a field.

For background information *see* AGRICULTURAL SOIL AND CROP PRACTICES; AGRONOMY; SOIL; SURVEYING INSTRUMENTS in the McGraw-Hill Encyclopedia of Science & Technology.   C. Gregg Carlson

Bibliography. B. Hoffmann-Wellenhof and H. Lichtenegger, *Global Positioning System: Theory and Practice*, 1992.

Solar activity

Solar activity is all forms of phenomena associated with the "active regions" on the Sun, which are associated with sunspots. Examples of solar activity are coronal mass ejections, flares, the 11-year-period solar cycle, energetic particles, and geomagnetic storms. Solar activity, although virtually impossible to forecast a month in advance, has succumbed to scientific methods on long time scales, much as seasonal climate forecasts are possible but weather forecasts beyond about 14 days are not. Moderately accurate solar activity forecasts on decadal time scales now seem possible. The workable methods fall into a class of prediction techniques called precursor methods, which have proved successful for two solar cycles.

Sunspots. The discovery of sunspots by Galileo in 1610 was followed by a dearth of solar activity, known as the Maunder minimum, for more than a half century when there were few sunspots at all. Subsequently, solar activity increased, but activity in the eighteenth and nineteenth centuries does not appear to have been as prominent as has occurred in the twentieth century. The **illustration** shows the record of solar activity from 1944 to 1996.

From the Earth, sunspots appear as small dark blemishes on the Sun's surface. They consist of an umbral (very dark) region and a penumbral (medium dark) region, in analogy to the regions of a shadow. Sizes range from small sunspot pores, a couple of thousand miles across, to giant spots, perhaps as

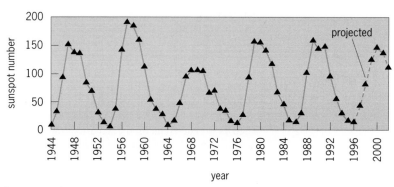

Sunspot numbers since 1944, as well as a projected curve.

large as 60,000 mi (100,000 km) across, many times larger than the Earth. The spots possess magnetic fields near a kilogauss, a thousand times larger than the Earth's. Such a magnetic field is sufficient to inhibit heat transport by convection into the photosphere (the surface of the Sun visible from Earth). This inhibition prevents the Sun's surface from radiating much light. It is a great puzzle since convection can be thought of as a "river of heat" flowing radially outward from inside the Sun and is extremely difficult to dam up. In fact, much of this energy makes its way around the spot to appear in regions on the Sun, called faculae, that radiate extra energy and hence are relatively brighter. How the magnetic field inhibits the outflowing energy is not completely clear; however, it may set up a cooling downflow of neutral hydrogen gas, which quenches the outward heat flux, much as water cools a fire.

Forecasting. Solar activity forecasting is important for space weather, which refers to the particulate and electromagnetic conditions impinging upon the Earth that are associated with solar outbursts from activity and sunspots. Solar activity affects space systems, power lines, and a number of advanced technological and communications systems. There may also be relevance to long-term climate change and other terrestrial phenomena affected by the Sun's variations. A wide variety of activity periods exist, from weeks to centuries, providing a rich spectral source to force terrestrial responses but making the solar cycle very difficult to predict.

Numerous prediction techniques have been arduously developed, but only with limited success. These may be classified as Fourier analyses, neural networks, curve fitting, planetary alignments, artificial intelligence, climatological, and "other." Aside from curve fitting and climatological, these methods have little justification for their use. Curve fitting, such as the McNish-Lincoln method, uses existing sunspot numbers to extrapolate future values, and works well when used in accord with the disclaimer "not to be used for more than one or two years into the future." Climatological simply means predicting the next cycle by an average value from a past number of cycles. This method also seems to work to some extent because, as with any geophysical phenomenon (for example, weather prediction), it always has a degree of persistence to it. Fourier analyses have coefficients as dependent upon ancient data as upon recent history. Hence the technique does not work well.

Nevertheless, some new methods may be gaining ground in the problem of understanding future solar activity. Some solar activity prediction methods, classified as precursor methods, have worked now for two solar cycles; they appear to be reasonably successful on decadal time scales. Precursors are early signs of the size of the next solar cycle's activity and manifest themselves before the main body of the solar cycle arrives. There are two kinds of precursor methods: solar and geomagnetic.

Solar precursors. The clue as to how the Sun broadcasts its future activity came from knowledge of solar dynamo theory. In a magnetohydrodynamic dynamo, any amplification of magnetic field occurs through the magnification of a preexisting field. As a result, one may ascertain the key solar fields to determine which ones would be amplified, and may use these to predict the size of the next solar cycle. As it turns out, from Babcock's picture of the solar cycle, the Sun's polar fields are the key. These fields will be amplified into future sunspots. They will produce flares, discharge coronal mass ejections (vast clouds of plasma ejected by the Sun) which result in geomagnetic storms, and occasionally damage spacecraft and electrical power grid lines. In this picture, the sizes of the Sun's polar fields near solar minimum are measured, and these fields are then used as the basis for estimating the next cycle's activity level.

Geomagnetic precursors. The geomagnetic precursor work began a few decades ago when it was found that variations in the Earth's geomagnetic field correlated extremely well with the Sun's future activity cycle. This was quite surprising, for it would seem that the Sun may affect the Earth, not the other way around, and the Earth cannot "know" what the Sun's activity level is going to be in the future. If it were not for the remarkably high correlation, one would simply dismiss the data as random. Nevertheless, the original correlative work showed many cycles of solar behavior following the terrestrial precursors, and was quite impressive. Researchers followed this lead and came to an understanding of the relationship.

The geomagnetic precursors work in a similar manner to solar precursors. They may be used to predict the size of the next cycle because they serve as a proxy estimator for the size of the Sun's polar field. They are linked to this field near solar minimum. During this time interval, the Sun's polar fields are swept toward low latitudes in interplanetary space by the solar wind. At this time, there is an absence of any significant low-latitude active region fields, and thus the interplanetary magnetic field has its origins in the Sun's polar regions. The Earth's geomagnetic fluctuations are then directly related to the southward component of the interplanetary

magnetic field and, as a result, these fluctuations serve as a good measure of the Sun's extended polar fields.

It was recently reported by the National Oceanic and Atmospheric Administration–Space Environment Center that the next solar cycle would peak in early 2000 and would reach a size of 160 ± 30 for smoothed sunspot number. This value was based predominantly on geomagnetic precursors. A solar precursor indicator provided a consistent, but mildly smaller, value of 130 ± 30 for sunspot number. The illustration shows a projected curve consistent with these predictions.

For background information *see* SUN; SUNSPOT in the McGraw-Hill Encyclopedia of Science & Technology.   Kenneth Schatten

Bibliography. J. A. Eddy, The Maunder minimum, *Science*, 192:1189–1192, 1976; K. H. Schatten et al., Using dynamo theory to predict the sunspot number during solar cycle 21, *Geophys. Res. Lett.*, 5:411, 1978; R. J. Thompson, A technique for predicting the amplitude of the solar cycle, *Solar Phys.*, (148):383, 1993.

Solution mining

The popularity of solution mining as a method of exploiting mineral deposits is increasing as the ore bodies progressively decrease in grade and increase in depth. With time, the ore near the surface of the Earth is exhausted, leaving the deeper and generally more complex ore to be mined. As a result, conventional mining must be replaced by innovative ore recovery methods.

Methods. Solution mining refers to the uses of a liquid solvent to extract the material of interest, which can be metals such as gold or copper, or industrial minerals such as soda ash, sulfur, or boron compounds. All forms of solution mining use a fluid of some type to extract and to concentrate the material of interest from the waste.

Metals recovered. Metals now being mined by solution techniques include gold, copper, and uranium. A number of industrial minerals generally involving evaporite are also being recovered by solution mining. These include boron, trona (soda ash), salt (sodium chloride), potash, and sulfur. Many other mineral materials of interest are being investigated to determine if a salable product can be recovered at a profit with the use of in-situ mining.

Advantages. Several advantages are found in solution mining methods as compared to conventional mining practices. The capital investment is generally much smaller because large earth-moving machinery for overburden stripping and ore extraction is not required. There is less environmental damage as compared to the large open pits or spoil piles from underground working. In-situ mining is safer. There are no risks from exposure to large earth-moving and rock-crushing equipment. Danger to employees from ground failure, ever present with conventional mining, are not associated with in-situ mining.

An important consideration is selection of a solution composition that can extract the material of interest and reduce the dissolution of extraneous material. This aspect can take years of research in order to design a correct leachate solution composition. To the extent possible, the reagent should be specific for the material of interest. The solution must also be able to react quickly and to provide a sufficient grade in the recovered solution to be profitable.

In-situ mining. In-situ mining is one form of solution mining that employs the technique of passing a fluid in the form of a leachate or lixiviant (mining solution) through the ore. The leaching agent can be water alone or water with additional components such as carbon dioxide or an acid. The leachate is injected into the ore through specially designed wells constructed with materials that are inert to the leaching fluid. As the solution works its way through the ore body, the material of interest is dissolved and carried to recovery wells, where the solution is then pumped to the processing, or refining, area. Because of the large volumes of solution involved, processing facilities are generally located close to the ore body to minimize fluid transport costs.

Boron example. One example of in-situ mining involves the recovery of boron values from an evaporite ore body. The ore body is located approximately 1400 ft (425 m) below the surface and averages 100 ft (30 m) in thickness. The ore body is encapsulated in clay, both overlying and underlying the ore. The deposit was formed by evaporation of water from boron-rich sediments that accumulated in a basin, leaving behind the enriched ore. Over time the ore body was covered by additional sediments, and it remained intact until it was discovered by explorational drilling and ground-water sampling.

To exploit this evaporite ore body, wells are placed into the ore zone by first drilling a 12-in. (30-cm) hole into the ground to a depth of 1500 ft (455 m) using a rotary drill. Next, a fiberglass well casing having a 7-in. (18-cm) outside diameter is placed in the hole to a depth of 1400 ft (425 m), thus leaving an open hole completion for 100 ft (30 m) in which the acid can contact the ore. Acid-resistant concrete is pumped between the earth and the casing and allowed to set up. These installation techniques result in the wells penetrating the deposit so that the mining fluid can be conducted into and out of the ore body. The concrete seal prevents mining fluid from contaminating ground water above the ore body. The fact that the ore body is encapsulated in clay ensures that no contamination will occur outside the area of the boron-containing unit.

Once the well is complete, a dilute acid solution of up to 5% sulfuric or hydrochloric acid, or a combination of both, is pumped into the well, where it reacts with the boron-rich ore, colemanite. After the ore is leached and boric acid is formed, it is pumped to the surface and treated in the processing plant. A number of processes can be used to recover the boric acid; these involve crystallization, ion-exchange concentration, or precipitation with calcium to yield calcium borate. After the product is formed and dried, it is sold primarily to the glass manufacturing industry, where it is used to strengthen glass formulations such as Pyrex.

A number of other industrial minerals are obtained by solution mining using techniques similar to those described above. These relate to soda ash (calcium carbonate) and potash for fertilizer usage.

Improving solution penetration. An important factor of in-situ mining is the permeability of the ore-containing host material. If the solution cannot penetrate the ore at a sufficient rate, the venture will fail economically. A number of techniques have been developed to improve the rate of solution penetration into the ore. These include fracturing of the deposit by using high-pressure fluid, explosives to loosen compacted material, and horizontal drilling.

Fracturing involves pumping fluid into the ore body at sufficient pressure to cause a break that will allow the solution to pass through the area. Occasionally material such as sand or glass beads is pumped into the broken areas to "prop" open the fractures and maintain the increased areas of flow.

Where explosives are used, they are placed in the well at the level of the ore zone and detonated to break up the mineral body and allow the solution to reach the areas of enrichment. Care must be taken not to damage the well with the downhole explosion. This can usually be accomplished by placing heavy mud over the explosives prior to detonation.

Increasing flow rate through the ore body can also be accomplished by horizontal drilling. This method involves drilling a vertical well to the top of the ore body, then rotating the drill bit to a horizontal plane and continuing drilling through the ore body in a level configuration. This allows an increased area of contact with the ore body. Both fracturing and horizontal drilling improvements were developed by the oil-well drilling industry and then adapted to in-situ mining.

Environmental protection. Another important factor in solution mining is environmental protection, which involves control of the extraction fluid. A number of techniques have been developed to determine the location, and then to control the distribution, of the fluid. These techniques include the installing of monitor wells to determine if the mining fluid is migrating out of the area of control. If the mining fluid is determined to be approaching the area limits, pumping rates are adjusted to retain the fluid in the problem area. Another common practice in solution mining is to maintain a small positive solution bleed in the system. This positive net removal of fluid, which removes more fluid than is injected into the aquifer, ensures that fluid is always moving into the area and not escaping. This bleed is then isolated in evaporation ponds, and it does not impact the environment.

For background information *see* SALINE EVAPORITE; SOLUTION MINING; UNDERGROUND MINING in the McGraw-Hill Encyclopedia of Science & Technology.   George J. Hartman

Bibliography. D. D. Rabb, Solution mining, *Min. Eng.*, 24(2):62–64; D. D. Rabb, *Solution Mining: A Review*, SME-AIME, September 1986; S. A. Swan and K. R. Coyne (eds.), *In Situ Recovery of Minerals II*, 1994.

Sonochemistry

When liquids are exposed to intense ultrasound, high-energy chemical reactions occur, often accompanied by the emission of light. There are three classes of sonochemical reactions: homogeneous sonochemistry of liquids, heterogeneous sonochemistry of liquid-liquid or liquid-solid systems, and sonocatalysis (which overlaps the first two). In some cases, ultrasonic irradiation can increase reactivity by nearly a millionfold. Especially for liquid-solid reactions, the rate enhancements via ultrasound have proved extremely useful for the synthesis of organic and organometallic compounds. Because cavitation can occur only in liquids, chemical reac-

tions are not generally seen in the ultrasonic irradiation of solids or solid-gas systems.

Cavitation. Because the wavelengths of ultrasound are so much larger than molecular dimensions, sound does not cause such chemistry in a direct interaction. Instead, sonochemistry and sonoluminescence arise from the physical phenomenon of acoustic cavitation: the formation, growth, and implosive collapse of bubbles in liquids irradiated with high-intensity sound. During the final stages of cavitation, compression of the gas inside the bubbles produces enormous local heating and high pressures (but with very short lifetimes, in otherwise cold liquids). In clouds of cavitating bubbles, these hot spots have equivalent temperatures nearly as high as the surface of the Sun (roughly 5000 K or 8540°F), pressures as large as at the ocean bottom (about 1000 atmospheres or 10^8 pascals), and lifetimes much less than a millionth of a second. If solids present in the liquid are irradiated with ultrasound, related phenomena can occur. When cavitation occurs near an extended solid surface, cavity collapse is nonspherical and drives high-speed jets of liquid into the surface. These jets and associated shock waves can cause substantial surface damage and expose fresh, highly heated surfaces. Ultrasonic irradiation of liquid-powder suspensions produces another effect: high-velocity interparticle collisions. Cavitation can accelerate solid particles to high velocities because of the shock waves it creates in a slurry. The resultant collisions can induce dramatic changes in surface morphology, composition, and reactivity.

Sonoluminescence. In general, sonoluminescence may be considered a special case of homogeneous sonochemistry, and recent discoveries in this field have heightened interest in the phenomenon. In clouds of collapsing bubbles, emission from the excited states of atoms and molecules (very much as in flames) can be observed. For example, high-resolution sonoluminescence spectra were obtained from cavitation clouds in silicone oil under argon. The observed emission comes from excited-state diatomic carbon (C_2), and was modeled as a function of rotational and vibrational temperatures to find an effective cavitation temperature of 5050 ± 150 K (8630 ± 270°F). Recent work on metal atom sonoluminescence from volatile organometallics, such as iron pentacarbonyl [$Fe(CO)_5$], accurately confirms this temperature. Under conditions where an isolated, single bubble undergoes cavitation, recent studies on the duration of the sonoluminescence flash suggest that a shock wave may be created within the collapsing bubble, with the capacity to generate truly enormous temperatures and pressures within the gas—much higher than those seen with interacting clouds of bubbles.

Ultrasound. In a sense, chemistry is just the interaction of energy and matter. All chemical reactions require energy in one form or another to proceed. To a large degree, the properties of a specific energy source determine the course of a chemical reaction. Ultrasonic irradiation differs from traditional energy

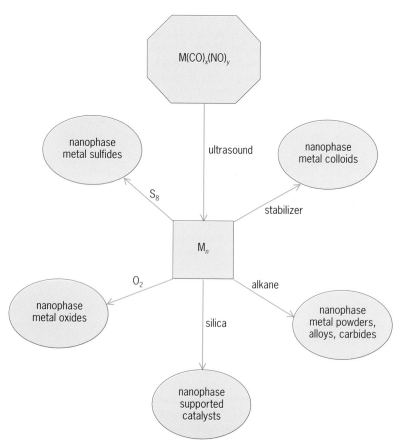

Fig. 1. Starting with volatile precursors, such as $M(CO)_x(NO)_y$ where M can be any of several metals, ultrasound can be used to break the precursor apart and liberate metal atoms that form small metal clusters of 100–1000 atoms. These clusters are then used to form various nanostructured materials.

sources (such as heat, light, or ionizing radiation) in duration, pressure, and energy per molecule. The immense local temperatures and pressures and the extraordinary heating and cooling rates generated by cavitation bubble collapse mean that ultrasound provides an unusual mechanism for generating high-energy chemistry. These unique conditions due to cavitation have been recently developed for the preparation of unusual, metastable inorganic materials.

Reactions. The predominant reactions of homogeneous sonochemistry are bond breaking and radical formation. The effect of ultrasound on aqueous solutions has been studied for many years. The primary products are H_2 and H_2O_2; there is strong evidence for various high-energy intermediates, including HO_2, $H\cdot$, $OH\cdot$, and perhaps $e_{(aq)}^-$. Recently there has been strong interest in the use of ultrasound to remediate low levels of organic contamination of water. The $OH\cdot$ radicals produced from the sonolysis of water can attack essentially all organic compounds (including halocarbons, pesticides, and nitroaromatics) and, through a series of reactions, oxidize them fully. The desirability of sonolysis for such remediation lies in its low maintenance requirements and the low energy efficiency of alternative methods (for example, ozonolysis, ultraviolet photolysis).

Synthetic routes. Also of recent interest is the development of sonochemistry as a synthetic tool for the creation of unusual inorganic materials (**Fig. 1**). As one example, the discovery of a simple sonochemical synthesis of amorphous iron helped settle the long-standing controversy over its magnetic properties. More generally, ultrasound has proved extremely useful in the synthesis of a wide range of nanostructured materials, including high-surface-area transition metals, alloys, carbides, oxides, and colloids. Sonochemical decomposition of volatile organometallic precursors in high-boiling solvents produces nanostructured materials (that is, built from nanometer-sized particles) in various forms. Nanometer colloids, nanoporous high-surface-area aggregates, and nanostructured oxide-supported catalysts can be prepared by this general route. The sonochemically prepared materials generally have very large surface areas that are extremely active as heterogeneous catalysts for a variety of industrial reactions, including hydrogenations and dehydrogenations, hydrodesulfurization, and carbon monoxide reductions. Heterogeneous catalysts often require rare and expensive metals. The use of ultrasound offers some hope of activating less reactive and less costly metals. Such effects can occur during the formation of supported catalysts, by activation of preformed catalysts, or through enhancement of catalytic behavior during catalysis.

Polymers. Sonochemistry is also proving to have important applications with polymeric materials. Substantial work has been accomplished in the sonochemical initiation of polymerization and in the modification of polymers after synthesis. The use of sonolysis to create radicals that function as radical

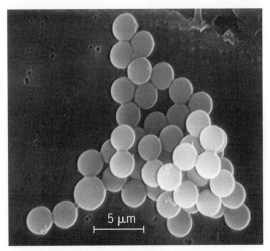

Fig. 2. Scanning electron micrograph of sonochemically synthesized hemoglobin microspheres.

initiators has been well explored. Similarly, the use of sonochemically prepared radicals and other reactive species to modify the surface properties of polymers is being actively developed. Another effect of ultrasound on long-chain polymers is mechanical cleavage, which produces relatively uniform size distributions of shorter chain lengths.

Protein microspheres. Sonochemistry has found another recent application in the preparation of unusual biomaterials, notably protein microspheres (**Fig. 2**). Using high-intensity ultrasound and simple protein solutions, an easy method to make both air-filled microbubbles and nonaqueous liquid-filled microcapsules has been developed. Sonochemically prepared microspheres are stable for months, and being slightly smaller than red blood cells, they can be intravenously injected and pass unimpeded through the circulatory system. The mechanism responsible for microsphere formation is a combination of two acoustic phenomena: emulsification and cavitation. Ultrasonic emulsification creates the microscopic dispersion of the protein solution necessary to form the proteinaceous microspheres. Alone, however, emulsification is insufficient to produce long-lived microspheres. The long life of these microspheres comes from a sonochemical cross-linking of the protein shell. Protein cysteine residues are oxidized during microsphere formation by sonochemically produced superoxide to create disulfide links between proteins (these same interprotein cross-links are responsible for the mechanical strength of hair, horn, and nails). These protein microspheres have a wide range of biomedical applications, including their use as echo contrast agents for sonography, magnetic resonance imaging contrast enhancement, and drug delivery.

Electrochemistry. Applications of ultrasound to electrochemistry have also seen substantial progress. Beneficial effects of ultrasound on electroplating and on organic synthetic applications of organic electrochemistry have been known for quite some time.

More recent studies have focused on the underlying physical theory of enhanced mass transport near electrode surfaces. Another important application for sonoelectrochemistry has been developed for the electroreductive synthesis of submicrometer powders of transition metals.

For background information *see* CATALYSIS; CAVITATION; SHOCK WAVE; SONOCHEMISTRY in the McGraw-Hill Encyclopedia of Science & Technology.

Kenneth S. Suslick

Bibliography. I. Hua, R. H. Hochemer, and M. R. Hoffmann, *Environ. Sci. Technol.*, 29:2790, 1995; R. B. King (ed.), Sonochemistry of transition metal compounds, *Encyclopedia of Inorganic Chemistry*, 7:3890–3905, 1994; T. G. Leighton, *The Acoustic Bubble*, 1994; K. S. Suslick, *MRS Bull.*, 20:29, 1995.

Space biology

In designing living quarters for people in space, it is important to provide as many characteristics of the Earth environment as possible. The internal air pressure of a space habitat is 14.7 lb/in.^{2} (101 kilopascals), the same as at sea level, which is not difficult to maintain. However, there is a great pressure differential between the inside and the outside (more than a ton per square foot of surface). As a consequence, space habitats must have strong construction, yet be light enough to be carried aloft in current rockets; only a cylindrical design meets this requirement. The temperature is kept at about 72°F (22°C), and the air consists of about 78% nitrogen and 22% oxygen. When these gases are released from their storage tanks, they contain no water vapor, so some water should be evaporated into the air to bring the relative humidity to about 30%, which most people find acceptable. Since a space habitat is a closed system, oxygen is added to the air as oxygen is used up, and carbon dioxide is removed from the exhaled air by circulating the air through canisters containing lithium hydroxide.

The habitat is wrapped with insulation to protect it from temperature changes. The inside of the habitat is warmed with electric heaters [it is very cold in space (−150°F or −101°C) when an orbiting habitat is in darkness, in the Earth's shadow]. Cooling the habitat is necessary because the sunlight generates heat, as do the people and equipment inside the habitat. Heat exchangers similar to small air conditioners transfer heat to a liquid that passes through large flat panels that radiate the heat into space. Once these basic needs are met, the special concerns in space are related to weightlessness, tightly confined quarters, and the inability to leave.

Physical environment. Weightlessness is not zero gravity, although people experience it that way. The Earth's gravity pulls a space vehicle orbiting at an altitude of about 200 mi (320 km) and a speed of about 17,500 mi/h (28,160 km/h) into a circular orbit. The centrifugal force of the orbiting vehicle pulls it away from the Earth with a force equal to gravity. The two forces balance each other, and persons and objects therefore appear to be weightless. This weightlessness is the primary difference between living in orbit and living on Earth.

Air close to the Earth's surface is denser than air above it because gravity pulls on all of the air so that the air above compresses the air below. When a person inhales cool air at room temperature, the air is warmed in the lungs and expands. When this air is exhaled into the denser air, it rises and is replaced by cool fresh air ready to be inhaled in the next breath. The rising air creates convection currents. However, convection currents do not occur in weightlessness because the warm air does not rise. Therefore, to prevent astronauts from suffocating by rebreathing their own stale air and to keep them cool, a system of fans and air ducts is used to move the air. These mechanical installations produce noise, and invariably space vehicles are noisier than rooms in buildings: the noise level in a typical living room is about 45 decibels, while the average noise level in space shuttles is about 72 dB—equivalent to driving on a highway with the car windows open.

Natural functions and activities. On Earth, people lie down to sleep for three major reasons: the heart does not have to work hard pumping blood up to the head against the force of gravity; the muscles that hold the body erect can rest; and falling is avoided as a person drifts into unconsciousness. In weightlessness, there is no up or down so it is impossible to fall; the muscles relax in any position; and the heart is not stressed. Thus, in orbit a lightweight sleeping bag attached to the wall is sufficient for sleeping. Also, people in orbit typically sleep about an hour less per night than they do on Earth. When a person relaxes in weightlessness, the body is pulled into the neutral body position by the natural tension of muscles, tendons, and ligaments (see **illus.**); the sleeping bag holds the arms down.

Eating in orbit works about the same as on Earth. Food items that hold together are easier to eat than foods such as peas which can come loose from a spoon if accelerated too quickly toward the mouth. Foods in liquid form must be drunk from a sealed container because in weightlessness liquids are not held in the bottom of vessels. Liquids that get loose are a serious problem because they become entrained in air currents and, for example, can be drawn into electronic or mechanical systems. Liquids are kept in plastic containers that collapse as the liquid is drawn out with a straw. Space straws have little turn-off valves. Otherwise, liquid on its way up the straw (and thus having momentum) would continue moving after the person drinking stopped sucking and would come out of the straw and float away.

Space toilets do not have water in them and must be used with a seat belt. A mild vacuum draws urine to a storage tank. A fan draws air in and downward into the toilet bowl from beneath the toilet seat, and fecal material is entrained in the air and carried to

Neutral body position, relaxed in weightlessness. *(After W. E. Thornton, G. W. Hoffer, and I. A. Rummel, Anthropometric changes in fluid shifts, Biomedical Results from Skylab, NASA, 1977)*

a plastic bag, where it and toilet paper are secured for storage. Urine is usually pumped into space, where it disperses, and solid waste is brought back to Earth.

All humans have competing needs for privacy and community. Needs for community are certainly met in the tight confines of current space stations, but privacy needs remain critical in maintaining good mental health. People are also territorial and need to have a place that belongs to them, one over which they have total control. Both privacy and territoriality can be achieved by having private staterooms that can be decorated to reflect individual tastes.

Humans have competing needs for stimulus constancy and novelty. They like things to remain much the same, yet if the rate of change falls too low they experience boredom. Russian scientists have found that morale on their space station *Mir* is greatly improved if there is sufficient interesting work to

keep people busy and if there are periodic flights of a resupply vehicle that brings news from home, fresh foods, videos, mail, and even one or two visitors who stay a week or two on the space station and then return with the supply vehicle.

Medical issues. The two major medical problems known to affect long-duration space travelers are loss of muscle mass, especially in the heart, and loss of calcium from the bones. On Earth, in a constant struggle with gravity, the bones bear a person's weight, the muscles hold the body erect and lift heavy objects, and the heart pumps blood in one direction while gravity pulls blood in the opposite direction. In space, the muscles do not have to work very much so they lose mass. Loss of muscle mass can be dramatically reduced by exercising daily; treadmills are often used because the person can wear a harness and be cinched down with bungee cords with a force equal to the person's Earth weight. Vigorous walking or running not only exercises the large muscles of the lower body and the heart but also puts loads on the large leg bones, slowing the rate at which they lose calcium. For long-duration space flights, a minimum of 1–2 h per day of heavy exercise is requried. However, people will still lose calcium and muscle mass over time. Some of those losses can be recovered by careful rehabilitation after returning to Earth. Such problems will remain until the day when large spinning space stations can provide an artificial gravity.

For background information *see* AEROSPACE MEDICINE; GRAVITY; SPACE BIOLOGY; SPACE STATION; WEIGHTLESSNESS in the McGraw-Hill Encyclopedia of Science & Technology.   Harvey Wichman

Bibliography. D. T. Damon, *Introduction to Space: The Science of Spaceflight*, 2d ed., 1995; P. R. Harris, *Living and Working in Space: Human Behavior, Culture and Organization*, 1992; K. M. Joels, G. P. Kennedy, and D. Larkin, *The Space Shuttle Operator's Manual*, 2d ed., 1988.

Space flight

The year 1997 exhibited a remarkable upswing in space activities over the several preceding years (**Table 1**), showing growth trends in operations and advanced developments. There were 85 successful launches, up from 69 in 1996 (**Table 2**). In the United States the development of the International Space Station reached a crucial point. In Russia, the continuing utilization of the space station *Mir* was marked by a series of events and emergencies requiring innovative maintenance and repair actions. A remarkable achievement was the landing of NASA's first robot explorer on Mars after a 21-year hiatus and the excursions of the small rover on the red plain of the landing site. The year also brought new discoveries by the Hubble Space Telescope after a new upgrade and by the deep-space probe *Galileo* at Jupiter, as well as the launch of the large probe *Cassini* to Saturn. *See* MARS.

Table 1. Significant space events in 1997

Mission designation	Date	Country	Event
STS 81 (*Atlantis*)	Jan. 12	United States	Launch of fifth *Mir* link-up; delivered Jerry Linenger and supplies; returned John Blaha (128 d in space) and cargo
Soyuz TM-25	Feb. 10	Russia	Launch of Mir 23 crew of three, with German researcher Reinhold Ewald, to replace Mir 22 cosmonauts
STS 82 (*Discovery*)	Feb. 11	United States	Launch of second servicing mission of Hubble Space Telescope; five spacewalks to upgrade it with two new instruments, exchange eight components, repair degraded insulation
Mir	Feb. 23	Russia	Flash fire in *Kvant 1* module, caused by malfunctioning solid-fuel oxygen generator candle; extinguished by crew
STS 84 (*Atlantis*)	May 15	United States	Launch of sixth *Mir* link-up; delivered Michael Foale and supplies; returned Linenger (132 d in space) and cargo
Mir	June 25	Russia	Collision of *Progress M-34* resupply drone with *Mir*; *Spektr* module damaged and decompressed; crew reestablished normal on-board conditions
Mars Pathfinder	July 4	United States	First Mars landing after 21 years; deployed *Sojourner* minirover; explored Ares Vallis for 2.5 months; sent back 16,550 images and over 15 chemical rock analyses plus weather data
Soyuz TM-26	Aug. 5	Russia	Launch of Mir 24 crew of two, to relieve Mir 23 cosmonauts; performed six spacewalks, including two into *Spektr* module to restore three-quarters power
Mars Global Surveyor	Sept. 11	United States	Second robot explorer arrives at Mars for cartography from orbit; begins one-year aerobraking procedure to establish final work orbit
STS 86 (*Atlantis*)	Sept. 25	United States	Launch of seventh *Mir* link-up; delivered David A. Wolf and supplies; returned Foale (144 d in space) and cargo
IRS-1D	Sept. 29	India	Third successful launch of four-stage Polar Satellite Launch Vehicle (PSLV); Earth-sensing satellite payload lost on Oct. 5 because of power problems
Cassini/Huygens	Oct. 15	United States/Europe	Launch of automated 6-ton (5.6-metric-ton) probe on 6.7-year mission to Saturn, via gravity-assist flybys of Venus and Earth; carries Titan entry probe
Ariane 5	Oct. 30	Europe	First successful launch of ESA's heavy-lifter Ariane 5 (*502*); some propulsion performance irregularities
SCD-2A	Nov. 2	Brazil	First test flight of Brazil's VLS launcher; failed 65 s after launch; environmental data-gathering satellite payload lost
Galileo	Dec. 8	United States	Jupiter probe begins Galileo Europa Mission (GEM) after primary 2-year mission ended Dec. 7; planned are 14 flybys of Europa, Callisto, and Io

Commercial companies engaged in providing space services with a variety of expendable carrier rockets displayed strong growth. Russia's success in marketing launch services reached a point where it appears that Russia is competing for market leadership with France (which uses the Ariane 4).

The United States' space shuttle and Russia's Earth-orbiting *Mir* carried out three rendezvous-and-docking flights, bringing the total flights of phase 1 of the International Space Station development program to seven, with two more scheduled for 1998. These missions conducted joint on-board science research preparatory to space station operations, gathered practical experience in cooperative on-orbit activities in the interest of risk mitigation, and tested assembly procedures for the space station construction phase.

Exceeding 1996's number of crewed missions by one, a total of ten flights from the two major spacefaring nations carried 58 humans into space, including 10 women. The total number of people launched into space since 1958 (counting repeaters) totaled 773, including 73 women (or 378 different individuals, including 32 women).

United States Space Activities

The four reusable shuttle vehicles of the United States Space Transportation System continued carrying people and payloads to and from Earth orbit for science, technology, and operational research. The International Space Station program dealt with technical and schedule problems, moving forward briskly toward inception of orbital assembly.

Space shuttle. During 1997, NASA completed eight space shuttle missions, one more than in each of the four preceding years.

STS 81. Atlantis, on its eighteenth flight, January 12–22, was launched on the fifth docking mission to *Mir* to replace astronaut John Blaha with Jerry Linenger as United States resident and to deliver supplies. During the joint flight phase (January 14–19), the largest transfer of cargo items so far took place, including water, United States science equipment, and Russian logistics.

STS 82. Discovery was launched on its twenty-second flight on February 11. Two days later, it caught

Table 2. Space launches and attempts in 1997

Country	Number of launches*	Number of attempts
United States (NASA, Department of Defense, commercial)	37	38
Russia	27	29
Europe (European Space Agency, Arianespace)	12	12
People's Republic of China	6	6
Japan	2	2
India	1	1
Brazil	0	1
Total	85	89

* Successful launches to Earth orbit and beyond.

up with and retrieved the Hubble Space Telescope for its second scheduled servicing mission since its launch in 1990. After the observatory was installed with the manipulator arm on a turntable in the cargo bay, alternating two-astronaut teams carried out five spacewalks totaling 33 h 11 min. They significantly upgraded the telescope's scientific capabilities by exchanging eight degraded or failed components and replacing two major instruments, the Goddard High-Resolution Spectrometer and the Faint-Object Spectrograph, with, respectively, the more advanced Space Telescope Imaging Spectrograph (**Fig. 1**) and the Near-Infrared Camera and Multi-Object Spectrometer (NICMOS). They also performed critical maintenance, including repair of sun-damaged

Fig. 1. Images of planetary aurora taken by the Space Telescope Imaging Spectrograph of the Hubble Space Telescope. This new instrument provides more than 10 times the sensitivity of previous Hubble instruments in the ultraviolet. (*a*) Jupiter; ultraviolet images of polar regions are superimposed on a visible-light image of the planet (*John Clarke, University of Michigan; NASA*). (*b*) Saturn (*J. T. Trauger, Jet Propulsion Laboratory; NASA*).

multilayer insulation with thermal blankets from an emergency repair kit. The Hubble Space Telescope was deployed and released on February 19, and *Discovery* landed on February 21. *See* INFRARED ASTRONOMY.

STS 83. Columbia's twenty-second flight lasted only from April 4 to 8. It carried the Spacelab module configured as the Microgravity Science Laboratory 1 (MSL 1) with 33 investigations in the areas of crystallography, combustion science, materials science, and life sciences. The mission was also to test some of the hardware, facilities, and procedures to be used on the International Space Station.

However, on April 6, voltage readings from one of the fuel cells showed anomalous behavior, indicating the potential for hydrogen-oxygen crossover and the risk of a fire or explosion. Shutdown and safing of the fuel cell was initiated, and the flight terminated early. When *Columbia* landed, approximately 15% of the MSL 1 objectives had been achieved, and the decision was made to refly the mission as soon as possible.

STS 84. Atlantis, on its May 15–24 flight, conducted the sixth *Mir* docking mission (May 16–21). Because preflight coordination of problem issues, crew exchange, and repair-related resupply on *Mir* were far more involved than for the previous shuttle docking flights, the mission gave the United States and Russia a new foundation for upcoming work on *Mir* and the future joint assembly of the International Space Station. During the shuttle's approach and departure from *Mir*, a new proximity sensor and avionics hardware using Global Positioning System (GPS) navigation and laser ranging was successfully tested. This technology will be applied to future Ariane 5–launched Automated Transfer Vehicle spacecraft for use with the space station. After docking on May 16, *Atlantis* remained linked to *Mir* for 5 days, transferring cargo and exchanging Linenger for Michael Foale, for another 4 months of continuing United States presence in space. A major European science facility, Biorack, was part of the Spacehab (double-module version) carried in the shuttle cargo bay.

STS 94. The *Columbia* mission of July 1–17 was the first reflight in the history of the shuttle program, after a record refurbishment and turnaround of Orbiter and Spacelab in only 84 days. It followed the same orbit as STS 83, with the same crew and payload, and was fully successful. The results from MSL 1 are likely to deeply influence current models and theories on the physics of combustion and other processes important to industry.

STS 85. On its August 7–19 mission, *Discovery* carried the CRISTA-SPAS (Cryogenic Infrared Spectrometers and Telescopes for the Atmosphere–Shuttle Pallet Satellite 2) on its second flight. The 7724-lb (3500-kg) satellite was released in orbit to measure infrared radiation emitted by the atmosphere; later it was retrieved with the shuttle's mechanical arm. Other payloads included the Japanese Manipulator Flight Demonstration, with three separate tests of a 5-ft (1.5-m) prototype robot arm being developed

Fig. 2. *Mir* space station photographed from the space shuttle *Atlantis* during a fly-around on October 3, 1997, following the conclusion of joint docking activities. One of the solar array panels on the *Spektr* module shows damage from the collision of the Progress resupply ship with *Mir* on June 25, 1997. *(NASA)*

flyer; and a Collaborative Ukrainian Experiment (CUE) for plant space biology research, particularly studies of the effects of microgravity on plant growth and pollination. The launch incorporated a new flight maneuver by which the shuttle, at about 6 min into the flight, rolled to a heads-up position. This maneuver allowed early acquisition of the Tracking and Data Relay Satellite System (TDRSS) in geostationary orbit in lieu of the Bermuda tracking station, a substitution which resulted in cost savings.

The Spartan satellite was deployed with the remote manipulation system. Intended for investigations of physical conditions and processes of the solar corona and the hot outer layers of the Sun's atmosphere, the spacecraft did not self-activate and began to tumble after a failed attempt to regrapple it with the mechanical arm. It was manually recaptured during a spacewalk which marked the first time that a manual retrieval was planned in space. A second spacewalk was conducted to further evaluate equipment and procedures for the International Space Station, including a telescoping crane for moving large Orbital Replacement Units, and a prototype autonomous, free-flying, robotic camera.

International Space Station. The International Space Station program achieved a number of milestones, reaching the critical juncture where station elements were made ready for transportation to the launch site. The program is divided into three phases: phase 1, the current shuttle-*Mir* program, phase 2 for space station assembly up to initiation of orbital research capability with a permanent crew, and phase 3 for further expansion and completion. A total of 45 assembly flights will be required, 33 of them to be launched by the United States shuttle and 12 on Russian boosters.

Phase 1. Phase 1 of the program, the joint United States–Russian effort on *Mir* to expand cooperation in human space flight, accomplished three successful shuttle-*Mir* missions. Phase 1 has provided essential opportunities to test assumptions and validate models in the actual environment that the space station will experience. The knowledge and experience gained has demonstrated its value in space station design decisions as well as in the planning and operational procedures for space station crews. For example, phase 1 operational lessons indicate that the station should be more dependent than past United States programs on in-flight service and maintenance as a key requirement for back-up options (redundancy) governing safety and operations. Other examples are the development of new procedures for docking, technical data exchange between control centers at Moscow and Houston, and design of stowage and inventory control technologies.

Phases 2 and 3. Completion of phase 2 will require 10 flights, including the delivery of the station's first two crews, five Russian Progress tanker missions, and a Soyuz escape vehicle change-out flight. By the end of 1997, design and fabrication of flight elements and software for the first eight United States assembly flights were essentially complete, with qualifica-

by Japan for its module of the International Space Station; the Technology Applications and Science 1 (TAS 1) package, with seven experiments for studies of atmospheric and topographic physics and of solar energy, observations of Comet Hale-Bopp's coma and tail, and testing of thermal control devices; and the International Extreme Ultraviolet Hitchhiker 02 (IEH 02), with four experiments to observe ultraviolet radiation.

STS 86. The *Atlantis* flight of September 25–October 6 was the seventh docking mission to *Mir* (September 27–October 3; **Fig. 2**). David A. Wolf was the next United States astronaut to stay on *Mir* for a long-duration mission, replacing Foale. Two astronauts performed a spacewalk to retrieve four suitcase-sized *Mir* Environmental Effects Payload (MEEP) experiments from the exterior of the Docking Module, where they had been attached by STS 76 crew members in March 1996. They also left a large solar array cover cap outside *Mir* for planned use in a future spacewalk as part of Russia's attempts to repair the damaged *Spektr* module, and evaluated the small jet-backpack called SAFER (Simplified Aid for EVA Rescue). *Mir* was resupplied with cargo, including a critical new computer.

STS 87. The *Columbia* mission of November 19–December 5 carried as major cargo the U.S. Microgravity Payload 4 (USMP 4); the Spartan 201-04 free-

tion testing under way. The main program focus continued to be on the first-element launch, the liftoff of the FGB/Control Module planned for summer 1998 on a Proton rocket from Baikonur, Kazakhstan. Node 1 and Pressurized Mating Adapters (PMA) 1 and 2 were to be on board the first shuttle assembly flight approximately 10 days later.

A cadre of 14 space shuttle astronauts were named in June to start intensive training in preparation for the spacewalks required for on-orbit construction of the station. In November, the first four three-member crews were named to live and work on board the station.

Advanced transportation systems. In 1996, NASA began a cooperative effort with industry to develop a reusable space launch vehicle to eventually take over launchings for a fraction of today's cost of space transportation, with turnaround times considerably lower than those of the space shuttle. Lockheed Martin is developing the X-33 as a technology demonstrator for a single-stage-to-orbit reusable launch vehicle. The smaller X-34 will test the feasibility of launching small commercial and scientific payloads aboard a reusable rocket.

During 1997, the X-33 encountered weight, cost, and schedule problems. However, a 10% scale model of the engine planned to propel the X-33, a linear aerospike rocket engine, was successfully flight-tested on October 31 atop a modified supersonic NASA SR-71 research aircraft. *See* AEROSPIKE ENGINE.

The X-34, being developed by Orbital Sciences Corporation, should be ready to begin test flights late in 1998. Its primary propulsion system, the 60,000-lb-thrust (267-kilonewton) Fastrac engine, is only the second United States–made rocket engine developed since 1973. In August, it successfully completed a critical series of static firing tests.

NASA is also developing a Crew Return Vehicle to eventually take over the emergency lifeboat function for the International Space Station from the currently chosen Russian Soyuz three-seater capsules. As a prototype test vehicle, NASA in 1997 began fast-track development of the X-38, a reduced-scale vehicle for drop tests from a B-52.

Boeing and Lockheed Martin began to study designs for a liquid-propelled fly-back booster for the space shuttle that would eventually replace the two solid rocket boosters. Four smaller companies are in various development stages of reusable launch vehicles.

Space sciences and astronomy. Several automated and remotely controlled research and exploration missions continued to provide a wide range of significant and, in part, revolutionary discoveries. Particularly notable was the landing of *Pathfinder* on Mars and the initiation of exploration of the planet by it and its minirover, *Sojourner*. *Pathfinder* was a mission of NASA's Discovery program. In 1997, NASA selected the fifth and sixth Discovery missions, a flyby of three near-Earth comets, and a flight to collect samples of solar wind.

Hubble Space Telescope. The performance of the Hubble Space Telescope in 1997 continued to meet and at times exceed expectations. Following the second shuttle servicing and maintenance operation in February, the telescope began delivering a stream of discoveries. Among them were the first direct evidence of a supermassive black hole in the galaxy M84, and an array of complex structures that result when massive young stars begin to violently eject material into the surrounding molecular cloud. Most remarkable are "bullets" of molecular hydrogen traveling at speeds up to and beyond 10^6 mi/h (500 km/s), which collide with slower-moving material and create bow shocks.

Subsequent discoveries included a new form of star birth in NGC 2264 triggered by a gale of high-speed particles from a young massive star, blast waves from Supernova 1987A traveling at up to $\frac{1}{20}$ the speed of light and colliding with a slower-moving outer ring of gas (**Fig. 3**), a 300-light-year-diameter dust disk and other complex structures around the double nucleus of the peculiar galaxy Arp 220, and a powerful twin-cone beam of radiation shooting from a supermassive black hole at the core of galaxy NGC 4151 and containing hundreds of gas blobs. Using the galaxy cluster CL1358+62 as a gravitational lens, Hubble revealed a galaxy far beyond the cluster, the most distant galaxy known.

Other images uncovered over 1000 bright, young star clusters bursting to life at the heart of a pair of colliding galaxies called the Antennae galaxies. Violence was also found to dominate the end of Sunlike stars. In a collection of detailed views, Hubble

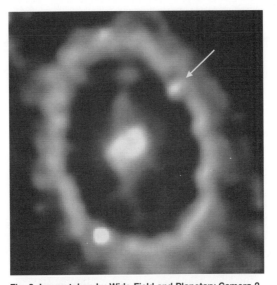

Fig. 3. Image taken by Wide Field and Planetary Camera 2 on the Hubble Space Telescope of Supernova 1987A in July 1997, a decade after the explosion. The glowing outer ring is gas which was excited by light from the explosion. The brightening knot on the upper right side of the ring (indicated by arrow) is the site of collision between the outward-moving blast wave and the innermost parts of this ring. Part of the shredded star is visible in the center. The bright dot in the lower left is a star which is not part of the system. *(NASA)*

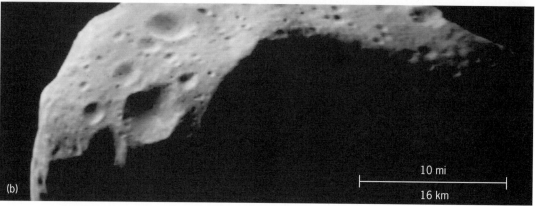

Fig. 4. Encounter of *Near Earth and Asteroid Rendezvous* (*NEAR*) spacecraft with the asteroid (253) Mathilde on June 27, 1997. (*a*) Comparison of an image of Mathilde taken by *NEAR* with images of Gaspra and Ida taken by *Galileo* spacecraft in 1991 and 1993, respectively. All three objects are presented at the same scale, but relative brightnesses have been altered. Mathilde is actually much darker than the other two asteroids and has more craters. (*b*) Portion of Mathilde viewed at closest approach, about 750 mi (1200 km). (*NASA*)

revealed surprisingly intricate glowing patterns that these aging stars spin into space.

Rossi XTE. The *Rossi X-ray Timing Explorer* (*RXTE*), launched by NASA in 1995, discovered a black hole exhibiting frame dragging, that is, literally dragging space and time around itself as it rotates. This phenomenon, known as the Lense-Thirring effect (predicted in 1918), is distorting the orbit of hot, x-ray-emitting gas near a black hole. *RXTE* also found a disk of matter surrounding a black hole that is periodically disrupted by gas jets from the black hole moving at nearly the speed of light. According to other *RXTE* observations, the luminous blue variable star Eta Carinae, one of the most massive bodies in the Milky Way Galaxy, may be a double star.

NEAR. The *Near Earth Asteroid Rendezvous* (*NEAR*) spacecraft, the second Discovery program mission, was launched by NASA in February 1996. On June 27, 1997, it flew within 750 mi (1200 km) of the asteroid (253) Mathilde. *NEAR* images (**Fig. 4**) showed that the asteroid's diameter is only 33 mi (52 km), smaller than estimated. Its dark surface

probably consists of carbon-rich material unaltered by planet-building melting and mixing processes. At least five craters larger than 12 mi (20 km) were found.

On July 3, the spacecraft's bipropellant engine was fired to head *NEAR* back toward Earth. An Earth gravity-assist flyby on January 23, 1998, sent the spacecraft toward its primary target, the asteroid (433) Eros. *NEAR* will reach this goal almost a year later, and then remain in orbit around Eros until the mission ends in February 2000.

ACE. On August 25, NASA launched the *Advanced Composition Explorer* (*ACE*) on a mission to study the chemical makeup of particles from the Sun and other galactic sources. *ACE* will be stationed about 10^6 mi (1.6×10^6 km) from Earth.

Galileo. In 1997, *Galileo* continued exploration of the planet Jupiter and its satellites. By measuring small changes in the spacecraft's trajectory, scientists can determine the gravitational fields of the satellites and their interior structure and density. Thus, Europa was found to have a metallic core and a layered internal structure similar to Earth's, while Callisto is a mixture of metallic rock and ice with no identifiable central core. The spacecraft found evidence of a volcanic eruption on Io that occurred between a flyby on April 4 and a passage on September 19.

Galileo's entry probe in 1995 had shown only dry air and a surprising absence of dense, thick clouds seen in earlier images. The orbiter now revealed wet and dry regions on the gas giant, leading to the conclusion that Jupiter is not as dry overall as first assumed.

December 7 marked the end of *Galileo*'s primary mission after 2 years of exploration in the Jupiter system, and the start of a 2-year mission extension called the Galileo Europa Mission (GEM). On December 16, *Galileo* performed another Europa flyby at just 124 mi (200 km) distance. The GEM plan includes eight flybys of Europa and four encounters of Callisto, and ends with two flybys of volcanically active Io.

Cassini. On October 15, NASA launched the 6-ton (5.6-metric-ton) spacecraft *Cassini* to the planet Saturn on a Titan 4B/Centaur rocket, beginning a 6.7-year journey involving multiple gravity-assist flybys of Earth and Venus. The deep-space probe carries 18 science instruments and 44 computers and processors within its engineering, science, and probe systems. *Cassini* is powered by radioisotope thermoelectric generators and heated internally by radioisotope heater units, which required presidential permission for launch. The approval was received on October 3 after completion of two separate review processes that addressed environmental and safety aspects of the mission.

Cassini will remain within the Saturn system for at least 4 years, completing 60 orbits of the planet. It consists of the orbiter-mothership and the entry probe *Huygens*, developed by the European Space Agency, which will separate from *Cassini* and parachute through the atmosphere of Titan, landing on the satellite's surface.

Ulysses. During 1997 the *Ulysses* spacecraft embarked on its second orbit of the Sun, to study the Sun's polar regions under conditions of high solar activity. Polar passes in 2000 and 2001 will occur close to the maximum of the solar cycle. Before that, *Ulysses* will make coordinated observations of the Sun's corona and the solar wind with the *Solar and Heliospheric Observatory* (*SOHO*) spacecraft.

Mars exploration. NASA's *Mars Pathfinder* mission probably attracted the greatest public attention of all space activities in 1997. Its companion craft, *Mars Global Surveyor*, arrived at the planet after a 10-month voyage. Meanwhile, NASA successfully tested two surface penetrators designed as miniature science probes for subsurface exploration of the Martian soil in 1999. Tests of an autonomous robotic rover named Nomad were under way, while NASA conducted preliminary remote-controlled runs of a six-wheeled prototype Mars rover for missions in 2001 and 2003.

The landing of *Pathfinder* on July 4 in the arid flood plain Ares Vallis was the first Mars landing since the *Viking* missions in 1976 and the first to use air bags to cushion surface impact. The subsequent operations by the station and its minirover *Sojourner* generated the heaviest stream of information ever sent by a planetary spacecraft to Earth. During 83 days of operation (nearly three times longer than expected), the mission returned 2.6×10^9 bits of information in the form of more than 16,000 images from the lander and 550 images from the rover, as well as more than 15 chemical analyses of rocks and data on winds and other weather factors.

Mars Global Surveyor was the first of the planned series of surveyor-type Mars explorers. It arrived at Mars on September 11, settling into an orbit of 156 mi (250 km) low point and 35,000 mi (56,000 km) high point with a 22-min burn of its main rocket engine. A few days later, it made the unexpected discovery of a planetwide magnetic field with a maximum strength not exceeding $\frac{1}{800}$ the magnetic field at the Earth's surface. With a series of several hundred dips into the outer reaches of Mars's atmosphere, the spacecraft is aerobraking itself with its solar panels into its final mapping orbit of 234 mi (374 km) altitude. One of its two solar panels, which had not fully deployed and latched after launch, showed slight movement during the first atmospheric passes. It was decided to slow down the descent and stretch out the braking process in order to avoid damaging this panel. Mapping is to begin in March 1999.

During the orbit-lowering phase, *Mars Global Surveyor*'s camera is already observing the surface. It has imaged a 4000-ft-high (1200-m) cliff in the Valles Marineris canyon covered in light-colored dust very much resembling snow in appearance and behavior. Pictures of Schiaparelli Crater detected small depressions with light-colored floors and dark cracks resembling dry lake beds. A laser altimeter measured the 60,000-ft (18,000-m) rise of the volcano Olympus Mons above its surroundings, detecting a steep slope that could indicate the area where the volcano collapsed in a landslide that deposited material for 300 mi (480 km).

Pioneer 10. At the end of 1997, *Pioneer 10*, launched in 1972, was over 6.2×10^9 mi (10.0×10^9 km) from Earth. NASA controllers had successfully maneuvered the spacecraft over that distance so that its main antenna again pointed toward Earth. Radio commands from Earth took 9 h 10 min to reach *Pioneer 10*.

Earth science. The year 1997 saw several Earth-observing missions of the civilian space program coordinated under the auspices of NASA's Mission to Planet Earth program. At the end of 1997, NASA changed the designation of this program to Earth Science.

Lewis. Launched August 22 from Vandenberg Air Force Base, the Earth-imaging satellite carried advanced remote-sensing instruments designed to analyze the spectrum of light reflected by Earth's land surfaces. However, after launch the spacecraft entered a spin that disrupted its power-generating capability, leading to loss of the mission.

TRMM. The *Tropical Rainfall Measuring Mission* (*TRMM*), a joint mission of NASA and the Japanese National Space Development Agency (NASDA), was launched on November 27 on a Japanese H-2 heavy booster from the Japanese launch complex on Tanega-Shima Island. It reached its orbit of 218 mi (350 km) altitude at 35° inclination. The satellite studies tropical and subtropical rainfall by using microwave and visible-infrared sensors and radar. The project also studies how El Niño–related rainfall anomalies correlate with other processes in the ocean and the atmosphere.

EOS. The first of NASA's Earth Observing System (EOS) spacecraft, *EOS AM-1*, reached a milestone in August when its last instrument arrived to complete module testing and integration of the instruments and the spacecraft. Launch was scheduled for June 1998.

Department of Defense activities. As an example of the civilian applications of military systems, President Clinton in March approved a national policy for management and use of the satellite-based Global Positioning System, aimed at balancing military and civil needs for the system. The widespread popular acceptance of GPS technology has far exceeded expectations.

Another example of military technology transfer is the application of the military *Midcourse Space Experiment* (*MSX*) to both Earth science and high-energy astronomy. Launched in April 1996 from Vandenberg as the Defense Department's first long-duration spacecraft designed to characterize ballistic missile signatures during the midcourse phase of missile flight, the satellite carried highly advanced remote-sensing instruments to gather a wealth of data for sharing with both civilian environmental scientists and researchers studying star formation and the structure of the Milky Way Galaxy.

Because of the rapid growth in commercial demand for launches, the Department of Defense in 1997 approved a plan to develop a second new family of Evolved Expendable Launch Vehicles (EELVs), in addition to the first line approved in 1996. The two families will comprise small-, medium-, and heavy-lift boosters for 2500–45,000-lb (1100–20,400-kg) payloads into low Earth orbit, costing 25–50% less to operate than current vehicles.

Military launches from Cape Canaveral and Vandenberg included three satellites for signal intelligence, reconnaissance, and early warning on three Titan 4 launchers; two navigation (*Navstar GPS*) satellites on Delta 2's; one communications satellite on an Atlas 2A; one weather satellite on a Titan 2; and two atmospheric physics research payloads on two air-launched Pegasus XL's.

Commercial space activities. In a commercial international joint venture, corporations from the United States, Ukraine, Russia, and Norway initiated Sea Launch, an ambitious project to develop a semisubmersible launch pad and command ship that would enable launches of major communications satellites into geosynchronous orbit from a non-land-based site. The Norwegian-built platform will float in the Pacific, near the Equator. The first launch planned is a Hughes *HS 702* communications satellite on a Ukrainian-built Zenit two-stage rocket, using a Russian-built Block DM upper stage from the Proton rocket.

In 1997, commercial launches of expendable space carriers totaled 19, with no failures. Seven Delta 2 vehicles, six Atlas 2A's, and one Atlas 1/ Centaur were launched. Pegasus XL took to the air four times in 1997, launched from an L-1011 aircraft. After its first launch attempt had failed in August 1994, the two-stage LMLV 1 succeeded on August 22, and the vehicle family was subsequently named Athena.

The development of large communications satellite networks advanced rapidly in 1997. By year's end, Iridium had 46 of a total of 66 satellites in space. Iridium expects to provide applications such as universal services for freely switching from a satellite link to a cellular link. Its closest competitor, Globalstar LPP, wants to establish a 48-satellite network.

The Teledesic network is to have 288 satellites in low Earth orbit, using the highly advanced Ka-band (at a frequency of 28 GHz). Along with corporate networks, Internet access could become the most important application of that new technology. Its competitor, Celestri system, would have 70 low-Earth-orbit satellites.

Of 36 planned Orbcomm satellites, 10 are now in orbit. Another small-satellite network, Ellipso, would employ 17 satellites in an elliptical orbit arrangement to provide cellularlike telephone service almost anywhere on the planet.

Russian Space Activities

While continuing to struggle with economic problems and severe financial shortages for its space program, Russia in 1997 showed no falling off in its space operations. Its total of 27 successful launches (out of 29 attempts) was higher than the previous year's 23 (out of 27 attempts): 10 Soyuz-U vehicles (two crewed), nine Protons (one failure), three Molniyas, two Tsiklons, two Kosmos 3M's, two Start 1's, and one Zenit 2 (failed). The partnership with the United States in the development of the International Space Station continued to gain substance. However, even with the increased logistics support of the United States shuttle, the 11-year-old space station *Mir* required increasing maintenance and repair, particularly after two serious emergencies in 1997.

Space station Mir. By the end of 1997, Russia's seventh space station, *Mir*, in operation since February 20, 1986, had circled the Earth approximately 67,775 times. It had been visited 33 times, including seven times by a United States space shuttle. To resupply the occupants, the space station was visited in 1997 by four automated Progress cargo ships, one more than the previous year. Despite these visits, *Mir*'s dependence on the space shuttle for its logistics continued unabated.

During 1997, three crew exchanges between visiting United States astronauts were completed. The United States crew members conducted a wide range of scientific research. On-board activities were frequently disrupted by systems anomalies endemic to the aging space station, which had exceeded its design life by 6 years. The cosmonauts, supported by their American guests and ground controllers, along with an effective spares management approach, proved able to cope with all anomalies. Two emergency events, however, were special: a small, intense, but contained flash fire on February 23 in the *Kvant 1* module, and on June 25 a collision of an automated supply ship, resulting in damage to *Spektr*, one of the seven building-block modules, and its depressurization. The crew had emergency return capability in a standby Soyuz ship at all times. NASA found the lessons learned from *Mir* maintenance and anomaly repairs to be an excellent preparation for the International Space Station, involving good response to emergency and contingency situations through joint problem resolution.

Soyuz TM-25 and Mir 23. Liftoff of the Mir 23 crew, Vasiliy Tsibliev, Aleksandr Lazutkin, and Reinhold Ewald (a German visitor), occurred on February 10, followed by linkup with *Mir* 2 days later. On February 23, a small flash fire broke out in the *Kvant 1* module when a lithium perchlorate "candle," a secondary oxygen-generating system, malfunctioned. The crew extinguished the flames within 90 s but had to wear breathing apparatus and subsequently filtering masks for a few hours because of smoke. Ewald performed 27 experiments in microgravity. He returned to Earth with Valeriy Korzun and Aleksandr Kaleri (the Mir 22 crew) in *Soyuz TM-24*, landing on March 2.

The two primary oxygen systems (based on electrolysis of wastewater) had failed previously, so that only one of the secondary systems burning chemicals remained until arrival of the crewless resupply ship *Progress M-34* on April 8. By then, other equipment failures on board added to concerns about crew safety. After *Progress M-34* unloaded 60 new candles and other cargo, repairs proceeded on coolant leaks in the thermal control system and on one of the primary oxygen units to restore it to partial operation. Replacement of the other oxygen unit with a new unit had to await the arrival of *Atlantis* on mission STS 84 in May. On April 29, Tsibliev and Linenger conducted a spacewalk during which they tested a new Russian spacesuit and installed and retrieved various equipment.

On June 25, six weeks after Foale replaced Linenger on *Mir*, the automated *Progress M-34* collided with *Mir* when Tsibliev attempted to link it to the station during a redocking exercise. The collision damaged one of *Spektr*'s four solar arrays (Fig. 2), dented a radiator, and punctured the hull, resulting in the *Spektr* module's depressurization—a major emergency. The crew was able to disconnect power and data cables and close the airtight hatch in time. During the subsequent weeks, on-board operations, including Foale's science research, were severely curtailed because of power shortage and were further beset by heart problems of the *Mir* commander and various subsystem malfunctions. Tsibliev and Lazutkin returned to Earth on August 14 in *Soyuz TM-25*, one week after the arrival of the Mir 24 replacement crew, after 184 days in space.

Soyuz TM-26 and Mir 24. *Soyuz TM-26* was launched on August 5 with Anatoly Solovyev and Pavel Vinogradov, a rested crew especially trained for repairing the damaged space station. Both crew members, assisted by United States astronauts Foale and Wolf, restored most of *Mir*'s on-board systems to normal operating conditions. They performed six spacewalks, two into the airless *Spektr* module to restore power and four outside the station.

Russian commercial activities. The Russian space program's efforts to enter the commercial market made remarkable progress in 1997, based on a space technology which is robust, versatile, and reliable. Between 1985 and 1997, 121 Proton and 338 Soyuz rockets were launched, with only 7 failures of the Proton and 9 of the Soyuz. The companies Khrunichev and RSC-Energia in Russia and Lockheed Martin in the United States have formed a joint venture as International Launch Services, which will use the Proton booster and Lockheed Martin's Atlas. Most of the Proton customers will be large western communications satellite companies. Of the nine Protons launched in 1997, six were for commercial customers.

European Space Activities

Aerospace reductions in Europe continued in 1997 because of lack of government funding for space projects in France and Germany, the two major member nations of the European Space Agency, and the apparent inability of industry, at least in Germany, to increase commercial space business by marketing its own products.

Ariane 4. With France's reliable Ariane 4 family of expendable launchers, the commercial operator Arianespace carried out 11 launches from Kourou, French Guyana, in 1997, one more than in 1996, for a total of 103 flights with only 7 failures. Ten of the 1997 flights carried a total of 16 commercial satellites, and one science satellite, *Equator*, was launched for the European Space Agency.

Ariane 5. The most significant event for the European Space Agency in 1997 was the success of the second launch of the Ariane 5 heavy booster, after the explosion of vehicle *501* in June 1996. The *502* took off on October 30, 1997, after several postponements. While going a long way toward qualification of the launcher, the vehicle's performance was marred by rolling and pitching motions that caused fuel sloshing in the propellant tanks. Tank sensors misread fuel levels and signaled the computer to shut off the Vulcain engine too early, causing an underperformance which the Aestus second stage was unable to compensate. The booster's payloads, the *Maqsat H* comsat dummy, the *Maqsat B* test package, and the educational *Teamsat*, ended up in an orbit much lower than planned.

Scientific spacecraft. The *Solar and Heliospheric Observatory* (*SOHO*), built by the European Space Agency, launched in 1995 by NASA, and operated from NASA's Goddard Space Flight Center, is the first spacecraft able to observe the Sun's deep interior as well as its stormy surface and atmosphere. In 1997, its observations suggested that the heating of the Sun's outer corona to about 3×10^6 K is due to electric and magnetic energy carried outward by "short-circuiting" magnetic loops arcing high over the surface. Beneath that surface, *SOHO* discovered streams of plasma, in motions similar to weather patterns in the Earth's atmosphere. The entire outer layer of the Sun is steadily flowing from the equator to the poles.

Observations of the European Space Agency's *Infrared Space Observatory* (*ISO*) have detected traces of hydrogen fluoride gas in interstellar space. This detection allows study of the chemistry of fluorine-containing molecules, in the conditions of space. *ISO* has observed the earliest stages of star formation, water vapor in dark clouds toward the center of the Milky Way, and disks of dust particles rotating around normal stars.

In 1997, the European Space Agency completed the mission of the *Hipparcos* astronomy satellite, launched in 1989. The result is the most precise compilation of stars ever assembled, with detailed position and distance data for 118,000 stars.

The European Space Agency also shares in the *Cassini* mission to Saturn with the Titan entry probe *Huygens*.

Space station participation. The European Space Agency's participation in the International Space Station program consists of the Columbus Orbital Facility research module, the Automated Transfer Vehicle as an upper stage of the Ariane 5, and two multiple coupling adapters, called Node 2 and Node 3.

Asian Space Activities

In 1997, space activities continued in Japan, the People's Republic of China, and India.

Japan. Japan's space activities reached a number of milestones, but also suffered a serious loss when its *Advanced Earth Observation Satellite* (*Adeos*), launched in 1996 as Japan's largest and most complex satellite, was lost on June 30 after a string of malfunctions. On November 27, the Japanese space agency NASDA launched its fifth H-2 carrying the NASA/NASDA earth science satellite *TRMM* and the Engineering Test Satellite *ETS 7* (*Hikoboshi*) with a small target satellite (*Orihime*) attached for subsequent rendezvous and docking experiments.

Japan successfully tested a new rocket, the M-5, on February 12, carrying the *HALCA/Haruka* (formerly *Muses-B*) science satellite into a highly elliptical orbit. After the H-2, the M-5 is the second rocket developed by Japan entirely at home. It can put up to 4400 lb (2000 kg) into low Earth orbit.

Muses-C is scheduled for launch in 2002 to return samples from the asteroid (4660) Nereus to Earth in 2006. NASA will provide an instrumented rover weighing only 2.2 lb (1 kg) and based on *Sojourner* technology.

The H-2A, which uses the more powerful cryogenic LE-7A engine, underwent its first firing tests. It is derived from the H-2 by the addition of a single liquid-propellant strap-on booster with two LE-7A engines. Meanwhile, Japan stayed on track in the development of its contribution to the International Space Station, the Japanese Experimental Module (JEM), along with its ancillary remote manipulator system and exposed facility.

China. The People's Republic's space program showed strong signs of recovery after its commercial launcher setbacks in 1996, when two Long March (Chang Zheng) 3 rockets exploded after liftoff, with casualties. During 1997, China succeeded in launching four Long March 3 and two Long March 2 rockets with no failures. They carried five communications satellites and the country's first geosynchronous weather satellite (*Feng Yun 2*).

India. On September 29, the Indian Space Research Organization (ISRO) launched its four-stage Polar Satellite Launch Vehicle (PSLV) carrying the Earth resources imaging satellite *IRS-1D* into a Sunsynchronous polar orbit. (It was lost on October 5 because of power problems.) The launch marked the third consecutive success for the 145-ft (44-m) booster, which develops more than 10^6 lb (4450 kN) of thrust.

South American Space Activities

Chile, Brazil, and Argentina continued to press ahead with efforts to expand their space launch and operations capability. Brazil's plan to become the ninth country capable of designing, developing, and launching a space vehicle suffered a setback on November 2, when the first Brazilian-made space launch vehicle, the 63-ft-tall (19-m), four-stage Satellite Launch Vehicle (VLS, for Veiculo Lancador de Satelites) was lost about 65 s after launch. Brazil is pressing forward to build three more prototype vehicles. On July 8, the Brazilian National Institute for Space Research (INPE) entered a cooperative accord with NASA to participate in the International Space Station, providing parts, subsystems, and components.

For background information *see* ASTEROID; COMMUNICATIONS SATELLITE; INFRARED ASTRONOMY; JUPITER; MARS; MILITARY SATELLITES; PARALLAX (ASTRONOMY); REMOTE SENSING; SATELLITE ASTRONOMY; SATELLITE NAVIGATION SYSTEMS; SPACE BIOLOGY; SPACE FLIGHT; SPACE PROBE; SPACE PROCESSING; SPACE SHUTTLE; SPACE STATION; SPACE TECHNOLOGY; SUN; X-RAY ASTRONOMY

Jesco von Puttkamer

Bibliography. *Jane's Space Directory, 1996–1997*; NASA Public Affairs Office, *News Releases '97*, 1997; SpaceVest and KPMG Peat Marwick, *State of the Space Industry: 1997 Outlook*, 1997.

Speech

One of the most investigated characteristics of speech production is its variability. The acoustic properties of a given speech sound (a consonant or vowel) and the associated movements of the vocal tract (the lips, jaw, tongue, velum, and larynx) exhibit variability from a number of sources. The factors that can influence the extent and degree of variation in articulation are extensive, ranging from the intent of the speaker's message to physical constraints imposed by the anatomy of the speech production mechanism. Identifying the specific factors is critical to understanding the nervous-system principles and processes underlying human communication.

Speech movement variations provide insight into the neural basis of human behavior and into the component processes (speech perception and production) for verbal interaction. The intent of speech is to communicate, and accurate information transfer is based on a balance between the speaker's encoding of the message and the listener's decoding ability. If these two systems are appropriately tuned, a predictability results that facilitates the communication process. One method to examine the interaction of these two processes involves speech movement variability under a variety of conditions. The amount and the temporal location of articulatory variation in the speaker's output may be directly related to the manner and the location of perceptual cues used by the listener.

The analysis of speech movement variation into its sources is critical to the development of theoretical models of speech production and to the development of improved speech synthesis. Knowledge of patterns of speech movement variation can be used in examining the specific effects of nervous-system damage due to disease, trauma, and developmental disorders, and ultimately can lead to more focused diagnosis and treatment of many speech and language problems.

Control principles. The variations present at all levels of empirical observation (acoustic, aerodynamic, kinematic, electromyographic) reflect characteristics of the speech motor-control process, involving the 45–50 muscles of the vocal tract that may be used for speech. The variations may represent output noise that requires little explanation. Alternatively, the variations may be systematic, and the source of the variations needs to be understood. Factors that may influence the form of speech movement variability range from the physical characteristics of the vocal tract to considerations of explicitly controlled optimizing (performance) functions. Optimizing criteria, such as economy of articulatory effort, minimization of kinematic (acceleration, jerk) or dynamic (muscle force) properties, or smoothness constraints, may be seen as global system properties in which a cost function is minimized presumably because of high energetic demands.

The quantal nature of speech suggests that the nonlinear acoustic-articulatory characteristics of the vocal tract may directly influence speech movement variations. There are regions within the vocal tract (quantal regions) in which small articulatory deviations have relatively large acoustic consequences (unstable regions), and regions in which very large articulatory changes have relatively small acoustic consequences (stable regions). Quantal considerations suggest that certain patterns of variations within and across languages may be governed by the nonlinear properties of the vocal tract. By implication, certain speech sounds may require more precise spatial control because the portions of the vocal tract responsible for their production are proximate to quantal (less stable) vocal tract regions. These considerations suggest that movement variations may be directly related to the characteristics of the controlled object (the vocal tract) itself. The precise role of control principles in explaining speech movement variations is currently unknown.

Contextual variation. The most prevalent source of speech movement variation is coarticulation, a basic property of speech production. Coarticulation is a phenomenon in which the articulator movements for a given speech sound vary systematically with the surrounding sounds and their associated movements. Because speech sounds are always produced in sequence, the surrounding phonetic context will always influence the kinematic and acoustic properties of any specific phonetic segment. Contextual variations have been at the heart of most theoretical issues in speech, frustrating the search for simple invariances that could provide a correspondence between phonological categories and acoustic and kinematic waveforms, and obscuring attempts at identifying the units of speech production. For example, different positions of the tongue and associated tongue surfaces are observed when a vowel (/ae/) is produced in the words "rack" and "sack" (**Fig. 1**). In the two contexts the spatial location of the

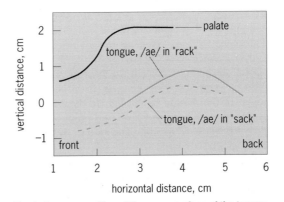

Fig. 1. Average position of the upper surface of the tongue for the vowel /ae/ in the words "sack" and "rack" from a single speaker. The position of the tongue surface was estimated from the position of four inductor coils affixed to the tongue from the front to the back and separated by approximately 1 cm (0.4 in.). The position of the hard palate is shown from behind the upper teeth to the extent of the palatine bone.

tongue is different, producing different acoustic properties.

Coarticulation at the level of movement kinematics has been reported in a number of speech articulators and in various experimental manipulations. While a range of accounts for coarticulation have been proposed, two views have dominated: context-invariant models, which involve the blending of the influences of discrete motor commands; and context-sensitive (look-ahead) models, which suggest planned adjustments in the motor commands. The major difference in these two views is the extent to which the reported patterns of context sensitivity are directly specified or planned in the neural control signals. In the context-invariant models coarticulation effects result from the interaction of adjacent segments, while in the context-sensitive approach the nervous system explicitly adjusts the movements because of the upcoming context. A fundamental difficulty in addressing these two explanations is that inferring control strategies from kinematic data alone requires knowledge of what aspects of the kinematic variation result from nonneural factors, such as biomechanical properties and dynamics.

Biomechanical sources. The human vocal tract displays a number of biophysical properties that influence speech kinematics. Whereas the tongue and lips are soft tissue structures that undergo substantial viscoelastic deformation during speech, the jaw displays a degree of anisotropic tension. Even seemingly homogeneous structures such as the upper and lower lips display different stiffness properties which may contribute to their differential movement patterns. The mandible is a rigid body exhibiting rotational and translational motion, while the tongue is a deformable, volume-preserving solid with a complex tissue structure and muscular organization. In addition to the structural arrangement of the vocal tract muscles for valving and shaping actions, the biomechanical properties of the tissue loads against which the different vocal tract muscles contract are extremely heterogeneous. For some structures such as the lips and vocal folds, inertial considerations are minimal, while for the jaw and the respiratory system inertia is a significant factor. Such considerations suggest that the kinematic and acoustic variability characteristic of speech production partly reflects the filtering of neural control signals by the biomechanics of the vocal tract. Recently, a physiological model of the motion of the human mandible and hyoid (the bone that supports the tongue and its muscles) was used to show that certain patterns of intra-articulator coarticulation could be explained, not by active movement planning, but by the dynamics of the system at the biomechanical level.

Anatomical sources. Variability may also arise from the anatomy of the speech production mechanism itself. Ignoring the nasal cavity, the human vocal tract extends in a superior-inferior direction from the hard palate to the larynx and in an anterior-posterior direction from the lips to the pharyngeal wall. The vocal tract proper is a nonuniform acoustic

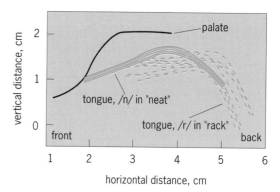

Fig. 2. Positional variation in the upper tongue surface within the vocal tract from a single speaker repeating the words "neat" or "rack" eight times. The position of the tongue surface was estimated from the position of four inductor coils affixed to the tongue from the front to the back and separated by approximately 1 cm (0.4 in.). The position of the hard palate is shown from behind the upper teeth to the extent of the palatine bone.

tube of approximately 17 cm (7 in.) in length and is bounded by hard and soft tissues providing constraints on articulator motion. One constraint that appears to substantially influence degree and extent of speech movement variability is the hard palate and teeth. All consonants of English are produced by constricting the vocal tract somewhere along its length. For example, the consonants /n/ and /r/ in the words "neat" and "rack" display different amounts of tongue positional variability because of the proximity of the tongue to the hard palate and teeth (**Fig. 2**). For the /n/ the amount of variability is quite small, apparently because of tongue contact with the hard palate and front teeth. The amount of variation seen for /r/ is substantial, because /r/ is produced farther back in the mouth with much less tongue contact with the hard tissues.

For background information *see* CONTROL SYSTEMS; SPEECH in the McGraw-Hill Encyclopedia of Science & Technology.   Vincent L. Gracco

Bibliography. F. Bell-Berti and L. Raphael (eds.), *Producing Speech: Contemporary Issues, For Katherine Safford Harris*, 1995; D. J. Ostry, P. L. Gribble, and V. L. Gracco, Coarticulation of jaw movements in speech production: Is context-sensitivity in speech kinematics centrally planned?, *J. Neurosci.*, 16:1570–1579, 1996; J. S. Perkell and D. H. Klatt (eds.), *Invariance and Variability in Speech Processes*, 1982.

Speech coder

The use of a digital representation for speech signals has many advantages. The signal can be more easily manipulated, combined with other signals such as video or data, and made less sensitive to transmission errors. A drawback of digital representations is that for high-fidelity reproduction the number of bits per second is high. A digital representation can be ob-

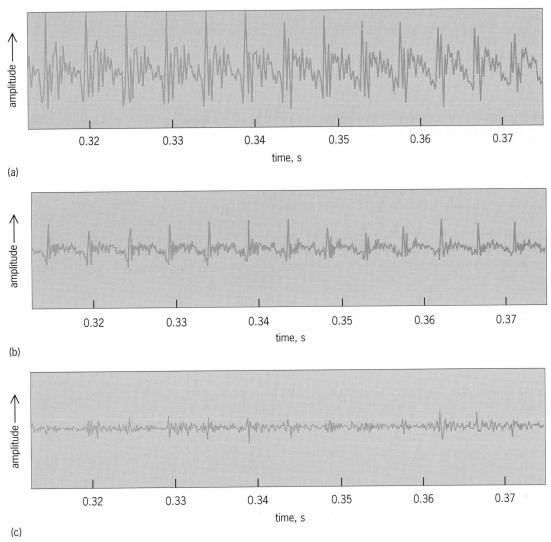

Fig. 1. Example of a 50-ms segment of (*a***) speech, (***b***) speech after short-term prediction, and (***c***) speech after both short-and long-term prediction.**

tained by sampling the analog signal with a frequency at least twice that of the highest frequency occurring in the signal. For each of the samples, the amplitude has to be encoded with a digital number. The most simple form of coding is pulse-code modulation (PCM), which requires 8–16 bits per sample. A telephone-bandwidth (200–3400 Hz) speech signal is typically sampled 8000 times per second by using 8–12 bits per sample. The resulting bit rate for the digital representation is 64,000–96,000 bits per second.

The objective of speech coding or speech compression is to reduce this high-bit-rate pulse-code-modulation presentation without a severe reduction in signal quality. The process involves an encoder, which converts the digital pulse-code-modulation signal into a low-rate digital signal or bit stream. This bit stream is either transmitted or stored. The decoder converts the bit stream into a digital pulse-code-modulation signal, which can subsequently be converted back to an analog signal for playback.

Speech-compression techniques. Speech compression is accomplished by taking advantage of both the redundancies and irrelevancies of the signal. The redundancy is due to the speech production mechanism, which consists of sounds generated by the vocal cords and modulated by slowly moving articulators (the mouth cavity, tongue, and so forth). Redundancy exhibits itself, for example, in the form of correlations between adjacent samples. This allows a more efficient representation by encoding the differences in amplitude instead of the absolute values of the signal. Other redundancies can be found by looking at blocks of samples with durations of 20–30 ms. For example, from examining the distribution of the energy as a function of frequency for a block of samples, it is observed that the spectral envelope changes in most cases only gradually from block to block. The spectral envelope in each block is due to the sample-to-sample correlations and can be efficiently represented with a linear predictor filter.

Another property of the speech signal is that for

sounds such as vowels (such as the "ee" sound in speech) the signal is highly periodic, meaning that the signal will look very similar in every pitch period. The pitch of a signal varies for different sounds and speakers. Typically, female talkers produce higher-pitched sounds than male talkers. This pitch-period redundancy can be effectively represented with a pitch or long-term predictor. The short-term and long-term correlations are removed by filtering the signal with the short-term and long-term predictors, respectively (**Fig. 1**).

The remaining (residual) signal does not show any obvious correlations and can be quantized with either a scalar quantizer (sample by sample) or a vector quantizer (which quantizes a block of samples). The filter parameters for both the long-term and short-term predictors, and the quantized samples, represented by the quantizer indices, form the coder parameters which are either transmitted or stored. The decoder filters the quantized residual through the inverse of short-term and long-term predictor filters to restore the correlations in the signal, thereby reconstructing the speech signal.

Use of signal irrelevancies. Irrelevancies of the signal refer to the fact that the decompressed signal will be played back to a human listener. The properties of the human hearing system are such that some distortions cannot be heard. As an example, a noise-like signal such as the "s" sound could be used in the word "speech." To represent the noiselike samples for this part of the sound requires many bits. However, noise could be taken from another source, such as a noise generator, and as long as the amplitude and the spectral shape are matched, it will sound the same. This is just a simple example. More complicated is masking, in which one sound is used to mask the distortion introduced by another sound. Unfortunately, the human auditory model and the way it treats distortions is not fully understood. Nevertheless, many models have been suggested and have been quite successful despite their shortcomings.

Analysis-by-synthesis. Ideally, it would be desirable to determine the coder parameters such that the perceived distortion is as low as possible. One powerful approach is to do analysis-by-synthesis. The consequence of choosing a particular value of a coder parameter is evaluated by locally decoding the signal and comparing it to the original input signal (**Fig. 2**). This comparison can be done directly on the waveform or on a modified version of the waveforms. The modification reflects the use of an auditory model to make the comparison more meaningful from a perceptual point of view.

CELP coder. A very successful realization of the techniques described above is the code-excited linear predictive (CELP) coder. This coder uses both short- and long-term predictors combined with vector-quantization techniques. It uses an analysis-by-synthesis approach to search for the best combination of parameters, and is very effective at bit rates between 8 and 16 kilobits per second (kb/s).

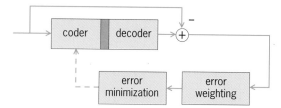

Fig. 2. Concept diagram of analysis-by-synthesis coding. The coder parameters are determined such that the coded signal can be said to be perceptually close to the input signal. *(After W. B. Kleijn and K. K. Paliwal, Speech Coding and Synthesis, Elsevier, 1995)*

System attributes. The applications of speech compression are numerous. They include network and wireless communications, Internet phones, videophones, and voice messaging (such as answering machines). Although the main attribute of a speech-compression system is speech quality for a given bit rate, additional parameters such as delay and complexity play an important part in the selection of a coding algorithm. The delay refers to the time it takes for a certain speech segment to go through a complete encoding-decoding process. Some of this delay is due to processing and transmission, but the coder needs to look at a block of speech in order to obtain efficient compression. This coder delay is called algorithmic delay and varies from 0.1 to 40 ms. The complexity is another important parameter. Many portable applications run on batteries, and a high complexity usually means an increased power consumption, which will reduce the talk time, that is, the amount of time that the phone can be in an active talking mode before the battery runs out. For Internet applications, the speech coder is implemented on a personal computer, and a high complexity would mean that the user could not talk and perform another computer task at the same time.

Quality can have many meanings, but implicitly most users expect consistency in the performance for a variety of signals. Most low-rate speech coders will do a decent job with clean speech signals, but will have difficulty with a combination of speech and background noise, or nonspeech signals such as tones or music that is played while the caller is placed on hold. In cellular and Internet applications, an additional requirement is that the coders should be able to survive transmission problems. In other words, if not all of the bits of the bit stream are received, it should still be possible to construct a speechlike signal. To combat random bit errors on the channel, the use of error-correction codes is necessary. More difficult is the problem of the loss of a complete frame (that is, 20–40 ms). However, the lower-rate coders parametrize the signal (with parameters such as energy and spectral shape), and as long as the decoder knows that a frame is lost or corrupted, simple repetition of the parameters has proven to be quite effective.

Standards. For most telecommunication applications, it is necessary to define standards. These stan-

Telephone bandwidth coding standards based on linear predictive analysis-by-synthesis				
Name*	Application†	Date	Bit rate, kb/s	Mean opinion score (MOS)‡
FS1016	Military	1988	4.8	3.2
GSM 6.10 FR	Cellular	1987	13	3.5
GSM 6.42 HR	Cellular	1994	5.6	3.4
GSM 6.60 EFR	Cellular	1995	12.2	3.9
IS-54 FR	Cellular (TDMA)	1989	7.95	3.6
IS-641 EFR	Cellular (TDMA)	1996	7.4	3.8
IS-96 VR	Cellular (CDMA)	1993	8/4/1	3.4
IS-127 VR	Cellular (CDMA)	1996	8.5/4/1	3.8
RCR STD27 FR	Cellular (Japan)	1990	6.67	3.2
RCR STD27 HR	Cellular (Japan)	1993	3.45	3.3
ITU-T G.728	Network	1992	16	4.0
ITU-T G.723.1§	Multimedia	1995	5.3/6.3	3.4/3.6
ITU-T G.729	Network/PCS	1996	8	3.8

* Most cellular standards have both a full-rate (FR) and half-rate (HR) coder. Replacements of the FR coders are referred to as enhanced full-rate (EFR) coders. Variable-rate (VR) coders switch between the bit rates indicated, depending on the type of signal. (VR is not part of the official name.)
† TDMA = time-division multiple access; CDMA = code-division multiple access; PCS = personal communications service.
‡ Numbers are for clear speech without background noise. Some other coder dimensions such as complexity and delay are not represented in the table.
§ Multirate coder, which is chosen to run at one of the bit rates indicated, with the corresponding MOS.

dards can be global, such as those defined by the International Telecommunications Union (ITU), or more regional such as ETSI in Europe, TIA in North America, and RCR in Japan. Most of these standards apply to cellular communications, but they are also used in videoconferences and military communications. Most are based on some realization of the CELP coding concept explained above (see **table**).

A quality rating can be given in terms of a mean opinion score (MOS) [see table]. This number is obtained by presenting coded speech utterances to a large listener panel, which rates the quality on a 5-point scale (1 = bad, 2 = poor, 3 = fair, 4 = good, 5 = excellent). The average scores represent the MOS rating. These numbers depend on the test material, talkers, listening conditions, and so forth.

Low-bit-rate and scalable coders. At lower bit rates, coding paradigms different from CELP coding seem to be more effective, and this is an area of current research. Depending on the application, very low bit rates (for example, 1000 bits per second) can be achieved, but the price paid is increased delay and complexity, and reduced robustness.

The use of speech coders for the Internet has put more research focus on scalable coders. These coders allow the use of the same coder structure at various bit rates. A special case is embedded coding, which allows the decoder to provide a lower-quality rendering of the signal even after the removal of bits from the bit stream. The Internet applications have also created a demand for low-bit-rate coders (8–16 kilobits per second) that can encode both audio and speech signals with high quality.

Most current speech coding research focuses on low-bit-rate coders, scalable coders, and universal speech and audio coders. It is also recognized that more efficient compression schemes can be realized only by understanding better the human auditory system, and research will continue on this topic as well.

For background information *see* DATA COMPRESSION; INFORMATION THEORY; MASKING OF SOUND; MOBILE RADIO; PULSE MODULATION; SPEECH; SPEECH RECOGNITION in the McGraw-Hill Encyclopedia of Science & Technology. Peter Kroon

Bibliography. W. B. Kleijn and K. K. Paliwal (eds.), *Speech Coding and Synthesis*, 1995.

Sperm

The majority of sessile marine invertebrates reproduce by releasing eggs and sperm (gametes) into the water column where they come into contact and fertilization occurs. This method is called free spawning. Each resulting embryo develops rapidly in the plankton, giving rise to a free-swimming larva. Depending on the species, this larva swims in the plankton for a few minutes up to several months before settling onto a substratum and metamorphosing into the adult form.

Free-spawning sessile marine invertebrates have evolved many mechanisms for maximizing the probability of gamete contact, and thus, fertilization success. These mechanisms include strategies that increase the concentration of gametes at spawning, and the evolution of gamete characteristics that enhance the probability of contact between eggs and sperm. Recent studies have shown that the sperm of some free-spawning sessile marine invertebrates display adaptations that may conserve their energy reserves until they are close to eggs, thereby maintaining sperm viability for extended periods in the absence of eggs.

Maximizing fertilization success. It is widely assumed that there has been strong evolutionary selective pressure to maximize the probability of gamete contact in sessile marine invertebrates. An example is the evolution of mechanisms that increase the concentration of gametes at spawning. Many free-spawning species exhibit synchronous spawning in response to environmental cues, including light, temperature, and the presence of gametes in the water column. Synchronous spawning increases the concentration of gametes in the water column, and thus the probability of fertilization success. Similarly, maximization of fertilization success is considered to be one of the selective pressures for the aggregated field distributions exhibited by many free-spawning sessile marine invertebrate species. Field experiments have shown that aggregation of adults increases the concentration of gametes, and fertilization success, at spawning. Perhaps the strongest evidence of the importance of fertilization success as a selective pressure comes from the evolution of sperm chemotaxis in many marine phyla.

Sperm chemotaxis is the directional orientation and swimming of sperm toward compounds originating from eggs and reproductive structures. Sperm chemotaxis has been demonstrated in four marine phyla: Cnidaria (hydroids, jellyfish), Mollusca (chitons), Urochordata (solitary ascidians), and Echinodermata (sea cucumbers, sea urchins, brittlestars, starfish). The adaptive significance of sperm chemotaxis is believed to lie in the increased probability of gamete contact, even when gamete concentration is low.

There have been few attempts to isolate and characterize the compounds that stimulate sperm chemotaxis; much of the work centers on sea urchins. This work has isolated compounds associated with sea urchin eggs that increase the activity level and respiration rate of sea urchin sperm on a species-specific basis. Thus, increases in sperm activity and respiration are characteristic of the chemotactic response in sea urchins.

Sperm chemotaxis is widespread in solitary ascidians, commonly known as sea squirts (**Fig. 1**). Though the compounds associated with ascidian sperm chemotaxis have not been isolated and characterized, the chemotactic response in these organisms also involves increased sperm activity. Recent studies have investigated the activation of solitary ascidian sperm in response to compounds associated with homospecific eggs and the relationship between sperm activity and longevity.

Ascidian sperm. Solitary ascidians are sessile filter-feeding marine invertebrates of the subphylum Urochordata, class Ascidiacea. They are commonly found attached to substrata in intertidal, subtidal, and benthic marine environments throughout the world. The majority of solitary ascidian species are found in shallow coastal waters, but they are also common components of the benthic fauna at depths greater than 2000 m (1.2 mi).

Solitary ascidians are free-spawning hermaphrodites, producing both egg and sperm. In some species, a single testis and ovary lie next to the stomach and intestine. The gametes produced by the testis and ovary are stored in gonoducts that run parallel to the intestine. The sperm duct can be clearly seen in species that have a transparent body wall. The

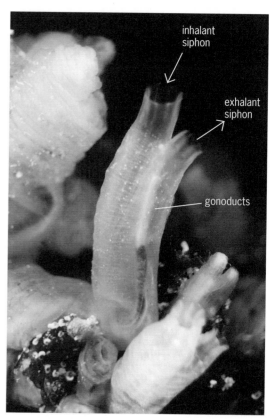

Fig. 1. Solitary ascidian *Ciona intestinalis*. (Photography by Troy Jantzen)

gonoducts open into a cavity close to the exhalant siphon. At spawning, the stored gametes are released from the gonoducts into this cavity and are swept into the water column by the feeding water current and contractions of the body wall (Fig. 1).

The longevity (and viability) of sperm from *Ciona intestinalis* and *Ascidiella aspersa* has been measured as a function of their ability to fertilize freshly extracted eggs at regular time intervals after exposure to seawater that has been incubated with homospecific eggs (referred to as egg water). Compounds that are responsible for the chemotactic response in sperm diffuse from the eggs into the seawater in which they are incubated. To compare the longevity of sperm exposed to egg water with sperm that are not, the longevity of sperm in plain seawater has also been measured. Measurements of the proportion of *C. intestinalis* and *A. aspersa* sperm active after exposure to homospecific egg water have been made simultaneously with measurements of sperm longevity.

Studies on the proportion of active sperm of both species show that it is substantially greater in homospecific egg water in comparison to plain seawater for approximately 1.5 h. After this period, the proportion of active sperm in egg water declines sharply, and is lower than in plain seawater after 2 h. After 3 h, there are no active sperm in egg water solutions, though the proportion of active sperm in

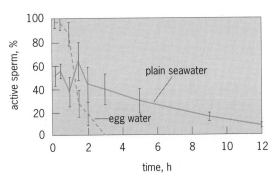

Fig. 2. Proportion of active *Ciona intestinalis* sperm in treatments over time. (The general trends are also representative of *Ascidiella aspersa* sperm.)

the plain seawater declines gradually over time and a small proportion remains active after 12 h (**Fig. 2**).

Simultaneous studies of sperm longevity have shown that sperm from both *C. intestinalis* and *A. aspersa* are viable in excess of 12 h in plain seawater. However, when sperm from these species are incubated in homospecific egg water, their viability declines rapidly. After 1.5 h, sperm incubated in homospecific egg water are no longer viable (**Fig. 3**). These findings suggest that there is a causal inverse relationship between sperm activity and longevity in *C. intestinalis* and *A. aspersa*.

Results of these studies suggest that the activation of nonmotile sperm by compounds diffusing from eggs provides a mechanism by which the energy reserves of a sperm are conserved in the absence of eggs, thereby maintaining sperm viability for extended periods.

Ecological implications. The evolution of a mechanism that enables sperm to conserve energy reserves may enhance fertilization success by prolonging sperm viability until gametes are brought into contact through water currents. Such a mechanism is unlikely to be of any advantage in environments where gametes are rapidly diluted by high levels of water turbulence. However, *C. intestinalis* and *A. aspersa* commonly occur in high densities and cover large areas of hard substrata in sheltered environ-

ments. These species are also reported to spawn synchronously in response to light. Therefore, the concentration of gametes may be high over an extensive area and, because they live in sheltered environments, may remain high for a considerable time. In such conditions, a mechanism that extends the period of sperm longevity, and hence the potential for fertilization success, may have substantial selective advantage.

Because the adult stages of solitary ascidians are sessile, the transfer of genetic material between populations (gene flow) has been assumed to be primarily mediated by the planktonic egg, embryonic, and larval stages. However, the eggs of both *C. intestinalis* and *A. aspersa* are surrounded by a viscous mucilage that readily adheres to available substrata. Studies have suggested that the embryos and larvae of these species may be frequently retained within this mucilage until settlement occurs. Therefore, the egg, embryonic, and larval stages of *C. intestinalis* and *A. aspersa* may not mediate gene flow to the extent previously thought. If this is the case, interpopulation gene flow may be significantly mediated by sperm, and the conservation of sperm energy may be important in facilitating this process.

Field conditions. Experiments on the inverse relationship between sperm activity and longevity have been conducted in the laboratory. Thus, the extrapolation of these results to the field needs to be viewed with caution. Further studies are therefore required to determine whether the inverse relationship between sperm activity and longevity in response to compounds associated with eggs occurs in field conditions, and if so, what are its ecological implications. Further studies are also needed to determine how widespread is the inverse relationship between sperm activity and longevity in free-spawning marine invertebrate species.

For background information *see* ASCIDIACEA; ECOLOGY; FERTILIZATION; INVERTEBRATE EMBRYOLOGY; SEAWATER FERTILITY; SPERM CELL in the McGraw-Hill Encyclopedia of Science & Technology.

Toby F. Bolton; Jon N. Havenhand

Bibliography. R. S. K. Barnes, P. Carlow, and P. J. W. Olive, *The Invertebrates: A New Synthesis*, 2d ed., 1993; T. F. Bolton and J. N. Havenhand, Chemical mediation of sperm activity and longevity in the solitary ascidians *Ciona intestinalis* and *Ascidiella aspersa*, *Biol. Bull.*, 190:329–335, 1996; D. R. Levitan, M. A. Sewell, and F. S. Chia, How distribution and abundance influence fertilization success in the sea urchin *Strongylocentrotus franciscanus*, *Ecology*, 73(1):248–254, 1992; R. L. Miller, Sperm chemotaxis in ascidians, *Amer. Zool.*, 22:827–840, 1982.

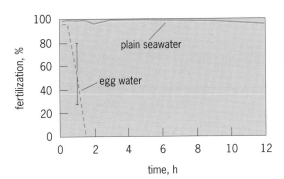

Fig. 3. Viability of *Ciona intestinalis* sperm in treatments over time. (The general trends are also representative of *Ascidiella aspersa* sperm.)

Stellarator

Ever since it was postulated in 1939 that stars obtain their energy from fusion reactions, continuous attempts have been made to harness this fusion, the main source of energy in the universe, in a controlled manner. However, it was realized in 1957 that to use fusion to produce electricity on Earth, even with the most reasonable fuel, a mixture of 50% deuterium and 50% tritium, the material would have to be heated to temperatures equivalent to at least 10 keV (approximately 10^8 K). The problem is how to isolate enough fuel (approximately 1-2×10^{20} particles/m³) at such extreme temperatures (1-2×10^8 K) from the surrounding environment for enough time (approximately 2-3 s) to allow a sufficient number of reactions to occur and make the overall energy production process efficient.

Magnetic confinement. One possible solution to this problem is magnetic confinement. Magnetic confinement takes advantage of the facts that at the high temperatures required for fusion any gas is in a fully ionized state (that is, a plasma), and that in the presence of magnetic fields the charged particles of the plasma can move freely along the field lines while their movement across the lines is restricted to circles in a direction dependent on their charge. A simple technique to isolate the fuel while it reacts is to close these lines upon themselves in a toroidal chamber so that, in the absence of collisions, the particles will be confined as long as the toroidal magnetic field is maintained.

Unfortunately, nature does not always favor simplicity. Some very simple calculations show that the curvature needed to close the lines gives rise to a drift in the particle orbits perpendicular to the field and its gradient. As the direction of this drift depends upon the charge of these particles, a natural separation of charge is introduced in the torus, with positive particles tending to move toward the upper part and electrons toward the lower. This creates an electric field which, when combined with the magnetic field, causes a discernible drift toward the outside of the torus. This drift is independent of the charge on the particles and results in all of the particles being pushed out of the confinement volume.

Fortunately, solutions to this problem do exist. For instance, it may be possible to prevent the magnetic field lines from closing upon themselves, so that they are allowed to ergodically cover a surface (that is, to cover the surface in such a way that each field line, if sufficiently extended, passes arbitrarily close to any point on the surface). In that case, the upper and lower parts of the torus will be connected, the electric field will be short-circuited, the drift due to the electric field will disappear, and confinement will be recovered. In principle, this solution is realized by superimposing a poloidal field on the basic toroidal field. The lines inside the torus are then forced to follow a helical trajectory.

Tokamaks versus stellarators. At least two closely connected families of magnetic confinement devices use this solution to produce a magnetic bottle, named tokamaks and stellarators. They differ only in the way in which the required poloidal field is produced (**Fig. 1**). In tokamaks the main confinement field is created by coils that are mounted perpendicular to the doughnutlike chamber. The transformer effect is used to induce a toroidal current in the plasma, thereby creating the required poloidal field. Stellarators rely exclusively on external coils to create all the fields needed.

At present, the tokamak (Fig. 1a) is without question the most advanced and best developed of all magnetic confinement experiments. However, there are certain inherent difficulties. For instance, the need to induce a current in the plasma by using the transformer effect makes the tokamak, in principle, a pulsed device. Moreover, this current is a source of free energy capable of inducing instabilities in the plasma, which limit the performance of tokamaks. Furthermore, if these instabilities cause a sudden loss of confinement—a disruption, in fusion terminology—strong and potentially damaging forces can be transmitted to the magnetic coils and the vacuum chamber. Thus, sophisticated control systems are required to avoid or limit this situation. Schemes

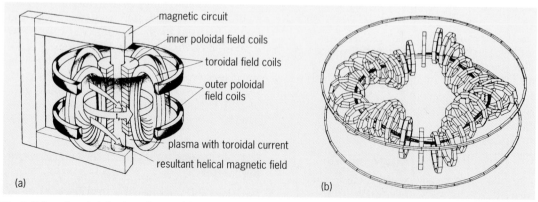

magnetic circuit
inner poloidal field coils
toroidal field coils
outer poloidal field coils
plasma with toroidal current
resultant helical magnetic field

(a)   (b)

Fig. 1. Tokamak and stellarator schemes. (a) Tokamak. The toroidal field is created by using external coils, and the required poloidal field is created by means of an induced toroidal current, I_p, flowing through the plasma. (b) Stellarator. All the needed fields (toroidal and poloidal) are produced by a combination of external coils, independently of the plasma. (*Asociacion Euratom CIEMAT*)

TABLE 1. Stellarators in operation

Device	Country	Major radius, m (ft)	Plasma radius, cm (in.)	Magnetic field, tesla	Power, MW	Operating since
Heliotron-E	Japan	2.0 (6.6)	20 (8)	1.9	5.0	1980
ATF	United States	2.1 (6.9)	25 (10)	2.0	3.0	1988–1995
CHS	Japan	1.0 (3.3)	20 (8)	1.5	4.0	1988
W7-AS	Germany	2.0 (6.6)	20 (8)	3.0	5.6	1988
H-1	Australia	1.0 (3.3)	20 (8)	1.0	0.2	1992
CAT	United States	0.5 (1.6)	10 (4)	0.1	0.1	1993
U-2M	Ukraine	1.7 (5.6)	20 (8)	2.4	0.4	1993
TJ-IU	Spain	0.6 (2.0)	10 (4)	0.7	0.4	1994
L-2M	Russia	1.0 (3.3)	12 (5)	1.5	1.0	1995
TJ-II	Spain	1.5 (4.9)	25 (10)	1.0	5.0	1997

exist to overcome these problems; nevertheless, the problems remain a limitation to realization of the idea.

Stellarators (Fig. 1b) provide a way to circumvent these difficulties. The removal of the need for current to flow through the plasma (so that a steady state is inherent) eliminates the free source of energy and its associated instabilities and disruptions. Magnetic properties are controlled externally, and achievable densities appear to be higher than in tokamaks. However, these advantages do not come without drawbacks. In particular, stellarator configurations are intrinsically nonaxisymmetric with the result that, in classical stellarators, any particle that becomes trapped in the helical ripples of the magnetic field can, without any collisions, escape from confinement in a time much shorter than that needed to heat the plasma. On the contrary, collisionless orbits in ideal (axisymmetric) tokamaks are, in principle, absolutely confined. Moreover, the inherent three-dimensional configuration of stellarators may complicate the design and construction of the coil structures, the tritium breeding blankets, and the impurity extraction systems of stellarator-based power plants of the future.

Development. Both concepts were conceived about the same time and are, in some ways, a reflection of the political competition of that time. The first tokamak was proposed in 1951 and constructed in Moscow. Since 1958, when secret fusion research was first disclosed and the tokamak concept was first described, the tokamak has been the principal and leading approach to magnetic confinement in all fusion programs throughout the world.

Stellarators have had a more difficult course of development. The first proposal to build a stellarator was also made in 1951, and the first stellarator was built at Princeton, New Jersey. However, the results of this first machine and its successors were disappointing. After it was announced, in 1968, that new records for temperatures (equivalent to 1 keV) and energy confinement times (10 ms) had been obtained in the Russian tokamaks T-3 and TM-3, the researchers at Princeton abandoned their stellarator idea (their machine had achieved temperatures equivalent to about 100 eV and confinement times

of about 1 ms) and converted their machines to a tokamak.

Fortunately for the concept, not everybody shared their disappointment. Some physicists realized that the problem with stellarators was their intrinsic three-dimensional geometry. In order to confine a fuel heated to a temperature of millions of degrees Kelvin, it is necessary to comply with very strict requirements on the artificial forces designed to contain such matter. Therefore, no errors can be allowed in the magnetic field structure. Not only the underlying idea but also its engineering must be perfect. To prove this point, small machines were built in Japan, Germany, and Russia. Stellarators continue to follow tokamaks on the road to better and larger confinement bottles.

Improvements. The 1990s have seen major increases in the level of stellarators research (**Table 1**). A medium-sized stellarator, Wendelstein 7-AS, has

Fig. 2. TJ-II stellarator during assembly, showing the peculiar helical vacuum chamber.

TABLE 2. Stellarators under construction or entering operation						
Device	Country	Major radius, m (ft)	Plasma radius, cm (in.)	Magnetic field, tesla	Power, MW	Foreseen operating date
HSX	United States	1.2 (3.9)	15 (6)	1.0	0.2	1988
LHD	Japan	3.9 (12.8)	65 (26)	4.0	>20	1998
W7-X	Germany	5.5 (18.0)	54 (21)	2.5	>20	2005

been in operation since 1988 in Garching, Germany. It has attained confinement properties equivalent to those achieved in similar-sized tokamaks (ion temperatures equivalent to about 1.6 keV, electron temperatures equivalent to about 3.5 keV, and confinement times of approximately 43 ms). It has produced, for the first time in stellarators, a high confinement mode, which until now had been the domain of tokamaks. Another medium-sized stellarator, TJ-II in Madrid, Spain (**Fig. 2**), began operation in 1997. In addition, two large superconducting stellarator projects are under development (**Table 2**): Construction of Wendelstein 7-X at Greifswald, Germany, began in 1997, and the Large Helical Device (LHD) near Nagoya, Japan, is expected to be ready for commissioning in 1998 (**Fig. 3**).

Two technological developments are responsible for this increased interest in stellarators. First, the advent of very powerful supercomputers has made it possible to design sophisticated magnetic traps with the right physical properties for the confinement of plasmas. It has even become possible to devise methods of confinement optimization wherein the design process begins with the specification of the desired physical properties of the

plasma, and then continues with the design of the needed modular coils to produce such properties. The superconducting modular coils of the new Wendelstein 7-X have been designed in this way, and the predictions for its energy and particle transport are similar to those of axisymmetric devices such as tokamaks.

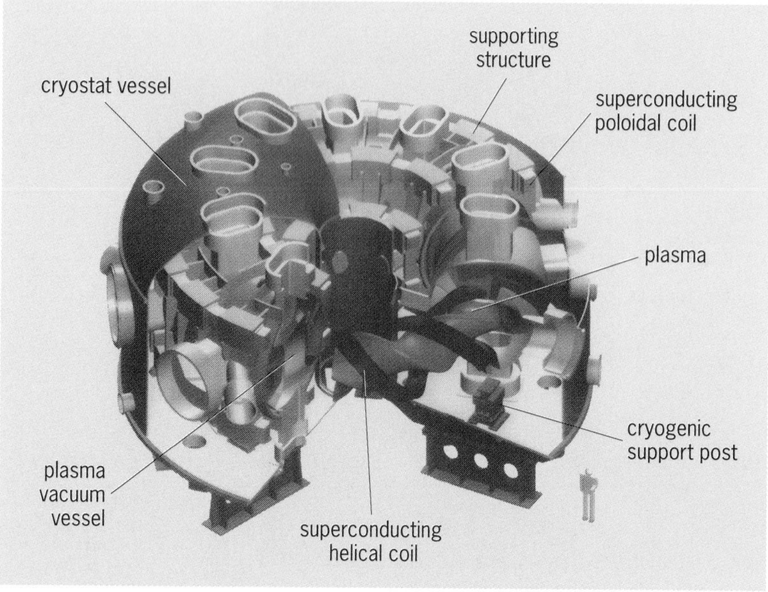

Advances in technology have enabled the attainment of designs requiring extremely tight tolerances and sophisticated construction techniques. For example, such advances have permitted the design and construction of the TJ-II, 5 m (16 ft) in diameter, with a helical copper coil capable of carrying an electric current with a density of 10^8 A/m^2 and with deviations of less than 1 mm (0.04 in.) from an ideal helix. Modular coils with sophisticated shapes have been working reliably since 1988 at Wendelstein 7-AS, and are now under design in superconducting form for Wendelstein 7-X. At the site of the Large Helical Device, 36 km (22 mi) of niobium-titanium (NbTi) superconducting cable have been wound in a helical coil of 3.9-m (12.8-ft) major radius and 0.975-m (3.2-ft) minor radius with tolerances of less than 2 mm (0.08 in.).

In spite of such progress, much work must be done before stellarators are at the developmental level of tokamaks. Fortunately, tokamaks and stellarators are similar in many ways, so it is likely that much of the technological experience gained in tokamak development, for example, in neutronics, tritium handling, and ignition physics, could be easily implemented in an ignition stellarator machine. Therefore, short cuts can be found in stellarator development, while the understanding of physics gained in present and future stellarators should be useful in tokamak development. The experimental work at stellarators, particularly the large, superconducting projects, will determine whether the advantages of a current-free, intrinsically steady-state, three-dimensional magnetic configuration are worth pursuing to achieve the long-term goal of an economically competitive and environmentally friendly fusion power plant.

For background information *see* MAGNETOHYDRODYNAMICS; NUCLEAR FUSION; PLASMA PHYSICS in the McGraw-Hill Encyclopedia of Science & Technology.

Carlos Alejaldre

Bibliography. C. Alejaldre and B. Carreras (eds.), *Transport and Confinement in Toroidal Devices*, 1992; F. Bauer, O. Betancourt, and P. Garabedian, *Magnetohydrodynamic Equilibrium and Stability*

Fig. 3. Drawing of the superconducting Large Helical Device (LHD).

of Stellarators, 1984; O. Motojima et al., Physics and engineering design studies on Large Helical Device, *Fusion Eng. Design*, 20:3–14, 1993; Special issue on stellarators, *Fusion Technol.*, vol. 17, no. 1, January 1990.

Synchrotron radiation

The Advanced Photon Source (APS) at Argonne National Laboratory near Chicago, Illinois, is the premier source of hard x-ray radiation in the United States. Along with its sister facilities, the ESRF (European Synchrotron Radiation Facility) in France and the Spring-8 (Super Photon Ring 8-GeV) in Japan, it is a third-generation photon source providing hard x-ray radiation (roughly at energies from 3 to 300 keV) of unprecedented brilliance and energy range. Researchers apply these x-ray beams to probe the structure and composition of matter in a wide variety of disciplines: materials science; biological science; environmental science; chemistry; geoscience; agricultural science; and atomic, molecular, and optical physics. *See* DIAMOND.

Central to the rapid growth of research in these fields is the synchrotron's high brilliance. This property enables the production of ultrahigh-resolution x-ray beams (whose energy variation is approximately 10^{-7} of the energy itself) that retain usable intensity (approximately 10^{9} photons per second). The high brilliance also enables the development of high-performance x-ray microprobes that provide elementally specific maps of biological, material, and environmental samples on submicrometer distance scales. The additional properties of variable polarization and pulsed time structure open new avenues of research in magnetic scattering and time-resolved structural studies on the nano- and picosecond time scales. User operations at the Advanced Photon Source commenced in late 1996, and much noteworthy research has already been conducted. Some examples will be discussed.

High-resolution spectroscopy. Submillivolt-resolution x-ray beams enable detailed studies of excitations and interactions in matter using inelastic photon scattering methods. The remarkable monochromaticity of the incident beam is achieved in two stages (see **illus.**). The first stage uses a standard two-crystal nondispersive geometry with silicon crystals in the (111) orientation, and reduces the relative bandwidth of x-ray from the undulator source, initially about 2%, to about 10^{-4}. The second stage is composed of two nested silicon crystals with asymmetry angles very close to the Bragg angle in a dispersive geometry, and reduces the relative bandwidth to about 10^{-7}. The high-angular-resolution (12.5-nanoradian) rotation stages for the nested crystal geometry provide the energy tunability for the incident beam. The scattered x-rays are energy-analyzed through resonant excitation of a nucleus using Mössbauer techniques. Through this method, called resonant inelastic nuclear gamma-ray scattering, it is possible to extract model-independent values of the phonon density of states in a variety of systems. A number of elements are accessible through this method, for example, iron, tin, dysprosium, europium, and krypton.

An elegant demonstration of the technique has been conducted on bulk and nanocrystalline iron. The nanocrystalline iron shows a distorted phonon density of states relative to the bulk material. While there is good agreement between the experiment and calculations for the bulk iron sample, the experiment on the nanocrystalline iron deviates significantly from the model calculations, with an enhancement of the density of states at low energy (less than 20 meV) and over the region between 55 and 75 meV. The origin of the deviations is not unambiguously established, but possibilities include, for the low-energy region, a change in

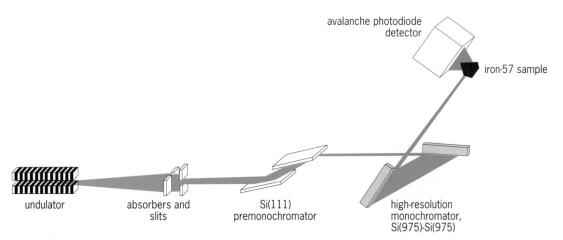

Apparatus employed for ultrahigh-resolution inelastic scattering. The bandwidth of x-rays from the undulator is reduced in two stages, and the highly monochromatic x-rays that result illuminate the iron-57 sample. Fluorescence from excited nuclei in the sample is detected.

the velocity of sound in the nanocrystalline material and, for the 55–75-meV region, a coupling of vibrational motion of iron atoms covalently bonded to oxygen atoms. This experiment confirms the enhancement of the density of states at low energy in nanocrystalline materials observed recently by neutron inelastic scattering, and provides greater detail on the high-energy tail (due to the excellent signal-to-noise ratio as compared to that of neutron scattering studies).

This method of inelastic nuclear resonant scattering will also be useful in applications other than the probe of bulk single-element materials. The element containing the resonant nucleus can be a useful probe of local vibrational structure in studies of, for example, thin films, buried interfaces, and iron-containing enzymes.

X-ray microprobe. The high-brilliance Advanced Photon Source undulator beams have been used in combination with x-ray microfocusing devices to develop an advanced x-ray microprobe that allows elementally specific maps in a variety of material, environmental, and biological systems to be obtained. The monochromatic x-rays are focused to a spot size of 0.33 micrometer with an intensity exceeding 5×10^{10} photons/(μm^2 s) within a 0.01% bandwidth. With solid-state detectors surrounding the irradiated sample, the x-rays emitted from different elements (in various chemical states) can be distinguished. This ability to produce spatial maps on a submicrometer scale with elemental- and chemical-state specificity promises to have wide-ranging impact on the understanding of fundamental processes at a cellular level.

A demonstration of the power of this x-ray microprobe has been the study of the distributions of phosphorus, sulfur, potassium, calcium, manganese, iron, nickel, copper, and zinc in a plant-fungus symbiotic system in its natural environment. Mapping the elemental distribution will provide insight into the uptake and transportation of nutrients through the plant-root–fungi system. This pioneering experiment demonstrated elemental detection sensitivity significantly better than 10 parts per billion and a minimum elemental detection limit of 0.3 femtogram, both of which are orders of magnitude better than those obtained with charged-particle microprobes. Studying the near-edge absorption spectrum with submicrometer spatial resolution (micro-XANES) allowed researchers to obtain the oxidation states of manganese (+2 or +4) at several locations in the root and fungal area. While the Mn^{2+} state is water soluble and useful to plants, the Mn^{4+} is insoluble and less important. Detection limits on the chemical-state specificity of Mn^{4+} were established by this experiment to be less than 50 parts per million, with an illuminated volume containing 30 femtograms. Future improvements are envisioned which will permit spatial resolutions of 0.1 μm and elemental sensitivity of less than 1 part per billion.

The x-ray microprobe combines the advantageous features of low radiation damage, high penetration power, chemical state analysis, and elemental analysis to provide a powerful tool with which to study many important questions in the life sciences, agriculture, microelectronics, geoscience, and various other disciplines.

Crystal structure determination. X-rays have long been used to determine the three-dimensional atomic structure of biologically important materials, a leading example being the model of deoxyribonucleic acid (DNA) deduced by J. Watson and F. Crick. Crystal structure determination proceeds through a number of steps. Crystals are grown, x-ray diffraction data are taken, phases for the x-ray scattering are determined, an electron-density map is generated, a model is proposed that conforms to the map, and that model is subsequently refined for best agreement with the observations. The advent of high-brilliance synchrotron radiation has significantly enhanced the speed and accuracy with which data may be acquired in the x-ray diffraction and phase determination steps. A similar breakthrough in crystal preparation, cryoprotection, allows crystals to be flash-frozen to about 110 K ($-260°F$) for x-ray diffraction. This means that crystals of about 10–50 μm in size, which are easily grown and well matched to undulator beam sizes, can be used to obtain complete data sets. The high-brilliance undulator radiation coupled with the technique of multiwavelength anomalous diffraction (MAD) has made it possible to solve crystal structures with unprecedented speed.

These techniques have been demonstrated in the determination of the three-dimensional crystal structure of free and nucleoside-complexed fragile histidine triad (FHIT). FHIT derives from a fragile site on human chromosome 3 that is commonly disrupted during formation of cancerous tumors. On the basis of genetic evidence, it has been postulated that the FHIT protein may act as a tumor suppressor. The structural analysis of FHIT identifies critical binding and catalytic sites. Phase information using the MAD technique was obtained on crystals of the selenomethionyl-FHIT protein and various ligand complexes. The selenium atoms served as the scattering centers for phase determination using the four-wavelength MAD technique. The four required wavelengths (pre-edge, edge, peak, and above-edge, referenced to the K-edge in selenium) were obtained with small variations of the gap width of the undulator. The structural data show that catalytic mechanisms in this protein are metal independent, contrary to earlier belief. The biomolecular structural information now available through these advanced techniques promises to significantly enhance the understanding and control of biological processes on a molecular level.

For background information *see* MÖSSBAUER EFFECT; PHONON; SYNCHROTRON RADIATION; X-RAY CRYSTALLOGRAPHY; X-RAY DIFFRACTION; X-RAY FLUORESCENCE ANALYSIS; X-RAY SPECTROMETRY in the McGraw-Hill Encyclopedia of Science & Technology.

Linda Young

Bibliography. B. Fultz et al., Phonons in nanocrystalline ^{57}Fe, *Phys. Rev. Lett.*, 79:937–940, 1997; C. D. Lima et al., MAD analysis of FHIT, a putative human tumor suppressor from the HIT protein family, *Structure*, 5:763–774, 1997; W. Yun et al., X-ray imaging and microspectroscopy of symbiotic associations of plants and fungi, preprint.

Television

Digital broadcasting of television signals offers advantages over the usual analog methods: enhanced picture and sound quality, ability to transmit higher-resolution and wide-screen images, and new opportunities for interactive television services. This article discusses the principles of digital video broadcasting and its worldwide implementation, and the digital television broadcasting system that is planned for the United States.

Digital Video Broadcasting

Since the invention of the transistor and its evolution into the semiconductor integrated circuit, there has been a steady move from analog to digital techniques in all branches of electronics. Apart from specialized applications in the defense sector, digital telephone exchanges were the first major example of this transition. The signal bandwidth required for telephony was typically 5 kHz, and this represented an achievable target for digital processing with the semiconductor technology available in the 1970s. The first impact of digital technology on consumer electronic products came with the compact disk in the 1980s, when digital processing could handle the bandwidth of 30–40 kHz required for high-fidelity sound recording and reproduction. Progress in digital technology accelerated in the 1980s, driven by the demand for personal computers, and enabled the move from analog to digital video.

This transition was a major challenge. A typical analog television signal in most terrestrial broadcast systems occupies 6–8 MHz of bandwidth, a thousand times that of a telephony signal. There are some differences between the bandwidths and formats of television standards adopted around the world, but in all the standards each television picture is composed of an array of distinguishable picture elements (known as picture cells or pixels), approximately 500×700 elements in size. For each pixel, the amplitude of the three primary colors (red, green, and blue) must be specified to an accuracy of around 1%, since this accuracy matches the resolution of the eye. Each pixel can be described by an 8-bit digital word for each color, and the resulting digital data in a single television picture comprise around 8 megabits (equivalently, 1 megabyte). Since complete television pictures (known as frames) are sent 25 or 30 times per second (depending on the standard used), the overall digital data rate required for transmission is around 200 Mbit/s.

Digital compression. Although these very high digital data rates could be transmitted around television studios on high-frequency cables or optical fibers, it was not economic to broadcast them or send them over telecommunication link networks. The way to achieve digital video broadcasting lay in reducing the amount of digital data without reducing the perceived quality of the television picture. Agreement on a technique for carrying out the data reduction (known as compression) on a single frame (equivalently, a single picture) of a television signal could result in mass production and hence reduced cost of the resulting digital technology for television sets.

Compression of single frames. Most pictures have some areas with very little detail, and when these are identified, the data sent can be reduced radically. The most common process for achieving this reduction uses the discrete cosine transform. A section of the picture, for example, an 8×8 matrix of pixels, is examined vertically and horizontally. The spatial variations in intensity of the primary colors across the matrix are analyzed in exactly the same way as Fourier analysis is commonly used to analyze waveforms in the analog domain. In areas of low detail, the whole matrix can be described by a very few discrete-cosine-transform coefficients representing the slow, low-order variation of the picture across this sector. Only in areas with a large amount of detail will more and higher-order coefficients be needed. The process is then repeated in blocks across the whole picture. The result of this work was the ability to compress pictures containing 1 megabyte of data by factors of at least 50 times to some 20 kilobytes with negligible perceived degradation of the picture. International standardization of the process was achieved in the mid-1980s by the Joint Photographic Experts Group (JPEG).

Video compression. The Motion Picture Experts Group (MPEG) continued this standardization work in the late 1980s and early 1990s for the specific application of digital video broadcasting. With continuous television pictures, there is added potential for compression because it is only the parts of the picture that move which change from frame to frame. The basis of video compression is therefore to subtract one frame from the preceding frame and transmit only the difference signal, representing the parts of the picture that have changed. A complete new frame is sent from time to time to avoid the buildup of errors. Additional compression can be achieved by detecting areas that move together (for example, a vehicle or a football) and representing the motion of the whole object by a vector, eliminating the need to describe the motion of each part of the object.

Again, the discrete cosine transform has been the most commonly used technique for video compression, but it is not obvious that this is the ultimate technique. When it fails, because of processing overload resulting from too much changing detail, the picture breaks up into an annoying block structure.

Other compression techniques, such as those involving fractals or wavelets, may offer improved performance in the future. The digital signal for the television sound channels, multiplexed with the video signal, was also the subject of international standardization—the MPEG Audio (or MUSICAM) system being adopted in Europe and the Dolby AC-3 system in the United States.

Progress. In 1992, the progress in digital compression was such that, from the original 200-Mbit/s studio data rate of digital television pictures, images of excellent quality could be delivered at 34 Mbit/s. By 1993, broadcasters were satisfied with the picture and sound quality at a data rate of 8 Mbit/s. With more recent progress in video compression, around 4 Mbit/s is deemed adequate for most picture material, with data rates as low as 1 or 2 Mbit/s being acceptable for news broadcasts and information services. This is a remarkable achievement, since at 2 Mbit/s only 1% of the original information is left in the television signal being delivered to the viewer.

Advantages of digital transmission. The early achievement of compression to a data rate of 34 Mbit/s was significant because it meant that a digital television signal could be transmitted in a satellite television transponder as a replacement for an analog signal. Digital transmission brings not only increased picture and sound quality, as a result of its high degree of immunity to electrical noise or interference, but also the ability to transmit higher-resolution and wide-screen pictures. After manufacture, digital receivers do not need adjustment throughout their lifetime and can provide a wide range of consumer-controlled functions through software control of the digital signal, just as in a computer. Also, since the digital signal can be a flexible mix of video, audio, and data, new types of service different from traditional entertainment television became possible.

Subsequent improvements in video compression meant that more than one television channel could be transmitted in a satellite transponder, and this capability radically changed the economics of satellite broadcasting. It made possible the satellite delivery of very large numbers of television channels to the home and allowed the growth of specialty or niche programming channels.

Implementation. In Europe, digital video compression was first used in 1993 to feed the head stations of cable networks. In the United States, which had not experienced analog direct-to-home satellite television to the same extent as in Europe in the early 1990s, a major new system provided over 100 channels of digital satellite picture and sound programming. By 1997, this system had reached over 3 million homes and was providing strong competition to established analog cable television operators. Apart from this initiative, the focus of digital video broadcasting in the United States has been on the terrestrial delivery of high-definition television to the public, as discussed below. In countries such as Thailand and South Africa, which previously had only terrestrial broadcast systems with a few analog channels, the technology and a liberalization of the regulatory regime has allowed a rapid expansion to a satellite-delivered, multichannel digital broadcasting environment.

Standards. International standards were needed not only for digital picture compression but also for transmission in order to avoid the complexity of different analog standards that had existed. A major initiative, started in Europe in 1993 but open to all countries, was the Digital Video Broadcasting (DVB) Project. This initiative brought together all those in the process of broadcasting, from program origination to consumer equipment manufacture. It adopted the MPEG standards for video-compression coding of normal (4 : 3 aspect ratio) or wide-screen (16 : 9 aspect ratio) pictures and went on to specify a whole family of standards for transmission over cable, satellite, terrestrial, and other media, as well as deciding how program guides and payment systems were to be set up.

Standards were decided according to the particular characteristics of the transmission medium. For satellite transmission, a quaternary phase shift keying (QPSK) standard was adopted; for cable transmission, quaternary amplitude modulation (64-QAM) was adopted. For broadband radio distribution, the same standards were specified. For terrestrial transmission, because of the already congested use of the frequency spectrum in Europe and in many countries elsewhere, the spread-spectrum technique of orthogonal frequency division multiplex (OFDM) was adopted. This technique divides the digitally compressed television signal across a large number of carriers (typically 2000 or more) spread across the 8-MHz frequency channel. It has great immunity to interference or ghosting and requires only low-power transmitters, making it possible to introduce digital television services in the existing frequency band used by analog services.

These standards are now being adopted in many countries preparing for the introduction of digital video broadcasting. Broadcasts that conform to these standards are already made by satellite in France, Germany, Italy, Spain, Thailand, Hong Kong, Brazil, and South Africa. Cable systems in such countries are steadily being converted, and the first digital terrestrial transmissions were scheduled to start in the United Kingdom in 1998.

Interactive services. The standards also specify the way in which a narrow-band digital return channel to the broadcaster (typically using the domestic telephone line with a computer modem operating at some tens of kilobits per second) may be implemented. This specification opens up new opportunities for interactive television services. New commercial ventures are being formed between broadcasters and suppliers of goods and services to allow the home television receiver to be used in banking, shopping, travel services, and the downloading of computer games, electronic journals, or large amounts of data from the Internet.   John R. Forrest

Digital Television Broadcasting in the United States

Planning a digital television broadcast system for the United States has entailed the adoption of a digital television standard and the study of issues related to implementing digital broadcast services.

Development. In the United States, the desire to increase the resolution of television by developing high-definition systems began to gain momentum in the late 1980s. In 1987, broadcasters petitioned the Federal Communications Commission (FCC) to consider the public-policy and technical issues related to a significant upgrade in the resolution of the NTSC (National Television Systems Committee) system used in the United States. The FCC formed the industry-staffed Advisory Committee on Advanced Television Service (ACATS) to consider the issues and provide advice.

A formal competitive testing process began in 1992 with two analog and four digital systems. The digital systems proved far superior, although the four digital contenders were found to have different areas of best performance. In May 1993, a consortium of the digital proponents formed the Grand Alliance to create a single system that would combine the best features of their contending designs.

Testing of the system resulting from the merged designs was completed by 1994. In November 1995, the ACATS recommended that the FCC adopt the digital television standard that had been documented by the Advanced Television Systems Committee (ATSC). This organization had been formed to establish voluntary standards for advanced television systems. The FCC adopted a technical standard for digital television in December 1996 and set service rules and channel assignments in April 1997.

Channels and stations. Each new digital television service must operate in a 6-MHz-wide channel. The temporary assignments for these channels will be located in the same very high frequency (VHF) and ultrahigh-frequency (UHF) bands that have been allocated for NTSC television. Both the new and current television services will operate for a period of years.

The FCC set up a staggered construction period for stations. Network-affiliated stations in the top 10 markets shall be constructed by May 1, 1999, and those in the top 30 markets by November 1, 1999. Remaining commercial stations shall be constructed by May 1, 2002, and noncommercial stations by May 1, 2003.

Digital broadcasting services. These include high-definition television, standard-definition television, and multiple ancillary data services.

High-definition television (HDTV). The new picture format offered by high-definition television allows for both high-resolution and a wide-screen presentation. High-definition television has almost six times the total picture resolution of NTSC television, ten times the color detail of NTSC, a wide picture (16 : 9 aspect ratio in contrast to the current 4 : 3), and multichannel digital compact-disk-quality surround sound. Sports programming is a prime choice for new production in high definition. Movies and television shows shot on 35-mm film are the easiest to convert to high-definition television because they have high resolution and aspect ratios consistent with the high-definition television formats. These formats are encoded in such a manner as to use up the peak capacity of the 19.39-Mbit/s channel, which would preclude transmission of any other television program at the same time.

Standard-definition television (SDTV). The ATSC DTV (Digital Television) Standard also supports the transmission of multiple lower-resolution digital television programs in the same digital stream or multiplex. The number of programs that can be transmitted at once is a function of the resolution and amount of action in the program. ''Talking heads'' can be encoded very efficiently, while motion and fine detail require more bits to avoid objectionable defects in the picture. Generally, it appears that between three and six standard-definition television programs might be transmitted at the same time depending on the program content.

Data services. Testing has shown that there are periods where the full data rate is not needed for the high-definition television program, and may be filled in by ancillary data services. (This available space is sometimes called opportunistic data capacity.) Such periods also can be expected when multiple standard-definition television programs are being broadcast. This feature of the system could be used to provide a wide variety of data to multiple premises, such as additional information about a product being advertised, a continuous stream of information such as the output of a stock-market ticker, or weather information. Retail sales support data service is another possibility; for example, pharmacies in a market may want to broadcast price changes or inventory data to all franchisees. Property managers may want to broadcast database updates on housing availability. There are potential applications in teaching, security, document imaging, and the updating of data at kiosks and automatic teller machines. A variety of interactive, medical, and publishing information could be provided by broadcasters. These data services might also be a path for more datalike information transfer to and from personal computers, such as Internet downloads or even program code updates.

Technical standards. Standards had to be established for video, audio, multiplex and transport systems, and radio-frequency transmission.

Video standards. The FCC adopted all parts of the ATSC DTV Standard except the constraints on the video formats. Generically, video formats include the specification of constraints on all scanning parameters, including the number of pixels (across) and lines (up and down) in a frame, frame (or field) rates, progressive and interlace scanning, and the picture aspect ratio. Thus, there are no federal regulatory requirements for limiting transmissions to include any particular set of picture elements. Constraints on allowed video formats are present in the ATSC DTV Standard, a voluntary industry standard

Video formats in the ATSC DTV Standard

Vertical lines	Horizontal pixels	Aspect ratio	Picture rate, Hz; scanning type*			
1080	1920	16:9	60; I	—	30; P	24; P
720	1280	16:9	—	60; P	30; P	24; P
480	704	16:9, 4:3	60; I	60; P	30; P	24; P
480	640	4:3	60; I	60; P	30; P	24; P

*I, interlaced scanning; P, progressive scanning. Picture rates can be the stated integer value or 1000/1001 times the stated integer value (for example, 59.95 Hz instead of 60 Hz).

that is embraced by both the broadcast and the consumer electronics industries. The FCC-mandated portion of the ATSC DTV Standard includes the modulation, error-correction, data-packet-structure, data-control, video-compression, and audio-compression elements in their entirety. The video-compression and data-transport structure in the ATSC DTV Standard is based on the international MPEG-2 standard discussed above. Multiple video formats are permitted in the ATSC DTV Standard to allow for selection of the optimal format for a given type of subject material (see **table**).

Audio standards. The standard for audio compression defined in the ATSC DTV Standard describes how to encode from 1 to 5.1 channels of audio inputs, supporting surround sound. The five channels are left, left surround, right, right surround, and center. The "one-tenth" channel is for low-frequency effects, not requiring as much bandwidth as one of the full channels. Additional services can provide alternative languages, narrative descriptions, enhancement for the hearing impaired, separate dialogue, commentary, and emergency and voiceover announcements.

Multiplex and transport systems. The video, audio, and ancillary data are put into fixed-size (188-byte) packets, per the MPEG-2 transport specification. This packetized data-transport system allows the transmission of virtually any combination of video, audio, and data packets with a total transport-stream data rate of 19.39 Mbit/s.

Radio-frequency transmission. The DTV Standard uses an eight-level, vestigial-sideband (8-VSB) digital modulation method. The incoming data stream is processed to add error detection and correction capability. The resulting data frames are transmitted as 8-level signals, or symbols, with three bits of data per symbol. The symbols are used to suppressed-carrier-modulate a single carrier frequency. Before transmission, the lower sideband is removed and a pilot carrier is inserted.

Station transition issues. Since the costs are large and the new technology must be learned, more stations will plan the conversion to digital broadcasting in phases. When each phase is complete, a new level of capability will be in place. Generally, digital equipment will first supplement NTSC equipment and then totally replace it. Particularly beyond the first phase, different stations will introduce new capabili-

ties in different sequences, with more or less equipment purchased and installed sooner or later, based on the needs of the local market and the implementation decisions for these later phases. For example, some stations may choose to provide only one standard-definition television format for local origination, and only pass-through syndicated or network programming, which may use other formats. Some stations may wish to use the digital television signal to provide multiple standard-definition television programs simultaneously, and would need to purchase equipment that would support that capability. Some stations might establish extensive supplementary data-transmission capability. These and other variations can significantly affect costs and construction periods.

Spectrum issues. The FCC has allocated 402 MHz of spectrum for television broadcasting, covering 67 channels (12 VHF and 55 UHF). This spectrum is shared among approximately 1600 full-service stations and many more translators and low-power secondary services nationwide. At present, there are no further spectrum allotments that would comply with the FCC's rules for consumer protection from interference.

To achieve the transition to digital transmission, broadcasters will double the number of stations on the air. Only with careful planning can this transition take place in the scarce amount of spectrum available. Broadcasters are unique among video service providers in that they do not have control over the television receiving conditions that consumers experience. Thus, it is doubly important that interference in the television band be minimized. The rights of consumers to receive interference-free services on both the more than 200 million television sets currently in use and the new digital television sets will be protected by carefully establishing the technical parameters for broadcast transmissions.

When enough consumers have migrated to digital television service (by buying either a digital television set or a digital-to-analog converter for an existing analog television set), and reliance on NTSC receivers drops acceptably low, NTSC service will be discontinued. At that point (targeted to be in 2006 by the FCC) it is expected that some stations will move their digital television operation to their old NTSC channel, some will keep their digital television on the same channel, and some digital television channels will be moved to channels near to other digital television channels. The characteristics of the digital television signal enable much closer packing of digital television services than NTSC services. This will yield some amount of contiguous spectrum nationwide for reallocation. The final all-digital television channel band has been set by the FCC to include channels 2 through 51.

For background information *see* ANALOG-TO-DIGITAL CONVERTER; DATA COMPRESSION; FOURIER SERIES AND TRANSFORMS; FRACTALS; INTEGRAL TRANSFORM; SINGLE SIDEBAND; TELEVISION; TELEVISION STANDARDS; WAVELETS in the McGraw-Hill Encyclopedia of Science & Technology.   Lynn D. Claudy

Bibliography. Advanced Television Systems Committee, *ATSC Digital Television Standard*, Document A/53, 1995; Advanced Television Systems Committee, *Guide to the Use of the ATSC Digital Television Standard*, Document A/54, 1995; Federal Communications Commission, *4th Report and Order: DTV Standards Adopted*, MM Docket No. 87-268, FCC 96-493, 1996, *5th Report*, MM Docket No. 87-268, FCC 97-116, 1997, *6th Report*, MM Docket No. 87-268, FCC 97-115, 1997; J. R. Forrest (ed.), Special issue on video broadcasting, *IEE Electr. Commun. J.*, 9(1):1–56, February 1997; J. Slater, *Modern Television Systems to HDTV and Beyond*, 1991.

Thymosin

Thymosin α_1 is a member of the thymosin family of biologically active peptides that help to regulate immune responses. These peptides are also called biological response modifiers. Thymosin α_1 is the most potent and extensively studied peptide isolated from the thymus to date. Its enhancing properties have provided novel therapeutic applications in the treatment of a number of infectious diseases, cancers, and immunodeficiency diseases.

The highest concentrations of thymosin α_1 are produced in thymus tissue. The peptide is produced in smaller amounts in other tissues, including the spleen and lymph nodes, and is also found in nonlymphoid tissues, such as the lungs, kidneys, and brain.

Chemistry. Thymosin α_1 was purified to homogeneity from a mixture of peptides. It is an amino-terminal acylated peptide of 28 amino acids with a molecular weight of 3108 daltons. It is postulated that thymosin α_1 is a proteolytic cleavage product of a larger parent molecule, prothymosin α. Prothymosin α is a 112-amino-acid protein which contains the thymosin α_1 sequence at its amino terminal. It was purified and sequenced, allowing for rapid chemical synthesis of the thymosin α_1 molecule.

Biological activities. Thymosin α_1 is classified as a biological response modifier on the basis of its effects on cytokine secretion, lymphocyte phenotypic markers, and lymphocyte functional activity, both in vitro and in vivo:

In vitro effects of thymosin α_1

Enhances production of interleukin-2, interferon α, and interferon γ in activated lymphocytes.

Enhances expression of high-affinity interleukin-2 receptors.

Modulates activity of terminal deoxynucleotidyl transferase bone marrow precursors and splenic lymphocytes.

Induces expression of receptors Thy-1 and Lyt-1, 2, 3 on bone marrow precursor cells.

Enhances natural killer recruitment and lytic activity.

Enhances mixed lymphocyte reactions by induction of T-helper-cell activity.

Antagonizes steroid-induced apoptosis of developing thymocytes.

Stimulates angiogenesis and endothelial cell migration.

Is chemotactic for endothelial cells and monocytes.

In vivo effects of thymosin α_1

Increases cytokine production, natural killer cell activity, and antitumor activity in immunosuppressed animals.

Enhances resistance to many viral, mycobacterial, and fungal pathogens in immunosuppressed animals.

Stimulates viral clearance in a woodchuck animal model of hepatitis.

Acts as an adjuvant to restore immune responses in aged and immunosuppressed animals.

Stimulates wound healing.

There is a report of an interesting antiviral action of thymosin α_1 in woodchucks infected with a hepatitis virus. This animal virus is similar to the human form of hepatitis B, and the antiviral effects of thymosin α_1 seen in infected woodchucks provided a rationale for the testing of thymosin α_1 as a treatment for hepatitis in humans. Thymosin α_1 also augments immune responses in aged and immunosuppressed animals, and it can act as an adjuvant for boosting vaccine responses to influenza vaccine and to the hepatitis B vaccine in humans.

Mechanism of action. Thymosin α_1 acts primarily by increasing the efficiency of the T-cell maturation process and by increasing the ability of T cells to produce cytokines such as interferon α, interferon γ, interleukin-2, and interleukin-3 following antigen or mitogen activation (see **illus.**). Thymosin α_1 also upregulates and increases high-affinity interleukin-2 cytokine receptors. The ability of thymosin α_1 to act on both lymphoid stem cells and more mature T cells to induce growth factors, such as cytokines and cytokine receptors, may be the reason why thymosin α_1 exhibits such a wide range of bioactivities, and may explain its synergism with cytokines such as interferon α and interleukin-2 in animal tumor model systems.

Glucocorticoid hormones and stress. Before knowing the important role of the thymus in immunity, it

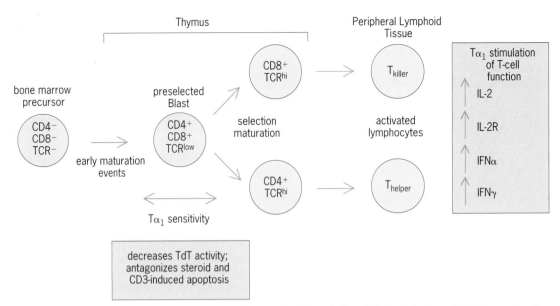

Mechanism of action of thymosin α_1. Thymosin α_1 influences the differentiation of pluripotent stem cells to thymocytes (T cells) and the maturation of T cells within the thymus. Thymosin α_1 specifically protects preselected CD4, CD8, double-positive T cells from steroid and antibody-induced apoptosis. Thymosin α_1 also stimulates T-cell function in the blood and peripheral lymphoid tissues.

was found that the thymus was sensitive to steroid hormones and was a good barometer of stress. For example, if a mouse receives a pharmacologic dose of a glucocorticoid hormone (5 mg), within 24 h the size of the thymus shrinks by 90% or more. The immunosuppressive effects of acute physiological stress is associated with stimulation of the hypothalamus-pituitary-adrenal axis and enhanced production and release of glucocorticoid hormones. The massive death of thymocytes that occurs is a programmed cell death (apoptosis), and it can be induced either by glucocorticoids or by specific antibodies to surface markers of thymocytes such as the CD3 antigen.

It has been found that thymosin α_1 antagonizes the steroid-induced apoptosis of thymocytes. This suggests that thymosin α_1 may function as a homeostatic regulator of glucocorticoid action within the thymus. Thymosin α_1 has been found to interfere with the steroid-induced death. Further, by using highly specialized and sensitive tests (such as cytometry and analysis of surface markers on T cells), it has been established that the thymosin α_1–sensitive cell is a CD4, CD8, double-positive thymocyte.

Quantitatively, over 90% of the stem cells that enter the thymus, if not selected, die there. There is an important although not clearly understood maturation process that occurs in the thymus. The process is regulated not only by factors produced within the thymus but also by other endocrine organs, such as the adrenals. The fact that thymosin α_1 can moderate one of the strongest external signals (glucocorticoids) of thymocyte apoptosis implies a homeostatic role for thymosin α_1 in helping to regulate the pituitary-adrenal-thymus axis and the response to stress. The role of thymosin α_1 in decreasing the ability of glucocorticoids to induce the apoptosis of thymo-

cytes is of physiological interest with regard to the known circadian rhythm of thymosin α_1 in the blood of mice which appears to be inversely correlated to glucocorticoid levels. In mice, it has also been observed that a mixture of peptides or thymosins produces a reversal of some of the immunosuppressive effects of glucocorticoids.

Therapeutic applications. Initially, efficacy of thymosin α_1 in cancer was studied in combination with conventional therapy (radiotherapy and chemotherapy). Later investigations using combinations of thymosin α_1 and interferon α in patients with progressive melanoma and lung cancer suggested that a better approach may be to use thymosin α_1 in combination with other biological response modifiers. This proved to be more effective in fighting tumors than the biological response modifiers alone. These studies indicated that the complex role of the immune system in cancer may require the use of biological response modifiers in combination and with conventional therapies.

Lung cancer. Thymosin α_1 has been used to treat non-small-cell lung cancer. This cancer accounts for the majority of lung cancer cases in the United States, for which treatments with radiation therapy and chemotherapy have generally been disappointing. When thymosin α_1 was used to treat people with inoperable lung cancer, an increase of T-cell levels and lymphocytes expressing the pre-T-cell and helper-T-cell surface markers resulted. The lymphocytes and T cells were originally depleted by other therapies. Further combinations to combat this type of cancer utilized thymosin α_1 in combination with chemotherapeutic agents, including cisplatin and etoposide, interferon α, and ifosfamide. The success of combination treatments indicates that if thymosin α_1 is to be effectively used in the treatment of cancer it may require adjuvant therapy with biological response modifiers and conventional therapies.

Malignant melanoma. Malignant melanoma is resistant to most forms of therapy. Thymosin α_1 in combination with chemotherapy and cytokine therapy for treatment of malignant melanoma revealed that these therapy regimens are more successful than more traditional treatments.

Primary immunodeficiency diseases. A number of severe immune deficiency diseases, such as DiGeorge syndrome, are now recognized to be genetic diseases characterized in part by an absence of the thymus gland, resulting in severe T-cell deficiencies, increases in opportunistic infections, and a general failure to thrive. Application of a partially purified thymic preparation suggested that the failure of synthesis and secretion of thymic peptides, such as thymosin α_1, by the thymus may play a vital role in immune abnormalities. The major immunomodulatory peptide in this mixture is thymosin α_1. The serum levels of this peptide are often low in children with DiGeorge syndrome. These observations suggested that thymosin α_1 may be useful in treatment of the major immune defects in this disease. Treatment with thymosin α_1 has shown improved T-cell and antibody responses, and it has resulted in a general improvement in the overall clinical condition of those afflicted.

Aging and immune senescence. Viral influenza and other infectious diseases remain a serious and growing source of morbidity and mortality. Among the elderly, these are a significant cause of illness and death. Predisposing factors to outbreaks of influenza are age-diminished antibody responsiveness to infection and vaccination. Thus, immune enhancement has been considered a method to increase antibody responses to vaccine administration in the elderly. A reason to consider thymosin α_1 for such a role is the fact that immune deficiency associated with aging is correlated with the gradual involution of the thymus gland. It has been shown that thymosin α_1 can reverse some of the immunosuppressive effects of aging and can increase a number of T-cell-dependent antibody responses. Following treatment with thymosin α_1, the percentage of elderly patients who developed influenza decreased in comparison with those not receiving this therapy.

Thymosins such as α_1 help keep the immune system active and may be a way of extending human life-span. Additional therapeutic applications of thymosins include AIDS, cancer, hepatitis B and C, and arthritis. The function of thymosins in the protection against infections in cases of immunodeficiency is of vital importance. As the thymus involutes with aging, secretion of thymosins decreases, as does protection against illness.

For background information *see* CELLULAR IMMUNOLOGY; HORMONE; IMMUNITY; THYMOSIN; THYMUS GLAND in the McGraw-Hill Encyclopedia of Science & Technology.   Allan L. Goldstein

Bibliography. C. A. Baumann, M. Badamchian, and A. L. Goldstein, Thymosin α_1 antagonizes dexamethasone and CD3 induced apoptosis of CD4$^+$ CD8$^+$ thymocytes through the activation of cAMP and protein kinase C dependent second messenger pathways, *Mech. Aging Dev.*, 94:85–101, 1997; A. L. Goldstein et al., Thymosin α_1: Current status of human trials and potential applications in clinical therapy, in H. R. Maurer et al. (eds.), *Thymic Peptides in Preclinical and Clinical Medicine*, W. Zuckschwerdt Verlag, Munich, 1997; J. A. Hooper et al., The purification and properties of bovine thymosin, *Ann. N.Y. Acad. Sci.*, 249:125–144, 1975; R. S. Schulof et al., A randomized trial to evaluate the immunorestorative properties of synthetic thymosin α_1 in patients with lung cancer, *J. Biol. Response Modifiers*, 4:147–158, 1985; K. E. Sherman et al., Combination therapy with thymosin and interferon for the treatment of chronic hepatitis C infection: a randomized, placebo-controlled double-blind trial, *Hepatology*, 27:1128–1135, 1998; D. W. Wara et al., Thymosin activity in patients with cellular immunodeficiency, *New Eng. J. Med.*, 292:70–74, 1975.

Transcranial magnetic stimulation

Transcranial magnetic stimulation (TMS) involves the use of a small electromagnet that is placed on the scalp and generates a magnetic field to stimulate the underlying superficial cortex. When the magnetic pulses are given in rapid succession (faster than 1 Hz), the technique is referred to as repetitive transcranial magnetic stimulation (rTMS); it can induce long-lasting effects (of neuronal activation or inactivation) in neural networks.

In 1831 M. Faraday discovered time-varying magnetic fields. These magnetic fields can generate magnetic changes that can be used as stimuli to influence living tissue. Magnetic stimulation was applied to the nervous system as early as 1896 by the physicist and physician J. A. d'Arsonval. Many attempts at examining the effects of magnetic stimulation on the nervous system followed. Work in 1975 led investigators to wonder if magnetic stimulation might have clinical utility. The outcome was the currently available magnetic stimulators suitable for both clinical and investigative applications in humans.

Research tool. A magnetic stimulator consists of a bank of capacitors and a stimulation coil (inductor). When a bank of capacitors is charged to about 4 kV and then discharged, it induces a current of up to 5000 A. This current passes through a copper coil (the stimulator pedal), creating a brief but intense magnetic field. The magnetic field, which is of a rapidly changing intensity, creates a linearly oriented current that is strongest below the coil's center. If the induced current is of sufficient strength, it will cause depolarization in the underlying tissue. Depolarization is likely to disrupt the ongoing physiological activity of the depolarized neurons, causing a short-lived, reversible lesion of this area. This capacity allows researchers to examine the functions of these brain regions in intact awake animals, including human subjects.

The two main types of stimulation coil are round, and butterfly or figure-8 shaped. Large round coils produce the strongest magnetic fields but result in nonfocal stimulation of a large volume of tissue. The figure-8-shaped coil consists of two small loops that intersect in the middle. The magnetic field is strongest under the intersection and produces a fairly focal stimulus. The figure-8 induced stimulus allows the technique to be more useful in examining the functions of relatively circumscribed brain regions.

Transcranial magnetic stimulation has been available since the early 1980s for investigative purposes in humans. It can be used to induce temporary functional lesions in specific areas of the brain. Researchers have used repetitive transcranial magnetic stimulation to investigate such phenomena as language, vision, and memory. More recently, repetitive transcranial magnetic stimulation has been used to study mood regulation in healthy subjects. For example, repetitive transcranial magnetic stimulation was administered over the right or left prefrontal region of the cerebral cortex of healthy adult volunteers. Left-sided stimulation resulted in increases in self-rated sadness, whereas right-sided stimulation caused increases in self-rated happiness.

Transcranial magnetic stimulation has potential as a method for studying both the anatomic and functional connectivity of the human cerebral cortex. Combining transcranial magnetic stimulation and positron emission tomography (PET) scanning permits direct stimulation of a selected cortical area while simultaneously measuring changes in brain activity, indexed by the cerebral blood flow. *See* POSITRON EMISSION TOMOGRAPHY.

Diagnostic tool. The application of a small, powerful magnet over the scalp to deliver a magnetic pulse to the cortical motor region induces involuntary finger and hand movement on the side contralateral to stimulation. With this technique, subclinical lesions of the motor pathways can be identified in patients suspected of having multiple sclerosis. Similarly, transcranial magnetic stimulation can be used to assure the intactness of the motor pathways connecting the brain to the extremities during spinal surgery. The fact that both the stimulation (at the head) and the recording of induced potentials (at one of the extremities) are away from the area of the surgery (usually the back) makes this technique ideal. Recent reports show that some anesthetic agents do not significantly affect the transcranial magnetic stimulation–induced potentials, thus allowing its use for this monitoring.

Epileptic patients whose seizures are unresponsive to treatment with medications may benefit from the surgical removal of pathological brain tissue that could be the origin of the epileptic attacks. Based on the assumption that the abnormal tissue needs less stimulation to produce abnormal epileptic activity than the surrounding healthy tissue, transcranial magnetic stimulation can be used to identify pathological brain tissue. In removing parts of the temporal lobe to eliminate an epileptic focus, the side (left or right) that is dominant for speech needs to be determined to guard against eradicating the speech areas. Transcranial magnetic stimulation can be used on each temporal lobe. Stimulating the dominant side results in speech arrest.

Dystonia is characterized by sustained involuntary muscle contractions leading to abnormal postures or movements generally occurring during voluntary activity. Electrophysiological observations suggest hyperexcitability in some brainstem and spinal-cord pathways. Research utilizing low-intensity transcranial magnetic stimulation suggests that the relationship between the induced motor potentials during rest and during voluntary contraction differs in patients with dystonia as compared with normal controls. The amplitude increase induced by voluntary contraction seems to be greater in the dystonic patients. Similar findings were reported in patients with Tourette syndrome.

Therapeutic tool. Transcranial magnetic stimulation has been used to enhance motor responses in Parkinson's disease patients. The beneficial effects on the motor activity of patients with Parkinson's disease are short lived, observed to last less than 2 weeks. Transcranial magnetic stimulation of the motor cortex is effective in decreasing tremors in these patients. This effect could be due to transcranial magnetic stimulation's blocking the action of a central tremor generator on the motor cortex, or to its influence on transcortical long-loop reflexes (which are also thought to mediate the tremors). Evidence for a transcortical or intracortical effect of transcranial magnetic stimulation comes from comparing its effects with those of electrical stimulation. Electrical stimulation of the motor cortex directly activates descending corticospinal pathways, whereas transcranial magnetic stimulation influences these pathways primarily transsynaptically, resulting in greater intracortical effects. The inability of electrical stimulation to influence parkinsonian tremors suggests that intracortical mechanisms, which can be influenced by transcranial magnetic stimulation, play an important role in generating these tremors.

Much excitement was generated by the potential therapeutic effects of transcranial magnetic stimulation in a number of psychiatric disorders, including depression, obsessive compulsive disorder, mania, and most recently schizophrenia. One promising therapeutic use of transcranial magnetic stimulation is in the treatment of depression. A number of case reports suggest that repetitive transcranial magnetic stimulation of the left prefrontal region has significant antidepressant effects. Daily left prefrontal repetitive transcranial magnetic stimulation was administered to six highly medication-resistant, depressed inpatients. Depression symptoms significantly decreased for the group as a whole. In a controlled study a number of cerebral sites (left prefrontal, right prefrontal, and central) were stimulated in the same individuals. Daily left prefrontal repetitive transcranial magnetic stimulation resulted in a significant decrease in depressive symptoms in

17 severely depressed patients, whereas stimulation of other regions did not have similar effects.

Only a handful of studies have attempted to elucidate the neurobiological mechanisms by which repetitive transcranial magnetic stimulation influences mood in either healthy subjects or clinically depressed individuals. Two possible general modes of action seem plausible: a direct local excitatory or inhibitory effect on the neural tissue being stimulated, and a neurohumoral mechanism through which neuroendocrine factors involved in the pathogenesis of mood changes are affected. The observation was made that repetitive transcranial magnetic stimulation applied to the left prefrontal region of healthy individuals causes increased sadness, but a decrease in depressive symptoms in clinically depressed patients. This suggests that the effects of repetitive transcranial magnetic stimulation may depend on the condition of the individual being stimulated. It is postulated that when repetitive transcranial magnetic stimulation is delivered to the left prefrontal region, it induces a transitory lesion (deactivates) and results in a temporary increase in sadness, much like a stroke affecting the same region. When repetitive transcranial magnetic stimulation is delivered to the same cortical region of a depressed individual, it seems to exert a more stimulatory effect, most likely through a deactivating effect on the mechanism contributing to the emergence of the depressive syndrome and resulting in a hypometabolic cortex.

Recent reports suggest that the rate of stimulation is a crucial determinant of the effects. Slow stimulation (about 1 Hz) may have more of an inhibitory result, described by the term quenching. This inhibitory influence is suitable for treating conditions such as movement disorders and seizures. Rapid stimulation may have more of an excitatory outcome, making it more useful in conditions such as depression, Parkinson's disease, and poststroke rehabilitation.

On the microscopic level, evidence for a direct effect on the tissues being stimulated was provided by R. H. Belmaker and his colleagues. They showed that acute repetitive transcranial magnetic stimulation caused an increase in dopamine content in the hippocampus and striatum, as well as an increase in serotonin levels in the hippocampus, of rats. Two rodent studies failed to demonstrate any pathological brain changes, whether gross anatomical or histological, after repeated repetitive transcranial magnetic stimulation. In contrast, one study reported the appearance of spaces without neuronal elements in the rat brain, and another reported inner-ear trauma in normal-hearing rabbits subjected to repetitive transcranial magnetic stimulation. The most frequently reported serious complication of repetitive transcranial magnetic stimulation was the precipitation of generalized seizures during administration. This complication tended to occur in less than 1% of subjects undergoing repetitive transcranial magnetic stimulation. Clinical implications of these findings are unclear.

Transcranial magnetic stimulation is a research tool that is promising for both psychiatry and neurology. In fact, it is helping clinicians as well as researchers bridge the gap between these two disciplines. In order to advance the science and facilitate collaboration between transcranial magnetic stimulation research centers, the International Society for Transcranial Stimulation was formed in August 1997 at a meeting in Interlaken, Switzerland.

For background information *see* BIOMEDICAL ENGINEERING; BRAIN; CENTRAL NERVOUS SYSTEM; COMPUTERIZED TOMOGRAPHY; ELECTROTHERAPY; MAGNETIC FIELD; MEDICAL IMAGING; NERVOUS SYSTEM (VERTEBRATE); NERVOUS SYSTEM DISORDERS; PARKINSON'S DISEASE; SEIZURE DISORDERS in the McGraw-Hill Encyclopedia of Science & Technology.   Nashaat N. Boutros

Bibliography. R. H. Belmaker et al., The effects of TMS on animal models of depression, β-adrenergic receptors and brain monoamines, *CNS Spectrums*, 2(1):26–30, 1997; N. S. George et al., Daily rTMS improves mood in depression, *NeuroReport*, 6:1853–1856, 1995; A. Pascual-Leone et al., Rapid-rate transcranial magnetic stimulation of left dorsolateral prefrontal cortex in drug-resistant depression, *Lancet*, 347:233–237, 1996; A. Pascual-Leone, M. D. Catala, and A. P. Pascual, Lateralized effect of rapid-rate transcranial magnetic stimulation of the prefrontal cortex on mood, *Neurology*, 46:499–502, 1996.

Tree

While large size can be advantageous for a tree, it also gives rise to problems. This article discusses the factors that determine the maximum heights of trees, and the mechanisms by which large trees survive high winds.

Maximum Tree Heights

In the evolution of tall stature in trees, both the tree species and the environment have been significant. Several physiological mechanisms limit tree height, such as the hydraulic capacity of the tree's vascular system.

Evolution of tall stature. For photosynthetic plants, growth and survival depends on the capture of solar energy; large size can be a great advantage in the competition among neighboring plants to intercept light. Early in the evolutionary history of vascular plants, xylem cells, which are responsible for water transport, became thickened and strengthened, allowing stems to support fairly large plants. Competition for light apparently spurred this evolutionary trajectory, leading eventually to secondary (radial) growth of xylem tissue (wood). By the time of the Carboniferous Period, 360–286 million years ago, the landscape was covered by dense forests of primitive trees, dominated by woody lycophytes, which reached heights of 40 m (130 ft) or more, along with 18-m-tall (60-ft) giant horsetails and fernlike trees reaching heights of at least 30 m (100 ft).

Today these primitive trees have been replaced by other woody species from two phylogenetic groups, the gymnosperms (most of which are conifers) and the flower-bearing angiosperms. The ability to form wood evolved independently in these two groups, and the anatomy of their wood is quite different. Both groups include species that achieve great heights. The largest trees in the world are conifers: the redwoods (*Sequoia sempervirens*) of the California coast reach heights of 117 m (384 ft). Attaining over 100 m (330 feet) is an angiosperm, *Eucalyptus regnans*, known in its native Australia as mountain ash.

Effects of species and environment. Unlike animals, plants continue to grow throughout their lives, but not to an unlimited size. Growth in height is most rapid during early life, tapering off with age until it nearly ceases (**Fig. 1**). The general form of the height growth trajectory is common to all woody plants, although the specifics vary greatly among species. Through mathematical modeling, height growth curves can be described quite well as the result of an evolutionary trade-off between advantages (the ability to compete for light) and disadvantages of tall stature.

The world's tallest trees grow in temperate regions with plenty of moisture and moderate temperatures throughout the year, such as the coastal area of northern California, the Valdivian forest of Chile, and the kauri forests of Australia. All of these forests are evergreen, potentially permitting year-long growth and photosynthesis. Trees in warm, humid, tropical regions also achieve great heights, though not so great as in the temperate regions, with some reaching 60 m (197 ft) or more. Almost any adverse environmental condition can limit height growth. In extreme cases, environmental constraints lead to whole forests of pygmy trees. High wind speeds, cold temperatures, drought, flooded soils, and poor soil nutrition impose strong limitations on tree height.

Height growth is under strong genetic control, but there are no general trends among closely related groups of plants for similar height growth potential. Within the genus *Pinus*, for example, some species are small shrubs (*P. mugo*) while others, such as sugar pine (*P. lambertiana*), can reach heights of 70 m (230 ft) or more. There is no relationship between maximum height and longevity of woody plants. Although many of the world's tallest trees have relatively long life-spans, the oldest trees, bristlecone pines (*Pinus aristata*), are short statured. With life-spans approaching 6000 years, these trees rarely achieve heights over 40 m (130 ft). Very tall trees require large trunks for mechanical support, but there is no relationship that holds across species between the maximum heights of trees and the stem diameters. The girth of baobab trees (*Adansonia digitata*) in Africa can nearly equal that of the California redwoods, but the maximum height of the baobabs is much less.

Physiological limits. Several physiological mechanisms limit tree height. One limitation is mechanical support. The allometry of trees (for example, the dimensional relationships between height and trunk diameter) must support the vertical mass and must resist forces of winds, which increase rapidly with height. Many trees, especially in the tropics, have evolved efficient means of mechanical support. Long, slender trunks are supported by radiating buttresses, sometimes reaching 10 m (33 ft) or more up the trunk. All mechanical support systems require considerable investment in nonphotosynthetic tissues.

Respiration. For years, many scientists assumed that the most important limitation to large size is the

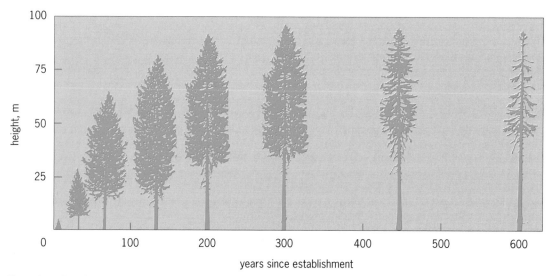

Fig. 1. Growth and development of Douglas-fir (*Pseudotsuga menziesii*) through a typical life cycle on a high-quality site. (After R. E. McArdle, W. H. Meyer, and D. Bruce, The Yield of Douglas Fir in the Pacific Northwest, USDA Tech. Bull. 201, May 1961)

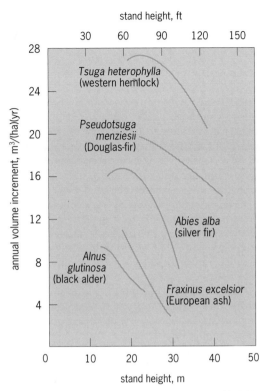

Fig. 2. Annual stem-wood production versus stand height for various example species from yield-table projections. *(After D. A. King, The adaptive significance of tree height, Amer. Natural., 135(6):809–829, 1990)*

growth in old trees lags well behind the cessation of height growth. Another explanation, the hydraulic limitation hypothesis, does account for the difference between height and diameter growth dynamics, and may apply to trees in all environments. According to this hypothesis, physiological activity of foliage is limited by the hydraulic capacity of the tree's vascular system, which supplies water and nutrients. Key to this hypothesis is the concept that leaf pores, or stomata, regulate both the loss of water (transpiration) and the uptake of carbon dioxide (for photosynthesis) as they open and close.

Xylem and hydraulics. The xylem in plants creates continuous columns of water from the roots to the leaves. Water is "pulled" through plants because of tension (negative hydrostatic pressure) in xylem water induced by the evaporative loss of water from leaves. For water to move from soil to leaves, the tension in the xylem of foliage must be greater than that of soil water. At the same time, there is a limit to the tension that the plant's vascular tissue can sustain without breaking (known as cavitation—the introduction and expansion of air bubbles that inter-

maintenance cost, or respiration, required by living biomass in very large stems and root systems. This respiration consumes the organic products of photosynthesis, leaving less for new growth in large trees. A great deal of evidence shows that wood production decreases substantially as trees grow in height (**Fig. 2**). However, direct measurements show that the respiratory losses from woody stems account for only a small portion of the reduced growth.

Old trees. One alternative explanation for reduced productivity as trees grow in height is that there is an endogenous senescence process. Indeed, the life cycles of annual plants are endogenously controlled, mediated in part by hormones. There are arguments for and against endogenous control of senescence in trees, but to date there is no conclusive evidence. Another explanation is that growth in older trees is limited by nutrient supply. In some older forests, nutrients become tied up in living plants and soil litter, reducing the availability of nutrients for new growth. However, the supply of nutrients is not limiting in all older forests, and the explanation cannot apply to individual trees growing in well-fertilized soils, such as in urban areas.

Mechanical support requirements, maintenance costs for large stems and roots, endogenous senescence, and nutrient limitations may all contribute to reduced growth in older trees, but none of these accounts for the fact that the slow-down in diameter

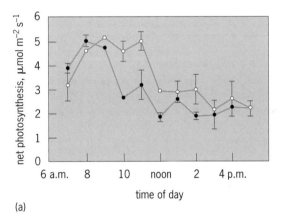

(a)

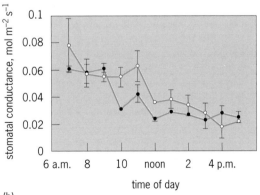

(b)

Fig. 3. Experimental measurements with *Pinus ponderosa* showing lower stomatal conductance and photosynthesis in older trees. (a) Diurnal course of photosynthesis and (b) stomatal conductance for 50-year-old (open circles) and 230-year-old (solid circles) trees growing in open conditions on the same site on a clear, mild summer day. *(After B. J. Yoder et al., Evidence of reduced photosynthetic rates in old trees, For. Sci., 40(3):513–527, 1994)*

rupt the water column), and there is good evidence that leaf stomata close as the tension of xylem water nears a critical level for cavitation. The critical tension that induces cavitation varies greatly among species. The xylem of riparian species, such as cottonwoods (*Populus*), cavitates very easily, whereas the xylem of species from dry climates, such as junipers (*Juniperus*), is much more resistant to cavitation.

As trees increase in size, the hydraulic resistance of the vascular path also increases. This is due to gravity, length of the pathway, resistances at branch junctures, and possible changes in rooting patterns. Thus, a large tree requires greater tension in its xylem to pull water from soil to foliage compared with a small tree of the same species growing in the same soil. Two results are possible. Either the growing shoots of the older trees would have less turgor pressure to drive cell expansion, or large trees might reduce the opening of their stomata to avoid xylem tensions that could cause cavitation. The stomatal closure would lead to lower photosynthesis per unit leaf area in the larger tree, resulting in lower growth. Experimental measurements with ponderosa pine showed precisely this response (**Fig. 3**). Either way, growth would be reduced in older trees, especially at tree tops and the tips of long branches.

Because hydraulic resistance varies greatly among tree species, even for trees of the same size, and because the vulnerability for xylem cavitation also varies among species, the hydraulic limitation hypothesis has the potential to explain why the maximum heights are so variable from one species to the next. In addition, environmental limitations to maximum height can be explained by their effects on photosynthesis, water use, or both. Many experimental observations support the hydraulic limitation hypothesis.
Barbara Bond

Surviving High Winds

A tree obtains energy by intercepting sunlight, which demands a large surface exposed to the sky. It competes with its neighbors for a place in the sun, each tree extending its trunk upward to minimize shading by the others. Its weight presents no serious problem; trees could grow much taller without crushing or buckling their trunks. Trouble comes from episodes of violent wind, when both leaf area and height become major liabilities. Under such conditions, trees function as giant levers, with the drag of their leaves high above the ground turning them around their bases and putting them at hazard of uprooting or breaking. Therefore, trees have evolved wind-resistant designs.

Roots as anchorage. For healthy trees in most places, uprooting appears to present a more serious problem than trunk breakage. At least four structural arrangements may keep roots firmly anchored in the soil. A given tree may use different arrangements or a varying mix of several as it grows from a sapling.

Compressive buttressing. Uprooting requires raising a large weight of roots and associated soil. Increasing the work involved in uprooting decreases the chance that a tree will blow over. For instance, a stiff, wide base puts some distance between the pivot point or axis of turning and the center of trunk and root mass (**Fig. 4***a*). Such a broad base requires a set of buttresses on the downwind (compression-loaded) side. On the upwind side the base and buttresses contribute weight that must be lifted as the tree is turned. Partly burying the broad base improves matters by using soil to increase the weight further. Beneath its base, the tree compresses the substratum, normally making the soil resist well. The arrangement requires that the trunk be stiff to minimize downwind drift of the center of gravity. Compressive buttressing may be the most important arrangement used by the large broad-leafed trees of temperate North America, and it is probably used by conifers that lack deep roots, as shown by the Sitka spruce.

Tensile buttressing. The most conspicuously buttressed trees, found in tropical rainforests, do not depend on compressive buttressing. Their buttresses may extend many feet upward and spread broadly, but they are too thin to compress without buckling. Instead, the buttresses work in the opposite way, resisting tension rather than compression, and transmitting the tensile forces on the upwind side of a trunk to the roots (Fig. 4*b*). Soil itself may have little tensile strength, but the tangle of roots beneath the surface in a rainforest can take substantial tensile loads. Stabilizing the center of gravity with a stiff trunk is less important than in compressive buttressing, a significant factor for the tall, thin trunks of the trees of a rainforest canopy.

Taprooting. An alternative to buttresses takes advantage of the good resistance of soil to being pushed on. If the trunk is continued downward as a stiff taproot, and if lateral roots near the soil surface fix the location of the tree, then pushing the trunk in one direction pushes the taproot in the other (Fig. 4*c*). The taproot must resist bending and be sufficiently broad to push against, rather than slip sideways through, soil. (Additional vertical roots often supplement the mechanical role of taproots.) Taproots may develop noncylindrical cross sections in response to wind from a prevailing direction.

Diagonal guying. Bamboo trunks (properly termed culms) use yet another arrangement, rare in true trees (Fig. 4*d*). As with tensile buttressing, tensile forces on the upwind side are transmitted through tension-resisting structures to lateral roots which, in turn, pull on a dense tangle of other roots. The diagonal guying of bamboo is relatively symmetrical above and below the lateral roots, with a taproot and a set of guying roots below as well as above. The scheme gains efficiency by using ropes rather than solid buttresses to take tension; in a tensile buttress the outermost part carries almost the entire load. But the ability of most true trees to grow in girth probably rules out guying ropes, which would have to be gradually shifted further upward and outward as the tree got taller.

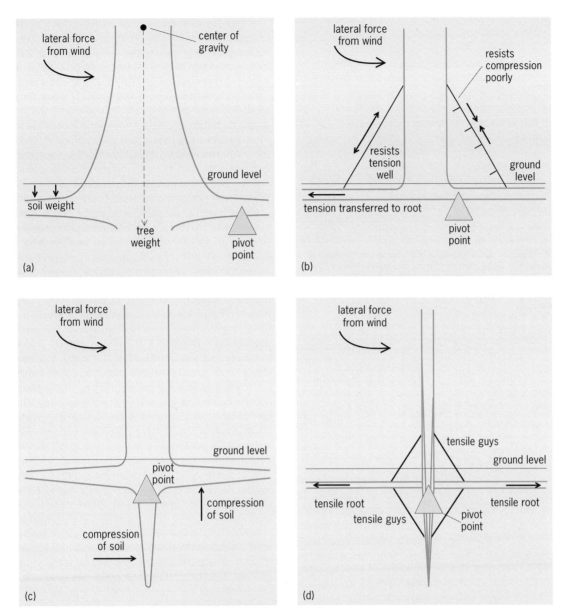

Fig. 4. Four ways to keep roots and ground together. (*a*) Compressive buttressing. (*b*) Tensile buttressing. (*c*) Taprooting. (*d*) Diagonal guying. *(After S. Vogel, Blowing in the wind: Storm-resisting features in the design of trees, J. Arbor., 22:92–98, 1996)*

Trunks and force transmission. Different arrangements for anchorage make different demands on trunks. Thus, only the compressively buttressed tree uses its weight in keeping itself upright. A hollow cylinder may resist bending almost as well as a solid one, but being lighter, it will be less useful. Furthermore, high stiffness keeps the center of gravity above the base. Maximizing weight and minimizing sway matter less for trees that use any of the other arrangements.

Wind on a tree imposes a bending load. If the tree is not perfectly symmetrical, wind imposes a twisting load as well. Bending is hazardous, since it may contribute to uprooting or direct breakage. However, twisting may actually be beneficial, since it may reduce the bending load itself by allowing branches and leaves to reorient in ways that reduce drag. The most straightforward way to increase bending resistance relative to twisting resistance is to use noncylindrical cross-sectional shapes. I-beams or cylinders with lengthwise grooves, for instance, bend with difficulty but twist easily. Most tree trunks, though, are almost circular in cross section.

Relative resistance to bending and twisting also depends on the material of a structure, and woods vary widely in their ratio of bending resistance to twisting resistance. Thus, trees manipulate the ratio by material rather than by structural alteration. It has long been known that cylinders of dry wood cut from the trunks of trees have ratios 5–15 times the values (around 1.3) for cylinders of simple materials such as metals. Such high values turn out to

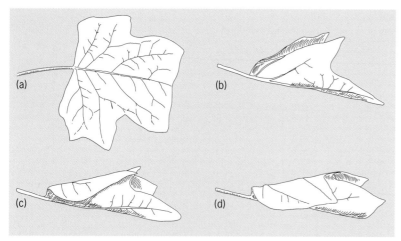

Fig. 5. Broad leaf of a tulip (yellow) poplar reconfiguring in the wind at wind speeds of (a) 0 mi/h or 0 m/s, (b) 11 mi/h or 5 m/s, (c) 22 mi/h or 10 m/s, and (d) 44 mi/h or 20 m/s. *(After S. Vogel, Life in Moving Fluids, 2d ed., Princeton University Press, 1994)*

characterize fresh, intact trunks as well. Indeed, the values for softwoods, hardwoods, and even bamboo culms are quite similar. Conversely, roots and vines have ratios of only 2–3, showing that high ratios of bending to twisting resistance are not intrinsic to wood as a material. Thus, even without noncircular cross sections, trunks twist more easily than they bend—behavior appropriate for their situation.

Leaves and drag minimization. Since a tree must expose a large area of leaf surface to sun and sky, a high drag exerted far above the substratum appears unavoidable. But in most places, high winds are intermittent and associated with the low light intensity of thick cloud cover. Perhaps leaves might reduce area and drag in high winds by taking advantage of their flexibility. Flexibility, though, is no automatic advantage, since flexible structures of great area normally suffer much more drag than do stiff ones. A flexible flag of ordinary shape encounters about 10 times the drag of a rigid weathervane of the same shape and area.

A tree handles the drag of its leaves in a more complicated way. For an ordinary, rigid object, drag increases in proportion to the square (exponent 2.0) of wind speed. The first indication that the drag forces on trees did not increase that way came from measurements on a pine in a large wind tunnel. Drag increased with an exponent of less than 1 (0.72) rather than the expected 2.0, at wind speeds up to 85 mi/h (38 m/s), when the tree started to shed pieces. As the wind increased, the tree reconfigured, with needles and then branches coalescing into clumps. Instead of being a pure liability, as in a flag, flexibility is put to use by leaves.

Broad leaves show more spectacular and at least equally effective temporary and reversible changes of form. In a high wind the leaves of a branch of holly turn sideways by bending their stems (properly termed petioles), ending up as a tightly pressed sandwich on top of their twig. Many kinds of leaves have relatively long petioles and stemward-protruding lobes on each side of the attachment of petiole to blade (**Fig. 5**). Those that have been tested in wind tunnels roll upward into cones whose open apices point upwind toward the stem and which become tighter as the wind increases. These cones are stable in even highly turbulent winds, they open and close quickly enough to respond to even brief gusts, and they achieve values of drag closer to that of a weathervane than of a flag. Drag even lower (relative to leaf area) is achieved by leaves that have leaflets extending to either side of a central shaft, at least in the species that have been tested (**Fig. 6**). The leaflets bend and curl upward, interacting to form elongate, hollow cylinders just above their common shaft.

Groups of leaves reconfigure as well, forming tight, conical clusters with lower overall drag (again relative to area) than individual leaves of the same species. Individual leaves of some trees, such as white oaks, are not especially effective in reconfiguration but do fairly well as groups. White oaks, in any case, may derive a compensatory advantage from their less extreme reconfiguration. In modest winds, they maintain their normal, skyward orientations when others, such as maples, have begun to curl and flutter. In general, some instability at low speeds seems to be associated with good facility for dealing with higher winds. The shimmering of quaking aspen leaves may just represent the low-speed instability associated with an especially good ability to reconfigure stably (in this case, as multileaf clusters) in strong winds. The closely related and similar-looking leaves of white poplar also shimmer and are particularly stable and damage resistant in high winds.

In order for leaves to reconfigure into clusters, their petioles must be able to twist. But to support protruding leaves, petioles have to resist bending. Thus, like trunks, they ought to resist bending more than twisting—which they do. While trunks get a high ratio by manipulating their material, petioles do so by adjusting geometry as well. Short petioles

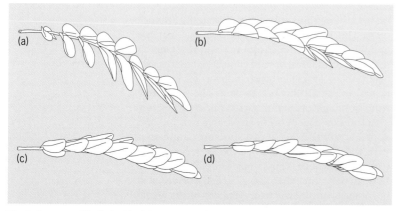

Fig. 6. Compound leaf of a black locust reconfiguring in the wind at wind speeds of (a) 0 mi/h or 0 m/s, (b) 11 mi/h or 5 m/s, (c) 22 mi/h or 10 m/s, and (d) 44 mi/h or 20 m/s. *(After S. Vogel, Life in Moving Fluids, 2d ed., Princeton University Press, 1994)*

in particular often have lengthwise grooves on top, side-to-side flattening, or other kinds of noncircular cross sections.

For background information *see* AERODYNAMIC FORCE; PLANT TISSUE SYSTEMS; ROOT (BOTANY); TREE; TREE GROWTH; TREE PHYSIOLOGY; XYLEM in the McGraw-Hill Encyclopedia of Science & Technology.   Steven Vogel

Bibliography. J. Bodig and B. A. Jayne, *Mechanics of Wood and Wood Composites*, 1982, reprint 1993; J. E. Gordon, *Structures, or Why Things Don't Fall Down*, 1978; D. A. King, The adaptive significance of tree height, *Amer. Natural.*, 135(6):809–828, 1990; C. Mattheck, *Trees: The Mechanical Design*, 1991; L. D. Nooden and A. C. Leopold (eds.), *Senescence and Aging in Plants*, 1988; M. G. Ryan and B. J. Yoder, Hydraulic limits to tree height and tree growth, *BioScience*, 47(4):235–242, 1997; S. Vogel, *Life in Moving Fluids*, 2d ed., 1994; R. H. Waring and J. F. Franklin, Evergreen coniferous forests of the Pacific Northwest, *Science*, 204:1380–1386, 1979.

Tuberculosis

In the early 1990s, some persons in New York City were diagnosed with a new, virtually untreatable form of tuberculosis. Called Strain W, it very rapidly killed 80–90% of those infected: most died within 4 months. All of the drugs routinely used to treat tuberculosis were useless. Strain W has now spread to at least 10 states and to France. By 1996 it accounted for one-quarter of the drug-resistant tuberculosis cases in the United States. This virulent outbreak demonstrates how multidrug-resistant tuberculosis is transforming treatment and control of the disease.

To be called multidrug resistant, a strain must be resistant to at least the two front-line tuberculosis drugs, isoniazid and rifampin. Just over 2% of tuberculosis cases in the United States now meet that criterion. The global picture is less clear, but the available studies suggest a larger problem. For example, rates of multidrug-resistant tuberculosis in San Diego County, California, were under 2%, but just over the border in Baja, Mexico, the rate was 22%. One-third of cases in Gujarat, India, were reported to be multidrug resistant. About half of the tuberculosis in Saudi Arabia is resistant to at least two drugs. How drug resistance arises, the basis of this resistance, and ways to combat it are all areas of active investigation.

Drug resistance. Resistance was noted just months after the first effective tuberculosis drug was introduced. Bacteria develop antibiotic resistance either through random mutation of genes on the chromosome or by acquisition of extra pieces of deoxyribonucleic acid (DNA) known as resistance plasmids. When simultaneous resistance arises to multiple antibiotics with distinct mechanisms of action, plasmids that confer multiple resistances are often involved. In multidrug-resistant tuberculosis, however, no resistance plasmids have ever been identified. Instead, all multidrug-resistant tuberculosis studied to date can be explained by the sequential accumulation of individual chromosomal mutations conferring resistance to each individual drug.

Resistance arises because in any large population of bacteria a few mutants exist that are insensitive to each potential drug. Consider a person freshly infected with tuberculosis. This person likely has inhaled very few (less than 100) bacteria, and probably all of these organisms are susceptible to tuberculosis drugs. However, by the time this person is sick enough to seek medical help, these few bacteria will have multiplied to a billion or more. Due to random mutation, about 10 of these organisms will be resistant to rifampin, at least 100 resistant to streptomycin, 100 to 1000 resistant to isoniazid. If only one drug is used for treatment, for example, isoniazid, nearly all the bacteria will be killed. However, those 100 isoniazid-resistant organisms will replicate unabated until the patient is again fighting billions of bacteria, all of which are now isoniazid resistant. Random mutation will ensure that this new infection includes about 10 more organisms that are rifampin resistant as well; they are the seeds of a multidrug-resistant infection.

Recognizing that a small fraction of any infection will resist each individual treatment, physicians quickly learned to treat tuberculosis with multiple drugs simultaneously. Current tuberculosis therapy generally involves four different drugs taken for at least 6 months. Such a long course of therapy involving drugs with noxious side effects is difficult for patients to complete. If therapy is stopped early or is erratic, the resistant organisms may not be completely eradicated and may emerge as a multidrug-resistant infection at a later date.

Drug resistance mechanisms. Using techniques of biochemistry and molecular biology, researchers have identified some mechanisms of drug resistance. To determine how an organism comes to survive antibiotic treatment, they often begin with a resistant strain, which can be either a laboratory isolate or a sample from a patient. In a typical experiment, recombinant organisms are created with DNA from the resistant strain, which is cleaved into numerous fragments, introduced into the sensitive strain, and then incubated in the presence of drug. Nearly all the introduced pieces of DNA are unrelated to antibiotic resistance; organisms receiving these fragments are killed by the drug. Eventually, the only surviving organisms are those that took up DNA related to antibiotic resistance, which can then easily be isolated and studied. Because the cloning techniques are powerful and because antibiotics are so effective, 10–100 million recombinant organisms can easily be screened in a single experiment. Once a mutation is associated with resistance, its importance is assessed by evaluating the frequency at which that mutation is found in resistant clinical samples. Often, multiple means of resistance to a single agent are identified.

Resistance to particular drugs. The drugs for treating tuberculosis include isoniazid, rifampin, streptomycin, and pyrazinamide.

Isoniazid. One of the most powerful and least expensive antitubercular drugs, isoniazid was introduced in 1953. Treatment failures from resistant isolates were noted in its first year of clinical use. Isoniazid is not inherently toxic to the tuberculosis bacterium; it must first be activated by the bacterial enzyme KatG. Virtually all isoniazid-resistant clinical isolates have alterations affecting KatG. Mutations in a second gene have been identified in roughly 10% of resistant strains, but most of these also carry KatG mutations so the relevance of the second gene to isoniazid resistance is unclear.

Rifampin. Along with isoniazid, rifampin forms the backbone of antituberculosis therapy. The basis of its rapid killing is its target. Rifampin binds to the portion of ribonucleic acid (RNA) polymerase encoded by the *rpo*B gene and inhibits transcription. More than 95% of rifampin-resistant tuberculosis bacteria have mutations in *rpo*B.

Streptomycin. Isolated from an organism growing in the throat of an infected chicken, streptomycin was the first antitubercular antibiotic ever described. It is still in worldwide use. Streptomycin acts by binding to the 16S ribosomal RNA of bacteria, preventing protein synthesis. The mutation most common in streptomycin-resistant tuberculosis bacteria, present in about 50% of resistant isolates, is in the *rps* gene, for ribosomal protein S12. In addition, about one-fourth of streptomycin-resistant strains carry mutations in the 16S ribosomal RNA gene, *rrn*.

Pyrazinamide. As with isoniazid, pyrazinamide must be activated by a bacterial enzyme (pyrazinamidase, product of the *pnc*A gene) before it is toxic to tuberculosis bacteria. Also as with isoniazid, at least 70% of resistant strains fail to activate the drug, carrying mutations that eliminate *pnc*A activity.

Treatment and control. Since multidrug-resistant tuberculosis can spread with alarming speed, control depends on the rapid identification and isolation of cases followed by effective treatment. To determine which drugs will be beneficial, organisms isolated from each patient must be tested for drug sensitivity. The standard method to determine sensitivity is to assess whether bacteria from the patient will grow under controlled conditions in the laboratory in the presence of various antimicrobials. Tuberculosis organisms grow very slowly, doubling only every 20 h in the laboratory; it may take 6–8 weeks to obtain results. During this time, a standard multidrug regimen (usually isoniazid, rifampin, pyrazinamide, and either ethambutol or streptomycin) can be started. The regimen is modified based on culture results. Tuberculosis is spread on respiratory droplets produced when an infected person coughs. Hospitalized tuberculosis patients are placed in respiratory isolation to minimize the risk of transmission to other patients and health care workers until treatment has rendered the patient noninfectious. At that point, the patient may be discharged from the hospital for the remainder of treatment.

Inadequate therapy, either with ineffective drugs or for insufficient time, greatly increases the risk that multidrug-resistant tuberculosis will emerge. Many experts recommend that a health-care worker carefully monitor tuberculosis patients in the community to ensure compliance. This program, called directly observed therapy, is cumbersome and expensive, but it has proven remarkably effective in halting the spread of tuberculosis and multidrug-resistant tuberculosis. For example, after instituting an aggressive directly observed therapy program in the early 1990s, New York City reduced its number of multidrug-resistant tuberculosis cases by 44%. The World Health Organization now recommends directly observed therapy as the worldwide standard of tuberculosis care.

Effective containment of multidrug-resistant tuberculosis requires extensive community surveillance of control programs. Currently, all documented cases of tuberculosis must be reported to the community health department. The tuberculosis patient's close and casual contacts must be tested to determine whether the disease has already spread. In addition, health departments collect data on the number of tuberculosis patients, initial drug regimen, susceptibility testing, and drug resistance. In this way, individual hospitals and physicians that fail to provide acceptable standards of care can be identified and the problems addressed. Particularly dangerous outbreaks can be identified quickly so that an appropriate response can be coordinated. Also, since multidrug-resistant tuberculosis is a menace the world over, the surveillance and coordination must be global. The World Health Organization and the International Union Against Tuberculosis and Lung Disease together are implementing a project to establish worldwide surveillance of tuberculosis drug resistance.

Another impact of the upsurge in multidrug-resistant tuberculosis has been increased interest in the biology of the pathogen. Research milestones, such as determining the complete genome sequence of the tuberculosis bacterium, are being reached. Progress can now be made on faster methods to diagnose tuberculosis and to determine drug resistance profiles, and on development of new drugs and a more effective vaccine. If well coordinated, the elements of multidrug-resistant tuberculosis control (rapid identification of infected individuals, patient isolation, direct observed therapy, surveillance of tuberculosis trends, and new research) raise the hope that this deadly disease can eventually be contained.

For background information *see* ANTIBIOTIC; BACTERIAL GENETICS; DRUG RESISTANCE; MUTATION; MYCOBACTERIAL DISEASES; PLASMID; TUBERCULOSIS in the McGraw-Hill Encyclopedia of Science & Technology.   David R. Sherman; Jeanette Farrell

Bibliography. T. R. Frieden et al., A multi-institutional outbreak of highly drug-resistant tuberculosis, *JAMA*, 276(15):1229–1235, 1996; M. Moore et al.,

Trends in drug resistant tuberculosis in the United States, 1993–1996, *JAMA*, 278(10):833–837, 1997; J. M. Musser, Antimicrobial agent resistance in mycobacteria: Molecular genetic insights, *Clin. Microbiol. Rev.*, 8(4):496–514, 1995; W. N. Rom and S. M. Garay (eds.), *Tuberculosis*, 1996.

Ultrasonic transducer

An efficient way to propagate energy from one medium to another is with sound. Acoustic transducers provide a means for redirecting energy over long distances. This energy redirection results in instrumentation that provides information for many everyday needs. The operating frequency ranges (and corresponding wavelength sizes) of the various applications provided by acoustic transducers (**Fig. 1**) serve to dictate the preferred transduction means. To couple transformations of energy from electrical to mechanical and then to acoustical (and vice versa), it is necessary to use active materials capable of transferring energy from one type to another. A common excitation mechanism is based on piezoelectric ceramics. Acoustic transmitters (projectors) operate by applying an electric field to the active materials within the transducer device to produce mechanical movement within the device such that

an acoustic pressure (sound) is output from the transducer. The converse is also true; that is, a sound impinging upon an acoustic receiver (a microphone for in-air detection or a hydrophone for underwater use) mechanically excites the active material in the transducer so that an electrical signal is generated and may be analyzed in terms of a local sound field. The active materials that convert electrical signals to mechanical vibrations and then to sound are the focus of most transducer research, which centers on developing such materials to achieve specific performance gains. Thus, the design of many transducers begins with the tailoring of the active material component with regard to its intended applications (Fig. 1). Among the active materials are piezoceramics, piezocomposites, electrostrictive relaxors, magnetostrictive alloys, and single crystals.

Piezoceramics. The most common active material is the polycrystalline, ferroelectric, ceramic compound lead zirconate titanate (PZT). Powdered forms of this compound with various compositions have been used since the 1960s; the selection of a specific type of compound is typically based upon the intended application. The electrically soft form is known as PZT-5, and it is the easiest to manufacture because of the low temperatures required for inducing the electric-field polarization of the crystal structure. It is typically found in sensor and ultrasonic

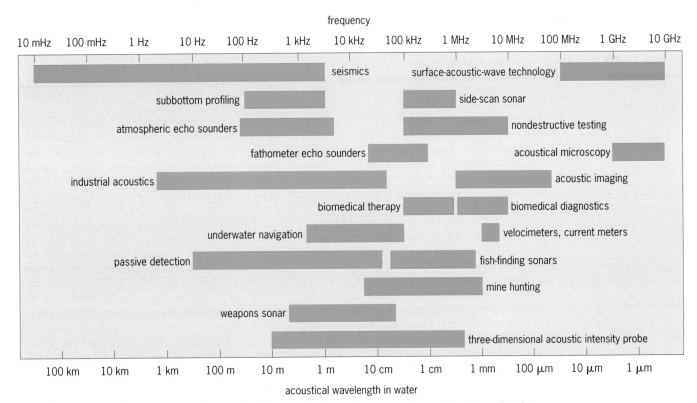

Fig. 1. Acoustic transducer applications, with operating frequency regions and corresponding underwater wavelengths. *(After J. F. Tressler, Capped Ceramic Underwater Sound Projector The Cymbal, Ph.D. Thesis, Pennsylvania State University, 1977)*

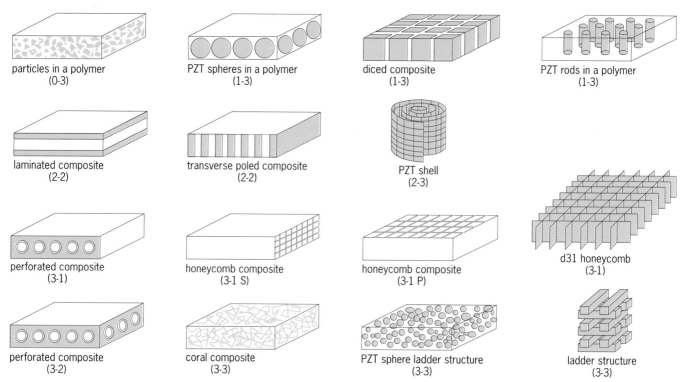

particles in a polymer
(0-3)

PZT spheres in a polymer
(1-3)

diced composite
(1-3)

PZT rods in a polymer
(1-3)

laminated composite
(2-2)

transverse poled composite
(2-2)

PZT shell
(2-3)

perforated composite
(3-1)

honeycomb composite
(3-1 S)

honeycomb composite
(3-1 P)

d31 honeycomb
(3-1)

perforated composite
(3-2)

coral composite
(3-3)

PZT sphere ladder structure
(3-3)

ladder structure
(3-3)

Fig. 2. Examples of the Newnham classification system for piezocomposites. *(After L. E. Cross, Ferroelectric ceramics: Materials and application issues, Ceramic Trans., 68:15–55, 1996)*

applications because of its high sensitivity and dielectric properties.

The compound PZT-4 is a versatile ceramic because it can withstand higher internal stresses than the soft compounds with minimal performance loss. It is often featured in transducers used for reciprocal applications (reception and transmission) as well as for operations at greater ocean depths, where increased hydrostatic capabilities are required.

The electrically hard form is PZT-8. It is the most difficult to manufacture because of the temperature elevations required for electric field inducement. It is found in applications requiring high electrical drives (such as low-frequency projectors) as well as those at ocean depths greater than 1000 ft (300 m), where hydrostatic pressure forces are often the limiting environmental factor.

With these three PZT types, it is possible to perform some engineering optimization (material tailoring) of acoustic transducer designs for specific applications, but because the PZTs are ceramics, they suffer from the mixing of transverse resonance frequency modes with bulk material properties. For operations at a specific acoustic mode, these effects may often be ignored, but for applications involving a broad spectrum of frequencies, pure ceramics are application limited.

Piezocomposites. Material studies since the late 1980s have focused on the shaping (usually cutting or machining) of piezoceramics. Cut or preshaped piezoceramics are then interleaved with a passive polymer or epoxy host matrix compound to form a composite active material. The new active materials, known as piezocomposites, are categorized by the Newnham classification system, which accounts for the number of axes along which the active and passive material components extend, respectively (**Fig. 2**).

For instance, one of the first piezocomposite materials consisted of a piezoceramic component shaped into a coral-type arrangement and then backfilled with an epoxy. This structure is referred to as a 3-3 piezocomposite because both the active (coral-shaped piezoceramic) and the passive (backfilled epoxy) materials extend along each of the three axes. This material had some performance enhancements in terms of sensor application, but to date its manufacture has been too cumbersome to be practical.

Another configuration developed was the 0-3 piezocomposite. This material, sometimes referred to as piezorubber (PZR), consists of small, piezoceramic particles (less than 10 micrometers in diameter) interspersed in a rubber base. The volume fraction of the piezoceramic is typically 60–80%, but the polymer matrix presence results in a highly flexible, rubberlike composite. Each of the individual piezoceramic particles is covered by the rubber compound such that the piezoceramic does not fully extend along any of the axes (thus the 0 of the 0-3 nomenclature), while the passive material (rubber compound) extends along all three axes. The 0-3 piezocomposite material is used for acoustic hydrophones and sensors as well as robotics applica-

Underground mining **385**

tions. It is commercially manufactured in sheet form and is available from manufacturers in Japan, the United Kingdom, and the United States.

A 2-2 piezocomposite configuration has been commonly used for ultrasonic transmitters and receivers in biomedical transducers. The 2-2 configuration consist of rows of solid piezoceramic separated by epoxy or polymer rows. This type of piezocomposite is now found in many biomedical and ultrasonic transducers because of its broad, clean resonance-frequency behavior and low cost.

Since the late 1980s, there has been concerted effort in the development of 1-3 piezocomposite materials. The 1-3 configuration has individual piezoceramic rods mounted in a polymer or epoxy host matrix and may be used for both receive and transmit applications. One attraction of this configuration is that the selection of the piezoceramic volume fraction and material type can be done with respect to the final application. For instance, acoustic receivers are often 15%-volume-fraction PZT-5 (or PZT-54), projectors are 40–60%-volume-fraction PZT-4 or PZT-5 (depending on their operating frequency and the hydrostatic pressure environment), and receiver/transmitters (transceivers) have piezoceramic volume fractions at 15–30% in between. The 1-3 piezocomposite is featured in transducers operating in the 10 kHz–1 MHz regions because of their performance advantages of good impedance matching with the medium (both water and biomedical), high broad-band response, and low lateral degradation effects. Also, because the 1-3 material is a piezocomposite, it can be shaped into geometries not possible with ceramics.

Previously the formation of the 1-3 configuration was obtainable only by machining out a piezoceramic disk or plate and then backfilling the cut regions with polymer. However, since 1992 an injection molding process has been demonstrated, and it is being used for commercial applications. This method has resulted in 1-3 piezocomposites with repeatable performance and lower cost. It is expected that most new acoustic transducers operating at 10 kHz–1 MHz frequencies will feature the 1-3 piezocomposite structure through at least 2007.

Electrostriction. In electrostriction the induced strain is related to the square of the electric driving field as opposed to the linear relationship of piezoelectricity. This means that the use of electrostrictive materials as the active transduction material requires an electrical biasing field. Recently, the use of a class of electrostrictive ceramics known as relaxors has been investigated because these materials have shown superior performance within specific ranges of frequency, temperature, and electric field. Present studies concern the broadening of these conditions as well as the development of methods for mass manufacture of transducers with repeatable performance.

Magnetostriction. Acoustic transducers featuring magnetostriction as the active means for transduction have been used since before World War I. The principle of magnetostriction is to place a magnetically oriented material within a coil, bias the material with a direct-current field (either through a direct current or through placement in a magnetic field), and drive the coil with an alternating-current field directed into the coil. In the 1970s, the finding of rare-earth–iron compounds with strains approaching 1% resulted in the design of magnetostrictive projectors for high-power, low-frequency underwater applications. Research continues into improving manufacturing methods and material quality.

Single crystals. Since 1995 there has been a return to the research of growing single crystals as active transducer materials. Although traditionally this use has been limited by environmental conditions (temperature, humidity, fragility, and so forth), relaxor ferroelectric single crystals have laboratory-demonstrated maximum strains greater than 1.2%. So far, this performance has been seen only under laboratory conditions, but over the next few years it is expected that research will be directed to exploitation of this potential.

For background information *see* CERAMICS; COMPOSITE MATERIAL; ELECTROSTRICTION; FERROELECTRICS; MAGNETOSTRICTION; MICROPHONE; NANOSTRUCTURE; PIEZOELECTRICITY; SINGLE CRYSTAL; TRANSDUCER; ULTRASONICS; UNDERWATER SOUND in the McGraw-Hill Encyclopedia of Science & Technology.

Thomas R. Howarth

Bibliography. L. E. Cross, Ferroelectric ceramics: Materials and application issues, *Ceramic Trans.*, 68:15–55, 1996.

Underground mining

Underground miners work in an artificial atmosphere which is likely to be subject to an inflow of contaminants. There are significant differences in the underground mining of flat-lying ore bodies such as coal seams, and steeply pitching ones such as veins of copper or gold ores; therefore, the ventilation systems need to be different. These differences arise from the geology and extent of the ore body, the applicable mining methods, and the nature of contaminants and their rates of emission.

The purpose of mine ventilation is to supply fresh air to the miners and to dilute and remove explosive and toxic gases and dusts from the mine workings. In very deep mines, heat and humidity control is as important for miners' health and safety as is the control of gases and dusts. The cause of major mine disasters such as explosions and suffocations has been traced to inadequate control of the mine air quality and quantity. As mines go deeper, as new technology is introduced to increase production, as the ability to monitor the various contaminants increases, and as the knowledge of the dose-response relationships increases, the understanding of the health and safety issues that can be addressed through mine ventilation is also increasing.

The fundamental principles of contaminant control in mine ventilation are prevention, removal, suppression, containment, and dilution. Often several principles are used in combination to maintain a safe and healthful atmosphere for miners. Circulation of adequate quantities of air to reduce the concentrations of toxic and explosive contaminants below permissible exposure limits (PEL) is the most versatile and the most used control technique in underground mines.

Coal mine ventilation. As coal mines go deeper, the adaptation of longwall mining as the principal extraction method is becoming standard. In recent years, the traditional United States method of retreat longwall mining with multiple-entry longwall gate development is also becoming the worldwide standard for achieving high productivity. The size of panels has been increasing, with panel widths in excess of 1000 ft (300 m) and panel lengths in excess of 16,000 ft (5000 m). The phenomenal increases in production (up to 6000–7000 metric tons per shift) from these highly productive systems are placing tremendous stress on the ventilation system for methane and dust control.

In terms of overall coal mine ventilation planning, the driving of a small-diameter (less than 10 ft or 3 m) drilled shaft at the back end of a bank of longwalls, and use of a fan to draw over 150,000 ft³ of air per minute (70 m³/s) through the mined-out areas (gob) are becoming essential to adequately ventilate long panels. The sealing of gob to reduce the methane accumulation and spontaneous combustion problems is also becoming an acceptable alternative to ventilating the gob. According to the most recent United States ventilation regulations, use of booster fans in underground coal mines is not allowed. In terms of longwall ventilation, the unidirectional Y-system of ventilation is more effective than the traditional U-system of ventilation (**Fig. 1**). The larger quantities of fresh air that can be delivered to the face and the simplicity of unidirectional flow are two advantages of the Y-system.

Respirable dust control. Respirable dust-related diseases remain the most pernicious industrial hazard. Airborne dust in mine atmospheres is associated with the occurrence of several occupational diseases, pneumoconiosis and silicosis being readily associated with coal dust and silica dust, respectively. In some cases, coal and sulfide dusts are also associated with explosions. The current United States respirable coal mine dust standard of 2 mg per cubic meter of air for 8 h per day or 40 h per week, established by the 1969 Coal Mine Health and Safety Act, is the most stringent in the world. The use of environmental control to decrease airborne dust concentration, as opposed to the use of respirators and work practices to reduce the exposure of the miners, is viewed as the major directive of the Coal Act. Therefore, the most common method for dust concentration control is dilution ventilation. Respirators or air stream helmets are provided for use as additional measures of protection to miners working in dusty areas.

The prevalence of simple coal workers' pneumoconiosis and progressive massive fibrosis is declining. The concentration data from the compliance sampling programs also indicate that, on the average, there is excellent compliance with the mandated levels. Clearly, good progress is being made in the control of airborne dust. There are, however, several less encouraging observations. The coal dust sampling program has revealed that as much as 30% of the samples are above the permissible exposure limit. Further, the high variability of the concentration data reveals a need to operate in general at lower average dust concentrations so as not to exceed the permissible exposure limit. Questions have been raised on the methods of sampling for compliance and of determining noncompliance. On the medical front, there is a call for taking a broader view of occupational lung diseases, including the increased risk of chronic obstructive pulmonary disease.

The National Institute for Occupational Safety and Health (NIOSH) recommends a permissible exposure limit of 1 mg/m³ for respirable coal mine dust as a time-weighted average concentration for up to 10 h per day during a 40-h week, measured according to the current methods. Questions have been raised on the NIOSH models, model assumptions, data, and analyses. Some questions have centered on age-related background x-ray abnormalities, wide variations in the classification of the source x-rays, nature of available data on exposures, effects of mineralogical and chemical composition of airborne dust in addition to concentration, performance of the human clearance mechanisms at low levels of exposure, smoking history, and length of working life. The question of whether the current permissible exposure limit on coal mine respirable dust is sufficiently protective cannot be resolved without better understanding of the disease process.

Methane drainage. The principal means for reducing methane concentration in mine air to below a safe limit (usually less than 1%) has been dilution ventilation, and the circulation of 5–20 metric tons of air per metric ton of coal mined has been usual. The extremely variable nature of methane emissions encountered during mining has been a major reason for the dangerous accumulations of the gas. As mines went deeper, the quantities of air required for dilution ventilation were becoming so large that the search intensified for removing the methane by other means. In the United States, spurred by the energy demand and tax incentives, coal-bed methane drainage technology and production saw major growth beginning in the 1980s. The most productive degasification methods are the vertical degas hole in virgin areas, in-seam horizontal drainage both before and during mining, and the vertical degas hole in mined-out areas (**Fig. 2**).

The amount of methane that can be drained from a particular coal seam is dependent on factors such as the gas content, permeability, methane reservoir

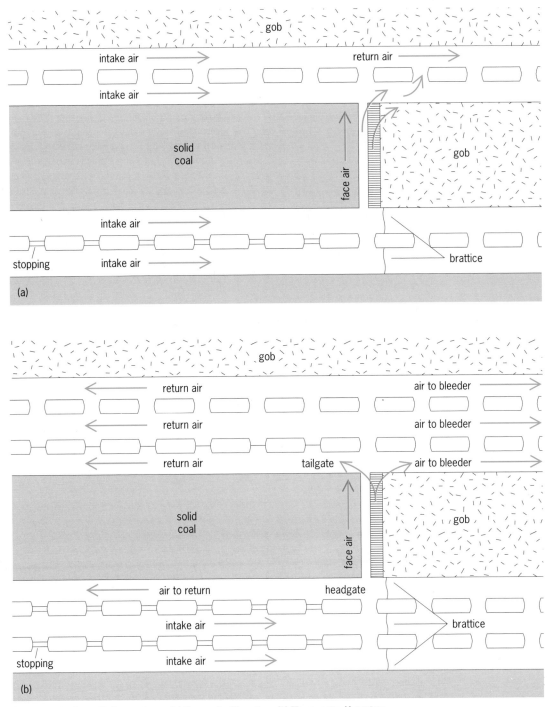

Fig. 1. Longwall ventilation systems. (*a*) Two-entry Y-system. (*b*) Three-entry U-system.

characteristics, method of methane drainage, location and timing of coal extraction, and method of coal extraction. Even where methane drainage is practiced to reduce emissions during mining, in most cases the trapped methane is vented to the atmosphere. It is estimated that the amount of methane emitted annually from coal mines worldwide is about 1300 billion cubic feet (37 billion cubic meters), out of which just over 211 billion cubic feet (6 billion cubic meters) is captured in drainage systems

and about 88 billion cubic feet (2.5 billion cubic meters) is utilized as an energy source.

Few mines can afford the establishment of a complete methane drainage and methane utilization program because of the high capital and operating costs, the lack of ready availability of a commercial gas distribution network to connect the mine methane drainage system, and the uneven quality of the drained gas. Where the area of the coal property is large and the seam gas content is high, methane

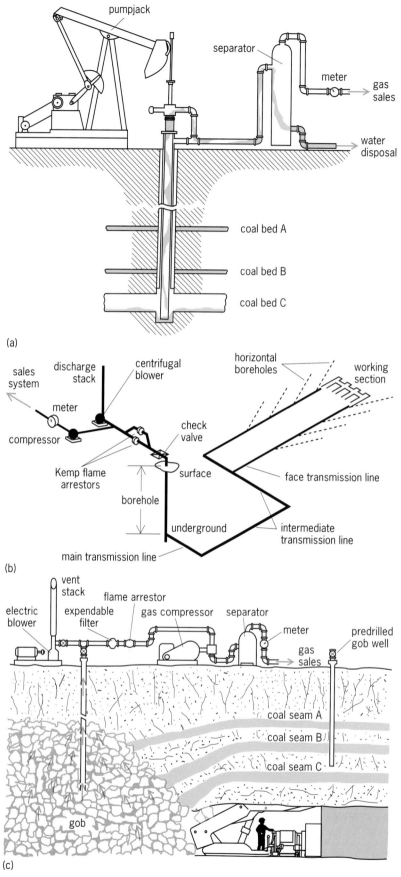

(a)

(b)

(c)

Fig. 2. Coal-bed methane drainage systems. (*a*) Premining vertical degas well. (*b*) Horizontal drilling during mining. (*c*) After-mining vertical gob degas well.

drainage can be a useful and profitable adjunct to mining operations. Methane drainage reduces the load on the ventilation system, enhances mine safety, and provides another source of revenue for mines.

Metal mine ventilation. Ore bodies that are steeply inclined present challenges not only to the selection of appropriate mining methods but also to the planning of ventilation of the mine workings. Special considerations arise from the source and nature of pollutants (the ore characteristics, diesel-powered equipment, heat and humidity, blasting, and so on) and the use of certain practices such as recirculation of air, underground fans, and mine cooling. The heat removal problem is acute in very deep mines because of the high virgin rock temperatures, and the decreased cooling effect of air due to increased autocompression as the air descends to the depths of workings. The capital and operating costs of the mine cooling system increase significantly with depth, and for developing an optimal system the design must consider both the refrigeration plant and the energy recovery components. There is a mine cooling system that incorporates a surface cooling plant and hydro hoists for energy recovery. The mean rock breaking depth is 11,000 ft (3400 m), and the average virgin rock temperature is 135°F (57°C). The heat load for a production of 180,000 metric tons per month is 54 megawatts. The reduction in heat load due to backfill is 6 MW. The cooling capacity of the surface air, after bulk air cooling is lost because of autocompression, leaves a total heat load of 48 MW to be removed by the mine cooling system. The ventilating air required is 1400 lb/s (640 kg/s), which requires approximately 20 MW cooling at the surface, provided by the bulk air coolers and refrigeration plants. The ratio of metric tons of water circulated for a metric ton of rock is 9.7. In terms of coefficient of performance, which is defined as the kilowatt cooling provided divided by the electrical input power, this system is reported to have the optimal performance among four cooling systems that were compared.

Diesel exhaust emission control. Diesel-powered equipment has been in use in underground mines since the late 1920s. In general, it is more common in underground metallic and nonmetallic ore mines than in coal mines. The potential for serious health and safety hazards from the gases, vapors, and particulates in the diesel engine exhaust, and from the storage, transportation, and handling of the diesel fuel is well known. The major pollutants in the exhaust are diesel particulate matter, nitric oxide, nitrogen dioxide, carbon monoxide, carbon dioxide, sulfur dioxide, and hydrocarbons. It has been recommended that the whole diesel exhaust be regarded as a potential occupational carcinogen, and that since diesel exhaust is a mixture of several contaminants it be regulated by using several mixed exposure-limit formulas, each of which addresses the contaminants affecting a specific body organ.

The diesel particulate matter consists mainly of insoluble carbonaceous soot, trace metals, sulfates, and organic compounds. In recent years, great attention has been directed to the control of these particulates, which are mostly of submicrometer size. Measuring exposure to diesel exhaust pollutants, particularly particulates, has been challenging. The three methods used at present for diesel particulate matter estimation in mine air are size-selective sampling, elemental carbon content, and respirable combustible dust content in noncoal mines.

The primary method for controlling the health effects of diesel emissions in underground mines has been dilution ventilation. In most cases, the volume of air required in a split with a single diesel engine or with multiple diesel engines is specified by regulations. However, proper selection and operation of the engine, use of cleaner fuels, aftertreatment of the engine exhaust, and good maintenance are necessary to reduce the volume and toxicity of the exhaust. The treatment of the engine exhaust prior to release into the mine atmosphere includes catalytic converters to reduce carbon monoxide and hydrocarbon emissions, and water scrubbers to cool the exhaust and to reduce the concentrations of hydrocarbon, sulfur dioxide, and diesel particulate matter. Water scrubbers are not effective in reducing the diesel particulate matter. Use of filters to trap diesel particulate matter is a recent development; types include ceramic monoliths, wire mesh, ceramic foam, matlike ceramic filters, and disposable pleated element filters. Efficiencies of particulate collection in excess of 85% mass are reported for some of these filters. Integration of the various control devices into a system has resulted in a significant reduction of carbon monoxide, hydrocarbons, and particulate matter in the exhaust before discharge into the mine atmosphere.

For background information *see* INDUSTRIAL HEALTH AND SAFETY; MINING; RESPIRATORY SYSTEM DISORDERS; UNDERGROUND MINING in the McGraw-Hill Encyclopedia of Science & Technology.

Raja V. Ramani

Bibliography. H. L. Hartman et al., *Mine Ventilation and Air Conditioning*, 1997; C. Hegerman, Optimizing the cooling of the Vaal Reefs, No. 11 Shaft underground environment and a description of refrigeration and energy recovery equipment use, *J. Mine Vent. Soc. S. Afr.*, 50(1):18–24, 1997; R. V. Ramani (ed.), *Proceedings of the 6th International Mine Ventilation Congress*, 1997; A. W. Wala (ed.), *Proceedings of the 7th U.S. Mine Ventilation Symposium*, 1995.

Vertebrate evolution

The earliest vertebrates with limbs and digits—tetrapods—had descendants that eventually colonized the land and diversified into all the vertebrate forms seen in the subsequent history of life on Earth. Dinosaurs, birds, lizards, bats, snakes, whales, humans, frogs, and salamanders are all tetrapods. The ancestors of tetrapods first appeared during the Devonian Period, about 380–350 million years ago—a period that is also remarkable for being the Age of Fishes. Tetrapods evolved from within a group of fishes called the lobe-fins whose other descendants include the living lungfishes and the coelacanth *Latimeria*. Among fossil forms, the tetrapods' closest relatives are the osteoleptiforms, whose other members are now extinct. Until very recently, few fossils representing this important stage in the history of life had been found, and ideas about how the transition from fish to tetrapod happened, where it happened, and in what sequence tetrapod characteristics arose, had to rely largely on speculation. More clues have now come to light, and it is possible to put together a few pieces in the jigsaw puzzle. The emerging picture is more complicated than expected, and there are still many questions.

Animals with limbs. The earliest unequivocal evidence for the appearance of animals with legs and digits rather than fins comes from Australia, and consists of fossil trackways, dated from the lower part of the Upper Devonian, the Frasnian. Two different kinds of animals are apparently represented, or at least two animals moving in different ways. One track shows drag marks from the animal's belly while the other does not. Both tracks show the characteristic alternating pattern of fore and hind limb impressions made by tetrapods. However, it is not clear whether these tracks were made by animals progressing on land, or whether either or both animals were partially supported by shallow water. Recently discovered trackways from Ireland may be even earlier than the Australian sets, from the Middle rather than the Upper Devonian, but the same problems of interpretation apply. It is not clear whether the limbs were used for walking on land or for paddling around in shallow water. No remains of the animals have been found, so that it is not known whether the limbs would have been capable of supporting the body on land.

Limb construction. The earliest remains which do provide evidence of limb construction in tetrapods suggests that land locomotion was not easily accomplished by any of them, if at all. From the top of the Upper Devonian (Famennian) of East Greenland come the two best-known Devonian tetrapods, *Acanthostega* and *Ichthyostega*. In *Acanthostega*, both fore and hind limbs were paddlelike, and show many primitive characters, including finlike construction of the forearm bones and a full complement of eight digits per limb. *Acanthostega* could not have made any of the known trackways unless supported by water, though the outward-facing digit impressions in the Australian tracks match the position in *Acanthostega*. *Ichthyostega* had a paddlelike hindlimb similar to *Acanthostega*, though bearing only seven digits, but its massive shoulders and forelimbs may have been used for dragging the body over mudflats, or simply for supporting the head and trunk clear of shallow water.

The third genus of tetrapod from this period, *Tulerpeton*, from Russia, shows limbs which more closely resemble those of later animals. The forearm bones are longer and more slender than those of either *Acanthostega* or *Ichthyostega*, but the wrists and ankles are not similar to those of the more conventional early tetrapods which first appeared in the next period, the Carboniferous. *Tulerpeton* had six digits on each limb, suggesting that in the earliest days of limb evolution the number of fingers or toes had not settled firmly into the tetrapod genome. It is not clear whether *Tulerpeton* would have walked on solid ground or paddled like its contemporaries from Greenland.

Some new fragments of tetrapods from other parts of the world have been found in the last few years. None of these shows complete limbs; in fact, many consist of only jaw fragments, which give no clues to locomotory capabilities. However, some partial limb bones are known from sites in Scotland and Latvia, and there is an isolated shoulder girdle from the United States. The Scottish animal, *Elginerpeton*, shows the earliest of the known body fragments, predating those from Greenland by as much as 10 million years. It seems to have been a large, flat-headed form whose pelvic girdle and hindlimb elements, though only partially preserved, suggest a paddler. The shoulder girdle from the state of Pennsylvania suggests that the animal had powerful shoulder muscles, but there is not sufficient evidence to distinguish whether these were used for walking or for paddling.

None of these discoveries supports the traditional view of the origin of tetrapods, in which ventures onto land were first made by the osteolepiforms, in their attempts to follow the drying watercourses postulated for the arid climate of the Upper Devonian. In that scenario, movement on land preceded the evolution of limbs. Judging strictly from the fossil evidence, the reverse may be inferred—that limbs evolved first for paddling in shallow, vegetation-choked water. This scenario would have allowed early tetrapods to invade aquatic habitats where free swimming with fins was hampered.

Dating. A problem with all Devonian tetrapod material is the uncertainty of dating. Most of the sites are dated indirectly, usually by reference to the associated fish species. For some localities, absolute radiometric dates (in millions of years) based on isotope analysis have been obtained for associated sediments, but often these dates give anomalous results, some much earlier than would be expected, others much later. This uncertainty makes it difficult to work out the actual sequence in which some of the animals appeared, and either may spread the events of the fish-tetrapod transition over a longer period or may telescope it into a much shorter one. The most reliable method of relative dating seems to be spore analysis of the associated floral communities. Spore analysis is just becoming available for the Greenland tetrapod horizons, but it tends to support the widely accepted Famennian date.

Two other perspectives can be taken which may help explain the evolution of limbs and tetrapods.

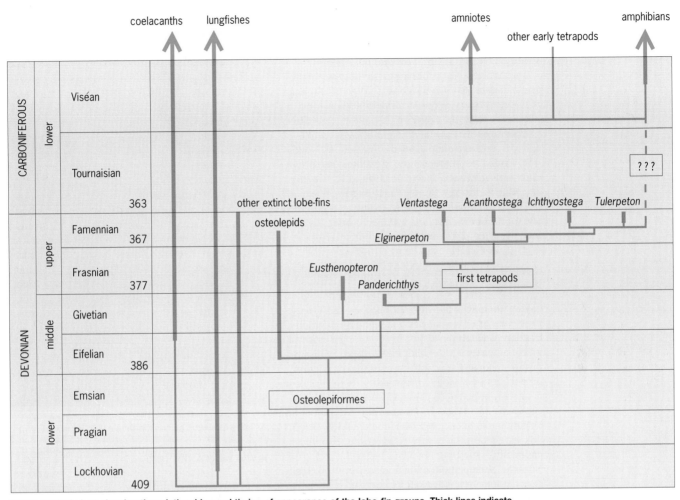

Stratigraphical chart showing the relationships and timing of appearance of the lobe-fin groups. Thick lines indicate known occurrence, and thin lines indicate inferred occurrence. Arrows indicate that these groups are still present. *Eusthenopteron* is a well-known osteolepiform whose structure is often used to compare fish morphology with that of an early tetrapod, while *Ventastega* is the Devonian tetrapod from Latvia. Dates (in millions of years) show the inception of the respective stages. *(After J. A. Clack, Devonian tetrapod trackways and trackmakers: A review of the fossils and footprints, Palaeogeog. Palaeoclimatol. Palaeoecol., 130:227–250, 1997)*

One is to look at the phylogeny, or family tree, of the lobe-fins and infer relative timing of appearance of the members (see **illus.**). Another is to look at the earlier parts of the Carboniferous Period for evidence of what happened next.

Lobe-finned fishes belonging to recognizable groups are first known from the Lower Devonian, but osteolepiforms, from which the tetrapods are thought to have evolved, are not found until the middle of the period. The most closely related osteolepiform group, the panderichthyids, have not been found before the top part of the Middle Devonian, implying that the split between them and tetrapods could not have occurred much before then.

Knowledge of the tetrapods of the Lower Carboniferous has been held back by the gap which appears in the fossil record of the group spanning the next 30 million years or so. Until recently, only a few isolated scraps were known from the lowest parts of this interval, called the Tournaisian and Viséan

stages. More finds are now being made in Viséan sediments from around the world, and it seems clear that by that time some fully terrestrial forms had evolved. Some bizarre forms had lost their limbs altogether and become snakelike in appearance. In addition, the foundations had been laid for the evolution of the lineages leading to modern amphibians (frogs, salamanders, and caecilians) and to amniotes (reptiles, birds, and mammals). Many of the adaptations to land living found today in these groups, such as mechanisms of air breathing, hearing, and land locomotion, could have evolved separately among ancestors in the Lower Carboniferous or even in the Devonian. However, until more tetrapod fossils from the Tournaisian and lower parts of the Viséan are found, it will not be possible to determine for certain either the ancestry and relationships between the animals or the sequence and timing in which these adaptations appeared.

This large gap has begun to be filled. Fossil tetrapods from the Tournaisian and from the lower Viséan are now beginning to be found, and when they have been thoroughly studied, should go a long way to help resolve some questions concerning the origin of limbs and life on land among vertebrates.

For background information *see* ANIMAL EVOLUTION; CARBONIFEROUS; DEVONIAN; EXTINCTION (BIOLOGY); VERTEBRATA in the McGraw-Hill Encyclopedia of Science & Technology.   J. A. Clack

Bibliography. P. E. Ahlberg, *Elginerpeton pancheni* and the earliest tetrapod clade, *Nature*, 373:420–425, 1995; P. E. Ahlberg and A. R. Milner, The origin and early diversification of tetrapods, *Nature*, 381:61–64, 1994; J. A. Clack, Devonian tetrapod trackways and trackmakers: A review of the fossils and footprints, *Palaeogeog. Palaeoclimatol. Palaeoecol.*, 130:227–250, 1997.

Veterinary paleopathology

Paleopathology is the study of diseases and disease processes in ancient individuals and populations, both human and animal. Justification for the study of paleopathology is threefold: information on disease processes for any era contributes to the overall body of medical knowledge; information about diseases in ancient populations can help to elucidate historical and paleontological questions; and differences in lesions and incidence between ancient and modern populations can help answer questions of modern pathology.

In the paleopathology of humans, both skeletal material and mummified soft tissues may be available for study. For ancient or extinct animals, there are, with few exceptions, only dental and skeletal remains. That shortcoming is mitigated somewhat by the fact that many animal skeletal remains preserved as fossils predate humans by millions of years.

Hard tissue lesions. Veterinary paleopathology is largely concerned with lesions of bones and teeth, hard tissues which undergo fossilization. These lesions may be classified as congenital or acquired.

Congenital. Congenital lesions, whether genetic or nongenetic, develop during intrauterine life. The majority of congenital lesions seen in ancient animals affect the teeth. Most of the dental defects which are seen in modern animals have also been reported in ancient animals.

An example of improper congenital development is a dystrophy, that is, improper development, of the upper molar teeth in modern horses which often causes clinical disease. It appears at about a 40% rate in modern population of *Equus* of whatever breed. The lesion is basically a congenital failure of proper formation of enamel and cementum, the significant abrasion-resisting elements of the equid tooth. The same lesion has been found in *Equus* from the Pleistocene (around 5 millions years ago) and *Hipparion* from the Miocene (around 10 million years ago). Perhaps this abnormality in modern horses is a trait persisting since the time that equids were evolving from low-crown (browsing) teeth to

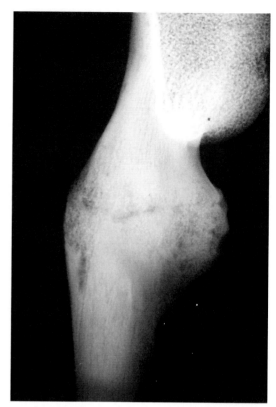

Fig. 1. Healing fracture of a rib of *Hipparion* (about 10 million years ago). Lacy-appearing callus is present on both sides, and the incompletely united fracture line is in the middle. *(From J. R. Rooney, Equid paleopathology, J. Equine Vet. Sci., 17:8, 1997)*

high-crown (grazing) teeth during the early to middle Miocene.

Acquired. Acquired lesions of bones and joints in ancient animals are largely of traumatic or infectious origin. Healed fractures, chronic joint damage, and healed ligamentous avulsions (tearing out of ligaments from their insertions into bone) of the digit are among the common lesions seen.

Ligamentous avulsions heal with formation of additional bone at the site of the avulsion and are readily recognized. Perhaps some of these lesions in ancient equids are related to instability of the digit during the evolution from the three-toed to one-toed condition. During this transition, the digit became progressively more upright and prone to instability.

Fractures can be identified in ancient animals only if healing occurred with the formation of callus at the fracture site. Fresh fractures present at the time that an animal died cannot be differentiated from fractures that occurred after death or during the millions of years in the substrate (**Fig. 1**).

Diseases. Chronic joint disease has been reported in a number of ancient animals, including horses, dogs, cattle, and dinosaurs. The diagnosis is problematic in many cases, being made on the basis of abnormal bone formation around the joint rather than on direct evidence of cartilage damage. Such bone formation around joints is part of the healing process

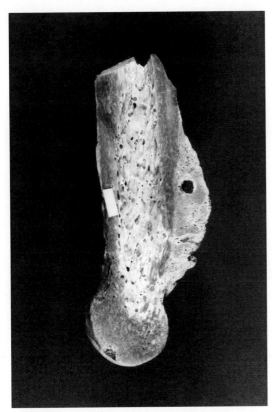

Fig. 2. Osteomyelitis in a metacarpal bone from a *Parahippus* (about 20 million years ago). The bone was split down the middle. The bulging whitish mass to the right is bone formed as reaction to bacterial infection. The hole contained a dried-out material which appeared to have been pus. *(From J. R. Rooney, Equid paleopathology, J. Equine Vet. Sci., 17:8, 1997)*

of arthrosis, but it is also the healing process of ligamentous avulsion. Great care is required to differentiate between the two causes. Cartilage is rarely preserved in ancient animals; therefore, it cannot be used to distinguish the presence or absence of arthrosis. In a large series of ancient equids, prior to the appearance of humans and the domestication of equids, clear-cut evidence of arthrosis was found in only one stifle joint.

The diagnosis of chronic joint disease is quite correct in oxen and horses of the Iron Age and under the control of humans. Lesions of the hock joints and pastern joints of the digit are the same as those seen in modern horses and oxen used for draft purposes.

In human pathology, certain systemic diseases such as chronic anemia and syphilis produce changes in bones. These changes have been described by paleopathologists in ancient human remains, although some of the reports are problematic. Similar bone changes associated with systemic disease have not been recognized in modern or ancient animals.

Osteomyelitis, a bacterial infection involving bone, has been seen in ancient animals. In some cases, both bone and joint seem to have been involved, just as in osteomyelitis in modern animals. In many cases, the disease process had obviously gone on for a considerable time, with evidence of extensive efforts to repair the damage (**Fig. 2**).

Comparisons with osteomyelitis in modern animal populations cannot be made. The reasons are that it is not possible to determine the frequency of such lesions in ancient populations, and few attempts have been made to determine the incidence in modern animal populations.

Tumors of hard tissues such as bones and teeth are not common in modern animals and are virtually unknown in ancient animals. There are a few reports of osteomas, which are benign tumors of bone. However, in fossilized material the distinction between bony lumps which represent healing of a traumatic or infectious process and osteoma can be very difficult.

Techniques for bone study. While many techniques are available for the study of bone disease in modern animals, only a few are useful in paleopathology. The basic technique is examination with the naked eye and careful description of the changes present. This is supplemented with examination of the bones and teeth with a low-power dissecting microscope. X-rays are of great value not only in evaluating the lesions apparent on gross examination but in detecting changes in the deep parts of bones.

Microscopic study of some lesions can be useful. For most lesions of ancient bones, it is necessary to prepare ground sections rather than standard histological sections. The same methods are used for fossil bone as for the preparation of thin sections of shells and rocks in geology. The older the bone, the more friable it is, so it must be embedded in plastic and ground down to be thin enough for moderate-power microscopic study. Magnifications greater than $100\times$ are usually not helpful for paleopathological work because of fossilization and artefactual changes, but such magnifications have been useful in some paleontological studies.

An interesting finding of veterinary paleopathology is that a number of lesions of bones and joints often seen in modern animals have not been seen in their ancient counterparts. In most of these cases, the presence of lesions in modern animals can be directly and indirectly related to domestication. An example is osteochondrosis, a developmental defect of those parts of bones forming the joints. This condition is seen in virtually all modern species, including humans, but has not been reported in any studies of fossil animals. The exact cause of osteochondrosis is still controversial, but it seems to be related to changes of conformation and rate of growth of the young animal. Humans influence conformation by genetic selection and influence rate of growth by intensive feeding practices.

Paleontologists recognize many of the abnormalities of animal bones and teeth. Very few of the resulting cataloged collections, however, have been systematically studied by veterinary pathologists trained to evaluate and diagnose bone and dental disease. Veterinary paleopathology is, in fact, a virtually virgin field for scientific investigation. Collaboration between paleontologists and pathologists could contribute a great deal to both paleontology and pathology and to medical science in general.

For background information see PALEONTOLOGY; PATHOLOGY in the McGraw-Hill Encyclopedia of Science & Technology.   James R. Rooney

Bibliography. R. L. Moodie, *Paleopathology: An Introduction to the Study of Ancient Evidences of Disease*, 1923; C. Roberts and K. Manchester, *The Archaeology of Disease*, 2d ed., 1995; J. R. Rooney, Equid paleopathology,*J. Equine Vet. Sci.*, 17:8, 1997; J. Siegel, Animal paleopathology: Possibilities and problems, *J. Archaeol. Sci.*, 3:349-384, 1976.

Volcanology

About 80% of the Earth's crust, the outermost layer, is of igneous origin, closely related to volcanism. Recent advances in volcanology include improved understanding of eruptive phenomena; refinements in techniques of volcano monitoring, data processing, and interpretation; demonstrated capability to mitigate volcano hazards; and direct assessment of the impact of large explosive eruptions on global climate.

Eruption frequency. Data show that 1511 above-sea volcanoes have been active during the past 10,000 years, 539 of these during recorded history; and that on average 50-60 above-sea volcanoes are active in any given year (about half represent continuations of activity and half are new eruptions). However, the vast majority of eruptions occur unseen along the global oceanic ridge systems that crisscross the deep ocean floor.

Analogous to the seismologists' Richter magnitude scale, volcanologists have devised the Volcanic Explosivity Index (VEI), a semiquantitative, open-ended logarithmic scale for eruption size (magnitude) based primarily on the volume of material erupted, as evidenced in nearly 5000 documented Holocene eruptions. As with the frequency-magnitude relationship observed for earthquakes, the frequency of eruptions follows an exponential decrease with eruption size (see **illus.**). While there are many thousands of eruptions with VEI less than or equal to 2, only a small number of eruptions are ranked as having VEIs greater than or equal to 5. The largest known historical eruption, the 1815 eruption of Tambora in Indonesia, is rated VEI 7, while voluminous pre-Holocene caldera-forming eruptions (as in Yellowstone in Wyoming) would rank VEI 8 or higher.

The hazards associated with eruptions include ash fall, pyroclastic flows, debris avalanches, mudflows, lava flows, tsunami, and volcanic gases and associated acid rain. The larger and more energetic the eruption, the greater the severity of these hazards and the attendant risk to people and societal infrastructure. Experience shows, however, that the number of fatalities and the amount of economic loss caused by eruptions are primarily dependent on factors such as the volcano's proximity to population centers, intensity of agricultural development, availability and efficacy of contingency plans, and success of volcanic emergency management, and not on eruption size alone. For example, in Colombia in 1985 the small Nevado del Ruiz eruption (only 0.007 mi³ or 0.03 km³ of magma erupted; VEI 3) killed more than 25,000 people, while the 1912 eruption of Novarupta in Katmai, Alaska, the largest to date in this century (approximately 4 mi³ or 13 km³ of magma; VEI 6), occurred in a remote, unpopulated

Period	Caldera system	Nature of unrest	Current status/remarks
1976–1995	Yellowstone (Wyoming)	During 1923–1976, limited leveling data indicate a net uplift of about 28 in. (0.72 m); the caldera rose another 7 in. (0.18 m) during 1976–1984, but during 1985–1993 the caldera subsided by 6 in. (0.16 m).	Yellowstone is a seismically active region, and the current subsidence trend apparently began following a seismic swarm in October 1985; measurements made in 1995 show another 0.8 in. (20 mm) of subsidence since 1993.
1980–1989	Long Valley (California)	Intense seismic swarms occurred in 1980, 1983, and 1989; cumulative uplift of about 24 in. (0.6 m) has occurred since 1980.	Unrest continues, with intermittent less intense seismic swarms; as of early 1997, the rate of ground uplift was slackening.
1982–1984	Campi Flegrei (Italy)	Energetic earthquakes caused collapse of older structures; the central part of the caldera rose about 71 in. (1.8 m), following an earlier uplift of 67 in. (1.7 m) during the period 1969–1972.	The caldera is located in a heavily populated region near Naples; although there were no fatalities from earthquake damage, nearly 40,000 people were evacuated temporarily; the caldera has not shown any significant unrest since the mid-1980s.
1983–1985	Rabaul (Papua New Guinea)	During the height of unrest, many thousands of earthquakes struck the region; total ground uplift was about 39 in. (1 m).	Emergency-management officials issued a Stage 2 alert in October 1983 and were prepared to evacuate local populations; unrest ceased shortly thereafter, but Rabaul erupted 10 years later; since 1994, sporadic weak eruptive activity has continued.

Recent volcanic unrest at calderas documented by volcano monitoring

region and caused no known deaths and only minimal property damage.

Caldera-forming eruptions. The potentially most hazardous but lowest-frequency volcanic events are huge explosive eruptions associated with caldera collapse. Such eruptions can eject as much as 240 mi³ (1000 km³) of magma from large systems, such as occurred three times at Yellowstone during the past 2 million years. Fortunately, during recorded history the world has been spared cataclysmic eruptions on the scale of Yellowstone; the geologically youngest, comparably large caldera-forming eruption, with a VEI greater than 7, took place about 75,000 years ago and expelled approximately 480 mi³ (2000 km³) of magma, producing the Toba caldera in Sumatra, Indonesia. However, during the 1980s volcano-monitoring data demonstrated significant volcanic unrest at four, geographically separated large caldera systems (see **table**): Yellowstone; Long Valley in California; Campi Flegrei near Naples, Italy; and Rabaul in New Britain, Papua New Guinea. Seismic swarms and significant ground uplift, ranging from about 2 to 6 ft (0.6 to 1.8 m), are interpreted by volcanologists to indicate subsurface movement of magma or increased fluid pressure within these volcanic systems. The intense seismicity and high rate of uplift at the Rabaul caldera prompted officials in 1983 to issue a Stage 2 alert, which implied that an eruption could occur within a few months. Local inhabitants and officials were prepared to evacuate and conducted exercises, but the anticipated eruption did not materialize and the alert was lifted in 1984 after activity substantially declined. However, in 1994 Rabaul did erupt, producing a modest-size (not caldera-forming) eruption that devastated the area but resulted in fewer than a dozen fatalities—owing to a swift self-evacuation of the local populace, who had learned well the lessons from the previous volcanic crisis.

Since the mid-1970s, vertical ground movements have been monitored systematically at the Yellowstone caldera. Leveling surveys indicate that between 1923 and 1976 the central part of the caldera rose about 2.4 ft (0.72 m); continued movement through 1984 resulted in an additional uplift of 0.6 ft (0.18 m). The monitoring data then showed no movement during the 1984–1985 measurement interval; since 1985, the caldera has been subsiding, by about 0.5 ft (0.16 m) through 1993, thereby nearly canceling out the uplift since the mid-1970s. Such movements are not fully understood by volcanologists. They may reflect a cyclical increase and decrease of the pressure in Yellowstone's hydrothermal system on a decadal scale related to the sealing of fractures by mineral deposition and attendant buildup of pressure to produce an uplift, followed by the reopening of the sealed fractures or the formation of new fractures to relieve pressure, thus causing subsidence. Such new fractures could then gradually undergo sealing by mineralization, thus setting the stage for renewed uplift.

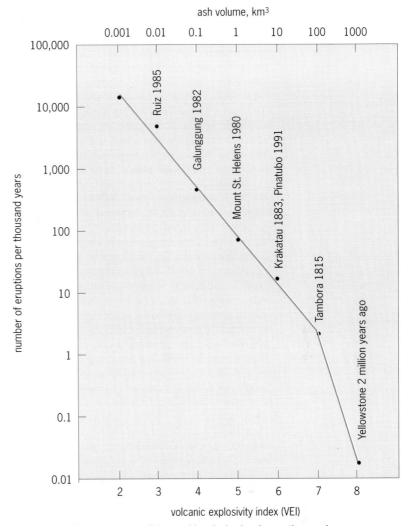

Magnitude and frequency of well-known historical volcanic eruptions and one prehistoric Yellowstone eruption for each VEI class. The line extending to VEI 8 is poorly constrained because of the low frequency of such events. *(After T. Simkin and L. Siebert, Volcanoes of the World: A Regional Directory, Gazetteer, and Chronology of Volcanism During the Last 10,000 Years, Geoscience Press, 1994)*

Climatic impact. Volcanic ash ejected high into the atmosphere by large caldera-forming eruptions can remain airborne many days, drifting with the prevailing winds before settling out to blanket areas hundreds of thousands of miles downwind. For example, the wind-blown ash from the eruption that formed the Long Valley caldera about 760,000 years ago has been found in traceable layers throughout the midwestern states nearly to the Mississippi River. Studies of recent explosive eruptions, such as at El Chichón in Mexico in 1982, and at Mount Pinatubo in the Philippines in 1991, demonstrate that volcanic gases injected into the stratosphere can form globe-circling volcanic clouds, composed of sulfuric acid droplets. These clouds form by the reaction of sulfur dioxide with water vapor, which can persist for as long as 5 years before becoming too dispersed to be detected.

A connection between volcanism and climate change is now well documented. The prevailing view among volcanologists and atmospheric scientists is that the size and duration of the stratospheric sulfur dioxide aerosol layer—not the much rapidly dispersed airborne ash particles—determine whether an explosive eruption might affect climate. This aerosol layer tends to cool the troposphere by reflecting solar radiation, and to warm the stratosphere by absorbing heat reradiated from the Earth. Mount St. Helens in Washington erupted in 1980 with minimal climatic impact, resulting in little or no change in average surface temperature for the Northern Hemisphere. The 1982 El Chichón and 1991 Pinatubo eruptions lowered temperature by 0.4–0.9°F (0.2–0.5°C), reflecting the significantly higher initial concentrations of sulfur in the magmas compared with that for Mount St. Helens. The Mount St. Helens and the El Chichón eruptions were about equal in size (VEI 5), whereas the Pinatubo eruption was considerably larger (VEI 6). The aerosol cloud produced by the 1815 eruption of Tambora Volcano, the largest in written history (VEI 7), resulted in the well-documented following ''year without summer,'' causing significant lowering (3.6–5.4°F or 2–3°C) of average summer temperatures in the eastern United States, Canada, and Europe. Data demonstrate that climatic effects induced by historical eruptions have been short lived, detectable for no more than a few years. Yet, extrapolating from the Tambora eruption, it is clear that much larger prehistoric caldera-forming eruptions, such as Long Valley, Yellowstone, and Toba, must have had proportionately greater, and probably longer-lived, impacts on global climate.

Monitoring and prediction. For active or potentially active volcanoes in densely populated regions, eruption prediction provides the only practical approach to reducing volcano risk, and volcano monitoring provides the only scientific basis for anticipating either an impending eruption or changes in ongoing eruptions. Although reliable long-term forecasts (months to years in advance) of eruptive activity still elude volcanologists, short-term eruption predictions (days or weeks in advance) are becoming possible at a few extremely well-monitored volcanoes. Even though the systematic measurements of volcanic seismicity and ground deformation are the most commonly used monitoring techniques, geochemical (for example, composition and discharge of volcanic fluids) and nonseismic geophysical (for example, gravity and electromagnetic fields) monitoring methods show great promise. Experience worldwide has shown that the optimum monitoring approach employs a combination of techniques rather than reliance on one.

Since the 1980 eruption of Mount St. Helens, monitoring techniques have been refined substantially, reflecting advances in electronics and data acquisition, processing, and interpretation. In the past decade, the increasing use of broadband seismometers in monitoring has greatly improved the characterization and interpretation of long-period earthquakes and volcanic tremor. The appearance of long-period signals has been shown to be a key diagnostic precursor to eruptive activity. Other recent advances include the development of personal-computer–based monitoring and data acquisition and analysis systems, real-time seismic amplitude measurement, and real-time measurement of the significant volcanic gases, such as sulfur dioxide and carbon dioxide. These portable and cost-effective systems serve as the core of mobile observatories, used with great success at Mount St. Helens, Redoubt Volcano in Alaska, Pinatubo, and elsewhere. For example, the rapid and effective deployment of a mobile observatory at Pinatubo provided the essential volcano-monitoring data, allowing volcanologists to forecast the escalation of activity culminating in the climactic eruption on June 15, 1991. These forecasts were used by emergency-management officials to carry out timely evacuation of areas around the volcano, saving many thousands of lives and billions of dollars of property.

Satellite-based geophysical and geochemical monitoring methods constitute another advancement in volcano monitoring, and in the 21st century these methods will greatly augment and perhaps supplant ground-based monitoring techniques at many volcanoes. Already proven satellite-based methods include the Total Ozone Mapping Spectrometer, which from space can measure eruptive sulfur dioxide emissions; and geodetic applications of the Global Positioning System (GPS), capable of the few-parts-per-million resolution needed for all-weather volcano monitoring. GPS monitoring of ground deformation is still largely conducted in a campaign mode, that is, periodic surveys of benchmarks, but ''continuous'' GPS monitoring can now provide daily determination of ground positions at selected volcanoes, and prototype ''real-time'' GPS systems are being tested at Augustine Volcano in Alaska and Long Valley caldera. Though still largely experimental, Interferometric Synthetic Aperture Radar (InSAR) is another promising space-geodesy technique, using repeat-pass radar images from Earth-orbiting satellites to map ground movements over the entire surface of a volcano. The InSAR technique has been used successfully at Mount Etna in Italy and is now being tested at Long Valley caldera and some other volcanoes.

Despite impressive recent advances in volcano monitoring and the successful eruption forecasts at Mount Pinatubo in 1991, it is still not possible to predict—routinely and reliably—large explosive eruptions at active and potentially active stratovolcanoes. The prediction of a gigantic eruption at a restless caldera system is even more formidable because the frequency of caldera-forming events is quite low (one per tens to hundreds of thousands of years) and their precursory patterns are uncertain. Within written history, humankind has never witnessed a huge caldera-forming eruption the size of those at Long Valley or Yellowstone in the geologic past. Yet, such infrequent but cataclysmic eruptions are certain to happen again. A major challenge for volcanologists is to recognize the onset and progression of volcanic unrest that might culminate in a large-volume caldera-forming eruption.

For background information *see* CALDERA; HOT SPOTS; VOLCANO; VOLCANOLOGY in the McGraw-Hill Encyclopedia of Science & Technology.

Robert I. Tilling

Bibliography. C. G. Newhall and R. S. Punongbayan (eds.), *Fire and Mud: Eruptions and Lahars of Mount Pinatubo, Philippines*, 1996; R. Scarpa and R. I. Tilling (eds.), *Monitoring and Mitigation of Volcano Hazards*, 1996; L. T. Simarski, *Volcanism and Climate Change*, Amer. Geophys. Union, Spec. Rep., 1992; T. Simkin and L. Siebert, *Volcanoes of the World: A Regional Directory, Gazetteer, and Chronology of Volcanism During the Last 10,000 Years*, 1994.

Water

Water is the subject of a great deal of modern research. Most properties of common liquid water cannot yet be calculated accurately even with the most sophisticated theories and the most powerful supercomputers available. The physical nature of water is truly unusual, relative to all other simple liquids. For example, water boils at an anomalously high temperature and freezes at a very low temperature, exhibits a density maximum (at 39°F or 4°C), and has an unusually high heat capacity. Its most common solid form, ice, floats on top of the liquid; there are more known forms of solid water (12) than of nearly any other substance. The underlying source of all of these unusual properties is the tendency for water to form four strong, highly directional hydrogen bonds with its neighboring molecules in condensed phases.

The cooperative behavior of these hydrogen bonds is being studied by a variety of modern experiments and new theoretical approaches. One of the most promising methods is to form solid and liquid water "one molecule at a time," that is, to generate water clusters, and to investigate the properties of these clusters at an extremely high level of detail, not accessible with bulk-phase studies. By examining sequentially larger clusters in this fashion, the measured properties, and perhaps even the general behavior of the clusters, might eventually be observed to converge to those of the bulk. Thus, a genuine "molecular-level" understanding of liquid water and ice would be achieved. Such studies of water clusters constitute a very active area of modern research.

The recently developed method of far-infrared-laser vibration-rotation-tunneling spectroscopy is a powerful probe of the structures, force fields, and dynamics of water clusters. In this technique, water clusters are produced and cooled to nearly absolute zero temperatures in supersonic molecular beams, and the bending and stretching vibrations of the hydrogen bonds between water molecules constituting the clusters are excited by the far-infrared laser. Precise measurements (to 1 part per million) are taken of the frequencies at which far-infrared-laser radiation is absorbed. These frequencies correspond to "natural" vibrational frequencies of the hydrogen bond network accompanied by an intricate fine structure from cluster rotation and hydrogen bond network rearrangement tunneling. From these data, and with help from advanced theoretical developments (for example, quantum Monte Carlo and other dynamic methods, electronic structure calculations, potential surface exploration methods, and permutation-inversion group theory), the properties and dynamics of these clusters can be characterized.

Structures. One of the essential features of water clusters extracted from analysis of the vibration-rotation-tunneling measurements is the cluster structure. The trimer-through-pentamer are cyclical water clusters, with each water molecule acting as both a single donor and acceptor of a hydrogen bond. The hexamer has a three-dimensional cage structure, although several other low-energy structures have been predicted (**Fig. 1**).

The water dimer (studied first by microwave spectroscopy methods) exhibits the archetypal features of a hydrogen bond. An oxygen-hydrogen (OH) bond in the donor molecule is directed at nearly 180° toward the oxygen on the acceptor, while both OH bonds on the acceptor point away from the hydrogen bond at nearly the "tetrahedral" angles found in ice and liquid water. The strength of the dimer hydrogen bond is about 5 kcal/mole (21 J/mole), although a precise determination of this important quantity has yet to be made. Polarization effects cause the dipole moment of an individual water molecule in the dimer to increase from 1.86 debyes for the isolated molecule to 2.06 D in the dimer, while in liquid water this polarization enhancement raises it by nearly 30% to 2.4 D. This polarization effect is a critical factor in the chemical behavior of liquid water.

The structures of large water clusters are determined by a competition between the tendencies to form the strongest possible (near-linear) bonds and the maximum number of hydrogen bonds (four per water molecule). For the trimer, tetramer, and pentamer, this competition results in cyclic structures, wherein each water molecule acts as both a single donor and acceptor of a hydrogen bond. The trimer and pentamer structure are chiral in that they have no symmetry. The pentamer ring structure seems to be rather special, as it has been identified as a building block of the hydrogen bond network in liquid water, in water aggregates surrounding certain proteins and nucleic acids, and in clathrate hydrates. This characteristic may result from the fact that the hydrogen bond angles are nearly optimal in the pentamer ring, creating an alternative to the normal (tetrahedral) way of building strain-free three-dimensional networks in solids and liquids.

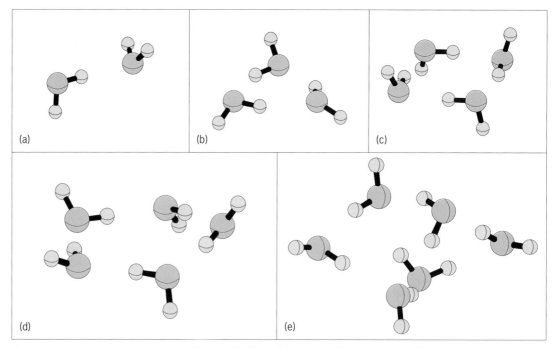

Fig. 1. Lowest-energy forms of the water (*a*) dimer, (*b*) trimer, (*c*) tetramer, (*d*) pentamer, and (*e*) hexamer, determined from vibration rotation tunneling spectroscopy.

The hexamer structure defines a transition point wherein three-dimensional networks become more stable than monocyclic rings, because they allow the formation of more hydrogen bonds. In the cage structure characterized by vibration-rotation-tunneling spectroscopy and theoretical calculations, the four equatorial monomers act as double donor–single acceptor, or vice versa, while the axial monomers remain single donor–single acceptors. Most theoretical calculations agree that this cage is indeed the most stable form of the hexamer. However, several other structures are predicted to lie very close in energy to this cage.

The water octamer has been partially characterized by a combination of laser vibrational spectroscopy experiments in the mid-infrared and electronic structure calculations, and some transitions observed by far-infrared vibration-rotation-tunneling spectroscopy have been ascribed to this cluster with-

out definitive assignment. The proposed structure is a very interesting one. Termed the molecular ice cube, it consists of two tetramer rings stacked on top of one another to form a distorted cube. There are two ways to do this, but the energies of the corresponding structures are too close together to distinguish between them. Future work on this system is likely to lend insights that will be of general importance for the understanding of water, because it is thought that clusters larger than the octamer will simply build on this cubic arrangement until they become quite large.

Dynamics. The internal dynamics characterized in the vibration-rotation-tunneling studies correspond to motions that occur in these clusters at essentially the zero of temperature, and it is important to understand these in detail before addressing the more complicated finite temperature dynamics. These motions occur by quantum-mechanical tunneling

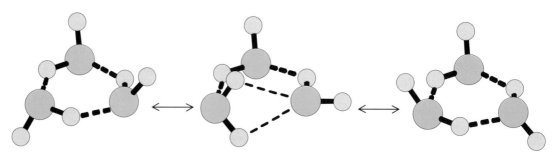

Fig. 2. Bifurcation tunneling pathway in the water trimer. The free hydrogen on one of the water molecules exchanges position with the hydrogen participating in the hydrogen bond. The transition state of this pathway involves two hydrogen bonds to a single acceptor, a bifurcated arrangement.

through potential energy barriers that constrain the water monomers to their minimum energy structures. These movements are an explicit consequence of the wave nature of matter, and cannot be reproduced in classical (Newton's law) computer simulations.

One such motion that is common to all clusters studied so far by vibration-rotation-tunneling spectroscopy is bifurcation tunneling (**Fig. 2**). It involves a hindered rotation of the donor molecule in a hydrogen bond such that its bonded and free hydrogens are interchanged. In the course of this motion, the donor actually forms two weak hydrogen bonds to a single acceptor, which is called a bifurcated hydrogen bond. The potential barrier impeding this motion has been calculated to be near 2 kcal/mole (8.4 J/mole)—much larger than the thermal energy available to liquid water at room temperature. Hence, this process is likely to be of general significance in aqueous dynamics. In fact, the vibrational motion corresponding to this bifurcation tunneling gives rise to the dominant feature in the infrared spectrum of liquid water, called the librational band.

A second motion common to all studied clusters larger than the dimer involves the "flipping" of a free hydrogen between equivalent positions in the structure, for example, from above to below the ring in the trimer. This is effected by rotation of a water molecule about its donor OH bond, which is impeded by a very small potential energy barrier (which could even be zero). This motion greatly affects the properties of the water clusters by inducing considerable vibrational averaging, but it is unlikely to be of much consequence in the bulk phases of water because these possess relatively few molecules with free hydrogens.

Force fields. Much effort is being applied to deduce a quantitative molecular force field which can better describe the condensed phase of water from these highly detailed studies of water clusters. By using numerical regression methods to fit the vibration-rotation-tunneling spectra to models of the cluster force fields, constructed from well-tested theories of intermolecular forces, the water pair potential can be extracted. This method has been applied for simpler hydrogen bonded systems (for example, HCl dimer), with the intent to determine the crucial three-body and four-body interactions that have previously eluded experimental study. These efforts will again require a close interaction between theory, experiment, and numerical methodology.

Concurrent with these efforts is the study of distortion in the strong chemical bonds of the water monomers constituting the clusters that is known to accompany hydrogen bond formation. This study is carried out in the mid-infrared region of the spectrum, wherein the water monomer stretch and bend vibrations lie, by a variety of spectroscopic techniques. Under development is a novel method for measuring such spectra called infrared cavity ringdown laser absorption spectroscopy.

For background information *see* CHEMICAL BONDING; INFRARED SPECTROSCOPY; LIQUID; MOLECULAR STRUCTURE AND SPECTRA; WATER in the McGraw-Hill Encyclopedia of Science & Technology.

Richard J. Saykally

Bibliography. J. D. Cruzan, M. R. Viant, and R. J. Saykally, Terahertz laser VRT spectroscopy of the water tetramer, *J. Phys. Chem. A*, 101:9022, 1997; J. K. Gregory et al., The water dipole moment in condensed phases: Insights through cluster studies, *Science*, 275:814, 1997; K. Liu et al., Terahertz laser VRT spectroscopy of the water pentamer: Structure and hydrogen bond network rearrangement dynamics, *J. Phys. Chem. A*, 101:9011, 1997; K. Liu, J. D. Cruzan, and R. J. Saykally, Water clusters, *Science*, 271:929, 1996; R. J. Saykally and G. A. Blake, Molecular interactions and hydrogen bond tunneling dynamics: Some new perspectives, *Science*, 259: 1570, 1993.

Water resource management

Water management involves the protection, development, and allocation of fresh-water resources for human and environmental uses. Water managers are challenged to provide adequate supplies for human and environmental health, food production, and industrial needs in the context of population growth, climate change, and intensified competition for the resource. Meeting this challenge will require, among other things, the utilization of economic and technical tools to increase the efficiency of water use.

Supply and demand. Current worldwide water usage is 35% of the 10,100 million acre-feet (12,500 km³) of annual global runoff accessible from reservoir storage, steady river flows, and ground water. Yet, even under conditions of apparent water abundance periodic shortages occur in the western United States, the Sahel (in Niger), and elsewhere. Water is not spread evenly across the globe and throughout the year is often not available when it is needed. Africa, much larger than South America, receives less than half as much annual runoff. South America receives most of its plentiful runoff between April and August. In Asia, 36% of global runoff is used to meet the demands of 60% of the world's population and of more than half the world's irrigated acreage (**Table 1**).

While demand for water varies regionally as a function of population, climate, and level of economic development, agriculture is the major user of water nearly everywhere. Of the 3,590 million acre-feet (4430 km³) of water withdrawn around the world in 1990, agriculture demanded 65%, while industry, municipalities, and reservoir losses accounted for 22, 7, and 6%, respectively. Water use in the agricultural sector is expected to increase, but will become less important relative to industrial and municipal demands.

Human needs. Meeting basic human water needs is critical for decreasing the prevalence of water-

TABLE 1. Global runoff by continent in 1995*

Region	Total annual runoff		Share of global runoff, %	Share of global population, %
	million acre-feet	km³		
Europe	2,630	3,240	8	13
Asia	11,800	14,550	36	60
Africa	3,500	4,320	11	13
North and Central America	5,030	6,200	15	8
South America	8,450	10,420	26	6
Australia and Oceania	1,600	1,970	5	<1
TOTAL	33,010	40,700	101†	~100†

* From S. Postel, *Dividing the Waters: Food Security, Ecosystem Health, and the New Politics of Scarcity*, Worldwatch Inst. Pap. 132, 1996.
† Does not add to 100 because of rounding.

related disease. One goal would be to provide 53 quarts (50 liters) per person per day, a suggested minimum for drinking water and food preparation, sanitation, and hygiene needs. While it is not known how many people receive this minimum, more than 1.1 billion people—many in the rapidly growing cities of the developing world—lack access to safe drinking water. The provision of universal access is made difficult by the lack of investment in necessary technology, infrastructure, and institutions, and often not by the lack of water. Thus, it is possible to compare two regions with similar climates but different economic characteristics and find disparate levels of access to water supply.

Environmental needs. Meeting environmental water needs is critical for preserving the integrity of freshwater ecosystems and the ability of the environment to support future human activities. Although difficult to ascertain, minimum stream flows and sustainable ground-water yields need to be determined. This is necessary to circumvent the ecological and economic consequences of the overuse of water resources. The collapse of fisheries in the Aral Sea and the permanent loss of ground-water storage capacity in the United States plains aquifer system suggest how grave these consequences can be. In addition, a number of water-pollution problems require attention, including acid deposition—a growing problem in China—and high levels of nitrates, metals, industrial organic pollutants, and salinity. The adverse ecological effects of these pollutants are often exacerbated by overfishing, introduction of nonnative aquatic species, dam construction, and destruction of wetlands.

Agricultural needs. The engine of global food production is kept in operation by a steady input of water. Rough estimates indicate that water use in agriculture must increase by 35% to meet the needs of the world's population in 2025. This will be an arduous task in regions where water supply is already insufficient to meet demands, and where

sources, such as the ground-water basins in the United States, China, and India, have begun to show signs of distress. Related to water insufficiency is the decreasing availability of productive land which, combined with less support for irrigation projects from governments and international agencies, has slowed the expansion of irrigated acreage to 1% per year. Thus, future food needs will likely be met by increasing yields on land currently under cultivation, in part by raising irrigation efficiencies beyond the current global 37%.

Unpredictable factors. Complicating water management even more are the unforeseen changes in population, climate, and competition. Population growth, predicted to increase from 5,850 million in 1995 to a minimum of 10,000 million in 2050, will have important consequences for the availability and use of water. Over 90% of this growth will occur in developing regions, where access to clean water and sanitation is already inadequate. Variation in regional precipitation patterns and soil moisture, stemming from temperature changes associated with climate change, will also affect both supply and demand. Competition over water resources within and between nations will increase as supplies are strained. The potential for conflict is particularly high where there is unequal access to water resources, where a downstream user has more power than an upstream user but relies heavily on imported supplies (**Table 2**), where the current supply is not enough to meet total demand, and where no treaty exists to allocate water among users. Rivers such as the Nile, Jordan, Ganges-Brahmaputra, and Tigris-Euphrates have been cited as potential battlegrounds in "water wars."

TABLE 2. Dependence on imported surface water in selected countries*

Country	Percentage of flow originating outside border
Turkmenistan	98
Egypt	97
Hungary	95
Mauritania	95
Botswana	94
Bulgaria	91
Uzbekistan	91
Netherlands	89
Gambia	86
Cambodia	82
Syria	79
Sudan	77
Niger	68
Iraq	66
Bangladesh	42
Thailand	39
Jordan	36
Senegal	34
Israel†	21

* From S. Postel, *Dividing the Waters: Food Security, Ecosystem Health, and the New Politics of Scarcity*, Worldwatch Inst. Pap. 132, 1996.
† Includes flow originating outside current borders; a significant additional share of Israel's fresh water originates from occupied, disputed territories.

Management tools. Constructing dams and diversion works, draining and filling wetlands and lakes, and channelizing rivers have been important for capturing and putting runoff to use. A boom after World War II was followed by a decline in construction of water projects during the 1980s because of environmentalist and local opposition, high project costs, and the fact that only marginal sites remained undeveloped. Some projects will continue to be necessary to meet multiple objectives of flood control, water supply, and irrigation. Alternatively, it might be possible to satisfy these needs with smaller-scale, community-managed projects, such as the irrigation systems that have been operating for more than 500 years near Valencia, Spain.

Desalination. Global desalination capacity has steadily increased since the 1970s and stands at more than 14,000 acre-feet (17 million cubic meters) per day. Most of this capacity is concentrated in Saudi Arabia, the United Arab Emirates, the United States, and other nations that can afford the high energy costs. Indeed, it is the cost of energy that will continue to limit the widespread applicability of desalination.

Efficiency. The best tools available to water managers are those that allow a given supply to be stretched further, such as conservation and recycling. In agriculture, where potential water savings are greatest, efficiency can be improved by detecting and fixing leaks in distribution systems, leveling fields for more even application of water, lining canals to prevent seepage, recapturing runoff for reuse, and controlling the timing and amount of water applied to fields. Designing projects so that farmers can have water when they want it, rather than on a rigid time schedule, is useful for increasing both irrigation efficiency and crop yields. Efficiency can be improved further by adopting more expensive irrigation technologies, such as subsurface "drip" systems which deliver water to the roots of crops and are 40–60% more efficient than traditional systems.

In urban areas, water can also be saved by fixing leaks in distribution systems. In cities where there are multiple-tap connections, the installation of low-flow toilets and horizontal-axis washing machines in residences, encouraged by incentives from water providers or required by efficiency standards, can lead to impressive water savings. Municipal wastewater can be reclaimed, that is, treated to an adequate level of quality and applied to another use, usually agriculture. Israel reclaims 65% of its municipal wastewater for use in agriculture, thereby providing 30% of all water used in its agriculture.

Economics. Pervasive subsidization of water use makes it difficult to implement efficiency measures. While subsidization of the cost of water is appropriate for situations where equitable access for the poor is an issue, economic pricing could help achieve efficiency in agricultural and urban sectors around the world. This would involve a determination of the true economic cost of supplying the water, rather than what is needed to merely cover the costs of operation, and charging the customer accordingly, often at different rates for different volumes. Economic pricing of water in a California irrigation district, based on a tiered rate structure, realized a 19% water savings in less than 5 years.

International cooperation. Information on international, national, and regional water availability and demand as well as environmental conditions should be shared freely in the international water management arena to promote cooperative problem solving. International agreements and accords in international river basins, as well as transboundary water management institutions, will be critical in preventing water-based conflict. International laws, such as those that define a right to water for basic human and ecosystem needs, may help prioritize water management activities.

For background information *see* IRRIGATION (AGRICULTURE); RESERVOIR; WATER CONSERVATION; WATER POLLUTION; WATER TREATMENT in the McGraw-Hill Encyclopedia of Science & Technology.   Anna Steding

Bibliography. P. H. Gleick (ed.), *Water in Crisis: A Guide to the World's Freshwater Resources*, 1993; L. W. Mays, *Handbook of Water Resources*, 1996; World Resources Institute, *World Resources, 1997–1998*, 1997.

Weather forecasting and prediction

Forecasts are commonly directed at severe weather events that pose a threat to life and property as well as at synoptic weather that affects everyday planning for the civilian population, military interests, and commercial interests.

Severe weather forecasts. Severe weather in the form of high-wind events, dangerous ice and snow storms, and heavy precipitation must be forecast in time for the public to prepare. The lead time for a warning depends on the time scale of the event being forecast, which is very short for tornadoes and longer for large-scale phenomena. In the case of a tornado, for example, an accurate warning an hour or less in advance constitutes a successful forecast, but that lead time would be completely inadequate for a hurricane, since it takes 24–36 h to prepare a much larger geographic area for the extremely high winds, rain, and possible storm surge.

Synoptic weather forecasts. These give the general distribution of high- and low-pressure systems, fronts, rainfall, and other weather features. Everyday planning, such as deciding to pack heavy coats for the family vacation across the country or to plant crops this week or wait until next week, requires that these daily forecasts extend from 1 day out to at least 1 week. Behind all types of weather forecasts presented to the public by radio, television, newspapers, and the Internet are a large number of activities involving collecting weather-related observations taken worldwide, using these observations to update the current state of the atmosphere (data assimilation), forecasting the future state of the atmosphere with sophisticated computer models and powerful supercomputers (numerical weather prediction), generating specific maps and other products that depict the forecast in ways that users can employ conveniently and efficiently, and disseminating these products efficiently and reliably. All these activities must be carried out operationally on a tight, regular schedule and with little, if any, disruption or loss of services for end users.

Forecast model development. With ever-increasing computer power, operational numerical forecast models have steadily improved in horizontal and vertical resolution and in the sophistication of the mathematical treatment of the physical processes included. Most large operational numerical weather prediction (NWP) centers have global forecast models with 50–100 km (31–62 mi) horizontal resolution and 30–50 vertical levels extending into the stratosphere. Recent improvements in the model physics have been in the treatment of ground-surface physical phenomena and the prediction of clouds. Surface physics now commonly includes multilevel soil models that predict soil wetness, evaporation from the soil and vegetation, and geographically varying surface drag. Many models forecast the cloud (liquid and ice) water content and include the radiative effects of the condensed water. There is increasing realization that interaction of surface winds from storm systems (for example, hurricanes and midlatitude cyclones) with the ocean can induce significant changes in the sea-surface temperature that can last for several weeks and feed back into atmospheric processes; these effects are included in forecasts out to 2 weeks.

Data assimilation. Major progress has occurred in developing data assimilation techniques for analysis of observations to produce initial conditions for numerical weather prediction models. As a result, very large gains in analysis and forecast accuracy have been made. Many operational NWP centers, for example, the National Centers for Environmental Prediction (NCEP) and the European Centre for Medium-Range Weather Forecasts, now use a three-dimensional (that is, x, y, and z) variational (3D-VAR) assimilation. Data assimilation is the process of combining observations irregularly spaced in space and time with information forecast forward in time with a weather forecast model to produce the best estimate of the state of the atmosphere (such as temperature, winds, humidity, and pressure) at any given time. An extension of 3D-VAR is four dimensional variational (4D-VAR) assimilation which includes the time history (for example, the past 6–24 h) of the fit to the model and the observations. This technique is much more expensive since the forecast model must be run forward and backward in time to arrive at the optimum minimization.

Measurements from more observational platforms are being assimilated, including radial velocities from the National Weather Service's WSR-88D Doppler radar, wind profilers, automated surface stations

(ASOS), and high-density wind data derived from geostationary satellites. Temperature and moisture information from polar-orbiting satellites is obtained as radiation emitted at certain wavelengths (that is, channel radiances), instead of as soundings that are retrieved from the radiances and a thermodynamic profile from a short-term model forecast. Plans for using advanced satellite instruments that measure radiation from more frequency bands affected by atmospheric temperature and moisture and from the Earth's land, ocean, ice or snow surface are being implemented. This process involves developing increasingly accurate and efficient techniques for solving the radiative transfer equation and specifying the surface emissivity of microwave radiation. Improvements in models and data assimilation have contributed immensely to increasing the skill of forecasts. In 1997, for example, forecasts at 5 days are as skillful as 3-day forecasts in 1987.

Ensemble forecasting. The pioneering work of E. Lorenz has demonstrated that the atmosphere is a chaotic system in the sense that small errors in initial conditions lead to larger forecast errors. For this reason, weather cannot be predicted beyond about 2 weeks, even with perfect forecast models. One successful approach to forecasting the chaotic atmosphere has been to construct an ensemble of model initial conditions and to generate forecasts from them that diverge from each other over time. The differences (spread) of ensemble forecast members should increase with forecast time, thereby indicating the chaotic nature of the modeling system, and represent the uncertainties of a particular forecast. Currently, the European Centre for Medium-Range Weather Forecasts runs a 50-member ensemble with initial perturbations generated from singular vectors, which represent the fastest-growing modes based on a linearized version of the forecast model. The National Centers for Environmental Protection run a 17-member ensemble with perturbations generated by the "breeding" method, which considers the nonlinear growth produced by the complete forecast model including physics. The techniques of both Centers select the perturbations that are most responsible for divergence among forecasts instead of relying on random initial differences that are not as effective in producing divergence among ensemble members. The mean of all ensemble members is generally a better forecast than each individual member, but the major advantage of ensemble forecasting is to provide measures of confidence for forecast events as well as fully quantitative probabilistic information to users. A forecast based on a 50-member ensemble not only is more accurate than a 17-member ensemble but also gives increased probabilistic information. However, to achieve this, more time and computer power is needed. Probabilistic forecasts reflect the degree of uncertainty in the evolution of the real atmosphere and, especially for difficult-to-forecast quantities such as precipitation, they may extend the useful range of forecasts by at least 1 day.

Hurricanes. Large improvements in operational forecasts of hurricane tracks employing numerical prediction over most of the world's ocean basins have occurred since the mid-1990s. At that time the NOAA Geophysical Fluid Dynamics Laboratory (GFDL) hurricane forecast system was introduced at the National Centers for Environmental Protection and at the Navy's Fleet Numerical Meteorology and Oceanography Center. The forecast model is a nested-grid (set of grids, one within the other, that have increasing resolution) system model formulated in latitude, longitude, and sigma coordinates with 18 vertical layers. The three horizontal grids have resolutions of 1, ⅓, and ⅙ degree, and the two innermost grids move with the hurricane. The initial condition for the hurricane model is taken from a global model that has much coarser resolution than the hurricane model. Thus, the representation of the hurricane in the global model is very poor. A higher-resolution vortex is produced by a version of the hurricane model; this vortex is axisymmetric (a function of radial distance from the hurricane center and height) but is basically compatible with the three-dimensional hurricane model in the sense that the wind, temperature, and humidity fields are generated by the same physics (that is, the representation of clouds, radiation, and surface fluxes in the forecast model). Therefore replacement with a vortex more consistent with the GFDL forecast model physics produces a more realistic initial condition and improved forecasts. Track predictions from the GFDL model are consistently superior to those from simplified dynamical models, statistical models, and previous operational models. In 1997, track forecasts for 3 days were as skillful as track forecasts for 2 days in 1987.

Most forecast quantities for hurricane intensity (for example, maximum wind) have been developed from statistical regression on predictors such as underlying sea-surface temperature, previous intensity, and storm latitudinal position. Intensity forecasts from the GFDL system are competitive in skill with those from statistical models, particularly when the short-term bias (average difference between forecast and observed intensity at 12 h) is removed. Improved intensity forecasts are a major focus for current research and development activities.

Tornadoes. Major progress has been achieved recently on forecasting the incidence of tornadoes by statistical regression using point soundings of forecast model output. Forecasts out to 24 h are useful for determining watch and warning areas. Both the National Centers for Environmental Protection Eta model and the Rapid Update Cycle are used for severe weather prediction. In combination with improved models, the WSR-88D Doppler radar and satellite imagery have resulted in increasing the lead time for significant weather events over the United States. Forecast of high winds, hail size, and other critical weather parameters are not currently feasible from operational numerical weather prediction models. Considerable progress, however, has been made in simulating convective storm structure and tornado vortices with very high resolution research models that could become operationally feasible to run on future computers. Limited-area models covering large fractions of North America and adjacent oceanic areas with 10 km (6 mi) resolution should be operational by the year 2000.

Quantitative precipitation forecasting. In the 1990s, progress has been made in the accuracy of quantitative precipitation forecasts. It has come from increased resolution of forecast models, greater sophistication of model physics, improvements to analysis systems that produce more accurate initial conditions, and additional observations from geostationary satellites, Doppler radar, and commercial aircraft. Because of increased computer power available at operational numerical weather prediction centers, and the maturation of techniques for generating ensembles, probabilistic quantitative precipitation forecasts can now be produced directly from ensemble model output that has been calibrated to deliver reliable probabilities (that is, such that the forecast probability of a particular precipitation amount matches the observed probability over a sufficiently large sample). Integration of probabilistic quantitative precipitation forecastings with hydrological forecast models for flood prediction is a major challenge that appears feasible by the year 2000. Since the 1970s, day-5 precipitation forecasts have more than doubled in accuracy, and ensemble probabilistic quantitative precipitation forecasts are able to signal major precipitation events as much as 7 or 8 days in advance.

For background information *see* ATMOSPHERIC WAVES, UPPER SYNOPTIC; DOPPLER RADAR; DYNAMIC METEOROLOGY; METEOROLOGY; WEATHER FORECASTING AND PREDICTION; WEATHER OBSERVATIONS in the McGraw-Hill Encyclopedia of Science & Technology.   Stephen Lord

Bibliography. E. Kalnay, Numerical weather prediction, *Comp. Phys.*, 9:488–495, 1995; E. N. Lorenz, Deterministic non-periodic flow, *J. Atmos. Sci.*, 20:130–141, 1963; E. N. Lorenz, The predictability of a flow which possesses many scales of motion, *Tellus*, 21:289–307, 1969; E. N. Lorenz, A study of the predictability of a 28-variable atmospheric model, *Tellus*, 17:321–333, 1965.

Web resources

In the past few decades, society has moved from information poverty to information abundance. Increasingly, documents become available on-line through the World Wide Web, Internet document repositories, digital libraries, and multimedia servers. A user with a Web browser and an Internet connection can now browse newspapers from around the world, collections of museums and art galleries, libraries of research articles, commercial content from companies in all industries, and countless pages of content self-published by authors of every type.

The abundance of information presents new challenges: finding information with desired content, identifying a desirable subset of information within the set of information on a given topic, and identifying new or current information from within the set of information on a given topic.

To address these challenges, researchers have developed several techniques for indexing, searching, recommending, and monitoring Internet content. These techniques can be classified by several key attributes. Techniques may gather information about the content and audience of a document through automatic classification, specification by the author, specification by an editor, feedback from readers, or a combination of these. Content classification systems may employ defined categories or hierarchies, or dynamic classification using keywords. Audience classification systems may employ defined audience categories, reader demographics, or individualized personalization. Reader interest may be specified for a particular request or as an ongoing profile, and the specification may be explicit or implicit. Identification of new content can be achieved by using preferences for newer material, explicit notification when a document is updated, or record-keeping of documents that have already been seen by the reader.

Explicit category hierarchies. Explicit classification requires the editor of a directory to specify a set of categories into which documents must be arranged. This technique has been used historically in a wide range of applications, such as arranging books in libraries or bookstores, subject-based telephone directories, and the classified advertising sections of newspapers. Several attributes distinguish on-line directories from other directories and from other online content-selection technologies:

1. A hierarchy of categories is specified for documents. A Web page, for example, may be listed under the category "Business and Industry/Companies/Internet/Directories." Depending on the number of entries in a category, levels may be collapsed together (for example, "Companies" may be displayed directly at the top level).

2. A Web page may appear in multiple listings within the hierarchy. Thus, an Internet directory specializing in automobiles may be listed under "Automobile/Directories" and "Internet/Directories."

3. An entire category may appear at multiple locations in the hierarchy. For example, the "Automobile/Directories" category may also be found by searching for "Directories/Consumer Products/Automobiles."

4. Listings are arranged into global, regional, and local directories, providing an additional dimension of categorization.

Classification is accomplished in two ways. Editors identify pages of interest and classify them. Page authors have learned to enter their pages, either directly or through a publicity service, to help potential readers find them. Users sometimes submit favor-ite page listings themselves, though editors are generally assigned to verify unsolicited listings.

Users attempting to find content of interest can browse the category listings directly or search the database either in its entirety or within a category.

Other services provide editor-selected or author-classified content. Like its noncomputerized counterparts, explicit classification is amenable to a wide range of editorial discretion. Many of the most popular sites on the Web are volunteer-maintained sites called launching pads that contain topical links assembled by the editor.

Automatic subject classification. Automatic classification uses the content and structure of a document to generate a searchable index of documents. On the Internet, these indexing services have three main components: document finding, index construction, and query processing.

Document finding. Document finding involves locating new and changed documents throughout the Internet. While some services index only documents that are explicitly selected or entered, most of the major indexing services attempt to find all known pages. The primary technique used is the crawler, which scans through known documents seeking references to other documents (that is, hypertext links). Crawlers may operate on several computers in parallel, with a coordinating database that ensures that documents are revisited on a regular schedule but not revisited so frequently as to waste network or processing resources. One challenge for document finding is the increasing prevalence of pages with content that is generated on demand. These pages are difficult to crawl to and through, since the information in them may change with each visit.

Index construction. Index construction involves scanning documents and storing sufficient information to determine whether and how well a document matches a user's query. The basic operation in index construction is to store the frequency with which nontrivial words appear in the text of a document. For example, this article would have a very high frequency for the word "document" and a low frequency for the word "thermodynamics." As part of the indexing process, words are commonly reduced to stem form. Words appearing in titles, headings, and keyword lists may be assigned higher frequency to reflect the importance of their use. More advanced index construction techniques augment the basic mechanism to include identification of structural features, such as Web-page addresses; identification of word adjacency, occurrences of common phrases, and other proximity conditions; and identification of proper nouns and, in particular, people's names.

Query processing. Query processing takes a user query and identifies both a set of documents that satisfy the query and a rank ordering of the documents that best match that query. While most search engines support advanced queries with logical operators as well as structural specifiers (for example, it is often possible to search for a document that has "plague" in a heading without the word "bubonic"), almost all user queries involve a simple list of words or phrases.

Identifying the document set for simple queries is easy. The difficult task is ranking them. Each indexing service has its own algorithm for assigning weights to the resulting documents, but some commonly used features include higher weights for documents that contain more of the specified search terms; for documents that contain more occurrences of the search terms, either in absolute terms or as a percentage of total document length; for search terms that appear in few documents; for documents in which search terms appear in titles, headings, and keyword lists; for documents to which many other documents refer (that is, authoritative documents); and for documents that refer to many authoritative documents (that is, launching pads).

Some indexing services retain a copy of each document that they have indexed, allowing them to perform more complicated searches, to detect changes in documents, and to display document contents even when the document itself is not available.

Collaborative filtering. One shortcoming of categorization and indexing systems is that they focus on a topic without much attention to quality or more narrow measures of interest. Collaborative filtering is the set of technologies that use readers' ratings of documents or items to identify specific ones that would be of interest to each reader. Expert recommendations such as movie reviews are a crude form of collaborative filtering. Voting-based recommendations are a more democratic, but still nonpersonalized, approach. Personal collaborative filtering involves identifying patterns of agreement among readers to find the opinions that are most likely to match those of the target reader.

For example, a collaborative filtering system that recommends jokes distributed on the Internet would examine reader ratings of those jokes to find readers who have similar preferences. The system could then recommend jokes for a reader by identifying the jokes that other readers with similar tastes preferred, or it could annotate each joke with a prediction that estimates the interest for that reader by combining the ratings of the readers with whom he or she agrees.

User ratings may be either explicit indications of preference or implicit measures that the system observes and interprets. Useful implicit measures include time spent reading a document; choosing to save, print, or forward a document; and economic decisions such as purchasing documents or items.

Subscription and push technology. Each of the three techniques discussed can be enhanced to provide a preference for new content, but none is specifically concerned with providing desired new content to readers from pages or sources that are regularly updated. Readers who have identified a source of valuable content that changes regularly will often benefit from a subscription or push model, rather than a browsing-based Web model.

Subscription services include general e-mail lists, notification lists where regular readers of a page can sign up to receive e-mail when the page has been updated, and recurring searches that inform the user when a new item meets the search criteria. Two good examples of the latter are reference library mailings that inform patrons of new journal articles of books, and a commercial book-watching service that can be used to notify readers when new books are available by a specific author or about a specific subject.

More recently, push technology has expanded beyond the e-mail model to provide integrated content channels that deliver news, entertainment, or other information as it is available or on a regular schedule. More advanced systems integrate channels of pushed content into Web browsers.

For pushing content to be efficient, it is necessary to identify the desired content and to avoid an excessively centralized architecture. Push technology meets these needs by providing varying levels of customization, including channel subscriptions, keyword selection, and personalization through collaborative filtering; and by distributing channels to regional redelivery centers.

For background information *see* LITERATURE OF SCIENCE AND TECHNOLOGY; MULTIMEDIA TECHNOLOGY in the McGraw-Hill Encyclopedia of Science & Technology.   Joseph A. Konstan

Bibliography. J. A. Konstan et al., GroupLens: Applying collaborative filtering to Usenet news, *Commun. ACM*, 40(3):77–87, March 1997; T. A. Letsche and M. W. Berry, Large-scale information retrieval with latent semantic indexing, *Inform. Sci.*, 100(1–4):105–137, August 1997; G. R. Notess, Searching the World Wide Web: Lycos, Webcrawler, and more, *Online*, vol. 19, no. 4, July–August 1995; R. Scoville, Find it on the Net, *PC World*, 14(1):124–130, January 1996.

Weightlessness

Crewed space flight, especially aboard spacecraft in low Earth orbit, is now commonplace. The space shuttle, able to carry the *Spacelab* module in its payload bay, provides an orbiting scientific laboratory in which scientists and astronauts can perform experiments in a low-acceleration (or nearly weightless) environment. Doing science in space is important for two reasons. First, as more people work and live in a weightless environment, practical knowledge of how systems, materials, and even the human body perform in and respond to extended exposure to low gravity is critical to continued space exploration. Thus, many applied-science experiments are performed aboard the shuttle to gain insight into the effects of long-term weightlessness. Second, the Earth's gravity is a dominant and pervasive force in ground-based laboratories and, in the case of experiments in fluids, can mask more subtle forces. In the relative absence of thermal and buoyant convection

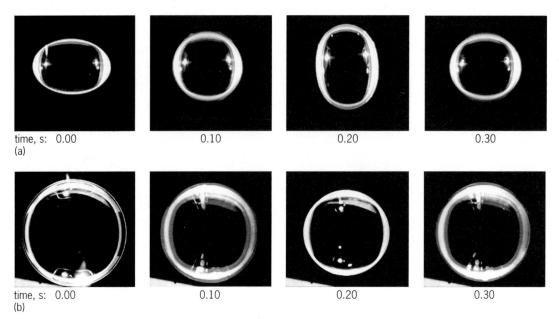

time, s: 0.00   0.10   0.20   0.30
(a)

time, s: 0.00   0.10   0.20   0.30
(b)

Fig. 1. Simultaneous views of a single cycle of a free oscillation of a pure water drop aboard the space shuttle *Columbia*. (*a*) Side views. (*b*) Top views. *(NASA)*

and their effects in orbit, surface tension becomes the dominant fluid force, and ideal experiments can be performed to provide absolute and rigorous tests of fluid-dynamic theories, which would be impossible on the ground. In one such experiment, liquid drops nearly 2.5 cm (1 in.) in diameter were allowed to float aboard the space shuttle, where they were deformed by an acoustic standing wave and then released to execute free oscillations about a perfect spherical equilibrium.

Weightless environment. *STS 73* (October 20–November 5, 1995) was the seventeenth flight of the space shuttle *Columbia*. The primary payload was the second United States Microgravity Laboratory, a *Spacelab* module housing a series of fluids- and materials-science experiments designed to take advantage of the small residual acceleration, approximately 10^{-6} g (the acceleration of gravity on Earth) or microgravity, afforded by low Earth orbit.

The terms microgravity and weightlessness refer to the net inertial force on the cargo (astronauts and payload) while the shuttle orbits at approximately 300 km (150 nautical miles) above the Earth's surface and at a velocity of 7.7 km/s (17,000 mi/h). Since the shuttle is not very far away from the Earth, it feels a strong gravitational pull, which is balanced by manipulating its high-velocity trajectory into a circle of nearly constant radius. The primary force in the lateral direction comes from the very small drag (approximately 10^{-6} g) due to the thin atmosphere the shuttle travels through. Thus the net force on the shuttle (and hence the inertial force on its cargo) is roughly six orders of magnitude smaller than the terrestrial pull of the Earth, and massive bodies experience effective weightlessness.

Importance of liquid drops. Surface tension is the name given to the everyday observation that liquids, in general, hold together and require external force or energy to pull apart. At the surface of a liquid, the outermost layer of molecules experiences an unbalanced force, preferentially pulling the molecule toward the bulk of the liquid. A familiar example of the effect of this relatively weak surface tension is the beading of water on a waxed surface.

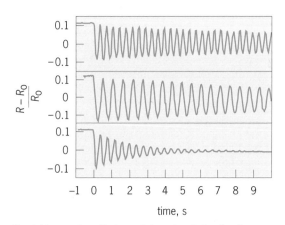

Fig. 2. Decay of oscillations of the azimuthal radius for 2.5-cm-diameter (1-in.) aqueous drops with an initial deformation of approximately 20%. The vertical scale gives the departure of radius, R, from its equilibrium value, R_0, as a fraction of equilibrium value. (Top) Pure water. (Middle) Water with 1.4×10^{-4} g/ml Triton-X-100 dissolved in the bulk. (Bottom) Water with 1.0×10^{-5} g/ml bovine serum albumin dissolved in the bulk. *(After R. G. Holt et al., Surface-controlled drop oscillations in space, J. Acous. Soc. Amer., 102:3802–3805, 1997)*

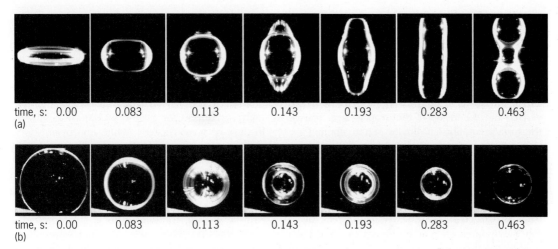

| time, s: | 0.00 | 0.083 | 0.113 | 0.143 | 0.193 | 0.283 | 0.463 |

(a)

| time, s: | 0.00 | 0.083 | 0.113 | 0.143 | 0.193 | 0.283 | 0.463 |

(b)

Fig. 3. Simultaneous views of a half-cycle of a free oscillation of a water drop in space with 1.4 × 10⁻⁴ g/ml of the nonionic surfactant Triton-X-100 dissolved in the bulk. (*a*) Side views. (*b*) Top views. (*NASA*)

On Earth, the force of gravity causes liquids to flow unless they are contained. But aboard the shuttle, the net inertial force is so small that surface tension is the strongest force, and a blob of liquid will form a sphere in order to pull itself into the most compact shape with a minimal surface.

The perfectly spherical liquid drop has long been an important idealization in physics. Studied not only for its intrinsic interest (rain, for example), the drop has served as a paradigm system for the Earth itself on the terrestrial scale, for the states and stability of atomic nucleii on the microscale, and for modeling stellar masses on the cosmic scale. The experimental conditions aboard the shuttle allow the physical realization of this ideal free surface, whose dynamics have been theoretically and mathematically modeled for over a century. The low-amplitude, surface-tension-driven oscillations of a pure liquid drop about a spherical equilibrium are so well understood, in fact, that any deviations from the theoretical predictions can be exploited to infer properties of multicomponent nonequilibrium solutions.

Thus it is useful to dissolve very small amounts of molecular species, called surfactants, which preferentially reside on the liquid-air interface, into an otherwise pure liquid drop. Not only will these surfactants lower the static surface tension (by positioning themselves between the host liquid molecules and weakening the intermolecular bonds), but they will have profound effects on the oscillatory motion of the drop. These effects are made manifest in the easily observable frequency and damping of small oscillations, and the deviations from the theoretical values for pure liquids can be related to the fundamental properties of the surfactant molecules. But these ideal experiments, can be performed only on the large (about 2.5-cm or 1-in. diameter) perfectly spherical drops that can be achieved aboard the shuttle.

Drop oscillations in space. In the experiments aboard the space shuttle, free oscillations of a water drop 2.5 cm (1.0 in.) in diameter were observed (**Fig. 1**). The drop equilibrium shape was spherical to within less than 1%, and the drop executed nearly perfect, low-amplitude oscillations. A slow 0.5-Hz rotation rate was imposed on the drop to gyrostabilize the symmetry axis. The measured frequency of 2.8 Hz and damping of 0.05 s⁻¹ are identical to the theoretical results for pure water within experimental error.

Oscillation decay curves were measured for three different types of 2.5-cm-diameter (1-in.) drops. The drops were acoustically squeezed, then released from the same initial deformation. One type of drop (**Fig. 2*a***) consisted of pure water, which has a surface tension of 72 millinewtons per meter. A second type of drop (Fig. 2*b*) consisted of water with 1.4 × 10⁻⁴ g/ml of the nonionic surfactant Triton-X-100 dissolved in the bulk, yielding an equilibrium surface tension of 31 mN/m. The third type of drop consisted of water containing 1.0 × 10⁻⁵ g/ml of bovine serum albumin, which is also a surfactant, dissolved in the bulk, yielding an equilibrium surface tension of 54 mN/m. The amounts of both of the surfactants were too small to affect the bulk properties of the drops in which they were dissolved, yet both the frequency and the damping of the quadrupole oscillations of these drops were very different from those of the pure water drops.

These phenomena can be explained by understanding how surfactants behave. First, since surfactants lower the surface tension, the force restoring the drops to spherical after the squeezing is released is weaker than that of pure water, and hence the restoring oscillations are slower than that of water. The Triton-bearing drop is much slower because it lowers the surface tension more. Second, during a quarter cycle of the oscillation, the drop surface stretches and creates fresh surface on parts of the drop. Since this will cause an uneven distribution of surfactant molecules on the surface, there will be a tendency for the surface to flow opposite the stretching. This increases the damping and causes the oscillations of surfactant-bearing drops (Fig. 2b, c) to die out more quickly than those of pure water (Fig. 2a). This excess damping will be less if the surfactant molecule can move rapidly between the surface and the inside of the drop to help restore the surface equilibrium. Bovine serum albumin is a large protein molecule which actually changes shape when it gets to the surface, and thus cannot move very rapidly either along the surface or between the bulk and the surface. The result is a dramatic damping of the oscillations (Fig. 2c). This effect has been recognized for centuries. Ancient Greek divers routinely poured olive oil on the surface of the sea in order to damp the surface waves and enable them to see into the water more easily.

When the initial deformation is very large, the oscillations become very nonlinear (**Fig. 3**). Such highly nonlinear oscillations are much more difficult to describe mathematically even for a pure liquid; nevertheless, they will provide a stringent test for theoretical models which incorporate both the fluid dynamics of a single-component liquid drop and the effects of surfactants dissolved in the liquid.

Applications. Over 100 h of drop oscillation experiments were conducted during the flight of *STS 73*. One goal of this research is to validate a theoretical surfactant transport modeling approach for the ideal case in order to be able to extend the modeling to include the effects of a constant high-amplitude acoustic field. This validation will allow research to be conducted in Earth-based levitators, where the acoustic field necessary to hold very small drops (1 mm or 0.04 in. in diameter) results in both a static deformation and a nonlinear, amplitude-dependent restoring force for oscillations, which can mask surfactant effects on the oscillations. Ultimately, the space experiments described here will yield information on surface diffusivity and frequency-dependent sorption rate constants for surfactants. Such information, incorporated into the theoretical model, will allow the prediction of macroscopic rheological effects in very practical industrial situations from the specification of fundamental structural and transport properties of a given surfactant species.

For background information *see* ACOUSTIC LEVITATION; ACOUSTIC RADIATION PRESSURE; DAMPING; SURFACE TENSION; SURFACTANT; VIBRATION; WEIGHTLESSNESS in the McGraw-Hill Encyclopedia of Science & Technology.   R. Glynn Holt

Bibliography. D. A. Edwards, H. Brenner, and D. T. Wasan, *Interfacial Transport Processes and Rheology*, 1991; H. Lamb, *Hydrodynamics*, 1945; Y. Tian, R. G. Holt, and R. E. Apfel, Investigations of liquid surface rheology of surfactant solutions by droplet shape oscillations: Theory, *Phys. Fluids*, 7:2938–2949, 1995; E. H. Trinh, R. G. Holt, and D. B. Thiessen, The dynamics of ultrasonically levitated drops in an electric field, *Phys. Fluids*, 8:43–61, 1996.

Wetlands

Water quality from point sources of pollution such as factories and city sewers has been regulated in the United States since the 1970s. Recently, nonpoint source effects on water quality have become important issues. Croplands and grazing lands are increasingly scrutinized for their contribution to nutrient loading of water bodies. While improvements in grazing management usually can reduce such loading, the nutrient loading contribution by grazing animals may be overestimated, and goals for reduction of nutrient loading may be unrealistic. Determining background levels is difficult but critical to setting realistic goals for nutrient loading.

Eutrophication. The process by which water bodies become rich in nutrients supporting abundant microbiotic growth is called eutrophication. This natural process can be accelerated by pollution or entry of excess phosphorus and other nutrients to shallow reservoirs or lakes. Nonpoint sources may equal or exceed the phosphorus load of point sources. Often the natural or background levels are unknown. The phosphorus load in a stream is a function of the geologic materials, soils, topography, vegetative cover, precipitation intensity, and water hydraulics. The contribution of phosphorus from natural sources can be difficult to differentiate from anthropogenic sources of stream phosphorus.

Phosphorus transport. Elevated phosphorus loading of wetlands, streams, lakes, and reservoirs can occur from nonpoint sources such as grazed uplands, wet meadows, seasonally flooded lands, and saturated wetlands. Erosion caused by livestock grazing or other activities will increase total phosphorus load in streams. However, herbivores can also harvest phosphorus from forage and export a portion of it from the watershed. Some land managers fail to recognize that phosphorus taken up by plants will continue to cycle through soil and water. Soluble phosphorus in water or phosphorus attached to soil particles suspended in water are the primary vectors of phosphorus movement in a watershed. Herbivores add another vector with more opportunities to export phosphorus from the watershed. Use of best-management practices such as rotational grazing, buffer strips next to wetlands, and proper irrigation management should reduce overland water flow and stream-bank erosion. Livestock grazing should harvest and remove a significant amount of phosphorus from an ecosystem by incorporating phosphorus into bone and tissue of growing animals and then exporting beef animals from the watershed.

Livestock grazing. Many high mountain valleys in the Northwest have subirrigated meadows which are typically used for summer grazing by cattle. During the spring cattle are moved into these watersheds, and in the fall they are moved out. Some riparian areas suffer from accelerated stream-bank erosion. Overland erosion rates may be as high as 0.1 ton/acre (200 kg/hectare) annually. Thousands of tons of sediment may be added annually to water bodies in moderate-sized watersheds (occupying more than 10,000 acres).

Grazing affects phosphorus cycling. A portion of phosphorus from plants is retained by growing animals and incorporated into bone and soft tissue or into milk of lactating females. Undigested nutrients are excreted from the body in feces and urine. Proper grazing management is essential to reducing nutrient loadings to streams. Total phosphorus concentrations in surface runoff from continuously grazed watersheds may be three times higher than those from rotationally grazed watersheds because of greater soil loss. Since vacation home owners and recreationists seek property near water bodies and want excellent water quality, the perception is that the environmentally correct solution is the removal of livestock grazing from the watershed.

Nutrient cycling. Transport of phosphorus by overland flow depends on desorption, dissolution, and extraction of phosphorus from soil, and mineralization of plant material and feces. Temperature, precipitation, presence of anaerobic soil conditions, and evapotranspiration rates further influence the process. Much of the phosphorus enters the wetlands as a pulse during snow melt. Also, as plants die or become senescent, leaves, stems, and roots decompose by weathering and microbiotic assimilation of nutrients. Nutrients are recycled to the soil, where they remain until absorbed by plants or are leached from the soil into water bodies. About 75% of total phosphorus may be leached from dormant or dead vegetation. Plant species composition, precipitation, and decay rate affect the phosphorus leached from plant material. Soil phosphorus loss is dependent on the capacity and charge of ion-exchange sites on minerals and organic matter, pH, and concentrations and interactions of other elements.

In a system without herbivores, nutrients cycle from soil to soil water, to plants, to litter, and back to soil. Erosion of soil or leaching through the ground water transports phosphorus to streams and reservoirs. When herbivores are added to the ecosystem, phosphorus may be found in more chemical forms with varying solubility. Urine and feces return unabsorbed or unretained phosphorus to the soil surface to continue cycling. Livestock grazing does not create phosphorus. Livestock consume forage containing phosphorus that is susceptible to loading streams, regardless of the grazing. There is a need to determine the forms, solubilities, and rates of phosphorus release from plant material versus animal wastes.

Patterns of dung and urine deposition are not uniform. Such patterns may be more distinct with sheep, where 1–2 lb phosphorus/acre (1–2 kg/hectare) annually may be concentrated at ridges where sheep camp at night. Theoretically, a best-management practice of high-intensity and short-duration grazing should provide more uniform dung distribution. However, phosphorus is still accumulated in areas closest to shade and water, as a result of urine and feces deposition by livestock and wild ungulates. If the only source of shade and water is near a wetland or stream, deposition of animal waste could be a significant contributor of phosphorus to the wetland. It is clear that any activity accelerating erosion will increase total phosphorus load. It is not clear what effects grazing will have on soluble-phosphorus loading to streams and reservoirs.

PURGE model. The Phosphorus Uptake and Removal from Grazed Ecosystems (PURGE) simulation model was developed to estimate phosphorus uptake by grass and phosphorus retention in bodies of grazing cattle. The variables include known, approximate, and assumed values based on measurements, the literature, and personal experience.

The net phosphorus absorption by cattle is about 90% efficient in young calves and 55% efficient in cows. The phosphorus concentration of forage can vary between 0.18 and 0.30%, depending on soil series, temperature, interactions with other nutrients, fertilizer treatments, soil moisture, plant species, and plant growth stage.

The phosphorus composition of bone and soft tissues in cattle is highly predictable, and therefore the phosphorus export is easily calculated from weight gain by cattle while on the pastures. Bone ash contains 16–17% phosphorus, making up 75–80% of total body phosphorus (in the skeleton and teeth). Using moderate values in the PURGE simulation, the model produced an estimate for phosphorus removed from the watershed of 22 tons (20 megagrams), or 1 lb phosphorus removed per acre (1 kg/hectare).

The PURGE model clearly demonstrates that grazing livestock which are gaining weight in soft tissue and bone (either calves or cows with developing fetuses) will export phosphorus from the ecosystem when cattle are removed from the area. Hypothetically, the amount of phosphorus exported is significant and could be equal to the average load entering the reservoir. However, whether this export of phosphorus actually reduces phosphorus loading to the reservoir depends on good grazing management to protect stream banks from erosion and to limit deposit of feces and urine in the water. When properly managed, grazing cattle can remove phosphorus from the ecosystem, but improperly managed grazing can simultaneously increase phosphorus loading to streams and reservoirs. Even at the above predicted rates of phosphorus export, erosion and large runoff events would produce big phosphorus loads because of the enormous mass of the phosphorus pool in soil and minerals.

Recommendations of best-management practices. Grass buffer strips between pasture and stream can be effective in reducing phosphorus transport from pastures by increasing infiltration and sedimentation and decreasing overland flow. Off-stream water development and fencing of riparian areas should reduce stream-bank degradation, and deposit of feces and urine near streams. High-intensity rotational grazing systems should provide for a healthier pasture. Since degraded water quality is detrimental to recreationists, wildlife, homeowners, and agricultural producers, best-management practices and other scientific tools should be used to reduce phosphorus loading. Grazing activities that accelerate erosion will increase total phosphorus loading because of phosphorus adsorption to soil particles. However, with proper grazing management, livestock grazing should be part of a long-term solution to excess phosphorus loading of streams and thus improve water quality.

For background information *see* AGRICULTURAL SOIL AND CROP PRACTICES; EUTROPHICATION; FERTILIZER; PHOSPHORUS; SOIL CONSERVATION in the McGraw-Hill Encyclopedia of Science & Technology.   Glenn E. Shewmaker

Bibliography. S. A. Barber, *Soil Nutrient Bioavailability*, 1984; D. C. Church (ed.), The macro (major) minerals, *Digestive Physiol. Nutrit. Ruminants*, 2:417–472, 1971; M. Stelly (ed.), Phosphorus nutrition of forages, *The Role of Phosphorus in Agriculture*, pp. 805–846, 1980.

Wideband optical amplification

Since the early 1970s there has been a general expectation that high-speed, long-distance communications would be dominated by optical-fiber technologies. This belief was based on the silica fiber's extremely low optical power loss and high information bandwidths (that is, data capacity) compared with coaxial cable. At an infrared wavelength of 1.55 micrometers, the loss minimum in silica fiber is as low as 0.2 decibel per kilometer (0.32 dB/mi), that is, less than 5% power loss after 1 km of light propagation (8% power loss after 1 mi). Furthermore, the fiber's data capacity in this low-loss region can be as high as 25,000 gigahertz of information, compared with the few kilohertz of information contained in a typical voice-generated telephone call. However, it was the lack both of a true all-optical amplifier and of the ability to transmit ultrahigh capacity on one fiber that made optical systems fall far short of the fiber's theoretical capacity.

That situation changed dramatically in the late 1980s. The advent of the erbium-doped fiber-optic amplifier (EDFA), which can amplify many signals simultaneously over a bandwidth greater than 3 terahertz (3000 GHz) heralded a revolution in capacity for optical communication systems. For the first time, amplification is truly all optical and covers a wide wavelength range. That, in turn, has made wide-bandwidth, all-optical, many-wavelength-channel multiplexing schemes practical. Such techniques allow the simultaneous transmission of many different channels, each of a different-colored wavelength, thereby greatly increasing the overall capacity of the fiber. Experimental systems have broken the terabit-per-second barrier over 150 km (90 mi) of transmission, with a bit of information being a transmitted digital 0 (light off) or 1 (light on) signal. Furthermore, systems transmitting 100 gigabits per second over thousands of kilometers are planned for commercial deployment.

The erbium-doped fiber amplifier is a key enabler for almost all fiber-based systems. In fact, much of the relevant advances in optical communication since 1987 can be traced to the incorporation of optical amplifiers.

Optoelectronic regenerators. Until 1987, no practical all-optical amplifier existed. Instead, optical signals were electronically regenerated every few tens of kilometers to overcome the optical fiber's inherent power attenuation as well as other losses originating from in-line components.

In optoelectronic regeneration, a weak optical signal is briefly stopped in its travel along a fiber to be detected, amplified, retimed, reshaped, and retransmitted at full strength, in perfect shape, and without any accumulated noises. Not only are electronic regenerators expensive, but they also waste time and power in converting the signal from photons to electrons and back again to photons. Moreover, the regenerator components limit a system's performance because each regenerator can operate at only one predetermined incoming bit rate, one data modulation format, and one wavelength of a single input channel.

The goal has been an all-optical amplifier. For optical communications, the ideal amplifier would function essentially as a transparent box that would accept parallel input optical signals over a broad range of wavelengths and amplify them simultaneously. Only with such wide bandwidth would it be practical to multiplex many channels at once and thus take full advantage of optical fiber's potential capacity. The ideal all-optical amplifier would provide gain to all the optical signals while being insensitive to their individual bit rate, modulation format, power level, or wavelength, and it would amplify them without introducing significant signal distortion or noise. It would be advantageous if the optical amplifier was also cheaper and more reliable than electronic regenerators.

Erbium-doped fiber amplifiers. In 1987, this list of objectives was almost completely fulfilled with the demonstration of the erbium-doped fiber amplifier. The erbium-doped fiber amplifier contains a meters-long length of silica glass fiber that has been filled with ions (atoms that have an electronic charge) of the rare-earth metal erbium. When the erbium ions are excited to a metastable higher-energy state in such a way as to create a population inversion (that is, there exist more atoms at the higher energy state than at the normal lowest-energy or ground state), the doped fiber acts not as a passive transmission medium but as an active amplifying medium. This amplification is achieved because a single incoming signal photon can stimulate an excited ion to fall to a lower energy level. The result is a new photon at the same wavelength and phase as (that is, coherent

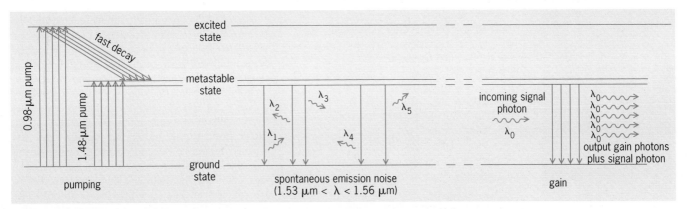

Fig. 1. Energy diagram showing amplification mechanism of an erbium-doped fiber amplifier. Illumination of the fiber amplifier with a pump laser excites erbium ions to a metastable higher-energy level, either directly or through an intermediate level. Spontaneous decay from this level emits photons with random wavelengths (λ_1–λ_5), directions, and phases, whereas stimulation by a photon causes a metastable erbium ion to emit photons with precisely the same direction, phase, and wavelength (λ_0). All these coherent photons constitute gain. (After A. E. Willner, Mining the optical bandwidth for a terabit-per-second, IEEE Spectrum, 34(4):32–41, April 1997)

with) the original incoming signal photon (**Fig. 1**). This process continues to produce many new coherent photons. The result is gain: A stronger signal comes out than goes in. In essence, the erbium-doped fiber amplifier acts as a laser, except that the optical signal makes only one pass through the active medium instead of being repeatedly bounced back and forth within it by external mirrors.

To pump the erbium ions to the metastable higher-energy state, infrared radiation from a diode laser emitting at 0.98 or 1.48 μm, wavelengths preferentially absorbed by erbium, is coupled into the erbium fiber. This coupling of signal and pump into the erbium-doped fiber is accomplished by using a three-port, wavelength-selective coupler (**Fig. 2**).

As the erbium ions in their metastable state have a typical lifetime of milliseconds, they eventually decay spontaneously to a lower energy level when not stimulated by an incoming signal photon. Such a spontaneous energy drop, however, emits a photon in a random direction and at a random wavelength and phase; that is, it produces incoherent radiation. Such spontaneous emissions, which exist

over the entire wavelength spectrum of the amplifier, are considered additive noise to the system. This behavior is similar to that of electronic amplifiers, which contribute noise along with gain to the signal.

There are three generic systems applications for optical amplifiers: (1) immediately following the laser transmitter, to act as a power amplifier; (2) inline at several locations along the transmission path, to compensate for periodic attenuation due to fiber, distribution-splitting, or component losses; and (3) directly before the receiver, to boost the signal for reception.

Advantages. The erbium-doped fiber amplifier has critical advantages over optoelectronic regenerators: (1) Erbium ions can amplify light between 1.53 and 1.56 μm, spanning the range in which the silica fiber has the greatest transparency (**Fig. 3**). This wide range allows the boosting of tens of different-wavelength signals simultaneously. (2) Erbium-doped fiber amplifiers can provide very high gain, routinely 100–1000 times the original optical signal. (3) The circular cross section of the erbium fiber means that

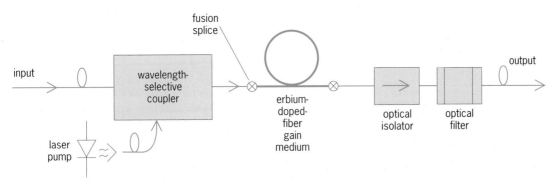

Fig. 2. Basic amplifier configuration in which a transmission fiber and a pump laser are connected to the erbium-doped fiber through a wavelength-selective coupler. The optical isolator allows only unidirectional propagation to prevent reflections back into the amplifier. The optical filter limits output of amplifier-generated spontaneous-emission noise. (After L. G. Kazovsky, S. Benedetto, and A. E. Willner, Optical Fiber Communication Systems, Artech House, 1996)

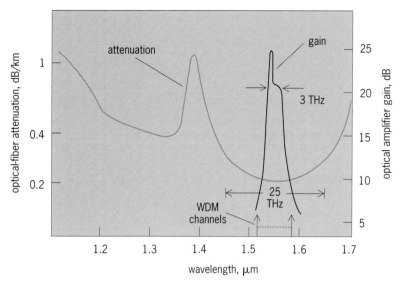

Fig. 3. Variation with wavelength of optical-fiber attenuation and of gain of an erbium-doped fiber amplifier. Proposed range of wavelength-division-multiplexed (WDM) channels is shown. The region of the fiber's greatest transparency coincides with the wavelength region (1.53–1.56 μm) of the erbium-doped fiber amplifier's greatest gain. *(After A. E. Willner, Mining the optical bandwidth for a terabit-per-second, IEEE Spectrum, 34(4):32–41, April 1997)*

the optical coupling between the amplifier and the circular transmission fiber is minimal. (4) Fiber amplifiers introduce very little noise. The amplifier noise figure, based on the spontaneous-emission additive noise, is 4–5 dB, nearly as low as the theoretical quantum limit of 3 dB. (5) The milliseconds-long lifetime of an erbium ion in its raised metastable state is quite long compared with the nanosecond time scale of an individual fast digital data bit. This means that, even when an intense incoming signal saturates and decreases the amplifier's time-averaged gain, there is still no perceivable fluctuation of the gain during the extremely short time of an individual bit.

Soon after being introduced, erbium-doped fiber amplifiers made remarkable achievements. In 1991, a fiber preamplifier enabled a receiver to recover digital bits having 20 times less optical power than could have been detected with the most sensitive optoelectronic photoreceiver. The next year, a cascade of in-line fiber amplifiers transmitted a single 5-gigabit-per-second channel uninterrupted along 9000 km (5500 mi) of fiber, representing transpacific transmission, without regenerating the optical signal.

Wavelength-division multiplexing. Throughout the 1980s, optical-fiber research focused on the higher-speed transmission of data over longer distances from a single laser source. This was accomplished by modulating an optical beam at a faster on/off digital bit rate in a simple time-multiplexing fashion. No matter how fast optoelectronic device technologies eventually become, however, they may never be practical much beyond the 100-gigabit-per-second range.

Therefore, a conceptually simple technique must be pursued in parallel if terabit-per-second optical communications are to be realized. Such a technique is the multiplexing of signals at many different wavelengths onto the same optical fiber, known as wavelength-division multiplexing (WDM). It dramatically enhances an optical system's capacity, proportional to the number of wavelengths. After the optical amplifier, this is the second key technology which has enabled terabit-per-second optical systems. In the most basic arrangement, the desired number of lasers, each emitting light at a different wavelength, are coupled into the same high-bandwidth fiber. At the receiving end, a narrow-band optical filter is used to select one of many incoming wavelengths so that only one signal is allowed to pass and be received. Typical interchannel wavelength spacings range 50–500 GHz.

There has been much progress in technologies that will enable wavelength-division-multiplexing systems. Examples of commercially available devices include (1) single-frequency semiconductor lasers that can be made to emit at one of many wavelengths; (2) tunable optical filters to reject unwanted signals and reduce spontaneous-emission noise generated by the erbium-doped fiber amplifier; and (3) wavelength multiplexers and demultiplexers, which can passively route a signal based solely on its wavelength to one of many destinations (analogous to a prism, which separates white light into different colors).

Another enabling technology is the optical amplifier. The erbium-doped fiber amplifier simultaneously provides gain to signals of many different wavelengths. One drawback of the fiber amplifier, however, is that the gain is not uniform over the amplifier's wavelength range. This lack of uniformity can become severe in a cascade of amplifiers, and the power differential among several channels can become intolerable. Fortunately, there are several techniques of selectively attenuating the wavelengths that have the highest amplifier gain, thus equalizing the overall spectrum.

Implementation of the most demanding high-speed, long-distance wavelength-division-multiplexing systems requires overcoming problems associated with nonideal properties of the fiber itself. These deleterious effects, which distort the well-formed rectangular bits, include dispersion and nonlinear effects. Significant success in managing such problems has been achieved by using two different types of fiber alternating along the transmission span, wherein the problems generated in one type nearly cancel the problems generated in the other.

Terabit-per-second transmission. Three remarkable terabit-per-second experiments were reported in 1996. All experiments were performed near 1.55 μm and used erbium-doped fiber amplifiers. Moreover, all results used wavelength-division multiplexing to varying degrees, with 50 channels each modulated at 20 gigabits per second using somewhat conventional technology, or 10 channels each at 100 gigabits per second using more exotic technologies. Subsequently, a 2.6-terabit-per-second result was reported. Other experiments involved sending 0.1 terabit per second over 9000 km (5500 mi). Since the performance of commercial systems has always lagged behind that of experimental demonstrations by about 5-7 years, commercially available terabit-per-second systems may be expected around 2002.

For background information *see* LASER; OPTICAL COMMUNICATIONS; OPTICAL FIBERS in the McGraw-Hill Encyclopedia of Science & Technology.

Alan Eli Willner

Bibliography. E. Desurvire, *Erbium-Doped Fiber Amplifiers: Principles and Applications*, 1994; L. G. Kazovsky, S. Benedetto, and A. E. Willner, *Optical Fiber Communication Systems*, 1996; T. Li, The impact of optical amplifiers on long-distance lightwave telecommunications, *Proc. IEEE*, 81:1568–1579, 1993; A. E. Willner, Mining the optical bandwidth for a terabit-per-second, *IEEE Spectrum*, 34(4):32–41, April 1997.

Zoonoses

Zoonoses are infections of humans caused by the transmission of disease agents that naturally live in animals. People become infected when they unwittingly intrude into the life cycle of the disease agent and become unnatural hosts. Zoonotic helminthic diseases, caused by parasitic worms, involve many species of helminths, including nematodes (roundworms), trematodes (flukes), cestodes (tapeworms), and acanthocephalans (thorny-headed worms). Helminthic zoonoses may be contracted from domestic animals such as pets, from edible animals such as seafood, or from wild animals. Fortunately, most kinds of zoonotic helminthic infections are caused by rare human parasites. *See* FOOD SAFETY.

Pet-borne infections. Dogs and cats carry several species of helminths that can infect humans. The closely related intestinal nematodes *Toxocara canis* and *T. cati* respectively parasitize dogs and cats as definitive hosts (in which the adult parasite lives). Adult worms living in the small intestine of the animal produce prodigious numbers of microscopic eggs that pass with the feces and embryonate in the soil. Eggs become infective after several weeks and may remain so in the soil for many months. Dogs and cats become infected in several ways. They may ingest eggs from the soil; hatched larvae either can develop to adults in the intestine or can enter tissues such as muscle and remain undeveloped. Virtually every puppy is born with *T. canis* acquired in utero from larvae in the mother's tissue. Nursing kittens become infected with tissue larvae of *T. cati* passed in the milk. Dogs and cats also can become infected by eating animals such as mice that have ingested *Toxocara* eggs from soil; the animals carry the larvae in their tissues, acting as paratenic hosts (in which the infective larva lives; when the paratenic host is eaten by the definitive host, the larva develops to the adult stage).

These *Toxocara* species can infect people who ingest soil containing embryonated eggs. Humans act as abnormal paratenic hosts to the larvae, resulting in a zoonosis called visceral larva migrans. The *Toxocara* larvae migrate within many different tissues over periods of months, causing a disease with varying signs and symptoms, but most often marked by enlargement of the liver, pneumonitis (lung inflammation), and a dramatic increase in the number of circulating eosinophil leukocytes. In a disease syndrome known as ocular larva migrans, single larvae of *T. canis* cause an inflammatory lesion in the eye. Visceral larva migrans caused by *Toxocara* is common in children of the United States; most infected children are less than 6 years of age, and commonly have a history of eating dirt. Human infection by these parasites could be prevented by early deworming of puppies and kittens, thus destroying the sources of eggs. There are no drugs with proven efficacy against *Toxocara* infection in people.

The hookworms of dogs and cats can infect people. *Ancylostoma braziliense* of dogs and cats, *A. caninum* of dogs, and probably other *Ancylostoma* species of these definitive hosts are capable of causing types of visceral larva migrans infections that are incompletely understood. Adult worms parasitize the small intestine of the definitive host. Eggs passing in feces quickly develop and hatch in the soil, where the microscopic infective larvae may live for a week or two. Larvae of *A. braziliense* enter people's skin from the surface of soil where cats or dogs have deposited feces, such as at beaches or under houses. The larvae cause a characteristic dermatitis known as cutaneous larva migrans (sometimes called creeping eruption) that is marked by progressive, linear, meandering tracks of inflammation that itch intensely and persist for several weeks. In some instances, skin infection is known to be followed by pneumonitis, with the larvae sometimes coughed up in the sputum. This infection is common on the southeastern seaboard of the United States. *Ancylostoma caninum* can also infect through the skin, resulting in a less characteristic and shorter-lived dermatitis; this species may subsequently enter deeper tissues, and sometimes matures in people, causing a characteristic inflammation of the small intestine. All of the *Ancylostoma* species of dogs and cats in the United States are probably capable of producing a type of visceral larva migrans infection in people who ingest the larvae in soil.

The larval form of a minute tapeworm of dogs, *Echinococcus granulosus*, can cause a potentially serious zoonosis. The life cycle of the parasite involves a dog as definitive host and a herbivorous intermediate host (in which larval forms grow and develop) [see **illus.**]. This tapeworm commonly occurs in geographic areas where sheep are raised. Sheep dogs acquire infection by eating the tapeworm's larval forms that live within the viscera of

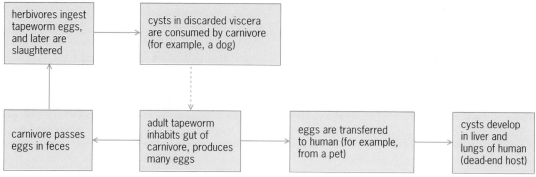

Life cycle of *Echinococcus granulosus*.

sheep, although the larval forms may also be found in other herbivorous mammals. The sheep, in turn, become infected by ingesting eggs from dog feces. Humans act as abnormal intermediate hosts by ingesting eggs and supporting the growth and development of the larval forms. These larval forms, known as hydatid cysts, are hollow and fluid filled. They are lined with a delicate membrane from which millions of microscopic tapeworm scoleces (heads) bud; each scolex will become an adult tapeworm in the intestine of a dog. Hydatids are slow growing, but may eventually become large enough (several centimeters in diameter) to cause disease by compressing adjacent tissue. Most hydatids are found in the liver and lungs, but they may occur in any tissue, including bone. The eggs of *Echinococcus* are immediately infective; people who have close contact with an infected dog are more likely to ingest eggs directly from the dog than from soil. The infection can be successfully treated with drugs and surgery.

A rare zoonotic helminthic infection in the United States is caused by the dog heartworm, *Dirofilaria immitis*. This parasitic nematode is known to occasionally infect people, who apparently serve as inadequate definitive hosts. The adult worms, which live in the right ventricle and pulmonary artery of the dog, have been found in pulmonary lesions in people. The worm is transmitted to people by the bite of the intermediate host, a mosquito, which has acquired the organism by taking a blood meal from an infected dog in which circulate embryonic larvae known as microfilariae.

Food-borne infections. The best-recognized example of a food-borne zoonotic helminthic disease is trichinosis, caused by the trinchina worm, *Trichinella spiralis*, a tiny nematode. People commonly become infected by eating inadequately prepared pork, but a sizable proportion of victims now contract the worms by eating the meat of wild carnivores, such as bear. An infected person supports two generations of trichina worms: the adult generation that develops in the mucosa of the small intestine, and a resulting larval generation that lives, and eventually dies, encysted in the striated muscles. Trichinosis is usually a mild disease, manifested by symptoms and signs of intestinal and muscular inflammation, but in heavy infections damage done by the larvae to the heart and central nervous system can be life threatening. Because of public awareness about properly cooking pork and federal regulations about feeding pigs, trichinosis has become uncommon in the United States, with an average of fewer than 60 cases reported annually.

People who eat inadequately prepared marine fish may become infected with larval nematodes. Adult *Anisakis* and *Pseudoterranova* (*Phocamema*) nematodes respectively parasitize the gastrointestinal tracts of porpoises and seals, among other marine mammal definitive hosts. The infective larvae are carried by paratenic hosts, marine fish and invertebrates. People may become infected by these nematode larvae (which do not mature in humans) by eating raw marine fish (in dishes such as sushi or ceviche) or poorly cooked, salted, smoked, or pickled fish. Several dozen cases have been reported in the United States. In the Asian area, where marine fish is preferentially consumed raw, this zoonosis is very common. Patterns of infection vary, but larval *Pseudoterranova* may ascend the esophagus into the pharynx hours to days following ingestion, to be coughed up by the temporary host. Both types of larvae may enter the mucosa of the gastrointestinal tract, causing inflammation and symptoms mimicking those of a gastric ulcer or appendicitis. Infections are not treatable with drugs, but they are typically short lived. Both species occur in a variety of marine fishes. Larval *Pseudoterranova* is common in codfish. In waters of the United States, larval *Anisakis* is particularly prevalent in some species of Pacific rockfish and salmon. Larvae of *Anisakis* typically occur in the viscera of fish, but may migrate into edible muscle before the landed fish is gutted. Fish that have been frozen at $-20°C$ ($-4°F$) for 60 h or cooked so that all the flesh has been heated to at least $60°C$ ($140°F$) for 1 min or more are safe to eat.

Wild animal–borne infections. Of the many potential (and rare) helminthic zoonoses from wild animals in the United States, *Baylisascaris procyonis* is particularly dangerous. The nematode is highly prevalent in raccoons, the definitive host; it uses rodents as paratenic hosts. The life cycle is simple: eggs pass in raccoon feces and are ingested by raccoons or by rodents. In raccoons, the hatching larvae mature. In mice, larvae migrate to the brain, causing the host to lose voluntary motor control and to stagger and spin about, which attracts the attention of the predatory raccoon. People ingesting the eggs of *B. procyonis* seem to act as abnormal paratenic hosts. Larvae migrate widely in the body and predictably enter the brain, causing severe and sometimes fatal pathological changes. Raccoon fecal masses, which may be deposited near dwellings, may contain very high numbers of embryonated eggs. Adoption of orphaned wild raccoons certainly should be avoided.

For background information *see* ACANTHOCEPHALA; CESTODA; FILAROIDEA; MEDICAL PARASITOLOGY; NEMATA; PARASITOLOGY; TREMATODA; TRICHINELLOIDEA; ZOONOSES in the McGraw-Hill Encyclopedia of Science & Technology.   Donald E. Norris

Bibliography. P. C. Beaver, The nature of visceral larva migrans, *J. Parasitol.*, 55:3–12, 1969; S. L. Gorbach et al. (eds.), *Infectious Diseases*, 1998; G. L. Mandell et al. (eds.), *Principles and Practice of Infectious Diseases*, 1990; F. A. Neva et al., *Basic Clinical Parasitology*, 1994.

Contributors

Contributors

The affiliation of each Yearbook contributor is given, followed by the title of his or her article. An article title with the notation "in part" indicates that the author independently prepared a section of an article; "coauthored" indicates that two or more authors jointly prepared an article or section.

A

Agarwal, Dr. Rajat. *Henkel Surface Technologies, Madison Heights, Michigan.* METAL COATING—coauthored.

Alejaldre, Dr. Carlos. *Head of the Research Unit, Asociación EURATOM-CIEMAT para la Fusión, Madrid, Spain.* STELLARATOR.

Allen, Dr. James F. *Department of Computer Science, University of Rochester, Rochester, New York.* NATURAL LANGUAGE TECHNOLOGY.

Anderson, Dr. David T. *Department of Chemistry, University of Pennsylvania, Philadelphia.* CHEMICAL DYNAMICS—coauthored.

Anderson, Prof. O. Roger. *Senior Research Scientist, Lamont-Doherty Earth Observatory, Columbia University, Palisades, New York.* AMEBA.

Angel, Dr. Ross J. *Bayerisches Geoinstitut, Universität Bayreuth, Bayreuth, Germany.* SILICON.

B

Bailey, Dr. D. K. *Department of Geology, University of Bristol, Bristol, United Kingdom.* CARBONATITES.

Bambach, Dr. Richard K. *Professor of Paleontology, Department of Geological Sciences, Virginia Polytechnic Institute and State University, Blacksburg.* MASS EXTINCTION—in part.

Bamber, Dr. Shaw D. *Department of Biological Sciences, University of Plymouth, Plymouth, Devon, United Kingdom.* CRAB—in part.

Baross, Prof. John A. *School of Oceanography, University of Washington, Seattle.* HYDROTHERMAL VENT.

Barton, Prof. Jacqueline K. *Arnold and Mabel Beckman Laboratories of Chemical Synthesis, California Institute of Technology, Pasadena.* DEOXYRIBONUCLEIC ACID (DNA)—in part.

Beasley, Prof. Donald E. *Department of Mechanical Engineering, Clemson University, Clemson, South Carolina.* FLUIDIZED BED.

Beck, James E. *Boeing Defense & Space Group, Rocketdyne Division, Boeing North American Inc., Canoga Park, California.* AEROSPIKE ENGINE.

Bell, Prof. James P. *University of Connecticut, Storrs.* METAL COATING—coauthored.

Beran, Dr. George W. *Department of Microbiology, College of Veterinary Medicine, Iowa State University, Ames.* FOOD SAFETY.

Bingham, Prof. Carrol. *Department of Physics and Astronomy, University of Tennessee, Knoxville.* PROTON RADIOACTIVITY.

Bird, Kenneth W. *Director, Marketing/Sales, SPF Corporation of America, Louisville, Colorado.* CORROSION—in part.

Birmingham, Dr. Jeannette M. *Society for Industrial Microbiology, American Type Culture Collection, Manassas, Virginia.* MUSHROOM—in part.

Boero, Dr. Ferdinando. *Professor of Zoology, Universitá di Lecce, Dipartimento di Biologia, Stazione di Biologia Marina, Lecce, Italy.* ONTOGENY.

Bolton, Dr. Toby F. *School of Biological Sciences, The Flinders University of South Australia, Adelaide, Australia.* SPERM—coauthored.

Bond, Dr. Barbara. *Assistant Professor, Department of Forest Science, Oregon State University, Corvallis.* TREE—in part.

Boutros, Dr. Nashaat N. *Associate Professor of Psychiatry, Director of Electrophysiology Laboratory, Director of Dual Diagnosis Clinical Research Program, School of Medicine, Yale University, New Haven, Connecticut.* TRANSCRANIAL MAGNETIC STIMULATION.

Bozer, Dr. Yavuz A. *Department of Industrial and Operations Engineering, University of Michigan, Ann Arbor.* MATERIALS HANDLING.

Bragg, Prof. Michael B. *Department of Aeronautical and Astronautical Engineering, University of Illinois at Urbana-Champaign.* ICING.

Bridgeman, Dr. Bruce. *Professor of Psychology and Psychobi-*

ology, Department of Psychology, University of California, Santa Cruz. PERCEPTION.

Browning, Dr. Michael. *Senior Lecturer in Immunology, Department of Microbiology and Immunology, University of Leicester, School of Medicine, Leicester, United Kingdom.* POLYMORPHISM (GENETICS).

Bult, Dr. Carol J. *Research Faculty/Program Manager, National Center for Geographic Information and Analysis, Department of Spatial Information Science and Engineering, University of Maine, Orono.* ARCHAEA.

Burgess, Dr. Dawn. *Department of Geophysics, Stanford University, Stanford, California.* EARTHQUAKE—coauthored.

Burstyn, Dr. Judith N. *Department of Chemistry, University of Wisconsin, Madison.* NITRIC OXIDE—coauthored.

C

Campbell, Dr. Eleanor. *Max-Born-Institut, Berlin, Germany.* ATOM CLUSTER.

Campbell, Dr. Lee Ann. *Professor of Pathobiology, Department of Pathobiology, School of Public Health and Community Medicine, University of Washington, Seattle.* ATHEROSCLEROSIS.

Cara, Dr. Andrea. *Research Assistant Professor, The Mount Sinai Medical Center, New York, New York.* ACQUIRED IMMUNE DEFICIENCY SYNDROME (AIDS)—coauthored.

Carlson, Dr. C. Gregg. *Professor, Plant Science, South Dakota State University, Brookings.* SOIL VARIABILITY.

Cassenti, Dr. Brice N. *United Technologies Research Center, East Hartford, Connecticut.* ANTIMATTER.

Chapell, Dr. Brian J. *Chemistry Department, University of Waterloo, Waterloo, Ontario, Canada.* CATALYST—coauthored.

Chen, Prof. Kang Ping. *Associate Professor, Department of Mechanical and Aerospace Engineering, Arizona State University, Tempe.* PIPELINE FLOW.

Chiocca, Dr. E. A. *Assistant Professor in Neurosurgery, Molecular Neuro-Oncology Laboratory, Harvard Medical School, Massachusetts General Hospital, Boston.* CANCER (MEDICINE)—coauthored.

Clack, Dr. Jennifer A. *Senior Assistant Curator, University Museum of Zoology, Cambridge, England.* VERTEBRATE EVOLUTION.

Clark, Prof. Rose A. *Department of Chemistry, Mathematics, and Physical Science, Saint Francis College, Loretto, Pennsylvania.* ELECTROCHEMISTRY.

Claudy, Lynn D. *Senior Vice President, Science and Technology, National Association of Broadcasters, Washington, D.C.* TELEVISION—in part.

Close, Dr. Laird M. *Assistant Astronomer, Institute for Astronomy, University of Hawaii, Honolulu.* ADAPTIVE OPTICS.

Cohen, Dr. Andrew S. *Professor of Geosciences/Joint Professor of Ecology and Evolutionary Biology, Department of Geosciences, University of Arizona, Tucson.* MACROEVOLUTION.

Conlisk, Prof. A. T. *Department of Mechanical Engineering,*

Ohio State University, Columbus. HELICOPTER AERODYNAMICS.

Cordani, Dr. John R. *Computer Science Department, James Madison University, Harrisonburg, Virginia.* COMPUTER SECURITY AND PRIVACY.

Cordero, Dr. Oscar J. *Assistant Professor, Department of Biochemistry and Molecular Biology, University of Santiago de Compostela, Santiago de Compostela, Spain.* HORMONE—coauthored.

Cronin, Prof. John R. *Department of Chemistry and Biochemistry, Arizona State University, Tempe.* AMINO ACIDS.

D

Davies, Dr. Matthew A. *National Institute of Standards & Technology (NIST), Gaithersburg, Maryland.* MACHINING—coauthored.

Deisboeck, Dr. Thomas S. *Research Fellow in Neurosurgery, Molecular Neuro-Oncology Laboratory, Harvard Medical School, Massachusetts General Hospital, Boston.* CANCER (MEDICINE)—coauthored.

Demianski, Dr. Marek. *University of Warsaw, Institute of Theoretical Physics, Warsaw, Poland.* M-THEORY.

Denton, Prof. M. Bonner. *Department of Chemistry, University of Arizona, Tucson.* ANALYTICAL CHEMISTRY—coauthored.

Devadoss, Dr. Chelladurai. *Department of Chemistry, University of Illinois, Urbana.* PHOTOCHEMISTRY—coauthored.

Donovan, Dr. John. *Principal Technical Specialist, The Boeing Company, St. Louis, Missouri.* PRESSURE-SENSITIVE PAINT.

Doolittle, Dr. Russell F. *Center for Molecular Genetics, University of California, San Diego.* EVOLUTION.

Dorey, Prof. A. P. *Department of Engineering, University of Lancaster, Lancaster, United Kingdom.* INTEGRATED CIRCUITS.

Dowling, Dr. Patricia M. *Associate Professor, Clinical Pharmacology, Department of Veterinary Physiological Sciences, Western College of Veterinary Medicine, University of Saskatchewan, Saskatoon, Canada.* ANTIMICROBIAL RESISTANCE.

Dugan, Dr. Frank M. *Collection Scientist, Mycology & Botany, American Type Culture Collection, Manassas, Virginia.* AIR POLLUTION, INDOOR.

E

El-Amine, Moustapha. *University of Sherbrooke, Sherbrooke, Quebec, Canada.* CALPASTATIN—coauthored.

Ergas, Dr. Enrique. *Attending Physician, Hospital for Joint Disease Orthopedic Institute, and Assistant Clinical Professor of Orthopedic Surgery, New York University, New York, New York.* PROSTHESIS.

F

Fang, Dr. L. *Department of Mechanical Engineering, Ryerson Polytechnic University, Toronto, Ontario, Canada.* CONFLICT ANALYSIS—coauthored.

Farrell, Jeanette. *University of Washington, School of Medicine, Seattle.* TUBERCULOSIS—coauthored.

Feld, Prof. Michael S. *Director, G. R. Harrison Spectroscopy Laboratory, Massachusetts Institute of Technology, Cambridge.* CLINICAL PATHOLOGY—coauthored.

Felsenfeld, Dr. Herbert W. *Emergency Department, Saint Francis Hospital & Medical Center, Hartford, Connecticut.* CHEMOTHERAPY.

Fichtali, Dr. Jaouad. *POS Pilot Plant Corporation, Saskatoon, Saskatchewan, Canada.* IMMUNOSELECTIVE ADSORPTION PROCESSES.

Fishman, Dr. Gerald J. *Space Sciences Laboratory, NASA-Marshall Space Flight Center, Huntsville, Alabama.* GAMMA-RAY BURSTS.

Foote, Dr. Mike. *Department of the Geophysical Sciences, University of Chicago, Chicago, Illinois.* BIODIVERSITY.

Forrest, Dr. John R. *FEng; Chelsea Harbour, London, United Kingdom.* TELEVISION—in part.

Fossum, Dr. Eric R. *Chief Scientist, Photobit Corporation, La Crescenta, California.* OPTICAL IMAGING DEVICES.

Fowler, Dr. Joanna S. *Chemistry Department, Brookhaven National Laboratory, Upton, New York.* POSITRON EMISSION TOMOGRAPHY—coauthored.

Fraundorf, Prof. Philip B. *Associate Professor, Department of Physics and Astronomy, University of Missouri, St. Louis.* SCANNING TUNNELING MICROSCOPE.

Freedman, Dr. Wendy L. *The Observatories of the Carnegie Institution of Washington, Pasadena, California.* COSMIC DISTANCE SCALE—coauthored.

G

Gambetti, Dr. Pierluigi. *Director, Division of Neuropathology, Institute of Pathology, Case Western Reserve University, Cleveland, Ohio.* PRION DISEASE—coauthored.

Gerard, Dr. Craig. *Associate Professor of Pediatrics, Children's Hospital, Perlmutter Laboratory, Boston, Massachusetts.* INFLAMMATION.

Giachetti, Dr. Ronald E. *Department of Industrial and Systems Engineering, Florida, International University, Miami.* MANUFACTURABILITY.

Glass, Prof. Charles E. *Department of Mining and Geological Engineering, University of Arizona, Tucson.* MINING—in part.

Goldstein, Dr. Allan L. *Department of Biochemistry & Molecular Biology, George Washington University Medical Center, Washington, D.C.* THYMOSIN.

Gracco, Dr. Vincent L. *Vice President, Haskins Laboratories, New Haven, Connecticut.* SPEECH.

Griffith, Dr. R. Harsh, IV. *Associate Professor in Neurosurgery, MGM Brain Tumor Center, Harvard Medical School, Massachusetts General Hospital, Boston.* CANCER (MEDICINE)—coauthored.

Gubser, Dr. Donald U. *Superintendent, Materials Science and Technology Division, Department of the Navy, Naval Research Laboratory, Washington, D.C.* HIGH-TEMPERATURE SUPERCONDUCTOR.

Guthrie, Dr. George D. *Department of Geology, Western Michigan University, Kalamazoo.* OPAL.

H

Hahn, Dr. David W. *Sandia National Laboratories, Livermore, California.* DIAMOND FILM.

Hale, Dr. Alan. *Director, Southwest Institute for Space Research, Cloudcroft, New Mexico.* COMET HALE-BOPP.

Hankley, Dr. William. *Department of Computing and Information Science, Kansas State University, Manhattan.* SOFTWARE ENGINEERING—in part.

Hartman, George J. *General Manager, Fort Cady Minerals Corporation, Newberry Spring, California.* SOLUTION MINING.

Harwell, Dr. Kenneth E. *Fellow, American Institute of Aeronautics and Astronautics, and Senior Vice President for Research, University of Alabama, Huntsville.* ARCJET.

Hassett, Dr. Daniel E. *Department of Neuropharmacology, The Scripps Research Institute, La Jolla, California.* IMMUNIZATION.

Havenhand, Jon N. *School of Biological Sciences, The Flinders University of South Australia, Adelaide, Australia.* SPERM—coauthored.

Helin, Dr. Eleanor. *Member of Technical Staff, Planetary Scientist and Astronomer, Geology and Planetary Section, Jet Propulsion Laboratory, California Institute of Technology, Pasadena.* NEAR-EARTH OBJECTS.

Heron, Dr. Carl. *Senior Lecturer in Archaeological Sciences, Department of Archaeological Sciences, University of Bradford, Bradford, West Yorkshire, United Kingdom.* ARCHEOLOGICAL CHEMISTRY.

Hipel, Prof. Keith W. *Chair, Faculty of Engineering, Systems Design Engineering, University of Waterloo, Waterloo, Ontario, Canada.* CONFLICT ANALYSIS—coauthored.

Hirsch, Dr. Peter M. *Electric Power Research Institute, Palo Alto, California.* ELECTRIC POWER TRANSMISSION.

Holt, Dr. R. Glynn. *Department of Aerospace & Mechanical Engineering, Boston University, Boston, Massachusetts.* WEIGHTLESSNESS.

Hossenlopp, Prof. Jeanne M. *Department of Chemistry, Marquette University, Milwaukee, Wisconsin.* CHEMICAL DYNAMICS—coauthored.

Hou, Dr. Hsing. *Senior Research Scientist II, Bristol-Myers Squibb Company, Syracuse, New York.* ANTIBIOTIC.

Howarth, Dr. Thomas R. *Naval Research Laboratory, Washington, D.C.* ULTRASONIC TRANSDUCER.

J-K

Jones, David A. *Department of Chemistry, University of Arizona, Tucson.* ANALYTICAL CHEMISTRY—coauthored.

Kellman, Prof. Michael E. *Department of Chemistry, University of Oregon, Eugene.* CORRELATION (PHYSICS).

Kerschhofer, Dr. Ljuba. *Bayerisches Geoinstitut, Universität Bayreuth, Germany.* OLIVINE.

Ketterle, Prof. Wolfgang. *Department of Physics, Massachusetts Institute of Technology, Cambridge.* ATOM LASER.

Kilgour, Prof. D. M. *Department of Mathematics, Wilfrid Laurier University, Waterloo, Ontario, Canada.* CONFLICT ANALYSIS—coauthored.

King, John F. *TRW Strategic Systems Division, Rosslyn, Virginia.* COMMAND AND CONTROL—coauthored.

Klassen, Dr. David. *Department of Astronomy, Center for Radiophysics & Space Research, Cornell University, Ithaca, New York.* MARS—in part.

Klein, Prof. Cerry M. *Department of Industrial Engineering, University of Missouri, Columbia.* INDUSTRIAL FACILITIES.

Klein, Dr. Stanley B. *Associate Professor of Psychology, University of California, Santa Barbara.* MEMORY—in part.

Klotman, Dr. Mary E. *Director, Division of Infectious Diseases, and Associate Professor of Medicine and Microbiology, The Mount Sinai Medical Center, New York, New York.* ACQUIRED IMMUNE DEFICIENCY SYNDROME (AIDS)—coauthored.

Knoll, Dr. Joan H. M. *Scientific Director of Clinical Cytogenetics, Department of Pathology, Beth Israel Deaconess Medical Center, and Division of Genetics, Children's Hospital, Enders Research Building, Boston, Massachusetts.* HUMAN GENETICS.

Konstan, Dr. Joseph A. *Department of Computer Science, University of Minnesota, Minneapolis.* WEB RESOURCES.

Kramer, Dr. John R., Jr. *Department of Cardiology, Cleveland Clinic Foundation, Cleveland, Ohio.* CLINICAL PATHOLOGY—coauthored.

Kroon, Dr. Peter. *Acoustics and Speech Research Department, Bell Laboratories, Lucent Technologies, Murray Hill, New Jersey.* SPEECH CODER.

Krumhansl, Dr. Carol L. *Department of Psychology, Cornell University, Ithaca, New York.* HEARING (HUMAN).

L

Layne, Dr. John E. *Department of Zoology, Duke University, Durham, North Carolina.* CRAB—in part.

Lehner, Dr. Paul E. *Chief Scientist, Information Systems and Technology Division, The MITRE Corporation, McLean, Virginia.* AUTOMATED DECISION MAKING.

Lester, Prof. Marsha I. *Department of Chemistry, University of Pennsylvania, Philadelphia.* CHEMICAL DYNAMICS—coauthored.

Lo, Prof. Yu-Hwa. *Associate Professor, Cornell University,*

School of Electrical Engineering, Ithaca, New York. SEMICONDUCTOR.

Loesch, Dr. Hansjürgen. *Fakultät für Physik, Universität Bielefeld, Bielefeld, Germany.* CHEMICAL DYNAMICS—in part.

Lopresti, Dr. Daniel. *Panasonic Information and Networking Technologies Laboratory, Panasonic Technologies Inc., Princeton, New Jersey.* COMPUTER STORAGE.

Lord, Dr. Steven. *National Centers for Environmental Prediction, Washington, D.C.* WEATHER FORECASTING AND PREDICTION.

M

Madden, Sean P. *Department of Chemistry, University of Arizona, Tucson.* ANALYTICAL CHEMISTRY—coauthored.

Madore, Barry F. *The Observatories of the Carnegie Institution of Washington, Pasadena, California.* COSMIC DISTANCE SCALE—coauthored.

Mallory, Prof. Frank B. *W. Alton Jones Professor of Chemistry, Department of Chemistry, Bryn Mawr College, Bryn Mawr, Pennsylvania.* PHENACENE.

Mansfeld, Prof. Florian. *Corrosion and Environmental Effects Laboratory, Department of Materials Science and Engineering, University of Southern California, Los Angeles.* CORROSION—in part.

Martinez-Carrera, Dr. D. *Head, Mushroom Biotechnology, College of Postgraduates in Agricultural Sciences, Puebla, Mexico.* MUSHROOM—in part.

Maryanski, Dr. James H. *Department of Health & Human Services, Food and Drug Administration, Washington, D.C.* FOOD BIOTECHNOLOGY.

Mata-Toledo, Dr. Ramon A. *Computer Science Department, James Madison University, Harrisonburg, Virginia.* SOFTWARE ENGINEERING—in part.

Meade, Dr. Thomas J. *Division of Biology, Beckman Institute, California Institute of Technology, Pasadena.* MEDICAL IMAGING.

Meese, Prof. Jon M. *Electrical Engineering Department, University of Missouri-Columbia.* OPTOELECTRONIC DEVICE.

Ménard, Dr. Henri-André. *Professor of Medicine and Cell Biology, University of Sherbrooke, Sherbrooke, Quebec, Canada.* CALPASTATIN—coauthored.

Messerschmitt, Prof. David G. *Department of Electrical Engineering and Computer Sciences, University of California, Berkeley.* COMMUNICATIONS.

Miles, Prof. Richard B. *Department of Mechanical and Aerospace Engineering, Princeton University, Princeton, New Jersey.* FLUID-FLOW VISUALIZATION.

Monplaisir, Dr. Leslie. *Assistant Professor, Department of Industrial and Manufacturing Engineering, Wayne State University, Detroit, Michigan.* COMPUTER-SUPPORTED COLLABORATIVE WORK.

Moore, Dr. James E., Jr. *Assistant Professor, Mechanical Engineering Department, Florida International University, Miami.* ARTERIAL BLOOD FLOW.

Moore, Prof. Jeffrey. *Department of Chemistry and Materials*

Science & Engineering, University of Illinois, Urbana. PHOTOCHEMISTRY—coauthored.

Mosbach, Prof. Klaus. *Pure and Applied Biochemistry, Center for Chemistry and Chemical Engineering, Lund University, Lund, Sweden.* MOLECULAR IMPRINTING—coauthored.

Muirhead, Dr. Brian K. *Mars Pathfinder Flight System Manager, Jet Propulsion Laboratory, California Institute of Technology, Pasadena.* MARS—in part.

Murdock, Prof. Larry L. *Department of Entomology, Purdue University, West Lafayette, Indiana.* AGRICULTURAL SCIENCE (PLANT).

N

Nagy, Prof. George. *Department of Electrical, Computer, and Systems Engineering, Rensselaer Polytechnic Institute, Troy, New York.* COMPUTERIZED DOCUMENT ANALYSIS.

Nellis, Dr. William J. *Lawrence Livermore National Laboratory, University of California, Livermore.* HYDROGEN.

Nelson, Dr. Philip. *Associate Professor of Physics, Department of Physics and Astronomy, David Rittenhouse Laboratory, University of Pennsylvania, Philadelphia.* DEOXYRIBONUCLEIC ACID (DNA)—in part.

Nicoletti, Dr. Paul. *Professor, Department of Pathobiology, College of Veterinary Medicine, University of Florida, Gainesville.* BRUCELLOSIS.

Nicolussi, Günther K. *Materials Science and Chemistry Division, Argonne National Laboratory, Argonne, Illinois.* RESONANT IONIZATION MASS SPECTROMETRY—coauthored.

Nogueira, Dr. Montserrat. *Professor, Department of Biochemistry and Molecular Biology, University of Santiago de Compostela, Santiago de Compostela, Spain.* HORMONE—coauthored.

Norris, Dr. Donald E. *Professor, Department of Biological Sciences, University of Southern Mississippi, Hattiesburg.* ZOONOSES.

Norris, Dr. Richard D. *Associate Scientist, Woods Hole Oceanographic Institution, Woods Hole, Massachusetts.* MASS EXTINCTION—in part.

Novas, Dr. Fernando E. *Museo Argentino de Ciencias Naturales "Bernardino Rivadavia," Buenos Aires, Argentina.* DINOSAUR.

Nur, Prof. Amos. *Department of Geophysics, Stanford University, Stanford, California.* EARTHQUAKE—coauthored.

O

Ohashi, Dr. Haruhiko. *Japan Synchrotron Radiation Research Institute, Kamigouri, Hyogo, Japan.* DIAMOND—coauthored.

Oldfield, Prof. James E. *Department of Animal Sciences, Oregon State University, Corvallis.* SOIL CHEMISTRY.

P

Palaszewski, Bryan. *NASA Lewis Research Center, Cleveland, Ohio.* PROPELLANT MODIFICATION.

Park, Prof. Duk-Won. *Department of Civil and Environmental Engineering, University of Alabama, Tuscaloosa.* MINING—in part.

Peach, Dr. Paul E. *Rehab Associates of South Georgia Inc., Albany, Georgia.* POLIOMYELITIS.

Peck, Dr. Jonathan P. *Aquila Mining Systems Ltd., Montreal, Quebec, Canada.* OPEN PIT MINING.

Pellin, Dr. Michael J. *Materials Science and Chemistry Division, Argonne National Laboratory, Argonne, Illinois.* RESONANT IONIZATION MASS SPECTROMETRY—coauthored.

Petty, Prof. M. C. *School of Engineering & Centre for Molecular Electronics, University of Durham, Durham, United Kingdom.* MOLECULAR ELECTRONICS.

Pohlmann, Prof. Kenneth C. *Chairman, Music Media and Industry, University of Miami, Coral Gables.* COMPACT DISK.

Pomeroy, Prof. Roland K. *Department of Chemistry, Simon Fraser University, Burnaby, British Columbia, Canada.* ORGANOMETALLICS.

Popper, Dr. Arthur N. *Department of Zoology, University of Maryland, College Park.* ANIMAL COMMUNICATION.

Pratson, Dr. Lincoln F. *Research Scientist, Institute of Arctic & Alpine Research, Department of Geology, University of Colorado, Boulder.* SEA-FLOOR IMAGING.

Prull, Dr. Matthew W. *Department of Psychology, Stanford University, Stanford, California.* MEMORY—in part.

Purcell, Dr. William R. *Program Manager, Civil Space Systems, Ball Aerospace & Technologies Corporation, Boulder, Colorado.* MILKY WAY GALAXY.

R

Raman, Dr. Shivakumar. *School of Industrial Engineering, University of Oklahoma, Norman.* MACHINING—in part.

Ramani, Prof. Raja V. *Professor and Head, Department of Mineral Engineering, Pennsylvania State University, University Park.* UNDERGROUND MINING.

Ramström, Dr. Olof. *Pure and Applied Biochemistry, Center for Chemistry and Chemical Engineering, Lund University, Lund, Sweden.* MOLECULAR IMPRINTING—coauthored.

Reinhard, David. *Irvin Aerospace Inc., Santa Ana, California.* AERODYNAMIC DECELERATORS.

Reynolds, Mark F. *Graduate Research Assistant, Department of Chemistry, University of Wisconsin, Madison.* NITRIC OXIDE—coauthored.

Richards, Dr. Paul G. *Lamont-Doherty Earth Observatory of Columbia University, Palisades, New York.* EARTH INTERIOR.

Richardson, Dr. Stephen H. *Professor of Microbiology, Department of Microbiology, Bowman Gray School of Medicine, Winston-Salem, North Carolina.* BACTERIAL GENETICS.

Riedel, Dr. Ralf. *Fachgebiet Disperse Feststoffe, Fachbereich Materialwissenschaft, Technische Universitaet Darmstadt, Darmstadt, Germany.* CERAMICS—coauthored.

Roesch, Dr. Maurie A., III. *Deputy for Systems Engineering, Systems Integration Group, TRW Strategic Systems Division, Rosslyn, Virginia.* COMMAND AND CONTROL—coauthored.

Rooney, Dr. James R. *Professor Emeritus, Gluck Equine Research Center, Department of Veterinary Science, University of Kentucky, Lexington.* VETERINARY PALEOPATHOLOGY.

Rothblatt, Dr. Martine A. *Executive Vice President, International Development, Sky Station International Inc., Washington, D.C.* COMMUNICATIONS PLATFORM.

Royse, Dr. Daniel J. *Professor, Department of Plant Pathology, Pennsylvania State University, University Park.* MUSHROOM—in part.

Ruby, Dr. Norman F. *Research Scientist, Department of Biological Sciences, Stanford University, Stanford, California.* HIBERNATION.

Ruwisch, Lutz. *Fachgebiet Disperse Feststoffe, Fachbereich Materialwissenschaft, Technische Universitaet Darmstadt, Darmstadt, Germany.* CERAMICS—coauthored.

S

Sage, Prof. Andrew P. *Founding Dean Emeritus and First American Bank Professor, University Professor, School of Information Technology and Engineering, George Mason University, Fairfax, Virginia.* INDUSTRIAL ECOLOGY.

Samson, Dr. Michel. *GERM-INSERM U, University of Rennes, Rennes, France.* HUMAN IMMUNODEFICIENCY VIRUS (HIV)—in part.

Sattentau, Dr. Quentin. *Centre d'Immunologie de Marseille-Luminy, France.* HUMAN IMMUNODEFICIENCY VIRUS (HIV)—in part.

Saykally, Prof. Richard J. *Department of Chemistry, University of California, Berkeley.* WATER.

Schatten, Dr. Kenneth H. *National Science Foundation, Arlington, Virginia.* SOLAR ACTIVITY.

Schmelling, Dr. Michael. *Max-Planck-Institut für Kernphysik, Heidelberg, Germany.* QUANTUM CHROMODYNAMICS.

Shannon, Prof. Robert. *Optical Sciences Center, University of Arizona, Tucson.* CONFORMAL OPTICS.

Sherman, Dr. David R. *PathoGenesis Corporation, Seattle, Washington.* TUBERCULOSIS—coauthored.

Shewmaker, Glenn E. *Biological Technician (Soils), Northwest Irrigation & Soils Research Laboratory, U.S. Department of Agriculture, Kimberly, Idaho.* WETLANDS.

Shirley, Donna L. *Manager, Mars Exploration Program, Jet Propulsion Laboratory, Pasadena, California.* MARS—in part.

Shobatake, Kosuke. *Graduate School of Engineering, Nagoya University, Furo-cho, Nagoya, Japan.* DIAMOND—coauthored.

Simoudis, Dr. Evangelos. *IBM, Almaden Research Center, San Jose, California.* DATA SYSTEMS.

Smith, Murdo J. *Manager, Commercial Business Development, International Fuel Cells Corporation, South Windsor, Connecticut.* FUEL CELL.

Smith, Dr. Scott. *University of North Carolina, Charlotte.* MACHINING—coauthored.

Snieckus, Prof. Victor. *Professor of Chemistry, NSERC/Monsanto Chair in Chemical Synthesis and Biomolecule Design, University of Waterloo, Waterloo, Ontario, Canada.* CATALYST—coauthored.

Sobel, Dr. Henry W. *Department of Physics and Astronomy, University of California, Irvine.* NEUTRINO ASTROPHYSICS.

Sperling, Prof. Daniel. *Director, Institute of Transportation Studies, University of California, Davis.* AUTOMOTIVE VEHICLE.

Steding, Anna. *Research Associate, Pacific Institute for Studies in Development, Environment and Security, Oakland, California.* WATER RESOURCE MANAGEMENT.

Suh, Prof. Nam P. *Ralph E. & Eloise F. Cross Professor, and Head of the Department of Mechanical Engineering, Massachusetts Institute of Technology, Cambridge.* DESIGN ENGINEERING.

Surewicz, Dr. Witold. *Institute of Pathology, Case Western Reserve University, Cleveland, Ohio.* PRION DISEASE—coauthored.

Suslick, Prof. Kenneth S. *William H. and Janet Lycan Professor of Chemistry, Professor of Materials Science and Engineering, Chemical & Life Sciences Laboratory, University of Illinois, Champaign, School of Chemical Sciences, Urbana.* SONOCHEMISTRY.

Swider, Raymond J., Jr. *GPS Product Team, Federal Aviation Administration, Washington, D.C.* LOCAL AREA AUGMENTATION SYSTEM (LAAS).

T

Thompson, Prof. Rodger. *Principal Investigator, NICMOS Project, Steward Observatory, University of Arizona, Tucson.* INFRARED ASTRONOMY—coauthored.

Tilling, Dr. Robert I. *Chief Scientist, Volcano Hazards Team, U.S. Department of the Interior, U.S. Geological Survey, Menlo Park, California.* VOLCANOLOGY.

Tiwari, Dr. Sandip. *IBM, Thomas J. Watson Research Center, Yorktown Heights, New York.* SINGLE-ELECTRON TRANSISTOR.

Torgerson, Dr. David F. *Vice President of Research and Product Development, Atomic Energy of Canada Limited, Chalk River Laboratories, Chalk River, Ontario, Canada.* NUCLEAR REACTOR.

V

Viemeister, Prof. Neal F. *Department of Psychology, University of Minnesota, Minneapolis.* AUDITORY PROCESSING.

Vogel, Prof. Steven. *Department of Zoology, Duke University, Durham, North Carolina.* TREE—in part.

Volkow, Nora D. *Chemistry Department, Brookhaven Na-*

tional Laboratory, Upton, New York. POSITRON EMISSION TOMOGRAPHY—coauthored.

von Puttkamer, Dr. Jesco. *Office of Space Flight, NASA Headquarters, Washington, D.C.* SPACE FLIGHT.

W

Weigel, Dr. Detlef. *Assistant Professor, Plant Biology Laboratory, The Salk Institute for Biological Studies, La Jolla, California.* PLANT DEVELOPMENT.

West, Dr. Charles P. *University of Arkansas, Fayetteville.* GRASS ENDOPHYTES.

Whitten, Patrick G. *Senior Project Manager, Wang Laboratories Inc., Cleveland, Ohio.* COAL.

Wichman, Dr. Harvey. *Professor of Psychology, and Director, Aerospace Psychology Laboratory, Claremont McKenna College, Claremont, California.* SPACE BIOLOGY.

Wilkes, Dr. Joseph E. *Senior Research Scientist, Bell Communications Research Inc., Red Bank, New Jersey.* RADIO COMMUNICATIONS.

Willner, Prof. Alan Eli. *Department of Electrical Engineering—Systems, University of Southern California, Los Angeles.* WIDEBAND OPTICAL AMPLIFICATION.

Winkler, Dr. Jay R. *Beckman Institute, California Institute of Technology, Pasadena.* PROTEIN.

Winter, Dr. John M. *Associate Research Professor, Department*

of Materials Science and Engineering, Johns Hopkins University, Baltimore, Maryland. NONDESTRUCTIVE TESTING.

Witten, Prof. Thomas A. *Department of Physics, James Franck Institute, University of Chicago, Chicago, Illinois.* CRUMPLING.

Wubah, Dr. Daniel A. *Associate Professor, Department of Biological Sciences, Towson University, Towson, Maryland.* FUNGI.

Y

Yellon, Dr. Steven M. *Professor of Physiology, Center for Perinatal Biology, Loma Linda University School of Medicine, Loma Linda, California.* MELATONIN.

Young, Dr. Linda. *Argonne National Laboratory, Argonne, Illinois.* SYNCHROTRON RADIATION.

Yule, Lauray D. *Steward Observatory, University of Arizona, Tucson.* INFRARED ASTRONOMY—coauthored.

Z

Zelefsky, Dr. Michael J. *Associate Professor, Radiation Oncology, Department of Radiation Oncology, Memorial Sloan Kettering Cancer Center, New York, New York.* CANCER (MEDICINE)—in part.

Zhang, Dr. Xu. *PPG Industries, Inc., Allison Park, Pennsylvania.* METAL COATING—coauthored.

Index

Index

A

A2100TM satellite bus 35–36

Aberration: conformal optics 105–108*

Acanthocephalans 413–415

Acanthostega 390

ACATS *see* Advisory Committee on Advanced Television Service

ACE see Advanced Composition Explorer

Acoustic transducer 383–385

Acoustic waves: nondestructive testing 258

Acquired immune deficiency syndrome (AIDS) 1–3*
  HIV-1 co-receptor 1–2
  human immunodeficiency virus 174–177*
  new therapies 2–3

Acremonium chrysogenum 24

Adansonia digitata 376

Adaptive differential pulse-code modulation 318

Adaptive optics 3–5*
  atmospheric limits on imaging 3
  new discoveries and capabilities 5
  technique 4–5

Addictive disorders 296–298*

Adenosine triphosphate synthase 257

Adenovirus: gene delivery 62

Adhesion molecules 175–176

Adjacency graphs 192

Adleman, L. 95

Adsorption: immunoselective processes 187–189

Advanced Composition Explorer 350

Advanced Earth Observation Satellite 354

Advanced Mobile Telephone Service 316

Advanced Photon Source 365–366

Advancing system: longwall mining 234

Advisory Committee on Advanced Television Service 369

Aerodynamic decelerators 5–8*
  applications 6
  Mars Pathfinder 214
  technology development 6–7
  types of decelerators 5–6

Aerodynamics: helicopter 165–167
  icing 183–185*
  trees in high wind 378–381

Aerospike engine 8–11*, 349
  advanced launch vehicles 11
  advantages 10
  altitude compensation 8
  comparison with conventional engines 8–9
  linear 10–11

Aging 228–229, 373

Agricultural science (plant) 11–12*
  biotechnology for plant transformation 11–12
  breeding for stored-grain insect resistance 11
  future 12
  gene selection for breeding insect-resistant plants 12
  traditional control of stored-grain insects 11

Agrostis 161

AIDS *see* Acquired immune deficiency syndrome

Air navigation: Local Area Augmentation System 199–200*

Air pollution, indoor 12–14*
  fungal allergies 12–14
  fungal detection and diagnosis 14
  indoor fungi 13
  mycotoxins and volatiles 13
  recommendations to reduce 14
  sampling of indoor environments 13–14
  standards for fungal exposure 14

Air pollution—*cont.*
  substrates for fungal growth 14

Air quality: benefits of electric vehicles 52–53
  coal 81–83*
  underground mining 385–389*

Aircraft: conformal optics 105–108*
  icing 183–185*
  spin/stall recovery 8

Alinda (asteroid) 249

Alkali metasomatism 66

Alkaline fuel cell 154

Alkaloids: grass endophytes 161–163*

Allen's Source (star) 196

Allergens: air pollution, indoor 12–14*
  food 151
  fungal 12–13

Allergic fungal sinusitis 14

Alper, Tikvah 257

Alpha-amylase inhibitor 12

Alternaria 12–13

Aluminum 304
  alloys 110–112
  -copper pretreatment 112

Alvinella 182

Alzheimer's disease 301

Ameba 14–16*
  feeding and movement 15
  habitat and salinity tolerance 16
  new marine testate ameba 15
  reproduction 15–16

American Standard Code for Information Interchange 96, 100

Amino acids 16–18*
  chirality 17–18
  formation mechanism 18
  origin of life 18

α-Amino-*n*-butyric acid 17

7-Aminocephalosporanic acid 24

7-Aminodecacetoxycephalosporanic acid 24

2-Amino-2,3-dimethylpentanoic acid 17